Guide to the Most
COMPETITIVE
COLLEGES

Seventh Edition

Edited by the College Division Staff of
Barron's Educational Series, Inc.

All inquiries should be addressed to:
Barron's Educational Series, Inc.
250 Wireless Boulevard
Hauppauge, NY 11788
www.barronseduc.com

Library of Congress Control No. 2011922228

ISBN-13: 978-0-7641-4599-5

PRINTED IN THE UNITED STATES OF AMERICA

9 8 7 6 5 4 3 2 1

❏ CONTENTS ❏

❏ INTRODUCTION ❏

We are proud to present this seventh edition of *Barron's Guide to the Most Competitive Colleges*. A school's inclusion is based on the standards of Barron's Selector Ratings in the comprehensive *Profiles of American Colleges*. These schools accept only the best and brightest students.

In the sixth edition, published in 2009, 80 eligible institutions were included. In this edition, we are happy to present 85 schools.

We turned to recent graduates or (in several cases) soon-to-be graduates of each of these institutions and asked them to write an essay on what it's *really* like on campus. We requested them to comment specifically on those aspects of campus life that would be of most concern to a college-bound student trying to decide which institutions should be sent applications.

Essays for schools previously listed were either rewritten by new writers or the factual information was updated by the schools to ensure its accuracy.

Geographic locations of the colleges range from California to Maine. Some are large, others small. Most are private, but state universities are also represented. And several of the service academies are represented as well.

The Most Competitive chart beginning on page 1113 shows at a glance how each of the most competitive schools stacks up against one another in areas such as acceptance numbers, test scores, and other comparisons.

Short biographies of the contributors are included in a special section. And, finally, for quick geographic locating, the book concludes with an index by state.

It is our hope that these perceptive essays will be helpful in guiding the college-bound reader to intelligent choices in the major decision-making area of college applications.

The College Division Staff
Barron's Educational Series, Inc.

PLEASE NOTE

Historical information regarding SAT scores is based on the newer test, based on a total score of 2400, where possible. Some historical data is based on the older 1600-point test.

For definitive information about a particular school's admission requirements, including the ACT, SAT, and the SAT Subject Tests, we recommend you visit the school's Web site or contact the school's admissions office directly.

THE MOST
COMPETITIVE COLLEGES

Amherst College Photo

 Amherst College
Amherst, MA 01002-5000

 (413) 542-2328
Fax: (413) 542-2040

 E-mail: *admission@amherst.edu*
Website: *www.amherst.edu*

 Enrollment

Full-time ❑ women: 875
❑ men: 869

INTRODUCING AMHERST

Within the culturally rich and naturally gorgeous Pioneer Valley of western Massachusetts sits the peaceful 1,000-acre campus of Amherst College. Stroll around on the grassy quads, peek inside the impressive yet mismatched buildings, and talk to the students in their purple Amherst gear on their way to and from their classes and club meetings, play rehearsals, and sports scrimmages. You'll start to sense why, ever since its founding in 1821, distinguished faculty and talented undergrads have flocked to "the College on the Hill," helping it develop its current reputation as one of the country's best liberal arts institutions.

Only recently, though, has Amherst articulated its ideals into an official Mission Statement:

> **"** *Amherst College educates men and women of exceptional potential from all backgrounds so that they may seek, value, and advance knowledge, engage the world around them, and lead principled lives of consequence.*
>
> *Amherst brings together the most promising students, whatever their financial need, in order to promote diversity of experience and ideas within a purposefully small residential community. Working with faculty, staff, and administrators dedicated to intellectual freedom and the highest standards of instruction in the liberal arts, Amherst undergraduates assume substantial responsibility for undertaking inquiry and for shaping their education within and beyond the curriculum.*
>
> *Amherst College is committed to learning through close colloquy and to expanding the realm of knowledge through scholarly research and artistic creation at the highest level. Its graduates link learning with leadership—in service to the college, to their communities, and to the world beyond.* **"**

True to this mission, Amherst values rigorous critical thinking, deep discussion, close relationships, and service to the greater good.

The name "Amherst" (with a silent *h*, please) may still conjure, in some people's minds, images of a snobbish haven for wealthy white men. However, this conception was never completely accurate (the college was founded explicitly for "the education of indigent young men of piety and talents"), and it certainly no longer applies: Led by former President Anthony W. Marx, Amherst has made a concerted—and already very successful—effort to be more visible and accessible to promising students from lower-income families and communities and from developing countries. Today's Amherst students are women and men of all colors and cultures (as reflected in the opening of a new Multicultural Resource Center). They come from nearly every U.S. state and dozens of other nations; from inner-city public schools as well as private prep schools and home-schooled backgrounds.

All these diverse young people come together to hone and use their talents in a community based on a love of all kinds of learning: literary, artistic, historical, scientific, and philosophical. Yes, they learn a lot from small classes with their accomplished professors and from the renowned speakers and performers who visit the college each semester. But as they live together in cultural theme houses, eat together in Valentine Dining Hall, compete together on Pratt Field, and sing together in *a cappella* groups, Amherst students learn just as much from one another.

There's talk of "the Amherst Bubble"—the students' feeling of privilege and shelter from "the real world" as they pursue their own interests and ideals, surrounded by the best and brightest at a school that, frankly, has more resources than most. But the college has been working harder and harder to bring the real world into the Bubble, and Amherst out into the real world, through a new Center for Community Engagement, free concerts, and museum exhibits that attract the public from miles around—even a class conducted in a local prison. And, over four years, Amherst prepares young adults to venture into the wider world with the confidence that they belong to a special community within it; with greater understanding of its complexities, problems, and possibilities; and with the right habits of mind to navigate and take the lead in improving it.

Of course, life in the Bubble isn't perfect—some students struggle academically or emotionally, and all have complaints from time to time. But there are always people and places to turn to for help (Resident Counselors, the Counseling Center, the Dean of Students' Office, the Campus Police, the Keefe Health Center), as well as ways to speak up and take action (forming a new student group, arranging a meeting with faculty or staff, writing to the school newspaper, talking to a Peer Advocate). Amherst students have a remarkable amount of freedom to chart their own courses, to decide how much to put into their time here and what exactly they want to get out of it.

And most will agree that they get a lot from Amherst. Of those who come in as first-year students, ninety-seven percent remain to graduate. Many graduates stay to work here, and some even come back as professors. Each year, more than sixty percent of alumni donate to their college, and hundreds return to campus for Homecoming and Reunion. Younger siblings often follow their big brothers and sisters here—and sons and daughters follow their parents—having seen how much they love Amherst. But not until they get here can they know all the many, many reasons why.

ADMISSIONS REQUIREMENTS

In a recent year, 7,679 applicants vied for spots in Amherst's incoming first-year class. The college accepted only 1,227—not quite sixteen percent (of whom 467 enrolled), making it one of the most selective schools of its kind in the nation.

Amherst requires applicants to report scores on either the SAT or the ACT, as well as on at least two SAT II subject tests. (International applicants for whom English is not a first language might have to take an English-proficiency exam as well.) The admissions office recommends taking four years of English, math through calculus, at least three years of a foreign language, at least two years of history and social science, and at least two years of natural science, including a laboratory course. Though an admitted student may not use Advanced Placement credits to count toward an Amherst degree, doing well in AP courses will likely help an applicant to get into Amherst in the first place and, in some cases, can entitle a student to skip certain introductory courses.

About thirty percent of each incoming class is accepted through Early Decision, and each year, a dozen or so transfer students from community colleges or other four-year schools are admitted as sophomores or juniors. First-year students must begin courses in the fall semester, but transfer students may begin in either the fall or the spring.

Several admissions officers examine and discuss each application, taking into account grades and test scores, teacher recommendations, two essays, and extracurricular activities. Rather than plugging each of these factors into a strict formula to get an objective rating, they do their best to consider each applicant as a whole person. They understand that everyone comes from a background having had a different set of academic, extracurricular, and personal opportunities and challenges, and they judge each applicant with his or her life story in mind as much as possible. Above all, they look for intellectually vibrant people who have challenged themselves academically and who have begun to develop interesting talents. They want each incoming class to include diverse perspectives and personal histories. Many who work in admissions are Amherst grads themselves, so they know what kinds of students will enrich and be enriched by the Amherst experience.

> **❝** *Here, I'll use myself as an example of an admitted applicant. I attended a mid-sized, middle-class, small-town public high school and was near, but not at, the very top of my class (perhaps in the ninety-fifth percentile for GPA). My standardized test scores were generally slightly below the average for admitted Amherst students. But I took three AP and many honors-level classes, played in the school band, was trained as a peer mediator, did volunteer work, and won several awards for writing and theater. I got two very enthusiastic recommendations from my favorite teachers and tried to put a warm and funny spin on my application essays. Amherst was my "reach" school—and I'm certainly glad it turned out to be within my reach!* **❞**

ACADEMIC LIFE

Academics at Amherst are a challenge. Each class requires hours of reading, writing, problem-solving, and conversation—and discussions often spill over from the classroom into the professors' offices, dining hall, and dorms. Every student will, at some point, have to question some preconceived notions, pull some all-nighters in Frost Library or a Merrill Science Center lab, and turn to someone for help. This can be jarring for anyone accustomed to breezing through high school classes and always being the smartest kid in the room.

But don't worry—the atmosphere at Amherst is one of more collaboration than competition. Once students surmount the major hurdle of being admitted, there is no cutthroat scramble to the top of the class. It's actually difficult to fail out of Amherst, especially with help available from Academic Peer Mentors, The Writing Center, and the Moss Quantitative Center.

And though the course load might sometimes feel like it's weighing you down, it also includes a lot of freedom and choice. Rarely at Amherst does a student have to take a class that he or she does not find interesting and worthwhile. And just in case, there's a two-week Add/Drop period at the start of each semester, so students can shop around for the right courses before committing.

Professors and the Advisor System

Amherst prides itself on the close relationships that students are able to form with faculty. The average class size is only seventeen students. Every professor holds regular office hours so that students may come in to get clarification on ideas and assignments. Many professors hire student research assistants. A program called TYPO (Take Your Professor Out) even lets students invite favorite professors to dinner at local restaurants. Some students suggest choosing courses based not on their topics, but on their teachers.

Each incoming student is assigned a faculty advisor—a particular professor who helps him or her choose each semester's course load based on interests, goals, and the ideal of a well-rounded liberal arts education. Once a student declares a major, he or she gets an advisor in that department. A student who chooses to do a senior honors project gets at least one special thesis advisor whose area of expertise most closely reflects the topic of the project.

Courses

To graduate from Amherst, a student must complete four courses per semester over eight semesters—thirty-two courses in all. Unlike most colleges, Amherst has no core curriculum. Other than the courses necessary for one's major, the only required course is a First-Year Seminar, and there are dozens of these to choose from.

Majors

Students may major in any of thirty-six different subjects or design an interdisciplinary major. (Amherst has a pre-law advisor and a health professions advisor to give guidance on fulfilling the requirements for admission to law school or medical school. However, Pre-Law and Pre-Med are not considered majors in and of themselves; the school requires an official departmental major in addition.) Many choose to double-major in combinations of any two subjects, and a few ambitious souls each year complete triple majors. Year after year, the most popular majors (in varying order) are economics, English, psychology, and political science, and the newest majors available are environmental studies and film and media studies. Depending on the department, a major will involve anywhere from eight to fourteen required courses and perhaps a comprehensive final exam or a senior project. It's not only allowed but common for a student to change majors once or twice over four years.

Interterm

Interterm is Amherst's name for the three-week period in January, between the fall and spring semesters. Students may stay home for Interterm, or they may return to campus to take noncredit courses or do research. Some also do urban education "Winternships" or other volunteer work. And every Interterm includes at least one colloquium in the new Amherst College Colloquium Series, in which well-known experts are invited to teach classes and debate divergent viewpoints on important and controversial topics. Past colloquium guests (for Interterm and during the spring and fall semesters) have included columnists David Brooks and E. J. Dionne, General Wesley Clark, and former New Jersey Governor Christine Todd Whitman.

- Anthropology 39: The Anthropology of Food
- Sociology 44: Sport and Society
- Astronomy 25: Galactic and Extragalactic Astronomy: The Dark Matter Problem
- Biology 39: Animal Behavior
- Black Studies 25: Women and Politics in Africa
- Economics 25: Environmental and Natural Resource Economics
- English 53: The Literature of Madness
- Geology 45: Seminar in Biogeochemistry
- Law, Jurisprudence, and Social Thought 20: Murder
- Mathematics 13: Multivariable Calculus
- Computer Science 24: Artificial Intelligence
- Music 37: Advanced Topics in Jazz
- Philosophy 69: Seminar: Well-Being and Well-Lived Lives
- Physics 14: Relativity, Cosmology, and Quantum Physics
- Psychology 34: Gender, the Brain, and Behavior
- Religion 41: Reading the Rabbis
- Russian 17: Strange Russian Writers
- Spanish 80: Latino Autobiography

Senior Honors

Roughly half of all Amherst students take on ambitious thesis projects—usually research papers; reports on lab experiments; or original works of art, literature, music, or drama—to serve as capstones for their college careers and earn them Latin honors. Any student who completes a thesis of acceptable quality may graduate *cum laude*; thesis writers whose GPAs are in the top twenty-five percent of the class might graduate *magna* or *summa cum laude*. All whose grades are in the top quarter, with or without a thesis, get English honors—they graduate "With Distinction." Amherst also has chapters of the national honors societies Phi Beta Kappa and Sigma Xi.

The Five College Consortium

Because Amherst works in partnership with the nearby University of Massachusetts Amherst, Hampshire College, Mount Holyoke College, and Smith College, an Amherst education includes the advantages of five very different schools in one. Amherst students can go to any of the other four campuses to take courses for credit; complete certificate programs in, for example, logic or international relations; audition for performances; attend parties, sporting events, and concerts; and hang out with friends. Just hop on the free bus!

Study Abroad

Though Amherst does not sponsor a study abroad program of its own, more than forty percent of students spend one or two semesters—usually in the junior year—living and studying in a foreign land. In recent years, students have ventured to the United Kingdom, France, Italy, Germany, Spain, Denmark, Uruguay, Ghana, South Africa, China, Japan, New Zealand, and more. Studying abroad can help fulfill the requirements for foreign language majors. Certain research assistantships, volunteer programs, and extracurricular groups provide chances to travel overseas as well.

> **"***I majored in English, with a concentration in creative prose writing. Through a program at Mount Holyoke, I also earned state certification to teach high school English. But I had enough time and freedom to take elective courses in psychology, theater and dance, anthropology, religion, astronomy, biology, and other departments.***
>
> *One of my friends pulled off a triple major, semesters in Italy and France, and a European Studies thesis based on her passion for the culinary arts. Another came in intending to major only in biology, but discovered an interest in history, and ended up doing a thesis on the history of science education in public schools. Yet another did two honors projects: a math thesis about knot theory and an original play about math.***"**

SOCIAL LIFE AND ACTIVITIES

Among classes, exams, and lectures, there is always something to do at Amherst. The campus boasts more than 100 student organizations. The roster of entertainers invited to campus in the past few years includes The Upright Citizens Brigade, comedian Margaret Cho, the Tokyo String Quartet, the Harlem Gospel Choir, The Amazing Whirling Dervishes, and rapper/actor/poet Mos Def. Every weekend, a student group called FLICS screens a different film free in Keefe Campus Center. Frost Library hosts a weekly Community Tea, Valentine Dining Hall periodically puts on a festive Luau, and every year, there's a Casino night to raise money for local charities. Of course, students throw various kinds of parties every weekend. And Amherst officially abolished fraternities and sororities several decades ago, but you'll still find a few unofficial ones if you look hard enough.

It's worth noting, though, that many of the most fun moments at Amherst happen not at the big special events, but in the course of day-to-day life. As the only dining hall on campus, Valentine is a hub for socializing; it's impossible to pass through without seeing someone you know, and quite possible to linger there for hours, eating and talking. Students make memories walking into town for coffee, playing video games in friends' dorm rooms, and sitting out in the halls before class.

A SAMPLING OF STUDENT CLUBS AND ORGANIZATIONS AT AMHERST COLLEGE

- ○ Amherst Christian Fellowship
- ○ Amherst Feminist Alliance
- ○ *The Amherst Student* (college newspaper)
- ○ Amherst Symphony Orchestra
- ○ Association of Amherst Students (elected student government)
- ○ Big Brothers / Big Sisters
- ○ Black Student Union
- ○ DASAC: Dancing and Stepping at Amherst College
- ○ Debate Society
- ○ FACE: Financial Aid & Class Equality
- ○ The Green Amherst Project
- ○ Habitat for Humanity
- ○ Hillel
- ○ The Men's Project
- ○ Mr. Gad's House of Improv
- ○ Pre-Business Group
- ○ Pride Alliance
- ○ *Prism* (magazine)
- ○ Progressive Student Alliance
- ○ Quiz Bowl
- ○ Sci-Fi / Fantasy Club
- ○ South Asian Students Association
- ○ Student-Athlete Advisory Committee
- ○ WAMH (campus radio station)

There's plenty of fun and enrichment off-campus, too. *The New York Times* has called The Pioneer Valley "arguably the most author-saturated, book-cherishing, literature-celebrating place in the nation." Community theater, amateur and professional music, and social dancing all thrive in the area.

And with sunny summers, famously brilliant autumn foliage, white winters, and lush spring grass, there are opportunities for all kinds of outdoor activities. (You haven't lived until you've sledded down Memorial Hill on a mattress or a dining hall tray!)

> **❝** *I was part of what I thought of as "the silent majority": Amherst College students who don't sing. Amherst is known as "The Singing College," and indeed, many of my friends participated in the Choral Society, the six a cappella groups, and the annual Interterm musical. And even though I can't carry a tune in a bucket, I faithfully attended and enjoyed all their shows.* **❞**

CHECK IT OUT! ATTRACTIONS IN AND AROUND AMHERST

○ **For Breakfast, Lunch, or Dinner: Antonio's, Baku's, Haymarket, India House, Judie's, The Lone Wolf, Stables, Thai Garden, The Whately Diner**

○ **For Dessert: Bart's, The Black Sheep, Flayvors of Cook Farm, The Henion Bakery, Herrell's**

○ **For Shopping: A.J. Hastings, Faces, Hampshire Mall, Holyoke Mall, Thornes Marketplace**

○ **For Books: Amherst Books, Food for Thought Books, Montague Book Mill, The Option*, Raven Used Books**

○ **For Entertainment: Academy of Music Theatre, Amherst Cinema Arts Center, Calvin Theater, Iron Horse Music Hall, Pleasant Street Theater**

○ **For Enrichment: Amherst College Museum of Natural History*, Bassett Planetarium*, Emily Dickinson Museum*, Eric Carle Museum of Picture Book Art, Mead Art Museum*, National Yiddish Book Center**

*(Owned and run by Amherst College.)

Athletics

Amherst is an NCAA Division III school and a charter member of the New England Small College Athletic Conference (NESCAC), with thirteen varsity sports teams for women and fourteen for men. The Lord Jeffs of men's basketball and women's ice hockey have recently had especially impressive seasons, while the men's football team carries on its legendary rivalry with Williams College. There are also six intramural sports for women and six for men, including rugby and Ultimate Frisbee. About one-third of the student body are varsity athletes, and as many as eighty percent play on the intramural teams.

Amherst's athletic facilities include Pratt Pool, Orr Rink, indoor and outdoor tracks, thirty-three tennis courts, baseball and softball diamonds, and a nine-hole golf course. More casual fitness buffs can simply work out in the Wolff Fitness Center, go for a walk in the bird sanctuary, or take any of several free, noncredit physical education classes.

FINANCIAL AID

Insufficient family income will never be an impediment to a qualified student arriving and thriving at Amherst. Even in these tough economic times, the college stands by its need-blind admissions policy. In fact, it has recently expanded the policy: Amherst is now one of very few schools to be need-blind for international students as well as Americans. The college has also replaced all loans with scholarships in its financial aid packages, so that no student need ever graduate with debt. If a student is on financial aid at Amherst, that aid also applies to studying abroad as well.

More than half of Amherst students take part-time jobs on campus, whether or not work-study is part of their financial aid packages. Jobs are available in Valentine Dining Hall, in Frost Library, in Keefe Campus Center, with the Physical Plant, and elsewhere. Many students spend at least one summer working on campus, in an office internship or a research fellowship. The Center for Community Engagement also offers Fellowships for Action, to support students who wish to spend the summer doing community outreach work, domestically or abroad.

GRADUATES

Throughout their college years, Amherst students can make use of the Career Center to begin networking and exploring job options. They can consult the Fellowship Office to find funding for further education. But the most useful tools they'll graduate with are sharp, active minds, knowledge of their own strengths and passions, and deep, durable relationships.

PROMINENT GRADS

- Henry Ward Beecher, 1834, preacher and abolitionist
- Joseph Hardy Neesima, 1870, first Japanese graduate of a Western college and founder of Doshisha University
- Melvil Dewey, 1874, inventor of the Dewey Decimal System
- Calvin Coolidge, 1895, thirtieth President of the United States
- Charles Drew, 1926, surgeon and inventor of blood banking
- Richard Wilbur, 1942, U.S. Poet Laureate and winner of two Pulitzer Prizes
- Joseph Stiglitz, 1964, Nobel Prize-winning economist
- Teller, 1969, illusionist (of Penn & Teller)
- Patrick Fitzgerald, 1982, U.S. District Attorney
- David Foster Wallace, 1985, author
- Jeffrey Wright, 1987, stage and screen actor
- Debby Applegate, 1989, Pulitzer Prize-winning biographer
- Lauren Groff, 2001, bestselling author
- Kimmie Weeks, 2005, founder of Youth Action International

In the years right after Commencement, many young Amherst alumni go on to graduate or professional schools. Some go to work for nonprofits, while others join the worlds of business or finance. Several each year might win prestigious national fellowships, such as the Watson, the Marshall, and the Rhodes. Quite a few stick around the college for a year or two as staff members.

As former students return to Amherst for their Fifth, Tenth, Twenty-Fifth, and Fiftieth Reunions, they may well find that they and their classmates have been elected to public office, started businesses, published books, and won prestigious awards—or else lived quieter lives as thoughtful, well-informed workers and citizens. As the college's 20,000 active alumni make clear, an Amherst education can form the foundation of myriad careers and life paths.

> **❝** *I'm surprised and pleased to find that much of what I consider to be "my Amherst education" has actually happened since I've graduated. I've kept in touch with a community of students and young alums online, and we still have the kinds of thoughtful, challenging (and often silly) discussions we had in the classrooms and dorms. I've watched my friends begin careers as teachers, preachers, lawyers, researchers, computer technicians, librarians, actors, and writers. I've met up with these friends again at Homecomings and Reunions. I've even returned to work at the college for several years. And throughout, I find that my world awareness, critical thinking abilities, and professional skills continue to expand, as does my web of connections to this amazing educational community.*
>
> *Amherst is still teaching me. At this school, getting one's B.A. might seem like the end, but it's just the beginning.* **❞**

SUMMING UP

Amherst College is not perfect, and it's not the right school for everyone. But if you're looking for a rigorous liberal arts education in a beautiful and lively region of the country; if you are comfortable in a tight-knit community where everyone is a friend or a friend-of-a-friend; if you want to work closely with accomplished professors and live, learn, and play with a wide variety of talented young scholars; if you believe in learning inside and outside of the classroom;

if you are willing to challenge yourself and open your mind to new viewpoints and opportunities, then you can't do much better than Amherst. There are so many reasons why it earns the loyalty of the vast majority of its students and alumni, and why we are so proud of its history and traditions.

And yet, Amherst is an institution that keeps striving to make itself even better. Since I arrived as a first-year student, and even since I've graduated, I've seen Amherst make improvements in all areas, from its wheelchair accessibility, to its environmental friendliness, to its Web site, to its financial aid. Professors keep creating new courses and breaking new ground in their research, and students keep forming new organizations and heading down new paths of inquiry.

This is what Amherst expects from its students and graduates: life-long discovery, expansion, and improvement, not just within our own intellects, but out into all aspects of the broader society. As our motto goes, *"Terras Irradient*—Let them bring light to the world."

❏ *Katherine Duke, B.A.*

BATES COLLEGE

Photo by Phyllis Graber Jensen

Bates College
Lewiston, ME 04240

(207) 786-6000
Fax: (207) 786-6025

E-mail: *admissions@bates.edu*
Website: *http://www.bates.edu*

 Enrollment

Full-time ❏ women: 928
❏ men: 810

INTRODUCING BATES

If you read about Bates you will see it is a welcoming, small, highly selective liberal arts college in Lewiston, Maine. But if you spend time at Bates and sit with students in the dining hall while they nurse tea, coffee, and conversations about environmental sustainability projects or the upcoming ski trip, you realize that it is also so much more. Bates is located in the vacationland state, and it is a mere thirty to forty minutes from sea, forest, and city. Simply put, you can have it all at Bates. For example, Bates is a small college, but you can make your experience as big as you want by traveling abroad or exploring Lewiston and Portland.

Bates is widely renowned as one of the first institutions to make SAT/ACT scores an optional part of the application process, but Bates has been leading since its inception. In addition to waiving SAT/ACT requirements before most other schools, Bates was one of the first schools to accept all students regardless of race, religion, or sex. There have never been fraternities or sororities at Bates so people tend to overlap. If you go to the newly constructed dining hall you will not only taste some of the best/healthiest food served in a college cafeteria, but you will also be hard pressed to find clear separations between the different types of students.

All students eat in one brand-new dining hall, which physically represents Bates' commitment to egalitarianism. There are no partitions separating students in the dining hall and there is no hierarchy of seating because Bates has always attempted to bring people together. Parties are required to have nonalcoholic drinks, clubs and organizations are open to all, and there are gender-neutral bathroom options in the newest dormitory.

Bates students come from all over the world and represent more than just typical categories of diversity. Bates is a place where a rower also sings in one of the *a cappella* groups on campus. It is a place where an honors thesis student is in a jam-funk band that plays covers of Britney Spears for the sake of irony. Bates is a place where common archetypes melt away and interests stretch across categories. It is the kind of college where contradictions flourish in the most positive way.

What makes Bates one of the top schools in the country is the family of students, faculty, and staff that fill the dorms, classrooms, and offices. Students come to Bates because of the resources and educational opportunities and stay because of the familial atmosphere. The people at Bates are so important because they contribute to and sustain a philosophy of intellectual curiosity, civic engagement, and egalitarianism.

Batesies are a passionate and progressive bunch, so even after the fall foliage has passed, this quaint and picturesque campus remains colorful and bright with student energy. Cookouts, clambakes, and camping trips characterize the fall, while sledding, snow forts, skiing, and extended dinners in the dining hall mark the winter. And as for spring and short term, well that deserves a section for itself.

> **❝** *Bates students are always willing to hang out and hash it out. Whether it's over an extended dinner in Commons, at the Ronj with a cup of coffee, or just outside the library—you can always find a familiar face to talk to about your day.* **❞**

—Katie Conkling, '09

At Bates, you will most likely know someone everywhere you go. Fortunately, even if you do not know anyone, students will smile when you walk down the quad and professors' doors are open and inviting. It is easy to take the necessary first step to get to know someone, speak up in class, or find the mentor support you need.

Bates is an environment that cultivates a type of confidence that affects every aspect of your life. The Bates climate encourages students to claim and build their own lives. Bates students manage and run the college radio station, coffee house, and the first-year outdoor orientation program Aesop. Residents in the arts and culture and environmental theme houses on Frye Street organize events such as movie and craft nights. Events vary, but they are all warm and inviting.

> **❝** *Running Aesop gave me the opportunity to have hands-on management experience that I would have never received had the program not been student run. Based on the college's egalitarian principles, many of the largest organizations on campus are entirely student run, such as the outing club, the radio station, and the on-campus coffee shop. Few, if any, colleges provide their students with these kinds of leadership opportunities, since the Bates Outing Club is the oldest student run outing club in the country, and Aesop is the only one of its kind still student run.* **❞**

—Graham Jones

The Diy (do it yourself) attitude affects the academic curriculum as well. Students have the option to design their own major if traditional majors like English or Physics leave them wanting more. Students have successfully designed majors such as Journalism and Pop Cultural Studies because, at Bates, if you can dream it, and want it badly enough, it will happen. Every single person at Bates, including classmates, faculty, and staff, is invested in making sure students thrive.

ADMISSIONS REQUIREMENTS ▬▬▬▬▬

Like many colleges in the New England Small College Athletic Conference (NESCAC), Bates is a highly selective institution and one of the most competitive colleges in the United States. The applicant pool, which is increasing every year, consists of highly motivated and talented students from around the world. However, there is not one standard of student. There are many routes to Bates College, and similarly there are many different types of students at Bates.

With the number of applicants increasing each year, and with a limited number of available spaces, the number of applicants who choose to apply during the Early Decision round is increasing. While an Early Decision application does not guarantee you admittance, it does significantly increase your chance of acceptance. If you are unsure of whether the Early Decision option is the right option for you, there are several other alternatives including: Regular Decision, Deferred Admission, January Admission, and Transfer Admission.

Testing

Unlike many other elite colleges in the United States, Bates does not require applicants to submit SAT or ACT scores. Even though most applicants have excellent standardized scores, the optional SAT/ACT policy illustrates that Bates understands that there is more than one way to measure intelligence.

Interviews/Essay

One of the reasons that Bates is such a diverse college is that the admissions staff is committed to carrying out the college's mission to foster an inclusive and heterogeneous community. Bates' ethos of diversity is one that informs the entire admissions process. Instead of just looking at the numbers, the Bates admissions staff also strongly considers a student's record of leadership and evidence of special talents. The Bates admissions staff is looking for students who can contribute to the community, and students who can learn from the community.

Admissions staff comes to understand applicants better through the essay and the admissions interview. The essay and interview are valuable components of the application because they also offer the admissions staff an opportunity to see more than a list of extracurricular activities and test scores. If you are strongly interested in attending Bates, it is highly recommended that you schedule an interview and distinguish yourself in your essay. Use the essay as a chance to stand out and disclose more than the common application allows.

> 66 *The interview is more just a friendly discussion and is not overly stressful. If interested in Bates, the interview is a must because it allows you to get a better idea of what Bates College is all about while giving the admissions officer a personal and individual view of yourself that they can't get on paper. Bates really wants to know what kind of person you are beyond the numbers and that is something that really stuck out to me during the process. Bates cares for its prospective students and doesn't just look at you as another statistic.* 99

—*Paul Lombardi, '11*

Since not every applicant has the means to visit the college, Bates also offers alumni interviews. Alumni interviews, which also factor into admission, allow students the chance to speak with a Bates alumnus, and to gain some insights into the character of a Batesie. Another way a student can come to understand the Bates experience without physically walking through the campus is by visiting the student blogs.

FIVE THINGS TO CHECK OUT IF YOU VISIT BATES

5. Frye Street houses
4. "New" commons
3. Nezinscot Farm
2. Walk around the "Puddle"
1. Sit on the steps of Hawthorne and survey the Quad

The admissions process can vary depending on your proximity to the college and your individual interests. However, the admissions team makes every effort to connect with each applicant, and to ensure that the applicant pool is going to thrive at Bates. The requirements for admissions are often discussed in terms of what is expected of the applicant, but what is most inspiring about the Bates admissions team is that they take it upon themselves to remain connected with the students they admit even after the acceptance letters are mailed.

ACADEMIC LIFE

> **❝** *During a visit to Bates after graduation, I went out to lunch with a former professor and current mentor and after talking about everything from the existential questions posed in the show* Lost *to my plans for next year, she asked, 'What was the greatest thing you learned during your time at Bates?' I replied, 'I learned how to think, question, and grow.'* **❞**

There is a theory that small liberal arts colleges like Bates do not teach you how to do any one thing, but rather prepare you for everything. While some graduate college with a single degree, Bates students graduate with a malleable skill set that can be applied to more than a dozen careers and top-tier graduate programs. When the curriculum, staff, and faculty are committed to teaching students how to think critically and how to analyze what is in front of them, students graduate prepared to meet life's challenges with confidence and grace. What can you do with a degree in Philosophy? Anything. What can you do with a degree in English? Anything.

One of Bates' greatest academic strengths is that Bates students are not competitive with one another. Bates students are some of the most talented and capable students in the United States, but they are also cooperative and relaxed. Classrooms at Bates are not contest grounds for intellectual one-upmanship. Instead, students literally feel that they can learn from everyone at every moment.

Faculty

There are few, if any, barriers at Bates. Students talk and learn from one another, and this spirit of shared learning and open dialog is one that also extends to the relationship between students and faculty. Faculty members do not lecture at an untouchable distance. Classrooms are intimate and a faculty member, never a teaching assistant, always leads classes. Most professors emphasize classroom participation. Students learn by talking their ideas out so students tend to evolve into confident public speakers. At Bates, the professor and student become well acquainted with one another over the course of a semester.

Students are always encouraged to visit professors during office hours, and while it is a good time to work out questions on readings, these meetings are also an opportunity to just chat about life. Because of the character of the student/teacher relationships, Batesies do not have to strain to find a professor capable of, or willing to, write a compelling recommendation. Evidence of the strong bond between students and faculty is the amount of alumni who keep in touch with faculty and stop by Pettengill Hall to visit teachers when on campus.

While most faculty members are constantly involved in researching and publishing, their first priority is the student and teaching. Bates faculty members genuinely care about the well-being of the student body and that manifests itself in and out of the classroom. To bridge the gap between research and teaching, professors invite students to assist in their research. Research assistant opportunities are typically uncommon at the undergraduate level, but at Bates, faculty members use them as opportunities to better prepare students for graduate studies.

Harward Center for Community Partnerships

Bates is not isolated from the community. It is a part of Lewiston-Auburn, and Lewiston-Auburn is a part of Bates. One of the ways that Bates remains connected with the community is through the Harward Center for Community Partnerships. The Harward Center is comprised of four program areas that focus on teaching students how to live socially responsible lives and behave as democratic citizens. Further, many professors use the Harward Center to integrate community involvement into their syllabus. The Harward Center is an excellent way for students and community members to volunteer and develop as civic leaders. For example, students are currently working on a mentoring and tutoring project with the Longley School in Lewiston.

Courses/General Education Requirements

Bates is committed to helping students claim their education, and therefore, Bates gives its students a lot of academic freedom. Students can choose among 32 majors, through 20 departments and 8 interdisciplinary programs, and they have the option to design their own interdisciplinary major with the help of an academic advisor.

However, the school does require that students design a curriculum that incorporates sciences, humanities, social sciences, mathematics, and the arts. In order to fulfill these requirements, students enroll in two General Education Concentrations (GECs) from outside their major. GECs are four linked courses that allow a student to focus on one topic or area of inquiry. Courses may come from different disciplines, or they may focus on a topic in a single department, program, or major. The goal of the GECs and the entire Bates course curriculum is to teach students about the connections between disciplines, reinforce strong writing skills, and provide students with college-level instruction in the sciences and quantitative analysis.

There are several ways to talk about and assess the academic life at a college. But if one really wants to tap into the academic climate, one has to look beyond a course list because the admissions materials cannot illustrate how Bates students listen to each other and talk about learning in the classroom, dining hall, and dorms.

Short Term

The 4-4-1 academic calendar allows students to step outside of their scholastic routine during the spring and to focus on just one class for five weeks. While some classes do meet in the classroom, many are experiential and allow the student to physically connect with what they are researching. Students learn about geology in Maine by hiking and kayaking. Students learn about anthropology and Jamaica by spending five weeks researching on the island. Students learn about theater in Europe by flying overseas. Known as "short term," this abbreviated semester is wildly popular at Bates because it allows students to thaw after a long winter. The reduction in course load decreases stress and makes even the most challenging class manageable. Two short terms are required, but most students participate in at least three.

Study Abroad

The Bates academic curriculum is designed to challenge students and to push students beyond their comfort zones. Many schools talk about the learning that takes place outside of the classroom, but at Bates the lessons outside the classroom span the entire globe. About seventy percent of the Bates student body studies abroad at some point during their college career and the lessons and knowledge gained through this experience is paramount. Students not only learn about different parts of the world while studying abroad, but they also learn about what they are capable of accomplishing.

> **❝**On December 10th, I caught a last-minute plane ride from Egypt to Jordan. I took a bus to Petra, saw one of the New Seven Wonders of the World, and took a ferry back across the Red Sea. There I caught a bus from the Egyptian Sinai through the desert and back to Cairo. In Cairo I took my finals, wrote a paper, and with a group of friends hired a private taxi to the Israeli border and headed to Jerusalem. By December I was dying to get into my advisor's office and tell him about my new views on Islam. **❞**

— Graham Jones, '09

Thesis

Thesis is the culmination of four years of academic growth and development. Almost every student, regardless of major, completes a senior thesis at Bates. Students work closely with one faculty member for either one semester or one academic year. Professors work hard to push your writing and develop your skills as a researcher and scholar. The caliber of writing usually allows students to use the writing as material for their application to graduate school. And in some cases, students publish segments of their thesis in scholarly journals. When you first come to Bates the thesis process can appear daunting, but by the time you are a senior you can rest assured that the Bates curriculum and faculty will have prepared you.

> **❝**I really appreciate that Bates requires a thesis because it offers me the opportunity to pick a topic that I am passionate about and delve deeply into that subject. It is a chance for me to take control of the educational experience and produce something original. And I know I will be able to look back and be proud of the work that I put into the process. **❞**

—Stephanie Howson, '09

> 66 *Batesies are social. We know how to organize and mobilize to have a good time and unwind on the weekends. Theme parties, impromptu dance parties, movie marathons, and student band performances are just a few examples of how we pass our time. The Bates student activity office organizes dances, concerts, and films on a regular basis. However, if you want to spend a Friday or Saturday night in the library catching up on work, you won't be looked down upon—but don't expect not to be tempted away.* 99

—*Katie Conkling, '09*

Balance is a key component of the Bates experience. Classes require students to devote a good deal of time to their studies, but even with a full course load of four classes, students find the time to enjoy a number of the 128 available extracurricular activities. Students practice with their bands in the new rock room, throw Frisbees on the quad, take day trips to Portland for the First Friday art openings, and organize weekend camping excursions to a nearby lean-to. Sports, clubs, service projects, and time with friends not only help the Bates community come together and share a part of themselves with other students, but they also help Batesies learn more about themselves.

Aesop

Even though the energy at Bates is pretty relaxed, movement characterizes the Bates student body. Activities begin almost immediately after stepping onto the campus and continue for four years. One of the most popular activities on campus is the first-year orientation program, Aesop, which is a manifestation of the college's longtime emphasis on individual initiative and personal responsibility. Students have been the sole organizers of Aesop for years, and students lead virtually all the trips. Trips vary in level of difficulty and range from kayaking to hiking and camping, but the spirit of shared learning is the thread that runs through all of the options. Aesop shows off Maine's beautiful mountains, forests, and ocean. Upperclassmen pass on insights into Bates' life around campfires, and first years can have a chance to take a deep breath before starting school.

> **“** *After my Aesop trip freshman year, I not only made a friend who I would later room with sophomore year, but I also made connections with seniors who helped get me a job at the student-run, on-campus coffee shop, The Ronj.* **”**

—Graham Jones, '09

Social Traditions

Some of the most enjoyable social activities at Bates are the quirky ones. The types of events that happen annually are the settings of epic and memorable stories year after year. Aesop is one of these activities, but it is not the only ongoing event that students and alumni remember fondly. Some of the other prime Bates events are puddle jump, Gala, a Mount David hike, a (legal) beer at the Goose, ocean clambakes, and Trivia Night. Even if swimming in freezing water or staying up all night to compete in the radio station's trivia bonanza are not what you consider fun, nearly everyone at Bates agrees that the President's Gala is one of the annual highlights. Whether you go to dance the night away in formal wear, chitchat with faculty, or just see how many chocolate-covered strawberries you can eat, the Gala is one of the most momentous events at Bates.

Sports/Clubs

Nearly seventy-five percent of the student body participates in either one of the thirty-one intercollegiate sports available to men and women or the sixteen intramural sports available to men and women. Students play on varsity sports as well as on intramural teams, and regardless of the season, it is common to see some Batesies doing something active.

> **“** *Strange things are always happening on Frye Street. This fall students built a half pipe for skateboarding and when it first snowed, they turned it into a ramp for skiing down Mount David.* **”**

—Graham Jones, '09

It is no big deal if you do not prefer traditional sports because there are plenty of organizations and activities that will promise to exercise your mind and body. The debate team is world renowned. Successfully competing in both the Ivy League circuit and in international competitions, the Bates debate team is one of the more exciting teams to watch. More importantly, if you want to do more than just watch, lack of experience is not going to come between you and the team. Due in large part to the college's commitment to egalitarianism, all clubs and organizations are open to everyone.

The absence of exclusive clubs and student organizations characterizes the entire college. No one will ever be turned away from an organization and no one will be turned away from a social event at Bates. Divisive issues such as alcohol tend not to isolate non-drinkers from drinkers because all Bates events serving alcohol are required to provide non-alcoholic options.

Bates is a place that facilitates choice. If varsity athletics are not your thing, you have intramural. If house parties with kegs are not your cup of tea, the Discordians, the chemical-free organization on campus, host events on a weekly basis. The choice is yours, and none of your social choices are binding. A far more difficult choice is deciding between breakfast at the Pop Shoppe in Lewiston or Nezinscot Farm in Turner.

FINANCIAL AID

The Bates tuition is by no means a small amount of money, but Bates does make a concerted effort to offer competitive financial aid packages to assist qualifying families with the cost of tuition. In addition to the financial aid packages, the financial aid office can provide information on student loan programs and available student employment opportunities on campus.

While the school follows federal guidelines for distributing financial aid, it approaches the matter by thinking about the individual. Every member of the admissions staff is knowledgeable about the financial aid policies and can concisely translate information that is otherwise confusing. The financial aid office and the admissions office attend to the matter of financial aid carefully, and it is common to see admissions personnel sending reminder e-mails to applicants regarding financial aid deadlines to ensure that students are not disqualified from the process.

Approximately forty percent of all Bates students receive some form of financial aid, and many students hold jobs on campus. On-campus jobs range from working in the library to working as a junior adviser. Pay varies, but wages are sufficient to cover weekly and incidental expenses of student life. In addition to putting some money in your pocket, campus jobs also provide students with skills for the working world outside of Bates. Whether that is learning how to manage a business through your work at the Ronj or how to research in a lab through your work as a research assistant for a professor, jobs at Bates give a student more than just expendable income, and none of the jobs encroach on the time one needs to devote to studies.

At first glance, the tuition at Bates can appear prohibitive, but there are several avenues for funding your education here. And as daunting as the process is, it is important to remember that the Bates tuition is not just securing you a four-year education. Rather, it is a lifelong investment. It is one that connects you with a network of successful alumni, gives you a skill set that will lead to your success, and provides you with experiences that you will never forget.

GRADUATES

You graduate from Bates College not only with a diploma and a leading education, but also with a place in a family. The network of Bates alumni is strong and the friendly spirit and "need any help with that" attitude that defines the campus atmosphere carries on after graduation. Alumni regularly come to campus to speak about career paths and employment opportunities. Bates alumni are willing to help in any way that they can, both on and off campus.

> ❝ *You always hear stories about how helpful Bates' alumni networks can be when searching the job market, [and] I decided to roll my dice and see what an e-mail, some sharp writing, and a Bates plug could do for me. Sure enough, upon writing one e-mail I get a response that says (to paraphrase) 'You're a Bates kid? Come in on Friday at 8 A.M.!'* ❞

—*Graham Jones, '09*

Batesies stick together and offer each other a support network both in college and afterward. Alumni in Boston, New York, and D.C. not only meet up after work for the occasional drink or kickball game, but also live together. Many schools fall back on the college maxim that the friends you make in college last a lifetime. But when you graduate from Bates, you also tend to make friends with Batesies who graduated before and after you. Despite age gaps, most Batesies have shared experiences like the climb up Mount David to watch the sunrise the day of graduation or the Senior Faculty Dinner.

SUMMING UP

When applying to college it is important to ask yourself what you want from your college experience. If you prefer intimate classes where you get a chance to learn by doing, then Bates could be for you. If you enjoy quirky and well-rounded people and small social gatherings, and do not mind silence after 1 A.M., then Bates could be for you. If you want to experience a New England fall, winter, and spring, but you also want the option to trek across Argentina or travel in Africa, then Bates could be for you.

There is no doubt that the college admissions process can appear daunting. There are an endless series of questions, and at times it can seem like there are no clear answers. But perhaps the best way to decide if Bates is a good fit is to come spend a day and a night on campus. Come see what a seminar on the philosophy of law is like. Experience what it is like to see a classroom of motivated students sit around a table and talk about what law means. Taste the savory goodness of the brick oven pizza or the fresh and nourishing offerings at the vegan bar in the dining hall. Get cozy with a book on the third floor of the library. Or just come lounge on the Quad in the fall. If you cannot make it out to Bates, then stream shows from the Bates radio station online, check out YouTube, and read the Bates blogs.

It is impossible to promise that Bates is right for everyone, but Batesies are definitely welcoming to everyone. Students are willing to answer any questions, and professors are usually happy to let a visiting student sit in on a class. Even when you are a visitor, Bates will make you feel like you are a part of the family. That is not just a small liberal arts college thing. That is a Bates thing.

❏ *Jordan Williams, B.A.*

PROMINENT GRADS

- ○ Benjamin Mays '20, Spiritual Mentor to Martin Luther King, Jr.
- ○ Edmund Muskie '36, U.S. Senator, Secretary of State, Author of Clean Air and Clean Water acts
- ○ Bryant Gumbel, '70, Television News Personality
- ○ Valerie Smith, '75, Princeton Professor of Literature
- ○ Stacey Kabat, '85, Documentary Filmmaker

Photo by Gary Gilbert

Boston College
Chestnut Hill, MA 02467

(617) 552-3100 / (800) 360-2522
Fax: 617-552-0798

Website: *www.bc.edu/admission*

 Enrollment

Full-time ❏ women: 4,761
❏ men: 4,410

INTRODUCING BOSTON COLLEGE

Boston College's distinctive approach to undergraduate education can be best understood through the motto of the University: "Ever to Excel." For more than 145 years, Boston College has maintained a commitment to excellence through the experiences and opportunities it offers its students both inside and outside the classroom. "Men and Women in Service for Others" has long been a phrase used to describe the focus of a Jesuit education, and the influence of the Jesuit focus is evident in all aspects of the university. Academically, in addition to maintaining the highest standards for its faculty and its students, Boston College's curriculum is focused on helping its students develop a consciousness of their identities and their responsibilities in today's society. Socially, Boston College provides a diversity of opportunities for its students to discover their abilities and their calling, including dozens of clubs and organizations representing artistic, athletic, cultural, ethnic, religious, and political interests; professional internships; volunteer programs; international study; and leadership opportunities.

Boston College draws inspiration for its academic and societal mission from its distinctive religious tradition. As a Catholic and Jesuit university, it is rooted in a worldview that encounters God in all creation and through all human activity, especially in the search for truth in every discipline, in the desire to learn, and in the call to live justly together. In this spirit, Boston College regards the contribution of different religious traditions and value systems as essential to the fullness of its intellectual life and to the continuous development of its distinctive intellectual heritage. While highlighting its Jesuit and Catholic traditions and principles, Boston College recognizes the importance of a diverse student body, faculty, and staff, and maintains a firm commitment to academic freedom, as the university encourages a communal effort toward the pursuit of its mission.

Location

Boston College's main campus is located on the border between the cities of Boston and Newton, six miles from downtown Boston, in a village known as Chestnut Hill. BC's location is one of its most attractive features. Students enjoy living and studying on a quiet campus featuring green lawns and beautiful English Collegiate Gothic buildings, and at the same time, having easy access to one of America's greatest cities. The Green Line of Boston's mass transit system, "the T," begins at the base of the main campus, and transports travelers to all parts of the city.

In addition to a plethora of opportunities for shopping, sightseeing, nightlife, professional sports, research, volunteering, internships, and employment, Boston is also America's largest college town. Boston College students often become acquainted with students from neighboring universities, including Harvard, M.I.T., Tufts, Boston University, and Northeastern.

Boston College also features a Newton campus, located approximately one-and-a-half miles west of the Chestnut Hill campus, which is the home of Boston College Law School, and also the home to more than 800 students in the freshman class. Shuttle buses travel between the two campuses, providing convenient access between them. Although undergraduate classes are held on the main campus, freshmen living on the Newton campus enjoy the unique "freshman-only" community that the separate location affords them. And, in 2004, Boston College acquired 43 acres of land in Brighton, adjacent to its main campus. Ambitious plans for academic and cocurricular facilities on the new campus are underway.

Size

In the fall of a recent year, approximately 9,100 undergraduate students enrolled at Boston College. However, the number studying on campus is somewhat smaller because many students choose to spend a semester studying abroad. Boston College is best classified as a "medium-size" university. Although the student body is much larger than any student would have experienced in high school, the overall population is much smaller than that of most of America's leading universities. In addition, the large number of full-time faculty at Boston College allows class sizes to be kept small; the student-faculty ratio is 13:1.

ADMISSIONS REQUIREMENTS

Boston College features four undergraduate colleges: the College of Arts and Sciences, the Carroll School of Management, the Lynch School of Education, and the Connell School of Nursing. Although applicants do not have to declare a major when they apply, they must designate the school to which they are applying.

Applicants typically have pursued challenging academic goals in high school; most have taken Advanced Placement classes, participated in numerous cocurricular and extracurricular activities, and have scored well on the SAT or ACT exams. Even among these students, Boston College is very selective. For the undergraduate class entering recently, approximately 30,000 students applied for 2,250 places.

While specific courses in high school are not required, students are recommended to pursue a strong college preparatory program, which should include four years of English, mathematics, foreign language, laboratory science, and social studies. Students applying to the School of Nursing are *required* to complete at least two years of laboratory science, including one year of chemistry.

There are two standardized testing options. Students may either take the SAT with writing test and two SAT Subject Tests; or, they may take the American College Test (ACT) with writing. Applicants must take all standardized tests by the December test date of their senior year of high school, and each applicant must have his or her test scores sent directly to Boston

College. These scores must be received by December 15. For the class admitted to Boston College in a recent fall semester, the majority of applicants scored between 1880–2150 (out of 2400) on the SAT, and/or between 28–33 on the ACT.

As mentioned before, the Boston College community reflects a diversity of talents, attitudes, backgrounds, and interests. Although diversity is sought in these areas, one common characteristic sought among applicants is a demonstrated interest in the Jesuit ideals of commitment and service to others. The Committee on Admission looks for applicants to demonstrate not only their academic abilities, but also their intellectual curiosity, strength of character, motivation, creativity, and devotion toward personal growth and development.

Freshman Applicants

To apply to Boston College, students must complete both the Common Application and the Boston College Supplemental Application. For students seeking to begin their academic career at BC in the fall semester, there are two admission options: a nonbinding Restrictive Early Action Program, and the Regular Decision Program.

Freshman applicants with superior credentials who view Boston College as a first choice should consider Restrictive Early Action. Students electing to use this option may not apply to an Early Decision program at another college. However, they are free to apply to other nonbonding Early Action programs. All application material must be sent or postmarked by November 1. Early Action candidates will be notified of their admission decisions before December 25.

All application materials for Regular Decision must be sent or postmarked by January 1. Candidates will be notified of admission decisions at the end of March.

Candidates wishing to apply for freshman entry in the spring semester must complete their applications by November 1.

Transfer Applicants

Boston College accepts transfer applicants each semester. Transfer candidates must also complete both the Common Application and the Boston College Supplemental Application. Students wishing to transfer into BC beginning in the spring semester must submit their application forms and the $70 fee by November 1; and those students seeking to transfer into BC beginning in the fall semester must hand in the forms and fee by March 15. In addition to high school records and standardized test scores, transfer applicants must furnish transcripts from all postsecondary institutions they have attended.

The Core Curriculum

Perhaps the most distinguishing feature of a Jesuit undergraduate education is the core curriculum, a tradition that Boston College has embraced since the school's founding in 1863.

Although the university has undergone many changes since that time, questions that have traditionally stood at the center of intellectual debate have remained salient. Many focus on issues such as the origin and destiny of existence, the principles of the physical world, the characteristics of human nature, the state of our society, and our attitudes toward the past. Because of the relevance of these questions to all academic pursuits, Boston College has retained its integrated core curriculum, allowing students to examine these questions during their years at the university.

Because each academic discipline examines these questions from a unique perspective, the core requirements are dispersed among the university's many departments. All students are required to take a full year of theology, philosophy, natural science, social science, and modern European history. In addition, one semester of study is required in fine arts, cultural diversity, English literature, English composition, and mathematics. The College of Arts and Sciences and the Carroll School of Management also require each student to demonstrate proficiency in a foreign or classical language. As students proceed through the core, the above-mentioned questions are addressed in depth, challenging undergraduates to formulate and reformulate their positions on the questions and issues that shape their lives.

> **❝** *I had never taken classes in philosophy or theology before, and wasn't sure how they would complement what it was that I thought I wanted to do. But looking back, I find that my interests (academically, professionally, and otherwise) have changed a great deal since I was a freshman in college. Had I filled my schedule with classes to prepare me for the career I sought when I was eighteen, I would have been quite disappointed when my path eventually changed course. But through the classes I took for the core, I was exposed to ideas that complemented all of the other classes I took in college, and in my grad school and law school coursework as well.* **❞**

Faculty

One of Boston College's greatest assets is the quality of its faculty. Although BC prides itself on its research accomplishments, the professors, lecturers and instructors at Boston College possess a common characteristic: all are devoted to the importance of their primary responsibility—teaching undergraduates. Unlike other research universities, at which many of the lower-division classes are taught by teaching assistants or part-time faculty, the bulk of the classes required in Boston College's core curriculum are taught by full professors who are distinguished in their fields.

> 66 *Although BC boasts a beautiful campus and first-rate facilities, in my opinion, the school's greatest asset is its faculty. You can tell that the reason they are at BC is because they want to teach undergraduates. My sophomore year, I had a history professor who had a reputation as a very tough grader. After receiving a grade on a paper that was lower than I expected, I went to his office to ask him for advice. I didn't expect the meeting to last more than five minutes. He invited me into his office, and after discussing the paper for a minute or two, he began to ask me questions about my academic interests and the career path I was considering. At the time, I wasn't sure, and I told him so. His response was brilliant. He said, 'Well, that's the reason you're here! One of the purposes of a liberal arts education is 'to liberate' you from the restrictions placed on your ability to learn about the world once you leave school and focus on a career. Use your time here to explore all that you can—you may not have many chances like this ever again.' I took his advice, and outside of my major, I took classes on Shakespeare, American architecture, Beethoven, World War II, and other areas in which I had a curiosity. That professor and I became close friends, and are still in touch today. Not only did I get an A in his class, the advice he gave me about how to approach my college career was among the best I had ever received.* 99

In lower-division "survey" classes in the history, natural science, and social science departments, classes are taught by full professors in a lecture hall setting two days a week, and are then broken up into smaller discussion groups on a third day. This format allows for general information to be communicated *en masse*, but also gives students and faculty a weekly opportunity to discuss what has been presented and to relate the material to more specific topics. In departments such as theology, philosophy, English, foreign languages, mathematics, and fine arts, classes are kept small to maximize the student's ability to comprehend and discuss the subject matter with other students and faculty members alike.

As students move from the core requirements to their upper-division electives, they find that the class sizes become even smaller. Each department offers seminar classes in which a professor and small groups of students examine specific academic issues in detail; the departments also allow students to earn class credit for "Readings and Research" in a one-on-one project with a faculty member. A popular cocurricular employment opportunity offered by all four schools is the Undergraduate Faculty Research Fellowships, in which students can earn money as they assist faculty members with their research. Faculty are also instrumental in helping students to win prestigious fellowships and other awards.

Course evaluations and surveys of graduating seniors demonstrate that Boston College students are quite satisfied with their professors; many have indicated that the student-faculty relationship at BC often transcends the classroom experience, as professors and students develop friendships that last well beyond the student's graduation.

Academic Resources

Boston College students have access to a multitude of resources to assist them in their academic pursuits. The university's network of libraries features the Thomas P. O'Neill, Jr. research library, along with eight other libraries featuring art collections, rare books, and professional resources for education, social work, theology, and law. These facilities also provide students with access to the Web and other on-line databases and applications, private small-group study rooms, and audiovisual equipment. Boston College's Academic Development Center, located in the O'Neill Library, provides free tutoring to students in all subjects, along with specialized services for students with learning disabilities.

Boston College's Student Affairs division includes several offices that serve students seeking academic support. Included among these is the Learning Resources for Student Athletes office, and the Learning to Learn program, which helps students improve their critical thinking and develop learning skills necessary to succeed in college.

The university has refurbished many buildings on campus to accommodate state-of-the-art classrooms, laboratories, computer facilities, and meeting rooms providing every Boston College student with a learning environment that complements the subject matter being taught. International study provides students an opportunity to integrate their majors with coursework abroad, giving undergraduates a global perspective on their fields. Similarly, service learning allows students to apply their enthusiasm for creating a more just world to their classroom work.

In addition, BC recently was named among the nation's "most wired" campuses by *PC Magazine*, for providing its student body and its faculty with access to the latest innovations in communication technology.

SOCIAL LIFE AND ACTIVITIES

Student Groups

While Boston College students share much in common when it comes to dedication to academics and service, the diversity of the student body is most recognizable in the multitude of student clubs, musical groups, and organizations on campus. Not only is there diversity in the types of organizations, which include groups devoted to athletics, music, culture and ethnicity, religion, politics, dance, literature, charities, social action, and community service, but diversity is also found among the groups within each genre. For example, for musical ensembles, there are *a cappella* groups, jazz bands, gospel choirs and liturgical music groups, a symphony orchestra, a marching band, and the university chorale.

Athletics

No BC student can deny that varsity athletics—especially football, basketball, and hockey—have a profound effect on the culture of the university. Freshmen find this to be the case when they experience the first home football game on a Saturday afternoon in September. The campus erupts in maroon and gold, the marching band can be heard from the early hours of the morning, and students, alumni, and fans from New England and around the country arrive to cheer on the Eagles.

Boston College's athletics programs serve many important functions at the university. For those who play sports, a team participation provides many students with opportunities to display their talents to a national audience, as all of BC's thirty-one varsity teams compete at the NCAA Division I level. For those who do not play on these teams, athletic events draw the campus community together, contributing to a spirit that is quite unique to Boston College. Among many other distinguishing characteristics, the presence of strong, major conference, Division I athletic teams, is yet another feature that allows Boston College to stand out among the other elite Catholic universities in the United States.

Recent success among many of BC's teams also plays a role in the popularity of athletics among Boston College students. In 2010, the Boston College men's ice hockey team won the national championship. The football team and the men's and women's basketball teams have earned national ranking. Since forming the Atlantic Coast Conference, BC has been competitive in all men's and women's sports. But at BC, excellence goes beyond the playing field, for Boston College maintains one of the highest graduation rates of any Division I university in the nation.

Many opportunities to participate in athletics are available for students who do not play varsity sports. Intramural and club leagues are sponsored by the university for more than forty men's, women's, and coeducational sports. The campus also offers a pool, basketball and tennis courts, indoor track, weightlifting facilities, and locker rooms. Free weights are also available in the residence halls on the Chestnut Hill campus and on the Newton campus.

Residence Life

Most students admitted to Boston College are offered three years of on-campus housing. Most live on campus for freshman, sophomore, and senior years, while spending junior year studying abroad or living off campus in a neighboring apartment.

> *Students frequently ask about a student body's 'diversity' when they are looking at schools. I've always found the term hard to define. The friends I made at BC came from all over the country. Some of their parents were business owners, some were teachers, some were in the military, some were farmers, and some were professionals. My friends were Catholic, Eastern Orthodox, Protestant, Mormon, Jewish, Hindu, and nonpracticing. Their ancestors were from North America, South America, Europe, the Middle East, Africa, and Asia. Some friends were more liberal, others more conservative; some politically active, and others not as involved. Today, my friends are doctors, teachers, lawyers, financiers, musicians, nurses, professors, students, college administrators, and computer programmers. This kind of diversity—in backgrounds, interests, beliefs, motivations, and aspirations—can't be appropriately expressed by a statistic. However, while there was no doubt that we were diverse in our differences, the best part of the BC student body was something we all had in common. The 'typical BC student' is bright, well rounded, ambitious, and concerned, and spending four years with people with these kinds of common characteristics was what made BC a great place to learn and grow over the course of my college career.* **"**

There are many on-campus housing options at Boston College. Most freshmen live in traditional dormitories with one or two roommates in a single bedroom. These residence halls are located on the Newton campus and on Chestnut Hill campus. Most sophomores live in four-, six-, or eight-person suites, featuring two, three, or four two-person bedrooms, a common living room, and a kitchenette. Most seniors live in four- or six-person apartments, which have two or three bedrooms and a full kitchen.

There are no fraternities or sororities at Boston College. The freshman residence halls on the Newton and Chestnut Hill campuses are arranged so that students not only feel as though they are part of a community in their dormitory, but also in their class.

FINANCIAL AID

BC is committed to admitting its students solely on the basis of their academic and personal accomplishments, and without regard to financial need. The exception is the Presidential Scholars Program, which offers full-tuition four-year scholarships to fifteen incoming freshmen, need.

To demonstrate need, students and families must fill out the Free Application for Federal Student Aid (FAFSA) and the Profile form, published by the College Scholarship Service. Boston College also asks parents and students to provide the university with copies of their tax returns and W-2 forms. Because of the limited amount of financial aid available, it is important for parents and students to follow the instructions carefully, and to provide the University with the information requested by the specified deadlines.

The Office of Student Services is providing students with quick and convenient access to answers for all of their financial and academic questions. Each student is assigned a counselor who works in the office, all of whom are available to discuss specific cases with parents and students. Although the application process is structured and formal, the financial services counselors at BC take a personal approach to help students and families afford their education at Boston College.

GRADUATES

Boston College's endowment now stands at $1.49 billion. Much of its growth can be attributed to the donations of many successful graduates who have given back to the school that gave so much to them.

The successes of Boston College alumni are beneficial, not only for the university, but also for current students looking for jobs and internships in the "real world." A common characteristic among BC graduates is a strong sense of loyalty to their alma mater. This loyalty is often expressed through the willingness of BC graduates to help current students, especially through job networking and career counseling.

Boston College places a great deal of emphasis on service to others. For Boston College graduates, the theme of service is reflected in the career paths chosen by its graduates. In business, education, research, nursing, social work, politics, law, entertainment, or community service, Boston College graduates are leaders in their fields.

SUMMING UP

Boston College stands out among its peers in American academe because of a distinctive approach to higher education. While upholding the standards of excellence that are expected of the nation's finest colleges and universities, Boston College's mission articulates another set of expectations for its faculty, staff, and students.

The personal development of every member of the BC community is the primary result. Because of this belief, Boston College emphasizes its dedication to the philosophy of *cura personalis*, or "care for the whole person." This dedication is recognized through the university's commitment to employing a distinguished learned faculty devoted to teaching undergraduates; through the resources it makes available for education outside the classroom; through the academic, social, and recreational resources and facilities it makes available to all members of its community; and through the holistic perspective it offers from its broad-based, spiritually focused, liberal arts curriculum.

Dedication to these goals, combined with the University's commitment to excellence in all aspects of its operation, has given Boston College recognition, not only as one of the nation's leading Catholic universities, but as one of America's finest providers of an undergraduate education.

❏ *Matthew J. Kita, A.B.*

Photo by Dean Abramson

 Bowdoin College
Brunswick, ME 04011

 (207) 725-3100
Fax: (207) 725-3101

 E-mail: *admissions@bowdoin.edu*
Website: *http://www.bowdoin.edu*

 Enrollment

Full-time ❏ women: 886
❏ men: 869

Part-time ❏ women: 6
❏ men: 1

INTRODUCING BOWDOIN

Bowdoin enjoys a reputation for academic prestige and rigor, but what truly distinguishes this small liberal arts college is its location in Maine. Just twenty-five miles up the coast from the comfortable city of Portland, Bowdoin's idyllic campus provides unique opportunities for an independent-minded student body. For more than 200 years, Bowdoin's world-class resources and tight-knit community have balanced tradition and innovation, a combination that continues to shape principled world leaders in every field.

Bowdoin is in the heart of Brunswick, a small town at the hub of several ocean peninsulas where retirees, fishermen, and pilots from the nearby naval air station make for an interesting milieu. Students and locals alike can take pride and enjoyment in the college's well-respected museums, frequent guest speakers, and outstanding hockey team. Bowdoin's dining service, recognized as one of the best in the country, puts on annual lobster bakes. Juniors and seniors can find great seaside cottages off campus, or choose from among a wide variety of housing options, which include dormitories with quads and singles, a sixteen-story tower of single-rooms, and college-owned houses and apartments. "The completely renovated bricks" are the six mid-campus dorms that house all first-years and foster tremendous class unity. Fraternities were abolished in 2000, and Bowdoin has now acquired all of the houses; today these houses have been renovated, and make up the College House system, a unique social and residential opportunity.

Thanks to ambitious fund-raising in the nineties, there are also handsome new dining, library, and Outing Club facilities. President Barry Mills, himself a Bowdoin graduate, arrived in 2001 and has worked to expand and diversify the student body. In recent years, as at many other colleges, the activist spirit ebbed; now, with political turbulence at home and abroad, Bowdoin is reemerging as a place of intense political discourse.

In addition to the 205-acre campus—known for its beauty—the college owns 120 acres of forest, fields, and wetlands along the shore of the Atlantic just eight miles from campus. This site, on picturesque Orr's Island (a short bridge connects the mainland) features Bowdoin's Coastal Studies Center, for research in ecology, geology, ornithology, and marine biology.

Bowdoin prides itself on its excellent faculty and its cutting-edge information and technology resources. There is plenty here to guide a motivated student in his or her explorations. Likewise, this is a place of many extracurricular passions. Sports are a popular part of college life here, but so are the Outing Club, the campus radio station, and a variety of volunteer programs, available through the new McKeen Center for the Common Good.

Nevertheless, this is primarily a venue for intense academic rigor (though the cutthroat mentality is virtually unheard of here). Although Bowdoin students do play hard, the spirit of the college—evident in the admissions criteria, academic program, and alumni achievements—is independent thinking. Bowdoin students are encouraged to choose their own paths, and that freedom of choice generates true intellectual growth.

ADMISSIONS REQUIREMENTS

Gaining admission to Bowdoin gets harder each year. In 2010, Bowdoin accepted 1,183 of 6,018 applicants. That's less than twenty percent. Of those accepted, 510 matriculated—a full forty-eight of them high school valedictorians. Since 1969 Bowdoin has made it optional to submit one's SAT scores, although most accepted students do, and the average score of that group is pretty high.

Bowdoin's admissions committee reviews grades, a personal essay, awards and honors, extracurricular activities and accomplishments, and teacher recommendations. Of special interest to the committee is a demonstrated willingness to seek out intellectual challenges in Advanced Placement and Honors courses. Interviews, while not required, are strongly encouraged, and can be arranged during a campus visit or in one's hometown with an alumni interviewer. If supplementary materials such as musical tapes or works of art help to flesh out one's basic application, then the committee encourages the applicant to submit these.

MATRICULATION BOOK

During the first week on campus, every new Bowdoin student signs the Matriculation Book. The book itself is laid out in the president's office on the desk of Henry Wadsworth Longfellow (class of 1825). Each new student meets the president before signing his or her own name. There is also a little bit of time to peruse past volumes, which are arrayed around the room, opened to the signatures of Hawthorne (1825) and former Secretary of Defense William Cohen (1962), themselves once fresh-faced and eager new students.

The entire admitted class begins in the fall, and generally includes only a very small handful of students who have transferred from other institutions. Some will have spent a day and night on campus the year before in order to sample the classes, the social scene, and the famously good food. Many will be international students, actively recruited by the college.

Early Decision

In addition to the Regular Decision program, there are two Early Decision programs at Bowdoin. The first requires that application materials be postmarked by November 15, and an applicant will receive notification a month later in mid-December. The second program has the same deadline as Regular Decision (January 1), but those applying under this program receive notification by mid-February. Both Early Decision programs are binding, and ask for one's signature to ensure that one enrolls at Bowdoin if admitted.

"To carry the keys of the world's library in your pocket, and feel its resources behind you in whatever task you undertake" is part of *The Offer of the College*, a sort of proto-Mission Statement, ubiquitous within the community ever since a former Bowdoin president penned it a century ago. Bowdoin remains true to this liberal arts ethos, with an academic program designed to broaden the range of the intellect rather than stuff it with facts.

Of the total, students must take one course on mathematical, computational, or statistical reasoning; one course on inquiry in the natural sciences; one course on "exploring social differences;" one course on "international perspectives;" and one course in the visual and performing arts. Courses are designed to help students hone their written and analytical skills, deepen their aesthetic judgments, use varied forms of informational resources, and create multifaceted solutions to complex problems.

ADMIRAL PEARY

Admiral Robert E. Peary made explorations of the Arctic, and found the North Pole in 1909. He and his assistant, Admiral Donald B. MacMillan, were Bowdoin graduates, (class of 1877 and 1898, respectively). Hence, the school mascot is the Polar Bear. The campus is home to the Peary-MacMillan Arctic Museum. Perhaps these reasons, plus Bowdoin's northern location, explain why Arctic Studies is stronger here. Students have approached that field from angles of environmental science, geology, and anthropology.

In addition, students are required to take one first-year seminar by the end of their second semester. These seminars provide an opportunity for students to take a small, seminar-style class about a topic of interest that is also directed toward building students' writing, critical reading, research, and analytic skills. The courses range widely; a few examples include: *Mass Media in American Politics; Seekers' Lives; Dreaming in the Middle Ages; Non-Violence, Nukes and Nationalism.*

Students are allowed to direct their own studies, taking classes in many different fields outside their major. Pursuing two majors is not all uncommon. Requirements for the major vary, but eight to ten courses is a rough standard.

Of the forty-two majors and forty-one minors available at Bowdoin, the most statistically popular are government, economics, and biology. Most students would agree that the film students, artists, and economics majors are discernable groups, and that there are some beloved professors in the Africana Studies and religion departments. Recent changes in the academic structure include the creation of two new programs: Latin American Studies and Gay and Lesbian Studies. New interdisciplinary majors have sprung up

(English and Theater is just one), and for a small college in Maine, there are particularly strong departments of Asian studies, neuroscience, and computer science (some interesting work with robots and artificial intelligence here has caught international attention).

Several years ago, the campus theater underwent renovation and is now a vibrant center for theater and dance on campus as well as a big draw for the Brunswick community. In 2007, the college's landmark Walker Arts Building reopened after a two-year, $20 million renovation. The building is the home of the Bowdoin Museum of Art, a teaching museum with a collection of more than 14,000 objects. It is one of the oldest collegiate art collections in the United States with works from the ancient world to the present. Also in 2007, Bowdoin opened a new 290-seat state-of-the-art recital hall. And in the 1990s a donation by Stanley Druckenmiller (class of 1975) made possible a new, state-of-the-art science building that is successful both as a research center and as an architectural triumph.

> **❝**I used the pass/fail option only once, in my first semester, because I wanted to try some unfamiliar subjects before I got too serious. I did have a friend who used it junior year, in a fifth class he took by special arrangement with the dean. This meant that in the spring of our senior year he had to take only three classes, which allowed him to spend the extra free time making trips up to ski at Sunday River, which was about ninety minutes away. I had an AP credit, so I also had just three classes; I joined my friend a few times, but mostly used that extra time working on finishing my honors project. **❞**

Along with introductory-level courses (average size of 30), freshmen (known as "first years" at Bowdoin) may end up taking the regular course offerings that are the bread-and-butter of upperclassmen. These classes have an average size of sixteen. Toward the end of the Bowdoin experience, most students are back in senior seminars—the small, upper-level classes designed primarily for majors. Students are permitted to take up to four classes on a "credit/fail" basis, which allows for a greater opportunity for pressure-free academic exploration.

Independent Study and Honors Projects

Independent study is very popular at Bowdoin, chiefly owing to the motivation of the students and accessibility of the professors. Such projects allow the student (typically a junior or senior, but not always) to choose a topic, set specific goals and schedules, and work closely with a professor. An independent study usually replaces one of the four classes the student would normally take, and works like a class credit toward graduation and, if applicable, the major.

Many projects begin as an extension of work that a student and professor explored earlier—or had to pass up—in a traditional classroom course. Sometimes students with similar interests will band together, find a professor, and use the independent study model to create what is for all intents and purposes a private class. Popular professors have been known to direct three or four projects in one semester, in addition to their classroom duties.

Some independent studies evolve into Honors Projects. This last feature of the curriculum, however, is much more involved than an independent study; a typical Honors Project spans two semesters, involves periodic oral defenses before the academic department, and may culminate in the publication of scientific data or a hundred-page paper. An Honors Project is always a solitary endeavor, and each department at Bowdoin encourages only the most motivated (i.e., graduate school-oriented) students to pursue such a project.

Independent studies and Honors Projects are among the most attractive features of Bowdoin College. It is rare, even at the highest academic levels, for students to enjoy such unfettered access to world-class faculty. Such close-quarter interaction is why intellectuals are drawn to small, elite colleges such as Bowdoin, and it is why they leave equipped with superior critical-thinking skills and broad knowledge of cultural, historical, and scientific fields.

Off-campus Study

Many Bowdoin students (about fifty-five percent) study off campus, usually abroad, for a semester or two of their junior year. Bowdoin sponsors a well-respected program known as the Intercollegiate Sri Lanka Education. Students participate in more than one hundred additional approved study-abroad programs.

Students less exotically inclined may also choose to study for a year at one of the schools in the Twelve College Exchange: Amherst, Connecticut, Dartmouth, Mount Holyoke, Smith, Trinity, Vassar, Wellesley, Wesleyan, Wheaton, and Williams.

Other possibilities, for students who want both a large university's resources as well as the liberal arts milieu, are the 3-2 engineering degree programs with Columbia, Dartmouth, The University of Maine, the California Institute of Technology or the 3-2 law program with Columbia.

Writing at Bowdoin

Naturally there is plenty of ambient literary energy at the school that produced Hawthorne and Longfellow, as well as hip, younger writers such as Jason Brown and Willing Davidson.

The Writing Project is a tutoring program in which students recognized for excellent writing serve as editors for their peers. These students are there to receive first drafts of papers and return them, prior to the due date, with nonjudgmental advice for revision.

The *Bowdoin Orient*, the student newspaper, enjoys the distinction of being the oldest continuously published campus weekly in the country; *The Quill* is a student-run literary magazine; and the *Bowdoin Forum*, initiated in the late nineties, is an annual compilation of essays by students, faculty, alumni, and staff, and its primary focus is an analysis of international events.

In addition to all of these outlets, the English department continues to be recognized as first-rate. Scholars such as Pete Coviello, Ann Kibbie, Anthony Walton, are outstanding in their fields.

SCIENCE BUILDINGS

Alongside a strong literary tradition, Bowdoin is also home to cutting-edge science. In the late nineties, Stanley Druckenmiller ('75) donated tens of millions for the renovation of Bowdoin's science buildings. Among the state-of-the-art research tools available there is a confocal laser-scanning microscope, made available in 2003 through a National Science Foundation grant. Bowdoin professors are leading scientific authorities on robotics and oil-spill cleanups, and places such as Caltech and Harvard Medical School always boast a handful of Bowdoin alums.

SOCIAL LIFE AND ACTIVITIES ▮▮▮▮▮▮▮▮▮▮▮▮

All kinds of off-campus activities are available within a short distance of the campus. Bowdoin is a short walk from downtown Brunswick, where students' favorite stops are two Indian restaurants, a small music store, a tea house, a popular bar called Joshua's, and a small movie theater filled with sofas and featuring indie films. A ten-screen cinema is a few miles from campus.

FAMOUS AUTHORS FROM BOWDOIN

In addition to Hawthorne and Longfellow, another icon of eighteenth-century American literature has roots at Bowdoin. Harriet Beecher Stowe wrote *Uncle Tom's Cabin* here in Brunswick (her husband was a Bowdoin professor). The book, which stirred the North's condemnation of institutional slavery, can be said to have done as much to have precipitated the war as another Bowdoin graduate did to end it; Joshua Chamberlain, class of 1852, accepted the Confederate surrender at Appomattox. Long famous among Civil War buffs as one of the only unambiguous heroes of the conflict, Chamberlain's bayonet defense of Little Round Top was popularly dramatized in *The Killer Angels*. The novel, by Michael Shaara, was the basis of the movie *Gettysburg*, in which Jeff Daniels, playing Chamberlain, gets big cheers around Brunswick when he mentions Bowdoin College.

The Outing Club arranges canoe trips, hiking, skiing, biking, and other outdoor activities. Many incoming students participate in preorientation trips that last three or four days, at which time new students bond with their classmates and enjoy Maine's woods and water.

Upperclass students at Bowdoin are allowed to have a car on campus. Cars are not allowed for first-year students. Those students who do bring cars to Bowdoin frequently find themselves leading trips to Freeport, just fifteen minutes down a country road. There students find a wide array of outlet shops, but the main draw is L.L. Bean, legendary for its gadgets, indoor fish pond, and for operating twenty-four hours—the midnight trip to Bean's is an age-old finals-week tradition.

On campus, the Smith Union is undeniably the hub of campus life. Here are the campus post office and bookstore, a café, and a three-story pub (bring ID). The building itself is an architectural master-piece, with a spacious central lounge filled with couches and sofas. Guest speakers are frequent here, as are musical performers and petition drives. Encircling this lounge is a ramp that takes students past art exhibits, the campus book-store, a game room, and meeting rooms. Smith Union is where Bowdoin feels smallest, and many students go there simply to socialize, since the whole student body seems to cycle through continuously.

Athletics

Bowdoin is passionate about athletics. One of the most striking aspects of the college culture, according to visitors, is how many students participate in intercollegiate and intramural sports. The school's gyms see a lot of daily use too; many men and women jog and lift weights. A new state-of-the art Health, Fitness, and Wellness Center opened in October 2009.

There are thirty varsity intercollegiate sports teams here; thirty-five percent of students participate. There are brand-new squash facilities, a new astroturf field, a boathouse, and indoor and outdoor tracks. Diving, swimming, and water polo teams share a sixteen-lane swimming pool. Cross-country and squash are dominant in their competitions. The ski team is Division I, but the hockey team, which plays in the brand-new Watson Arena, is central to Bowdoin pride. The Colby-Bowdoin matchup is not to be missed.

Club sports like crew and rugby are also popular, and intramural competition (usually dorm vs. dorm) is common on Bowdoin's thirty-five acres of fields. Bowdoin is not a "jock" school, but it's fair to say that there aren't many idle bodies here.

> **"** I lived off campus my senior year, in an old hunting lodge that had been rented to Bowdoin seniors since the seventies. We were on our own island, attached to the mainland by a causeway that flooded and stranded us only once or twice a month. We paid $1,500 a month, among six of us, which was a little bit more than what seniors paid on campus, but which was totally worth it. We got solitude and social autonomy and a great venue for some unforgettable parties. We made sure to pass the lease off to kids we knew so that we could come visit after graduating. **"**

The Social Scene

When Bowdoin phased out the fraternity system in 2000, the change turned the college social scene and housing situation upside down (over a third of the student body had been involved with the system, which was coeducational by the end). The college acquired most of the vacated houses, did extensive renovations, and turned them into the nonexclusive College House System, which provides students with many of the benefits of the old fraternity system, such as leadership opportunities, party venues, self-governed houses, and links with students of all four classes.

Now, from the day students set foot on the campus, they are affiliated with one of the "Social Houses"; each House is paired with one of the first-year dorms. First-years use the house as a gathering place, and have the option to live there over the next three years.

Although parties no longer revolve around fraternities, beer remains a staple of the Bowdoin social landscape, both at the Social Houses and several off-campus residences. Drugs are uncommon at Bowdoin, in comparison to many colleges.

Living on the Water

Aside from the first-year dorms and the College Houses, Bowdoin has a broad spectrum of housing opportunities. Every spring a lottery system, complicated but fair, determines where students will live. Many sophomores end up in apartments in self-selected groups of three and four. Most of the students living in the sixteen-story Coles Tower (there are four suites per floor, with four rooms in each) are juniors. Seniors often live in one of two clusters of condominium-like apartments, located beside the athletic fields, and nestled in the pines.

> ❝ I made a lot of money one summer working on a lobster boat. I was a sternsman (all lobstering vessels have a captain and a sternsman) and I hauled up traps, checked them, and baited them. I woke up according to the tides, and I perpetually reeked of rotten fish bait, but it was an incredible experience; I ate a lot of seafood, got to be around Brunswick through a summer, and made a pile of money. I also got to see the coast of Maine from a native's perspective; this is something that you sometimes miss when you're wrapped up in campus life, which gets pretty insular. ❞

Students also explore off-campus housing opportunities. There are literally hundreds of seaside cottages within twenty minutes of the campus, and many of these are owned by retirees who spend only the summer in Maine. That means relatively low rent and a once-in-a-lifetime opportunity to live on the coast. A handful of coveted leases are handed down perennially between Bowdoin students, but a little searching is generally rewarded.

FINANCIAL AID

The college is committed to making a Bowdoin education available to students regardless of their financial situation. Financial aid at Bowdoin is *need-based*, which is to say that award packages are not dispensed according to academic or athletic merit. These packages include some combination of grants and student employment. In 2008, Bowdoin replaced student loans with grants for all students.

For the class of 2013, for example, forty percent of all Bowdoin first-years received need-based scholarship aid. The average first-year award is $35,470. The average portion that is in the form of a grant is $35,007, and the average work contract is for $1,800.

The amount of financial aid given to each individual student is dependent on the financial situation of the student's family. Need is determined by an evaluation of financial-resource statements that the applicant submits to the Student Aid Office, and decisions are made annually on an individual basis. Financial aid extends to the semesters during which a student recipient studies off campus (in the United States or abroad). Furthermore, the college is able to offer some scholarships for postgraduate study at other institutions.

Some sixty percent of Bowdoin students work in part-time jobs on campus. Clerical work in an academic department, shelving books in the library, and driving the campus shuttle are some examples. There are plentiful off-campus jobs too.

The deadline for financial aid applications is February 15.

GRADUATES

Bowdoin conferred 456 bachelor degrees in 2010. Most students stay on a pretty regular course through the school (eighty-eight percent graduate in four years, and ninety-two percent in six). In one recent class, eighty-nine percent of graduates responding had either enrolled in graduate school or found employment in their field.

So it can safely be said that, in addition to intangible rewards, the Bowdoin degree opens a lot of doors in the academic and professional world; the small class size means that Bowdoin's reputable professors are able to offer warm recommendations for their departing students.

The Career Planning Center

The Career Planning Center offers a wealth of resources for job searches, graduate school applications, and underclassmen seeking summer internships. The staff helps Bowdoin

○ **Franklin Pierce, President of the United States**

○ **Nathaniel Hawthorne, Novelist**

○ **Henry Wadsworth Longfellow, Poet and Linguist**

○ **Major General Oliver Otis Howard, Union Army Officer and Founder and President of Howard University**

○ **Brigadier General Joshua Lawrence Chamberlain, Savior of the Union and Governor of Maine**

○ **Admiral Robert E. Peary, First Man to Reach the North Pole**

○ **Harold Burton, Chief Justice of the U.S. Supreme Court**

○ **Alfred Kinsey, Author of Seminal Works of Sexual Psychology**

○ **William S. Cohen, Secretary of Defense in the Clinton Administration**

○ **George Mitchell, Diplomat and Former Senate Majority Leader**

○ **Joan Benoit Samuelson, Gold Medal Winner in the First Women's Olympic Marathon**

○ **Kenneth Chenault, Chairman and CEO, American Express**

○ **Cynthia McFadden, Co-Host, ABC News Nightline**

○ **Reed Hastings, Founder and CEO, Netflix**

students refine their résumés and interviewing skills. One-on-one interview training with alumni, which might include videotape posture analysis, is also available. The Center indexes research on thousands of internships across the country. Even for students without specific ambitions there are workshops to help make important postgraduate decisions. The CPC publicizes the visits of recruiters and hosts review test-prep courses for the GRE, LSAT, and MCAT. At the Center, alumni offer job counseling, networking, and informational interviews. Even after graduation, alumni can still use the Career Planning Center resources, such as a newsletter with job postings and contacts within the alumni network.

SUMMING UP

Every other Friday at noon, the Bowdoin community convenes to hear a faculty member or guest speaker deliver a talk. The question-and-answer period that follows is often animated and memorable. Recent speakers have included Edward Albee, Doris Kearns Goodwin, George Will, Judy Fortin, Salman Rushdie, Paul Rusesabagina, Robert F. Kennedy, Jr., and Bill Bradley. This "Common Hour" is emblematic of the ideal for which Bowdoin has strived for over two centuries: a place where a variety of people can engage each other directly in intellectual exploration.

Bowdoin College is the perfect choice for young men and women who want more from an education than simply grabbing a credential and moving on. Working much more closely with their professors and peers than most of their Ivy League counterparts get to do, Bowdoin students learn to develop and explore previously untapped academic, cultural, political, and artistic interests that they retain for the rest of their lives. Bowdoin students also can enjoy pinetrees, snowstorms, and quick jaunts to the craggy shoreline, while staying connected to the world at large.

A "first-year" who enters Bowdoin today will find a school with strong traditions such as lobster bakes and hockey. That same student will also find that the abolition of fraternities has left the student body with a unique opportunity to determine the shape of the school's social scene and residential plan.

Students who benefit the most from Bowdoin are those who seek out new challenges and opportunities, who are willing to take risks, and who take pride in achieving their goals. The student community is competitive but the cutthroat careerism of some of the larger schools of this academic caliber is unheard of at Bowdoin. Students at Bowdoin know how to relax, look around, and appreciate the gifts of place and community.

After more than two centuries of shaping the world's leaders in business, diplomacy, education, social activism, medicine, and law, the school has perfected the craft of offering a rigorous, broadening curriculum to students from diverse backgrounds. Bowdoin graduates walk away with something special.

❏ *Nathaniel Vinton, A.B.*

BRANDEIS UNIVERSITY

Mike Lovett

Brandeis University
Waltham, MA 02454

(781) 736-3500
Fax: (781) 736-3536

 Enrollment

Full-time ❑ women: 1,795
         ❑ men: 1,425

Part-time ❑ women: 15
         ❑ men: 5

INTRODUCING BRANDEIS UNIVERSITY

Founded in 1948, Brandeis is one of the youngest top-tier universities in the nation that is rated most competitive. In this respect and others, Brandeis has achieved in decades what other universities have taken centuries to accomplish. The university is named for the late Louis Brandeis, the first Jewish associate justice of the United States Supreme Court, and reflects the ideals of academic excellence and social justice he personified. These principles continue to shape every aspect of the university's character.

One of the many reasons Brandeis has rapidly risen through the ranks is because its founders, including Albert Einstein, modeled it after the best of three centuries worth of American colleges and universities. It balances the feel of a small liberal arts college with the resources and faculty of a major research university. As a result, Brandeis students not only have remarkable faculty,

but they actually have the opportunity to create personal and close working relationships with them, something few other colleges can offer to the same degree.

This balance between a small liberal arts college and large research university is reflected again in both Brandeis's student population and its location. The Brandeis paths are filled with familiar smiles, but the undergraduate population is big enough to meet new people daily. While the community is fairly small, every state and over one hundred countries are represented at Brandeis. Since more than eighty percent of students live on campus, there is extraordinary exposure to a wide variety of different cultures, backgrounds, and perspectives. The campus is surrounded by the safe streets and great restaurants of Waltham, Massachusetts, but with easy access to Boston, including free shuttles and a train stop adjacent to campus, giving students the best of the big city as well.

No description of Brandeis would be complete without paying homage to the rich activist history and to the student body's dedication to social justice. Brandeis was a frequent destination of Martin Luther King, Jr., and others during the civil rights movement because of its activism. Brandeis students led the National Student Strike to protest American Foreign Policy during the Vietnam War. The history of Brandeis is filled with passionate students advocating change. The traditions of social activism and social services continues today.

Brandeis students work hard and play hard. While Brandeis has been able to rise through the ranks with the highest of academic standards, extracurricular activities, athletics, and parties have a presence on campus that can entangle even the strongest of wills. One factor that distinguishes extracurricular life at Brandeis from many other schools is that while nearly every conceivable interest is available on campus, students can be actively involved in multiple activities, not just one: A student can be an editor of *The Justice*, the independent student newspaper, play soccer with the Brandeis Football Club, and be a class senator, all at the same time. If you matriculate to Brandeis, regardless of your major you will attend at least one Pachanga—a clublike party put on by the International club that frequently attracts well over a third of the student body—see the statue of Louis Brandeis transmogrified into a variety of different characters such as a giant chicken or WWF wrestler during your stay, and sled down a snowy hill on a cafeteria tray in the dead of winter.

The founders of Brandeis succeeded in creating a university modeled after the best parts of other universities. Strong academics, a commitment to social activism, a robust student life, and a great community all contribute to the wonderful experiences and bountiful opportunities Brandeis offers. While other universities have multiple-century head starts, Brandeis continues to rise because of the quality of the experience.

ADMISSIONS REQUIREMENTS

The Brandeis admissions process is designed to attract exceptional students with a broad range of interests and backgrounds. Brandeis looks for accomplished students who possess special talent or individuals who have used their resources well. Brandeis seeks students who are best prepared to embrace the university's academic rigors and contribute to campus life in diverse ways.

Qualified candidates tend to take the most challenging courses their secondary schools offer. The Admissions Office looks closely at involvement with Advanced Placement and Honors classes. The admission committee carefully considers recommendations from professors, headmasters, or other mentors. They are also interested in applicants' extracurricular involvement and/or volunteer work.

Admission into Brandeis is very competitive. Approximately ninety-three percent of Brandeis matriculants are from the upper quintile of their high school class and the median SAT score is 1367 (based on 1600). In a recent year, Brandeis had approximately 7,600 applicants and each undergraduate class is comprised of only 700–750 students. If Brandeis is your unwavering first choice you will find yourself in good company upon arrival. Last year, approximately twenty percent of the incoming students were accepted Early Decision.

The Office of Admissions

The members of the Admissions staff at Brandeis are very friendly and helpful. They know applying to college can be stressful, so they do what they can to make it as "applicant-friendly" as it can be. Tours are offered year-round and are given by student volunteers who try to give prospective students and their families a feel for life on campus. Visitors can sit in on classes and can stay overnight with student hosts. The university also hosts a yearly Open House that exhibits a sample of life at Brandeis through discussion panels with professors, a mini club fair, and presentations on what prospective students might expect.

The Application

The application attempts to glean the most information it can from applicants while steering clear of unnecessary forms or requirements. Brandeis accepts the Common Application on-line and in hard copy.

The university pays close attention to the secondary school record and, in general, recommends a course of study that includes the following:

- Four years of English
- Three years of foreign language (including, whenever possible, study in your senior year)
- Three years of college preparatory mathematics (prospective science concentrators should study mathematics for four years)
- A minimum of one year of science
- A minimum of one year of history

Aside from a student's academic record, Brandeis requires the following four components from students who are applying:

1. SAT and two SAT Subject tests OR the ACT
2. An essay
3. Two letters of recommendation
4. An interview (recommended)

Academic records and standardized test scores should be taken seriously because they are an important tool for admission; however, Brandeis is looking for students who have more depth than these numbers alone might communicate. Recommendations and the personal statement are important windows for the Admissions Office into the character of applicants. A strong recommendation and well-written personal statement will add depth to your application and, in turn, the Admissions Office's understanding of you.

Brandeis encourages but does not require a personal interview with a member of the admissions staff. Meeting with an admissions officer gives applicants a chance to learn more about specific opportunities of personal interest at Brandeis. At the same time, the interview lets an admissions officer get to know an applicant better by giving applicants an opportunity, through informal conversation, to communicate aspects of themselves that may not have an appropriate outlet in the written forms and school transcripts. If an on-campus interview is not possible, applicants can arrange to meet with an alumni admissions counselor. Alumni conduct interviews on campus and in cities throughout the world, and communicate their impressions to the Brandeis Admissions Office.

Finally, Brandeis has a need-blind admissions policy. This means that applying for financial aid does not influence Brandeis's decision regarding a domestic student's admission to the university during the Early Decision and Regular Decision admissions cycle. The Brandeis Office of Admissions reaches its decision, then notifies the Office of Financial Aid if the student has been admitted. Even Brandeis's admission policies reflect the philosophies its founders set forth. The university is committed to bringing together a student body that embodies excellence, social activism, inclusiveness, and a reverence for learning regardless of financial background.

ACADEMIC LIFE

Academic life is one of the aspects of Brandeis that make it really shine in comparison to other top-rated colleges and universities. Brandeis attracts the most prestigious professors because of the attractiveness of its resources as a research institution. In a major study of higher education, "The Rise of American Research Universities" by Graham and Diamond, Brandeis was named the number one rising research university in the nation. When normalized for size, the Brandeis faculty rank number two out of the 3,000 colleges in the United States in the percentage of faculty who are members of the top three scholarly societies in America, namely the Academy of Science, the American Academy of Arts and Sciences, and the American Association for the Advancement of Science. However, prestigious faculty are not the only factors in making Brandeis stand out: The intimate learning environment that students share with their accomplished professors is exceptional. Other universities may have prestigious faculty, and other liberal arts colleges may have small classes, but having top professors in a small classroom is a rare luxury.

> **❝** *The one-on-one experiences with professors are really what makes the Brandeis experience special. I was able to attend a conference on Civic Engagement with one of my professors and at the conference present a paper I wrote to his peers. While a grad student is frequently common, my thesis advisor was also the chair of the department. The relationships with professors and peers contributed to the best learning experiences of my life.* **❞**

This dynamic between professor and student translates into the classroom and beyond. World-renowned professors doing research at a university with small classes means exceptional research opportunities. Brandeis offers first-year students the unusual opportunity to be able to participate in a research lab assisting professors. Through students' stays at Brandeis they are presented with a number of opportunities to participate in research with their professors. Some examples that extend beyond the lab include working with national and international organizations and traveling to other countries to assist in the field. The product of this cooperation between professor and student is an opportunity-filled academic experience. Brandeis is the youngest institution to earn recognition by Phi Beta Kappa, in part, because of this successful dynamic.

The Curriculum

The College of Arts and Sciences (CAS) is the core of the University. CAS is comprised of twenty-four departments and twenty-four interdepartmental programs, which offer thirty-nine majors and forty-four minors. The departments and interdepartmental programs are divided among four schools forming broad groupings among the disciplines: the School of Creative Arts, Humanities, Science, and Social Science. Interdepartmental programs pro- .

FACULTY/CLASS SIZE

- ○ 352 full-time faculty
- ○ Ninety-six percent of full-time faculty hold a Ph.D. or the highest degree in their field
- ○ Forty-one percent of faculty are women
- ○ Twenty-four fellows of the American Academy of Arts and Sciences (thirteen emeriti)
- ○ Nine members of the National Academy of Sciences (five emeriti)
- ○ Three members of the Institute of Medicine, National Academy of Sciences
- ○ Twenty-two fellows of the American Association for the Advancement of Science (fourteen emeriti)
- ○ Five Howard Hughes Medical Investigators
- ○ Three MacArthur Fellows
- ○ Student-to-faculty ratio: 8 to 1
- ○ Two thirds of all courses at Brandeis enroll nineteen or fewer students; median class size is seventeen

vide structured opportunities to explore areas of study that are interdisciplinary in scope. The broad range of departments and interdepartmental programs offer students and faculty the opportunity and formal structures needed to explore fields in-depth and across disciplines. The structure and offerings of CAS encourage and inspire students and faculty to pursue a true liberal arts education through university requirements and continuing research endeavors. The CAS's offerings are bolstered by the university's established graduate schools whose classes are open to undergraduates.

This broad range of offerings provide classes in almost every conceivable discipline. For students who aren't sure what they want to major in, Brandeis provides variety that smaller liberal arts colleges can rarely offer. For students who know (or think they know) exactly what they want to major in on their first day of class, the depth of the course selection will more than fulfill their interests.

Requirements

Flexibility and an interdisciplinary approach characterize the entire curriculum at Brandeis. Studying ideas from a variety of academic perspectives gives you the ability to form your own critical viewpoint and synthesize knowledge in new ways. To earn a Bachelor of Arts or Bachelor of Science degree at Brandeis, students must complete thirty-two semester courses, which include the required courses of your major and the general university requirements:

- One university seminar
- Three writing-intensive courses (one of which may be a writing-intensive university seminar)
- One quantitative reasoning course
- A three-semester foreign language sequence (or the equivalent)
- One course in nonwestern and comparative studies
- Two semesters of physical education
- At least one course from each of the four schools at the university—Humanities, Social Science, Science, and Creative Arts. (Courses taken to fulfill requirements listed above may also count for this requirement.)

The University Seminar in Humanistic Inquiries (USEM) is a hallmark of the Brandeis curriculum, designed specifically for first-year students and intended as a foundation for their studies at Brandeis. USEMs are small seminar-style classes, taught by distinguished faculty. They are interdisciplinary in subject matter and develop critical thinking and writing skills through close analysis of significant texts. They typify the intimate classroom environments with accomplished faculty that Brandeis works hard to create.

At Brandeis, you can design an academic structure for yourself, combining majors and minors that can either focus your interests through a multidisciplinary approach to a particular area of study, or broaden your view by exploring an eclectic array of interests in a personal journey of academic discovery. It is possible to earn two degrees simultaneously—a dual bachelor's/master's degree—in most programs at Brandeis that offer graduate study.

Brandeis also has an expansive study abroad program. It is not required, but more than twenty percent of juniors study abroad. Brandeis offers students from all majors opportunities to study in more than sixty-two countries, in many centers of learning that have centuries-old reputations for academic excellence.

Brandeis's requirements are not difficult to fill. Courses can double count for the core curriculum, distribution, and concentration requirements. This allows for many courses taken to be elective courses. In comparison to other universities, Brandeis's requirements are light, but they ensure that students leave with a true liberal arts education.

SOCIAL LIFE AND ACTIVITIES

Central Perk, the coffee shop in the Emmy Award winning show "Friends" (created and produced by Brandeis graduates Marta Kauffman '78 and David Crane '79) is modeled after Cholmondeley's, the campus coffeehouse at Brandeis. How many colleges have a social scene that receives nods on prime-time television weekly (daily if you include reruns)? It is located in Brandeis' genuine castle that serves as a residence hall for upperclass students and whose unique wedge-shaped rooms overlook Boston. While students probably won't see Jennifer Anniston or King Arthur on campus, students have a good chance of finding lifelong friends, their knight in shining armor, and much more.

Location

Brandeis is in the city of Waltham, an inner suburb of Boston, located nine miles upstream on the banks of the Charles River. The city is a popular dining location for residents of Boston and Brandeis students alike because of the wide variety of ethnic restaurants in its downtown. A cinema in town, specializing in independent and foreign films allows students to catch the best of Sundance as well as French, Italian, and Japanese films. For students who would like to spend some time in a big city, Boston is just a shuttle ride or commuter rail away. An on-campus commuter rail stop provides access to the Boston subway system all day seven days a week. Starting Thursday and running until Sunday, Brandeis provides free shuttles to and from Cambridge and downtown Boston.

Residence Life

Although students visit Boston many times during their four years at Brandeis, most are quite content to stay on campus because it is almost always bustling with activity. Approximately ninety-nine percent of first-years and eighty-two percent of all students live on campus in Brandeis's twenty-four residence halls in nine quads. Rooms range from traditional dorm rooms (lofted rooms and doubles) to suites, townhouses, and apartments. First-year students at Brandeis are housed either in Massel or North Quadrangle, right on campus, convenient to classroom and dining options. Each quad is supervised by a professionally trained director, assisted by resident advisors who are upperclass Brandeis students. Most residence halls are coed, though single-sex areas are available. First-year students are housed in either double or lofted rooms. Upperclass students are eligible to live in single rooms, suites, or apartments, including the castle. Part of the reason campus living is so popular is because more than half of the rooms on campus are singles. A brand-new residence hall housing 220 students opened in the fall of 2003—perfect timing for the lucky incoming class.

In the residence halls a variety of programs are offered—movie nights, ice cream parties, and informational talks on subjects such as safe sex, current events, and local issues. Big screen TVs, kitchens, and foosball tables can be found in nearly every quad lounge, which are popular hang-out spots well into the wee hours of the morning. In first-year quads, milkshakes, smoothies, and snacks are also available well into the night. Most students become confident that the quad, building, and even the hall they live in is the best in the university. Playing fields and basketball courts are adjacent to many of the residence halls, creating a perfect environment for pick-up games at virtually any hour. Every dorm room is equipped with a high-speed Internet connection, ideal for accessing multimedia, playing multiplayer computer games, or accessing Brandeis's 1,000 electronic journals and publications.

Dining

It will probably be difficult to find college food that is as good as home cooking, but Brandeis will certainly give your folks a run for their money if not for the food, for the convenience. Usdan Cafe and The Boulevard, located in the Usdan Student Center offer cook-to-order, "grab-and-go stations," and late night pizza delivery. If students are really hungry, they can go to Sherman Dining Hall's all-you-can-eat facility, which serves both kosher and nonkosher foods. All the dining locations provide generous vegetarian options and a station in Sherman always provides vegan food. Brandeis accommodates every dietary restriction; students need only speak with the dining staff. Some dining options include the ability to order from off-campus restaurants such as Dominoes. By using "Who Cash" in participating area restaurants, students add even more variety to the Brandeis diet.

The newly renovated "Stein," located above the Sherman Dining Hall, is a modern pub serving lunch and dinner entrees, as well as sandwiches, soups, salads, and homemade desserts.

Clubs and Organizations

The new Carl and Ruth Shapiro Campus Center, a $25 million addition to Brandeis's already dynamic campus, is the hub for student activity on campus. Open around the clock, seven days a week, it houses a cafe, a state-of-the-art student theater, lounges, function rooms, computer clusters, and offices for student organizations, all built around a soaring art-filled atrium.

At most campuses students must choose between serious involvement in one club or involvement in many with a selection of clubs to choose from. For example, at a big school being an editor of the student newspaper is often the exclusive post a student can hold. In contrast, a small school might welcome participation in many clubs, but might not have a selection that includes a radio station or the resources a bigger school might have to make the experience as worthwhile. Brandeis manages to deftly walk this line, making clubs and organizations an exceptionally popular outlet to have fun and learn. With more than 175 clubs and organizations, it is safe to say that every student participates in club life in some way.

Students can write for *The Justice*, the inde-

CLUBS AND ORGANIZATIONS

- Total student clubs and organizations: 250+
- Community service clubs: six
- Cultural awareness groups: twenty-one
- Performing groups: thirty-two including three comedy troupes, six dance troupes, ten instrumental groups, and thirteen vocal groups
- Religious groups: five
- Sports and games clubs: thirty-nine
- Student leadership/activism groups: twenty-three
- Student publications: eleven
- Student service organizations: thirteen
- Television station BTV and radio station WBRS

pendent student newspaper, or one of the ten other student publications. They can join the campus radio or television station and host a live talk show. They can join the debate team and win first place again in North American parliamentary debate. Students who dare can go skydiving, scuba diving, or mountain climbing all with a full or partial subsidy from Brandeis. The entertainment of theater groups, comedy troupes, and about a dozen *a capella* groups is enjoyed daily. Multicultural events fill the academic calendar and add richness to campus life. They include: Asian Awareness Week, Black History Month, Caribbean Week, Chinese New Year, Culture X, Hispanic Heritage Month, Kwanza, Mela, and the Vietnamese Spring Festival. Dozens of athletic clubs provide instructors that will show students how to improve their game in everything from rugby and Ultimate Frisbee to Tae Kwon Do and kick boxing. Religious groups provide everything from a gospel choir and Friday night shabbat dinners to a Muslim prayer room.

> **66** *It seemed that there was always something happening on campus. Whether it was a famous speaker, a club meeting, a party, an* a cappella *performance, or a rally, there was always some event to go to.* **99**

With almost two dozen activist groups, students will find a strong and active community with a great history of national advocacy. Brandeis students led The National Student Strike against the Vietnam War and convinced the Board of Trustees to be one of the first universities to divest from apartheid South Africa.

Athletics

Brandeisians love athletics. If you are looking for Division I athletics Brandeis is not for you, but if you are merely looking to enjoy either competitive or recreational play Brandeis will more than suit your needs. More than 1,000 students participate in intramural and club sports every year. Brandeis has ten men's varsity sports, ten women's varsity sports, and one coed team (sailing). The Gosman Center is one of the largest multipurpose indoor athletic facilities in the East. It has a 70,000-square-foot field house; a 200-meter six-lane track, three indoor tennis courts, ten outdoor tennis courts, squash courts, weight training rooms, and fencing, dance, and aerobic facilities.

Creative Arts

Students interested in the arts will find a supportive community with top-notch resources. Brandeis's music department was founded by Leonard Bernstein and there are seventy musical performances annually. The theater department hosts six major productions each year and several student-run theater groups put on productions each semester as well. With two major state-of-the-art theaters (one opened last year) and several minor spaces, the university has quality theater resources. The Rose Art Museum, an art destination of many Bostonians, is located on campus, making museum openings especially convenient for Brandeis students. The museum boasts the largest, finest, and most comprehensive collection of twentieth-century modern and contemporary art in New England. Beyond the museum, the campus is dotted with sculpture by professionals and students alike year-round through permanent exhibits and art festivals.

> **❝** *When Charlton Heston visited campus, I can still remember that well over 1,000 students were either standing in line for the event, chanting in protest or support, or pretending to lie dead on the ground with blood-stained shirts to dramatize gun violence. The best part was after he left when students and NRA members engaged in long and productive discussions about gun rights and gun control. The event really captured both the openness to ideas and dedication to fostering dialogue that Brandeis cherishes.* **❞**

The college experience can in many ways teach you more than your classes. Brandeis's supportive environment, so full of opportunities, virtually assures that you will maximize your college experience.

FINANCIAL AID

Approximately sixty percent of incoming undergraduates received some form of need-based financial aid during a recent academic year. Need-based financial aid is a combination of loans, work-study, and grant awards that are offered to students whose families demonstrated financial eligibility for assistance. Need-based aid is available from federal, state, and private sources, including Brandeis. To apply for need-based financial aid, students must submit the CSS/Financial Aid PROFILE and, if applicable, the Business/Farm Supplement and Noncustodial Parent's Statement along with their application.

In addition to its deep commitment to need-based financial aid, the university maintains its own strong scholarship program. Brandeis scholarships are based primarily on academic merit and are used to enroll the very best class possible with the scholarship funds available. To be eligible, applicants must complete the CSS Profile.

Financial aid counselors work with students and their families to create a financial aid package that suits their needs. If necessary, they help find additional scholarships or loans to supplement Brandeis grants. Approximately 200 students in a recent first-year class of 837 received scholarship awards ranging from $5,000 per year for four years, up to $27,000 per year for four years. In a recent year Brandeis awarded undergraduate students more than $27.9 million in scholarship/grant assistance.

GRADUATES

The ability to think creatively, solve problems logically, and communicate effectively defines a liberal arts education. A bachelor's degree from Brandeis signifies exceptional achievement in all of these skills compounded with a commitment to social justice. The successes of Brandeis alumni suggest that this is a winning formula.

Alumni can be found in nearly every profession or field of work. Notably, eighteen alumni serve as presidents of colleges or universities in the United States or abroad. Ten percent of Brandeis alumni are physicians. Brandeis graduates are presidents of fifty hospitals or HMOs. Of the 2,300 Brandeis alumni in the legal profession, seventy-five are district attorneys and thirty have gone on to become judges.

Brandeis graduates are among the highest echelons of graduate school applicants. In a recent year, Brandeis seniors achieved an eighty percent acceptance rate to medical school, while the national average is forty-seven. They also enjoyed a ninety-four percent acceptance rate to law school, besting the national average of seventy-eight percent. Brandeis graduates were accepted to an average of four law schools of their choice, as compared to the national average of 2.3.

One small part of graduates' success is the assistance they receive from the Hiatt Career Center. It provides career counseling and a range of services for undergraduates and alumni. It directs students to internships related to their interests during the academic year and throughout the summer. The Center hosts Alumni Network Events at Brandeis during which students can meet with alumni to explore a wide variety of postgraduate careers; a Shadow Program allows students to spend a day in the workplace with a Brandeis graduate to explore a particular career field; the Hiatt Alumni Career Network gives students access to thousands of alumni volunteers who offer to share advice about utilizing a liberal arts degree in a broad variety of careers; and Alumni Network Events on campus and in New York offer prearranged interview days in Boston, New York, and Washington, D.C. Beyond all this, Hiatt offers resources and assistance on standardized tests, résumé preparation, interview techniques and much more.

SUMMING UP

While most American universities were named for a location or major benefactor, Brandeis was given its name seven years after Justice Louis Brandeis died. He is the namesake solely for who he was and the ideals for which he stood. In design, Brandeis was modeled after the best parts of the best American colleges and universities. The founders managed to combine the best qualities of location, size, offerings, and campus life to maximize the university's potential. As a result, in its short life span it has been able to create an experience that places it among the best colleges. The university fully embraces the mission of a liberal arts college with renowned research. The success of its graduates is perhaps the best indicator. A Brandeis degree can take its graduates anywhere they want to go. While not a household name in America, it is a name that is known and respected in both academic and professional circles. It is a name that allows its graduates to compete for the most sought-after jobs and most selective graduate schools. However, the value of a college experience is not in the diploma that hangs on the wall; it is based on the quality of the experience.

❏ *Joshua F.A. Peck, B.A.*

BROWN UNIVERSITY

Photo by William Mercer

 Brown University
Providence, RI 02912

 (401) 863-2378
Fax: (401) 863-9300

 E-mail: *admission_undergraduate@brown.edu*
Website: *www.brown.edu*

Enrollment

Full-time ❑ women: 3,177
❑ men: 2,909

Part-time ❑ women: 7
❑ men: 9

INTRODUCING BROWN UNIVERSITY

Brown University, a member of the Ivy League, is a high-caliber institution that is low on pretension. With no core requirements, Brown's innovative curriculum takes academic decisions out of the ivory tower and puts them in the hands of students. Each student becomes the architect of his or her own education. The result is a community of self-motivated learners who relish the chance to discover and explore their true passions.

On the whole, Brown students are more collaborative than cutthroat. The university attracts some of the highest achievers from the United States and abroad, but in the Brown environment, these students value learning from and working with their peers over vying for grades. Brown students can also be an eclectic, creative bunch. The typical Brown student is atypical. As one student puts it:

> 66 *The main thing I love about Brown is that everyone is here to learn. There is a lot of passion in the student body. People come here because they have a love of learning and want to expand their minds—consequently, grades are not considered as important as they might be at other schools.* 99

—*Elizabeth Gilbert, '08*

For some, the academic and social freedom can be intimidating, but Brown works hard to provide a system of advising to help students find their way. Students get the most support through one-on-one mentoring relationships with faculty members. Professors are easy to approach and devote considerable personal attention to undergrads. It is not uncommon for students to form close bonds with professors and stay in touch with them long after they graduate. With 682 regular, tenured, and tenure-track faculty, the largest number in Brown's history, the current student-to-faculty ratio stands at nine to one. In fact, Brown has expanded its faculty by more than twenty percent since 2001.

Students also tend to form close ties to Brown's host city, Providence, Rhode Island. An artsy, midsized city, Providence has undergone a transformation over the past decade. The refurbished downtown area boasts a beautiful walkway along the Providence River, several small-scale concert venues and theaters, and the easily accessible Providence Place mall, complete with a movie megaplex and a vast array of shops and restaurants. All of these entertainments are within walking distance or a short trolley ride from College Hill. Closer to campus, students frequent the coffee shops and eateries on Thayer Street and Wickenden Street and enjoy the brick sidewalks and large Colonial and Victorian houses that give this section of Providence, known as the East Side, a distinctly New England feel.

Many students first get to know Providence through community service projects. Nearly 70 percent of Brown students contribute time and skills to the local community. This community involvement is a hands-on form of student activism, as students work to effect change locally through grass roots organizing.

Large-scale political activism is rare or nonexistent on Brown's campus. While Brown's liberal curriculum attracts a predominantly liberal student body, both sides of the political spectrum are represented, and protests are few and small. Students are most vocal about issues directly affecting the Brown community. Brown adopted a need-blind admission policy in 2003. Information about applicants' financial means is excluded from admission decisions for first-year students who are U.S. citizens or permanent residents.

Campus activities and clubs offer another outlet for students' diverse interests. From musical groups and sports teams to campus newspapers and literary societies, Brown students make involvement in extracurricular activities a major part of their educational experience. Freshmen and sophomores usually dabble in a variety of clubs. By junior year, many students have focused their involvement on one or two organizations where they take on leadership positions such as team captains or editors. Alternatively, many students add to the activities on campus by starting their own organizations.

> 66 *The people at Brown are intelligent and talented; that's almost a given at any university of Brown's caliber. What makes Brown different is that everyone here has something more—something other than intellecutal capacity that makes them unique, independent individuals.* 99

—*Diane Mokoro, '11*

Brown offers bright, self-directed students the freedom and support they need to realize their full academic potential. Students shape their own learning experience while enjoying collaborative working relationships with professors and peers alike. They also know how to balance rigorous academics and community involvement with a social life for a well-rounded collegiate experience. In a 2009 senior survey, 91 percent of graduating students reported that they would encourage a high school senior like them to attend Brown.

ADMISSIONS REQUIREMENTS ▬▬▬▬▬▬▬▬▬▬▬▬▬▬▬

Each year Brown's admissions process seems to get more selective. In a recent year, Brown accepted 2,816 of 30,132 applicants. Students seeking admission must meet high academic standards. While more than half of the entering class attended high schools that do not report a rank-in-class, 93 percent of freshmen from high schools that do report rank were in the top 10 percent of their class and had SAT scores of at least 600 in reading, math, and writing.

But meeting these requirements alone does not ensure acceptance. There is no one formula for gaining admission to Brown. Admissions officers look at many different aspects of an applicant's profile in addition to his or her academic record. Brown, like most competitive colleges, looks for students who have the whole package—exceptional academics, leadership in outside activities, commitment to the community, and a certain intangible spark that can come across in an applicant's essay or recommendations.

Geographic and Ethnic Diversity

Brown's admissions committee also tries to foster geographic and ethnic diversity in the student body. For this reason, students who come from underrepresented regions, such as the Midwest, may have an easier time getting in than students from the Northeast. The university also actively recruits international students and values the diverse perspectives they bring to the community. At present, Brown enrolls approximately 5,900 undergraduates from all 50 states and over 90 countries. Ten percent of undergraduate students hail from abroad.

The university has an equally strong commitment to promoting ethnic diversity. About 30 percent of undergraduates are people of color. Over the years, the university has established programs to provide a network of support for the minority community on campus. Minority Peer Counselors or MPCs are a group of Arab, Asian, Black, Latino, Multiracial, and Native American undergraduates who provide academic and personal counseling to first-year students of color. They also conduct workshops in freshman dorms throughout the year to promote understanding on campus.

Student groups based on cultural background are another source of support and community for minority students and are very popular. They provide a venue for students from similar backgrounds to hang out and get to know each other, and they also host events on campus, such as performances or panel discussions, that let students share their heritages and raise awareness about issues affecting their community.

Application Process

Brown's application process is fairly standard. Applicants submit academic transcripts, recommendations, test scores for the SAT or ACT, two SAT Subject Test scores, and a personal essay.

Once students have assembled all of their materials, they can submit their applications to Brown by one of two deadlines: the Early Decision deadline or the Regular Decision deadline. Students choosing the Early Decision option apply by November 1 and receive decisions by mid-December. This option is reserved for applicants who have selected Brown as their first-choice college and will attend Brown if admitted as an Early Decision candidate. The Regular Decision admissions deadline is January 1, with a notification date of April 1.

> *Brown is about making choices—your own choice. The university provides advice and guidance, but ultimately your own internal decisions form your learning world. Here you are viewed not for what you can be inside an institution but instead for who you are as a student and a person. A Brown education becomes what you make of it and what you want it to be, and it's that freedom of choice that makes Brown so special.*

—Sam Speroni, '11

ACADEMIC LIFE

Requirements

Brown stands out from other competitive colleges in its emphasis on student choice. While most schools have distribution requirements that all students must take to graduate—usually a series of introductory-level courses in different fields of study—at Brown students are free to imagine and build their own. To graduate, students need to pass thirty courses, demonstrate competency in writing, and complete the requirements for their concentration (Brown's term for a major).

Some might fear that students would abuse this system and miss out on all that a liberal education has to offer. But Brown students are inherently motivated to explore a curriculum which is constantly in flux. The school assigns academic advisors to help students consider their academic programs carefully, and students invest an enormous amount of effort in planning their course of study each term. Even without requirements, most students choose a well-rounded selection of classes, and they are more eager to put time and energy into classes they've chosen.

At the end of the sophomore year, students begin to focus their studies on one of Brown's seventy or so concentration programs. Requirements for concentrations vary greatly. Some departments, such as Africana studies, have as few as eight required courses, while some Sc.B. programs may require as many as twenty-one courses. Students also have the option to double-concentrate or create their own concentration in collaboration with a faculty advisor.

> 66 *Applying Early Decision to Brown was the best choice I ever made. My experience here at Brown has been everything I hoped it would be. There is an incredible support system in place for freshmen that makes them feel welcome and at home when they arrive, and a rich student and campus life with opportunities for all students to get involved with whatever they are interested in. All the students I have met here are bright, interesting, and passionate people, the kind of people I want to be surrounded by and live with for four years.* 99

—Beth Enterkin, '07

Academic Advising and Support

While Brown students enjoy tremendous freedom in shaping their course of study, they do not have to go it alone. All incoming first-year students are assigned an academic advisor, a faculty member or administrator with whom they meet during orientation and throughout the year. Some academic advisors teach in the Curricular Advising Program (CAP). This program allows freshmen to take a class with a professor who will also serve as their advisor.

The CAP program has garnered mixed reviews from the student body. While CAP advisors are generally encouraging and supportive, they often know a lot about their department but are less helpful when giving advice about courses outside of their area of specialty.

Fortunately, there are many other opportunities for students to receive guidance. Brown faculty members, on the whole, are accessible and eager to help students. Many advising relationships develop informally as students get to know their professors. Most incoming students take a first-year seminar, which allows them to work closely with a faculty member and other students interested in the same topic. Faculty Advising Fellows, who host meals and social gatherings provide support and mentoring in Advising Central. Fellow students are also on hand to help. Resident Counselors, upperclassmen who live in freshman dorms, have already navigated through their first year of decisions, and they can be an invaluable resource to the freshmen they mentor. Sophomores get an added level of support through Randall Advisors, faculty members who work particularly with sophomores to review their educational goals and from Community Advisors in the residence halls. And once students declare a concentration, Concentration Advisors help students further hone their course of study.

Classes

Class size and format vary at Brown depending on the department and type of course. Most classes are small in size (about 30 to 40 students) and are taught in a seminar style with an emphasis on student participation. Introductory lecture classes and lab classes for sciences tend to be larger (one hundred students or more) but usually include smaller section meetings during the week where students can get more individual attention.

A shopping period at the beginning of each semester allows students to check out a variety of classes before finalizing their schedule for the semester. Students often use the shopping period to compare different courses and see which professors they prefer.

As with concentrations, students also have the opportunity to design their own classes. Student-created classes develop as collaborations between a small group of students and a faculty advisor and are known as Group Independent Study Projects, or GISPs. GISPs are a perfect example of what happens when you give motivated students the freedom and resources to pursue their true passions. Many GISPs encompass several fields of study and result in innovative research or help extend Brown's interdisciplinary course offerings.

The Brown-RISD Dual Degree Program began in 2008 to provide students with a range of opportunities to develop and integrate academic and artistic work. The Dual Program is five years in length. Students may receive a Bachelor of Arts (A.B.) degree from Brown and a Bachelor of Fine Arts (B.F.A.) degree from RISD. Prospective students must apply and be accepted to both institutions, and then be approved by a separate Brown/RISD admissions committee.

Grades

Most Brown students are inherently motivated to take their studies seriously, but they are not overly concerned with grades. Overall, grading at Brown is fair. Students receive an A, B, or C for passing work and an NC, or No Credit, for failing work. Professors maintain high standards for A and B level work in all disciplines, though professors in the sciences may grade more harshly.

Pass/Fail Grades

The S/NC grade option at Brown, which stands for satisfactory/no credit, is intended to encourage academic risk-taking. Since students can opt to take any course S/NC, they are more likely to venture outside of their comfort zones academically without fear of sullying their transcripts with a low grade. For example, a history concentrator may decide to take a competitive physics course S/NC or an economics concentrator might try art history without having to worry about grades. Most students view the S/NC system as a nice option but still take the majority of their courses for a grade. Very few students abuse the system.

PLME

One final aspect of academic life at Brown is the Program in Liberal Medical Education (PLME). This program provides a unique path to medical education. Students apply to PLME as high school seniors and, if accepted, are guaranteed spots in Brown's medical school upon graduation, provided they maintain a certain GPA. As undergrads, PLME students are just like other members of the class. They are encouraged to take full advantage of Brown's liberal arts offerings, and many end up concentrating in the humanities before continuing on to medical school. Ultimately, this eight-year continuum of liberal arts education and medical education encourages PLME students to develop into well-rounded scholars who view medicine as a humanitarian pursuit rather than a trade.

RECENT INDEPENDENT CONCENTRATIONS AT BROWN

- Humanistic Healthcare
- American Deaf Studies: Linguistic and Cultural Identities
- Gastroanthropology
- Philosophy, Politics, and Economics (PPE)
- Sustainable Engineering and Architectural Design
- Animation Theory and Practice
- The Musical Dimensions of Contemplative Studies

Units

The freshman unit marks the beginning of every Brown student's social life. It comprises 40 to 60 students who live together in the same freshman dorm. Brown intentionally tries to maximize diversity in these groups, so students from one unit represent many different ethnicities, geographic backgrounds, and interests.

People tend to bond quickly with their unit mates, and units often travel as a pack during the first few months of freshman year. Members of the same unit will eat together in the campus cafeterias or turn out in large numbers to support one of their unit mates at a performance or sporting event.

Many Brown students make lifelong friends in their freshman unit, and some even meet their future spouses. Overall, the unit setup provides first-years with a feeling of community and gives students a chance to make a diverse group of friends whom they might not otherwise encounter.

> *As a first-year student at Brown, I was a little worried about coming to Providence from deep south Texas. But I soon found that social life is just as active on campus as off. Comedy, parties, music, movies on the green—anything you might want can be found at Brown University. You never have to leave the campus!*

—*Meagan Brooke Garza, '08*

Fraternities and Sororities

Units are the first social group at Brown, but it isn't long before students begin to find their way to other campus groups and activities, such as fraternities and sororities. Unlike many college campuses, Greek life plays a small role in Brown's social scene. Ten percent of students belong to the ten fraternities and three sororities on campus. Of the fraternities, two are coed and tend to throw less traditional frat parties around themes such as swing dancing. The more traditional frats and sororities throw the majority of big public parties on campus. These parties can draw a crowd, but many students move on to other social options after their first year or two on campus.

Other Social Activities

The alternatives to frat parties are as diverse and creative as Brown's student body. Cultural events are a particularly big draw. Students pack theater productions, dance performances, *a cappella* concerts, and improv comedy shows. There is also an on-campus music venue called The Underground. Funk night at The Underground is popular among freshmen and sophomores, while upperclassmen frequent the Graduate Center Bar, known for its dungeonlike atmosphere, pool tables, and dart tournaments.

> ❝ *No matter how much you stood out in high school, at Brown you blend right in. For many people Brown will be the one time in their lives they will be just like everyone else around them for a change.* ❞

—*Michael Thompson, '07*

Off Campus

Off campus, students enjoy the cultural and culinary offerings of Providence. A near-perfect college town, Providence is small enough to feel homey but large enough so there's always something going on. Recently, Providence has gone through a much-touted cultural renaissance. There's a thriving arts community that plays host to many quality theater productions and offbeat performance art. There are also several concert venues and jazz clubs and, for more mainstream entertainment, the massive Providence Place mall has a megaplex movie theater as well as an Imax theater.

Providence is also home to some of the best restaurants in New England. Freshmen find that Family Weekend is a perfect time to try some of the city's pricier establishments, such as the famed Italian restaurant Al Forno, while seniors who are off meal plan frequent South Providence's pan-Asian hangout, Apsara.

- Thayer Street—the main drag, home of the Brown Bookstore, the Avon Movie Theater, and countless restaurants and coffee shops
- Wickenden Street—like Thayer, but artsier and a few blocks farther from campus
- Atwells Avenue—Providence's answer to little Italy
- Waterplace Park—downtown's stage for free concerts and drama
- Blackstone Boulevard—a road near campus with a great jogging path

Dating

The dating scene at Brown is somewhat lacking; it seems that people are either in a serious relationship or they're single. There's not a lot of casual dating. Brown students tend to hang out in groups, and couples usually stay connected with their group of friends.

Sports

Brown offers a wide range of varsity sports (37 different teams) and has decent facilities for a school its size. In general, sports at Brown, like Greek life, are in the background. Attendance at games is low. Athletes tend to support other athletes and students support their friends who play sports, but rarely does the whole campus rally around a sporting event.

There is, however, a strong sense of community among athletes, and students who do attend games get caught up in the school spirit and cheer loudly. Many games are also attended by the very enthusiastic Brown Band. The world's first ice-skating band, the Brown Band performs postgame ice shows that are a highlight of the hockey season.

Groups

In addition to athletics, students can participate in a wide variety of activities. There are more than 400 student organizations at Brown including theater and dance ensembles, music groups, community service organizations, faith-based groups, student government, and much more. Involvement in campus groups is a major part of the Brown experience. Most clubs give students the option to get involved in a small or large way, and most students are actively involved in at least one club or volunteer activity. Students enjoy the opportunity to try new things, and they often find that campus groups provide their first introduction to a potential career path. For example, Andrew Barlow, class of 2000, served as a writer and editor for the campus humor magazine during his years as a student, and since graduation, he has published humor pieces in *The New Yorker*.

FINANCIAL AID

In February 2008, the Corporation of Brown University approved a new financial aid policy that eliminates loans for students whose family incomes are less than $100,000, reduces loans for all students who receive financial aid, and no longer requires a parental contribution from most families with incomes of up to $60,000.

Students receive financial support both through financial aid and scholarship grants. Forty-three percent of Brown students receive some sort of aid. For the class of 2014, the average financial aid package totaled over $35,940.

Many students work part-time jobs as part of their work-study program or to make some extra spending money. Food service jobs are the most common, but there are also job opportunities in academic departments, libraries, or other campus facilities. On-campus jobs pay an hourly wage that typically increases as a student logs in a number of hours or rises to leadership. The average yearly earnings from campus employment is approximately $1,450.

The deadline for submitting financial aid forms is November 1 for Early Decision applicants and February 1 for regular applicants, and financial aid awards must be renewed each year.

GRADUATES

Over ninety-five percent of Brown students graduate in six years. Then they are faced with the anxiety of figuring out what to do next. Fortunately, Brown provides a support network to help seniors make post-graduation plans.

About a quarter of Brown graduates go directly to graduate or professional school after graduation. These students receive guidance from professors in the field and often attend the top schools in their discipline. Nearly 80 percent of Brown graudates pursue graduate or professional study within ten years of completing their Brown degree.

Deans

For students who pursue professional tracks in law or medicine, there are deans at Brown who specialize in counseling prelaw and premed students. They guide students through the process of deciding whether or not law school or medical school is the right next step for them, and if students decide to apply, they help them navigate the involved application and interview processes.

There are also deans who help students apply for research awards, scholarships, and fellowships. Historically, this support has helped Brown students fare very well in competitions for highly selective post-graduate awards, such as the Fulbright, Rhodes, and Marshall scholarships.

> **“** *Brown's culture creates a unique environment on campus. The students are interesting and passionate, and there are many professors who are incredible mentors. The open curriculum and the freedom to explore new ideas enable me to craft a personalized educational experience, one that I could not have gotten anywhere else.* **”**

—*Sharon Langevin, '09*

Job Hunting

Career Services is the most valuable resource for students who look for employment directly after graduation. Each year, many finance and consulting firms recruit Brown seniors through interview sessions at the Career Development Center.

SUMMING UP

Brown University provides bright, self-directed students with the freedom and resources to realize their full academic potential. By removing the confines of a core curriculum, Brown lets students, with the help of faculty advisors, select a course of study that best matches their interests and passions. From the beginning of their college careers, students learn how to discover and pursue their academic interests.

As students explore Brown's offerings, they have access to the full resources of the university, most notably, the faculty. Thanks to small classes and dedicated faculty, students develop close mentoring relationships with their professors. There are even university grants designated for undergraduate research with professors, a benefit usually reserved for graduate students.

Although Brown students are high achievers who embrace academic rigor, they are more collaborative than cutthroat. Brown's liberal curriculum and grading system help create an atmosphere where students value learning for learning's sake and enjoy working with their peers rather than competing for grades.

Brown students also know how to balance their studies with extracurricular and social activities. Involvement in campus groups lets students try things they've never done before, such as hosting a radio show or organizing a political rally. Brown students are also willing to try new things socially. While many schools' social scenes revolve around drinking and partying, Brown's social options are as diverse and creative as the student body itself.

Brown is a school that nurtures the student as an individual. Students accept responsiblity for their education and are encouraged to chart their own course, and the professors who help them along the way also get to know them as people. Students graduate from Brown with a stronger sense of who they are and the conviction and skills to go on to pursue their true passions.

❏ *Michelle Walson, A.B.*

PROMINENT GRADS

- Mary Chapin Carpenter, Country Singer-Songwriter
- Ira Glass, Host of National Public Radio's "This American Life"
- John Hay, Personal Secretary to Lincoln and Secretary of State under Presidents McKinley and T. Roosevelt
- John Heisman, the Trophy's Namesake
- Charles Evans Hughes, Chief Justice, Supreme Court
- John F. Kennedy, Jr., Publisher
- Laura Linney, Oscar-Nominated Actress
- Horace Mann, Educator
- Joe Paterno, Football Coach
- Tom Scott and Tom First, AKA "Tom & Tom," Creators of Nantucket Nectars
- John D. Rockefeller, Jr., Philanthropist
- Ted Turner, Media Mogul
- Thomas Watson, Jr., Former IBM Head
- Craig Mello, 2006 Nobel Laureate
- Jim Yong Kim, President Darmouth College
- The late Richard Holbrooke, Special Representative to Afghanistan and Pakistan for President Obama
- John Krasinski, Actor
- Lynn Nottage, 2009 Pulitzer Prize winner

BRYN MAWR COLLEGE

 Bryn Mawr College
Bryn Mawr, PA 19010

 (610) 526-5152, (800) BMC-1885
Fax: (610) 526-7471

 E-mail: *admissions@brynmawr.edu*
Website: *www.brynmawr.edu*

 Enrollment

Full-time ❑ women: 1,283

INTRODUCING BRYN MAWR

Your first glimpse of Bryn Mawr is unforgettable. At the end of a winding Montgomery County road, the wooded manses will give way to a spectacular view of the famed collegiate gothic architecture. From across a hilly expanse of lawn, you will glimpse Pembroke Arch, gateway to the main campus, where the mighty spire of Goodhart Auditorium peeks above the towers of Thomas Great Hall. This is Bryn Mawr College where women have been offered the finest liberal arts education imaginable since 1885.

When Dr. Joseph Taylor, a Quaker physician from New Jersey, founded Bryn Mawr he intended it to be a trailblazing institute of higher learning for young women, with particular emphasis on the sciences. It was also the first women's college to offer the Ph.D. Bryn Mawr, Welsh for "big hill," is one of the four remaining independent Seven Sisters of the Ivy Leagues, those late nineteenth-century colleges built exclusively for women when coeducational environments were not yet in vogue.

Today, Bryn Mawr is known for its vast array of rigorous academic programs, including thirty-six majors and thirty-eight minors to choose from. Indeed, Bryn Mawr's strong reputation in all liberal arts disciplines places it among the top schools in the country. Approximately 1,300 undergraduates comprise the student body in addition to the co-ed postbaccalaureate program ("post-bacs") and assorted grad students from the Graduate School of Social Work and Social Research and the Graduate School of Arts and Sciences.

Its intimate size is perhaps one of Bryn Mawr's greatest strengths as a liberal arts institution, offering as close to "one on one" instruction as it gets in the United States. While the English tutorial system is very much alive on campus, as exhibited by seminar classes of eight to fifteen students and more traditional lecture-style classes with typical enrollment of twenty to forty students. There are also independent studies available to upper-level undergraduates in which you truly do get to work with one or two advisors on a self-designed extended project. The student-faculty ratio is an astounding eight to one so you're definitely going to get a lot of face time with your professors. All the more reason to make sure you've read the material in preparation for each class! Your professors and your peers expect you to come to class ready to engage in lively discussion, so don't be shy. If there's one thing a Mawrter is not, it's a wallflower, but we are a supportive bunch and understand that this is quite a change from high school.

Situated on one-hundred and thirty-five pastoral acres, Bryn Mawr occupies a lovely niche of the Main Line, just eleven miles west of central Philadelphia. Easily accessible by car and train, Bryn Mawr is convenient to several notable shopping and recreational destinations; most famously, perhaps, the King of Prussia Mall, which rivals the Mall of America in sheer size. Of course, the historical city of Philadelphia with its 250,000 college students and numerous museums, restaurants, and nighttime hotspots is of great appeal to Mawrters who want to cut loose on the weekends and socialize off campus. As an added bonus, Bryn Mawr is part of a college consortium with Haverford, Swarthmore, and the University of Pennsylvania. Students may take courses at any of the four schools, but the relationship with Haverford is an especially close one. Majoring at either institution, participating in

Bi-College (bi-Co) programs and events is the norm and encouraged. Between Haverford and Bryn Mawr there are more than 3,000 cross-registrations per year. Within the college consortium there are more than 5,000 courses to choose from. (Yes, ladies, there might just be a member of the opposite sex in your eighteenth-century satire class.)

ADMISSIONS REQUIREMENTS

So why Bryn Mawr? Let's cut to the chase. You're a smart girl, a young woman on the brink of choosing a school at which you'll be spending the next four years striving toward a degree. Make the informed decision. Choosing Bryn Mawr means making an intense intellectual commitment; a decision you can handle by the looks of your strong high school record (the most important factor in considering an application—ninety-six percent of freshwomen are in the top twenty-five percent of their classes), your consistent involvement in select extracurricular activities, and your individual potential to thrive here.

This is not to slight standardized test scores (they do count for something!) In fact, the median SAT scores for incoming freshwomen are 680 reading, 670 writing, and 630 math. As for the rest of it? Don't sweat it. The very fact that you're even considering Bryn Mawr speaks volumes about your character. You have the brains, you have the drive; all you need is a killer essay to prove that you belong in that select group of three-hundred and fifty first-years. That insatiable desire to grow will shine through and then it will become clear that Bryn Mawr is the only place for you.

ACADEMIC LIFE

It is impossible to describe the typical first-year course load, as freshwomen have surprising freedom when choosing their classes. For a detailed list of requirements, see the sidebar. Each student, like it or not, participates in the somewhat stressful "shopping period" at the start of the new semester. This privilege can be a curse when it means that rosters are not finalized until a class is lotteried by necessity (admittedly a rare occurrence outside of in-demand History of Art and Creative Writing, which keep class sizes under sixteen) if there are too many people preregistered for it. Worst case scenario, an underclasswoman is asked to register again the next time the course is offered. If you plan accordingly, you will have no regrets when it comes to squeezing in every course you eagerly highlighted in the catalog you received during Customs Week (first-year orientation).

Many Mawrters opt to major and minor, or double major, double major or even double major with a minor or concentration.

Honor Code

The Honor Code looms over all campus activity. Bryn Mawr is a community founded on the honor and integrity of its members. We take responsibility for our judgments, actions, and for our student community. Personal integrity is such a key part of life at Bryn Mawr that exams are either self-scheduled or given without the use of a proctor. While not officially a part of the honor code, there is little discussion of grades or GPA standing among students. Why? Because Bryn Mawr encourages competition with the self and only the self. You're here to learn, not gossip and undermine others. GPAs are not weighted, there is no curve, and you get what you deserve, end of story.

This honor code extends into social life as well and covers all things under the Golden Rule of "do unto others." It's common sense. Don't steal, don't lie, and rest assured, if you are caught you will go to the Honor Board and that is a very public process. Quakers don't hold back. Additionally, to maintain these basic rights, Bryn Mawr makes good use of its Self Government Association, or SGA, the oldest in the nation, founded in 1892. Plenary, a tedious but necessary convening of the entire student body (at least two-thirds in attendance is needed to make Quorum) is held twice a year. You meet, you listen, and you vote on current issues. It is a privilege and one of the standouts of academic and campus life. Overall, BMC is a very liberal environment but no one will force her views on you unless solicited. Mawrters respect one another for their differences, as well as their similarities.

FIRST YEAR SCHEDULE

The normal course load is four classes per semester, but many students take advantage of Bryn Mawr's diverse offerings by taking a five-course load sometime after their first semester.

SEMESTER I
Elements of Probability and Statistics (Q)
CSEM: Querying Gender in Literature
Intermediate French
Early Modern Drama (III)
African Dance (PE)

SEMESTER II
How Things Work: Conceptual Physics
  (II w/ lab)
Shakespeare (III)
Intermediate French
Writing for Children (Creative Writing)
Methods of Literary Study
Intramural Volleyball (PE)

*Clearly this individual is a future English major with an overachiever's proclivity towards masochism. A schedule like this is approved only after speaking with your Dean at length. It happens often because at Bryn Mawr, the name of the game is "intense intellectual commitment." Anthro majors will sometimes take up to three languages during their four years; physics majors spend their winter/summer breaks doing research in labs; the drive to learn about the world is unparalleled and uncontainable within 8 short semesters of college.

It's not uncommon for Mawrtyrs to double or triple up on majors and minors. And if you don't see it here, you can design your own.

- ○ Africana Studies
- ○ Anthropology
- ○ Architecture
- ○ Arts Program
- ○ Astronomy at Haverford
- ○ Biology
- ○ Chemistry
- ○ Classical and Near Eastern Archaeology
- ○ Classics
- ○ Comparative Literature
- ○ Computer Science
- ○ East Asian Studies
- ○ Economics
- ○ Education
- ○ English
- ○ Environmental Studies
- ○ Film Studies
- ○ French and French Studies
- ○ Gender and Sexuality
- ○ Geology
- ○ German
- ○ Greek, Latin, and Classical Studies
- ○ Growth and Structure of Cities
- ○ Hebrew and Judaic Studies
- ○ Hispanic and Hispanic-American Studies
- ○ History
- ○ History of Art
- ○ International Studies
- ○ Italian
- ○ Linguistics at Swarthmore
- ○ Mathematics
- ○ Middle East Studies Initiative
- ○ Neural and Behavioral Sciences
- ○ Peace and Conflict Studies
- ○ Philosophy
- ○ Physics
- ○ Political Science
- ○ Psychology
- ○ Religion at Haverford
- ○ Romance Languages
- ○ Russian
- ○ Sociology
- ○ Spanish

Advisors and Faculty

At Bryn Mawr, you're treated as a peer and an adult. This can be an adjustment for many freshwomen, some of whom have never even done their own laundry before. You are assigned a Dean, alphabetically, and he or she will act as your chief academic advisor for the first two years before you declare a major at the end of your sophomore year. Once you have a major, your class year will be assigned an advisor or you can choose a mentor, usually a professor with whom you have worked closely in the past, to see you through scheduling for the remainder of your time at Bryn Mawr. Your support network of faculty and staff is more than happy to find the time to meet with you. Office hours are a hallmark of the collegial give-and-take present at Bryn Mawr that you'd be hard-pressed to find elsewhere. It is not uncommon for professors to invite students to their homes, to meet in town at Starbucks, or in one of the cafes on campus, or just to lend a sympathetic ear after class. These bonds you create, departmentally and otherwise, you will nurture for the rest of your life.

After cramming in four to five academic classes per semester and one or two gym credits, you're probably wondering where you go to learn everything you need to know. Bryn Mawr has numerous quiet lounge/study spaces or loud and social spaces, depending on how much work you actually plan to do. The campus center is a popular nocturnal perch where two men named Ben and Jerry are always available and your best friend is just a cozy chair away. Try the gourmet sandwiches and assortment of bubble teas if you plan to make a night of it.

> **❝** *In the fall of my senior year I took a class called Eating Culture and on the very first day the professor posed a deceptively simple question: Are we what we eat, or do we eat what we are? This is what a Bryn Mawr class will do—force you to stop and think about something you have always taken for granted, to ask questions for which there are no easy answers. Throughout the semester, as we read and cooked, sampled the fruits of our labor and analyzed them, I thought back to that first day again and again. At the end of the course, I still didn't know how to respond to the initial question. But it didn't matter; if there's one thing I learned here it's that not having a short and simple answer to a question doesn't mean you don't understand; it means that you* do. **❞**

—Hannah Wood, '08

Labs and Libraries

For those times when only silence will do, there's a computer lab and three libraries on campus; Canaday is the largest, housing the rare books and general collections (hello, English majors), Carpenter, the Classics and Art History Library, is the belle of the architectural ball, built in 1997, and finally, there's Collier Science Library (no mystery there). Bryn Mawr houses over one million volumes; an astounding number for a college of its size. There is a wonderful electronic resource called Blackboard where profs post course syllabi, assignments, PDFs of that night's reading and even facilitate discussion groups. You get all the biblio-perks of the Tri-Co, as well, meaning you can order a book from Harverford or Swarthmore via EZ Borrow and it arrives, in most cases, the next day. They even e-mail you to tell you it's in. This is handy for seniors in thesis mode and for special projects but be warned, you can't keep it just because you ordered it. If someone requests it, you need to turn it in and then a book war ensues.

Academics at Bryn Mawr are rigorous. This accounts for the tee-totaling vibe on campus, though Bryn Mawr is not technically a "dry" school, and means that even on a warm spring evening toward the end of the year, the dutiful scholars will be click-clacking away on their laptops, sprawled on the lawn (there's wireless on Merion Green) or bent over Proust, sunning on Carpenter Beach. Mawrters take breaks, for sure, whether it be Pilates in the gym, a quick run to Starbucks, or a good movie in the dorm living room. Mawrters know how to kick off their shoes but only after an honest day's work. Here it's work hard, play hard, and one need only look to the Great Kate as an example.

Tired of studying for final exams, Katharine Hepburn famously stole away to the Cloisters Fountain, stripped down to her birthday suit, and plunged into the icy waters for a refreshing dip. Many students honor Kate with a ritual skinny dip before graduating, though the fountain is now chlorinated and nudity is optional. (I recommend doing this under cover of darkness, as there are 360 degrees of classrooms surrounding the cloisters but hey, if you feel lucky…)

FINANCIAL AID

So you've been accepted? Congratulations! Before you freak when you look at the yearly tuition bill (and please save your parents a heart attack, too) know that a majority of the student body receives need-based financial aid. While Bryn Mawr doesn't operate on merit-based scholarships, need-based financial aid and the college meets 100 percent of student's demonstrated needs. In addition to Federal Aid and Bryn Mawr grant aid, seventy percent of the student population holds down a campus job through the work-study program. For more information, contact a representative from the Financial Aid Office. It doesn't come cheap but believe me, you *can* afford a Bryn Mawr education and it's worth every penny in post-grad paybacks.

SOCIAL LIFE AND ACTIVITIES

Dining Services

During your time at Bryn Mawr you will grow and in more ways than one; dining services sees to that freshman year, as your waistline bears the effects of five-star meals in your choice of two full-service dining halls and two student-operated cafes. The food is truly spectacular, offering award-winning creations for all tastes—vegan, vegetarian, or carnivorous. Haffner is home to the rotating "international bar" where you can sample such delicacies as Pho noodles or Tapas. Erdman is the largest of the halls, open for three meals a day. Inside its cavernous halls you'll find a spectacular offering of ice cream and fro-yo (with toppings) and a short-order line for when all you really want is a good burger.

Fitness Center

Never fear: there is a newly renovated fitness center to take care of the aforementioned "growth," not to mention twelve varsity athletic teams, a rugby club, and, oh right, that pesky Phys. Ed. Requirement (see sidebar or details). Active minds need active bodies so put down that book and join a dance or yoga class, if the commitment of Division III sports isn't for you. And once you curb your enthusiasm over the free-for-all dining experience, the growing is more figurative than substantive.

Student Body

Bryn Mawr challenges you in unexpected ways, both academically and interpersonally. Campus life is a close-knit network of relationships that encourages you to coexist with women from multifarious backgrounds and viewpoints, some of which you may never have been exposed to before. With more than forty-nine states and forty-three countries represented in the student body, you're sure to meet some incredible young women with whom you'll forge a lasting bond of friendship. To help ease the transition from high school to college, Bryn Mawr's Residential Life department sorts incoming students into hall groups throughout the thirteen residence halls, each a uniquely charming building in varying architectural styles, matching them with roommates based on a compatibility questionnaire. A hall group consists of ten to twenty-two freshwomen living in traditional doubles, triples, or quads (and in some dwindling cases, singles) who are watched over by two upperclasswomen called Customs People.

Customs People

The Customs People are usually energetic sophomores or juniors who encourage socializing on the hall during orientation week and carry out the role of "big sister" and counselor throughout the year. They are also the sources behind "hall teas," a hangover from the days of petticoats and, well, high tea, though now the ritual frequently revolves around junk food or hot cocoa before packing the frosh off to study. As far as dorm life is concerned, you couldn't ask for a better setup than Bryn Mawr. It's all women sharing the bathroom, which is about as close to collegiate heaven as it gets. But be advised, despite the Victorian grandeur, traditional bunk beds are still a part of the first-year experience if you're placed in a triple or quad, but there are also perks such as oversized window seats with sweeping views of campus, or ornate (nonworking) fireplaces. Remember: John D. Rockefeller's niece went here so you know the digs are pretty sweet.

The Customs People are overseen by one Hall Advisor, generally a senior, who is the equivalent of an RA at larger universities. She is more of a "hall mother," responsible for the practical things such as hall maintenance and checking in with the housekeeper, coordinating Hell Week events with the other HAs in the building, and overseeing the traditions budget for the year. There are also class quotas on each hall to ensure that no dorm or section of a building is exclusively for freshwomen or exclusively for seniors. There's a little Quaker process called Room Draw that sees to that. (Freshwomen don't go through it until the end of their first year.) It is worth noting that your hall group is your introduction to life on the Mawr and many Mawrters form the closest bonds with their original hall mates, while others remain friendly over the next three years but move on to live with other people. It all depends on the luck of the draw but the personal evaluations help the process of matching up roommates. Plus, it's a nice confidence boost to have a built-in network of upperclasswomen when you're just a "froshling" on campus.

There are nearly one-hundred clubs and student-run organizations available for the joining. Part of the beauty of self-government is the privilege of a healthy activities budget so if, by some miracle, you don't see the club for you already listed, you have the opportunity to create your own. From political and religious groups to community service and culturally based clubs, there's something for everyone. In addition to student-run activities, the Residential Life office sponsors some pretty amazing day-trips to New York, Philadelphia, a shuttle to King of Prussia Mall, event nights with Karaoke, Guitar Hero, and perhaps Wii, so you don't even have to leave campus if you don't want to. There are humanitarian-minded weekends of service sponsored by community service organizations that anyone can participate in. The options are all there but you have to take the initiative.

Career Development Office

Similarly, Bryn Mawr's Career Development Office is an oft-overlooked gem that has access to several databases listing over 2,000 internships and externships with alumnae. Take advantage of this incredible resource during your first two years and you'll be happy you did when it comes time for the real job hunt. While Bryn Mawr doesn't generally offer academic credit for summers of service, you make up for it in real-world contacts that will open doors you didn't even know existed. There's free peer counseling or you can schedule an appointment with a career coach to go over interviewing skills and resumes. The bonds of sisterhood truly do extend into the workplace and you're sure to meet some incredibly talented and accomplished Mawrters along your life's journey, beginning with apprenticeships and leading to bigger and better things beyond.

> **"** Katharine Hepburn once remarked that Bryn Mawr 'isn't nylon, isn't plastic, but is pure gold.' During my four years there, I met the most intelligent, dedicated, and determined women (whether in the classroom, the chem lab, or rowing on the Schuykill) with whom I had ever or will ever come in contact. They became some of my best friends. I also had the oppportunity to lead discussion in small, intensive English classes and pursue original research as an undergraduate with various faculty members supported by the college's Hanna Holborn Gray Fellowship. These experiences more than prepared me for graduate education and my future responsibilities teaching undergraduates of my own. If you want the best and brightest, the pure gold standard, you should absolutely choose Bryn Mawr. **"**

—Christin Mulligan, '07

Traditions

Traditions are an integral part of the Mawrter's experience and essential to understanding the bonds of sisterhood. A word of caution: Some people take them really, really seriously and others don't get into it at all. In typical Bryn Mawr spirit, you will never be forced to participate in anything that makes you uncomfortable but you should definitely give them a shot. The main traditions are as follows: Parade Night takes place the first night of classes when unwitting first years run the gauntlet through sophomores spraying water guns/throwing water balloons, "sympathetic juniors" toss candy at you to make it all better, and seniors stand around in various states of sobriety because they are "apathetic" and have seen this three times before. It's wacky, it's fun, it's a bit of light humor to start the year off right.

The next tradition is appropriately placed around Halloween. Lantern Night brings out the witch in every woman, as we dress up in seriously antique "bat robes" from the turn of the century, chant Greek hymns to the goddess Athena, and prepare to receive the ultimate emblem of Bryn Mawrterdom—the mighty lantern. Each class is assigned a color corresponding to the four elements (light blue for air, dark blue for water, green for earth, and red for fire.) The panes of glass in your lantern will match your class color and make you a bonafide, recognizable Bryn Mawr alum when you take it out into the world. This is a highly symbolic evening, as it is your official welcome to the class of 20__. Many people lose it, emotionally, so tuck some tissues into your little bat wing.

A few other favorite traditions include the mother of them all, Hell Week, where freshwomen prove if they really have what it takes to stick it out for another three years (just kidding! It's fun!) as their sophomore "hellers" give them tasks to complete, ranging from the daring to the moderately humiliating. Example: Ever proposed to your calculus professor in front of a roomful of peers? This is a true bonding experience, rewarded with a pancake breakfast at IHOP after you run your buns off at the crack of dawn on a Saturday morning to the Haverford Duck Pond. Did I mention this is *fun*? Finally, there's May Day to close out the year.

On the first Sunday after classes end in spring, Mawrters and their professors take to Merion Green to welcome in the May with ye olde faire on the lawn. There are four poles erected for the four classes, each with appropriately colored ribbon, and there's a "May Hole" for the more progressive-minded where you can toss flower petals and listen to Dar Williams until your heart is content. It's a daylong picnic with performances and music and merriment culminating in a feast to rival Henry VIII's finest, as well as a midnight screening of "The Philadelphia Story."

From the moment you arrive on campus, the observant freshwoman will note the many owls carved into the stone archways throughout the forty campus buildings. The owl is Athena's totem, an emblem of wisdom. Athena is Bryn Mawr's patron goddess and indeed, her effigy stands in the far right corner of Thomas Great Hall. It is a copy of the original statue from antiquity that was damaged by some errant Haverfordians in the 1970s. The

- ○ Emily Green Balch, 1889, Winner of the Nobel Peace Prize
- ○ Ume Tsuda, 1892, the Founder and First President of Tsuda College, Tokyo
- ○ Nettie Stevens, Ph.D., 1903, the First Person to Observe that the X and Y Chromosomes Determine Gender
- ○ Marianne Moore, 1909, Poet
- ○ Katherine Sergeant White, 1914, the Co-founder of *The New Yorker* Magazine
- ○ Dorothy Klenke Nash, 1922, the First Woman Neurosurgeon in the United States
- ○ Katharine Hepburn, 1927, the First Woman to Receive Four Academy Awards (Double Major in History and Philosophy)
- ○ Hanna Holborn Gray, 1950, the First Woman President of a Major American University (Former President of the University of Chicago)
- ○ Alice Rivlin, 1952, the First Woman to Head the Congressional Budget Office and commission on Budget and Financial Priorities, Also Known as the Rivlin Commission
- ○ Susan Band Horwitz, 1958, the Person to Discover How a Derivative of Yew Tree Bark Could Be Used to Slow Tumor Growth, Paving the Way for the Development of the Anticancer Drug, Taxol
- ○ Shirley Peterson, 1963, the First Woman to Head the Internal Revenue Service
- ○ Drew Gilpin Faust, 1968, the First Woman President of Harvard College
- ○ Allyson Y. Schwartz, M.S.S., 1972, Member of the U.S. House of Representatives, 13th Congressional District of Pennsylvania (Pennslvania's Only Female Congresswoman)
- ○ Rhea Graham, 1974, First Woman and First African-American to Serve as Director of the U.S. Bureau of Mines
- ○ Candace Beebe Pert, 1970, a Psychoneuroimmunoloigst at NIMH and Developer of Nontoxic AIDS Therapy
- ○ Sari Horwitz, 1979, a Two-time Pulitzer Prize-winning Journalist for the *Washington Post*
- ○ Julie Beckman, 1995, Won the Nationwide Competition to Design a Memorial to the victims of the September 11 Terrorist Attack at the Pentagon
- ○ Maggie Siff, 1996, Actress Who Currently stars in TV's, *Mad Men* and *Sons of Anarchy*

original Athena survived the misguided prank and now rests safely in a niche high above Carpenter library.

GRADUATES

Bryn Mawr graduates go on to make their meaningful contributions to the world in nearly every discipline under the sun. We are writers, actors, nonprofit founders, CEOs, scientists, teachers, and more. BMC alums have a nearly eighty percent acceptance rate into law schools and just over a seventy-five percent acceptance rate into medical schools. With a solid liberal arts education, Mawrters are equipped to set the world on fire and that's exactly what we do. Thinking back to that application crunch time not so long ago, I am reminded of a quote so apt it feels like a custom epitaph from E. B. White:

"I have known many graduates of Bryn Mawr. They are all of the same mold. They have all accepted the same bright challenge: Something is lost that has not been found, something's at stake that has not been won, something is started that has not been finished, something is dimly felt that has not been fully realized. They carry the distinguishing mark—the mark that separates them from other educated and superior women: The incredible vigor, the subtlety of mind, the warmth of spirit, the aspiration, the fidelity to past and to present. As they grow in years, they grow in light. As their minds and hearts expand, their deeds become more formidable, their connections more significant…I once held a live hummingbird in my hand. I once married a Bryn Mawr girl. To a large extent they are twin experiences. Sometimes I feel as though I were a diver who had ventured a little beyond the limits of safe travel under the sea and had entered the strange zone where one is said to enjoy the rapture of the deep."

SUMMING UP

Bryn Mawr is an investment on several levels. In order to make the most of it, you're going to have to work. You better believe we earn that title of "Mawrter." Everyone struggles through a class or two during their time at BMC. This may not be something that a high school honors student is prepared for at the end of her senior year, but it makes your multilayered liberal arts education all the richer for the effort. The truth is, when you finally pass through the stone arches at the end of your undergraduate career, you aren't leaving with a mere diploma. You leave Bryn Mawr with a purposeful vision of your life and a desire to make a meaningful contribution to the world. You leave Bryn Mawr with your lantern, a light bearer, ready to illuminate the way for others to follow.

❏ *Sarah Caldwell, A.B.*

Bucknell University
Lewisburg, PA 17837

(570) 577-1101
Fax: (570) 577-3538

E-mail: *admissions@bucknell.edu*
Website: *www.bucknell.edu*

 Enrollment

Full-time ❏ women: 1,822
❏ men: 1,747

Part-time ❏ women: 67
❏ men: 41

INTRODUCING BUCKNELL UNIVERSITY

Located along the banks of the Susquehanna River in central Pennsylvania, Bucknell is just a few hours' drive from some of the liveliest urban centers in the country: Washington, DC; Baltimore; Philadelphia; Pittsburgh; New York City. But chances are you won't miss the hubbub of the big city once you arrive on campus. While Bucknell has earned a national reputation as a leader in academics, athletics, social responsibility, extracurricular activities, and student engagement, ask a student or alum what it was that drew them to the university, and they'll probably tell you that, first and foremost, it was the beautiful, pristine campus that attracted them to Bucknell. Set on 450-acres that adjoin the quaint town of Lewisburg, Bucknell's buildings are a combination of historic gems and new, state-of-the-art facilities.

> 66 *Walking around campus, you usually see someone that you know, some-one who looks familiar, and someone who you've never seen before. The size of the campus is just perfect.* 99

—*Jennifer Kawczenski, '03*

Since its founding in 1846, Bucknell has been recognized as an elite private liberal arts college. Originally dubbed the University at Lewisburg, the school was renamed for William Bucknell, a charter member of its Board of Trustees, in 1886. The university was an early advocate for admission of women and minorities: the first female graduated from Bucknell in 1885, the first African-American in 1875, and the first international student in 1864. Offering over fifty majors and sixty minors in its two colleges—the College of Arts and Sciences and the College of Engineering—Bucknell has established itself as a place of academic rigor and social variety.

Bucknell students take their academic advancement very seriously. The university is in the top four percent of the most selective colleges in the nation. All students are required to take a foundation seminar class in their first semester on campus; many also opt to join one of seven residential colleges, theme-based living and learning environments that combine classroom and co-curricular activities. Students also take a capstone course, either within their majors or across multiple disciplines, during their senior year. Bucknell student-athletes rank in the top eight in the nation in graduation rates over a four-year period.

In addition, the university offers a number of options for students to pursue independent research projects, scholarly studies, and coauthoring of papers for scholarly journals and conferences. Bucknell professors are committed to excellence in both teaching and research. Ninety-seven percent of full-time faculty members hold a Ph.D. or equivalent degree, and the student-faculty ratio is 10:1. The school's academic program is based in the liberal arts and works to equip students with critical-thinking, independent analysis, and problem-solving skills.

But while the primary goal of the university, and of any other higher education institution, is to provide a firm academic foundation for its students, Bucknell is unique in its ability to do so in a social environment that has so much to offer. Bucknell blends its rich heritage and competitive academics with a vibrant Greek life, a wide range of varsity and intramural sports, and numerous clubs and activities (and if you don't find something you like, no problem—just create a new one). A Bucknell student is likely to be involved in an assortment of activities at any given time, from Ultimate Frisbee to comedy improv, from the Culture Couture fashion club to the BU jazz band, from the Japan Society to the Debate Team. The university provides all this in a community-oriented, collegial environment where individual goals and achievements blend with school spirit and common support.

> 66 *Five years after graduating from Bucknell, I can still recall many of the lectures I sat through, the sporting events I attended, the conversations I had with professors and friends. This, to me, is what Bucknell is all about—providing a foundation that is solid and rich, with the liveliness and excitement to last a lifetime. While Bucknell's academic reputation is constantly increasing, it is the combination of so many different opportunities at the university that makes it the ideal match for the student who wants to try it all, in a place where he/she is provided with every chance to succeed.* 99

ADMISSION REQUIREMENTS

There is no secret recipe for getting accepted to Bucknell. Admissions decisions are based on a variety of factors, including academic excellence (AP and Honors courses are key), extracurricular activities, and "evidence of special talent." Of course, special talent can be interpreted in a number of ways, but the admissions officers are very adept at identifying individuals who will excel at Bucknell and contribute to the university's academic and cultural excellence.

Bucknell has always had tough admissions standards, and has recently been propelled into one of the top four percent of the most selective schools in the nation (those offering admission to thirty percent or less of applicants). The university received 7,572 applications for the class of 2013, and offered admission to just 29.8 percent of those applying. About 920 students make up the most recent freshman class, which is slightly larger than usual. Approximately fifty-nine percent of incoming freshmen were in the top ten percent of their graduating high school classes, twenty-eight of whom graduated first in their classes. Twelve were National Merit finalists.

Bucknell requires students to submit SAT or ACT scores including the writing component. For the most recent freshman class, the middle fifty percent of admitted students posted an SAT reading score of 600–680, and an SAT math score of 630–720.

Diversity at Bucknell

Bucknell has made a number of efforts to increase the diversity of its students in recent years. The school has appointed a Chief Officer for Diversity and Equity, and the overarching Plan for Bucknell includes several initiatives to diversify the campus.

Bucknell's student body includes more than one hundred international students representing forty-two nations.

Application Process

Bucknell offers an early decision program in addition to its regular admission process. Early decision applications should be completed and submitted by November 15; regular decision applications are due January 15 for fall entry (there is a $60 application fee). Notification of early decision is sent December 15; regular admission notifications are sent April 1. All entrance exams should be taken before January 1. Applications are accepted online.

Bucknell also accepts transfer students, who must have a minimum GPA of 2.5 in courses comparable to those at Bucknell. SAT or ACT scores are required for transfers. A minimum of sixteen credit hours are required, though thirty-two hours are recommended. Students are accepted on a space-available basis.

Getting into Bucknell is a wonderful feeling. You realize that your hard work and dedication in high school have paid off, and that you are on your way to establishing yourself at one of the premier institutions in the country. Whether you've known what you want to do with your life since you were ten, or have no clue what course of study to take, Bucknell provides a variety of classes and a multitude of resources, making academic decisions both thoughtful and fun.

Bucknell offers more than fifty majors and sixty minors in its two schools, the College of Arts and Sciences and the College of Engineering. All students must complete a Foundation Seminar in their first semester on campus; other requirements for the College of Arts and Sciences include two courses in the arts and humanities, two in natural science or mathematics (including a lab science), two social science courses, one course in diversity, the environment, global connections, or quantitative reasoning, and a culminating seminar or experience during senior year. This may sound a bit abstract and extensive, but the university offers such interesting, multilayered courses (many of which fulfill more than one requirement), following the required course of study still leaves students with plenty of time to complete major and minor requirements, and even allows students to pursue classes that they find compelling outside of their majors. In addition to the requirements listed, Bucknell also calls for students to have a minimum writing competency for graduation. Popular programs of study include biology, management, and mechanical engineering.

> **❝** *My courses at Bucknell, whether requirements or fun options, were always thought-provoking, engaging, and interesting. I overwhelmingly liked and respected my professors, and felt that I was constantly being presented with new and incisive ways of looking at the material being studied. Oftentimes, the information that we discussed in an English class was also being studied in one of my history or French classes, and in each instance the conversations were both reinforcing and uniquely perceptive.*
>
> *I can still go to museums and remember terms and techniques discussed in the one art history course I took sophomore year. My interests were in the humanities, and yet I had the opportunity to be a teaching assistant for introductory biology. From my foundation seminar to my capstone course, I always felt that I was getting my money's worth from a Bucknell education.* **❞**

Bucknell's engineering program is highly acclaimed, which is especially notable for a school whose main focus is in the liberal arts. Engineering students are required to complete the Exploring Engineering course in their first semester. A total of thirty-two courses and a minimum GPA of 2.0 are required for engineering students to graduate. The university's management program is also noteworthy. As part of a hands-on, practical approach to

POPULAR MAJORS

- ⭕ Economics
- ⭕ Business Administration
- ⭕ English
- ⭕ Biology
- ⭕ Psychology
- ⭕ Management
- ⭕ Mechanical Engineering

learning, the management and engineering departments offer a summer program called the Institute for Leadership in Technology and Management (ILTM), in which students attend workshops by faculty and corporate leaders, travel to industrial and business sites, and work with companies on real-world management and technological projects.

Special academic programs at Bucknell include a Washington semester, internships, study abroad, a five-year dual engineering/arts degree, and student-designed majors. There are twenty-three national honor societies on campus, including Phi Beta Kappa, and fifty-five departmental honors programs. Students can also design their own majors and minors, provided they receive departmental and university approval.

UNIQUE ACADEMIC PROGRAMS

- ⭕ Common Learning Agenda
- ⭕ Seminar for Younger Poets
- ⭕ Philip Roth Writer-in-Residence Program
- ⭕ Stadler Semester (for Poetry)
- ⭕ Poet-in-Residence Program
- ⭕ Institute for Leadership in Management and Technology
- ⭕ Presidential Scholars Program
- ⭕ Undergraduate Summer Research Program

Faculty

Bucknell's faculty members represent some of the brightest, most forward-thinking individuals in their fields. Ninety-seven percent of full-time faculty at the university hold a Ph.D. or terminal degree. Faculty members are regularly published in academic journals, make presentations at professional meetings worldwide, and receive prestigious research grants and awards. The student-faculty ratio is 10:1, and faculty members are known to go out of their way to offer one-on-one assistance to students.

> 66 *In my four years at Bucknell, I was privileged to learn from and work with a number of devoted and energetic faculty members, in a rich variety of fields. I always felt I had sufficient access to professors outside of the classroom, and was able to discuss concepts at length in an open, collaborative environment with them. I had several classes with fewer than ten students in them, and felt very much a part of the academic process at the university.* 99

Academic Resources

Though its campus is small, Bucknell offers a number of state-of-the-art resources to contribute to students' academic growth. The Ellen Clarke Bertrand Library houses over 900,000 total volumes, including books, magazines, periodicals, CDs, DVDs, and microform items, among others. There is a learning resource center, and computerized library services include interlibrary loan, database searching, Internet access, and laptop Internet portals. It also includes a Special Collections and University Archive section. Nearly all of the campus has wireless capability with the exception of only a few outdoor areas.

Bucknell has a renowned art gallery, radio station, observatory, primate center, greenhouse, performing arts center, writing center, environmental and public policy centers, photography lab, and engineering structural test lab. Its poetry center, the Stadler Center for Poetry, recently celebrated its twentieth anniversary and is one of only a few poetry centers in the United States.

SPECIAL FACILITIES
○ Outdoor Natural Area
○ Primate Facility
○ Uptown (Alcohol-Free Night Club)
○ 7th Street Café (Coffee Shop)
○ Tustin Theater
○ 18-Hole Golf Course
○ Photography Lab
○ Race & Gender Resource Center
○ Multimedia Lab
○ Conference Center
○ Craft Center
○ Herbarium
○ Engineering Structural Test Lab
○ High Ropes Course

Study Abroad

Bucknell ranks in the top twenty among bachelor's institutions nationwide in the number of students studying abroad, with about 300 juniors and first-semester seniors studying in another country each year (more than forty-five percent of eligible students). Students travel to more than sixty countries and focus on a variety of study programs. Bucknell-run programs include Bucknell en France (in Tours, France), Bucknell in London, Bucknell en España (in Granada), and Bucknell in Barbados (near the capital city of Bridgetown). The university also has summer programs in a variety of locations, such as Northern Ireland, Barbados, and the U.S. Virgin Islands.

Bucknell also offers students the opportunity to volunteer in Nicaragua through its popular program called the Bucknell Brigade. Founded in 1999 to provide emergency relief following Hurricane Mitch, the Brigade travels each year to Nueva Vida, a facility built from Brigade donations outside of Managua. During their trip, students and staff work together to provide residents with medicine and supplies, and to assist with manual labor projects, while learning about micro-enterprise initiatives, grassroots development, and the history and culture of Nicaragua. While not a program of study abroad, the Brigade has become a popular way for students to spend Spring Break, and is most certainly a learning experience for those who participate.

Greening the Campus

Bucknell students and leaders are very dedicated to making the campus more environmentally efficient. The university has implemented a Campus Greening Initiative to promote sustainability and environmental literacy among all members of the university community. The Initiative provides curricular and extracurricular programs using the campus as a learning environment and aims to transform the university's green footprint.

A recent assessment project implemented by the Greening Initiative provided a thorough understanding of the strengths and accomplishments of the program thus far, as well as a blueprint for future improvement. The university's power plant, which provides ninety-five percent of Bucknell's power, converted from coal power to natural gas more than ten years ago. While the school has undertaken a number of new construction projects and renovations over the last several years, its energy use has remained relatively consistent, reflecting the move to more efficient practices.

While there still remain weak spots in terms of greening the campus, Bucknell is dedicated to continuing to look for new ways to promote sustainability and provide real-world examples of environmental responsibility for students to take with them after they leave campus.

SOCIAL LIFE AND ACTIVITIES

Bucknell's distance from major metropolitan areas and the insular nature of its campus would seem to indicate that finding things to do outside of the classroom is somewhat difficult. However, the university provides a wide variety of opportunities for students to participate in clubs, activities, athletics, and volunteer organizations. The Bucknell student's social life is truly self-determined, and can be just as full and rewarding as those of students at big-city schools.

There are more than 150 clubs and organizations on campus at Bucknell, including music groups, varsity and club sports, performing arts organizations, ethnic groups, gay and lesbian clubs, honor societies, political associations, service groups, a student-run newspaper, and religious clubs, among others. New groups are constantly being created, and dormant ones brought to life again. Bucknell students are very active in volunteer organizations—eighty-five percent of seniors participate in some form of community service.

Bucknell also hosts a number of outside performance groups and speakers throughout the year. The 1,200-seat Weis Center for the Performing Arts regularly holds theater, music, and dance events, as well as political and social lectures and commentaries from some of the world's leading authorities in their fields. The Bucknell Forum series has featured such prominent speakers as Jim Kramer, Doris Kearns Goodwin, F.W. deKlerk, and Tim Russert. The Janet Weis Fellow in Contemporary Letters award brings noted authors to campus each year, including past winners Toni Morrison, John Updike, Salman Rushdie, Tom Wolfe, Joyce Carol Oates, Derek Walcott, and David McCullough.

Other popular activities on campus include the Chrysalis Ball, the student-initiated gala festivities each spring; the Christmas Candlelight service, the Emmy-nominated holiday event featuring the Rooke Chapel Choir and the Rooke Chapel Ringers; readings from world-renowned poets at the Stadler Poetry Center; rotating exhibits at the Samek Art Gallery; and annual student productions of theater and dance shows.

Fraternities and Sororities

Bucknell has a highly active Greek life. There are twelve national fraternities on campus, drawing fifty-four percent of eligible men, and eight national sororities, drawing fifty-three percent of eligible women. Fraternity and sorority rush occurs first semester of a student's sophomore year. These Greek organizations provide students with the opportunity to meet new people, develop their leadership skills, and participate in a number of community service projects.

Most weekends feature a number of fraternity parties and dual fraternity-sorority social events. However, although fraternity and sorority life is vibrant at Bucknell, students who choose not to go Greek are at no disadvantage when it comes to their social lives. They can still attend Greek-sponsored events and participate in a variety of fraternity and sorority functions.

Athletics

Bucknell has thirteen varsity sports for men and fourteen for women, along with twenty-two intramural sports for men and twenty-one for women. Eighteen co-recreational sports are also available. Bucknell is a member of the Division I Patriot League, and has won the Patriot League President's Cup, the league's all-sports trophy, in sixteen of the last twenty years. Rival schools include Colgate, Holy Cross, Lehigh, Lafayette, and American. Bucknell ranks among the top schools in the nation in student-athlete graduation rates, according to recent NCAA surveys. In addition, Bucknell ranks fifth nationally in terms of the number of student-athletes named to national Academic All-America teams.

Bucknell's athletic facilities are state-of-the-art for a university of its size. The campus boasts an athletics and recreation center with an Olympic-size pool, a 16,000-square-foot fitness center, a 4,000-seat basketball arena, a 13,000-seat stadium, hockey and lacrosse fields, baseball fields, and recreational fields for soccer, softball, and other activities, as well as tennis courts, a dance studio, climbing walls, and an 18-hole golf course.

> *" Bucknell provided me with the rare opportunity to compete in Division I collegiate baseball while acquiring a first-rate degree. While my postgraduate path and that of many of my teammates has not included baseball, some have had the opportunity to play professionally. I believe those who participate in athletics at Bucknell embody the true meaning of the student-athlete. "*

—*Brad Gething, '01*

Many Bucknell students played varsity sports in high school, and often choose to take advantage of the university's extensive intramural and club sports program. Students can join men's, women's, or co-recreational teams, including basketball, golf, volleyball, squash, softball, bowling, and tennis, to name a few. There are also more than 30 club sports for students who want to participate in the competitive team atmosphere of athletics without the commitment of a varsity sports program.

FINANCIAL AID

Kiplinger's Personal Finance recently ranked Bucknell in the top fifty nationally in terms of best value for private colleges. That said, the university recognizes that quality education has become increasingly difficult to afford for many families. Bucknell has a wide-ranging financial aid program to help students cover the costs of their education. The university offers eligible students a number of financing options, including scholarships, loans, grants, and on-campus employment opportunities.

In 2009–2010, sixty-one percent of full-time freshmen and continuing full-time students received financial aid. The average financial aid package for Bucknell freshmen in 2009–2010 was over $25,000.

Over one-third of Bucknell students work part-time while on campus. Through the Federal Work-Study program, students can find jobs on campus and work eight to ten hours per week while classes are in session. There are also jobs available for students who do not participate in the Federal Work-Study program.

Additional information and specific financial aid package options are available at the university's Financial Aid Office's Web site.

GRADUATES

Bucknell graduates are some of the most successful in the nation. According to an August 2008 report in *The Wall Street Journal*, Bucknell ranked first among liberal arts schools in terms of the mid-career salary rates of its graduates. (The study was performed by PayScale Inc., an online compensation provider.) Bucknell graduates also rank in the top twenty nationwide for the number of graduates who go on to earn doctorates.

Ninety-one percent of Bucknellians graduate within five years, which is among the highest rates in the country. Within six months of graduation, more than twenty-five percent of students are typically enrolled in graduate school, and almost sixty percent had found employment. The school hosts a number of career and graduate school fairs throughout the academic year, where students can meet and network with alumni and company representatives from a variety of industries, an occasion that often leads to internship and career opportunities.

Bucknell's Career Development Center is dedicated to providing students with an array of services, and can be extremely helpful to students in finding internships and jobs after graduation, as well as continuing career advice and assistance to alumni. The Center's services include career counseling, assessment testing, employment and networking fairs, internships and externships, job shadowing, resume assistance, interview preparation, and graduate and professional school information.

SUMMING UP

There are many colleges and universities in the United States that provide a solid academic foundation, an array of activities and social organizations, a chance to study abroad, and an array of services and networking after graduation. However, Bucknell graduates overwhelmingly agree that their school excels at all these things and more, in a spirited, social, engaged environment that allows students to connect to each other, to their professors, to their community, and to themselves.

Bucknell is a school suited to students who want a small, intimate campus that fosters a sense of community and school pride. While there are none of the perks associated with big-city colleges, students can enjoy the charms of a small town. The movie theater is on the historical register, one of the few art deco theaters in the country that are still in operation. There is a Victorian parade the first weekend in December and the annual Arts Festival in April. The university does an excellent job of providing cultural, educational, political, and literary events and speakers that allow students to broaden their perspectives and capitalize on their academic opportunities. Students at Bucknell are rewarded when they are motivated, active, and ambitious—and most Bucknell students are all these things. They come from different backgrounds and have many different goals for success, but their shared experience during their four years at Bucknell unites them in ways that are at once evident and unexplainable.

In the end, Bucknell is a school that provides its students with a rewarding, engaging all-around education. Bucknell students and graduates are among the most accomplished, thoughtful, dedicated, hard-working, and successful in the country. And, most of them will agree, they are also among the luckiest.

❏ *Kristi Johnston, B.A.*

CALIFORNIA INSTITUTE OF TECHNOLOGY

Caltech Photo

 California Institute of Technology
Pasadena, CA 91125

 (626) 395-6341
Fax: (626) 683-3026

 E-mail: *ugadmissions@caltech.edu*
Website: *http://www.caltech.edu* (general)
http://www.admissions.caltech.edu
(Undergraduate admissions)

 **Enrollment**

Full-time ❏ women: 359
❏ men: 592

INTRODUCING CALTECH

Caltech's scientific reputation ranks it among the world's preeminent research universities, but with only about 300 professorial faculty and 951 undergraduates, Caltech's small size sets it apart from its peers. Caltech is the place where Linus Pauling determined the nature of the chemical bond, where Theodore Von Kármán developed the principles that made jet flight possible, where Charles Richter created a logarithmic scale for the magnitude of earthquakes,

More Ph.D.s than undergraduates—
campus population in 2010:
○ **Professorial faculty: 299**
○ **Emeriti faculty: 104**
○ **Research faculty: 69**
○ **Postdoctoral scholars: 549**
○ **Visiting faculty: 185**
○ **Staff: 2,734**
○ **Graduate students: 1,179**
○ **Undergraduate students: 951**

where Nobel Laureate in physics Richard Feynman—one of the most original thinkers of the twentieth century—spent the better part of his preeminent career, and where physicists and engineers are currently working toward the first detection of gravitational waves. However, Caltech is also a place where approximately 75% of students participate in on-campus research before they graduate, where eighty-five percent of students participate in intramural or intercollegiate athletics, and where students have lived under a student-run honor system since the 1920s. The Caltech undergraduate experience is a fusion of two seemingly incompatible institutions: a multibillion-dollar research university and an intimate small-school community.

As a high-powered research institution, Caltech has produced some of the greatest scientific achievements of the past century. Caltech's undergraduate program trains scientists and engineers for the great discoveries of the next. In class, you don't just learn the answers to questions in your textbook; you learn to ask your own questions and are challenged to find the answers. Professors often treat students as intellectual peers, and while this creates a very demanding curriculum, it also gives students the opportunity to actively participate in cutting-edge research. Many undergraduates work as research assistants on campus, and more than 300 participate in the Summer Undergraduate Research Fellowships program each summer. Many of these students will be named as authors or coauthors of articles in major scientific journals, a rare honor for undergraduates. This unadulterated exposure to the real world of science means that Caltech graduates are well prepared for a career in research. A higher percentage of Caltech graduates go on to receive Ph.D.s than do graduates of any other university.

Although the science at Caltech is very serious, student life at Caltech is well-rounded and even a little quirky. Almost all students at Caltech are members of one of the seven houses on campus. The house, the modern-day remnants of long-lost fraternities, perpetuate a long list of offbeat traditions and are the center of year-round intramural sports competitions. The beautifully landscaped campus of lush, open lawns, cool ponds, and winding pathways fosters a relaxed Southern California lifestyle. On an average day, you might find professors and students sharing coffee at an outdoor table or students teaching each other to juggle. At night, you might find a game of Ultimate Frisbee on the athletic fields or students grabbing a midnight snack at the coffeehouse. There are more than eighty student clubs on campus, eighteen varsity sports, two jazz bands, a symphony orchestra, a concert band, numerous choral groups, and an active theater arts program. Caltech students work very hard on academics, but they're also very good at finding diversions and, fortunately, there's no shortage of activities from which to choose.

ADMISSIONS REQUIREMENTS

Caltech is not for everyone, and getting in is not easy. By campus tradition, the target size of the freshman class is always 215—the number of seats in the original physics lecture hall. Compare that to the fact that over 4,000 applications were received and 674 letters of admission were sent in 2009; do the math and you'll see that it is a highly selective process. Although there are no strict requirements for test scores, the academic achievements of the freshman class are always very high. The middle SAT scores range from 700–770 Verbal, 770–780 Math, 700–800 Critical Reading, and 680–770 Writing; ninety-nine percent graduated in the top tenth of their high school class.

> **❝**As a Caltech alum, I often speak to high school students about admission to Caltech, and they always ask, "How can I be sure that I will get in?" My answer, of course, is that there is no sure way, but there are definitely things that you can do to increase your chances. Take the most challenging courses offered at your high school. Look for ways that you can express your love of science outside of school. Ask for recommendations from teachers who really know you and what makes you tick, and who are willing to write about you in depth. And finally, spend time on your application essays! Your essays speak for you to the admissions committee, and they want to hear what you have to say, not what you think they want to hear.**❞**

—*Debra Tuttle, '93*

> *The key to admission to Caltech is passion. An applicant must demonstrate a passion for learning, for life, and for science through activities outside the classroom. We focus more on how you spend your free time than on your test scores and class rank, because being successful at Caltech takes more than brains and more than diligence; it takes a love for what you are doing.* **"**

—*Jialan Wang, '04*

Although those numbers look daunting, there is no blueprint for getting in to Caltech. The admissions process at Caltech is not formulaic. The Undergraduate Admissions Office has only six admissions officers, but they get help from faculty and students in reading applications. The Freshman Admissions Committee includes sixteen faculty and sixteen undergraduate students. Each member of the Admissions Committee brings his or her own personal experiences of Caltech, and they work together to find and admit those students who fit best with Caltech. There are a few qualities that Caltech always looks for in its applicants: a strong *interest* in mathematics, science, or engineering, high academic *ability*, and demonstrated *initiative* in their approach to learning.

The goal of the Admissions Committee is to admit students who will become the "creative type of scientist" that Caltech seeks to produce. Members of the committee find these students by carefully reviewing the more subjective parts of the application—essays, choice of high school curriculum, extracurricular activities, and teacher evaluations. Caltech also encourages prospective students to attach a research paper to their application, which is one of the best ways to evaluate how well an applicant will do in a research-oriented environment. Caltech loves to find students who take an active role in their own education, and who pursue opportunities to learn both in and out of the classroom.

The only absolute requirement for coming to Caltech is a passion for science. Through Caltech's core curriculum, students who enroll don't get to choose whether or not they take science classes. This does not mean that applicants need to be one-dimensional; Caltech students are actually required to take more humanities courses than science majors at most other schools. A strong love of science is a must, though; those with just a casual interest need not apply.

The academic experience at Caltech is unlike that of any other university in the world. Every student has to learn the fundamentals of each major aspect of science while staying well rounded with a required number of humanities courses. Homework is done in collaborative groups and tests are almost all take-home. Participation in scientific research is easily accessible to every undergraduate and world-renowned faculty members interact with students on a daily basis. With big-time scientific research happening in an intimate small-school environment, the academic environment at Caltech is like no other.

When freshmen arrive at Caltech, they are all enrolled in math, physics, and chemistry courses. This is the beginning of the core curriculum, which is the heart of a Caltech education. Every undergraduate, whether majoring in biology, economics, literature, or chemical engineering, has to take five terms of physics, two terms of chemistry, one term of biology, two terms of introductory laboratory, two terms of science writing, twelve terms of humanities and social sciences, three terms of physical education, and one term of freshman "menu" course.

Options

At the end of the freshman year, students must declare an option, Caltech's version of the major. There are options in every aspect of science and engineering, with the most popular being physics, engineering and applied science (which includes computer science), biology, chemistry, mechanical engineering, mathematics, and electrical engineering. A few students each year graduate with degrees in history, economics, or literature, but they are very different from their peers at other universities—through the core curriculum, all humanities and social science majors will have taken differential equations and quantum mechanics. Changing options is generally very easy, and double options are pursued by a few students each year. Every few years, a student designs his or her own curriculum and graduates under the Independent Studies Program.

AWARDS AND HONORS FOR CALTECH FACULTY AND ALUMNI

- Nobel Prize: 31 recipients, 32 prizes
- Crafoord Prize: 6 recipients
- National Medal of Science: 55 recipients
- National Medal of Technology: 12 recipients
- California Scientist of the Year: 15 recipients
- Fellow, American Academy of Arts and Sciences: 87 faculty
- Member, National Academy of Sciences: 75 faculty
- Member, National Academy of Sciences, Institute of Medicine: 4 faculty
- Member, National Academy of Engineering: 31 faculty

Classes

The major distinguishing characteristic of academics at Caltech is that it's very hard. Often unnoticed is the fact that Caltech students tend to take more classes than their peers at other universities. Caltech operates on a trimester system, with three terms a year that are each eleven weeks long. In addition, Caltech students take an average of five classes each term, while students at other universities generally take only four classes. After four years at Caltech, students almost always find themselves well ahead of their peers in the first year of graduate school.

The Honor System

The fast pace of Caltech is more than almost any student can handle on his or her own, but fortunately, nobody is expected to study without help. Collaboration with peers is strongly encouraged under Caltech's more than eighty-year-old Honor Code. Instead of strict rules handed down from the administration, Caltech students are held responsible for their own actions and are on their honor not to cheat, plagiarize, or steal.

The greatest benefit of the Honor System is the fact that no tests are proctored. In fact, almost all quizzes, tests, and exams are take-home. The professor will set some ground rules for each test, and each student is responsible for respecting the given time limit and whether the test is open- or closed-book. Students are allowed to take tests wherever and whenever they want; some students sit in the privacy of their own rooms with their favorite CD or album playing, some prefer the quiet desks in the library, and some even take their tests out on the lawn or at the beach. Rather than having to wake up at 9:00 A.M., students can take their tests after dinner or even late at night; the professor won't care as long as it is turned in by the stated deadline.

The Honor System also applies to homework, where students are generally free to share their answers with each other. As long as each student understands everything written on his or her own paper, the professor will give full credit. This atmosphere of collaboration virtually eliminates competition between students for grades. Every Caltech student is happy to help a friend with a lab or homework assignment because some day, he or she may need the favor returned.

Scientific Research

This training in the Honor System is part of Caltech's strong focus toward scientific research. In the scientific community, researchers share their results openly and are held on their honor to conduct experiments with integrity. Undergraduates can experience this firsthand in numerous research opportunities on campus. The most popular way to do research at Caltech is through the SURF (Summer Undergraduate Research Fellowships) program. SURF provides grants of over $5,000 to students who want to do research with a faculty member over the summer. Each "SURFer" must write his or her own proposal, submit progress reports through the summer, write a final paper, and present his or her research on SURF Seminar Day. Over the years, SURF has become an integral part of the Caltech experience. Last summer, more than thirty percent of the student body stayed on campus as part of the ten-week SURF program. In the most recent graduating class, more than seventy-four percent of students had spent at least one summer in the SURF program.

Staying on campus over the summer is not the only way Caltech students can do research. The SURF program also pays for students to go to other universities over the summer—every year a few take this opportunity to travel to Europe. Caltech has instituted exchange programs with Cambridge University and the University of Copenhagen, which allow students to spend a term studying abroad. Students can stay on campus and receive hourly pay as research assistants during the school year or over the summer, and many labs are happy to hire undergraduates. Students can also earn academic credit by doing research as a senior thesis or to displace another requirement in their major. With so many laboratories at Caltech doing high-level research every day, the opportunities for undergraduates are seemingly limitless.

Laboratories

Some of the most advanced laboratories in the world are run by Caltech. The Jet Propulsion Laboratory (JPL) is the largest of these facilities. Located about fifteen minutes northwest of campus, JPL is NASA's center for robotic exploration of the solar system. It has been run by Caltech since the 1930s and is the place where *Voyager I* and *II*, now heading toward the edge of our solar system, were designed and built. JPL also produced *Galileo*, which orbited Jupiter and its moons, and the highly successful *Cassini*, which is now orbiting Saturn, its rings and moons. JPL was also in the news for the multiple probes it has sent to Mars: *Global Surveyor*, the *Pathfinder*, *Odyssey*, and rovers *Spirit* and *Opportunity*. A van runs daily between Caltech campus and JPL, and many undergraduates make the trip throughout the summer.

Telescope Facilities

Caltech also operates several telescope facilities, including the Palomar Observatory north of San Diego housing the 200-inch Hale Telescope, and the Keck observatory on the summit of Hawaii's dormant Mauna Kea volcano, home of the world's largest optical and infrared telescopes. Caltech also operates the Owens Valley Radio Observatory, a collection of radio telescopes 250 miles north of campus. On the Caltech campus, there are 0.35-meter and 0.25-meter telescopes atop the Caltech astrophysics buildings that are used for undergraduate classes. Also, plans are underway at Caltech, in collaboration with the University of California, to design and build the Thirty-Meter Telescope, the world's most powerful telescope.

LIGO

In conjunction with MIT, Caltech operates the Laser Interferometer Gravitational Wave Observatory (LIGO), a facility dedicated to the detection of cosmic gravitational waves. LIGO is the largest project ever funded by the National Science Foundation, and consists of two widely separated installations within the United States—one in Hanford, Washington, and the other in Livingston, Louisiana. They are each massive L-shaped structures with four-kilometer-long arms held in a vacuum, the largest high vacuum ever constructed. A one percent-scale prototype sits on Caltech campus, and a few undergraduates work there every summer, experiencing the cutting edge of experimental physics.

Other Facilities

Caltech is also home to Nobel Laureate Ahmed Zewail's Laboratory for Molecular Sciences, the headquarters of the Southern California Seismic Network, and a new initiative to improve voting technology. A new nanotechnology center and a state-of-the-art MRI facility are two more projects that are keeping Caltech at the forefront of scientific research.

Caltech students have the unique privilege of learning in the midst of advanced scientific research. Many other universities perform high-level research, but nowhere else can students so easily walk into the laboratories. On a campus where the Ph.D.s outnumber the undergraduates, anyone who wants to participate in research needs only to ask. Research experience is the best possible training for those going to graduate school, and Caltech students have an easy time gaining that edge.

> *Tech is not full of people who lock themselves in their rooms and study. There is something for everyone here. Plenty of people go out clubbing on the weekends, and yet these are the same people who do interesting summer research in cutting-edge fields like quantum computing.*

—*Kutta Srinivasan, '04*

Houses

Social life is generally not one of the reasons a high school student chooses Caltech, but every year, freshmen are surprised to find an active social scene centered around the seven undergraduate houses. Blacker, Fleming, Lloyd, Page, Ricketts, Dabney, and Ruddock House are descendants of fraternities that dominated the campus in the 1920s. This fraternity lineage is most obvious at family-style house dinners each night. Student waiters set the tables, serve food, and refill drinks; everyone must ask permission to get up from the table, and dinner ends with announcements from the house officers. Dinner is certainly not a formal affair though; each house adds its own quirky rules; for example: no "nerd talk," and no freshmen sitting at corners. Breaking the rules results in a variety of interesting punishments and the nightly ritual serves as an entertaining diversion that makes each house seem more like a family.

> ❝ The houses are microcosms within Caltech. There are enough different personalities within the houses that almost everyone can find someplace to fit in. I have found that the house system is a wonderful way to establish a family-like support network. Even from the beginning, I have felt like I was a part of what was going on and that people cared about what was going on in my life. ❞
>
> —Aimee Eddins, '04

During the first week of classes each year, freshmen are assigned to houses in a process known as rotation. A toned-down version of a fraternity rush, each freshman visits each of the seven houses and submits a list of preferences at the end of the week. Upperclassmen from each of the houses then get together and assign each freshman to a house in an all-night meeting. The end of rotation marks the beginning of a week of initiations, when freshmen can be found trading water balloons, and moving furniture across campus at the request of upperclassmen. This gives freshmen their first taste of Caltech pranking, and after this shared experience, each house is drawn together as a tight community.

Getting into a house gives each freshman an instant circle of friends and a constant source of social activity. Each house hosts one large "interhouse" party during the year, as well as many smaller parties. Every house elects a social team that plans other events such as ski trips, concerts, and trips to various L.A. tourist locations, but most social activity isn't incredibly organized. Nightly, students can be found relaxing and socializing in the common areas of the house, getting to know the group of people who will be their neighbors for four years.

Athletics

While academic competition is almost nonexistent, the seven houses engage in constant competition through a year-round schedule of interhouse sports. The houses play softball, soccer, swimming, track, basketball, tennis, Ultimate Frisbee, and football, earning points for compiling the best record in each sport. The house with the most points at the end of the year wins the interhouse trophy. The games are competitive, but everyone gets a chance to play—eighty-five percent of students play in interhouse sports before they graduate.

Intercollegiate sports are open to almost any student who can commit to daily practices, and almost thirty percent of the student body plays on Caltech's eighteen NCAA, Division III teams. There is cross-country, soccer, basketball, baseball, fencing, and more, but for over a decade now, no football team. There are also a wide variety of physical education classes for students to fulfill their PE requirement, ranging from traditional sports to yoga, scuba diving, and rock climbing.

Other Activities

Many Caltech students happen to be talented musicians, so the school sponsors a variety of music and arts programs. There is a concert band, two jazz bands, chamber music, a symphony orchestra, men's and women's glee clubs, and a theater program that performs three shows every year. A growing number of arts programs at Caltech are now being organized by students. There are several *a capella* groups, multiple rock bands, dance troupes, and a literary magazine, all run entirely by students.

These groups are just a sampling of the more than eighty student clubs on campus. Caltech students run a cheerleading squad, chess team, entrepreneur club, student investment fund, amateur radio club, science fiction club, ethnic organizations, religious groups, and many more. The Caltech Undergraduate Research Journal is now distributed at numerous universities across the country and has won top awards.

Student Government

All these clubs operate with little or no oversight from the faculty or administration and are an example of Caltech's long tradition of student self-governance. Many aspects of this self-governance have been alluded to elsewhere in this essay, and it is an integral part of student life at Caltech. Student government bodies decide who lives in the dorms, discipline students in cases of cheating, fund the majority of student activities, and choose representatives that help read admissions applications.

Student government is centered around a nonprofit organization known as the Associated Students of Caltech (ASCIT), Inc. Completely independent of the Institute, ASCIT publishes the student newspaper, yearbook, student handbook, and literary magazine. ASCIT is also in charge of administering the Honor System: suspected cases of cheating are investigated and adjudicated by the Board of Control, a committee of twelve students. Student representatives, along with faculty members, also sit on the Conduct Review Committee, which rules on disciplinary matters for undergraduates. Those students are just a few of the more than sixty student representatives on various Caltech committees that review academic policies, set the dinner menu, make admissions decisions, award merit scholarships, and determine academic ineligibility, to name a few examples. Caltech students are allowed to participate in almost every administrative decision that affects student life, which is a rare privilege in the present-day big business of higher education.

> 66 *Whatever you want to do, Caltech will always be very understanding and supportive. If you're interested in extracurricular activities, it's simple to get involved in clubs or student government. If you're interested in sports, you can participate on a team or just play recreationally in interhouse sports. If you have a hobby that isn't already at Caltech, you can easily start a new club. Since there are so few students, one person can make a big difference. While I've been here, I've seen students start an undergraduate research journal, a cheerleading squad, and a community service group that didn't even exist when I was applying.* 99

—*Janet Zhou, '04*

Traditions

This level of influence allows students a high degree of independence from Caltech administration. Over the years, students have been able to shape their own unique way of life without much administrative interference. This has created many quirky traditions, one of the wackiest being senior Ditch Day, which was featured on the *Tonight Show* with Jay Leno. One day every May, all the seniors ditch their classes and leave campus. Many years ago, underclassmen began to prank seniors' rooms while they were gone. The seniors countered by "stacking" their rooms, creating barriers to keep students from getting in on Ditch Day. Over the years, these stacks have become more elaborate, and now most take the form of an all-day scavenger hunt, where students run around campus collecting clues that will unlock the seniors' rooms. The Institute has relented to the students, and now cancels classes every year for Ditch Day. Every year, this creates some unexpected sights, which can really be understood only by those going through it. Ditch Day is somewhat representative of the entire student experience at Caltech; it is quirky and unpredictable, and is exactly what Caltech students enjoy.

FINANCIAL AID

Caltech financial aid has long held to a simple policy: "If you are an admitted student whose family has insufficient financial resources to pay for all or part of your educational expenses, Caltech will provide you a financial aid award that will meet Caltech's calculation of your financial need and so make it possible for you to attend." This has created a tradition of Caltech providing unparalleled opportunities to excellent students, regardless of their families' economic circumstances.

Applying for first-time financial aid is a simple process that mirrors that of other universities. Every applicant must fill out the Free Application for Federal Student Aid (FASFA) and the College Scholarship Service (CSS) Financial Aid PROFILE Application. These documents enable the Financial Aid Office to determine the amount that the student and his or her family can reasonably be expected to contribute toward a Caltech education. Any difference between that amount and the cost of attending Caltech is considered the student's financial need, and the Financial Aid Office will prepare a student aid package consisting of a combination of scholarships, grants, loans, and work study that will fully meet that need. The sum of a student's contribution along with the financial aid award covers the entire cost of attending Caltech: tuition, room and board, student fees, health insurance, money for books, extra meals, and personal expenses, even travel money if you live far away. There aren't any hidden costs.

Caltech tuition is already well below the cost for its peers, but the Financial Aid Office makes the additional effort to make it affordable for everyone. Most students are very satisfied with their financial aid package.

> **❝** *I knew that Caltech would be expensive, but the good thing is that Caltech's price tag includes everything: tuition, room and board, student fees, health insurance, money for books, extra meals, and personal expenses, even travel money if you live far away. There aren't any hidden costs.* **❞**

—*Debra Tuttle, '93*

Caltech strives to be fair and generous with its financial aid. A student's financial standing never factors into the admissions decision. The admissions process is completely "need blind" for domestic students and applications are evaluated separately from financial aid applications. Caltech also never uses financial aid as a bartering tool to attract students. All awards are based on need alone, and no award will ever be increased to match an offer from another school. If a student receives an outside scholarship, it will go toward reducing a student's loan or work study, rather than reducing scholarship or grant awards. If a student's financial circumstances change, Caltech is very willing to reevaluate the family's current, revised financial status.

Work-Study

Many students receive federal work-study as part of their financial award, and it is very easy to find opportunities to work on campus. The number of job opportunities far outnumbers the number of students on campus. The Financial Aid Office is very flexible with switching between loans and work-study, and many student work off a significant portion of their costs before they graduate. Some of the best-paying jobs are research assistant and teaching assistant. Students can also earn work-study by performing community service such as tutoring, reading to kids, or feeding the homeless. Other students work as office assistants, tour guides, ushers, or waiters. Many of these jobs have very flexible hours and pay reasonably well.

Scholarships

Caltech gives many scholarships that are need-based, but in recent years, several donations have allowed Caltech to give a limited number of merit-based scholarships to incoming freshmen. These merit awards come in a range of values. There is no separate application for the merit awards; all admitted students are automatically considered. There are also a number of upperclass merit awards given to sophomores, juniors, and seniors on the basis of academic excellence. These awards cover up to the full cost of tuition, and the Scholarships and Financial Aid Committee awards them to many outstanding continuing students each year.

GRADUATES

Thirty-two Nobel Prizes have been awarded to Caltech alumni and faculty. A Caltech education primes students for a career in scientific research, and a majority of graduates follow that path. On average, about half of Caltech graduates go on to earn a Ph.D., which is a significantly higher percentage than any other university. These are the students that Caltech is designed for—those who will dedicate their lives to the study and teaching of scientific knowledge. Caltech graduates are very successful in competing for fellowships and more than twenty each year win national and international awards.

Most freshmen enter Caltech dreaming of a professorship or a career in scientific research, but by the time graduation comes around, many find their interests are elsewhere. These students go into a variety of fields they never considered when they were in high school.

About twenty-five percent of graduates each year go straight into the workforce. Even when the economy is down, Caltech students don't have much trouble finding excellent jobs. More than one hundred companies recruit on campus each year; in a recent year graduates received offers that averaged about $71,000 and several graduates received offers in excess of $80,000. Most job offers come from the engineering and computer science industries, but an increasing number of recruiters come from the financial sector, insurance industry, and management consulting firms. More and more companies have found that the prob-

- ○ Frank Capra, Film Director
- ○ Linus Pauling, Chemist, Political Activist, two Unshared Nobel Prizes: Chemistry and Peace
- ○ Arnold Beckman, Chemist, founder of Beckman Instruments, Inc.
- ○ Vernon Smith, Economist, Nobel Prize for Economics
- ○ Ben Rosen, Cofounder of Compaq Computer Corporation
- ○ Gordon Moore, Cofounder of Intel Corporation
- ○ David Ho, Biologist and Physician

lem-solving skills, technical background, and mathematical ability of Caltech graduates apply to a wide range of activities.

This still leaves a group of graduates that doesn't fit into a particular mold. Although Caltech does not have a premedical program, each year graduates get into the top medical schools and go on to earn M.D.s. A growing number of graduates are applying to law school even though there are no prelaw majors. A few students each year join the Peace Corps, travel around the world, go into teaching, or start their own businesses. The rigorous education that Caltech provides does more than train students for scientific research; it teaches skills that are valuable in almost any field.

To graduate from Caltech is to be part of an elite club of a little more than 20,000 living alumni. As an extension of the intimate culture of Caltech, the alumni network is very close-knit and supportive. Many Caltech alumni look to hire other alumni, and all are happy to help in job searches or provide business contacts. Many graduates find their way back into the Caltech community; twenty-five current faculty members earned their undergraduate degrees at Caltech.

SUMMING UP

Most things at Caltech are not truly unique; there are many small schools where undergraduates live in an intimate environment, and there are many world-class research institutions where undergraduates have the opportunity to learn science and do research.

However, Caltech is the only place where these two ideas coexist on a single campus. They come together with great success, as Caltech consistently ranks among the top schools in the world. This makes the California Institute of Technology truly special and very difficult to describe on paper.

One big thing that nobody realizes until they step onto campus is how beautiful the landscape is. The student houses are flanked by brick pathways lined with orange trees on one side and olive trees on the other. Palm trees dot the campus and quiet ponds are home to lily pads, turtles, and bullfrogs. Every few weeks, a couple takes advantage of this scenery and gets married on campus; many more use Caltech as a backdrop for their wedding photos. This may have inspired the producers of *The Wedding Planner* to bring Jennifer Lopez on campus. Caltech students also recognize their campus in *Legally Blonde*, *Orange County*, and many other movies, as well as a host of TV shows including *Numbers*. Located a few miles from Hollywood, Caltech is a prime site for filming on location. The northern and western sides of campus are decorated with roses, which reveal another often forgotten aspect of Caltech: It is located in Pasadena, California, home of the Tournament of Roses. Each year, the Rose Parade marches within a few blocks of campus and all Caltech women are eligible to enter tryouts for Rose Queen.

This relatively small school is filled with surprises, and four years isn't nearly enough time to uncover them all. Caltech is a small school where there is big science. Its students are high achievers, but forego competition for an Honor System. Its beautifully landscaped campus shares space with cutting-edge scientific facilities. It is a place where Nobel Prize winners are spotted wearing shorts and T-shirts. It has innumerable extracurricular activities. It employs more Ph.D.s than there are undergraduates. It requires its literature and economics majors to learn quantum physics. It provides a top-notch education and charges less tuition than most peers. Can all of that exist at one place? At Caltech, it has existed for more than 100 years.

Coming to Caltech is certainly not for everyone, but for those who truly love science, there is no better place. The Caltech undergraduate experience is a wild and amazing ride, and there is never a shortage of things to do. Four years at Caltech forever changes the way every student looks at himself or herself, and most graduates agree that it is one of the most exciting periods of their lives. The shared journey bonds students together, and many make friends that last a lifetime. For all graduates, it is an experience they will never forget—once a Techer, always a Techer.

❑ *Ted Jou, B.S.*

Carleton College
Northfield, MN 55057

(507) 222-4190
Fax: (507) 222-4526, (800) 995-CARL

E-mail: *admissions@carleton.edu*
Website: *www.carleton.edu*

👫 Enrollment

Full-time ❏ women: 1,023
         ❏ men: 963

INTRODUCING CARLETON COLLEGE

Driving down rural Highway 19 in southeast Minnesota amidst farms and cornfields, it's hard to imagine that one of the country's best liberal arts colleges lies just out of sight. Nestled in the small town of Northfield, Carleton attracts a talented, diverse, and intelligent group of students, many of whom were initially considering matriculation at the Ivies. In fact, what sets Carleton apart from its East Coast counterparts is that the campus atmosphere, while intensely intellectual, is at the same time laid-back and friendly. Strangers really do smile at each other in passing, and even in the middle of finals or midterms, Carls can be seen tossing a frisbee in the middle of campus or building snow forts in the subarctic Minnesotan winters.

In typical Carleton style, the college just celebrated the 140th anniversary of its founding with celebratory cupcakes during the half-time of its homecoming football game. Although the rural college still maintains its Midwestern humility, its student body hails from forty-nine states, the District of Columbia, and more than thirty foreign countries. Carls come from a wide range of socioeconomic, ethnic, religious, and cultural backgrounds, so there really isn't a "typical" Carleton student. Carls often discover their classmates' unique perspectives not just in the classroom but also in late-night conversations with their roommates, over a team dinner after sports practice, or on walks with friends in the college's arboretum.

ADMISSIONS REQUIREMENTS

For a small private college in the Midwest, Carleton has boasted acceptance rates in the past few years that are as selective as those of its East Coast counterparts. Getting into the college is not an easy feat, and in 2005, around thirty percent of people who applied to Carleton were admitted. What does it take to get into such a place—high SAT scores? Perfect GPAs in Advanced Placement classes? Good recommendations? Maybe. Since the college prides itself on its diverse and well-rounded student body, admissions officers don't just look for one outstanding quality in an applicant.

There are, however, certain qualities in any application that admissions officers do look for, and aspects about an accepted student that will set him or her apart from less qualified applicants. In order to select a group of students for an incoming class who will take full advantage of all that Carleton offers, admissions officers will review applicants' academic backgrounds, standardized test scores, school and community involvement, and other unique accomplishments. Regarding the application-reading process, Dean of Admissions Paul Thiboutot reflects, "If I think about twenty-plus years of reviewing, there is an interplay among our evaluation of the strength of curriculum taken and grades obtained, impressions from the essay and overall assessment of the person's engagement in the larger life of their school."

One of the most important parts of any student's application is his or her high school transcript. Admissions officers want to see that a student has taken challenging academics like honors, International Baccalaureate, or Advanced Placement classes, even if it means that the student has a lower GPA than if he or she chose to take easier courses. A broad range of harder courses on a transcript shows that an applicant is academically curious, can handle a Carleton-size course load, and is up for a challenge. Good grades aren't everything, but they are something, and admissions officers will take them into consideration. Want to secretly hide away all of your ninth grade English and history grades? Take heart, admissions officers also look favorably upon academic improvement over the course of an applicant's high school career. Keep in mind that officers also note any declining grades, especially in applicants' senior years, so don't succumb to any acute cases of "senioritis" yet.

Dean Thiboutot stresses that another extremely important aspect of the application is the essay. He states, "I know that a lack of effort in writing an application essay can have a negative impact in those final close deliberations or vice versa," since it allows admissions officers to really "get a glimpse" of the applicant's interests, sense of humor, ideas, and perspective on life. The essay also is a chance for applicants to show that they can communicate well in writing—a skill that will become invaluable at Carleton, even for budding math and science majors. You don't have to produce a work worthy of a Pulitzer, but it would be a good idea to enlist a few teachers, parents, and/or friends to read through your essay before you submit it.

Despite what some students may think, Carleton is not just about academics. It makes sense then that students' extracurricular activities and involvement in their school and neighborhood communities are also important parts of their applications. Carleton will probably not accept a student just because of perfect grades and a perfect SAT score if the student doesn't show that he or she has other interests besides coursework. A perfectly "well-rounded" student doesn't have to be the editor of the school newspaper, a varsity team captain, or the founder of a neighborhood charity organization (although it helps if you are any one of these), what is important is that a student shows a genuine interest in his or her community and/or enjoys helping and teaching others. Dean Thiboutot stresses that the admissions staff tries to undertake "a holistic evaluation of an individual, keeping in mind that we are not admitting some robot-like academic machine, but a human being with a host of interests, talents, and qualities that will be developed in the classroom and beyond at Carleton, from dining room conversations to exchanges while tossing a Frisbee."

Admission officers also consider teacher recommendations, the college counselor recommendation, and standardized test scores. Carleton requires either the SAT or the ACT with writing and recommends that students take the SAT subject tests (scores on these tests can generally only help an applicant). Students for whom English is a second language should take the TOEFL.

If you can visit Carleton or contact an alumni admissions representative in your area, a good idea would be to schedule an interview. Carleton encourages but does not require admissions interviews, and the absence of an interview is not held against an applicant in any way. The interview is "a chance to meet someone who knows the Carleton experience well and can share reflections on that experience and answer question and hopefully deepen a prospective applicants understanding of the college," Dean Thiboutot explains. Because of this purpose, interviews are pretty informal meetings and are definitely more like conversations than interrogation sessions. When preparing for an interview at Carleton, forget about your canned answers and instead think about what really interests you and why you care about it so much because that's what your interviewers will really want to know about you.

Early Decision

Carleton has two Early Decision options for those who are certain that Carleton is their top-choice school. Early Decision is a binding agreement, and accepted Early Decision students will have to withdraw all other applications and not submit new ones. The Fall application deadline is November 15, and decisions will be mailed by December 15. The Winter deadline is January 15, the same as the Regular Decision deadline. Winter Early Decision will be notified by February 15. Regular Decision will be notified by early April, and no later than April 15.

ACADEMIC LIFE ▬▬▬▬▬▬▬▬▬▬▬▬▬▬▬▬▬▬

Academics are at the heart of students' liberal arts experience. Since Carleton is solely a full-time undergraduate institution, its academic programs are of course focused on undergrads, unlike many prestigious universities. Carls can choose from thirty-four majors and have the option of choosing one of sixteen concentrations, which is similar to an interdisciplinary minor. All Carls graduate with a Bachelor of Arts degree.

Distribution Requirements

Since Carleton is a college of liberal arts and sciences, students are expected and required to complete a wide range of courses in varied subjects. The college's distribution requirements are designed with the intention that all students' four-year academic experience will have breadth as well as depth. Everyone must take two courses in arts and literature (art and art history, dance, English, music, theater, classical and modern literature), two courses in humanities (history, philosophy, and religion), three courses in the social sciences (economics, educational studies, linguistics, political science, psychology, sociology, and anthropology), and three courses in math and the natural sciences (biology, chemistry, geology, physics and astronomy, mathematics, computer science, and specific psychology courses).

Students must also pass a writing requirement by taking a designated writing-intensive course and submitting a portfolio of samples of their writing by the end of their sophomore year. Carls also must fulfill the RAD (Recognizing and Affirming Differences) requirement, which basically means taking a class that focuses on a subject from a non-Western European perspective. Finally, all students must take four physical education courses, which can range from rock climbing to contact improvisation to ice skating.

"Distros," as these requirements are commonly called, represent about a third of the classes students will take at Carleton. Many Carls fulfill the distribution requirement without even thinking about it, and since there aren't any specific classes that all Carls are required to take, each student's course schedule can be incredibly personal and flexible.

Working Toward a Major

While distros are a great way for students to achieve a good breadth of knowledge, the major is an opportunity for them to study extensively in one subject that truly interests them. Many students have very vague ideas about a potential major when they arrive at college. Thankfully, Carls don't have to declare a major and an optional concentration until the spring of their sophomore year, so they have plenty of time to dabble.

Every major and concentration has its own distro requirements and required number of credit hours. Most majors require students to complete introductory courses (100 levels) in order to take intermediate (200 levels) and advanced courses (300 levels). Most students will also have to complete a methods course in their major during their sophomore or junior years and a Senior Seminar. Some will have to go through a petition process to complete a special major and/or double major. All students will meet with an assigned advisor from the faculty in their major to further discuss and plan their academic path.

The Senior Integrative Exercise, or "Comps"

In their senior year, students will cap off their major by completing a senior integrative exercise, or the comprehensive project. Carls fondly call this beast "Comps." Comps can take on many different forms, even within a certain major. They can be long exams, an in-depth research paper, an original thesis, a body of original artistic work, or student-conducted scientific or psychological research. Seniors love to gripe about comps, but secretly most enjoy the challenge of an extensive project that culminates their four years of academic study.

Academic Strengths

In the past decade, Carleton has been known for its strength in the physical sciences, and biology in particular has been one of the most popular majors with recent classes. About eleven percent of students in the class of 2006 were biology majors, and fifty-three percent of that entire class took at least one biology course during their Carleton careers. But biology isn't the only popular major at Carleton; political science/international relations, economics, English, and psychology also regularly make their way onto the top majors list. These top five majors are popular for a reason: students are attracted to the depth of study in which they can engage in each department, and the quality of professors and the breadth of subjects they teach.

Geology, a small but very strong department, has the amazing ability to attract students to its major. Few students come to Carleton intending to major in geology, but after taking a few introductory classes filled with plenty of hands-on field trips, many are hooked. The geo majors are a tight-knit group, and one can expect to see many of them literally camped out in their lab in the first floor of the Mudd Science Hall, entrenched in their research.

The arts of Carleton are receiving much attention. The initiatives being discussed will tie the arts into other aspects of the curriculum and provide new facilities. A planning committee has recommended the college create a center for visual and narrative arts featuring classrooms for campus-wide use: support services for visual and narrative production, studio arts, art history, cinema and media studies, English, and theater and dance; and a teaching art museum. The committee has also proposed the Perlman Learning and Teaching Center. The recommendation also calls for the development of an integrated music building that combines the teaching of music with performance space. Cinema and media studies (CAM) is now a major and will increase its course offerings and study-abroad programs.

The Trimester System

Carleton differs from the semester schedule of many other colleges of its size and caliber, and instead operates on a three-term system. The terms, conveniently named

"Fall," "Winter," and "Spring," are ten weeks long, and students will usually take three classes each term. Three classes seem like it would make for a relatively "light" course load, but when a semesters-worth of information is crammed into ten weeks, most Carls will agree that three classes is more than enough. The advantage of the trimester system is that it allows students to focus intensely on a few subjects for short bursts of time instead of spreading out their concentration to four or five classes that seem to last forever. Classes usually meet three days a week for seventy minutes or twice a week for an hour and forty-five minutes, so each class is incredibly important and bring something new to the course of study.

For four years, Carleton students will look at the world in ten-week increments: the first week is always an adjustment period, the fifth week is "crunch time" for midterm papers and exams, and things really pick up during the eighth and ninth week in anticipation of finals. The great thing about trimesters is that Carleton students are rewarded at the end of each term with a significant break. A six-week long break follows fall term, spanning from Thanksgiving to the beginning of the New Year. A two-week long spring break follows winter term, and, of course, the end of the spring term marks the beginning of summer.

The Classroom Environment

Since classes do meet for a significant amount of time, many students feel a particularly strong bond to their classmates and professors after ten weeks. Statistically speaking, the student-to-faculty ratio is nine-to-one, and the average class size is eighteen, with sixty-three percent of class sections having under twenty students. These stats show that Carleton students will (whether they like it in some cases or not) be an integral part of each class they take. Some introductory courses are more lecture-based classes and will have upwards of fifty students, but students in these large classes are split up into much smaller groups for the more hands-on laboratory sections.

Most classes are, however, discussion-based classes where each student is expected to participate regularly. In these classes, students help each other learn and will often meet in groups outside of classes to help each other study for exams or to critique each others paper's or projects.

> **❝** *One of the best things about an introductory religion class I took was the study group that a few other students and I formed. We'd meet regularly in the library or at a local coffee shop and just discuss the material until we knew it all inside and out. We even met a few times without studying in mind, just to catch up.* **❞**

Most Carleton professors are "accessible," meaning that they schedule ample time outside of class to meet with students and discuss anything from an upcoming paper to a theory that was glossed over in the last class. Some professors will even require their students to meet with them at least once so that they can connect and make the subject meaningful to everyone. Even though Carleton profs are brilliant and often critically acclaimed experts in their fields, most have chosen to teach at a small liberal arts school because they want to teach and interact with their students.

Learning Outside of the Classroom

When most people think of college academia, they usually conjure up visions of students sitting at desks in front of chalkboards, furiously taking notes, or students holed up in the college library, practically drowning in papers and books. While you can see plenty of scenes to match these visions at Carleton, much of the learning that occurs at the college happens in nontraditional settings, like on field trips, in study groups, or even in conversations that take place at a professor's house. Environmental biology courses will often take frequent trips to study the ecology of Carleton's 880-acre arboretum (or Arb), geology students will take frequent trips to South Dakota's "Badlands," educational psychology students will tutor in area schools, and sculpture students will install their works in public spaces across campus and in downtown Northfield.

Even Farther from the Classroom: Study Abroad

If there's one thing that Carleton students like to do, it's explore. About two thirds of students study abroad at least once during their time at college in over a hundred programs in forty-five different countries. It's not that Carls are dying to get away from campus (although doing tropical field research in Costa Rica might beat trudging to class in a Minnesota winter), it's probably more that Carls value a challenging, real-life experience away from the comforts of home. Many students choose to go on Carleton-sponsored programs, and each year faculty members lead groups of fifteen to thirty students to destinations around the world for ten weeks. These programs let students take a wide range of classes that help to fulfill requirements in their major, while at the same time allowing them to experience the subject they are studying on a more first-hand basis.

> **66** *My favorite class was a program run by a Carleton professor in Ireland; we worked with an Irish scholar on James Joyce's* Ulysses. *It was one of the greatest intellectual challenges I've ever had, and I learned so much about Ireland, Joyce, and crazy indecipherable prose.* **99**

—*Derek Zimmerman, '07*

If you want to get a little farther away from Carleton for a term, your options certainly aren't limited to the college's programs. Carleton is a member of several off-campus consortia, like the Associated Colleges of the Midwest and the Higher Education Consortium for Urban Affairs. You can also choose to participate in one of the many national and international college abroad schools, and programs like the Sea Education Association and The School for International Training are popular among students. Since the majority of Carleton students do go abroad, the Off-Campus Studies Office is very experienced at answering questions related to anything from credit transfers to host families to passports.

Technology Inside and Outside the Classroom

If you get a chance to walk around campus between classes, you'll probably see a fair number of students running to check e-mail at one of the many public computer labs around campus, or pulling out laptops to surf the net at Wi-Fi hubs in the Sayles-Hill Student Center or in the McKinley Gould Library, also known as the Libe. Many students will be rushing to post comments for a class on Moodle, Carleton's course-management system. Through Moodle, classes can create on-line forums for further discussion or questions outside of the classroom. All Carls also have access to a central server where they can access useful course materials, and more and more students can access most or all of their readings for certain classes on-line.

Carleton is both Mac- and PC- 'friendly,' although most classroom computers are Macs. Most students do own a computer, and laptops are useful, especially when they want to escape from distracting roommates and retreat to the depths of the Libe to write a paper. There are, however, plenty of computers around campus for student use, although finding an unused one can become quite a challenge during finals. If computers decide to revolt right before comps are due, workers at the Student Computing Information Center, or the SCIC, are there to help.

Academic Intensity—What to Expect

Most students at Carleton are academically curious and came to the college with the goal of satisfying that curiosity, not the goal of making straight As or being in the top of their class (although someone's got to do it). For some, this atmosphere is a dramatic shift from their cutthroat college-prep high schools, but in most cases, it's a welcome change. Students do worry about doing well in their classes, but "doing well" means really learning and manipulating the subject matter. Carleton has been called "a work hard, play hard" school, and it is not uncommon to see the student center filled with people typing furiously on their laptops or groups putting together a presentation at four in the morning during a finals period, or even during a particularly busy week. Another strange phenomenon about Carleton is that the person you least expect to be a physics whiz or heart-wrenchingly good writer, often is.

Social Life and Activities

If you think that the process of "getting an education" at Carleton only applies to hours spent in the classroom or studying in the Libe, think again. Much of the "learning" that happens at Carleton occurs during the conversations between classes with a floor-mate, in late-night broomball competitions, or while trying to organize a campus-wide event with a group of friends. But really, what does happen when you get a community of almost 2,000 incredibly interesting and talented young people together? Something pretty interesting.

Residence Halls

Carleton is first and foremost a residential campus, so all first-year students and the majority of all students live in the nine residence halls (or dorms) on campus. Every dorm is coed and mixed by class year. Freshmen will live in one of seven dorms (they don't live in two dorms because their layout isn't conducive to proper freshmen "floor bonding") and will be assigned to one or two roommates. Living in close quarters with a diverse group of people for an entire school year can be a challenging, yet ultimately rewarding experience. Dorm floors become small communities of their own, and many of them band together in intramural broomball games or as cast and crew of an annual campus-wide video-making competition called DVD Fest.

The chief overseers of the floor living communities are Resident Assistants, or RAs. RAs are upper-class students who have all applied for the job and have been trained to handle many of the situations that might arise in a dorm environment. Two RAs are assigned to live on each dorm floor, and they are good resources for first-year student making the transition to life at college.

Upper-class students progressively get more living options as their seniority grows. After their first year, students can apply to live in special interest houses like the Sustainable Living house or the Jewish Interest house. Some juniors and seniors can apply for Northfield Option, which means that they can live in privately owned houses or apartments in town. A few lucky seniors (and maybe some very lucky juniors and sophomores) get to live in college-owned townhouses, the cushiest campus living.

Clubs and Activities

At the beginning of every school year, each student is given a *Lagniappe,* Carleton's very own daily planner. It's a good thing to have around campus because schedules can get complicated very quickly. Besides class periods, assignment due dates, and readings to follow, a Carleton student will probably want to keep track of things like club meetings, performances, volunteer events, intramural games, and dates to hang out at the local coffee shop. All students are part of the Carleton Student Association (CSA), and elected officers form a student government that influences college policy and allocates funding to student organizations. There are over 150 "official" student organizations on campus to satisfy just about everyone's interests, whether it be religious, athletic, political, artistic, cultural, intellectual, or just plain goofy. If there isn't a club for a particular group of Carls, they can easily start their own.

Students often find a sense of camaraderie in the club that they join because they are drawn together by a collective enthusiasm, and sometimes passion, for a particular subject or cause. Because students have a broad and often unique range of interests, it's hard to peg people into certain groups. The captain of the rugby team might also be involved in the outdoor enthusiast association and the campus alliance against gun violence, or the awkward guy who helps you out with your calculus homework is also a member of a comedy improv group.

> 66 *Being Nigerian means so much to me and I wanted to make sure that I did not forget that when I went to college. Joining AFRISA [African Students Association] was like meeting all of my brothers and sisters and getting to know a place I had not seen in so long. Its role is to make sure that the spirit of Africa that lives inside every African student on campus has a voice . . . and that voice is heard.* 99

—*Love Anani, '07*

Community Involvement

Northfield's population of just over 17,000 people includes students from the town's two colleges, and this inclusive measurement goes to show how much the town relies upon college students to be involved residents. But what does it mean to be a Carleton student and also live in a small town in the middle of cornfields? First off, there's plenty of opportunity to get invested in a small but vibrant community. Carleton's Acting in the Community Together (ACT) office is a place that helps students find service opportunities in the Northfield area. From playing with puppies on Friday afternoons at the local animal shelter to traveling to rural Arkansas to help out with a Habitat for Humanity project during spring break, the ACT office gives Carls plenty of opportunities to get involved and stay involved.

Many students work as peer leaders in many different offices on campus. Carleton's Resident Advisors, Intercultural Peer Leaders, Gender and Sexuality Center Associates, Student Wellness Advisors, Chaplain's Associates, and Student Departmental Advisors are constantly working to make Carleton a welcome and inclusive campus for all students. They frequently host guest speakers, panel discussions, open houses, movies, and other events to educate and inform the entire campus community.

Fine Arts

Two of the largest student organizations are KRLX, Carleton's very own radio station, and Ebony II, a dance troupe open to anyone (like just about all Carleton groups). Over 200 students are involved in each club each term—as DJs, newscasters, and engineers for the round-the-clock FM station, or as dancers in one or many of the Ebony II shows that debut near midterms. Students wanting to get more involved in dance can try out for Semaphore Repertory Dance Company, take classes ranging from ballet to moving anatomy, or even apply for a special major. Every year a few students also apply for special majors in theater, and there are many opportunities for Carls with a wide range of abilities and interest levels to get involved in theatrical productions. Every year students write, direct, and perform in a program of one-act plays or put on larger faculty-directed Players shows that go up in the large Arena Theater. Students can also participate in a number of CSA-sponsored theatrical and comedy groups that usually perform several times a term.

If there's one thing there isn't a lack of on campus, it's singing groups. There are seven a cappella groups, many of which you can sometimes hear practicing in dorm stairwells singing anything from The Postal Service to traditional Irish airs. There are also a number of choir ensembles, as well as an orchestra, a symphony band, a jazz ensemble, an African drum ensemble, and many other smaller groups for those who are musically inclined. Those who are interested can learn how to play the sitar, as Carleton offers music lessons to both beginners and advanced musicians for many different instruments.

Carleton offers a wide range of publications to inform, entertain, and educate the student body. The campus' weekly newspaper, *The Carletonian*, has been an independent source of news since 1877. From the wacky and often cynical articles in the *Carleton Literary Association Paper* (the *CLAP*) to the heated political debates published in the *The Observer*, there's something for everyone. There are also several more artistic and literary journals around campus for students to debut and share their work.

Athletics

A good majority of students will play varsity, club, or intramural sports during their time at Carleton because, really, Carls would rather be *in* the action than just watching it. Whether its varsity soccer or intramural dodgeball, Carleton students will support their teammates and make lasting friends inside and outside the field, court, or pool.

There are twenty-one NCAA Division III varsity teams at Carleton who compete in the Minnesota Intercollegiate Athletic Conference, one of the strongest Division III sports conferences in the country. Men's and women's basketball, men's and women's swimming and diving, and women's soccer and volleyball have been particularly successful in the past few years. While varsity sports are a large commitment, student athletes are no different than their classmates—they're still the students singing in a cappella groups, finishing late-night projects in the lab, and laughing with friends over French fries in Sayles. Some sports teams can be a bit insular, but many athletes would argue that sports teams become close groups of friends, almost families of their own.

If a sport isn't played at the varsity level at Carleton, it's probably a club sport. Club sports range in intensity, but most seem to strike a balance between serious competitive play and just having fun. Some of the most intense club sports are the Ultimate Frisbee teams. Both Syzygy, the women's squad, and CUT, the men's squad, have made it to the national championships year after year. Other popular club sports are men's and women's rugby, cycling, hockey, lacrosse, and equestrian teams.

Most students get involved in intramural leagues, which are truly open to any student with any type of sports ability. One of the most beloved intramurals is broomball—the perfect excuse to run around late at night in subfreezing weather and not feel cold. For those not wanting to brave the cold more than they already have to, there are also frisbee, sand volleyball, 3 on 3 basketball, dodgeball, indoor soccer, and tennis intramural leagues as well.

Many students will do a pilgrimage to Carleton's fairly new Recreation Center, especially in the winter months. The Rec Center features a fully equipped fitness center, as well as a climbing wall, a bouldering gym, multipurpose courts, racquetball and squash courts, and a dance/yoga studio. Students can sign up to take classes like yoga and kick boxing through the Rec Center. There are also two lap-swimming pools on campus available for student use. In the fall and summer months, Carls will take advantage of the seemingly endless running trails in the 880-acre Cowling Arboretum, or Arb (President Oden claims to have run on every single one of them). In the winter, students can check out cross-country skis from the Rec Center and explore the miles of trail while hurling a few snowballs at friends. Whatever the sport, Carleton students will stay active all year long and make like they're having fun doing it.

Making the Most of Campus

Since Carleton is a full-time residential college, the social scene is very campus-centric. In any given week or weekend, there are countless speakers, exhibits, community meetings, movies, presentations, gatherings, festivals, performances, and parties to attend. Sometimes it can be quite overwhelming. If there's one thing Carls know how to do, it's how to have fun, both inside and outside of academic activities.

Carleton does a good job of providing various types of events and social opportunities for its eclectic student body. The social atmosphere on campus is pretty laid back, and most feel that they're free to do what they want, with whom they want, and when they want. On a Friday night, Carls can watch and talk about Anime movies, sled down icy hills on lunch trays, or

○ **Late Night Breakfast:** On the last night of reading days before the first day of finals, staff members, like the Dean of Students, serve all Carleton students plates of scrambled eggs, pancakes, and cinnamon rolls to refuel those needy brain cells.

○ **Schiller:** Forty years ago the bust of Friedrich von Schiller was stolen from the Office of the President. Students steal the bust from one another, knowing that whoever has possession of it must show it at campus events. Rumor has it that Schiller's taken trips around the world in his 40 year vacation.

○ **Rotblatt:** In 1964, a group of sophomores created a new intramural softball league and named it after ex-White Sox pitcher Marvin J. Rotblatt. The tradition of playing an annual game of one inning for every year Carleton has been in existence began in 1967. Every spring assorted loonies still gather in an attempt to complete a marathon game.

○ **Dacie Moses House:** Dacie Moses, a long-time employee at Carleton, was known for inviting students to her house for cookies and conversation. She donated her house where, now, two students live each year. It is still a shared gathering spot. Whether to bake cookies (which must be left for all to enjoy), share brunch, or maybe catch one of the a cappella groups practicing, this house provides a sense of "home" for many.

catch up with friends at a party, among a million other activities. There aren't any sororities or fraternities on campus, and the vast majority of social events on campus are open to all students. Members of the CSA-sponsored "Party Crew" will even help any group of students put on a unique all-campus party, whether it's a Bar Mitzvah or a Luau on Mai Fete Island.

The social atmosphere on campus is pretty liberal, and xenophobic, homophobic, sexist, and racist attitudes are not tolerated inside or outside the classroom. But students aren't just tolerant, and the college itself makes an effort to help student organizations that foster campus inclusiveness. In fact, Carleton was one of the first colleges in Minnesota, and perhaps the United States, to give institutional support to a campus Gender and Sexuality Center and the Queers and Allies House. Since Carls are such a diverse bunch, it can sometimes be difficult to truly understand a roommate or a classmate, or even a group of peers, but it's a challenge that students want to tackle (and do) on a daily basis.

FINANCIAL AID

Regardless of what a prospective student is looking for in a school, a college's financial aid policy can sometimes outweigh almost any other aspect of the institution when that student is deciding to apply. Carleton knows this fact, and the Office of Student Financial Services claims that no student should hesitate to apply to the college because of its cost.

Carleton has a need-based financial aid policy, meaning that there is an expectation that the family will contribute as much as they can toward the cost of education. Of course, this contribution varies with each family. For the 2007–2008 school year, all Carleton students who demonstrated financial need had those needs met. Half of Carls receive need-based aid, and more than $37.3 million was awarded to Carleton students in 2007–2008. Nearly two thirds of that money was funded by Carleton grants and scholarships, which do not have to be repaid. Outside aid comes from federal and state grants and national, regional, and local scholarships. In each class, Carleton sponsors seventy-five or more National Merit and National Achievement Scholarships. Carleton does not, however, offer scholarships for athletics, the arts, or academic performance, since most students would be eligible for one of those anyway. Carleton also participates in the Federal Supplemental Education Opportunity Grant (SEOG), Federal Pell Grant, Academic Competitiveness Grant (ACG Grant), and National Science and Mathematics Access to Retain Talent (SMART) Grant programs, as well as the Perkins Loan Program, the Stafford Student Loan program, SELF Loans, and a number of other loan programs.

Most of Carleton's financial aid packages consist of grants from Carleton and outside sources, a loan, and a work contract. Almost 82% of all students work on campus, most as a part of the work-study program through their financial aid. First-year students don't work more than eight hours a week, and upper-class students don't work more than ten hours a week. Most students find that their work is manageable and often a rewarding part of their overall Carleton experience. From working in the Burton dining hall dishroom to writing press releases for the Media Relations office, students are an important part of the "nuts and bolts" of the college's operations. Because students only work part-time and loans are generally about $4,000, the bulk of financial aid awarded to students comes from Carleton's grants—

a testament to the fact that the college seeks to provide educational opportunities to academically qualified students, regardless of their financial situations.

GRADUATES

After four years at college, students sometimes struggle to realize that they will have to continue with life outside of the "Carleton bubble." After initially having to get over the fright of reality beyond dorm life, ten-week terms, and dining hall meals, most Carleton alums realize that their undergraduate education has provided them with the tools to succeed in "the real world."

More than half of all Carleton alumni earn advanced degrees, with approximately seventy percent going on to graduate schools within five years of getting their Carleton diplomas. Many Carleton grads do not go straight to grad school and instead decide to enlist in programs like the Peace Corps, AmeriCorps, and Teach for America. They also might work for a few years to gain some practical experience before considering more school. Some Carls see the few years after graduation as a time to pursue a passion that they discovered and fostered while at Carleton. Many Carls also take advantage of postgraduate fellowships, like the Watson, Mellon, and Fulbright fellowships. These competitive opportunities are definitely once-in-a-lifetime experiences.

PROMINENT GRADS

- Thorstein Vehlen, 1884, Economist
- Pierce Butler, 1887, U.S. Supreme Court Justice
- Michael Armacost, '58, Former U.S. Ambassador
- Barrie Osborne, '66, Film Producer
- Dr. Mary-Claire King, '67, Medical Genetics Researcher/Professor
- Jane Hamilton, '79, Novelist
- Jonathan Capehart, '89, Pulitzer Prize-winning Journalist

66 Mostly, I feel really lucky to have something in my life that I'm that passionate about and to be able to really pursue it. I don't feel like I chose—I didn't have a choice. I can never not be dancing—it's like I'm addicted to taking dance classes. When I realized I could never go even for a couple weeks at winter or spring break without dancing, I realized this was maybe something I should consider making the focus of my life. 99

—Laura Grant, '06

Carleton alumni have a strange, yet wonderful, knack for congregating in certain areas around the United States, including the Minneapolis area, New York City, and San Francisco. In fact, Carleton's alumni network is incredibly strong, and the fact that Carleton continually ranks high among the nations' private liberal arts schools in alumni giving shows how much Carls care about their college community, even after leaving Northfield. The alumni network is an amazing resource for recent grads to have, no matter where in the world they're living or what kind of career they decide to pursue.

SUMMING UP

> **"** *My mom really wanted me to go to a school in the Midwest, and I wanted to get away from Nebraska; we were looking at schools and I figured that Carleton was probably the best school in the region. My grades weren't stellar, so I figured I'd apply early decision to Carleton and if I got in, then that would be a great stroke of luck. And voila, I matriculated.* **"**

—Derek Zimmerman, '07

The decision to come to Carleton is different for every student, but whatever the reason, not many people end up at the college by mistake. Some students will arrive for the first day of their freshman year in full Knights apparel, knowing the ins and outs of the academic system and the Ultimate Frisbee team's record since 1983. Others will need time to adjust to the small college community and the Minnesota winters. Regardless of background, Carleton is a great fit for students who want a small liberal arts college atmosphere, and a student body filled with a diverse, eccentric, and fun-loving people.

Prospective students who visit the campus in the summer will have a hard time envisioning what the college is all about because Carleton is really defined by the students, staff, and faculty who populate it. All of these people come together to make the college a supportive, intellectual, and challenging environment in which to live and learn. Carleton students don't just "get" an education, they have to make it their own—but there is no dearth of peers, professors, and other members of the Carleton community to help students on their way. Graduating seniors and alumni know that there is a great deal of truth in President Oden saying that "from the first day forward, you become a part of Carleton, and Carleton becomes a part of you."

❑ *Erika Lewis, B.A.*

Courtesy of Carnegie Mellon University

 Carnegie Mellon University
Pittsburgh, PA 15213-3890

 (412) 268-2082
Fax: (412) 268-7838

 E-mail: *undergraduate-admissions@*
andrew.cmu.edu
Website: *www.cmu.edu/admission*

Enrollment

Full-time ❑ women: 2,468
❑ men: 3,483

Part-time ❑ women: 36
❑ men: 36

INTRODUCING CARNEGIE MELLON

Carnegie Mellon University is consistently recognized as one of the premier research universities in the world. While the university is often associated with computers and engineering, others think of it as a university that specializes in art and drama. In reality, Carnegie Mellon is about all those things and more—creating students who can view life through a wide variety of lenses and who leave here prepared to make an important and lasting impact on society. The students here are as different from each other as you can get, yet everyone still finds ways to interact. There are students here from halfway around the world; there are students here from two miles away. There are undergraduate and graduate students from all fifty states and more than 100 foreign countries. Some people are here building complex electronic and robotic devices, and some are making beautiful art. The one thing that everyone does have in common is that they're committed to what they're doing, and they work hard.

Carnegie Mellon, located about five miles from downtown Pittsburgh, is surrounded by three culturally active, residential neighborhoods. Pittsburgh has come a long way from its industrial past. Forbes magazine recently named Pittsburgh "America's Most Livable City" based on employment opportunities, income growth, cost of living, crime rates, and artistic/cultural opportunities.

In 1900 Andrew Carnegie, a Pittsburgh industrialist and philanthropist, founded Carnegie Institute of Technology and Margaret Morrison Women's College to educate the sons and daughters of local working class families. In 1967 Carnegie's institutions merged with Mellon Institute, founded by Andrew Mellon, and formed Carnegie Mellon University. There are now seven colleges and schools within the university: Carnegie Institute of Technology (engineering) (CIT), Mellon College of Science (MCS), School of Computer Science (SCS), Tepper School of Business (Tepper), College of Humanities and Social Sciences (H&SS), College of Fine Arts (CFA), and the H. J. Heinz III College (policy and information systems).

Students embody a wide array of backgrounds and cultures. Carnegie Mellon's goal is to create an atmosphere that cultivates a sense of community while also embracing each student's individuality. Students at Carnegie Mellon represent all 50 states and more than 45 nations. The university offers degree programs in 12 countries, including its undergraduate campus in Doha, Qatar. Nearly one-third of the university's students are from outside the U.S., representing nearly 100 countries and giving Carnegie Mellon one of the largest international student populations in the U.S. Carnegie Mellon also boasts an influential, global alumni base in nations such as China, India, Japan, Singapore, South Korea, and the United Kingdom, among many others.

Carnegie Mellon has an incredibly distinctive history and, luckily, many of the traditions live on.

One of the rituals that students take part in is the painting of the fence. When Carnegie Mellon was still divided between men and women, the two schools were literally separated by a ravine. The one footbridge that connected the two campuses was where all of the men and women met in their free time. Then, when the College of Fine Arts building was built, the builders leveled a hill and filled in the ravine. The students of both schools were so disappointed that the administration built a fence in the bridge's place, but this was not a good idea because the fence really had no point. The night before it was to be torn down, a group of fraternity brothers painted the fence to advertise a party. The party was such a huge success that it became a tradition to paint the fence. Today, anyone can paint the fence. The only rules are that the fence must be painted, with a paintbrush, between midnight and 5:00 A.M., and whoever paints the fence must guard it for twenty-four hours or as long as they want their painting to stay. The fence paintings range from messages from fraternities advertising parties to happy birthday wishes to friends.

Carnegie Mellon is also one of the only universities that uses bagpipes to greet its first-year students on the first day and say farewell to graduates at commencement. Carnegie's Scottish heritage is celebrated even today. The name of our marching band, the Kiltie Band, says it all; every member of the band wears authentic Scottish garb (yes, including kilts). Carnegie Mellon is one of the few schools in the United States that offers a music degree in bagpiping. If you're not interested in majoring in it, there's also a bagpipe club (no kidding).

> **❝** *I never realized how different my college experience was from that of my friends. I never knew how many different people could live together on one campus. Like a lot of other people that have never really left home, I just figured everybody would be more or less like me. I was so wrong. But I've learned so much from just being here that I wouldn't trade it for anything.* **❞**

ADMISSIONS REQUIREMENTS

To be considered for admission to Carnegie Mellon, you must submit the following items:
- Common Application
- Carnegie Mellon Common Application Supplement
- Official high school transcript
- All score reports for standardized testing (SAT, SAT Subject Tests, ACT, etc.)
- Secondary School Counselor Evaluation
- Teacher Recommendation
- Arrange for an audition or portfolio review, if necessary

If you are an applicant whose native language is not English, you must submit the results of the other required standardized tests. Once you submit your application, we invite you to track the progress of your materials by visiting Where Am I in the Process (*http://my.cmu.edu/portal/site/admission/home/*).

ACADEMIC LIFE

At Carnegie Mellon, music, molecular science, acting, analysis, opera and organic chemistry, among other class choices, weave in and out of the lives and minds of Carnegie Mellon students on a daily basis, creating a lifelong foundation for learning.

One way that Carnegie Mellon students delve into their interests is through undergraduate research. Undergraduates are building mobile robots, creating documentary films, investigating cultural trends, and developing new digital communications technology. The Undergraduate Research Office supports student research in every field of study. Students receive small Undergraduate Research Grants (SURG) to cover research expenses, summer fellowships for full-time summer research, and Presentation Awards to support students presenting at academic conferences. In May of each year, Carnegie Mellon holds a campus-wide celebration of undergraduate research, the Meeting of the Minds.

> 66 *When I was getting ready to come here, I was really worried because I thought I wouldn't be able to handle the work load. All I had heard was how hard it was and how much everybody had to work. Now that I look back on it, I do have a lot of work to do, but it was as if I was eased into it. I'm used to it. Plus, all of my friends have the same amount of work to do, so I don't feel that I'm the only one studying so much.* 99

Although Carnegie Mellon is an extremely competitive school, students learn early that they need to help and support each other to succeed. People are willing to explain a difficult concept or give constructive criticism because they know that at some point they will probably need the same favor.

In many cases, professors or teaching assistants organize review sessions prior to exams. In addition to this, many students take it upon themselves to start their own study groups.

Classes and Faculty

With more than 90 majors and minors available, Carnegie Mellon offers you the opportunity to choose a program and change the world. The Carnegie Mellon education is complete with hands-on experience and groundbreaking research with real world application—even in your first year.

At Carnegie Mellon, you are more than a number. A 10-to-1 student-to-faculty ratio gives students the opportunity to learn directly from individual professors in a team environment. And Carnegie Mellon's world-renowned faculty members are committed to your education, and are often available after hours for additional academic help. Carnegie Mellon faculty and alumni are recognized as international leaders in many fields. The university has been home to 18 Nobel Prize winners.

There are more than 50 academic, research, and administrative buildings, three libraries, and a first-of-its-kind wireless network. While the Pittsburgh campus is rich in history, Carnegie Mellon is also known for employing leading-edge technology. Our students have unparalleled access to state-of-the-art equipment.

Students are also encouraged to solve problems by collaborating with peers across disciplines and across campuses. Global exchanges generate new ideas at Carnegie Mellon, and students are encouraged to take advantage of countless study abroad opportunities.

> **"** *When I was looking at schools, I was intimidated by Carnegie Mellon's reputation. I came for a visit and was really surprised to find that the students were normal people—their rooms were messy and they procrastinated, just like me! Since I've been here, I've found teachers and classmates to be very supportive. It's an intense environment, but I don't feel I'm in it alone.* **"**

The course load and the kind of work you do depends on what college you're in and what you're majoring in. Computer science majors will obviously spend a lot of time at their computers, while architecture majors will spend a lot of time in their studios. While one person is working on problem sets every night, another will be writing a long paper. Everyone will say that his or her work is the hardest, but the truth is that everyone is doing the kind of work they enjoy (or they should be). It's impossible to classify the class work here into one category. Every class has its own pattern.

Fellowships and Scholarships

Students interested in applying to competitive scholarship and fellowship programs find support at the university's Fellowships and Scholarships Office (FSO). Staff members help students identify external scholarships that best match their financial needs and interests in areas such as study abroad, graduate study, and research. The FSO helps students prepare competitive applications, practice interviews, and navigate national selection processes. Carnegie Mellon students have won many national and international awards, including 24 Fulbright, 15 Goldwater, five Truman, three Rhodes, three Udall, and one Marshall scholarships.

Study Abroad

Students and alumni often report that studying abroad has been one of the most valuable experiences of their lives. The Office of International Education provides resources for students interested in studying abroad during the academic year, as well as short-term study, internship, or volunteer opportunities during the summer and semester breaks.

Computers

You would expect Carnegie Mellon to be one of the world's most wired campuses and it delivers. It's not uncommon to see students connected anywhere, anytime on the campus. At Carnegie Mellon, a reliable and fast-wired network links all residence, academic, and administrative buildings on campus. An expansive wireless network spans 4.2 million square feet of the Pittsburgh campus, connecting over 56,000 computers and mobile devices. Seventeen public computer labs (clusters) offer approximately 400 Macintosh, Windows, and Linux computers, and over ninety software titles on three operating systems. A pool of publicly available Linux computers offer remote access to e-mail and other services or tools. Carnegie Mellon also has a state-of-the-art multimedia studio with equipment for animation and computer modeling, music composition, digital video, imaging, and sound recording, a large format color printer, and an equipment lending service. The Blackboard course management system enables faculty to securely manage and deliver course materials to students. The Carnegie Mellon (*C@CM*) course helps new students understand the computing environment and available resources. An excellent technical Help Center Staff is available Monday–Friday in person, by phone, or by e-mail to answer computing related questions.

The Campus: New Buildings and New Options in Housing and Dining

Carnegie Mellon is technically a neighborhood within a city of neighborhoods. The campus is self-contained and surprisingly open, perhaps because of the university's commitment to green initiatives. In recent years, the shape of the campus has changed to include a new west campus featuring the Gates Center for Computer Science and the Hillman Center for Future-Generation Technologies. Important additions in teaching and office space were made in buildings housing the social sciences, business, and the sciences. Construction and renovation on campus emphasizes a green approach, and Carnegie Mellon is distinctive in the number of green buildings, including Stever House, the nation's first green dorm.

All first-year students are required to live in university housing. Housing Services guarantees housing for all four years if you remain in the university housing system, which about 75% of students do. There is a variety of housing options with various amenities available, including laundry facilities in some residence halls. Carnegie Mellon owns 25 residence halls and apartments on and off campus. Different housing options, like standard, prime suite-style, and special interest, are available. All residence halls contain wireless internet. Greek Housing is available for members within the Greek community.

All first-year students are also required to have a meal plan. Dining Services offers several meal options to choose from that can be used at various locations both on- and off-campus. Carnegie Mellon's Dining Services also has made it a priority to implement programs and practices that are healthier for students and the environment through a sustainable dining program. This includes local food purchase of fair trade products.

Carnegie Mellon has a safe campus, patrolled by police and security officers who travel the area on foot, by car, and by bike 24 hours a day. There are programs encouraging safe walking and a campus shuttle service that travels to areas near the campus. A campus emergency alert system uses voice and text messages and web updates to keep the community updated on any emerging situations.

Unwinding On and Off Campus

All work and no play? Not a chance! Although the academic environment can get fairly intense, Carnegie Mellon students definitely know how to unwind. After a full week of classes and schoolwork, everybody's ready to relax and have some fun. A common stereotype of Carnegie Mellon students is that they can never tear themselves away from their computers. While everybody here has probably had a few weekends when they spent much of it working, it is much more common for students to find other, non-work-related things to do, with world-class museums, more trees per square mile than almost any other city in the nation, and food options from every cuisine imaginable. Pittsburgh is a manageable international city with a small town feel. In fact, some of the richest cultural offerings in Pittsburgh are actually on the Carnegie Mellon campus. Students from the College of Fine Arts offer plays, concerts, operas, and gallery shows. Whether you're a sports fanatic, enjoy the outdoors, or want to take in some culture, Pittsburgh has something for you. With downtown only five miles from campus, you'll soon learn firsthand why Pittsburgh is rated one of the most livable cities in the country. You can find shopping, restaurants, movie theaters, coffeehouses, museums, and nightlife—and this is all within walking distance. Beyond that, it is easy to catch a city bus going downtown or to a nearby shopping mall. Students have free access to public transportation with their ID cards. Pittsburgh is full of things to do, from the cultural to the just plain fun. You can go to the symphony one night and then attend a Pittsburgh Steelers football game or go to a Pittsburgh Penguins hockey game the next. The possibilities are endless.

Athletics

Carnegie Mellon's team name is The Tartans. Carnegie Mellon is a member of Division III in the NCAA and of the University Athletic Association. Students have an opportunity to participate in non-varsity intercollegiate athletic competition and formalized group instruction. Club Sports are recognized student organizations that establish their own leadership structures, membership requirements, competition schedules, dues, and fundraising events. The clubs provide social, competitive, instructional, and safe environments based on the common interests of the participating members. The Club Sports program strives to provide a dynamic learning environment while promoting sportsmanship, skill development, and camaraderie through sport and play.

Organizations

Beyond sports, there are more than 225 student organizations on campus. There is a club here for everyone. Students are celebrating ethnic heritage through Bhangra in the Burgh, hosting concerts and comedians through the Activities Board, participating in service projects through Amnesty International, playing video games with the Online Gaming Society, promoting green practices with Sustainable Earth, shaping campus policies through Student Government, and reporting on the latest news at *The Tartan* newspaper, cmuTV, and

WRCT-88.3 FM. If there isn't a group that matches your interests, you can gather some friends and propose a new organization to the Committee on Student Organizations.

> *I had been involved in drama in high school, but I knew I wouldn't be able to take part in the drama productions here because I wasn't a drama major. I was so excited when I found out about Scotch and Soda, a group of nondrama majors who put on shows throughout the year. I've met some of my best friends through S&S.*

Scotch and Soda, an amateur theater group, has a long tradition at Carnegie Mellon. Throughout the year the group produces two full-length shows and several one-act plays.

Fraternities and Sororities

Throughout the year, the fifteen fraternities and eight sororities on campus plan various social and charitable events open to the entire campus. These events include the Greek Sing talent show and Almost Midnight Breakfast before finals. The Greek system makes up about 19 percent of campus. If a student chooses not to join the Greek system, he or she will have no problem having a social life.

Spring Carnival

Each spring, the campus comes together for Carnegie Mellon's annual Spring Carnival. Many alumni return to campus for reunions and to interact with current students. This three-day event includes shows, concerts, and contests. The two biggest elements of Spring Carnival are Booth and Buggy. Each student organization has the opportunity to build a large, elaborate booth corresponding to the carnival's theme.

> *Buggy has been one of the highlights of my life at Carnegie Mellon. At first, I wasn't sure about it. Everyone seemed to know exactly what they were doing but I had no clue. However, the first time I pushed, the whole team ran along beside me cheering—after that first push, I felt like a pro. I've also made a lot of friends through Buggy. There's a lot to be said about the friends you can make getting up at 5:00 A.M. on a weekend.*

These same organizations build buggies, high-tech soapbox derby cars, to race through Schenley Park. The buggies look like torpedoes on wheels and are driven by the smallest student (usually a female) that the organization can find. People push the buggies up the hill and then let them coast through the park (some get up to speeds of thirty-five to forty miles per hour).

FINANCIAL AID

The total cost of a year at Carnegie Mellon, including tuition, room and board, books, etc., during a recent year was about $52,800. With a price tag like this, it's obvious that many students will need some kind of financial aid. Depending on your financial need, your financial aid package might include a combination of grants, loans, and work-study. About seventy-two percent of the freshmen who entered in a recent year received some sort of financial aid. The average need-based package was $22,943. Although you are not guaranteed financial assistance, most people who are eligible and in need receive it.

My parents own a small business and don't have a lot of extra money. When I applied to Carnegie Mellon, I was worried that the cost would be too high for them to afford. If it wasn't for the financial aid, there is no chance that I would be here. I've talked to several of my friends about this and many of them are in the same position.

Work-study gives students the opportunity to have on-campus jobs in order to make money to pay some of their college expenses. These jobs include positions in offices, food service, the child-care facility, and the library, to name a few. These jobs usually don't take up more than ten to fifteen hours a week and they allow the student to make extra money that they might need to buy books or for other necessities. Since there are so many jobs available, students may work on campus even if they don't qualify for need-based work-study.

GRADUATES

There are more than 84,000 Carnegie Mellon alumni in nearly 130 countries around the world. Alumni have won Oscars, Tony Awards, Emmy Awards, and Grammy Awards, as well as Nobel Prizes. The goals achieved and backgrounds of these alumni are as diverse as when they began their careers at Carnegie Mellon. Like most, very few go immediately to the top; but many of these graduates are used to working hard to achieve their goals. After four years at Carnegie Mellon, these graduates know how to get the job done. An experienced Career Center staff works with students throughout the year on job interviewing skills and to bring recruiters to campus. Because of the university's reputation for preparing students with real-world and practical experience, Carnegie Mellon ranks among major employer's top U.S. colleges and universities from which to hire recent graduates. In addition, approximately one-third of Carnegie Mellon graduates enter graduate school directly.

There is a large network of Carnegie Mellon graduates organized all over the world. This network helps fellow alumni who decide to relocate or need advice concerning a job. It is also an invaluable resource for meeting people in your field. The one thing that all Carnegie Mellon alumni do have in common is the pride and tradition of being part of this network. You could go anywhere in the world and be able to chat with alumni about Spring Carnival or Schenley Park.

SUMMING UP

Carnegie Mellon has, in a word, everything—there is nothing that you could not find at Carnegie Mellon. Walking across the Cut (the grassy area in the middle of campus), you can see people studying, playing Frisbee, reciting poetry, sleeping . . . the list could go on and on. The people who end up coming to Carnegie Mellon are from all over the world, with different cultures, different beliefs, and different interests. But they all exist together. People say that going away to college is as educational outside of the classroom as it is inside. This has never been truer than it is at Carnegie Mellon.

PROMINENT GRADS

- Matt Bomer, television/film actor
- Holly Hunter, television/film actor
- Ted Danson, television/film actor
- Zachary Quinto, television/film actor
- Iris Rainer Dart, bestselling novelist, including *Beaches*
- Erroll B. Davis Jr., academic chancellor and CEO
- Jeffrey Housenbold, CEO, Shutterfly
- Stephanie Kwolek, inventor of Kevlar, recipient of National Medal of Technology
- Rob Marshall, theater and film director and choreographer, including *Chicago*
- John Nash Jr., mathematician, Nobel Prize winner, and subject of the film, *A Beautiful Mind*
- Gela Nash-Taylor, founder of Juicy Couture clothing line
- Randy Pausch and Jeff Zaslow, co-authors of *The New York Times* bestseller, *The Last Lecture*
- Stephen Schwarts, musical theater composer/lyricist including *Godspell*, *Wicked*, and Disney's *Pocahontas*
- David Tepper, president and founder, Appaloosa Management
- Andy Warhol, pop artist

There is so much here, it can be very intimidating at first. Where do I go? What do I do? How do I make friends? It's impossible to know exactly how to approach it. Fortunately, somebody has already planned this. For the first week that freshmen are on campus they are involved in, as many students would tell you, the best orientation anywhere. Through the entire week, students take part in planned activities, learn how to deal with being away from home, and meet more people than they could ever remember. This orientation is just the beginning of the series of support systems that exist here. No matter what you're doing, there will always be somebody there to help you. There are programs here ranging from peer tutoring to peer counseling. If you have a problem that you don't think a peer can help you with, the professors and other staff are always willing to try to help you. Basically, no matter what's going on, if you look for help, you'll find it.

The students that attend Carnegie Mellon are motivated, driven, and goal-oriented. Everyone here knows that everyone else has worked hard to get here. They're all in the same boat, and this brings everyone closer together. College is about the things you learn and the friends you make in the process. You'll have both at Carnegie Mellon.

> 66 *There isn't anybody who goes here—or has ever gone here—who won't tell you that everything about this place is intense. People work hard. They have goals and dreams. But they also have friends and fun. Don't ever let anybody tell you that it's too hard.* 99

❏ *Jessica Demers, B.A.*

 Case Western Reserve University
Cleveland, OH 44106

 (216) 368-2000 (general information)
(216) 368-4450 (admission)

 E-mail: *admission@case.edu*
Website: *www.case.edu*

 Enrollment

Full-time ❑ women: 1,718
❑ men: 2,367

Part-time ❑ women: 88
❑ men: 54

INTRODUCING CASE WESTERN RESERVE UNIVERSITY ▬▬▬▬▬

Rated the best university in the state of Ohio and one of the best universities in the country, Case Western Reserve University has gone through more than one crisis of identity in the last few years. It is best known as a top-notch research university. The class of 2009 fondly called it "Case" and joked about the "fat-man-and-surfboard" logo (two interlocking letter C's meant to represent the university's tie to the local Cleveland community). The class of 2010 called it "Case," too, but got rid of the washed-up fat man in favor of a new "sunrise" logo that symbolizes the school's mission of forward thinking. Now, most of its students know it as "CWRU." Whatever you call it, one thing remains constant about Case Western Reserve University: its respect for academic exploration and commitment to innovation.

A first visit to Case would ideally happen in the spring or summer, since Cleveland's "lake effect" winters turn the campus into a snow globe, minus the cute penguins and reindeer. Weather permitting, the campus is extremely walk-able, with wide sidewalks and lush, manicured grounds. Signage is big at Case, so it's hard to get lost. The university makes visitors feel welcome by hosting special events such as campus tours and new student orientations. Case students show their hospitality by serving as guides for campus tours or by hosting prospective students for overnight stays. Visitors have the opportunity to sit in on classes and lectures, eat at the campus dining halls, check out the residential halls and facilities, or talk to one of the expert counselors in Undergraduate Admissions.

My first visit to Case was in March. There was snow on the ground, but the sun was out, and I could see hints of spring between the patches of white. I remember being impressed with how big the campus seemed and how quiet it was, despite being so close to downtown Cleveland. All of the people we passed on the sidewalk looked busy. Case had a special energy that drew me in. It seemed like everyone was going somewhere.

There's a lot to be proud of at Case. First founded in 1826, Case Western Reserve University, as we know it today, was officially formed when two schools, Case Institute of Technology and Western Reserve College, federated in the late 1960s. Case Western Reserve University has a long history of pushing its students to academic excellence. This has earned the school a reputation for holding its students and faculty to high standards. Case's motto, *Think beyond the possible*, encourages students, faculty, staff, and alumni to embrace creative thinking and meet new challenges with excitement.

It's All about Location

Case's 155-acre campus is nestled in the heart of Cleveland's University Circle, a hub of educational, cultural, social, and medical institutions. The Circle is filled with things to do. Wade Oval, for instance, treats residents to free live jazz in the summer and the chilly thrills of a festive ice rink in the winter. Case students have endless options for recharging in the Circle. They are sure to find inspiration in one of the Cleveland Museum of Art's 42,000+ pieces, or they can take a study break with some fragrant herbal tea and a piece of baklava at Algebra Tea House.

University Circle has seen major changes in recent years because many of the institutions that call the Circle home have expanded. Case hasn't been left out of this exciting development. New buildings have sprung up all over campus in order to accommodate the interests of an ever-diversifying student body. A pleasing juxtaposition of progress and tradition is created on campus by the conglomeration of chic modern buildings and stately remnants from the school's heyday as the old Western Reserve University. For example, the Mandel Center for Nonprofit Organizations, with its clean lines and façade of large windows, recently gave the North Side of campus a facelift. It is a surprising find after a stroll between Mather Quad's weathered stone buildings.

Its quiet campus and location make Case feel more residential than urban, but the university is just five miles east of downtown Cleveland. The city is mid-sized, and it's easy to navigate by car or public transportation. If students crave more action than the neighborhood community immediately surrounding the campus offers, they can hop on the RTA's train system or board one of its Healthline buses and arrive in the center of the city in a matter of minutes. With landmarks like the Rock and Roll Hall of Fame and local treasures such as the Playhouse Theater or the West Side Market, there is always something new to do downtown. Cleveland is a sports fan city, and Case students often take advantage of the opportunity to cheer on the Browns during football season, the Indians during baseball season, or the Cavaliers during basketball season.

Case's location isn't all about fun and games, of course. By and large, Case students are ambitious individuals who are serious about reaching their goals. They often venture into the city in search of internships or summer jobs, and many students volunteer with local schools and other organizations. Innovative technology, research, and social services flow from the university to better the community, too. Case's estimated economic impact on the Cleveland area which it calls home is an estimated $1 billion.

The Learning Environment

Students and faculty at Case are extremely focused on learning. Courses at Case are rigorous, and since most students take advantage of résumé-building extracurricular activities, leadership roles, and professional opportunities, the workload can be quite demanding. There are some tried-and-true tricks to surviving Case with your GPA intact, such as budgeting your time wisely and finding a study buddy. The rest is trial-and-error, according to Anna Handorf, an energetic member of the Class of 2012, who is double-majoring in biology and psychology, minoring in chemistry, and following a premedicine curriculum. Anna has got a lot on her plate, but she has figured out a system that keeps her on top of her studies. "For me, it's all about keeping a balance between classes, homework, and extracurricular activities," she explains. "I need to keep really busy or I just procrastinate and barely get my work done on time. When I'm busy, I'm forced to use the little free time I have to really focus. I tend to study alone. I like to spread out and isolate myself so that I can really focus. I like to lie down on the floor when I study—it's kind of weird, but it's how I study best!"

When your own methods for cracking the physics homework that was due yesterday aren't enough, sometimes it helps to ask the expert: your professor. Case faculty and staff have done an excellent job of creating a strong support system for students. Professors hold walk-in office hours and, as a general rule, respond with near immediacy to e-mail when students have questions about coursework.

Free tutoring in nearly all required courses, counseling for matters such as effective study strategies and time management, and guidance for students with disabilities are all offered through Educational Student Services (ESS). One of the best surprises about the tutoring services at ESS is that they are offered by students. Struggling to figure out your microeconomics homework? Who better to turn to for help than a fellow student who aced the class and with whom you can relax and be yourself? If you're trying to find answers to questions about life outside the classroom, Case has your back on that, too. The Career Center offers free career counseling, hosts Career Fairs for forward-thinkers, and connects undergraduates with alumni who can offer professional advice. Support is always available, and it's not hard to find.

Support Staff

Just as critical to students' success as the supportive staff and faculty are the resources and technology available for student use. Kelvin Smith Library—or KSL as it is more commonly known—is the main library on campus. The library allows 24-hour access to students. During the week of final exams, it isn't uncommon to spot groups of students armed with books, notes, iPods, and Starbucks coffee cups holding last-minute study sessions as late as 3:00 A.M.

KSL is also popular for its technology services. The Freedman Center in KSL offers digital library, language learning, and multimedia services. The Center also lets students check out audio and video recording equipment for free or use computer software such as InDesign. Helpful staff members are always on hand to guide students through tricky tech issues.

The supportive learning environment at Case is enriched by a diverse student body, which represents approximately 100 countries and all 50 states. As the international student population at Case has grown, the university has become increasingly sensitive to the cultural, social, academic, and emotional needs of these students. Students have also dedicated their time and energies to celebrating differences at Case by starting student groups that advocate diversity such as CWRU LGBT Center, Indian Student Association, and Asian American Alliance, to name just a few.

ADMISSIONS REQUIREMENTS

To become a CWRU Spartan, you need three things: an on-line application (including a transcript with prerequisite coursework and a personal essay), an interview, and a passion for learning. The application process is competitive, but getting your foot in the door at this prestigious school is not impossible. Case accepts around seventy percent of its applicants.

Most undergraduate applicants are among the top students in their high schools. The average SAT score for an incoming freshman is between 610-700 in critical reading, 650–750 in math, and 600–690 in writing. Average ACT scores range from 28 to 32.

With such great high school credentials and test scores, prospective students could go to college just about anywhere. Why choose Case?

> **"** *CWRU had a very strong engineering school, but also gave me [the] option to take classes in multiple disciplines if I wanted to explore my creative side. [The] urban setting as well as relatively small and personal class sizes also attracted me to the university.* **"**

—Marissa Morgan, '11

The university celebrates incoming students' post-college plans with professional advising and programs like the Pre-Professional Scholars Program (PPSP), which offers conditional admission to one of CWRU's professional schools in medicine, dental medicine, law, or social work to a select group of first-year applicants.

Case students hit the books notoriously hard. Where are the best spots for getting your nerd on around campus?

○ **Kelvin Smith Library:** Kelvin Smith Library, aka "The Lib," aka "KSL," has a lot of nicknames. This popular spot offers plenty of high-speed computers and comfortable seating. You can avoid distractions in a silent study space, or head to a private room for group work. Open 24/7, KSL can accommodate even the worst procrastinator's (lack of) schedule.

○ **Wade Lagoon:** Students sprawl out on the grass near this man-made lagoon wedged between the Cleveland Museum of Art and Euclid Avenue. Savvy studiers bring a blanket and a picnic basket and set up camp under the shady willow trees.

○ **University Coffee House:** Located conveniently near the freshman dorms, this Starbucks-alternative is popular because of its affordable yet tasty menu offerings and low-key atmosphere. It's not uncommon for professors to hold office hours, study sessions, and even classes upstairs.

○ **Nord Hall:** Although the School of Engineering officially occupies this building, students of all majors frequent Nord. Some come for class, but most show up for Einstein Brothers' Bagels, naps on the oversized furniture on the ground floor, a visit to the computer lab, or brief study sessions with friends.

○ **SAGES Café in Crawford Hall:** This is Case Quad's best-kept secret. In addition to the near-guarantee that the student barista won't pass judgment when you order a sixth cup of coffee before a final exam, you are also usually guaranteed silence and your own sofa. Tutors, especially members of the SAGES Peer Writing Crew, also hang out here, so your chances of running into a helpful study buddy are high.

○ **Wade Commons:** Another location highly trafficked by tutors, a lot of students come to Wade for homework help or exam reviews. Clubs and Greek societies rent out rooms in Wade for social activities, so it's a good choice for those who want to study and socialize.

ACADEMIC LIFE

When I was a freshman at Case in 2006, upperclassmen joked that we had an Ethernet internet system second only to NASA's. While the NASA comparison might be an exaggeration, Case is unmistakably a techie-friendly place. Professors use technology to shake up the classroom, and, thanks to go-green initiatives, on-line class discussions and assignment submission have become commonplace.

Case's emphasis on technology won't surprise those who are familiar with the university's reputation as a science school. Future doctors, dentists, researchers, and engineers flock to Case because of this reputation. In September 2010, a report released by the National Science Foundation ranked the school 26th in the nation as a recipient of federal funding for research. Case receives close to $400 million each year in external research awards, meaning that research opportunities abound for students and faculty members who are interested. The university's semiannual magazine, *Think*, celebrates the power of thought and showcases some of the most important research happening at the university. *Discussions*, a student-run research publication, which is part of Case's undergraduate Media Board, honors student research at the university.

So much focus on the sciences at Case might leave students and faculty of the humanities on campus sidelined, waiting bitterly for someone to give them the kudos they deserve. But Case's culture of learning, which encourages interdisciplinary curiosity, prevents that from happening. It's not strange to see a poetry course on a future chemist's schedule, or for a music major to waltz into an economics class. The curriculum is flexible in terms of required courses, so double-majoring is no phenomenon at Case. With seventy-five programs of study to choose from, Case students can make their education truly their own.

Of course, education is not limited to the classroom. I learned just as much outside of Case's many classrooms as I did in them. Case professors encourage students to take charge of their own learning, and there's a certain accountability that comes with that kind of freedom. The independence made class more fun, and it helped prepare me for a lot of the professional work I would do after graduation.

The Seminar Approach to General Education and Scholarship (SAGES) program, an alternative to freshman composition courses, is mandatory for all students and was designed as a launch pad for experiential learning. SAGES aims to cultivate students' analytical and communications skills—transferable skills many students use in their future careers.

Over seventy-five percent of students take advantage of research, internships, co-ops, clinical work, service learning, and study abroad opportunities. Malavika Kesavan, a member of the Class of 2011 and biology major, spent a semester abroad at University College Dublin in Ireland.

> 66 It was a really good experience, because it opened up my horizons. I was able to meet a lot of different people. In terms of academics, the system [in Ireland] is really different. It was interesting, and a lot more self-taught than I expected. 99

Malavika was "surprised" by the distance her Irish professors maintained from their students because, at Case, professors make themselves very accessible. Overall, Malavika described the study abroad experience as formative and said she appreciated the diversifying effect it had on her academically.

There are more than 2,700 Board-approved faculty members molding bright minds on campus. Case's small class sizes, especially in humanities classes, mean that students are almost always engaged in meaningful dialogue with knowledgeable, supportive faculty members. "One person who has provided excellent mentorship throughout my undergraduate career has been Dr. Alan Levine," says Chairut Vareechon, a Class of 2010 Case alumni and current research assistant at the university. "It was his immunology course and ongoing advice that led me to a career in biomedical research."

While proactive faculty members ensure that there is ample opportunity to find a mentor at Case, an estimated sixty percent of Case's students are graduate-degree-seeking students who are more than happy to reach out to younger students.

SOCIAL LIFE AND ACTIVITIES

Although it has been the butt of its fair share of "nerd school" jokes, Case has gotten much cooler in the last few years. There are over 150 active student organizations for students to get involved in. It you can't find a club to suit your fancy, it's not hard to step it up and start your own. You can also join the twenty-seven percent of students who go Greek with one of the campus's twenty-three fraternities and sororities. Iva Jeras, a fourth-year nursing student and member of the Class of 2011, shares her sorority experience.

> **“** *I'm happy I joined because I got to meet a lot of new people who I wouldn't have met otherwise and who became some of my best friends. They're the ones who pushed me to do better in school and were always there if I need anything.* **”**

With such a wide range of backgrounds and interests represented in the student body, it's easy to find someone you can connect with as long as you're willing to back away from the computer game and look.

In their downtime, Case students can rock out on campus with concerts sponsored by the University Programming Board (UPB). Watch your friends "break a leg" on stage at a Footlighters theatrical performance. If you need to burst the "Case Bubble" and break away from campus for the evening, Cleveland has a lively music scene and great restaurants. Dine in style downtown at famous chef Michael Symon's restaurant Lola or take a ten-minute stroll off campus to Cleveland's Little Italy for pasta and cannoli. Getting to know and love the city is part of Case culture. In 2009, Case was named a top ten "best neighbor" school by "Saviors of Our Cities: A Survey of Best Neighbor College and University Civic Partnerships," which recognizes universities for the positive impact they have on their urban locales.

Case students stay fairly active, and you can almost always spot someone tossing around a Frisbee or going for a jog. Case is a charter member of the University Athletic Association, a part of the NCAA's Division III conference. The campus boasts ten athletic facilities and fields. Twenty percent of students play a varsity sport, including basketball, baseball, cross country, football, soccer, swimming, tennis, track and field, volleyball, and wrestling. A whopping seventy percent of students play intramural sports.

FINANCIAL AID

Education is an investment, and with the economy in trouble, students and their families are nervously fingering their thinning wallets. A world-class education is not cheap, no matter where you go. After tuition, housing, books, fees, and travel, an average year of schooling at Case adds up to about $52,453.

Luckily, a generous alumni network and a small student body mean that it is normally possible for qualified applicants to afford a Case quality education. Need-based aid, like loans, grants, and work study, as well as merit-based scholarships and special awards are all available. The counselors in the Office of Financial Aid are quick with advice and information. The Office of Student Employment helpfully posts job listings, ranging from research assistants to peer tutors, for all students who want to earn some extra cash. Case ranks thirty-fifth among American universities for best value, determined by the school's ratio of cost to quality of education.

Kevin Reuning stayed busy during his time at Case; he majored in political science and math, with a minor in economics. Even with two majors and a minor, Kevin held down a work study job at the Francis Payne Bolton School of Nursing as an administrative assistant.

> **“**My boss was really good about having an open schedule," he recalls, "just as long as I got stuff I needed to get done done. It gave me spending money. **”**

Campus jobs—especially work study jobs—tend to pay decently, averaging around $10 an hour. Many students choose to work so that they can fund their social life. "College was paid for, but the fun wasn't," Kevin laughs.

GRADUATES

Case is honored by a network of over 100,000 alumni who live all around the world. Case encourages its alumni to keep in touch. There are ten organizations under the Alumni Association of Case Western Reserve University that graduates can join. In 2010, the university awarded 978 undergraduate degrees, 62 certificates, 989 master's degrees, and 781 doctorates.

CBS Evening News anchor Katie Couric spoke at the Class of 2010 Commencement Convocation. Couric's message to graduates heading out to face a sickly economy was optimistic. "The good news," she said, "is you're graduating from a truly outstanding institution and are well-equipped to face the world."

Elizabeth Hilow is testing Couric's theory. Hilow graduated in 2010 after simultaneously earning a B.A. in religious studies and a master's degree in bioethics through Case's rigorous Integrated Graduate Studies program. She sums up her Case experience,

> **“**I think I actually appreciate Case more not being there. I realize now how unique the opportunities I had were and how many unique and exquisite people I met along the way. I'm looking at jobs, and I'm realizing that Case put me in a good position for that. **”**

Case has a long tradition of successful alumni, including bestselling author Dr. Michael Palmer and creator of Gmail, Paul Buchheit. Among its current and former faculty and alumni, Case honors fifteen Nobel laureates, including Albert Michelson, who received the prize in 1907 and was the first-ever American scientist to do so. Excellence has become an institution at Case, and it has set a precedent for achievement that Case Spartans are proud to uphold.

SUMMING UP

A college experience at Case can hold you hostage for twenty-four hours in Kelvin Smith Library with your nose buried in one of the 2.75 million books in its collection, or it can send you to Bangladesh for two weeks to study social development and micro-financing. You can spend Friday night playing videogames at an LAN party in your dorm, or you can gather a group of friends for dinner and dancing downtown. Study the sciences, study the arts, or create your own combo! An education at Case Western Reserve University, like so much else in life, is what you choose to make of it. Explore, engage, and push yourself!

❏ *Kayla Gatalica, B.A.*

CLAREMONT MCKENNA COLLEGE

 Claremont McKenna College
Claremont, CA 91711

 (909) 621-8088
Fax: (909) 621-8516

 E-mail: *admission@cmc.edu*
Website: *www.cmc.edu*

 **Enrollment**

Full-time ❏ women: 580
❏ men: 673

INTRODUCING CLAREMONT MCKENNA

Recognized as one of the nation's most prestigious liberal arts colleges, Claremont McKenna College sets itself apart from its counterparts by its focus on leadership. The college's mission statement is to train "leaders in the making" and leadership is stressed everywhere, from the classroom to dorm life to athletics. Many students pursue the "Leadership Sequence," which includes courses focusing on leadership across disciplines, in addition to their major.

> **❝** *CMC encourages students to pursue their interests and then provides the resources for them to succeed. CMC offers countless opportunities for students to engage in research, to travel abroad, and to create their own sponsored internships. I would not have been able to so thoroughly pursue my own interests without CMC's vast and readily accessible resources. The best part is that the career services office is fully equipped and prepared to serve students of every interest.* **❞**

—*Brittany Pineros, '11*

One of the admissions criteria is leadership potential and the "typical" CMC student excelled academically in high school and also participated in some sort of leadership role, whether yearbook editor, swim team captain, or orchestra section leader. Students selected for the McKenna Achievement Award are chosen for their leadership activities in high school.

Consequently, CMC students are "doers." They apply what they have learned in the classroom at one of the college's ten research institutes or through internship programs. They participate in more than 200 student organizations that support student activities from skiing to vegetarian cooking. They play on one of CMC's twenty-one Division III athletic teams. They study abroad in more than fifty countries internationally and have performed volunteer work at a high rate compared to other colleges nationwide.

More than thirty percent of students graduate with a degree in economics, with government, international relations, psychology, and science rounding out the top five. However, CMC's liberal arts curriculum requires that students complete a broad distribution of courses across departments, including mathematics, literature, and foreign language. More than half of students choose to pursue dual or double majors, allowing for combinations like biology and international relations, or economics and psychology.

Due to CMC's practical and pragmatic approach to the liberal arts, employers note that CMC students are well-prepared for the work world. They are trained to think analytically and to present their ideas both orally and in written form. Writing skills are stressed from the Freshman Humanities Seminar through the mandatory senior thesis, in which students present their senior research project in a paper which may range from fifty to hundreds of pages. Also, CMC students are taught to present their ideas orally through oral exams and research presentations, as well as through in-class debate with professors or fellow students.

With approximately 1,250 students, CMC has a community feel. It is not uncommon to attend a class dinner at a professor's home in the nearby Claremont Village, and strong friendships are formed between students, starting from the ten-day freshman orientation including WOA (Wilderness Orientation Adventure) and lasting far beyond graduation day. More than ninety-eight percent of students live on campus for all four years and the dorms serve as hubs for on-campus social life, hosting various themed parties throughout the year, and for student government. The Associated Students of Claremont McKenna College (ASCMC) is one of the most popular on-campus organizations, as more than one-third of the student body serve in student government as dorm presidents, class representatives, and student senators.

Location and the Claremont Consortium

Claremont McKenna is located on a fifty-acre campus in the convenient and safe college town of Claremont, thirty-five miles east of downtown Los Angeles. CMC is close to two major freeways, and for beach lovers, Laguna Beach and Santa Monica are each about an hour away; nature enthusiasts often head to Joshua Tree National Park for camping and hiking; and on weekend evenings many students make the forty-minute drive west to Hollywood or Universal City. It also is not uncommon for students to take weekend trips to San Francisco, San Diego, or even Las Vegas!

CMC is also unique through its inclusion in The Claremont Colleges consortium. As part of the consortium—a group of five undergraduate colleges and two graduate institutions—located in one square mile—the atmosphere is that of a small college within a larger university. Students take classes, socialize, and participate in activities across the greater Claremont community but always have the home base of CMC. The consortium makes CMC an ideal choice for students who want a small college experience academically but also want the resources that a larger university would provide. Dining halls and libraries are open to all students and it is easy to take classes that may not be offered at CMC at one of the consortium colleges.

ADMISSIONS REQUIREMENTS

CMC is highly selective and traditionally accepts approximately sixteen percent of applicants. What is this selectivity based on? There are the usual traits—each entering class includes its fair share of valedictorians and National Merit Finalists, and the median combined SAT score is around 2100. In addition, though, CMC seeks students who will be engaged learners and active members of the CMC community. Admission officers look for students who have shown leadership potential, self-motivation, and interpersonal skills, and emphasis is placed on extracurricular involvement and how these activities could translate into success in the classroom and in the CMC community.

> 66 *We're not trying to maximize pure intellectual performance. Certainly, we want to have good grades, test scores, and recommendations, but we balance it a lot with other considerations. It is ultimately important whether or not the student is a good fit for CMC, and vice versa.* 99

—*CMC VP & Dean of Admissions, Richard Vos*

CMC's small size allows the Admission Office to build a comprehensive class made up of individuals who will be well suited to the CMC community and CMC's educational style. The admission officers will try to "get to know you" as they consider your admissions materials. The components of your application that allow your personality to shine through, such as your essays, along with other factors such as your test scores, will all be considered. One recent graduate recalled being amazed when, during her first semester at CMC, one of the admission officers approached her in the dining hall to tell her how much she had enjoyed the student's personal statement.

It is equally important for you as an applicant to get to know CMC to determine that CMC is the best fit for you.

The Admission Office regularly offers tours of the campus and it is also possible to arrange an overnight stay in a dorm. Those who may be unable to visit the campus can write directly to current students with any questions that they may have by using the "Ask a Student" section of the Admission Office Web site.

Curriculum and Standardized Tests

An applicant's high school education must have included four years of English, three to four years of math, at least three years of a foreign language, at least two years of science, and one year of history. All high schools are different however, and the availability of advanced, honors, or AP classes at your school will be taken into account. Steady improvement over the high school career is considered, and slacking during the senior year is not viewed favorably. Admission Dean Vos said, "That last year is crucial because students who carry their grades through to the end will likely be people who see projects through and complete tasks to the best of their ability."

The SAT is required. The median SAT score for the entering class in 2010 was 700 on the Critical Reading portion and 710 on the Math portion. These are median scores, however, not hard-and-fast standards that all candidates must achieve and the Admission Office requests that applicants submit all scores earned for each and every time that an applicant has taken the SAT. Interested students should plan to take the exam during their junior year, or between October and January of the senior year.

Recommendations and Essays

It is also necessary to include three recommendations, one from a high school guidance counselor and two from teachers. Two essays must also be included. These essays include a personal statement and an analytical essay, and are one of the most important components of your application. The personal essay is an opportunity to show your personality and highlight your special achievements or personal experiences. The analytical essay should identify a person who has shaped current events and culture.

Interviews are offered on campus and with alumni in metropolitan areas. This interview is another opportunity for applicants to demonstrate the qualities that can set them apart from other candidates.

Admission Plans

There is a binding Early Decision plan for students who view CMC as their top choice; it should be filed by November 15th. About one-third of the freshmen class is accepted through Early Decision. Regular fall semester applicants should submit their applications by January 2.

ACADEMIC LIFE

CMC students know that big is not necessarily better. The small size of Claremont McKenna allows for an academic environment that is rigorous, yet personalized, as students can count on a great deal of interaction with their professors. In fact, student participation is expected at CMC, where the average class size is seventeen students.

Majors

CMC students are known for their eclectic choice of majors as many students pursue a double major or a dual major. (A student with a double major fulfills all course requirements in both majors while a student with a dual major fulfills slightly fewer courses than a full major in both departments.) Students are also allowed to complete a major at one of the other Claremont Colleges that may not be offered at CMC. Another option is the self-designed major, which must be planned with direction from a faculty advisor.

Requirements

CMC has various general education requirements that all students, regardless of major, must fulfill. These include three semesters of social sciences, two semesters each of science and humanities courses, and one semester of literature, math (calculus-based), and world civilization. Additionally, all students must either demonstrate proficiency in a foreign language or complete three semesters of foreign language study.

An additional requirement for all CMC students is the senior thesis, a major research paper or project designed by the student. Normally completed during the senior year and overseen by a faculty advisor, this one- or two-semester venture is usually on a topic of interest within the student's major field of study. Social science and humanities students usually write thesis papers ranging from thirty to hundreds of pages, science students design and carry out experimental research, and often students choose to do a creative project such as a short film or a novel.

> **"** *The opportunities for students to interact with faculty at CMC are beyond what I could have hoped for. Whether it's collaborating on research, publishing papers, traveling to professional conferences, or even grabbing a cup of coffee, our professors' investment in their students is immense. They truly want to involve themselves in our lives and careers, often going out of their way to help us succeed academically and professionally.* **"**

—Tessa Dover, '11

Professors

Do not choose CMC if you want to go through four years of college as an anonymous student in the back of the classroom. The vast majority of CMC professors want to hear your ideas and opinions, they want you to ask questions, they hope that you will come to their office hours, and they would like to know how you are doing outside of school as well. It is not uncommon to find professors eating lunch with students in the dining hall and students are often invited to professors' homes for class gatherings.

Feedback

However, the payoff may not be initially in terms of grades. The bar is set high and new students may not also receive the straight As that they earned in high school. Students must challenge themselves to master material and improve their knowledge and they do so in an environment that is collaborative and supportive. Competition with one's fellow student is virtually unheard of and most CMCers note that there is a sense of solidarity when exam or term paper time rolls around.

Grades at CMC are based on a 12-point, rather than 4-point scale, with 12 being an A, 11 equal to an A–, 10 is a B+, and so forth. The Dean's List credits students who have achieved a GPA of 10.0 or higher during the previous semester, and the Distinguished Scholar List is a mark of achievement for those who earned a GPA of 11.0 or higher.

Because there is a special emphasis on writing as part of a CMC education, first-year students may be dismayed when they receive their first papers back. CMC professors work to improve their students' writing through the application of proper grammar, the use of effective techniques, and clear structure. A popular government professor requires first-year students to review effective writing techniques before writing their first paper of the semester. The Writing Center is a unique resource that offers writing help and specialized workshops for students who would like extra help. Writing at the college level can seem daunting at first but CMC grads report that their training in writing has served them well in their professional lives.

Throughout their college career students can count on the advice and guidance of their faculty advisor. Students are assigned faculty advisors in their interested field of study at the beginning of their first year, with the option of changing advisors if desired.

Research and Other Programs

CMC students have more opportunities to participate hands-on in original research than at any other liberal arts college nationwide. While a number of American universities house research centers, work at these centers is usually reserved for professors and graduate students. Students at CMC are able to gain valuable experience in their chosen field by initiating research projects, supervising fellow student researchers, publishing in academic journals, organizing and participating in conferences, and attending group study trips organized by the research institutes.

Another integral component of the CMC experience is the Marian Miner Cook Athenaeum, the "intellectual hub" of the College. Every night during the academic year, students have the opportunity to dine with leaders from politics, science, the media, literature, and beyond, and then participate in a lecture. Recent guests included Thomas Friedman, Roxana Saberi, Fareed Zakaria, and W. S. Merwin.

- ○ Family of Benjamin Z. Gould Center for Humanistic Studies.
- ○ H.N. and Frances G. Berger Institute for Work, Family, and Children.
- ○ The Center for Human Rights Leadership.
- ○ Reed Institute for Applied Statistics.
- ○ Henry Kravis Leadership Institute.
- ○ Keck Center for International and Strategic Studies.
- ○ Roberts Environmental Center.
- ○ Lowe Institute of Political Economy.
- ○ Henry Salvatori Center for the Study of Individual Freedom in the Modern World.
- ○ Rose Institute of State and Local Government.

Off-Campus Experiences

Students have the opportunity to participate in a domestic exchange at either Haverford or Spelman colleges. The Washington, D.C. semester includes a full-time internship with an elected official, government agency, or public interest group, courses with CMC faculty, and a major research paper requirement. This experience infects many students with the "DC bug" and has led to the start of many students' future careers in Washington.

Study abroad programs are offered in more than fifty cities.

CMC also offers students many opportunities to complete internships in cities around the world, in Washington, D.C., and in locations closer to home through opportunities such as the McKenna International Internship program, the Community Service Internship program, the Uoroboros Fellowship, and other internship opportunities offered through the various research institutes.

❝ I studied in Oxford and had a wonderful time. This was my first trip outside the United States, and it really showed me what the United States is like from a different cultural viewpoint. Being in the UK for an election as well, showed me how they see and interpret the U.S. and U.S. policy abroad, especially in Europe. ❞

Special Degree Programs

CMC offers many special degree programs that allow students to combine fields of study or to accelerate the completion of their undergraduate and postgraduate degrees through various partnership programs. Politics, Philosophy, and Economics (PPE) is an interdisciplinary major modeled after an Oxford University program in which students participate in small seminars and tutorials with faculty. The Environment, Economics, and Politics (EEP) major is a unique interdisciplinary program that trains students to analyze and develop policy solutions for environmental issues. CMC offers several accelerated degree and cooperative programs with graduate schools that allow CMCers to combine their study at CMC with eventual postgraduate study. Through the Robert Day School of Economics and Finance, seniors may apply to remain at CMC for an additional year to earn a Master's Degree in Finance and recognition as a Robert Day Scholar. Additionally, CMC offers the Robert A. Day 4+1 B.A./M.B.A. with the Drucker School of Management at Claremont Graduate University and a 3+3 B.A./J.D. with Columbia Law School. CMC students interested in engineering may participate in accelerated programs in Economics/Engineering or Management/Engineering by combining a B.A. from CMC with a B.S. from a top engineering school like Columbia University of Harvey Mudd College.

SOCIAL LIFE AND ACTIVITIES ▰▰▰▰▰▰▰▰▰▰▰▰

As a residential liberal arts college, CMC has a vibrant social community in addition to the strong academic culture. Extracurricular activities and social life at CMC are part of the experience. They are a way to meet new people, develop friendships, take a break from studying, follow hobbies, and develop a support system.

Clubs and Organizations

There are a wide variety of clubs, sports teams, and other organizations for CMC students to choose from. Everything from orchestra, to the Claremont Colleges Debate Union, to religious and ethnic organizations, to the student newspaper, to karate, is available.

It is also always possible for students to develop new clubs themselves if they find that a niche is lacking at CMC. Students can apply for money from the student activity fund and charter a new organization. In recent years, students have founded clubs and organizations focused on everything from human rights to vegetarian cooking to boxing.

CMC also hosts International Place (I-Place), the heart of the international program at The Claremont Colleges, which provides support to international students and hosts monthly luncheons with presentations on international politics and culture.

The Associated Students of CMC often hosts concerts in Claremont Bridges Auditorium. Recent concerts have included Claremont native Ben Harper and the Black Eyed Peas.

Community Service

Many CMC students take part in community service, ranging from tutoring to working on Habitat for Humanity projects. CMC clubs and sports teams are also active in service projects. An annual community service project is also part of the freshman orientation.

Every year two students serve as community service coordinators organizing service projects in the local community.

Dorms

CMC does not have fraternities or sororities and the vast majority of students (over ninety-eight percent) choose to live on campus. As a primarily residential campus, the heart of CMC social life is the college's thirteen dorms and student apartments. Divided into North Quad, Mid Quad, and South Quad, each grouping of dorms has a different feeling and most students develop an allegiance to one residential area. In their fourth year, students can choose to live in on-campus student apartments located on the eastern edge of CMC's campus. Dorms often host parties that range from simple gatherings to themed affairs including disco parties and costume parties. Popular themed parties include Mardi Gras and Monte Carlo, complete with blackjack tables.

Off-Campus

The "Village" of Claremont is only a five-minute walk from campus and offers restaurants, coffee shops, shops, and a local farmers market. All that southern California has to offer is only a car or train ride away from Claremont. Weekends often find students heading into L.A. (forty minutes away by freeway and by Metrolink commuter rail train) or to nearby beaches. Claremont is served by Ontario International Airport—only fifteen minutes from campus—so going home for vacations is never a problem.

FINANCIAL AID

Claremont McKenna has a need-blind, meet-full-need admission policy, a practice shared by only a select few colleges and universities nationwide. Your application for admission will be reviewed without regard for your ability to pay, and all admitted students' determined financial need will be accommodated.

Financial aid supports over sixty percent of students who are enrolled at the college. While most student aid is need-based there are also merit scholarship programs. One exciting scholarship is the McKenna Achievement Award, a $10,000 scholarship renewable for all four years, which is awarded to fifteen incoming first-year students who have demonstrated outstanding academic and personal achievements during their high school careers. The average financial-aid award for 2010–2011 is $37,600. Family incomes of students qualifying for financial aid range from $0 to six figures.

All students who wish to apply for financial aid must file the Free Application for Federal Student Aid (FAFSA) and the Financial Aid PROFILE form that is processed by the College Scholarship Service (CSS) in order to be considered eligible. The deadline for these forms usually occurs soon after the admission application is due.

GRADUATES

CMC graduates leave Claremont with a sense of direction as they move into the workforce or on to graduate or professional degree programs. On-campus recruiting by firms, graduate schools, and the local and national government takes place throughout the senior year and the majority of CMC students have a job lined up by the spring.

> *In talking with students who attend top colleges across the country, I have yet to encounter a similar degree of generosity and support for the interests of students. CMC seeks to make leaders that will leave their mark on society and thus do all that they can to provide students with a well-rounded education that can hardly be gained anywhere else.*

—*Joanna Respold, '07*

CMC students are also competitive in the field of postcollege scholarships and fellowships such as the Fulbright, Rhodes, Marshall, and Truman. Claremont McKenna College was ranked tenth, nationally, among undergraduate colleges for the number of Fulbright Scholars it produces, according to a national ranking published in 2010 by *The Chronicle of Higher Education*. Eight CMCers from the class of 2010 were awarded Fulbright scholarships that year.

The CMC Career Center is a helpful resource throughout the process. Professional career counselors and student assistants are on hand to help fine-tune resumes, practice interviewing skills, search for internships, and also keep alumni informed about career development opportunities.

CMC alumni stay in close touch through the Alumni Office, which organizes nationwide events, publishes a newsletter, and sponsors class reunions.

SUMMING UP

What kind of college education do you want? Claremont McKenna College is not for everyone; it is for students who would like to be challenged, who would like to know their professors and have their professors know them; it is for those who hope to build relationships in a small setting, but still have all of the options that a larger university would afford them, it is for students interested in developing the skills to pursue a life of leadership in their intended fields. And the sunshine of Southern California doesn't hurt either.

CMC students are smart and many of them had their choice of top-ranked schools. But they chose CMC. Students choose CMC because they believe that it will be the best school for them, in terms of education and environment. This is apparent when you meet the students—they are active in campus life. The campus is crowded on weekends, attendance at Athenaeum lectures and sporting events is high, and—a rarity on some college campuses—students attend class regularly. They also know that CMC supports them, their education, and their future career development.

❏ *Sarah Ciaccia, B.A.*

COLBY COLLEGE

Colby College
Waterville, ME 04901-8841

(207) 859-4800, (800) 732-3032
Fax: (207) 859-4828

E-mail: *admissions@colby.edu*
Website: *http://www.colby.edu*

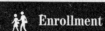 **Enrollment**

Full-time ❏ women: 985
       ❏ men: 840

INTRODUCING COLBY

Colby College sits up on Mayflower Hill like an illustration in a fairytale. Like Baba Yaga's house on chicken feet, or the gingerbread cottage, something about the campus just screams out to be drawn in pen and ink and printed in a nice leather-bound volume. It is, in good ways and bad, the "Ivory Tower on the Hill."

The feel of the physical campus is an oft-cited reason current students give for deciding to apply to Colby. One presumes it is also a reason why some high school students choose not to apply. Those who love it say it looks exactly like what a college is supposed to look like. Those who don't take issue with the cookie-cutter nature of the architecture. The college moved in the 1940s, and, as a result, many of the buildings were built at the same time.

> 66 *[Colby's] remote location and small size actually proved to be a tremendous benefit. The professors are caring and inspirational, the location is serene, and the student body is close (maybe since they must huddle together for warmth). A small school created the community I always wanted . . . and allowed me a safe place to become myself.* 99

—*Maya Klauber, '08*

Waterville, Maine, is unfortunately best described as a failing former mill town. There are hints that a renaissance is just around the corner, but even with that, it will be a while until the town is truly dynamic. Again, some students like the town, its history, and possibilities; others just don't go there. Geographically, Waterville occupies an enviable position of being both remote and central. Within an hour and a half's drive are the Maine coast, Sugarloaf (favorite ski mountain of the Colby community), Freeport (where L.L. Bean has its flagship store), and Portland, a small dynamic city of restaurants, art, and live music. Drive another two hours and you're in Boston. Montreal is also within easy driving distance, and closer than that are the Maine North Woods, western Maine mountains, and more lakes and rivers than there's time to paddle. On the other hand, it's possible to go for months without leaving campus. There are events every weekend night, lectures most weeknights, and an astonishing amount of live music.

By the numbers, Colby is very much like its brothers and sisters in the NESCAC league. Classes are small, professors are friendly and interested in being good teachers, and students are intelligent. It's easy to put Colby students in boxes, and in some ways the school is very cliquey. But, because the school is small, a given student will fall into any number of boxes, which breaks down any attempt to categorize. You end up with biology-loving basketball players, Chinese/physics double majors, and poet lumberjacks (called woodsmen at Colby).

> 66 *I came to Maine a city person, someone who felt most at home on the subway into Boston or shopping in Manhattan. I thought I'd have a hard time adapting to Waterville, which isn't what you'd call 'cosmopolitan.' I soon learned, though, that there were a lot of other reasons to love central Maine. During my freshman year, I learned to snowshoe, cross-country ski, and down-hill ski, and took my first winter hike. Now it's difficult for me to imagine living in a place with smoggy air and busy streets.* 99

—Nina Gold, '09

There are definite pros and cons to having a small number of students, almost all of whom live on campus. Secrets stay secret for approximately forty-five seconds, and you have to work pretty hard if you want to avoid an ex. On the other hand, seeing your friends takes very little effort. It is impossible to walk across campus without seeing someone you know well, and while eating alone is always an option, it is almost never the only one.

While Colby concerns itself with fostering diversity of students and opinions, it is hampered by its location, and its size. Fifty-two percent of the student population is from the Northeast, and a sizeable number of those students are from twenty minutes outside of Boston. That said, the other forty-eight percent are from all over. International students make up around ten percent of the population, and they form a real and inclusive community. In addition, Colby admissions works hard to attract students from all around the United States. It is possible at any school to go through four years and never step outside your comfort zone, but it is also possible to make friends from Bulgaria, Belarus, and Brunswick, Maine. Like any school, so much of the Colby experience is what you make of it.

Colby may differ from other small liberal arts colleges very little on paper, but it is home to a tight, spirited, unique community. It is not a place to go if you want to spend your weekends clubbing, but if community, access to the mountains, and professors who invite you to their homes all sound important, Colby might just be the right choice.

Food at Colby

Colby is home to three very distinct dining halls and a cash snack bar. Each has its own style and clientele, something that both increases food choices on campus dramatically, and causes arguments around 5:30.

- Foss: The Foss dining hall caters largely to vegetarians and international students. Lines are always long, and vegan soy-balls are often available. Food is a little spicier than other dining halls, and the people who eat there are often fiercely loyal. Fosstafarians will wait in incredibly long lines and often don't make dinner dates, knowing exactly where all their friends will be.

- Dana: Dana dining hall caters to people who like the option of pizza and hamburgers at every meal. Often overlooked, the food is usually quite delicious, and the salad bar extensive. Dana regulars include varsity teams, less devoted Fosstafarians, and a certain coterie of "normal folks."

- Roberts: Bob's is Colby's newest dining hall, and offers full meals on square plates. The food is good, always interesting, and beautifully presented. Bob's has legendary breakfast omelets and is favored by students from all classes and cliques.

- The Spa: Colby has a cash snack bar where students grab food if their eating schedule is out of whack, if they're trying to work in the student center, or if they just want a snack. Students can use one meal credit a week at The Spa, for a breakfast, lunch, or dinner special. There is also a grab-and-go lunch option offering salads, sandwiches, and/or soups that students may take any day.

ADMISSIONS

Like all of the institutions in this volume, admission to Colby is competitive. In a recent year, the college had 4,520 applicants, 1,544 of whom were admitted. 480 matriculated, and, of those, 212 were Early Decision applicants. Colby's admissions materials are actually rather specific about what makes a strong applicant: "In making admission decisions, we seek excellence—in academics, art, music, theater, research, work experience, publications, leadership, public service, and athletics. We value diversity throughout the college and seek candidates from all parts of the country and the world." In other words, academics are important, but extracurriculars play a big part of the admissions decision.

In terms of standardized testing, Colby requires either the American College Test (ACT) or the SAT or SAT Subject Tests in three different areas. While there is no minimum score, 680 (per section) has been the average mean SAT score for students accepted in the last few years. International Students are also asked to submit a Test of English as a Foreign Language (TOEFL) or IELTS score.

Interviews

While not necessary, admissions interviews are strongly suggested, both as an opportunity to ask questions, and as an opportunity to meet someone affiliated with the college. Interviews are available on campus with admissions staff or off campus with alumni interviewers until January 15th.

ACADEMIC LIFE

Life at Colby is academic by definition. Days and meals revolve around class times, and homework is at least in the top five most popular activities. Colby classes are hard, rewarding, and seldom a waste of time. People don't go to school because it's the only thing to do in the winter; they go to school because that is why they live in Waterville, and because for the most part, class is fascinating.

Colby offers forty-four majors (and thirty minors) with biology, economics, International studies, and government graduating the highest percentage of students any given year. Colby lacks a film major and an English minor, but almost everything else is covered. Students who don't like to be put in boxes have the option of making their own box, with the Independent Major program, and every year a handful of individuals take advantage of that offer, to create personal majors in geography, medieval and renaissance studies, environmental education, or something else.

Faculty

Departments and majors are important, but in many cases they take a backseat to the individual faculty who populate the departments. Colby boasts a world-class faculty, professors dedicated to teaching as much as to climbing in their fields, and it makes a difference. It is not uncommon to see professors in their offices well into the night, at the campus pub with seniors, and it is difficult to graduate without being invited to at least one professor's house for dinner or class discussion. The student-faculty ratio is 10:1, so most classes are small and it is easy to get to know one's teacher. The warmth and generosity of the faculty with their time and their knowledge is often a big factor for students to decide to go to Colby.

> 66 *It's normal, not the exception, to call most professors by their first names, and we're constantly encouraged to get to know them. For me it's easier to relate to the subject matter when I have a personal relationship with the teacher, and Colby makes it easy.* 99

—*Jake Obstfeld, '09*

Core Requirements

Colby sits somewhere in the middle of the spectrum when it comes to graduation requirements: not as rigorous as St. John's (in Maryland), and certainly not as "loosey goosey" as Brown. Most students complete all but a handful of the ten or so classes in the distribution requirement by simply choosing classes they like, or by completing their major. For the nontechnically inclined student, the quantitative and lab science requirement can be a drag, but friendly faculty try to soften the blow by offering "Chemistry for Citizens" and "Mathematics as a Liberal Art," for example. Keeping students on track to complete their requirements is one of the most important functions of the academic advisor.

Study Abroad

Around two-thirds of Colby students study abroad in their junior year through the Office of Off-campus Studies. While programs have to be preapproved by the college, they range geographically from Mexico to Madagascar to Morocco. Study abroad has an amazing impact on the social lives of second-semester juniors and seniors. People talk about what they've seen, cook dinner for each other, and sometimes even buy better beers. But it also splits the junior class and, for students going abroad in different semesters, makes it hard to stay in touch with friends. Overall, the program is a very positive one, but, like anything, it comes at some costs.

Colby maintains its own study-abroad programs at universities in Dijon, France, and Salamanca, Spain. In addition to providing a Colby-out-of-Colby experience for juniors, the Dijon and Salamanca programs are also open to entering first-years. Every year approximately forty first-years forgo their first semester at Colby and instead study abroad. They come back for Colby's January term having missed much of the drama of freshman fall, but also orientation, and everything else. On the other hand, they've missed much of the drama of freshman fall, and in most cases are close friends with their twenty or thirty fellows. Friends are easy to make at Colby, and generally the "mid-year admits" don't suffer for their decision. There is even a winter COOT to help them settle in. While certainly not for everyone, the freshman study-abroad program is well attended and well liked, and part of what sets Colby apart from the pack.

> ❝ COOT...puts small groups of freshmen with two student leaders who take them backpacking or canoeing or base camping. In my case, we hiked all day, ate PB&Js, cooked dinner over a camp stove, and slept in tents. Nobody showered. Everybody smelled bad. It was awesome, mostly because after the first day, nobody was worried about embarrassing themselves. This is the strength of COOT: that a bunch of insecure freshmen can stop feeling scared and alone and start feeling like a group of friends. It's also nice that they have extremely enthusiastic leaders to give them pointers on campus life and assure them that college is a wonderful experience. ❞

—*Nate Lifton, '08*

COOT

Another thing that sets Colby apart is the Colby Outdoor Orientation Trip. Student leaders take small groups of first-years outdoors, and create lasting bonds in the process.

Though the program has seen some changes in the last few years, the core components remain. There are rigorous trips backpacking in the Mahoosuc Mountains, and there are somewhat slower trips, floating down the Saco River. Other COOT trips offered include trail work, community service, wellness, local foods service, and theater. If nothing else

COOT offers a chance to learn about the Colby culture from nice, honest, and generally awesome people, make good friends, and ease into college life. A newer component of orientation is the Colby Community Involvement Trip (C2IT).

January Semester

The January term usually known as Jan Plan is one of the things that makes Colby, well, Colby. Though it shortens winter break considerably, Jan Plan allows Colby students to do whatever they can think of, as long as they can find a valid academic reason for doing it. Professors offer intensive classes in everything from volcanology to photography. Some students take requirement-fulfilling classes, while others take classes not offered during the normal school year, such as furniture making or blacksmithing. Each year, a few lucky students travel abroad with Jan Plan Colby programs to teach music in India, learn about the Chinese economy hands on, or work on biology projects in the Galapagos. Otherwise busy students take advantage of guitar or voice lessons, and many opt to get off campus. Jan Plan is an optimal time for a short internship, or an independent project. In recent years, more than one student has made a ski movie, and two roommates who had decided not to study abroad took the month to ride the length of Vietnam on a Soviet motorbike. Recent internship locations include Comedy Central, the Maryland State House, and the headquarters of the New England Patriots. Jan Plan is what one makes it (though faculty approval is needed). Students must complete three approved Jan Plans to graduate.

Public Affairs and Civil Engagement

The Goldfarb Center for Public Affairs and Civil Engagement sponsors lectures, lunches, and student projects, but for a lot of students, civil engagement goes far beyond that. The Colby Volunteer Center boasts 284 volunteers and sends students to where they're needed in the community. During 2009–10, 190 Colby students contributed more than 3,800 hours to community organizations through the Colby Volunteer Center, and 200 students participated in one-day service events. Three hundred and seventy students mentored children through Colby Cares About Kids (CCAK), and 255 students participated in 16 civic engagement courses. Altogether, Colby students contributed more than 28,000 hours of service to local communities.

> **"** *Every CCAK relationship between a student and his mentor is both test-ing and richly rewarding. I quickly learned that I would need to earn the trust and candor of my new mentee, and at first with him, just maintaining a con-versation was emotionally draining, since he was very reluctant to share any-thing personal. In time, though, I gained his trust, and the characteristic, awkwardly silent lunchtime that followed our standard recess game of HORSE (which he usually won) transitioned into a comfortable and often very engaging conversation over the daily matter of interest, which ranged from our families to the virtues of square pizza.* **"**

—*Luke LaViolet, '08*

SOCIAL LIFE AND ACTIVITIES

There are people at Colby who are so busy they have to schedule dinner dates weeks in advance, and there are people whose plans stay the same from day to day and usually involve watching TV, playing video games, and eating pizza. The choice is completely per-sonal, but Colby does its best to make sure there's something for everyone to do. The begin-ning of the year activities fair can be a little overwhelming, and first-years often end up signing up for more clubs than there are days in the week, but things quiet down over the semester and years, and most people seem to find a niche they like.

> **"** *Students at Colby used to create mix CDs to be played during meals in the dining halls. One night during dinner, 'Call on Me,' a techno song that was popular on campus at the time, came on. Heads at every table began to bob in time to the song's catchy baseline. Suddenly, one student stood up and began to dance. People at every table followed his lead—first busting moves at their seats, then on the dining hall stage. At Colby, students are comfortable enough to be themselves and enjoy the company of those around them.* **"**

—*Nina Gold, '09*

Colby does not lack for student clubs and organizations. Into Japanese drumming? The Taiko Club already has that handled. Want to give back to the community? Check out the Colby Volunteer Center. Like to play outside? Join the Outing Club. Can't find a club to join? Start one. Want to run around? Play a sport.

Athletics

Colby gets a rap for being a jock-y school, and rightly so. Around half of the student population competes in one form or another, with varsity teams competing in the NESCAC conference. Colby has thirty-two varsity teams, and all are Division III (with the exception of the Nordic and alpine ski teams, which compete in Division I). It also has thirteen club teams, from sailing to badminton to rugby. Of the club teams, the woodsmen's team stands out as something that makes Colby a little bit different. Students (many of whom have never held an ax before) compete in old-time lumber sports such as chopping, sawing, and fire building, and welcome anyone to the field to try it out. The general sportiness of the school means a couple of things. Around one in eleven men are on the football team, the Alfond Athletic Center (usually just called the gym) is nearly always full, and four o'clock is not a good time to schedule a group meeting. But it also means that the gym is state of the art and that people can generally catch a ball if you throw it at them. To some extent, it doesn't really matter. If you're an athlete, chances are good you'll find a community of athletes who will join you in your endeavors. If you shudder at the thought of organized sports, you won't be alone, and you might be a good candidate for iPlay, Colby's intramural sports league, where every year teams play flag football, field hockey, three-on-three basketball, dodgeball, broomball, and softball. iPlay games are laid back, and often played in bare feet. In other words, there's something for everyone.

Weekends

Weekend activities are another place where there's something for everyone. The Outing Club (a chem-free club by charter) runs trips most weekends, and the Student Programming Board (SPB) has an ample budget to make sure there's something to do every single weekend night. From intimate concerts in the coffee house to campus-wide dances in the student center, campus events has it all. Still, many people prefer to stick to the dorms, and there's a sizable party scene. Unlike schools with fraternities or common houses, Colby's parties are generally smaller and it's rare to not know your host. For many Colby students, Friday and Saturday are a time to relax and cut loose (at the same time, if that's possible) and Sunday is the day to spend in the library, trying to get ready for the next week.

> 66 *Colby's residential focus breeds a New England prep school social atmosphere that is great to be a part of but out of touch with reality. That said, Colby's greatest asset that sets it apart and balances the sometimes infantilizing culture of residential life is its location. If students take the time and initiative to explore Waterville, the Belgrade Lakes, and the mountains and rivers of central and western Maine, their social and academic bubble will be balanced with a good dose of local culture. Getting a job in town or spending weekends in the Maine woods makes it easier to appreciate the wealth of opportunity the school provides without remaining cloistered on the Hill.* 99

—*Chris Zajchowski, '07*

Residences

Colby is a residential college, and a spot in a dormitory is guaranteed all four years. All residences are co-ed, and all except one complex (the Alfond Senior Apartments) are mixed among classes. Upperclassmen are allowed to live off campus, and each year approximately five percent of students choose to live in Waterville or neighboring Oakland. Each dorm develops its own culture, though some are perpetuated by preference and stereotype. Foss and Woodman dorms (where the vegetarian-friendly Foss dining hall is located) have reportedly had a crunchy vibe since at least 1974. Other personalities have changed. Roberts Row used to house Colby's seven fraternities. With the Greek ban in 1984, all that changed, and now the buildings are small dorms with a focus on communities, which is a big part of why they have been chosen to host Colby's experiment in Dialogue Housing.

Dialogue Housing

Since 2005 Colby has been experimenting with themed dorms, in the Dialogue Housing program. Because of the new nature of the program, there have been a lot of changes year to year, but it looks as though it's here to stay. So far, Colby has allowed for a "green" dorm, an art and music house, and a Spanish-speaking floor of a larger dorm among others. The idea is that by living together, students with similar priorities will be able to continue discussions outside of the classroom, and put on events to involve the larger campus community. Dialogue Housing is currently not open to first-year students.

> 66 *Looking back on my two years in Colby's Environmental Dialogue Housing, referred to as the 'Green House,' I remember a community of engaged students coming together to make lifestyle changes and provide positive change on campus. Were we perfect at this? No. There is a strong need for the college and students to agree on a long-term vision for the Green House. Whether it will represent what can be done now or what could be done in the future seems uncertain. Ultimately, the Green House offered me an invaluable experience and I believe it stands as a powerful symbol of change at Colby.* 99

—*Joel Alex, '08*

FINANCIAL AID

As of 2010, Colby's comprehensive fee, which includes tuition, room and board, was $51,990, plus a variable $1,600 for books and materials. However, Colby is committed to working with admitted students on financial questions, and promises to meet full calculated financial need. In 2008 the school replaced loans within aid packages with grants. This can represent a large and welcome savings for middle-income students. Student loans are still available to supplement the college package. For the class of 2013, thirty-eight percent of students received grant aid.

International Admissions

Many of Colby's international students come to Waterville from the United World College (UWC), a secondary school with campuses around the world. Colby was one of the five pilot colleges for the Davis United World College Scholars program, which, through the generosity of Shelby and Gale Davis, has brought more than 220 international students to Colby since the program's inception in 2000. Calculated financial needs are met

- Doris Kearns Goodwin, 1964, Historian, Pulitzer Prize Winner
- Elijah Parish Lovejoy, 1826, Abolitionist
- Dan Harris, 1993, ABC News anchor and reporter
- E. Annie Proulx, 1957, Pulitzer Prize-winning Author of *The Shipping News* and *Brokeback Mountain*
- Eric S. Rosengren, 1979, Current President and CEO, Federal Reserve Bank of Boston
- Stuart Rothenberg, 1970, Editor and Publisher of *The Rothenberg Political Report*, CNN Political Analyst, and Syndicated Columnist
- Tom Silverman, 1975, Founder of Influential Hip-Hop Record Label Tommy Boy Records
- Cecily von Ziegesar, 1992, Novelist, Creator of "Gossip Girl" series
- Pete Rouse, 1968, President Obama's Chief of Staff

for admitted international students, whether they come from the UWC or other secondary schools. Enrolled international students who qualify for need-based Colby grants may also recieve assistance for summer living expenses and transportation to campus at the time of enrollment. Colby is not need-blind.

GRADUATES

Colby graduates go on to do pretty much everything. Many head to Boston or New York, living together, working together, and often drinking together. Some opt to stay in Maine, and others pursue dreams and ambitions across the globe. Around twenty percent immediately head to graduate programs, and eventually around seventy-five percent earn a graduate degree. Picking up a copy of the Colby Magazine, one will find stories about alumni who are now professors, CEOs, writers, and media personalities. Notable graduates include TV personality Billy Bush, and prominent banker Robert Diamond, currently President of Barclays PLC.

A good number (around thirteen percent) of Colby graduates marry each other, and Lorimer Chapel, on campus, is available for Colby weddings. But in addition to nuptials, the Colby network is there for graduates all around the world. From organized events to a hand-up in the job market, graduates are eager to meet students and other graduates, making the Colby Alumni Network feel a lot like family sometimes.

SUMMING UP

At first blush, Colby may appear to be just another small East Coast liberal arts college, but it is very much its own institution. Jan Plan is one of the things that sets it apart, and the first semester-abroad program for freshman is another. Colby is a cold place for much of the year, but the faculty, staff, and students who make up the community are as warm as the air is chilly. The number of students studying abroad creates disconnects within classes and among friends, but it also enriches the community as students bring their experiences back to campus. Some people drink a lot, though probably not more than any other school. The administration does its best to curtail underage drinking while keeping the campus social and friendly, and (losing battle or not) does a pretty good job. It is true that sports are big at Colby, but they rarely define one's entire social life. It is possible to be friends with soccer players and pottery club members, and nobody is going to tell you what to do. The town may not be as cute as some, but it is steeped in the history of the Industrial Revolution and poised for a twenty-first-century renaissance. Colby students are smart, friendly, engaged, interested, and interesting. People hold doors open, lend their cars to friends, and volunteer in the community. Colby is a great place to major in creative writing and an equally great place to do undergraduate research in the sciences. Healthy science budgets and no graduate students mean that if organic chemistry is your thing, you'll have plenty of time in the lab. If you have a very specialized interest, in an arcane subject, you might find Colby a little small, but for most students, that's not really a problem. In the end, Colby is a good place to spend four years, and for a lot of people, it's a great place.

❏ *Martin Connelly, B.A.*

COLGATE UNIVERSITY

 Colgate University
Hamilton, NY 13346

 (315) 228-1000
Fax: (315) 228-7544

 E-mail: *admission@mail.colgate.edu*
Website: *www.colgate.edu*

 Enrollment

Full-time ❑ women: 1,525
❑ men: 1,343

Part-time ❑ women: 10
❑ men: 6

INTRODUCING COLGATE

When visiting Colgate University's campus, nestled in the Chenango Valley of Central New York, it is impossible not to be struck by the school's setting. It sits amid the rolling hills of a region that features more scenic vistas than traffic lights. The campus is a strikingly beautiful accent to the region—its majestic, gold-tipped Memorial Chapel is visible from surrounding hillsides for miles around. Oak-lined drives, a picturesque on-campus lake, and impressive stone architecture complement the school's remote location to create a profound atmosphere of knowledge.

Since the school's founding in 1819, Colgate's students have taken advantage of their location and its bountiful resources while pursuing their studies at the highest level. Today, Colgate's undergraduates can be found doing everything from studying in the state-of-the-art library facilities, to mentoring local children, to conducting ground-breaking research about endangered Central New York plant species. The Upstate Institute, one of the university's premier programs, is designed to support high-level academics and civic engagement simultaneously by providing and funding opportunities for students to engage in research in the Central New York region.

> ❝ *What others perceive as the isolation of the campus leads to a deep knit, very human community. Along with the village, we know that we are the only ones here and that our community is precisely what we will make of it.* ❞
>
> —*President Jeffrey Herbst at his inauguration ceremony, 2010*

While students develop a very strong sense of local connectivity through such activities, they are also encouraged to explore their global sense of place, an opportunity that most of the student body takes advantage of, with more than sixty percent of students participating in at least one off-campus study experience. Even when on campus, students are building their global perspective by interacting with a diverse population. Students may learn as much from their classmates and the social networks they build as they do from their professors. In 2010, individuals from forty-eight states and thirty-six countries could be found attending Colgate, each bringing unique perspectives, traditions, and backgrounds to share with classmates. Colgate has resources including a dedicated cultural center, Dean of Diversity, and multicultural wellness plan that all work together to encourage a healthy interest among students in different ways of living, an interest that serves all students well in an increasingly global world.

> ❝ *After my experience with Colgate's Upstate Institute, I felt connected to not just the town that Colgate's in, but the region. I was not just going to a school, but living in a community.* ❞
>
> —*David Ryan Pokorny '10*

It is all a part of Colgate's educational philosophy, which is designed to help students find their passions and explore them to the fullest extent. At its foundation is the Liberal Arts Core Curriculum. This program ensures that students are exposed to some of the most integral features of a classic liberal arts curriculum, as well as more progressive curriculums and teaching methods. Although the Core represents only five of the thirty-two courses the typical student will take at Colgate, in many ways the program epitomizes Colgate's character—a deep respect for tradition balanced by the aspiration to remain at the forefront of education in the modern world.

Due to the school's unique size, Colgate blends the best of a small college atmosphere with big university resources. Students are never instructed by teaching assistants, instead always receiving instruction directly from their professors in class sizes averaging only nineteen students. Likewise, research opportunities, office hours, and fieldwork opportunities with Colgate's world-class staff are reserved almost exclusively for undergraduates.

What Colgate students bring to the table is impressive. They are best described as ambitious, curious, and adventuresome, striving for success in all of their many endeavors. In 2010, Colgate's Division I athletic program featured a graduation rate of 100 percent, the highest of any Division I program in the country. Clearly, whether students are competing on the field, participating in international community service expeditions, or creating art projects for display around campus, they settle for nothing less than their best. And with everything from a student-run radio station to a community garden on campus, students are free to pursue excellence in almost any passion they might discover.

The end result of Colgate's intensive undergraduate experience is an individual prepared to face the challenges of a rapidly changing world. At the same time, the bonds established on that hillside in Central New York have created a fiercely passionate alumni body that is sincerely interested in being a part of the education of Colgate's next generation, as they themselves strive to be lifelong learners.

ADMISSIONS REQUIREMENTS

Just as Colgate's alumni strive to be lifelong learners after graduation, Colgate is looking for prospective students who have demonstrated a commitment to their own education. It would be impossible to define a prototypical candidate for admission at Colgate, but those who challenge themselves to achieve excellence in the classroom, in extracurricular and athletic activities, and in the community certainly stand out during the admission process. To learn about its applicants, Colgate uses The Common Application with a supplemental application, the most significant piece of which is a 250-word essay.

Standardized testing is certainly a part of the admission process—and is required—but that score is by no means the definitive factor in the admission decision. Recognizing that oftentimes students have different testing styles, Colgate accepts either the SAT or the ACT, and encourages prospective students to try to see if they excel at one over the other. Colgate will accept the highest scores achieved in each section of the SAT Reasoning Test or the highest ACT composite score, should applicants choose to sit for an exam more than once. Also, note that the writing sections of the SAT and the ACT are not considered as a part of the admission process.

That being said, applicants' high school transcripts will play a major role in the admission process. Academic achievement is clearly important, but this means more than just grades. When reviewing an applicant's transcripts, Colgate likes to contextualize grades—has the student been challenging himself or herself academically? That means enrolling in AP, IB, and honors-level courses, when offered. Colgate also recognizes that many applicants attended high schools that do not offer many higher-level courses, and will not hold that against those applicants. The people in the admission office are looking to see whether students challenge themselves given the available resources.

This philosophy extends outside the classroom as well. If you played a sport, let Colgate know! If you edited the school newspaper, speak up! If you worked twenty hours a week as a waiter while you were in high school, highlight this experience on your application. Remember, it isn't about how many activities you are involved in; rather, it is about commitment, growth, and how you impact your community. The fuller picture you can paint of yourself, the better. Students that come to Colgate are joining a tight-knit community with students, faculty, alumni, and the local Hamiltonians. How you integrate into and contribute to your high school and hometown communities is a critical part of the admission decision at Colgate.

Early Decision, Regular Decision

Early Decision at Colgate is an excellent option for those students who have no doubt that they want to join Colgate's community. There are two options available. Early Decision I (binding) applicants can apply by November 15, and will receive a decision in mid-December. Early Decision II (binding) is an option for students who may decide later that they want to apply ED to Colgate, or who applied for Regular Decision and wish to change their decision plan to Early Decision. Applicants who apply to Colgate by the January 15 deadline have until March 1 to change their decision plan to Early Decision II. They will then receive a decision letter within four weeks of the completion of their application.

ACADEMIC LIFE

The heart of a Colgate education is obviously academic. Colgate offers fifty-one majors, and several additional minors. To graduate, students must earn thirty-two credits. Anywhere from eight to sixteen of those credits are dedicated to a student's major, and the Liberal Arts Core Curriculum requires an additional five credits for completion. Courses are generally one credit each, meaning students average four courses per semester. This leaves a large number of credits with which students may pursue minors, second majors, and elective courses.

Engagement

Perhaps the greatest strength of Colgate's academic program is its intense student engagement. With a student to faculty ratio of 10:1, an average class size of only nineteen, no teaching assistants, and a requirement that professors host weekly office hours, Colgate students are afforded incredible personal access to a host of world-class scholars. Professors take advantage of the small class sizes and their students' enthusiasm to implement creative instructional methods. Geology classes examine the various materials used to make gravestones in Colgate's cemetery; Jewish Studies classes may travel to New York City to observe thriving modern Jewish communities firsthand; and Biology labs can be seen exploring the forests around campus.

Colgate's commitment to intensive student engagement also manifests itself in undergraduate research opportunities. From colonial Jamaican history, to cutting-edge behavioral studies, Colgate professors are conducting field-leading research with plenty of opportunities for their students to get involved. Often students are conducting research as early as their first year on campus. This does not mean simply conducting menial tasks

Colgate takes great pride in having developed and maintained a program of study that ensures that students develop a foundational knowledge of the world around them, take the opportunity to explore a diverse range of academic studies, and have ample opportunity to focus on their interests. Requirements of that program include

○ **Legacies of the Ancient World:** The study of texts from the ancient Mediterranean and Near Eastern world that have had lasting influence.

○ **Challenges of Modernity:** An interdisciplinary study of primary texts from the period between 1750 and the present that help illuminate the realities of the modern world.

○ **Communities and Identifies:** A variety of courses studying in depth the community of a specific area, ranging from The Caucuses to Japan.

○ **Scientific Perspectives on the World:** A variety of courses in which students observe how scientific methods apply to an issue in society.

○ **Global Engagements:** A designation for many courses across disciplines in which students analyze the conditions and effects of cross-cultural interaction.

Areas of Inquiry (six courses total):

– **Human Thought and Expression (at least two courses):** Can be fulfilled by courses from a variety of humanities disciplines and departments

– **Social Relations (at least two courses):** Can be fulfilled by courses from a variety of social science disciplines and departments.

– **Natural Sciences and Mathematics (at least two courses):** Can be fulfilled by courses from a variety of natural science and mathematics disciplines and departments.

as part of professors' larger projects, either. Each year, Colgate students who invest the necessary time and effort may publish papers in scholarly journals, or present their research at major academic conferences around the world.

> *Presenting at the AGU (American Geophysical Union) conference in San Francisco was an amazing experience. I was one of only a handful of undergraduates, constantly surrounded by 16,000 professional geologists. It was impossible not to immerse myself in the scientific conversations around me.*

—*Katie Garman, '10*

The First-Year Seminar (FSEM)

Colgate's academic opportunities are vast, and studying at Colgate is very different from high school. To aid students in that transition, all first-year students must enroll in a First-Year Seminar (FSEM) during their first semester. How the transition is designed depends on the professor teaching the course. Some will slowly and deliberately introduce the opportunities and resources available to students, while others will open the semester full throttle, challenging students to explore their new environment. Either way, students have the reassurance that they are exploring alongside their first-year peers. FSEM courses are capped at eighteen students, may be part of Colgate's Core or areas of inquiry requirements, and are offered in an array of subjects from Conserving Nature, to Masters of the Short Story, to Mind & Brain in Meditation.

> **❝**My FSEM was easily more work than any other class I took freshman year, but suddenly being faced with all that work after graduating from high school was a very good introduction to college life. It was beyond my expectations going in, and it was easily one of the best classes I took at Colgate. **❞**

—*Kathleen Onorevole, '10*

Off-Campus Study

Another great strength of Colgate's academic experience is its Off-Campus Study Program. Just as the university encourages students to become active members of the campus, local, and regional communities, Colgate recognizes that modern students must also be global citizens. Therefore, the university offers more than twenty off-campus study programs for students to choose from. These programs are to destinations as diverse as Beijing and Jamaica. Colgate's National Institutes of Health (NIH) Study Group in Bethesda, Maryland is the NIH's only undergraduate research partnership, and allows Colgate students 30+ research hours weekly at the world-renowned research facility. Each of Colgate's off-campus study programs is led by a Colgate professor, so students have direct access to Colgate support while off campus. Programs are also specifically designed to allow the easy integration of earned credit into students' transcripts. For some courses taught at Colgate, there are also "extended studies" available, in which students will cap a semester of study on campus with two to three weeks of study while traveling after the semester. Extended studies are great opportunities for students who wish to study off campus but who may not be able to commit to a full semester away due to other obligations. Students receiving financial aid from Colgate can apply that aid to one semester program and an extended study. Finally, if a student would like to participate in an off-campus study program not offered by Colgate, the off-campus study office will work with that student to arrange for the transfer of credit and necessary paperwork, although Colgate financial aid will not cover such outside programs.

SOCIAL LIFE AND ACTIVITIES

There is plenty to keep Colgate students busy when not studying. Involvement in organizations and initiatives outside the classroom is an integral part of a Colgate education. Extracurricular activities allow students to develop as leaders, organizers, team members, and citizens. Students may join any of the more than 180 groups registered with and supported by Colgate's Center for Leadership and Student Involvement. These groups have access to extensive resources that support everything from a state-of-the-art radio station to the nation's oldest college weekly, *The Colgate Maroon-News*; to an equestrian club that frequently competes with top varsity squads. Getting involved is as easy as checking out the activities fair at the beginning of each semester.

SOME WEEKEND ACTIVITIES

- ○ **Late 'Gate**—This is actually a student-run organization dedicated to throwing a variety of healthy nighttime activities, such as the popular "Late Skate" roller skating event.
- ○ **Sporting events**—Whatever the season, every weekend features home Division I sporting events. Whether it is football, basketball, volleyball, or anything else, student tickets are always free.
- ○ **Bowling**—Reid Athletic Center has several lanes on campus at an extremely affordable price. Enroll in one of Colgate's bowling classes to master the techniques needed to beat your friends.
- ○ **Turning Stone**—This resort and casino in Oneida is only a half-hour from campus and frequently hosts big-name concerts and events.
- ○ **Glendening Boathouse**—During the warmer months, go kayaking with friends total free of charge.
- ○ **Midnight Movies**—Several times a semester when big films are released, students can purchase discounted tickets from a showing at 11:59 P.M. on Friday night at the Hamilton Movie Theater. Free pizza, popcorn, or posters.

The Colgate community is truly in tune with student interests and desires largely because it is organized and directed by students. The Student Government Association is elected by the student body to represent the students to the school's administration. The Budget Allocations Committee is a group of students entrusted with managing and distributing the entire student activities budget to the various organizations on campus. When students step foot on campus they are not just joining a student community—they are actively defining it.

○ "Slices"—Officially The New York Pizzeria in downtown Hamilton, this pizza joint has been serving up the perfect slice, plain only, to hordes of Colgate students for decades.

○ Take 2 Movies—Every Friday and Saturday in Colgate's largest lecture hall, students can see a double feature on the big screen of films out of theaters but not yet on video—totally free.

○ The Frats—Colgate's Greek system features some of the best BBQs, parties, and concerts on campus. If nothing in particular is going on, who says you can't lounge on a couch in the front yard?

○ The Barge Canal Coffee Shop—Hamilton's hub. The Barge expertly combines great coffee, a cozy feel, and frequent performances by local and regional musical talents.

○ The Palace Theater—This theater in downtown Hamilton hosts everything from *The Vagina Monologues* to visits with Santa. Keep an eye on the schedule and there is sure to be something of interest.

○ "The Jug"—Officially The Old Stone Jug, generations of Colgate students fondly remember this part-bar, part-club, nighttime hot spot as all-fun.

○ Gilligan's Island—Located just a short drive south in the town of Sherburne, this burger and ice cream joint is a staple. Attend Colgate athletic events and you may earn yourself a coupon for some free ice cream!

A Multicultural Campus

Twenty-six percent of the Class of 2014 self-identified as being from a multicultural background, making it the most diverse class in Colgate's history. Because Colgate draws students from many locations and backgrounds, cultural exploration is one of the driving forces behind the social scene. To facilitate cultural exploration, Colgate features the ALANA (African, Latin, Asian, and Native American) Cultural Center. This professionally staffed center on campus supports an array of cultural clubs and events. Throughout the year, ALANA hosts BBQs, lectures, and travel opportunities that allow students to learn more about their classmates and the world around them. Events like the South Asian Cultural Club's Bhangra nights are some of the most popular of the year.

Colgate's multicultural campus also includes great religious diversity. Colgate supports students of every faith with an active Office of the Chaplains that not only strives to meet the religious needs of the campus, but to facilitate interfaith activities. Worship, prayer, reflection, and meditation spaces are available to students in Colgate's Memorial Chapel, the Saperstein Jewish Center, and Chapel House, a unique space for reflection that must be experienced to be truly understood.

Downtown Hamilton

Hamilton may not be big, but it has a flavor and personality that rivals any city in the country. Local businesses and restaurants line the five streets that meet in one of the world's most interesting five-way intersections at the heart of town.

There is no shortage of places to eat in Hamilton. When students need to take a night off from on-campus dining options, Hamilton offers everything from Chinese, to Mexican, to sushi, to pizza. Lunchtime favorites include wraps at the Parkside Deli, or during the warmer months, a hot dog from the stand on the village green.

> **"** *I see it as Colgate is a part of the community, and the community is a part of Colgate.* **"**

—*Sasha Ivanov, '11*

That village green represents the core of the Hamilton community. It is a park area that stretches from downtown Hamilton almost to the edge of Colgate's campus. Many community events, including "cabin fever" festivals in the winter and a weekly concert series in the summer, take place on the green. On Saturday mornings from spring through fall, students can take advantage of Colgate's rural location by picking up fresh produce and local goods at the green's popular farmers' market.

There is a vibrant nightlife downtown as well. The Hamilton Movie Theater has been providing entertainment to residents and students since 1895, and today is an affordable option for both box office hits and indie flicks. Dancers can hit up the Old Stone Jug, a legendary Colgate hot spot. Those looking for a more relaxed musical experience may try the Barge Canal Coffee Shop, which frequently hosts live music and open mic nights.

The walk from Colgate's campus to the center of Hamilton takes only ten to fifteen minutes, and Colgate also provides free shuttles. Due to the close proximity, many students consider the village and the university to be part of a single unit. The university encourages this sentiment to the extent that Colgate's bookstore is located in one of the central downtown storefronts, and university and town leaders frequently collaborate in support of community events.

Greek Life

Colgate's Greek life system dates to 1856 and remains as an influential, but by no means overpowering, feature of the Colgate community. Featuring six fraternities and three sororities, approximately thirty percent of Colgate students join a Greek letter organization during their time at Colgate. There is no divide between students in the Greek life system and those who remain unaffiliated, largely due to a delayed recruitment system in which students are not eligible for recruitment until the fall of their sophomore year. This allows students to fully integrate with the Colgate community and build a network of friends before being faced with a decision about whether to join a Greek letter organization.

Members of the Greek life system can be spotted organizing fundraising events and activities for charitable causes throughout the year. The organizations also host many popular social events and concerts, which are open to all students regardless of affiliation. Because all Greek life houses are owned by Colgate, social events are registered and coordinated with the university. This system has allowed Colgate to maintain its historic Greek life system as a healthy social option for those who wish to participate, without it coming to dominate the campus's social scene.

Community Service

Students interested in focusing on community service can check out the Center for Outreach, Volunteerism, and Education (COVE). This professionally staffed organization is an umbrella group providing guidance, training, and support for all of Colgate's student-led community service groups.

> **❝** *Volunteering through the COVE, I met people I wouldn't have met otherwise. I also definitely worked on my organizational skills, public speaking, budget and time management, and other skills you might not necessarily learn in a classroom. What I think makes community service at Colgate so effective is how well community partners work with students to make the groups and projects as effective as they can be.* **❞**

—*Sasha Ivanov, '11*

Involvement opportunities at the COVE range from playing bingo with senior citizens on a weekly basis to "alternative spring breaks," which are week-long service trips to locations such as New Orleans and the Dominican Republic. An impressive number of students take advantage of the opportunities available through the COVE, and if students notice any opportunity that is missing, they will find ample support in turning their visions into new organizations.

Artistic Life

Each spring, art projects start popping up all over campus as students place the fruits of their artistic labors on display. Throughout the year, projects are also on display in the galleries of Colgate's Little Hall, and students are hard at work bringing their visions to life in the university's Ryan Art Studio and Paul J. Schupf '55 Studio Art Center. Instructed by world-class artists, and privy to the advice and counsel of world-famous visiting artists, Colgate students have the opportunity to take their creative expression to the next level.

Colgate also has innumerable musical opportunities. Singers may choose to join one of Colgate's four *a capella* groups, the university chorus, or even the Student Musical Theater Company. Students who play instruments may wish to check out the University Orchestra or the Jazz Band. Informal student bands also took a step forward recently, organizing the first ever 'Gatestock, a weekend-long music festival featuring student musicians.

Theatrically, Colgate has something for every interest. The University Theater program and the Masque and Triangle, a student dramatic society, offer a variety of performances throughout the year. On any given weekend, students may participate in or attend a One Night Stand (staged reading), a 24-Hour Burn (the writing, production, and performance of a play in just 24 hours), or a performance of the hysterical Charred Goosebeak (improv comedy troupe). One of the most popular events of the year is Colgate's Dancefest, staged at the end of every semester, and featuring all of Colgate's dance groups, from ballet to belly-dancing.

Athletics

A thletics are an integral part of Colgate's identity. Part of the Division I Patriot League, Colgate's varsity student-athletes perform at the highest level both academically and athletically. The student-athlete lifestyle is demanding, but Colgate provides the resources and support that its student-athletes need, including quiet study spaces at athletic facilities, a faculty body that is willing to accommodate demanding travel schedules, and coaches who are willing to accommodate demanding academic schedules. Colgate's student-athletes are quick to point out that while balancing academics and athletics is difficult, their experiences are an integral part of their practical education, and the bonds they forge with their teammates will last a lifetime.

> ❝ *The support that we get from both our coaches and our teachers is far and above what I would assume student-athletes get at other schools. Both our coaches and our professors are super accommodating. I think at big Division I schools you often miss that, and you become more of an athlete-student than a student-athlete. I think Colgate does a good job at giving you the best of both worlds.* ❞

—Emma Eckerstrom '12

Students don't need to be varsity athletes to stay active at Colgate though. There is a slate of student-led club sports teams that participate in intercollegiate contests, as well a thriving intramural program that features leagues for people of all skill-levels. To stay fit outside of team athletics, students can hit up the state-of-the-art athletic facilities at the Trudy Fitness Center, which just opened in 2011, join Colgate's famous Outdoor Education Program, hit the on-campus cross-country trails, or in warmer months check out Colgate's Glendening Boathouse on nearby Lake Morraine.

FINANCIAL AID

Colgate provides its students with one of the best liberal arts educations in the country, including access to state-of-the-art facilities and resources, and instruction from world-class scholars. A concern for many students and their families is how they are going to finance such an education. To resolve this concern, students should turn to Colgate's Financial Aid office.

Colgate offers a limited number of athletic scholarships, and no merit-based awards, but it does commit to meeting 100 percent of admitted students' demonstrated financial need upon application for aid. Colgate meets this commitment with a mix of grants (money that does require repayment), loans, and work-study. Typically grants constitute the largest portion of a financial aid package, and the average package for the Class of 2014 came to $40,217. Upon graduation, aided students from the Class of 2010 had an average indebtedness amount of $13,304. Though this is not an insignificant amount of money, it is very competitive relative to the statistics at Colgate's peer institutions.

To receive financial aid, applicants must complete the Financial Aid PROFILE, which is submitted online through the College Scholarship Service (CSS). Once admitted, students who are awarded aid and have decided to attend Colgate must also file the Free Application for Federal Student Aid (FAFSA). These forms must be resubmitted each year, as each student's financial need is reevaluated and their aid package is adjusted accordingly. Note that the financial aid process is slightly different for international students, who are advised to contact Colgate for more information.

GRADUATES

Some will say that it is the tight-knit community; some will say it is the incredible growth they experienced on campus; and some may just say there is something in the air. Whatever the cause, it is undeniable that Colgate inspires a lifetime of passion in its alumni body. For the rest of their lives alumni remain involved in regional alumni clubs, and many are regular attendees at Homecoming and class reunions. When former students hear the word Colgate, or see the name in the subject line of an e-mail, you instantly have their attention.

Career Services

Current students can leverage that intense passion for the university as they begin to think of their own postgraduation plans. Through Colgate's career services office, a student may arrange a shadowing experience or informational interview with an alumnus in almost any industry. Alumni may be found doing everything from teaching at an elementary school, to developing cutting-edge green initiatives, to producing television shows. By e-mailing, shadowing, and speaking on the phone with these alumni, current students can hear first-hand accounts and get expert advice regarding industries in which they are interested. Alumni also frequently advertise job postings specifically to Colgate students through the resources available at the career services office.

- Adam Clayton Powell '30, civil rights leader and former New York congressman
- Dr. H. Guyford Stever '38, former director of National Science Foundation and former presidential adviser
- Andy Rooney '42, *60 Minutes* commentator, columnist
- Gloria Borger '74, CNN senior political analyst, columnist
- Broken Lizard Comedy Troupe '90, '91, '92, of *Super Troopers* and *Club Dredd* fame
- Francesca Zambello '78, leading American opera and theatre director
- Drew Esocoff '79, director of *Sunday Night Football* on NBC
- Joe Berlinger '83, documentarian of *My Brother's Keeper* and *Crude* fame
- Adonal Foyle '98, former NBA player and founder of nonprofit, nonpartisan "Democracy Matters"
- Paul Ridley '05, rowed solo across the Atlantic Ocean

Each January, more than 100 alumni voluntarily return to campus during the university's winter break for Colgate's Real World program. It is an optional program attended by most of the senior class, in which alumni with real-world experience share advice with students about the job search process and particular industries, as well as answer student questions. It provides a venue for students nervous about their post-college plans to find answers and support, and it is an incredible networking opportunity for everyone involved.

Alumni Life

Colgate makes an effort to remain connected to its alumni long after they have received their degrees. All over the country, alumni clubs are active in hosting trivia nights, send-off parties for incoming Colgate first-year students from their respective regions, and more. Colgate reaches out to its alumni via more traditional methods, such as its world-class alumni magazine, *The Colgate Scene*, but also in increasingly new and innovative ways. To learn more about how Colgate engages its alumni and more about the school in general, check out the university via social media on Twitter, Facebook, Flickr, and YouTube.

SUMMING UP

The student experience at Colgate is truly unique. Students arrive at the university each year from locations all over the country and from all over the world. Students at many other schools may spend four years studying next to each other without ever truly developing their sense of community, or a sense of place. At Colgate however, students immediately join an established, engaging, and vibrant community of students, professors, and community members. Students will both impact and be deeply impacted by this community in their four years of study.

Of course, this is all in support of Colgate's academic program, which somehow manages to counterintuitively be both time-honored and cutting-edge. As students at Colgate study many of the great classics and cultures of the world, they are also given free rein to explore, become experts in, and conduct groundbreaking research in fields as diverse as chemistry and peace and conflict studies. In the end, the students that walk across the stage at graduation have not been given an education by anybody; a Colgate degree is something that is crafted by the student. Colgate gives students the best resources with which to learn—including top-notch faculty members for guidance, state-of-the-art facilities for study and research, and a body of classmates that will challenge and inspire one another—but ultimately it is up to the student to utilize these resources and find success. The number of students who succeed in this endeavor at Colgate is a testament to the quality of person that finds their way into the Colgate community.

Inside the classroom, and inside the residence hall; competing in Division I athletic contests, and cheering in the stands; performing community service, and performing theater; exploring other cultures, and building their own—no matter what it is that Colgate students are doing, they do it with a passion that is hard to adequately capture. Glimpses of what makes Colgate so special are visible in the impressive photographs of the hillside campus, or in images of Colgate's traditional torchlight processional as the graduating seniors carry their figurative flames of knowledge with them down the hill. But to be truly appreciated, one simply must be a part of the fully transformative experience that takes place during four years on that hillside.

❑ *Jason Kammerdiener, B.A.*

 The College of New Jersey
Ewing, NJ 08628

 (609) 771-2131
Fax: (609) 637-5174

 E-mail: *admiss@tcnj.edu*
Website: *www.tcnj.edu*

 Enrollment

Full-time ❏ women: 3,625
❏ men: 2,668

Part-time ❏ women: 84
❏ men: 78

INTRODUCING THE COLLEGE OF NEW JERSEY

Located just a stone's throw from the state capital of Trenton, New Jersey, TCNJ exudes the ultimate collegiate ambiance and energy. With its classic Georgian Colonial architecture, wide brick pathways, and vibrant green lawns dotted with books and blankets on warm afternoons, visitors to campus might think that they've accidentally wandered onto the set of a quintessential college movie.

> ❝ *Growing up in suburbia, I'd always imagined myself cutting ties with my small-town past and reinventing myself as a big-city college girl, but my parents encouraged me to keep an open mind about TCNJ, a mid-sized school just about an hour from home. Initially, I only agreed to take a tour of TCNJ to rule it out, but as soon as I stepped foot on the campus, I grudgingly admitted that my parents were onto something. The campus, the residence halls, the academic programs...despite what I thought I had wanted, it all just seemed to fit. A second visit sealed the deal. Ultimately, I ended up applying Early Decision—and not applying anywhere else.* ❞

Long considered the college of choice for many of New Jersey's best and brightest students, this in-state secret is out, and the rest of the nation is taking notice: TCNJ provides a world-class education at a public school price, even garnering the label of "the hot college" from *The New York Times*.

The college was established in 1855 as the New Jersey State Normal School, the state's first teacher training institute. In its first year, the school welcomed 15 students at its one-building Trenton campus. Today, nearly 7,000 graduate and undergraduate, full- and part-time students take a range of classes offered in seven schools on the college's 289-acre campus.

The campus itself is a quiet oasis within bustling Ewing Township, closed to outside traffic and encircled by Metzger Drive, a two-mile loop popular with joggers, walkers, and bikers. An abundance of trees and the bordering Hillwood Lakes—Lake Sylva and Lake Ceva—give the campus a natural, pristine feel, despite its location in the heart of suburban New Jersey. There's never a shortage of geese to feed, and at dusk, it's not uncommon to see deer darting into the woods.

More than half of TCNJ students, and nearly all freshmen, choose to live on campus in an array of residence hall arrangements. Residential life at TCNJ goes far beyond simply sharing a bathroom or living space. On-campus living is heavily focused on community-building, providing new students with a supportive and hospitable home away from home. Several days before upper-class students arrive and classes begin, incoming freshmen participate in Welcome Week, a whirlwind five days of floor-bonding and community-building activities, and an integral part of the college's award-winning First Year Experience (FYE) program. Highlights include a local community-service project, volleyball tournaments,

T-shirt decorating, and PlayFair, best described as the biggest ice-breaker you'll ever experience. (It's not a bad idea to have a list of fun facts about yourself on hand.)

One of the first people you'll meet during Welcome Week is your Community Advisor, or CA, an upper-class student who oversees your area of the residence hall. Your CA is your connection to campus resources, as well as a wealth of must-know information, such as which pizzeria will offer the most prompt delivery for your 2:00 A.M. study session. Think of your CA as the cool older sibling you never had.

You'll also get to know your floor's College Ambassadors, typically identified by their striped rugby shirts and infectious enthusiasm. Your Ambassador will be your host—and get you excited—for a number of Welcome Week activities.

66 TCNJ's Welcome Week really helped me to ease comfortably into college. I had plenty of time to get to know my roommates and neighbors, and to just all-around adjust to my new surroundings. I'd never in my life met so many people in such a short period of time! Thanks to events like PlayFair, I was able to extend my social circle beyond my freshman floor—and I can safely say that I've high-fived every single person in the Class of 2010. By the convocation ceremony, I knew I'd made some lifelong friends.

Simply put, I had a great time at Welcome Week. Yeah, some of the activities were kind of cheesy, but I'm so glad I put any apprehension aside and threw myself into the unknown. Those first few days at TCNJ were an experience that I will always remember fondly. 99

—*Caitlin Levins, '10*

Though TCNJ students take their studies seriously, the fun and camaraderie don't stop when classes begin. Throughout the year, there are plenty of opportunities to set aside the books for a bit and participate in a variety of school activities and Residence Life programming, such as bus trips to football games, on-campus comedy shows, and concerts from popular music acts, to name just a few options. And even though freshmen aren't permitted to keep a car on campus, the free "Loop" bus offers service to local malls, movie theaters, and grocery stores several evenings a week.

With its impressive academics, active campus community, and bargain price, it's no wonder that more than ninety-five percent of freshmen decide to continue their education at TCNJ beyond their first year.

ADMISSIONS REQUIREMENTS

Many current TCNJ students made the decision to apply after talking to older siblings and friends, checking out the Web site, or scouting the rankings in college guides. For others, it took a visit to campus to seal the deal.

Visiting Campus

Prospective students are encouraged to take advantage of campus tours, offered several times per week all year long. During a campus tour, you'll receive a presentation from an admissions counselor and an hour-long tour of the campus led by the same College Ambassadors you'll meet during Welcome Week, should you choose to attend TCNJ.

A few times a semester, the college holds campus "open houses" to give prospective students the chance to chat with current students, faculty, and administrators. The open house schedule includes a campus tour, an admissions presentation, and an information fair with faculty from all of TCNJ's academic departments. For an even more true-to-life TCNJ experience, you can also request to sit in on a class, or to stay overnight with a current student.

If you're interested in taking a tour, attending an open house, or just want to receive more information about the application process, it's recommended that you register for the college's mailing list at *www.tcnj.edu/~admiss*. Once you're registered, you'll be able to RSVP for prospective student events and receive information about the academic, residential, and social opportunities available to TCNJ students.

The Application Process

After you've made the choice to apply, the process is fairly standard. Prospective students are required to submit an application (the Common Application is accepted), academic transcripts, official test scores (SAT or ACT), two or three letters of recommendation, an essay, a list of activities or a résumé, and a nonrefundable application fee. (Certain majors may have additional requirements; check the Web site for more information.) The entire application process can be completed online if you'd like, although mailing it all in the old-fashioned way is perfectly okay, too.

It's important to note that hard-copy applications for admission and course catalogs are no longer mailed to recipients—but no worries, these materials can be downloaded from the TCNJ Web site.

Getting In

Just like every other school you're looking at, there's no magical combination of grades and test scores that will guarantee you a spot in TCNJ's incoming freshman class. One of the most crucial elements of an application is a strong high school transcript. The classes you take in high school (and their difficulty—special emphasis is placed on honors and Advanced Placement courses), your grades, your GPA, and your class rank are all weighed heavily during the decision-making process, more so than your standardized test scores. Eighty-seven percent of current freshmen were in the top fifth of their graduating classes, with ninety-eight percent in the top two-fifths.

As TCNJ becomes the top choice of many applicants, it also becomes less of a "safe school" option, with a current acceptance rate of around forty-six percent. Bottom line: if you're sure that TCNJ is the place for you, admissions officials recommend you apply Early Decision.

ACADEMIC LIFE

At TCNJ, you have your choice among seven schools and more than fifty majors and programs of study. Your classes will be instructed by a member of TCNJ faculty—virtually no classes are led by graduate students or teaching assistants. With an average student-to-faculty ratio of thirteen to one, you'll play an active role in each class meeting, and have the opportunity to get to know your professors first-hand. Rarely, if ever, will you meet in a lecture hall. Your professors will know your face and name.

While it might sound intimidating to not be just another anonymous face in an enormous lecture hall, the small class size is highly beneficial to your academic growth. TCNJ professors are always available during office hours. Take the time to connect with your class instructors on a personal level. You never know when you might need some academic guidance or a letter of recommendation.

Internship and Research Opportunities

Your learning experience won't be limited to the classroom. Several hundred companies actively recruit TCNJ students for jobs and internships, and the school's location just about midway between Philadelphia and New York places students just about an hour away from an abundance of internship and job opportunities.

Internships and jobs are plentiful in nearby cities and communities, but real-life work experience can also be acquired without ever leaving campus. Nearly every academic department offers independent study options and research projects each semester. Some students choose to assist professors in their research; others, under the tutelage of their advisers, embark on their own personal research projects.

While I knew I wanted to work in the media industry postgraduation, I was unsure about what specific career path I was meant to follow. With my adviser's encouragement, I applied and interviewed for a variety of communications-related internships. TCNJ's proximity to New York, arguably the media capital of the world, allowed me to pursue two internships with a popular cable television network, and a whirlwind semester-long stint at a weekly celebrity magazine. All three positions taught me more about working in the media industry than any course I'd taken—and how cool is it that I earned class credit by interviewing a supermodel and working on a TV shoot with a rock 'n roll legend?

With New York just a train ride away, I still got the big-city experience I'd always wanted…though I'm still figuring out that whole career-path thing.

Liberal Learning

While the number of credits required for graduation varies from major to major, all students must earn at least one hundred twenty-eight semester hours, with a minimum overall GPA of 2.0. The general TCNJ undergraduate education consists of a "liberal learning" curriculum of thirty-two to thirty-four course units. These courses span a variety of topics, including diversity and community engagement, natural, physical, and social sciences, humanities, and the arts. While students must meet specific academic requirements to graduate, there are a number of classes to choose from to fulfill each requirement.

> 66 *Taking classes across the academic spectrum allowed me to pursue scholarly interests outside of my major. After taking a class called The Politics of Sexuality in order to fulfill the liberal learning gender requirement, I was so enamored with the subject matter that I took on a minor in women's and gender studies. My internship with a cable network piqued my interest in film production, and I added a minor in communications. The liberal learning curriculum opened my eyes to what else is out there beyond my major, and allowed me to develop marketable skills in addition to pursuing my interests.* 99

First-Year Requirements

As a part of TCNJ's comprehensive "First Year Experience," students are required to complete a First Seminar, an academically exciting and challenging small, seminar-style class. Students can choose whatever seminar focus interests them most—and you're guaranteed to be interested in at least one of these unique topics. Subjects range from Walt Whitman to tourism to cultural history and the science of food.

Community service, or civic engagement, is also a crucial element of the First Year Experience. Students participate in their choice of more than thirty community service projects in the Ewing/Trenton area. In addition to fulfilling an academic requirement, students form a solid connection with their new home away from home. Many choose to continue serving the community long after the requirement is met.

Some of the student organizations you might be surprised to find at TCNJ include

○ **ACTION:** A coalition of political activists striving for change at TCNJ and beyond.

○ **ORDER of the Nose-Biting Teacups:** A Harry Potter appreciation and community service club.

○ **Manhunt:** Manhunt members rule the night with their nocturnal cross of tag and hide-and-seek.

○ **PEANUTS:** A much-appreciated acronym for "Planning Exciting Activities for a Never-ending Utopia for TCNJ Students," PEANUTS is responsible for events such as white-water rafting and "Natural High Olympics."

○ **TCNJ Swing:** Its goal is to preserve, maintain, and celebrate the historic legacy of swing dancing.

○ **Water Watch:** This environmental organization is dedicated to improving water quality in the Trenton area.

Honor Societies

Ranging from Iota Iota Iota (women's and gender studies) to Beta Gamma Sigma (business and administration) and beyond, TCNJ is home to fifteen national honor society chapters. In 2006, the college was selected in Phi Beta Kappa, an honor for which fewer than ten percent of higher education institutions are selected. Forty departments offer their own honors programs.

Facilities

TCNJ students have access to truly impressive, state-of-the-art academic facilities. In January 2010, the Art and Interactive Multimedia Building was completed, providing a 70,000 square foot facility that houses studios, classrooms, computer labs, offices, and display space. The art history, digital arts, fine arts, graphic design, interactive multimedia (IMM), and photography departments all reside in this building. For the fall 2010 semester, Eickhoff —TCNJ's main dining facility—welcomed students with a completely renovated eating space that features freshly prepared and made-to-order meals that will satisfy any craving from pasta to burritos to freshly made sushi. There is even a separate space especially for gluten-free foods and students with foods allergies. In 2006 construction on a 135,000 square-foot library was completed. In addition to housing traditional library collections and services, the building accommodates twenty-four group study rooms, a café, a late-night study area, and a 105-seat multipurpose auditorium. Its five stories are packed with more than half a million volumes, almost twenty thousand periodicals, one hundred public computers, printers, scanners, copiers, and cozy nooks perfect for a quiet study session (or a quick nap). Most areas inside the library, as well as the outdoor Alumni Grove just beyond the library's front door, have wireless access. TCNJ recently broke ground on a new education building, scheduled to be completed by the start of the fall 2012 semester.

You'll be amazed at how many resources are at your fingertips at TCNJ. Take advantage of them, and you'll be sure to achieve academic success.

SOCIAL LIFE AND ACTIVITIES

In recent years, TCNJ has shaken off the "suitcase school" image of the past. While it's true that most students hail from the Garden State, more than half of TCNJ students reside on campus, and on any given weekend, most of them are sticking around town. And why wouldn't they?

Like many colleges, TCNJ doesn't permit first-year students to keep a car on campus, but you're hardly stranded on the college's grounds. The "Loop" bus service provides free transportation to area malls, movie theaters, and grocery stores several evenings a week. There's an NJ Transit bus stop just outside of the Brower Student Center, offering service to a number of local attractions, including the closest NJ Transit train station. Public transportation offers easy access to the museums, restaurants, theaters—and general excitement—of New York and Philadelphia.

For those interested in getting off campus but still keeping it local, there are many restaurants and shops in Ewing proper and on the nearby Route 1 corridor. Minor-league baseball and hockey games are only a short drive away in Trenton.

Thanks to TCNJ's many active student organizations, there's almost always something cool happening on campus any given night of the week. Concerts, lectures, late-night pizza parties—you name it, and it's probably on the schedule.

Athletics

TCNJ, home to eighteen varsity sports teams, is a National Collegiate Athletic Association powerhouse. In the past thirty years, TCNJ has earned thirty-eight Division III titles in six different sports. The college has also amassed thirty-two runner-up awards. With the support of an excellent coaching staff, many TCNJ student athletes have earned All-American and all-conference honors.

VARSITY SPORTS
Women's
○ Basketball
○ Cross Country
○ Field Hockey
○ Lacrosse
○ Soccer
○ Softball
○ Swimming and Diving
○ Tennis
○ Track and Field
Men's
○ Baseball
○ Basketball
○ Cross Country
○ Football
○ Soccer
○ Swimming and Diving
○ Tennis
○ Track and Field
○ Wrestling

In addition to the various NCAA titles and honors, TCNJ athletics also enjoy a solid and enthusiastic fan base, with the annual Homecoming celebration bringing out students and alumni alike to support the college's football team.

Athletic participation isn't limited to those competing at the varsity level. The college is home to eighteen club sports, ranging from such diverse options as rugby and ice hockey to fencing and Ultimate Frisbee. Intramural sports such as flag football, volleyball, basketball, and softball are also offered.

Clubs and Organizations

There are almost two hundred clubs and organizations at TCNJ, ranging from the Asian American Association to Zeta Phi Beta Sorority, and a new club is probably forming at this very moment. If no existing organization embodies exactly what you're looking for, you're welcome to request campus funding and start your own club.

About twenty-five percent of TCNJ students belong to a sorority or fraternity. While there are no official Greek houses on campus, there's a strong off-campus presence if you choose to seek it out.

It's fairly safe to say that no matter what your background or your interests, you'll feel at home and find your niche at TCNJ.

FINANCIAL AID

TCNJ offers a world-class, first-rate education at a bargain public school price. But as college costs continue to rise, many students find themselves seeking ways to manage the financial burden of a college education. In a recent year, about two-thirds of full-time freshmen received some form of financial assistance.

TCNJ's Office of Student Financial Assistance counsels students on the various resources, such as work-study programs, scholarships, loans, and grants, that are available to fund their college educations.

To be considered for most types of assistance, you must first complete either the Free Application for Federal Student Aid (FAFSA) or the Renewal FAFSA. The FAFSA is required for consideration for any need-based and/or federal aid at any American college or university. (Learn more at *www.fafsa.ed.gov.*) The priority filing date for TCNJ is March 1. Getting your application and supporting documents to the federal processor by that date labels your application as a "priority" when it's received by the Office of Student Financial Assistance, meaning that, although there are no guarantees, you may have a better chance of receiving funds that are awarded on a "first-come, first-served" basis. Once your application is received, you'll be notified of the amount of need-based aid for which you qualify. For more information, visit the Office of Student Financial Assistance online at *www.tcnj.edu/~sfs/aid/*.

Even with the support of financial aid, the cost of attending college can seem overwhelming. But there are options beyond just need-based aid and federal assistance. Many students are the recipients of private scholarships, secured with the help of high school guidance counselors or by searching online scholarship databases. In addition to padding their pockets, students can pad their résumés with the on-campus work-study program. Certain positions in residence life even provide free room and board. Off-campus, there are lots of businesses that are happy to hire hardworking college students and are willing to work with their flexible schedules.

Another financial aid option for some New Jersey state residents is the Educational Opportunity Fund (EOF). The EOF program provides financial assistance, as well as personal and academic support, to motivated state residents who have the potential for academic and career success, but come from backgrounds of "historical poverty" and who "have lacked access to quality education preparation," according to the EOF mission statement. You can find more information and see if you're eligible at *www.tcnj.edu/~eofp*.

GRADUATES

The sky's the limit for TCNJ graduates. Thanks to the impressive education under their belts, former students have gone on to work in the corporate, nonprofit, and governmental sectors, and have embarked on successful graduate school careers at the nation's top law, medical, and graduate schools.

The Office of Career Services offers a variety of workshops on career and major exploration, résumé writing, interviewing skills—including the cringe-inducing, yet enormously valuable, videotaped mock interview—and internship and job search preparation.

The LionsLink system, powered by the NACElink network, is TCNJ's online recruitment program. This recruitment tool, used by many top-tier universities around the nation, allows students

NOTABLE GRADS

- Chris Smith, NJ Representative to U.S. Congress
- James Florio, Former Governor of New Jersey
- Holly Black, Author, *The Spiderwick Chronicles*
- Ty Treadway, Actor/Television Host
- Tom McCarthy, Announcer, Philadelphia Phillies
- Derick Grant, Harlem Globetrotter

and alumni to submit résumés to potential employers. Whether you're looking for an internship to add to your résumé or a full-time permanent position, LionsLink is a convenient one-stop shop.

TOP EMPLOYERS

In recent years, some of the top employers of TCNJ grads have included...
○ Johnson & Johnson
○ State of New Jersey
○ Americorps
○ Ernst & Young
○ Bloomberg LP
○ US Army
○ Liberty Mutual
○ KPMG
○ Hospital of the University of Pennsylvania
○ Deloitte

With eight hundred companies recruiting on campus in a recent year, many students have jobs lined up well before graduation. Currently, TCNJ grads are writing award-winning children's books, researching potential cures for cancer, and editing video for some of your favorite television shows, just to name a few. Your possibilities are endless with a TCNJ degree.

SUMMING UP

With its pride in its humble Jersey roots and its rise to prominence on the national stage, perhaps TCNJ is the college equivalent of Bruce Springsteen or Jon Bon Jovi. If you choose to attend TCNJ, you'll be welcomed into a community of learners and friends, dedicated to the pursuit of excellence in all aspects. Don't be dissuaded by its size or its location—just remember that at TCNJ, you're getting world-class, Ivy-caliber education at a public school price. Take advantage of all the academic, social, and professional developments that come your way, and a successful college career is guaranteed. Come graduation, you won't believe the doors that will open for you with a TCNJ degree in hand.

❑ *Nicole Levins, B.A.*

COLLEGE OF THE HOLY CROSS

College of the Holy Cross
Worcester, MA 01610

(800) 442-2421 or (508) 793-2443
Fax: (508) 793-3888

E-mail: *admissions@holycross.edu*
Website: *www.holycross.edu*

 **Enrollment**

Full-time ❏ women: 1,582
❏ men: 1,315

Part-time ❏ women: 17
❏ men: 18

INTRODUCING HOLY CROSS

Why Holy Cross? Commonly asked of students on "The Hill," this question seems to be simple and certainly it has no shortage of enthusiastic replies.

Many students choose Holy Cross for its prestigious academic reputation. The small class sizes, dedicated faculty and staff members, and rigorous curriculum make it an enticing choice for excellent high school students from across the country and around the world. A true liberal arts college, Holy Cross educates its student body to be better thinkers, writers, speakers, readers, and perhaps most importantly, better doers. It doesn't matter what path of study or course load students take because all offer challenges and the opportunity to become effective learners.

Other students are drawn to the Jesuit heritage of the school. The only exclusively undergraduate Jesuit Catholic college in the country, Holy Cross has flourished into a prominent and selective college since its establishment in 1843. Benedict Joseph Fenwick, the second bishop of Boston, founded the school as a community in which the Jesuit ideals of educational integrity and social justice could thrive. While the school has expanded from its original one-and-a-half buildings and all-male student body, those ideals are still firmly rooted in Holy Cross. Students are urged to strive for more and live up to the college's mission of becoming "men and women for others."

Still others visit and are so enamored of the campus that they cannot imagine school anywhere else. Many students and their families are impressed with the campus' buildings, beautifully landscaped grounds, and its modernity amidst all its tradition. State-of-the-art athletic facilities and technologically advanced academic buildings neighbor historic, ivy-covered halls. The campus supports wireless internet access in addition to the hundreds of available computers in libraries, labs, and common areas. There are two multi-sport recreational facilities, four extensive libraries, performance and gallery spaces, a bustling campus center, and a brand new science complex. A quintessential New England college and a registered arboretum, Holy Cross is breathtaking any time of the year. An autumn stroll down tree-lined Linden Lane, the main entrance to the campus, or past Fenwick's flushing ivy shows foliage at its brightest. Springtime brings a burst of life to Holy Cross, with students flocking outside for studying or relaxing or to enjoy the courtyards, flower gardens, and open green space on the college's award-winning campus. Even winter has stunning beauty, blanketing the campus in pristine snow, though it never stays that way for long. Holy Cross sits on 174 acres atop Mount St. James overlooking the city of Worcester, and the Hill provides some of the best sledding around. Regardless of the season, few people are disappointed with the remarkable campus.

Some students come to Holy Cross for the upkeep of a proud tradition or an opportunity to forge strong loyalties. For generations, students have dedicated themselves to intellectual challenge, high standards, and open dialogue, and in doing so create lifelong bonds with their peers. Each year, students are still drawn to Holy Cross to find these ideals and this type of living-learning community. To facilitate the intellectual discourse and scholarly exploration, all first years enroll in Montserrat, a program that immediately immerses students in an intensive academic experience complemented with extracurricular activities and a supportive living environment. The program is designed to help students make connections between what they're learning in the classroom and their lives outside of it, and to integrate the two in a way that enhances their education.

Other responses to "Why Holy Cross?" include its active student population, unique opportunities such as Study Abroad or Spring Break Immersion Trips, and its impressive Division I athletics. Whatever their responses and reasons, students are satisfied with their choice to attend Holy Cross, as demonstrated by the college's ninety-six percent freshman retention rate. Holy Cross gives students the opportunity to explore beyond their known interests and pursue more. Holy Cross encourages its students to practice *cura personalis*, or care of the whole person. This focus sets Holy Cross apart and allows students to develop all aspects of their lives.

> ❝ *HC is a place where people prioritize well-being in all senses: intellectually, emotionally, physically, and spiritually. Sometimes this comes out as 'work hard, play hard,' but it was great to be at a place where people love life!* ❞

—*Rebecca Krier '09*

Students who choose Holy Cross also choose a holistic approach to education, which will follow them long after they head out the wrought-iron gates and into the world.

ADMISSIONS REQUIREMENTS

In recent years, more than 6,500 students apply annually for fewer than 730 places in the first-year class at Holy Cross. Though the personalized admissions process allows Holy Cross to consider candidates with a wide variety of interests and backgrounds, students who have consistently demonstrated excellent academic achievement and success throughout high school have a greater chance of gaining acceptance to the college. Nearly all students entering Holy Cross achieved grades that put them at or near the top of their class. Most have experience with Advanced Placement and honors coursework.

Accepted students tend to share several other characteristics besides academic accomplishments. They view activities not as a checklist of items, but as ways to pursue what really matters to them. By engaging intensely in a few activities, they better demonstrate leadership and passion. Many students have also been involved in service activities that have positively affected their communities. Most candidates have an interview, which allows them to better demonstrate their openness to different viewpoints, willingness to become engaged in the college community, and their commitment to helping others.

Rather than relying on a preset formula for admissions, Holy Cross' selection committee tries to have a clear understanding of each candidate. By focusing on each student individually, the selection team is better able to identify those candidates who will thrive at Holy Cross not only academically, but also socially and spiritually.

Admission Requirements

All prospective students must complete the Common Application and an essay. They must submit their high school transcript, two letters of recommendation (one from a teacher and one from a guidance counselor), and an application fee. The submission of standardized test scores (SAT I, SAT II, ACT) is optional.

While not required, the Admissions Office *strongly* urges students to visit the Holy Cross campus and complete an interview. Campus interviews are conducted by the Admissions Committee, which is comprised of admissions counselors and trained members of the current senior class.

> **"** *I chose HC solely based on how I felt when I toured the campus. I remember standing on Fenwick Porch, overlooking the city of Worcester, thinking that my possibilities and potential would be endless here.* **"**

—Lauren Courtney '09

Early Decision

Exceptional high school seniors who have identified Holy Cross as their first choice are encouraged to apply Early Decision. An Early Decision application demonstrates one's commitment to and excitement about attending Holy Cross. Admissions counselors spend a considerable amount of time reviewing a candidate's application. Additionally, this option alleviates the stress of the college search process, as candidates will be notified of a decision within three to four weeks after the school receives all necessary materials. Upon acceptance, Early Decision applicants are expected to enroll at Holy Cross, subject to financial aid determinations, and to withdraw all pending applications at other colleges due to the binding nature of the decision.

The rigor of Holy Cross academics encourages both cooperation and competition. Students often collaborate and challenge each other to achieve more. It's not unusual to come across study groups in the dorm common rooms or students working together outside of Cool Beans, the on-campus café. The classes at Holy Cross also encourage students to take on life's bigger questions and challenges by emphasizing fundamental skills such as critical thought and analysis. The liberal arts approach to education allows students to pursue their passions and find their vocations instead of pigeonholing them in a career track.

> **"** *The emphasis on critical thinking, analytical skills, and interpersonal skills enabled me to be very marketable. The education I obtained at HC has opened doors to numerous possibilities. I was hired right out of college in a terrible economic environment and now have been accepted to graduate school. HC has provided a solid foundation for continuing my education.* **"**

—Maryanne O'Brien '08

Programs of Study

All programs of study at Holy Cross lead to a Bachelor of Arts degree. Students can choose from twenty-six majors in the fields of humanities, social science, science and mathematics, and arts. Additionally, there is the option of a student-designed major. Students' interests can be combined or expanded by means of a double major, a minor, or a concentration. For those planning a career in law, engineering, business, education, or medicine or other health professions, Holy Cross offers focused pre-professional programs to help students prepare for success after graduation.

EXAMPLE MONTSERRAT SEMINARS

- ○ Hearing the Divine
- ○ Science and Religion
- ○ Writing the Self in Fiction
- ○ When Worlds Collide
- ○ Cuisine, Culture, and Identity
- ○ History, War, and Memory
- ○ Nature Poetry
- ○ Islam and the West: Encounters
- ○ The Biology of Consciousness
- ○ Made in America/Made in Society
- ○ Freedom and the Meaning of Life
- ○ Disaster Economics

Common Requirements

Academic exploration is fundamental in a liberal arts education, and Holy Cross creates opportunities for students to access all areas of study with open-mindedness. Although there is no core curriculum or specific sets of classes required by the school, students must fulfill some flexible common requirements to expose them to the different areas of study:

- The Arts and Literature (one course in each)
- Religious, Philosophical, and Historical Studies (one course in each)
- Cross-Cultural Studies (one course)
- Social Sciences (two courses)
- Language Studies (two courses in a language other than one in which a student possesses native fluency)
- Natural and Mathematical Sciences (two courses, of which one must be a natural science)

This academic framework is designed to offer students exposure to a variety of disciplines with the flexibility to choose what will both interest and challenge them. All classes train students to think critically, read analytically, write clearly and effectively, and communicate purposefully. The focus of these fundamental skills provides Holy Cross graduates with an educational foundation that will help them become successful in almost any career path.

Students do not need to wait until the upper levels to find meaning in their education. Instead of letting first-year students get lost in an academic shuffle, Holy Cross provides opportunities for intimate seminars, stimulating discussions, and authentic learning through Montserrat, the first-year experience at the college. The program is grouped into clusters: the natural world, the divine, the self, global society, and core human questions. Students have the unique opportunity to not only take classes with members from their cluster, but also live in the same dorm building with them. This helps promote a welcoming and intellectually challenging environment for first-year students. All students must take two courses (one each semester) of interdisciplinary Montserrat seminars from within their cluster.

Holy Cross students take four classes as a full course load for the semester; students may spend fewer than fifteen hours a week in class, but they are expected to do much of their reading and learning outside of the classroom. Most classes come with a weighty reading list on the syllabus, and while some majors are definitely more reading and writing intensive, it is not uncommon for any professor to go through seven or eight texts in a semester. Due to the large volume of work required outside of class, students either develop excellent time management skills early or learn to deal with pulling regular all-nighters.

Faculty

Without question, one of the best things about a Holy Cross education is the outstanding faculty that students work with.

> 66 *The professors at Holy Cross are first-rate, and are some of the most intellectually stimulating people I've ever met. At Holy Cross, the status quo is regularly being challenged . . . students are constantly exposed to various political, religious, and cultural forums that frequently make them reevaluate (and sometimes question) their own views.* 99

—*Sean Coombs '10*

Professors at Holy Cross are extremely accomplished and experts in their respective fields, but it is their dedication to student relationships that keeps them in high esteem. They are committed to their students, as demonstrated by their accessibility through regular office hours and flexible appointments. Many have an open door policy, and as a result, it isn't uncommon to see clusters of students waiting patiently outside of the faculty offices. Some professors even hold classes in their homes or invite students over for a home-cooked meal and a review session. The faculty challenges students and pushes their thinking beyond their comfort zone, to consider the position of others, and to make personal discoveries about their own learning.

Classes

When one walks into a classroom at Holy Cross, it's clear that a love of learning from both professors and students drives instruction. Due to the small average class sizes (fewer than twenty students) and a student-faculty ratio of 11:1, students receive a personalized education with individual attention. Intense discussion characterizes the Holy Cross classroom, and students are expected to not only show up prepared for every class, but also actively participate. Upper level seminars offer an even more intimate setting, with some courses capped at twelve to allow for a better, more meaningful exchange among participants. Students often contemplate the day's lesson long after they've stopped taking notes. Professors quite intentionally use their courses as catalysts to spur student thinking beyond the gates of Holy Cross.

> **"** *I'd never come into contact with poverty and injustice the way I did through Holy Cross. This allowed me to develop and discover a social awareness that in many ways is the lens through which I see the world. From politics to education to theology to ethics, I find my mind centered around wondering if it's bringing about a more just and equitable existence for people or whether it's marginalizing.* **"**

—*David Floyd '09*

Special Opportunities

Close faculty and administrative relationships and high levels of academic autonomy afford Holy Cross students the opportunity to pursue learning outside of the classroom. By their junior year, many students are collaborating with Holy Cross professors on extensive research projects and independent studies that are often presented in academic journals or at national symposia. Around 190 students each year complete off-campus, academic internships through the Center for Interdisciplinary and Special Studies. In a recent study conducted by the Institute of International Education, Holy Cross also ranked first in student participation among baccalaureate institutions with long-term study abroad programs. Each year, more than two hundred students spend a summer, semester, or an entire academic year exploring other parts of the world.

> **"** *When I think back to Holy Cross, I immediately think of the extracurricular stuff, but the academics really grounded my whole experience. The opportunity to develop a thesis and present it culminated my HC experience and the knowledge I gained from this process is vital to my future studies, school related or not.* **"**

—*Abigail Parsons '09*

20 full year, 10 semester, 8 summer

Academic Year Programs
○ Australia—University of Melbourne
○ Cameroon—The University of Central Africa, The Catholic Institute of Yaoundé
○ England—Oxford University, Mansfield College; Oxford University, St. Edmund Hall; University of Leicester; University of Sussex; University of York
○ France—Université de Bourgogne, Dijon; Université de Strasbourg
○ Germany—Otto-Friedrich Universität, Bamberg
○ Ireland—National University of Ireland, Galway; University College, Cork; University of Dublin, Trinity College
○ Italy—Università di Bologna; Università di Firenze
○ Japan—Sophia University, Tokyo
○ Scotland—University of St. Andrews
○ Spain—Universidad de León; Universitat de Les Illes Balears, Palma; Universidade da Coruña

Semester Programs
○ China—CET Beijing, CET Harbin, CET Shanghai
○ El Salvador—Casa de la Solidaridad (through Santa Clara Univ., California)

○ Greece—College Year in Athens (CYA)
○ Indonesia—Universitas Sanata Dharma
○ Ireland—University College, Dublin
○ Italy (Classics Majors Only)—American Institute of Roman Culture (AIRC), Intercollegiate Center for Classical Studies—Rome (ICCS, through Duke Univ.)
○ Peru—Pontificia Universidad Católica del Perú, Lima (can also be academic year)
○ Sri Lanka—ISLE Program (through Bowdoin College, ME) School for Field Studies (Environmental Programs)— Australia, Costa Rica, Kenya/Tanzania, Mexico, Turks & Caicos
○ Organization for Tropical Studies—Costa Rica; Cape Town, South Africa

Summer Programs
○ Jerusalem
○ London
○ Moscow
○ Paris
○ Peru
○ Rome
○ Southeast Asia
○ South Africa

SOCIAL LIFE AND ACTIVITIES

While the challenging and often heavy workload keeps Holy Cross students busy, most still find time to get involved on campus or in Worcester. Due to the school's small size, students are better able to form meaningful, lasting connections. These extensive friendships make the campus a lively and social place to be. Students meet up between classes for chats and chai lattes at Cool Beans. Crossroads, in lower Hogan, or Lower Kimball both offer great places to lunch with friends. Kimball Dining Hall brunch is the place to socialize on weekends and take a breather from the "work hard, play hard" mentality that so many students take on. Although much of the student body migrates to the adjacent neighborhood and other off-campus destinations for any number of celebrations, there is no pressure to drink. Wherever they flock to, students just want to take a break to relax and enjoy one another's company.

The Hogan Campus Center serves as a hub for many of the over ninety clubs and organizations at Holy Cross. Students can pursue their passions or explore new things by involving themselves in activities. Holy Cross offers a wide variety, from Multicultural Peer Educators, to *The Crusader* newspaper to Campus Activities Board. If there's a special interest or hobby not available at Holy Cross, the Student Affairs staff will help create it. It's really easy to get involved with things like GESSO student art club or Eco-Action, and it's a great way to not only make friends, but to truly personalize Holy Cross.

Holy Cross also offers many social and entertainment options throughout the year right on campus. There are several class-sponsored dances, student theater productions, concert performances, stand-up comedy acts, guest speakers, and theme nights. Seelos Theatre beneath Kimball Dining Hall shows free movies during the week.

Athletics

Holy Cross has a legendary tradition that student-athletes strive to honor. About one-quarter of the population competes as varsity athletes, but almost all of Holy Cross students participate in athletics in some capacity. There are twenty-seven varsity sports, all but one of which compete in the NCAA Division I level (I-AA for football). The Crusaders are primarily members of the Patriot League, and often have competitive schedules and impressive results. Holy Cross student-athletes keep academics and personal growth at the forefront of their college experience, and this commitment constantly earns Holy Cross national recognition for its high student-athlete graduation rates. Both men's and women's basketball and men's hockey have recently advanced to NCAA tournaments. Athletic events and strong tradition help contribute to the intensely fierce school spirit; it's not uncommon to see purple-clad students trek up to the Hart Center or down to Fitton Field during inclement weather to cheer on the 'Saders.

There are also more than twenty intramural and club sports, ranging from Ultimate Frisbee to co-recreational floor hockey. Most students also frequent the Hart Center to use its pool, track, workout facilities, or to take an exercise class like kickboxing or yoga.

Off Campus

For those seeking a break from campus, the college's central Massachusetts location provides an excellent base to explore New England. Worcester is home to many great eateries; its most well known area is Shrewsbury Street, which is lined on both sides with excellent restaurants. Blackstone Valley in nearby Millbury offers some chain restaurants, shopping, and a movie theater.

Both Boston, MA and Providence, RI are less than an hour away and provide excellent shopping and diverse cultural and historical opportunities. The Student Government Association offers free shuttle services to both cities on the weekend. A weekend getaway can easily be arranged in New York City or in any of Cape Cod's quaint villages. There are also orchards, mountains, lakes, and state parks near Holy Cross that offer quality skiing, rock climbing, kayaking or canoeing, camping, or simply a quiet stroll through nature.

Giving to the Community

Students at Holy Cross take the school's commitment to producing "men and women for others" quite seriously. The values-based education at Holy Cross keeps students thinking constantly of others, as demonstrated by their commitment to giving back in Worcester and beyond. Student Programs for Urban Development (SPUD) is an umbrella

Worcester was once home to one of only ten companies in the nation that made diner cars. The Worcester Lunch Car Company operated from 1906 to 1961, and though the company no longer exists, Worcester's reputation for fantastic diner food is still going strong. No student at Holy Cross should graduate without tasting some of the city's history at these local eateries.

- ○ The Boulevard, or "The Bully," serves diner staples 24 hours a day, which makes it a great place to stop when you need a break from that all-nighter.
- ○ Right across the way from the Bully is Parkway Diner. This diner not only offers traditional breakfast fare, but also inspired Italian dishes.
- ○ Located right across from the former Worcester Lunch Car Company on Southbridge St., Miss Worcester is the closest diner to Holy Cross.
- ○ Just a block from Miss Worcester is Corner Lunch, which was originally parked in Babylon, New York before heading to Worcester.
- ○ Green Island Diner, also close to Holy Cross, dishes up breakfast-only starting at 4 A.M. for early birds or night owls.
- ○ Rebuilt after the 1999 Worcester Cold Storage fire destroyed it, Kenmore Diner originally served late-shift crews, which is perfect for those late-night weekend adventures.
- ○ Ralph's Chadwick Square Diner, or Ralph's, as everyone in Worcester knows it, isn't really a diner anymore. It's now a hotspot for great live music and good burgers.
- ○ Worcester's newest diner, Blanchard's 101 Diner, may have only opened in 2008, but it was one of the last lunch cars produced in Worcester. It wasn't finished until it was purchased a few years ago.

organization composed of forty student-run programs throughout Worcester. As the largest student club on campus with over 700 participants, SPUD allows students to tutor in public schools, visit the elderly, serve food to the homeless, work with domestic violence victims, and many other opportunities. Each year, one in ten students dedicates their spring breaks to immersion trips in areas of Virginia, Kentucky, West Virginia, New Orleans, or New Jersey. Holy Cross also offers international immersion programs in Kenya, Jamaica, and Mexico. They not only do service work, but experience life from a different perspective to better enable themselves to work with others, not just for them.

Faith

Participating in religious life at Holy Cross is by no means mandatory, but a good portion of the student body actively participates in some aspect of faith life on campus. In fact, it's not uncommon to find the chapel filled for the late Sunday night service. The Jesuit priests and lay chaplains offer support to those who wish to explore or expand their spirituality while at Holy Cross. Faith life can be explored through immersion trips, liturgy services, Christian Life Communities, and perhaps most popular, through retreats. Over 400 students take advantage of the Escape retreat for first-years only, Manresa weekend retreats offered several times during the year, and five-day silent retreats known as the Spiritual Exercises offered twice yearly.

> 66 *The Jesuit philosophy, which I was never exposed to before Holy Cross, allowed me to be a much more open-minded person. I was a little wary about attending a Catholic school because I'm not particularly religious, but I soon discovered that HC is not by any means preachy about religion.* 99

—*Joseph Puleo '10*

FINANCIAL AID

Tuition, room and board, and other fees total approximately $50,850; the cost of attending Holy Cross should not prevent anyone from applying. Holy Cross accepts students regardless of their ability to pay and then meets one hundred percent of their need, as calculated according to national financial aid criteria. Nearly two-thirds of students receive some form of assistance, typically in a package that combines scholarships and grants, loans, and work-study employment.

To apply for financial aid, an incoming student must indicate on the admissions application that he or she would like to be considered for Holy Cross financial aid. To be considered for both Federal Student Assistance and Holy Cross scholarships, a student must both file a Free Application for Federal Student Assistance (FAFSA) and register for the College Scholarship Service (CSS) by filing a PROFILE document. The financial aid forms must be completed by the deadlines listed on the Holy Cross website.

GRADUATES

Since the focus of the Holy Cross education centers on critical skills and values, graduates can enter a variety of occupational and educational fields with confidence.

Law, medicine, and business are among the most common professions sought by Holy Cross students. Law schools accept HC students at a rate of eighty-four percent, and medical schools at seventy-eight percent. An increasing number of students are also pursuing other graduate studies.

Still others choose to continue being "men and women for others" by pursuing social service work full-time. Among the nation's Jesuit colleges and universities, Holy Cross consistently sends the highest number of graduates to serve in the Jesuit Volunteer Corps, a yearlong national service program. Many students also serve in organizations like the Peace Corps, Teach for America, AmeriCorps, VISTA, Jesuit Volunteers International, and Teaching Fellows.

PROMINENT GRADS

- Robert Cousy, '50, Hall of Fame Celtics basketball player and professional basketball coach
- J. D. "Dave" Power III, '53, Founder, J. D. Power and Associates
- Anthony Fauci, M.D., '62, Director, National Institute of Allergy and Infectious Diseases
- Billy Collins, '63, U.S. poet laureate, 2001–2003
- Chris Matthews, '67, Host, *Hardball* on MSNBC and *The Chris Matthews Show* on NBC
- Hon. Clarence Thomas, '71, U.S. Supreme Court justice
- Edward P. Jones, '72, 2004 Pulitzer Prize-winning author of *The Known World*
- Mary Agnes "Maggie" Wilderotter, '77, Chairperson and CEO, Frontier Communications
- Mary Berner, '81, President and CEO, Reader's Digest Association
- Carolyn Risoli, '86, President, Marc Jacobs
- Jon Favreau, '03, Chief speechwriter for President Obama

> * HC helped me to understand my own core values and beliefs, and allowed me to realize how I can apply those morals to both my career and my personal life.*

—Justin Rucci '09

Holy Cross graduates leave with more than an excellent education; they also leave with strong loyalties to the school and community. They "bleed purple" and it shows. They are very generous with alumni participation in fund-raising, constantly setting new records for donations. Additionally, they provide an extensive professional network and are more than willing to talk to current students and recent graduates to offer guidance and career advice.

SUMMING UP

Students who choose Holy Cross choose a superior intellectual, social, and spiritual experience. They choose an education that doesn't stop after they step out of the classroom, or even graduate from the college. They choose to be challenged and pushed by faculty and peers to achieve more. They choose to forge lifelong friendships with their peers. They choose to become men and women for others. And they choose to let this four-year experience last a lifetime. So why choose Holy Cross? Come and find out.

❏ *Ali Lincoln, B.A.*

COLLEGE OF WILLIAM AND MARY

 College of William and Mary
Williamsburg, VA 23187-8795

 (757) 221-4223
Fax: (757) 221-1242

 E-mail: *admission@wm.edu*
Websites: *http://www.wm.edu*

 Enrollment

Full-time ❑ women: 3,153
❑ men: 2,623

Part-time ❑ women: 45
❑ men: 29

INTRODUCING COLLEGE OF WILLIAM AND MARY

Visitors and tourists alike wander through William and Mary's campus on a daily basis. They amble around an old campus walking under a canopy of trees and on top of hundred-year-old bricks. Everyone stops to admire the Crim Dell, W&M's supremely photogenic lake in the middle of campus. Surely, anyone who visits Williamsburg and has a look at William and Mary's campus leaves knowing that it is a gorgeous and pleasant place; that it's the home of one of America's oldest and finest universities.

And these visitors are correct. W&M is the second oldest college in America, founded in 1693. It is known as the "Alma Mater of a Nation" as the Tribe credits four American presidents and sixteen members of the Continental Congress in the ranks of alumni. These visitors will also certainly notice that W&M is not stuck in the past. Anyone who walks around campus will hear tales of more than eighty Fulbright Scholars since the year 2000. A tourist might stroll past a club meeting, ranging from Belly Dancing to the Wizards and Muggles appreciation club. They'll even see evidence of the Tribe athletic teams truly defining the term "student athlete," winning championships and scholarships at the same time.

Yet, these visitors, like most people who come to look at William and Mary, are missing the best part of campus! Actually, it's hard to blame them, since the best part of William and Mary can't be experienced just by a casual stroll through the grounds. In fact, the best part about William and Mary isn't even visible at all. What defines the William and Mary experience, what will make your next four years outstanding beyond imagination, is the community spirit that reaches from every person to every corner of campus.

This family spirit lies in the interactions between students and professors. The relationships formed extend far beyond the classroom, reaching into real collaborative research and lasting friendships. W&M students aren't confined to doing menial research; they regularly publish professional articles side-by-side with their professors.

The W&M life-blood pulses and thrives in our residence halls, governed by a policy of self-determination. Self-determination allows your hall, the people you live with, to determine the rules that you will live by. I'm sure Thomas Jefferson, Class of 1762, is smiling at this adaptation of democracy to the policies governing your new home.

The community shows its strength in our students helping friends and strangers, on campus and off. One doesn't have to look far to find students volunteering and helping others; the majority of W&M students volunteer on a regular basis. But the students' volunteering interests aren't confined to typical pursuits; it reaches even to the incoming freshman each year. Hundreds of upperclassmen move down to Williamsburg a week early for the sole purpose of helping incoming freshmen carry their things into their rooms, and settle in their new homes!

Our community shows off its muscle in our athletic teams. Our varsity athletes truly define the phrase "student athlete." The Tribe is *the* Colonial Athletic Association (CAA) powerhouse among all sports, having won more than eighty conference championships. But this athletic prowess does not come at the expense of academic success, no not at all. The Tribe athletic teams can claim a 95 percent graduation rate, fourth best among all Division I schools in the country. "Student-Athlete" indeed.

But, what if a student isn't interested in participating in sports at a varsity level, just for recreation? No problem. The campus recreation center has just finished a renovation project that doubled its size. Recently, *Men's Health & Fitness Magazine* ranked W&M as the seventeenth fittest college in the country, highlighting our healthy options available at all dining halls. Our spirit certainly runs strong through many different kinds of athletic endeavors.

W&M's community spirit whips through campus like a winter wind. It moves, it morphs, it pervades. It runs from every dorm to classroom to concerts to coffeehouses. The spirit burns inside every member of the Tribe, bursting through in the form of smiles, laughs, and friendships formed. This community spirit shows in our acceptance and tolerance of others. There is no other university in the country like William and Mary. It is singularly unique in the combination of personal attention, extraordinary academic opportunities, research capability, and on-campus student community.

The community spirit, the fire inside William and Mary students' hearts, can be yours. But just touring the college, just visiting and admiring the pretty buildings, won't reveal to you the true extent of our community. This spirit, this fire, is best experienced from within, as a member of the Tribe.

ADMISSIONS REQUIREMENTS

Admission procedures at William and Mary take into account many different factors from your high school years. But simply put, William and Mary is looking for the best students in the world who are looking to challenge themselves and grow in all facets of their life. The classes you took and the grades you earned are important, but so are the characteristics that tell us more about the kind of person you will grow to be, like leadership, creativity, and character.

Many students ask, "What classes should I be taking?" William and Mary does not have a magic formula of the specific classes you need to be taking to gain admission. However, the typical admitted William and Mary students challenge themselves in every opportunity during their high school years. Most admitted students take the strongest and most rigorous course of study their high school offers. This usually includes four years of English, four years of math, four years of a foreign language, three to four years of history, four years of science, and other elective courses. Honors, Advanced Placement, and International Baccalaureate courses all entail rigorous study and are therefore recommended whenever possible. The Admissions Office recognizes that course offerings are not consistent between schools so exceptions to this rule of thumb always exist.

All applicants must take the SAT or ACT as part of a complete application. SAT subject tests are fully optional. All testing must be completed by January of the senior year so that scores will be reported to William and Mary in time. Students who enter William and Mary must also meet proficiency requirements in foreign language and writing by time of graduation. However, you can exempt yourself from these ordinarily required courses if you have already satisfied the requirements in high school! You can satisfy the foreign language requirement by successfully completing four years of one foreign language or a minimum score of 600 on the SAT Foreign Language subject test (650 on the Latin test). A student can gain exemption from the writing requirement by scoring well on the AP or IB English Exam.

But these aren't absolutely the most important parts of the application. William and Mary knows that you are more, so much more than just classes, grades, and test scores. You have a whole life outside of classes where you have done some amazing things. To William and Mary, the intangibles that make you *you* are just as important as grades and scores. The admissions committee certainly takes this into account when considering each student's admission. But the committee needs your help. In the application, you should present your activities, accomplishments, interests, and values. Try to really convey who you actually are and what you will add to William and Mary's community of scholars. A large opportunity for this is the essay section. The Common Application (of which William and Mary is an exclusive user) essay section is also a large opportunity to creatively and appropriately enlighten us about your intangibles.

For the simple fact that William and Mary is included in this book, you know that we are labeled "Most Competitive." Each undergraduate class is comprised of between 1,400 and 1,500 students, of which 65 percent are Virginians. In recent years, the Admissions Office has received over 12,000 applications for each class. While those numbers might be intimidating, don't be discouraged. The Admissions Office encourages everyone to apply!

If you have decided that William and Mary is the only place for you, that it is your absolute first choice, and that you want to become a new member of the Tribe more than anything else, then you might want to consider our Early Decision plan. Early Decision at William and Mary is binding, which means that if you are accepted, you agree to attend. The application deadline for Early Decision is November 1, and notifications will be sent one month later, on December 1.

Regular Decision applicants must postmark their applications by January 1 for freshman, March 1 for fall-term transfer applicants, and November 1 for spring-term transfer applicants.

A university's charge is not just to teach facts, formulas, and procedures. The true mark of a university is how well it can help to mold and meld the nubile minds of freshmen into cogent, prepared, and mature adults ready to start the path towards leading the future. Many universities accomplish this, but to varying degrees. William and Mary meets this charge to the highest degree.

Here, in our school's academic setting, you will, without a doubt, be challenged on a daily basis. However, do not confuse the word "challenged" with "unbelievably difficult." Believe me, if you are admitted, we know you can do the work that lies ahead of you. But at William and Mary, challenging means more than this. It means you will have extremely dedicated faculty members seeking to draw out your best. It means you will have peers who are just as excited as you are about classes and studies. It means you will have the opportunity to, and many times be expected to, develop original and innovative research that is graduate level at many other schools. In short, the academics at William and Mary will challenge every inch of what you can do.

Faculty

William and Mary encourages students to develop a very well-rounded educational base. It requires that students take classes in all of the different types of disciplines, but leaves the students a lot of flexibility when it comes to choosing which specific courses to take. For example, the requirements don't say students must take one course in the English department; one of the requirements is for students to take one course in literature and history of the arts, of which many English department courses qualify.

> ❝My freshman seminar was in the music department and was called "Sound and Image." The course explored the relation between the two, specifically sound and music used in movies. We watched plenty of films for the course and spent time training our brains to listen to movies rather than watch movies. It was a fascinating process, and I can credit that course with advancing my writing and critical thinking skills more than any other course I took at W&M. ❞

Because of William and Mary's smaller size, most classes are small enough for students to interact regularly with the professor and with fellow classmates. The student-to-faculty ratio is eleven-to-one, the lowest of any public school in the country! Here are some more stats to further set your mind at ease: Introductory courses are taught by professors, not graduate students, and your professors are really committed to teaching you, not just to completing their research. These are all things that might not be true at larger universities. See, you really won't be just a number at William and Mary!

Special mention must go to our professors. The dedication of the William and Mary faculty to teaching was recently ranked third in the country, and first among public schools in a national poll. For W&M professors, research and publication are important, but teaching always comes first. William and Mary undergraduates do the kind of research and work with their professors that is rarely seen at other universities until work begins for the Ph.D.

Another special facet of the William and Mary education is the freshman seminar, guaranteed and required for all first-year students. The classes, taught by full-time professors, are all topical in nature and work to greatly advance students' writing and critical thinking skills while also providing an in-depth examination of the subject. One of the best facets of these seminars is that the maximum number of students allowed in them is fifteen. Past years have seen seminars like "Reading the Romance Novels," "Emerging Disease," and "The Six Wives of Henry VIII." Many graduates have fond memories of their freshman seminar, and many credit it with introducing them to their major, research interest, or faculty advisor.

Majors

William and Mary offers about forty undergraduate majors, as well as an opportunity for students to create their own major combining various disciplines. There are also many opportunities to explore personal interests in one's major through independent study, senior honors projects, and even collaboration on scholarly publishing with professors. Recently, the most popular majors have been in the School of Business Administration, psychology, government, English, neuroscience, and biology.

Also, in William and Mary's academic system, students are encouraged to explore all facets of our academic offerings. This also makes it very easy for students to double major or have a minor and still graduate in four years. Double majoring is very popular at W&M and allows many students to gain a more specific skill-set that might take a graduate degree at other colleges.

SOCIAL LIFE AND ACTIVITIES

Obviously, the focus of transforming and molding young minds into educated adults is not contained within the classroom walls. A large part of learning in college comes outside of the classroom. What you do outside of those fifteen to twenty hours a week you spend in class really matters and can truly have an impact on the kind of person you develop into. Simply put, ordering pizza, watching movies, and playing video games is not the best way to spend all of your extracurricular time as an undergraduate. Thankfully, William and Mary recognizes this and has more than you could possibly ask for to make your life at college more fun than you can even imagine.

One of the most popular ways to enrich your life outside of classes is by getting involved with any of our more than 400 student organizations, all of which are organized and run solely by students. William and Mary has a wide and varied selection of groups to capture the interests of most students. Walking across campus, you might run into the Club running team out for a run, an a capella team staging an impromptu concert, the geology club digging up some treasures, or even the Wizards and Muggles fan club staging a mock-quidditch game! W&M also has several service-oriented clubs, cultural groups, social fraternities and sororities, literary magazines and newspapers, yearbook, student government, and many performing groups. The point is William and Mary has a club for every kind of interest you could have. If by some chance we don't, then you have the opportunity to create the club with some friends.

> *In your freshman year you'll have a roommate that is usually matched up with you by the Office of Residence Life. It's a scary thought to live with somebody you haven't met yet, but they have a great track record and do an amazing job of matching up roommates.*

Something else that must be mentioned: William and Mary is not a commuter school; that is to say, on the weekend, our students do not vacate the grounds to go back home. People live here, stay here, and have their friends here on campus. The residence hall is the basic organizing unit of W&M dormitories, and coincidentally, it is where most students meet their best friends. Many students spend the weekend hanging out and relaxing with their friends all over campus and off campus too.

Without doubt, one of the most exciting days of the whole school year at William and Mary is freshman move-in day. All 1,350 or so freshmen, in the peak of Virginia's summer heat, move into their campus dorms at the same time; sounds stressful and hectic right? To make the process easier for you and your family, hundreds of William and Mary upperclassmen move back down to campus early just to come and help incoming freshmen move in.

The largest source of weekend events is the campus events programming group, AMP. They are responsible for bringing hundreds of events to the campus with something going on every weekend and most weeknights. Every year, AMP brings comedians, hypnotists, prominent speakers, entertainers, new movies, debates, and lots of concerts to campus. Recent years have seen bands like Wilco and The Roots, comedians like Jon Stewart and Tracy Morgan, and speakers like Former UN Secretary General Kofi Annan and Archbishop Desmond Tutu come to Williamsburg!

William and Mary performing arts also doesn't disappoint when it comes to social life fun. The theatre department puts on several high-quality productions each year, including many that are student-directed. The campus also has a wildly popular improvisational theatre group (think *Whose Line Is It Anyway?*) that perform all over campus, much to the delight of students, faculty, and staff. William and Mary is also fortunate enough to have so many student-run a capella student groups that you might think there is a concert going on every night of the week!

For students interested in Greek organizations, William and Mary does not disappoint. About thirty percent of the William and Mary student body is in one of fifteen social fraternities or twelve social sororities. Think you know all there is to know about Greek organizations after watching some Hollywood movies? Think again! William and Mary Greek organizations not only serve a social purpose but also commit large amounts of time to philanthropic endeavors. Every Greek organization puts on philanthropy events all through the year. These events are hugely popular and regularly raise thousands of dollars for the organizations' charities.

Athletics at William and Mary are also a big draw for students. Students at W&M say they all have Tribe Pride running through their veins and bleed William and Mary's colors, green and gold! At the varsity level, the Tribe is, statistically and historically, the best overall team among all sports in our conference, the Colonial Athletic Association. In the past years, you might have seen many of our teams streaking up the Division I Top 25 in men's and women's cross country, men's gymnastics, women's field hockey, men's and women's soccer, and women's tennis. Not interested in varsity sports? No problem. There are opportunities for you to compete against other colleges in our club sport program, or just relax and have some fun with intramurals. Overall, eighty percent of W&M undergrads participate in intercollegiate sports, club sports, and/or intramural programs. Also, *Men's Health* recently named William and Mary students some of the fittest in the country.

For off-campus entertainment, there is more than you might think. True, Williamsburg is no New York City. But there is much more to the town than just touristy Colonial Williamsburg. Some of the more popular and student-friendly places in town are the delis.

These three bars/restaurants are right off campus and, according to the students, have the best sandwiches and cheese fries for miles around! They are great places to hang out with friends and watch a game, listen to live music, or just talk and unwind from the school week. Williamsburg also has numerous coffee shops, movie theatres, and restaurants, all right off campus. And how many colleges can claim to have Busch Gardens right in their backyard! You want a night out in the big city? No problem: Norfolk, Virginia Beach, and Richmond are all less than an hour's drive away.

Finally, one of the biggest extracurricular pursuits for W&M students is community service. More than 70 percent of William and Mary students participate in public service activities during their time on campus, contributing over hundreds of thousands of volunteer hours every year. W&M students' character really shows through when you see that our largest fraternity on campus is actually a coed service fraternity that is dedicated to service projects on campus and off.

FINANCIAL AID

One of the things that makes a William and Mary education so special is not only the benefits outlined above, but also its comparatively low price tag in relation to schools of the same caliber. As an example, *Kiplinger* recently ranked William and Mary fourth on the 50 Best Values in Public Colleges!

Nonetheless, the cost of a college education today is a difficult burden to bear for many families. Many students rely on financial aid for assistance in their quest for higher education.

At William and Mary, financial assistance can come in different forms, but most aid is distributed in the form of grants, loans, and work-study opportunity packages. William and Mary uses the Free Application for Federal Student Aid (FAFSA) to determine each student's unique need. Each student's financial need is not just based on family income. It also takes into account family size, number in college, assets, and many other variables. FAFSA forms for all applicants are due March 1.

An additional financial aid package includes the Gateway William and Mary initiative. Gateway William and Mary is a financial aid packaging tool serving students from the Commonwealth of Virginia who come from low-and middle-class families with a less than $40,000 annual income. Undergraduate students within the Gateway program are eligible for financial aid that uses grant monies to meet 100% of their demonstrated financial need—so they are able to graduate from college with little to no debt! This shows that William and Mary is committed to giving every admitted student, regardless of their socioeconomic background, the opportunity to achieve an education from one of the top rated institutions in the country. In some cases, families that come from exceptionally low income households may not have to contribute any money to cover the cost of attending William and Mary. The FAFSA form would determine if the family is eligible for this type of financial aid packaging.

William and Mary has three main merit scholarships. The William and Mary Scholars Award is available to approximately forty students who will greatly enhance the diversity of the student body. Awards are equal to the value of Virginia tuition and fees for four years. The second main award is the Monroe Scholars program. Approximately five percent of the entering freshman class is designated as a Monroe Scholar. Beyond academic benefits, recipients are provided a $3,000 research grant to pursue a specific academic interest. Both of these programs require no separate application.

The third main award is the Murray Scholars Program. Endowed by a multimillion dollar alumni gift, the Murray Scholars Program will provide four students per year with extensive benefits, including in-state tuition, fees, room and board annually, two separate $2,500 research grants towards their academic research interests, and the kind of academic attention reserved at most universities exclusively for graduate students. Finalists for the Murray Scholars Program are selected from the application review process and would be asked to come to campus for scholarship competition.

Federally funded grants such as the Pell Grant and the Supplemental Educational Opportunity Grant are available at William and Mary, as are federally sponsored loans such as the Perkins Loan and the Stafford Loan. The State Council of Higher Education for Virginia (SCHEV) awards the Virginia Transfer Grant for minority transfer students. Some academic departments give scholarships to students who demonstrate outstanding scholarship in that field. There are several other unique opportunities for assistance such as $1,500 scholarships offered by the Order of the White Jacket for students who are working in food service to help put themselves through school.

GRADUATES

It is quite understandable that your immediate focus is on getting in to William and Mary, and not particularly on what you will do after you graduate. However, the opportunities available to you post-W&M, and how we help prepare you for that time, is an important facet to consider in any school. William and Mary, in fact, does not disappoint in this respect.

To be competitive after graduation these days, more is required than just a diploma and good grades. Nobody will hand you a job just for that. Sorry. You must develop and demonstrate skills that do not come easily: leadership as well as humility, self-reliance and also the ability to work in a team, self-awareness while also being internationally knowledgeable. William and Mary is the place where you can learn and develop these skills. Memorizing some formulas won't cut it, in the real world or at William and Mary. Here, students are given the well-rounded background they need to live life to the fullest once they graduate.

- Carter Braxton, Signer of the Declaration of Independence
- Glenn Close, Actress
- Benjamin Harrison, Signer of the Declaration of Independence
- Thomas Jefferson, Third President of the United States
- Linda Lavin, Actress
- James Monroe, Fifth President of the United States
- Darren Sharper, NFL Football Player for the Minnesota Vikings
- Jon Stewart, Comedian, host of *The Daily Show with Jon Stewart*
- John Tyler, Tenth President of the United States
- George Wythe, Signer of the Declaration of Independence
- John Marshall, Supreme Court Justice
- Robert Gates, Former Director of CIA, Current U.S. Secretary of Defense
- Perry Ellis, Fashion Designer
- Mark McCormack, Founder of IMG, World's Largest Sports Marketing Agency

As for what our graduates do after graduation, William and Mary students are known for their passion in learning and education. Towards this end, between one third choose to go directly to graduate school. Acceptance rates for graduate schools (including medical schools and law schools) are fifteen to twenty percent, above the national averages. Students with a B or B+ average have a seventy-five to eighty-five percent acceptance rate for medical school, far above the national average.

Interested in a job after graduation? The college will give you more help than you can imagine in finding one. The Career Center brings approximately 750 employers to recruit on campus each year. They also host over a hundred sessions each year to help students with resume and cover letter writing as well as job searching. Not ready for graduation you say? They also coordinate internships on campus and will help you prepare for and land that connection-making summer internship you can only now dream about. Also, many of the companies who recruit at William and Mary have a large body of W&M grads already employed. They know the caliber of our students and come looking for more!

SUMMING UP

A former President of William and Mary loved to end all of his speeches, e-mails, and official communication with the phrase "Hark Upon the Gale." The phrase comes from the refrain of William and Mary's Alma Mater:

William and Mary loved of old, Hark Upon the Gale!
Hear the thunder of our chorus, Alma Mater Hail!

The word *hark* can be interpreted two ways, as "to listen" and "to think back on something." The word *gale* is usually defined as a "very strong wind" but can also mean "a noisy outburst." So one can interpret this in two ways, both seem quite appropriate to the college. Hark Upon the Gale! Listen to the strong wind! Remember our actions! Put in more direct terms: Feel our impact!

William and Mary is a university that has a very strong impact: an impact on the nation and local community, the alumnae, the current students, and you, the future students.

❏ *Matt Scranton, B.A.*

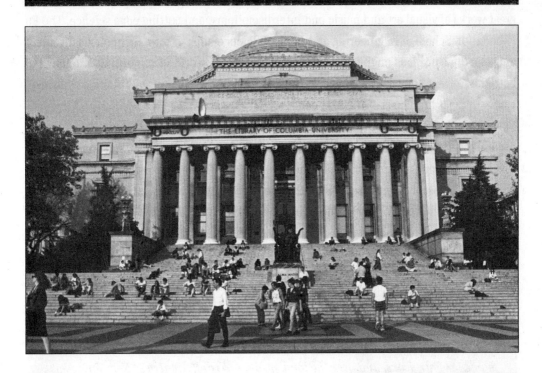

 Columbia University
New York, NY 10027

 (212) 854-2522

E-mail: *ugrad-ask@columbia.edu*
Website:
http://www.studentaffairs.columbia.edu/admissions/

 Enrollment

Full-time ❑ women: 2,647
❑ men: 3,020

INTRODUCING COLUMBIA UNIVERSITY

Founded in 1754, Columbia University has grown from a small liberal arts college, Kings College, to a large and dynamic research university in one of the world's most vibrant and exciting cities. Alma mater to Alexander Hamilton, Lou Gehrig, Tony Kushner, Maggie Gyllenhaal, and Barack Obama, Columbians also invented FM radio and designed the New

York City subway system. Columbia College, a small liberal arts college, has a unifying, discussion-based Core Curriculum with a focus on classic texts in literature and philosophy, great works of visual art and music and interdisciplinary, and cutting-edge science. The Fu Foundation School of Engineering and Applied Science aims to train technologically adept and socially conscious engineers, able to design for the world of tomorrow. Graduates of both the College and the Engineering school graduate with the critical thinking skills necessary to meet the needs of the 21st century.

The diversity of the undergraduate student body plays a crucial role in the Columbia experience. Over half of undergraduates self-identify as students of color and approximately seventeen percent are international students. With all fifty states represented, as well as ninety countries, the conversations in the dining hall and the residence halls are always diverse and exciting. Whether it's debating how Machiavelli's *The Prince* relates to current events or the most efficient way to design a water filtration system, Columbia students are never afraid to express an opinion, and always willing to listen to those around them.

> 66 *One of my favorite Columbia memories is at the end of graduation. Clad in my Columbia blue cap and gown, I took a last look around at the place I called home for four years, and over the loud speakers Frank Sinatra's "New York, New York" was playing. I thought about the nervous excitement during orientation, when two floor mates and I decided to take the bus to the Met and buy posters for our rooms. I thought of the countless papers I had written about politics, history and philosophy, the friends I had made from all over the world, the Congressional campaign internship, the all-night bike tour of New York City where I watched the sunrise on the Promenade in Brooklyn Heights. Sinatra sang "If you can make it here, you'll make it anywhere..." and as I prepared for my next adventure teaching English in Japan, I was confident that no matter what came next, I would make it.* 99

Walking through the wrought-iron campus gates, the contrast between the bustling city outside and the wide open green lawns and intimate community inside is striking. With guaranteed housing for all four years, Columbians take advantage of the 500 campus organizations ranging from Amnesty International to WKCR, Columbia's radio station, to the

Black Students Organization to a dozen a cappella groups. On a Friday afternoon you might find yourself tutoring local middle school students, and then taking in a Division I basketball game with some of your floor mates that night. The world comes to Columbia—world leaders, artists, musicians, inventors, scientists—all at events open to students. In recent years speakers have included Microsoft founder Bill Gates, musician Wynton Marsalis, Hillary Clinton, former Czech Republic President Vaclav Havel, and the Dalai Lama. Add to this film screenings, concerts and intramural sports, and sometimes the biggest challenge is deciding what *not* to do.

Campus life is only the beginning. Columbia is located in Morningside Heights, a college town nestled on the upper west side of Manhattan. The majority of the Columbia faculty lives right in the neighborhood and students often bump into their professors at the Hungarian Pastry Shop, at West Side Market, or Book Culture. Morningside Heights also houses such other icons of higher learning as Bank Street College of Education, Union Theological Seminary, and the Manhattan School of Music. Indeed, strolling along Amsterdam Avenue you might just bump into a future teacher, rabbi, musician, or even a future president. Home to numerous ethnic restaurants, bars and bookstores, on a given night students can take in a jazz show or a poetry reading, and then have a Broadway shake and cheese fries at Tom's, of *Seinfeld* fame.

As much as can be found within blocks of campus, a Metrocard will get you, within minutes, to the center of the most cosmopolitan and dynamic city on the globe. There, you might secure an internship with any number of leading publishing houses, law firms, museums, financial institutions, or theaters. But the allure of New York City extends well beyond its professional offerings. With free entrance to dozens of museums, discounted tickets to off-Broadway and Broadway plays, operas and concerts, New York is a mecca of art and culture that serves as the perfect backdrop to a Columbia education. Add to that the Knicks, Astroland, Bronx Zoo, Central Park's Great Lawn, the Mets, the Hayden Planetarium, Chelsea Piers, and Katz's Deli, just for starters, and there can be little doubt that New York is truly an embarrassment of riches.

ADMISSIONS REQUIREMENTS

There is no one student profile that embodies the successful applicant to Columbia College or The Fu Foundation School of Engineering and Applied Science (SEAS). The admissions committee seeks representation in each class from all walks of life and experience. Each year Columbians are drawn from myriad different geographic, social, economic, and ethnic backgrounds that are reflected in the unique voices and perspectives they exhibit in and out of the classroom. Apart from good grades in a rigorous high school curriculum, admissions officers seek candidates who have made an impact on those around them, whether through performing community service, performing in the orchestra, or performing on the sports field. Special attention is paid to the applicant's level of intellectual engagement; the application requires students to indicate the books they have read for pleasure, the print and electronic publications they read regularly, and the films, concerts, performances, or exhibits they have attended.

The admissions process is highly competitive. Together, the two schools received more than 26,000 applications last year, for a first-year class of 1,380. For all applicants, intellectual curiosity and a passion for learning are a must. Beyond this, the admissions committee reviews each application holistically, weighing and accounting for each of the qualities demonstrated in each student's application. Engineering candidates must demonstrate a deep and sincere interest in the field. Regular Decision applications are due by January 1 of the senior year, and students are notified in early April.

Recommendations for Admission

The admissions committee does not require a specific minimum ACT or SAT score or GPA. It is recommended, however, that students' high school curricula include

- four years of English, with an emphasis on writing
- three years or more of a foreign language
- three, but preferably four, years of a social science
- three or more years of math
- three years or more of a lab science such as chemistry (students interested in engineering, science, or medicine should take as much math and science—particularly calculus, chemistry, and physics—as is offered in their high school curricula)

In addition to this coursework, applicants are required to sit for either the SAT or ACT and two SAT subject tests. Also expected are letters of recommendation from a guidance counselor or college advisor, as well as two from teachers of academic subjects, and a personal essay. Columbia utilizes The Common Application and requires a supplement, which gives students ample opportunity to share their unique achievements, interests, and goals. Interviews are available with Columbia alumni across the globe, and candidates are contacted by an alumni representative committee member after the first part of the application is received.

Early Decision

Students for whom Columbia is their first choice may apply Early Decision, submitting their application by November 1 of the senior year. Applicants who apply early are notified of a decision by mid-December, and, if admitted, are obliged to accept the offer and withdraw their applications from other schools.

ACADEMIC LIFE

> **"** At Columbia I could engage with the most important ideas of our time with professors and peers who had the same enthusiasm for thought and problem solving. Through the Core Curriculum I learned to expand myself beyond subjects; take intellectual risks, and think about issues from different perspectives. Columbia is a place that values questions as much as answers; it is thought becomes practice in any number of student-initiated ventures. It is a total academic experience. **"**

—Keith Hernandez, '07

Columbia College students begin their college career learning and interacting in intimate discussion-based seminars typically taken during their first two years. These courses, in literature, philosophy, music, and art, part of the Core Curriculum, create a space for lively debate and exchange of ideas. Beginning in 1919 as a course on War and Peace, the Core has evolved into a curriculum that unites the entire undergraduate population, not just with each other, but with alumni from across the years. In one seminar, Literature Humanities, students are transported into the writings of Plato and Homer, Shakespeare and Sophocles. There is something spectacular about debating the ideas of Madison, Burke, Hobbes, and Marx with classmates from across the globe, each with their own spin on these works and how they relate to the modern world.

The City

For Art and Music Humanities students, New York City serves as an extension of the classroom. With world-class museums such as the Metropolitan Museum of Art and MOMA, as well as countless smaller galleries, students study visual art close up, discerning

- African Studies
- African-American Studies
- American Studies
- Ancient Studies
- Anthropology
- Applied Mathematics
- Archaeology
- Architecture
- Art History
- Art History and Visual Arts
- Astronomy
- Astrophysics
- Biochemistry
- Biology
- Biophysics
- Chemical Physics
- Chemistry
- Classics
- Classical Studies
- Comparative Literature and Society
- Computer Science
- Computer Science—Mathematics
- Creative Writing
- Dance
- Drama and Theatre Arts
- Earth Science
- East Asian Studies
- Economics
- Economics—Mathematics
- Economics—Operations Research
- Economics—Philosophy
- Economics—Political Science
- Economics—Statistics
- Education
- English
- Environmental Biology
- Environmental Chemistry
- Environmental Science
- Ethnicity and Race Studies
- Evolutionary Biology of the Human Species
- Film Studies
- Financial Economics
- French
- French and Francophone Studies
- German Literature and Cultural History
- Hispanic Studies
- History
- History and Theory of Architecture
- Human Rights
- Information Sciences
- Italian Cultural Studies
- Italian Literature
- Jazz Studies
- Latin American and Caribbean Studies
- Linguistics
- Mathematics
- Mathematics—Statistics
- Medieval and Renaissance Studies
- Middle East and Asian Languages and Cultures
- Modern Greek Studies
- Music
- Neuroscience and Behavior
- Philosophy
- Physics
- Political Science
- Political Science—Statistics
- Portuguese
- Psychology
- Regional Studies—East/Central Europe
- Religion
- Russian Language and Culture
- Russian Literature and Culture
- Slavic Literature and Culture
- Slavic Studies
- Sociology
- Statistics
- Sustainable Development
- Urban Studies
- Visual Arts
- Women's and Gender Studies
- Yiddish Studies

brushstrokes from double exposures. Likewise, music students enjoy an embarrassment of riches at their disposal: opera at Lincoln Center, classical and avant garde concerts at Carnegie Hall, jazz and more contemporary offerings at New York City's smaller music halls and clubs.

Engineering

For Columbia engineering students, the curriculum is similarly structured to provide students with a foundation from which to build and grow. In addition to enrollment in half of the liberal arts Core, engineering students begin their coursework with a solid foundation in calculus, physics, chemistry, and economics.

A cornerstone of the Columbia engineering curriculum is a core service-learning design class, *Design Fundamentals Using Advanced Computer Technologies*. The only one of its kind required nationally, the course is designed to give first-year SEAS students an authentic window into the life of an engineering professional. In small groups, students work to solve a real-life problem of a company or organization, using the state-of-the-art Botwinick Multimedia Learning Laboratory. Past projects include the design of accessible playground equipment for children with disabilities and the development of a mixed-use bus stop that monitors environmental conditions for risks to asthmatics. Students also often partner with global organizations, working on projects in Haiti, Guatemala, and South Africa. At the end of the project, students present their product to their client. The experience is designed to cultivate in engineers an awareness of the impact of their designs on the world around them.

COLUMBIA ENGINEERING DEPARTMENTS AND MAJORS

- Applied Physics and Applied Mathematics
- Biomedical Engineering
- Chemical Engineering
- Civil Engineering and Engineering Mechanics
- Computer Engineering Program
- Computer Science
- Earth and Environmental Engineering
- Electrical Engineering
- Industrial Engineering and Operations Research
- Material Science and Engineering Program
- Mechanical Engineering

Major

Following exposure to a number of academic disciplines and departments, Columbia students declare a major during their sophomore year. At this point students examine a specific area or areas of academic study more fully. The result of the Columbian's at once broad

○ Columbia faculty supervises more than $1 billion in sponsored research

○ Nine current faculty are Nobel Laureates, part of a cumulative total of eighty Nobel Prize winners in the Columbia family, past and present (including faculty and alumni)

○ 143 are members of the American Academy of Arts and Sciences

○ Thirty-eight are members of the Institute of Medicine of the National Academies

○ Twenty of the National Academy of Engineering

○ Forty-three of the National Academy of Sciences

○ Four have won the National Medal of Science

○ Thirty have won a MacArthur Foundation Award, popularly known as the "genius grant."

and narrow education is a "jack of all trades, and a master of one." Columbia College students choose from almost 100 wide-ranging majors, with new programs, like the recently added Sustainable Development, being developed every year.

Faculty

Columbia boasts a world-class faculty, committed to undergraduate education. Whether they are innovative scientists, critically acclaimed artists, or widely respected public intellectuals, faculty members are accessible and very involved in the life of Columbia undergraduates. As a result of Columbia's intimate classes (almost eighty percent of classes have twenty students or less and the student-to-faculty ratio is six-to-one), students develop relationships with their teachers that then extend outside the classroom, and continue past graduation. Whether during an all-night bike tour of New York City, during an aerobics class, or at a review session over pizza at the apartment of their engineering professor, students and faculty have the opportunity to relate as neighbors and friends, as well as teachers and students.

66 Columbia offers a number of joint programs, including a 3-2 Combined Plan, in which students complete three years at a liberal arts institution, two years at SEAS, and graduate with both a BA and BS in five years. There is a five-year program offered with the School of International and Public Affairs, allowing students to complete both an undergraduate and MIA and MPA. Finally, Columbia offers a joint program with Juilliard, allowing exceptionally talented Columbia College student access to instrumental and voice instruction through both an Exchange and Joint Degree program. 99

A GLOBAL COMMUNITY

Located at the crossroads of the world, Columbia attracts an incredibly diverse student body, eager to learn from each other and the city around them. With all fifty states represented, and more than one hundred and fifty countries represented among faculty and students, nearly every interaction in and out of the classroom provides an opportunity for cross-cultural dialogue. The Office of Multicultural Affairs, which advises nearly 50 cultural and identity-based student organizations, provides a space for students to both embrace their own unique cultural heritage and explore others. Additionally, Earl Hall is the home for the nearly forty religious and spiritual organizations, and the Office of the University Chaplain works to promote intercultural and interfaith dialogue and programs on matters of justice, faith, and spirituality.

COLUMBIA AROUND THE WORLD

Columbia offers hundreds of study abroad options, including the Columbia-sponsored programs below:
- Columbia University in Beijing at Tsinghua University
- Berlin Consortium for German Studies (BCGS)
- Kyoto Consortium for Japanese Studies (KCJS)
- Columbia-Penn Program in Paris at Reid Hall
- Summer Business Chinese and Internship Program in Shanghai
- Italian Cultural Studies in Venice

This exploration also happens in the classroom, often facilitated through interdisciplinary studies promoted by the Center for the Study of Ethnicity and Race. Finally, Columbia students have a long-standing commitment to service and activism, in an effort to constantly improve both the school and the surrounding community. Whether through Community Impact (consisting of nearly 1,000 Columbia student volunteers) or one of the many activist or service groups, Columbia students leave their mark.

> **❝** *One of my fondest memories of Columbia was the first time I walked out of a World Leaders Forum event in Low Library and looked toward South Field. On the steps of Low Library, a new friend and I saw a group of students having sandwiches over a conversation about Aristotle, another group taking turns playing a guitar, one student typing a paper on her laptop, and another student reciting lines of poetry from a play. Just beyond the field stood all of the first-year residence halls, and behind us was the president of Pakistan gathering his belongings. It was right then that I realized how incredibly special Columbia is: the world was literally set at our doorstep, and there was no way we could turn it down since we knew that Columbia believed in us.* **❞**

—Brian Smith, '09

Residence Life

With guaranteed housing for all four years, nearly all Columbia undergraduates live on-campus. First-year students all live in one of five dorms that form a U around Columbia's South Field, ensuring ample opportunities for pick-up Frisbee, impromptu study sessions, or debates over dinner in John Jay Dining Hall. The housing options are incredibly diverse, including single rooms, even for first-year students, apartment-style suites, and a Living and Learning Center where residents live together around a common theme, academic or otherwise. Residence Life staff, deans, faculty members, and other students work together to provide a stimulating yet comfortable home, housing programs on topics as varied as career development and current events. Finally, with a myriad of dining options right on campus, students grab a latte and bagel right before class, some sushi before their volleyball practice, and then a late-night snack of cheese fries at JJ's Place.

Organizations and Clubs

One of the biggest challenges at Columbia is choosing which student organization or club to join—with nearly 500 student organizations to choose from there is truly something for everyone. From *a cappella* to anime, debate and dance, Columbians are among the most active and engaged college students in the country. There are groups that represent every political orientation, religion, and ethnic background, as well as career and academic interest.

> **❝** *SEAS offers students the opportunity to become involved in any number of the 500 activities on campus. I knew engineers who were involved in everything from the Columbia Daily Spectator newspaper to the King's Crown Shakespeare Troupe to the Society of Automotive Engineers. Columbia Engineering gave me the opportunity to access the resources of a large research university without sacrificing the small school feel of SEAS.* **❞**

—*Elizabeth Strauss, '08*

Athletics

Whether you are an avid sports fan, recreational martial artist, or a serious varsity athlete, Columbia has something for you. With a number of Olympians and Olympic medalists, past and present, there are also more than eighty club and intramural sports in addition to the thirty varsity sports.

As an original member of the Ivy League, Columbia competes in NCAA Division I sports. Men's varsity teams compete in baseball, basketball, cross-country, fencing, football, golf, rowing (heavyweight and lightweight), soccer, squash, swimming and diving, tennis, wrestling, and track and field, as do women's varsity teams in archery, basketball, cross-country, fencing, golf, field hockey, lacrosse, rowing, soccer, softball, squash, swimming and diving, tennis, volleyball, and track and field.

Columbia students cheer on their Lions at Baker Field, Manhattan's only football field, or at the pool or on the basketball court. It is not unusual to see the cross-country teams running through Central and Riverside Parks in Columbia blue.

New York City

Being a college student in the Big Apple presents infinite possibilities. While there are some weeks when Columbia students stay busy on campus and Morningside Heights, eventually the rest of New York City beckons. In addition to being an extension of the classroom, the city is the center of commerce, culture, and art, providing professional and social opportunities for all.

Columbia students take advantage of internships in a wide variety of industries, often found with the help of the Center for Career Education. With few classes held on Fridays, students can be found in the city's law firms, art galleries, laboratories, non-governmental organizations, and publishing houses, gaining real-world experience and begin networking and building relationships while still in college. Whether interning at MSNBC, for the Mayor of the City of New York, or working at a cell and tissue engineering lab, these experiences help students to better understand their career options and give them a leg up when looking for employment after graduation.

New York City is more than a place to work, of course. Even on a student budget, there are lots of ways to take advantage of the city's many diversions. The city's numerous ethnic neighborhoods are home to cheap eats, and the Columbia University Arts Initiative (CU Arts) regularly provides free and reduced price tickets to cultural events all over the city. Opera, jazz, theater, art galleries—every weekend there is somewhere new to explore, all a subway ride away.

> 66 *Sophomore year, I spent almost every Thursday afternoon at the Museum of Modern Art. With your Columbia ID you get free admission to the museum so I decided to take advantage of it. I would bring a book I was reading for my Contemporary Civilization class and sit in front of a brilliant piece of art for hours and hours. It was a dream that could only be realized in NYC and as a Columbian.* 99

—*Tiffany Sanchez, '10*

FINANCIAL AID

For many families, one of the first questions when considering a school like Columbia is "Can we afford it?" Fortunately, Columbia has long been committed to making sure that all admitted students, regardless of their family's economic situation, can attain a Columbia education. Columbia meets the full demonstrated financial need of every admitted student through need-based grants and work-study. Nearly half of all undergraduates receive some form of need-based aid and Columbia has the highest percentage of Pell Grant recipients of any Ivy League university.

With a need-blind admissions policy, the Office of Admissions does not consider a student's ability to pay for tuition and fees when reviewing his or her application. This policy applies to U.S. citizens and permanent residents, citizens of Canada and Mexico, and persons granted refugee visas by the United States. Although a large number of foreign students apply and receive substantial financial aid, financial need is taken into consideration at the time of admission for international students.

> **"** *Everything about Columbia excited me as a high school student: the Core Curriculum and the small class sizes, the internship and cultural opportunities of New York City, as well as the vibrant campus life. As the daughter of a teacher and a nurse, I was concerned about whether I would be able to afford a school like Columbia. Despite some concerns by my parents, I applied for Columbia Early Decision, and was pleasantly surprised when I received a financial aid package we could work with. Yes, I worked over summers and had a work-study job during the school year. But Columbia made my dream possible, and for that I will always be grateful.* **"**

—*Adina Berrios Brooks, '98*

Recently Columbia has made some significant enhancements to its financial aid policy. These include

- The elimination of loans for all financial aid recipients, regardless of their family income.
- Families with calculated incomes below $60,000 and typical assets no longer are expected to make a parental contribution, and those with incomes between $60,000 and $100,000 and typical assets have significantly reduced parental contributions.
- To support students pursuing study abroad, research, internships, and community service opportunities, Columbia offers the opportunity to apply for additional funding and exemptions from academic year and summer work expectations.

These initiatives continue Columbia's longstanding efforts to create a diverse community, with students from every socioeconomic, racial, and ethnic background, all fifty states, and from all over the world.

GRADUATES

Columbia's Office of Career Education (CCE) works with students and alumni to develop the skills required to better understand the career development process. Whether students are wondering how to get started; looking for an internship; thinking about graduate school; seeking advice on interviews or resumes; looking for a part-time or full-time job; or in their first or senior year, Career Counselors are available to meet with students individually to discuss their career issues. Additionally, CCE works with more than seven-hundred organizations to recruit talented individuals interested in careers in a wide range of industries and professions.

PROMINENT GRADS

- Edwin Armstrong, Inventor of FM radio
- Art Garfunkel, Musician
- Lou Gehrig, New York Yankees
- Allen Ginsberg, Poet
- Alexander Hamilton, First U.S. Secretary of the Treasury
- Oscar Hammerstein, Composer
- Langston Hughes, Author
- John Jay, First Chief Justice of the Supreme Court
- John Kluge, Entrepreneur, Philanthropist
- Alfred Knopf, Publisher
- Tony Kushner, Playwright
- Michael Massimino, NASA Astronaut
- Barack Obama, President of the United States
- Richard Rodgers, Composer

Columbia alums give back to their school in ways big and small. Columbia College alumnus John Kluge gave a $400 million gift in 2007 to the university to be used toward expanding financial aid. Alumni like actor Matthew Fox, CC '89, and Attorney General Eric Holder, CC '73, returned to give the Class Day keynote address. Others return to campus to mentor current students or participate in panel discussions or informal events that relate to their professional work. Columbia's Young Alumni works to bring alums from the prior ten years together, through social and professional events on-campus and around the world.

SUMMING UP

Through a combination of rich academic offerings, New York City's infinite career and cultural offerings, and a vibrant campus life, Columbia students have access to, literally, the world. These opportunities compel students to find balance—to do cancer research in the lab in the morning, throw a Frisbee on the lawn in the afternoon, and then check out the latest off-Broadway play in the evening. This exercise serves Columbia graduates well as they head out into the world.

For Columbia College students, the Core Curriculum provides a foundation for becoming a critical thinker and global citizen. By delving into some of the world's most significant works of literature, philosophy, art, and music, students graduate with the deep sense of what has come before. This Core experience is then matched by the more than ninety majors taught by Columbia's world-class faculty. Of course, whether a student studies the humanities, arts, social, physical, or life sciences, New York provides an ideal extension of the classroom.

Our engineers have exposure to that same liberal arts core, but add to it cutting-edge technological prowess and real-world experience through the service-learning course taken by all first-year engineering students. Whether developing the next artificial heart or designing advanced water filtration for developing countries, Columbia engineers leave with a sense of the tremendous impact one person can make.

With all this to take advantage of, Columbia seeks to put together a class of students who have already begun to make an impact in their school and community. The comprehensive application process provides ample opportunities for applicants to paint a rich picture, including their aspirations and interests. Once admitted, Columbia's Office of Financial Aid and Educational Financing will work with the student and the student's family to finance all four years of the student's education.

Four years at Columbia sometimes does not feel like nearly enough. With a diverse and vibrant student body, a rich academic experience, and New York City just outside the gates, it is easy to want it never to end. But when it does, graduates find they are ready for the next step, as Columbia has prepared them to do whatever it is they set their mind to do.

❏ *Adina Brooks, B.A.*

Columbia University/Barnard College
3009 Broadway
New York, NY 10027

(212) 854-2014
Fax: (212) 854-8220

E-mail: *admissions@barnard.edu*
Website: *http://www.barnard.edu*

 **Enrollment**

Full-time ❏ women: 2,350

Part-time ❏ women: 60

INTRODUCING COLUMBIA UNIVERSITY/BARNARD COLLEGE

"Changing the world, one woman at a time," Barnard College continues to lead the way for women's education. With a new president at the helm and even bolder initiatives, the campus is poised like never before to empower young women to meet the challenges of a diverse, global community.

Launched in fall 2009, Barnard's Athena Center for Leadership Studies investigates the ideas at the forefront of women's leadership—what it means to lead, to motivate, to collaborate, and to excel. It is quickly becoming the premier interdisciplinary center devoted to the theory and practice of women's leadership. More globally, academic symposiums held in Beijing, Dubai, and Johannesburg have provided unique perspectives on women's voices, leadership, and life experiences within a political, historical, and cultural context, while increasing recognition of the Barnard name abroad.

Bold initiatives also involve campus changes, including a brand new multi-use student center, the Diana Center. This state-of-the-art facility sits at the crossroads of the campus, and serves as the nexus of student life, extending the College's cultural and intellectual reach beyond the walls of the classroom. The plan to "Build Tomorrow's Barnard" also includes renovations to campus residence halls and labs, with forward-thinking design, embracing sustainability and community needs. Not bad for a college whose mission is to educate and support the growth of some 2,300 students, all of whom are motivated and talented, all of whom are women.

Paradoxically, it is easy to forget that Barnard is a women's college, what with the intellectual excitement and the variety of activity on the campus. Barnard's unique relationship with Columbia University means that Barnard's women have access to a coed experience at all times, but on their own terms. It also means that the Barnard faculty and administration have as their main focus and attention the female Barnard student body, not the coed masses across the street (literally—Columbia's campus is just on the east side of Broadway). Therefore, the Barnard student is taught by faculty members rather than teaching assistants. These scholars are experts in their fields and have immeasurable resources that they share with their students. Or, as one young alumna put it:

> 66 *As a graduate student at [Ivy League School X], I advised undergrads on their senior theses. I tried to be helpful, but I only know so much. My thesis advisor at Barnard was the chair of her department, a wealth of information, and an all-around inspiration.* 99

Add to this wonderful mixture Barnard's New York City location—now considered the safest major city in America by the FBI—and one begins to see what all the fuss is about. A stroll down Broadway, a bus ride uptown, or a subway trip to Greenwich Village enables students to experiment in the most diverse cultural laboratory this side of the United Nations (where students regularly intern). The glamor of Fifth Avenue and the glitter of Broadway are equally accessible. And, as in any urban setting, opportunities abound to make a difference in the community: Barnard women serve as legal advocates to the homeless, tutors in the America Reads program, and providers of hot meals through the Community Lunch Program.

ADMISSIONS REQUIREMENTS

Barnard is, quite simply, "hot," which is both exciting and daunting. Everybody and her sister seems to be applying, creating a stir among prospective students and the admissions staff. Receiving more than 4,600 applications in 2010, the largest number in the College's history, Barnard continues to be the most sought after women's college in the world. Barnard also yields nearly fifty percent of the women admitted, a clear sign of keen interest and a more "self-selecting" applicant pool. Applicants who visit campus connect with the unique and contradictory charms that are Barnard: small and large, college and university, campus and city, all women and in a coeducational community, a blend of attributes which creates opportunities for Barnard students to shape their experience.

Getting into Barnard isn't all that easy, but there is no single criterion a student can point to and know, "This is the reason I was admitted." The application process is the usual, including personal data, high school transcripts, official copies of standardized test scores (either the SAT plus two SAT Subject tests or the ACT with Writing, and three recommendations—one from a guidance or college counselor and two from teachers [in academic subject areas]). Applicants may be deferred to the general application pool if they are denied admission. The regular deadline for application is January 1.

The admissions staff at Barnard works hard to make sure that each student offered admission will thrive in her own way. The ideal applicant to Barnard has a solid record, pursues diverse interests, and shows promise that she will take advantage of the breadth and depth of experiences the college and New York City will offer her.

The High School Record

The high school record is the single most important part of the application. While overall achievement (that is, high grades) is important, the admissions staff makes it very clear that they care about a student's demonstrated effort to challenge herself in the classroom. This means an A in a less rigorous class doesn't mean as much as a B+ in one that is more rigorous. In addition, course availability is taken into consideration. For instance, if a particular high school offers twenty-five ways to exceed the minimum graduation requirements, and an applicant avails herself of only one or two, she doesn't seem to indicate that she'd take advantage of the thousands of opportunities that await her upon matriculation at Barnard. On the other hand, an applicant taking the only two AP courses available at her high school can't be expected to do any more, but those courses are important measures of her success. In addition, because the college expects students to study a broad range of subjects, evidence of that interest—four years of English, social studies, and math and at least three years of science and foreign language—is very important.

Other Criteria

That is not to say that the Barnard experience is solely an academic one! The college takes pride in the amazing collective talent of its actors and athletes, debaters and dancers. Indeed, its strength comes from its unparalleled diversity—students hail from forty-eight states and fifty countries, from around the corner and around the world. Over forty percent of Barnard students identify themselves as Asian American, African American/Black, Latina, or Native American. Participation and leadership in extracurricular activities—clubs, teams, youth groups, or community service opportunities—are part of the admissions picture. Holding down a part-time job is also considered in this category, as some high school students are active contributors to their family's overall earnings. Multiyear commitment to an activity is always a plus; it shows your ability to stay with something for longer than it takes to get your picture taken for the yearbook. A liberal arts college wants to educate students to be good citizens, not simply good scholars. Participation in the community, which often translates into activity and volunteer participation, is a reality at Barnard, a positive reality.

Standardized Tests and the Essay

Now, about those pesky standardized tests. They are required, they count for something, and it's a good idea to do your best on them. They are the one measure that can be used to compare students no matter where they're from. That said, as the official admissions materials state, "no preconceived profile of an ideal student population limits the number of applicants accepted from any one group." So when it's time to fill out the personal part of the application, students should feel free to show some personality and let their individual quirks and interests peek through. The essays are a student's golden opportunity to express herself, her views, and her goals—and not knowing exactly what to do with one's life is a terrific place to start as a Barnard first-year student!

ACADEMIC LIFE

The admissions staff brings in class after class of students who dive into the curriculum. Graduation requirements ensure that a Barnard degree means something; all students must be competent in writing, quantitative reasoning, and in a foreign language. Beyond the depth provided by a major field (from which there are about sixty to choose, or students may combine or design their own), distribution requirements called "The nine ways of knowing" guarantee exposure to the humanities, social and natural sciences, visual and performing arts as well as to a variety of cultures and societies. Several of the requirements overlap, however, and students always have a choice as to how to fulfill them. Although all students must take First-Year English, there are several topical areas from which to choose (The Americas and Women and Culture are two of them). Its companion course, First-Year Seminar, is taught by faculty from all departments, allowing every first-year student the opportunity to discuss and write about subjects ranging from Chaos or Memory to Immortality, Death, and the Meaning of Life and from the Art of Being Oneself to Utopias of Love. Both of these courses are limited in size to promote active participation, lively discussion, and plenty of personal attention from the professors.

Faculty

Again and again, Barnard students and alumnae praise their academic experiences at the college.

> *Faculty members are great. They provide so much encouragement, are more than willing to provide a recommendation or just some encouragement and ideas. One history professor even helped me get my first real apartment!*

This kind of testimonial is available from virtually every Barnard student. Their close and productive relationships with the highly acclaimed Barnard faculty make Barnard a singular institution. Barnard students frequently collaborate with faculty as research assistants, so it is not unusual to hear a senior describe her work with an anthropology professor, or a junior discuss her experiences in the biology laboratory. Not long ago, a group of Barnard students traveled to Bangladesh to conduct research with a Biology professor and collaborated with scientists at the University of Dhaka. This type of collaboration enables the completion of high-level research but the scientists also learn about each others' cultures.

During their first two years, Barnard students receive counseling from faculty advisors and the Dean of Studies Office.

> **❝** *My advisor helped me figure out what courses would be most useful to me in choosing a major and at the same time satisfying my general requirements. He also suggested I become a calculus tutor and helped me secure a summer internship at CBS news.* **❞**

Advisors are well versed in Barnard's policies and regulations, working closely with the Deans' Office and the Registrar to ensure that all students are on the right track for graduation. At the end of the student's second year, advisors are prepared to assist with the transition into the major. From then on, students are advised by a faculty member in their major department; a double major will have two advisors. Students can decide whether they want to establish a close relationship with their advisors or keep it strictly business. Advisors are prepared to provide the necessary and required parts of the job, but they have chosen this role because they want to be available to students in a more personal way and have small advising roles. It is therefore not unusual for an advisor to write graduate school or other critical recommendations for students they never actually taught, but who they have come to know well over the course of several years together.

Partnership with Columbia

Barnard's partnership with Columbia means that the curricular offerings of one of the country's top research universities are available for the asking; courses in all departments are available for cross-registration. About equal numbers of Barnard and Columbia students do this, indicating a true academic parity between the two schools. Some celebrated professors have become major attractions; for example, Barnard's Richard Pious and Janet Jacobson are quite sought after, both as noted scholars in their fields (the American presidency and Feminist Theory, respectively) and as regular teachers of first-year students in introductory courses. Barnard students especially join their Columbia counterparts in courses taught by luminaries such as Robert Thurman in religion. While some departments are particularly focused on one campus or the other (theater at Barnard, for example, or computer science at Columbia), the offerings by popular departments such as English, history, and political science amount to nearly twice the number of courses as would be available otherwise. In every case, academic advisors can help students make informed choices about their course selection.

Senior Theses or Projects

Each Barnard student's academic endeavors are capped off by a significant culminating experience, which comes in the form of a senior thesis, project, or exam in her major. Preparing for and completing this terminal work presents true challenges, but that's part of the Barnard way. It understandably unifies the class; the buzz of activity in the library, labs, and studios keeps the midnight oil burning senior year. The idea is that if a student can succeed in such a project, she can do it in just about any field she chooses after Barnard. All things being equal, an art history major could just as easily land a financial services job as an economics major; they both certainly have the verbal, research, and critical thinking skills such a position might require.

Joint Programs

Other academic attractions include joint programs with the Juilliard School and the Manhattan School of Music, the Jewish Theological Seminary, and various graduate and professional schools of Columbia University such as the School of Engineering, the School of International and Public Affairs, the Law School, and the Dental School. While entrance into these programs is quite limited and often extremely competitive, the students who participate in them not only benefit themselves, but they contribute an extra degree of depth and diversity to their Barnard classrooms.

> **"** After spending the spring term at the London School of Economics, I was feeling rather 'out of the loop' at Barnard. When I attended Dean Szell's special meeting in the fall, my advisor helped me realize that I wasn't the only one feeling this way. **"**

Exchange and Overseas Programs

About thirty-five percent of Barnard's graduates participated in study abroad, whether it was for a semester or two. Barnard's official exchange programs in the United States include Spelman College and the Columbia University-Howard University Exchange Program, while overseas programs are located in more than fifty countries, including Argentina, Australia, Cuba, England, France, Germany, Italy, Japan, Kenya, Russia, and Spain. Students on financial aid are covered for any study abroad opportunity; however, Barnard students' diverse interests take them to such far-flung places as Russia, Israel, the Cameroons, Nicaragua, and Australia. The world, as they say, is their oyster. The Dean of Study Abroad meets with students individually and in groups, providing information and guidance before and after the experience.

These kinds of touches mark the Barnard experience from start to finish. Whether it's the personal letter sent by the first-year class dean upon matriculation or the handshake from the college's president at graduation, the Barnard faculty and administration make a concerted effort to ensure that each student's experience at Barnard is individual and special.

SOCIAL LIFE AND ACTIVITIES

Past president and Barnard College alumna Ellen Futter often characterized Barnard by saying, "This is *not* a cloistered enclave," thus coining a slogan for the ages. While students find campus activities galore, they have never-ending access to the unquantifiable offerings of what is arguably the world's greatest city; moreover, the college tries to make the city's offerings affordable for the usually cash-strapped undergrad. Discount vouchers to first-run films and the performing arts supplement the popular Urban New York program, which takes students to events such as *In the Heights* on Broadway, opening day at Yankee Stadium, the New York Philharmonic, and even the circus, all for the price of the subway. Each trip is escorted by a member of the college or university faculty or administration, providing an extra opportunity to get to know a key member of the community in a relaxed, sometimes unconventional, setting.

Most students worry, to some degree or other, about making friends in college. If they can be generalized in any way, Barnard friendships are built to last. That said, the need for privacy inherent in living in New York City means that personal space is valued and respected. People don't run right up to you to get to know you here, but don't mistake that for unfriendliness. Attend any club meeting, event, or party and you're sure to make a new acquaintance.

Whether it's the woman in your sponsor group during orientation, the friend of a friend from high school or summer camp who lives down the hall, or the person who wants to have coffee after orchestra practice, student life lends itself to the friendship-making process.

Housing

Barnard's residential focus means a great deal of programming takes place in the dorms. First-year students are clustered together in the quad, a grouping of (surprise!) four halls that situated on the south end of the main campus houses a total of about 900 students. The main dining room is located here, in Hewitt Hall, with a second dining option located in the Diana Center, and Liz's Café, also in the Diana Center, is open late into the evening for that much-needed burst of energy courtesy of Starbucks Coffee. Beyond the quad, which primarily features the traditional corridor style of dormitory living, upperclass students live in suites of various configurations in seven other residence halls surrounding the main campus. In every hall, Resident Assistants (RAs) sponsor floor programs and study breaks to foster social connections; movie nights and guest appearances by various peer education groups and speakers offer something for just about everyone. After the first year, students select their own living space through a lottery process. In addition, they may enter the lottery in groups, sometimes with their Columbia friends, for suite living on either campus. Another more competitive option is to participate in Special Interest Housing, meaning that students come together around a theme such as Community Service, Foreign Language, or Environmental Awareness, and sponsor programs in their residence hall for everyone's benefit. The Housing Office offers forums early in the spring semester to help explain the various options.

Outside Groups

The amount and quality of activity sponsored by and for the college is inspiring. While the faculty and administration present lectures and readings by prominent and emerging scholars and artists, students themselves create and invite a great deal of programming. Thus, you're likely to find both a classical musical recital and a concert by an alternative band, with a *Barnard Bulletin* (a news weekly) reporter on hand to interview the talent and audience as well. Barnard's radio station, WBAR, broadcasts a college/alternative format and there are traditional activities such as the yearbook and student government (called SGA), which is responsible for the eighty or so student organizations. Cultural organizations and various other community groups come under SGA's umbrella.

That said, there are another 400 plus groups at Columbia, giving Barnard students the opportunity to work on a daily paper (the *Spectator*) or a jazz-oriented radio station (WKCR), to get involved in religious, volunteer, and political organizations (most of which are jointly sponsored by Barnard, but whose offices are physically located on the Columbia campus), and clubs galore.

The Greeks

The Greek system, including both sororities and coed fraternities, is open to Barnard students who want to experience more "traditional" collegiate life. Those who take part in them tend to rave about their experiences; however, the SGA constitution prohibits groups that limit their membership and therefore does not recognize the Greek system. There's hardly a more concrete example of how student life at Barnard offers something for everyone!

Productions

Dance, theater, and musical productions abound. From improv comedy to *a cappella* singing, Barnard women regularly appear on stage. Two annual events are Acapellooza, an *a cappella* jamboree hosted by Barnard's own Bacchantae, which features groups from the university and selected others and results in a professional-quality CD, and Broadway Tonight, a benefit performance of Broadway selections that teams up Barnard students with professionals from the Great White Way. Off stage, students provide technical support and packed houses. This is one talented group of students, and a group appreciative of the efforts of their peers.

Athletics

Those who prefer their thrills on a court, arena, or stadium can participate on a number of levels. Barnard varsity athletes compete in Division I archery, basketball, soccer, field hockey, crew, tennis, lacrosse, cross-country, track and field, swimming and diving, softball, fencing, golf, and volleyball as part of the athletic consortium with their counterparts from Columbia College and the School of Engineering. We're talking Ivy League here—no athletic scholarships, just sheer love of the game. Club sports such as Ultimate Frisbee, sailing, and rugby offer unique opportunities for intercollegiate competition and comraderie. Intramurals provide a great way to let loose, either in indoor soccer, basketball, or volleyball. Finally, many students work out on their own or with friends by running in Riverside Park, taking yoga, or swimming a few laps in the Barnard pool. While obviously not an outdoorsy, let's-go-skiing-this-afternoon campus, Barnard students enjoy breaking a good sweat.

Off Campus

And, all right, let's not forget Barnard's location. From poetry readings to film screenings, cafés and restaurants to galleries and museums, concert halls to night clubs, this is the city that never sleeps and always has something to offer. Parades, street fairs, festivals, and impromptu concerts are year-round occurrences. Professional sports teams have crosstown rivals, bookstores have cappuccino, and there's nothing quite like a trip to Central Park, whether it's for a visit to the zoo, rollerblading around the Loop, or ice-skating at Wollman Rink. Even the lifelong New Yorker will find herself traveling to new places and trying new foods with her Barnard friends—and a welcome number of area restaurants deliver to the residence halls for snacking on sushi, tandoori, pizza, lo mein, or simply a nice deli sandwich.

FINANCIAL AID

Private colleges are expensive. Barnard's tuition falls in line with its peer institutions, but that doesn't make the bill much easier to swallow. Unlike many schools, however, Barnard admits students on a need-blind basis, meaning that students are admitted regardless of their ability to pay. Moreover, they are met with a full demonstrated-need financial aid package in keeping with the federal government's formulas—once the Financial Aid Office has calculated the amount that a student and her family are able to contribute, it offers a package to make up the difference. Approximately fifty-three percent of the student body receives some form of financial assistance.

Generally speaking, this package has three parts. First, all students are expected to borrow money, but Barnard does not expect both the student and her parents to take out loans or liquidate their assets. And, Barnard's Office of Financial Aid has been particularly effective in decreasing the use of expensive private loans. Next, students are asked to work during the school year to contribute to their own education, with work-study awards focused on first-year and sophomore students in particular to assist in their getting to know the campus and its functionings; upperclass students are encouraged to find off-campus jobs relating to their majors or career interests. Summer earnings are also expected after the first year. Finally, the college provides grants—funds that need not be repaid—to bridge the gap. Forty-one percent of the student body receives grant monies from Barnard.

New York state residents who meet certain financial and academic criteria may apply as Higher Education Opportunity Program (HEOP) students. This program, sponsored by New York State but largely funded by the college itself, provides intensive preenrollment preparation for Barnard academics as well as special counseling and support during all four years. About twenty-five students are admitted each year under the HEOP program and their graduation rate is on par with the overall Barnard student population.

GRADUATES

Barnard women are staunch and loyal supporters of their alma mater, leading to an "oldgirl" network that spans the country and the world. Organized Barnard Clubs in many regions sponsor faculty lectures and receptions for admitted students, but even more prevalent is the individual connection—the women who make themselves available to assist current students and fellow alumnae through informational interviews, internships, job contacts, and relocation support.

Several times a year, alumnae appear on panels to discuss their career paths, in fields ranging from psychology to law, from education to arts management. The BEST program, sponsored by the Career Development Office, not only organizes these panels and helps seniors with résumé and interview tips, but also offers workshops on building a business wardrobe, following proper etiquette at business meals, and even how to find a New York City apartment.

Thanks especially to the high standards and personal encouragement of the faculty, Barnard is one of the leading producers of Ph.D.s in the country. The most recent study of private undergraduate colleges and universities (done by Franklin and Marshall College for the period between 1920 and 1995) ranked Barnard third overall—second in the fields of psychology and foreign languages, third in anthropology and sociology, and fourth in English—in the number of its graduates receiving PhD.s. Not women graduates, *all* graduates. In terms of medical doctors, Barnard ranks fifth in the country in the number of women who become physicians, behind much larger institutions such as Cornell, Harvard, Stanford, and the University of Michigan. While no studies have been done on the field of law, Barnard boasts a remarkable array of graduates who go on to become lawyers and judges.

A recent graduate who is currently earning her Master's in International Affairs at Columbia recently said, "At Barnard, I learned I could do anything!" and this sentiment seems to echo through the generations. Barnard alumnae have authored more than 4,100 books and such best-selling novelists as Erica Jong, Mary Gordon, and Edwidge Danticat are among the ranks. In journalism, eight Barnard alumnae have won or shared the Pulitzer Prize, including Anna Quindlen and Natalie Angier at *The New York Times*, Eileen McNamara at the *Boston Globe*, and most recently, Jhumpa Lahiri for her book, *Interpreter of Maladies*. In broadcast news, Latino USA and PBS newsmagazine *NOW's* Maria Hinojosa and National Public Radio's Susan Stamberg are prominent contributors to their fields.

Former Dean of the College Virginia Gildersleeve helped to charter the United Nations; alumnae Jeane Kirkpatrick and Sylvan Foa became its first female ambassador for the United States and its first female spokesperson, respectively. While their names may be less recognizable, the women who lead Rockefeller and Company and the Ford modeling agency, the American Museum of Natural History, and one of the founders of the National Organization for Women all graduated from Barnard. But whether they have made big names for themselves or have pursued goals more privately, Barnard women make a difference in the world, an aspiration inculcated in them during their years on campus.

SUMMING UP

Barnard's unique position as a small independent college for women closely linked to a first-rate research university and located in one of the world's major cities offers an extraordinary and unparalleled opportunity for those young women smart and savvy enough to avail themselves of it. The internship possibilities and cultural offerings of New York City are second to none, and the intimacy of the Barnard campus and student body provides a perfect home base from which to explore Manhattan. It is a literal and metaphorical oasis, a place where students can relax and learn to express themselves more and more fully.

Often described as "the best of both worlds," Barnard students have the advantages of a women's college—its nurturing and inspiring faculty, the sisterhood that stems from a unity of purpose in studying the liberal arts—while at the same time having full access to the facilities, activities, and social life of a large, coed, multipurpose university. Columbia provides research facilities, graduate programs, and a diversity of talents and backgrounds that no other small college can offer.

A recent article in *Town and Country* magazine featured women from the colleges still affiliated by their Seven Sister history. The interviewer asked a Barnard senior which one part of her education she would use most if she were stranded on a desert island. The student's response?

> *Barnard does not educate women to live on desolate islands. Barnard educates women to make a real difference in the real world.*

As this particular alumna now holds a master's degree in Public Policy and is currently spending a year in China as a Luce Fellow, she is certainly living up to the ideal she expressed.

Whether your interests lie in the humanities, the social and natural sciences, or the arts, Barnard College offers a fertile training ground for young minds and ideas. The intellectual debates that begin in the classroom and extend into a dining hall or dorm room are reflective of the involvement and curiosity of the student body. Close academic relationships with faculty and peers, and a supportive environment that actively and tacitly provides a foundation for the intellectual and social development of an extraordinary group of young women makes for a wonderful home base from which to explore Columbia University, Morningside Heights, New York City, and the world. Small wonder it is experiencing such a surge in interest and excitement!

> *The spirit of the Barnard pioneers who were the founders of the College continues to evolve every year as new women join Barnard, not because attending a women's college is the only choice any longer or a limiting choice in the current climate, but because they have the liberty to choose.*

—*Debora Spar, President, Barnard College*

❑ *Catherine Webster, B.A.*

COLUMBIA UNIVERSITY, SCHOOL OF GENERAL STUDIES

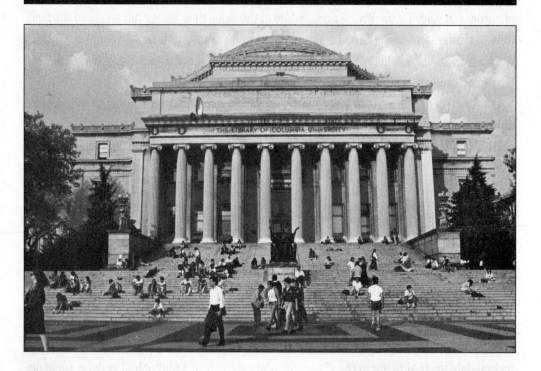

 Columbia University
408 Lewisohn Hall
New York, NY 10027

 (212) 854-6316

 E-mail: *gs-admit@columbia.edu*
Website: *http://www.gs.columbia.edu*

 Enrollment

Full-time ❏ women: 395
            ❏ men: 523

Part-time ❏ women: 289
            ❏ men: 254

INTRODUCING COLUMBIA UNIVERSITY

Founded in 1947, in large part to accommodate the wave of veterans returning from World War II, the School of General Studies of Columbia University (GS) is the finest liberal arts college in the United States devoted to returning, adult, and nontraditional students who seek a rigorous undergraduate education. GS students take the same classes, with the same professors, and earn the same degree as students in Columbia's other undergraduate colleges.

As one of the world's leading research centers, Columbia University offers a distinctive and distinguished learning environment. Undergraduate colleges at Columbia include GS, Columbia College, a liberal-arts college for traditional students, and the Fu Foundation School of Engineering and Applied Science; affiliated institutions include Barnard College, a liberal arts college for women, and The Jewish Theological Seminary.

The Students

What exactly is a nontraditional student? It's a difficult question, particularly since, according to Department of Education figures, seventy-three percent of all college students are nontraditional, and the GS student body provides no easy answers. Some GS students attend part-time while working, performing, or raising a family, while others enroll full-time and immerse themselves in the Columbia undergraduate experience. The commonality shared by all GS students, apart from a desire to earn a bachelor's degree in

WHY GENERAL STUDIES?

The name "School of General Studies" is rather unfortunate, because, as most GS students are quick to point out, there's nothing general about us. GS evolved out of Columbia's extension program, which offered degrees in "general studies." "School of General Studies" was adopted to maintain a sense of continuity and to establish GS as a full-fledged undergraduate college based in part on the model of medieval universities, which, because they catered to a diverse, international group of scholars, were known as studia generalia (vs. the more parochial studia particularia).

a dynamic, challenging academic environment, is that they have interrupted their educations for at least one year. In every other respect, each GS student is unique, making GS one of the most diverse colleges in the nation and, moreover, a place where diversity is defined by standards that are themselves diverse.

> *The guiding philosophy of our school is to question the mainstream idea of what makes a successful college student. Instead of requiring that all of its students take the same path to get here, GS actively seeks out students who have taken different paths. If one of the goals of diversification is to expand the perspectives and backgrounds within a given community, what better way to achieve it than by including individuals who have transcended tradition and convention?*

—Pavan Surapaneni, '06

Like New York City, GS is home to a wide spectrum of peoples and personalities: world-class dancers, athletes, models, musicians, and actors, veterans and refugees, entrepreneurs, firefighters and police officers, community activists and computer programmers, writers and welders, bankers, bike messengers, and baristas, professionals returning for a second degree and parents resuming their education, students who have never been to college and those who are transferring from community colleges and Columbia's peer institutions, representing each of the 50 states and every corner of the world—all in search of a rich, vigorous education that prepares and inspires.

The Campus

Stepping off Broadway and onto College Walk can be disorienting for the first-time visitor, simply because the Columbia campus is unlike any other space in New York City. Located on thirty-six acres in the northern Manhattan neighborhood of Morningside Heights, the campus was designed by the renowned architect Charles McKim in a monumental neoclassical style well suited to the neighborhood's nineteenth-century nickname, "America's Acropolis."

> 66 *The first time I walked on campus, Columbia had me in its grip. I knew I had to come here. Later I became a student tour guide to help pass on that feeling.* 99

—*Erich Erving, '06*

Glance to the north and you'll see Low Library, modeled on the Roman Pantheon and the Baths of Caracalla (which housed libraries and were the sites of public lectures, in addition to their more obvious function). Beneath Low Library—no longer a library, but the university administration building and site for special events, such as the annual awarding of the Pulitzer Prize—is Low Plaza, an open space ideal for socializing that has been called an "urban beach" and named a "Great American Public Place."

Glance to the south and you'll see the tall Ionic columns of Butler Library, the university's main library, which houses two million of Columbia's nine and one half million volumes. The main study spot on campus, Butler has a serious façade—literally: the names of ancient and modern writers, orators, and philosophers are inscribed on its frieze—and, with Columbia's academic demands, you will spend a not inconsiderable amount of time there or in one of the university's twenty-five other libraries. Of course, everyone else is there too, so this is not an isolating experience; rather, the libraries are places where the entire university comes to work, socialize, and procrastinate together.

The City

James Thurber once wrote to his *New Yorker* colleague E. B. White that "[t]here is nothing else in all the countries of the world like New York City life. It does more to people, it socks them harder, than life in Paris, London, or Rome, say, possibly could." A fundamental characteristic of GS students, whether they are lifelong New York residents or moving to the city for the first time, is an openness to the whole experience of New York City life, with all its vicissitudes.

New York City offers unparalleled and inexhaustible cultural and recreational opportunities, but as a GS student your interaction with the city won't be strictly extracurricular. You'll have the option to study with some of the leading members of New York's arts community, retrace Walt Whitman's steps in "Whitman and New York," or learn about Manhattan from Peter Minuit to the present day, including a professor-led bike ride through the city, in "History of the City of New York." You'll also visit some of the city's outstanding museums and performance spaces through core courses in art and music.

Of course, as an elite university in an international city, Columbia is also uniquely poised to reach far beyond the borders of its hometown. Through initiatives such as the Committee on Global Thought, which counts among its members Joseph Stiglitz and Orhan Pamuk, Nobel laureates in economics and literature, respectively, and the World Leaders Forum, which, since its founding in 2003, has brought leaders from more than forty countries to campus, including the Dalai Lama, Vladimir Putin of Russia, and Pervez

PASSPORT TO NEW YORK

Columbia students with a valid ID card can obtain free admission to the museums listed below (and many others).
- American Folk Art Museum
- Asia Society
- The Cloisters
- Solomon R. Guggenheim Museum
- International Center of Photography
- El Museo del Barrio
- Museum of Chinese in the Americas
- Museum of the City of New York
- Museum of Jewish Heritage—A Living Memorial to the Holocaust
- Museum of Modern Art
- Metropolitan Museum of Art
- Museum of Television and Radio
- National Academy Museum
- New York City Police Museum
- New York Historical Society
- PS1/MoMA
- Schomberg Center for Research in Black Culture
- Whitney Museum of American Art

Musharraf of Pakistan, Columbia has become increasingly connected to institutions and scholars throughout the world. GS students complement this outward extension by bringing their distinctive experiences to Morningside Heights and, in doing so, are playing a unique and significant role as Columbia becomes a global university.

> 66 *Everyone knows Andy Warhol's soup cans—but seeing an entire wall of them at MoMA is a different experience altogether. Similarly, I'd listened to some of Morton Feldman's compositions on my iPod, but I didn't realize how quiet and textured they were until I heard them played by a full orchestra at Carnegie Hall. For some things you really do have to be there.* 99

ADMISSIONS REQUIREMENTS

The fact that its students are fully integrated into the larger undergraduate community makes GS unique in nontraditional education; it also makes admission very competitive, since GS students are expected to perform at the same level as students in Columbia's other undergraduate colleges, which are among the nation's most selective.

In many respects the GS admissions process resembles the standard model: applicants must submit standardized test scores, transcripts from every academic institution attended (high school and college, if applicable), two letters of recommendation, and the official GS application. At the same time, however, the GS admissions committee is aware that in many cases traditional admissions metrics do not sufficiently convey a nontraditional student's ability to succeed.

> 66 *When I found out that Columbia considered me an adult and that I would have to apply to GS, I was a little taken aback. I had been out of school for five years, but I had no wife, no kids, no mortgage—and certainly no adult-level income. I eventually came to terms with being a quote-unquote grown-up, but even so, I knew that I wanted the full academic experience: I didn't want to be pandered to with night classes, cut-rate tuition, a separate faculty, or anything else that might diminish what I knew I could accomplish. GS was exactly what I was looking for.* 99

Consequently, the committee makes a determined effort to engage applicants in a dialogue in order to produce a more comprehensive profile: in addition to such traditional measures of academic success as test scores and grade-point averages, this profile includes work experiences, past academic accomplishments, personal achievements, and depth of commitment to a demanding program of study.

ADMISSIONS DEADLINES

Fall
Early Action: March 1
International Students: April 1
Regular Decision: June 1

Spring
International Students: August 15
Early Action: October 1
Regular Decision: November 1

Summer
April 1

At the heart of this profile is the autobiographical essay. Both an occasion for reflection and a chance to indulge your deepest egocentric impulses, the autobiographical essay is the best opportunity to explain your nontraditional path and why GS is the place for you.

If you decide to apply, you'll have a variety of options, all designed to accommodate a nontraditional applicant pool. If your SAT or ACT scores are older than eight years, you may instead take the General Studies Admissions Exam. You may apply to begin in the fall, spring, or summer terms, and admission deadlines fall later in the admissions cycle (see sidebar), although applicants requesting consideration for financial aid and/or housing are encouraged to apply Early Action. Should circumstances prevent you from matriculating as planned, deferrals of up to a year are available.

Transfer Students

There is no separate admissions process for transfer students; in fact, most GS students have previously attended college elsewhere and matriculate with at least some transfer credit. GS students can transfer up to sixty credits (out of 124 needed to graduate) and are notified upon admission how many of their credits will transfer. Transfer-credit guidelines are available for review on the GS website (*www.gs.columbia.edu*).

International Students

International students representing more than eighty countries comprise approximately twenty-four percent of the GS student body. The admissions process for international students differs in a few important respects: deadlines fall earlier (see sidebar), and English-language testing may be required. Visit the GS website (*www.gs.columbia.edu*) for a full explanation of international applicant procedures; additional resources are available on the International Students and Scholars website (*www.columbia.edu/cu/isso*).

Academic life at Columbia is, to borrow a title from University Professor Simon Schama, an "embarrassment of riches." You can choose from more than seventy majors (or design your own), embark on a study-abroad program virtually anywhere in the world, and study with a distinguished faculty. GS students also contribute immeasurably to the university by bringing their pasts into the classroom; you might be reading *The Iliad* with a military veteran just back from Iraq, or learning about sustainable development with grassroots environmental activists.

The Core

GS students arrive at Columbia with varying degrees of academic preparation; some have never attended college, while others have already earned a bachelor's degree (or, in some cases, advanced degrees). One thing that unites them, however, is the Core, a series of distribution requirements designed to encourage critical thinking in a number of disciplines. GS students fulfill requirements in science, literature, humanities, social sciences, art, music, and cultural diversity, and demonstrate proficiency in a foreign language. In some cases, core requirements can be fulfilled through exemption exams or with transfer credit for equivalent courses taken at another institution.

Advising

Nontraditional and traditional students on their own for the first time will inevitably have different concerns, and accordingly, GS has a full staff of school-specific advisors who work exclusively with GS students and are well equipped to offer counsel in a variety of areas, from making the transition to Columbia to finding child-care options or balancing a career with studies. GS also provides preprofessional and fellowship advising, as well as tutoring and study-skills workshops throughout the year through the GS Academic Resource Center.

> **❝** *I have a great relationship with my advisor. He has helped me with both academic affairs as well as administrative issues. Having this support is key to balancing a successful student life.* **❞**

—*Michael Rain, '09*

Special Programs

For more than fifty years, GS has been home to the Joint Program with Albert A. List College of The Jewish Theological Seminary. Students in the Joint Program earn two bachelor's degrees: one from GS and one in a Judaic studies program from List College. Similarly, students can pursue a dual BA with the renowned French Univeristy, Sciences Po, where the first two years are spent in France and the next two years are spent in New York City. GS students also have the option to pursue dual-degree programs with many of Columbia's graduate schools, including the 3-2 engineering combined plan (three years at GS, two at the School of Engineering and Applied Science).

The Faculty and the Classroom

As a premier research university in New York City, Columbia consistently draws some of the world's leading scholars. The Columbia Faculty of Arts and Sciences, which offers instruction to students in GS, Columbia College, and the Graduate School of Arts and Sciences, among others, includes members of the American Academy of Arts and Sciences and the National Academy of Sciences and National Medal of Science and MacArthur Foundation Award winners, in addition to nine Nobel laureates (out of seventy-nine in the University's history).

Just as important, however, is Columbia's commitment to undergraduate education, demonstrated by the student-faculty ratio, which is seven to one. Columbia's course offerings range from large lecture classes to small seminars to individual independent studies.

> *Most of my classes were seminars, where I had to be prepared for every session; even in lecture courses, the professors would quiz us on the reading or start a discussion. Columbia's definitely not a place where one can just absorb information passively. Of course, no one I've met here would ever stand for that.*

SOCIAL LIFE AND ACTIVITIES

The GS student body is a mixture of recent transplants and longtime New Yorkers, with an average age of twenty-nine. Some GS students step on campus only to attend classes and then return to their everyday lives, while others structure their lives around being a Columbia undergraduate. Whatever level of engagement you choose, you won't have any trouble meeting people. Most new students join Storybook, an online community specifically for newly admitted GS students, and meet their classmates before Orientation. The on-campus hub for GS student life is the GS Lounge, a space for studying and socializing that is open twenty-four hours and specifically dedicated to GS students.

Housing

Housing is often a concern for GS students relocating to New York, given the unique (to say the least) nature of the New York real estate market. Full-time GS students are eligible for university-owned or -leased apartments, but quantities are limited, with priority given to students who apply early and are moving from great distances; approximately forty percent of all eligible students live in university housing.

> 66 *Finding an apartment wasn't easy, but that's how New York is. If I wanted easy, I would've stayed in Kansas. I spent an entire week hitting refresh on craigslist and looking at apartments—a minor inconvenience, when you consider all the advantages that New York offers. And it paid off: I found an affordable, rent-stabilized place close to campus. It can be done; keep the faith!* 99

Student Organizations

GS students are fully integrated into the Columbia undergraduate community and can choose from more than two-hundred organizations that include everything from fraternities and sororities to student-run publications, service initiatives, and businesses to cultural, religious, activist, and performance groups. If the organization you envision doesn't exist, you always have the option to create it: some of Columbia's most distinctive organizations were started by GS students, including the U.S. Military Veterans of Columbia University and the Columbia Ballet Collaborative.

> 66 *The GS Gala is one of those unique events that allows students to interact at a completely different level than in University Writing, or passing each other on College Walk, or discussing Oscar Wilde in a study group in Butler Library. It's a chance for students to step out of their day-to-day wardrobe and put school work on hold, in order to get all dressed up and enjoy a well-deserved, elegant night out.* 99

—*Elizabeth Hollister, '07*

Many GS students participate in student government through the University Senate and the General Studies Student Council, which represents the student body to the GS administration and across the university. The student council also sponsors a number of social events throughout the year, including the GS Gala, a formal held annually in Low Rotunda.

Sports

As a member of the Ivy League, Columbia competes at the NCAA Division I level. The university also offers a number of club and intramural sports opportunities. GS students are eligible to join any of Columbia's teams (subject to NCAA regulations), and many do; in fact, in recent years GS students have competed on the varsity volleyball team and placed second in the national equestrian championships (as well as competed on the U.S. Olympic skeleton and ice dancing teams).

FINANCIAL AID

There is no way around it—a GS education is expensive. While admission is need-blind, applicants should be aware that, in most cases, they will need to take out loans in order to attend GS.

Aid is available, however, and GS has recently taken steps to enhance its financial aid program; additionally, Columbia is currently in the midst of a capital campaign that includes a stated goal of raising $15 million for GS financial aid. Approximately seventy percent of all GS students receive some form of need-based financial aid, merit scholarship, or both. Many students also receive outside scholarships or grants from private organizations, such as the Jack Kent Cooke Foundation and the Charlotte W. Newcombe Foundation.

Need-based Aid

Need-based aid includes grants, loans, and the Federal Work-Study Program. To receive need-based aid, you must complete the Free Application for Federal Student Aid (FAFSA), which will determine your Estimated Family Contribution (EFC), the key to your eligibility for federal aid. The EFC is based on your tax return, so if you've been working full-time, you may see a high number; after you're admitted, however, you can apply to have your eligibility reevaluated due to a change in financial circumstance, since, as a student, your annual income will be lower (much, much lower).

The FAFSA is also the primary factor in determining your eligibility for New York State aid, which could include either the Tuition Assistance Program (TAP) or Aid for Part-Time Study (APTS).

Institutional (Merit-based) Aid

At GS institutional aid consists of merit-based scholarships, which are awarded to new and continuing students who demonstrate academic achievement. In general, the level of support increases as students progress through their degree programs. Students must reapply for financial aid every year, so be sure you have everything turned in by the deadline.

> **❝** *I was fortunate in receiving generous scholarships, but they didn't cover the entire cost of attendance. I considered GS as an investment in myself, and I think that paying my own way made me take my education more seriously.* **❞**

Program for Academic Leadership and Service

The Program for Academic Leadership and Service is a scholarship opportunity for first-generation college students with significant financial need who are members of historically underrepresented groups at Columbia. The PALS scholarship covers full tuition and entails a service requirement of fifteen hours per semester, although most PALS scholars exceed that through their work on a number of service initiatives, including the annual No Limits Conference, which brings area high school students to campus to highlight the importance (and possibility) of higher education.

> **❝** *PALS is unmatched in the Ivy League. The unparalleled financial aid package and the opportunity to work with New York City public school students have made my Columbia education the most fulfilling experience of my life.* **❞**

—*Adrienne Herrera, '09*

GRADUATES

Approximately seventy percent of all GS graduates earn graduate or professional degrees, either immediately after graduation or at a later date. Some GS graduates pursue fellowship opportunities, while others resume previous careers or begin new ones in a wide variety of fields.

Both students and alumni have access to the Center for Career Education, which capitalizes on New York's status as an industry center by offering a robust series of information panels, on-campus recruitment events, and internship opportunities. Throughout the year the center also sponsors a number of career fairs that focus on green jobs, not-for-profit and public service opportunities, international organizations, and government careers.

As a GS alum, you'll be part of a global network that includes not only GS graduates, but alumni from all of Columbia's undergraduate, graduate, and professional schools. You can stay connected to the university as a member of the Recent Alumni Leadership Committee, or by joining one of the regional chapters of the Columbia Alumni Association, which holds events throughout the United States and in many foreign countries. Alums who remain in New York can participate in the Columbia Alumni Arts League, which offers discounted tickets to cultural events and spotlights alumni working in the arts.

PROMINENT GRADS

- R.W. Apple—New York Times chief correspondent and associate editor
- Isaac Asimov—author
- Baruj Benacerraf—Nobel laureate, medicine
- Trent Dimas—Olympic gold medalist, gymnastics
- Jerry Ford—co-founder of Ford Models
- Alicia Graf—dancer, Dance Theatre of Harlem and Alvin Ailey Dance Theatre
- Jane Jacobs—activist, author of *The Death and Life of Great American Cities*
- Donald Judd—artist
- Simon Kuznets—Nobel laureate, economics
- Federico Garcia Lorca—poet and dramatist
- Tim Goebel—"Quad King" Olympic Bronze medalist, figure skating
- Stewart Rawlings Mott—philanthropist, member of Richard Nixon's enemies list
- Jacques Pepin—chef
- Anthony Perkins—actor, best known as Norman Bates in *Psycho*
- Thomas Reardon—architect of the Internet Explorer browser
- Gil Shahan—award-winning violinist
- Kristi Zea—Academy Award-nominated art director and producer

Any college has the power to help shape a life: taking a certain class, discovering a certain interest, meeting certain people—any or all of these can launch a trajectory that might last a lifetime. But GS, with its unique student body and academic rigor, has a singular opportunity to transform a life.

> 66 *When I arrived at GS the highlight of my professional career was a particularly well-received Jamba Juice run. Of course I always knew that I could do more, if given the opportunity; GS gave me the opportunity. Glancing around at Commencement I saw my classmates: a former member of Guns N' Roses who's now in medical school, the chief architect of Internet Explorer, and a retired New York City firefighter who worked in the recovery effort at Ground Zero, and so many other people with amazing stories. I found myself marveling at the fact that we were all together, in one place; that's when I realized fully just how special this school is.* 99

❏ *Robert Ast, B.A.*

CONNECTICUT COLLEGE

Vickers and Beechler Photography

Connecticut College
New London, CT 06320

(860) 439-2200
Fax: (860) 439-4301

E-mail: *admission@conncoll.edu*
Website: *www.conntcoll.edu*

Enrollment

Full-time ❏ women: 1,129
❏ men: 710

Part-time ❏ women: 29
❏ men: 38

INTRODUCING CONNECTICUT COLLEGE

In his Commencement speech to the class of 2010, economist Jeffrey Sachs advised students, "Your liberal arts education has empowered you to be effective citizens of the world." In this moment, Sachs unknowingly captured the essence of the Conn College mission: to build a community of informed and empowered students, allowing them to become individuals who will eventually make contributions as "effective citizens of the world."

In a community of fewer than 2,000 there is, surprisingly, no "typical" Conn student. Rather, points of difference like the tradition of shared student governance and an honor code, the opportunity for a self-designed major, the five interdisciplinary certificate centers, the legacy of eco-consciousness, and the funded internship program run by career services come together to create a unique environment that attracts students from all different backgrounds—and all over the world.

Conn College is based on a scenic, waterfront campus just outside of New London, Connecticut. While the setting is very New England, rowers and sailors have easy access to Conn's waterfront located on the Thames River, and less athletically inclined students can enjoy the beautiful view of the Long Island Sound from the campus greens or the short drive to several points of beach access. A 750-acre arboretum satisfies those students that like to hike or boulder, and provides a convenient outdoor classroom for environmental science and botany classes.

In fact, outdoor classes are fairly common scenes at Conn. On the first beautiful day of spring, the campus greens are filled with students sitting in circles around their professors, listening intently to the day's lesson. That professors are able to do this speaks volumes about the student-faculty relationship; with a 9:1 student-faculty ratio, my professors always knew my name and had the time to sit down with me outside of class to discuss my progress or answer any questions that I might have. Since my first year at Conn, the faculty has further personalized the academic experience by moving freshman seminars (small classes taught by academic advisors and taken the first semester of freshman year) into the common rooms of residence halls. In my former res hall, Jane Addams, students would frequently be seen lounging with their professors before classes, or grabbing a quick lunch afterwards in our small dining hall.

Conn offers forty-seven majors to its students, a very broad educational menu for a college of its size. What is particularly striking though, is not the breadth of its offerings, but their *strength*. A close friend (a biology major and dance minor) went on to do scientific research for Columbia University, while I entered the world of magazine publishing. Another friend interested in human development and education was accepted into Teach for America. Our interests and courses of study could not have been more diverse, but we found ourselves equally prepared to pursue careers in our fields of interest upon our graduation from Conn. And that is what is so special about a Conn College education: just as there is no typical student, there is no typical education. The faculty and staff work together to make an individual experience for each student that leaves them uniquely prepared to take on the world after graduation, and be the "effective citizens" that Jeffrey Sachs proclaimed us Conn grads to be.

ADMISSIONS REQUIREMENTS

Despite stiff competition (5,300 applicants for a targeted class of 490–500 students), Conn's application process is, in the words of the Admissions office, designed to be "holistic." Admissions officers are not just looking for students with good grades and test scores, but they're searching for new members that can contribute a wide range of interests, expertise, and worldviews to the Conn community.

Common Application

Connecticut College accepts the Common Application, which can be submitted online or through the mail. Conn's Supplement to the Common Application, also found online, seeks to reveal things about students' personalities and experiences that might not otherwise be well-represented with questions like "Please share something about yourself that you have not addressed in the Common Application and that may not be revealed in a recommendation." Conn's Admissions process is now test-optional (this includes both the SAT and ACT), although students who are not native English speakers are required to submit the TOEFL or its equivalent. Regular Decision applicants must submit a Common Application, Supplement, and all relevant materials to Admissions by January 1, and are notified of the status of their candidacy in late March/early April. While interviews are not required, they are highly recommended. Interviewing is seen as a mutually beneficial process: it puts a personal stamp on a candidate's application, and allows a prospective student to meet a current Conn student or Admissions staff member that can offer a real perspective on what student and academic life is really like.

Early Decision

Early Decision is a popular choice for students applying to Conn. There are two rounds offered: Early Decision I has a deadline of November 15, and applicants are notified in mid-December. Early Decision II requires submission of all application materials by January 1, with notifications sent out in mid-February.

Distribution Requirements

In the spirit of a true liberal arts education, there is no core curriculum—specific classes required of all—at Conn. Rather, a series of General Education distribution requirements seeks to broaden academic interests and perspectives. Students are required to take at least one course in each of the following seven disciplines in order to graduate: Physical and Biological Sciences, Mathematics and Formal Reasoning, Social Sciences, Critical Studies in Literature and the Arts, Creative Arts, Philosophical and Religious Studies, and Historical Studies. Conn students must also complete a foreign language requirement, and two courses designated as writing-intensive.

Despite hugely varied educational options for a college of its size (forty-seven majors and more than 1,000 courses in thirty departments), Conn is no slouch when it comes to academics: a student-faculty ratio of 9:1 keeps classes small and personal, and ninety percent of faculty members have a doctorate or the equivalent.

A special academic offering for first-year students is the Freshman Seminar. A wide variety of courses cater to many interests, help introduce students to academic life at Conn, and seminar professors often serve as students' academic advisors prior to declaring a major. "Food in Art, Culture, and Cinema," for example, is a course that enables one to cook a medieval meal, create a photographic food diary of the food that one eats for two weeks, and learn about the enormous cultural influences and implications that food has had throughout history. There is also a seminar called "Glow," in which one spends a semester studying bioluminescent organisms that culminates in a trip to Vieques, Puerto Rico to swim in bioluminescent lakes and do lab research on site.

> 66 *Those wary of General Education requirements, fear not: my first semester at Conn, I took an introductory sociology course as part of my distribution requirements and wound up majoring in the discipline. And despite a strong personal aversion to mathematics, I found my Mathematics from a Cultural Perspective to be manageable and more applicable to my interests than statistics or calculus.* 99

Study Abroad

Conn places a strong emphasis on the study of foreign languages and cultures, and has a vested interest in incorporating the experiences and expertise of international students into its curriculum. A 2009 recipient of the Paul Simon Award for Campus Internationalization, Conn was recognized for the exceptional opportunities that it provides to its students in terms of international study and research. More than half (fifty-five percent) of Conn students will study abroad at some point during their junior year through affiliated programs in more than fifty countries around the world. Conn also offers a unique study abroad option known as SATA, or Study Away/Teach Away. Through SATA, a small group of Conn students travel with one or two Conn professors to a host institution in a foreign country, living and working together for a semester. While the selection of SATA offerings changes yearly, popular options in the past have included India, Vietnam, South Africa, and Rome.

Interdisciplinary Centers

In addition to a broad range of majors and departments, the college also offers five different interdisciplinary certification programs. Students apply to these certificate programs during their sophomore year, and admission is highly selective. In order to earn certification through these five interdisciplinary centers, students must complete a three-year course of study (combined with their chosen majors and/or minors), a summer internship, and a senior integrative project. The five interdisciplinary centers are the Holleran Center for Community Action and Public Policy, the Toor Cummings Center for International Studies and the Liberal Arts, the Goodwin-Niering Center for the Environment, the Ammerman Center for Arts and Technology, and the Center for the Comparative Study of Race and Ethnicity.

Holleran Center

Holleran Center for Community Action and Public Policy—following Conn's legacy as a "college with a conscience"—is a top producer of Peace Corps and Teach for America inductees, and President Higdon himself served in the Peace Corps. This interdisciplinary center focuses on creating "just and equitable communities through programs that cultivate intellectual and ethical judgment." Students in PICA study human rights issues and health care reform, among other contemporaneous social matters. Recent PICA internships have included organizations such as Rwanda Women's Network; The Fund for

American Studies—AIDS Alliance for Children, Youth and Families; and Rain Forest Action Network.

Toor Cummings Center

Toor Cummings Center for International Studies and the Liberal Arts: Students participating in this certification program (CISLA for short) are required to achieve written and oral proficiency in a foreign language and complete an eight-to-twelve week internship in a foreign country, among other challenges. Members of CISLA are still encouraged to study abroad, and in fact many remain in their host countries to complete their summer internships after the conclusion of the semester. Examples of past foreign internship experiences include learning about the politics of medicine in China.

Goodwin-Niering Center

Goodwin-Niering Center for the Environment: It's no small wonder that Conn recently received a B+ on their environmental score card. The college has had a historical interest in protecting and promoting an environmentally friendly agenda. From the 750-acre arboretum campus to the on-campus Sprout garden, environmental activism is part of a typical Conn student's education. Students in the Goodwing-Niering center build upon this legacy by bringing together the social sciences, humanities, and arts in the service of addressing contemporary ecological issues. Goodwin-Niering students have completed internships with CT Department of Environmental Protection, Assistance and Pollution Prevention Unit/EPA of Boston, Gandoca Sea Turtle Conservation Project WIDECAST, and The Chancellor's Urban Education Leaders Internship Program (UELIP) in Washington, DC.

Ammerman Center

Ammerman Center for Arts and Technology: Students in the Ammerman Center for Arts and Technology (also known at CAT) attain proficiency in various technological mediums, merging them with art forms of the individual's choice through on-campus research, internships, and a senior integrative project. Examples of CAT internships include Lucas Films production internship, *Wine & Spirits* magazine design and post-production internship, Sound Spectrum software design internship, and Arthur Lubetz Architects architectural internship.

Comparative Center

Comparative Center for Race and Ethnicity: The newest of the five interdisciplinary centers, CCSRE is committed to exploring "social, historical, cultural, religious, and political contexts" that have contributed to the creation of the racial and ethnic groups we observe today. Students in the Comparative Center for Race and Ethnicity study issues such as immigration and labor, the legacy of slavery in America, race and gender in the workplace, diasporas, and collective memory and historical traumas.

> **“** *Conn's emphasis on interdisciplinary studies extends well beyond the interdisciplinary certification programs, and even students that choose not to apply to one of the Centers will be called upon to bring together several disciplines consistently throughout their academic careers. During an introductory environmental studies class in my sophomore year, I was required to research forms of sustainable energy, create a lesson plan to teach the concept to third graders, and go into a New London school to put my plan into action. It was a rewarding experience, both for my classmates and the kids that we taught.* **”**

Certificate Programs

In addition to the interdisciplinary centers, Conn offers teaching and museum-studies certifications, earned in addition to the major course of study. Through the teaching certification program, Conn students can graduate fully qualified to teach in primary or secondary schools. The museum-studies certificate program provides training in museum skills and operation, and offers hands-on experience at the campus's Lyman Allyn Art Museum.

Honor Code

The Honor Code is one of the defining features of a Connecticut College education. Chartered in 1922, it encourages responsible citizenship, academic integrity, and self-governance. Incoming students are required to attend a seminar on the Honor Code and sign a matriculation pledge that includes its stipulations. Many professors require students to write out the honor pledge on exams or papers and sign them before turning in their work. In return, students are often entrusted with self-proctored or take-home exams and self-scheduled finals.

> **❝** *As a prospective student, an honor code was something that really appealed to me, and stood out as a point of differentiation. Higher education for me meant taking on a great deal of responsibility—for my academic and social well-being. The honor code really does impact daily life at Conn, and for the most part promotes an atmosphere of intellectual, academic and social integrity.* **❞**

FULBRIGHT SCHOLARSHIPS

Conn's commitment to research, the liberal arts, and the creation of global citizens is demonstrated by the high percentage of graduates that have been awarded Fulbright Scholarships, prestigious grants that provide funding for students to live, teach, and work in a foreign country for a year. The Chronicle of Higher Education has named Conn as one of the top producers of students awarded Fulbrights, with eighteen winners in the past four years. Conn's 2010 winners and projects were

- Lynne Stillings, Fulbright-mtvU research award to study music in Indonesia
- Ivy Chippendale, researching Sicilian food culture, as it relates to HIV-opportunistic illness specific to Palermo, Italy.
- Jacob Daniels, teaching in Vietnam.
- Johanna Gregory, teaching German and an afterschool program focusing on American influences on German pop-culture and slang in Germany.

Conn's 2009 winners and projects were:

- Jessamyn Cox, teaching English and an afterschool program in American Art in Germany.
- Soren Gabrielsen, teaching English at a German school.
- Lucy McAllister, teaching English and publishing an environmental newspaper in the English language in Germany.

SOCIAL LIFE AND ACTIVITIES

As a former tour guide, I can attest to the fact that the number one question prospective students have when visiting campus is, "What's the social life like here?" The answer is: pretty vibrant. A small, accessible campus where ninety-eight percent of students choose to live for all four years makes for a tight-knit community with a plethora of extracurricular and social options. The college provides a variety of social spaces, from the Oasis in Cro (a café with late-night snacks available), to Coffee Grounds (a student-run coffee shop in one of the dorms). SAC, the Student Activities Committee, is devoted to conceiving of and executing a wide variety of on-and-off campus activities and performances to keep students involved and entertained.

Clubs and Activities

There are currently eighty clubs and club sports on campus, all of which are student-led. Examples of current clubs include the Renewable Energy Club, the Feminist Majority, WCNI-FM radio station, Connecticut College Republicans, Hillel,

Human Rights Now, Spectrum (ending homophobia through education and advocacy), Habitat for Humanity, MOBROC (Musicians Organized for Band Rights on Campus), and the campus's six *a cappella* singing groups. Don't see something you like? Students are encouraged to start their own clubs and organizations to better serve the interests and needs of their peers.

Despite the campus's central location between New York and Boston, and its proximity to local hotspots like New London and Mystic, the vast majority of the student body is found on campus on weekends. SAC organizes weekly activities like TNE's (Thursday Night Events) and FNL's (Friday Nights Live) as a way to kick back after a long week of hard work. Thursday Night Events are hosted in each of the dorms throughout the year, and range from screenings of popular movies to cookouts where all are invited. FNL's are free live performances from student-booked bands, held nearly every Friday night in Crozier-Williams Campus Center. In addition to weekly events, annual favorites include Camelympics (yearly inter-dorm competitions in everything from Quidditch to Wii Golf), Festivus (a holiday celebration for the rest of us), and Floralia (an all-day outdoor music festival to celebrate the conclusion of the academic year).

Dorm Life and Housing

There are twenty-three residential halls on campus, all of which are within ten minutes walking distance from classes and require no public transportation. While freshmen live in doubles, triples or quads, the vast majority of upperclassmen live in singles. A variety of theme housing options are available, including Knowlton House, a language dorm; Earth House with eco-friendly living; and Burdick, designated "quiet" housing. There is also apartment-style housing available for upperclassmen.

All dorms have common rooms, where students are invited to lounge, and where freshman seminars take place. Many dorms also have a dining hall, so students don't have to brave the cold winter weather or rain in order to grab a meal with friends.

Athletics

Connecticut College offers twenty-eight Division III varsity teams that compete in the NESCAC (New England Small College Athletic Conference) with schools such as Amherst, Bates, Bowdoin, Colby, Hamilton, Middlebury, Trinity, Tufts, and Williams. Varsity teams participate in sports ranging from basketball to squash to water polo.

Club sports are an attractive option for students that want to participate in athletics, but not at the varsity level. More than seventy-five percent of Conn's student body participates in athletics at the club level, with team offerings including golf, equestrian, sailing (nationally ranked!), and diving. Intramural sports are another option; more than 1,000 students, faculty and staff compete during the four mini-seasons held during the academic year.

Athletic facilities include a newly renovated fitness center, a pool with one- and three-meter diving boards, a 1,000-seat gymnasium, squash and racquetball courts, a turf field, and a waterfront with rowing and sailing docks.

> **“** *Despite the small-school athletics stereotype, Conn students are enthused when it comes to rooting for their fellow Camels. A series of three regulation-sized greens in the middle of campus make athletic games like soccer super-accessible to fans, and enthusiasts can often be seen hanging out of dorm windows, cheering on Conn teams.* **”**

FINANCIAL AID

Connecticut College recognizes the value in making education accessible to all of those that seek it. Forty-five percent of Connecticut College students receive more than $27.5 million dollars in need-based aid per year. Eighty-five percent of this financial aid budget is in the form of grants—an average of $26,700 from Conn)—money that does not need to be paid back. Conn also offers work-study jobs in many different departments on campus.

For more information, contact the Admissions office or go to *http://finaid. conncoll.edu/*

GRADUATES

Even after graduation, Conn students are, well, CONN-ected to the school, whether it be through alumni giving, networking and internship programs, or visits back to campus for Fall Weekend. While some might see smaller schools—and therefore smaller alumni bodies—as a disadvantage, my personal experience has been a positive one. The intimate community that Conn fosters makes for alumni that have likely shared activities, classes, and even beloved professors and staff members. These serve as important building blocks for fostering and nurturing effective networking relationships.

- Tim Armstrong '93, AOL Chair and CEO
- Jim Berrien '74, Mother Nature Network, President and Chief Operating Officer, Chair of the College Board of Trustees
- Ted Chapin '72, Rodgers and Hammerstein Organization, President/Executive Director
- Peggy Charren '49, Founder, Action for Children's Television
- Charles Chun '90, Actor
- Karen Church '90, CBS Television, Vice President for Talent and Casting
- Clap Your Hands Say Yeah, Alec Ounsworth '00, Lee Sargent '00, Robbie Guertin '02, Tyler Sargent '00, and Sean Greenhalgh '02, Musicians
- Michael Collier '76, Poet, Director of the Bread Loaf Writers' Conference at Middlebury College
- Sloan Crosley '00, Writer and Essayist
- Anita DeFrantz '74, Olympic Medalist, Rowing; Vice President of the International Olympic Committee
- David Dorfman '81, Dancer, Professor of Dance at Connecticut College
- Lee Eisenberg '99, Television Screenwriter (*The Office*)
- Vincent Farrell '96, Spike TV, Director of Production
- Sean Fine '96, Sundance Award-Winning Documentary Filmmaker, Oscar Nominee (*War/Dance*)
- David Foster '77, Director of the Harvard Forest
- Susan Froshauer '74, Rib-X Pharmaceuticals, President and CEO
- Marie L. Garibaldi '56, First Woman to Serve on the New Jersey Supreme Court
- Vance Gilbert '79, Musician
- Joshua Green '94, Senior Editor, *The Atlantic Monthly*
- Amy Gross '63, *O, The Oprah Magazine*, Editor-in-Chief, 2000–2008
- David Gross '88, Commissioner of the Major League Lacrosse
- Agnes Gund '60, Museum of Modern Art, President Emerita
- Dorcas Hardy '68, Commissioner of the Social Security Administration 1986–1989
- David Haussler '77, University of California-Santa Cruz, Director of the Center for Biomolecular Science and Engineering
- Bruce Hoffman '76, Terrorism Expert
- Judy Irving '68, Emmy Award and Sundance-Winning Filmmaker
- Lashawn R. Jefferson '88, Human Rights Watch, Former Executive Director, Women's Rights Division
- Drew Ketterer '71, Attorney General, Maine, 1995–2000
- Barbara Shattuck Kohn '72, Principal, Shattuck Hammond and Partners, and former Chair of the College Board of Trustees
- Susan Kronick '73, Federated Department Stores, Vice Chair
- Jay Lauf '86, Publisher, *The Atlantic*
- Linda Lear '62, Author, Environmentalist
- Andre Lee '93, Film Producer
- Trish May '75, Venture Philanthropist; Athena Partners, Founder and CEO
- Suzi Oppenheimer '56, New York State Senator
- Leland Orser '82, Actor
- Estelle Parsons '49, Academy Award-Winning Actor
- Mary Lake Polan '65, Stanford University School of Medicine, Chair and Professor Emeritus, Department of Gynecology and Obstetrics

- Christof Putzel '01, Broadcast Journalist, Winner of Student Academy Award for AIDS Documentary, *Left Behind*
- Luanne Rice '77, Novelist (*Sandcastles, Beach Girls*)
- Peter Som '93, Fashion Designer
- A.B. Stoddard '89, Journalist, Political Commentator
- Sally Susman '84, Pfizer Inc., Senior Vice President and Chief Communications Officer
- Susan Thomases '65, Attorney, Former Presidential Adviser
- Ellen R. Vitetta '64, University of Texas Southwestern Medical Center, Director of the Cancer Immunobiology Center
- Jessie Vogelson '96, Film and Television Producer (*No End in Sight*)
- Kevin Wade '76, Screenwriter (*Working Girl, Meet Joe Black*)
- Patricia Wald '48, Federal Judge, retired; Member of the International Criminal Tribunal for the Former Yugoslavia and Member of the Iraq Intelligence Commission
- Marion Rockefeller Weber '60, Philanthropist and Initiator of the Flow Fund Circle
- Kimberly Williams '90, NFL Network, Chief Operating Officer
- Tim Young '92, Olympic Medalist, Sculling

CELS

Alumni also play a key role in the Career Enhancing Life Skills program. The CELS funded internship program is a unique opportunity for a small liberal arts college, but one that provides incalculable benefits for undergrads. After taking a series of seminars covering topics from how to write a cover letter to how to interview, Conn students become eligible for a grant of up to $3,000 to help offset the costs of an unpaid internship between the summer of their junior and senior years.

CELS counselors help students find and apply to these internships, many of which are furnished by Camel alumni across the United States and the world. As a part of the CELS training, students are encouraged to write to alumni, to network, and ask for advice on future careers. Alumni are responsive and interested, and many approach the CELS office year after year with internship or job leads, or to come back to campus to speak to students.

❝ *When I first toured Conn, my parents breathed a sigh of relief at the emphasis Conn places on career goals. My internship with a travel magazine was an invaluable experience, and led to employment after graduation with the same company.* ❞

Just as there is no "typical" Conn student, there is no typical "Conn" experience. The range of academic, extracurricular, and social offerings make for a community with a diverse range of interests and expertise. Camel alumni are found all across the world, engaging in professions that range from acting to writing to dance to politics. Despite these varied passions and professions, Conn students –former and current—all have one thing in common: they attended an institution with a vested interest in helping its students discover what they love, and help them turn it into a career. Conn is a place for exploration, and for making career dreams into a reality.

> ❝ *When I entered college, I didn't know where life would be taking me. I hoped, though, that I would leave a better educated, more well-rounded, and "effective" citizen, ready to take on the working world. My professors, mentors, and the CELS office helped me to accomplish that and more.* ❞

❑ *Arielle Shipper, B.A.*

**Cooper Union for the Advancement
of Science and Art**
New York City, NY 10003

(212) 353-4120
Fax: (212) 353-4342

Website: *http://www.cooper.edu*

 Enrollment

Full-time ❑ women: 367
❑ men: 601

Part-time ❑ women: 4
❑ men: 27

INTRODUCING COOPER UNION

The founder of Cooper Union, Peter Cooper, had a vision to offer an education that was "as free as water and air." Established in 1859, Cooper Union is the "only private, full-scholarship college of higher learning in the United States dedicated exclusively to preparing students for the professions of architecture, art, and engineering."

Cooper Union sits in the heart of the East Village of Manhattan and offers more than an exceptional classroom education to its students of art, architecture, and engineering. The institution's campus *is* New York City, a city alive with the sounds, smells, and events of the culturally, ethnically, and racially diverse population. It is not uncommon for a professor's assignments to extend outside of the classroom and incorporate different aspects of the city. During my freshman year, the assignment for my engineering design class was to design an effective system to allow for subway transfers on one subway line in lower Manhattan. Architecture students are often given assignments of photographing buildings and bridges for class. Art students frequently take class trips to view different installations in the plethora of great museums, studios, and galleries of Manhattan.

From helping in local soup kitchens, to the sorority's annual scavenger hunt, to dinners in Chinatown, the various student organizations also offer students the chance to experience New York City. Cooper students become a part of New York City by giving back to their community; it's not uncommon for a student organization to sponsor a volunteer outing or a food/toy drive to benefit New York City residents. After September 11, students organized a "penny drive," which raised over five hundred dollars for the local fire company. Aside from having its students explore the city, Cooper brings the city's culture to the school with various lectures in its historic Great Hall and Wollman Auditorium, and art and architecture exhibits in its galleries.

> **❝** *As a high school senior, I was told by my guidance counselor to contact the deans and department chairpersons of schools that I would like to attend. I contacted quite a few schools, and I must admit that the attention I received from the chair at Cooper was exceptional. Since I had swimming practice after school, the chair set aside time at night to speak with me. I had mentioned that I wanted to visit the grounds over the weekend and the chair called me back a few days later to give me instructions on obtaining access to the buildings and gave me his home number in case I had any trouble entering the buildings. Early the following week, he called to ask me what I thought and to see if I had any questions. Consistently throughout our conversations, I could tell that the chair really cared about the students and the institution.* **❞**

The education in each of the three schools—Engineering, Architecture, and Art—is stellar. The professors succeed in bringing out each student's creative problem-solving abilities in different ways. At Cooper, it wasn't only what I learned, but how I learned, and how I learned to think and analyze. The professors and administration actively reach out to their students. It's not uncommon for a professor to help a student in the evening or for faculty to attend a basketball game or a student performance. After my four years, I realize that the professors and administration really care; they are an integral part of the Cooper community.

The Cooper community is quite diverse; the students represent different ethnic, religious, racial, socioeconomic, and geographical backgrounds. This diversity is represented in the multitude of clubs and organizations that represent the student body's various interests and range from ethnic and religious clubs, to professional societies, to sports, to special interest groups.

Peter Cooper's legacy lives on as Cooper Union continues to provide students with the unique opportunity of attending a distinguished full-scholarship small institution with all the benefits of the wonderful big city!

ADMISSIONS REQUIREMENTS

Admission to Cooper Union is highly selective. Most students, albeit bright, intelligent, and talented, when asked why they think they were accepted, will most likely say they fell through the cracks! However, deep down, we Cooper students know that each one of us was hand-picked for our special talents in our chosen field. The key to being accepted to Cooper Union is showing that you posses the skills and qualities necessary to excel in this first-rate academic institution, skills and qualities that range from talent, to intelligence, to motivation, to dedication.

Admissions requirements for each school vary; however, all applicants must take the SAT or ACT, complete sixteen to eighteen high school academic credits, and graduate from an accredited secondary school. In addition, engineering applicants must take SAT Subject Tests in mathematics I or II and physics or chemistry. Applicants must also complete an application with essays that enable them to describe themselves to the admissions committee. Art and Architecture applicants must complete a home test that shows their unique abilities to the admissions committee.

Cooper Union is comprised of these schools—Engineering (The Albert Nerken School of Engineering), Architecture (The Irwin S. Chanin School of Architecture), and Art, each offering an unparalleled undergraduate education. Cooper Union grants the following bachelors degrees: B.S., B. Arch., B.E., and B.F.A. Architecture and the engineering schools also offer graduate programs. The engineering school has B.E. degrees in chemical, civil, electrical and mechanical, as well as a B.S. in general engineering. The engineering school offers a Masters of Engineering Degree and the architecture school offers a Masters of Architecture II degree. The art school offers a B.F.A., which provides both a general visual arts education and a focused preparation for future artists and designers. The architecture school offers a five-year program leading to the Bachelor of Architecture, the first professional accredited degree. Cooper Union's engineering school is ABET-accredited, the architecture school is NAAB-accredited, the art school is NASAD-accredited. It is quite a challenge, although not impossible to switch between schools so you should choose wisely, and know that whichever school you study in, you are getting a first-rate education.

Faculty

Professors at Cooper are scholars in their field who have graduated from excellent institutions worldwide—some even graduated from Cooper themselves! Aside from their academic merit, professors care about their students. Their relationship with students motivates and drives the students. For the most part, professors are easily accessible and ready to help. It's not uncommon to see professors in the halls on a weekend, or to e-mail a professor a question on a weekend and get a quick response. In fact, I was visiting my architecture roommate in the "studio" where all architecture students "live" during their Cooper years, and walking through this large room, with desk upon desk upon desk, was one of their professors ready to help if anyone needed it. One of my professors agreed to hold early morning study sessions so we could get a head start before the lecture, and hold study sessions in the evening too, so we could review and ask questions. Although this was not my best or favorite subject, his willingness to help motivated me to continue studying.

Fellow Students

Student relationships with one another also drive motivation. Due to small class sizes, students become very fond of their classmates; they are usually their study partners, as well as their best friends. As a freshman, I was told, the only way to survive at Cooper is to work with others—and that was true. So, I give that same advice to freshmen. Students at Cooper want to help each other. It's rare to find a student who will not share notes or help. After being sick, I returned to school to find that a classmate had already photocopied the class notes and put them in my mailbox. That's camaraderie! I fondly remember my study sessions with my peers as we worked hard trying to solve problem sets. Today they are my closest friends.

> 66 *Throughout the three schools class sizes are extremely small, which helps foster the unique teacher-student relationship. Additionally, classes rarely have TAs, and if a class has a TA, the TA is only there to complement the professor and help. In my years at Cooper, I had only one TA!* 99

Core Classes

Each school sets its own core classes for each major; the humanities department also has a set of core liberal arts classes required for each student, regardless of the major. These classes include literature classes and history classes. Additionally, students are required to take a certain number of elective humanities and social science courses. For some majors, humanities elective credit may be fulfilled with a language course. Cooper Union offers access to a wide range of language courses from the traditional French and Spanish to the more unusual Japanese or Hindi. Students may also participate in courses at the New School University. Although Cooper is not a liberal arts institution, it places great emphasis on the humanities and social science courses, and hires professors from prestigious liberal arts institutions to teach classes.

In the engineering school certain core classes are required for every engineering student, including: physics, chemistry, physical chemistry, calculus, probability, differential equations, computer programming, and design principles. Students are given the opportunity to perform research in such areas as chemistry, environmental engineering, and biomedical engineering. Art students must be proficient in such courses as drawing, color, two-dimensional design, and three-dimensional design. Architecture students are required to take such courses as design structures, mathematics, and physics. For some majors, electives within the major are required. Study abroad programs for summer and semester study are available for more majors and provide a unique and interesting way to continue studying your own discipline while exploring a new culture.

Graduation Requirements

The requirements for graduation in each school vary. Art students must complete 130 credits, including 41 liberal arts credits. The five-year architecture program requires 160 credits, with about 40 in liberal arts and electives. The engineering requirements include 135 credits, with 24 credits in liberal arts and social sciences.

Since Cooper prides itself on a fair education for all, there is no grade inflation. If you graduate above 3.0, you are definitely in the minority. After a few tests, where the class average is only forty or fifty percent, you quickly learn that it's not the grade on your exam that matters, but what you will be able to accomplish with what you've learned when you are faced with challenges outside of the classroom setting.

Senior Project

Each school requires a senior project. Engineering senior projects range from designing an ethylene plant to designing a car, and anything and everything in between. Some of these projects are entered in competitions, and many receive recognition. Each art student is given the chance to display his or her work in a senior show. Students present work ranging from paintings, to drawings, to movies. In their fifth year, architecture students enroll in their senior thesis class, which prepares them for work after graduation.

With small classes, friendly helpful professors, plenty of research opportunities, and bright and helpful peers, the opportunities for academic growth are endless.

SOCIAL LIFE AND ACTIVITIES

It's true that the workload at Cooper is challenging, but Cooper students do know how to have a good time. I can honestly say I was never bored at Cooper—between academics, campus organizations, and exploring Manhattan, every minute was occupied.

Housing

The Cooper residence hall, home mostly to freshmen, with a few upperclassmen, gives students their first opportunity to build a community at Cooper. Friendships start in the dorm and last a lifetime. Housing is apartment-style with three-, four-, and five-person apartments. The dormitory has a recreation room where many organizations hold meetings, a study lounge with the Hall and Resident Assistant offices, and a laundry room. Ethernet access is available in all the apartments. Resident Assistants with extensive training are available in an emergency, or simply to talk. During the first few weeks of the semester, RAs help bring out the community within the dorm, and try to foster that throughout the year with various activities and meetings.

Like a rite of passage, after the first year, most students move out of the dorm into apartments in the surrounding areas. Some students venture into Brooklyn or Queens. Living off campus affords students freedom, but not without many new added responsibilities. Having your own apartment, paying rent, electricity, and phone bills can be quite an adventure, and a lot of responsibility too! But, it is a growing experience, preparing oneself for the "real world."

Activities and Organizations

Campus events and activities range from lectures, to plays, to gallery openings, to Greek parties sponsored by the various student organizations. Student organizations and clubs range from student government, to literary and artistic groups, to religious and cultural organizations, to Greek societies, to professional societies.

Every year, the South Asia Society, along with other ethnic and cultural clubs, organizes the Annual Culture Show, where student groups perform pieces representing world cultures, and there is also an international food fair, where students can sample food from different parts of the world. Donations collected during this event are given to UNICEF. South Asia Society also holds a Diwali Celebration for the Indian New Year with traditional Indian food and music. Hispanic Heritage night is a popular event sponsored by the Society of Hispanic Professional Engineers and !Enclave! Café Night, a relaxing night of varied performances from Cooperean and city residents, is sponsored by the Black Student Union. Also popular is the Soulsa Dance sponsored by Enclave and the Black Student Union, with Caribbean and Latin food on the menu. Kesher-Hillel, the Jewish Student Union, also draws a large crowd as it holds its semiannual Shabbaton to celebrate the Jewish Sabbath.

From the beginning of the year, many students look forward to Dean Baker's annual ski trip at Mount Sutton in Canada. Over a hundred students and their friends cross over the American-Canadian border for a week of skiing and fun. This trip was so popular that the dean started an alumni trip during President's Day weekend.

The February Celebration is also a favorite among Cooper Students. It's the annual semiformal where students get the chance to dress up and dance the night away with their friends.

The Cooper Dramatic Society works hard to put on a performance each semester.

Greek societies usually provide a social outlet for students. There are two national fraternities—Zeta Psi and Tau Delta Phi—and one local sorority—Delta Eta—on campus.

Usually, there is one Greek-sponsored party on campus per semester. But the Greeks tend to throw off-campus parties too. Greeks sponsor events such as TechnoBowling, Chilli Night, and Lipsync.

Students appreciate the larger community and do give back to the community with penny drives, fund-raising activities, and various volunteer opportunities.

Athletics

Cooper students play as hard on the field as they work in the labs and studios. As Dean Baker puts it, Cooper students have: "No gym. No courts. No fields. No pool. No time. No money. No EXCUSES!!" Yet, year after year, Cooper receives many accolades for its athletic programs; Cooper teams and players have been featured in the *New York Times*, ESPN Magazine's *The List*, *Glamour* Magazine, and on HBO's "Real Sports with Bryant Gumbel." Last year, three of Cooper Union's sports teams won Hudson Valley Atlantic championships.

There are both intercollegiate and intramural sports. There are five intercollegiate men's teams and two women's teams. There are twelve intramural coed teams. The basketball team makes its annual trip to California to play Caltech. Some home basketball games honor a graduating senior, and these games are followed by food and festivities. The soccer and tennis teams also draw small crowds of cheering fans.

> ❝ *I wouldn't want to be anywhere else. I wouldn't be able to do all the things I've done at another place.* ❞

Off Campus

Cooper Union is located in the best city—a city that never sleeps. Off-campus adventures can be exciting. The opportunities to explore New York are endless; trips to Chinatown or Little Italy can be culturally stimulating. Additionally, students frequent coffee shops, restaurants, museums, galleries, bookstores, movies, theaters, and concerts. There are farmers markets in Union Square, and street performers in Washington Square Park. Street fairs line the streets throughout Manhattan during the spring, fall, and summer. And, with New York's public transportation, you can be anywhere in just a few minutes.

FINANCIAL AID

Cooper Union is a private institution; however, thanks to Peter Cooper who believed education should be as "free as water and air," Cooper is tuition free. All U.S. resident students are admitted under a full scholarship, which covers the $35,000 tuition. However, there is an additional student fee that must be paid each semester. Students must also pay for housing (dorms or off-campus apartments), food, books, and expenses.

The financial aid counselors really help to ensure that students receive the most aid possible so that they can attend Cooper without having to worry about how they will finance their education. In fact, almost half of the incoming freshmen receive financial aid, and a substantial number of upperclassman receive aid. The average financial package is approximately $3,500. (Remember, each student also receives a full-tuition scholarship.) Aid is offered in the form of scholarships and need-based grants, loans, and work-study programs. Approximately one-quarter of the students work part time on campus, and some also work off campus. The average financial indebtedness of the 2009 graduate was about $12,717.

GRADUATES

Students graduating from each school pursue different paths, but what's true for graduates from any major at Cooper is that upon graduation, they have attained the necessary skills in their field to conquer anything the future may bring. Cooper provides the basis for which all future possibilities are endless. Some students continue their education at Cooper and pursue a master's degree. Others enroll in other prestigious universities to pursue higher-level graduate education in the arts or engineering fields. Others enter medical school or law school. Many return to school for M.B.A.s after working for a few years. Some students begin applying their newly acquired skills and find jobs in the "real world."

Cooper has a career counseling department actively helping students find jobs upon graduation. Also, the Career Services department helps underclassmen find summer internships and school-year internships; these internships will be valuable assets in preparing students for work upon graduation. During the 2009–2010 academic year, over 100 companies recruited on campus and others recruited through the school's on-line recruiting system. Alumni are also active in the recruiting process. Many students find jobs through a network of alumni who return and recruit graduates. Alumni return each year to help in the annual Networking Dinner and Mock Interview nights sponsored by various professional societies and Career Services. Career Services sponsors the ever-popular Etiquette Lunch, where graduating seniors learn the art of interviewing while eating.

Those who do not find jobs right away may travel and explore new and exciting areas, others apply and receive Fulbright scholarships, thirty-one since

2001. Some join various organizations helping others. One engineering student in my graduating class went to teach English in Japan.

As I said, for Cooper graduates the possibilities are endless.

SUMMING UP

Cooper Union in the heart of Manhattan's East Village is a small school with a community atmosphere. Its excellent teachers and wonderful opportunities provide its students with an unrivaled education. Its classrooms, labs, and studios are filled with top students who come to develop into top scholars in their fields, without compromising their social science and humanities education. In addition to the education, students are exposed to new and exciting people, cultures, events, activities, and experiences, which enable them to grow and learn socially. After graduation, the Cooper connection continues to help its alumni grow and develop in their major; the strong Cooper Union network of alumni helps students find job placement in the engineering, art, and architecture circles. As you can see, the name Cooper Union is the key to success in the art, architecture, and engineering worlds.

❑ *Dalia Levine, B.E., Ch.E.*

Photo by Charles Harrington

Cornell University
Ithaca, NY 14853

(607) 255-5241

E-mail: *admissions@cornell.edu*
Website: *http://admissions.cornell.edu*

 Enrollment

Full-time ❑ women: 7,019
❑ men: 6,916

INTRODUCING CORNELL

When the name Cornell comes up in conversation, people who've been there usually exclaim, "It's so pretty there," and after a visit, it is easy to agree. Cornell sits on founder Ezra Cornell's farm, overlooking Cayuga Lake, in the Finger Lakes region of New York State. The campus covers 745 acres with classic ivy-covered buildings and contemporary research labs. Ezra Cornell's educational philosophy, "I would found an institution where any person can find instruction in any study," is the guiding force throughout campus where any person is free to found any organization, play any sport, practice any religion, and do just about anything they want without too much trouble.

Cornell students are proud of the fact that the university has been open to all kinds of students from the beginning. By 1870, Cornell was the first major university in the eastern United States to admit women. And Cornell led the way in welcoming students of varying ethnic backgrounds as well. The nation's first African-American fraternity, Alpha Phi Alpha, was founded at Cornell in 1906. In addition, Ezra Cornell was determined that Cornell graduates would enter the world both well educated and useful, accounting for the university's emphasis on a superb liberal arts program and equally outstanding applied programs in areas such as engineering, business, and agriculture.

> 66 *Whenever my schedule got way too crazy and it seemed like I wasn't going to make it, I took the time to put everything in perspective. Sitting at the top of Libe Slope and taking in the breathtaking view of Ithaca and Cayuga Lake, or standing in the middle of the suspension bridge and jumping up and down to make the whole thing shake while watching water cascade over the falls, was the best cure for anything that was getting you down.* 99

In fact, Cornell offers seven undergraduate colleges: the College of Agriculture and Life Sciences; the College of Architecture, Art and Planning; the College of Arts and Sciences (the traditional liberal arts college); the College of Engineering; the School of Hotel Administration; the College of Human Ecology; and the School of Industrial and Labor Relations. Students in all the colleges come from a wide range of backgrounds, and from all fifty states and more than 120 countries. It's a high energy, eclectic mix that gives Cornell its distinctive flavor.

Libraries

The twenty on-campus libraries provide the best places for studying in whatever kind of atmosphere suits you best. The two most popular libraries are Mann and Uris. Mann is located on the Ag quad and is most frequented by students in Ag and Hum Ec. Uris Library is located on the corner of the Arts quad looking down the hill, affectionately known as Libe Slope. Uris can get pretty social at night, but within the library, the

A.D. White Library, with its balconies and alcoves, provides a classic academic aura for studying. It's nice and quiet studying among the books in the stacks. The best-known spots in Uris are the Fishbowl and the Cocktail Lounge where wine isn't served, but wines may be studied.

ADMISSIONS REQUIREMENTS

Here's what it boils down to: If Cornell accepts you, you can make it. Every fall, thousands of applications pour into the Admissions Office. Over 30,000 students apply for admission to one of the seven colleges. The Undergraduate Admissions Office collects and keeps track of all the applications and, once they are complete, funnels the applications to admissions offices in each college for decisions. The Common Application and short Cornell Supplement are used in all the colleges (interviews and portfolios are required for some). An applicant's first encounter with the uniqueness of Cornell's colleges is at this stage when applicants must decide which of the colleges to apply to. For example, one can major in biology in both the College of Agriculture and Life Sciences and in the College of Arts and Sciences. In the Ag school, bio focuses on the natural world. In Arts and Sciences, biology can be studied with anything from classic civilizations to anthropology to linguistics. (Don't worry—internal transfer between schools is possible if you decide you don't want to study biology and want to try meteorology or theater arts instead.)

CORNELL LIBRARY TREASURES

- A copy of the Gettysburg Address handwritten by Abraham Lincoln in 1864, one of only five copies in existence.
- A vellum copy of the 13th Amendment to the United States Constitution, signed by Abraham Lincoln and members of the Senate and House who voted for the joint resolution, one of three copies known to exist.
- A complete set of the Shakespeare folios.
- The "Jade Book" of the second Manchu emperor K'ang-hsi (reigned 1662–1722), inscribed in Chinese and Manchu in blue and gold on ten tablets of solid jade.
- A witchcraft collection containing 3,000 books and manuscripts, one of the most comprehensive collections available for the study of European witchcraft.
- Five manuscript volumes of the famous Chinese fifth-century encyclopedia, *Yung-lo ta-tien*.
- Cornell's Human Sexuality Collection, established in 1988 to record and preserve the cultural and political aspects of sexuality, one of the few collections of its kind.

> *The transition to Cornell was not easy. I knew that my classes were going to be much more difficult than in high school. For the first semester, I struggled a little and did my best. A number of my friends also found the course work challenging, but we stuck together and gave each other confidence. The foundation of support has led to great friendships, and these friendships are what make the Cornell experience so great.*

Requirements for admission vary by school and program, but basically excelling in any college preparatory course load in high school is a step in the right direction. The SAT or ACT with writing is required. SAT Subject tests are specified by college and division. AP credits are accepted but will count differently depending on your major and score, so don't think you're home free just because you got a 5. Applicants who go to small high schools that don't offer AP classes shouldn't be concerned about being at a disadvantage. Some freshmen arrive with fifteen to twenty AP credits under their belt, and yes, they will probably be able to start out in higher level classes or maybe finish a semester early, but the majority of students have only a few, if any, AP credits and still graduate in good standing after four years.

Important Factors

One of the best things about Cornell admissions is that they look beyond the numbers. Special talents and leadership records are just as important as your SAT scores. Three percent of incoming students with an exemplary leadership record in high school are selected as Meinig Family Cornell National Scholars. Students who held jobs during their high school academic year may be selected as Cornell Tradition Fellows, an undergraduate loan replacement fellowship. In order to continue to be a Fellow, students must work, keep a certain GPA, and be involved in public service activities. Upperclassmen can apply to be Cornell Tradition Fellows in the spring of each year. The Hunter R. Rawlings III Cornell Presidential Research Scholars program is designed to recognize, reward, and encourage students who have demonstrated academic excellence and true intellectual curiosity. These scholars are assigned a faculty mentor in freshman year and are given special opportunities (some paid) to participate in research as undergraduates.

Interviews

Regardless of whether the college you're applying to at Cornell requires an interview or not, the Cornell Alumni Admissions Ambassador Network offers the opportunity for applicants to meet with alumni in their local area for a casual exchange of information.

The most important thing to remember is that if you get accepted to Cornell, the people who read the application believe you can make it and be a success. There's no need to change from the person you were in high school. Your record there led admissions officers to believe you would be a success at Cornell, too.

ACADEMIC LIFE

Regardless of which undergraduate college you technically enrolled in, you can take classes from every school on campus, and there's no need to search in order to find the popular ones. The legendary Psych 101, incessantly discussed in tours and information sessions, is held in Cornell's biggest classroom, Bailey Hall, with a mere 2,000 of your closest friends. Despite its size, Psych 101 is educational and interesting. Offered only in the fall, one class in the semester is a live demonstration of a psychic telling one student everything about his or her life.

> 66 *When I took Psych 101, Professors Bem and Maas selected Mindy from the class for their demonstration. Four years later, I would still hear people say, "There's that girl from Psych 101." In a class of 2,000, who says you don't get to know your classmates? Interested? It's offered Mondays, Wednesdays, and Fridays at 10:10 A.M.* 99

Other popular classes, though smaller in size, are Human Sexuality offered in Human Ecology, and Introduction to Wines in the Hotel School, which once a week offers an hour of tasting wines from around the world.

Class Size

Cornell is big, and you have to accept this fact to be happy there. Classes vary in size, but in freshman year, you will most likely have a couple of classes with at least 200 people. Depending on what you are studying though, it is possible that you may never have a class bigger than fifty people. Popular intro classes, such as Government 111 and Chemistry 207, can easily have 400 or more students in the class, but, as you move into upper-level classes, the numbers get much smaller. Language classes and first-year writing seminars usually aren't much bigger than twenty students per section. Most large intro classes will also have a mandatory discussion section held during the week, led by a TA (teaching assistant) or the professor, with many fewer students, rarely over twenty-five per section. These sections provide students with a time to ask questions and get to know the teaching assistants. TAs can be very helpful and are usually very willing to meet with and help the students in their section. Being nice to your TA will come in very handy when you need help on papers or problem sets. Faculty are accessible and friendly too if you make the effort to get to know them. Don't be shy!

Degrees

There are seemingly, to quote late Cornell professor Carl Sagan, "billions and billions" of programs of study at Cornell. There are more than eighty majors at the university, and you can graduate with a B.A., a B.S., a B. Arch, or a B.F.A., or any combination. Bachelor's degrees are awarded to any field from animal science, or operations research, to ancient civilizations, textiles and apparel, and mechanical engineering. The largest enrollments (by major) are in biological sciences, applied economics, and engineering.

> 66 Believe it—you can major in anything and any combination of things you can find. Friends of mine had majors in classic civilizations, historic preservation, and linguistics and psychology. 99

Clearly, there are no boundaries to what you can study, even if it includes subjects that have never been put together as a formal major or your areas of interest are in more than one at Cornell's colleges. That's one of the benefits of going to a school with a great deal of academic flexibility.

Required Courses

As for what's actually required of all students, the list is pretty short. Entering freshmen must take and pass the swim test, take two semesters of first-year writing seminars and two semesters of physical education. Now, there's no need to worry about these three requirements in the least. Seminars offered across the curriculum by the award-winning Knight Institute for Writing in the Disciplines are as varied as majors. Writing seminars are offered on such topics as:

- African-American Women Writers
- The Personal Essay
- From Fairy Tales to the Uncanny
- Contemporary Moral Problems

There are just as many phys ed classes to choose from to fulfill that requirement including the (extremely popular) ballroom dancing, tae kwon do, rock climbing, intro to ice skating, badminton, squash, Swedish massage, yoga, scuba diving, running, skiing, golf, and riflery.

Study Away

Getting tired of being on campus but think transferring is a little too drastic? It's easy to study somewhere off campus and still graduate on time. You can study abroad in more than fifty countries, such as Spain, Sweden, Australia, and France. Engineers can take part in a co-op program and spend a semester and a summer earning some serious money in real-world work experiences. The Cornell in Washington program gives students in any college the opportunity to live inside the beltway at Dupont Circle in the Cornell Center (a four-story building with three floors of apartments and one of classrooms and a computer lab), take classes with Cornell faculty and visiting professors, and have an internship in the nation's capital. Urban Semester gives students a chance to spend a semester in New York City working and studying.

You can also spend a summer at Shoals Marine Lab on Appledore Island off the coast of Maine. Undergraduate students can earn a semester's worth of credit studying topics related to marine biology and ocean ecology, and participate in research projects—sometimes on the station's research vessel. Adventurous Cornellians also take part in archeological digs around the world and more locally in New York State.

Undergraduate Research

Cornell is one of the top research universities in the world, and hundreds of undergraduates participate in faculty research projects every year. It isn't hard to find a project. It can be as easy as talking with a faculty member after class about getting involved in his or her research. There are also structured undergraduate research programs on campus, such as the Hughes Program in biology or the research teams (such as Robocup) in the

- Cornell's chimes, dedicated in 1868, were the first to peal over an American university.
- Cornell awarded the first Bachelor of Veterinary Science in 1871, the first Doctor of Veterinary Medicine in the United States in 1876, and the first DVM degree to a woman in 1910.
- Cornell granted the first Bachelor of Mechanical Engineering degree in 1871.
- Cornell appointed the first professor of American history in an American university in 1881.
- Cornell endowed the nation's first chair in American literature.
- Sigma Xi, the national science honor society, was founded at Cornell in 1886.
- Alpha Phi Alpha, the nation's first black fraternity, was founded at Cornell in 1906.
- Cornell offered the first college-level course in hotel administration in 1922.
- Cornell established the first four-year school of Industrial and Labor Relations in 1945.
- Cornell developed CUinfo, the first campus-wide information system, in 1986.

College of Engineering. Some students even get their names on research papers and present their results at conferences. It's a wonderful way to meet professors and other student researchers, and it looks great on your résumé!

SOCIAL LIFE AND ACTIVITIES

Housing

All freshmen have a similar first-year housing experience, living together in residence halls located on North Campus. Some returning students elect to live in residence halls on West Campus, but about half of Cornell students live off campus in sorority or fraternity houses, in Collegetown, and in the surrounding areas. There are a variety of off-campus options to choose from, from high-tech (and expensive) apartment buildings to three-story Victorian houses with six apartments that include oddities like oval windows, sinks in hallways, and sit-down showers.

Parties

The university offers a lot of music, theater, dance, and films, but if you're looking for other social activities, trust me, you'll find plenty. As each weekend approaches, one is faced with an immense variety of choices. Since one-third of the campus is Greek (fraternities and sororities), there are always a collection of fraternity open parties, crush parties, after hours, and formals to attend. Fraternities are housed both off and on campus in just about every direction, so there is bound to be one nearby. Many other options exist outside of the Greek realm and cater to a variety of interests. Cornell supports more than 600 student organizations and clubs—and if you can't find one you want to join, you can create your own! In addition, Cornell's extensive intramural sports programs will help you let off steam in competitions involving everything from giant slalom skiing to inner tube water polo.

Campus Activities

Just glance at the *Daily Sun* on Friday and you'll find a plethora of activities going on all over campus. On any given weekend, you can attend a concert, a varsity sporting event, intramural games, an ethnic festival, or listen to a speaker. Because of its size, there are always lots of people at whatever event you attend, and you'll definitely meet someone with interests similar to yours:

- Diwali, a celebration of the Indian New Year—"the festival of lights"—takes place every fall. It's put on by the Society for India and the Cornell Indian Association and features traditional Indian food and a performance of skits, traditional and modern dance, and instrumental music.
- In the spring, the Festival of Black Gospel brings famous gospel singers to campus and unites regional gospel choirs, like Cornell's own Pamoja Ni, in song and spirit.
- One weekend every year, Lynah Rink is packed solid to watch the hockey team play their biggest rival, Harvard. Smuggled in under jackets and in shirts, fish of every size and color as well as some frozen fish sticks and lobsters become airborne when Harvard players skate onto the ice.
- Some years, Bailey Hall is packed with over 1,800 *a cappella* fans for Fall Tonic, the all-male Hangovers annual concert. Visiting *a cappella* groups who perform during Fall Tonic are undoubtedly amazed at the number of people at the concert and often mention that there are more people in the audience than students at their own school. We are dedicated fans and strongly support the groups or teams we enjoy!

Volunteering

Volunteerism runs like a raging river through Cornell as thousands of Cornellians find extra time in their crazy schedules to help others. The Public Service Center, mobilizes over 3,000 student volunteers each year in both one-time and ongoing projects. That's over 170,000 hours each year of service to the community. During Into the Streets, a national day of service, there are close to 500 volunteers who work with thirty local agencies. On that one Saturday alone, Cornellians do over 2,500 hours of service in the greater Ithaca area. Cornell's record of public service is one of the things that Cornell's president admires most about the university.

Movies

In the evening and weekends, Cornell Cinema offers at least four different films, playing either in the theater at the Straight (Willard Straight Hall, the student union) or in Uris Auditorium. Both are on central campus and are a short walk from any dorm or apartment. The movies can be classics that you never thought you would see on the big screen, movies that have just left theaters across the country, and foreign films. Every so often, the student film classes show their own interesting (and often experimental) work.

Sports

Sports at Cornell may not draw the television coverage of the Big Ten, but there are many teams doing an excellent job representing Cornell, and you have to admire student athletes for their hard work and hectic schedules. Hockey tickets are the only tickets that aren't free to students, and many games sell out. Cornell has varsity teams in basketball, cross-country, indoor and outdoor track, soccer, squash, tennis, polo, lacrosse, field hockey, rowing, gymnastics, and hockey. Known as the Big Red, Cornell teams are of championship quality.

FINANCIAL AID

Cornell's need-based admissions policy makes it affordable to attend. Paying for college is often a burden for a family, and Cornell's philosophy is that the burden shouldn't be one that kills you. About fifty-five percent of Cornell undergrads receive some form of financial aid. Students always gripe about financial aid, but on the whole, Cornell assists those families who really need help paying for college. There are also plenty of on campus and off campus jobs to be had as well as temporary jobs for crunch times.

> **"** My financial aid package was excellent. I was a Cornell National Scholar and came out owing only $5,000. But my parents made sacrifices and so did I. My mother went to work while I was in school to help pay for my college. (She hadn't worked before.) Yes, I was in debt. My take on it is this: Education's supposed to be hard; not impossible, but not a free ride. **"**

The simplest way to think about it is this: If Cornell accepts you, they will find a way for you to meet your financial obligations. Financial aid packages are usually made up of some combination of grants, loan, and work study. Adjustments can also be made to your financial aid package during the school year if your family's financial situation changes.

Cornell's financial aid system is 100% need based. Cornell (and all other schools in the Ivy League) doesn't give merit or athletic scholarships. Cornell is also 100% need-blind when it comes to admission. Your need for financial aid does not influence your admission decision at all at Cornell.

The most important thing to remember is that paying for college isn't meant to be easy. It can put a strain on your resources. But you will receive a top-quality education, and as alums will tell you, the name alone will take you far in life.

Need-based aid also gives Cornell the kind of diverse community it needs to be a great institution. The mix of income levels and socioeconomic backgrounds at the university makes it a truly interesting and stimulating place.

Work-Study

When parents think about paying for college, work-study is always on the top of their lists. Work-study is a great thing. Your employer only has to pay half of your wage; the other half is paid by the government. Therefore, employers LOVE work-study students, and there are usually enough jobs to go around. Granted, it may not be your dream job, but in most jobs, there is plenty of room for advancement, and your salary usually advances, too. If the job is in research or something related to your major, it gives you additional experience that makes you even more marketable once you leave. There's a student employment office to help you out, and job postings on CUinfo, Cornell's computer information system.

❝ When I first started hunting for a job, it was the worst. Every place I inquired at was full and none of the available jobs fit in with my class schedule. It seemed hopeless. I called my mother in tears and told her I didn't want to be on work-study anymore. Then I found a job at the Undergraduate Admissions Office as an administrative assistant. The job had great (and flexible hours), and an understanding staff. I stayed there for the rest of my four years, became a student personnel assistant—which meant I hired and coordinated all the students for the building—and still had a job after taking a semester off to go to Washington. The job gave me excellent experience that I put to good use after I left Cornell. ❞

GRADUATES

Friends who have had long hair since freshman year are getting haircuts and buying suits. Résumés are spilling off printers everywhere, and reality is starting to set in. What time is it? It's the fall of senior year, and recruiters are swarming over the campus. There are job fairs and information sessions every week, and everyone is talking about how to survive an interview. Cornell brings in recruiters from more than 700 nationally prominent companies and 160 grad and professional schools each year.

PROMINENT GRADS

- Adolph Coors, '07, Beer Baron
- E.B. White, '21, Author
- Allen Funt, '34, TV Personality
- Harry Heimlich, '41, Developed the Heimlich Maneuver
- Kurt Vonnegut, Jr., '44, Author
- James McLarmore, '47, Burger King Founder
- Ruth Bader Ginsburg, '54, Supreme Court Justice
- Toni Morrison, '55, Author, Nobel Prize Winner
- Janet Reno, '60, Former U.S. Attorney General
- Lee Teng-Hui, '68, Former President of Taiwan
- Christopher Reeve, '74, actor
- Pablo Morales, '94, Olympic Medalist

Of those who aren't interviewing for jobs, many of them are interviewing for graduate school. People are leaving left and right to go to med school, grad school, and vet school interviews—senior year of high school all over again, except much more intense. There's a breather after all the applications and interviews are over, but the decision letters start coming in the spring. There will be much rejoicing, but there may be disappointment, too.

In addition to the main Career Services Office, each of the undergraduate colleges also has a career services center where students can go for career planning and information, job search strategies, and advising. Cornell alumni around the world network with current students to help them find jobs and offer externships to sophomores, juniors, and seniors who want to experience the real world of work. Placement rates into medical, veterinary, and law schools are considerably higher at Cornell than the national average for other colleges and universities. Cornellians are definitely successful, and their years of hard work pay off well when they go job hunting.

Public Service Continues After Graduation

Cornell's record of public service holds true after graduation as well as during the undergraduate years. Cornell traditionally ranks in the top ten schools nationally in the number of alumni who are accepted into Peace Corps training. Many more work with

AmeriCorps and VISTA in their postgraduate years. There are thousands of opportunities out there, and Cornellians are experiencing them every day.

SUMMING UP

Seven undergraduate colleges; 4,000 courses to choose from; more than eighty majors. After four years at Cornell, anyone is prepared to be a success in the real world. With the help of faculty and your fellow students, you'll find yourself evolving intellectually and personally throughout your years at the university into a person ready to take on any challenge. You may travel far after graduation, but you will always be a member of the Cornell family. The opportunities provided to you on 745 beautiful acres are unique and unlike those available anywhere else. Cornell has been called by more than one Cornellian, "the best place on earth to be."

Cornell gave me three priceless things. First, I got an amazing education. Second, I had a broad range of experiences that helped me grow into an independent adult. And finally, Cornell gave me an incredible bridge to the future. I will always look back on my days at Cornell with fondness and pride.

❏ *Laura Barrantes, B.A.*

DARTMOUTH COLLEGE

Photo by J. Mehling

 Dartmouth College
Hanover, NH 03755

 (603) 646-2875

E-mail: *admissions.office@dartmouth.edu*
 Website: *http://www.dartmouth.edu/apply*

 Enrollment

Full-time ❑ women: 2,077
❑ men: 2,119

INTRODUCING DARTMOUTH

If you're thinking of going to Dartmouth, the only Ivy League school to call itself a college, here's a few things to expect:

- First, you'll love green eggs and ham (and the color green, in general).
- You'll be tempted to learn new languages and you'll probably study abroad at least once.
- You'll always be taught by a professor.

- Your summer vacations are portable. You can transfer your "Leave Term" to the winter to avoid New Hampshire weather or compete for an internship in the fall and then return in the summer to study.
- If you learn to ski, you'll do it at the Dartmouth skiway.
- You'll wonder why every school doesn't have a version of "Camp Dartmouth" on a mandatory summer term.

Founded in 1769 by the Reverend Eleazar Wheelock for the expressed purpose of educating Native Americans and all those seeking education, Dartmouth is the ninth oldest college in the United States. It's also one of the most beautiful. Nestled between the White Mountains of New Hampshire and the Green Mountains of Vermont, the 269-acre campus has its share of picture-perfect scenery. In fact, visiting the campus for a commencement address in 1953, Dwight Eisenhower commented that "this is what a college ought to look like." Affectionately termed "the college on the hill," Dartmouth's central green is adjacent to the cozy town of Hanover, New Hampshire. On campus, brick dorms and administrative buildings are adorned with ivy, and Baker Library's tower presides majestically over it all. If you listen carefully, every day at 6:00 P.M. the bell tower plays a recognizable melody. Selections range from show tunes to Beethoven.

Dartmouth, however, has a lot more going for it than aesthetics. A bona fide "college" rather than university, Dartmouth prides itself on this distinction. The whole issue was decided in 1819, during the now-famous "Dartmouth College Case," in which Daniel Webster, class of 1801, successfully convinced the Supreme Court that Dartmouth should remain a private institution instead of becoming a property of the state of New Hampshire. In what is an oft-quoted line around campus, Webster summed up his argument by saying, "It is, sir, as I have said, a small College, but there are those who love it." From then on, Dartmouth has fondly referred to itself in the same way.

ADMISSIONS REQUIREMENTS

Dartmouth's admissions process is highly selective. The applicant pool has grown significantly in recent years and of the 18,778 students who applied for admission to the class of 2014, eleven and a half percent were accepted. The middle fifty percent of admitted students scored between 670 and 790 on the math, verbal, and writing sections of the SAT and between 29 and 34 on the ACT.

Admissions, however, is not based on book smarts or academic standing alone. What distinguished the exceptional applicants admitted from the thousands of other qualified candidates is intellectual curiosity, and academic or extracurricular passion, and an eagerness to be a positive member of a diverse and international community. In essence, Dartmouth is looking for students who will add to the community, inside or outside of the classroom.

Dartmouth uses the Common Application for admissions. There is one particularly unique supplement to the Common Application that Dartmouth requires, however. In addition to two teacher recommendations, you'll also need to solicit one of your more eloquent friends to write a peer evaluation. Dartmouth realizes that the best way to understand how you might interact in our community is to see how your peers in your own environment evaluate your contributions.

Alumni Interview

Conducted by one or more alums in the applicant's home district, this personal conversation allows the student to convey their interests in the admissions process in ways that a written application might not easily facilitate. Dartmouth does not require an interview, nor does it favor students who have one with alumni.

Early Decision

Finally, here's one more bit of advice. If you're completely psyched to go to Dartmouth, apply Early Decision by November 1. If admitted, you'll be finished with the entire college application process in time for the holidays. Keep in mind that the Early Decision admissions process is binding, meaning that you have to go if you are admitted. Although the percentage of applicants accepted for Early Decision is typically slightly higher than that of the normal applicant pool, the selection process is comparably competitive.

ACADEMIC LIFE

Despite three top-notch professional schools (the Dartmouth Medical School, The Amos Tuck School of Business Administration, and the Thayer School of Engineering), as well as twenty-five other graduate programs in the arts and sciences, Dartmouth prides itself on what seems to be an almost singular focus on undergraduates. Dartmouth students, consequently, have a unique advantage. All classes are taught by professors and not graduate students. Not surprisingly, Dartmouth consistently gets high rankings for its quality of teaching, as well as for the level of interaction between faculty and students.

The Dartmouth Plan

The Dartmouth plan is a unique year-round calendar. Dartmouth's academic year is divided into four ten-week quarters (called fall term, winter term, etc.), and students typically take three classes in each. This schedule works particularly well because not only is it difficult to get bored after a mere ten weeks, but students enjoy being able to focus on just three subjects at a time.

In order for the logistics of this to work out, students are required to spend at least nine terms on campus, including fall, winter, and spring of their freshman and senior years, as well as the summer between sophomore and junior year. Often a favorite term, "sophomore" as it is called, summer allows for a less crowded campus, afternoons of studying outside in weather that's finally warm, and a chance to bond with classmates. Students then get to decide what they want to do with the other terms; choices range from staying on campus to doing a transfer term at another university to taking part in one of Dartmouth's forty-eight off-campus programs in twenty-one departments in twenty-three countries. Sixty percent of the student body will go abroad at least once during their four years.

> **❝** I chose Dartmouth in large part because of its Russian department, and spent the spring of my sophomore year on the Dartmouth Foreign Study Program at St. Petersburg University in Russia. We were in Russia at a time when the country was changing every day and it was an unbelievable experience to witness these changes firsthand—and to have the language ability to speak to people about how their lives were affected. After it was all over, I came back to Hanover and shared what I had learned with my classmates. **❞**

The Curriculum

The requirements for the Bachelor of Arts degree at Dartmouth are designed to promote the overall goals of a liberal arts education: the deep analysis of a single discipline (the major); the broad introduction to several fields (the distributive requirements); and the integrating force of interdisciplinary work.

The Major

About one-third of the student's curriculum will be in his or her field of major study, elected before the end of the sophomore year. Dartmouth offers 56 standard majors, as well as nearly limitless possibilities for special majors, designed to meet diverse student needs. Options include: a Modified Major (work in two departments with emphasis in one); a Dual Major (completion of the requirements for two Departmental Majors, which may in themselves be quite dissimilar); a Special Major (accommodates students who wish to design special interdisciplinary or interdivisional programs of study involving two or more departments of programs); and a Major/Minor. In addition to the above majors, there are interdisciplinary programs in a number of areas.

The General Requirements

All Dartmouth students study a broad spectrum of courses fundamental to higher learning and basic to a liberal arts education. Of the 35 courses needed for graduation, students must take ten courses distributed across eight intellectual fields; three courses that emphasize three different cultural perspectives (North American, European, and Non-Western); and one course that is interdisciplinary in its focus. A single course may satisfy two or even three of these requirements. In addition, a course that falls within a student's major may also be used to satisfy these requirements.

Distributive Fields
- Arts
- International or comparative study
- Literature
- Philosophical, religious, or historical analysis
- Social analysis
- Natural science
- Quantitative or deductive science
- Technology or applied science
- The Culminating Experience

Each academic department and program includes among its major requirements a culminating activity, normally undertaken during the senior year. All students will take a course—or engage in an independent study project—that permits them to pull together the work of their major and add to this some intellectual or creative activity of their own. The culminating experience could take one of several forms, including a thesis, a paper, an exhibition, or a performance.

The Language Requirements

All students are expected to become proficient in a least one foreign language. Unless exempted on the basis of SAT Subject Tests, Advanced Placement tests or departmental placement exams, students complete their language requirement by studying a language on campus or by participating in a Dartmouth Language Study Abroad program.

> **“** When I realized that I needed to fulfill an art distributive, I wasn't sure what I was going to do. I'm not exactly artistically inclined, but I found the perfect class. I enrolled in Greek Tragedy, which provided a unique alternative. Instead of creating or studying art in the forms of paintings or sculptures, we studied the art of performance in Ancient Greece. It suited me perfectly. **”**

Faculty

Dartmouth has an incredibly strong faculty and student-faculty relationships are excellent. Classes for the most part are small. In fact, sixty percent of classes have twenty or fewer students, while only two percent of courses have over 100 students. The most popular departments at Dartmouth are History, English, Government, Economics, Biology, and Psychological and Brain Science.

Foreign Language Program

One particularly innovative academic program is Dartmouth's unique approach to foreign language instruction. The brainchild of famed professor John Rassias, the program is designed to make students comfortable speaking their new language. Each day, in addition to a regular class period, students have a one-hour "drill," which meets at 7:45 each morning. (Those who can't hack the early hours can elect to take a 5:00 P.M. drill instead.) There, they meet with an upper-level teaching assistant who puts them through the rigors of conjugating verbs and practicing dialogue. The session, accented by liberal amounts of pointing and clapping on the part of the instructor, is incredibly fast-paced and lively.

> *Although taking—and then teaching—drill got me up at 6:30 A.M. for most of my college career, I'm convinced that Dartmouth is an ideal and nurturing environment for anyone hoping to learn another language. Hundreds of students flock to drill each day to witness Professor Rassias's unique "in your face" approach, which is probably part of the reason I fared so well in my foreign language classes. It gave me such a good foundation, in fact, that now I'm fluent in French, in graduate school for Spanish literature and education, and learning Italian in my spare time.* 🙾

Research Opportunities

With over $200 million invested annually in grant-funded research, world-class laboratory facilities, and strong support among the faculty for student research, the opportunity to participate in faculty research proves to be an invaluable compliment to classroom learning for many Dartmouth students. Because Dartmouth's graduate student population is relatively small, Dartmouth undergraduates enjoy access to funding for research and in many cases serve as co-authors on faculty publications.

> *As a Presidential Scholar research assistant, I had the opportunity to assist my government professor on an article he was writing about the timing of presidential economic initiatives. He involved me almost every step of the way, providing me with first-hand exposure to the correct methodology for conducting political science research. I am currently using this knowledge to further my own research on media coverage of women gubernatorial candidates. In fact, my thesis proposal on this topic was accepted at the Midwest Political Science Association's Annual Meeting, and I presented my results at their annual convention in Chicago.* 🙾

In addition to participating in faculty-led research, many students pursue their own endeavors, often with funding from their department, the College, or outside agencies. Dartmouth students also pursue more than 1,000 independent studies for academic course credit during each academic year. Through this close collaboration with faculty mentors, many students find that their professors transcend the role of "instructor" and become colleagues and close friends. Forty percent of students pursue independent research.

Funding Sources
- Dean of Faculty Office
- Dickey Center for International Understanding
- Rockefeller Center for Public Policy and Social Sciences
- First Year Office
- Office of Residential Life
- Academic Departments

Formal Research Programs
- First-Year Summer Project
- Women in Science Project Research Assistantship
- Presidential Scholars Programs
- Senior Fellowship Program

66 *Participating in the Senior Fellowship Program allowed me to study the life and work of a woman named Theodate Pope Riddle, one of the nation's first women architects. Because I was required to take only a couple of classes during the year, I had the chance to visit Riddle's buildings and travel to museums to do archival research. I also learned a lot from my advisor, a professor who specialized in architectural history. By the end, I had written a biography that was more than 200 pages long and produced an accompanying video documentary.* 99

Research Funding

It's not just senior fellows who fare well with research, either. As students will attest, funding at Dartmouth for almost any sort of academic endeavor is readily available. Much money is doled out by the Rockefeller Center, named for Nelson Rockefeller, class of 1966. The center houses the departments of economics and government, and has financially supported everything from internships at the U.S. Embassy in Ecuador to research on Dartmouth's role in the Civil War. The center also draws a number of prominent speakers for panels and discussions. In recent years, it has hosted former Prime Minister of Israel Ehud Barak, chairman of the Pakistan Press International Foundation Owais Aslam Ali, Pulitzer-prize winner Laurie Garrett, and former Secretary of Labor Robert Reich, '68.

Libraries

The final thing to know about Dartmouth academics is that students spend a lot of time in one or more of Dartmouth's nine libraries, which contain over two million printed volumes. Baker is the largest and is an architectural wonder. The wood-trimmed Tower Room is a popular studying spot, as is the reserve corridor, which is framed by the murals of Mexican artist José Clemente Orozco. Painted between 1932 and 1934 when Orozco was the artist-in-residence, the famed murals depict the barbaric nature of the colonization of the New World. Dartmouth also has related libraries for biomedical science, math, business, physical science, engineering, art and music, and English. One thing to check out is the Sanborn English Library in midafternoon; every weekday at 4:00, students break for tea, cookies, and talk.

SOCIAL LIFE AND ACTIVITIES

With everybody going to and fro so often, it might seem that Dartmouth would have a hard time fostering a sense of community on campus. Ironically, the opposite is true. Bonding begins early, in fact, before students even officially matriculate at Dartmouth. Over ninety-five percent of the incoming class elects to participate in a first-year trip sponsored by the Dartmouth Outing Club. Each group of eight to fifteen "first-years," led by an upperclassman, faculty member, or school administrator, take to the woods for three days of hiking, canoeing, biking, and rock climbing. There are few rules, but one remains firm: no showers. After the three days are over, students convene at the Moosilauke Ravine Lodge on Dartmouth's Mt. Mousilauke (still no showers) to practice singing the alma mater, learn the Salty Dog Rag, and pay tribute the Theodore Geisel, a.k.a. Dr. Seuss, class of 1925. (This is also where the green eggs and ham come into play.)

Dorm Life

Besides first-year trips, Dartmouth has an impressive network set up to unite incoming students. Organized by residence, each dorm floor has a U.G.A. (undergraduate advisor) who organizes movies and ice cream sessions, plus dorm formals and barbecues. Dorm life tends to be incredibly social during first year, although it undoubtedly lessens as the years go on. Surprisingly, however, even after first year, eighty-seven percent of students remain in the dorms. Many Dartmouth students are surprised to find that the dorms, for the most part, are far more spacious than other living quarters. More than one person typically would share more than one room, and private bathrooms (although not showers) are not uncommon. Plus, many have fireplaces, which is an especially appealing feature as you're living through a long Hanover winter.

As if freshman trips, hall-bonding, and a host of common interests weren't enough, there's one more thing that tends to unify a diverse group of undergraduates: a fondness for their school. Student satisfaction ratings are among the highest in the country, and tend to breed an odd phenomena: the "I-love-everything-that's-green-and-related-to-Dartmouth" mentality. At first, anyway, it seems exceedingly hard to find anything you *don't* like. Of course, Dartmouth students do not love it blindly. In the past years, issues of race and sexuality have sparked debates, as has the age-old issue of whether or not the Greek system should be abolished. And despite impressive numbers of students of color (they compose approximately twenty percent of the student body) and international students (they compose more than seven percent of the student body), Dartmouth continually strives toward a communal balance of supporting affinities and interests with the institutional need of integrating students to enrich the intellectual discourse. As a perfect example, Dartmouth supports affinity housing (such as Cutter-Shabazz for students interested in learning more about African-American issues), but has the housing available to all students with genuine interest. Though Dartmouth issues reflect the issues in society, the sense of community yields a dialogue that is open and respectful. It is safe to say that Dartmouth students have a very real affinity for their school—not only during the years they attend, but in the years to follow.

Sports

More than seventy-five percent of the campus participate in either intercollegiate, club, or intramural sports programs. The athletic center's modern facilities include two pools, basketball courts, squash and racquetball courts, an indoor track, a brand new 16,000-square-foot recreational fitness center, a ballet studio, and a gymnastics area. Outside, there are tennis courts, an outdoor track, and the football stadium. Dartmouth also has its own skiway about twenty minutes from campus, and buses run to and from it six days a week during the winter. If you decide you want to ski, you can get a season pass to the skiway, a seasonal bus pass, and rent skis, all for under $200.

> **❝** My skiing lessons were Tuesday mornings, and as I was headed up the lift, I always used to think how crazy it was that I was here skiing, when almost everyone else I knew was either in class or at work. Was I spoiled! **❞**

Tucker Foundation

A host of other popular programs falls under the auspices of the Tucker Foundation, which organizes all the volunteer activities on campus. About one-third of the students devote time to programs like Big Brother/Big Sister, Adopt-A-Grandparent, Students Fighting Hunger, and Habitat for Humanity. To facilitate volunteering, the Tucker Foundation has cars that students can use to travel to their activities.

In addition to organizing—and often funding— volunteer activities, Tucker is also the umbrella under which all the campus religious organizations fall. Most recently, Dartmouth dedicated the new Roth Center for Jewish Life, which will provide space for Jewish religious services, an annual Holocaust commemoration, and social events.

Racial/Ethnic Groups

D artmouth students also spend a lot of time participating in groups organized by particular racial or ethnic affiliations. Groups such as the Afro-American Society, The Dartmouth Asian Organization, The Korean-American Student Association, Africaso, Al-Nur, La Alianza Latina, and Native Americans at Dartmouth all have large memberships. The Dartmouth Rainbow Alliance, Dartmouth's gay and lesbian organization, also tends to be a vocal force on campus.

Publications

W orking on student publications is also popular. *The Dartmouth*, said to be the oldest college newspaper in the country, resides in the same building as Dartmouth's AM and FM radio stations, which are completely student-run. The newspaper is supplemented by a number of specialty publications, including the *Stonefence Review*, a literary magazine, *Sports Weekly*, *Main Street* (the Dartmouth Asian Organization's publication), *Black Praxis* (the Afro-American Society's publication). *Woodsmoke*, an outdoors magazine, and *The Dartmouth Review*—the reason that so many outsiders mistakenly think of Dartmouth as a conservative bastion, *The Dartmouth Free Press*—the liberal campus newspaper, and *The Dartmouth Independent*, which strives to present varying viewpoints on pertinent issues.

Campus Committees and Groups

Students also serve on campus committees, in the student government, and in organizations that try to educate the campus about problems that affect the Dartmouth campus, such as alcoholism, sexual assault, and eating disorders.

Many also sing in one of the eight *a cappella* groups on campus. For those who don't sing, attending their shows is a favored pastime. (About now, you're probably beginning to understand why that daily planner comes in handy.)

Hopkins Art Center

The Hopkins Center, or the "Hop," designed by the architect who was responsible for both Lincoln Center and the U.N., is the hub of the arts on campus. Interestingly, it's also the home of the campus mailboxes. They were put there, goes the rationale, so that students would be forced to take notice of all of the Hop's artistic offerings. Besides housing three departments (art, music, and drama) and a jewelry studio, the Hop has incredible films, plays, and concerts. In a recent term, for example, the Hop played host to:

- Ang Lee (on campus for the U.S. debut of *Crouching Tiger Hidden Dragon*)
- Wynton Marsalis
- Itzhak Perlman
- Oliver Stone

The hop also features movies; for a $20 pass, you could conceivably see about thirty-plus films per term.

Hood Museum

Dartmouth's other cultural center is the Hood Museum, which houses over 60,000 college-owned artifacts. The collection, which draws over 40,000 visitors annually, is particularly strong in African and Native American Art, nineteenth- and twentieth-century painting, and contemporary art.

Parties, Carnivals, and Fun

OK, so Dartmouth students are busy, you say. But do they have any fun? The resounding answer to that question is yes. Dorm parties are a big deal first year, as are Homecoming (fall), Winter Carnival (winter), and Green Key Weekend (spring). Each fall, it's the responsibility of the first-year class to build a big wooden structure in the center of the green—and make sure that it's still standing on Friday night for the big bonfire. On that night, there's also an alumni parade, many speeches no one hears, and lots of parties. Winter Carnival, perhaps Dartmouth's most famous social tradition, is complemented by a huge snow sculpture on the green, and for the very brave, a dip in the local pond.

Besides the dorms, fraternities, sororities, and coed houses there are central party areas. No one joins a fraternity, sorority, or coed house until sophomore year, but those who do generally form close relationships with the people in them. The merits of the primarily single-sex Greek system are heavily debated on campus, although for the time being it seems to be here to stay.

For those who aren't into the Greek scene, there is a host of other social opportunities. The college often sponsors comedy clubs, hypnotists, concerts, and something called "casino night," which tends to be incredibly popular with the high rollers on campus. And, contrary to popular belief, people do date at Dartmouth. However, the on-again, off-again nature of the D-plan—you're there for nine months, and then gone for six—has been known to put a crimp in many a budding romance. Sorority and fraternity formals are popular date functions. Finally, right outside campus is the quaint town of Hanover, which has one good movie theater, a few bars, and a ton of reasonably affordable restaurants.

> 66 *People always asked me what I found to do in Hanover, but the truth was, I was busy all the time. I loved the fact that my friends and I couldn't go anywhere particularly exotic: it made us all so much closer to one another. Had there been the distraction of a big city, I'm not sure I would have formed the fabulous friendships that I did.* 99

FINANCIAL AID

Dartmouth offers its students and their families one of the most comprehensive financial aid packages in the Ivy League. 46.3% of a recent class is receiving need-based scholarships from Dartmouth, with an average scholarship of $35,504, and a total of $82.2 million in financial aid awarded.

The school recently announced a number of exciting new enhancements to Dartmouth's Financial Aid program for current and prospective students. This latest initiative provides free tuition for students who come from families with annual incomes below $75,000 with typical assets, replaces loans with scholarships for all scholarship recipients, assures need-blind admission for all students, and replaces one "leave term" earning expectation with additional scholarship dollars.

GRADUATES

According to a 2010 nationwide salary survey Dartmouth graduates have the highest median salary, $123,000, 10–20 years out of college. On average, Dartmouth churns out large numbers headed for lucrative jobs in investment banking and consulting; recently, more than 200 companies looked to Dartmouth to recruit prospective employees.

Of course, not everyone from Dartmouth heads off to the world of big business. Medical school and law school are both popular options for many recent grads, as are M.A.- or Ph.D.-tracked graduate programs. In a recent year, about twenty-five percent of the senior class was headed right back into school. Additionally, by the time they've been out of school for five years, about seventy-three percent will have gone back to some school.

The working crowd, meanwhile, tends to be attracted to jobs in education, social services, advertising, and publishing. Others teach English in foreign countries or head off to parts unknown with the Peace Corps.

Even with so many varied directions, the one thing you can be almost sure of with most Dartmouth graduates is that they'll come back to Hanover at some point. Dartmouth has an incredibly strong alumni network, and Homecoming and reunions are always well-attended. The alumni magazine is one of the strongest in the country. Each class produces a newsletter several times a year.

Dartmouth graduates don't just stay in touch with each other, either. They also stay in touch with the college. Over two-thirds of alumni contribute to Dartmouth's alumni fund, making Dartmouth's endowment one of the largest in the country. Alums also keep up with recent graduates. Dartmouth's Career Services keep extensive files on alumni who are willing to be contacted about their jobs, and the networking connections are consistently strong. Dartmouth graduates tend to like their school, and like others who went to their school.

> 66 *Since I've been out of college for over a year, I'm surprised in a way by how involved I still am with Dartmouth. I recently attended the twenty-fifth Anniversary of Coeducation and was heartened simply by the sight of so many bright, articulate women who shared my alma mater. Dartmouth has exposed me to so many wonderful ideas and people that I'm realizing it's something I never want to give up.* 99

SUMMING UP

If Dartmouth isn't the ideal campus, it's pretty much as close as you can reasonably get. With its northern location, year-round calendar, and focus on the undergraduate experience, Dartmouth is perhaps the most comfortable of the Ivy League schools. Its intimate atmosphere breeds some of the highest student satisfaction rates in the country, which is probably partly due to the fact that everything balances so well. Dartmouth students are some of the smartest in the country, but they also like to have a lot of fun. The Dartmouth community is incredibly close-knit, yet, thanks to the fact that different students and professors come and go each term, it never feels stifling. Hanover is a beautiful, rural locale, yet the school manages to attract first-rate speakers, performers, and intellectuals. In fact, you'd probably be exposed to about as much culture at Dartmouth as you would in any major metropolis. It's just that Hanover is a heck of a lot quieter. Student activities see high participation rates, but the school is small enough so that you never get lost in the crowd. And finally, the school has just enough surprises so that even when you're feeling stressed, there's always something to appreciate.

Finally, Dartmouth is an intellectual powerhouse that offers incredible on-campus and international opportunities. Besides those tangibles, however, Dartmouth offers something ineffable. As evidenced by the fact that everyone puts their arms around one another as they sing the alma mater, there is something very special about going to school up in the mountains. Perhaps, in fact, this appeal is best summed up by the alma mater's cryptic last line, which speaks to the permanency of the Dartmouth experience. Dartmouth students, it proclaims, find themselves with "the granite of New Hampshire in their muscles and their brains." Go to Dartmouth, and by the end, you'll understand what that phrase means. I know I do.

❏ Suzanne Leonard, B.A.

DAVIDSON COLLEGE

Photo by Billy Howard

Davidson College
Box 7156
Davidson, NC 28035

(1-800) 368-0380, (704) 894-2230
Fax: (704) 894-2016

Website: *http://www.davidson.edu*

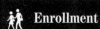 **Enrollment**

Full-time ❏ women: 887
　　　　　 ❏ men: 858

INTRODUCING DAVIDSON COLLEGE

Founded in 1837 with the belief that a strong liberal arts education prepares students for lives dedicated to leadership and service, Davidson continues to instill a sense of honor and responsibility in each individual who passes through its hallowed halls. Retaining the highest degree of selectivity and scholarship, Davidson enrolls students with academic promise, strength of character, dedication to service, and an open-minded diversity of interests.

Students exhibit enthusiasm for learning not only in the classroom, but also in the everyday adventures that shape a college experience. A single day may transport a Davidson student from reflections in a discussion-based Gandhi seminar to the neuroscience lab for cutting-edge research on Alzheimer's disease. After class, community organizations welcome students as mentors to local children and volunteers at a free medical clinic. And whether scoring on the Division I playing field or rolling kayaks on the lake, Davidsonians are constantly on the go, thriving in an environment that encourages vigorous and engaged learning both inside and outside the classroom. Although faculty, staff, and community provide an invaluable support network, Davidson students are independent, creative individuals who thrive on giving back to their community.

Situated on a 450-acre arboretum in a picturesque town of 9,100 residents, Davidson's ideal location draws a geographically diverse student body of approximately 1,650 students from forty-seven states and thirty-six countries. Students celebrate opportunities for meaningful relationships and cross-cultural discussion. Close proximity to the booming metropolis of greater Charlotte balances the benefits of a small college town setting with easy access to all the cultural and professional opportunities that the city has to offer. The school's ideal location on Lake Norman offers a network of cross-country trails, and central access to both the mountains and the Carolina coast. In addition, approximately seventy percent of the student body will study abroad at some point during their Davidson career. Extensive travel, study, and service encourage students to reflect on their position as local and global citizens.

Davidson's Honor Code serves as the foundation for a strong environment of academic and personal freedom. Take-home tests and self-scheduled exams enhance classroom study by combining an interactive, discussion-based classroom atmosphere with an evaluation based on knowledge and thought, not test-taking know-how. A signature on the Honor Code pledge represents dedication to a place where unlocked doors signify the immense trust that governs each interaction; through the Code students cultivate a unique sense of responsibility to the greater community.

> *" My favorite Honor Code story happened in the Baker Sports Complex. Over my four years at Davidson, I swam laps in the pool in the Sports Complex each morning. I kept my goggles, swimsuit, and towel in a locker in the locker room and I never thought to put a lock on my locker. In the rush of graduating, I forgot to clean out my locker. When I returned two years later for Homecoming, I went to visit my old locker. Although a little dusty after two years, I discovered all of my belongings just as I had left them. Indeed, the most important aspect of my four years at Davidson was the Honor Code. There is an immense sense of freedom derived from living and learning in a community where you know that you are trusted and you know that you can trust those around you. "*

E. H. Little Library houses extensive resources including 631,000 volumes and an inter-library loan system that allows students to have access to virtually any resource their academic explorations may require. A comprehensive collection of journals is housed on-line, permitting students to access resources from personal WIFI Internet connections in their room or a library computer. High-tech music and art slide libraries complete with sound recordings, music scores, music reference works, multimedia listening stations, DVDs, and videotapes supplement the main library. The Sloan Music Center, complete with sound-proof practice rooms, electronic music and recording studios, and performance space complements the light-filled visual arts center and Duke Family Performance Hall. Students drawn to the sciences thrive in extensive research facilities and state-of-the art laboratories. Internet access is comprehensive, with two wireless facilities and personal Internet ports for each student. Nationally recognized for its careful roommate pairing system (welcome to the world of the Myers Briggs personality test), Davidson's highly residential campus houses ninety-four percent of the student body in doubles, singles, suites, and apartments.

ADMISSIONS REQUIREMENTS

Davidson seeks to gather an intellectually rigorous, well-rounded, open-minded community of learners with the highest degree of academic achievement and promise. In evaluating a student's application for admission, the Office of Admission and Financial Aid examines both academic performance and potential. Each application is carefully reviewed, with special attention paid to the rigor of the high school record, contributions to school and community, recommendations from teachers, counselors, and peers, essays, and test scores. Admission to Davidson is highly selective with about one third of the applicants earning a place.

Nearly three-quarters of first-year Davidson students have graduated in the top tenth of their high school classes, with a strong academic curriculum of at least sixteen credits (four English units, three units of math, two units of the same foreign language, two units of history/social sciences, and two sciences). Suggested high school courses may include additional courses in science, history, mathematics (ideally through calculus), and foreign language, with competitive candidates acquiring twenty academic credits during high school. The middle fifty percent of those accepted score 640–740 (writing), 650–750 (critical reading), and 650–740 (math) on the SAT; the middle fifty percent of ACT scores fall between 28 and 32. Standardized test scores continue to play a role in the admission process but are not used as a single factor in the decision-making process. While SAT Subject Tests are not required, they are recommended, with one in mathematics and one other of your choice strongly encouraged.

Students may receive credit for AP classes with a score of a 4 or a 5 in the academic areas (or a 3 in Calculus AB and BC) or for higher-level examinations in the International Baccalaureate Program.

An important factor in the evaluation of a student's high school curriculum is the amount of rigor present. While a strong GPA certainly plays a role in the evaluation process, course choice has significant impact on the evaluation of the application. Strong applicants also demonstrate a loyal commitment to school and community activities. As an applicant approaches the Davidson admission process he or she should understand that admission counselors seek not only academic motivation and potential but also personally compelling students who will contribute significantly to the Davidson community both inside and outside the classroom. Thus, in addition to placing emphasis on academics, each admission counselor works to evaluate the whole person in areas including leadership, personal character, service, and motivation. Personal recommendations often contribute keen insight to this side of the admission process. In an ever-increasingly diverse society, counselors are also aware of students who represent diverse ethnic, cultural, economic, and religious backgrounds as well as evaluating the differences among secondary schools.

Decision Plans

Because first-year students are admitted for the fall semester, standardized tests should be taken no later than November of the senior year. Students are welcome to apply to Davidson under either one of the two Early Decision Plans or under Regular Decision. Both

Early Decision Plans are binding, and therefore, students who make Davidson their first choice are encouraged to apply. Early Decision candidates should take standardized tests no later than October of their senior year. The first Early Decision deadline is November 15, with notification in mid-December. The second Early Decision Plan deadline is January 2, with notification in early February. A requirement of the Early Decision plan is the Early Decision candidate's agreement stating that Davidson is the student's first choice and if accepted he or she will enroll and withdraw any other applications from other colleges and universities. The Regular Decision plan requires that students submit application materials to Davidson no later than January 2; admission decisions are mailed by the first week of April. In addition to accepting its own application, available in both a paper and electronic form, Davidson encourages the use of the Common Application, provided the student completes the necessary supplementary information.

Campus Visits

Although Davidson does not require a campus visit for admission, it is strongly recommended. Sometimes the deciding factor in the college decision, the campus visit provides valuable insight to a student's process and allows him or her to have direct contact with members of the Admission and Financial Aid staff. The Office is open from 8:30 A.M. to 5:00 P.M., Monday through Friday, and selected Saturdays throughout the year. Students are encouraged to call and schedule an appointment ahead of their visit. Tours and information sessions are offered daily in both group and individual settings.

Prospective applicants are welcome to visit classes and encouraged to have conversations with faculty, coaches, and current students. Seniors are invited to stay overnight in the residence halls on selected evenings. To schedule time on campus, please call the Office of Admission and Financial Aid at least one week prior to your planned visit.

ACADEMIC LIFE

Dedicated to a traditional liberal arts and sciences curriculum combined with the most up-to-date methods in research and technology, Davidson's academic strength lies in an interdisciplinary course of study. Students, motivated by strong ambition and inspiring faculty, choose from a myriad of academic opportunities. With special emphasis placed on writing, analytical and critical thinking, and eloquent communication skills, classroom learning extends beyond the traditional college lecture into a rare undergraduate experience of intellectual discourse.

A strong core curriculum encourages students to choose initial courses in literature, foreign language, writing, history, natural sciences, mathematics, social science, religion and philosophy, and fine arts. In addition, a cultural diversity and physical education requirement remind students of Davidson's dedication to the whole person. Thorough and rigorous examination of each area in a discussion-based environment affords students the opportunity to not only strengthen their academic foundation, but also discover new areas of intellectual pursuit. Flexibility and individualized guidance characterize an advising system that works with students from orientation to postgraduation. Cutting-edge research gives students a competitive margin over their counterparts with exposure to graduate study technique and methods in a fully undergraduate environment.

At Davidson, learning is approached as a lifelong endeavor, placing great importance of molding students into global citizens with the skills to lead in whatever field they choose to pursue after graduation. Challenging the mind and engaging the heart make Davidson's classroom environment a unique and highly stimulating place to pursue academic study. The results are priceless; not only do students leave with an exceptional liberal arts education, but they are highly sought after by businesses and graduate, and professional schools, and regarded as some of the most highly competitive candidates in the workplace and beyond. Davidson students truly are the "go-to" leaders in their communities.

Students choose their major from twenty-one disciplines by the end of their sophomore year, with the possibilities of double majoring or minoring in a second area.

Concentrations provide the opportunity to pursue more specific interests through interdisciplinary study in an area such as Gender Studies, Applied Mathematics, Computer Science, Genomics, and International Studies. In addition to the strong traditional liberal arts curriculum, Davidson offers students the opportunity to engage in professional programs in the areas of Prelaw, Premedicine, Preministerial, Education, and the dual degree Engineering Program.

Faculty

Although some students will tell you that the most passionate intellectual discussion often takes place at 3:00 A.M. in the residence halls, an outstanding faculty is truly the core of what makes Davidson a premier institution of higher education. Noteworthy achievements and credentials aside, the most exceptional characteristic of each faculty member is an absolute passion for and dedication to undergraduate learning. Full professors in each classroom (nearly 100 percent of whom hold Ph.D.s in their area of study) facilitate learning in a dynamic discussion-based environment. The absence of teaching assistants and graduate students creates an atmosphere of engaging intellectual challenge that encourages students to pursue their interests to the highest degree.

Individual attention heightens the effectiveness of Davidson's average class size of fifteen students, with some seminars numbering as few as five. Independent research projects ground students in a practical experience, which few of their counterparts at larger colleges and universities can boast; students geared toward graduate study and other postgraduate pursuits benefit greatly from an in-depth approach to study alongside accomplished faculty scholars.

Open office hours, meetings held at the local coffeeshops, and faculty and staff who serve as activity advisors fully incorporate educators into the Davidson student life. Students find their professors accessible and eager to engage their minds in the current issues of the day and the past events that have shaped history. A student-to-faculty ratio of 10:1 ensures highly personalized attention with relationships that often stretch beyond the classroom walls. Several students note professors' willingness to open up their homes for dinner discussion and advising meetings. From the moment students set foot on campus their Davidson experience is shaped with the help and insight of a faculty advisor. Each works to ensure success from class selection to the graduate study that eighty-five percent of alumni undertake at some point.

STUDY ABROAD

In addition to a plethora of options available through agreements with other colleges, universities, and international programs, several students choose to study on one of Davidson's own programs: fall semester in India and Nepal; year or semester in Tours, France; year in Wurzburg, Germany; summer in Cambridge, England; summer at The University of Cape Coast, Ghana; summer premed program in Kikuyu, Kenya; summer program in Mwandi, Zambia; summer archeological dig in Cyprus; summer in Moscow, Russia; summer in Monterey, Mexico; spring semester in Classical Humanities in Greece, Sicily, Italy

Off-Campus Study Programs

In a community where a global perspective is valued, seventy percent of students are eager to pursue a portion of their studies abroad. Davidson sponsors a wide variety of programs, taking students from the monasteries and museums of India and Nepal to the storied history of Cambridge University and over to Kenya for medical studies and volunteer work. Although Davidson programs span the globe, students are permitted to enroll in non-Davidson programs through the Office of Study Abroad, an important part of the Dean Rusk International Studies Program. The Dean Rusk International Studies Program, named for former Secretary of State and Davidson graduate Dean

Rusk, supports a wide variety of international opportunities both on and off campus. Throughout the year, the community is enriched by visits from international speakers and government officials and conferences organized through the Dean Rusk Program. A generous monetary pool also allows students to dream up independent global adventures and academic experiences with more than $100,000 in grants given annually for international pursuits.

> **"** *I arrived at Davidson with the study skills to make the grade; I left with a fiery passion for the written word. My advisor was not only an accomplished scholar in her chosen area of study but a true mentor who listened, challenged, and led me in an intellectual journey to push toward the outer reaches of my potential.* **"**

SOCIAL LIFE AND ACTIVITIES

Davidson students' only limitation to the pursuit and cultivation of their passions is the short twenty-four hours in each day. Building on a diverse array of interests and talents, the Davidson student body dedicates time and energy to lead over two hundred student organizations. Active in a variety of ways, students learn not only the importance of community involvement, but effective leadership skills through involvement in student government policy, campus life, the organization of campus events, and promotion of social causes and multicultural interests.

Supported by outstanding facilities, student activities and gatherings are enhanced by the Alvarez College Union. Fueled by a constant buzz of activity, this student haven boasts a twenty-four hour a day workout facility, a rock-climbing wall (part of the popular Davidson Outdoors organization, which hosts a variety of trips and training sessions in everything from hang gliding on North Carolina's Outer Banks to skiing in West Virginia to canoeing in the Everglades), the Duke Family Performance Hall (which hosted the Royal Shakespeare Company in an ongoing campus residency), and a cafe and grill open to students and the surrounding community. The Union Board works to keep minds engaged outside the classroom with recent speakers including Gloria Steinem, Cornel West, Marian Wright Edelman, Jane Goodall, and Annie Proulx. Music enthusiasts also find a haven in the concert committee, active in not only bringing local acts to campus but also supporting diverse acts from Ludacris to Counting Crows. Both the *Davidsonian* and *Libertas,* Davidson's premier publications, hold offices in this space. From an active SGA that governs everything from the tax activities council to the Vamonos Van, students have endless opportunities for involvement.

Patterson Court

Comprised of thirteen houses, the self-selecting Patterson Court social system is unique to Davidson College. Unlike a traditional Greek system, students join houses through a self-selecting process that invites each student to spend time in the houses before choosing membership in an organization. The majority of houses (eight national fraternities for the men and four eating houses for the women) are single-sex, with two of the houses offering open membership to both sexes (one coed house and the Black Student Coalition). Houses offer the opportunities for social interaction, shared meals, and service projects. The houses also support court-wide projects such as the annual Project Life Pasta Dinner (to benefit Bone Marrow Transplants) and the recent Habitat for Humanity Gala (in conjunction with the Union Board and several other campus organizations to support a Davidson College Habitat House). About sixty percent of the women and forty percent of the men choose to join a house.

> 66 *Perhaps the best thing about Davidson is not the opportunities that already exist, but those that you, with a little determination and creativity, create on a daily basis. As a prospective student I searched out female* a cappella *groups on each campus I visited. Although Davidson was the only campus without an existing group, I wasn't deterred. By the end of my freshman year The Davidson Delilahs were headlining concerts alongside the established male* a cappella *group and by midway through my junior year I was working in a recording studio on our first CD!* 99

Music and Theater

Bolstered by state-of-the-art facilities in both music and theater, the performing arts enjoy great popularity at Davidson. Students gain valuable performing experience through active participation in the writing, directing, and producing of theatrical productions. An annual visiting Artist Series and plethora of events enhance the cultural community. Through ensembles, performances, lectures, individual instruction, and academic courses, the theater and music departments provide both the college and the community with invaluable resources that strengthen the human spirit and intellect. Whether jamming with a group of friends on your freshman hall or listening to the *a cappella* concerts under the stars, participating in an opera workshop, or performing in the improv comedy group, there is a hardly a student that remains untouched by the vibrant cultural pulse of these departments.

Community Service

Davidson's commitment to community service is reflected in the twenty-six student-run programs that comprise United Community Action. From day one, the Freshman Service Experience introduces students to service in and around the Davidson community with a focus on poverty, the environment, children, and senior citizens. Reflecting the diversity of the student body, opportunities range from scaling roofs with Habitat for Humanity, translating for recent immigrants at a local medical clinic, and working with CROP to organize an annual hunger-awareness week. Four annual grants for environmental service and summer programs total upwards of $75,000 to make student projects a reality.

Athletics

Success and high levels of performance stretch beyond the classroom walls to the Division I playing field. Twenty five percent of Davidson students engage in rigorous competition with the same tenacity that they approach their academic studies. Davidson students balance their hard work with fierce efforts on the fields; eighty percent are involved in athletics at either a club or intramural level. Size doesn't stunt the high level of performance students bring to the playing field, evidenced

PROJECT LIFE

Project Life was formed in 1989 by a group of students honoring a friend who had a bone marrow transplant. This exemplary Bone Marrow Registration program enables the typing of all new students through the raising of $25,000 annually. In thirteen years, Davidson has added over 4,000 names to the national registry, with at least eighteen matches as a result. Project Life serves as a model program for other colleges.

by the many conference championships captured by Davidson varsity teams in recent years. Often pitted against larger universities, Davidson succeeds in not only making the Division I experience a reality but coupling it with the finest academics around.

FINANCIAL AID

As an institution that practices need-blind admission, Davidson is committed to making education affordable to all qualified applicants, thereby supporting a diverse community from which all students benefit. In accordance, all application decisions are made without regard for a student's financial situation.

Davidson offers both need-based and merit-based financial aid to its applications. Approximately one third of the student body receives some sort of need-based aid, usually in the form of grants, loans, and work-study positions. At the heart of Davidson's financial aid philosophy is the Davidson Trust. Through the Davidson Trust 100 percent of demonstrated need is met through grants and student employment. No loan component is included. Of course, families may choose to take out loans as a means of personal financing.

To apply for financial aid, applicants will complete the College Scholarship Service/Financial Aid PROFILE Application and the Free Application for Federal Student Aid (FASFA). These forms are available through high school guidance offices and Davidson sends these forms to each applicant. The timetable for need-based aid is as follows:

Early Decision:	CSS/Financial Aid PROFILE Application	November 15
Regular Decision:	CSS/Financial Aid PROFILE Application	February 15

Merit scholarships are also available in varying dollar amounts to stellar applicants, regardless of need. Characteristics including outstanding academic and leadership potential, ability, character, and potential contributions to the Davidson community all play a role in the selection process. No application is necessary for general merit aid. A small pool of special application scholarships recognize excellence in specific academic and art areas that require the submission of a portfolio, writing sample, or an audition or interview, which take place during Scholars Weekend in April.

GRADUATES

In an increasingly educated and specialized society, some question the value of a liberal arts education; citing the pressure to specialize in one single track, thereby imaginably increasing their marketability in the professional world. At Davidson, the community remains fiercely loyal to the ideals of a liberal arts education, which allows students to not only build skills in a highly focused area but also attain a broader foundation that makes them both versatile and desirable in today's society.

To ask what the "typical" Davidson graduate pursues in his or her post-Davidson life is to open a floodgate; graduates pursue innumerable paths but share the common motivation not only to reach for the highest realms of the professional world but also to give back to the community. Although popular professional paths center on traditional fields such as medicine, law, and business, a strong number of students also pursue the ministry, academia, and nonprofit fields. Graduates are often known as the "go-to" people in their communities, emerging as leaders and facilitators—they are the people who others look to in order to get things done. With strong writing and communication skills, extensive leadership experience, and a vested interest in their communities, Davidson alums find themselves recruited by the top organizations in a spectrum of industries. A rich history of graduate fellowships also paves the way for students (twenty three Rhodes Scholars!) to make possible the continuation of their studies at the graduate level.

An extensive alumni network and the Career Service Office allow students maximum exposure to opportunities for internships and jobs both during their Davidson experience and in their postgrad lives. Beginning in the freshman year and continuing through graduation, Career Services plays a significant role. Offering career workshops, alumni panels, and professional job fairs throughout the year increases the exposure students have to the working world and allows them to explore various fields while still under the guidance of the professional Career Services Staff. In addition, the extensive and varied experience of the faculty lends itself to concrete career advising.

Fortunately for current students and the institution, Davidson alums are passionate about their alma mater and are notorious for their willingness to help fellow Davidson graduates explore different career and life paths. A Davidson connection is one of the strongest a graduate can have and a strong ally in an anonymous world.

SUMMING UP

Davidson's application asks two simple short answer essay questions. The first deals with its foundation: the Honor Code. The second cuts straight to the heart of it all: Why Davidson? Why, after all the colleges and universities you have explored; why, when there are so many fine institutions of higher education available to you; why will you choose Davidson? The answer? It is not in the million dollar facilities for art, sciences, and athletics. It is not in the fully wired network that allows students access to equipment, materials, and facilities rare at institutions ten times our size. It is not even the fact that Davidson does your laundry (although, admittedly, that doesn't hurt . . .).

It is the people. At the true heart of what makes Davidson unique is the community. There is no question, from the staff that rise before the sun to the students who dance until dawn, that the individuals that Davidson draws from all over the country are unique. Without these extraordinary human beings, dedicated to "lives of leadership and service" the physical beauty of the Davidson campus would be just that, fleeting, ephemeral, and empty. With these individuals, Davidson becomes a remarkable microcosm of society in which people truly believe that they can make a lasting difference in the lives of others.

Grounded in the ideals of Honor Code and anchored in a tremendously talented faculty, Davidson retains simple, basic values that embrace a commonality of spirit and celebrate the differences of each individual. *Let learning be cherished where liberty has arisen* continues to serve as Davidson's motto and perhaps even more true for those who have studied in its halls, liberty arises through the mind-opening collaboration and challenge this dedicated group of scholars brings to daily life.

As a student who didn't know a whole lot about Davidson before visiting, I sometimes wonder what life would have been like had I stayed on my New England-centered path in the college search. The thought that I would have chosen otherwise makes me more than grateful that Davidson entered my life when it did. Simply put: Davidson is different. Without hesitation I wholeheartedly encourage you to seriously consider Davidson, but be forewarned—it may just change your life.

❏ *Page Neubert, A.B.*

Photo by Les Todd

 Duke University
Durham, NC 27708

 (919) 684-3214
Fax: (919) 681-8941

 E-mail: *undergrad-admissionse@duke.edu*
Website: *http://www.duke.edu*

 **Enrollment**

Full-time ❑ women: 3,250
❑ men: 3,250

INTRODUCING DUKE

The heat around Duke University comes from more than just its steamy southern North Carolina climate—a sense of energy and intellectual dynamism emits from this campus. The daring and exuberance of this young university, founded in 1924, has propelled it to the upper echelon of higher education in the United States and around the world. Duke students, both new and old, see themselves as forces for positive change. Dukies are a bold bunch with creative and analytical minds, helpful hands, and an unmatched willpower to succeed.

Blue Devils excel at many activities and skills, but athletics in particular have always accompanied Duke's strong academics. Duke's teams have won twelve NCAA team national championships: the women's golf team has won five, the men's basketball team has won four, and the men's soccer (1986), women's tennis (2009), and men's lacrosse (2010) teams each have one under their belts. Historically, Duke's major rival has been the Tar Heels of the University of North Carolina at Chapel Hill, especially in basketball. This is not to say that Dukies are not competitive and successful off the field too. Duke has produced forty-three Rhodes scholars, including twenty-two in the past fifteen years, as well as twenty-two Marshall scholars. Students achieve high honors in both arenas. Just ask Parker Goyer, Duke's most recent Rhodes scholar, who was also a varsity tennis player.

A liberal arts education and experiential learning undergird the undergraduate experience, no matter if a student is in the Trinity College of Arts and Sciences or in the Pratt School of Engineering. Duke undergrads take a wide variety of courses across intellectual disciplines. Students expand on knowledge gained in class through internships, service-learning courses, and "DukeEngage," a funded summer service program that sends students to areas of need around the globe. Duke undergrads can also avail themselves of the resources and opportunities of Duke's nine graduate and professional schools, which include specialized studies in business, divinity, engineering, the environment, law, public policy, medicine, and nursing. About half conduct at least one research project with a professor during their time at Duke.

The range of academic possibilities available at Duke's campus is reflected most dramatically by its architecture. On West Campus, gothic spires and a green quad frame the majestic 210-foot-tall Duke Chapel. From there, one can see the high-tech 300,000 square-foot French Family Science Center standing adjacent or look over to the world-renowned Duke Medical Center. First-year students will find themselves nestled in the residence halls of Duke's Georgian architecture on East Campus, replete with their own performance spaces, athletic facilities and a library for the newest Blue Devils.

Individual students and their interests vary as much as the campus. Students find that the Duke experience has something for everyone: Division I athletics and popular intramural leagues; a wide range of majors and certificates; a vibrant collection of extracurricular clubs from majors' unions to five *a cappella* groups; fraternities and sororities; political unions and cultural and religious groups. Similarly, Duke students are as diverse as their interests and reflect the global view of the university. They come from across the United States and thirty-six other countries, with ten percent of the most recent class being international and half of minority background. More than half receive some form of financial assistance.

> 66 *While at Duke, I also was able to polka dance in an international festival, participate in a national rights movement conference, and be on two national award-winning a cappella CD's. Where else can you have all of these momentous experiences while pursuing a first-class education?* 99

—*Michael Silver, '09*

Moreover, Duke is a global university that prides itself on its diverse faculty and students who tackle global issues and look for ways to serve an ever-more interconnected world. This happens within classrooms and out, with half the students studying abroad and several hundred embarking to destinations around the world through DukeEngage. Yet students do not always have to look far to be able to explore; many find outlets for their varied interests and diverse cultures in their cosmopolitan surroundings. Durham forms the hippest corner of the larger Research Triangle metropolitan area, which includes Raleigh and Chapel Hill and nearly two million residents. The area is brimming with award-winning restaurants, local museums, and art galleries. Duke students also have access to facilities, classes, and events at both UNC-Chapel Hill and North Carolina State University.

The diversity of backgrounds and interests doesn't prevent Duke students from creating a united "blue" front when it comes to school pride; this is especially true during basketball season. During games, the student body melts into a sea of blue, collectively termed the "Cameron Crazies." This heart-pounding vigor spills over into all aspects of academic and campus life.

STUDENT BREAKDOWN

Fall 2010
- Total Undergraduates 6,500
- Male to Female Ratio 1:1
- African-American 10%
- Asian-American 22%
- Hispanic/Latino 7%
- Caucasian 47%
- Foreign 7%
- Other/Unknown 7%

ADMISSIONS REQUIREMENTS

Each year, over 25,000 students from around the world apply to Duke for a class of 1,700. A walk around campus during Blue Devil Days for admitted students easily conveys the diversity of applicants, and talking to the students would demonstrate that Dukies are a unique bunch—handpicked to be exact. While admitted students at Duke have impressive academic credentials, like most top-tier institutions, grades and test scores are far from the only factors in the selection process. The Admissions Office focuses on six areas:

- quality and rigor of secondary school academic program
- academic record
- recommendations from teachers and counselors
- extracurricular activities and accomplishments
- standardized testing (SAT, ACT)
- application essays

Most admitted students possess strengths in nearly all of these areas, but each student's individual strengths and personality are weighed heavily. This personalized admissions process is designed to ensure that a student's entire life portrait is taken into consideration during admissions.

Dukies love to talk about Duke. Current undergrads staff campus tours and events for admitted students, giving them and their families a chance to ask current students about their lives at Duke. The Admissions Office can also arrange overnight stays with current students during the school year. This provides prospective students with a chance to stay in the dorms and experience "a day in the life" of a Duke student.

ACADEMIC LIFE

Students at Duke entering either Trinity College of Arts and Sciences or Pratt School of Engineering are required to take thirty-four semester courses across departments. Prospective students should be aware that both Trinity and Pratt, like most elite programs, accept only a limited number of AP and IB credits. However, a Duke education means more than required coursework. Mentored research, internships, study abroad, and DukeEngage service trips buttress the academic requirements with real-world experience.

Majors

Students in Trinity College pick among forty-three designated majors from traditional English or chemistry programs to biophysics or Asian and Middle Eastern studies. Students who find this number limiting can design their own majors through Program II. The most popular majors are economics, psychology, biology, public policy, and political science. Blue Devils may also tack on one or more of the university's sixty minors and certificates such as the popular "Markets and Managements" and "Global Health" certificates. Pratt students choose among five engineering disciplines, with biomedical engineering being the most common. Engineers may also take on second majors or minors in Trinity College. Of course, classes in either school are open to interested undergrads.

> 66 *Public policy is the only major at Duke that requires students to complete an internship. While most Duke students do internships, public policy students get the added advantage of a dedicated staff member whose job it is to help secure you an internship. Public policy majors also come in with a wide variety of interests from international development and domestic politics to health and social policy. As a result, students are encouraged to supplement their public policy major with another major or minor. Public policy students especially seem to embody the idea of wanting to positively change the world* 99

—*Jin-Soo Huh, '09*

Faculty and Programs

Duke strives for the intimacy of a liberal arts college with the resources of a major research university; that is, Duke wants to place some of the world's leading researchers into close contact with the brightest youth. Duke retains over 1,700 tenured or tenure-track faculty across its ten schools with another thousand or so researchers, lecturers, and experts participating as faculty. Duke's faculty-student ratio is a staggeringly low eight students for each faculty member. This results in smaller class sizes and personal attention to each student. Over fifty percent of undergrads graduate having conducted mentored research under a professor in either independent coursework or on an honors thesis.

Moreover, professors and academic advisors work at great length to empower students in shaping their own academic and professional lives. Duke tries to forge a sense of academic camaraderie between students and faculty from the beginning of freshman year. Each August, arriving students find faculty members greeting them as fellow residents in their dorms. Each East Campus residence hall houses a faculty member who regularly hosts events and advises students on their academic trajectory. Similarly, during orientation, the Faculty Outings program allows professors to introduce the newest residents of Durham to their favorite spots, including historic monuments, art galleries, and cafes. The Chautauqua Lecture Series for first-years brings celebrated professors into residence halls for regular dinners among the students. A quarter of first-years also participate in the Focus Program, which places students in themed course clusters for the semester in topics such as "Muslim Cultures" or "Exploring the

Mind." For example, in the "Global Health" cluster, students take courses in biology, psychology, and public policy. Each week, all the students and all their professors join in a catered meal for further discussion of the week's lessons. Several clusters take research and field trips to impress upon students the hands-on component to a Duke education.

> **❝** *I have one professor that I think hung the moon. My marketing professor goes above and beyond to make himself available to his students. He has been a mentor to me both within and outside of the classroom, helping me work through academic and extracurricular challenges, and has also provided guidance as I navigate the career search process. Everyone needs to have a professor like George at some point in their college career.* **❞**

—*Stephen Temple, '11*

All of these programs have the intended purpose of showing the newest Dukies that they are not merely students, but fellow researchers alongside their professors. First-years who have built lasting relationships with faculty members are ushered more easily into research projects early in their academic life. Students are also given ample opportunities to take their learning out of the classroom into the world. Opportunities such as DukeEngage in India, research fellowships, internships in the Medical School, and courses with service components in Durham are meant to parallel and enhance the skills gained in class. What better testing grounds for a mechanical engineer than a water-purification system in Africa? Is there a better complement to courses on emerging markets than working with micro-finance NGO's in a developing world? These university-funded programs not only enhance coursework, but they also translate into unique and marketable skills to employers and graduate schools.

> **❝** *We strike a balance. Yes, school is "super" important, but so are life and knowing not to take yourself too seriously. Duke students realize this, and so we live our lives instead of letting them pass us by...I was part of a club sport and it practically ruled my life. I loved it!* **❞**

—*Catalina Blanco, '10*

SOCIAL LIFE AND ACTIVITIES ▰▰▰▰▰

Students have said that Blue Devils keep to the three S's: study, socialize, and sleep. Although you might want to add "sports" or "saving the world" to the list, it nevertheless captures the energy and restlessness of Duke's campus. When students are not occupying themselves with their studies, you'll often find them at a meeting of one of Duke's 400 student clubs and organizations. The myriad of student groups reflects the diversity of Duke students and their interests from cultural groups such as the Black Student Alliance or the Sabrosura Latin dance troupe to more leisurely groups such as the Duke Political Union or the Ultimate Frisbee team. Curricular and extracurricular often blur at Duke: social groups such as Engineers without Borders coalesce around academic and personal interests, while two of the biggest parties of the year take place in Perkins Library and the Nasher Museum of Art, respectively. Yet, Dukies are rarely one-dimensional, and it is as common for science majors to join dance groups as for a Theater Studies major to perform in one of Hoof n' Horn's annual musicals.

NATURE LOVERS

Although Duke has an urbane locale, it's a great school for nature lovers. West Campus boasts fifty-five acres of gardens with thousands of species of plants and migratory birds. In addition, the 7,200-acre Duke Forest abutting campus provides ample trails for biking or hiking. The forest also contains the university's lemur preserve, which houses the largest population of lemurs outside of Madagascar. The Atlantic and the Appalachians are both within driving distance of campus, so students often opt for weekend getaways. To help out, the university loans outdoor gear, including camping equipment and bikes, for free. Students wishing to combine their love of nature with their academics can spend a semester on the beach at Duke's Marine Laboratory in Beaufort, North Carolina. First-years may participate in either of Duke's "outdoorsy" pre-orientation programs, Project WILD or Project WAVES, in which incoming students spend two weeks bonding and learning either in the woods or at the beach.

Athletics

Many students choose to participate in athletics, from fitness or recreational classes to intercollegiate sports. Blue Devils are also avid, if not rabid, fans—they proudly sport the name "Cameron Crazies," after the Cameron indoor basketball stadium. Student spectators pack the seats for almost all of Duke's sporting events and make their presence noisily known. During basketball season, students camp for tickets outside of the stadium in a tent-village named for basketball coach Mike Krzyzewski or K-Ville for short. All sporting events tickets are free for students, but the high demand for seats at a UNC game drives over 1,000 students each year to take up temporary residence for the best spots.

Besides the Division I NCAA sports, Duke has a range of both club sports and intramural leagues, which cover the gamut of sports from traditional soccer and basketball leagues to the more exotic sailing and *Quidditch* teams. Campus is also replete with state-of-the-art athletic facilities on both West Campus and East Campus. Recently a smaller workout facility was built adjacent to the Central Campus pool, providing fitness facilities on all of Duke's campuses. The Washington Duke Inn golf course, adjacent to campus, likewise offers golfers a nearby spot to play. For much of the year, campus greens are the primary locations for casual athletics. It is common on a spring day to see students running through the gardens or holding an impromptu Ultimate Frisbee match.

Residences

Duke considers living on campus central to its undergraduate experience. Around eighty-five percent of the students elect to live on campus for all four years, and on-campus living is required for the first three years. All first-years live together on Duke's East Campus, which is a short walk or bus ride from main West Campus. First-years enjoy a sense of community from having their own "home." Freshmen do not suffer from a lack of amenities on East though; academic spaces, a library, a full recreational sports center, tennis courts, two coffee shops, and a dining hall surround the residence halls. East is also within walking distance of the dining and shopping of eclectic Ninth Street and of downtown Durham.

Most upperclassmen live on Duke's West Campus in the historic Gothic dorms or they may opt for apartment-style living on Duke's Central Campus. Scattered among the quads are restaurants, study spots, and spaces for relaxation ranging from billiard rooms to sound-proof musical spaces. Duke's free printing service, E-print, is the most used and cherished of residence hall niceties. In the fall of 2012, Duke's newest residence hall in Keohane quad, nicked-named K4, will add one hundred and fifty more beds and social spaces to West Campus.

Duke also offers traditional fraternities and sororities as well as selective and theme living groups. Living groups and fraternities have residential spaces in the dorms called "sections." While the neighbors of fraternities may not always appreciate them, living within the dorms makes fraternities at Duke more inclusive than "frat houses" at other schools. Although a majority of the students do not belong to Greek organizations or themed communities, these groups heavily shape the social scene on campus. Needless to say, students have many options for on-campus activities beyond their living groups, many of which are expressive of their creativity and desire to relax, including movies, concerts on campus, "Disney sing-alongs." Large-scale events shape much of the student calendar, from SpringInternational (Epcot on a quad) and "Midnight Breakfast" during finals to the epic "Last Day of Classes" concert (affectionately called LDOC). LDOC has recently landed acts such as Kanye West, Girl Talk, Ben Folds, and Flogging Molly. And of course, all of campus shifts into high gear for basketball season.

Beyond campus, Blue Devils inhabit the rustically chic city of Durham, currently undergoing heavy revitalization. Intermixed with historic Southern charm and barbeque joints are trendy sushi bars and studio lofts enclosed in former tobacco warehouses. Downtown Durham offers a range of restaurants from pubs to French bistros. Downtown also sports Durham Bulls (Durham's minor league baseball team) as well as the Durham Performing Arts Center, which regularly brings concerts and shows to the Bull City. Arguably Durham doesn't provide as lively a social scene of clubs and bars as other university locales. Luckily, Dukies are only a hop, skip, and a jump away from the quintessential American college town of Chapel Hill. The free Robertson bus runs every thirty minutes between Duke and UNC-Chapel Hill campuses, bringing the town's famous Franklin St. a little closer to fun-seekers.

FINANCIAL AID

Duke and its community are dedicated to keeping education accessible, and for this reason Duke is one the United States' "need-blind" colleges. A family's ability to pay is not a factor in determining admission to Duke. In fact, admissions officers never know whether an applicant has requested aid. Recently, Duke eliminated parental contributions for families who make less than $60,000 a year and requires no family contribution for students from families with incomes below $40,000.

Students receive their financial aid analysis with their acceptance letters. Duke meets one hundred percent of demonstrated financial need for U.S. citizens and permanent residents. The university also provides a limited number of need-based financial aid available for foreign students. Demonstrated need is calculated using federal guidelines through information provided on the FAFSA form. The Financial Aid Office works with each family to try and make the most reasonable package of aid for their needs. Roughly half of Duke undergrads receive financial aid of some sort. Aid usually consists of a package combining federal and university grants, loans, and work-study funds.

Financial aid is renewed annually, which adds a degree of bureaucracy and paperwork to the process, but Duke has tried to make this process as seamless as possible. Many requirements can now be done online which has greatly reduced any uncertainty about packages and disbursement.

Payment Plans

Duke offers a payment plan called Tuition Management Systems (TMS). TMS allows students and parents to make monthly payments over the course of the year rather than making a large, single payment or taking out excessive loans. For families not qualified for aid who wish to spread out the payments over an extended period of time, Federal Stafford and PLUS loans are available directly through the university. Federal PLUS loans are available for eligible families to borrow up to the full cost of attendance, minus financial aid received, at a preset interest rate. The Financial Aid Office and Duke's Bursar happily aid parents and students in choosing options that work best with individual needs.

Merit Aid

Duke has a limited number of merit scholarships, along with its athletic scholarships. While many of the students who are accepted to Duke are eligible for scholarships at other schools, they often are not offered a scholarship at Duke because of the quality of the student body and the relatively few number of scholarships available. All applicants are considered for each scholarship for which they might be eligible. Full-tuition scholarships include the A. B. Duke Scholarship, B. N. Duke Scholarship, Reginaldo Howard Scholarship, University Scholars Program, and the Robertson Scholars Program. Unlike many of its peers, Duke also offers three ROTC programs (Army, Navy, and Air Force) for interested students. All three programs provide packages of aid and scholarships.

GRADUATES

Approximately sixty percent of graduates enter the workforce directly after graduation, translating the skills acquired in college into many different careers. Just as there is no typical Duke student, there is no typical post-Duke career. The Duke brand and the real-world experience that comes with a Duke education make graduates desirable as employees and future leaders, in both the private and public sectors. The stereotype that Duke students go only into medicine, law, or work on Wall Street still holds some truth, but increasingly students are flocking to civic jobs and non-profit work as well as independent entrepreneurial ventures. (That said, the large consulting, investment banking, and accounting firms still recruit heavily at Duke each year.) The expansion of the Sanford School of Public Policy with programs like the Entrepreneurial Leadership Initiative explains part of this trend. Many are surprised to find out that now, along with financial institutions such as Goldman Sachs, Teach for America is one of the largest employers of Duke graduates. The Duke Career Center enthusiastically supports students with any career aspirations and helps them translate their skills and coursework into meaningful careers. The Career Center takes a holistic approach to the process of finding a job and shaping a career. Freshmen are encouraged to meet with a career counselor to begin exploring opportunities at Duke that may aid a student. In the end, most find that the Duke name on their resume serves them well. Besides their wits, Dukies have a reputation for being well rounded and more personable than their peers at other academic powerhouses; this translates into a flexibility that many employers appreciate.

- Dan Abrams, News anchor and former General Manager of MSNBC
- Johnny Dawkins, Stanford basketball coach and former NBA player
- Elizabeth Dole, former U.S. Senator
- Melinda Gates, co-founder of Bill and Melinda Gates Foundation
- Grant Hill, NBA player
- John Mack, former CEO of Morgan Stanley
- Peter Nicholas, founder and Chairman of Boston Scientific
- Mike Posner, musician
- Reynolds Price, author
- Charlie Rose, PBS news anchor
- David Rubenstein, co-founder of The Carlyle Group
- Alan Schwartz, CEO of Bear Stearns
- Robert Steel, former CEO of Wachovia
- William Styron, author of *Sophie's Choice*
- Karl von der Heyden, former CEO of RJR Nabisco and Vice Chairman of Pepsicorp
- Richard Wagoner, former CEO of General Motors
- Judy Woodruff, CNN news anchor

Graduate and Professional Schools

A third of Duke graduates move directly to graduate school, with most attending law or medical school. Duke provides ample resources that prepare its students for competitive admissions to America's top graduate schools. Trinity College operates three advising offices specifically for students hoping to attend law, business, or medical/healthcare-related school. Engineering students have access to these resources as well as counseling on admissions to engineering graduate programs, including Duke's "4+1" Masters in

Engineering Science program. This individual support and the strong reputation of a Duke degree yields considerably higher acceptance rates for Duke students against national averages: ninety-four percent of those who apply to law school using Duke's Prelaw Advising Center are admitted (compared with the national average of fifty percent); eighty-four percent of those who apply to medical school are admitted (compared with the national average of forty-eight percent). These offices steer students toward graduate programs best suited for them as well as advise throughout the entire process, from test preparation to editing of admissions essays. Once accepted, these offices and their deans aid students in choosing the school they should attend. The support and counseling of these offices does not end at graduation; the offices don't hesitate to help recent alumni looking for guidance on admission to graduate school.

SUMMING UP

Duke is a hard place to pigeonhole, and Dukies take it as a point of pride that we are not so easily categorized either. Campus itself best captures the multivalence of the Dukie. It is sunny and relaxed, with more than the occasional party, yet it is also the center of cutting-edge research and learning. An engineering major may go from his job at the DIVE, Duke's virtual reality lab, to grabbing a beer at the weekly E-Social for engineering faculty and students. At the same time, a club lacrosse player may head from practice to an investment club meeting. Dukies can rarely be reduced to stereotypes. They come from all backgrounds and life experiences and bring with them different interests and trajectories.

As a relatively young university, Duke itself has yet to succumb to a rigid mold or stereotype. Duke and its community retain a strong sense of youth and the unlimited possibilities that come with it. This translates into a place that isn't defined by its traditions, but rather its tradition is constant redefinition—why shouldn't the brightest students be out in the trenches serving the world? Why shouldn't a cultural anthropology major become a best-selling rapper? One recently has. This notion of progress and youth permeates the Duke experience and all the students and alumni who live. Duke asks its students not to consider what kind of man or woman a Duke education makes, but to ask themselves what they may make of themselves with a Duke education. In less than a century, this philosophy has put Duke on a par with much older institutions as well as produced thousands of leaders for positive change around the world. They've been heads of Fortune 500 companies such as Pfizer, General Motors, Morgan Stanley, Bear Stearns, and Kraft Foods. Others have been policy shapers and newsmakers: governors, senators, and presidents of two nations (Richard Nixon and Ricardo Lagos of Chile). Some have been news reporters: MSNBC's Dan Abram, CNN's Judy Woodruff, and PBS's Charlie Rose. Students, though, brag more about basketball than the accomplishments of Duke's celebrated alumni. Where Duke and its students have been always comes second to where they might be going next.

> **❝** *Duke will go wherever its students take it. An admissions letter is an invitation to reinvent Duke as much as it is to reinvent yourself. Similarly, Blue Devils put the excellence and boldness honed at Duke to use in reshaping the world. The four years at Duke are intended to be formative in the sense that students leave with the ability to adapt, excel, and have fun in whatever they choose to do with their lives.* **❞**

❏ *Norman Underwood, B.A.*

EMORY UNIVERSITY

 Emory University
Atlanta, GA 30322

 (1-800) 727-6036
Fax: (404) 727-4303

 E-mail: *admiss@emory.edu* or visit
    www.emory.edu/home/admissions
Website: *http://www.emory.edu*

 Enrollment

Full-time ❏ women: 3,926
          ❏ men: 3,216

INTRODUCING EMORY

The white marble buildings and manicured lawns are the first clue when walking onto Emory's campus that it's not a typical college. Aside from the gorgeous setting that's fifteen minutes northeast of downtown Atlanta, Emory's combination of diversity and academic excellence drives its students to be successful and have fun. Since its inception as a small Methodist college in Oxford, Georgia, in 1836, Emory has become a nationally ranked research university. The school offers a broad liberal arts education and sets students on a track for success in a wide array of fields. Emory's connections to well-known businesses and organizations, such as the Centers for Disease Control, The Carter Center, and Coca-Cola, help the university attract applicants from more than fifty countries and rank among the nation's elite universities. Emory is known for its commitment to creating positive transformation in the world; it expects its students to do well and also do good for the world.

Emory is always changing and that's directly seen by the constant development on campus. The university continues its commitment to providing students with state-of-the-art facilities, including the completion of a $14.8 million expansion/renovation of the Cox Dining Hall, and a $20-million Sorority Housing Complex that features ten townhouses on Eagle Row. Additionally, new residence halls are under construction with nine freshman living complexes being built in eight years. Four of the nine new residences halls are currently open, with the remaining five to be completed in the next five years. Emory is also particularly proud of the new Psychology building and the recently completed Oxford Road Building. The Oxford Road Building is home to the Office of Undergraduate Admission, a three story Barnes & Noble, and expansive Starbuck's, and has a private parking deck for the Emory community and visitors. Other outstanding facilities include the Cox Hall computer lab which lets students create interactive projects with SmartBoards and DVD production software, and the Math and Science Center helps students study constellations in the high-tech planetarium. The forty-two-acre Clairmont Campus offers apartment-style housing to juniors and seniors, and each apartment is equipped with a washer/dryer unit, full kitchen, and individual rooms with full-size beds. The Student Activity and Academic Center (SAAC) on Clairmont lets students soak up rays beside the Olympic-size, heated outdoor pool, play sand volleyball, or study on the plush leather couches. The 90,000-square-foot Schwartz Center for the Performing Arts allows students to enjoy an orchestra concert, dance performance, or theater reading. These additions combined with the pedestrian-friendly, auto-restricted zones make Emory accessible and facilitates all students' unique interests.

Aside from the innovative buildings and designs, students' serious drive for excellence sets Emory apart from other schools. All Emory undergraduates can choose from more than seventy majors, fifty-eight minors, combined bachelor's/master's degrees, preprofessional programs, and a dual degree program in engineering with Georgia Tech. Fifty-two percent of Emory students have dual majors and/or minors. Many students come to Emory already sure that they want to pursue a terminal degree, and forty-three percent of a recent graduating class went on to a graduate program in medicine, law, business, sciences, or the humanities within six months of graduation.

Students enjoy Emory outside of the classroom as well. There's always an on-campus lecture by a renowned writer, a unique sub-Saharan art exhibit, or a band concert featuring popular artists, such as O.A.R., Common, The Roots, Kid Cudi, B.O.B and Guster, that students can attend. Undergrads can also step off campus to attend a Falcons game, visit the Atlanta Botanical Gardens, or enjoy a meal at a trendy restaurant in Buckhead or Virginia Highland. For weekends and breaks, Emory's location makes it convenient for students to take road trips to the coast of Georgia, the Panhandle of Florida, or the Louisiana bayou. Whatever the event, Emory students can always find the perfect mix of academic, cultural, and entertaining events on and off campus.

> *During my four years at Emory, it always astonished me how people reacted when they heard I attended this university. Whether it's my father's coworker or a random person I met at an internship or in a doctor's office, the 'wow' reply never ceased to amaze me. People were taken aback by Emory, and recognized the institute as a respected, forward-thinking school. I am proud to say I attended one of the top twenty schools in the nation. As a graduate now, I constantly run into people through my new job who ask where I went to college and still receive that 'wow' or 'great school' comment. There's nothing better than hearing a stranger be impressed by my collegiate choice.*

ADMISSIONS REQUIREMENTS

Emory's admission process is fairly standard. Applications must include test scores (SAT or ACT), an essay, and a counselor recommendation. Since the numeric information conveys little about a student's personal ambitions, passions, or interests, it's important for an applicant to give the admissions committee some sense of his or her personal qualities in the essay portion of the application. What sets an Emory student apart isn't so much his or her academic strengths, since all of Emory's accepted applicants are strong students, but the combination of talent, energy, and ambition that's apparent in Emory's student body. The admissions committee carefully considers students' high school curriculum and grades, and looks for students to have taken challenging coursework including Advanced Placement, International Baccalaureate, or honors courses based on the context of their school. Within the application, a varied extracurricular portfolio including commitment and leadership assists in illustrating students' character. For the 2009–2010 year, 15,550 students applied and twenty-eight percent were admitted. Of those, approximately ninety-eight percent were in the top fifth of their class, twenty-five percent scored above 33 on the ACT, and the SAT average was a 1960–2220.

Decision Programs

The Regular Admission deadline is January 15, but many students choose to apply through Emory's Early Decision program. In a recent year, thirty-eight percent of all enrolled students were admitted through Early Decision. Early Decision applicants have two chances to apply: the first deadline is November 1 and the second is January 1. This flexibility allows applicants to consider all aspects of other schools before making their decision. Applicants should seriously consider their decision to apply early, because both Early Decision options are binding and Emory expects accepted applicants to withdraw other applications. Although the Early Decision option is a big commitment, it's also a good way for a student to demonstrate his or her desire to attend Emory. Students will hear from the Admissions Office by December 15 if they applied in November and by February 15 if they applied during the second Early Decision round. (Don't forget that your financial aid forms must also be filed early if you choose this path.)

Campus Visit

The Admissions Committee and most Emory students agree that a visit to Emory's campus is essential for prospective students, as such a visit provides a chance to get a sense of the school before making a decision. The Admissions Office can help those interested in visiting by arranging class visits and providing contact information for students to meet with specific professors or program directors. For those who want to just tour the campus, the admissions staff offers visits between Monday and Saturday, and often recommends that students visit during the week if possible in order to get a sense of the Emory community and a collegian's weekday schedule. Recently, Emory instituted a new program for Saturday tours, Alumni Lobby Hosting, where recent alumni join admissions staff and current students for a meet and greet with prospective students and their families. In this way, Saturday vistors have a unique opportunity to engage in conversations with alumni. This program is followed by a student-led tour of the campus. Students can also take a virtual campus tour on the Web and view YouTube videos. Be sure to check out the Schwartz Center and Clairmont Campus while online. For a virtual tour visit *www.emory.edu/WELCOME/VirtualEmory*.

> *I still remember how relieved I felt, knowing I had an excellent college to attend in the fall. When the rest of my friends worried in April, I was able to sit back and await their decisions, without worrying myself.*

ACADEMIC LIFE

At Emory, students take their academics seriously and professors expect a lot from them. With a student-faculty ratio of seven to one, students have abundant access to their professors, whether it occurs during office hours, through individual appointments, or in the classroom. Professors are more than willing to work with students' schedules and genuinely care about their pupils' performances. Expert faculty who love to teach choose Emory for the opportunity to work with intelligent and ambitious students. The academic environment is friendly and collaborative, albeit competitive, as students support and push one another to perform their best. Students can always find a colleague to investigate a sociological theory with, or can consult an upperclassman teaching aide about a math quagmire. With the recent technology additions, Emory professors are implementing and maximizing the potential of group projects, allowing students to split up work and present material in innovative ways.

The university's Writing Center continues to be a successful part of Emory's academic life and allows students to bring outlines or rough drafts to selected undergraduate and graduate students to help them sharpen their writing skills.

What's more, Emory knows how much its students like to be connected, and in addition to being wireless, there are kiosks around campus to allow students to stop and check their e-mail or surf the Web briefly between classes. The school's computing services help students sift through various computer quandaries and will make on-campus trips to your dorm room to personally fix your computer glitch. Learning Programs provide a range of academic support resources to enrich students' educational experiences—from online study tips, to individual academic consultation, science mentoring, and technology workshops. Whatever a student needs academically, Emory offers a plethora of support that is easily accessible and shows the university's commitment to educating its students.

Advising Systems

Emory College of Arts and Sciences offers numerous advising resources with which students connect to help them plan and achieve their academic goals. First-year students are matched with faculty advisers, who work closely with them to select classes, develop their schedules, and plan their academic goals through the Pre-Major Advising and Connections at Emory (PACE) program. These relationships offer students insight and guidance as they discuss ways to engage in the Emory curriculum and identify educational opportunities. In conjunction with faculty, peer advisers provide student perspectives on academic and campus life and help with the transition to college. Once students choose their academic concentrations, they find one or two faculty members to advise them within their areas of interest. Faculty members devote significant time to mentoring their advisees and, as a result, often write recommendations for internships, scholarships, and jobs.

The Academic Advising Program in the Office for Undergraduate Education (OUE) supplements the faculty advising system. Academic advisers in OUE are available for individual academic advising appointments and can explain and interpret academic policy, as well as connect students to campus resources and services. The OUE Advising Program sponsors many programs, including drop-in advising events, major fairs, and panels that foster intellectual community among students, faculty, and staff. OUE also coordinates and participates in other advising programming, including Second Year at Emory (SYE) and the Pre-Health Advising Office.

Majors

Emory students' majors and minors run the gamut, as four of the university's nine academic divisions offer undergraduate degrees in almost any concentration. Emory College is the largest with 5,300 students, offering liberal arts classes with popular majors such as biology, economics, psychology, political science, chemistry, international studies, and history. Students can attend Emory College freshman through senior years. Students also have the opportunity to attend Oxford College, on Emory's original campus in Oxford, Georgia, about forty miles from Atlanta. Approximately 850 students attend Oxford for freshman and sophomore years, and then continue on to Emory for junior and senior years. The Nell Hodgson Woodruff School of Nursing has about 220 students pursuing a bachelor of science in nursing, and the Goizueta Business School includes 500 students pursuing a bachelor of business administration degree; you can apply to either school from Oxford or Emory College after your sophomore year. Emory is known for producing future doctors and lawyers, along with students who pursue Ph.D.s in the humanities or start nonprofit organizations. The diversity among majors and concentrations is indicative of the school's variety and global awareness—its study abroad components further demonstrate students' desires to explore global places. With the help of CIPA (Center for International Programs Abroad), the majority of students have international experiences by studying abroad. CIPA offers comprehensive assistance in planning a student's time abroad, either for a year, a semester, or a summer. Advisers help students through all facets of the process—from choosing the right program, through the application process and pre-departure preparations, to the transition back to campus upon their return. Advisers are also available to talk about such issues as cultural adjustment, financing an experience abroad, or the transfer of credits toward the Emory degree. Emory's programs allow students to spend a semester or year in Europe, Latin America, Asia, Africa, or Australia, or summers in locations such as Beijing, Cape Town, Buenos Aires, or Vienna. Students can also conduct research or community service while abroad. Wherever a student chooses to go, Emory can help make studying abroad a life-altering experience.

SOCIAL LIFE AND ACTIVITIES

There are plenty of activities to keep Emory students entertained, both on and off campus. Students maintain a good balance of academics and amusement through involvements in numerous organizations. Students perform through Theater Emory, write opinions for *The Emory Wheel*, and read books to inner-city children through Volunteer Emory. Off campus, students can intern at the Centers for Disease Control or CNN, or spend an autumn afternoon at Piedmont Park. Well-known guests are invited to speak year-round; Maya Angelou, Naomi Wolf, Kenneth Cole, the Dali Lama, Alice Walker, and Margaret Atwood have made recent appearances on campus. One of the special events specifically orchestrated for first-year students is the annual Carter Town Hall Meeting, in which former president Jimmy Carter addresses questions asked by the new students about foreign policy, national issues, local politics, as well as personal issues in a relaxed environment. He's also been known to lecture to certain political science classes and offers many internships to Emory students through the Carter Center, located a few miles from campus.

Athletics

There's a long-standing joke among Emory students that the football team is still undefeated. That's because Emory, a Division III school in the NCAA, doesn't have a football team. But that doesn't stop students from gearing up for sporting events. There are eighteen intercollegiate sports at Emory, including basketball, soccer, volleyball, tennis, swimming, and diving. Emory's varsity athletic successes have proved that the college is both an academic and athletic powerhouse.

Consistently ranked one of the top Division III athletic programs in the country, Emory students continue to excel both inside the classroom and on the playing field. Emory's athletic program posted an eighteenth-place finish out of over 310 Division III athletic programs in the 2009–2010 Directors' Cup standings. The Directors' Cup ranks the best overall athletic programs in the nation. The Eagles had four overall top-ten finishes in the 2009–2010 Directors' Cup standings: men's tennis (fifth), men's swimming and diving (third), women's swimming and diving (first), women's tennis (second). For those not on varsity teams, Emory has over forty intramural or club sports for students to engage in. The competitive intramurals can make any student think he or she is at a championship game, as fraternities, sororities, and other clubs and organizations go head to head in flag football, soccer, and softball among other sports. Sometimes these can be the most exciting games to watch! The primary gym, the Woodruff Physical Education Center, boasts an Olympic-size swimming pool, a 3,000-seat gymnasium with four basketball courts, an indoor and outdoor track, rock climbing wall, and an impressive array of exercise equipment. Students can take yoga, step aerobics, kick boxing, and spinning classes, as well as dance and weight training through the university's physical education system. On the Clairmont Campus, basketball courts, outdoor tennis courts, sand volleyball courts, and a weight room equipped with cardiovascular machines open until midnight, let students sweat a bit at any hour they need a break.

Unofficial Mascot

To spur school spirit, Emory's students flock to Dooley, the unofficial mascot. Though the Emory Eagle is the official mascot, Dooley illuminates students' enthusiasm through his unexpected and impromptu visits all over campus. Dooley is a skeleton that is always accompanied by black-clad, white-gloved bodyguards who relay his messages to the student body. The saga says that Dooley was adopted in the early years of the university when some Emory students developed an unusual attachment to a lab skeleton in one of their classrooms. Ever since, Dooley has been the spirit of students and he always dons a skeleton-painted shirt, dapper top hat, and long black cape. His identity is a strictly kept secret and students never know when or where he'll appear. He's present at major student events, leaning on his cane while crossing the floor, and will show up unannounced in any classroom during the school's annual Dooley's Week. During his week, he's given license to release any class he chooses with a slow wave of his arm and a message from one of his escorts. He always departs with the same motto: "Students may come and students may go, professors may come and professors may go, presidents may come and presidents may go, but Dooley lives on forever."

Greeks

Another aspect of Emory's activities is the Greek system. About thirty percent of undergrads pledge one of the fifteen fraternities or thirteen sororities. Emory's Greek life is known to be laid back, fun, and productive; Greeks often are seen organizing a run for cancer, cooking dinners for ill children, and raising money for various charities. Students go through Greek recruitment second semester, which gives students the chance to experience the Emory community, meet classmates, and engage with the city of Atlanta. One unique aspect of Emory's Greek life is that it's not exclusive; many students who pledge an organization say their best friends aren't in a fraternity or sorority.

Activities On and Off Campus

Aside from Greek organizations, Emory offers a plethora of activities for undergrads to enjoy on campus. Students go to parties, attend film screenings, see concerts on campus, and attend presentations from world-renowned faculty and guests. Undergrads can always find a friend to toss a Frisbee with, watch a band concert on McDonough Field, or nosh on free food at a club meeting. For a break, students can grab a gourmet cup of coffee in the recently renovated café on the top floor of the Michael Graves-designed Michael C. Carlos Museum, or listen to a poetry reading outside Cox Hall. Off campus, Atlanta provides plenty of adventures for undergrads. Students can go to Six Flags over Georgia for the day, dance at a trendy club in Buckhead, grab eclectic food on Ponce de Leon, or attend a show at the Fox Theater. Some of the most popular off-campus activities include attending a Braves game, visiting the local Sweetwater Brewery, and wandering around the High Museum of Art.

Dining

Emory has a plethora of dining options to choose from; whether you want farm fresh or a meal on the go, Emory has you covered. The renovated Cox Hall is home to Chick-fil-a, Freshens, and Pizza Hut, just to name a few. Zaya's is a huge hit with those who like to stay up late as it is open until 2 A.M. seven days a week. The Dobbs University Center (DUC) is home to Einstein's and the undergraduate cafeteria. Emory provides seven different meal plans that vary in cost and services and have been specifically tailored to meet the needs of the entire student body. Most meal plans come with a certain amount of DUC meals, and all plans come with Dooley Dollars which can be spent in lieu of cash at the twenty-seven a-la-carte food locations across campus. If you ever run out of Dooley Dollars you can replenish them with Eagle Dollars; both are tracked via your EmoryCard.

EmoryCard

An EmoryCard is a cross between an ID and a debit card; you will need it to get into the library and you can also buy food or coffee with it. The EmoryCard is just as valuable off-campus as well because many local businesses offer discounts when one is presented. In addition, many local restaurants provide complimentary items or discounts if you bring your EmoryCard with you.

FINANCIAL AID

Emory is committed to helping its students find a way to finance their education. Last year, sixty-two percent of undergraduate students received some sort of financial aid. Through on-campus jobs, grants, loans, or scholarships, the Emory administration works with students to help them finance their education with as little stress as possible. If you wish to be considered for financial aid, be sure to fill out the CSS/Profile and FAFSA forms, and submit tax documents by the appropriate deadline. Early Decision applicants must turn in their forms with their applications. Emory encourages all applicants to spend the time to apply for financial assistance as it devotes a portion of its sizable resources to student support in the financial realm. Emory recently developed and launched its Emory Advantage program, which is designed to reduce the debt burden for undergraduate domestic students from families with annual total incomes of $100,000 or less who demonstrate a need for financial aid.

Aside from Emory scholarships and programs, the school acknowledges National Merit Scholarships, the HOPE Scholarship for Georgia residents, and funding for summer and study abroad programs.

Emory's large endowment can be credited to the Candler and Woodruff families, the early owners of the Atlanta-based Coca-Cola Company. The university has been associated with the families and the company ever since Atlanta pharmacist Asa Griggs Candler sent a keg of Coca-Cola syrup to his son at Emory in 1895. Today, several buildings on campus are named after members of the Candler and Woodruff families and Emory doesn't serve any beverages that aren't Coke-produced on campus. An urban legend still circulates among students that a couple of seniors placed a Pepsi vending machine on the quadrangle one year, sending the administration into a frenzy, and they immediately ordered the removal of it. Resident Advisors even joke that they'll make periodic dorm raids to make sure that students are drinking the "right" cola.

Merit Scholarships and Programs

One of Emory's financial aid strengths is the plethora of merit scholarships it makes available to students each year. The most prominent of these is the Emory Scholars program, which students must be nominated for, and includes the most prestigious award, the Woodruff Scholarship. The Woodruff Scholarship offers selected students full tuition, room, and board for their four collegiate years. Emory Scholars receive extremely generous awards and the university program currently has over 300 students in the Scholars program. The Admissions Office receives more than 2,800 nominations for the scholarships that are renewed each year for students' four-year stints at Emory. Scholars have access to a number of special academic and cultural opportunities, ranging from research grants and funding for study abroad programs to small "coffee talk" discussions with speakers invited to Emory. They frequently attend events in Atlanta, such as the Atlanta Symphony and Ballet, as well as sporting events, concerts, and funded group dinners. For those not initially selected as Scholars, there's also the possibility of becoming an Emory Scholar after one's freshman or sophomore year by receiving the Dean's Achievement Scholarship. Around sixty of these scholarships are available each year, and recipients usually have a college G.P.A. of 3.9 or higher.

One of the other unique programs available at Emory is the Community Building and Social Change Fellows Program. Emory alum and world-renowned fashion designer Kenneth Cole built the program with social consciousness in mind to give undergraduates the opportunity to help build communities and spur social change in the Atlanta area. The CBSC is a twelve-month program that gives students the opportunity to work with professors and community partners to rebuild inner-city neighborhoods and promote community initiatives.

Another opportunity for Emory seniors is the Robert T. Jones Scholarship which enables recipients to live and study in St. Andrews, Scotland, for one year. In addition to this internal award, Emory works hard to help students win outside scholarships, such as Fulbright fellowships, Luce scholarships, and James Madison scholarships.

In addition to offering scholarships, Emory holds copious meetings throughout the year to coach students in the scholarship/award application process. Emory students can engage in mock interviews, essay workshops, and hear from scholarship recipients on how to strengthen their applications. Administrators, professors, and career counselors are more than willing to help Emory students throughout the processes and students are encouraged to apply for these awards. Those interested in learning more about these programs and others can visit *http://college.emory.edu/current/achievement/scholarships/index.html*.

> **❝** *The Atlanta Ballet, a Counting Crows concert, the NCAA Elite Eight games, and stimulating conversation at the Atlanta Fish Market with other scholars are just a few of the occasions I enjoyed while participating in the Emory Scholars program. Emory Scholars have an impeccable academic background and drive, which the program supports through an array of academic, research, and study abroad opportunities. I received supplementary scholarship money to study abroad the summer before my senior year, and I applied this toward linguistic studies in Spain. The program allows Scholars to leave an individual, lasting mark; by the time I graduated, I had sat on the advisory board, created new Emory Scholars events, and interviewed potential incoming scholars. These qualities make the Emory Scholars program truly unique among the merit-based scholarship programs offered at the country's top schools.* **❞**

—*Rachel, Emory Scholar, '04*

GRADUATES

Emory graduates are among some of the most successful alumni nationwide. Many graduates go on to become doctors and lawyers, while others pursue Ph.D.s in the humanities, join the Peace Corps, or work on political campaigns. Emory's Career Center is very active and can assist students by hosting career fairs, critiquing personal resumes, and helping Emory's graduates attend the school or land the job of their dreams. The Career

- The Indigo Girls—Amy Ray and Emily Saliers, musicians
- Kenneth Cole, Fashion Designer
- Sam Nunn, Former U.S. Senator
- Reverend Bernice King, Daughter of Martin Luther King, Jr.
- Newt Gingrich, former U.S. Representative
- Ashley Puleo, Miss USA 2004 Pageant Second Runner-up
- Paul Amos II, President Aflac
- Kristian Bush, Singer, Songwriter, and Guitarist for the band Sugarland
- Ely Callaway, Founder of Callaway Golf

Center also helps students find summer or semester internships that can lead to potential full-time jobs. Whatever the desire, advisors are available to help undergraduates and alumni get in touch with staff and make use of their resources. More than 250 companies recruit on campus each year, and motivated students can usually find a postgraduation position in Atlanta or beyond. Or, if a career isn't the initial desire of grads, the Career Center helps student hone in on postcollegiate study. Of the 2010 graduating class, forty-three percent were enrolled in graduate school post-graduation. Whether it is medical school or graduate school for art history, the Career Center will keep students' recommendations on file and send them out when requested to help ease the application process.

For more information on these services, visit the Career Center's Web site: *http://www.career.emory.edu/*

SUMMING UP

Emory offers a unique, fantastic education to those who're ready for a diverse and demanding education. Although Emory is probably not for everyone, students who thrive on full schedules, big ambitions, and a work-hard, play-hard attitude will find themselves at home here. Emory offers a challenging, but supportive environment with great intellectual and cultural resources. Students learn a number of theories, but most important, they learn how to think critically for themselves. But facts and figures can offer only so much information; it's impossible to describe the special atmosphere at Emory. Students find it difficult to quantify fond memories of ordering Everybody's pizza at three in the morning while studying for a midterm, grabbing a drink with friends to celebrate a new job in Buckhead, or caravaning to the coast for a weekend getaway during fall break. Graduates will always have a soft spot for something—a cold Coke or a burrito from Willy's—that reminds them of their alma mater. Emory is more than a college education; it's a glimpse into the copious opportunities of the real world that are framed by an outstanding network of professors, researchers, athletes, and artists. Whether a student wants to become an archeologist, doctor, politician, or writer, a solid Emory education will get him or her on the right track. The diversity of the school in the heart of Atlanta produces the comfort and adventure of a quintessential college experience that lucky students will have the chance to encounter.

> 66 *Emory changed my life. The knowledge that was imparted to me, the friends and professors that I had the pleasure to meet, and the amazing experiences that I was fortunate enough to take part in transformed me throughout the entirety of my undergraduate career. I am blessed to be able to call Emory my alma mater. I give back to the school in any matter, and as frequently as possible, yet I will never be able to repay the debt of gratitude that I feel.* 99

❑ *Brock Cline, B.A.*

FRANKLIN & MARSHALL COLLEGE

 Franklin & Marshall College
Lancaster, PA 17603

 (717) 291-3953
Fax: (717) 291-4389 (877) 678-9111

 E-mail: *admission@fandm.edu*
Website: *www.fandm.edu*

 Enrollment

Full-time ❑ women: 1,205
❑ men: 1,083

INTRODUCING FRANKLIN & MARSHALL COLLEGE

Over the past few years, the face of Franklin & Marshall College has changed rapidly. Renovation is complete on the Patricia A. Harris Center for Business, Government, and Public Policy, nestled snugly in the shadow of the recently completed Barshinger Life Sciences and Philosophy building. From the windows of the ultra-modern College Row apartments one can watch yellow CATs scurrying like sunspots across verdant fields, preparing the land for an eventual new football stadium and athletic fields. Sipping coffee and reclining in a high-backed, riveted leather chair in the fire-warmed Jazzman's coffeehouse, it is easy to forget that the addition is less than a decade old. But change at F&M is not superficial. From the cutting-edge psychology facilities to faculty and student growth to the latest Apple Macintosh computers in the computer labs, F&M is striving to create an epi-center of modern education in the heart of Lancaster, Pennsylvania.

In light of this apparent flux, one would be inclined to think that little is constant at F&M. However, two things remain unchanged: quality education and respect for tradition. Inside the Druker Humanities Common a sharp eye can pick out embell-ishments to the modern architecture. While F&M is involved in expanding and improving its physical presence, the education F&M provides needs no improvement. F&M has always been dedicated to fur-nishing a superior liberal arts education through indi-vidual attention to the students. With a ten-to-one student-to-faculty ratio, relationships form fast, last long, and challenge the traditional master/pupil dynamic. Ninety-one percent of F&M faculty have earned Ph.D.s, or other terminal degrees in their respective fields.

However, world-class facilities and faculty do come with a price. An F&M student is expected to be exemplary in all things, not just academics: Athletes, like F&M's women's lacrosse team, are not just hardworking players, but Division III cham-pions. Students like Ben Burghart don't just travel the globe to study abroad but also to teach and build schools in Bremen Esiam, Ghana. Students who wish to break earthly bonds can study the stars at the Grundy Observatory on Baker Campus. In short, F&M offers you opportunity. All the school asks is that you seize it.

NEW BUILDINGS ON CAMPUS

○ **Barshinger Life Science and Philosophy Building—$48.7 million—**Houses Philosophy, Psychology, Biology, and two unique interdisci-nary programs, Biological Foundations of Behavior and Scientific and Philosophical Studies of the Mind.

○ **Klehr Center for Jewish Life—$2 million—**Built to replace the old Hillel House, the Klehr center sponsors events such as Shabbat dinner and weekly "cafés," gatherings where students discuss current events, upcoming holidays, Jewish ideals, "and, of course, eat!" Dean Ralph Taber, Director of the Klehr Center for Jewish Life.

○ **Ware College House Commons—$1.5 million—**Built to bolster community in the college House system, this sleek structure boasts a quiet study library, a kitchen, several conference rooms, and a large hall for meals or movies.

○ **College Row—$30 million—**200,000 square foot upperclass housing, and retail establishments. College Row boasts spacious apartments ranging from singles to quads with all the amenities of home. The first floor houses venues such as the restauraunt Iron Hill Brewing Company and fine clothier Fillings at College Row.

The students at F&M are keenly aware of the myriad possibilities F&M makes available, and as such, student life tends to take advantage of as much as possible. "Work hard, play hard" is the students' motto. In everything from who scored higher on last week's test to who can prepare the best *confit de canard* to who can best quote *Family Guy*, F&M students relish a challenge as the opportunity to prove their excellence. If you are looking for a school at which one can disappear, F&M is not the school for you. If you are looking for a school at which you will be challenged, where you will be required to grow and mature, and where you will be given all the nurture and support you need to do so, look no further than Franklin & Marshall College.

ADMISSIONS REQUIREMENTS

Franklin & Marshall College demonstrates the dedication to individual attention one expects from a private liberal arts school. The admissions process typically begins with a small guided tour of the campus by a knowledgeable underclass student, followed by a one-on-one interview with a member of the admissions team.

FRANKLIN & MARSHALL CLOTHING

In 2003 Franklin & Marshall College entered into an agreement with the already popular Italian clothing line Franklin and Marshall. F&M agreed to license their name to the company, already prevalent across Europe, especially with UK youth, though the clothing company usually opts to omit the ampersand. Franklin and Marshall clothing uses a modified version of F&M's crest during the school's days as an all-male academy as well as retro images from F&M yearbooks to create an authentic-feeling line of stylish collegiate apparel. Can't make it to Europe? Stop in the F&M bookstore to browse the latest from Franklin and Marshall.

Long walks across the meticulously landscaped greens, peeks into the intimate classroom settings, and a taste of the dining services' chow are usually enough to get the student started on the application process.

Typically, the staff member who meets with the student to discuss Franklin & Marshall assists the student with any hiccups in the application process, which can be done online or submitted in hard copy.

The goal of the admissions staff is to help one decide if F&M is the right school for the student, before admissions decides if the student is right for F&M.

In the 2009–2010 year 44.7 percent of applicants were accepted, with average SAT scores slightly above 1300. Prospective students may choose to submit two recent graded writing samples in lieu of standardized test scores.

Requirements

Franklin & Marshall also requires a high school transcript, recommendations from two teachers and a counselor, a personal essay, and the supplement to the Common Application. F&M recommends four years of English and math, three or four of foreign language, three each of lab science and history, and one or two courses in art or music. For students demonstrating an advanced understanding, F&M offers the option to test out of certain math and science degree requirements, and the option to test out of certain foreign language requirements after being accepted to F&M.

Transfer students must present a minimum of four course credits completed at an accredited university, a dean's form, recommendations from two faculty members, and a letter explaining the reason for transfer, as well as the regular admissions materials. Sixteen of thirty-two courses required for the bachelor's degree must be completed at F&M.

First year students are admitted for the fall and spring, with Early Decision deadline being November 15th and January 15th, and regular decision February 1st. Notifications for Early Decision are sent out December 15th, Regular Decision April 1st.

AP and CLEP credits are accepted.

ACADEMIC LIFE

Academic life at Franklin & Marshall begins in the same personal setting as social life. First-year students are enrolled in a seminar-style class with other students from their College House. From the beginning, F&M students are encouraged to discuss their ideas, to share insights, to engage knowledge on a constant basis. One professor who shares the dual roles of class proctor and first-year adviser conducts the seminar. The small class size prevalent at F&M is especially apparent in this seminar, fostering an organic relationship that allows the professor to better advise the student through the potentially treacherous first year.

From the beginning students are free to make their way through a myriad of paths toward a B.A. degree. F&M offers many popular majors, such as Biology, English, Geology, Chemistry, Psychology, and Business, Organization and Society, as well as more traditional liberal arts pursuits: Philosophy, Religious Studies, Classics, Sociology, Anthropology and, of course, the Fine Arts. Franklin & Marshall also offers a plethora of language study programs, some for a major, such as German and Spanish, and others for a minor, like Japanese and Arabic.

> 66 *Chinese Ink Painting was one of the most unique class experiences at F&M. Not only did I learn the technique of Chinese ink painting, but also the mentality behind it. This led to my development on two levels: first, the physical skills required to produce a work of art and second, the mental state required to understand the 'why' behind the paintings.* 99

—*E. Kahn, '08*

To facilitate the education process F&M offers 3-2 degree programs with five schools, including Duke and the Pennsylvania State University College of Engineering and cross-registration with the Lancaster Theological Seminary and Millersville University. F&M offers the opportunity to study urban planning and architecture at Columbia University, theater in Connecticut, and oceanography in Massachusetts. Franklin & Marshall also offers the opportunity to study abroad in more than 200 countries, such as the Czech Republic, Denmark, England, France, Germany, Italy, India, Japan, and Turkey.

General Education

Franklin & Marshall also encourages educational exploration, with the general education distribution requiring one course in arts, humanities, social science, non-Western cultures, and two natural sciences, including a lab. To fulfill these requirements F&M offers courses in everything from Chinese Ink Painting to Astronomy, from Symbolic Logic to Jack Kerouac. To satiate the students' ravenous desire to expand their knowledge, more esoteric courses are offered on a wide range of specialty subjects: Cognitive Neuroscience, Statistics, Stochastic Processes, History of the Blues, and Sociology of Medicine, to name just a few.

Classes

The small size of F&M's student body lends itself to an intimate classroom setting, with class sessions being more conducted by the professor than being taught. The close relationships between peers and between students and professors promote progress and a genuine exchange of ideas. The F&M classroom is closer to a group of close friends discussing cherished ideals than a megaphone speaking to masses of dozing coeds. Elementary topics are breezed over, complex ones elaborated.

> **❝** *I'm still good friends with my freshman seminar adviser. We talk about school sure, but we also text random lolz; sometimes we'll get a drink. It's a unique relationship that only a school like F&M could provide.* **❞**

—*Nicholas Novak, '08*

The Library

Let's face it; if you're at F&M you're going to be spending a lot of time in the library. For those desiring a work space with a little extracurricular stimulation, the Fackenthal Library has everything you need. Long tables on the mezzanine overlook the first floor for people watching, picture windows on the ground floor pour in sunlight filtered through foliage, perfect for drifting through daydreams. Soundproofed rooms make even the rowdiest study party library-friendly, and truly large gatherings can always take up roost in the lavishly appointed Academy Room. Of course the Shad-Fack isn't all fun and games. A vast collection of reference materials, two computer labs, three floors of quiet study, wireless Internet throughout, and Jazzman's just a skip away make the Shad-Fack the perfect place to camp out during a particularly tough week.

For those seeking study environs with less distraction, the Martin Library of the Sciences provides the ideal serious session setting. Half the size of the Shadek-Fackenthal library, but with twice the computers and a strict decibel limit, as well as most of F&M's scientific and medical texts and open doors until 2 A.M., the Science library is the choice of pre-med and physical science students.

Psychology majors might finish lab work after hours in the Barishinger Life Sciences and Philosophy building, while the avid polyglot practices conjugation at the language labs located in the basement of Stager Hall. F&M is filled with nooks to hit the books, whether you're a lone wolf or social butterfly.

Faculty

At F&M approximately two-thirds of students have at least one one-on-one course experience with a faculty member. Many take a capstone course, which usually involves the student and a small group of peers undertaking an intensive research project under the guidance of a faculty member or two. The capstone courses encourage peer editing and review and allow the students to express the width and breadth of their newly garnered knowledge.

SOCIAL LIFE AND ACTIVITIES

By now it's been made clear that F&M students are no slouches, but all work and no play makes for some seriously stressed students. Thankfully there's a lot to do around the F&M campus, so students who work hard can have a chance to play hard too.

> *Being a part of the Chessmen at F&M provided the kind of support similar to the keystone in a well-constructed archway. It taught me not only to have the confidence to express myself onstage, but to inspire those around me to do the same. The Chessmen transcend being just another student group to being a part of you that will remain for years to come.*

—Drew Degen, '08

As well as the lavishly appointed common rooms found on virtually every floor in every housing building, F&M and the surrounding areas furnish many options for simply hanging out. Jazzman's café provides large leather chairs, toasty fires, and roasted coffee in the blustery months, while warmer weather may inspire a trip to Dosie Dough's, a locally owned, locally grown bakery. The perfect deli sandwich can be found at Thomas' Campus Deli (the Manheim is recommended for the brave). For those seeking finer fare, there's always the sustainable, organic restaurant John J. Jefferies, located at the Lancaster Arts Hotel, just a few blocks from campus, where the bison tartar dances across the palate. Those looking for an artistic bastion close to home will relish the company and the student art lining the halls of the Arts House, while the more adventurous might mosey down to Gallery Row on First Friday, when more than eighty local artist galleries and shops, including vintage clothing and record stores are open late. Lancaster County takes great pride in inspiring creativity and nurturing artists, as well as being fun for more plebeian pursuits. For the upcoming gourmand, Central Market offers the freshest and most delicious bounty Lancaster County has to offer. Sports fans make sure to check out the Clipper Magazine Stadium, made possible by the success of *Clipper Magazine*, started in part by F&M grads Steve Zuckerman and Ian Ruzow.

Clubs and Societies

Like any college F&M has its own cosmos of clubs and societies, everything from the Gourmet Society to the Chessmen and Sweet Ophelia, F&M's *a capella* groups, from the Black Student Union to Hillel, dance, debate, drama, and of course a chapter of Phi Beta Kappa. For the student on the lookout for the ever-elusive "free food," look no further than the next gathering of the Writers Commune at the Philadelphia Alumni Writers House, a place where students gather at all times of the day and night to laugh, talk, be. Those looking for a little privacy can curl up in the Zen garden adjacent to the International House or up a tree in Buchanan Park, abutting the southern end of campus.

Theater and Art

Franklin & Marshall also sponsors student theatrical productions in the Green Room Theatre, located on campus, or for more esoteric productions the Other Room Theatre, just three blocks off campus. Exhibits at the Philadelphia Museum of Art, student and otherwise, guest speakers such as Eric Schlosser of Fast Food Nation, Judy Wicks, founder of Philadelphia's White Dog Café, or literary luminary David Foster Wallace, bands such as the White Stripes at the Chameleon Club, or the Roots right on campus, and free movies on the green are all offered as rewards for the arduous work required at F&M.

Greek Life

Greek life plays a role in the social scene of F&M, with twenty-eight percent of men enrolled in seven national fraternities and twenty-three percent of women belonging to three national sororities. Since re-recognition of the Greek system in 2004, Greeks haven't just been about partying. Greeks sponsor everything from Delta's beanbag toss at the Spring Art Festival to Chi Phi's annual Run/Walk for Cancer and the famous duo of Chi Omega and Kappa Sigma's annual haunted house, open to the public at the Kappa Sigma House in the North Charlotte Street Historic District. Of course that's not to say that the doors don't open once in a while: fraternity parties offer a chance for students who wouldn't normally interact to socialize on an equal footing.

Athletics

The dedicated will find their place among F&M's division champion Women's Lacrosse team or the D1 wrestling squad. With twenty-seven intercollegiate and thirteen intramural sports offered to men and women, there's a sport for everyone, from golf to frolf (Frisbee golf), squash, and crew, and if nothing else jog out to southern practice fields to throw around with Deep Blue, F&M's Ultimate Frisbee team. Sports facilities include a 3,000-seat gym, 4 squash courts, a wrestling room, fifty-four acres of playing field, a 400-meter all-weather track, a strength center, and tennis courts. The Alumni Sports and Fitness Center houses a fitness and aerobic center, five multipurpose courts, two jogging tracks, and an Olympic-size pool.

Festival

Finally what would a year be without at least a couple of all-out bashes to look forward to? When the weather turns friendly there's the Spring Arts Festival, where student bands perform, display their art, and celebrate the sublime clime of F&M in the spring. The school closes down a few blocks of West James Street for an afternoon and the food, music, and fun don't stop. In the middle of the reading days before finals week there's always the delicious Flapjack Festival, all you can eat pancakes served by your favorite professors and deans. And of course, the all-time campus favorite: just as exams end and as you click "send" on that final paper, the curtains come up and the yellow lights go on at the Lancaster County Carnival, complete with cotton candy and funnel cake, Ferris wheels and tilt-a-whirls. Truly the finest way to celebrate a job well done!

FINANCIAL AID

At a school as costly as Franklin & Marshall College it should come as no surprise that fifty-six percent of full-time students receive some form of aid and forty-one percent of students receive need-based aid. Average aid packages are at around $25,000 for need-based and $11,000 for non-need-based. F&M offers a plethora of avenues through which aid can be obtained. From awards for academic excellence to rewards for community service, work-study programs, and federal loans, F&M is committed to exploring every avenue of aid for its students. Forty-four percent of undergraduates work part-time. School-sponsored work-study opportunities include jobs such as answering phones at the information desk, checking out and shelving books at one of the libraries, and painting dorm rooms over the summer with Facilities & Operations. Lancaster County offers boundless employment possibilities, from retail at the Tanger Outlets to working with chefs at the Zagat-rated Gibraltar's restaurant or efficiency consulting with Armstrong Industries, as well as the less-taxing clerical positions available everywhere from Royer's Florist to the Beer & Beverage Shoppe.

F&M and its impressive alumni provide several options for outstanding scholarships. From the coveted and exclusive Marshall Fellowship for Academic Excellence to the William H. Gray Scholarship for students from underrepresented ethnic backgrounds who demonstrate academic strength, leadership ability, and strong moral character, aid is there for those who need it.

However, if one exhausts all available options and is still unable to afford tuition, deans and prefects employ an aggressive outreach process to ensure that students seek out assistance from the Financial Aid Office. In fact, there are additional funds for students who experience changes in family income during their time at the college.

As a rapidly growing school F&M has increased tuition by at least $1,000 every year since 2003 and some students have found that their financial aid packages do not increase to match this inflation. The college changed this policy beginning with the class of 2013, so that grant aid will increase with tuition.

Fortunately the Financial Aid Office is extremely helpful, located centrally between the Philadelphia Alumni Writers House and the Phi Kappa Tau fraternity on scenic College Avenue. The staff at the Financial Aid Office is willing to work with every family, from assisting in loan applications to reviewing FAFSA forms before they are submitted and writing aid decision appeals, to help Franklin & Marshall students. However, their reach extends only so far and once all alternatives have been explored, there is little else they can do.

It is recommended that students plan for the rising cost of tuition when considering F&M, and those lucky enough not to have such concerns should capitalize on that fact. Education is expensive, but ignorance more so, and it cannot be contested that the education F&M offers is worth every dime.

The average indebtedness of a 2008 graduate was $27,152. F&M is a member of the CSS (College Scholarship Service), and requires the CSS profile of FAFSA, and, if applicable, business/farm supplements and noncustodial parents' statements. The deadline for filing a financial aid application for first-years is February 1st.

GRADUATES

As a school that prides itself on academic and extracurricular excellence, Franklin & Marshall also boasts an impressive record of graduate employment and graduate school acceptance.

Between July 1st, 2009 and June 30th, 2010, a total of 467 bachelor's degrees were conferred in forty different majors, the most popular being Government and Business, Organizations and Society with about eighteen percent apiece. The next most popular major is English, which comes as no surprise considering the phenomenal English department faculty. In fact, alumni were so grateful to the department that in 2004 they opened the Philadelphia Alumni Writers House, a building beautiful both inside and out.

LIST OF NOTABLE GRADUATES

- Mary Schapiro, '77, Chairwoman of the Securities and Exchange Commission (SEC)
- Kenneth Duberstein, '65, White House Chief of Staff under President Ronald Reagan
- William H. Gray, '63, former U.S. Congressman from Pennsylvania, former President of United Negro College Fund
- Roy Scheider, '55, Actor (*Jaws*, *All That Jazz*) (1932–2008)
- Bowie Kuhn, '48, Commissioner of Baseball (1969-1984)
- Franklin Schaffner, '42, Oscar-winning Film Director (*Patton*, *Planet of the Apes*) (1920–1989)

Indeed, Franklin & Marshall alumni often express their gratitude for the school that enabled their success through monetary donations. Buildings such as the stellar Alumni Sports and Fitness Center, complete with Olympic-size swimming pool, two indoor tracks, and five multipurpose courts, owe their existence to generous F&M alumni and the school that allowed them to achieve success. It is the superior education F&M provides that allows already gifted students to actualize their ambitions, to succeed with such magnitude, such enormity.

Given the rising cost of education, both monetarily and temporally, America has seen an increase in the average number of years students require to graduate. To accompany its already sterling reputation for graduate employment, seventy-nine percent of F&M students graduate within four years or less, eighty-four percent in five or less, and eighty-five percent in six years or less.

Graduates from F&M enjoy a wide range of careers, from rappers like Spliff Star to Mary Schapiro, appointed chairwoman of the SEC by President Barack Obama. Truly, with an F&M education, anything is possible!

Franklin & Marshall offers a premium education and a superior social atmosphere, as well as student services second to none. Whether it is the Kosher International Vegan Organic (KIVO) option in the dining hall, school-sponsored trips to NYC to see Broadway plays at huge discounts, buses to the enormous and enormously famous Lancaster County Outlets and the King of Prussia Mall, access to school-owned automobiles and bicycles, or dining hall specials where F&M hosts chefs from schools across the Northeast to compete with the students as the judges, the accoutrements to an F&M education are almost enough in themselves to warrant application to Franklin & Marshall College. But don't forget that the education is world-class as well. At F&M one will find all that is needed to flourish emotionally, physically, spiritually, and academically. F&M asks that you give your best and offers its best in return.

❏ *Nicholas Novack, '08*

THE GEORGE WASHINGTON UNIVERSITY

The George Washington University
Washington, DC 20052

(202) 994-6040
Fax: (202) 994-0325

E-mail: *gwadm@gwu.edu*
Website: *http://www.gwu.edu/~go2gw*

 Enrollment

Full-time ❏ women: 5,329
　　　　　❏ men: 4,198

Part-time ❏ women: 248
　　　　　❏ men: 280

INTRODUCING THE GEORGE WASHINGTON UNIVERSITY

At the George Washington University, our location in the heart of Washington, D.C. is not just *where* we are, it is also a large part of *who* we are. Our namesake, President George Washington, envisioned a world-class university situated in the nation's capital that would bring together students from all backgrounds and teach them to become global leaders. Nearly 200 years later, we are that university, home to students and faculty from every state and more than 130 countries, who learn and work together and who take full advantage of our global setting to enrich the classroom experience.

GW's renowned faculty embodies the richness of the curriculum, and includes a Pulitzer Prize winner, former White House staff members, diplomats, and other leading experts in business, science, arts, and the humanities. Each semester, professors create vibrant learning communities in which students experience the traditional modes of instruction but also hands-on training from some of the most influential leaders of our time. In fact, GW is the only university in the country to have the honor of hosting the entire First Family, as well as Vice President Joe Biden and Dr. Jill Biden, countless Members of Congress, Nobel Prize winners, more than a dozen current and former heads of state, journalists, artists, scientists and inventors, CEO's, and icons from nearly every field of endeavor.

The foundation of the GW academic experience is built on the belief that learning does not—and should not—end at the edge of campus. Instead, GW students utilize Washington, D.C. as an extended classroom unlike any other university. For example, GW students have exclusive opportunities to take classes at the Smithsonian Institution. They also work closely with their professors to conduct research at the National Institutes of Health, or attend symposiums at the World Bank, the State Department, or the Kennedy Center. GW's deep connections with many of the most powerful and influential institutions and corporations in the world provide unparalleled opportunities to apply knowledge gained in the classroom to tackle real-world challenges.

Despite all that they do throughout D.C., GW students still find time to be part of a close-knit, diverse campus community. Students live on campus in one of thirty-one on-campus residence halls and seventeen townhouses. Each GW student has a Guide to Personal Success, who works to help with the transition to college and provides support through the freshman year. GW students are also firmly committed to service, and the GW community recently exceeded First Lady Michelle Obama's challenge to complete 100,000 hours of service in a single academic year, which resulted in her keynote address at Commencement.

The Campus

Chartered by Congress in 1821, GW moved to its current location in the Foggy Bottom neighborhood in the early 1920s. The Foggy Bottom campus is surrounded by the Potomac River, the Kennedy Center for the Performing Arts, to the West; the White House and the World Bank to the East; Pennsylvania Avenue to the North; and the U.S. Department of State and Lincoln Memorial to the South. In 1998, the twenty-six-acre Mount Vernon Campus became a part of the university, located amid the rolling green hills of Foxhall Road. The Mount Vernon Campus offers several residence halls, academic buildings, and outdoor athletic facilities surrounded by embassies and diplomatic residences. Both campuses are close to all the conveniences of city living and are connected by shuttle service twenty-four hours a day.

In addition, GW has a visible presence throughout Northern Virginia, having offered educational programs in Virginia for over fifty years. The Virginia Science Technology Campus located in Loudoun County is home to GW's School of Nursing, several high-tech research labs in a range of emerging industries as well as a myriad of graduate programs in a variety of fields.

ADMISSIONS REQUIREMENTS

Admission to GW is highly selective with more than 21,000 applications for 2,350 spaces, resulting in a 31.5 percent admit rate. Of those admitted, the average SAT score is 1960 and nearly three-quarters rank in the top ten percent of their graduating class. Quality academics, an unparalleled location, and amazing professional opportunities combine to make the school very attractive to students all over the country and the world. This mass appeal provides for the incredible diversity found at the university—diversity in thought, in religion, in demographics, and in disciplines, a fitting match for one of the most culturally diverse places in the world.

Requirements

The Admissions Office looks to select and enroll students for the freshman class who are not only scholars, but who will be active contributors to the GW community. In doing so, a number of factors—academic performance, extracurricular involvement, and excellence in academic pursuits—are considered. Students are encouraged to visit the university's website for a description of the application process and a listing of required documents. Potential applicants may consider from one of three application options—Early Decision 1 or Early Decision II with application deadlines of November 10 and January 10, respectively; or Regular Decision with a deadline of January 10.

Visiting GW

A campus visit is a very important aspect of the college application process because it allows prospective students to learn first-hand about GW's engaging college experience and the vibrant city that awaits them. The Admissions Welcome Center is located on our Foggy Bottom Campus, but visitors can take advantage of a variety of visit options on the Mount Vernon campus as well. Interested students should consult the website for the daily visit schedule, as well as open houses, interviews, and other visit opportunities.

ACADEMIC LIFE

GW students are energized by the academic rigor of the university. Professors challenge students to think critically in a dynamic and engaging classroom environment. By encouraging intellectual curiosity, professors empower students to work toward solving real-world problems. GW students learn from experts in their fields who draw on personal and professional experiences that highlight material covered in class. Theory-in-action is a core element of GW's academic personality, and undergraduates are actively engaged in their own discovery through research and internship opportunities.

This also means that students have special learning opportunities and often have a front row seat to history-making events. For example, you may be taking a journalism class taught by former CNN Washington bureau chief Frank Sesno, see him commenting on current events on network evening news, and then be invited to a televised town hall he is moderating between Secretary of State Hillary Clinton and Secretary of Defense Robert Gates. From students who were able to discuss Haiti's reconstruction with top officials just weeks after the massive earthquake, to others who traveled to the Vancouver Winter Olympics and South Africa's World Cup to learn about sports marketing, GW puts students in the thick of the action.

At GW, students have access to the world of Washington that no other school can match. Students and faculty integrate the classroom and campus experience with the full range of scholarly, professional, and cultural activity. This integrated approach to education not only benefits student academic performance but also provides a vast network of contacts and resources that benefit them both professionally and personally.

Because of our location and intensive academic program, GW attracts people who want to make a difference in the world. In many GW courses, students learn while helping others. The array of service-learning courses span the disciplines and deepen the academic experience through service to local communities and organizations. For example, students of Professor Perillan's Advanced Spanish class work with local nonprofit groups to assist non-English speakers with a variety of social services. These academic experiences help prepare the forty percent of our graduating seniors who go on to careers in nonprofits, government, and education.

As the most comprehensive university in the District of Columbia, GW offers a wide range of academic fields from which to choose. Students experience both the breadth and the depth of disciplines in GW's flexible curriculum. GW's eighty-eight majors and fifty-seven minors span six undergraduate schools, including:

- Columbian College of Arts and Sciences (includes School of Media and Public Affairs)
- Elliott School of International Affairs
- School of Business
- School of Engineering and Applied Science
- School of Nursing (second bachelor's degree program)
- School of Public Health and Health Services

GW's highly competitive graduate programs collaborate with both undergraduate students and the community to address national issues and train future leaders. In addition to the six schools listed above, GW graduate programs are also available in:

- School of Medicine and Health Sciences
- Law School
- Graduate School of Education and Human Development
- College of Professional Studies (includes the Graduate School of Political Management)

Writing Programs

In an effort to help students prepare for their academic careers and create a more scholarly environment in class, the university has created one of the most rigorous writing programs in the country. The program includes courses for freshmen designed to introduce students to the norms of academic and publishable writing, as well as upper-level classes for juniors and seniors known as Writing in the Discipline courses. These classes focus on the particulars of writing in certain fields and provide students with the practice needed to be comfortable participating in scholarly research, publication, and peer review during their careers.

Faculty

Acornerstone of every GW student's academic experience is his or her relationship with faculty. Internationally recognized for leadership and scholarship, GW professors are deeply committed to teaching and research. The university boasts ninety endowed faculty positions, more than fifty-five current and former Fulbright scholars, and several members of the National Academies. In the last decade, six GW faculty members have been awarded the Carnegie Foundation's prestigious "Professor of the Year" Award, more than any other DC-based institution.

> ### FACULTY COMMITMENT
>
> GW's faculty actively seeks ways to make the academic experience current and relevant for our students. This commitment includes changes in curriculum to meet employer demands, introduction of new interdisciplinary courses, and designing evaluation standards and assignments to test students on their reasoning skills.

At GW, the faculty excel at integrating cutting-edge research and professional experiences into classroom instruction. Professors expertly link theory with practice, inspiring students to pursue their academic passions. As educators, the professors at GW guide students to become thoughtful individuals, accomplished leaders, and involved citizens.

The Faculty in Residence and Faculty Guide programs enhance students' experience outside of the classroom and are designed to enhance the life of students in each residence hall. These faculty members support the academic mission of the university by facilitating educationally purposeful programs outside of the classroom. Faculty Guides and Faculty in Residence hosted over 200 programs during the 2009–2010 academic year.

Classrooms and Facility Space

GW's intimate learning and research environments are enhanced by state-of the-art technology. Over the past decade, GW has constructed or renovated more than a dozen academic buildings, recreational sites, and residence halls, including two Gold LEED-certified residence halls, South Hall on the Foggy Bottom campus, and West Hall on the Mount Vernon campus. The newest teaching technologies are standard in all GW classrooms. More than fifty-six percent of the undergraduate courses have fewer than twenty students, and almost twenty-five percent have fewer than ten students.

Resources

The university offers a number of resources to support the academic mission for undergraduates. The Gelman and Eckles libraries offer more than two million volumes, subscribe to hundreds of periodicals, and provide a number of study and group meeting spaces. Additionally, the local consortium of libraries gives GW students access to more than five million volumes in the D.C. area. Staff throughout Student and Academic Support Services work closely with students in various capacities to assist with their GW questions. The Study Abroad Office is another resource for students interested in academic study overseas. Annually, about half of the junior class spends at least one semester abroad. Additionally, the Writing Center on campus is a free student resource that offers peer mentoring and collaborative learning to help students improve their own writing. For international students, the International Student Office offers assistance to help students transition to their new home.

Special Programs

At GW, freshmen who want to expand their interests may apply for admission to a number of specialized programs designed to augment their traditional classroom experience. Many of these programs offer co-curricular experiences, residential housing options, and specialized coursework. All programs are fully integrated into the general curriculum.

SPECIAL PROGRAMS

These programs include
- University Honors Program
- Seven-Year BA/MD Program
- Scholars in Quantitative and Natural Sciences
- Presidential Scholars in the Arts Program in Theater, Art, Dance, Music, and Fine Arts
- Elizabeth Somers Women's Leadership Program
- Dean's Scholars in Shakespeare
- Combined BA/MA programs

SOCIAL LIFE AND ACTIVITIES

GW students are active, concerned, and passionate about the causes they believe in, and our campus activities reflect those passions. Our Student Activities Center sponsors major events centered on social justice, culture, entertainment, and the arts. GW capitalizes partnerships across the district to provide speakers, programs, workshops, and professional development.

GW even has its own metro stop, and students enjoy getting out into the city. However, filling your social calendar with activities right here on campus is equally as easy to accomplish. The fun begins within the residence halls, as GW Housing Programs provide some of the most attractive and modern residence halls in the country and also hosts a number of in-house programs for freshmen.

Students can choose to take part in Living and Learning Communities. GW Housing Programs provides opportunities for students to engage in topics around civic engagement, sustainability, and the performing arts.

> 66 *GW affords the opportunity to conduct service around all 8 wards of the District of Columbia, across the country and around the world. We attract and cultivate a population of students that care about their communities and want to give back which is creating a generation of civically engaged scholars and leaders.* 99

—*Darnell Cadette, '10*

Athletics

The Lerner Health and Wellness Center is a state-of-the-art wellness and workout facility with everything from Pilates and yoga to weightlifting and squash. The facility as well as the athletic fields at the Mount Vernon Campus are the perfect places for the 1,000 to 3,500 students who passionately participate in the wide range of intramural and club sports. Those interested in playing Division I NCAA sports will be pleased to see the selection GW offers of 22 intercollegiate varsity sports. With a recent multi-million dollar renovation, the Smith Center hosts some of the most exciting basketball action in the D.C. area.

Student Organizations

GW students continue to build their leadership skills and knowledge outside the classroom through the many diverse student groups and activities that make the campus come alive. Students have many options to follow their passions, by participating in over 400 student organizations or joining one of forty-three national sororities and fraternities including 12 multicultural Greek organizations. GW is also home to a very active student government and award-winning student newspaper (*The Hatchet*).

The GW community also shows its spirit for our NCAA teams at a series of special events during Spirit Week. Colonials Invasion gives coaches and players a chance to rally fan support for the upcoming basketball season. Students can join the "Colonial Army" and become one of the thousands of fans sporting buff and blue hats and cheering on our teams.

Other long-standing GW traditions include: Colonial Inauguration, GW's award-winning undergraduate orientation program and Colonials Weekend during October when students, alumni, family, and friends come together for a weekend of events and world-class entertainment. Past Colonials Weekend performers include Jimmy Fallon, Jerry Seinfeld, Jon Stewart, and Whoopi Goldberg. These are just some of the traditions that build GW spirit.

Arts and Entertainment

Arts and entertainment options abound on campus, as well. Students can cheer on friends at many performing arts events, at Betts Theatre or the new Black Box Theater on the Mount Vernon campus. The Program Board brings big-name acts to campus for events including Fall Fest and Fountain Day. Recent headliners have included Kanye West, the Black Eyed Peas, and Maroon 5. Those interested in art, theater, and dance are treated to a continuous host of performances in Lisner Auditorium, one of Washington's most popular venues. Student organization partnerships with the Multicultural Student Center and University faculty bring world-class writers and cultural leaders to campus, including: Pulitzer Prize winner Junot Diaz, Dr. Michael Eric Dyson, Nikki Giovanni, M.C. Lyte, and Dolores Huerta.

Beyond Campus—D.C. Life

For those ready to venture beyond campus, the city represents the ultimate playground for a college student! Less than five minutes from campus, students can attend free concerts at the Kennedy Center. Cultural institutions such as the Smithsonian Institution, the Corcoran Art Gallery, and Ford's Theater are just steps from Foggy Bottom. Students often find themselves visiting not just for pleasure, but also as part of coursework or internships. In addition, there are dozens of event venues that are a short Metro ride from campus.

A lot happens here! For foodies and fashionistas, the Foggy Bottom area is surrounded by neighborhoods known for their culinary treats. Walking through Dupont Circle or Adams Morgan, you'll likely find it hard to resist the smells of Malaysian, Italian, Indian, Thai, and Spanish cuisine. Hop on the Metro to U Street for some of the best jazz on the East Coast or the legendary 9:30 Club, home to some of the most popular bands in the country. Grab the Blue Line Metro to Eastern Market and enjoy fresh seafood, vegetables, pastries, and fine local artwork. Socially or professionally, the city offers an infinite number of possibilities.

FINANCIAL AID

We are committed to helping families meet the costs of a GW education. Over the last five years, the amount of funding available for undergraduate financial aid has increased forty-seven percent, ranking GW fourth in the *U.S. News & World Reports'* list of schools with the most need-based financial aid awarded.

GW also offers a fixed-price tuition program, which means that tuition for each undergraduate will remain unchanged for up to five years. For example, the graduating class of 2010 paid the same tuition in 2010 as it did when it arrived at GW in the fall of 2005. Students attending similar institutions experienced a tuition increase on average of roughly fifteen percent over the same four-year period.

The Office of Student Financial Assistance works tirelessly to help students secure aid in the form of institutional and federal grants, work study, and federal loans. To be considered for need-based financial assistance, students must submit the Free Application for Federal Student Aid (FAFSA) and the CSS Profile. In addition to need-based assistance, the university also offers academic-based scholarships for which all students are considered at the time of admission.

VETERANS

GW has a long history of educating and supporting student veterans. The first recipient of the 1944 GI Bill was a GW student named Don A. Balfour. In 2010 alone more than 550 student veterans are enrolled at GW, including more than 300 who are taking advantage of the Yellow Ribbon Program, part of the GI Bill passed after 9/11, which provides returning veterans with enhanced access to private colleges and universities.

As one of the leading participants in the program, GW has budgeted up to $2.8 million for the program in 2010–2011, which will be matched by the Department of Veterans Affairs. Veterans who qualify for GW's Yellow Ribbon Program receive about a seventy-one percent discount on full-time graduate tuition and a one hundred percent discount of undergraduate tuition.

The university also was recently was named a top "military friendly" school by *GI Jobs* magazine; GW also ranked twenty-one out of 4,400 colleges in the "Military Times' Best for Vets" college rankings, including fourth in the nation among private universities.

GRADUATES

With a community of more than 225,000 alumni in 150 countries around the world, GW graduates make use of their comprehensive academic training to propel them into careers and activities that give back to the local and global communities. The link between real-world opportunities found only in Washington, D.C. and rigorous classroom learning has come to define GW, and prepares our alumni to be engaged citizen leaders. Their time on campus also forges enduring bonds of friendship and pride that last throughout their lives.

- Dr. Ralph A. Alpher, BA '43, MA '45, PhD '48, Physicist, Published Big Bang Theory
- Chris Anderson, B.S. '81, Author of *Free: The Future of a Radical Price* and Editor of *Wired* magazine
- The Honorable Eric Cantor, B.A. '85, House Majority Leader
- Abby Joseph Cohen M.A. '76, President; Global Markets Institute, Goldman Sachs
- Dr. Scott Cowen, M.B.A. '72, D.B.A. '75, President, Tulane University
- The Honorable Tammy Duckworth, Assistant secretary for Veterans Affairs
- Dr. Anwar Mohammed Gargash, B.A. '81, M.A. '84, Minister of State for Foreign Affairs, United Arab Emirates
- Edward "Skip" W. Gnehm, Jr., BA '66, M.A. '68, Former U.S. Ambassador to Jordan and Kuwait; GW Kuwait Professor of Gulf and Arabian Peninsula Affairs
- The Honorable Daniel Inouye, J.D. '52, Senate President Pro Tempore
- Madeleine Jacobs, B.A. '68, Hon. Dr. Sc. '03, Executive Director and CEO of the American Chemical Society
- Scott Kirby, M.S. '93, President, US Airways Group, Inc.
- Randy Levine Esq., B.A. '77, President, NY Yankees
- Dr. William P. Magee, M.D. '72, Co-Founder and CEO, Operation Smile
- Jacqueline Kennedy Onassis, B.A.,'51, Former First Lady
- General Colin Powell, M.B.A., '71, Former Secretary of State
- The Honorable Harry M. Reid, J.D., '64, Senate Majority Leader
- The Honorable Mary L. Schapiro, J.D., '80, Chairman, Securities Exchange Commission
- The Honorable John W. Snow, J.D., '67, Former Secretary of the Treasury, Chairman, Cerberus Capital Management
- Kenneth W. Starr, B.A., '68, President, Baylor University
- Van Toffler, B.A. '80, President, MTV Networks Music/Logo/Films Group
- The Honorable Mark Warner, B.A., '77, U.S. Senator
- Kerry Washington, CCAS B.A. '98, Actress
- Ellen Zane, B.A. '73, CEO, Tufts-New England Medical Center
- Rachel Zoe, CCAS B.A. '93, Celebrity Fashion Stylist

Our alumni include former secretaries of state, top White House officials, thirteen Members of Congress, presidents of foreign countries, award-winning journalists, four-star generals, successful social entrepreneurs, CEOs, and individuals who have made an impact on our society's culture like Ina Garten (aka The Barefoot Contessa) and actress Kerry Washington.

GW is also proud that it is the #1 provider of Peace Corps volunteers in the country among medium-size universities. In the past decade, 499 graduating seniors have gone on to serve in the Peace Corps. In addition, GW is one of the top producers of Fulbright scholars in the nation.

GW's students are able to learn how to succeed in the classroom and how to transition that success into every aspect of their lives. They are assisted in achieving their personal and professional goals in the academic setting and beyond through close relationships with faculty members and our career centers. GW's career centers have strong relationships with top employers through partnership initiatives, programs, and events. They directly connect approximately 5,000 students with almost 600 employers annually through a robust on-campus interviewing program, employer information sessions, career/internship fairs and industry expos. A sample of employers who regularly recruit on campus include Bloomberg, Booz Allen Hamilton, Deloitte, the Federal Bureau of Investigation, IBM, Johnson & Johnson, Peace Corps, Teach for America, and the U.S. Department of State.

SUMMING UP

With a strong commitment to excellence and innovation, the George Washington University is an institution constantly moving forward. The university's premiere location provides outstanding opportunities for social and professional engagement. GW faculty help create a learning environment that challenges, motivates, and equips students to enter successful careers at home and abroad. Indeed, GW's dynamic classroom experiences and unrivaled connections to the world's most influential organizations and institutions enable our students to complete their studies with a clear sense of where their talents can have the greatest impact—and give them a head start on getting there.

As you think about colleges, there is certainly no better institution than GW to help you prepare for your future, whatever you study. Indeed, in a city shaping the future, GW is a university where faculty and students not only study the world but work together to change it.

❏ *Brian Hawthorne, B.A.*

GEORGETOWN UNIVERSITY

 Georgetown University
Washington, DC 20057

 (202) 687-3600
Fax: (202) 687-5084

 E-mail: *guadmiss@georgetown.edu*
Website: *http://www.georgetown.edu*

 Enrollment

Full-time ❏ women: 3,913
❏ men: 3,202

Part-time ❏ women: 183
❏ men: 135

INTRODUCING GEORGETOWN

The nation's oldest Catholic university, Georgetown University, is a vibrant, student-centered institution dedicated to educating a diversity of students in the Jesuit tradition. Committed to engaging people in open dialogue, Georgetown considers the undergraduate experience a vital component of its mission. Georgetown is one of the few schools of higher education that effectively combines the benefits of a large research university with the community and uniqueness of a small liberal arts college.

Georgetown offers a superb faculty and cutting-edge research opportunities while encouraging intentional reflection on questions of faith, meaning, and truth. Drawing on their broad exposure to the liberal arts, students engage the faculty and each other through critical thinking and thoughtful debate. Georgetown's four undergraduate schools include the Georgetown College of Arts and Sciences, the School of Nursing and Health Studies, the Walsh School of Foreign Service, and the McDonough School of Business. Academic life at Georgetown is rigorous and driven by a belief in holistic education. The institution focuses on the whole person, simultaneously fostering intellectual, spiritual, and social development.

> **66** *My earliest memory of Georgetown begins with crossing the Potomac River and driving into the District of Columbia. The lampposts lining the Key Bridge were adorned with flying blue and gray balloons—I felt like the entire city was welcoming the new class of Hoyas! And so began my Georgetown experience, a time of challenging classes and professors, life-changing relationships, and inspiring conversations and events. From the time I spent my days in New Student Orientation until the day that I walked across the Commencement stage, Georgetown remained the driving force behind my development as a reflective human being dedicated to a life of service to others.* **99**

Drawing students from all fifty states and more than 120 countries, Georgetown continues to fulfill its foundational commitment to diversity. By encouraging spiritual inquiry and development in all faiths, it has attracted students of every religious tradition and background since its founding in 1789. Georgetown University offers academic programs in arts, humanities, sciences, international relations, nursing and health studies, business administration, law, and medicine. In addition, Georgetown prides itself on a multitude of volunteer opportunities and student activities complete with cultural, political, academic, and social organizations.

Due to its prominent position overlooking the Potomac River, Georgetown University is often affectionately called the Hilltop. It sits on 104 acres of land, a mere mile and a half from downtown Washington, D.C. Although Georgetown relishes its appeal as an urban institution, it still provides the feel of a small residential campus. Its sixty buildings include six libraries with over two million volumes, two dining halls, athletic facilities, and residence halls and apartment complexes featuring high-speed Internet access. Washington, D.C. is a fantastic city for students, offering museums, galleries, libraries, theaters, concerts, sports events, and festivals—many of them free-of-charge and easy to access via Georgetown transportation shuttles and public Metro system. Of course, Georgetown students are often drawn toward the political action in the city. Rallies, protests, political campaigns and activities, and internships abound in our nation's capital, and Georgetown often plays host to American and world leaders and international summits.

ADMISSIONS REQUIREMENTS

Georgetown is one of the most selective universities in the country, and it has seen a consistent increase in the number of applications over the last ten years. In a recent year, 18,619 applications were received, and 3,683 applicants were accepted. Approximately forty percent of accepted students ranked first, second, or third in their high school class. An outstanding high school academic record, challenging academic program, solid SAT or ACT scores, leadership and extracurricular experience, and a unique and sincere essay are necessities. Most applicants also utilize the alumni interview as a way to demonstrate their distinctiveness and desire to enroll. Georgetown is definitely looking for more than an exceptional academic background; the school is seeking creative students with a diversity of interests.

Applicants must choose one of the four undergraduate schools when applying. The application essay and other admissions requirements may differ with each school. In general, applicants' secondary school education should include a full program in English, a minimum of two years each of social studies, modern language, and mathematics, and one year of natural science. There are additional school-specific recommendations as well. Applicants are also asked to submit the results of at least three SAT Subject Tests. Candidates for the Walsh School of Foreign Service or the Faculty of Languages and Linguistics (a part of the Georgetown College), for instance, should include a modern language test among these two.

Georgetown University is proud of its "need-blind" admissions policy; an applicant's ability to pay tuition costs is not a factor in the admission's process. This ensures that all qualified persons have access to a Georgetown education, regardless of financial status. All regular decision applications must be received by January 10; transfer applications are due by March 1. Georgetown also offers an Early Action Program for interested students; these applications are typically due by November 1. Although the students accepted through the

Early Action Program will be notified of their admission in December of their senior year, they, too, have until May 1 to decide if they will enroll, and they are not obligated to accept the offer of admission. Students not accepted in the Early Action program are included among the regular decision applicant pool. Generally, fifteen percent of these applicants are accepted after the regular decision review. First-year accepted students are also given the option to defer their enrollment for one year.

> 66 *I still remember the first time I walked through the Healy Gates to visit Georgetown's campus. It was alive with activism and discourse. Students read along Copley Lawn, faculty members walked through the hallways engaged in debate, and the Healy Clock Tower provided a symbol of Georgetown's international presence. I knew without a doubt that I would attend Georgetown. It remains one of the most significant decisions of my life.* 99

The Office of Undergraduate Admissions provides daily campus tours and information sessions for students and families. The student-led tours are an excellent way to get a sense of the Georgetown campus and overall student life. You can sit in on a class, eat a meal in one of the dining halls, or just chat with students, faculty, and staff. Applicants may download information and an application from the Office of Undergraduate Admissions web site (*http://www.georgetown.edu/undergrad/admissions*).

ACADEMIC LIFE

Georgetown consists of four undergraduate schools: the Georgetown College of Arts and Sciences, the School of Nursing and Health Studies, the Edmund A. Walsh School of Foreign Service, and the Robert Emmett McDonough School of Business. All of these schools also offer graduate degrees. In addition, there are graduate programs at the Georgetown University Law Center and the Medical Center. Despite their enrollment in one undergraduate school, students enjoy a shared educational community, taking courses in other schools and living and socializing with students from every major and background. Although required to remain in their chosen school for at least one year, students may opt to transfer to another undergraduate program. Most students, however, spend the entire four years in their original school.

> *Georgetown educates women and men to be reflective lifelong learners, to be responsible and active participants in civic life, and to live generously in service to others.*

—*Georgetown Mission Statement*

The Jesuit tradition ensures that students are instilled with a sense of responsibility for their community—both local and global. Accordingly, Georgetown is committed to offering students a comprehensive liberal arts education, not mere preprofessional training. All Georgetown students are required to complete the six-course liberal arts core curriculum. This includes two courses each in English, Philosophy, and Theology. There are additional school-specific course requirements as well. The Walsh School of Foreign Service, for instance, requires two courses in a regional history and four courses in economics; the McDonough School of Business, for example, requires two courses in Accounting and a course in the Social Responsibilities of Business.

Majors

Although all are shaped by Georgetown's commitment to a liberal arts education and social responsibility, the four undergraduate programs offer a variety of majors and concentrations. The Georgetown College offers majors in: American Studies, Anthropology, Arabic, Art History, Biology, Biochemistry, Chemistry, Chinese, Classics, Comparative Literature, Computer Science, Economics, English, French, German, Government, History, Interdisciplinary Studies, Italian, Japanese, Linguistics, Mathematics, Medieval Studies, Philosophy, Physics, Political Economy, Portuguese, Psychology, Russian, Sociology, Spanish, Studio Art, Theology, and Women's Studies. The College also offers minors in a variety of disciplines including Art, Music, and Theater, Environmental Studies, and Justice and Peace Studies to name a few. This diversity of offerings allows students to engage in a wide range of ideas and values.

The School of Nursing and Health Studies offers both a Nursing major and a Health Studies major that includes Science, Health Systems, and International Health tracks. Like all of the undergraduate programs, there is an emphasis on the liberal arts and sciences in conjunction with theory and clinical practice. Celebrating its centennial in 2003, the School of Nursing and Health Studies continues to produce the future leaders of the health care industry.

Established in 1919, the Walsh School of Foreign Service, the oldest school of its kind in the United States, offers concentrations in: Culture and Politics, International Economics, International History, International Politics, International Political Economy, Regional and Comparative Studies, Science, Technology and International Affairs, and individualized courses of study. All of these concentrations are multidisciplinary, engaging fields that range from economics, history, and government to sociology, philosophy, and the fine arts. The school also features extensive certificate programs that are open to students enrolled in the other three schools. These may be region-specific such as the Latin American Studies Certificate program, or discipline-related such as the International Business Diplomacy Certificate program.

The McDonough School of Business offers concentrations in: Accounting, Finance, International Business, Management, Marketing, and individualized courses of study. Business students are highly encouraged to obtain a minor within liberal arts as well. Above all, the McDonough School produces socially responsible women and men within the business community.

Faculty and Class Size

Georgetown faculty members are both cutting-edge researchers and top-notch teachers. All professors keep weekly office hours and meet regularly with students. Average class sizes echo this commitment to students by boasting an introductory lecture average of thirty-four, a laboratory average of eighteen, and a regular course average of twenty-nine. There are virtually no courses taught by graduate students, although smaller discussion sections for larger classes might be led by teaching assistants.

Georgetown's location in the nation's capital ensures that it will attract some of the world's most notable politicians, scholars, and humanitarians. It is not unlikely to see former ambassadors or world-renowned linguists teaching undergraduate courses. Georgetown's faculty boasts some of the world's leaders in all fields, and their expertise is often solicited by congressional hearings, foreign governments, and the media. Above all, however, our faculty members are widely recognized for their commitment to undergraduate teaching.

Study Abroad Opportunities

The study abroad experience is one that many Hoyas decide to pursue. With more than ninety summer, semester, and academic programs worldwide, Georgetown's division of Overseas Studies offers extensive international programs with direct matriculation, that is, students are enrolled in their host university as normal students. This creates a more authentic cultural immersion. Drawing from the Jesuit philosophy, these overseas opportunities encourage students to reflect on their identities and on their roles as responsible citizens of the world. Approximately fifty percent of the junior class opts to study abroad for at least part of the junior year. Many programs include a home-stay option for interested students, and others may travel to one of the two Georgetown-owned villas in Florence, Italy, or Alanya, Turkey. These programs offer students a chance to study with Georgetown's own professors in another country.

> 66 *I had the extreme good fortune to study for a semester in Auckland, New Zealand. It was truly a life-changing experience; one in which I learned more about myself and other cultures that I had previously thought possible. Many of my friends still refer to their time abroad as wonderful periods in their lives, allowing genuine reflection and practical learning opportunities.* 99

SOCIAL LIFE AND ACTIVITIES

Georgetown is fortunate enough to combine the benefits of an active campus life with the opportunities of a vibrant city like Washington, D.C. The Georgetown neighborhood alone provides countless restaurants, bars, and shops. The nation's capital provides an abundance of cultural and political activity with the Smithsonian Institution, the Kennedy Center for the Performing Arts, the Cherry Tree Blossom Festival, art exhibits, concerts, protests, rallies, and lectures. Many students expand their educational pursuits by obtaining internships in nonprofit organizations, media organizations, congressional offices and committees, think tanks, and a variety of other institutions. Washington, D.C. also features professional sports teams and seven other colleges and universities. Although Georgetown does not have any social fraternities, sororities, or eating clubs, the vibrant social scene centers on student organizations and campus events and the surrounding Washington, D.C. communities.

There is a high level of student activism signified by the more than 180 student organizations registered through the Office of Student Programs. There is an abundance of cultural, political, intellectual, and social groups on campus. Georgetown students participate in more than four campus media publications, a television station, and a radio station. Georgetown's Outdoor Education program offers rock-climbing, kayaking, hiking, and outdoor training programs. In addition, the Georgetown Program Board serves as the main source of campus entertainment by providing free weekly movies, large-scale concerts, comedy shows, and trips around the D.C. area. Students certainly have no trouble finding a group to suit their interests.

> **❝** *One of my fondest memories of Georgetown and Washington, D.C. begins with obtaining free tickets to a Kennedy Center performance of Harper Lee's* To Kill A Mockingbird. *A few friends and I received free tickets from the university president's office, and we trotted down to the theater. As we made our way to our seats, we began to realize that everyone around us was wearing a congressional pin. We had managed to get ourselves into the congressional viewing of the play! They had even postponed the congressional session so that the members could all attend; we were as mesmerized by the performance as we were by our fellow theater-goers.* **❞**

As mentioned above, student organizations often have a significant social component. Events such as the Holiday Gala, Business School Ball, D.C. A Cappella Festival, Late Night at Leavey, the Halloween screening of *The Exorcist* (which was filmed at Georgetown), and Diplomatic Ball are just a few of the annual events that mark a typical Hoya's semester. Georgetown also serves as a host to a myriad of lectures, panel discussions, and forums through the student-run Lecture Fund. Past speakers include former President Bill Clinton (SFS '68), Senator Hillary Rodham Clinton, Dikembe Mutumbo (COL '91), Hamid Karzai, Patricia Ireland, Reverend Al Sharpton, former Secretary of State Madeleine Albright, and former Justice Sandra Day O'Connor. All of these events are open to all Georgetown students.

The Georgetown University Student Association functions as the student government on campus. Its representatives and committee members serve as the liaison between the student body and the university administration. One of the greatest aspects of Georgetown is the amount of student ownership over the campus culture. For business-minded undergraduates, there is a multimillion dollar corporation, Students of Georgetown, Inc., that remains the largest completely student-run company in the country.

The Office of Performing Arts houses a number of student arts-related organizations. There are dance companies, an improv troupe, numerous *a cappella* groups, bands, the orchestra and choir, and three dramatic societies that produce multiple shows per semester. There is a one-act festival for student-authored scripts, an Independent Film Festival, and an annual HoyaStock battle of the bands. In addition, cultural organizations such as the South Asian Society produce performances like their Rangila show. Its 700-seat venue sells out within minutes every year!

In keeping with the Jesuit philosophy of service to others, Georgetown's Center for Social Justice contains the Volunteer and Public Service Center (VPS) where students can engage in a variety of volunteer activities. Students tutor at area schools and community centers, work at soup kitchens and shelters, and build houses through Habitat for Humanity and the Spring Break in Appalachia program. VPS is definitely one of the more active areas of campus, with more than twenty-five community service organizations. Indeed, more than 1,400 students are currently involved in weekly service projects in Washington, D.C. alone. Georgetown also provides the opportunity for service-learning credit by combining community service with academic coursework.

> 66 *The last day of classes during each spring semester has been declared 'Georgetown Day' by the entire campus community. It is one of the most lively days of the year, full of celebration and activity. Student performers take multiple stages, grills produce burgers and hot dogs, faculty's children jump and play within the Moon Bounce, and pride fills the air. The Hilltop community comes together in celebration of all that is wonderful about Georgetown. We plant blankets along the lawn, watch and listen to our fellow Hoyas, and chat with friends. Year after year we remark, 'It never rains on Georgetown Day.' Indeed, it never will.* 99

The Jesuit tradition is one that values diversity and the spiritual development of students of all faiths and backgrounds. Accordingly, the Hilltop also has a very active Campus Ministry with full-time chaplains including Catholic priests, Protestant ministers, Jewish rabbis, and a Muslim imam. Students can join any number of Campus Ministry organizations centered on particular religious affiliations. There are also vibrant retreat programs with a variety of faith-based and non-faith-based retreat opportunities.

Athletics

The Georgetown athletics department boasts twenty-two varsity sports teams. These include women's basketball, crew, field hockey, golf, lacrosse, sailing, soccer, swimming/diving, tennis, track, and volleyball. The men's varsity programs include baseball, basketball, crew, football, golf, lacrosse, coed sailing, soccer, swimming/diving, tennis, and track. Although well known for the men's varsity basketball program, Georgetown has an honored athletic tradition in multiple sports. A member of the Big East Conference in our Division I programs, the Georgetown Hoyas are always serious contenders and thrive on their academic excellence.

Georgetown students also enjoy an active intramural sports program. Indeed, over forty percent of all Georgetown students participate in an intramural sport at some point in their college career. There are a number of club sports teams as well. These include lacrosse, rugby, soccer, volleyball, water polo, field hockey, softball, and Ultimate Frisbee. Yates Field House serves as the main recreational facility with indoor tennis, basketball, squash, racquetball, and volleyball courts, an indoor track and swimming pool, golf practice facilities, free weights, cardiovascular equipment, weight machines, saunas, and a wellness center. There are aerobics, spinning, cardio-kickboxing, and yoga classes on a regular basis. All of these facilities are available to all students.

FINANCIAL AID

As previously mentioned, Georgetown is proud of its "need-blind" admissions policy. Once a student is accepted, Georgetown is committed to meeting his or her full financial needs. Thus, the university wants qualified students to attend and enrich the Georgetown community, regardless of their ability to pay for tuition and other associated costs. Although yearly tuition is about $36,000 (for a recent year) with room and board costs of approximately $10,000, students usually receive grants, loans, and federal work-study opportunities to alleviate the financial burden. In fact, each year, more than fifty-five percent of the undergraduate students at Georgetown receive some form of financial assistance. In a recent year, Georgetown undergraduates received $38 million in grants, scholarships, employment, and loans. The average Georgetown-funded grant award per recipient was $17,325.

> 66 *Georgetown University is proud to be among the few educational institutions in the United States that practice need-blind admissions and meet 100 percent of the demonstrated financial need of eligible undergraduates. We believe these programs help us to enroll and retain the most talented students who enhance the Georgetown educational community in endless ways.* 99

—*Patricia McWade, Dean of Student Financial Services*

- William Jefferson Clinton (SFS '68), Former President of the United States
- Antonin Scalia (C'57), Supreme Court Justice
- George Tenet (SFS'76), Former Director of Central Intelligence Agency
- General James Jones (F'66), Commandant, Marine Corps, NATO Commander
- Andrew Natsios, (C'71), Administrator, U.S. Agency for International Development
- Gloria Macapagal Arroya (SFS'68), President of the Philippines
- Francis A. Keating II (C'66), Governor of Oklahoma
- Charles Cawley (C'62), Chairman and CEO, MBNA Bank of America
- Ted Leonsis (C'77), President and CEO, AOL Interactive Properties; Majority Owner, Washington Capitals Hockey Team
- Philip Marineau (C'68), President and CEO, Levi Strauss & Co.
- Stuart Bloomberg (C'72), Chairman, ABC Entertainment
- Jonathan Nolan (C'98), Author of Memento
- Margaret Edson (G'92), Pulitzer Prize-Winning Author of Wit
- Maria Shriver (C'77), First Lady of California and best-selling author
- Malcolm Lee (C'92), Director, The Best Man and Undercover Brother
- Antonia Novello (Hospital Fellow '75), Physician, Former U.S. Surgeon General
- John J. Ring (C'49; M'53), Former president, American Medical Association
- Solomon Snyder (C'59, M'62), Neuroscientist
- Joan Claybrook (L'73), President, Public Citizen
- Robert M. Hayes (C'74), Founder, Coalition for the Homeless
- Anthony Shriver (C'88), President, Best Buddies International
- Paul Tagliabue (C'62), Commissioner, National Football League
- Carmen Policy (L'66), Former President, Cleveland Browns Football Team
- Patrick Ewing (C'85), Professional Basketball Player and Coach
- Alonzo Mourning (C'92), Professional Basketball Player
- Dikembe Mutombo (SLL'91), Professional Basketball Player

Like most institutions, applicants are asked to complete the FAFSA and PROFILE forms and indicate Georgetown University as a recipient of the processed information. The Office of Student Financial Services also helps families plan to allocate existing family resources. The Office offers monthly payment plans, low-interest supplemental loans, and updated links to external scholarship programs.

GRADUATES

A Georgetown education is definitely a significant investment—one well worth the time, heart, and energy. Graduates leave the Healy Gates as intellectual, thoughtful, and reflective critical thinkers. Hoyas live out the Jesuit philosophy through their actions as responsible citizens of global society. Many graduates enter the Peace Corps, Jesuit Volunteer Corps, or programs such as Teach for America. Others head to Wall Street or Capitol Hill. Most alumni eventually go on to graduate work and become lawyers, doctors, and scholars.

Prominent Hoya alumni can be found as leaders in business, politics, social action, education, entertainment, the media, and professional sports. Graduating from Georgetown University insures lifelong membership in the global Hoya community. The Georgetown family offers any number of benefits and connections. Most importantly, however, it links you to the mission of Georgetown and its reputation as a premier institution of higher learning.

SUMMING UP

With its exhilarating location and a milieu characterized by activism, diversity, open dialogue, and academic rigor, Georgetown University offers students an unique opportunity. There is a vibrant campus life with volunteer programs, athletic teams, performing arts, and student organizations, in addition to the countless social and educational opportunities in the greater D.C. area. Whether interested in arts, humanities, sciences, international relations, nursing and health studies, or business administration, Georgetown emphasizes the benefits of a liberal arts education. With a student-centered mission, Georgetown offers a premier faculty dedicated to teaching. Its superb academic programs, dedication to service, commitment to diversity, and location in our nation's capital, ensure that Georgetown will attract the country's most outstanding applicants.

Attending Georgetown is an amazingly formative experience. It is marked by significant relationships, personal challenges, and incredible learning opportunities. Georgetown prepares its students as leaders—people with a strong moral character, a reflective nature, intellectual prowess, and the tools necessary to tackle both the personal and professional tensions of life. Grounded in the Catholic and Jesuit tradition, the Georgetown community is committed to diversity and the holistic development of students from all faiths and backgrounds. Membership in the Georgetown family ensures meaningful friendships, professional connections, and a common dedication to a life of service to others.

❏ *Meaghan M. Keeler, B.S.*

HAMILTON COLLEGE

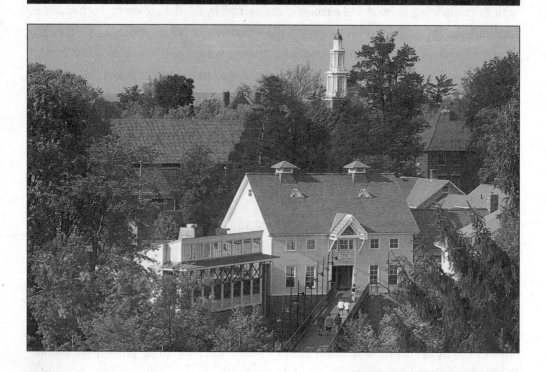

 Hamilton College
Clinton, NY 13323

 (315) 859-4421 or (800) 843-2655
Fax: (315) 859-4457

 E-mail: *admission@hamilton.edu*
Website: *www.hamilton.edu*

Enrollment

Full-time ❑ women: 983
❑ men: 861

Part-time ❑ women: 12
❑ men: 5

INTRODUCING HAMILTON COLLEGE

No matter when you arrive at Hamilton College, your first drive up College Hill Road will make a significant impression on you. If it's summertime, you'll probably be amazed by the number of people you see bustling around. Many students choose to stay on campus during the summer to conduct research with professors, work in one of the offices, or help out with the various camps that Hamilton hosts. If your arrival takes place during the spring or fall, you'll likely be caught off guard by Hamilton's breathtaking campus—the tree-lined paths and stone and red brick buildings are especially gorgeous when flowers are blooming and leaves are either sprouting or turning an astonishing blaze of reds, oranges, and yellows. And if it's wintertime, you're definitely just praying your car triumphs over the snow and makes it up the hill! But whatever the season, you'll probably be greeted by at least one passerby on campus, and you may begin to understand exactly what it means to be a part of the Hamilton College community.

Hamilton College is a small liberal arts institution set atop a rather large hill in the middle of Central New York. Because of its location, Hamilton almost demands that its students become part of a vibrant and close-knit campus community. At Hamilton, there's no big city full of distractions to pull you away from the dorms (where you'll likely live for all four years), and there's nowhere near enough people on campus to let you even consider being anonymous. At times, particularly during the winter, this situation can be a bit frustrating, to say the least. But, because it absolutely necessitates that students get to know each other and become involved in campus life, it is also precisely this situation that leads to the creation of the unique Hamilton community that many Hamilton grads yearn for even years after they've left the Hill.

THE SACERDOTE SERIES: GREAT NAMES AT HAMILTON

Once or twice a year, participants in the Sacerdote Great Names Series come to Hamilton to give a speech, participate in a question-and-answer session, meet with selected students, and, generally, teach a class or two.

2010—Condoleezza Rice, former Secretary of State
2008—Jon Stewart, *The Daily Show*
2006—Aretha Franklin, musician
—Al Gore, former Vice President of the United States
2005—Tom Brokaw, NBC News
2004—William Jefferson Clinton, Former President of the United States
2003—Bill Cosby, Comedian, actor, and author
2002—Madeleine Albright, Former Secretary of State (March)
—Rudolph Giuliani, Former Mayor of New York City (September)
2001—Jimmy Carter, Former President of the United States
2000—Desmond Tutu, Archbishop of Capetown, South Africa
1999—Lady Margaret Thatcher, Former Prime Minister of the United Kingdom
1998—F.W. de Klerk, Former President of South Africa (April)
—B.B. King, Musician (October)
1997—Elie Wiesel, Author
1996—Colin Powell, Former Secretary of State (April)
—James Carville and Mary Matalin, Political Strategists (October)

History, Tradition, and the Future

As a newcomer walking around Hamilton's campus, you'd probably notice that the parts of campus you see on your left look quite different from those that you see on your right. This is because College Hill Road once ran between two separate colleges. On the right lies the north side of campus and the origins of Hamilton College. Founded by Samuel Kirkland in 1793 as the Hamilton-Oneida Academy and chartered as Hamilton College in 1812, the Hamilton of today (which was once all male) is the third-oldest college in New York State. On the left lies the south side of campus, which used to be Kirkland College, an independent, experimental, all-female college that was founded by Hamilton in 1968. The two schools merged in 1978, but the vastly different architecture—stone and red brick vs. poured concrete—makes their history hard to forget.

Hamilton does not encourage its students to forget its long history. Hamilton has worked hard to preserve and promote the ideals of both Hamilton and Kirkland Colleges. From the Hamilton side comes the current emphasis on developing writing and speaking skills, and a strong association with science, social science, and government service. From the Kirkland side comes a keen interest in the arts, a more liberal view of what a college education should include, and a strong emphasis on interdisciplinary studies. In many ways, Kirkland complemented Hamilton very well, and students today benefit from a greater diversity of academic offerings due to Hamilton's continuous incorporation of both schools' strengths.

Since 2000, the college has invested more than $140 million in new and renovated facilities for science, the social sciences, fitness, and student activities. New space for the arts is planned. One of Hamilton's biggest assets is its careful blend of tradition and progress—it is truly a college that knows where it has been and eagerly anticipates where it is going.

Hamilton Students

So, if Hamilton is moving rapidly toward the future, who is going to take it there? The answer: its 1,800 students, 62 percent of whom come from public high schools and 38 percent of whom come from private high schools. Hamilton students originate in 49 U.S. states and 45 countries, and the student body is 4.6 percent international, 3.9 percent African-American, 0.5 percent Native American, 7.6 percent Asian/Pacific Islander, 5.0 percent Hispanic, and 67.2 percent Caucasian.

Basically, regardless of their backgrounds, Hamilton students have several traits in common and, as such, comprise a unique group. They tend to be fairly conservative people who highly value a strong liberal arts education and a commitment to excellence. They appreciate being seen as individuals, and not just as numbers, in a close-knit and vibrant community. And they have a wry sense of humor about, and a curious appreciation of, their rural surroundings and often less-than-favorable climate. Ultimately, they are intelligent, well-rounded people who tend to look back fondly on their time "on the Hill."

ADMISSIONS REQUIREMENTS

Hamilton is need-blind in admission and meets the full demonstrated need of every student. As a small liberal arts institution that takes great pride in its commitment to personal instruction and independent research, the size of each entering class is kept relatively small, with a target of 480 students. At the same time, because Hamilton is growing in notoriety, the number of applications the Admissions Office receives each year keeps increasing, and Hamilton's acceptance rate is now around twenty-nine percent.

So, how do you get yourself noticed (and accepted!)? When making its decisions, Hamilton's Admissions Office looks first and foremost for students with a proven record of academic achievement and for those with strong academic potential. In fact, eighty-three percent of accepted students ranked in the top ten percent of their high school classes.

Hamilton also seeks out well-rounded and involved students, so a strong activity resume demonstrating your leadership skills, extracurricular involvement, athletic accomplishments, or community service may make up for a slightly lower GPA. Additionally, it never hurts to showcase your special talents or interests, so if you have tapes of your athletic, theatrical, or dance performances, or if you have samples of your art, photos, poems, stories, or music, feel free to send them along. (Contact the Admissions Office or check the Admissions pages on Hamilton's web site for the preferred format of these submissions.)

In terms of actual admission requirements, Hamilton is like most colleges in that it accepts the Common Application and requires a $60 application fee (unless waived), a school counselor evaluation, a teacher evaluation, a personal statement, your choice of standardized test scores, and a midyear grade report. Hamilton also requires that students submit a graded sample of their expository writing, such as an analytical essay or a research paper (but not lab reports or creative writing), and that they complete Hamilton's own supplement to the Common Application. An interview is not required, but is strongly recommended.

Because Hamilton believes that students can demonstrate their academic potential in a variety of ways, it no longer requires that applicants submit scores from the SAT test (though roughly sixty-four percent of all accepted students have submitted scores, with the middle fifty percent scoring between 1370 and 1480, based on 1600). Instead, for students applying, Hamilton now simply requires either the SAT, ACT, or three AP/IB, or SAT Subject Test scores: one that reflects quantitative skills, one that reflects verbal and writing skills, and one test of the student's choice. (The Admissions Office can provide a list of tests that satisfy the quantitative and verbal requirements.) And when in doubt, you can submit a variety of tests and The Admission Committee will select the best scores from among them.

At the heart of Hamilton's academic mission lie two main goals:

1. Develop well-rounded, accomplished, critical-thinking individuals who continually thirst for knowledge and who are ready for nearly any challenge the "real world" might throw at them.
2. Produce students who are able to express themselves clearly and effectively through written and oral communication.

No small challenge. But Hamilton has a long history of accomplishing both of these goals, chiefly through its dedication to the quintessential liberal arts education. At Hamilton, students are encouraged to take a wide variety of courses in a number of disciplines so that they may develop the most balanced, informed perspective on life they can. In so doing, they become better prepared to meet life's challenges because they are able to examine and analyze almost any issue from a variety of viewpoints, which is far more effective than seeing only one.

Consequently, although Hamilton students select their concentrations (typically one or two subject areas out of about forty options) and their minors (one discipline out of about forty-five options) during the second semester of their sophomore year, many spend their first couple of semesters—and many semesters beyond that—taking a variety of courses, a good number of which probably seem entirely unrelated to their intended or declared concentrations. An economics concentrator, for example, may take dance or biology classes, and a religious studies major might find himself or herself in a calculus or a French class. The excitement and challenge for most students is figuring out how these seemingly disparate disciplines overlap, and the biggest reward tends to come when they realize they're using information or perspectives they gained in one area of study to inform or improve upon their work in another.

The Open Curriculum

In a continuing effort to help students acquire the most solid education possible, Hamilton recently did away with distribution requirements and, instead, established an open curriculum. In this way, students have more responsibility, as well as more freedom, in obtaining the education they desire.

Writing Skills

Because one of Hamilton's primary objectives is to produce students who write well, all students are required to pass at least three writing-intensive classes, each taken during a different semester, during their first two years of study. In these classes, the majority of grades that students accumulate tend to come from writing papers, and students generally have the opportunity to revise most, if not all, of these papers to ensure that they understand the processes and principles behind good writing.

Academic Atmosphere

The Honor Code

Because Hamilton is a school that takes academics quite seriously, all incoming students must sign the school's Honor Code, which basically says that students pledge to maintain academic honesty at all times. Students are thereby treated more or less as adults and their honesty is trusted and respected. As a result, professors do not generally feel obligated to police exams and may assign take-home exams that students are on their honor to complete fairly.

STUDY OFF-CAMPUS

Because Hamilton is so committed to the concept of a liberal arts education, it offers—and strongly encourages—a variety of options to get students off the Hill and out into the world. Nearly half of all students study away from campus, and Hamilton has its own programs in Paris, Madrid, Beijing, New York City, and Washington, D.C. Hamilton also encourages its students to seek out other schools' programs if they wish to go elsewhere in the world.

Collaborative Atmosphere

At the same time, although the Honor Code is quite serious and academics are rather rigorous, the general academic atmosphere on campus is far more collaborative than it is competitive. Many students hold themselves to high academic standards, so a certain degree of competition is created that way, but few, if any, students engage in the type of cut-throat academics that are rumored to be typical of many academically prestigious institutions. Hamilton students are much more likely to get together at Café Opus, the campus coffeehouse, for a group study session or to lend each other their notes to study from than they are to steal each others' class materials. Because of this cooperative atmosphere, many students make some of their best friends by working on group projects or having late-night study sessions.

> **❝** *I find my relationships with a lot of my professors to be collaborative. It feels more scholar-to-scholar than teacher-to-student. This relationship keeps me invested in my coursework because I feel like my professors truly value my thoughts.* **❞**

—Ann Horwitz, '06

And this cooperative atmosphere tends to extend to professor-student relationships as well. In fact, as previously mentioned, close professor-student relationships are one of the hallmarks of a Hamilton education. Currently, Hamilton employs 184 full-time faculty (ninety-four percent of whom hold the most advanced degree in their fields), and maintains a student-faculty ratio of 9.4:1. Accordingly, thirty-one percent of all classes have ten or fewer students, and seventy-four percent have twenty or fewer students. Students therefore have ample opportunities to engage in their education and almost have no choice but to participate in class. After all, it's hard to slip through the cracks or fade into the background in a class of fifteen students!

SOCIAL LIFE AND ACTIVITIES

Hamilton students know that mixing work and play is the key to a rich, fulfilling college experience, and it is this universal commitment to balance that makes Hamilton the vibrant community that it is. Although Hamilton students take their studies seriously, most are involved in at least one extracurricular activity that gets them out of the library at crucial times and allows them to meet other students with similar interests.

> 66 *Some of the best conversations I had at Hamilton took place in my professors' homes. Professors became more friends than teachers at times like these, and discussing academics, careers, or life in general tended to be easier and more interesting outside the formal atmosphere of classrooms and offices. Meeting a professor's family is a very pleasant and personal aspect of a small college—and when I discovered that my French professor's nine-year-old twins spoke French ten times better than I did, it motivated me to work much harder in her class.* 99

—Jane Simmons, '04

Athletics

For about thirty percent of the student body, the extracurricular activity of choice is playing on a sports team. Hamilton sponsors twenty-eight varsity sports (fourteen men's, fourteen women's), which are affiliated with the NCAA Division III, and the New England Small College Athletic Conference.

Even though Hamilton's organized athletics do not dominate life on campus, approximately sixty percent of students participate in intramurals at one point or another. Hamilton sponsors about fifteen intramural activities and over a dozen club sports each year, and because Hamilton is such a small school, it is relatively easy for anyone to set up an intramural league or pick-up game.

Clubs and Organizations

Other students occupy their time by joining one (or several!) of Hamilton's approximately 120 clubs and organizations. These groups cover just about any interest under the sun, so there really is something for everybody. These clubs and organizations plan and participate in their own events, and many also hold a variety of social functions—both with alcohol and without—that are open to the entire campus.

> *Activities are very accessible to everyone on campus. Unlike at larger schools where you can't work on the newspaper unless you're a journalism major or you can't debate unless you're pre-law, at Hamilton hard work and interest can usually make up for no prior experience.*
>
> —*Alex Sear, '05*

In addition, because Hamilton is so small and nonbureaucratic, if a particular interest isn't already represented by a club or organization, a dedicated student should have no trouble *starting* a group to reflect that passion. Within the past several years, for example, over two dozen new groups have cropped up. In fact, Hamilton students are so open-minded about extracurriculars that interested students have started up a "varsity streaking team" that actually travels to other colleges and (for better or worse!) has gained national attention. On the other hand, though, because the school is so small, when interest in some of the smaller organizations begins to wane, certain groups may go dormant until someone new revives interest.

Entertainment

Because Central New York is not exactly an entertainment mecca, many groups work to bring diversions to campus. The Emerson Gallery, Hamilton's on-campus art gallery, for example, spices up its regular offerings of primarily American, British, and Native American work by bringing lecturers and special exhibitions, and the Department of Theater and Dance brings a variety of solo performers and ensemble groups. (Note, too, that student exhibitions in art and performances in theater and dance are also quite common, either as part of class requirements or as part of the fun had by some of the more artistic extracurricular groups.) Moreover, a variety of student groups work to bring guest-lecturers that pique their own interest and that might not correspond with the offerings of any one particular department.

Music

The Campus Activities Board (CAB) generally brings comedians and larger-name musical acts to the Tolles Pavilion, and those coordinating the Acoustic Coffeehouse series ensure that interested students can sip free coffee while taking in the soulful stylings of well-known artists as well as up-and-coming stars. Within the past few years, the likes of The Kooks, LCD Soundsystem, Passion Pit, Gym Class Heroes, Citizen Cops, Jamie Lidell, and Ellis Paul have all graced the Hamilton stage.

Music makes its way to the Hill in a variety of ways outside of CAB and Acoustic Coffeehouse events, too. The Music Department brings visiting artists and lecturers, the school runs eight different ensemble groups that perform regularly, and students taking classes in the music department also give the occasional recital. Additionally, Hamilton is home to four student-run *a cappella* groups that perform several times each semester: Special K (all female), the Hamiltones (coed), Tumbling After (all female), and the Buffers (all male).

Greek Life

Currently, the school recognizes nine fraternities and seven sororities, some of which are national and some of which are local. Unlike at many colleges, though, frats and sororities at Hamilton do not have their own houses, a situation that some students feel is beneficial for Hamilton's social life because it means that societies do not tend to isolate themselves from the rest of the campus community by having friendships, living arrangements, and social events that revolve entirely around the society. On the other hand, some students *do* feel that there is a real divide between Greek-affiliated students and Independents. This ongoing debate creates an interesting Greek/non-Greek dynamic on campus at times, and conversations revolving around fraternities and sororities can become quite heated. Regardless, fraternities and sororities do tend to contribute substantially to Hamilton's social scene by throwing parties, coordinating lectures, and organizing philanthropic events.

Parties

In terms of the late night social scene, there are usually a variety of parties—both with and without alcohol—that students can attend. As mentioned before, many different clubs and organizations hold parties, and most of these gatherings tend to be open to the entire campus. They also very often have a theme, and many Hamilton students seize the opportunity to venture out to the local Salvation Army for appropriate (and cheap!) attire for the evening.

Bon Appétit!

You might not think about it much—or you might not have considered it at all—but the quality of the food in the dining halls is a very important aspect of college life. After all, you're most likely going to be eating this food two or three times a day, at least five or six days a week, for four years. That's a lot of meals. Fortunately, Hamilton's food service provider, Bon Appétit, does a great job of making a variety of fresh and largely healthy dishes for the Hamilton community. Sure, they have some "misses," but the majority of the time the food is quite good, particularly for college standards.

THE WEATHER OUTSIDE IS FRIGHTFUL . . .

No doubt about it—Hamilton can be a cold place. In fact, from October until at least March, there's a very good chance of there being a heaping helping of snow on the ground. The following are some Hamilton favorite ways to stave off a whopping case of Seasonal Affective Disorder.

○ Recruit some friends and build a snowman… or snowwoman.
○ Rent some gear from the Hamilton Outing Club and go snowshoeing in Root Glen.
○ Take bets on the amount of time that will pass before the next avalanche of snow careens off the roof of Kirkland, Dunham, or Root Hall.
○ Two words: snow angels.
○ Ski.
○ Steal (er, borrow) one of the plastic trays from the dining hall and go sledding behind Bristol Campus Center.
○ Snuggle up in your dorm room with a warm blanket, a cup of hot chocolate, and a good book.
○ Watch the snow fall. Wax poetic.
○ Get involved in "Feb Fest," Hamilton's annual winter carnival. The week of festivities features concerts, snow-sculpture contests, snoccer (snow-soccer) and snow-football tournaments, all-campus snowball fights, wine/beer/chocolate tastings, and a variety of other events that all aim to alleviate the winter blues.

But what's even more impressive about Bon Appétit is its connection to the students. If you have a favorite recipe from home that you're just dying to have on campus, bring it in and Bon Appétit will look into making it. If you're sick of seeing only apples, oranges, and bananas as your fruit options, let them know and you might walk in to find kiwis, mangos, plums, and pears the next day. And if you and your friends want to have a picnic in the pavilion, just give Bon Appétit the meal card numbers of everyone involved and they'll set you up with hamburger patties for grilling, buns, chips, sodas…the whole shebang.

Although Hamilton and the surrounding area certainly can't offer the same variety of restaurants as, say, New York City, Hamilton students have nevertheless found some surprisingly unique and tasty places that are great for a study break, a relaxed Sunday brunch, or a weekend dinner out with family or friends.

○ The Only Café: Comfort food prepared in a home-y setting. There's no set menu; the chef makes what he feels like making that day, from mac 'n' cheese to pulled-pork pizza.

○ The Phoenician: Family-owned restaurant with authentic Lebanese food.

○ La Petite Maison: Fine, sophisticated French cuisine. Popular on Family Weekend.

○ The Rio Grande (or "Tex Mex," as it is more commonly known around campus): Moderately priced Mexican food. Perfect for Friday and Saturday night dinners.

○ Nola's, formerly the Adirondack Coffeehouse: Small café and coffeehouse with homemade soups and salads. Located just down the Hill on Park Row in Clinton.

○ Breakfast at Tiffany's: Known for its hit-the-spot, early morning (think 2 A.M.) eats.

○ Piggy Pat's Barbecue: Their motto is "Put some South in Yo' Mouff"…'nuff said.

And if you've got a craving for Italian or Indian food, just take a drive into Utica and explore the many options the city has to offer.

It's a small detail, but it's just one more aspect of Hamilton that makes the on-campus community feel a little more like home.

FINANCIAL AID

Admittedly, Hamilton is an expensive school. Very expensive. Fortunately, though, every year, Hamilton offers financial aid to about fifty percent of its students via scholarships, loans, and campus jobs. In 2009–2010, for example, the average financial aid package for a Hamilton student was $32,580. This award was paid toward an estimated student budget of $51,500, and was calculated to take into account expenses such as books, personal needs, and travel, in addition to tuition, room, and board.

GRADUATES

Thanks to their broad liberal arts backgrounds, Hamilton graduates go on to engage in a wide variety of pursuits. In terms of statistics, in recent years, around seventy percent of graduating seniors chose to take jobs and about twenty-one percent chose to enter graduate or professional school immediately after graduation and two percent pursued fellowships (Watson, Fulbright, etc.). About thirty-seven percent obtained an advanced degree within five years of graduation.

The Career Center

One resource that helps prepare students for their post-Hamilton pursuits is the Career Center. Students may make appointments at the Career Center at any point during their time at Hamilton and, in fact, are encouraged to do so as early as their first year of studies. During these appointments, students meet one-on-one with either a career counselor or a Career Center intern, depending on their needs, and they discuss a wide variety of topics, including career assessment materials, graduate school applications, cover letters, interview strategies, finding an internship, and networking to find a job. If students so request, they may schedule a "mock interview" to prepare for either graduate school or professional interviews.

The Career Center also arranges lunches featuring Hamilton alumni who have returned to campus to talk about their current careers, how they have gotten to this point in their careers, and the industry in which they work in general. The lunches not only help prepare students for continuing their education or entering the professional world, but they provide valuable networking experiences as well.

Alumni Relations and the "Hamilton Connection"

These meetings are not the only way that members of the Hamilton community network with each other, however. Hamilton has alumni associations that plan outings and events in many large cities throughout the United States. And because Hamilton is such a tight-knit community, alumni actually attend these events, which is not always the case with alumni of larger colleges and universities. These events are great ways for recent grads to make contact with older, more established alumni, and they provide a venue in which newer alums can network to find a job, make new friends, or learn about the city to which they have just moved.

PROMINENT GRADS

- ○ Elihu Root, 1864, U.S. Senator, U.S. Secretary of War, Secretary of State, Winner of the Nobel Peace Prize
- ○ James S. Sherman, 1878, Vice-President of the United States
- ○ William M. Bristol, 1882, cofounder, Bristol-Myers Co.
- ○ Ezra Pound, 1905, poet
- ○ B.F. Skinner, 1926, behavioral psychologist
- ○ Paul Greengard, 1948, 2000 Nobel Prize Winner in Physiology or Medicine
- ○ Thomas E. Meehan, 1951, Tony Award-winning playwright (*The Producers, Hairspray*)
- ○ Robert Moses, 1956, Leader of the Civil Rights Movement (1960s), currently a pioneer in algebra education (The Algebra Project)
- ○ Edward S. Walker, Jr., 1962, Professor at Hamilton, Former U.S. Ambassador to Israel, Egypt, and the United Arab Emirates
- ○ A.G. Lafley, 1969, former President and CEO, Procter & Gamble
- ○ Kevin Kennedy, 1970, Managing Director, Goldman, Sachs & Co.
- ○ Melinda Wagner, 1979, 1999 Pulitzer Prize in Music Composition
- ○ Mary Bonauto, 1983, Civil Rights Attorney (gay marriage amendment)

Other times, older alumni will simply make the effort to connect with more recent grads on their own. When Elizabeth Backer, '04, a public policy concentrator, began her first day of work at a market research company in Boston, for example, the company's HR department sent out an e-mail introducing her as a new hire. Within hours, Liz received an e-mail from Andrew Stockwell, '96, a new colleague who wanted to take Liz out to lunch based purely on their Hamilton connection.

SUMMING UP

The bottom line is this: Your Hamilton experience is what you make of it. If you intend to spend your four years shuffling to and from class with your head down, making the occasional trip to the library or dining hall, and staring forlornly out your window at the snow, you're going to have a miserable and isolating time indeed. But if you're willing to take some risks, join some groups, go to some parties, and really, truly engage with some professors (inside *and* outside of class), you're almost bound to have a rewarding experience. You'll grow from being an uncertain, freshman to a senior who has gained some incredible friends and experiences and loves where you are.

> *It's the things that weren't expected or immediately perceived at Hamilton that were the most important to me. It's the four-hour-long dinners in the dining halls that no one wanted to be the first to leave…the first walk in Root Glen in the spring…the sentence that your professor casually tosses over her shoulder that makes you adopt academia as your new religion…the omelet that you waited 30 minutes in line for on a Sunday morning because the Omelet God was working that day. It's the late nights spent chatting with friends, the play you buy tickets to so you can cheer on your friend who you ran lines with for three months…I never imagined myself doing stand-up comedy, working in Admissions, or majoring in a subject that would require me to learn another language and use quantum physics, but four years on the Hill can encourage you to take some bizarre, wonderful, and relatively risk-free challenges that can change your life.*

—*Jane Simmons '04*

❑ *Jennifer Kostka, B.A.*

 Harvard College
Cambridge, MA 02138

 (617) 495-1551
Fax: (617) 495-8821
E-mail: *college@fas.harvard.edu*
 Web site:
http://www.admissions.college.harvard.edu

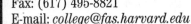 **Enrollment**

Full-time ❏ women: 3,350
❏ men: 3,350

INTRODUCING HARVARD COLLEGE

Tour guides leading visitors around the Harvard campus are quick to mention that Harvard, founded in 1636, is the oldest college in the United States. In historic Harvard Yard, tour guides explain that Hollis Hall, a red brick structure built in 1763, housed Washington's troops during the Revolutionary War. In front of Widener Library, tourists learn that Harvard's library system is the largest university system in the world, containing more than ninety libraries, over sixteen million volumes, and some 100,000 periodicals.

○ Harvard's Widener and Pusey Libraries contain millions of volumes on more than 57 miles of bookshelves.

○ Harvard's libraries contain more than just books: a set of Harry Houdini's handcuffs; Charles Dickens's walking stick and paper knife; T.S. Eliot's panama hat; a set of George Washington's pistols.

Harvard's age and outstanding physical resources are among the college's most distinctive features. Yet, few Harvard alumni will say that the best part of their Harvard experience was the fact that the college is the oldest in the country. It is more likely that they will mention the environment of daily life as the distinguishing aspect of their experience, an environment characterized by the cities of Cambridge and Boston, a unique residential life system, and the people who make Harvard tick.

Harvard has called Cambridge, Massachusetts, home for all of its 360-plus years. Cambridge, located along the Charles River a few miles from downtown Boston, boasts beautiful tree-lined streets as well as numerous shops, cinemas, restaurants, music stores, coffeehouses, bars, theaters, and bookstores.

In addition, the city of Boston is only a $1.70 trip away on the subway. The Boston area is home to more that forty colleges and universities and some 200,000 college students, five professional athletic teams, and all of the resources of a large city in a historic, scenic, and pedestrian-friendly package.

"I think the best thing about student life at Harvard is that, in a typical discussion, the topics of conversation could be anything from Kant's philosophy on morals to the thorough pummeling the New England Patriots received at the hands of the Green Bay Packers in last week's football game. It is really gratifying to be able to engage in a serious intellectual conversation whenever and with whomever one pleases. Also, because the Harvard community is saturated with such amazing talent, the atmosphere of high achievement and hard work around campus tends to motivate each of us to strive to be our very best."

Harvard students also enjoy the world beyond metropolitan Boston. The mountains of New Hampshire and the Maine seacoast are each a short drive away to the north; the beaches of Cape Cod are a short drive south of Boston.

Harvard students are amazing in the diversity of their backgrounds, interests, and perspectives. Students come from all fifty of the United States as well as more than seventy foreign countries, and nearly seventy percent of them come from public high schools. The college is entirely coeducational and has been since 1977, when Harvard and Radcliffe joined forces in a unique partnership. (Radcliffe was completely assimilated by Harvard in 1999.) Students hail from many different religious, ethnic, and socioeconomic backgrounds. It is impossible not to feel energized by the presence of so many different people and ideas.

Harvard's location, its residential system, and its many human resources create a unique environment for the college years. Regardless of your interests or goals, daily life in this environment is challenging, inspiring, and, in Boston-speak, "wicked fun."

ADMISSIONS REQUIREMENTS

Getting into Harvard is extremely competitive. Only seven to ten percent of the applicants in the past few years were admitted, yet more than eighty-five percent of the applicants were academically qualified. Harvard attracts some of the best students in the world: most admitted students rank in the top ten to fifteen percent of their high school graduating classes, with over 2,500 applicants for the class of 2014 being valedictorians of their high school classes. Statistics like these can be intimidating, but remember that a little over 2,000 people received good news from Harvard last year. It's hard to get in, but it's not impossible.

If you decide to apply, do your best to present yourself to the Admissions Committee with a complete, concise application. Keep this in mind if you are thinking of applying:

- Harvard accepts the Common Application and the Universal Application, but does not even have its own institutional form. The Common Application is fairly straightforward: send a transcript, write an essay on a topic of your choice, fill in some biographical information, provide a summary of your extracurricular life, and ask two teachers and a counselor to fill out recommendations. Harvard does have its own application supplement to be completed in addition to either the Common Application or the Universal Application. An alumnus interview is also a required component of the application. After you send in your application materials a volunteer from your local area may contact you to arrange the interview. Harvard requires students to submit either the SAT or ACT with writing and any three of the SAT Subject Tests. Finally, a Secondary School Report and Mid-Year School Report must be filled out by your college advisor or school counselor.
- Harvard College no longer offers an Early Action program, as of fall 2007. The Regular Action deadline is January 1; decisions are mailed in early April.

- In making its decisions, the Admissions Committee considers all aspects of a person's candidacy. You will be evaluated on your academic performance and potential, your extracurricular talents, and your personal strengths. First and foremost, the committee wants to be confident that you can handle the Harvard coursework. Your high school transcript is important here; take the toughest classes your school offers and in which you can excel. Once it has been determined that you could swing it in Harvard's classrooms, the committee will look for what distinguishes you from the thousands of other qualified candidates. Some applicants set themselves apart from the rest of the pool based on their extraordinary academic promise. Others are distinguished because of their well-roundedness or their specific talents beyond the classroom. Personal qualities are an important component in every decision.

There is no formula through which one is admitted to Harvard. The committee reads every application with great care and strives to identify and admit those students who will make an impact during their college years and beyond. Be yourself on the application and in the interview and let your strengths, talents, and accomplishments speak for you. You certainly can't get in if you don't apply.

ACADEMIC LIFE

Students at Harvard enjoy a great variety of academic offerings and resources. Pursuing their A.B. or S.B., undergraduate students choose from about 3,500 classes every year and over forty fields of concentration (or majors). Throughout the course of eight semesters, students are required to take and pass thirty-two semester-long courses to graduate. The concentration accounts for roughly half of the course load over the four years. Students major in such fields as engineering, folklore and mythology, computer science, linguistics, economics, history and literature, and biological sciences, to name just a few. Some students design their own concentrations or pursue joint concentrations in two different disciplines.

The General Education Curriculum

The remaining half of the curriculum is divided between electives and a new General Education curriculum. With the help of your advisor, you decide when to take General Education courses and which ones to take. Many students take more than they are required to take for their diploma. They are lively and interesting courses; they provide an opportunity to explore areas outside of your concentration.

Electives

The last part of the curriculum is composed of electives, which allow students to explore any other interests they might have. For example, some students concentrate in a nonscience discipline and use their electives to complete the premedical requirements. Others become fluent in a foreign language or take studio art classes as electives. Many students use their electives to take classes that will be fun and that will provide them with a different academic experience or choose from a "minor" field.

The curriculum offers students a great deal of choice and flexibility, and it includes special opportunities such as cross-registration at M.I.T. and study abroad. In a recent year, Harvard students studied in thirty-five different countries in Europe, Asia, Africa, and Latin America. Physical resources, such as the world's largest university library system, enhance the curriculum by providing students with world-class facilities. Yet it is the human resources, namely the faculty and students at Harvard, that have the largest influence on the academic experience at the college.

Faculty

The student body benefits from a great human resource—the faculty. For the most part, the professors are kind, approachable people, as well as remarkable scholars. They make themselves available to students through office hours, by leading students in research, and by chatting informally before or after class or in the Yard during the school day. The enthusiasm of the professors is a perfect complement to that of the students they teach.

The Harvard professors are superb scholars, but they also prove to be caring and devoted teachers. Ninety-eight percent of the faculty teach undergraduates, and the average class size is smaller than you might imagine (about sixteen or seventeen students, according to a recent survey). Students take advantage of the small class sizes provided by numerous seminars and tutorials. Many students are involved in research at some point during their college years, which might include one-on-one work with a professor. A senior thesis project is an option for most concentrations, although a few of the departments do require a thesis.

> 66 *My favorite professor is Peter Burgard, who is also the Head Tutor for my concentration (German Cultural Studies). As a freshman, I took one class each semester with Professor Burgard. He really seemed to care about what we thought of the class by periodically asking the students for feedback. Professor Burgard encouraged us to see him during office hours, which I frequently did. He was always very helpful in answering my questions, and he helped me to think about which classes would be most beneficial for my interests, in addition to providing information on study abroad programs.* 99

Freshman Seminars

Freshman Seminars bring together faculty members and small groups of freshmen to investigate specialized topics. Most members of the entering class take advantage of this early opportunity to work closely with professors in an area of mutual interest. Some recent Freshman Seminars:

- Child Health in America
- The Genome and Society
- Cyberspace in court: Law of the Internet
- African Musical Tradition
- Public Policy Aproaches to climate change
- Complexity in Works of Art. *Ulysses* and *Hamlet*
- AIDs in Africa

Academically, the experience at Harvard depends to a certain degree on what you decide you want to do with your time in Cambridge. Small classes, accessible, friendly professors, helpful advisors, and top-notch physical resources are yours to enjoy; ultimately, it's up to you to take full advantage of the opportunities.

Residences

The exciting atmosphere of the area surrounding Harvard's campus complements the college's unique residential system. Students are guaranteed on-campus housing for each of their four years at the college, and about ninety-eight percent of them choose to live on campus. First-year students live in Harvard Yard, the historical, academic, and administrative center of the campus. This first year is fun, and living with all of your own classmates in the heart of the campus is a great way to create class unity and to adjust to college life in a friendly, supportive environment.

> " *The housing system is an enormous part of my life here. I have forged some of the most wonderful friendships with the people from my freshman year entryway. The house masters and tutors really create a family atmosphere. It's a good feeling to be able to go to the dining hall and know among all those eating there—there is certainly not a dearth of friends.* "

Sophomores, juniors, and seniors reside in one of the twelve residential houses, which are large dorms accommodating 350 to 500 students. Each House has its own dining hall, library, computer lab, weight room, music practice rooms, and other facilities. Faculty members are in residence as well as a team of advisors or tutors. House spirit is strong, as students represent their houses on intramural sports teams and spend hours socializing in the house dining halls and common areas. In sum, while students at Harvard College enjoy all of the resources of a university, the residential system provides the feeling of a smaller college. The communities of the Yard and of the houses give students access to one another, and to the educational benefits of the college's diverse population.

Harvard Square

The second tier of social life, after the houses, is Harvard Square and Cambridge. On the weekends, students flood the Square, taking full advantage of this unique urban atmosphere. Even during the week, the Square offers a refreshing break from the books; a study break might include a movie, a cup of coffee with a friend, or an hour of listening to Cambridge's fantastic street musicians.

The City of Boston

The final tier of the social life at Harvard is the city of Boston, where students might attend the theater, go to museums or concerts, visit other local colleges, or walk and shop in the city's historic neighborhoods. While the Harvard campus itself provides all students with social options, many do like to explore the surrounding environment in their free time.

Student Organizations

Harvard students like socializing and relaxing, but they also tend to be busy, as most are involved in two or three extracurricular activities. All told, there are more than 450 official student organizations on campus, including five orchestras, two jazz bands, a marching band, a gospel choir, a glee club, over ten *a cappella* groups, both a daily and a weekly newspaper and dozens of other political and literary publications, more than sixty theater productions per year, and student government, debate teams, religious groups, and minority and other public service organizations.

> ❝ I'd like to say I chose Harvard because I thought it was the best fit for me in terms of size, location, student-professor ratio, etc. I have to honestly admit, however, that I came here mostly because of Harvard's reputation. I knew my academic needs would be met here but was actually worried I wouldn't be musically stimulated. My worries were unfounded, however, because Harvard gave me musical opportunities that I probably wouldn't have found at another institution. Not only was I able to sing a lead in an opera, but was able to sing solos with full orchestras and tour around the world. Only at Harvard are undergraduates given this much opportunity at such a young age. ❞

Athletics

Harvard boasts forty-one varsity athletic teams, more than any other college or university in the country. If you don't think of Harvard as a jock school, think again. In recent years, Harvard athletes have won Ivy League championships in men's and women's soccer, women's basketball, men's tennis, baseball, football, men's and women's squash, and men's and women's crew. Harvard athletes have earned NCAA Division I championships in women's lacrosse, men's and women's hockey, crew, and squash. In addition, intramural, club, and recreation-level sports are extremely popular; about two-thirds of undergraduates are involved in some sort of athletic endeavor. You can take aerobics, learn a martial art, row novice crew, or play soccer for your house or dorm intramural team. Even if you are a non-athlete, you'll probably enjoy the Ivy League rivalries and the school spirit they inspire. The Harvard-Yale football game continues to be one of the highlights of the school year.

The example of athletics demonstrates the scope of extracurricular life at Harvard; it is astounding if not sometimes overwhelming. You will probably never be able to take part in as many activities or groups as you would like; however, you can rest assured that the opportunities for involvement will be numerous regardless of your level of ability.

The energy of Harvard's campus is one of its most distinctive features. That energy originates from the wide range of extracurricular and cocurricular activities and from the committed, enthusiastic students who keep them going. Some people perceive all Harvard students to be "grinds," interested only in their academic pursuits. This is one of the biggest myths about Harvard. Daily life is full of occasions for involvement, and it's hard, if not impossible, to find a Harvard student who isn't passionate about something beyond school work.

> 66 *My problem is trying to narrow down what I really want to do extracurricularly because there are so many groups and programs that interest me. I am currently involved in varsity cheerleading, the Black Students Association, undergraduate recruiting, and the Undergraduate Admissions Council. I have also been involved in the Harvard Entrepreneurs Club and tutoring elementary school students. I find that I need to be involved in activities; it's just an important aspect of who I am.* 99

FINANCIAL AID

Harvard is committed to a need-blind admissions process. This means that an applicant's candidacy for admission will be evaluated without regard for the family's ability to pay. So, let's say you've been admitted; now, how to foot the bill? College is expensive, and Harvard is certainly no exception. Fortunately, Harvard is also generous in its use of funds to support students.

Once you have been admitted, Harvard will meet your family's demonstrated need to make it possible for you to matriculate. All of the financial aid is based solely on need. Harvard believes that all of its students make valuable contributions to the college; therefore, the college offers no merit-based scholarships. In addition, as part of the Ivy League, Harvard offers no athletic scholarships.

Approximately seventy percent of Harvard students receive some form of financial assistance. In recent years, the average scholarship was $37,000; the average financial aid package, including a grant, a loan, and a campus job, totaled over $40,000. In 2008–2009, Harvard distributed more than $150 million in financial aid, including over $125 million in direct need-based scholarships to undergraduates.

Harvard's Financial Aid Initiative (HFAI) has eliminated parental contribution from families earning $60,000 or less. Families with income of $180,000 or less with typical assets are now expected to pay an average of up to ten percent of their income.

Applying for Financial Aid

Logistically, it's important to have your act together and to submit all of the forms required for a financial aid application on time (by February 1 of your senior year).

- You will need to fill out the CSS Profile, a form that you actually file directly with the College Scholarship Service. Don't forget to designate Harvard as one of the schools to which you are applying.
- You need to fill out the Free Application for Federal Student Aid (FAFSA), a form that is available in your school guidance office.
- You are also required to submit your own and your parents' federal income tax returns.
- Students applying from countries other than the United States should fill out Harvard's own Financial Statement for Students from Foreign Countries instead of the CSS Profile. This is the only difference for international students in the financial aid process.

The financial aid officers are some of the most helpful people at Harvard. They want to work with you and your family to make it possible for you to come to Harvard once you have been admitted. Stay organized so that you always give the Financial Aid Office the most accurate, up-to-date information. It's also a good idea to photocopy all of the forms you submit as part of your financial aid application.

GRADUATES

Harvard's liberal arts curriculum provides students with a base on which to build their futures. Students graduate from Harvard with a comprehensive understanding of their concentrations, and with an appreciation for other disciplines. In recent years, the most popular concentrations have been economics, government, and biology. This may reflect many students' interest in business, law, and medicine, respectively. But many graduates who were government concentrators are not aspiring lawyers; they are pursuing various career paths. The message here is that it is impossible to generalize about Harvard students and graduates.

Students receive excellent career counseling from the Office of Career Services, where they are encouraged to explore possible career paths. More than 300 companies recruited on campus in a recent year. These facts illuminate the degree to which students are exposed to different possibilities before they leave Harvard.

- John Adams, President of the United States
- John Quincy Adams, President of the United States
- Leonard Bernstein, Composer, Conductor
- e. e. cummings, Poet
- W.E.B. DuBois, Educator, Writer
- T. S. Eliot, Poet
- Ralph Waldo Emerson, Writer, Philosopher
- Al Gore, former Vice President of the United States
- Oliver Wendell Holmes, Jurist
- Henry James, Author
- Tommy Lee Jones, Actor
- John Fitzgerald Kennedy, President of the United States
- John Lithgow, Actor
- Yo-Yo Ma, Cellist
- Franklin Delano Roosevelt, President of the United States
- Theodore Roosevelt, President of the United States
- George Santayana, Author
- Henry David Thoreau, Writer
- Paul Wylie, Skater

The commencement ceremony is Harvard's most spectacular annual event. I remember every detail of that day vividly—the beautiful crimson, black, and white flags and banners in Harvard Yard, the music, the smiling graduates draped in caps and gowns, my own friends and family sharing in my excitement.

When you think of Harvard, think of its many resources, both human and physical. Think of Cambridge and Boston and New England. Think of the vibrant extracurricular life. Think of the special benefits of the residential system.

At the same time, Harvard isn't the ideal school for everyone. For one thing, Harvard is urban and it might not be a good place for those looking for a small, quiet, college town. Cambridge has a lot of trees and lawns and a beautiful river, but it also has traffic and a lot of general activity. Harvard might not be great for those who want a small college environment. Although the college is considered medium-sized, you probably won't be able to learn everyone's name. Moreover, although you will work closely with an advisor, Harvard is more suited to those who are excited about taking some of the responsibility and initiative to make their education a success. Finally, Harvard might not be a good choice for you if you have a clear idea of what field you want to pursue in college and want to pursue a strictly professional program. Having said that, come visit Harvard. It's worth seeing as an historic site even if you never decide to apply.

> ❝ *What is so great about Harvard? More important than the prestige (though perhaps because of it), it is the resources and opportunities that Harvard places within your reach that shrink your four years into fleeting moments. What you have at Harvard is an unmatched opportunity to discover and rediscover, in and outside class, who you are and what motivates you.* ❞

❏ *Brooke Earley, A.B.*

Photo by Chuck Chaney

 Harvey Mudd College
Claremont, CA 91711

 (909) 621-8011
Fax: (909) 607-7046

 E-mail: *admission@hmc.edu*
Web site: *http://www.hmc.edu*

 Enrollment

Full-time ❏ women: 322
❏ men: 450

INTRODUCING HARVEY MUDD COLLEGE

Harvey Mudd College is a highly selective private coeducational undergraduate college of engineering, mathematics, and science that could well be billed as "one of the best colleges in America that most people have never heard of." The college does not show up in the Final Four or try to market itself as the Harvard of anywhere. What it does do is attract some of the nation's brightest students and offers them a unique, rigorous, and liberal technical education that is as good as or better than the more famous colleges that some turn down to matriculate here. There are three key aspects of HMC that set it apart from other top colleges and give the school its reputation as a leader in Science, Technology, Engineering, and Mathematics (STEM) fields. Harvey Mudd College is an intensely small college; it offers majors only in engineering, science, and mathematics, and it prides itself on having humanities and social sciences requirements that it hopes will produce "leaders with an understanding of the impact of their work on humanity."

For most prospective students Harvey Mudd College seems like a big enough place engulfed in the larger Claremont Colleges Consortium. In reality, HMC is a close-knit community, a place where everybody knows your name, or at least everyone recognizes your face. The entire student body of around 772 "Mudders" is smaller than the high school graduating class of many incoming students. With ninety-six percent of the school living in the eight dorms (and the other four percent often crashing with friends on campus), getting to know your fellow Mudders is easy. The core math and science curriculum ensures that most freshmen are taking a nearly identical set of classes. All of this community interaction means that the same group of people you sit with in class in the morning will be eating with you in the dining hall at lunch, dropping by your room to work on homework that evening, playing intramural innertube water polo with you later that night, and going out to have a good time together on the weekend. And it stays that way for four years. With this amount of intimacy, Mudd is a good place to make great friends and a terrible place to make any enemies.

With no graduate students, no TAs, and a faculty dedicated to a high level of student interaction, few Mudders fall through the cracks or blend into the woodwork. The administration and staff take an active role in campus life. The chef in the dining hall and the building attendants on the night shift are some of the best-liked and most well-known personalities on campus, regularly chatting with students and offering a chance to be "chef for a day." Faculty/staff/student interaction is supported on all levels through "Friday Forums" (where all are invited to discuss current campus and world issues) and the Campus Activities Planning (CAP) Committee, a student group that sponsors trips to cultural and fun events throughout Southern California. It is common for any student to converse freely with the president of the college, go sailing, surfing, or hiking with a professor, or drop in to the office of the dean of students to talk about which campus policies need to be reformed. This camaraderie and immediate access to the people who make the college run (from the maintenance staff to the professors to the president) gives Harvey Mudd College a sense of community unthinkable in the large research-oriented institutions.

Some students find HMC's small size a bit smothering, and most students need to take a break from the college every now and then. For these Mudders, the other four undergraduate colleges in Claremont provide a convenient outlet. Within the five undergraduate colleges and two graduate institutions in Claremont, there are innumerable clubs, organizations, concerts, art shows, sports teams, and coffeehouses to take your mind away from the academic rigor of a small engineering and science school. Anyone with a car has the unlimited distractions of Los Angeles just a quick freeway drive away. Students looking for nationally televised football games, fraternity/sorority parties, and large government-funded research laboratories, however, will be sorely disappointed if they come to Harvey Mudd College. What can be found instead are afternoon pick-up football games, impromptu dorm parties, and small well-stocked labs where talented faculty involve their undergraduate students in every aspect of their research.

ADMISSIONS REQUIREMENTS

Getting into Harvey Mudd College can be as much fun (and as difficult) as graduating from the place. Over the past several years, HMC's Office of Admissions has worked hard to put a human face on the sometimes cold and judgmental world of college admissions. The school's clever "Junk Mail piece" (a satirical mailing introducing Harvey Mudd College to prospective students), adds much needed levity to the college recruiting process, poking fun at the way most schools try to market themselves, while at the same time drawing in the type of savvy but not humorless student that Harvey Mudd seeks to attract.

> **❝** *I got way more personal attention from the Admission Office at Harvey Mudd College than any other college I applied to. I liked the fact that every letter I received was signed in ink, not laser printed or photocopied. Any time I had questions I was able to talk to someone directly and not just get brushed off in favor of some pamphlet dropped in the mail. I felt that I was a welcome part of the college before I ever saw the campus.* **❞**

Harvey Mudd College is a highly selective college and the applicant pool is dominated by students in the top ten percent of their high school class. Each year around one-fourth of the incoming class is made up of students who were National Merit finalists or who were #1 or #2 in their high school class. As opposed to some larger schools, the HMC Office of Admissions avoids hard-and-fast admission minimums or formulas. Instead, the staff at HMC favors reading each application and determining if the individual applicant is the sort of student who will thrive at Mudd. The staff does, however, insist that every incoming freshman at Mudd has had chemistry, physics, and calculus as part of a rigorous and successful high school career.

SAT scores among applicants tend to be extremely high. Aptitude in math and science, as measured by curriculum and grades, but also scores, is considered very carefully in the selection process. A very heavy emphasis is also placed on communication skills. The ability to move easily between different disciplines and ways of thinking is also valued. HMC produces excellent problem solvers who can think, write, and express themselves, as well as perform laboratory research and engineering calculations.

The college has been successful in adding more diversity to its student body in the last several years; for example, entering classes have included about forty percent women students, and the 2014 entering class comprised more women than men—fifty-two percent women for the first time in the college's fifty-five year history. Extracurricular activities, unique talents, interests, hobbies, and a diversity of geographic and cultural backgrounds are all taken into consideration in the admission process, although academic aptitude remains the essential component in each admission decision. Interviews are encouraged, although visiting the campus and experiencing its unique atmosphere is highly recommended for prospective students.

ACADEMIC LIFE

Although Mudders tend to be extremely talented and have widely varying interests and hobbies, everyone's course load at HMC revolves around a heap of rigorous courses in engineering, science, and math. The core curriculum demands that every student take courses in physics, chemistry, biology, computer science, engineering, and a lot of math. Coincidentally, these are the same six fields that you can choose to major in at Mudd. Students with a distaste for one of these fields will find themselves sitting in tough classes with high expectations, a motivated professor, a steep grading curve, and a room full of classmates who are engrossed in the subject matter. Almost everyone will be surprised by the level of challenge in at least one such course during the freshman or sophomore year before settling into classes of individual interest or which are required for their chosen major.

Humanities and Social Sciences

The significant humanities and social sciences requirement (around one-third of the total graduation requirements) makes the curriculum at Harvey Mudd College far more interesting and challenging than the typical tech school. Mudd has been described as "a liberal arts college of science and engineering." Indeed, the educational approach at Mudd is to provide young scientists and engineers with a broad, liberal education including courses in a variety of technical and nontechnical fields. Although no one without a strong affinity for the sciences and engineering should enroll at HMC, those who have little appreciation for fields outside of math and science would be frustrated here.

Few Mudders can fill the requirements for their technical classes anywhere other than HMC, but it is common for students to take advantage of the vast course offerings in the humanities and social sciences at the other four undergraduate colleges in Claremont. The Claremont Colleges Consortium provides Mudd students with a wide array of course offerings including music, fine arts, and foreign languages. The strong academic programs at the other colleges in Claremont allow Mudders to study nontechnical fields in depth and even double major if they so desire.

> **❝** *One of my classmates double majored in chemistry at Mudd and literature at Scripps College; another was the concertmaster for the Pomona College orchestra and double majored in music. Next to them I felt like an academic slacker completing my physics major from Mudd with an economics concentration.* **❞**

Some of the best and most interesting "HSS" (humanities and social sciences) professors in Claremont, however, teach right here at Harvey Mudd College. These professors teach here out of the sole desire to teach Mudders, for they will never have their students major in their fields of interest, which makes their devotion to the college unique. Every student is required to take several of these classes on HMC's campus. Though the humanities courses offered at Mudd may seem limited to some, the department listens to student interests and desires and hires new faculty based upon this feedback. Recently, a professor of Chinese Language and Culture joined the faculty to meet an increasing demand for language classes on campus. Other popular classes include an annual Shakespeare seminar, The Media Studio (a course in media production), and an economics course entitled Enterprise and Entrepreneurship. At the end of each semester the computer labs are filled through the night with as many students writing humanities term papers as students running computer simulations of chemical processes.

Majors

After three well-regimented semesters of the core curriculum, students complete their career at Harvey Mudd taking classes in their major and completing the humanities requirements. The six majors at Harvey Mudd are all academically broad in their own right. The most popular major, engineering, shuns the specialization seen in other top engineering programs for an emphasis on core design principals, mathematical modeling, and a cross-disciplinary "systems" approach to the ever-broadening field of engineering. The chemistry, physics, and biology majors are largely focused on producing top-caliber graduate students who will go on to become career scientists, although in recent years more and more Mudd science majors are studying and pursuing applied fields. A math and computer science joint major and a "chemistry and biology" joint major lead students into an exciting and evolving new area of study. A mathematical biology joint major opens the door of opportunity to an emerging and critical area of future endeavor.

All students at Mudd must have a concentration in a humanities or social sciences field in addition to their technical major. This concentration (which may as well be termed a mini-minor) may be in any nontechnical field from dance to political science to religious history. The vast array of course offerings in Claremont gives Mudd students a lot of options in choosing their HSS course of studies, although students must take about half of their nontechnical courses from HMC faculty members.

Projects

As students enter their senior year, they are required to undertake a year-long project to demonstrate their knowledge and abilities to the faculty, while learning how to budget and develop a lengthy project. For the majority of science and math majors, this involves a theses research project where students design and formally propose projects under the guidance of a chosen professor. Many students choose to begin research as early as their freshman year, and often these students continue this research for their theses. The facilities are first class, from the high tech NMR machine in the chemistry department to the laser scanning confocal microscope in the biology department to the magnetism lab in the physics department. (Even more, students have access to these facilities around the clock thanks to the college's Honor Code.) Both professors and students alike consistently win awards for undergraduate research and publish in the top scientific journals in their fields.

Engineering and Computer Science majors, as well as those who prefer applied areas of study to theoretical endeavors, will take part in Clinic projects as their Capstone research experience.

The Clinic Program (pioneered by HMC more than forty years ago) brings blue-chip corporate sponsors to campus to "hire" teams of four to six HMC engineering, math, physics, and computer science majors for one-year projects that solve a problem or fill a need for the company. The Clinic projects, both domestic and international, give students at Mudd the opportunity to deal with the real-world issues of working with a client, facing deadlines, writing reports, presenting and defending their work, and finding solutions to problems that do not appear in a textbook. The nature of the Clinic projects varies widely both in scope and in subject matter. Recent projects have included a device to measure whether nuclear sites have weapons-grade or research-grade material inside, to camera boards on the latest deployment of two miniature satellites called picosats that took photographs of the Space Shuttle Discovery (STS-116) in December 2007, to designing the next generation of surfboards. Numerous patents have come out of work done by HMC Clinic teams over the years, and many companies return to sponsor Clinic projects year after year, in part to recruit HMC undergrads for future employment.

The Honor Code

Every HMC student commits to a robust, student-administered Honor Code. The Honor Code is a statement of integrity and honesty and is taken very seriously by all members of the community. It engenders a high level of trust between faculty and students. Open-book, un-proctored, and take-home exams are all common at Mudd, and cheating of any kind is simply not tolerated. Students are encouraged to study and work in groups, but are also instructed to acknowledge their classmates who help them on homework assignments. Mudders scorn cut-throat competition; a big reason they chose to attend HMC was so they could learn from and live with very bright peers who want to work in an atmosphere of collaboration and camaraderie.

Course Load

A typical course load at Mudd is five courses per semester. At least one lab per semester and one or two HSS classes per semester is the norm. Those who choose to double major often enroll in six classes each semester. Those who can get away with taking four classes (through summer school, advanced placement, or sheer luck) are teased by their friends for slacking off. At the other four undergraduate colleges in Claremont, and many other private colleges, four classes per semester is the accepted norm.

Grades

The grading scale at HMC can be harsh, although most Mudders exaggerate the cruelty of their grades. GPAs average around 3.3 at graduation, although many freshmen and sophomores suffer through much lower GPAs in the core curriculum before pulling them up during their junior and senior years. HMC does not inflate grades, but neither does the college wish to weed anyone out. Students who do not perform well in classes are given several notices with ample time to correct their behaviors. They can seek counsel from faculty who are readily available and who want them to succeed, and can always lean on a classmate or upper-class student for help.

> **❝** *Struggling through freshman physics was one of the best things that ever happened to me at Mudd. Although it was a real blow to my ego at the time, it forced me to get serious about my homework and not let things slide until an exam came along as I had in high school. The study habits I adopted in order to get through physics became part of my routine for every class and helped me keep my grades up for the rest of college—although to this day I still hate physics.* **❞**

Midterms and finals, almost always administered without a proctor, can be very tough. The freedom a student has to take an exam "home" gives license to the faculty to provide some extremely challenging problems, intended to determine what a student has mastered and perhaps what they can deduce on their own. Class average scores of fifty to sixty percent on an exam are common with some students who had 4.0s in high school scoring in the twenty to thirty percent range. Fortunately, most of the faculty at HMC grades on a sliding scale and there is an abundance of Academic Excellence seminars available for students who fall behind in their studies or wish to go beyond the course material.

Freshmen at Mudd do not receive letter grades for their first semester classes in order to give incoming students a chance to adjust to high academic expectations as well as the transition to life at a residential college. An Associate Dean of the Faculty serves as ombudsman for students, making sure exam schedules are coordinated to spare the students from having to face exams or major assignments due on consecutive days. This Associate Dean also meets with faculty in each department regularly and intervenes with individual students to make sure that no one "slips through the cracks."

Students at Mudd are expected to work hard, study hard, and do an abundance of homework each of their four years at HMC (and few take more than four years to graduate). The work load is heavy, but the competition between students is not. Studying in groups is standard, peer tutoring is widely offered on both a formal and informal basis, and the faculty keep long office hours and offer extended review sessions before exams.

SOCIAL LIFE AND ACTIVITIES

Dorms

Social life at Harvey Mudd revolves around eight on-campus dorms in which nearly the entire student body resides.

Each dormitory at HMC has a distinct personality and set of traditions. The social atmosphere in any given dorm (and indeed on the entire campus) evolves somewhat with every group of new students, but there is some continuity in the types of students found hanging out in certain dorms at Mudd year after year. Dorm stereotypes are plentiful: West Dorm is rowdy, East is secluded and quiet, South is eclectic, North is where the athletes live, etc. HMC is small enough (and homogeneous enough) that students are generally comfortable regardless of which foreign dorm they end up in for a review session, study break, or weekend party. Of course, many students take up residence in a dorm that is not their first choice, and Mudders tend to have friends scattered across multiple dorms; most students at Mudd reside in more than one dorm over the course of their four years.

The dorms are all coed and include a mix of students from all classes. Freshmen are required to live on campus with a roommate and are placed in all eight dorms. The quad dorms, the four older dorms on campus, are named for the four points of the compass although in a Mudd-esque twist of logic, South Dorm is north of West Dorm and west of North Dorm. The quad dorms are each constructed in the early 1960's vintage cinderblock style that dominates the architecture on the campus. The atmosphere tends to be more social in the quad dorms, even if less aesthetic than the newer dorms, where suite arrangements are typical and students are more likely to stick with their closest friends. All of the dorms have central lounges with TVs and DVDs (perfect for weekend movie festivals). On any Friday or Saturday evening, you are likely to see residents of any dorm banding together for a giant picnic on large hibachi-style barbecues in the dorm courtyard. A wireless network covers the entire campus.

The Linde Activities Center (LAC), located amidst the dorms, is also a staple of fun and work. The center includes a weight room, a movement room for martial arts, pilates, dance, yoga, etc., a competition court for volleyball, basketball, etc., a room for table games like foozball, air hockey, pool, a TV room with satellite and DVDs for smaller gatherings. Two meeting rooms and a large computer room reside upstairs.

The proctors (seniors trained in first aid, crisis management, and handing out candy) are placed in each dorm. The roles of the proctors are to mentor those in need and maintain a sense of community within the dorms; they aren't rule enforcers and disciplinarians. There is little non-student presence on campus after hours, except for one faculty member in residence and the bike-pedaling Claremont College campus safety force. Mudd students enjoy a tremendous amount of freedom, and necessarily, responsibility. There are a host of official and not-so-official student government organizations on campus that set student policy, organize events, discipline those who step over the line, and promote the general welfare.

Parties and Competitions

Parties of all sizes, from small spontaneous gatherings to well-hyped five-college extravaganzas, take place at frequent intervals in the dorms on the HMC campus. Mudd parties are reputed throughout The Claremont Colleges to be the biggest, most creative, and most fun parties in Claremont. Parties must serve attractive alternative non-alcoholic drinks in addition to any alcoholic offerings. As on most college campuses, alcohol is noticeable although drinking and driving is not, since all of the parties are within walking distance on campus. In truth, HMC's rigorous academic curriculum ensures that students who do not understand when to stop partying and start studying will not last very long on the campus.

There is a sizable portion of the student body at Mudd that does not drink at all and there are always a myriad of nonalcoholic events at HMC including regular movies, concerts, and off-campus trips. "Jay's place," an on-campus pizza parlor and pool hall, is a popular hangout seven nights a week, occasionally offering up live music and other events. Mudders are as good at coming up with creative and unique extracurricular activities for themselves as they are at throwing parties. The Etc. (extremely theatrically confused) Players produce original plays as well as old standards as often as they can get a willing cast together (three or four times a year). Other Mudd clubs plan outdoor events like the

Delta-H (which means "change in height") club, and coordinate volunteer opportunities for Mudders looking to use up the last remaining ounce of their valuable spare time.

The annual class competition event is a giant relay race that crisscrosses the campus with representatives from each class performing in such events as whistling with peanut butter in one's mouth, computer programming under pressure, running a seven-legged race, and stuffing a textbook into a milk bottle. Faculty and staff serve as judges for the events, although stretching the rules is a time-honored tradition. After the race is over (it takes about thirty minutes), the entire campus settles in for a picnic and celebration of all things great about being at Harvey Mudd College.

Sports

Despite the emphasis on academics, Mudd is a very athletic campus. Many Mudders achieve in varsity sports, although for some students it is difficult to find time to participate in the NCAA Division III athletic program HMC shares with Claremont McKenna and Scripps Colleges. Intramural sports are popular, with inner-tube water-polo as the clear favorite. Intramurals help promote dorm rivalries. They rarely require a great deal of skill, and always provide fun stress relief. There are plenty of club sports to go around like the fencing club or cycling or badminton, and several are extremely successful: the Ultimate Frisbee team is well regarded regionally, while the ballroom dance team and rugby teams (one each for men and for women) enjoy national reputations. Pick-up games of volleyball, basketball, soccer, and Frisbee are daily occurrences at Mudd, as most students are looking for any chance to put aside their homework, soak up some sun, and release some stress. HMC is near Mt. Baldy, one of Southern California's highest peaks, which means that quality mountain biking, hiking, and skiing are less than a half hour away.

Trips

Claremont is well located for weekend and spring break road trips. Los Angeles, Las Vegas, the Joshua Tree National Monument, Santa Barbara, San Diego, and Tijuana are all within three hours by car. San Francisco, the Grand Canyon, and resort towns in Baja are all popular locations, well within the reach of road-tripping HMC students with a few days break. Perhaps the most popular road trip among Mudd students, however, is to DonutMan (a.k.a. Foster's), home of world-famous strawberry donuts. Mudders make the fifteen-minute drive late at night, bypassing numerous other inferior donut shops along the way. This is the popular eating spot for Mudders who are studying late (or taking a break from studying late).

FINANCIAL AID

Harvey Mudd College is, unfortunately, an expensive place to go to college. The school is young (founded in 1955) and has an impressive endowment for its age, but does not bathe in the financial resources that much older institutions enjoy. However, most of the students (around eighty percent) receive financial aid of some form. As at other prestigious private institutions, students and parents alike can accrue a sizable debt over their four years at HMC. The consistency of Mudd graduates being placed in high-paying jobs and prestigious graduate school programs, however, makes all of this debt much easier to stomach and faster to pay off.

Fortunately, HMC is the type of small institution that can give students personal attention, even in financial aid matters. It's common for parents to call and discuss their child's financial aid package with the college's Office of Financial Aid or with the college vice president overseeing the financial aid office. Mudd will work with parents and students to adjust financial aid awards and to establish payment plans that help ensure that any student who has been admitted to HMC has every opportunity to attend the college.

GRADUATES

Perhaps the greatest testament to Harvey Mudd College is the success of its alumni body. Mudd has produced a greater percentage of graduates who go on to receive Ph.D.s (nearly forty percent) than any other undergraduate institution over the last several years. Mudders are in such demand that those who decide to enter Ph.D. programs usually are completely funded for their graduate studies. And many Clinic sponsors offer jobs to Mudders before they have even graduated. A respectable percentage of HMC alumni own their own businesses and alums litter the faculty ranks at top colleges across the country (including five who teach at HMC). HMC alumni have diverse endeavors. Not bad for a college with around 4,500 total alumni, fewer than many universities produce in a single year.

About forty percent of the students at Mudd step directly into the top graduate programs in the country. Students from all majors regularly make the choice to go immediately to graduate school out of Mudd, but the chemistry and biology majors are especially valuable commodities and generally can write their own ticket into the graduate program of their choice. In the past several years, numerous highly prized NSF fellowships, Churchill scholarships, Hertz Fellowships, Thomas Watson Fellowships, and two Rhodes Scholarships have been handed out to Harvey Mudd College graduates.

Due to the HMC Clinic Program and the continuing success of Mudd alums in the work force, dozens of companies come to campus each year to recruit HMC engineering, physics, computer science, and math majors. HMC graduates leave college with a set of skills and experiences that are unique to the Mudd philosophy of education, and invaluable to employers. These experiences include working in randomly selected teams of peers, tackling open-ended problems with no clear solution, exploring the intersection of different technical fields, and generally working hard with limited resources under tough deadlines and related stress.

> ❝ *In my first year out of Mudd working for a big Silicon Valley software firm I was amazed at how most of the guys I started with would complain about the long hours and difficult project assignments that they felt were way over their heads. All I could think was 'this stuff is fun and interesting and a hell of a lot easier to manage than my clinic project back at Mudd was.' I was certainly challenged in my new job but I wasn't overwhelmed like the other new guys.* ❞

A few Harvey Mudd College graduates go on to business, law, or medical school, although most pursue more traditional careers in engineering, science, and math. Medical school applicants from HMC often face the disadvantage of a lower GPA than most of the competing applicant pool who have not endured HMC's rigorous curriculum and grading curve. A growing number of Mudd students are pursuing volunteer service appointments upon graduation including programs in the Peace Corps, AmeriCorp, and Teach for America.

SUMMING UP

Harvey Mudd College is a distinctly small school where some of the top undergraduates in America come together to study engineering, science, and mathematics in an academically rigorous, but extremely fun, environment. The technical curriculum is broad with an emphasis on the humanities and social sciences as well as core science, math, and engineering principals. The residential campus is vibrant with a student body that is widely talented, dynamic, and quirky in addition to being academically gifted. HMC is bolstered by its participation in The Claremont Colleges Consortium, which gives Mudd students access to academic resources, course offerings, athletics, and other opportunities that could not otherwise be supported by a small technical college. The student-run Honor Code demands integrity and honesty from every student. In addition, the general pace and atmosphere of the college demands a healthy sense of humor in addition to a healthy work ethic and a strong affinity for engineering, science, and math.

❏ *Erik Ring, B.S.*

Haverford College
370 Lancaster Avenue
Haverford, PA 19041-1392

(610) 896-1350 (admission)
(610) 896-1000 (general info)
Fax: (610) 896-1338

E-mail: *admission@haverford.edu*
Web site: *http://www.haverford.edu*

 Enrollment

Full-time ❏ women: 652
❏ men: 538

INTRODUCING HAVERFORD

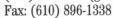

   Once a well-hidden gem tucked away in leafy, suburban Philadelphia, Haverford is
breaking out of obscurity and into the forefront of the country's top liberal arts colleges. And
why not? Haverford embodies what most people associate with college: an arboreal campus
dotted with historic stone halls, professors and students chatting away on the steps after class,
people reading or throwing a Frisbee on the main green. But there are many things about

Haverford that go beyond that, that break the mold and make it a unique place. An Honor Code brings trust and respect to the campus community both in the classroom and at Saturday night parties. Only 1,100 students means that even intro courses average fifteen or fewer students, giving you close contact with a challenging and accomplished faculty. And Haverford has the top collegiate varsity cricket team in the nation (also the only one). It's no wonder Haverford is no longer a secret.

The college covers 204 acres about ten miles from Center City Philadelphia; however, you could easily be convinced that you were in the middle of nowhere. Shrouded by a wall of trees on all sides, the campus consists of rolling fields with buildings concentrated around a square in the middle. The campus itself is an arboretum, and there is a duck pond (complete with ducks). Founded in 1833 by members of the Society of Friends, Haverford was intended for Quaker men, but soon thereafter opened its doors to all comers (except women, who were admitted in 1980). The Quaker tradition is strong but not overbearing in typical Quaker fashion. Meeting is held weekly for those who choose to attend, and aspects such as consensus decision-making and the Honor Code are direct results of the Quaker background.

Liberal arts is the important thing to remember when talking about academics. Haverford is truly committed to the idea, meaning that physics majors cannot hole themselves up in lab for four years, just as philosophy majors will end up stepping into the Marian E. Koshland Integrated Natural Sciences Center more than once or twice during their college career. A few basic requirements, such as a year of foreign language, freshman writing, and a social justice class, are designed to ensure this, but don't prove to be restrictive. That's not to say Haverford students will do well only in Trivial Pursuit; the past few classes have produced prize-winning physicists and published economists, among others. Be prepared to roll up your sleeves right away—the work is rigorous to say the least. The thirty-page reading assignment that you were shocked to get in high school will seem like a night off.

Of course it's not all work and no play. Haverford offers a broad range of activities for such a small college. More than three quarters of the student body plays sports at either the varsity, club, or intramural level. Students can choose from more than 100 clubs and groups ranging from theater to the Zymurgy Club (beer-making). Haverford also has the highest per capita number of *a cappella* groups in the nation, making for a lot of harmony on campus.

The surrounding towns offer the usual fare of movie theaters, restaurants, book stores, and twenty-four-hour Wawa convenience stores, which come in very handy when you want a hoagie at 2:30 A.M. Downtown Philadelphia is a fifteen-minute ride away on the local train; Swarthmore and Bryn Mawr can be reached through regular van and bus service.

The Honor Code

Underlying life at Haverford is the Honor Code, one that goes beyond not copying off your neighbor's exam book. All incoming students have to sign the Code, pledging to live by the academic and social responsibilities it assigns to all students and faculty. What this translates to is take-home tests, and unproctored, self-scheduled final exams that can make the stress-induced angst of finals week a bit easier to take. The more blurry and controversial side of the Code is its social expectations. The basic premise is that all students must treat each other with respect and work out their differences through dialogue. Enforcing such a vague idea can be difficult. The social Honor Code has been a big topic of discussion the past few years at Plenary, the town-meeting style biannual gathering. The Code is a work in progress, constantly being changed and remolded by students who propose amendments and then plead their case at Plenary. All resolutions are put to a vote, and if passed, become part of the Code.

If what you are looking for is academic excellence combined with a strong sense of community, then look no further. A strong emphasis on the liberal arts and the trust and respect implicit in the Honor Code teach Haverford students not only how to be a complete intellectual package, but also how to be humane and thoughtful in their social interactions.

ADMISSIONS REQUIREMENTS

Gaining admission to Haverford is not an easy task, but it's also not one that should be discouraging. Fewer than thirty percent of the students who apply are accepted, but being in the top of your class with great SAT scores doesn't guarantee you a spot nor does that C+ you got in tenth grade geometry seal your fate. The Office of Admission uses the numbers as a benchmark, but is also interested in more than just an applicant's statistics. It is looking for students who will not only excel in the classroom, but also contribute to the Haverford community, either on the athletic field, on stage, at club meetings, or even in a conversation in the dining center. So keep up the piano lessons, join the French club, and maybe take a weekend day or two to volunteer.

Now for the numbers. A total of 3,403 students applied to Haverford during a recent year; 862 were accepted, from which 323 chose to attend. Of those who enrolled, ninety-three percent were in the top fifth of their high school class, and eighty-five percent were ranked in the top tenth. The median range for Verbal SAT was 640–740; median range for Math was 640–720. Women make up fifty-five percent (174 students) of the class of 2010, and thirty-three percent of the class are students of color. Almost all the enrolled students have been officers of one or more school organizations or have lettered in a sport, illustrating the emphasis Haverford places on complete candidates.

The Office of Admission requires the standard materials from applicants: SAT (or ACT) and SAT Subject Tests, high school transcript, recommendations, and a personal writing sample. Haverford uses the Common Application exclusively along with a one-page supplement. Interviews are required for students living within 150 miles of Haverford, and are strongly encouraged for those outside of the radius. Any additional material sent with an application is welcomed, but make sure it is relevant to your admissions information. You might want to hold onto the tape of you scoring the winning goal in last week's soccer game. If you're seriously considering Haverford, an overnight visit is also a good way to get a good feel for the place. Admissions has a cadre of nonthreatening hosts ready to show any prospective students around for a night.

Haverford has been making a concerted effort to increase the diversity of the college. Close to thirty percent of the students are students of color, and Haverford offers need-based scholarships such as the José Padín Fund for students from Puerto Rico and the Ira DeA. Reid Fund for minority students. The college has also been addressing other areas of diversity, including class differences while many Haverford students come from upper middle-class backgrounds, the Office of Admission is trying to affect change by seeking out talented students from lower income families. This is a difficult task because it means putting a heavy burden on the already limited amount of financial aid the college can provide, but one that Haverford has committed to.

ACADEMIC LIFE

The freshman orientation week used to include a session with a long-time chemistry professor on balancing work. The bow-tied chemist would break down, to the hour, the daily schedule of the average Haverford student in an effort to impress upon the freshmen the amount of planning they needed to keep up with their studies. Eight hours a day were allotted for sleeping, three for meals, four for class, and three for any extracurricular activities, which, according to his calculations, left a reasonable six hours of the day for homework. Needless to say, this left many already apprehensive freshmen wondering what they had gotten themselves into.

While few if any Haverford students follow these recommendations for time budgeting, they take their studies very seriously. There are no stereotypical students; the captain of the basketball team might also be a philosophy major who reads Kant when not at practice. The work load is heavy, and often the faculty members seem to forget that you aren't taking only one course each semester. The library is one of the most popular places during the week, which also makes it one of the most social spots on campus. Students looking for some serious studying can hole themselves up in one of the numerous carrels that are scattered throughout the stacks, leaving the main floor for those more interested in being seen.

The cutthroat competition that is rampant in high school does not carry over to Haverford. With the academic responsibility of the Honor Code as a backdrop, the academic life at the college is refreshingly noncompetitive; that is, people are only interested in their own work and don't snap their neck trying to see how their neighbor did on an exam. Haverford supports this by intentionally avoiding a competitive environment; there is no dean's list or honors program.

> **66** *I remember the summer after my freshman year at Haverford, returning home after one of the most stressful years of my life. It was the first time that I had really been home since the school year began, and the first time I had seen many of my high school classmates since graduation. I was really taken aback when one person asked me what my GPA was. Maybe I was reacting as any Haverford student, not used to asking people about their grades, and not being asked about mine, or maybe I thought it was a judgment of my success in college. The fact is I had become part of a community in which grades are not the measure of a person's worth (nor a point of competition or separation within the student body), a community that looks at each member as an individual and values what that individual brings to the community. I am a lot more than the ten-page paper I stay up all night writing, and I am glad to be at a school where the community (and not just my close friends) realizes that.* **99**

The Value of Liberal Arts

Haverford heavily stresses the value of liberal arts, meaning that there is a set of academic requirements. Students must take at least three credits (one class equals one credit) in each of the three major disciplines: the social sciences, humanities, and natural sciences. A semester of freshman English is required for all first-year students, and two semesters of a language are necessary to graduate unless a student can test out of the requirement. There is also an oft-forgotten gym requirement that can haunt seniors who need gym credits to graduate. Students can choose from thirty-two majors, including those at Bryn Mawr College.

The bi-college relationship with Bryn Mawr is designed so that the two colleges offer more together than they could individually. For example, Bryn Mawr offers a major in growth and structure of cities while Haverford provides astronomy. Some majors, such as comparative literature, are bi-college, sharing faculty and campuses. Class size is generally small, averaging fifteen to twenty students. Introductory courses can reach thirty and the occasional survey course can reach seventy-five students. However, by the time students are seniors, they have most likely been a part of more than one seminar that numbered from five to ten.

Faculty

Small classes mean that students come into close contact with professors, and Haverford has some of the best around. Not only are many at the top of their fields, but they are also interested in teaching as well as research. The biology faculty welcomes juniors into their labs over the summer to assist them in their research, and many biology majors use that experience as part of their thesis or to get published. Most Haverford professors encourage classroom discussion, which both enlivens courses and means that if you haven't done the reading for the day, there's nowhere to hide. Professors are very accessible, with ample amounts of office time, and they are willing to stay after class to talk. Many live on campus. Faculty members will invite students over to their homes for dinner, and some hold class in their living rooms.

Study Abroad

By junior year, many students feel the urge to try something new for awhile and to meet some new people. Study abroad programs are enormously popular and the junior class is gutted each semester when students head off for all corners of the globe. The most popular programs are the European ones, but Haverford has also established ties with universities in Nepal, Ghana, Japan, and Chile, among others. Junior year abroad serves two purposes: students get to see the world, and they also tend to return to campus with a fresher view of the college after their time away.

The Haverford experience begins with Customs Week, basically five days of intensified summer camp. Freshmen are divided into groups of ten to fifteen according to their dorm and hall, which becomes their Customs group. Upperclass students, usually sophomores, guide first-year students through a gauntlet of games, get-to-know-you activities, and general orientation to the college. The week includes a dorm Olympics, where each of the three freshman dorms compete against each other in games ranging from the human knot to egg tossing. Customs groups tend to be tight-knit during the first semester, usually traveling *en masse* to and from the dining center. This mentality can slow down the process of meeting new people, but it also is easier to make some close friends within the group.

Housing

For those who enjoy their personal space, housing at Haverford is ideal. Many of the dorms have single rooms, usually grouped together in suites with a common room. Except for freshman year, there is a good chance that a student can go through most of college without having to share a room. If you are looking for a college roommate with whom you can share stories at your twenty-fifth reunion, the several houses on campus and the Haverford College Apartments (HCA) are the way to go. HCA is a complex located on the edge of campus. It houses a third of the freshmen and a large part of the sophomore class. Apartments are shared by three or four students, each with two bedrooms, a bathroom, and a kitchen. The only drawback is that you have to clean the bathroom yourself. HCA develops its own social scene throughout the year, since the third of the student body that lives there creates its own special camaraderie.

Parties and Bars

Haverford has no Greek system, but party-goers still tend to gravitate toward the several houses on campus for their Friday and Saturday night activities or to Lloyd dorm for traditional Thursday night parties. The same scene can get old midway through the first semester, so the more adventurous and legal fun-seekers head out to some of the area bars. Actually, most don't make it any further than the five-minute walk to Roache and O'Brien, more affectionately known as Roaches. About the size of your average walk-in closet, Roaches is a bizarre mixture of seedy locals and Haverford students, complete with a life-size poster of Willie Nelson, a jukebox that hasn't changed a record in twenty years, and a bartender who dishes out insults along with drinks. It's no wonder why it is such a popular hangout. Bryn Mawr is also five minutes away by Blue Bus, the shuttle that runs between the two campuses. Haverford men have the distinct advantage of the famed 3:1 ratio, that is, three women between the two schools for each Haverman, although this is no guarantee that romance will be found. The dating scene can get a bit claustrophobic at a school as small as Haverford, and a general complaint is that there is no casual dating—most relationships tend to be intense. However, many students find their future spouses in the bi-college community.

Traditions

The college also has some long-standing traditions, the most notable being Class Night, a variety show in which classes compete with each other to put on the most ridiculous and often offensive skit. Alums will get teary-eyed remembering their Class Night shenanigans, but in the past few years, participation has flagged, and some classes don't get organized enough to put in an entry.

Going Off Campus

Finding places to go off campus is not too hard. Vans run between Haverford and Swarthmore every day, and UPenn is a twenty-minute car ride away. Right across the street from Haverford is a commuter train stop that goes directly into Center City Philadelphia, opening up a whole world of restaurants, theaters, clubs, sports, stores, parks, and, of course, historical Philadelphia. New York is also a one-hour ride away and Washington, D.C. can be reached in two hours. Or, if you're interested in risking your student job earnings, Atlantic City is only an hour away.

Sports

Athletics are a big draw at Haverford, ranging from the varsity athlete to the intramural badminton player. Forty percent of the students play intercollegiate sports and another fifteen percent play on club teams. There are twenty-one varsity teams that compete in the NCAA Division III and in the Centennial Conference, which includes schools such as Swarthmore, Bryn Mawr, and Johns Hopkins. While some teams are up and down each year, both the men's and women's track teams are perennial powerhouses, advancing to the national championships virtually every year. The college does not have a football team, so Haverford has a unique Homecoming with soccer as the centerpiece of the weekend's events. One requirement to play or watch sports at Haverford is a passionate hatred for

Swarthmore. The academic camaraderie is left at the door whenever there is a game against Swarthmore, and the schools compete for the Hood Trophy, given annually to the winner of the most games.

Clubs or Groups

If you're looking for a club or group to join, there is a smorgasbord to choose from. Interested in boats? Sign up for the sailing club. Want to learn how to make films? Try the Bi-College Filmmaking Club. If you have an interest that you want to pursue or organize, the college will help you get it started.

Haverford shares a weekly newspaper with Bryn Mawr, and the entirely student-run *Bi-College News* is a favorite Saturday morning brunch reading material. Lighted Fools is a popular student theater group that produces several comedy skits each semester, and Horizons Unlimited Musical Theater puts on two musicals each year. Four campus *a cappella* groups regularly square off against each other in joint concerts as does the Bi-College Chorale.

In accordance with its Quaker roots, Haverford also encourages students to take part in service activities. The 8th Dimension Office is a resource for students looking to do some volunteer work, and the office has a goal of getting every student to take part in at least one activity before graduation. That goal has never been realized, but a good number of Haverford students do take time out to volunteer. This can simply be spending one Saturday afternoon helping to fix up an abandoned row house in Philadelphia, or a Big Brother/Sister pairing that lasts for all four years of college. The Quaker student group on campus also runs several service events and each spring break Haverford sends small groups of students throughout the country to help build or repair housing for low-income families.

FINANCIAL AID

Haverford is not cheap. With a price tag that is just over $40,000 a year, many students need help to cover their expenses. The Financial Aid Office is as generous as it can be, providing aid of some form for thirty-five percent of all freshmen and forty-one percent of the entire student body. Admission is need-blind, and financial aid is addressed only after a student has been accepted.

Financial aid decisions are made solely according to a need-based allocation formula developed by the college. In other words, Haverford does not offer any financial aid on the basis of academic, musical, athletic, or any other merits.

Financial aid at Haverford comes primarily in the form of grants and scholarships. The college has around 120 scholarship funds that students are awarded as part of their aid packages, and can be general or directed at students with particular interests. Campus jobs are plentiful, and range from monitoring the field house during evenings to writing press releases for the Public Relations Office. Students often use work-study as résumé-builders for summer internships or even jobs after graduation. Students receiving financial aid are given preference in hiring for campus jobs.

GRADUATES

The real test of the value of a Haverford education and experience comes after students walk across the stage to receive their diplomas. For some it is directly on to graduate or professional school, while others want to take some time to breathe before continuing their education. Roughly fifteen percent of all graduating seniors head straight for school right after college, with four percent attending law school and five percent going on to medical school. Another thirty-five percent spend some time in the work world before going back to school within five years of graduation. Those who do start the nine-to-five life do so in a wide variety of fields. Recent graduates tend to find jobs in business, education, scientific research, and journalism—basically most types of employment. Some students receive fellowships for overseas programs. Haverford is a perennial recipient of at least one Watson Fellowship, which provides money for a student to pursue a self-designed research project overseas. Recent grads on Watson Fellowships have played baseball in Russia and traveled throughout Scotland taking photographs.

PROMINENT GRADS

- John Whitehead, '43, Former Deputy Secretary of State
- Gerald M. Levin, '60, Former Chairman and CEO, Time Warner
- Joseph Taylor, '63, Nobel Laureate in Physics
- Norman Pearlstine, '64, Former Editor-in-Chief, Time Inc.
- Dave Barry, '69, Humorist

The bi-college career development office has a wealth of information on jobs, careers, and internships for those who get over the apprehension of even thinking about finding a job. Recruiters from many major companies and firms come on campus each year in search of future employees, and job-seeking students are also able to interview off-campus through programs established by career development. Those who try the word-of-mouth approach of networking can draw upon an alumni body of roughly 12,000, a small but tight-knit and very accomplished group eager to help out a fellow Haverfordian. Younger alumni tend to congregate in the major cities of the East Coast, a large contingent move a whopping ten miles away to Philadelphia, many succumb to the lure of New York, and Washington, D.C. is often referred to as Haverford's southern campus because of the large number of alumni living there.

SUMMING UP

Haverford offers its students an experience that they will carry with them long after graduation. It is also a rare example of a school where the word community can be used without stretching the truth. With only 1,100 students, most of whom know everyone on campus, Haverford is like a small town, and even has Plenary, its own form of the old-fashioned town meeting. This is exactly what some students are looking for, while others find it too stifling. Whatever their perception on the size, most would agree that the best aspect of the Haverford community is the healthy environment, one with intelligent, thoughtful, and respectful people.

> **❝** *I never really appreciated the effect that Haverford had upon me until I graduated. Comparing myself now to who I was when I arrived as a freshman is like looking at two different people. When I was a student, I never took the time to step back and realize what a fantastic experience I was having; I was more concerned with my work, my social life, the here-and-now. It wasn't until I left the comfort zone of college and joined the "real world" that I began to realize what Haverford had done for me. Not only was my brain crammed with more information than I knew what to do with, but I also had picked up a lot of valuable tools. I could write, express myself, carry on an intelligent conversation, and think critically. I found myself more aware of the world around me and how I could affect it. The Honor Code had opened my eyes not only to larger-scale social issues, but also to my interactions with people on an everyday basis. I would say the best thing Haverford did for me was to make me a complete person.* **❞**

And let's not forget education—Haverford offers one of the best around. Top-notch professors challenge the limits of their students, and classes are intimate academic experiences only a small college can offer. Students work hard, but in return are given the best available resources, the opportunity for independent work, and a thorough education. Haverford will forever remain committed to the liberal arts, choosing to produce intelligent, capable people rather than those trained to occupy a niche.

Each year Haverford sends its graduates out into the world, and in the fall, welcomes another batch of freshmen. While the faces are constantly changing, the college remains the same, and so do the values and education it imparts to its students. Trust, respect, and excellence will forever be the cornerstones of the Haverford experience.

❏ *Steve Manning, B.A.*

The Johns Hopkins University
Mason Hall/3400 N. Charles Street
Baltimore, MD 21218-2683

(410) 516-8171
Fax: (410) 516-6025

E-mail: *gotojhu@jhu.edu*
Web site: *http://apply.jhu.edu*

 Enrollment

Full-time ❏ women: 2,348
❏ men: 2,617

INTRODUCING JOHNS HOPKINS UNIVERSITY

If one were to poll the 1,300 students in Johns Hopkins University's most recently admitted class, virtually every individual would name a different reason for selecting Hopkins. Some would doubtlessly cite top-ranked programs and world-class faculty, while others might offer up the lush campus grounds, the startling variety of activities, or simply the "feel" of the place. Contrary to popular opinion, there isn't only one select type of student who finds Hopkins fascinating. Similarly, there isn't only one select type of student for whom Hopkins is an excellent fit. While the university continues to conduct leading work in the field of medicine, budding scientists and future physicians are *not* the only intellectuals best served by the undergraduate experience; in fact, prospective students do themselves an injustice by stopping there! With numerous well-respected (and highly ranked) programs in the Humanities, the Social Sciences, and Engineering, a Johns Hopkins education promises excellence in every discipline.

> **"** *Hopkins was the last stop on my long list of senior year college visits. New Haven, New York, New Jersey—up and down the Turnpike, these cities and the institutions within them each bore witness to the team of my mother's and my, 'positive attitude,' and Polaroid camera respectively in tow. Although a large part of my visit to JHU was given over to an Admissions Office open house program, my decision ultimately hinged on the most quintessential of campus visit options: the overnight stay. Shepherded from a cappella concerts and improv comedy to an evening game under the lights and several late-night parties, I found myself mentally bumping Hopkins to unforeseen heights on my college hierarchy. Blame it on the eclectic energy and powerful voices of the Mental Notes, clad in their signature Hawaiian shirts; blame it on the oversized Blue Jay mascot stalking the sidelines. From the words of a winning departmental chair (who sold my mom) to the welcoming wisecracks of upperclassmen (who sold me), conversations with campus personalities radiated a warmth and sincerity far beyond what I expected from one of the nation's preeminent research universities. I believed it then and I believe it now, nearly six years later: While a Hopkins education may be considered a rarefied experience, the people are what make the place so extraordinary.* **"**

Founded in 1876 by railroad magnate and philanthropist Johns Hopkins, the institution was the first of its kind in the United States. Curiosity and independence were the watchwords for this new establishment, headlining a tradition of exploration and inquiry that continues even more strongly today. Material examples of this educational philosophy are evident in the university's open curriculum, the availability of undergraduate research opportunity, and the amalgam of student organizations, ever in flux. This philosophy encourages students to take responsibility for their own education in a uniquely powerful way—those who are willing to ask questions and to dig deeply make the most of the Hopkins legacy.

The Campus

Hopkins undergraduates spend the majority of their four years on the Homewood Campus, a 140-acre swath of green in northern Baltimore City. Only three miles from the city center and tourist district, bordered by two busy thoroughfares, Homewood is an accessible, urban campus with a surprisingly rural feel. Georgian structures and fleets of sweeping marble stairs lend a collegial uniformity to the extensive, pedestrian grounds. Dotted with lampposts and a variety of flowering trees, the campus is an aesthetic triumph (and as such, is often a surprise to visitors expecting the raw, the gritty, or the hectic).

Boasting a modest population of approximately 5,000 undergraduates, Homewood houses both the Krieger School of Arts and Sciences and the Whiting School of Engineering. Relatively compact departments and their corresponding faculty cohorts create an intimate learning environment, lending courses the air of a much smaller liberal arts college.

The Hopkins Umbrella

Still, don't be fooled! New arrivals to Homewood will soon discover what locals have learned long ago: the "Hopkins umbrella" stretches far and wide, encompassing a good deal of Baltimore and the world beyond. Free shuttles run from Homewood to the Schools of Medicine, Nursing, and the Bloomberg School of Public Health in East Baltimore, after making a stop at the Peabody Institute Conservatory of Music just south of campus. The Nitze School of Advanced International Studies (also known as SAIS) is based in Washington, D.C., and maintains campuses abroad in China and Italy. Students also have access to the School of Education, The Carey Business School, and finally, the Applied Physics Laboratory. Some of these divisions offer specific undergraduate programs, while the remainder provides opportunities for post-graduate studies, independent research, or employment. Ultimately, no interdivisional work is mandatory; however, if a student seeks adventure away from the Homewood quads, the rest of the university and all of its resources are waiting.

At Hopkins, students need not choose between the rural or urban, the small or expansive; the university somehow manages to provide and to be something slightly different for everyone. With that said, be forewarned: Hopkins students don't view these, or any other defining features, as "compromises." They fully feel as though the best of all worlds is accessible.

Last year, the number of applications submitted to the Office of Undergraduate Admissions increased approximately fifteen percent, making the highly selective process that much more challenging. Still, gaining admission to Hopkins isn't impossible and numbers aren't everything. In order to matriculate a highly diverse and well-crafted class each year, Hopkins admissions counselors have the luxury of reviewing each applicant individually. A 4.0 GPA and flawless standardized testing won't guarantee admission; students must demonstrate a promise of contribution in and outside of the academic arena. From artists and athletes to class leaders and community citizens, students with commitment and passion consistently prove most successful in the application process.

Applying

Prospective students have several application options and submission deadlines from which to choose. Hopkins accepts the Common and Universal College Applications; both are available online and in paper form. Similarly, students can choose between an Early Decision and a Regular Decision program with deadlines of November 1 and January 1, respectively. While Regular Decision is much more flexible, Early Decision is binding, and thus best suited to those students who are sure Hopkins is their top choice.

Applications are evaluated using a number of specific components, some more academic and others more extracurricular in nature.

- Within the academic sphere, the transcript will prove the most helpful. Not only will it demonstrate how well a student has done, but also (and perhaps more importantly), it will indicate how challenging that student's course load has been. Raw grades and class rank don't tell the whole story; an assessment of rigor, or difficulty, in a curriculum demonstrates that student's investment in the act of learning.
- Standardized testing is also considered an academic component. Though by no means the final word on a student's intellect or abilities, the SATs and ACTs provide some consistency between applicants.
- The summation of extracurricular involvement is weighed very significantly in the selection process. While some students choose to use the space allotted in the application to detail their activities, others enclose a resume or extended list. Regardless of the method used, this description of involvement is an essential indicator of contribution at the collegiate level. The admission committee is looking for variety and diversity of activity, but also for leadership and commitment.

- Essays are the best opportunity to share something new or something unique that may not be readily available in other parts of the application. While admissions counselors hope to see strong writing, they are most concerned with content and learning more about an applicant's interests inside and outside of the classroom.
- Three recommendations are required, two from a teacher or instructor and one from a guidance counselor. These should supplement the essay in detailing the character of the applicant.

Keep in mind that the admissions committee takes great care to understand the differences between schools, towns, states, and regions. Not every student has access to the same opportunities; all the committee asks is that an individual has delved deeply in that which is available.

ACADEMIC LIFE

Within the School of Arts and Sciences and the School of Engineering, the philosophy of education manifests itself in numerous ways. Students are given the opportunity to both focus and expand their academic interests through traditional coursework, independent research, internships, and study abroad experiences. In and outside of the classroom, within Maryland or overseas, Hopkins students are hard at work fulfilling the mission of JHU's first president, Daniel Coit Gilman: "[t]he object of the university is to develop character... Its purport is not so much to impart knowledge to the pupils as to whet the appetite, exhibit methods, develop powers, strengthen judgment, and invigorate the intellectual forces." Once students have gained admission to Hopkins, it's up to them to best utilize what they've earned.

Open Curriculum

At Hopkins, work within the classroom is divided into two loosely defined areas: departmental requirements and distribution credits. Unlike many of its peer institutions, Hopkins doesn't instate any type of core curriculum. The only "must-take" classes fall within students' self-selected majors or minors, allowing individuals the opportunity to craft a changeable course of study that meets their needs.

Major and Distribution Credits

With thirty-seven majors in Arts and Sciences, thirteen in Engineering, and forty-one minors ranging from Anthropology to Theatre Arts and Studies, students have a great deal from which to choose; however, due to the absence of a core curriculum, most aren't limited to one field or one major. More than two-thirds of Hopkins undergraduates complete a double major or minor in four years. It's also very easy to shift between majors or schools if the need arises. As Hopkins students become accustomed to the wide variety of academic options at their disposal, changes inevitably occur.

> **"** *One of my good friends began his time at Hopkins with interests in computer science; however, after taking several Chinese language and cultural courses, he decided to add a double major in East Asian Studies. After graduating last May, he accepted a teaching position in Beijing, China, and loves it.* **"**

While majors and minors encourage intellectual focus (and occupy the majority of students' time and energies), part of an average semester is usually given over to "distribution" credits. These courses, taken in areas outside of the major field of study, provide the opportunity to expand and explore. Though technically required, they maintain balance in a curriculum, offering the new, the diverse, and the challenging.

> **"** *As an English and history of art double major, I was obviously oriented toward the humanities; however, I wasn't prepared to sacrifice my fascination with the natural sciences as I moved into college. Hopkins allowed me to do both. From 'Gen. Bio.' and Biological Anthropology to an engineering course on art historical preservation and conservation, I was able to self-tailor my curriculum to my interests.* **"**

Consequently, students do receive a liberal arts education at Hopkins; however, their collective experience is marked by greater freedoms and increased autonomy. The structure is there, but the specifics are up to them.

Satisfactory/Unsatisfactory

Another way in which the university encourages academic investigation is through its current system of covered grades.

During the first semester of freshman year, students will register for and participate in courses as they normally would; however, the final grades they receive will be covered, appearing on their transcripts as either "S" or "U," "satisfactory" or "unsatisfactory."

The rationale for this system is twofold: first and foremost, it encourages freshmen to sample a diverse array of courses without the threat of poor performance as a deterrent. Second, and perhaps more subtly, it supports the notion that college isn't just academics; it is an all-consuming, holistic experience and it should be treated as such. The first semester of freshman year is filled with stimuli. There are friends to meet, clubs to join, a campus to comprehend, and a city to explore, not to mention a series of rigorous courses with which to grapple. "S/U" allows students to enjoy the immersion process while slowly, humanely, preparing them for their next seven semesters.

Research

There is little doubt that the average university student could be kept busy with courses alone, yet would class hours, problem sets, exams, and papers really provide enough intellectual fodder for the Hopkins undergraduate? From the look of it, apparently not— more than two-thirds of JHU students will conduct meaningful research by the time they graduate.

Research is the real meat of the undergraduate diet. Substantial, sus-

EXAMPLES OF UNDERGRADUATE RESEARCH BY DEPARTMENT
○ **Anthropology:** Women's Movement and Reproductive Health in India
○ **Civil Engineering:** The Qualifications of 19th-Century American Truss Bridges as Structural Art
○ **Film and Media Studies:** "2:37 A.M." A Film
○ **History of Art:** Visions of the Virgin
○ **Near Eastern Studies:** "The Investigation of New Kingdom Occupation at the Temple of Mut in Luxor, Egypt"
○ **Neuroscience:** The Role of Perivascular Cells in HIV Associated Dementia
○ **Political Science:** Thwarting the Terrorist Threat: Lessons from the Israeli-Turkish Experience
○ **Writing Seminars:** "Lost Writers and their Lost Works"

taining, it isn't just theorizing—it is the direct application, the fleshing out, of those theories. With a broadly based definition encompassing classical laboratory work, self-crafted classes, honors theses and capstone projects, internships, and study abroad experiences, an independent research opportunity is one of the university's signature offerings.

Hopkins undergraduates can become engaged in research as early as freshman year and in every major. Academic advisors, faculty, and departments all help students find topics and projects right for them. While some students choose to contribute to the work of a professor or colleague, others design their own projects with assistance from a faculty mentor.

Many undergraduate research projects are realized with help from fellowships, grants, and additional funding. Incoming freshmen have the opportunity to submit proposals for a Woodrow Wilson Undergraduate Research Fellowship when they apply for admission to the university. If selected, students receive a stipend of up to $10,000 to conduct original work. Current scholars benefit from the Provost's Undergraduate Research Awards (PURA), a program that sponsors around fifty students a year and provides grants of up to $2,500. Although these are only two examples, they demonstrate the administration's serious dedication to undergraduate research, both in theory and in practice.

Internships, Study Abroad, and Intersession

Though internships and study abroad experiences aren't commonly categorized as research, they do incorporate the element of experiential learning so critical to a Hopkins education. By investigating a profession or exploring a city, a country, or a culture, Hopkins students can test what they've learned in the classroom through direct, on-site application.

The Office of Academic Advising and the Career Center each provides resources for students interested in pursuing formal internship programs or more casual career exploration. Examples of recent internships include work at the American Enterprise Institute, Microsoft, Amnesty International, the Metropolitan Museum of Art, National Public Radio, the United States Congress, the World Health Organization, and Yahoo Inc. Internships can be conducted for university credit, for a salary, or simply, for the experience itself.

> **"** While I didn't personally choose to study abroad, my junior year was filled with comings and goings as friends traveled to all parts of the globe. Glowing reports of art history in Scotland and robotics in Japan were sent via e-mail; others went rafting in Australia and hiked Machu Picchu in Peru on days when classes weren't in session. More than simply an academic experience, study abroad fostered a genuine kind of growth and change in those who chose to take it on. Even now, some just can't let it go—my suitemate who went to Barcelona is still talking about it! **"**

Study abroad opportunities, like internships, are easily coordinated and readily available. Hopkins students can work with the Office of Study Abroad or organize something independently; with several campuses abroad and nearly 400 students living and working overseas each year, the university maintains a highly respected international presence.

For those students who feel as though adequate time for these options isn't available during the academic year, Intersession provides an excellent outlet. Similar to the "J-Terms" or "Wintersessions" offered at other institutions, Intersession is a three-week block of time tacked onto the end of mid-year vacation. Students can stay home if they wish; however, a good number choose to return to campus. One- or two-credit classes are offered, allowing students to lighten their course loads for spring; recreational courses are also available, along with time for research, internships, or short study abroad adventures. Popular offerings include a renaissance art program in Florence, Italy, a behavioral biology trip to the Galapagos Islands, and a financial course that culminates in a trip to New York City.

> " At every stage, on every level, Hopkins students are actively involved in the acquisition of knowledge. I wanted a place where the students were genuinely interested in learning…not just a place for people who were 'smart.' Here, professors don't expect you to [only] know what they taught. They expect you to take what they taught and teach yourself. It's a place where [people] are only limited by themselves. "
>
> —Sarah David, '07

SOCIAL LIFE AND ACTIVITIES

Clubs and Organizations

With more than 360 clubs and organizations from which to choose, students are provided with everything and anything extracurricular. Offerings range from publications to political organizations and from cultural and religious groups to club sports teams and community service. Like their varying memberships, these activities reflect the diversity of the Hopkins community.

Founded, led, and governed by students, these organizations, not surprisingly, retain a great deal of autonomy. While there should be something for everyone, in the event that there isn't, any group of students, large or small, can request funding to begin a club of their own. As a result, the greater body of extracurricular activities is ever evolving. Introduced at an expansive, open-air fair that traditionally follows the week of freshman orientation, student groups vie for the attention of new members.

> 66 *I don't believe I'll ever forget my first activities fair. As I browsed up and down the rows of folding tables, sense and sensibility were assaulted—literally! Back issues of* The News-Letter *were thrust into my arms, already filled with flyers from the Outdoors Club, Student Council, and the Admissions Office. I offered up my contact information in exchange for handfuls of Lifesavers or Tootsie Rolls, along with promises for fun times in the future. Though I probably signed up for too much, I soon became convinced that at Hopkins, there was rarely a dull moment.* 99

Arts and Music

With Peabody Institute just down the road and the Mattin Student Arts Center located right on campus, students are surrounded with opportunities for the fine arts at Hopkins. Although Peabody does offer several options for undergraduate degrees, interested students are able to pursue coursework, ensemble participation, and private lessons in a more informal way. Membership in the Hopkins Symphony Orchestra, the JHU Band, the assortment of *a cappella* groups, and other music organizations on campus is a popular pursuit and generally available by audition. In addition, concerts given at Peabody and at Homewood are available for Hopkins students free of charge. The Mattin Center provides an assortment of art and dance studios, a black-box theater, darkrooms, a digital media lab, music practice rooms, and multipurpose meeting space for student groups. From the Johns Hopkins University Theatre and Witness Theater, to the Gospel Choir and the Indian Cultural Dance Club, the variety of organizations dedicated to the arts fosters Homewood's collective creativity.

Athletics

With varsity, club, and intramural options available at two interconnected facilities on the north end of campus, athletics are a priority for more than three-quarters of the students at Hopkins. Nine varsity teams for women and eleven for men compete at the Division III level, while both men's and women's lacrosse contend in Division I. Despite excellent performances from many of its Division III teams, few Hopkins sports fans would argue with the fact that men's lacrosse, National Champions in 2005 and 2007, is the great love of the institution. From the opener straight through to Homecoming and the season's end, the Blue Jays pack the stadium; thousands upon thousands of pennant-waving, sign-wielding, blue-painted students, faculty, staff, and alumni fill the stands, ready to cheer their team to victory.

For the more casual participant, club and intramural teams offer numerous ways to get in shape or to stay active. With both traditional and more eclectic options available (inner tube water polo comes immediately to mind), competition is friendly and open to all. A *de facto* home base for these groups, the Ralph S. O'Connor Recreation Center offers basketball, volleyball, racquetball, and squash courts, weight and fitness rooms, several studios of various sizes, and a two-story climbing wall.

Campus Events

On several occasions throughout the academic year, Hopkins students convene as a community to learn, to listen, and on many occasions, to kick back and relax. On balmy days in the fall and spring, "the Beach," an extended, grassy space between the library and North Charles Street, is packed with students. Armed with blankets, books, radios, and Frisbees, groups convene to soak up the sun en masse. The Hopkins Organization for Programming, or the HOP, brings comedians and other performers to campus, while coordinating with Student Council to organize casino nights, club nights downtown, and concerts. Friday Night Films shows movies, often working in conjunction with the JHU Film Society.

Incoming students and upperclassmen alike anticipate Orientation, a week-long affair that precedes classes. Organized by a large executive staff and several hundred volunteers, its academic sessions and social events are well attended by all. The fall semester also witnesses a weekend-long Fall Festival, plus Culturefest and the Milton S. Eisenhower Symposium. Culturefest, a week-long series of lectures, discussions, and social activities, seeks to promote appreciation for diversity and tolerance, while the M.S.E. Symposium, the longest student-run lecture series in the country, increases campus and community awareness of national issues. Recent topics have included: "A Transition Between Generations in a Changing America" and "The Global Network: America's Changing Role in an Interconnected World." Past speakers have included Maya Angelou, Rubin "Hurricane" Carter, Ann Coulter, Kareem Abdul Jabbar, Patricia Ireland, Spike Lee, Nelson Mandela, Bobby McFerrin, Michael Moore, Will Ferrell, and Valerie Plame Wilson.

The second semester at Hopkins is equally full as activities capitalize on Baltimore's temperate climes. Students enjoy socializing at Spring Fair, an enormous student-run carnival complete with rides, "fair food," craft booths, and live entertainment. The complexity of the event's many components requires assistance from a staff of sixty coordinators and more than 200 student volunteers. Traditionally following Fair weekend, Homecoming brings generations of alumni back to Homewood. Convening for brunches, luncheons, the big game, and a good dose of nostalgia, families and friends mingle with current students in celebrating Hopkins.

Greek Life

I came to Hopkins thoroughly ambivalent toward anything 'Greek.' With a mother who served as the president of her sorority years ago, I felt as though my own collegiate experience would be perfectly satisfying without the influence of sorority life. Though this mindset did follow me through to graduation, I was pleasantly surprised to find a much less intense, much more welcoming group of organizations than originally expected.

With eleven fraternities and twelve sororities, the Hopkins Greek System and its process of rushing and pledging is much more of a "match to be made" rather than a means of establishing one's social status. Events are usually open to everyone; weekend fraternity parties and community service activities include members and nonmembers alike. While naturally these groups attract different types of students and boast varying campus reputations, all seek to serve their members through academic, social, and community-minded outlets. As such, they provide well for those students seeking a Greek system; however, rarely is being "Greek" all that one is or all by which one will be defined.

Residences

For a student's first two years at Hopkins, on-campus housing is required and guaranteed. As a result, social activities tend to revolve around, or at least stem from, life in the dorms. Students are able to select their preferred living arrangements from a series of options: basic doubles, singles, and suite-style rooms are available during the first year, while larger apartments supplement the second year's offerings. During this time, individuals live, dine, study, and relax together; lasting friendships are made, strong social networks are formed, and commonalities are discovered, even between the most disparate of personalities. With the advent of junior year, most students move off campus to apartments or row houses with friends. Though university-owned housing is available, the Off-Campus Housing Office is accessible to assist students. Few residences are more than two or three blocks from Homewood, encouraging continued involvement in club meetings, concerts, sporting events, and parties. The university has also just completed construction on Charles Commons, a 300,000-square-foot upper classman housing, dining, and retail complex. Still, the move off campus will have many upperclassmen looking increasingly toward greater Baltimore for the weekend's social activity.

Charles Village and Baltimore

Campus and all of its facilities are located in Charles Village, one of the many small neighborhoods that compose Baltimore City. Consisting of several main roads intersected by residential streets, the area caters to college students and local residents alike. Restaurants and small shops supply ready stomping grounds for those eager to grab a bite or a cup of coffee. The Baltimore Museum of Art, or the BMA, is adjacent to campus; with free admission for Hopkins students, there's really no good excuse for missing the latest exhibition.

Students also have access to greater Baltimore, an extensive yet easily navigable city. From the northern suburbs' malls and movie theaters to the historic neighborhoods near the harbor, students quickly learn what to do and where to go. Just south of campus, Mt. Vernon and the arts district house Peabody, the Meyerhoff Symphony, the Lyric Opera, and the Walters Art Museum. Further south, the Inner Harbor and tourist district lie within easy walking distance of Camden Yards, home of the Orioles, and M&T Bank Stadium, home of the Ravens. Canton, Federal Hill, and Fell's Point are favorite haunts of the fun-loving, each offering slightly different hybrids of the bar/club/restaurant mix. Finally, for the truly ambitious, Washington, D.C., Philadelphia, and New York City are only brief train rides away!

FINANCIAL AID

Though a Hopkins education could hardly be called inexpensive, the Office of Student Financial Services seeks to make the experience affordable for students and their families. Forty-eight percent of all undergraduates receive some kind of financial assistance. The university is committed to funding as much of a family's "demonstrated need" as possible, a figure determined using national and institutional criteria. Although the majority of aid offered is need-based in nature, limited merit scholarships are available. Approximately twenty Hodson Trust Scholarships of $25,500 are offered each year, along with two full-tuition Westgate Scholarships for engineering students. The university has also recently partnered with Baltimore City public schools in offering full tuition scholarships to eligible city students admitted to the university who are also city residents.

GRADUATES

Life after college isn't as terrifying a thing as it might appear; after years of working and living independently, most Hopkins students are more than prepared to meet postgraduation challenges. Assisted by the Office of Academic Advising, the Career Center, and the Pre-Professional Advising Office, students who know what they're looking for (and students who don't) are provided extensive resources to help them along.

PROMINENT GRADS

- Woodrow Wilson, Ph.D., 28th President of the United States
- John Astin, actor, Most Notably of *The Addams Family* (TV)
- Michael Bloomberg, Mayor of New York City; President and CEO of Bloomberg Financial Network
- Rafael Hernandez-Colon, Former Governor of Puerto Rico
- Russell Baker, *New York Times* Columnist and host of Masterpiece Theatre
- Antonia C. Novella, Former Surgeon General of the United States
- Wesley Craven, Director of *Nightmare on Elm Street* and the *Scream* films
- Jody Williams, 1984 Nobel Peace Prize winner
- Corbin Gwaltney, Founder-President of *The Chronicle of Higher Education*

The Hopkins emphasis on lifelong learning isn't a fiction; more than eighty percent of Hopkins students continue on to earn graduate or professional degrees within ten years of graduation, the highest percentage in the nation. Similarly, for students interested in professional institutions, the rate of acceptance is equally impressive. Approximately ninety percent of medical school applicants who participate in the premed advising process are accepted, which is more than twice the national average; similarly, ninety-two percent of those who apply to law school are accepted.

The Alumni Association for the Johns Hopkins Institutions provides numerous resources for the recent graduate. With career networking and professional development opportunities, social activities, and events for young alumni, the association is the tie that binds hundreds of thousands of members in more than thirty-five United States chapters and more than twenty international clubs. Wherever they go, wherever they find themselves, Hopkins alumni can always rely on support from their own. Indeed, as the T-shirts given out by the athletic association proudly read, each graduate is "forever a Blue Jay."

SUMMING UP

While most alumni would probably agree that Hopkins provided well for them both academically and socially, the university isn't resting on its laurels. Within the past several years, eight new buildings have been added to campus and several additional initiatives are well underway. From Clark and Hodson Halls to state-of-the-art new chemistry and computational sciences buildings, facilities for research and teaching have grown larger and glossier. Through the construction of the new arts and recreation centers, the rich extracurricular lives of Hopkins students have been not simply acknowledged, but commended and encouraged; their existence makes good on the notion that a Hopkins experience isn't solely academic. Mason Hall, a new quad area, complete with academic facilities and the university's visitor center, and Admissions Office fleshes out the south end of campus.

All told, these additions are indicative of a reflective, self-evaluative university that doesn't feel immune to critique. Hopkins embraces change per se, but perhaps more importantly, recognizes the need for an evolution that builds upon distinctive features and existing traditions. As noted by the second president of the university, Ira Remsen, in regard to campus construction, "[o]ur general plan should determine the style of architecture and arrangement of buildings appropriate to the gradual development of the campus so that in years to come the groups…will form a symmetrical whole." This passage is easily applied to the university at large; in reinventing its various parts, attention to the greater whole—the bigger picture—isn't just a priority, but a consistent practice.

❏ *Amy Brokl, B.A.*

KENYON COLLEGE

Kenyon College
Gambier, OH 43022-9623

(800) 848-2468
Fax: (740) 427-5770

E-mail: *admissions@kenyon.edu*
Web site: *www.kenyon.edu*

 Enrollment

Full-time ❑ women: 844
❑ men: 787

INTRODUCING KENYON COLLEGE

When Kenyon College founder Bishop Philander Chase first smoked the ham (smoked the what?!?), he had no idea what he was getting himself into.

It was the late 1820s and the location was Gambier, Ohio. The dinner Bishop Chase held that night for the handful of young men recently enrolled at this, the Bishop's fledgling college, would be the first of many intimate meals taken on this Midwestern hilltop. Today, 1,600 students from all over the world inhabit Kenyon, and as any current student will proclaim, intimate meals on the hilltop continue.

Kenyon, one of the strongest small liberal arts colleges in America, is a place where tradition and innovation constantly renegotiate their boundaries; a place where a professor of classics can attain the rock star status not seen since life in Ancient Greece; a place where "learning in the company of friends" is not only reality, it is a bona fide credo.

More than eighty percent of students at Kenyon come from outside the state of Ohio. A roommate is more likely to hail from Boston than from Cincinnati. Students at Kenyon are an eclectic group, and the college does an excellent job of providing for its unique community. A vigorous and varied social life exists on the 1,000-acre campus, which stretches throughout the rolling hills and quaint farm towns of Knox County, Ohio. The city of Columbus sits forty-five minutes to the south, offering up the closest urban experience for students. And while taking advantage of the art museums, good ethnic food, and international airport located in the city is always tempting, Columbus is not a place students go on even a weekly basis. Students happily call the town of Gambier their home. Campus life is self-contained, and Kenyon is committed to funding the kind of intellectual and social activities that effectively pierce the serenity of the mid-Ohio calm.

Thoreau would have loved this place. Instead of using Walden Pond for leisurely walks and self-meditation, students make do with the nationally recognized Kokosing River and the surrounding Kokosing Valley, which serve as the natural centerpiece of Kenyon's strong environmental science program. To boost the quality of science research and instruction available to its undergraduates, Kenyon has constructed a multimillion dollar science complex on campus. Both the natural surrounding and the man-made facilities that now exist demonstrate a strong commitment to science education at Kenyon. This has led to a host of multimillion dollar research grants from the likes of the Howard Hughes Medical Institute and the National Science Foundation, intended to promote collaborative research among students and faculty.

But of course, labs are not for everyone. In that case . . . there's always English. Nearly thirty percent of Kenyon students call the English department home, and for good reason; Kenyon's literary tradition dates to the 1940s and 1950s, when Kenyon served as the birthplace of modern literary criticism. The father of this movement, poet and critic John Crowe Ransom, as well as other imposing figures in the literary world, such as Peter Taylor '40, Robert Lowell '40, and E. L. Doctorow '52, all figure prominently in Kenyon's contributions to modern literature. One of the many legacies of this storied group of English giants can be seen in the *Kenyon Review*, one of the nation's foremost literary journals, known throughout the world for publishing the next generation of literary figures well before major publishers lavish them with book deals. The real plus for students is that the *Review* hires a number of interested students to assist with the publication of the journal. As one may imagine, this is a coveted position for any student seeking a future in the world of writing, and it's available only to Kenyon students.

As a liberal arts and science college dedicated to the intellectual and personal stimulation of undergraduates, Kenyon works hard to ensure that students are happy. In doing so, the institution places an emphasis on hiring staff and faculty who are committed to the college well beyond their standard nine-to-five work day. Kenyon faculty and staff members can often be seen attending football and basketball games with their spouses and children on the weekends, leading extra study sessions in the evenings prior to midterm exams, and attending the myriad lectures, concerts, and panel discussions held for students throughout the year. If Kenyon is about anything, it is about engagement on that most personal of levels: the human level.

ADMISSIONS REQUIREMENTS

Kenyon has seen a meteoric rise in applications in the last ten years, and, consequently, it has had to become much more selective in its application process. Although in recent years the college has accepted between thirty and forty percent of its applicants, it would behoove prospective students to do what Kenyon students already do best: be themselves.

Kenyon takes most of the typical things into consideration: scholastic record, extracurricular activities, letters of recommendation, and SAT or ACT exam scores. So, in other words, take hard classes, be a change agent, study for those standardized tests, and ask the teachers who like you to write you a recommendation letter or two. Oh, and don't miss the deadline. And even then, there is no guarantee.

> 66 My Kenyon interviewer did not ask me whether I had taken calculus or not, he asked me what I thought about why we study history and 'what makes history so special anyway?' Honestly, I'd never thought of that before. I just studied it because it was what the teacher told me to do, and I thought that's what I had to do. I realized then that Kenyon encourages students to think through even the most basic assumptions about life. If this was the admission officer talking, I couldn't wait for the professors. I submitted my application a week later. 99

Kenyon admission officers work hard throughout the year to recruit and shape a class that is diverse, inquisitive, talented, and earnest in their love of learning. Kenyon does not admit students based on specific departmental requirements; rather, it seeks students with wide-ranging intellectual curiosity. Students who do well in the admissions process at Kenyon are able to demonstrate that they have both the intellectual stamina to succeed in a classroom filled with discussion, and the social bravery to immerse themselves in a completely participatory community. Most students who are admitted have exceeded the minimum admissions requirements of four years of English and math, three years of foreign language, science and social studies, and one year of fine arts coursework. Most students have also visited the campus, either in the summer of their junior year or during the fall of their senior year, and many students interview, either on campus, or with an alumnus in the many cities around the country where they are offered.

> 66 *My high school years brought a yearning to flee as far from home as possible, and so initially I decided Kenyon wasn't for me. That is, until I visited. When I visited, I sat in on an English class with Ellen Mankoff, and the vibrant discussion that she facilitated was amazing. This model of discussion mixed with lecture was what really impressed me most.* 99

—*Dayne Baughman, '08*

If students have done particularly stellar work in an area of the performing or creative arts, the Admission Office will accept an arts supplement, such as slides or an audition tape for voice or instrumental music. These are optional and will be used in the review process if submitted. Kenyon pursues a holistic review process for its applicants. No stone is left unturned. Admissions officers are committed to thinking about whether students will benefit from four years in the Kenyon community and thus, "student fit" is an important X factor.

Quintessential Kenyon: Understanding Fit and Match

Kenyon students enjoy "the journey." They appreciate what it takes to be successful in life, and they know how to work hard to accomplish goals. But, they are not resume chasers. Internships might be important to some, and are available, but figuring out a personal *raison d'etre* is a compelling use of time for most Kenyonites. They are thinkers of a grander sort; they are intellectual altruists. Above all, they are smart, thoughtful, and usually willing to see Kafka as just as good a potential roommate as their "buddy down the hall." This sort of intellectual thoughtfulness permeates the mind of every Kenyon student. It describes the physics major and the philosophy major alike—these idiosyncrasies are well understood by Kenyon admissions officers and they look for this "fit" in every applicant.

Visiting Campus

Visits are highly encouraged. Students interested in applying in one of the two Early Decision rounds of admission are strongly encouraged to visit campus prior to submitting an application. During a visit, prospective students can spend the night in the residence halls, sit in on classes where they have a particular curricular interest, have an interview, and/or watch an in-season team practice their sport. Kenyon admissions welcomes visitors all year round, and sponsors Visit Days programs during select weekends in the fall and spring of every year.

ACADEMIC LIFE

Academic offerings at Kenyon are broad and far-reaching. It is common for first-year students to sample many academic disciplines before deciding on a major. By the end of the second year, all students will have settled into a particular department and declared a major or two. But after choosing a specialty, professors expect students to draw from the various traditions, disciplines, and research projects conducted in more disparate academic areas when speaking up in class. Talk about Boaz in Playwriting 101. Talk about Lincoln in an English seminar. Talk about Pythagoras in a human sculpture class. Others will relate, connections will be made, and professors will smile.

Learning in the Company of Friends

The academic environment at Kenyon is a synaptic fireworks show. Kenyon is truly a place where students are not intimidated from talking philosophy in the lunch line and bioethics in the math lab. Interdisciplinary studies have seen an explosion of growth in the last few years, with programs such as scientific computing, law and society, and international studies, which allow students to pursue work at the intersection of multiple disciplines simultaneously. With a ten-to-one student-to-faculty ratio, a library with more than a million volumes, and wireless access all over campus, doing homework is hardly a problem.

Professors at Kenyon are loath to assign anything but an essay. Let something be stressed: at Kenyon you will learn how to write. Sure, there are some disciplines that will ask you to write less than others, but Kenyon's philosophy is very clear: even math majors need to communicate their theorems. In order to do that, they must learn the most basic art of communication: writing. Regardless of the topic of the class, writing is an essential component of doing well at Kenyon. It is very common to have at least two to three hours of homework for every one hour of class time during the week. In some upper-level classes or for a seminar class that meets only once a week, it might be three to four hours to every one hour of class. Kenyon faculty expect students to come to class prepped and ready to engage, and one way to ensure that this happens is to assign a lot of work between classes.

> **“** *I remember very clearly that it was on September 7 of my sophomore year that I decided to be a history major. Professor Reed Browning had just brought in birthday cake for the celebration of the 467th birthday of Elizabeth I, and I thought, wow, this guy is crazy, I want him to be my advisor. So, I majored in history.* **”**

Advising

A good many Kenyon professors are great lecturers, but most would cringe at the thought that they would be known more for what *they* say rather than for what they get their students to say. Most Kenyon faculty members realize mentorship is a large part of the job description here. The classroom environment serves as an extension of the professor's office, and the college expects all professors to hold office hours at least twice a week. Additionally, all work well with e-mail, and responses are generally timely. In addition to serving students in the classes that they teach, Kenyon faculty have advisees who are majors in their particular department, as well as first-year students who are entering the college without any clear direction.

Freshman advising takes up a large portion of a faculty member's time in the very early stages of every semester, but students are expected to make connections with a faculty advisor if they need assistance during another part of the year. Faculty are always available, and students are treated as adults. It's quite well known that setting up a meeting on campus is as easy as sending an e-mail. Professors will go out of their way to help. Kenyon faculty are teacher-scholars who uphold the teacher side first. They do not mind staying late after class. They do not mind being stopped in the bookstore. Most do not even mind a phone call at their home at 9 P.M. They *want* their students to get this stuff. They don't mind going the extra mile (or four) to make it happen.

In addition to faculty advisors, freshmen on campus also receive an upper-class counselor. These are current Kenyon sophomores or juniors who help acclimate new students. They work in tandem with faculty advisors to get students enrolled in their first two semesters' worth of classes. They also serve as an immediate social contact, helping introduce newbies to the social scene and plugging them in to any activities that they might wish to pursue. The upper-class counselor stays with a preselected group of four to six students for their entire first year at the college, meeting with them periodically throughout the year to check in on both academic and social concerns that new students may have.

Studying Abroad

As if living in rural Ohio isn't enough excitement, Kenyon also encourages students to go to other places, meaning . . . Madrid, Nanjing, and Cairo, among others. Study abroad, either in an international program or one located in the United States, is a popular option for Kenyon students, and more than fifty percent of them will choose to participate. In addition to the 150 or so programs available to students, Kenyon runs three of its own programs that are tremendously popular. They are the Kenyon-Honduras program in anthropology and archaeology; the Kenyon-Exeter program, based in England and focusing on English literature; and the Kenyon in Rome program, devoted to the study of art history and other subjects. Because the curriculum is developed by each department, and because the courses are led by Kenyon faculty themselves (unlike the other abroad programs), majors in the various departments frequently take advantage of these programs.

SOCIAL LIFE AND ACTIVITIES

"Bells, bells, bells, the tin tinabulation of the bells bells bells . . ."

—Edgar Allan Poe really gets Kenyon College

At five o'clock every Friday afternoon, the Kenyon peelers fill the air with sound. From high atop the steeple of the only chapel on campus, a relic from the days when Kenyon held close ties to the Episcopal Church, Kenyon students understand what it all means: The weekend is finally here.

The Weekend

Social life at Kenyon is best described as organized chaos. The weekend is essentially strung together via a patchwork of structured programming and spirited random events, all coalescing to create what amounts to a whirlwind of young bodies flowing in and out of campus buildings for a full forty-eight hours. After 4 P.M. on Sunday, though, it's usually study time.

And who says the middle of nowhere isn't fun? A given weekend in Gambier might include both a Chanticleer concert and a fraternity toga party, as well as a talk by *Times of London* columnist Andrew Sullivan and a sold out performance of Marsha Norman's play *'Night Mother*. The great thing about this is that the same students will attend all four events. Kenyon students are an eclectic bunch, and they revel in the intellectual and social diversity that Kenyon's generous budgets allow. Whether it's bringing in major political speakers like John Kerry, sponsoring a weekend full of Diwali festivities, or paying for transportation to a community service activity, Kenyon administration is sensitive to the fact that, because everyone lives on campus, and, because it's not easy to get into a major city, that social life must be well funded. And it is.

> 66 *Kenyon offers so many opportunities to get involved and to take on leadership responsibilities. What I loved about the activities at Kenyon is that you could be involved in a bunch of things that had nothing to do with one another and it was not only okay, it was celebrated. The clubs and activities are really the lifeline of Kenyon.* 99

—Taryn Myers, '03

It's Not All About Books: This Place Is Fun

Life on campus is helped along by the more than 150 clubs and organizations. Popular clubs include many publications, such as *The Kenyon Collegian*, the college's only weekly newspaper; *Persimmons*, a creative writing journal; and *The Observer*, Kenyon's more right-leaning political journal. Music-based organizations such as the Kenyon Chamber Singers and the ten other student music ensembles, including seven strong *a cappella* groups, are also favored, as are drama and dance groups such as the Fools On the Hill and the Kenyon Musical Theater Society, and the community service clubs such as Circle K, Habitat for Humanity, and APSO, the Appalachian People's Service Organization, which sponsors a major service-learning trip to that region every semester. The local volunteer fire department sponsors Emergency Medical Technician (EMT) training to willing students and welcomes students who obtain EMT certification as members of the local ambulance and fire service. Student government is also a popular option. In addition to the First Year Council and Upper Class Council, current students are invited to participate on Board of Trustee committees, academic department student advisory boards, and administrative level committees that examine everything from study abroad policy to student activities budgets.

Greek Life

Nearly thirty percent of men and ten percent of women belong to a Greek organization on campus. These fraternities and sororities are frequent sponsors of campus social activities, and their parties are a fixture on the Friday night calendars of a majority of Kenyon students. Because of the close-knit nature of the campus community, parties are rarely exclusive, and the attitude is welcoming. Greeks at Kenyon view themselves not as secret "skull and bones societies" (my apologies to Yale) but rather as clubs and organizations just like any other on campus. While sometimes a bit cliquish in the dining halls, the vast majority of fraternity brothers and sorority sisters do not maintain exclusive ties with their organizations. Just like other Kenyon students, it is common to see frat boys running with a diverse circle of friends and serving in leadership roles within the Kenyon community that help to foster, rather than hinder, campus dialogue.

Athletics

There must be a word about fitness. The word is KAC. The Kenyon Athletic Center opened in January 2006 to applause from the entire community. This behemoth of a building is the center of the Kenyon athletic department. At the same time, it serves nearly 1,000 students who visit its 263,000 square feet of space every day for recreation and fitness purposes. It's kind of like a mothership with squash courts (and swimming pool, huge fitness room, full indoor track . . . well, you get the idea).

Varsity athletes—men are the Lords and women are the Ladies—compete within the North Coast Athletic Conference (Division III), the first conference in the country devoted to giving equal emphasis to men's and women's sports. Approximately thirty percent of Kenyon's student body participates on the twenty-two varsity sports teams, while nearly thirty-five percent more are involved in intramural competition. Kenyon leads all NCAA Division III institutions with a total of fifty-seven national championship trophies and top-three with fifty-three NCAA Postgraduate Scholarship award winners. Many of these championships belong to the Kenyon swim team, which has dominated for over three decades. The men's team has won thirty-one consecutive NCAA Division III national championships, and the women have won twenty-three of the last twenty-seven NCAA Division III national championships. And just in case anyone is wondering, the average GPA of a Kenyon swimmer last year was nearly a 3.5.

FINANCIAL AID

Let's face it, the cost of colleges like Kenyon can pose a challenge. The good news here is that Kenyon places a high value on making it affordable. And yes, there are scholarships. And yes, there are also loans.

The Financial Aid Office at Kenyon is a small, friendly office staffed with people who understand the phrase "extenuating circumstances." This is a good thing. It will mean that financial matters will not be maddeningly bureaucratic. It will mean mom and dad will be able to know someone's first name, so that making "that call" will be a bit easier.

> ❝ *I feel that financial aid is one of the places where Kenyon really shines. It was no more difficult applying for aid to study abroad than it was applying for aid any other semester. The staff was most helpful, and answered all of my many, many questions almost as quickly as I could ask them. In fact, there was a problem with one of my loans being credited to Kenyon—the bank scheduled disbursement weeks after I was set to leave for my study abroad in Spain—meaning that I would not have access to the money once I was overseas. But I called, and they were able to handle the problem in one afternoon and made sure that I had access to the loan funds before I left.* ❞

—*Dayne Baughman, '08*

Like most private colleges in America today, Kenyon sounds expensive. Total charges this year were about $50,000. Kenyon does meet one hundred percent of a family's demonstrated financial need, which means that, after all the dust clears, if you need money to attend Kenyon after mom and dad pony up their piece, then Kenyon will provide it in the form of a financial aid package.

In fact, nearly half of Kenyon students receive need-based financial aid. And the average package is about $30,000. U.S. residents must fill out two forms on-line: The Free

Application for Federal Student Aid (FAFSA) and the CSS PROFILE, available from the College Board. International students must fill out the International Student Financial Aid Form, also available on the College Board web site.

Scholarships

Kenyon sponsors several of its own merit scholarship programs. The Kenyon Honors Scholarship, the Kenyon Science Scholarship, and the Kenyon Trustee Scholarship are all offered to students regardless of financial need. They range in dollar amounts from several thousand dollars up to half tuition. Music and art scholarships recognize demonstrated achievement in these arts. Additionally, Kenyon sponsors the Distinguished Academic Scholarships, which are separate and decent-sized merit scholarships awarded to students who have demonstrated excellent leadership in high school. Kenyon is also one of the few schools in the United States that offers aid to international students. There are different forms that must be filled out, but Kenyon's commitment to diversity is strong, and this commitment manifests itself in many forms, including international student financial aid.

GRADUATES

After leaving the somewhat coddled life on Gambier Hill, alumni are thrust into the real world of quarterly performance evaluations and monthly rent payments, all of which seemed completely unthinkable only six months earlier. Alumni quickly learn that Kenyon has taught them many things, but that chief among them, it has taught them to think critically and to communicate effectively.

One of the best things about being an alumnus of Kenyon is that it means one is not alone. The Kenyon alumni network includes over 15,000 other alums who are always eager to help younger alumni find jobs, apartments, and internships. Nearly eighty percent of graduates go directly into the workforce after graduation from Kenyon, while the rest go on to graduate school. However, within five years of graduation from Kenyon, a full seventy percent of Kenyon graduates reenter graduate school to work toward an advanced degree of some kind. Law, business, and medical degrees are common; Ph.D. programs are very popular as well.

And for those who don't work right away, there's always travel. Kenyon is frequently listed among the top ten Fulbright-producing colleges in the nation. In fact, in the last five years, Kenyon students have been named Beinecke Fellows, Fulbright Fellows, Mitchell Fellows, Truman Fellows, Marshall Scholars, Jack Cooke Scholars, and Luce Fellows, allowing them to travel, teach, or attend graduate school at little or no cost.

SUMMING UP

Kenyon is an institution where tradition still holds a coveted place in the hierarchy of things. The college does its best to ensure that matriculants understand that they are part of something bigger and more profound than themselves. Kenyon does pomp and circumstance very well. Kenyon maintains its modern sensibilities, but it does not mind being old fashioned if the reasons are warranted. It blends what it had with what it has. It constantly reminds students that life is not about having the right answers but about asking the right questions. It will turn the eighteen-year-old mind inside and out until it has been thoroughly cleansed of everything that it thought was true.

Kenyon is not a place for intellectual sponges. Do not attend a class just to soak up a professor's thoughts from the back of the classroom. Do not think that the dictionary, the thesaurus, or the lab coat are anathema to an education. Hiding is not an option. Be prepared to speak up. Be prepared to attend dinner in the home of a professor. Come equipped to argue over the finer points of things like Western values, nanotechnology, and the 2008 election. And don't worry, you'll find someone who knows a little about them all . . . guaranteed.

It is a place where students engage the community in an attempt both to add to it and to leave their mark. Kenyon celebrates the individual, and it encourages everyone to live an examined life. The Ohio calm will allow plenty of time for contemplation, relaxation, and maturation. Kenyon wants students in the classrooms and the laboratories by day and in the lecture halls, concert halls, and theatres by night. Kenyon is a place where putting forth great effort will meet with great reward. It remains a place where the students, the buildings, and the weather constantly change, but where the questions people ask do not. Kenyon College is a small place that likes to think big.

❏ *Adam Sapp, B.A.*

LAFAYETTE COLLEGE

 Lafayette College
Easton, PA 18042

 (610) 330-5100
Fax: (610) 330-5355

 E-mail: *admissions@lafayette.edu*
Web site: *http://www.lafayette.edu*

 Enrollment

Full-time ❑ women: 1,105
❑ men: 1,257

Part-time ❑ women: 23
❑ men: 29

INTRODUCING LAFAYETTE

There is a little known theory about Lafayette. It doesn't involve mathematics or chemistry, but it may describe the actions of thousands of people over more than a hundred and seventy-five years. No scientists, anthropologists, or philosophers have been consulted, but after reading this essay, the theory may get their support. The theory is simply this: There's a certain type of magic you will find at Lafayette. That's right—magic. There is no name for it, and no proof that the magic is in the water or in the air, but anyone who graduated from Lafayette knows it's there. How else can you explain why such miraculous things happen at this college?

The heart of the magic is that year after year, the most involved, active, and focused students begin their college careers at Lafayette. And during their four years at the college, these students exchange their own interests, enthusiasm, and passions with other students. It's this connection, and the brilliance of the students, faculty, and administration that allows students to leave their mark, make a difference, and continue to contribute to the college long after graduation.

A Rich Legacy

When the 19-year-old Marquis de Lafayette asked the King of France to finance his journey to assist in America's fight for freedom, the king refused. Lafayette secretly purchased his own ship, adding the words *Cur Non* ("Why Not") to his family crest to serve as his motto. The Latin phrase *Cur Non* guides Lafayette College today in challenging students to move beyond the comfort of their familiar environments and experiences.

One of America's oldest colleges, Lafayette has roughly 2,400 students and more than 200 full-time faculty. With 47 majors in the humanities, social sciences, natural sciences, and engineering, 250 student organizations, and an amazing campus, rich in academic, residential, and recreational facilities, Lafayette offers all the benefits of larger schools with the student-centered approach of a small, undergraduate college. It does this through collaborative, high-impact learning, enabled by committed teachers and scholars and an extraordinary campus and facilities, for the benefit of involved, focused, and active students.

In Easton, Pennsylvania, on top of a steep hill, sits a well-manicured, tradition-soaked, 110-acre campus. Although its geographic location doesn't allude to it, Lafayette knows no boundaries—and neither do the students. That's what makes this college so special.

> **"** *As you drive up the hill to the college for the first time, you can only see hints of the old buildings hanging over the cliff. But once you reach the top, you become immersed in the Lafayette lingo and way of life. The school lets you grow but nurtures you at the same time.* **"**

There are hundreds of small liberal arts colleges sprinkled across the Northeast. For a long time the reputation of Lafayette was that the college was just one of the many schools to offer a solid academic experience on a beautiful campus. But over the past decade, Lafayette has distinguished itself as a well-resourced college dedicated exclusively to undergraduates, where students work in teams with others across different majors to solve real-world problems.

As Lafayette has gained national notoriety, however, the school still maintains the same sort of nurturing educational experience it always prided itself on. And that is why, to this day, the number of students hovers only around the 2,400 mark.

Here are the numbers that mean something to you:

- More than 6,000 apply to fill only 620 first-year class spots.
- The average SAT score was Verbal—630, Math—660.
- Sixty percent of the first-year class was in the top ten percent of their graduating class.

But please realize that it isn't all about numbers at Lafayette. In fact, the Admissions Department indicates that aside from test scores and GPA, it is very interested in "evidence of special talent, and personality/intangible qualities." While you're calculating your highest combined SAT score, why not think about things that really matter at Lafayette:

- Can you make a difference?
- Are you ambitious?
- Do you have the makings of a student leader?
- How can you impact your academic department?
- How will you leave your mark?

Interviews

Although interviews are not required, you are strongly encouraged to have one. While your application may mention the clubs and community service you participated in during high school, an interview is the perfect opportunity to let your personality and drive shine through. And even if you're not ready to be a future world leader or business tycoon, the Lafayette admissions staff is very adept at seeing the special sparkle in someone even before they recognize it themselves.

If you cannot get to the campus, Lafayette has more than 600 Alumni Admissions Representatives (AARs) who interview candidates in their home areas throughout the country. Interviewing with an alumnus may not only be more convenient for you, but it's a great way to see how influential the college has been on a student years after graduation.

Student Representative Program

The best way to see Lafayette is to participate in the Student Representative Program. A current student will be assigned to spend the day and night with you, taking you to classes, meals, and social activities. The Student Representatives volunteer to host prospective students overnight, with the hopes of sharing the magic of Lafayette with others. No doubt, after spending a day and night on campus, you will have a definite idea of whether the school is right for you.

Early Decision

If Lafayette is your first choice, you should consider applying under Early Decision. The priority deadline is November 15, with notification by December 15. Students who decide later that Lafayette is their first choice may convert a Regular Decision application to Early Decision by February 1. Applicants admitted under the plan must withdraw applications to other institutions. And if you are a financial aid candidate, you are bound to Lafayette only if your financial need is met.

While many Lafayette students come from the northeastern United States, the student body represents more than forty U.S. states and territories and fifty-five countries including Argentina, Australia, Bahamas, Brazil, China, Egypt, France, Ghana, Hungary, Kenya, Pakistan, Russia, Saudi Arabia, Sri Lanka, Turkey, and Zimbabwe.

ACADEMIC LIFE

To fully appreciate Lafayette, you really need to take advantage of all that the faculty has to offer. One of the greatest gifts that the faculty has given is student focused, student-directed learning. Lafayette is not about boring lectures and unavailable professors. Rather, Lafayette has built a strong reputation in the liberal arts, sciences, and engineering, because of its focus on the student. This unusual combination of strengths continues to define Lafayette's special role among the top liberal arts colleges in the nation.

Students can choose from forty-seven majors in four main categories: engineering, humanities, natural sciences, and social sciences. If Africana Studies, Neuroscience, or Environmental Science don't interest you, you have the flexibility to design your own major.

The current curriculum has been designed to allow students to experience greater depth in their learning, by requiring only four courses per semester.

One of the main focuses of the academic program is to create well-rounded thinkers. To accomplish this, Lafayette has introduced new areas of learning and has enhanced the current curriculum.

Faculty and Seminars

Small classes are one of the most valuable benefits of a small college, and at Lafayette, the professors are as dedicated to the introductory courses as they are to independent research. In fact, all senior faculty teach beginning as well as advanced courses. And the student/faculty ratio of 10 to 1 guarantees that no students have the opportunity to hide from interactive learning. Lafayette has committed to increase its faculty size to reduce the student/faculty ratio to 9 to 1.

There is no better example of how important this attention to students is than the first-year seminars. Limited to sixteen students per seminar, this series of courses of varying topics is designed to introduce first-year students to the value of small-class learning. Furthermore, the courses give students an opportunity to be comfortable among their peers and prepare them for the many other student-directed learning experiences that are ahead of them.

In fact, students use these skills each year as they present papers at the annual National Conference on Undergraduate Research. Lafayette's delegation is one of the largest among all the institutions that participate, including ones several times the size of Lafayette.

Renovations and Improvements

The college has an impressive endowment of more than $640 million. New or renovated academic buildings completed recently include Hugel Science Center for Chemistry, Physics, and Biochemistry; a renovation of Skillman Library; Oechsle Hall for Psychology and Neuroscience; Williams Visual Arts Building; a completely renovated Acopian Engineering Center; a Ramer History House; and Kirby Hall of Civil Rights for Government and Law. An experimental black box theater, state-of-the-art film theater, sound stage, and high-tech media and teaching lab are some of the exciting facilities planned for the new Williams Arts Campus at the base of College Hill, where the campus meets downtown Easton. The arts campus will be a vibrant new gateway to Lafayette and the city, and provide exciting new academic and cultural opportunities for students and the community.

Writing and Technology

No matter whether you decide to be an engineering, psychology, or business major, writing will be a major focus of your studies. The Writing Program is intended to help integrate the practice of writing into courses throughout the college. The program trains selected undergraduates as Writing Associates (WAs), assigning them to specific courses in the college's general curriculum and in a wide variety of disciplines. Through the Writing Program, everyone who graduates from Lafayette enters the world with an impressive understanding of the written word, and is able to leverage writing skills as an effective communication tool.

VAST (Values and Science/Technology) courses provide an exploration of math/natural science and humanities studies that look at the way technology and science impact our world. The courses are designed to engage students in problem solving using a multidisciplinary perspective. In particular, there should be strong evidence of both humanistic and scientific approaches to the chosen problem or issue. In essence, VAST courses are less about teaching content, and more about teaching a process of thinking.

Special Programs

The EXCEL Scholars Program is Lafayette's paid research assistantship program. Students do undergraduate research working one-on-one with a faculty member. Each year, more than 200 students gain this invaluable experience. Besides the stimulating academic challenge, they have the opportunity to apply techniques and knowledge learned in class to a specific problem.

Lafayette encourages students to consider the international dimension as an integral part of their education. Lafayette students may select from faculty-led programs offered in cooperation with European and African institutions. A Lafayette faculty member accompanies students and teaches one or two courses in these semester-long programs.

Another alternative learning opportunity is the Interim program. Last year, more than 150 students studied in Australia, Ecuador, Egypt, France, the Galapagos Islands,

Madagascar, New Zealand, South Africa, and Turkey during the winter break. The concentrated, three-week courses earn the same credit as a semester course.

> ❝ *The fact that, as B.S. majors, we were required to take various liberal arts courses such as English and foreign languages was very beneficial. I have met many people who had very "narrow" educations from wonderful schools—extremely knowledgeable about science but very lacking in communication and writing skills.* ❞

SOCIAL LIFE AND ACTIVITIES

·For the 2,400 students at Lafayette, there are more than 250 student-run organizations, five fraternities, six sororities, and more than forty intramural sports, so the average student could easily be the photo editor of *The Lafayette*, the drummer of the pep band, a DJ on the college radio station, and the vice president of a fraternity. In fact, ninety percent of all first-year students end up graduating from Lafayette—and as any student knows, it's not just the academics that help retain students. Rather it's a combination of academics, recreation, leadership activities, and fun that makes college a well-rounded experience. And Lafayette makes sure that every angle is covered.

Sports

The Allan P. Kirby Sports Center includes 110,000 square feet for recreational sports, including two indoor basketball courts, an elevated jogging track, an indoor inline skating rink, six-lane pool, thirty cardiovascular machines, spacious weightlifting area, a thirty-five-foot rock climbing wall, six racquetball courts, and a café. There is also an entire floor of the center dedicated to pool tables, foosball, and Ping-Pong. The most dramatic feature of the center is its wall of windows that face the varsity football field, Fisher Stadium. Lafayette's facilities for football recently underwent dramatic transformation with new spectator seating, lights, a FieldTurf field, a new varsity house, and improved restrooms and vending areas.

Lafayette's NCAA Division I intercollegiate athletics program includes 23 sports.

As soon as you come on campus in the fall, students will be already talking about the annual Lafayette-Lehigh matchup. This year marks the 146th meeting, making it the most-played rivalry in the nation. And it is therefore one of the oldest college party events in the nation too, as students and alumni from both Lehigh Valley schools make it a day to remember.

Community Service

Lafayette has a very active Community Outreach Center, with numerous and diverse programs. You'll easily find one that fits your interests and schedule. Every year, more than 900 students give more than 33,000 hours of community service. Lafayette also participates in the America Reads program, providing reading tutors for young children. One of the most exciting programs is Alternative Spring Break. Groups of students travel to various locations during the January interim session or spring break such as Johns Island, South Carolina; a Navaho reservation in New Mexico; Atlanta, Georgia; and Honduras to help communities with painting, home repairs, tutoring, or environmental work. You can volunteer for any of the center's programs or create one of your own.

Greek Life

Part of the Lafayette Experience is Greek life. There are five fraternities and six sororities. Approximately thirty percent of Lafayette students belong to a Greek organization, but that certainly doesn't limit non-Greeks from getting involved in the system. Part of the magic at Lafayette is that social events are hardly ever restricted, and those who are not Greek don't let that stop them from taking advantage of the parties and events that the houses sponsor. Furthermore, sorority and fraternity rush (the period of time when you learn about joining a house) doesn't take place until sophomore year, giving first-year students a whole year to get acclimated to college life before being thrust into the Greek system.

Off Campus

As the town of Easton continues to rebuild itself, more and more local pubs and bars are extending the social scene away from the fraternities and sororities and "down the hill." But there is much more to do on campus than go to parties. The award-winning activities planning organization, LAF, brings comedians, musicians, and other entertainers to campus each week. Recent shows have featured Bela Fleck and the Dave Mathews

Band. And there are also the much talked-about yearly events, such as Homecoming, the Lafayette-Lehigh Football Game, and All-College Day, which all involve a lot of outdoor parties, bands, and Lafayette spirit.

On-Campus Living

Living at Lafayette has taken on a whole new meaning in the past few years. While everyone is guaranteed housing for all four years, the options for living continue to expand. An exciting addition to Lafayette's residential campus is the newly-opened Sullivan Lane complex of four buildings and a parking garage. Designed to promote a distinctive integration of living and learning, the buildings are particularly well suited for living groups that are centered on academic or cocurricular interests.

Year after year, the most desirable place for underclass students to live is South College. But since everything is within ten minutes walking distance, you are never too far away from anything to make one residence hall more desirable than others. First-year students receive first choice for housing, and many of the top picks are South, McKeen, and Ruef Hall. Each room includes a bed, a desk, and a chest of drawers. As you can imagine, you will want to decorate your room to reflect your personality but any questions that you could ever have about your room and Lafayette in general can be answered by your Resident Advisor, an upperclass student who is highly trained and dedicated to making your experience complete.

After your first year, your living options increase to fraternities, sororities, college-owned off-campus houses, and specially designed learning-living houses. The most prominent of these houses is McKelvy House, which is home to the McKelvy Scholars Program. This program encourages academic excellence and facilitates the exchange of ideas among students. Students are nominated by the faculty to reside in the house, where students participate in discussions and other intellectual activities, including the production of a scholarly journal titled *The McKelvy Papers*. Living in the McKelvy House is highly coveted by students, and the program was featured on CBS News' *Sunday Morning*.

> 66 *One of the best things about Lafayette is how responsive the college is to meeting students' needs. If you want to make something happen, all you need to do is ask. Lafayette is small enough that the faculty and administration are very responsive, and large enough to have the resources to get things done.* 99

FINANCIAL AID

There is really no way around saying this: Lafayette is expensive, more than $50,000 a year. But that doesn't mean that affording Lafayette is impossible. In fact, about fifty-four percent of students receive aid. The president and trustees do realize that many families would have to channel some magic just to afford the school so the college is constantly increasing the amount of financial aid and scholarships that it awards to students.

Lafayette awards more than $35 million in financial aid. In the class of 2014, forty-eight percent received college-awarded financial aid in the full amount of demonstrated need. Awards directly from Lafayette ranged from $500 to $38,500 per year. Additional amounts from federal, state, and private sources are available up to the full cost of attendance.

Even students whose families are expected to pay the full cost of college can take advantage of payment plans that apportion costs into more manageable monthly amounts, or loans with reasonable rates that provide cash-flow relief.

Lafayette offers special education opportunities and more than $1 million in scholarships to the most academically promising applicants. These awards are made to accepted students who have demonstrated academic excellence and intellectual curiosity. These students are designated as Marquis Scholars. They receive an annual minimum award of $20,000 (totaling $80,000 over four years).

GRADUATES

The Lafayette magic follows students even after graduation. Talk to Lafayette graduates and they can recount times when they have been in odd places and encountered other Lafayette alumni or stories of running into alumni almost every week in New York City, where many alumni seem to relocate after graduation. But even more important is that Lafayette grads continue on to do great things. Lafayette graduates know that they have a responsibility to impact the continued value of their degree by giving back to the college. Alumni volunteer their time helping in admissions, providing interships and externships for students, and by helping students make career and graduate school decisions.

You are not on your own after graduation. Lafayette helps you make specific plans for graduate or professional school and for the world of work. You will gain experience during your four college years in applying your knowledge through undergraduate research, independent studies, community work related to your academic field, and internships. Through this special four-year career development program, Lafayette students work with an advisor to create an action plan to help them achieve their goals. Through the Career Services office, Gateway provides a wide range of informational and counseling services as well as access to a network of Lafayette alumni who can provide practical advice based on their own experiences. Students who sign up for the program are paired with a professional career advisor. Together they work out an action plan based on the student's interests and goals. Students have the opportunity to be matched with alumni for work-related experiences and networking in a specific career field. In addition, students registered with Gateway are linked to the Career Vault. Through this online job database, students will be notified when Career Services receives information about a job vacancy that matches their skills. Internships are an excellent way to gain experience in a field of interest. Most students participate in these during the summer or over the January interim session.

Faculty members and the Career Services office provide information on these opportunities, some of which offer academic credit. A major value of an internship is the on-the-job experience—an accomplishment sought by employers and graduate school admissions committees.

In addition to internship opportunities, Lafayette students have the chance to participate in a special program made possible by alumni volunteers. Lafayette alumni (and parents) offer more than 200 on-site job experiences called "externships." Students spend two to five days, during January interim sessions, shadowing an alumnus or alumna in a profession that they are interested in pursuing. For instance, one student assisted the supervising researcher at the National Marine Fisheries Service in Honolulu, Hawaii; another spent a week with a pediatrician in New Jersey; and another reviewed civil cases and observed a trial with a New York City law firm.

Approximately thirty-seven percent of all Lafayette graduates earn advanced degrees. Some prefer to work before pursuing graduate study, but about one of every four Lafayette graduates goes directly to graduate or professional school.

All academic departments provide graduate school counseling for their majors, but the college also offers specific assistance to those headed for professional schools.

SUMMING UP

The best thing about Lafayette is that it will prepare you for your future in a way that no other college can. The sky's the limit; if you want to try something new, create a new organization, research with a professor, create a major, or travel abroad, people at Lafayette will encourage and help you.

Lafayette is the perfect mix of independence and nurturing. You will become an independent thinker, an amazing writer, act in a play, sing in the chorus, play new sports, and of course, make long-lasting friendships. Lafayette will teach you how to think, how to be resourceful, and how not to let any obstacle keep you from your dreams—and that's all part of the magic.

❏ *Jodi Morgen, B.A., M.A.*

LEHIGH UNIVERSITY

Photo by Douglas Benedict

 27 Memorial Drive West
Bethlehem, PA 18015

 (610) 758-3000
Fax: (610) 758-4361

 E-mail: *ori@lehigh.edu*
Website: *www.lehigh.edu*

 Enrollment

Full-time ❑ women: 2,281
❑ men: 1,960

INTRODUCING LEHIGH UNIVERSITY

Founded in 1865 by Asa Packer, an industrial pioneer, Lehigh University is a premier research institution nestled on South Mountain in Bethlehem, Pennsylvania. As a coeducational, nondenominational, private school, it offers a distinct academic experience deeply rooted in school pride and rich tradition. Students at Lehigh enjoy a vast and multidimensional college experience. There are three undergraduate schools—the College of Arts and Sciences, the College of Business and Economics, and the P.R. Rossin College of Engineering and Applied Sciences—offering ninety majors and more than twenty cross-disciplinary programs. Additionally, the three undergraduate schools offer graduate programs, as does Lehigh's College of Education.

No matter in which college students decide to enroll, they are assured of a top-notch education both on and off campus. With a student-to-faculty ratio of ten to one, students have close relationships with their professors and often take advantage of opportunities for extra help and clarification. Lehigh prides itself not only on preparing students for their future endeavors in the classroom, but also off campus. Students and faculty take the learning experience outside of the classroom and into the surrounding neighborhoods. From studying the business trends of local shops and restaurants, to measuring the toxicity levels in nearby creeks, and to studying the rich history of the City of Bethlehem, the opportunities to practice classroom lessons in a real-life setting are everywhere.

> **“** *For a final class project my senior year, I used the reporting skills I gained in the Journalism department to learn more about Bethlehem Steel, once the second largest steel producer in the United States and national treasure. I sharpened my writing, reporting, and research skills and developed an interest in American industrial history. I met with past Bethlehem Steel employees, local businesses affected by the plant, and I learned about the future of the landmark. It's safe to say that at Lehigh, I didn't just listen and take notes, I lived the lessons.* **”**

The Bethlehem community and Lehigh have an intertwined relationship that encourages students to participate in the surrounding neighborhood. Since Lehigh first opened its doors in 1865, South Bethlehem has provided an outstanding home for the university, and thus encourages the Lehigh community to step off campus and take part in the tradition. Students are patrons of the quaint boutiques and restaurants and some hold part-time jobs. They attend street fairs and festivals as well. According to most students, the Bethlehem Celtic Fest on the north side is a highlight of the fall semester and the Chili Fest on the south side is a staple in April. Not only do students, faculty, and staff take advantage of all Bethlehem has to offer, they take part in the revitalization of the city, contributing more than $1 million worth of community service each year. When freshmen first arrive at Lehigh, the orientation program brings them into the surrounding neighborhood in order to feel an immediate connection to Bethlehem.

While students are busy participating in events and activities off campus, the level of student involvement on campus is just as impressive. From Greek life, to athletics, to peer tutoring, and to Student Senate, there is something for everyone. Community service events can be found daily, organized speakers visit campus almost weekly, and there is always an event to attend on the University Center front lawn where students come together to just enjoy themselves. Students rarely leave campus on the weekends, and if the sponsored activities aren't reason enough to stick around, the unbelievable scenery and fantastic views from South Mountain make Lehigh's campus a picturesque setting straight out of a painting. And while South Mountain does present it's challenging hills, the joke on campus is that the dreaded "freshman 15" is purely a myth at Lehigh. Over a century and a half after its founding, Lehigh University remains a staple in the Lehigh Valley. Once an industrial pioneer's dream, it is now one of the most prestigious and respected research universities in the country.

ADMISSIONS REQUIREMENTS

When freshmen arrive on Lehigh's campus, they are welcomed with the mantra that they are a part of the biggest and brightest class yet. Lehigh's student body is composed of some of the most intelligent and gifted individuals from all over the world. Admission to Lehigh is highly selective and is based on advanced placement or honors courses, evidence of special talent, and a leadership record.

Students apply directly to their chosen college; however, the ability to transfer from school to school is certainly feasible if one decides to change his of her field of study. The SAT or ACT is required for all applicants, and candidates should have completed four years of English, three years of math, and two years each of a foreign language, science, and social science. Most students present four years each of science, math, and English. An on-campus interview is available and AP credits are certainly accepted and encouraged.

Lehigh accepts the Common Application with an additional supplement application. There is a heavy focus on the admissions essay as a way to grasp the individual talents of each applicant. Prospective students utilize this space to point out ways in which they will be able to contribute to the community and why Lehigh is the perfect fit for them.

Lehigh University is home to four fine research institutions—the College of Arts and Sciences, the College of Business and Economics, the P.C. Rossin College of Engineering and Applied Sciences, and the College of Education (offers only graduate programs). In total, Lehigh grants twelve degrees in the undergraduate and advanced levels. The three undergraduate schools award B.A., B.S., B.S.B.A, and B.S.E. degrees, while all four graduate colleges award master's and doctoral degrees.

Lehigh boasts an average class size of twenty-seven, and in total, eighty percent of all classes have fewer than thirty-five students. While the larger, introductory classes such as Calculus, Economics, and Sociology hold a few hundred students, they are broken down into smaller recitation sections to complement the lectures. These recitations are facilitated by T.A.s who have a strong standing at the university and come with high recommendations from the professors. No new material is ever taught during these sessions; rather, they provide extra help and review of the week's lectures.

Faculty

Faculty members at Lehigh are world-class scholars known for their excellence in research and practice. The majority of Lehigh's faculty members are permanent full-time employees and ninety-nine percent of them hold doctorate degrees or the highest-level degree in their designated field. Sixty-nine percent of full-time faculty members are tenured, having undergone a rigorous academic review and establishing themselves as prominent members of the Lehigh community.

In addition to their academic accomplishments, Lehigh faculty members are dedicated to seeing their students succeed. Whether holding weekend help sessions, inviting students for dinner, or keeping their office doors open, the professors at Lehigh go the extra mile to offer a helping hand to their students. The low student-to-faculty ratio makes it possible for students at Lehigh to build lasting relationships with their professors. In fact, the lessons learned from faculty will stay with students forever, as their words of wisdom not only serve as day-to-day lessons, but inspirational messages.

> 66 *As an accounting major, I had a tough course load taught by professors who cared about each individual student. All of my professors knew my name and I was able to discuss my coursework with them as well as job opportunities upon my graduation. My professors encouraged me to follow the path that was best for me to take, and now I am very pleased with my decision to defer my job offer and earn my Master's degree at Lehigh.* 99

—*Lauren Harte, '10*

Fellow Students

The competition on Lehigh's campus motivates students to invest a significant amount of time in their studies. While the workload is more rigorous in some majors than others, no matter what course of study students select, in many respects, it is the close relationships that they have with each other that drives their desire to succeed academically. There is a bit of competition on campus in terms of grades; however, students use this to work together in groups to study, solve problems, and develop presentations together. There is even a peer tutoring center on campus that matches students who have successfully completed a class with those who might be struggling. Lehigh students find that by working with fellow classmates, they can be exposed to a different view of the material and receive an alternative means of help and mentorship. Additionally, it is not rare for an academic department to match an older student with a younger student to help foster relationships within the field. Some students take advantage of these programs and can use these relationships for networking purposes after graduation.

Presidential Scholarship

While most Lehigh students have an inherent drive to succeed academically, the university provides an additional incentive for those undergraduate students who complete 92 credit hours with a GPA of 3.75 or higher. The Presidential Scholarship rewards these students with one full year of on-campus study for free. Presidential Scholars work toward a second baccalaureate degree, master's degree, begin doctoral studies, or just continue in their fields of interest. The program was founded in 1997 by former Lehigh president Peter Likins to reward and acknowledge the accomplishments made by Lehigh's undergraduate students. This scholarship is just an extra opportunity for undergraduates to take advantage of furthering their education while establishing themselves in the Lehigh community.

> *The beauty of the Presidential Scholarship is that it awards students who have proven their ability to dedicate themselves to their studies the opportunity to structure their own free year.*

—Imani Hamilton, '10

Graduation Requirements

The graduation requirements at Lehigh vary based on the department, but each student must complete two semesters of English, at least thirty credits in their chosen major, a minimum of 121 credit hours, and a GPA of at least 2.0. Many academic departments at Lehigh require students to intern in their chosen area of study in order to gain real-world practice before actually venturing out into a permanent working environment. Each student is assigned an advisor to help guide class selections and courses of study in order to meet all graduation requirements. Students find this to be extremely helpful because while these professors won't hold their advisees' hands, they serve as an excellent resource in helping their students choose the right paths for them, and making sure they take the necessary steps to get there.

SOCIAL LIFE AND ACTIVITIES

One thing at Lehigh is for certain: students know how to work hard and play hard. With such rigorous work and study schedules, students have learned to blow off their steam through Lehigh-organized functions and both on- and off-campus parties. No matter what extracurricular activities students want to engage in, there is something for everyone to maintain an active and fulfilling social life.

Freshmen Move-In

The social life at Lehigh begins the day freshmen move into their dorms. First-year students are welcomed to campus by upperclassmen representing a handful of organizations from every corner of the university. As soon as the new students drive onto campus and they're directed to their residence hall, a swarm of upperclassmen take it upon themselves to bring all their belongings to their new rooms while engaging in conversation and answering any questions.

Housing

Students are required to live on campus their freshman and sophomore years; however, there are options available for upperclassmen housing. The living and learning atmosphere provided by the housing options creates an immediate community on the Lehigh campus, fostering relationships among students not only for the remainder of their college experience, but also for the rest of their lives. Freshmen dorms are divided into small groupings of communities. Upper and Lower Cents are essentially quads of dorms located close to the Rathbone dining hall, while M&M, Dravo, and Richards are separate housing communities. All freshmen dorms are set up in traditional dormitory style as a hall of rooms share a communal bathroom. Some dorms are co-ed by room, some by floor, and some by wing. Students fill out their rooming applications prior to coming to campus and they can request roommates or go potluck. Most students who choose to be randomly matched with a roommate are pleased with the outcome, but, if the situation is totally unbearable, Lehigh will make accommodations for a move. Upperclassmen housing is either traditional dormitory, apartment, or suite style. The housing system is based on a lottery, and groups of students who choose to live together select their building preferences on campus. While on-campus housing is mandatory for freshman and sophomore years, students almost always receive a room assignment if they choose to remain in the dorms beyond the two required years.

Each floor within the residence halls has a resident advisor known at Lehigh as a Gryphon. In Greek mythology, Gryphons were the keepers of the gold, and at Lehigh, students are as valuable as gold, while their R.A.s are their protectors. These Gryphons are a part of the Residence Hall Association where they are in charge of bringing bonding programs and group activities to the living communities. Barbecues, field trips, and movie nights are common programs brought to the dorms fostering long-term relationships that last throughout the college experience at Lehigh.

Activities and Organizations

Students get involved at Lehigh the day they arrive, and there are hundreds of ways to find a niche on campus. Lehigh's activities and organizations help students to grow, mature, discover a passion, develop leadership skills, and forge enduring relationships. With over 150 clubs on campus, there is usually something for everyone and the process to begin a new club is easy and flexible. From Student Senate for those with a thirst for leadership, to academic groups looking to extend their classroom experience beyond the walls of a lecture hall, and to the Green Action Club promoting environmental causes through education, protests, and direct action there is certainly a place on campus to fit any passion. Student organizations at Lehigh are an integral and active part of campus life. They provide students with a wealth of opportunities to develop and enhance their Lehigh experience.

The student-run Club Fair at the beginning of the school year is an excellent way for students to find groups that are right for them. The lawn in front of Lehigh's University Center is packed with tables representing clubs, organizations, Greek affiliates, and local vendors for those students looking to find their place. This is the event where newcomers are first invited to meetings and gather materials to learn more about what's offered at Lehigh. With this annual club fair, students never feel as though they miss out on any opportunities.

Greek Life

Greek Life is a prominent part of the Lehigh community. Thirty-eight percent of men on campus are affiliated with twenty-one national fraternities and thirty-nine percent of women belong to nine national sororities. The Greek community at Lehigh is responsible for many community service projects, campus outreach programs, and especially leadership development opportunities that enable members to go out in the Lehigh and Bethlehem communities to share the ideals that they represent through their organizations. It isn't rare to find a group of sorority members tutoring students at a local elementary school or an entire fraternity spending time at a soup kitchen.

The recruitment process at Lehigh takes place at the beginning of the second semester, giving students ample time to decide if a Greek affiliation is right for them. In addition, those who decide to participate have a few opportunities to get to know the organizations through open houses, bagel brunches, and presentations. Women's recruitment takes place during the final week of winter vacation, while men undergo the process during the first few weeks of the semester. The majority of students who are affiliated with a residential fraternity or sorority live in the houses their sophomore and junior year, fulfilling the university requirement to live on campus their first two years at Lehigh. While living together in large, renovated houses on "The Hill," the Greek community has built a tight bond that has been a part of Lehigh since the first organizations arrived on campus.

There is also an extensive social life associated with the Greek community. From sponsored, registered parties on campus to off-campus date nights and formals, the "Hill" is always abuzz with things to do on the weekends. In addition, when the weather is good in the Lehigh Valley, one can find barbecues all over the Hill.

Athletics

The majority of the Lehigh community is involved with athletics in one way or another. When last estimated, eighty percent of students participate in a varsity, club, or intramural sport or are dedicated fans of the teams. With eleven intercollegiate varsity sports for men and twelve for women, athletic talent is all over campus and is celebrated throughout the community. Most athletic events take place on Lehigh's Goodman Campus in Saucon Valley, but for the most part, students can take part in athletics no matter where they are at Lehigh. The athletic facilities include a 16,000-seat stadium, a 6,500-seat arena, a gym, a champion crosscountry course, a field house with basketball and tennis courts, swimming pools, a track, indoor squash and racquetball courts, playing fields including astro-turf for field hockey, football, lacrosse, and soccer, weight rooms, a fitness center, climbing wall, and an indoor tennis center. Student athletes at Lehigh are proud of their teams and often wear athletic apparel to show their pride to other students. Most important, the athletes at Lehigh uphold high standards set forth by the department and especially their coaches in order to represent Lehigh to the best of their ability both on and off the field.

> **❝** Athletics at Lehigh allows you to be competitive on and off the field, but coaches stress the importance that education comes first. **❞**

—*John Henry McNierney, '10*

Lehigh-Lafayette

Just down the road from Lehigh lives its biggest rival—Lafayette College. As the oldest college rivalry in the country, the heat between the two schools is one of the most noted aspects of Lehigh's school pride. Specifically, the football rivalry sparks one of the most popular events of the year as the matchup has been played annually since 1884. Every year, the weekend before Thanksgiving, the hosting school switches off as students, alumni, and friends flock to the stadium to cheer for their favorite team. Leading up to the event, Lehigh hosts a slew of activities to get the campus community excited for the game. There's a Turkey Trot 5K run across campus, bed race competition, and a banner contest where groups on campus show their creative pride. If anything, Lehigh-Laf (as it's commonly referred to) is a highlight of the fall semester to which the entire community looks forward.

FINANCIAL AID

Lehigh University is a private institution, but the belief is that a Lehigh education should be an attainable goal, no matter what a student's financial circumstances may be. In fact, when Asa Packer founded Lehigh in 1865, tuition was completely free! With this in mind, Lehigh has a deep and long-standing commitment to need-based financial aid and continually seeks new ways to provide access to a Lehigh education for all admitted students.

Lehigh's Office of Financial Aid is an excellent resource available to students and even prospective applicants. The counselors help each individual, and direct him or her toward grants, loans, and even scholarship opportunities. During the 2009–2010 school year, forty-six percent of all full-time freshmen and forty-five percent of continuing full-time students received some form of financial aid while forty-five percent of all full-time freshmen and forty-four percent of continuing full-time students received need-based aid.

In addition, there are plenty of work opportunities on and off campus. Work-study is available for students on a financial aid plan, and there are plenty of jobs in the surrounding Bethlehem area. It's not rare to find students with jobs at the local pizza parlor or in a quaint boutique on the north side. During the 2009–2010 school year, twenty-six percent of undergraduate students worked part-time.

GRADUATES

No matter what degree they receive or what major they master, students graduate from Lehigh with a keen understanding and preparedness for their future endeavors. Many students continue their Lehigh education in a graduate program to receive their master's or begin doctorate studies, while others enroll in prestigious institutions all over the world to study other fields. Some students choose to take a few years off before they enter the

○ **Lee Iacocca, '45,** Former chairman of Chrysler Corporation

○ **Scott Belair and Richard Hayne, '69,** Co-Founders of Urban Outfitters, Anthropologies, and Free People

○ **Donny Most, '72,** Actor/Director, played Ralph Malph on Happy Days

○ **Tucker Quayle, '96,** Son of former vice-president Dan Quayle

○ **Jim Davidson, '85,** Actor on Pacific Blue

"real world" and travel, volunteer, or simply take a break. I think what's most impressive, however, is that a huge percentage of students are able to land jobs upon graduation from Lehigh. According to the Office of Admissions' website, ninety-five percent of Lehigh's 2009 graduating class found jobs or other career-related opportunities within six months of Commencement, and many students found these through on-campus interviews. Specifically, fifty-six percent of the class found permanent employment, thirty-three percent sought further education, while six percent pursued military service and other activities.

Students at Lehigh owe a lot of their postcollegiate success to the university's Career Services center. From on-site resume building, to career counseling, and to interview workshops, the Career Center is equipped to help all students as they seek employment. Not only do students take advantage of the services provided by the Career Center, LUCIE, an online job search engine, is a popular way for students to browse through openings or on-campus interviews. LUCIE is a constantly updated list of opportunities, and all students have log-ins to the service and can apply to jobs directly through the site. In fact, almost 3,000 on-campus interviews were conducted during the 2008–2009 school year and many of these students set these up through LUCIE.

> ❝ *In this tough job market, employers are starting to recruit less from Ivy League, high academic-focused schools, and looking for more of the well-rounded applicants from schools like Lehigh. I am now working in a very competitive rotational program for a large government defense contractor and live 1,500 miles from home. I am proud of how well Lehigh prepared me for this job and life after school, and I will never forget my time there.* ❞

—*Nick Anderson, '10*

With a Lehigh education under their belts, students can pursue just about any dream they set their mind to. No matter what their focus might have been during their time at Lehigh, they will graduate knowing that the academic and extracurricular programs set them up for greatness.

SUMMING UP

Nestled in the heart of the Lehigh Valley, Lehigh University is a mid-sized school with an extremely close-knit community. With its outstanding academic and extracurricular opportunities, students not only find their niche during their college experience, but they excel in every aspect of it. The friendly academic competition inspires and motivates students to work hard in their chosen field of study, and with the endless amounts of clubs and activities, students really find their places on campus. After graduation, Lehigh students take the knowledge and experiences they gained during their undergraduate career and excel in the "real world." No matter what they set their minds to, a Lehigh student is given the tools necessary to succeed after college.

❑ *Rebecca Raphael, B.A.*

MACALESTER COLLEGE

 Macalester College
Saint Paul, MN 55105-1899

 (800) 231-7974
Fax: (651) 696-6724

 E-mail: *admissions@macalester.edu*
Website: *macalester.edu*

 Enrollment

Full-time ❏ women: 1,162
　　　　　 ❏ men: 825

Part-time ❏ women: 22
　　　　　 ❏ men: 24

INTRODUCING MACALESTER

In the 137 years since its founding, Macalester has come a long way from its Scottish roots. Affectionately nicknamed "Mac," Macalester seeks to educate thoughtful and responsible global citizens by integrating the traditional values of an academically excellent small liberal arts college with an emphasis on internationalism and civic engagement. Convincing Mac students of the importance of internationalism and civic engagement is simple—a visit to campus makes this instantly clear. Outside of Old Main and Carnegie

Hall, you will see students continuing classroom discussions about international economics with their professors. At the Campus Center, you will likely overhear students arguing about emerging U.S. policies in English and many other languages. On the sidewalk leading from the DeWitt Wallace Library to the Olin-Rice science complex, you will see colorful messages chalked by students about social/political rallies and student organization meetings. In the student newspaper, *The Mac Weekly*, you will read convincing but conflicting columns expressing opinions about proposed Macalester administrative decisions. At the Civic Engagement Center, you might hear stories of a Mac student inspiring an immigrant child to take her studies seriously so that she might one day attend the college of her mentor. If you stay up past midnight, you might find a group of first-year Genetics students in "The Link" between the Library and Old Main working feverishly to finish a lab report for the next morning. However, Macalester is not just a constant barrage of academic and sociopolitical engagement. In fact, you are just as likely to hear students outside of Old Main discussing the outcome of last night's soccer game (Mac won by a landslide, of course). Outside of the Campus center, you might hear Jordanian and African students planning a trip to the nearby Mall of America. Chalked messages around campus might advertise the coming Trads and Sirens concert, where students line up outside of the concert hall hoping to get a seat at the popular *a cappella* show. Or, you might be lucky enough to catch the biannual Mock Weekly, where *Mac Weekly* writers parody their normally serious journalism. In the Civic Engagement Center, you might hear a student bragging about this year's massive yield at the community garden where they volunteer. And, if you visit the campus center just before midnight, you will find chatting students ordering chicken strips and smoothies during a late-night study break.

> **"** *Late one Saturday morning, a few weeks after arriving at Macalester, I awoke to the distant sound of song. It wasn't long before I realized that the song was Mac's fight song 'Scotland the Brave' played on our official instrument, the bagpipe. At the time, I knew the song only as a tune, but soon I was 'loudly and proudly calling Scotland the brave' with my fellow Fighting Scots at any and every opportunity. I still regret not taking advantage of the free bagpipe lessons that Mac offers to any interested student so that I might have been able to make Macalester proud with my own piped rendition of 'Scotland the Brave.'* **"**

Because of its small size and location in a large city, Mac successfully combines the intimacy of a top-tier small liberal arts college with the excitement, engagement, and opportunities of a large metropolitan environment in a way that few other top liberal arts colleges can. Admittedly, Macalester's brand of liberal arts education is not for everyone. However, if you like the sound of a college where academics, internationalism, and civic engagement collide in the everyday life of students, then Macalester just might be the place for you.

ADMISSIONS REQUIREMENTS

As one of the top small liberal arts colleges in the nation, admission to Macalester is highly competitive. Dramatic increases in numbers of applications received, without concurrent increases in size of the student body, over the past decade have led to greater selectivity with each passing year. However, because Macalester's name recognition is not as widespread as many coastal schools with which it competes for students, applicants to Macalester are highly self-selected. Many applicants learn about Macalester because of the exceptional academic reputation that it holds within academic communities. Typical applicants to Macalester have put a great deal of thought and research into which colleges best suit their academic and cocurricular needs. The result of all of these factors is that, although admission to Macalester is academically competitive, the percentage of applicants who are admitted to Macalester remains high relative to the Ivy League.

Requirements

Macalester's application process is designed to give admissions officers at the college a view not only of the achievements of the applicant, but also of the passions, potential, and future goals of the applicant. For this reason, personal statements and the recommendations of teachers and counselors, along with the academic choices and accomplishments of the applicant, form the basis for selection of a student body. Because of the small size of the school, the admissions committee at Mac has the luxury of being able to review all applications completely and thoroughly. The statement that there are no formulas for admission or cutoffs is really true in the case of Macalester admissions. However, as one of the most academically competitive liberal arts colleges in the nation, outstanding academic and cocurricular performance in high school is certainly a prerequisite for admission; this necessity for academic excellence is reflected in the achievements of the entering class each fall. In particular, it is expected that applicants have taken full advantage of the academic and extracurricular opportunities afforded to them at their high school.

Students applying to Macalester must submit the Common Application and Macalester Supplement. Either the SAT or ACT is required for admission, and SAT Subject Tests are recommended. Interviews for admission also are advised. An excellent interview can separate one applicant from a sea of otherwise academically similar applicants. One-on-one interviews are offered on campus from April through January. Off campus interviews are offered on selected dates in many U.S. cities and internationally.

ACADEMIC LIFE

Curricular Requirements

Academic life at Mac can be at once overwhelming, exhilarating, and exhausting. Macalester is first and foremost an intensely academic environment, even outside of the classroom and laboratory. Showing a deep commitment to the liberal arts, Macalester requires students to undertake rigorous coursework in a variety of fields. Macalester's graduation requirements result in a curriculum that represents the best of the liberal arts; both breadth and depth of study are reflected in every student's coursework. The first requirement that entering Mac students encounter is the first-year course. The first-year course serves as a home base for the entering student. First-year courses are offered in every conceivable area of study, from "Big Bang Physics" to "Legal and Political Advocacy." Many first-year courses are residential, meaning that the sixteen students in the course live together on the same dorm floor. In this way, the courses help foster friendships and provide instant study groups. The first-year course professor also acts as a student's academic advisor until a major is declared in the sophomore year.

Other unique requirements are the domestic and international diversity requirements. These requirements can be fulfilled by designated courses in a variety of departments, such as "Jazz and the American Experience" and "Medical Anthropology." Macalester was one of the first schools to institute diversity requirements, and they continue to blend in with Mac's emphases of internationalism and multiculturalism. Although Mac has many curricular requirements, and holds rigorous major requirements, many opportunities exist for students to broaden their education with elective courses. Whereas most students welcome the opportunity to expand their academic horizons, there are always a number of students who complain about certain "unnecessary" requirements. Invariably, they are the ones who, at graduation, express only regret about choosing to take another chemistry course rather than a Shakespeare seminar.

> *Choosing classes each semester was always a difficult task. With so many interesting classes to choose from, it constantly seemed like there were at least three times too few spots in my schedule. However, at the end of the process, I always felt that the mix of classes suited my needs perfectly.*

In short, it is the diversity and rigor of Macalester coursework that transforms high potential into great minds. However, both students and faculty are never completely satisfied with the college program. Because of this, requirements at Macalester are constantly evolving as students and faculty continue to improve the educational experience.

Classroom Experiences and Professors

The level of teaching at Macalester is outstanding. Mentorship relationships formed between students and professors are commonplace at Mac and are a critical part of the Macalester experience. Small classes at Mac mean that professors and students know each other well. Even classes that are normally taught lecture style, such as developmental biology, are enhanced by the inevitable discussion that results in classes smaller than ten or fifteen students. Professors at Macalester are deeply committed to undergraduate education, and it shows. Although all Macalester faculty members are accomplished scholars and scientists, their primary commitment is teaching undergraduates. This is the real distinction between a Macalester education and the education one might receive at a large institution. Professors motivate their students to achieve inside and outside of the classroom, and they truly care about the well-being of students.

Individualized Research

Mac's academic environment consistently fosters creative, critical thought and research among its students, as evidenced by the large number of Mac students who produce independent projects with their professors. The opportunities and funding for student research are tremendous and available to any qualified student. Nearly ninety students at Mac are awarded research grants each summer. As expected, Mac students produce, and often publish, works in classical liberal arts fields such as Literature, Religious Studies, and Classics. Possibly less expected, however, is Macalester's strength in the social, physical, and biological sciences, stemming from a strong teaching and research faculty and resulting in excellent student research. Also, the state-of-the-art research facilities are a plus. Because of Mac's excellent science professors and small class sizes, students are taught more than just facts—Mac students are taught how to be scientists, in that they are encouraged to be both critical and creative.

Opportunities for individualized interdisciplinary research at Macalester are also exceptional.

> 66 *My senior year at Mac I created an interdisciplinary honors project that encompassed my studies in classics and political science. I looked at the influence of ancient religion and gender on modern war, not exactly your everyday subject matter. My professors at Mac, from both disciplines, wholeheartedly supported my research. They were always available to me for questions, advice, and creative criticism. They truly cared about my project and me. Having met professors from other schools and visited other college classrooms, I believe that the opportunity to pursue this kind of creative research with kind and encouraging faculty is rare at most schools. At Mac though, it is just part of our everyday experience.* 99

Senior Honors Thesis

All majors require a senior capstone experience and many students choose to undertake a senior honors thesis. The senior honors thesis represents at least one full year of individualized research under the tutelage of one or more chosen thesis advisors. Many honors theses are the result of multiple years of research, especially in the laboratory sciences. The honor's thesis process culminates in public defense of the thesis to a committee of at least three faculty members. A completed thesis is bound and stored in the school library for use by future students.

Off-campus Study

The huge number of businesses, hospitals, and law and government offices centered in the Twin Cities provides students with endless opportunities for internships during the summer and academic year. Some typical sites for off-campus internships include 3M, Best Buy, Federal Reserve Bank, Merrill Lynch, the State Capitol, and numerous hospitals and law firms. Over 300 students complete an internship through the internship program every year; some even receive academic credit for their work. Internships completed for academic credit range from apprentice papermaker (Art) and naturalist (Environmental Studies) to investment analyst (Economics) and architectural computer imaging intern (Computer Science).

Study Abroad

Furthermore, two out of three Macalester students study abroad during their undergraduate career. The range of study abroad opportunities available to students at Mac is so vast that choosing just one can often feel overwhelming. However, the International Center at Mac is well equipped to match students with a study abroad program where they can fulfill their pre-med requirements, sharpen their German, and volunteer at a hospital in Hamburg. Over 300 students study abroad each year in nearly 50 countries, from Argentina to Vietnam. These students return from their journeys eager to share the unique perspective they gained through both service and cultural immersion. Study abroad is considered by Mac to be a critical component of educating global citizens.

Steering Committees

Students at Macalester are never shy about expressing their opinions on any and every possible subject, especially administrative decisions of the college. Fortunately, these opinions don't fall on deaf ears. Many students have the opportunity to serve on faculty selection, admissions, and curricular renewal committees (to name a few). Student involvement on decision-making bodies demonstrates that the school values the opinions of its students. Many students will tell you that they not only sat on these committees, but that they also influenced the course of action the committees took. Experiences like these are invaluable to students who will stay in academia and those who will go into the job market.

SOCIAL LIFE AND ACTIVITIES

Location, Location, Location

Mac's leafy fifty-three acre campus in residential St. Paul looks like the traditional college campus. Campus buildings frame three large, grassy quads, where you are just as likely to see students reading Sartre as playing Ultimate Frisbee. Mac invests heavily in building and updating academic and residential structures, including a new Athletic and Wellness Center that opened in 2008 and the Institute for Global Citizenship in 2009. Although this investment results in outstanding academic and nonacademic facilities, it is the world outside of campus that highlights the many advantages of Mac's location. At Mac's front door, Summit and Grand Avenues provide pleasant scenery for outdoor activities and more restaurants and shops than any student could possibly need. The many restaurants that line Grand Avenue range from dirt cheap to quite expensive. Literally feet from the campus, students can always be found studying at Dunn Brothers or Coffee News. You also might see someone grabbing a kebab at Shish, a Mediterranean grill. Occasionally, you will find students at the more expensive restaurants on a date or out for a nice evening with friends. Summit Avenue boasts incredible Victorian mansions, the best walking/jogging/biking route to the Mississippi River, and a view of the Minneapolis skyline. The greater Twin Cities, with a metro population of almost three million, provide students with endless volunteer, internship, and additional social opportunities.

Civic Engagement

SCOTTISH ROOTS

Official Macalester
- Mascot: The Fighting Scot
- Instrument: The Bagpipe
- Fight Song: "Scotland the Brave"
- Plaid: The Clan MacAlister Tartan
- Student Nicknames: Scots, Fighting Scots

Mac students are heavily involved in community service; over half of enrolled students participate each semester. One of the advantages of being in an urban environment is that there are numerous opportunities for different types of community service that positively impact the Twin Cities. The popular and well-run Center for Civic Engagement ensures that students get connected with the type of community service that interests them most, whether it be volunteering at the Center for Victims of Torture, teaching English as a Second Language to Somali immigrants, or tutoring middle-school kids in chemistry.

Through its commitment to civic engagement, Macalester instills the nobility of service in its graduates for a lifetime. In short, Mac is an environment that encourages engagement in sociopolitical action. The college succeeds in instilling its core values in students of all disciplines—thus, graduating a class of future leaders in science, politics, medicine, economics, and academia who share a commitment to service and value an international perspective in an increasingly global society.

> **❝** *Macalester's Community Service Office was an invaluable resource for me as an undergraduate. Whether I wanted a one-time event or a weekly volunteering opportunity, a staff member was always available with opportunities to compliment my academic program and interests in child psychology. I took advantage of several one-time events in addition to volunteering on a weekly basis at an afterschool reading program for at-risk students, a residential treatment program for children with emotional and behavioral problems, and an experimental afterschool program to reduce weight stigmatization among fifth and sixth grade students.* **❞**

Student Groups

Although the richness of the Twin Cities offers students both rewarding and fun activities, Macalester's own campus life offers many opportunities for students. More than 100 student organizations exist at Mac ranging from *a cappella* singing groups to the WMCN-91.7 FM. In tune with Mac's international emphasis, some of the most popular student organizations are Macalester International Organization (MIO) and Model United Nations. Notably, both organizations are open to domestic and international students. The men's and women's *a cappella* groups The Traditions (Trads for short) and The Sirens belt *a cappella* renditions of Madonna's "Like a Virgin," Ben Folds Five's "Kate" and some satirical originals. Groups such as the Macalester African Music Ensemble enjoy widespread recognition throughout the Twin Cities. Many students write, edit, or take photographs for the student newspaper *The Mac Weekly.* Mac also has a very active student government (MCSG) in which many students participate. MCSG, among other things, provides funds to form new groups, as evidenced by the recent forming of the coed *a cappella* group "Scotch Tape."

Internationalism and Multiculturalism

Macalester has one of the highest percentages of international students of any college in the nation; twelve percent of the student body hails from overseas (eighteen percent if you count dual citizens). Mac is also the first college in the country to fly the flag of the United Nations and is the alma mater of recent Secretary-General of the U.N. and Nobel Peace Laureate, Kofi Annan. The large number of international students at Mac provides a unique and diverse perspective that pervades the academic and social lives of students in all disciplines.

The International Center at Mac is often the starting point of international activities on campus. However, it does much more than help international students acclimate to American life and arrange study abroad programs. It also reaches out to the global community by organizing programs such as the Macalester International Roundtable where top research scholars and Mac students and professors gather for a week of discussion and debate on an internationally relevant topic.

The Lealtad-Suzuki Center (in the Department of Multicultural Life) and a Dean of Multicultural Life provide international multicultural programming. Although the center for multiculturalism plays a large role in making Mac an inviting place for students of color, it also focuses on welcoming any group of students that is traditionally underrepresented, such as students of varied religions, gender identities, cultural backgrounds, and their allies.

Athletics

Division III athletics at Mac are an important part of student life, of particular note are men's and women's soccer, cross-country, and men's basketball; each of which has featured All-American players and consistently compete in the postseason. Many club teams, such as men's and women's Rugby and Ultimate Frisbee are also popular among students. Although Mac values its students' athletic abilities, academics come first. Coaches are aware of the values of the school and the fact that students have chosen Mac for its excellent academic opportunities. They push their players hard to improve on the field, track, and court while maintaining excellence in the classroom. The consistent presence of "M Club" members (a club of Mac alumni who were scholar-athletes) at a variety of sporting events creates a sense of athletic history that benefits scholar athletes in business and in life.

Housing and Dining Options

Like many liberal arts colleges, first- and second-year students are required to live in Mac's dormitories to enrich the community experience among students. Dormitories are constantly being renovated by the college. On-campus housing is coveted by many upperclassmen. Housing for upperclassmen is offered on a lottery basis; approximately half of upperclassmen live in college-owned dorms, houses, and apartments. Many juniors and seniors prefer to live in nearby apartments, and the neighborhood that surrounds the college offers many affordable rental properties within a few blocks of campus. The college also offers many specialty housing options. At the veggie co-op students cook their own vegan/vegetarian food. Hebrew House residents, who make up diverse faiths, immerse themselves in Jewish traditions, make kosher food, and host Shabbat services. Chinese, French, German, Japanese, Russian, and Spanish houses also are offered as places where students can live and dine with native speakers and be immersed in a foreign language.

Students who live on campus eat in Café Mac in the Campus Center, where the dining options are palatable and abundant. Cuisine choices are split into the four corners of the compass, North (Smorgasbord and Mediterranean), East (Asian), South (Latin American and Subcontinental), and West (Burgers, Chicken, and Fries). Also included are fruit and cereal at all meals and a salad bar, fresh soup, and wood oven-baked pizza at lunch and dinner. From made-to-order omelets, French toast, and fresh strawberries in the morning, black olive and mushroom pizza and a fruit salad at lunch, to chicken curry, broccoli, and wontons for dinner, the culinary options really are endless. Vegetarian and vegan options are also available at every meal. Visitors to Café Mac are always impressed by the choices and quality of food served, and many students who live off-campus choose to eat at Café Mac during the day. Furthermore, many students and faculty get individually priced meals, coffee, smoothies, snacks, and desserts at the Grillé outside of the cafeteria.

Leisure Activities

Because there are no fraternities or sororities at Macalester, student get-togethers often consist of small- to medium-sized gatherings in dorm rooms or small- to large-sized gatherings off-campus. Although Mac students work hard, and there are always a substantial number of students who are studying on Friday and Saturday nights, Mac students also know how to relax and have a good time. Options for relaxation on the weekend vary from watching movies with a few friends at a Mac Cinema showing to attending a campus-wide event to a gathering with a group off-campus. First-year students quickly realize which types of activities suit them best and attend accordingly. Various student organizations host dances, concerts, and other cultural events during the week and weekend. Students also venture into the Twin Cities for entertainment. Many students visit museums, such as the Walker, attend concerts at First Ave, professional sporting events, and plays at the Ordway or Guthrie. Some students explore the bar and club scenes of Minneapolis and St. Paul, ending up at noticeable places such as the Groveland Tap, W.A. Frost, the C.C. Club, or Bryant Lake Bowl. Either way, if one wants to escape the walls of the college, there are many different activities to be found.

The most referenced motto of Macalester admissions and financial aid is "excellence and access." Essentially, this means that the administration is committed to making a Macalester education accessible to all academically distinguished students. The bottom line is that if you are admitted to Macalester, the school will make sure that you can afford to attend, without draining your life savings or drowning in student loans. The cost of a Macalester education is subsidized by more than 16,000 dollars per student through the endowment; thus, even though tuition, room, and board totals $49,000 per year, Macalester actually spends approximately $63,000 per student, per year. Approximately sixty-five percent of students receive some form of need-based financial aid, totaling more than thirty-seven million dollars a year (eighty-four percent of which is in the form of grants or scholarships). A financial aid package usually consists of a combination of grants, work-study, and loans. Work-study jobs can often be one of the highlights of a Mac education.

> ❝ One of the best things about having a job on campus is how many great work-study opportunities exist. During my time at Macalester, I was able to act as a teaching assistant for four different classes in my major, and was offered other opportunities to act as an assistant outside my major. These experiences deepened my understanding of the subject matter, my relationships with professors, and strengthened my drive to continue my studies in pursuit of a professorship where I can teach undergraduates. ❞

Scholarships

Macalester offers only a few merit-based scholarships. Although almost all students who are admitted to Mac would receive large merit scholarships from many other institutions, students choose Mac because they recognize the value of an excellent education that suits their particular needs. Money not spent on merit-based scholarships can be used to provide excellent faculty and facilities. Furthermore, forgoing most merit-based aid allows more money to be put into need-based financial aid, thus encouraging socioeconomic diversity on campus. Indeed, Mac is one of the most socioeconomically diverse top-tier liberal arts colleges in the nation.

Students and parents must fill out both FAFSA, and the more detailed College Scholarship Service (CSS) financial aid profile. Tax returns for both the applicant and applicant's parents also must be submitted. The Financial Aid Office then calculates an amount that the family can comfortably afford. Macalester figures out how to fill the gap between what the family can afford and the total cost using grants, loans, and work-study. Surprisingly, because of Mac's commitment to generous financial aid, the out-of-pocket cost of a Macalester education to many students can be less than that of a public university that does not have comparable financial resources and commitment to financial aid.

GRADUATES

Civic Engagement

Macalester, in its classes and social environment, instills in its students a feeling of responsibility to use their education and privilege to change the world for the better. Many recent graduates volunteer with AmeriCorps, Peace Corps, or Teach for America en route to their chosen careers. In the long term, many Mac graduates enter service-oriented professions such as nonprofits and government. However, this sense of commitment to a better world manifests itself in the career and life choices of all graduates. For example, an alumnus who enters the field of law might do *pro bono* work for an NGO, or for refugees; or a surgeon might join Doctors Without Borders, or volunteer his or her services to victims of land mines.

> 66 *When applying to graduate school, I was a little bit nervous about the outcome. However, once I had met my competitors during interviews, I realized that no one had the depth and breadth of preparation I had received at Mac.* 99

Graduate and Professional Studies

A Macalester education also prepares students for successful entry into graduate and professional education. Many Mac alums who have attended and excelled in these areas strengthen Mac's reputation at the best graduate and professional schools.

Macalester students attend the best graduate and professional schools, and they excel. There is no better preparation for graduate or professional study than the high-quality liberal arts education that one receives at Macalester. A Macalester education prepares students so well for graduate and professional study that top programs look for Macalester graduates during the selection process. Furthermore, a Macalester education instills excellent analytical and practical skills, as well as the creativity that is necessary to stand out in academia.

Career Paths

Macalester graduates follow many different paths after graduation. Mac graduates are leaders in academia, government, law, medicine, and business. A large number of graduates work for national and international nonprofit organizations and other nongovernmental organizations. Others stay in academia, enter government, and some enter the private sector. However, no matter what path they take, Macalester students invariably initiate and execute change for the better. Furthermore, no matter how far removed from Mac one becomes in distance or in time, the excellent Career Development Center at Mac is a great resource for all things related to finding a job in the "real world," including job listings, résumé preparation, interview skills, and alumni networking.

Global Networks

Alumni networking plays a powerful and positive role in the career paths of many Mac graduates. Mac students abound in major cities across the globe. The Macalester experience is so transforming, that alumni feel a lifelong bond. This leads to lasting business, academic, and personal relationships among Mac alums of different generations. Due to the international blend of students and international emphasis at Macalester, alumni connections are global. Because of the large number of international students at Macalester, and the penchant Mac grads have to pursue advanced degrees or careers abroad, you would be hard pressed to find a Macalester graduate who does not have friends in Africa, Western and Eastern Europe, Asia, and South America. Graduates will confirm that it is great to have a friend from Mac to visit while you are on business in Hong Kong, at a lecture in Stockholm, or working with Doctors Without Borders in Swaziland. As a graduate of Macalester, you will be continuously surprised with when and where you run into other Mac alums. A recent issue of the Mac alumni magazine includes letters from alumni reporting chance meetings of fellow Scots in Sweden, Iceland, New York, Oregon, and Vietnam.

SUMMING UP

Macalester College is an academically distinguished small liberal arts college located in a friendly yet interesting neighborhood in St. Paul, one of Minnesota's Twin Cities. The combination of urban location, academic excellence, internationalism, and civic engagement make Mac unique among the top liberal arts colleges in the nation. Macalester's ideal environment, outstanding facilities and professors, and exceptional and engaged students create a vibrant milieu where the lines of classwork, community service, research, and play often blur. Although the resources and opportunities available at Mac would make any college great, it is the student body that makes Macalester truly exceptional. Mac students (and alumni) recognize the value of immersion in a traditional small liberal arts setting. They are deeply concerned with the affairs of their college, nation, and world, and they are committed to stewarding their college, countries, and continents, into a more promising tomorrow. Who knows that such a great college exists in the middle of St. Paul, Minnesota? Lots of people know, including other liberal arts college students and professors, as well as admissions officers at top medical, law, and graduate schools who enthusiastically admit so many Mac graduates. The thousands of alumni who are leaders in academia, government, medicine, law, business, and nonprofit organizations in every major city worldwide know, too. Undoubtedly, a Mac education is the ultimate preparation for success in graduate studies and any number of careers. But more importantly, Mac is an environment of life-altering enlightenment, life-changing experiences, and lifelong friendships.

❏ *Noah Palm, B.A.*

Photo by Donna Coveney

 Massachusetts Institute of Technology
Cambridge, MA 02139

 (617) 253-3400
Fax: (617) 253-4076

 Website: *mitadmissions.org*

 Enrollment

Full-time ❏ women: 1,943
❏ men: 2,342

Part-time ❏ women: 5
(special) ❏ men: 9

INTRODUCING MIT

The MIT educational experience is like a series of "ah-ha!" revelations that students build into an arsenal for attacking problems—and it will happen to you no matter what you major in. Everyone—this includes philosophy majors as well as physics majors—must take a year of calculus, a year of physics, a term of chemistry and a term of biology. There are other institute-level requirements (such as eight humanities, arts, or social science classes and a laboratory course) but it's really the science core that sets a quantitative ability standard for all undergraduates. This standard makes MIT students extremely attractive to graduate schools, professional schools, and potential employers. And it provides for an unusual sense of community—how many other schools can you name where *everyone* is able to solve a reasonably complex kinematics problem?

This doesn't mean that the only people who belong at MIT are mathematicians, physicists, and engineers. Quantitative thinkers don't necessarily manipulate equations for a living, and there's certainly a need for more of them in policy-making positions. John Deutch, an MIT alumnus and professor, lamented the lack of technical literacy in the higher levels of government during his tenure as Director of the CIA:

> **❝**...*probably two people in the Cabinet could solve quadratic equations. If you include deputies, you might have four. And three of them will have gone to MIT.* **❞**

ADMISSIONS REQUIREMENTS

> **❝***From the time Early Action applications arrive in early November, until Regular Action decisions are made in early March, each admissions staff member will have read close to 950 applications. It seems that most MIT applicants have high standardized test scores and very good grades. Our pool is very self-selecting, so a lot of the applicants are quite similar. We turn down a surprising number of straight-A students.* **❞**

The take-home message is that you need to be distinctive. MIT is fortunate enough to be able to pick and choose from a very large pool of academically superior applicants. Distinction comes in many forms; athletes, musicians, chess players, and debaters are all distinctive if they achieve at a high level. Applicants who work on a farm for thirty hours a week and still manage to get straight As are distinctive. Students who have gone out of their way to take college courses or participate in independent research are distinctive. And of course, *extreme* academic talent or achievement is distinctive.

A word about how MIT defines "extreme" for academics—straight As and 800s on your SATs are *not* enough to guarantee admission (more than a third of MIT applicants have at least one 800). MIT is far more likely to admit a student with scores in the 700s, a few Bs in English classes, and an Intel science fair project that made it into the semifinals. Why? Because the Intel applicant has demonstrated initiative, a passion for learning, and a degree of competence in a very competitive field. That last bit is important. No matter how brilliant you are, if the Admissions Committee can't see your brilliance, then it won't help your application one iota. And the SATs alone are not enough to prove brilliance.

So, if you're truly gifted academically, make sure that the committee has some way of knowing that you

- Participate in the American Mathematics Competition, USA Biology Olympia, or similar competitions.
- Get into an academic competition or science fair at the state (even better, national) level.
- Find a local university professor and get involved in independent research. It helps if you include a letter of recommendation from that professor with your application.
- For those of you who spend a solitary forty hours a week hacking on the internals of some compiler, *please* make sure that you have some way of providing verification of this work in your application.
- Get your independent programming projects supervised by teachers at your high school and then choose these supervisors to write your letters of recommendation.

This touches nicely on another point: how to present yourself in the application. Pick teachers who know you well (preferably, ones who like you) to write your evaluations. Ask them to relate some anecdote that they think captures you as a student. It's very difficult to get a feel for an applicant from a list of adjectives; "intelligent," "motivated," and "curious" all have different meanings, depending on who is using them. A story, on the other hand, provides context for the reader of the application, and has the nice side effect of making you appear more of a living, breathing, human being.

Description of Activities

Also, when you list your extracurricular activities, be very descriptive. The Admissions Committee probably doesn't know a lot of specifics about your high school, so if you write that you are the president of the National Honor Society, the reader doesn't know if there are five people in the NHS or 500. Detail is good. Detail is also important in writing your application essays. Expounding on some formative event in your life is a reasonable start, but remember that you're not just telling a story—you're trying to convince the reader why you belong at MIT with thousands of other students. Show off your creativity. If you choose to take a humorous route, be witty, not just funny. Above all, try to display some element of intellectual curiosity in your writing. Speak to the reader.

The Interview

As for the interview, it can be a mixed bag. In most cases, the interview lasts for about an hour and consists of fairly low-stress questions. The questions will probably be reasonably vague (as in, "Why do you want to go to MIT?"), so it helps to think about these types of questions in advance. You should also come up with a set of meaningful questions to ask, something beyond "How good is the food?" because it will indicate to the interviewer that you're serious about your decision to apply. Questions turn the interview into a two-way conversation, which will help to make it less stressful. In reality, a negative interview report is unlikely to hurt your application very much, but a good interview can give you an extra edge in gaining admission.

Highlights

There are a few more highlights you should probably know about the MIT admissions process.

- Of the 16,632 applications received in a recent year, 1,676 students were admitted, so competition is tough.
- MIT is Early Action, not Early Decision (if you're admitted early, you don't have to enroll).
- MIT admissions are need-blind, so the admissions staff has no idea how much your parents make or whether you're applying for financial aid.
- MIT is looking to build a diverse class, including diversity of ethnicity, socioeconomic status, geography, and interests—both academic and non-academic.
- Finally, international applicants go through a more competitive admissions process.

All of this factual information, plus a lot of other detail, can be found on the MIT admissions website.

ACADEMIC LIFE ▰▰▰▰▰▰▰▰▰▰▰

First, a general overview. MIT is divided into five schools: Architecture; Engineering; Humanities, Arts, and Social Sciences; Management; and Science. Within those schools there are twenty-two academic departments (such as Brain and Cognitive Science, Economics, and Mathematics). Most departments offer several majors, all of which are variations on a theme. Students aren't expected to declare a major until the end of their freshman year, so you don't need to apply to a particular school or department as an undergraduate; when you're admitted to MIT, you're admitted to all of MIT. Here's one student's perspective on the importance of this:

> 66 *It didn't really occur to me that the lack of administrative hassle would turn out to be such a vital thing. I switched majors twice: from architecture to biology and from biology to chemistry, and each time all I needed to do was get a signature from my advisor. I was horrified to hear stories from friends at other colleges who needed to write a long petition to switch majors, or go through a mini-admissions process to get into another department. If I had been asked to choose a major straight out of high school, it would have been a random choice, at best.* 99

This lack of bureaucracy pervades MIT's entire approach to education. With the exception of a few humanities courses, students never have to deal with being lotteried out of oversubscribed classes. You can add a class as late as five weeks into the term and drop a class as late as five weeks before the end of the term. After freshman year, there are no limits on the number of classes you can take per term as long as your advisor approves the decision (which is a rubber-stamp process for students who are performing well). Many students double major. Undergraduates can also register for graduate-level classes, which offer a very different type of educational experience: most graduate courses meet in a small room with very few students and one professor. The topics in these courses are usually closely related to the professor's current area of research, and the class feels more like a discussion than a lecture.

Classes

As for the undergraduate classes, there's a lot of variation in the presentation format. Most of the freshman science core courses consist of three lectures and two recitation sections per week. Lectures for these courses can have more than 100 students, but recitations are limited to about twenty students per instructor, giving a lot of opportunity for individualized instruction. Departments also offer variants on the basic core courses, so while the standard freshman calculus class has the format described above, the theoretical version of freshman calculus has far fewer students in its lectures. In addition to the other flavors of the science core classes, MIT has different versions of the freshman year program itself. Concourse, the Experimental Studies Group (ESG), the Terrascope Program, and the Media Arts and Sciences (MAS) Freshman Program, all offer alternative, innovative approaches to teaching the freshman curriculum. These programs are limited in size (between twenty-four and sixty students in each) and are first-come, first-served, so if you're interested in learning more about them, do your research before showing up on campus.

Credit

The institute gives Advanced Placement and International Baccalaureate credit for some classes if you score well enough on your AP exams, and in many cases will accept transfer credit from another college. Advanced standing exams are also offered by MIT, and if you pass them you receive credit. More than three-quarters of MIT's enrolling freshmen receive some sort of advanced credit, but no matter how much credit you have, MIT does not offer sophomore standing to first-term freshmen (although second-term sophomore standing is offered in the second term).

Grading

There is a limit on the number of classes freshmen can take and there is one other major difference between the first term of the freshman year and the remainder of the MIT undergraduate experience: Pass/No Record. This refers to the grading system used for freshmen. If you earn an A, B, or C in a course, it appears as a P on your transcript. Ds and Fs do not appear on the external transcript at all—it will simply look as though you had never even registered for the course. There are three reasons why MIT has this system of grading: to level the playing field for students from different high school backgrounds; to get students acclimated to the MIT way of thinking and problem solving; and to allow students to explore a little (academically or otherwise) without fear of receiving a bad grade.

Many prospective students want to know if the freshman year is difficult. "Different" would be a better word. Generally speaking, if you're bright enough to be admitted to MIT, you're more than bright enough to handle the material. For students with advanced high school preparation, most of the core classes will feel like accelerated versions of the material in high school with slightly more complicated homework, longer tests, and some interesting stories thrown into the lecture. If you're truly bored with the standard fare, try one of the theoretical versions of calculus or physics; even the brightest, most academically prepared students find these courses to be quite challenging.

> **❝** *I had never touched a computer before coming to MIT, so the first time I took a programming class, I had a lot to learn: how to use a text editor, how to move files around—some really basic stuff. Many of the other students in the class had been programming for years, which was sort of intimidating, and on the first problem set, I spent all night (from 5:00 P.M. to 8:00 A.M.) in front of a computer and accomplished literally nothing. I was going to drop the class, but a friend offered to come in and show me the essentials, so I took her up on the offer. We spent about four hours working, and it was enough to give me an overview of what I needed to do. I stayed with the course, and ended up earning an A in it. Looking back, it's hard for me to imagine why I thought it was so complicated at first, but I guess that's because I actually learned something.* **❞**

IAP/UROP

There are two other very unique elements to MIT academics: the Independent Activities Period (IAP) and the Undergraduate Research Opportunities Program (UROP). IAP takes place during January, and it's like a miniature, optional, month-long term. Students can decide for themselves whether they want to be at MIT for those four weeks, but the vast majority of students stay. Some students choose to do a wide variety of one-day seminars and projects, some students take classes (often for credit), and others work. Here's a small sampling of the noncredit activities offered during IAP: the 19th Annual Paper Airplane Contest, Basic Darkroom Techniques, Blackjack 101, Computers and the Human Genome Project, Hebrew Reading Literacy in Eight Hours, Intro to British Politics, Practical NMR Spectroscopy. For-credit classes included: Intro to Special Relativity, Special Problems in Architecture, IAP Japan Workshop (which included a three-week stay in Japan), Intro to Neuroanatomy, Experiencing Health Policy: A Week in D.C., Foreign Currency Exchange, Intensive German. There are hundreds of course offerings during IAP; for a complete listing of last year's activities as well as detailed descriptions of the events, check out *web.mit.edu/iap*.

The majority of students who work during IAP will probably do so through UROP, which is quite arguably one of the best things about MIT. In this program, undergraduate students work on a research project at MIT. UROP isn't limited to a select few, nor are the projects watered-down pedagogical tools. More than eighty percent of all students choose to get a UROP at some point in their undergraduate careers. The projects themselves are ongoing research efforts, so undergraduates work together with professors, graduate students, and "postdocs." With a little motivation, undergraduates can even coauthor research papers with the group, and there's no better way to cultivate a good faculty reference for later use. UROP enables students to interact with professors as colleagues, not just teachers; it also gives undergraduates an excellent sense for what graduate studies in a particular field would be like. On top of all this, students actually get paid for their work in UROP so they don't have to choose between meeting financial need and doing undergraduate research. For a listing of current UROP openings and their descriptions, look at *web.mit.edu/urop*.

> *" The summer after my freshman year, I got a UROP with the Communications Biophysics Group working on a speech aid for deaf-blind people. We built a device that decomposed sound waves into different spectral regions, and then mapped each region to one of twelve buzzers. When you strapped the device on your forearm, you were able to 'feel' people talking. The engineering was cool, but working with the deaf-blind test subjects was probably the most interesting part. They had been deaf and blind since birth, yet could speak pretty well and were able to 'hear' me talk by placing their hand across my face. Listening to their perceptions of the world was absolutely fascinating. "*

SOCIAL LIFE AND ACTIVITIES

Housing

MIT's housing system has a lot to offer: a diversity of experiences; a place truly to call home; active communities, with opportunities to connect with undergraduate students of all years, as well as faculty and graduate students. But most of all, it offers the freedom to choose housing most appropriate to you and that best suits your personality and lifestyle.

All freshmen are required to spend their first year at MIT living in one of MIT's twelve undergraduate residence halls. However, this doesn't mean that the decision of where to live is going to be simple or boring—in fact, quite opposite is true. MIT has an amazingly diverse residential community. Each residence hall has a different flavor, and most floors within these houses have distinct cultures. For example, there is an all-women's residence hall; a residence hall that is world famous for its architectural significance; a residential hall that wired its laundry and bathroom facilities to the Internet. There are also four cultural houses that celebrate the languages, foods, and customs of different cultures.

On-campus housing is guaranteed for freshmen and for upper-class students for eight consecutive semesters. After the freshman year, many students will take the opportunity to move into one of MIT's many fraternities, sororities, and independent living groups (FSILGs). Today, there are twenty-six fraternities, six NPC sororities, six living groups, and four office support for several metro-wide NPHC and NALFO fraternal groups. Each fraternity, sorority, and living group has its own unique characteristics. However, each group's primary purpose is to foster brother/sisterhood and camaraderie, and provide a supportive and healthy environment for its members.

Loyalty to one's living group is common at MIT. Undergraduates find that the residence halls and FSILGs are a great support network, academically, socially, and otherwise.

Athletics

MIT has an amazingly large athletics program—there are thirty-three varsity sports—the most intercollegiate offerings of any Division III School in America. In many of these sports MIT is quite competitive. Athletics at MIT are accessible; it is not uncommon for a person with no rowing experience to join the crew team as a freshman and then stay with it at the varsity level for four years (the Charles River is literally across the street from MIT). Club and intramural (IM) teams are also very common; there are more than 680 IM teams participating in twenty-three different sports and thirty club teams. D-league ice hockey is a great example of the IM spirit. It's hockey for people who don't necessarily know how to skate. The A-league teams, however, are considerably less forgiving.

Student Activities

There are more than 500 student activities at MIT, including cultural groups, student government, journalistic organizations, performance groups, and clubs for people interested in games. Getting involved at the institute is very easy—just ask. MIT students are about as anti-elitist as people can get; they're usually thrilled to find someone else who's interested in what they do. They're also enthusiastic teachers, so even if you know nothing about a particular game or skill, you'll probably be able to find someone who will spend hours showing you the ropes. Free of charge.

MIT students are famous for the elaborate practical jokes, or hacks, that they manage to pull off. Cars, telephone booths, makeshift houses, and plastic cows have all appeared on the tops of MIT buildings at various points throughout MIT history. While many hacks require what seems to be a small miracle of engineering, others are just really good ideas put into action. The history of MIT's hacks is chronicled in four books and on the web at *http://hacks.mit.edu.*

FINANCIAL AID

MIT recruits and enrolls talented and promising students without regard to their financial circumstances through a need-blind admissions policy. So once you've been admitted to MIT, the Institute wants to make sure you can get there. Financial aid is widely available and is provided to all students requiring assistance. Sixty-two percent of students receive scholarships based on need totaling $83 million.

On average, most students do not need to borrow, and those who do tend to graduate with less than $10,000 in debt. Last year, more than half of the graduating class left with zero debt. The median debt at graduation was at $9,966 or fifty-four percent less than it was ten years ago.

As an MIT grad you'll literally have the potential to change the world—and companies know it. The job placement rate for MIT students is incredibly high compared to other universities and the average starting salary for students graduating with a bachelor's degree is $67,270. Basically we're determined to make sure that what you get from MIT (and we're not just talking money) is a whole lot more than what you pay for.

PROMINENT GRADS

- Richard Feynman, '39, Nobel Prize Winner in Physics
- I.M. Pei, '40, Architect
- Sheila Widnall, '61, Former Secretary of Air Force
- Shirley Jackson, '68, U.S. Nuclear Regulatory Commission
- Heidemarie Stefanyshyn-Piper '84, Astronaut
- Alex Rigopulos '92, CEO of Harmonix (Guitar Hero, Rock Band)

GRADUATES

Many extraordinarily bright people have attended MIT. The institute has had more than its share of Nobel Laureates, National Medal of Science recipients, and the like. Rattling off a long list of MIT's all-time stars would be interesting but probably wouldn't tell you much about how the average graduate fares.

MIT students have very high acceptance rates into postbaccalaureate programs, and about fifty percent of graduating seniors choose to go directly to graduate studies. Industry and government employers heavily recruit students seeking jobs after graduation. A nice side benefit of MIT is the name recognition—simply saying you're a graduate commands a certain level of respect. Of course, it also sets a pretty high expectation level for your abilities.

MIT prepares its graduates to be more than just cogs in the machine, unless you like being a cog, in which case that's your choice.

MIT graduates excel at whatever they choose to do, primarily because they can often think circles around people with less quantitative backgrounds. While they're here, students may complain about the work load, but it's unlikely that you'll ever hear the phrase "I regret getting an MIT degree."

SUMMING UP

If you're still trying to figure out whether MIT is the place for you, consider the following two questions: Does "fuzzy thinking" bother you? Do you want to learn how to critically assess problems in whatever discipline interests you (whether it's mechanical engineering or political science)? If you can answer both with an enthusiastic "Yes!" then there's no better place for you academically than MIT.

❏ *Stacy McGeever, B.S.*

Photo by John McKeith

Middlebury College
Middlebury, VT 05753

(802) 443-3000
Fax: (802) 443-2056

E-mail: *admissions@middlebury.edu*
Website: *www.middlebury.edu*

 Enrollment

Full-time ❏ women: 1,259
　　　　　 ❏ men: 1,246

Part-time ❏ women: 21
　　　　　 ❏ men: 5

INTRODUCING MIDDLEBURY COLLEGE

Tucked away in a charming town in Vermont's picturesque, bucolic Champlain Valley, Middlebury College—ranked among the country's finest liberal arts schools—boasts post-card-perfect vistas. The jagged, often snow-capped Adirondack Mountains to the west and the rolling Green Mountains to the east provide a dramatic backdrop to an equally lovely campus. Gazing out of one of the towering windows in the college's state-of-the-art science building, students take in the student-run organic garden and the barns and silos of the college's farming neighbors in the distance.

But make no mistake: the College on the Hill is no provincial outpost. Though students routinely embrace their rural locale, volunteering with migrant farm workers or reading up on rural geography, they are just as likely to take to the stage in one of the college's five top-notch performing spaces, or team up with a chemistry professor for cutting-edge research. It's here, in a setting that prospective students and seasoned Middlebury students alike find breathtaking, that students dive into a curriculum steeped in the traditions of the liberal arts. That curriculum guarantees that Middlebury is populated by English majors with a soft spot for oceanography, or economics whizzes with a talent for photography. They do so in state-of-the-art classrooms and laboratories: take the $40 million, more than one-million-volume library that opened in 2004, or the newly renovated center for the humanities finished in 2008.

If you ask most students, though, Middlebury's sparkling amenities and stunning vistas pale beside the college's true draw—the intellectual and social vitality the community fosters in classrooms and dining halls, on highly competitive sports fields, and in paint-splattered artists' studios. These students will rave about their close relationships to their professors, who as often as not turn out to also be friends, or hiking buddies, or teammates in games of pick-up basketball. They'll tell you about a particularly heated debate at a seminar table, or a wet, cold, and downright fascinating lab expedition to band local birds. These same students will likely admit that they've never worked harder in their lives, but almost universally, they'll say that they wouldn't have it any other way.

With the lakeside college town of Burlington only thirty-five miles away, and Boston and Montreal well within striking distance, the college's "country mice" aren't entirely cut off from the occasional hubbub of city life. What the college's rural setting does offer, though, is a sense of community both reassuringly close-knit and vibrantly diverse. With often-posh on-campus housing guaranteed for students for all four years, ninety-seven percent of students live on campus, and this is no suitcase campus. Come weekends, students stay put—and with good reason. As most Middlebury students will tell you, the problem isn't ever a question of finding something to do. On the contrary, most students lament that there isn't enough time in a week, or a semester, or even a four-year stint at the College on the Hill to take advantage of everything the college has to offer.

Their best advice: dive in, head first.

ADMISSIONS REQUIREMENTS

To Choose and Be Chosen

If there were a recipe that guaranteed admission to Middlebury, someone would have cracked it by now. The fact of the matter is that there is no clear-cut formula that distinguishes Middlebury students in the making. The admissions committee at the college, holed up in the cozy Emma Willard House on the periphery of campus, considers a range of factors in evaluating candidates, and those factors tend to value individual quirks and strengths over empirical gauges of potential. That said, Middlebury does recommend that candidates for admission complete the following college preparatory coursework:

- Four years of English
- Four years of a foreign language
- Three or more years of laboratory science
- Four years of mathematics and/or computer science
- Three or more years of history
- Some study of art, music, or drama

Middlebury is among the few colleges that do not require the SAT for admission, instead allowing applicants to designate a representative sample of standardized tests from among the SAT, ACT, or SAT subject exams. If choosing to submit SAT subject exam scores, students should choose three subjects to highlight. (These exams, the college suggests, should be taken by December of the student's senior year or earlier if applying for Early Decision.) As this policy suggests, admissions officers at Middlebury are looking at the whole student rather than numbers on a page.

In this spirit, the admissions team welcomes materials that speak to a candidate's ability beyond the scope of mere test scores. The most important factors, they say, are a student's enrollment in advanced placement or honors courses during high school, recommendations by teachers and other school officials, and evidence of special talents. But in addition to this usual portfolio of high school grades and achievements and teacher recommendations, admissions officers also consider the optional dance and theater videos, artwork, or music compilations that some students choose to submit as well. Admissions officers are quick to say that it's these materials, as well as students personal essays and interviews, that often prove most illuminating.

As is the case at almost all prestigious colleges these days, Middlebury receives far more applications from qualified applicants than it can possibly accept. Given this reality, Dean of Admissions Bob Clagett has been known to send a note to prospective students explaining the difficult task facing admissions officers every year. Denial from Middlebury isn't a vote of no-confidence in an applicant's academic or extracurricular ability, Clagett says; it's a reflection of the ever-escalating applicant volume at a college that has established itself as among the nation's finest.

Students' Backgrounds

Middlebury received 7,984 applications for admission to the class of 2014, and accepted 1,529. (Of those accepted, 685 chose to enroll at the college.) An additional 1,958 students were placed on the waiting list.

Of students selected, eighty-six percent ranked in the top percent of their high school classes. Those students who elected to enroll at Middlebury last fall joined a student body 2,500 strong. Six percent of Middlebury students are Vermonters, but the college is home to students from all fifty states. If you make it to Middlebury, chances are strong that you'll stay here; only three percent of full-time freshmen do not continue after their first year, and ninety-two percent of freshmen go on to graduate from the college.

The college still contends with age-old stereotypes about the makeup of its student body, and like many elite New England colleges, Middlebury was historically regarded as a haven for well-to-do, white New Englanders. The school still contends with a reputation for homogeneity but the student population is still a vivid, international bunch squirreled away in the hills of Vermont. That diversity comes in part through programs such as the Posse Program, now in its twelfth year, which handpicks students from urban environments and gives them the scholarships—and institutional support—they need to succeed at Middlebury.

But Middlebury also attracts a great many international students; ten percent of the student body is made up of foreign nationals, in fact. These students, hailing from seventy countries, contribute to the college's vibrant cultural life. What this means is that the myth of the prototypical Middlebury student these days is just that—a myth. The college wants students from Nepal and North Dakota, aspiring poets and cross-country skiing enthusiasts, logrolling champions and budding scientists. The bottom line is this: Middlebury College wants students with broad-based interests and experiences, and a passion for learning, who will jump at the chance to invigorate campus life—and themselves—across four years of study.

The Feb Program

Middlebury students in the making do have one more decision to make before submitting their applications to the college: we're talking about the "September preferred" or "February preferred" dilemma. (Amid those checks and blanks, the college also provides an option for students with no preference for either September or February admission.) The so-called Feb Program is one academic path that sets Middlebury apart from its peer institutions. The program evolved in the 1970s as a novel way to fill places vacated by students studying abroad in the spring. Over time, the program grew to be a beloved fixture of the Middlebury community. Every February, just as Vermont winters seem their coldest and grayest, an infusion of fresh energy and new faces bursts onto campus in the form of around one-hundred eager first-year students.

> **❝** *I wasn't a Feb, but I had a heavy dose of Feb-envy, which 'Regs' will often reluctantly 'fess up to if pressed hard enough. I was chomping at the bit to make it to college, and was excited to start in September. That said, a part of me has always wished I had spent that first semester traipsing the world or interning in D.C., and earning my membership in the ranks of Middlebury's Febs. Their enthusiasm, by and large, is infectious.* **❞**

These "Febs," as they're dubbed, swear by their experience. Many use their gap semester to travel, work, or study abroad, and Febs argue that these experiences enrich their college careers. Many arrive on campus with thrilling stories to share with new friends, and their midyear arrival fosters a warm camaraderie among Feb classes. They take great pride in their Feb status, donning traditional "Feb" sweatshirts emblazoned with their "class year," for instance, 2012.5, for students who enrolled a semester after fellow first-years slated to graduate in May 2012.

The Feb experience culminates four years after their arrival on campus in a winter celebration. In addition to a ceremony at the college's hilltop Mead Chapel, Feb graduates don their caps and gowns and participate in a collective "ski down" at the college-owned Snow Bowl. The Feb Program isn't for everyone; some high school graduates are simply too antsy to wait out a semester before starting college, but for independent-minded students with big ideas for a gap semester, the Feb Program offers a flexible, nontraditional entrance to college.

Decisions, Decisions

Admissions applications have two parts with two different deadlines. Regular applications are due December 15 and 31. For candidates who are certain that the college is their first choice, Middlebury offers a binding, Early Decision program that telegraphs one's commitment to Middlebury and offers the promise of early notification from the Admissions Committee, which may choose to accept, reject, or defer a decision until the usual April 1 deadline. Early Decision 1 applications are due November 1 and 15; Early Decision 2 are due December 15 and 31.

In addition to Febs and "Regs," as September students are dubbed, Middlebury usually enrolls a handful of transfer students (5–15); however, none were enrolled in 2010–2011. Application deadlines for transfer students are February 15 and March 1 for fall admission and November 1 and 15 for spring admission.

ACADEMIC LIFE

Middlebury's curriculum values breadth and depth. In addition to diving into their own chosen area of study, students are required to sample courses from seven of eight "core" areas: literature; the arts; philosophical and religious studies; historical studies; physical and life sciences; deductive reasoning and analytical processes; social analysis; and foreign languages. (In addition to these eight core subjects, students also must satisfy regional distribution requirements.)

66 *I'm a huge fan of Middlebury's 'breadth and depth' approach to learning, particularly because it pushed me toward classes and departments I might not otherwise have explored. During the fall of my junior year I tried my hand at oceanography. Our class spent our weekly lab sessions on nearby Lake Champlain, collecting data from the deck of a lobster-boat-turned-research-vessel. On a cool October afternoon, as the Green and Adirondack mountains to the east and west turned gold with fall colors, I stood at the helm of this little dinghy with my professor and thought, This is what college is about!* 99

Coming over the Middlebury Gap toward the Champlain Valley, drivers cresting Route 125 will pass a cluster of brightly colored buildings painted in yellow and green. This is Middlebury's Bread Loaf campus, a picturesque mountain retreat that was at one time a haunt for poet Robert Frost. In the winter, Bread Loaf is transformed into a winter wonderland paradise, the headquarters of the college's Nordic ski touring center. But in the summer, the campus—complete with several cabins, a historic inn, a beloved barn, and well-worn theater—is home to the oldest and most famous writers' retreat in the country.

Come August, famed poets, writers, and journalists from around the world, including, in recent years, Edward Hirsch, Susan Orlean, Randall Kenan, and Scott Russell Sanders, converge at Bread Loaf for the venerable conference, which Frost himself jump-started in the 1920s along with colleagues such as Willa Cather and Louis Untermeyer. Despite concessions to convenience, the campus has changed little in the last half century. Today, the two-week conference is chock full of readings and lectures, workshops and hikes, friendly meals and blazing bonfires. Students of all ages come to study writing, and every year, a handful of talented young Middlebury students are granted full scholarships to the conference. It's a once-in-a-lifetime opportunity for aspiring writers.

But don't fret—those requirements don't translate into English 101 or Freshman Biology. Need to take a literature course, but not thrilled about Chaucer and Milton? Try "Maritime Literature," or "Science Fiction." Looking to fulfill a science requirement, but cringe at memories of high school chemistry class? Students in an Introduction to Astronomy class study the night sky every fall from a rooftop observatory atop the college's Bicentennial Hall.

Middlebury, after all, is a school that values choice; professors and advisors trust students to chart their own academic paths, providing guidance along the way. The framework of the college's core subject and regional requirements simply provides a rough outline for those paths.

The First-Year Seminar

All students at Middlebury kick off their academic careers with a "first-year seminar," a class designed to foster the close student-professor interaction that marks a Middlebury education. In a small class, made up of no more than fifteen students, freshmen huddle around a table with their professor in classic seminar style. Because students choose from a long list of possible seminars, and because professors design these classes based on their own research interests, the writing-intensive seminars naturally engender spirited conversation. Hope Tucker, professor of film and media culture, taught a class about what can be learned from "dead technologies," from passenger pigeons to the Brownie camera, while a professor in the music department led students in a song-writing workshop. Geologist Pat Manley looked at geology through the lens of national parks, and noted biologist Steve Trombulak introduced his seminar to ecology and conservation in Vermont.

In addition to fostering academic curiosity and the rigorous, in-depth exploration of a single subject, first-year seminars also inspire tight-knit communities. Professors serve as their students' academic advisors until the students declare their academic majors—something students aren't required to do until the end of their third semester. Because each seminar belongs to one of the college's five residential "commons," students also live in close geographic proximity to one another. (For more on the commons, see Middlebury's "Social Life and Activities.") Though the heart and soul of first-year seminars is in the classroom, that spirit frequently carries over into friendship and collaboration outside of the classroom—not to mention cozy fireside dinners at professors' homes.

Faculty

The close student-professor relationships that first-year seminars encourage don't grind to a halt after a student's first semester—far from it. One thing that students often extol when speaking about their alma mater is their close relationships with their professors. Middlebury professors are among the leading scholars in their fields and all boast impeccable credentials, but the college is first and foremost a teaching college. That means that professors are hired and reviewed not just on the basis of their scholarship, but also on their skill at the front of a classroom. At the end of every semester, just as professors tally students' grades, students have the chance to give their professors feedback, too. Every class ends with an anonymous review, which is typically used in tenure review discussions for faculty members. The job falls to one or two students in each class to hand-deliver these reviews to administrators at "Old Chapel," a hub for the college's movers and shakers. Students—and faculty members—take this stuff seriously.

Perhaps most importantly, students have access to these professors. Though language classes have native-language assistants, and professors occasionally hire students on as research assistants or tutors, classes are always taught by professors. And these classes tend to be small ones; the average class size at Middlebury is nineteen students. Even larger courses, like introductory courses in popular departments, often top out at forty or sixty students, and typically break down into smaller "discussion sections" of ten or twenty students—all led by a professor.

Just as professors wow students in the classroom, students frequently marvel at the dedication these teachers put in after hours. Professors routinely fire off lengthy e-mails and meet students at the Grille to discuss an assignment over coffee. Many open their homes to their classes at various points during the semester. At a school where students have a reputation for working hard, this sort of reciprocal dedication does not go unnoticed.

The Liberal Arts

If you're intent on picking up Chinese or diving in to Arabic, or any of the other ten languages the college teaches, there's no better place to start than Middlebury. (It's not a coincidence that teachers, government agents, and top-notch students from around the world join Middlebury undergraduates on campus during the summer for the selective "No English Spoken Here" immersion language programs.)

But Middlebury's well-deserved reputation for foreign language study doesn't begin to capture the scope of its academic strengths. The college offers forty-six majors and programs and nearly limitless academic options. Among the most popular departments every year are economics, psychology, and English and American literatures, but many students choose to participate in interdisciplinary programs that pull on courses from many departments. Take the International Studies (IS) program, for example, which combines foreign language study, regional specialization, time abroad, and a disciplinary focus. It's a sort of build-your-own-major approach to international affairs, which means a mouthful for IS majors trying to explain their own majors. Think: East Asian studies with a sociology focus, paired with Chinese language study in Hangzhou. What about European studies with a focus in human geography, topped off with a semester spent mastering Italian in Florence?

Another popular interdisciplinary choice is the college's program in environmental studies. Middlebury was a pioneer in this field, launching the first undergraduate program for environmental studies in 1965, and today the college remains well ahead of the curve. As is the case with the IS program, students choose a disciplinary specialization in addition to completing a prescribed selection of core courses. As one of the most popular departments at the college, ES attracts chemists and geologists, writers and musicians, literary analysts and historians, all of whom want to match their passions with a study of the natural world. These students are on the cutting-edge of their field. Middlebury graduates with a passion for the environment have gone on, in recent years, to lead the youth climate movement, spearheading the Step It Up and 350.org movements, and founding companies such as Brighter Planet, which designed and markets a carbon offsets credit card.

Middlebury students and recent graduates take off for the Appalachians, where they campaign against mountaintop-removal coal mining, or participate in international climate change talks in locales as far-away as Poland.

The hub of the environmental program is the Franklin Center for Environmental Studies at Hillcrest, an old farmhouse on campus that was remodeled in 2007. But the Franklin Center is only one of Middlebury's top-notch facilities. While still preserving the buildings that lend the college its historic character, Middlebury has added a fleet of new and recently remodeled buildings to its campus roster in the past several years. There's the state-of-the-art McCardell Bicentennial Hall, where students pair up with faculty for hands-on research in the sciences. The building was completed in 1999, in time for the college's bicentennial anniversary in 2000, and now houses the geography, psychology, chemistry and biochemistry, and biology departments, among others.

The college built a new library in 2004 (which is supplemented by an additional music library at the Center for the Arts and a science library at Bicentennial Hall) that houses thousands of volumes, technological tools, multimedia facilities, extensive support services, and boasts a comfortable café and lounge. In 2008 the college finished construction on the old Starr Library, now the Axinn Center for Literary and Cultural Studies. Just like the surrounding hills and mountains of Vermont, many of Middlebury's buildings are visually breathtaking.

Thinking Global

Middlebury's renowned language and international studies programs translate into another hallmark of the Middlebury education—the junior semester (or year) abroad. During the 2009–2010 school year, more than 400 Middlebury students studied abroad in more than forty countries and at more than ninety different programs and universities. The college itself administers schools abroad in Argentina (Buenos Aires and Tucumán), Brazil (Florianopolis, Belo Horizonte, and Niterói), Chile (Concepción, La Serena, Santiago, Temuco, Valdivia, and Valparaíso), China (Hangzho and Kunming), Egypt (Alexandria), France (Bordeaux, Paris, and Poitiers), Germany (Berlin and Mainz), Italy (Ferrara, Florence, and Rome), Japan (Tokyo), Mexico (Guadalajara and Xalapa), Spain (Córdoba, Getafe, Logroño, and Madrid), Russia (Irkutsk, Moscow, and Yaroslavl), and Uruguay (Montevideo). Students are also allowed to participate in select outside programs, participating in programs in places such as Kenya, Madagascar, South Africa, New Zealand, Greece, and the United Kingdom, to name just a few.

Study abroad means different things to different students. For many, it's a way to live the language they've been studying for several semesters, or in some cases, several years. For others, it's a chance to travel, or put anthropology and sociology skills to work observing a new culture. For everyone who goes abroad, it's a nice change of pace from Middlebury's admittedly isolated campus.

> 66 *Studying abroad in Mainz, Germany, the German I studied at Middlebury certainly got a workout! That came in part from my full immersion in the local university; by the end of the semester I was giving oral reports to my native speaker classmates and typing up fifteen research papers* auf Deutsch. *But to be perfectly honest, that wasn't nearly as instructive as navigating my way downtown on my trusty German bicycle, plopping down in a café under the shadow of the city's cathedral, and watching the world go by.* 99

Winter Term

Finally, no rundown of the Middlebury academic experience would be complete without mention of the college's Winter Term, or "J-term." This is the "1" in Middlebury's "4-1-4" schedule; after completing four courses during the fall semester, students return to campus for a one-month interlude before the spring semester kicks up. This is an integral part of the college's academic schedule, and one students look forward to with relish. It's a much-needed reprieve from a student's typical course load, and frees Middlebury students up to try their hand at something new or burrow deeper into an existing passion. Classes meet at least eight hours a week, and span the academic spectrum. Students taking a first-year language are often required to use J-term as a bridge to a second semester of language study. Other students might opt to jump-start their majors by taking a compressed version of organic chemistry or first-semester psychology. But just as often, students take a risk and try their hands at something new. Maybe that's a creative writing course, or an art class dedicated to oil painting. Maybe it's an in-depth look at the Lewis and Clark expedition, or a crash course in local politics. The college draws on faculty talent to teach these courses, but also invites outside scholars, artists, authors, and professionals into the classroom.

> **66** *During one standout J-term, my professor—a New York poet—suggested our class take advantage of a clear night and a full moon with a midnight snowshoeing adventure. It was my first time on snowshoes, but we had a blast. I never thought I'd be an outdoorswoman, but I left Middlebury nonetheless with a newfound love of snowy vistas and winter sports.* **99**

J-term can be surprisingly demanding, but inevitably, students spend more time outside of the classroom than in. What this means is that January is a wonderful time to explore Vermont in the winter. Students huddle onto the shuttle bus to the college-owned Snow Bowl or cross-country ski touring center, or borrow snowshoes from the wildly popular Middlebury Mountain Club. Workshops in everything from wine tasting to digital photography to sign language to Thai cuisine also crop up, many of them student-led.

SOCIAL LIFE AND ACTIVITIES

Though the sleepy village of Middlebury winds down most evenings around 8 P.M. (save, of course, the local pubs and pizza shop), the campus is alive every night of the week with things to do, places to be, and people to see. Walking up the hill from town en route to a WRMC 91.1 FM-sponsored concert, you'll pass the German House in the historic (and recently renovated) "Deanery," where students of German and their professors chat away over *kaffee und kuchen*, a reception that will likely give way to a party later in the evening once faculty members call it a night. At the nearby Weybridge House, on the corner of College and Weybridge Street, residents of the house cook up a nightly feast of local and organic vegetarian fare, and pile into a cozy kitchen for communal meals. Once you make the trek onto the college campus proper, you'll meet up with students on their way from a crowded dorm room to the Mahaney Center for the Arts, where dance majors are giving a recital. Others are queuing up outside of the Black Box Theater in Hepburn Hall, where tickets are always at a premium and students vie for a spot on the evening's wait list.

Continue past the Gamut Room, a student-run social place hosting a student band for the evening and serving up cocoa. Meanwhile, at the McCullough Social Space, things get going late; the pulsating music of a Friday or Saturday night dance party wafts out over the quad well past midnight. And the Grille, a hot spot for coffee fixes and late night snacks, is a popular destination at any time of day. Finally, out of breath and shivering, you arrive at Coltrane Lounge, where radio station DJs are manning the door. Inside you're greated by the sounds of Andrew Bird, the Books, Girl Talk, indie darlings Menomena, or any number of bands that played at the college recently.

This is all to say that it's hard to be bored here; in fact, you'd have to try pretty hard.

The Social Houses

Middlebury did away with single-sex fraternities and sororities in the early 1990s, so anyone hoping for a classic Greek system will be disappointed at Middlebury. That said, if the idea of such organizations appeals to you, check out the college's social house system. Tucked away in a wooded grove on one side of the campus, these co-ed organizations are Middlebury's own take on the Greek experience. The social houses throw regular parties that are open to the college community, but parties are just the start. The close-knit houses also host barbeques, volunteer in the community, and start up teams for the college's annual Relay for Life. Students may pledge a social house after completing one semester at college, and sometimes students join the organization and still live in the dormitories if they so choose.

Social house involvement runs the gamut at Middlebury. Some students find that belonging to a social house is a great way to plug into a smaller, supportive environment, and many members find their closest friends at the social houses. Other students are perfectly happy to head to parties on the weekend, but steer clear otherwise. Still other Middlebury students have little or nothing to do with social houses. It's a sliver of the student population that actually pledges a social house, but the rule of thumb is this: it's there if you're interested, but not omnipresent if you're not.

The Commons System

Every student, upon arriving at Middlebury, finds him- or herself a member of a "Commons," like it or not. The Commons System describes Middlebury's way of building smaller communities—residential and academic—within the school's larger residential system. Commons affiliations are determined for first years and sophomores by residence hall assignments. Each Commons has its own dean, faculty head, self-governing council, and residential assistants, not to mention its own unique character. A little over twelve years old, it's still a relatively new system at the college, and for every student who dives into the Commons System wholeheartedly there are some who are quick to point out the setup's flaws.

That said, the system does strive to build strong residential communities and provide students with support from deans and administrators who know them personally. Commons deans are the go-to people when a student is struggling in school or with a personal issue. The Commons also have financial clout on campus, and often fund lectures, visiting performers, outings, and social events. Cook Commons hosts a fall festival on Battell Beach every year, complete with pie-eating contests and apple bobbing, and Ross Commons throws a popular "Viva Ross Vegas" nightclub event each year. The Commons are the source of many fun traditions. Some are small and intimate, and others large and vibrant, but they are all driven by students and their interests.

Student Organizations

Middlebury boasts nearly 160 student organizations, and if you're the average Middlebury student, it might feel some days like you belong to each and every one of them. Far from lazy, Middlebury students occasionally teeter at the brink of being overwhelmed by academic, social, and extracurricular pressures. Most like it that way, though. Each semester kicks off with an activities fair in which group leaders peddle their wares. Dancers in the "Lindy Hop" swing dance club demonstrate their moves while the radio station recruits new DJs. There's the African running choir Mchaka-Mchaka, which dashes through campus one night per week chanting traditional songs in the dark, and a slew of magazines, political organizations, musical groups, and

Middlebury students take their studies seriously. When it comes time to let loose, though, they do so in high style. Among the quirkier fads to take root on campus recently is Quidditch, that broomstick-toting, Snitch-snatching game of "Harry Potter" fame.

The "Intercollegiate Quidditch League" started off humbly enough, when a few students in one of Middlebury's first-year dormitories rounded up the custodial staff's brooms, took to the sprawling green Battell Beach, and hashed out the rules for a "Muggle" version of the Harry Potter sport. They recruited a cross-country runner to play the part of the Snitch, devised a few goals out of hula hoops, and went so far as to fashion their own cloaks, some out of bedsheets or wall hangings.

In the last few years, Quidditch at Middlebury—and at colleges around the country—has taken flight. Though originally the stuff of children's literature, intercollegiate Quidditch is no child's play. The games can get rough, and victory at the now traditional "World Cup," which last year hosted nineteen teams, is taken pretty seriously.

Running around on a broomstick might not be everyone's cup of tea, but that particular hobby is indicative of Middlebury students' fun-loving streak. Depending on the season, students are often spotted around campus playing bocce, sculpting sledding courses, or, yes, chasing the Snitch. After all, it turns out that many Middlebury students take their "work hard, play hard" reputation just as seriously as they do their studies.

volunteer services. Among the most popular of the student groups is the self-proclaimed "Sunday Night Group," which piles into the grand salon of the Chateau every—you guessed it—Sunday night to brainstorm ideas for fighting climate change on campus, across the state, and throughout the country.

> **❝** *My favorite nights at Middlebury were invariably spent in the basement of Hepburn Hall, where the newspaper staff put together the college's weekly publication. Over pizza, we debated editorial topics, wrestled with layout dilemmas, and hurried to meet press deadlines. Working on* The Campus *wasn't always a cake walk, but nothing compared to the feeling of picking the newspaper up off the newsstand every Thursday morning to read over breakfast in the Proctor Lounge.* **❞**

For the artistic set, there are student organizations galore. Middlebury boasts strong academic programs in the visual and performing arts, but there are also several *a cappella* groups on campus for which students can audition, and an inevitable slew of campus bands each year. Dance fanatics find their home in "Riddim," the world dance troupe; every semester, their shows inevitably sell out, and student fans are left trying to smuggle themselves into their much-anticipated performances.

Athletics

Middlebury might be a Division III school, but this is the little engine that could on the athletic fields. Middlebury has perennially competitive teams in its New England Small College Athletic Conference (NESCAC), and athletics are a way of life for many Middlebury students. Sometimes that means competing on a varsity team, but just as often it means taking off for the Snow Bowl, playing Ultimate Frisbee on Battell Beach, or joining a feisty intramural hockey team.

> **❝** *Cheer, boys, cheer for Middlebury's here,*
> *Fight, boys, fight, fight with all your might,*
> *Cheer, boys, cheer, for Middlebury's here,*
> *It's going to be a hot time in the cold town tonight!*
> *Hey, hey, hey!* **❞**

—*Middlebury College Fight Song*

The Panthers field thirty-one varsity teams and about twenty-four intramural teams. Between these two programs, a significant percentage of students participate in athletics. Others are staunch fans, pouring into the student section at the Chip Kenyon Arena to cheer on the men's and women's hockey teams, typically powerhouses in their division. There's an impressive trophy case to boast of their success, but plenty of other teams at the college are equally competitive. In recent years, Middlebury has won national championships in men's hockey, women's hockey, women's lacrosse, men's lacrosse, women's cross-country, men's soccer, field hockey, and men's tennis.

Just like the teams themselves, the college's athletic facilities are top-notch, too. There are two field houses on campus, gyms, a swimming pool, a fitness center, indoor and outdoor tennis courts, playing fields, an 8-lane 400-meter track, and an eighteen-hole golf course. Parents, alumni, and town fans frequently pack into the 3,500-seat stadium or 2,200-seat hockey arena. Up the mountain, about twenty minutes from campus, the college owns and maintains alpine and Nordic ski areas.

For non-varsity athletes, there are plenty of intramural and club sports to keep students active. Ultimate Frisbee is a favorite for many; students bedecked in outrageous practice gear, often culled from the college's own recycling center, practice on Battell Beach and travel to tournaments as far away as Georgia. There's also crew, rugby, and many other sports. The Middlebury Mountain Club, billed as the largest club on campus, provides a recreational outlet for students looking to get outside. They lend out equipment and organize hikes and overnight trips to the Green and Adirondack Mountains.

FINANCIAL AID

A Middlebury education costs a pretty penny, but luckily the college cushions the sticker shock of its $52,120 (2010–2011 comprehensive fee) education with need-based financial aid. A candidate's decision to apply for financial aid has no bearing on the admissions decision. When a student factors in the additional costs of traveling to and from Vermont, and purchasing textbooks every semester, a $52,120 comprehensive fee might seem unmanageable. Students and families can take heart, though, in the fact that the college has a commitment to meet each student's full demonstrated need, as calculated by the Student Financial Services. (The college requires that students applying for regular admission submit the College Board's college scholarship service (CSS) profile by February 1.)

Aid packages typically combine grants with federal and institutional loans, and are guaranteed to remain consistent over the course of all four years, provided a student's family's financial circumstances do not change. Thirty-seven percent of incoming freshmen in 2010 received financial aid. (On average, freshmen receiving aid received $32,498 in need-based scholarships or grants, and $3,748 in loans and work-study jobs.) The operative word, when it comes to financial aid at Middlebury, is *need*. The college does not award athletic or academic scholarships. That said, students may still apply for outside scholarships to offset their college expenses.

Regardless of whether or not a student is eligible for financial aid, all students are able to work part-time on campus. A special office for student employment helps collect and advertise these positions, which range from paid research assistantships with professors to the popular job of manning the front desk at the library. Other students trundle into town to wait tables at a nearby restaurant (or the college's trendy town-gown bar, 51 Main), or work at any of the boutiques on Middlebury's quaint Main Street.

GRADUATES

Attending Middlebury earns one admission into a small but tight-knit community, both on campus and in cities and countries around the world. Running into a Middlebury student, current or past, is a treat, and most Middlebury students recognize that spending four years on this snowy campus in central Vermont is a sort of badge of honor. A Middlebury degree signifies a bond with all who came before, or who came after.

❝ *As I embarked on the stressful task of job-hunting during my senior year at Middlebury, I was bowled over by the support and enthusiasm I received from strangers I met through the Middlebury alumni network. All we had in common was a name on our diplomas, but that didn't stop professionals from going out of their way to tell me about their lives and their jobs, and dole out useful advice. What I realized is that, after leaving Middlebury, it's hard not to look back on the place and its people with exceptional fondness.* **❞**

What that means is that the Middlebury alumni network is a powerful asset. Alumni are scattered around the world and found in all industries. There are budding journalists in Gaza and heads of major national news organizations. The former governor of Vermont is a Middlebury alum, and so is a selectman on a local town selectboard. Financiers, bankers,

- Julia Alvarez, Author of *How the Garcia Girls Lost Their Accents* and *In the Time of the Butterflies*
- Ari Fleischer, Former White House Press Secretary
- Felix Rohatyn, Financier and Former Ambassador to France
- Jim Douglas, former Governor of Vermont
- Aditya M. Raval, White House Producer, BBC, and Baghdad Bureau Chief, BBC
- Eve Ensler, Playwright, Author of *The Vagina Monologues*
- Chris Waddell, Para-Olympic Gold Medalist
- Adrian Benepe, New York City Commissioner of Parks and Recreation
- Sabra Field, Woodcut Artist
- Donald Yeomans, Senior Research Scientist at NASA's Jet Propulsion Laboratory and an Expert on Asteroids and Comets
- James Davis, Founder of the New Balance Athletic Shoe Company
- Rep. William Delahunt, Congressman from Massachusetts
- Rep. Frank Pallone, Congressman from New Jersey
- Jacqueline Phelan, Three-time National Championship Mountain Bike Racer
- Anais Mitchell, Folk Singer and Songwriter
- Shawn Ryan, Television Executive Producer of *The Shield* and *The Unit*
- Snake Jailbird, fictional character and criminal on animated television series *The Simpsons* who repaid his Middlebury College student loans after robbing Springfield landmark Moe's Tavern.
- Jane Bryant Qinn, Personal Finance author

lawyers, a gold medalist Para-Olympian, an opera singer, and a Bollywood music composer are all linked by their Middlebury degrees. It's not the quantity that counts, to dust off a well-worn cliché; it's the quality.

SUMMING UP

Middlebury students agree: this place is an extraordinary one. The campus is beautiful, the social life vibrant, the caliber of student (both personally and academically) unmatched. Middlebury students are typically quite humble about their achievements, having opted out of a big school with a big name for a reason, but they're a talented, diverse crew. You won't discuss SAT scores over lunch at the dining hall; instead you'll talk about who you are, where you came from, and what is happening in the world beyond Vermont. For all of the campus's amenities, stunning vistas, and topnotch facilities, this is what makes Middlebury ultimately so special. Come see for yourself.

❑ *Kathryn Flagg, B.A.*

NEW YORK UNIVERSITY

Courtesy of NYU

 New York University
New York, NY 10012

 (212) 998-4500
Fax: (212) 995-4902

 Website: *admissions.nyu.edu*

 Enrollment

Full-time ❑ women: 12,648
❑ men: 8,167

INTRODUCING NEW YORK UNIVERSITY

If you stroll through Washington Square Park—the heart of Greenwich Village and unofficial quad of New York University's New York campus—on any weekday morning, it's impossible to miss the hundreds of bright-eyed, energetic college students headed to their first class of the day. If you squint just a little, it's almost possible to imagine this busy, urban "quad" to be in some rural area surrounded by endless miles of cornfields. If you stand on the southeast corner of the park, in the shadow of NYU's Bobst Library and the

Kimmel Center for University Life, you might just hear a century's worth of academic ghosts whisper, "This is college." For a moment, you think, "This is how I always dreamed college would be."

But then reality sets in and you realize that the voices you hear do not belong to former NYU scholars, but to performance artists slamming poetry near the park's fountain, and the imagined cornfields have dissolved into an unobstructed view of fabulous Fifth Avenue, with its impressive buildings and flurry of activity. NYU definitely offers a collegiate experience, but there is nothing typical about it. And NYU students don't want it to be. They are happy to exchange cows and barns for Broadway and Wall Street. Wrought iron and ivy become much less significant when prospective students learn about all that NYU and New York City have to offer.

NYU is a private research university with two portal campuses—one set in the Greenwich Village neighborhood of New York City, the other recently opened in the dynamic modern city of Abu Dhabi, in the United Arab Emirates. The university was founded in 1831 by Albert Gallatin, America's fourth Secretary of the Treasury and a man known for radical ideas and innovation. He knew, even then, that the way to maintain a steadily evolving modern society was through higher education. NYU has kept that tradition alive by offering more than 230 innovative and unique programs of study at its ten different schools, colleges, and programs: The College of Arts and Science, The Global Liberal Studies Program, The Liberal Studies Program, The Stern School of Business, The Steinhardt School of Culture, Education, and Human Development, The Tisch School of the Arts, The Gallatin School of Individualized Study, The College of Nursing, The Silver School of Social Work, and The Preston Robert Tisch Center for Hospitality, Tourism, and Sports Management. Each one offers major courses of study in distinctive subject areas. The benefit of having such a wide range of programs to choose from is that students are allowed and encouraged to pursue seemingly disparate interests across the ten schools, colleges, and programs. In addition to these, the Polytechnic Institute of NYU—the second oldest private engineering college in America—will soon be NYU's school of engineering and technology.

The strength of NYU's academic programs attracts very driven and ambitious students to each discipline, which makes for an interesting and diverse student body. For instance, several years ago a business student at Stern and a drama student at Tisch got together and created the Stern Tisch Entertainment Business Association (STEBA), a thriving NYU club that wants its members to learn about and make contacts in the entertainment industry. As different as these two camps of students may appear, they are truly members of a unified, academic community. NYU students like to recognize the traits they share and are proud of these qualities. The caliber and the personality of each individual, in addition to the open-minded and proactive nature of fellow students, makes NYU the amazing place it is and will continue to be.

So the next time you find yourself in Washington Square Park, observe the students who are on their way to class. They're probably a bit edgier and may walk with a bit more purpose than most college students. Just take a look around you to see why this is the case. These people have chosen to attend a Global Network University that has portal campuses in both Manhattan's Greenwich Village and Abu Dhabi, as well as NYU's 10 global academic centers worldwide—they know what they want and know that NYU is the best place to find it. This time, don't squint and try to make the school and its neighborhood look typical. Open your eyes and take in the reality of what NYU is: a fantastic university in two of the greatest, most vibrant cities in the world.

ADMISSIONS REQUIREMENTS

Applicants often seek definitive numbers and statistics to quantify an acceptable NYU student, but no such absolute profile exists. NYU aims to create a holistic application review process, learning as much as possible about a person from the application materials he or she provides. That being said, NYU is unquestionably a highly competitive institution. Even well-rounded, three-dimensional students must be at the top of their high school class while enrolled in a challenging curriculum composed of honors, AP, and/or IB courses. Solid performance on the SAT or ACT is a must for all applicants, and two SAT Subject Tests are required except for applicants who must submit a portfolio or audition as part of their admissions requirements. Applicants whose native language is not English must submit results of the Test of English as a Foreign Language (TOEFL).

With just over 37,000 applications for a recent academic year, there certainly wasn't a shortage of qualified students. Many applicants are academically talented, so admissions officers must rely on personal characteristics to distinguish students within the applicant pool. They want to see hard evidence of leadership, commitment, and drive in how you choose to spend your free time. It does not matter if your preferred activity is ballet or a part-time job—the committee would like to see applicants who have been seriously involved in extracurricular activities and leadership roles while in high school. A stellar teacher evaluation, responses to several short-answer questions, and a thoughtful, personal essay that showcases a meaningful aspect of the applicant will also help set you apart from the crowd.

Procedure

NYU offers two kinds of application processes for prospective students: Early Decision and Regular Decision. Students who know that NYU is their first choice school may want to consider Early Decision. It is a binding agreement, which means that if you are admitted to the university, you will withdraw all other applications and accept NYU's offer of admission. NYU recently began offering two rounds of Early Decision to accommodate applicants. Students interested in applying Early Decision I must submit all necessary materials to the Undergraduate Admissions office by November 1 and can expect to hear of their decision beginning December 15. Early Decision II applicants must submit their materials by January 1, and will receive acceptance notification beginning February 15. Regular Decision requires applications to be submitted by January 1, and notification of their acceptance will arrive on or around April 1.

Certain programs at the University have unique components to their admissions process that other programs may not. Some require the submission of supplementary information, an essay, a portfolio or even an audition, so please read through your application instructions carefully. The goal of the admissions process is to succeed in choosing students who will thrive at NYU. Obviously, the best students start with the best applicants; those who submit a complete, correct, and intelligent application on time will make a favorable impression where it counts the most.

ACADEMIC LIFE

The academic environment varies widely depending on which school, college, or program of the university students attend. While this is the case, all NYU students share one common experience—the work is intense. Whether a student is perfecting moves in a dance studio, teaching inner-city youth at a public school, or researching the genetic makeup of mutant worms, they are engaged in a rigorous learning environment for most of their waking hours. The amazing thing is that NYU students would not have it any other way. These fiercely independent students crave new ideas and constantly push themselves further. They want to learn in order to be successful, more informed people who are not afraid to put in the hard work it takes to achieve their goals.

Walk through the Tisch School of the Arts at night, and you'll find a surprisingly large number of students tucked away in studios, individually honing their craft. Stand in the atrium of Bobst Library and you'll see twelve stories of students studying. Because their education means so much more to them than a letter grade ascribed to their work, NYU students are ambitious scholars, scientists, teachers, and artists of their own accord.

> **❝** *I think what makes the academic experience so unique at NYU is the accessibility of culture. Students don't just sit in class staring at reproductions of paintings in books, nor are they limited to literary readings at the student center. They can visit original works of art at the Metropolitan Museum, or drop by poetry clubs and author readings at bookstores and cafes any night of the week. Professors seem to share a love for the city, and are creative in the endless ways they incorporate the city as a learning tool. The experiential education you receive at NYU is incomparable.* **❞**

—*Emily Krasner, '07*

Core Curriculum

Regardless of school, college, or program affiliations, most students at the university participate in the core curriculum called the Morse Academic Plan (MAP). Each college within the university uses this core a bit differently, but the structure that it provides is universal. While the aim of MAP is to provide a strong, liberal arts foundation, it also allows students the freedom to tailor their program to their individual interests—to experiment with and investigate what truly fascinates them. Requirements for the MAP program are broken down into specific subject areas. To fulfill the Expressive Culture requirement, for instance, students may choose from a variety of classes ranging from courses that deal with anything from Jewish culture, to political culture, or artistic culture. At NYU, students are encouraged to explore many different academic pursuits while laying a foundation for more complicated and specific coursework that accompanies their chosen major.

Internships

Internships play a huge role in the life of an undergraduate at NYU. Nearly eighty-seven percent of undergraduates hold at least one distinct internship or part-time job (and usually more) by the time they graduate. The Wasserman Center for Career Development manages CareerNet, a database of approximately 20,000 internships available exclusively to NYU students and alumni. These internships are quality positions that offer real-world work experience, not simply making copies and getting coffee. Wasserman has forged relationships with major businesses, theaters, schools, community organizations, museums, and hospitals in order to make these opportunities accessible to students. (These include Comedy Central, JP Morgan, the American Museum of Natural History, *Rolling Stone*, and Memorial Sloan-Kettering Cancer Center.) Many organizations have a long list of past interns from NYU and they keep coming back for more.

Faculty

Primarily a research university, NYU attracts many prominent scholars and researchers in any given academic pursuit. Among them you'll find CEOs and Fulbright Scholars, as well as Nobel and Pulitzer Prize recipients and Oscar and Emmy Award winners. They are revolutionary scholars, experts, and working professionals who are very much immersed in their fields. These are the leaders who teach NYU's undergraduates. All faculty members teach at least one undergraduate course per year—even the current NYU president and former dean of the NYU School of Law John Sexton teaches a Freshman Honors Seminar. The NYU faculty enjoys and takes pride in teaching and advising its undergraduate students.

In the classroom, it's easy to recognize the faculty's commitment to their individual fields. They are enthusiastic while introducing new material and show a genuine interest in fostering class dialogue. They want to learn from their undergraduates and will often cite their students as a source of inspiration for a new article or project. It is not uncommon to hear a professor say, "I had never thought of it that way" during a round-table discussion with his students. Together, students and professors engage in the material very seriously, which always makes class a worthwhile, and sometimes breathtaking, experience. While there may be lectures that students must take at the introductory level, the preferred method of instruction at NYU is the seminar, where a small group of students and a faculty member exchange thoughtful discourse.

Students are also members of NYU's distinctive global network, giving them unparalleled opportunities to study abroad. They can choose to study at one or more of the university's ten global academic centers—in Accra, Ghana; Berlin, Germany; Buenos Aires, Argentina; Florence, Italy; London, England; Madrid, Spain; Paris, France; Prague, Czech Republic; Shanghai, China; and Tel Aviv, Israel or in any of the many exchange programs the university has established with 16 outstanding urban research universities around the world. Additionally, ground was recently broken on NYU's global academic center in Washington, D.C., and plans are underway for a new global academic center in Sydney, Australia. Each international program provides a rich curriculum in which students—who have access to portable financial aid—can complete some of their general degree requirements and, in many fields, take courses in their own major. In fact, a number of NYU's schools, colleges, and programs offer specific curricula and majors with an international focus. Additionally, in fall 2010 NYU opened NYU Abu Dhabi, a highly selective liberal arts, sciences, and engineering college in the United Arab Emirates. It is the first campus of its kind, and is the only comprehensive liberal arts college in the Middle East that is fully operated by and integrated into an American private research university. In short, taking advantage of any one of these programs gives students the kind of cultural awareness and independence that only studying globally can make possible.

Undergraduate Research

NYU has so many faculty members doing postgraduate research right on campus that undergraduates wanted in on the action. For example, the College of Arts and Science created the Dean's Undergraduate Research Fund (DURF), a program that lets undergraduates pitch research ideas to the DURF committee, and if the proposal is considered worthwhile, receive funding for the project. Research projects may be done individually or in conjunction with a faculty member. CAS students' research projects really run the gamut—they range from studying Irish Literature in Belfast or tracing neurons of rat amygdala, to an analysis of the stained glass art of John La Farge or the development of contour detection and how it affects our visual world. Students who are granted funding must write a paper on their findings, present it at the annual research symposium held on campus each spring, and publish their abstracts in *Inquiry*, the NYU research journal.

SOCIAL LIFE AND ACTIVITIES

There is *always* something to do at NYU. This is not an overstatement in the least; in fact, it may be an understatement. The NYU campus in New York resides in and is part of Greenwich Village, the most hip, vibrant, young, eclectic, bohemian neighborhood in all of New York City. Being a college student in this creatively charged neighborhood, in the city that never sleeps, is a win-win situation. Students at NYU are never bored; they never grapple with the age-old question, "What should I do tonight?" Instead, they are faced with the challenge of juggling a social life with schoolwork. The catch phrase here is time management—NYU students choose and create a social hierarchy, attempting to fulfill their overwhelming number of commitments by the end of the night.

A Typical College Experience

Students who yearn for the typical college experience can still find it at NYU. There is an on-campus Greek system that, because of the high premium placed on real estate in the city, operates from designated floors in certain NYU residence halls. Greek letters adorn sheets hung from windows in otherwise innocuous-looking buildings as opposed to being firmly mounted on the front porch of an *Animal House*-style frat house.

Although Greek life does not dominate at NYU, university clubs and organizations are hugely popular. The NYU Office of Student Activities boasts a roster of nearly 400 student-run clubs ranging from the more serious breed, such as community service organizations, religious clubs, and political activism communities, to the light-hearted and fun, including the yo-yo club and the soap opera watchers club.

NYU also has sports. In fact, it has twenty-one intercollegiate teams that compete in the NCAA Division III. Throughout the year, as a member of the University Athletic Association (a remarkable athletic conference that believes academics and athletics are not mutually exclusive), the NYU Violets compete against seven other private, distinguished research universities such as Brandeis, Carnegie Mellon, and Emory. Students interested in sports may join the competitive level for maximum commitment or can choose from more than 300 intramural sports teams, and 25 intercollegiate club sports, five of which recently qualified for national competition. For a good workout, NYU students can take advantage of their memberships to the Coles Sports Center and the Palladium Fitness complex, premier NYU recreation centers.

Many students at NYU, not just drama majors at Tisch, are interested in the performing arts. There are literally hundreds of opportunities for non-drama majors to be involved in theatrical productions. The College of Arts and Science has CAST, a theater group that is open to talented students within the college who, in addition to their studies, want to perform in a production. The Steinhardt School of Culture Education and Human Development invites students to join their *a cappella* groups and jazz bands, and there is an all-university gospel choir. If you want to be involved in something extracurricular, as most NYU students are, there are plenty of outlets to help you do so.

An Atypical College Experience

At NYU, you will find many students who enjoy the traditional college experience. They love to curl up on a couch in the student lounge of their residence hall with a bunch of other eighteen- to twenty-two-year olds, order pizza, and watch a bad movie. But at the same time, there is an entire world outside just waiting to be explored. The Greenwich

Village neighborhood alone reveals countless treasures: art galleries and cafés, ethnic restaurants and gourmet food shops, secondhand bookstores and antique shops, specialty music stores, and art movie houses. Beyond the Village there are new neighborhoods to discover, each offering their own cultural surprises. You can shop on Fifth Avenue, catch a Broadway show in Times Square, attend an art gallery opening in SoHo, and see the latest exhibit at the Guggenheim in the same day. At NYU, all of New York City is at your doorstep; you simply have to walk outside to experience it.

From the very first day of orientation, NYU encourages new students to venture out into New York City and conquer their fears of the great unknown. Students attend events and outings that make them feel comfortable in their new home away from home. The university does everything in its power to ensure that you are safe in your travels on and off campus.

FINANCIAL AID

No doubt everyone knows that NYU and New York City are expensive places to live and study. It should come as no surprise that tuition for one academic year (including housing, meal plan, and fees) is around $53,000. Fortunately, the university understands that spending this amount of money on higher education is a major financial commitment. Therefore, NYU's financial aid policy is quite simple: If students find that NYU is the best institution to meet their educational needs and interests, the NYU Office of Financial Aid will work with students and their families to help make NYU an affordable option. In fact, seventy percent of full-time freshmen receive some form of financial aid.

Students seeking financial aid from NYU should apply for assistance by submitting one form: the Free Application for Federal Student Aid (FAFSA). Students are encouraged to fill out the FAFSA via the Internet, which is the fastest and easiest method of applying for financial aid. With the information you provide on the FAFSA, the U.S. Department of Education uses a federally mandated formula to assess a family's financial status and determine the amount of money the government feels each can contribute to higher education. The NYU Office of Financial Aid then creates an individual financial aid package based upon the amount of financial need estimated by the government. Packages can include need- and/or merit-based scholarships, state and/or federal grants, work-study, and student loans.

NYU gives hundreds of millions of dollars in aid to undergraduates each year. A large percentage of this aid comes to students in the form of grants and scholarships. All admitted students are automatically considered for every scholarship they qualify for—there is no separate application process. NYU participates in a variety of payment plans. They range from interest-free prepayment plans to extensive loan programs that allow families the option to finance the cost of an NYU education over many years.

When it comes to financial aid, the bottom line is that NYU really makes a conscious effort to help individuals and families offset the cost of higher education in any way possible. The staff at the NYU Office of Financial Aid is friendly, extremely knowledgeable, and always willing to provide sound financial options.

GRADUATES

NYU graduates are doing some great things out there in the real world. The university's Wasserman Center for Career Development reports that typically approximately ninety percent of the class are employed in full-time positions or enrolled in graduate programs within six to nine months after graduation—a statistic that speaks volumes about the type of preparation NYU provides to its students.

A large percentage of NYU grads enter medical, law, or dental school, and with acceptance rates of eighty percent, they are obviously ready to attend some of the top schools in the country. Stern School of Business students often work on Wall Street and Madison Avenue for Fortune 500 companies. Tisch School of the Arts is stocking Broadway with many recent grads and current students who perform in major roles on the stage. Every year Los Angeles receives a high influx of film grads working on major motion pictures or television shows. The Steinhardt School of Culture, Education, and Human Development offers New York schools accomplished grammar, high school, and special education teachers. Hospitals nationwide are staffed by graduates of the College of Nursing. These are just some examples of the kinds of futures NYU graduates are pursuing when they leave the university. No matter what your specific interest is, at NYU you'll learn what you want and how to get it.

Attaining these desirable positions and acceptances to top graduate programs are not simple tasks. For example, the preprofessional advising center in the College of Arts and Science helps to prepare future lawyers and doctors. Advisors meet with students throughout their four years at NYU, in order to help them secure positions in their graduate program of choice.

The Wasserman Center lends a helping hand to students interested in pursuing a career upon graduation. The staff at Wasserman believes that preparation for a career or an advanced degree does not begin during spring semester senior year, but starts as early as freshman year. Students get a taste of their field and how it functions in the real world through internships, which also allows them to network and make important connections with potential employers. Often, these internships lead to full-time positions after graduation. Wasserman also offers résumé building and interviewing workshops and hosts massive recruitment fairs on campus twice a year, as well as approximately 18,000 full-time job listings available in their CareerNet database. Wasserman really does as much as it can to prepare students for whatever path they may choose after graduation. It is common for NYU students to drop by Wasserman and ask a counselor for help to secure a political position in Washington D.C. or a seat in the entering class of the NYU School of Law. Without hesitation, students always receive valuable words of advice and a "let's do it" attitude.

SUMMING UP

NYU is a private, research university that has two portal campuses—one in Greenwich Village, the heart of New York City, and one in Abu Dhabi, the vibrant capital city of the United Arab Emirates. All its academic programs include a strong liberal arts foundation as well as many areas of preprofessional specialization. The academic, research, study abroad, and internship possibilities are seemingly endless. The social life is exciting and varied. NYU graduates are extremely successful. Taken alone, these facts somehow overlook the true essence of what NYU is really about. Is it important to know that you will receive a top-notch education? Yes. Should you be aware that your degree will help land you a great job or acceptance into a graduate program? Yes. But there is so much more to NYU that can only be discovered once you set foot on campus.

> *NYU and New York City enhance each other, and that is what makes being here so unique. The friendships and connections I cultivated here were invaluable to my career, ones I would be hard-pressed to have made elsewhere. NYU taught me to think critically about our global world in the classroom, then enabled me to apply those lessons due to the university's sheer proximity to so many professional opportunities. Studying in the heart of such a dynamic, diverse city is nearly unquantifiable in excitement, exposure, and inspiration. Whatever you want, it's here waiting to be sought out and made the most of.*

—Julian Cyr, '08

So I took my own advice and set foot on campus. I sat in the unofficial "quad" and tried to summarize NYU. But to harness all that NYU is and quantify it into something tangible is impossible, because NYU is not one thing. It's not simple or usual; it defies definition, which is the allure of this university. The fact that NYU does not lend itself to categorization is the exact reason why people want to attend. Those who come here refuse to be defined or to limit themselves. They are searching for an institution of higher education as energized and open-minded as they are. At NYU, people find their passion and their voice, and begin to carve out a unique space in this world.

❑ *Eric Muroski, B.A.*

Northwestern University
Evanston, IL 60204-3060

(847) 491-7271

E-mail: *ug-admission@northwestern.edu*
Website: *www.ugadm.northwestern.edu*

 Enrollment

Full-time ❏ women: 4,115
        ❏ men: 3,705

Part-time ❏ women: 125
        ❏ men: 95

INTRODUCING NORTHWESTERN

There's a T-shirt with a phrase on it that applies to most Northwestern University students: "Plays well with others." Although Northwestern undergraduates are unquestionably intelligent and academically driven—approximately eighty-six percent of them graduated in the top ten percent of their high school class—they are also a remarkably collaborative group.

As a result, you'll find Northwestern students working together on everything from scientific research projects with outstanding faculty members to a seemingly infinite number of student-organized *a cappella* and theater groups to the nationally known Dance Marathon, an annual thirty hours of nonstop dancing fund raising event for a designated charity. You'll also find students engaged in community service projects and internships throughout the Chicago metropolitan area where Northwestern is located.

> *❝ My Northwestern education encompassed so many components that it is difficult to avoid pigeonholing it into preconceived stereotypes. I had small classes, great research opportunities, and caring professors, but I also took part in Division I football games and a vibrant campus that never lay dormant. The intellectual atmosphere drove me to question my assumptions about the world around me, while the social atmosphere was just a lot of fun. Chicago offers everything you need from a city, while Evanston offers everything you need from a college town and then some.*
>
> *I visited other universities that claimed to have it all, but each was lacking in some component of the environment I desired. Northwestern didn't flinch in any of its attributes, rather, I grew to like them more as I learned more about them in my four years there. Looking back, I still can't imagine going to college anywhere else. ❞*

—*Braxton Boron, '08*

Part of that cooperative ethic stems from Northwestern's academic culture, which encourages collaborative learning in an unusually broad range of disciplines for a school of its size. Students can explore academic subjects in six undergraduate schools, regardless of major, either through academic programs such as dual degrees or simply by taking electives. Regardless of academic discipline, you're likely to end up in classes where you'll not only have a chance to voice your opinion, you'll be expected to do so. That means you're an active participant in your education, not a passive note-taker.

And part of this sense of community also results from the often-unplanned interactions that occur when you get 8,300 intelligent, involved students together in one place. Whether it's debating the merits of a particular viewpoint in class, hanging out at any of Evanston's half-dozen coffeehouses near campus, or riding the free university shuttle bus together to catch events in neighboring Chicago, Northwestern students generally cram as much into their lives as possible. If you want solitude, you can definitely find it at Northwestern—the campus' mile-

So why is a private university in the Chicago metro area named Northwestern? When it was founded in 1851, the university's founders intended it to educate the children of those living in the states that had been carved out of the Northwest Territory, which was created by Congress in 1787. The vast region included all the land between the Ohio River, the Mississippi River, and the Great Lakes. The area ultimately became the states of Ohio, Michigan, Indiana, Illinois, Wisconsin, and a portion of Minnesota, and was known for decades as simply "the Northwest." Today Northwestern attracts students from all fifty states and approximately 50 foreign countries.

long shoreline of Lake Michigan is a favorite place, especially in good weather—but if you're someone who enjoys "playing well with others," Northwestern is a good fit.

ADMISSIONS REQUIREMENTS

Admission to Northwestern isn't easy. The university accepts only about 25 percent of the 25,000 students who apply each year. Good test scores are a basic requirement, of course, but a more important factor is how well you did in a challenging high school program. If you've taken advantage of the most demanding courses offered in your school, such as AP and Honors courses, and excelled in them, that carries a great deal of weight. In addition, Northwestern wants to hear your individual voice. The essay is the place to do this. The essay is a chance for you to give Northwestern a better feel as to who you are and whether you'd be a good match for the university. The application also includes an activity chart that allows you to show important interests you have outside the classroom, so be sure to complete that portion as well.

❝Given the caliber of Northwestern students, it becomes easy to take excellence for granted. Luckily, the admissions staff at NU applies the same rigorous standards to more than 25,000 applicants in crafting next year's freshman class. Though its students claim a diverse body of interests, you can be sure that each possesses the passion to dream big and the skills to put that passion to work. My three best friends were a political junkie, a theatrical director, and a Minnesotan hockey player, but despite our different proclivities, we were able to uplift each other and broaden our own interests as well. This desire to improve oneself and one's surroundings is found within every student here, and it is this shared heritage that keeps Northwestern's standards so high year after year. ❞

—Braxton Boron, '08

Admission to Northwestern is "need-blind," meaning that an applicant's ability to pay is *not* considered when the application is being reviewed. Approximately forty-five percent of Northwestern students receive university-funded grants and 60 percent receive some form of financial aid: grants, loans, and/or work-study jobs. All awards are based on financial need (see the Financial Aid section for more information).

Tests

Northwestern requires that you submit the results of either the SAT or ACT. The middle of 50% range of scores for admitted students is 670–750 for the SAT Critical Reading, 690–780 for the SAT Math and 30–34 for the ACT. While not required, the results of any Advanced Placement, International Baccalaureate, or SAT Subject Tests that you have taken also are considered. If English is not your primary language, you must submit the results of the Test of English as a Foreign Language (TOEFL) as well.

Early Decision

If you believe strongly that Northwestern is the university you would most like to attend, you should consider applying by November 1 under the Early Decision plan, which allows you to receive a decision in December. Do this only if you're sure Northwestern is your first choice— by applying under this binding admission option, you agree to withdraw all applications at other colleges, initiate no new applications, and enroll at Northwestern if you're admitted.

> **"** *Perhaps the best word to sum up academic environment at Northwestern is simply 'hard' Buzzwords like rigorous and stimulating certainly apply, but don't be fooled for a minute into thinking that you can get by with merely giving the right answer on a test. Classes are demanding and unyielding, so you will have to yield to them. Granted, this process will include the occasional all-nighter in the library curled up with Tolstoy or Spinoza—and, oh yeah, that 20-page paper that you really should have started yesterday. Since Northwestern is on the quarter system, classes will move at a ridiculous pace, but they also end sooner. The additional courses allow higher flexibility for double (or even triple!) majoring. This process takes some time, of course, but why would you want to attend a world-class university without becoming a world-class individual in the process? When I left Northwestern, I had not merely gained insights into how to pass a class; rather, I had gained a new way of understanding the world around me.* **"**

—*Braxton Boron, '08*

Choosing Courses

With a full-time undergraduate population of about 8,300, Northwestern provides personal attention and flexibility that is rare in larger institutions. Students also benefit from superior academic advising, career counseling, and student services.

NORTHWESTERN'S SCHOOLS AND COLLEGES (WITH YEAR OF FOUNDING)

- ○ Judd A. and Marjorie Weinberg College of Arts and Sciences (1851)
- ○ School of Communication (1878)
- ○ School of Continuing Studies (1933)
- ○ School of Education and Social Policy (1926)
- ○ Robert R. McCormick School of Engineering and Applied Science (1909)
- ○ Graduate School (1910)
- ○ Medill School of Journalism (1921)
- ○ School of Law (1859)
- ○ J. L. Kellogg School of Management (1908)
- ○ Feinberg School of Medicine (1859)
- ○ Henry and Leigh Bienen School of Music (1859)
- ○ Northwestern University in Qatar (2008)

Yet the size of the student body and an easily navigated campus may be the only things about Northwestern that feel small. The broad range of academic opportunities is unmatched in other schools of similar size. In fact, students at Northwestern have a larger pool of courses to choose from—about 4,000 each year—than at most other institutions of comparable size. Undergraduates benefit from the fact that Northwestern is home to six strong and distinctive undergraduate schools that will prepare them for the work place or graduate study.

Also making it easier to customize a Northwestern education is an academic calendar of three quarters each year (with a fourth quarter of optional summer study)—instead of two semesters—that allows you to take four courses per quarter. It's an ambitious curriculum that means that you have to hit the ground running in each of your courses. But it also ensures that you'll have a solid foundation in the liberal arts and a thorough education in your chosen field. And it allows you to explore interests and subjects you might not have thought about before you came to Northwestern.

As a prospective undergraduate, you'll apply to one of Northwestern's schools that offer undergraduate programs. At the center of Northwestern is the oldest, largest, and most comprehensive of the undergraduate schools, the Judd A. and Marjorie Weinberg College of Arts and Sciences. Enrolling more than half of the undergraduates, Weinberg combines the vigor of a leading liberal arts college with the resources of a major research university.

Northwestern's other colleges and schools—McCormick School of Engineering and Applied Sciences; School of Education and Social Policy; Medill School of Journalism, School of Communication; and Bienen School of Music—offer outstanding preprofessional programs in their respective fields. Regardless of what area you choose, you will enjoy an unusual degree of access to top faculty and personal attention—in classrooms, around seminar tables, and in conversation with academic advisers from the university's many disciplines. You will also be able to work in the laboratories of prominent scientists, study with award-winning scholars, and engage with speakers from around the world.

Special Programs

In addition to the opportunity to customize academic programs, Northwestern also offers several specialized programs for undergraduate students. Among these is the Honors Program in Medical Education, in which a select group of students complete three years of undergraduate study and in the fourth year are admitted to the entering class of Northwestern's Feinberg School of Medicine. Or, as juniors, students may enroll in specialized undergraduate certificate programs in Financial Economics or Managerial Analytics offered by Northwestern's Kellogg School of Management, one of the top business schools in the world. Many students also take advantage of undergraduate research programs, which provide funds for students to conduct in-depth study, either during the year or over the summer, into a particular topic under the guidance of a faculty member.

> ❝ *What began as a tangential lunchtime conversation about the possibility of musicians learning video-game systems faster than average eventually became my summer job, my first academic conference presentation, and my senior thesis—all thanks to the Office of Fellowships. When I found out about the Undergraduate Research Grant program, I was skeptical that anyone would want to fund research about video games (or that the project was even possible). But when I talked to one of the professors about it, he agreed to advise me on the project and helped me develop the software system to record controller data for the games I would need. When I found out that I had won one of the grants, I was ecstatic—I hadn't expected to spend the summer running test trials of Mortal Kombat II, but at Northwestern, these things really do happen.* ❞

—*Braxton Boron, '08*

> *While Northwestern believes in core values as part of the liberal arts education, it trusts its students enough to allow them to learn these through subjects which appeal to them. Thus, instead of a rigid 'core curriculum,' Northwestern offers distribution areas of many classes which rely on the basic principles it hopes to impart. Don't like Differential Equations? You can take a Logic or Game Theory class instead. Instead of slogging through Bio 101, I took Astrobiology 111, where I learned about the search for life on other planets. I learned much more about how life develops in the context of a subject I liked rather than something that was forced upon me. Many of my friends discovered their future major by being adventuresome with their distribution requirements, and I highly recommend it as well.*

—*Braxton Boron, '08*

UNDERGRADUATE RESEARCH

Northwestern students have the opportunity to engage in major research projects while still undergraduates working closely with top faculty members. Following is a sample of some of the topics explored by undergraduates who received research grants recently:

- ○ Humanizing Deindustrialization: The Cultural Narrative of Pittsburgh's Steel Workers in the Post-Industrial America.
- ○ Creation of an MRI Phantom for Quantifying Liver Iron Content in Iron Diseases
- ○ World of Warcraft: American Social Fantasy Play
- ○ Achievability of Our Moral Ends in Immanuel Kant's Critique of Judgement
- ○ Relationship between HIV/AIDS Prevention and Christian Influences in Uganda
- ○ Language Learning and the Effect of Phonological Tone Awareness
- ○ Exercise and Chronic Pelvic Pain: A longitudinal Study in Women's Health
- ○ Epithet and Characterization in Homer's Odyssey
- ○ Fabrication of a Nanodiamond-Polymer Drug Delivery Platform for Directed Post-Operative Chemotherapy

Study Abroad

Every year, nearly 600 students from all of Northwestern's six undergraduate schools participate in overseas educational opportunities. With affiliated programs at approximately 100 institutions, Northwestern students literally have a world of choices. While Europe remains a popular location, a growing number of students choose to study in Africa, Asia, and South America. Some programs are university-based, meaning that students live in one place and take courses at a university. Others are field-based, focusing more on fieldwork and independent research projects.

> **&&** *The stereotypical collegiate experience probably proscribes large survey classes as an underclassman, followed by smaller upper-level classes later on. Certainly I experienced smaller classes within my major—by my senior year, I was the only undergraduate in a graduate-level seminar in which each student was expected to give a presentation on her research every week. When your classmates have worked in industry before returning to grad school, it sort of spurs you on to a higher work ethic.*
>
> *But I wouldn't say that my classes were impersonal even as an underclassman. My sophomore year, I was the only student enrolled in a Music Theory survey course, but the professor continued on, giving me a personal lecture every period that quarter. Even in the large lecture halls, my friends and I would sit right in front of our favorite philosophy professor as he was addressing a hundred or more students. Any time we had an insight or objection, we could ask him about it, and he would gladly banter back and forth with us—it felt more like a dinner table discussion that a lecture, and I learned the subject matter better as a result.* **&&**

—*Braxton Boron, '08*

Faculty

Northwestern has nearly 1,000 full-time faculty who teach in its undergraduate college and schools. One of the hallmarks of Northwestern historically has been that almost all faculty members teach undergraduate students; that remains true today. That means you'll be taught, mentored, and advised by MacArthur Fellowship recipients, Tony Award honorees, National Medal of Science winners, and members of numerous honorary and professional societies.

SOCIAL LIFE AND ACTIVITIES

Lakefront Living

Most undergraduates at Northwestern live on the Evanston campus in one of the residence halls, residential colleges, sororities, or fraternities. Some of the halls and residential colleges, and almost all the fraternities and sororities, are in older, ivy-covered houses. Other residence halls and residential colleges are new and feature apartment-style suites with individual bathrooms. Several of the residence halls/colleges overlook Lake Michigan, and all are within easy walking distance of the main classroom buildings.

> ❝ *Every student defines his or her Northtwestern experience in a different way. You could stay on campus every night for four years, and not run short of edifying experiences to fill your time. There is a new theatrical production opening almost every weekend, world-class concerts through the week, and exhibits, performances, outreaches, and activism of every kind happening constantly on Northwestern's campus. That being said, there is also the wide world of Chicago at your doorstep, and I for one could not resist the allure of the Chicago Symphony Orchestra, the Art Institute, the Cubs/White Sox rivalry (take your pick), the Lyric Opera—the list goes on and on. The real key to your time here is to balance the wealth of opportunities you have with actually staying caught up with classes—those things you come to college for, remember?* ❞

—*Braxton Boron, '08*

Regardless of where students live, they can enjoy Northwestern's beautifully landscaped lakefront campus that stretches for a mile along the shore of Lake Michigan. That location can bring some fairly chilly winds in winter, but it also means an endless horizon to the east, a private beach and boathouse where you can take sailing lessons, and plenty of open space where you can soak up the sun in the spring and fall.

RESIDENTIAL COLLEGES

Northwestern's eleven residential colleges provide housing and specialized programs that allow students and faculty to pursue a common interest outside the classroom. Here are some of the disciplines covered by res colleges:

- **Business (Commerce and Industry)**
- **Communication**
- **Cultural and Community Studies**
- **Humanities**
- **International Studies**
- **Performing Arts**
- **Public Affairs**
- **Science and Engineering**
- **Women's Studies**

Activities

Over-opportunity-ed. That was how one student described her undergraduate experience at Northwestern.

Students tend to be active, engaged, and involved. That means, at least for most students, that their most important accessory is their day planner (either paper or electronic), followed closely by their cell phones/PDAs because they keep rescheduling all their commitments.

For many students, those commitments include not just academic studies, but other activities as well. Northwestern has more than 300 extracurricular groups on campus, ranging from cultural groups to religious and spiritual groups to dozens of music and small theater groups open to nonmajors. Every fall during the first week of classes, the Student Activities Fair showcases these organizations, giving new students a chance to find out more and choose which ones they'd like to join. With enthusiastic members promoting each group, it's easy to jump into lots of organizations. If you're really good at time management, you can pull it off, but be prepared for some late nights—many groups start their meetings/rehearsals/practices at 9 or 10 P.M.

66 No decision influenced my collegiate experience as much as my choice to live in Chapin Hall, the Humanities Residential College. As a high school senior, I had little idea what constituted the humanities—I was mainly just drawn to Chapin's very large rooms. In my time there, the Chapin community provided me with friendships and memories that can only be forged out of a thousand little experiences: the late night political discussions in the common room, the poetry readings, the video game tournaments, the film screenings, the soccer games (either organized intramurals or impromptu matches in the guys' hallway). Each residential college has associated professors who eat with its members, allowing a quick way to get into upper-level classes, obtain research jobs, or just gain perspective from some of the most intelligent people you will ever meet. By the end of my first year in Chapin, I felt less like an individual in a building and more like a member of a family. 99

—*Braxton Boron, '08*

Community Service

Another key interest for Northwestern students is community service. Approximately 3,000 students perform some sort of community service each year, ranging from tutoring at local schools to service projects in Chicago. The largest student group on campus is the Northwestern Community Development Corps, which serves as an umbrella organization for many of the service groups on campus. In addition, the web site at *http://www.volunteer.northwestern.edu/* matches up students with volunteer opportunities in the community.

Sports

Northwestern is a charter member of and the only private university in the Big Ten, one of the premier Division I athletic conferences in the country. Sports at Northwestern are not just for watching, however, as club and intramural sports attract approximately 2,000 participants each year. Approximately forty sports clubs compete, including crew, Ultimate Frisbee, ice hockey, equestrian, water polo, cycling and a host of others, many of which compete at the highest levels. Intramural offerings range from casual softball leagues to competitive basketball, and many of the outdoor sports are played on Northwestern's lakefront fields.

> **"** *Northwestern teams are powerhouses in many sports: the women's lacrosse team has captured the NCAA championship four years in a row, the women's tennis team dominates the Big Ten, having won the title for 10 straight years, and the swimming, wrestling, and soccer programs are among the strongest in the country.* **"**

—*Braxton Boron, '08*

Evanston and Chicago

Evanston isn't a typical college town. While Northwestern is a vital part of the community, it doesn't dominate the city of 75,000 that adjoins Chicago as a large university in a small town does. So you won't find a large area of somewhat shabby student apartments just off campus or rows of bars catering to the just-of-age (or perhaps not) crowd.

Instead, Northwestern's campus is bordered by a neighborhood of beautiful old homes and a vibrant downtown. Downtown Evanston has dozens of interesting locally owned shops and more than sixty restaurants, ranging from student budget-friendly cafés to fancier places that are great for Family Weekend. Within walking distance of the campus is an eighteen-screen movie theater, with six of the screens devoted to showing independent and foreign films. Best of all, the theater—and almost all the stores and restaurants downtown—offer a discount if you show your WildCARD, the Northwestern student ID.

Then there's Chicago, one of the world's truly great cities. The third-largest city in the country, a place with world-class museums, an incredible theater scene, ethnic restaurants, and nightlife galore. Students can take advantage of such great opportunities as the Chicago Art Institute's free admission day and student-discount tickets to the Chicago Symphony (as cheap as $10), and, of course, a Cubs game at Wrigley Field.

66 *For a small-town kid, the allure of a city like Chicago is hard to describe. I remember arriving at Northwestern for the first time and seeing Chicago from campus and feeling that perhaps I was finally an adult. In my first two years at Northwestern, I explored Chicago thoroughly—the concerts, the parks, the independent theater companies, and the museums (especially free ones). I worked at restaurants downtown, recording studios, and even the finish line of the Chicago Marathon. In my later years, I found appreciation in exploring the outer reaches of Chicago land, attending video game concerts in Rosemont or biking the lakefront trail to Highland Park. I can't say enough about Evanston itself, which is less like a suburb and more like its own city on the outskirts of Chicago. The restaurants, used book stores, coffee shops, and fabulous lakeside parks always gave me plenty to do without ever jumping on the El.* 99

—*Braxton Boron, '08*

Getting to Chicago is easy. The CTA rapid transit ("the El") has three stops near campus and even runs express from Evanston during rush hours. In addition, the university runs a shuttle bus on weekdays between the Evanston campus and the Chicago campus (home to the law school, medical school, and part of the business school), which is only two blocks from Chicago's Michigan Avenue, one of the best shopping streets in the world. And on Saturdays, a free shuttle bus runs between the Evanston campus and downtown Chicago, providing easy access to Michigan Avenue, Millennium Park, the Art Institute, and other cultural attractions.

FINANCIAL AID

Financial aid at Northwestern is awarded on the basis of family need. Recipients of need-based financial aid come from a wide range of income backgrounds, so if you're not sure whether you'd qualify for need-based aid, go ahead and apply. To do so, you must complete the Free Application for Federal Student Aid (FAFSA) and the College Scholarship Service Financial Aid PROFILE. Northwestern awards more than $80 million in grant assistance to undergraduate students each year.

PROMINENT GRADS

- ⭕ Christine Brennan, Columnist, *USA Today*; commentator, ESPN
- ⭕ Steven Colbert, The Colbert Report
- ⭕ Douglas Conant, President and CEO, Campbell Soup Co.
- ⭕ Rahm Emmanuel, Former Chief of Staff for President Barack Obama
- ⭕ Joe Girardi, Manager, New York Yankees
- ⭕ Heather Headley, Tony-Award winning Actress; Star of *The Lion King* and *Aida*
- ⭕ David Schwimmer, Actor
- ⭕ David Skorton, President, Cornell University
- ⭕ John Paul Stevens, U.S. Supreme Court Justice
- ⭕ George Stigler, Economist, Nobel Prize Winner
- ⭕ Julia Wallace, Editor, *Atlanta Journal-Constitution*
- ⭕ Michael Wilbon, Columnist, *Washington Post*: co-host, *Pardon the Interruption*
- ⭕ Mary Zimmerman, MacArthur Fellowship recipient, Tony-Award-winning Director, and Northwestern Professor of Performance Studies

❝I was initially a little wary about attending Northwestern, knowing that my family's finances were going to be strained with three children in school at once. But when I met Northwestern's financial aid department, I was blown away. Every member of the staff is knowledgeable and caring; they immediately explain the system to you so that you understand your options. Since most of Northwestern's aid is need-based, they paid for most of my family's financial contribution without making us sell our house or take on renters. Best of all, I was able to meet my contribution with other scholarships and a work-study job, all without taking out any loans.❞

—*Braxton Boron, '08*

GRADUATES

Northwestern alumni and their employers regularly comment on how much they value a Northwestern education.

> *No amount of praise for Northwestern's programs will carry much water if the final product—its graduates—does not measure up. I was a regular at the Office of Fellowships throughout my senior year—flushing out what I had done academically and what I still wanted to do. Their guidance was crucial in forming my essays and applications for graduate school, and their work shows in the Rhodes and Fulbright scholarships my classmates have already won. In addition, the University Career Services Office does a great job of helping graduates enter the workforce smoothly. My friends working with consulting firms, helping after-school programs, and starring on Broadway are but a fraction of the NU graduates all around the world.*

—*Braxton Boron, '08*

Few students view graduation as the end of their education, however. The majority of Northwestern's undergraduate alumni eventually go on to earn advanced degrees.

Northwestern alumni, numbering approximately 200,000, include leaders in business, government, law, medicine, media, education, and the performing arts. In addition, alumni are engaged and active in their communities and their professions.

SUMMING UP

There really isn't such a thing as a "typical" Northwestern experience, mainly because there are so many different types of people here. That's probably a good thing, although it makes it hard to characterize the institution. In the end, Northwestern students can make their time here be pretty much anything they want, given the range of choices that exist. For most students, that means four years of a great education—and some really fun times with good friends.

> **❝** *I first visited Northwestern in seventh grade, when my older brother was visiting prospective colleges. I had visited many other universities and found them quite intimidating. I had thought that college was just an enemy to be defeated, but Northwestern felt more like home. By the end of the tour, my brother was still undecided, but I'd already made up my mind. Four years later, I felt more homesick leaving Northwestern than I had coming there.*
>
> *Like my parents prepared me for college, Northwestern prepared me for the real world, and yet it is so much more than the skills I gained from it. The most important lesson it taught me was to be extremely picky about the way you live your life—after all, you only get to do it once. Wherever your life takes you, it should always be painful to leave because you need to become a part of a place to grow there. Northwestern has a lot of environment to offer, but in the end you have to interact with that environment to make the next four years the best of your life.* **❞**

—Braxton Boron, '08

❏ *Kristen Acimovic, B.A.*

Oberlin College
Oberlin, Ohio 44074

(440) 775-8411 or (800) 622-6243
Fax: (440) 775-6905

E-mail: *college.admissions@oberlin.edu*
Website: *http://www.oberlin.edu/coladm/*

 Enrollment

Full-time ❏ women: 1,574
❏ men: 1,268

Part-time ❏ women: 24
❏ men: 44

INTRODUCING OBERLIN COLLEGE

Think one person can change the world? So do we.

When a pair of Yankee missionaries founded Oberlin College in 1833, they envisioned an institution built on high intellectual standards, a liberal education for all, excellence in teaching, and a commitment to the social and moral issues of the day. For the past 171 years, Oberlin has honored this mission, encouraging students to use their liberal arts education and change the world, one Obie at a time.

Today, Oberlin College's 440-acre campus sits next to, and has inexorably meshed with, the city of Oberlin, Ohio. A small town by definition, Oberlin (with a population of 8,600) is thirty-five miles west of Cleveland, Ohio. At first glance, the town's tree-lined square and old-fashioned business district may evoke memories of a sleepy Mayberry, but the annual fall migration of college students revitalizes the town with their youthful energy.

> **66** *The most impressive aspect of an Oberlin College education is the genuine rapport that exists between the diverse student communities. Obies come from every corner of the globe to share an intellectually stimulating atmosphere, where they are encouraged to be socially and civically engaged through a myriad of extracurricular activities.* **99**

The small-town atmosphere is an attractive draw for many students, who (because of the town's proximity to the college) often forge lasting bonds with local residents. Whether it's over a cup of coffee at the Java Zone, participating in annual events such as the Big Parade, or during a city- and campus-wide effort to register voters, students and "townies" band together to form an experience that is uniquely Oberlin.

Oberlin College's commitment to the surrounding community has introduced countless students to the idea of service and learning. In fact, the college's addition of academically based community service courses to the curriculum encourages students to take what they have learned in the classroom and apply it to real-world service situations. Students in these classes work with local community partners to strengthen the programs that are vital to Oberlin's diverse population.

With its emphasis on academics and social justice, it's no surprise that countless Oberlin grads have gone on to make a significant impact in the fights against poverty, racism, gender inequality, and other important social and political issues. Whether as doctors, lawyers, business executives, educators, politicians, or volunteers, Obies have left their mark on society by holding themselves to a higher standard and living Oberlin's ideals long after they've graduated.

Oberlin's founding fathers would be proud.

Oberlin's competitive admissions process attracts a cross section of intelligent, forward-thinking students, including the 5,824 who applied for one of the 742 coveted spots in the class of 2008. With sixty-seven percent of first-year applicants in the top tenth and eighty-five percent in the top quarter of their senior classes, prospective Obies have all their academic bases covered.

Oberlin's application process is fairly standard, calling for transcripts, recommendations, and a personal essay. The average test scores among successful applicants are 690/660 for the SAT I and 29 for the ACT. Oberlin requires the writing sections of both the SAT and the ACT. (Note: Oberlin requires either the SAT or the ACT, but recommends the SAT Subject Tests.) International students who apply to Oberlin must submit their TOEFL scores. Oberlin's admissions counselors (who are often Oberlin alumni) also consider a student's advanced placement and honors courses, leadership record, and extracurricular and volunteer accomplishments.

Although Oberlin does not require its prospective students ("prospies," as they are affectionately nicknamed) to schedule an on-campus interview, one is strongly recommended. Oberlin's admissions counselors are more likely to recognize the intangible qualities that define an Obie during a face-to-face interview. All prospies are encouraged to visit Oberlin during the academic year, to meet current students, and attend the classes that interest them. This candid look at campus life offers prospective students a clear picture of the Oberlin experience.

Students unable to schedule a campus interview can arrange one with Oberlin alumni in their hometown. Simply call Oberlin's Office of Admissions (1-800-622-OBIE) to request an off-campus interview or visit the office's web site (*http://www.oberlin.edu/coladm*) for further information. All alumni interviews must be scheduled by January 2.

Oberlin's Application

When applying to Oberlin, all prospective students must submit a two-part application. The easiest way to complete the first part of the application is to submit it online. But you can also submit an online request for information, e-mail an admissions counselor, or telephone the office directly to ask for an application packet.

The second part of Oberlin's application includes the Common Application and its personal essay, as well as the "Why Oberlin" essay and some supplemental forms. Prospies may submit the Common Application and the "Why Oberlin?" essay online.

- ○ **Secondary School Record: Very Important**
- ○ **Class Rank: Very Important**
- ○ **Recommendation(s): Important**
- ○ **Standardized Test Scores: Very Important**
- ○ **Essay: Important**
- ○ **Interview: Considered**
- ○ **Extracurricular Activities: Important**
- ○ **Talent/Ability: Important**
- ○ **Character/Personal Qualities: Important**
- ○ **Alumni/ae Relation: Considered**
- ○ **Geographical Residence: Considered**
- ○ **State Residency: Considered**
- ○ **Religious Affiliation/Commitment: Not Considered**
- ○ **Minority Status: Considered**
- ○ **Volunteer Work: Considered**
- ○ **Work Experience: Considered**

Admissions Deadlines for First-Year Students

If Oberlin is your top college choice, consider applying as an Early Decision candidate. The admissions committee considers the enthusiasm of Early Decision candidates a plus during the selection process, giving these applicants a slightly better statistical chance of gaining admission to Oberlin than a Regular Decision candidate.

Oberlin offers two Early Decision options. Early Decision I candidates must submit their applications by November 15, while the applications for Early Decision II must be postmarked by January 2. Students applying under the first program will receive their notification (admission, deferral, or denial) by mid-December. Early Decision II applicants will receive their notification by February 1.

All first-year, Regular Decision candidates must apply to Oberlin by January 15. They will receive notification of their status from the Office of Admissions by April 1.

Admissions Deadlines for Transfer Students

Oberlin enrolls first-year students during the fall semester *only*; however, transfer students may enroll during either the fall or spring semesters. Oberlin College defines a transfer student, for admissions purposes, as a student who has been enrolled in a degree program at another college or university or who has earned more than thirty semester hours of college course credit.

Transfer applicants must apply to Oberlin by March 15 for enrollment the following fall and by November 15 for enrollment the following spring. Notifications for these applicants are mailed in mid-December and at the beginning of April.

Deferred Enrollment

Oberlin also offers a deferred enrollment plan. Students admitted to the Division of Arts and Sciences can request deferred enrollment for up to one year. A written request for this status should be submitted to the Dean of Admissions, detailing the student's plan for the coming year. Approved deferral requires the student's commitment to enroll, as well as a deposit to secure a place in the following year's class.

The Oberlin Conservatory of Music

In addition to the College of Arts and Sciences, the campus is home to the Oberlin Conservatory of Music. Founded in 1865, the Conservatory is known throughout the world as a professional music school of the highest caliber. It is the oldest continuously operating conservatory in the United States, and is the only major music school in the country linked with a preeminent liberal arts college.

The Conservatory provides preprofessional training in music performance, composition, music education, electronic and computer music, jazz studies, music theory, and music history to approximately 595 students. The Conservatory offers the following degrees: Bachelor of Music, Performance Diploma, Artist Diploma, Master of Music in performance on historical instruments, and unified five-year programs leading to the BMus and MM in conducting, teaching, education, and opera theater.

Oberlin also offers a double-degree program for students admitted to both the Conservatory and the College of Arts and Sciences. Students in the five-year program earn a BMus in the Conservatory and a BA in the College.

The Conservatory is housed in a complex of three soundproof and air-conditioned buildings designed by Minoru Yamasaki that includes Bibbins Hall (the teaching building), the central unit (the rehearsal and concert hall building), and Robertson Hall (the practice building). The central unit also houses the Conservatory Library—one of the largest academic music libraries in the country. It includes a collection of more than 121,000 books and scores, 47,000 sound recordings, forty-two listening stations, and six audiovisual listening rooms.

Admission to the Oberlin Conservatory of Music

Like students applying to the College of Arts and Sciences, those seeking admission to the Conservatory of Music must submit their scores from either the SAT or ACT exams. Applicants whose first language is not English should submit the results of the TOEFL exam. Unlike the College of Arts & Sciences, however, the deadlines for the Conservatory application, as well as all supplemental material are November 1 for Early Review and December 1 for Regular Review.

Prospective "Connies" must also audition as part of the application process. Students audition in their principal medium (instrument or voice) unless applying for admission as a composition or electronic and computer music major (in which case they must submit their original compositions). All applicants are encouraged to audition in person, but may, if necessary, attend any one of the regional auditions that are held throughout the country during the months of January and February. Prerecorded auditions are allowed if travel to Oberlin or a regional audition is cost-prohibitive.

ACADEMIC LIFE

Oberlin's many departments and programs offer a mind-boggling number of courses, allowing each student to design a personalized educational program. Students can choose from more than forty disciplines (majors), or create a specialized course of study through the Individual Majors Program.

Selecting a major encourages students to study a particular discipline in depth. At Oberlin, students are not required to declare a major until the end of their sophomore year, which gives them time to explore new areas of study and discuss their interests with faculty advisors. The most popular majors at Oberlin are English, politics, and biology.

Students in the College of Arts and Sciences are required to take and pass 112 credit hours before receiving their B.A. Approximately half of these credits must be earned in the student's major field of study, while the remaining half are divided between the Divisions of Arts and Humanities, Social and Behavioral Sciences, and Natural Sciences and Mathematics. In addition, students must earn writing and quantitative proficiency certification, take a minimum of three courses dealing with cultural diversity, and complete three winter term projects.

Faculty

Oberlin's professors are both scholars and teachers. Like professors at major research universities, they contribute to their discipline through writing and research. But unlike the faculty of major research institutions, Oberlin professors teach everything from first-year courses to advanced seminars, without the aid of TAs. All professors keep regular and frequent office hours, coordinate and supervise independent study projects, and view the education of undergraduates as the most important role of their careers.

Faculty members also act as mentors to their students, especially when guiding their academic development. Since the college's founding, countless professors have collaborated on important research projects with their students. Some of the more recent collaborations include the study of smog pollution, the use of three-dimensional imaging technology to reconstruct archeological finds, and the publication of a dictionary that traced slang usage on campus through a decade's worth of students.

> **❝** *In a liberal arts setting, research is a pedagogical tool—not always just an end product in itself. That research produces results is a good thing, but—more importantly—it offers me an opportunity to teach students the substance of the discipline, as well as its techniques.* **❞**

The Honor System

Every student at Oberlin is familiar with the college's Honor Pledge, which reads: "I affirm that I have adhered to the Honor Code in this assignment." This pledge, formal and archaic as the phrasing may sound, is a very real part of campus life.

Oberlin's Honor Code is part of its student-administered Honor System and is based on the assumption that academic honesty lies at the heart of academic enterprise. The system applies to all work submitted for academic credit, including quizzes, exams, papers, and laboratory assignments. Each assignment must include the Honor Pledge and the student's signature in order to affirm the integrity of their work.

NUMBERS

○ **Total Number of Female Professors: 117**
○ **Total Number of Male Professors: 171**
○ **Total Number of Professors: 288**
○ **Faculty to Student Ratio: 9 to 1**

First-Year Seminar Program

Oberlin's first-year seminar program (FYSP) gives students the opportunity to experience liberal arts learning at the onset of their college careers. Each seminar brings together faculty members with a small group of students to investigate specialized topics. This format encourages students to test new ideas, learn from their peers, and get to know professors well in a small classroom setting, while at the same time honing their critical thinking, writing, and discussion skills.

Winter Term

Oberlin students spend the month of January pursuing projects of their own design. Individual or group-oriented, on or off campus, career-related or just for fun, winter term projects provide an opportunity to fully explore a unique educational goal. Winter term encourages students to discover the value of self-education by emphasizing creativity, intellectual independence, and personal responsibility. Many of the concerts, theatrical productions, films, lectures, forums, and discussion groups that take place during January are part of on-campus winter term projects.

The Experimental College (ExCo)

Oberlin's Experimental College, or ExCo, began in 1968 as an experiment in alternative education. Four decades later, ExCo is still an integral part of campus life, with more than sixty courses offered each semester.

ExCo is a student-run organization, headed by a volunteer committee that is responsible for choosing the curriculum and maintaining the integrity of the program.

ExCo is open to everyone in the Oberlin community, including students, faculty and staff members, and townspeople. Likewise, anyone who proves to be an expert in a particular subject can teach a class, as long as it is judged to have educational merit and a reasonably serious purpose.

ExCo reflects the current academic, intellectual, social, ideological, philosophical, political, emotional, sexual, and fashion trends of the Oberlin community. The most recent ExCo curriculum has included courses on grassroots organizing, environmental justice, Cantonese language, Indian film, Hip-Hop dance, sketch comedy, vegetarian cooking, knitting, and rock climbing.

Students may receive up to five credits toward graduation through the Experimental College, or they may take as many courses as they'd like for no credit. ExCo instructors receive credit for teaching ExCo courses.

SOCIAL LIFE AND ACTIVITIES

Residence Halls

Oberlin is a residential campus; all first-year students and the majority of other students live in the residence halls on campus. Housing options include single-sex and coed dorms, on-campus apartments, language houses (i.e., French House), special-interest houses (i.e., Afrikan Heritage House), and co-ops (Tank Hall). On-campus housing is guaranteed for four years and is assigned by lottery.

Student Cooperative Housing (Co-ops)

The Oberlin Student Cooperative Association (OSCA) provides students with an alternative to traditional college housing and dining options. Student-owned and operated, Oberlin's co-ops cultivate community by encouraging members to take responsibility for their own living environments. Co-op members share cooking, housekeeping, and maintenance tasks, and use a participatory, demo-cratic approach to settling co-op policy and resolving disputes. All co-op duties involve flexible hours and take into account students' class schedules, interests, and skills.

Athletics

Whether they're playing varsity sports or intramurals, Obies find the camaraderie, competition, and physical challenge of athletics the perfect complement to their academic pursuits. The College sponsors twenty-two varsity sports (eleven for women and eleven for men), fourteen club sports (including Ultimate Frisbee, scuba diving, martial arts, and cheerleading), and an ever-changing roster of intramural for both students and college employees.

Student Organizations

With more than eighty student organizations to choose from, Oberlin has something for everyone. Students can write for *The Oberlin Review*, sing *a cappella* tunes with the Obertones, toss a Frisbee on Tappan Square with members of the Flying Horsecows, or get active in politics with the OC Democrats.

Many student groups celebrate the diversity of cultures, ethnicities, and identities that can be found on campus. At Oberlin, student groups exist for those of African, Caribbean, Chinese, Korean, Latino, and Philippine descent, as well as for those who are Muslim or Jewish. Other groups exist for those who identify themselves as lesbian, gay, bisexual, or transgendered.

Music at Oberlin

Music and Oberlin are practically synonymous. Each year, the Conservatory hosts more than 400 concerts, including performances by faculty members and students, as well as guest appearances by visiting artists. Oberlin's annual Artist Recital Series brings premier, internationally renowned performers to campus, while alumni musicians frequently return to perform or teach master classes.

But the Conservatory isn't the only musical game in town. The Student Union brings big-name acts such as Bela Fleck and Rufus Wainwright to Finney Chapel's stage, while the Cat in the Cream Coffeehouse opens its doors to popular folk artists such as Sujan Stevens as well as to local and campus bands. And don't forget the 'Sco, where Oberlin's DJs spin everything from rap to rock, and where '80s night has achieved near-cult status.

Films, Theater, and Dance

An average year at Oberlin includes more than 200 film showings, two operas, and more than 60 theater and dance productions. Aside from the performances sponsored by the Theater and Dance program, many student organizations stage their own productions, and student filmmakers regularly hold screenings of their original works.

Volunteer Activities

Oberlin's long history of social engagement lives on in today's students, fifty-five percent of whom participate annually in volunteer activities. The Center for Service and Learning (CSL) organizes many of these service opportunities by pairing student volunteers with local community partners. The CSL also develops programs that combine community involvement with students' intellectual and artistic pursuits, and sponsors conferences and other events to nurture the relationship between the college and community.

FINANCIAL AID

With a price tag of $43,146 a year, many applicants may think that an Oberlin education is out of reach. But that's not true. Oberlin's historic dedication to an economically diverse student body means that nearly all funding from the Office of Financial Aid has been committed to students and families in financial need. Financial aid at Oberlin is need-based. It includes a combination of grants, loans, and student employment.

In a recent year, approximately sixty percent of Oberlin's students received a total of nearly $40 million in need-based financial aid. The average first-year award for that year was $22,500, which included an average of $17,500 in grants and $5,000 in loans and work-study earnings. A student's financial aid eligibility extends for eight semesters (ten for double-degree students) or until graduation, whichever comes first.

Financial aid applications are mailed to all prospective students with Oberlin's admissions material. Oberlin uses the College Scholarship Service's (CSS) PRO-FILE form, as well as the Free Application for Federal Student Aid (FAFSA) to calculate family contributions and financial aid awards for all first-time applicants. The College also considers parental income and assets, benefits, noncustodial parent information (if appropriate), awards from outside agencies, and a student's expected savings from summer employment when awarding aid to each student.

Approximately fifty-seven percent of all Oberlin students work part-time jobs on campus or in the surrounding town. Many opportunities exist for students to fulfill their work-study contracts, such as shelving books in the library, doing clerical work in an academic department, or earning money by working in one of Oberlin's cafeterias.

The deadline for financial aid applications is February 15.

GRADUATES

Oberlin College graduates have gone on to make lasting impressions in the sciences and humanities, often receiving praise and recognition along the way. Oberlin can claim three Nobel Prize winners and seven MacArthur Fellows as alumni, as well as numerous Javits, Mellon, and Watson Fellows, Marshall and Goldwater Scholars, and Fulbright Grant recipients.

Many Obies have gone on to earn Ph.D.s at the nation's most esteemed graduate and professional schools. In the last two decades, more Oberlin students received Ph.D.s than did students from any other predominantly undergraduate liberal arts college in the country. Not only do Obies attend the nation's top graduate schools, they teach there, too. Oberlin graduates can be found teaching at almost every one of the nation's top sixty colleges and universities.

SUMMING UP

Oberlin is a small community. On or off campus, it's easy to get to know your classmates and professors, and to form lasting ties with local residents. While some people might find a small-town atmosphere confining, a visit to Oberlin and the surrounding campus would most probably change their minds.

With a world-class Conservatory and some of the most forward-thinking members of their fields teaching in the College of Arts and Sciences, life at Oberlin is anything but dull. The constant stream of concerts, operas, theater productions, dance recitals, poetry readings, distinguished speakers, and other campus visitors creates a cosmopolitan climate that rivals that of a university in a big city. Not to mention all the impromptu gatherings and groups that evolve as students come and go, creating a vibrant, intellectually charged environment that is uniquely Oberlin.

An Obie's connection to campus doesn't stop after graduation. Oberlin alumni are a fiercely loyal crew, returning year after year to celebrate Commencement/Reunion Weekend and staying in touch with classmates through regional alumni groups. It's an old joke that an Obie can spot a fellow Obie a mile away, but there is some truth to that statement. Oberlin graduates can be found in all walks of life and at all corners of the globe, and they are always happy to share their memories about their alma mater with prospective students, or to reminisce about sunny afternoons in Wilder Bowl.

❑ *Sue Angell, B.A.*

Occidental College
Los Angeles, CA 90041

(323) 259-2700; (800) 825-5262
Fax: (323) 341-4875

E-mail: *admission@oxy.edu*
Website: *www.oxy.edu*

 Enrollment:

Full-time ❑ women: 1,170
　　　　　❑ men: 905

Part-time ❑ women: 10
　　　　　❑ men: 4

INTRODUCING OCCIDENTAL COLLEGE

　　The phrase "urban oasis" is often used to characterize Occidental, and in many ways it's an apt description of the liberal arts college situated on 120 acres in Los Angeles, just eight miles northeast of downtown. Students stroll about in nearly perpetual summertime and do their reading sprawled on the grass by the quad; classes often migrate outdoors. And yet insofar as "oasis" conjures a disconnect from the world beyond, it's misleading; Oxy students and faculty are deeply involved in wider cultural and civic life.

Oxy graduates are rightfully proud of their intellectually rigorous and broad liberal arts education, and will tell you that the work here is highly demanding. Current students love to gripe—and alumni, to brag—about the comprehensive exams or theses that all thirty-three majors require prior to graduation. And yet learning at Oxy is far from a harsh and competitive exercise; with a student-to-faculty ratio of ten to one, and a faculty as stirred by teaching as by their own research, it's impossible not to get to know your professors on an individual level. Professors regularly mentor students who choose to embark on independent patterns of study, sponsor student research and grant applications, and hang out with students at barbecues or even invite them to holiday dinners. It's learning in the truest sense, the sort that mingles lectures with life, and an education here inspires in students real intellectual curiosity—a majority of students go on to attend grad school, and they are highly competitive for national honors and awards (Occidental is one of the country's top producers of student Fulbright Award winners).

> **"** *At Oxy, professors knew me on a first-name basis. I had their home phone numbers and could call in the middle of the night, tell them I'm applying for this or that scholarship, last-minute, that I need a letter of recommendation. I developed this great relationship with the Bio chair; she didn't say, 'You're an English major, you can't do a research project on biodiversity.' I went to a sustainability conference in Vietnam. None of my requests to do undergraduate research were ever turned down.* **"**

—*Libby Evans, '06*

Diversity, in all its forms, is a fundamental value at Occidental, and its 2,102 person student body is one of the most racially, geographically, and socioeconomically diverse in the nation. In our increasingly interconnected world, intellectual muscle is most useful when combined with cultural and social literacy, and in this sense Oxy students learn much from each other. More than three quarters of students receive financial aid, and elite prep school graduates blend with those from inner-city public high schools. Almost every world religion is represented—more than a dozen Protestant denominations, plus Catholics, Jews, Muslims, Hindus, Buddhists, and Sikhs—and all are welcome to worship at the nondenominational Herrick Chapel. First-year students share a residence hall with the people in their core classes, and classroom discussions spill into the dorms. There is a feeling of community and camaraderie among students and a common desire to unite the intellect with the heart, theory with practice, to make a difference in the world.

Some eighty percent of students live on campus, while some upperclassmen choose to find housing nearby. Most venture out regularly into LA, on organized excursions or on their own, partaking in the endless panorama of music, theater, art, dance, food, nightlife, and culture. It's a quick drive to the coast—to some of the most famous beaches in the world—or to the Angeles National Forest where students often go to hike and perhaps take a dip in the natural pools around Switzer Falls. Campus, all the while, remains as busy as ever: a quarter of students participate in twenty-one intercollegiate sports and hundreds more compete in intramural and club sports such as rugby, lacrosse, and Ultimate Frisbee. Some one hundred clubs sponsor all manner of events. Theaters on campus hum with student plays, dance productions, and concerts.

ADMISSIONS REQUIREMENTS

This is the section that sets hearts racing and palms sweating. "*If only* I had started taking SAT prep courses in middle school," you think. "*If only* I had joined fifteen clubs and sports teams instead of twelve. *If only* . . . " As is the case with the rest of the schools listed in this book, the admissions statistics at Occidental are impressive and daunting. The acceptance rate currently hovers around forty-two percent and will likely continue to fall, as it has nearly every year for the past decade. More than ninety percent of

---

FILMING LOCATION

First-time visitors to the picturesque Occidental College campus may encounter déjà vu—the place seems perennially familiar. This makes sense given that Oxy has been a popular film and TV location for more than eighty years, beginning with MGM's *Cup of Fury* in 1919. Its proximity to Hollywood and its unique and beautiful campus make Oxy a favorite of directors and location scouts. Students often drop by the shoots to watch the process unfold in front of their eyes—before seeing it again on-screen. You might recognize Occidental from such movies as (from old to new):

- ○ *Horse Feathers* (1932) with the Marx Brothers
- ○ *She Loves Me Not* (1934) with Bing Crosby and Kitty Carlisle
- ○ *That Hagen Girl* (1947) with Shirley Temple and Ronald Reagan
- ○ *Pat and Mike* (1952) with Katharine Hepburn and Spencer Tracy
- ○ *The Tall Story* (1960) with Jane Fonda and Anthony Perkins
- ○ *Midnight Madness* (1980) with Michael J. Fox and Pee Wee Herman
- ○ *Real Genius* (1985) with Val Kilmer
- ○ *For the Boys* (1991) with Bette Midler and James Caan
- ○ *Clueless* (1995) with Alicia Silverstone
- ○ *Jurassic Park 3* (2000)
- ○ *Orange County* (2002) with Colin Hanks and Jack Black
- ○ *The Kids Are All Right* (2010) with Annette Bening and Julianne Moore

Or from such TV shows as *NCIS*, *Monk*, *Dragnet*, *The West Wing*, *Charmed*, and *Beverly Hills 90210*.

---

accepted students in the class of 2014 were in the top quarter of their high school class. Keep in mind, however, that a student's place on the statistical continuum is only one factor among many; Occidental evaluates applicants in a holistic manner that takes into account the whole person, the wide variety of passions and circumstances that GPA and SAT scores do not reflect. Students here often recall being pleasantly surprised by an admissions process that viewed them as human beings rather than reducing them to the sum of their statistically measurable parts.

Occidental seeks to enroll students who bring to the table a wide variety of talents and experiences, and who possess the intellectual curiosity and muscle necessary to take full advantage of its rigorous and stimulating liberal arts education. Competition for admission to Occidental and other top colleges is fierce and becoming fiercer, which can have the unfortunate effect of transforming high school into an anxiety-ridden experience. Too often in high school, frantic and shallow resume-building takes the place of other more valuable modes of exploration and maturation. Enrolling in every AP course and participating in a full load of extracurricular activities can be positive, certainly—but not if doing so impinges significantly on your ability to pursue your truer interests. Oxy is most interested in students who excel from a place of personal authenticity, rather than boilerplate candidates whose search for collegiate prestige undercuts their individuality. This does not imply that test and GPA scores don't count—they do—but there are also candidates who stand out from the crowd by capitalizing on their own uniqueness.

It goes without saying, then, that applicants to Occidental should opt for honesty and openness. Don't attempt to shoehorn yourself into the role you think Oxy wants you to play, which will inevitably cause you to come off as wooden and uninspired. Writing the essays will of course be challenging, but it shouldn't prove unduly painful. You've already done the heavy lifting—years of coursework, sports games, club meetings, living life—and here's your chance to tell your story to a friendly audience. The application for fall admission—Oxy uses the Common Application accompanied by a supplemental form—is due on January 10. Early Decision applications should be filed by November 15. Either the SAT or ACT is required (average SAT verbal score was 640, math, 650; writing, 650; ACT, 29). High school course requirements include four years each of English and math, three each of foreign language and science, and two each of social studies and history. The writing sample and interview are voluntary, but they will help the admissions committee get to know you—and therefore are a very good idea.

Academic work at Occidental is consistently challenging, but not in a dry and overly cerebral way. Students are encouraged to integrate life experience into intellectual conversation and to apply academic ideas toward understanding and navigating our complex and interconnected world. The broad diversity of the student body is of great service in this regard, and all are encouraged to engage the alternate worldviews of their peers—particularly in first-year cultural studies seminars and colloquia, which set the tone for the rest of the Occidental experience. First-year students choose from seminars in a variety of disciplines, each designed to examine large liberal arts questions; recent subjects include: "The Politics of Art in China" (art history and the visual arts), "Magical Realism and the Fantastic in Latin America" (English and comparative literary studies), "Why Crickets Sing: An Introduction to the Interdisciplinary Study of Music" (music), and "Science and You—A Needlessly Complicated Relationship" (science). Seminars are capped at 16 students, all of whom live together in the same dorm.

66 *My freshman year I lived in a dorm at the top of campus, and in the morning a bunch of us would head down the hill together to our core seminar, an art history course called 'Reading and Writing about Visual Experience.' That stroll, and lunch afterwards in the quad, was as much a part of the seminar as was our time in the classroom. I don't mean to imply that we spent our days and nights engaged in a formal debate about Griselda Pollock's feminist critique of modernist art history—but rather that as our intellectual and personal lives intertwined, conversation bridging the two realms began to feel natural and fluid. Late on a Tuesday evening a few of us might've been tossing a Frisbee in the hallway at the dorm, laughing about an improv show we'd seen earlier that evening, and brainstorming ideas for a paper contrasting the scholarly worldviews of Michel de Certeau and Dick Hebdige. Occasionally, our professor would come to us instead of the reverse, trekking up the hill and holding class or office hours in the common room of our dorm—and we scarcely had to change out of our pajamas.* 99

The first-year cultural studies seminars and colloquia, and the communities surrounding them, are an essential part of the college's Core program, which is designed to support rich liberal arts values throughout the Occidental experience. Students at Oxy become conversant across a wide breadth of academic disciplines and learn to approach their chosen field from an interdisciplinary perspective that also takes into account the intermixture of cultures, languages, religions, and historical narratives that constitute the world today. One society or set of ideas is hardly understandable these days in isolation from its neighbors, as underscored by our increasingly effective and affordable technologies of communication and transportation, and postmodern interpretations of self and country. As such, the Core program emphasizes global literacy and requires that all students take at least three courses that touch on at least three disparate geographical areas, for instance, Africa and the Middle East; Asia and the Pacific; Europe; Latin America; and the United States. Further, all students fulfill requirements in the fine arts and in the sciences, mathematics, or other courses that address formal methods of reasoning; they also become proficient in one or more foreign languages. Finally, students must demonstrate proficiency in writing, a skill that develops organically given the large amount of writing that many classes require.

Of course, this liberal arts framework would be meaningless without stellar teaching, which is the fundamental ingredient of an Occidental education. Professors engage passionately in their own research, but their first and foremost responsibility is in the classroom. Consequently, Oxy attracts professors who genuinely love to teach and who bring with them an infectious enthusiasm for the subject at hand. Class size is small—average lecture size is 21; laboratory, 16; regular course, 17—and discussion is integral to many courses. No introductory courses are taught by graduate students. Professors are very much part of campus life outside of the classroom, and you will often find professors and students ambling about together, engaged in lively intellectual conversation. Few professors adhere strictly to posted office hours and will generally tolerate—if not welcome—unarranged knocks on their doors.

> 66 *The professors are the best part about Oxy. I went to a high school where my graduating class was nineteen kids. I was close to my teachers there, but I was even closer to my professors at Oxy. In fact, I still keep in touch with my professors, all the time, and they're still there for me two and a half years after I graduated. I have a couple of professors to thank for helping me get the job I have now, as an assistant producer at National Public Radio. They knew me well enough to make strong recommendations, and helped me get good journalism internships when I was in school. Of course, you have to show initiative—but if students show initiative, the support is there for them.* 99

—Ben Bergman, '04

Students at Occidental commonly seek out internships and independent research opportunities, and faculty serve as willing mentors and advocates. Over the past five years, more than 560 Occidental students have received funding to undertake joint summer research with faculty, which often results in coauthored publications in peer-reviewed journals. Occidental traditionally sends more student presenters to the Southern California Conference on Undergraduate Research than any other participating school, and over the past five years has sent 150 students to make presentations at the National Undergraduate Research Conference. Undergraduate students from all majors are invited to pursue research opportunities that at larger universities are typically open only to high-achieving graduate students, and the college is routinely recognized for excellence in this realm, such as by the National Science Foundation, which conferred on Occidental its Integration of Research and Education Award in 1998. As far as internships go, opportunities in Los Angeles are limited only by the imagination, and students fan out to a wide array of organizations, such as the *Los Angeles Times*, NASA's Jet Propulsion Laboratory, UCLA Medical Center, and DreamWorks Studio.

As an institution dedicated to educating citizens of a pluralistic world, Occidental encourages all students to participate in off-campus study. Each year, roughly a third of the junior class heads off to more than fifty programs in dozens of countries; a student might study tropical biology at a field research station in Costa Rica, perhaps, or research international development and democratization in Hanoi, Vietnam. Some students choose to take part in domestic exchange options, such as the semester-long Occidental-at-the-United Nations program, one of the few of its kind in the country, in which students live and take classes in New York City while interning in the U.N.-related organizations and NGOs. Students who wish to pursue research abroad may also participate in off-campus summer research programs. Occidental is one of a dozen institutions selected to participate in the

RESEARCH OPPORTUNITIES

Students at Occidental have access to a wide breadth of research opportunities and funding sources as early as their freshman year. For instance, Oxy is one of only a dozen institutions selected to participate in the Richter Summer Research Program, which has awarded more than $1 million in research grants to students since 1969. Oxy students of all majors may apply to receive Richter grants to support independent research or creative work abroad; past projects include:

○ Gender Inequality in South Korea
○ The Role of Russian Art as a Bridge Between Western and Eastern Art
○ Community-Based Conservation for the Protection of Sharks in Costa Rica
○ Reconciling Tradition and Trend-Hip Hop/Flamenco in Spain
○ Human Capital Development in Zambia

Richter Summer Research Program, which funds independent research projects or creative work; recent Richter projects by Occidental students include "Media Freedom in Post-1997 Hong Kong," "Illicit Asian Art Trade, London, England," and "Ideology and Normalcy, Paris, France."

Even when abroad, students remain solidly connected to the Occidental community back in Los Angeles. Friends and professors clamor for updates—with pictures, if possible. It wasn't long ago, after all, that these savvy world travelers were arriving to that first freshman seminar, then heading back to the dorms with their sixteen pals. It's remarkable how enduring those friendships can be. And likewise, the Occidental ethos—defined differently by whomever you ask, but certainly including intellectual curiosity, cultural engagement, and service to the community—sticks with students and continues to influence them, whatever direction they may take.

SOCIAL LIFE AND ACTIVITIES

Living in Los Angeles is inextricably part of the Occidental experience, and even the most extroverted students find that by graduation they've exhausted only a fraction of the resources the city has to offer. A student interested in museums, say, might begin by exploring the Norton Simon Museum, home to one of the world's finest collections of European, American, and Asian art, situated just a few miles from Oxy in bustling Old Town Pasadena. In the months and years following, he or she might spend time at the LA County Museum of Art, the Japanese American National Museum, the Getty Center and the newly redesigned Getty Villa, UCLA's Hammer Museum, the Museum of Neon Art, and countless other museums and art galleries throughout the city. The theater and music scenes are equally robust, as you might expect in a city brimming over with world-class actors and musicians. Thousands of restaurants serve up every possible type of cuisine, and bars and nightclubs run the gambit from kitschy karaoke dives to swanky Hollywood hot spots. Some students have cars, while others catch Bengal Busses—free shuttles named for the Oxy mascot, a Bengal tiger, that ferry students to and from rotating destinations throughout the city. An Oxy club, Arts L.A., sponsors biweekly outings to museum exhibits, plays, film festivals, and other arts events.

Walking is also a very good option. Occidental is nestled in the northeastern Los Angeles neighborhood of Eagle Rock, which has become increasingly hip in recent years, with colorful boutiques and eateries joining such long-time student hangouts as the burrito joint Señor Fish and the Italian restaurant Casa Bianca, serving arguably the best pizza in Los Angeles. (New restaurants aside, some Oxy students claim that the tastiest food comes from homegrown "taco trucks" that set up shop each evening on nearby avenues.) The area immediately surrounding Oxy is mostly residential, a multicultural and mixed-socioeconomic neighborhood where many professors choose to live. Students are actively involved in the Eagle Rock community, particularly those affiliated with the Occidental Urban and Environmental Policy Institute, a college major which also serves as an umbrella organization for a variety of research and advocacy programs addressing work and industry, food and nutrition, housing, transportation, regional and community development, and urban environmental issues.

Regardless of the many adventures to be had in this vast metropolis, however, the Oxy campus remains filled with life; drop by for a visit, and you'll understand why students choose to stick around. The campus itself is airy and beautiful, a pocket of tranquility amid urban sprawl, and given the small student body it's rare to go anywhere on campus without bumping into friends. Come mealtimes, students choose between two dining options: the Tiger Cooler, popular for lunchtime and late-night snacking, is a grill serving all manner of hot and cold sandwiches, wood-fired pizza, sushi, smoothies, and frozen yogurt. The Marketplace, where most students take dinner and breakfast, is organized by station; for instance, there are stations for deli, home-style, grill and wok, and pasta, as well as a bakery and a fully stocked salad bar. Much of the food at the Marketplace is cooked-to-order—try the salmon and asparagus over rice, a perennial favorite. Suffice it to say that students remain well and happily fed.

The college maintains a full schedule of programs and entertainment, such as student plays and other theater productions held in two large theaters or outside in a Greek-style amphitheater, movies, concerts given by students and professional musicians, wildly popular dance productions, a variety of lecture series, and on-campus parties such as the elaborate casino-style themed shindig, "Da Getaway." There are always plenty of unofficial parties and get-togethers on and off campus, including those thrown by Oxy's modest Greek community (ten percent of men belong to fraternities; fifteen percent of women, to sorori-

BIRTHDAY DUNKING

Students at Occidental learn quickly that when your birthday rolls around, it's best to wear something that will survive a drenching. You never quite know when it's coming, but at some point on your birthday, friends may nab you, carry you down to the Gilman Fountain at the front of campus, and gingerly (it's shallow!) toss you in. Campus safety officers apparently dislike this tradition, but they don't do much to stop it. The good news is that this is sunny Los Angeles, so you can air dry on grassy slopes nearby while you plot your revenge.

ties). Clubs and groups meet all over campus; find your interest among the many choices— chess, choir, orchestra, improv comedy, musical theater, either side of the political spectrum, student government, photography, forensics, Occidental College Radio (KOXY), religious communities. Student publications include the *Occidental Weekly* newspaper, yearbook, and various literary magazines. Students interested in investing can apply to serve on the board of the Blyth Fund, a six-figure portion of Occidental's endowment managed solely by students. Opportunities for quietude and relaxation mingle with the hustle and bustle; enroll in Tai Chi, actually a course in the theater department, or head down to the gym for a yoga class, kick back poolside, or stroll up a dirt pathway to the highest point on campus, a rustic eminence dubbed Fiji Hill. Here you can listen to owls hoot and gaze out across the elegant downtown skyline, the San Gabriel Mountains, or the coast.

Student athletes abound at Occidental, and there are resources for athletes of every level. The college is a member of NCAA Division III, and some twenty-five percent of students participate in women's and men's varsity sports such as basketball, cross-country, golf, soccer, softball, baseball, swimming, tennis, track and field, volleyball, and water polo. Many others play in intramural leagues, and the fields around campus teem with all sorts of balls, sticks, and discs (rugby, lacrosse, Ultimate Frisbee). Surfers lug their boards seaward, and broomball players clear out residence hall common rooms for their gregarious and popular matches.

Athletics are an integral part of the well-rounded Occidental education—"the sweatiest of the liberal arts," one coach calls them—but even top varsity players are expected to keep scholarship on the front burner. Through all that studying, however, teams manage to excel—take the men's basketball team, for instance, which in 2003 became the first in the history of the NCAA Division III tournament to advance from Oxy's conference to the Elite 8. Oxy's football team has won the conference championship for four of the last six years. The Oxy athletic program has produced All-Americans numbering in the hundreds, dozens of Olympians, world record holders and national champions, and professional athletes and coaches. Alumni remain enthusiastic boosters of the athletic program and through the Tiger Club raise hundreds of thousands of dollars each year in support of Occidental athletics.

FINANCIAL AID

The price tag of an Occidental education can be intimidating, but keep in mind that almost eighty percent of students receive some form of financial aid, which renders the cost comparable to those of public institutions. Oxy is dedicated to maintaining a socioeconomically diverse student body, and financial difficulties should not keep anybody from applying. Students hail from a smorgasbord of backgrounds, and those arriving via public high schools actually outnumber their prep school peers. Applicants are automatically considered for a variety of merit-based scholarships, from the Margaret Bundy Scott scholarship ($20,000 annually) to the Achievement Scholarship ($5,000 annually). Merit scholarships are highly competitive and are awarded to students who have demonstrated outstanding academic and extracurricular achievement. Need-based assistance comes in the form of grants, work-study, and student loans. It's important that applicants file the requisite forms on time; the Free Application for Federal Student Aid (FAFSA) and the College Scholarship Service (CSS) Profile are due on February 1, while the Cal Grant application, required of California residents, is due on March 2. In 2009–2010, the average award was $31,883, and the average financial indebtedness of a 2009 graduate was $17,561.

> **❝** *My family was in an unusual financial situation when I applied to Occidental, and it looked on paper like we could afford to pay more than we actually could. If the financial aid office had relied strictly on numbers in putting together my award, I probably would not have been able to attend Occidental. Instead, a financial aid counselor suggested that we submit a letter fleshing out our financial picture, and then promptly responded with an award that was commensurate with the reality of our situation. As is the case with administrators and professors throughout the college, financial aid officers treated me as an individual and sought to understand the nuances of my circumstance. It felt as if we were working together to make this happen, with plenty of goodwill on both our parts.* **❞**

GRADUATES

Describing Occidental alums is no easy task; just as the school seeks to enroll a rich diversity of students, so too do graduates head off to follow their bliss in every conceivable direction. While generalizations in this realm tend to be inexact, it is safe to say that most students leave Oxy with a keen sense of the world's multilayered complexity and a framework through which to navigate that complexity, an enduring intellectual curiosity, and a sense of empathy and social responsibility. The focus at Occidental on merging education with action, theory with practice, produces graduates who are raring to apply their expertise in the real world, and they are highly competitive in the workforce, landing top jobs throughout the public and private sectors. When given the choice, Oxy grads will often pass up a high-paying job for one offering a clear benefit to community and society, and each year a good many choose to exercise those muscles in the Peace Corps and in nonprofit organizations the world over.

Occidental alumni achieve highly in a range of fields and are generally united in their ambition to use scholarly expertise to address real-world problems and concerns.

Writers and Journalists:

○ Steve Coll, '80, a Pulitzer Prize-winning Staff Writer at *The New Yorker*

○ Bill Davis, '80, President, Southern California Public Radio

○ Erik Eckholm, '71, Bureau Chief, *New York Times*

○ Patt Morrison, '74, Columnist, *Los Angeles Times* and Emmy-winning Public Radio Host

○ Rosalind Wiseman, '91, Author of *Queen Bees and Wannabes: Helping Your Daughter Survive Cliques, Gossip, Boyfriends, and Other Realities of Adolescence,* which inspired the movie *Mean Girls.*

Business Leaders:

○ Stephen Cooper, '68, "Turnaround Specialist," Former CEO of Krispy Kreme Doughnuts

○ W. Don Cornwell, '69, CEO of Granite Broadcasting

○ Bruce Fabrizio, '74, President and CEO, Sunshine Makers, Inc.; Founder of EGBAR Foundation (Everything's Going to Be All Right), a National Environmental Education Curriculum for Children

○ J. Eugene Grigsby, '66, President and CEO of the National Health Foundation

○ June Simmons, '64, President and CEO, Partners in Care Foundation, a Nonprofit Dedicated to "Creating Meaningful Change in Health Care Policy and in the Delivery of Health Services"

While some graduates go directly into the workforce and stay there, a majority head to grad school, eventually winding up in academia, education, law, medicine—an array of professions too numerous to mention. Oxy students and grads also contend successfully for national fellowships such as the Fulbright, Marshal, Rhodes, Truman, Luce, Watson, and National Science Foundation Fellowships. Whatever students choose to do with themselves, involvement with Oxy rarely ends on graduation day. Freshman year dorm mates have evolved into lifelong friends, professors are now enduring mentors. These relationships will continue to mature and evolve. Alums form the backbone of Oxy GOLD (Graduates Of the Last Decade), whose chapters, spread across the nation, sponsor all manner of mixers, meals, and events. The Oxy Career Center and other on-campus organizations remain invaluable resources for graduates.

SUMMING UP

The college application process often evokes more angst than excitement about the future, and all that worrying can seriously dampen the high school experience—but need this be the case? One Oxy freshman published an essay in the *Los Angeles Times* arguing for a different vision: "This rat race deserves the rotten reputation it has earned. I've been in the trenches—I graduated from high school last year and am a college freshman now—and I'm here to say there is another way: Follow your heart *and* get into the college right for you." Most folks at

Occidental would echo that sentiment. Students at Oxy are encouraged to appreciate the innate value and joy in education, rather than seeing it as merely a precursor to future prestige. High school students might consider embracing a similar mindset. At least, know that if you choose to apply to Occidental, you will be evaluated as a unique participant in a wonderfully complex world. There is no universal yardstick by which to measure us all.

Oxy is a small, diverse, vibrant intellectual community, set in one of the most stimulating and creative cities in the world. The combination of its mission and location produce "an institution with intimate scale and infinite scope," as former Oxy president Ted Mitchell describes it. Los Angeles serves at once as a playground and a laboratory for students and faculty, while campus remains alive with energy and activity. Students immerse themselves in a chosen discipline— and simultaneously receive wide liberal arts training that puts individual phenomena and ideas into context. They participate in a multitude of sports and clubs, conduct independent research, and study abroad all over the globe. It is a uniformly full and meaningful experience for most students. That said, no single college is right for everyone, and whoever is interested in Oxy is advised to come for a visit, if possible. Arrange with the Admissions Office for an overnight stay in the dorms, if you'd like, or just drop by and have a look around. Knock on doors, chat with students and professors, visit classes, lounge about on a bench with a book, and enjoy the sun.

❏ *Steven Barrie-Anthony, B.A.*

PROMINENT GRADS

Science and Medicine:
- G. Brent Dalrymple, '59, Awarded the 2003 National Medal of Science, Professor Emeritus and Former Dean of Oregon State University's College of Oceanic Atmospheric Sciences
- Richard Casey, '80, Cofounder, Los Angeles Eye Institute
- Eleanor Helin, '54, Principal Investigator for the Near Earth Asteroid Tracking program (NEAT) at the Jet Propulsion Laboratory
- Doug McAdam, '73, Director of the Stanford University Center for Advanced Study in the Behavioral Sciences
- John McCosker, '67, Chair of the Department of Aquatic Biology, California Academy of the Sciences
- Kimberly A. Shriner, '80, Founder of The Phil Simon Clinic; Infectious Disease and HIV Specialist

L. A. Luminaries:
- Alice Walker, '69, Commissioner of the First Five California Children and Families Commission
- Ian Montone, '89, Worldwide Manager of the White Stripes and Other Artists and Owner of Monotone, Inc.
- Steve Roundtree, '71, President of the Los Angeles Music Center

Politics:
- Jack Kemp, '57, Played Professional Football Before Going on to a Career in Politics as a Congressman, Secretary of Health, Education and Welfare, Vice Presidential Candidate and Codirector of Empower America
- Barack Obama, '09, U.S. President, Began His Political Career at Occidental before Transferring to Columbia University

PITZER COLLEGE

Photo by Gabriela Contreras

Pitzer College
Claremont, CA 91711-3908

(909) 621-8129
Fax: (909) 621-8770

E-mail: *admission@pitzer.edu*
Website: *www.pitzer.edu*

Enrollment:

Full-time ❏ women: 596
❏ men: 420

INTRODUCING PITZER COLLEGE

Pitzer College is the youngest highly competitive liberal arts college in the country, with a progressive spirit that matches its success. Other liberal arts colleges pride themselves on the longevity of their edifices, the strength of their traditions, and the constancy of their vision. Pitzer, in contrast, has undergone continuous change since its founding in 1963 as a women's teaching college. It became coeducational in 1970 and has since broadened its academic foci to encompass the complete liberal arts education. Few original buildings constructed during the 1960s and 1970s remain standing, having been supplanted by modern structures including several LEED Gold-certified residence halls. The students themselves have changed, too: fifty-five percent of the most recent first-year class of this once-local school are not California residents, including dozens of international students. Because of the prevalence of change and the high degree to which students are involved in shaping college policy, the future of Pitzer is a constant topic of conversation on campus.

The entire campus population, from students and staff to professors and the president, is on a first-name basis with each other (no exceptions). Professors host students in their homes (usually walking distance from campus) so frequently as to make the event commonplace. Every semester during finals week, the president and her cabinet serve anxiety-ridden students comfort food for a late-night snack. For one hour during this tense time, a first-year student can politely tell the Dean of Faculty, "Just one more empanada for me, thank you."

ACADEMIC LIFE

Buttressing all of this do-gooder feel-good homey-ness is a body of resources fit for a university fives times Pitzer's size. These resources are derived from the Claremont Consortium, the closest-knit set of liberal arts colleges in the country. In contrast to other American liberal arts consortiums, like the far-flung Seven Sisters or the Tri-College Consortium, the Claremont Colleges are inextricably intertwined. (A passing airplane pilot unfamiliar with the colleges might wonder why the university below has five distinct architectural styles.) When Planet Pitzer feels too small, Pitzer students need only step across the street in order to venture out into a friendly universe of 4,000 similarly intelligent and passionate college students.

The individual resources and facilities of Scripps College, Harvey Mudd College, Claremont McKenna College, and Pomona College, combine for unparalleled access to information and services. Campus Safety, the Chaplains' Office, the Chicano/Latino Student Affairs Office, the Office of Black Student Affairs, and Student Health and Counseling services are all shared.

This interdependence also applies to academics. Claremont Colleges students enjoy easy registration away from their home campus, and Honnold-Mudd Library serves all Claremont University Consortium students with more than two million volumes and access to dozens of electronic databases. The annual "Turf Dinner," put on by upperclassmen every September, showcases the dozens of five college student organizations that bring all

Claremont students together. Often the strongest personal relationships across colleges are built from these organizations. And, of course, all seven dining halls across the Claremont Colleges are open to all Claremont College students.

Pitzer's academic program is defined by its interdisciplinarity and its extraordinary flexibility. Students strive to achieve Pitzer's stated educational objectives: breadth of knowledge, understanding in depth, critical thinking, interdisciplinary perspective, intercultural understanding, and social responsibility. To graduate from Pitzer, a student has to complete thirty-two credits in a system in which almost all courses at the Claremont Colleges count for a single credit. There are only five distribution requirements, all of which can be satisfied in dozens of different ways. For example, most Pitzer students fulfill the "interdisciplinary and intercultural exploration" requirement by studying abroad for at least a semester, but they can also enroll in a coordinated set of courses that discusses another culture from multiple perspectives. The science and mathematics requirements are, frankly, lax, but many students take several math or science courses even if they have nothing to do with their major.

The most structured requirement is perhaps the first-year writing seminar, in which incoming first-year students choose from one of more than a dozen courses taught by established Pitzer professors who go through the nuts and bolts of academic writing.

The final hallmark of Pitzer academics is the ease with which students can cross-register at other Claremont Colleges. Pitzer students can not only easily enroll in other courses—they can also major in a discipline housed at another college if it is not offered at Pitzer. This allows a student who is passionate about the intercultural and social aspects of Pitzer to pursue every possible academic field.

SOCIAL LIFE AND ACTIVITIES

Pitzer is located in perhaps the best rendition of a New England-style college town on the West Coast. "The Village," as it's known, is directly southwest of the Claremont College and boasts a calculatedly charming array of restaurants, sports bars, bakeries, hair salons, pharmacies, and specialty stores. The "new" Village, which was completed just a couple of years ago, brought in a jazz club, a movie theater, cheap and trendy restaurants, and a central courtyard with modern fountains that quickly became a makeshift venue for live musical performances by local bands.

Claremont is the easternmost town in Los Angeles County, giving credibility to Pitzer students' claims that they go to school "in LA." Claremont-dwellers can reach one of the most exciting urban centers in the world by walking to the local MetroLink stop, which leads directly into downtown Los Angeles. Those with cars can take the 10 west, through downtown, until it empties into the beaches of Malibu. Driving northeast from Claremont for twenty minutes drops you on Mount Baldy of the San Gabriel mountains, which allows students to lounge on the tree-dotted grassy mounds while they look up onto a snow-capped peak.

The Inland Empire may get a bad rap for its cuisine, but Pitzer's off-campus eating options are plentiful, unpretentious, and cheap. Pitzer is within easy walking or biking distance to Trader Joe's, Target, In-N-Out Burger, Chipotle, and Legend's Burgers. One Claremont favorite is Sushi Cruise, a cheap sushi joint shaped like a massive boat, which regularly draws students and professors alike to sample sashimi and sake bombs. The famed fresh strawberry doughnuts of Glendora's "The Donut Man" attract patrons from as far as Malibu, but are just a forty-five minute bike ride from campus (a bit of a trek, but it's open all night).

Claremont also has a big-league concert venue in its backyard: the Glass House in Pomona has hosted Girl Talk, Rilo Kiley, No Doubt, OK Go, Bad Religion, Pavement, Chromeo, NOFX, TV on the Radio, the Black Keys, and hundreds of others. Within a fifteen-mile radius is an enviable supply of massive shopping malls and outdoor shopping complexes (although many Pitzer students express an inexplicable aversion to such commercialized diversions).

A unique aspect of Pitzer's location is its proximity to struggling communities. The nearby city of Ontario is home to Pitzer's Ontario Program, which studies the local government of that city through the lens of local leadership and social responsibility. Pomona Valley Hospital provides future physicians access to internships that provide access to medically underserved communities.

ADMISSIONS REQUIREMENTS

Successful applicants emphasize their commitment to Pitzer's core values through their essays, résumé, and interview. It is simply not sufficient to match the median GPA and SAT score of the incoming class; applicants must show how they will contribute to that class. Applicants who apply as if Pitzer is a "safety school" will not be admitted if they do not demonstrate that they understand the Pitzer ethos.

- ○ Amazing Race LA
- ○ Angeles High Country Backpacking
- ○ Athletes Trip
- ○ Cuyamaca Backpacking
- ○ Developing Leadership Vision
- ○ High Sierra Backpacking
- ○ Jennie Lakes Backpacking
- ○ Kayaking Catalina
- ○ LA Arts & Culture
- ○ LA Food & Coffee Culture
- ○ Mind/Body Adventure
- ○ Pedal to the Pacific
- ○ Sailing to Catalina
- ○ Sespie River Fishing & Fun
- ○ Social Justice in Action
- ○ Southern California Surf
- ○ S.T.A.G.E.
- ○ Sustainability in Action

Pitzer stresses interviews. Every Early Decision applicant is required to interview, and interviews are all but absolutely required for all other applicants. Because some applicants may not be able to visit campus for reasons physical or financial, Pitzer now accepts video interviews through a service called MyCollegeI. This allows students to express their creativity and philosophy from anywhere in the world.

Pitzer's optional standardized testing policy allows applicants greater flexibility in representing their diverse academic abilities, talents, and potential. Pitzer allows students to forego submitting their SAT or ACT scores by meeting any of several conditions: graduating in the top ten percent of their class, earning an unweighted cumulative grade-point average of 3.50 or higher in academic subjects, submitting at least two Advanced Placement test scores of at least four (one must be in English or English Language, and one in mathematics or a natural science), submitting at least two International Baccalaureate exams: one must be in English 1A and one must be in the Mathematics Methods (Standard Level or a higher-level course in mathematics), or submitting two exams: one junior or senior year graded, analytical writing sample from a humanities or social science course, and one mathematics examination, preferably a final or end-of-semester exam in the most advanced mathematics course possible (at least at the algebra II level). The samples must include the teacher's comments, grades, and the assignment. Many applicants take advantage of this opportunity to demonstrate their intellectual potential in a more personal way.

Immediately west of campus is the W.M. Keck Science Center, which serves Claremont McKenna College, Scripps College, and Pitzer College. This massive, state-of-the-art complex houses laboratories, classrooms, and research areas, hosts twenty-five faculty members from all three colleges, and offers more than fifty science courses—dozens each semester. In keeping with Pitzer's emphasis on interdisciplinarity, biology, chemistry, and physics constitute a single academic department. Each year about fifty students are granted a Bachelor of Science through the Keck Center.

> **❝** *I found that one of the things most undersold in the brochures and campus tours is how it's not only possible but amazing to have a 5C major and take classes at the other colleges. I was a religious studies major, and our senior seminar consisted of about fifteen of us from the other 5Cs. Especially as we began to work on our theses, I could see the influence each of the schools had had on us, but we were all united by our major and had learned to draw on the unique aspects of each of our schools (such as a gender studies perspective from Scripps and political influences from CMC). In the end, my thesis advisors taught at CMC and Pomona, and I loved not only representing Pitzer but seeing the connections with the other fields from other schools.* **❞**

—*Jessica Fitting, '10*

A linguistic study of Pitzer might find the phrase "social responsibility" used more often than any other. Even in fields seemingly removed from bright-eyed idealist impulses, impact on community is part of class discussions.

Pitzer's Community Engagement Center (CEC) is one hub for connecting students with avenues of exploring social responsibility in real communities. One flagship program enables Pitzer students to tutor and mentor youths incarcerated in a juvenile detention facility in nearby La Verne. Through the "Borrowed Voices" program, these youths express their own thoughts and feelings at a Spoken Word event on Pitzer's campus. Other CEC programs forge similar off-campus/on-campus connections: Students who commit their time to the Pomona Economic Opportunity-Day Labor Center work too. Pitzer students donate more than 100,000 hours to community service annually through the college's Community Engagement Center programs and partnerships.

RECENT FULBRIGHT DESTINATIONS

- Cyprus
- Malaysia
- Colombia
- Thailand
- Bosnia-Herzegovina
- Korea
- Spain
- Peru
- Nicaragua
- Hungary
- Malta
- Georgia
- Nepal
- Mexico
- Slovakia
- The Philippines
- Portugal
- Macau
- Indonesia

A key aspect of Pitzer's commitment to intercultural understanding is its outstanding track record in facilitating international experiences for its students. More than seventy percent of Pitzer students study abroad during their time in college, many for an entire year. For those students who are unable to study abroad during the academic year, as some student-athletes are, there are summer programs to Japan, Costa Rica, and other locations. When Pitzer-affiliated programs don't fit a student's academic plan or cultural interest, the Office of Study Abroad works with a student to craft an experience that does.

> 66 *The summer after my freshman year, Pitzer paid for me and six other students to travel to a small town in Mexico for a month and study healing with a* currandera. *We studied healing philosophies, healing practices, and learned from the Temixco culture. Only at Pitzer would this happen.* 99

—*Sarah Maibach, '13*

Social life at Pitzer is as varied and exciting as any metaphor to that effect. There seems to be at least one social event, barbecue, dance party, academic lecture, off-campus adventure scheduled for every minute of every day. The Claremont Colleges offer at least one outlet for revelry per night. Student party planners across the 5Cs seem to have a flair for the elaborate, and at least one party per weekend requires a creative costume. Official Pitzer parties tend to be more organic, the favorite being "Groove at the Grove," which is usually a couple of kegs, a DJ, and a couple of hundred dancing students spilling out from the steps of the Grove House onto the surrounding courtyard and lawn of Brant Clock Tower. On less structured nights, students hop from suite to suite until they reach a critical mass of people. While some ambitious first-years make it a point to party each consecutive night until they just can't take it anymore, the demands of many course loads force students to choose just one or two parties per week. And, every year, a few ambitious seniors make it their mission to party in Las Vegas or Hollywood as many times as humanly possible. But the particular balance of studying, partying, relaxing, and extracurriculars is up to the individual student.

One flagship student organization is Pitzer Outdoor Adventures, which organizes trips to the plethora of natural attractions in the southern California area. Every week, a POA meeting in the Grove House finalizes trip rosters, solidifies trip logistics, and approves future outings. Students active in POA go on several trips a year, but many students wait until they hear of that perfect blend of destination and difficulty before they sign up.

The Green Bike Program is another flagship student organization. The GBP was founded in 2001 by a small group of Pitzer students and professors as an attempt to counter Los Angeles' notorious car culture by encouraging eco-friendly transportation around The Claremont Colleges.

Bikes

The GBP loans bikes to students for any set period of time, repairs broken bikes, and raffles abandoned bikes off to students each semester for free. Due in part to the GBP's efforts, bike culture at Pitzer is huge. There is a dedicated group of hardcore cyclists on campus who regularly take long-distance bike trips, bike up and down Mount Baldy—even play bike polo at a nearby sports field on campus. Anyone associated with the Claremont Colleges can bring his or her bike to the shop for repairs. Finally, the GBP is a de facto social hub of campus. Because of its prime location on Pitzer Road, right in the middle of everything, it is a common sight to see, at 2:00 P.M. on a Tuesday, a group of students blasting a stereo while chatting, sipping lemonade on a makeshift couch, and fiddling with bicycle parts.

This incredible degree of hands-on student-involvement is reflected, first and foremost, in its student government. Pitzer enjoys one of the largest student government bodies in academia, with a ratio of student-to-senator at about 1:20. Student Senate is comprised of class and residence hall representatives and members of committees that address the various facets of college life. For example, one of the busiest is the Aesthetics Committee, which reviews student mural proposals. At Pitzer, new wall murals are painted several times per year.

> 66 *The murals at Pitzer are what really clicked with me when I visited the campus. I had toured over 25 campuses along the east and west coast. Most schools are just buildings. Pitzer's walls have life.* 99

—*Leslie Ching, '11*

College Council meetings are held once per month. Policy proposals that concern the entire college, such as the approval of a new academic major, are discussed by the community. Students, faculty, and staff all have voting power and the opportunity to make themselves heard on any issue, and College Council votes are binding on college policy. Only at Pitzer College do students have the opportunity to impact the functions of the college so directly.

> 66 *After interacting with anarchists, socialists, neo-liberals, libertarians, and realists on a daily basis, I feel as though a career with the UN would be just like any another day at Pitzer.* 99

—Chase Dyer, '11

Student housing at Pitzer is unique among comparable liberal arts colleges, even for Claremont. There is no "party" dorm, "jock" dorm, or "science" dorm. The campus culture is completely defined by the passions and personalities of the students who inhabit it. Thus, the interdisciplinary emphasis carries over from academic life into social life.

> 66 *The Pitzer Activities Committee (PACT) puts on a lot of events for free or reduced price, and I consistently had amazing experiences with Pitzer people on them. One of my favorite (though silliest) moments my senior year was going to a Medieval Times dinner show with my friends on a PACT trip. After watching some jousting and eating a medieval feast with my hands, the announcer said there was a group from Pitzer College at the show—all my fellow Pitzer students around me started cheering and screaming until our voices went hoarse and then he repeatedly returned to our section just because we screamed so loud! That was Pitzer pride to the max.* 99

—Jessica Fitting, '10

Residences

The first-year class resides in a cluster of four three-story residence halls called Atherton, North Sanborn, East Sanborn, and Pitzer Hall. The architecture of the "New Dorms," as they are known colloquially, is such that each hall faces inward toward each other and on the Gold Student Center swimming pool. There is no sorting hat at Pitzer. (If you really want to split hairs: North Sanborn enjoys unobstructed views of the San Gabriel mountains; East Sanborn has the clearest sight lines toward every other residence hall; Pitzer Hall is technically closest to the Pitzer dining hall; and Atherton boasts a music practice room, the mail room, and a classroom.) Because the differences between each residence hall are largely superficial, each incoming student starts his or her college career on equal social footing.

Off-Campus

The Pit-Stop Café, which opened in the Fall of 2010, feeds the hungry people passing through Scott academic courtyard coffee drinks, gourmet sandwiches, wraps, salads, fruit cups, fruit juice, freshly baked pastries, and bagels.

In the heart of the new residential complex is a completely student-run restaurant, the Shakedown Cafe. The Shakedown's menu changes according to the availability of fresh ingredients and the whims of the student chefs, but can generally be counted on to whip up a solid pad thai or chicken burrito. Students can gain valuable experience in food preparation.

Mentors

Critical to the first year experience is the students' first-year mentor group. The Housing Coordinator leads a small committee of people that match incoming first-year roommates "by hand," based on the housing forms completed by each student. These roommate pairs are combined into four-student clusters that share a bathroom. These clusters are further aggregated into groups of ten to eighteen students who constitute a mentor group and an older first-year mentor. Mentors are embedded in the first-year residence halls right next to their "mentees" in order to help students transition to the lawless autonomy of college life. If a first-year student has a serious problem, the mentor is expected to know about it and guide him or her to the resources to help face it. Over three years as a first-year men-

RECENT FIRST-YEAR SEMINAR COURSES

- ○ Rock in Las Americas: From "Refried" Elvis to Punk
- ○ Immigration and Race in America
- ○ California's Landscapes: Diverse Peoples and Ecosystems
- ○ Eradicating Poverty
- ○ On the Trail of the Vampire
- ○ Colonization, Racialization, and Renewal: Indian Nations of Southern California
- ○ Documentaries and the Politics of Dissent
- ○ Living Emma Goldman's Life
- ○ Character Ethics: From Confucius and Aristotle to Jane Austen
- ○ Science of Identity
- ○ Social Justice in Contemporary Europe
- ○ Gene Dreams: The Social Consequences of Genetic Determinism
- ○ Curating: Past & Present

tor, I personally helped my mentees deal with problems ranging from drug and alcohol dependency, mental illness, to social anxiety, as well as mundane, and much more common, issues like roommate communication and choosing classes. Because they live next to each other, students within a mentor group often become inseparable.

GRADUATES

Pitzer College's motto translates to "Mindful of the Future," and the futures of Pitzer graduates are bright. A result of Pitzer's global emphasis is its unparalleled performance in securing J. William Fulbright Scholarships for its students. For the past two years, Pitzer College students were awarded Fulbrights at the highest number per capita in the country. Fully ten percent of the graduating class of 2010 was awarded a Fulbright scholarship—to locales such as Indonesia, Colombia, Spain, and Korea. Pitzer students are also successful in securing positions with Teach for America, the Sacramento Fellowship programs, the Watson Fellowship, and others. The Career Services Center also works hard to connect alumni to graduating seniors.

FINANCIAL AID

Thirty-seven percent of the class of 2014 received financial aid, and Pitzer is committed to meeting one hundred percent of every student's demonstrated financial need. The average cumulative debt after four years of study is $16,000. Pitzer's Financial Aid Office uses the FAFSA and the CSS/Financial Aid PROFILE to determine the amount a student's family can contribute toward the cost of a Pitzer education. Each student is expected to provide between $1,550 and $1,900 for books and personal expenses. Many students work several hours per week in "work-study" positions, which can range from supervising the

Gold Student Center, to re-shelving books in Marquis Library, to assisting in one of the many community engagement programs based on campus.

SUMMING UP

Pitzer is a different sort of liberal arts college. Social responsibility is a key phrase, not an afterthought. International experience is the rule, not the exception. Pitzer is a place where life doesn't fit into neat little boxes: we blur the lines between off-campus and on-campus, between global and local, between academic and social, between individual and community. Because Pitzer was founded in a tumultuous time in American history, it has seen more than its share of physical, topographical, and philosophical change. The real bedrock of Pitzer College is shared values of intercultural understanding, social responsibility, autonomy, and academic excellence. These values reach far across the boundaries of a residence hall, a college, even a country.

❏ *Amy Jasper, B.A.*

Photo by Philip Channing

Pomona College
Claremont, CA 91711

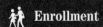

Enrollment

(909) 621-8134

Full-time ❏ women: 765
        ❏ men: 770

E-mail: *admissions@pomona.edu*
Website: *http://www.pomona.edu*

INTRODUCING POMONA COLLEGE

Walking onto Pomona's campus, it is easy to see the similarities between Pomona and the New England liberal arts colleges that inspired it. Los Angeles filmmakers have often used the college as a "stand in" for the campuses of East Coast colleges, featuring Pomona's architecture in *Pearl Harbor* and episodes of *The Gilmore Girls*. Of course, the students sunbathing, studying, and throwing Frisbees on Pomona's main quad in January illustrate one key difference between this college and its peers. Moreover, the Doric columns of the Carnegie Building are not far from the solar panels and rooftop greenhouses of the Seaver biology building, a testament to the meeting of old and new taking place at Pomona.

In 1887 a group of New England Congregationalists founded Pomona College. Their hope was to bring the intellectual rigor of the finest colleges of the East and Midwest to California. The unfinished hotel that housed some of Pomona's first students still stands today, serving as Pomona's admissions building. Like a traditional liberal arts college, Pomona prides itself on small classes, discussion-based education, and the relationships between students and faculty. Walking through Pomona's tree-lined walkways, it becomes clear that Pomona is a small school with big resources. The college builds or renovates at least one academic building and one dorm every year, and the administration has committed itself to building only LEED standard green buildings since 2003.

Pomona College is a coed, residential, nonsectarian liberal arts college located thirty-five miles east of Los Angeles. At Pomona, talented students enter a dynamic community with first-class faculty, melding some of the best qualities of small schools and research universities. The college brings together world-class teachers, a diverse student body, and an administration committed to its students, and places all of this in the sunshine of Southern California.

The Consortium

One of the keys to Pomona's ability to combine big school resources with small school feel is the consortium of colleges to which it belongs. The college grew significantly in the early twentieth century, and administrators faced the challenge of expanding Pomona to serve a larger and more diverse group of students while maintaining the character of a small school. While the liberal arts schools of the East gave the first model for Pomona, the college used Cambridge and Oxford as models to found a consortium of colleges that was new in the United States. Today, Pomona is the largest and most academically diverse of the Claremont Colleges, which include four other liberal arts colleges and two graduate schools. Not only can Pomona students walk to the adjacent schools, but they can also enroll in classes at the other colleges and take advantage of consortium resources such as a 2.5 million-volume library. The consortium also allows Pomona to feel more like a large or small school, depending on the student. Some people spend four years focusing on getting to know 1,535 at Pomona, while others branch out to the more than 5,500 across the consortium.

ADMISSIONS REQUIREMENTS

One question that comes up often on Pomona tours is "How competitive is Pomona?" The answer depends on what you are asking. As an elite liberal arts school, it is no secret that admission to Pomona is competitive. However, the competitive side of Pomona's applicants seems to be left in the admissions office, as Pomona students are often found studying in groups or serving as subjects for each other's psychology studies. It is challenging to get into Pomona, but the campus atmosphere is laid-back once you get here.

POMONA'S MASCOT

Pomona's mascot is the sage hen, a local desert bird. The full story of Pomona's mascot remains shrouded in mystery, though some claim that a uniform misprint changed the Pomona College "Huns" into the "hens," and a surprise winning season cemented the name. As a result, fans at sporting events chant "Chirp! Chirp! Chirp!" as they cheer for their friends.

Starting with the basics, Pomona requires the Common Application, official transcripts, SAT or ACT scores, and two teacher recommendations. Pomona has its own supplements to the Common Application for both the applicant and the applicant's high school. The individual supplement asks for a little more personal data as well as one more writing sample that the college strongly encourages students to submit. Pomona also provides the opportunity for applicants to complete special supplements for the arts, sciences, or athletics. Videos of theater performances, slides of paintings, and athlete profiles are assessed by Pomona faculty, who then submit their evaluations to the admissions committee.

Interviews

As a small college, Pomona prides itself on treating students as more than the weighted sum of their GPAs and test scores. Students are encouraged to submit a photograph with their application to remind admissions officers of the person who is applying to Pomona. Perhaps the best chance to come off the page is by interviewing at Pomona. Applicants can interview when they visit Pomona, though the most relevant conversations usually occur after a student has completed junior year. Students interviewing on-campus meet with an admissions officer or with a Pomona senior to talk about their high school experiences, their passions, and what they hope to do in college. Those who cannot come to campus can interview with an alum in their area. If you plan to interview off-campus, be sure to make that appointment early in your senior year.

Requirements

Just as there is no ideal Pomona student, there is no formula for getting into Pomona. Pomona expects applicants to have taken four years of English, three years of math and foreign language, and two years of lab science and social science. There is no magic number of AP or honors courses, but most students who are admitted to Pomona have taken full advantage of the academic challenges that their high school has to offer.

Talking with Pomona students, one is as likely to meet a semiprofessional cyclist as a state Scrabble champion, so it's not surprising that no particular combination of cocurricular activities are the "right ones" for Pomona. Many of Pomona's applicants have been involved with high school sports, publications, arts, or clubs. More than a laundry list of activities, though, Pomona looks for those students who have demonstrated a commitment to their interests by creating something new or taking on leadership.

Last, know that you have some options when applying to Pomona. Pomona offers three application deadlines: two Early Decision options and one date for regular decision. Early Decision applicants get a decision within seven weeks of the application deadline, while regular decision applicants find out in the spring. While Early Decision has a slightly higher admit rate, the pool is also more competitive. The main benefit of applying early is finding out where you're going to college before everyone else does.

ACADEMIC LIFE

Probably the most significant thing that separates Pomona from some of the other schools in this book is the size of the college. With only 1,500 students total, Pomona is a small college. At Pomona, the average class size is fifteen students and there is one faculty member for every seven students. Even introductory science classes, which are "large" by Pomona standards, break out into small lab sections. The classroom dynamic can vary quite a bit, depending on the professor and the students in a given class, but the vast majority of classes place a premium on student participation. If you learn best by being involved in the process, you want to be at a school like Pomona.

> **❝** *One slogan that speaks to the Pomona College education is 'size matters!' In my second semester at Pomona I took an English class with twelve students and a computer science class with five people. Beware though: with only four other people in the class, there is no 'back of the classroom' to hide in!* **❞**

What it really takes to be successful at Pomona is the willingness to take advantage of the relationships and opportunities that the college offers. Walking into a professor's office to discuss a paper assignment can be the beginning of a relationship that leads to a summer research opportunity, and it is the student who is willing to take advantage who makes the most out of Pomona. You see, there aren't any graduate students at Pomona, which means two things: One, every single class at Pomona is taught by a professor, not a grad student; two, Pomona undergrads end up working as research assistants for their professors, which becomes a huge advantage when they apply to graduate school. In fact, Pomona further encourages student research by funding summer research performed by students and Pomona professors. Students spend their summers at Pomona doing everything from synthesizing experimental pharmaceuticals to translating Frenchwomen's Civil War diaries.

> **❝** *One of the things that I didn't appreciate about Pomona until I got there was the influence that small, discussion-oriented classes had on my education. When I compared notes with friends at other prestigious schools, I found out that they expected to spend their first year or two in lecture halls where professors spoke through a microphone to a crowd of note-takers. To most university students, a discussion session means a break-out session led by a graduate student. At Pomona, academic dialogue is the norm. My college education took place around a small table with faculty and students who were interested in hearing my voice, and it made all the difference.* **❞**

For a school that prides itself on its small size, Pomona offers its students a surprisingly wide array of academic options. The college boasts forty-five academic majors in the natural sciences, humanities, social sciences, and arts. Of course, Pomona students can also design their own major with the help of an advisor and the approval of the college, which has led to the creation of such innovative programs as Peace Studies and Social Justice through Dance. Even the "standard" majors at Pomona benefit from the college's broad strength. Majors such as cognitive science, environmental analysis, and politics, philosophy, and economics take advantage of Pomona's versatility and ask students to think beyond the conventional boundaries of academic disciplines.

The academic breadth available to Pomona students is increased by the school's membership in the Claremont University Consortium. This partnership of five colleges and two graduate schools opens up possibilities to Pomona students. Students at Pomona register for classes at the same time as students across the consortium, and they have access to most of the classes being offered at all seven schools. Students use cross-registration in a variety of ways, from looking for a specialized computer science class at Harvey Mudd to shopping for a statistics class at Pitzer that doesn't meet as early as its Pomona counterpart. Pomona students can take up to half of their classes off Pomona's campus, though the average student takes only a few beyond Pomona's gates.

Given the broad strength of Pomona's programs and the diverse interests of the student body, it shouldn't be surprising that Pomona's most popular major changes virtually every year. Pomona students tend to move around as well: it takes only a one-page form to change a major, so the average Sagehen changes major 2.5 times!

When they enter Pomona, first-year students are paired with an academic advisor based on his or her academic interests as well as personality. While many students go on to change their major and their advisor several times (it's the same one-page form to do both), the relationship between student and advisor is usually a special one. It is not at all unusual to see academic advising taking place over a milkshake at the Coop Fountain, where faculty are given coupons to take students out to eat.

> *After dropping into my psychology professor's office hours a few times, I found myself with an offer to join her research lab as a second-semester freshman. The ability to get involved with research as an undergrad is one of the best parts of being at a school with no graduate students.*

General Education

Pomona recently revised its general education requirements with the goals of providing the most possible openness to its students while maintaining the breadth of a liberal arts education. As a result, Pomona enforces a Breadth of Study requirement for its graduates. While at Pomona, students must take one course in the arts, one in the natural sciences, one in the social sciences, one in mathematics or formal reasoning, and one in history, culture, or ethics. Pomona's academic departments are grouped into these five areas, and students can take any class within the area to satisfy their breadth requirement. For example, one could satisfy the science area requirement by taking "Biology, Gender, and Society," "Topics in Neuroscience," or "The Physics of Music." Likewise, Pomona students can fulfill their math requirement with a course in calculus, statistics, or formal logic. There is no such thing as a GE course at Pomona, so students have a choice in every course that they take.

The result of the broad-based general education system is a lot of academic freedom for students. Pomona requires thirty-two course credits for graduation, and thirty of those courses have to be taken at the Claremont Colleges. It is often possible for students to fulfill several breadth of study courses within their major, freeing up time to minor, double major, study abroad, or take classes for interest. Pomona students must also show proficiency in a foreign language, which can be demonstrated by passing an upper-division course or with an AP, IB, or SAT exam score. Students must also take a semester of physical education, which can be fulfilled by taking anything from ballroom dance to Pilates to archery.

> 66 One of the best teachers I experienced at Pomona was Zayn Kassam. Zayn's religious studies classes were exactly what I wanted from my education: her challenging discourses regularly spilled out into lunch tables, or onto the discussion board on the class website. Of course, Zayn openly refused to lead class discussion, asking every student to take a turn moderating a class. Though she is a nationally awarded teacher, Zayn understands that her strength is not organizing others, but pushing the interpretations and biases that students bring into the discussion. Zayn became the most spirited participant in her own classes, making each person consider their role in the communal meaning-making that we participated in. 99

The most distinctive and well-loved of Pomona's academic requirements is the Critical Inquiry Seminar. During their first semester at Pomona, students must take one of thirty or so seminars offered exclusively to first-year students. The topics for Critical Inquiry Seminars are chosen by the professors who teach them. Often these professors will choose to teach something that they are passionate about, so topics for seminars include "Baseball in America," "Music and the Order of the Universe," "The Graphic Novel," and "Light, Perception, and Art." Though the topics can be lighthearted, first-year seminars are designed to be an introduction to academics at Pomona. Critical Inquiry seminars have low enrollments, usually fewer than fifteen students, and ask students to engage with each other in discussion.

Study Abroad

One of the particularly strong opportunities that Pomona offers its students is its study abroad program. Every year, about half of Pomona's juniors spend a semester abroad in one of fifty programs in thirty-one countries. Pomona also allows students to petition to study in non-Pomona programs, opening the doors for Pomona students to go virtually anywhere on Earth. Pomona's study abroad office keeps a library of books about the countries that it serves, as well as an extensive list of program reviews from past students that include course evaluations, budgets, and recommendations for travel.

> 66 *During my junior year, I spent a semester at Cambridge University in England. The program was a great combination of an academic challenge, a cultural experience, and an opportunity to travel through Europe during the five-week intersession.* 99

For students studying abroad, Pomona tries to make the program as simple and seamless as possible. There is no added cost for studying abroad and financial aid applies. You just pay Pomona tuition as usual and the study abroad office will take care of tuition, housing, and fees, and they will write you a check for your plane tickets. Unlike some other study abroad programs, Pomona also makes sure that your courses from study abroad translate into Pomona credits when you return.

For a number of students, the journey to studying abroad begins in Oldenborg. Oldenborg, or "The Borg," as it is more commonly known, is a combination of a dorm and an international studies hub. Oldenborg houses mostly sophomore students, who live in "halls" grouped by language. The Russian hall, for instance, houses students interested in Russian language and culture, and meets regularly for conversation classes with a foreign language resident who is a native speaker. The hall might also meet to watch a soap opera in Russian or to cook some perogies. Pomona offers language halls for Spanish, French, Chinese, Japanese, Russian, and German, and there are two "theme halls" that students propose each year (past themes include "Middle Eastern Language and Culture" as well as "Dead Languages").

Even for those who don't want to spend a year living in "The Borg," Oldenborg offers an international relations speaker series, an international movie theater, summer travel grants, and a dining hall where the only language that is not allowed is English. And yes, "The Borg" is said to be the inspiration for the twisting halls of the Borg Cube in the *Star Trek* universe.

SOCIAL LIFE AND ACTIVITIES

Campus Life

The thing that eventually sealed my decision to come to Pomona was the feeling that the college was not just a school, but a community. It's hard to quantify, but when you take 1,500 smart, talented people and steep them in Southern California sunshine, something special happens: for instance, no one really talks about grades at Pomona. Sure, there are always a few whispered conversations when papers are handed back, but most of the time Pomona students assume that everyone is working, that everyone is going to struggle with something, and that everyone gets the grades that they get. Stress happens at Pomona too, but Pomona students seem to have a sense of perspective that keeps things in balance.

When speaking about campus life at Pomona, it bears remembering that Pomona is a residential college. That means that most students at Pomona live on campus all four years. As a result, most of what happens at Pomona, well, happens at Pomona. The town of Claremont isn't a college town by any stretch of the imagination, though a new development at the western edge of town has brought movie theaters and more nightlife to the sleepy community. Still, the Claremont Colleges provide most of their own entertainment, which isn't a bad thing. The five colleges host a substantial number of lectures, guest speakers, and musical events during the week, and the consortium opens up to feel more like one big college on the weekends.

Residential Life

The beginning of Pomona's residential college environment is the sponsor group program. The Pomona College housing form, in sharp contrast to other schools, is a full three pages and includes multiple choice, ranking, and essay questions. No, this isn't the last test from the admissions department, but rather the information that a group of juniors and seniors will use to put together the housing for Pomona's first-year students. Most first-year students get roommates, though about twenty percent of first years end up with single rooms. Pomona takes things a few steps farther than "smoking or nonsmoking," asking its incoming students about their sleep schedules, study habits, and taste in music. Because of the extensive housing form, Pomona has an extremely low rate of roommate "breakups," and most people get along well with their first roommate.

Sponsor Groups

After the roommates are in place, Pomona places its first year's "sponsor groups," which are groups of twelve to twenty students whose interests and personalities are similar. The sponsor group is a sort of instant social group when you arrive on campus. Every sponsor group is different, but often, sponsor groups will eat meals together and organize activities throughout the first year. Some sponsor groups hang together through all four years at Pomona. Also living in the sponsor groups are two sophomore "sponsors" who serve as informal mentors through the first year.

Though sponsor groups are only set up for first-year students, Pomona students are guaranteed housing on campus for all four years. Most students choose to take advantage of this because housing in Claremont is not appreciably more affordable, and the majority of campus life takes place on campus. For dorms, the housing at Pomona is pretty good, particularly because Pomona renovates at least one dorm every year. About sixty percent of Pomona's rooms are singles; there are no triples on campus.

SPONSOR GROUPS

The sponsor group has its own language at Pomona. "Sponsors" are the sophomores who live with their "sponsee" freshmen. Your sponsor's sponsors are your "grand-sponsors," and their "sponsees" are your "spaunts" and "spunkles." Relationships between members of the same sponsor group are generally frowned upon, and are given the term "sponcest."

Food

Another reason why Pomona students tend to stay on campus is the food. No, seriously. Obviously, eating in a cafeteria for four years is going to wear on everyone at some point, but the overall quality of Pomona's food is excellent. Every meal features a made-to-order grill, salad bar, pizza, and soup, and some kind of exhibition like custom pizza or custom stir-fry. Make-your-own sandwich day is a big favorite, featuring freshly baked bread, deli meats, and flavored mayonnaises.

The best part of Pomona's meal plan is that meals can be taken at any of the dining halls in the five colleges. Many students are willing to walk a couple of blocks to get a change from the regular fare, and a favorite dining hall is a common subject of debate on campus. Many students try to hit the best of each campus, hitting Harvey Mudd for steak night, Scripps for sushi, and Pomona for Sunday brunch. If that weren't enough, the dining hall menus for the consortium are posted online.

By far and away, though, the most important meal of the day at Pomona is snack. Four nights a week, Frary dining hall opens its doors to give studying students a bowl of Cheerios, some nachos, or a cup of coffee. For some, snack is a chance to grab free calories and a break from the books, and for some it is the social event of the day. The seven *a cappella* groups on campus take advantage of hungry students and the acoustics on the steps outside Frary to give evening concerts. Picture yourself at Pomona, bagel in one hand, watching Men's Blue and White, the oldest all-male *a cappella* group west of the Mississippi, performing Justin Timberlake. This is Pomona.

Cocurricular Activities

Honestly, I'm not even going to try to list the number of clubs and activities at Pomona. There is a conscientious eating club and a meat club. There are numerous campus publications, from poetry journals to newspapers. Pomona's musical ensembles are a great place to start understanding how campus activities work at Pomona. Like most small colleges, Pomona graduates only five or so music majors each year. However, Pomona's music department produces a concert choir, chamber choir, orchestra, concert band, jazz band, and Balinese Gamelan, as well as numerous student ensembles. At Pomona, most of the students who play in the orchestra aren't music majors, but just students who love music. The same goes for programs such as theater, dance, and athletics. The Claremont Colleges Ballroom Dance Company has won six national championships, but the only dance major at the Claremont Colleges is at Scripps. Pomona is a place where you expect to see biology majors writing entertainment columns and anthropology majors singing in a musical.

Athletics

Like other activities at Pomona, sports are a place where Pomona students excel, but not the only focus on campus. Pomona teams up with Pitzer College to compete as a

Division III varsity program, and Pomona's teams regularly play for national champi-onships—though you probably haven't seen them on ESPN. Most of the people who fill the stands at Pomona-Pitzer games are there to cheer on their friends rather than to take part in a collegiate rite of passage.

The games that tend to involve the whole campus are games with consortium rival CMS. Claremont McKenna, Harvey Mudd, and Scripps field varsity sports, and the games between Pomona-Pitzer and CMS are hotly contested and well attended.

Outside the varsity sports scene, Pomona also fields a full complement of club and intramural sports. A number of club sports draw from all five colleges, offering students every-thing from men's Ultimate Frisbee to women's rugby. Finally, Pomona puts on several intra-mural sports each semester. In these informal contests, friends, sponsor groups, academic departments, and even *a cappella* groups face off in spirited competition. While dodge ball and home run derby are enjoying upstart popularity, Pomona's favorite intramural activity is inner tube water polo. For those not familiar with the game, imagine two teams rowing inner tubes across a pool while trying to throw a ball into a goal. You have to see it to believe it.

Off-Campus Activities

With Pomona's proximity to Los Angeles, a lot of people want to know how often the average Pomona student gets off campus. The answer depends on the student. Some students take advantage of internships in the Los Angeles area, go to art openings down-town, and regularly venture out to see concerts at the Hollywood Bowl or House of Blues. Other students content themselves with working in a professor's research group, going to the Pomona College Museum of Art, and seeing Lewis Black, Gavin DeGraw, or Bill Clinton when they come to campus.

For the student who wants to get out, Pomona is a great jumping-off point for adven-tures in the Los Angeles area. Students can drive or take commuter rail into Los Angeles, and Pomona offers a shuttle that takes students to sporting events, shows, and other events, often with discounted tickets. Pomona's biggest off-campus group is called On the Loose. OTL, as the club is commonly known, is an outdoors club that organizes and outfits student adventures to go hiking, biking, climbing, camping, or even orienteering. The club trains leaders for trips, provides gear rentals, and even has access to vehicles so that stu-dents can enjoy the outdoor activities that Southern California has to offer.

Even for those who prefer not to sleep in tents, the outdoors has something to offer every Pomona student. Many take advantage of the sunny weather to do homework outside or to exercise regularly. The real proof of Pomona's fantastic geography is a tradition called Ski-Beach Day. Once a year, a busload of Pomona students take advantage of Pomona's central geography by driving up to the mountains to ski in the morning, then down to the beach for sun and a bonfire at night.

FINANCIAL AID

Pomona's financial aid policy is very simple and it's one of the best things about the college. Even with the declining economy, Pomona has increased its commitment to student aid, replacing the loans in their financial aid packages with grant aid. Graduating from college loan-free means that Pomona graduates are able to immediately begin careers and adventures rather than worrying about how to pay off their debts. Pomona admits its students need-blind, meaning that financial need has no bearing on a student's chance of being admitted to Pomona. By putting its endowment to work, Pomona allows its admissions office to choose the best students it is able to, then offers admitted students one hundred percent of their demonstrated financial need.

Talking with Pomona students, many were attracted by Pomona's reputation, but it was often the financial aid package that sealed the deal. By the numbers, Pomona's tuition is over $46,000, but the average student pays under $17,000 after need-based aid. Pomona offers a few merit-based scholarships through the National Merit program, but most of the aid at Pomona is directed toward making Pomona's education affordable to the greatest number of students possible.

GRADUATES

For those who are interested in getting out into the world, the Career Development Office offers comprehensive career counseling to Pomona students and graduates. By taking advantage of a network of alums, Pomona is able to offer its students advising, internships, and a lot of information about the world beyond Ponoma. This office also brings graduate school admissions officers, corporate recruiters, and informational panels about fields such as educaiton, journalism, and finance to campus. The CDO offers mock interviews, career inventories, and even etiquette courses to help students put their best foot forward as they leave Pomona's gates.

> **❝** *It is hard to generalize about what one does with a Pomona College education. During the first year out of Pomona, I can remember checking in with one friend who was teaching English in Korea on a Fulbright grant, one who was doing research for National Science Association, one attending UChicago Med School, one doing strategy for the presidential campaigns, one designing educational computer games, and one backpacking through South America. In recent years, the college has seen record numbers of students winning prestigious Fulbright Fellowships. The Career Development Office (CDO) counsels and prepares students to compete for this kind of post-baccalaureate fellowship, and a surprising number of Pomona's students spend a year doing research abroad after they leave Pomona.* **❞**

While students go on to do many different things, often a Pomona College degree isn't the last one. Many Pomona students find their way to graduate school within two years after graduating, taking advantage of Pomona's unusually strong reputation with graduate programs and their hands-on experiences as undergrads. Programs such as Pomona's pre-med group start meeting with students as freshmen to talk about course requirements and test preparation.

The relationships that one forms with faculty at Pomona also prove helpful when applying to graduate school as Pomona professors give great advice and can write personal recommendation letters. Particularly as they are graduating without student loans, Pomona students now have even more freedom to take interships or go on adventures in the wider world.

FAMOUS GRADUATES

- ○ Scott Olivet '84—CEO of Oakley Sunglasses and Fashion
- ○ Bill Keller '70—Pulitzer Prize Winner and Executive Editor of *The New York Times*
- ○ Catherine Porter '62—President of the Modern Language Association
- ○ Brendan Milbrun '93—Member of the Band Groovelily
- ○ Roy Disney '51—Former Vice Chairman of Disney
- ○ Kimberley Dodgson Labinger '80—California Teacher of the Year
- ○ Sylvain White '98—Filmmaker, Director *Stomp the Yard*

SUMMING UP

One of the things that most people applying to Pomona have to overcome is the "what's Pomona" experience. When you're having the recurring "So, where are you applying to college?" conversation and you list the schools you're applying to, your Great Aunt Harriet is going to tell you she's never heard of Pomona. Considering that it often competes for students with the big-name colleges, it *is* a surprise that more people haven't heard of Pomona. Still, let's remember that this isn't a popularity contest: you're choosing a place to spend four years of your life and finding the right place is going to determine what those four years are like. Clearly the college guides know about Pomona. Clearly graduate schools know about Pomona. The fact that Pomona's retention rate is often the highest in the country means that students know that Pomona is something special.

❏ *Nick Creech, B.A.*

Photo by Robert P. Matthews

Princeton University
Princeton, NJ 08544-0430

(609) 258-3060
Fax: (609) 258-6743

E-mail: *uaoffice@princeton.edu*
Website: *www.princeton.edu*

 Enrollment

Full-time ❏ women: 3,090
❏ men: 3,244

INTRODUCING PRINCETON

Princeton is home to a dynamic, diverse community of intellectuals who pursue their passions with unparalleled zeal. Founded in 1746, the university excels both as a major research institution and as a liberal arts college, making it one of the most respected centers of higher learning in the world. Because Princeton does not have an extensive graduate school system, lavish amounts of attention and resources are bestowed upon a relatively small under-graduate population. Basically, if you have a good idea, whether it's for an independent research project, a campus event, or your own personal growth, Princeton will provide you with the support and funding to make it happen.

Princeton boasts top-notch... well, everything. The campus, which is frequently ranked among the most beautiful in the country, features an art museum, a state-of-the-art music center, a visual and performing arts center, several theaters, an observatory, a plasma physics lab, a center for environmental and energy studies and eleven libraries containing more than seven million volumes. The university recently renewed its commitment to the sciences with the opening of a new Gehry-designed science library, and it plans to expand its arts offerings through the recently inaugurated Lewis Center for the Arts. A low faculty-student ratio of 6:1, coupled with the advising program, preceptorial system, and faculty office hours, means that undergraduates get remarkable access to luminaries such as Cornel West, Joyce Carol Oates, ten Nobel Prize winners, and twenty-two MacArthur "genius" grant recipients. The university also has a state-of-the-art computing system, a number of academic support centers, a campus healthcare facility, extensive recreation offerings, and a dedicated staff to ensure that students' needs are met around the clock. "Princeton runs like butter," summed up one recent graduate.

That said, gaining access to all that Princeton has to offer isn't easy. With an admit rate below ten percent, Princeton is one of the most selective universities in the country. In a recent year, ninety-seven percent of admits ranked in the top decile of their high school graduating classes, and three-fourths had SAT scores higher than 700 in all three sections. However, Princeton isn't just looking for brainy kids who test well; the admissions office ranks "advanced placement or honors courses," "recommendations by school officials" and "personality/intangible qualities" as its top three admissions considerations.

Princeton offers eighty departments and interdepartmental programs within two bachelor's degree programs: bachelor of arts (A.B.), and bachelor of science in engineering (B.S.E.). Because of the university emphasis on a broad liberal arts education, course requirements tend to be relatively easy to fulfill, which gives students the flexibility to delve into their own academic interests. Independent study is one of the pillars of Princeton academic life. Depending on their major, students must complete a number of independent projects during their time at Princeton, culminating in the production of a final thesis or project in their senior year.

Campus Life

Princetonians work hard, but they also play hard. Campus life is vibrant, owing to the fact that the vast majority—ninety-eight percent—of students live on campus. Contrary to popular belief, Princeton has a diverse student population; in a recent year, thirty-seven percent of students identified themselves as minorities (including African American, Asian American, Hispanic, and American Indian). Students hailed from all fifty states and more than ninety-five foreign countries. As a result, entertainment options on campus are varied, and there is never a shortage of things to do. You're as likely to find a hip-hop conference or *capoiera* performance as you are to stumble across an *a capella* arch sing.

Tradition

But that's not to say that all tradition is lost. In fact, it's quite the opposite. Princetonians embrace and cherish the university's time-honored rituals, from parading through the FitzRandolph Gate at the beginning of each year to celebrating the start of spring with concerts on the lawns of the university's Eating Clubs, large houses where upperclassmen take their meals and socialize. Each year, before Commencement, thousands of alums descend onto campus for one of the largest Reunions celebrations in the country to reminisce about their college years and salute the new class of graduates. In the sea of orange and black, you can see Princeton in a nutshell—alive and accomplished, with a deep-rooted respect for the past coupled with an eye to the future.

ADMISSIONS REQUIREMENTS

Like other highly selective schools, there is no exact formula for getting into Princeton. During the last admissions season, 26,247 students applied, 2,309 students were admitted, and 1,313 enrolled. To gain one of the coveted admit spots, find a way to make your application stand out. Princeton is looking for "a varied mix of high-achieving, intellectually gifted students from diverse backgrounds." They want students who have excelled both in and out of the classroom. In your application, emphasize your special talents, leadership experience, extracurricular activities, community service, and even your quirks. "Show us what's special about you," the admissions office invites prospective students.

The only admissions requirements are the official application form and scores for the College Board SAT or ACT (with writing where offered) and two SAT Subject Tests. Students who plan to pursue an engineering degree should take one Subject Test in either physics or chemistry and one in either Level I or Level II mathematics.

While there are no fixed high school course requirements, the university expects that students will have completed four years of English, mathematics, and foreign language, and at least two years of laboratory science and history. Many applicants have also taken courses in the visual and performing arts. Honors, advanced placement (AP) and dual-enrollment courses show that the applicant has challenged himself or herself and are a definite plus.

> 66 *I'm convinced that the key to getting into Princeton is writing a great essay. In addition to the academic requirements, the admissions office is looking for people who are passionate, articulate, and unique. The essay is the only way to showcase your personality, so take advantage of it! Be witty, be fun, and most of all, be honest. Don't pretend that all you do is read Dickens and listen to NPR when you're really a Perez Hilton junkie. Find a way to spin your quirky interests the right way!* 99

How to Apply

This writer recalls painstakingly writing out her essay, but now, Princeton has embraced technology as part of its admissions process. Applicants can apply using Princeton's online application or by submitting the Common Application along with a Princeton supplement. Purists can also apply using the paper versions of both applications.

In a highly publicized move, Princeton eliminated its Early Decision program in 2008 in an effort to balance the admissions playing field. Now, prospective students adhere to a single application timeline. Applications are due on January 1, and decisions are usually sent out by the end of March.

Bridge Year Program

In 2008 the university announced the launch of Princeton's new Bridge Year Program, a pre-collegiate enrichment year for admitted students who wish to spend a year in public service abroad before starting college. Through this program, Princeton partners with reputed international organizations to place students in service projects around the world, and it provides need-based funding to applicable students. The aim is to provide incoming freshmen with a break from the rigors of high school and help them develop an international perspective and commitment to public service.

Your academic experience at Princeton is truly what you make it. While some students choose to cruise by taking intro and pass/fail courses, others opt to fight their way into upper-level graduate courses. Most students aim for a balance, challenging themselves with a mix of large lecture courses and small seminars relating to their major or concentration, interspersed with distribution requirements and random courses they take just for the fun of it.

Princeton's course catalog offers hundreds of courses in thirty-four degree-granting departments. Students can also work toward a certificate in forty-six programs, from Creative Writing to Robotics and Intelligent Systems. Various interdisciplinary councils and centers also offer courses.

Because of Princeton's emphasis on the liberal arts, you won't find many practical preprofessional or vocational course offerings. Instead, you'll find titles such as "Ancient Greco-Roman Medicine," "The Making of the Ottoman Balkans, 1350–1500" and "Roll Over Beethoven: Black Rock and Cultural Revolt." Aspiring lawyers tend to major in Politics or the Woodrow Wilson School of Public and International Affairs, while pre-med students often study Molecular Biology or History of Science, but there are many exceptions to the rule. In truth, it doesn't really matter *what* you major in at Princeton, and the university urges students to sign into smaller departments such as Anthropology and Slavic Languages and Literatures, where they can receive more personalized attention.

Off Campus

While the university encourages students to broaden their horizons by spending time in foreign countries, most students are either unable or unwilling to study abroad during the academic year because of departmental requirements or fear that they'll "miss out" on part of the Princeton experience. As a result, many use their summers to pursue academic interests abroad. Through Princeton programs, students can study marine biology in Bermuda or pick up extra Italian credits in Macerata, a medieval town on the Adriatic coast. Programs such as Princeton-in-France or Princeton-in-Washington assist students with summer internship placements and offer support and social activities. The Office of International Programs also offers grants to fund summer language study, and juniors and seniors can apply for thesis funding to cover research-related travel.

Students who do study abroad during the academic year tend to go through Princeton-affiliated programs and exchanges; the programs at Oxford, Cape Town, and Melbourne are among the most popular. The university also allows students to receive credit for approved foreign programs, and students on financial aid continue to receive support abroad.

Special Schools

Princeton has a handful of special undergraduate schools; in addition to the School of Engineering and Applied Science, students can enter the School of Architecture or the Woodrow Wilson School of Public and International Affairs, which aims to prepare students "for leadership in public and international affairs." The Wilson School, also called "Woody Woo," is the only undergraduate degree program at Princeton that involves a competitive admissions process.

Graduation Requirements

Students must complete all general education requirements, departmental requirements, junior independent work, a senior thesis or substantial research project, and a final departmental examination before they can be awarded a diploma. Students in the A.B. program must take a minimum of thirty-one courses: one course each in epistemology and cognition, ethical thought and moral values, historical analysis, and quantitative reasoning, and two courses each in literature and the arts, science and technology (with laboratory), and social analysis. In addition, all A.B. candidates must take an introductory writing seminar and demonstrate proficiency in a foreign language.

Engineering students must take at least thirty-six courses and have a slightly different set of requirements, but they are also obliged to fulfill the writing requirement and take a number of courses in the humanities.

Classes

Princeton has a variety of course types, and the nature of the course determines for how long and how often the class meets per week. An environmental studies class might consist of two hour-long lectures, an hour-long precept, and a three-hour-long laboratory, while a humanities seminar will meet for a three-hour discussion session once a week. Many classes incorporate a preceptorial component, which allows students to further explore the readings and topics of the course in small discussion groups. A unique feature of the Princeton academic experience, the graded precepts force students to be knowledgeable enough about the material to engage in lively discussion and debate, and they are led by the professor who teaches the course, other faculty members, or graduate students.

> **❝** *If none of the titles in the course catalog appeal to you, design one yourself! For a class project, a friend of mine decided to put together the curriculum for a course on Latina literature. She created a syllabus, drafted a proposal, and found a professor willing to facilitate. The university was impressed by her initiative and implemented the course the following semester!* **❞**

Academic Support

Students at Princeton come from all academic backgrounds, so it's no surprise that many find it difficult to adjust to the rigors of a Princeton education. Luckily, there are a number of excellent support services available. The McGraw Center for Teaching and Learning offers workshops and individual consultations to teach study strategies, time management skills, and other tools to help students develop as learners, while the Writing Center helps students master college-level writing skills through one-on-one sessions with qualified (and patient!) writing coaches. Academic advising is available to all freshmen and sophomores through the residential colleges, and the masters and directors of studies in the colleges are often happy to lend advice on classes and majors.

The university also understands that many students experience emotional and psychological difficulties during their time at Princeton. For this reason, free counseling, support groups, and other services are available at University Health Services. No matter what your problem, Princeton will help you address it so that you don't fall behind.

Papers and the Thesis

Princeton is one of the few universities that make independent work a mandatory requirement for all undergraduates. All students must write a senior thesis, or in the case of engineers, complete a substantial independent project. During their senior year, students work one-on-one with a faculty advisor to develop and write a comprehensive departmental thesis, which generally runs between fifty to one hundred pages, on the subject of their choice. Most majors also require that students complete one or two independent papers or projects their junior year, which help to prepare students for the daunting task of undertaking the thesis.

> ❝ *I think the key to having a positive thesis experience is choosing a topic that you're passionate about. I chose to write my thesis for the History department on the contentious relationship between the United States and Guam, a tiny U.S. territory in the middle of the Pacific that I call home. I voraciously consumed every bit of information on the subject, and I even received a grant from my department and the Dean of the College to return to the island to conduct research and interviews. My advisor guided me in fleshing out my ideas so that I could explore issues I had grappled with all my life in an academic context. In the end, after many sleepless nights fueled by pizza and coffee, I produced a one-hundred-and-two-page thesis. It's an achievement that truly makes me proud.* ❞

SOCIAL LIFE AND ACTIVITIES

Students often refer to Princeton as the "Orange Bubble." Indeed, it's easy to forget the outside world once you step on the five-hundred-acre ivy-strewn collegiate Gothic campus. Because university housing is guaranteed for all four years, most students live on campus and stay on campus.

When students do venture out through the FitzRandolph Gate, it's into the genteel township of Princeton, New Jersey, located about an hour south of New York City and an hour north of Philadelphia. Charming and elegant, downtown Princeton consists of a cluster of restaurants and small businesses targeted to well-heeled day-trippers and returning alums. Princeton has a little something for everyone, except, perhaps, for students. The whole town shuts down around 10 P.M., and the few bars open past that are exceedingly strict about IDs.

Residential Colleges, Dorms, and Clubs

Student life begins in the residential colleges. All freshmen and sophomores live and take their meals in one of six colleges, each of which houses approximately five hundred students and is comprised of dormitories, dining halls, lounges, study spaces, game rooms, and extra amenities such as volleyball courts and dance studios. Each college also has its own residential college council, which hosts fun study breaks, plans large alcohol-free parties, and organizes subsidized trips to athletic events, Broadway plays, and amusement parks. Three colleges—Whitman, Mathey, and Butler—are four-year colleges that cater to a select number of juniors, seniors, and graduate students in addition to underclassmen.

- ○ Terrace Club
- ○ Tower Club
- ○ Quadrangle Club
- ○ Ivy Club
- ○ Cottage Club
- ○ Cloister Club
- ○ Cap & Gown Club
- ○ Charter Club
- ○ Tiger Inn
- ○ Colonial Club

Most juniors and seniors live in upperclassmen dormitories and take their meals in one of ten eating clubs lining Prospect Avenue. The eating club system is truly unique to Princeton and has been around for more than a century. Each club is housed in a stately mansion, which serves as a dining hall and hangout for between 120 and 180 upperclass members. Not only do students eat there, but they also party there. On weekends and most weeknights, "The Street" of eating clubs is the social epicenter of campus and comes alive with music, activity, and boisterous students. In many ways, the social function of the eating clubs takes the place of an active Greek scene. A number of fraternities and sororities exist on campus as well, although they are not officially recognized by the university.

Some students decide that the eating club scene is not for them, and there are a number of alternatives. Many continue taking meals in the four-year residential colleges, and some join co-ops, where members work together to shop for food and prepare meals in a laid-back setting. Others choose to stay independent of the system and are given preferential treatment in the housing lottery so that they can live in campus apartments equipped with kitchens.

Extracurricular Activities

The typical Princeton kid is a multitasking overachiever, juggling schoolwork with campus leadership, community service, student employment, and an active social life. The university strongly encourages this kind of involvement and provides generous resources to enable campus life to flourish. Students seeking to get involved can choose from hundreds of activities, from intramural sports teams to improv comedy troupes to organizations such as the Juggling Club and the Redhead Society.

- Anime-Manga Princeton: holds weekly screenings of Japanese animation
- Colosseum Club: throws late-night, action-packed events such as dodge-ball, laser tag, and NERF fights
- Figure Drawing Club: holds weekly drawing sessions for beginners and full-fledged artists alike
- Flavor: throws huge dinners catered by ethnic food restaurants
- Greening Princeton: organizes weekly farmers markets in the fall and spring
- Ignite: hosts groups of underprivileged youth on campus to spark their interest in attending college
- Jadwin Jungle: men's basketball fan club, which offers students special seating, free food before games, and a host of other benefits for a small fee
- Juggling Club: dedicated to the art of juggling, welcoming beginners enthusiastically
- Princeton Capoeira: spreads Afro-Brazilian culture through native martial arts dance
- Redheads Society: formed "with the purpose of sharing and enjoying their redheaded experience"
- Subtitles: hosts themed movie screenings, including late night excursions to see new films at the nearby Garden Theatre
- Surf Club: competes against other Ivy League schools in area tournaments
- Tasters: holds wine-tasting events for students over 21
- Union of Multiracial and Multicultural Students: brings together a diverse group of students for cross-cultural discussions

Athletics

The Princeton Tigers have a tradition of excellence in the Ivy League, and as a result, Princeton's campus is exceedingly active. About twenty percent of undergraduates compete in intercollegiate sports (twenty for men, eighteen for women), and Princeton's basketball, lacrosse, squash, and field hockey teams are particularly strong. Many students also play one of Princeton's nearly forty club sports, which include rugby, ballroom dancing, and Ultimate Frisbee. Those who aren't athletically inclined can be found working out diligently in Dillon Gym or cheering on their athlete friends from the stands.

Arts

The arts scene at Princeton is thriving thanks to an initiative to expand the university's art offerings. Under the new Lewis Center for the Arts, students can explore creative writing, musical performance, theater, dance, visual arts, and the interdisciplinary Princeton Atelier, both academically and through extracurricular activities. Actors and producers hone their craft by joining companies like the Princeton Triangle Club (musical comedy), Theatre Intime (dramatic theater) or the Princeton Shakespeare Company. Dancers have more than a dozen troupes to choose from, featuring an array of styles, from traditional Mexican folk (Ballet Folklorico) to breakdance and urban arts (Sympoh). Musicians have no shortage of outlets: the Orchestra, Jazz Ensemble, the Wind Ensemble, the Glee Club, the Chapel Choir, and more than a dozen traditional *a cappella* groups.

Media Organizations

Princeton has an abundance of incredibly gifted writers, as evidenced by the large number of famous authors and journalists that have stepped through its gates. Luckily, there is also an abundance of publications that will publish anything and everything students can produce outside their already heavy academic writing load. Many aspiring journalists earn their chops at *The Daily Princetonian*, the university's student-run daily. Students can also write for other campus publications, such as the *Nassau Literary Review*, the nation's oldest student-run literary magazine; the *Nassau Weekly*, an off-beat and often provocative humor weekly; or *Greenlight*, Princeton's self-ordained version of *The New Yorker*. Princeton also has its own campus radio station, WPRB, and a fledgling Princeton Student Television Network.

Organizations

At Princeton, there is truly an organization for everyone. You can flex your leadership capabilities by participating in the Undergraduate Student Government, or bond with like-minded College Democrats or College Republicans. Learn about different cultures by joining one of the dozens of ethnic and international associations, or find community service opportunities by joining the Student Volunteers Council. And if you don't find a group you like, start an organization of your own—dozens do it every year!

FINANCIAL AID

Princeton has one of the best financial aid programs in the country, which gives talented students from all economic backgrounds the chance to get a top-notch education. Admission to the university is need-blind, and Princeton promises to meet one hundred percent of each admitted student's financial need. The school uses its own financial aid application to assess student need, and the resulting assistance is often quite generous. The average financial aid package is $38,350, which covers tuition, and sixty-two percent of the class of 2014 received some form of aid. Typical financial aid packages are composed of grant aid; a self-help component that often involves student employment; and a summer savings requirement, which can be subsidized if the student is unable to earn the full amount. Princeton's groundbreaking no-loan policy, implemented in 2001, replaced all loans with grants that never have to be paid back. As a result, recent graduates have the freedom to pursue their passions without the burden of debt as a barrier.

> **❝** *I'd say funding is definitely one of the biggest perks of attending Princeton. The need-based financial aid grant package means that ANYONE can afford to attend the university, as long as he or she can get in. Plus, the school has the resources to fund student projects, language study, and travel. One of my friends recieved a $4,000 grant to backpack around Central America all summer studying murals!* **❞**

GRADUATES

Princetonians can be found in all fields, all around the world. In an exit survey of the class of 2010, 71.5 percent of students said they intended to enter the working world right away and 24.4 percent planned to pursue further education. Of those going to graduate school, 15.4 percent planned to go into medicine, 8.1 percent were entering law school, and the rest were pursuing master's degrees or doctorates in other subjects. A handful of others said they planned to travel, try out for professional sports teams, or join the military after graduation.

> **❝** *The common conception is that after graduation, all Princetonians participate in a mass exodus to Wall Street. For my group of friends, this couldn't be further from the truth. Many took advantage of Princeton's international postgraduate fellowship programs, such as Princeton-in-Asia, Princeton-in-Africa, and Princeton-in-Latin America. One friend shuffles between refugee camps in Ethiopia, another sends updates of her wilderness adventures in Nepal, and one spearheaded a performance of the 'Vagina Monologues' in Bangkok. Others decided to take public interest fellowships through Princeton's Project 55, working in schools and nonprofits around the country. Still others were awarded Fulbright or Rhodes scholarships or decided to join Teach for America. And me? I decided to travel the world after graduation, visiting everyone!* **❞**

Princeton provides a wealth of resources and post-graduate opportunities for students. Recent graduates can work for international nonprofits or schools around the world through Princeton-in-Asia, Princeton-in-Africa, and Princeton-in-Latin America, or provide domestic service through Princeton Project 55 fellowships. The Program in Teacher Preparation trains and places students interested in education, while the Princeton Army and Airforce ROTC prepares students for military service.

The Office of Career Services serves as a valuable resource for students, providing programs, counseling, and workshops. Students can join pre-professional organizations like the American Society of Mechanical Engineers and the Minority Business Association, or link up with alumni willing to give career advice (or jobs!) through the Alumni Careers Network. Hundreds of companies participate in on-campus job fairs, and many, particularly banks and consulting firms, work tirelessly to recruit students through swanky info sessions and private receptions.

One thing's for sure—no matter where they are or what they do, most Princeton alums find a way to stay connected to the university. Each spring, thousands of alumni return to campus for the largest Reunions celebration in the country, and many participate in class committees, regional associations, and affiliated alumni groups. Alumni can even take onsite or online classes through the Alumni Association's Education Program, or participate in family educational trips, with titles such as "Peru's Treasures" and "Tuscany Family Escape," with fellow alums through Princeton Journeys. Because of the unwavering loyalty of Princetonians near and far, the school consistently has one of the highest alumni giving rates in the country.

PROMINENT GRADUATES

- James Madison, 1771, Fourth President of the United States
- Woodrow Wilson, 1879, Twenty-eighth President of the United States
- Adlai Stevenson '22, Governor of Illinois, Ambassador to the United Nations, and Presidential Candidate
- Jimmy Stewart, '32, Actor
- John Nash, PhD '50, Mathematician and Nobel Prize Winner in Economics
- Sonia Sotomayor, '76, Supreme Court Justice
- Ralph Nader, '55, Green Party Presidential Candidate and Consumer Activist
- Steve Forbes, '70, President and CEO of Forbes, Inc.
- Queen Noor (Lisa Halaby), '74, Former Queen of Jordan
- Eric Schmidt, '76, CEO of Google
- Meg Whitman, '77, Former CEO of eBay
- Elena Kagan, '72, Supreme Court Justice
- David Remnick, '81, Editor of The New Yorker
- Michelle Obama, '85, First Lady of the United States
- Brooke Shields, '87, Actress
- Dean Cain, '88, Actor
- Wendy Kopp, '89, Teach for America Founder
- Moshia Hamid, '93, Novelist

So what is it that makes Princeton distinctive, that consistently puts it at the top of every rankings list known to man? What is it that created Princeton's exceedingly loyal alumni base and keeps them coming back for more each Reunions season? What is it about that name, *Princeton*, that inspires feelings of honor and tradition, and that strikes fear into the hearts of high school seniors everywhere?

Surely, it's a combination of things—the thrill of stepping through FitzRandolph Gate on the first day of freshman year, the often breathtaking beauty of campus during the change of seasons, the memories made during late-night study breaks, the pride of completing a senior thesis. An undergraduate education at Princeton is truly something special, and those lucky enough to experience it firsthand look back on their college days with a mixture of wistfulness and awe, this author included.

❏ *Jessica Arriola Marati, B.A.*

Reed College
Portland, Oregon 97202

(503) 771-7511
Fax: (503) 777-7553 or (800) 547-4750

E-mail: *.admission@reed.edu*
Website: *www.reed.edu*

 Enrollment

Full-time ❏ women: 781
❏ men: 627

INTRODUCING REED COLLEGE

Reed means being smart. Smart, in the biggest, most complicated, inspiring, and open sense of the word. Smart in the sense of taking risks, of seeking challenges, and of seeing in any answer an infinite array of more interesting questions. Smart in taking nothing for granted, and asking every day, "What does it mean to learn, to communicate ideas, to seek understanding?"

The 1,408 students who congregate on Reed's 119-acre campus share a singular passion for learning in an academic environment that is as known for its intense intellectual rigor as it is for its out-of-the-box, open-minded, and liberal students. For many, Reed's mixture of classical learning and independent living seems like a contradiction in terms; for those who see college as an adventure for the mind, as a challenge for the self, and as an opportunity to learn not for profit but for the intrinsic value of knowledge, Reed makes perfect sense.

What, then, of a school that seeks to capture and cultivate smartness?

Intensity can exist without senseless competition. At Reed, grades exist, but they aren't reported on individual assignments or placed on report cards. Students produce work because they value success as a measure of understanding. Classrooms come into being as spaces for discussion, where professors, called by their first names, guide student-driven inquiry. There are no honors programs, no dean's lists, or any exclusive club, organization, fraternity, or sorority—no NCAA or varsity athletics, either.

Trust creates true community. Students, faculty, and staff alike are governed by the Honor Principle, an unwritten commitment that takes the place of arbitrary rules and regulations. You're expected to act honestly and with regard for the community in all matters, academic as well as social. From the college's founding, this has meant that tests and examinations need not be proctored; you're as likely to take your chemistry test in the library as you are to take it on the front lawn. In all matters, students must engage disagreement rather than support divisiveness. An all-student judicial board, chosen by student representatives, provides for true peer review.

Fun exists. Reedies take learning seriously, but they also, refreshingly, remember not to take themselves too seriously. There's a college newspaper as well as a comic book library. And each year, students celebrate the Seventh Annual Nitrogen Day, a tribute to that element's unique triple bond.

And while Reed can't claim responsibility for Portland, the city that hosts the college's splendidly green campus is also known for its smartness. An award-winning public transportation system connects you to a vibrant downtown and to the city's many neighborhoods, whether you want to eat a great meal, go to a concert, or explore Forest Park's many miles of hiking trails.

ADMISSIONS REQUIREMENTS

For more than ten years now, Reed has openly refused to participate in annual college rankings, a fact that captures the college's attitude toward admission. Rather than rely on arbitrary numbers, presumptions of status and prestige, and the notion that colleges, like toasters or television sets, can be ranked from best to worst, Reed wants to be judged on its merits and chosen by students with a true interest in the education it offers. There is no one single Reed, either, in numbers, guidebooks, or online message boards, so you should explore as many angles of vision as possible to discover the school's distinctive character. Ideally, a campus visit offers the most comprehensive picture. You can meet students, go on a tour, and find out that the food is actually quite good. During the school year, you can sit in on classes and spend a night in the dorms. If you're not able to get to Portland, you should see if an admissions representative is traveling to your area, as interviews are offered in cities across the country in late summer and throughout the fall. Alumni interviews are also widely available. Check out the school's Web site, including the trees of Reed which document over 100 species of trees found on campus as well as individual student and professors' pages. There are as many sorts of Reedies and Reed experiences as there are students on campus, so look to discover and enjoy both diversity and coherence in your explorations.

On the college's end, Reed seeks to admit students with the same desire and ability for smartness that underlies the existing community. For starters, this assures that getting in is not a numbers game. Nor is it a matter of finding that most perfectly "well-rounded" person, as if the spherical was somehow the most nobly lived life. Reed is notable for "taking risks" with applicants who may be far from perfect on paper, but who have demonstrated in any number of ways their readiness and ability for success at Reed.

66 *When I was looking at schools, Reed was the one college that didn't try to impress me with how hard it was to get in, or to suggest that only some cadre of saintly elite might be worthy of admission. Everyone I spoke to wanted to know what I was interested in, how I thought about things, and why I wanted to go to college. Reed didn't mix up education with pretension or exclusivity; it just asked that I be interested in ideas, want to learn, and be willing to share in challenging work. It seemed so simple an idea yet Reed was the only place I could find such honesty. And they had fun, too.* 99

What Is Important?

A t the same time, there are some familiar truisms that, much more often than not, carry the day. The better you do in high school, especially taking the most challenging courses offered by your school, the better your chances for admission. There are no specific curricular requirements, though it's recommended that you have multiple years of coursework in all the major core subjects such as English, social studies, math, science, and foreign language. Involvement and extracurricular activities matter, though demonstrable passion, intellectualism, commitment, and thoughtfulness of involvement always triumph over resume building. Diversity of background, experience, and identity, including race, ethnicity, and gender play an important role in admission and in the larger Reed community.

Applying

First-year students can apply to Reed under either the November 15 or December 20 Early Decision options, both of which are binding, or at the January 15 Regular Admission deadline. Transfer students are to submit applications by March 1. If you're certain that you want to attend Reed, applying Early Decision can give your application added advantage in demonstrating your commitment. All admission options require the general Common Application form and supporting materials such as teacher recommendations and so forth. Also required are results from either the SAT or ACT and the Reed supplement form, a graded writing sample, and an essay that answers, "Why Reed?" This last piece is quite important; you should use your essay to demonstrate your understanding of the school, most importantly by showing how you imagine yourself at Reed. You're not being asked to write propaganda; instead, have fun and describe the potential adventures, challenges, and successes that draw you to the college.

ACADEMIC LIFE

Legends abound as to the amount and the difficulty of the work at Reed. Some have used the metaphor of boot camp. Those less militaristic and more existential have offered the myth of Sisyphus. Don't be afraid, though, of the hyperbole. There's no doubt that the academics are hard, that expectations are high, and that people take thinking seriously. At the same time, you're aren't thrown in the deep end and expected to know everything on the first day of class. Above all, you need to be interested in and engaged by learning. With that in mind, you'll find the challenges and satisfaction of studying at Reed to be as amazing as anything you might imagine.

Reed values the classical model of a liberal arts education, based on a requirement structure meant to ensure both breadth and depth in each student's program of study. Tradition also reigns within the college's department structure, with very few "interdisciplinary" or topical majors offered. The professors at Reed feel seriously that students need a grounding in their chosen major, with a comprehensive introduction to the various methods and theories of that discipline, past and present. This preparation gives you a solid foundation for the challenges you'll face and the independence you'll be given in upper-division coursework. Such focused introductions don't breed singularity of thought, however. Instead, they provide the basis for seriously considering similarities and differences in the various ways scholars both ask and answer questions. With this preparation, it's no wonder that Reed graduates have such a fantastic track record for success in graduate school.

Classes, Professors, and Evaluations

One of the greatest parts of learning at Reed comes in the small, conference-based classroom environment that predominates on campus. Conferences at Reed average fifteen students, and all are taught by members of the faculty. You're expected to be as active, involved and engaged as anyone around the table, including the professor. For starters, you can abandon the high school foolishness of hand raising. All students, shy and extroverted alike, develop their skills as conference participants during their time at Reed. Each meeting offers its own vibrancy and originality, and above all, you are learning how to think in harmony with others, how to ask questions and articulate your ideas.

Faculty at Reed are called by their first names, and this openness exemplifies the interest and support they offer students. You have a faculty member as an academic advisor from the day you step on campus, and you can easily change advisors if your interests shift or you develop a connection with another professor. Every professor hosts many office hours each week, and e-mails receive quick yet thoughtful replies, sometimes even at two in the morning.

Because letter or number grades are not noted on your assignments, faculty evaluate your work with extensive and detailed comments. The criticism is as plentiful as it is constructive. You're called to task on the strength and logic of your arguments, on the evidence you used or might have used. And you're also given encouragement to further your strengths and develop your own original questions, in the classroom, library, and laboratory.

> 66 When I started at Reed, I figured I would check my grades at the end of first semester, just to get a sense of how I was doing. When the time came, though, I had no interest in asking. My whole sense of not only how I learned, but why I was in school, what it meant to be successful, had begun to change. After four years, I can't imagine what it would be like to know your grades while in school, to be in an environment where people talked about or even worse were competitive about them. 99

Humanities 110

The summer before you arrive at Reed, the alumni association sends you a copy of Richmond Fagle's verse translation of Homer's *Odyssey*. With this text, new Reedies begin the shared and enduring experience of the required year-long introductory humanities course that focuses on ancient Greece and Rome with a new emphasis on the larger Mediterranean contexts from which they emerged. Course material consists mostly of primary sources in all classical fields, including art, with a minimum of secondary sources. Hum 110, as the course is known, has two distinct components. First, three times a week, the entire first-year class comes together for a lecture from one of the twenty or so faculty members drawn from a variety of departments who are teaching the course. You hear well-researched and thought-provoking talks that cover a given text or combination of works, offering useful contextual information as well as arguments on how you might develop your own interpretations. Second, each student is a member of a small, fifteen-student conference, led by one of the professors in the course. Conferences can vary in character depending on the home discipline of the professor, who might be a philosopher, political scientist, or art historian, yet all share the same syllabus and paper deadlines. In Hum 110, you learn as much about the classical humanities as you do about writing well, receiving academic feedback on your work, and participating in the conference environment.

Group Requirements

Part of attending Reed means having a broad interest in ideas and learning, and the curricular group requirements provide structure for ensuring breadth in each student's education. A total of ten of the thirty units required for graduation are given to these requirements; most semester-long courses are valued at one unit. Two units must be taken from one department within each of four groups: literature, arts, philosophy, and religion; history, the social sciences, and psychology; laboratory courses in physics, chemistry, or biology; and, mathematics, foreign language, logic, or linguistics. In addition, students must also complete two more units in any single department outside the students major department. Though there is no specific order or timeline for taking these requirements, most students concentrate

on them during their first two years at Reed, the advantage being that you gain exposure to a variety of different fields before choosing a major at the end of sophomore year.

Studying Off Campus

Close to thirty established foreign and domestic exchange programs allow Reedies the opportunity to study away from campus for either a semester or a full year. All of the programs are arranged in coordination with the faculty to support an aspect of the college's academic program. For instance, if you're studying Islam in the religion department, you might choose to take a semester intensively studying Arabic at the Al Akhawayn University in Morroco. Some programs offer more general opportunities for your exchange program, such as a year at Wadham College, Oxford, or at Ireland's Trinity College. Because each program has a direct tie with Reed, students are assured that they will have a meaningful experience, and years of established relationships give Reedies access to the fullest privileges at partner institutions. In addition, the International Programs Office will work with students to craft any number of additional opportunities that suit a student's particular interests. Unlike the established programs, however, those that you devise on your own are not covered by the college's financial aid packages. Because of the general curricular requirements that each student needs to complete, fitting a study abroad year into your time at Reed can take some planning, so it's worthwhile beginning to develop your plan for an exchange early on in your time at Reed. Many Reedies also choose to take time off to travel rather than participating in an official program, and the college is very flexible in granting leaves of absence. While a very different sort of experience, an independent adventure can often provide for some refreshing time away from the routines of a traditional academic semester.

The Junior Qualifying Examination

Before students can begin their senior year, they must pass a junior qualifying examination proctored by their major department. The "qual," as it's known, can vary widely in format from department to department, yet all are designed to test students' initial mastery of the skills and methods of their chosen field. The exams don't generally target a specific body of information that you need to cram into your brain in order to get through the test. Mostly, they are concerned with seeing if you've begun to get a handle on the way scholars in your department do research and communicate their findings, and the various methods and traditions that inform their work. Some departments, such as history and English, require specific Junior Seminar courses that play a role in preparing students for the exam. In all cases, the faculty of each department meets to discuss students' performance on their exams, as well as their work in the courses they've had up to this point. With solid focus and preparation, the vast majority of students pass their qual outright the first time they take the exam. Some receive what is called a conditional pass; in this case, you need to meet a specific stipulation, such as retaking a particular section of the exam or taking a class in a particular area. For students, the qual serves as a good time to think about your particular interests in your major, and look toward a topic you might like to explore in your senior thesis.

The Senior Thesis

Your thesis is a defining experience of your time at Reed. Along with two or three other classes in your senior year, you are given the opportunity to embark on a sustained and original piece of scholarship on a topic of your choice in your major. You have an advisor specifically for your thesis, and you're given the independence to shape your inquiry in a manner you find most engaging. Depending on your field, you usually complete one of three types of theses: experimental, research-analytical, or creative. Generally, those in the sciences take the experimental route; they get lab space for the year where they can base their work. If you're writing in literature, the humanities, or social sciences, you get a thesis desk in the library. Studio space in the art building or access to the theater or dance studio is given to those who do a creative thesis in the arts.

Wherever your thesis project lands you, the space inevitably becomes a home away from home, with decorations, stashes of food, reminders to call your family, and an accumulation of coffee cups that helps as a material reminder of your progress. There are also funds available if your project requires travel away from campus, such as visiting an archive, doing fieldwork, or using lab equipment that's not available at Reed.

Thesis means getting your hands dirty as a scholar, and Reedies produce amazing work that expresses their passion for thinking, for developing their ideas, and sharing them with others. Many a late-night conversation revolves around how everything in the world can be explained through your topic; the brilliance of this is that you present your case as eagerly as you listen to your friends explain theirs. Thesis gives you frustration and revelation and challenge, and ultimately, an unmatched experience for seeing how much you are able to accomplish through the cumulative education you've received in your time at Reed.

All theses are due to the college registrar by three o'clock on the last day of the semester, an event that is marked by Thesis Parade, an extraordinary celebration in which the community fetes all the seniors who have completed their projects. In the spring semester, the annual weekend-long Renaissance (Renn) Fayre celebration follows this ritual event. Later, during exam week, all students present their work for oral examination by a panel or four or five faculty members, including their thesis advisor. Tradition dictates that students bring plentiful refreshments for their orals board, and respond to two hours of faculty questioning. Orals mark the final completion of your thesis, confirmed with a handshake and congratulations from your advisor.

SOCIAL LIFE AND ACTIVITIES

Reedies' passions extend far beyond the classroom, and the myriad organizations, activities, and events occurring on campus testify to their creativity and involvement. Campus life occurs within these webs of interest, with people engaging one another in refreshingly

Over twenty acres of Reed's campus are dedicated to a natural plant and wildlife habitat forming the headwaters of Crystal Springs Creek, the only natural lake remaining in inner Portland. Currently, the college is engaged in an ongoing restoration project to remove invasive plant species and return the canyon to a more natural state. The canyon's waterway has been restored, including the installation of a fish ladder, in the hopes that salmon may again return to this site to spawn. Each year, Canyon Day brings members of the community together to get their hands dirty and celebrate this amazing part of campus. Every day, too, students enjoy exploring the canyon, whether for a biology research project or a relaxing and meditative middle-of-the day walk. To learn more, visit the canyon Web site at *web.reed.edu/canyon.*

genuine terms. With no exclusive clubs or organizations, such as fraternities, sororities, and NCAA athletics, community at Reed has a true sense of openness and opportunity.

Residences

Though it's not technically a requirement, pretty much every first-year student lives on campus. Dorms vary in size and location on campus, and generally the word actually designates the specific floor on which a student lives rather than an entire building. All dorms have students from every class year, and except for one all-women's floor, are coed. Most first-year students share what's called a "divided double," composed of an inner and outer room, the latter with a door to the hallway. On average, the rooms are generously large, and give you the benefit of both having a roommate and also getting your own space. Upper-class students have single rooms and participate in a housing lottery that decides who gets to pick their room on campus first—those with fireplaces tend to get snapped up early. Some dorms have designated themes, recently including film appreciation, community service, and one called "Running with Scissors" that sponsored lots of children's games. Language houses, each with a native speaker in residence, exist for the five modern languages taught at Reed. The college also owns a number of apartments on the west edge of campus, and this is a popular alternative to the dorms, one that doesn't require students to stay on campus. All dorms have upper-class students serving as house advisors, usually called dorm "moms" and "dads."

About a third of students live off campus, a number of them in "Reed Houses" near the school. Original names such as "The Fridge" or "Red Barn" offer testimony to their having been occupied by Reedies for as long as anyone can remember. Most students walk, bike, or bus to campus, but there are no restrictions on having a car. Reed provides a nightly van service that will take you to your off-campus house until 2:30 each morning.

Funding Poll

At the beginning of each semester, the student senate initiates a funding poll, and any organization that wants student body funds—new or well established—must submit an entry in the poll. Every student on campus has a chance to vote preferentially on all of the proposals. Groups that receive the most student support receive priority in presenting their ideas to the student senate during funding circus, which in turn divvies up close to $200,000 each year. This open and directly democratic system reflects the autonomy given to students in governing campus life, and also assures that anyone with an idea has a chance to see it happen. Groups such as the campus newspaper, radio station, multicultural resource center, outdoor club, and political organizations always receive significant support. More exceptional groups have been created under banners such as the Ladies Pie Society, Carnivorous Alternatives to Vegetarian Eating, and Defenders of the Universe.

> 66 *I've always been amazed by how much goes on at Reed. It's sort of like an incubator for people's passions, and that means it's never boring. One weekend a group of students turned the student union into a Nerf palace. Another group brought a mechanical bull to campus, for anyone who wanted to give it a whirl. And these are the same people who are licensed to operate the nuclear reactor, who have spent time researching plant fauna in Nepal, who developed a community exchange with a town in Nicaragua. As involved as I was, I also would just smile at the fact that so many people where getting to see their ideas take shape and participate in so many different activities.* 99

Athletics

Playing sports at Reed means having fun more than anything else. A few competitive teams exist, most notably the very successful female rugby team, along with Ultimate Frisbee, basketball, and squash. While there certainly isn't any jock culture on campus, Reedies do a good job of staying active, though generally through life sports such as tennis, squash, or hiking. Reed students must fulfill a general physical education requirement as well, and the available courses defy anything you might have found in high school gym class. Offerings include yoga, skiing at nearby Mt. Hood, canoeing, juggling, dance, SCUBA certification, and much more, assuring that there is something to suit everyone's interest.

Honor Principle

Reedies enjoy a remarkably large amount of freedom when it comes to campus life. Very few rules exist, and students respect this privilege by taking an active responsibility for their own conduct. The honor principle originated, and still thrives, as a hallmark of academic honesty. Professors opt not to proctor examinations, for instance, as an indication of the general trust extended to students for completing all of their work honestly and in good faith as assigned. More broadly, the honor principle has become a terms to designate the way of life agreed upon by all community members. Not a code of conduct to be adhered to—in fact, the honor principle isn't codified or written down at all—students instead have a responsibility for being aware of their actions and of the comfort and well-being of those around them.

The City of Portland and Beyond

One of the greenest, most vibrant, and livable cities in the country, Portland provides an exceptional backdrop to the experience at Reed. The college itself is located in a residential area about five miles from the city center. Downtown, along with the many great neighborhoods around the city, can easily be reached by public transportation. The city has also won awards for being one of the most bicycle-friendly in the world. Opportunities for cultural and artistic activities abound, from opera to Indy-rock, along with an almost endless number of great, inexpensive restaurants. Beyond the city, you can be skiing at Mt. Hood in about two hours, where the college has a cabin that's free for community members' use. Seventy-five miles east, the Oregon coast offers astounding views and lends itself to picnics and hiking adventures. From the Columbia River gorge to the many wilderness areas all around Portland, the opportunity for outdoor activities is beyond comparison.

FINANCIAL AID

The best colleges and universities tend to be very expensive, and Reed is no exception to that rule. At the same time, the college is extremely committed to making its education accessible to students from all economic backgrounds. To do this, Reed offers entirely need-based financial aid that covers tuition, room, board, college fees, and other related expenses, and will meet one hundred percent of the demonstrated financial need of all accepted students. Need is determined by the Financial Aid Office using information from the FAFSA and Profile forms. Over half of current students receive aid, which is composed primarily of grants; it also includes loans and, in addition, gives students the opportunity to use any campus job toward their small work-study contribution. The average aid package is well over $30,000. Another benefit of being a small school, Reed's Financial Aid Office can take the time to assist each student in maximizing the available resources for studying at Reed.

GRADUATES

Reed graduates take on the world with the same intellectual, creative, and open-minded energy that defined their undergraduate education. Success for Reedies means finding satisfaction and fulfillment in the challenges of the world, and little judgment exists as to whether that ought to mean starting your own organic farm, becoming a professor, or making your way in the marketplace. While there are no business or preprofessional programs on campus, many alumni have made successful careers in business, law, and medicine. Nearly ten percent of alumni are practicing artists or have direct involvement in the arts. A large contingent of graduates work for nonprofit and nongovernmental organizations, from international agencies such as the United Nations to smaller community-driven efforts. Most often, Reedies pursue careers in education at all levels and in any manner of ways.

GRAY FUND

In the early 1990s, Betty Gray, a long-time Reed benefactor, donated many millions of dollars for sponsoring fun activities on campus and adventures around the Northwest. A student, faculty, and staff committee plans events that have included David Sedaris, Dave Eggers, and Ira Glass to campus. Additionally, the Gray Fund sponsors trips almost every weekend, from white-water rafting adventures to trips to the Oregon coast or an afternoon at the art museum or movies. And the best part is, all trips are completely free—usually with an abundance of great food, too.

Almost three years after finishing Reed, I am still struck by how transformative an experience I enjoyed while in college. The amount of possibilities I see in the world, the amazing diversity of friends I made who have found such interesting paths to follow, make me realize exactly how Reed empowers your education. The personal rewards of independent thinking, of being critically aware, provide a bridge between the academic and the practical, the theoretical and the everyday. That bridge isn't handed to you; it's something that you begin building at Reed and continue to recognize in everything you do, always finding innovation and insight in whatever challenges you confront, whether at your job, taking action in your community, or simply continuing to explore the world.

No matter what path is chosen, Reed graduates more often than not attend graduate school, regularly gaining acceptance to the best programs in the country. In fact, nearly three out of every four alumni have earned a graduate degree, and one quarter of all graduates have a Ph.D. Reed's tremendous legacy of academic and intellectual achievement has included widespread recognition for its alumni, including thirty-one Rhodes Scholarships, sixty-four Watson fellowships, twenty-five Mellon awards, and two MacArthur "Genius grants."

SUMMING UP

Reed offers a distinctive liberal arts education for students who seek smartness in its many forms. First and foremost, you've got to enjoy academic work and find fulfillment through intellectual inquiry. Reed mixes irreverence, creativity, and a dedication to community in a way that makes education an ongoing and open question. The combination of classical learning with extensive personal freedom fuels a continuous creation of diverse and meaningful experience. Smart, liberal, and passionate, Reedies shun consumption and senseless competition and embrace production and collegiality, limited only by their imaginations.

❏ *Christopher Moses, B.A.*

 Rensselaer Polytechnic Institute
Troy, NY 12180

 (518) 276-6216
Fax: (518) 276-4072

 E-mail: *admissions@rpi.edu*
Website: *www.rpi.edu*

 Enrollment

Full-time ❏ women: 1,495
❏ men: 3,862

INTRODUCING RENSSELAER POLYTECHNIC INSTITUTE

Rensselaer Polytechnic Institute has undergone what can only be described as a "renaissance." From its roots as the oldest technological research university in the English-speaking world, RPI has launched an ambitious agenda of renewal and growth. The university has transformed itself through expanding research initiatives, massive campus building projects, and growing academic programs. Breathtaking new facilities, such as the Curtis R. Priem Experimental Media and Performing Arts Center and the Center for

Biotechnology and Interdisciplinary Studies, have set the tone for a new vision for Rensselaer as a premier research university in the twenty-first century.

RPI is located in New York State's Hudson-Mohawk Valley, just a few miles north of the capital city of Albany. The university sits on a 275-acre hilltop in the city of Troy, overlooking the Hudson River. Troy provides easy driving access to New York, Boston, and Montreal, as well as the beauty and recreation of the nearby Adirondack Mountains. The campus community is one of intellectual discovery, research, and bold exploration; from engineers and scientists to artists and entrepreneurs. Students at RPI are ambitious, original, fun, and intelligent with a global perspective and sense of citizenship. The university offers academic programs across a wide range of disciplines: engineering, the sciences, business, architecture, information technology, humanities, social sciences, and the arts.

RPI was founded in 1824 as "The Rensselaer School," the first academic institution of its kind. Stephen Van Rensselaer, visionary of the Erie Canal, created the school for the instruction of "the application of science to the common purposes of life." That mantra has propelled Rensselaer forward as a unique institution of higher education for more than 180 years. Over time, RPI graduates have done amazing things, from building the Brooklyn Bridge to masterminding the first moon landing. They have established and led successful enterprises, from Texas Instruments (inventors of the first silicon transistor) to Vicarious Visions (creators of *Guitar Hero*). At Rensselaer, students walk in the footsteps of pioneers—and become pioneers themselves.

If you have those kinds of ambitions, you will find great satisfaction at Rensselaer Polytechnic Institute. You will enjoy access to world-class research facilities, and work alongside exceptionally talented researchers on challenges that range from eradicating cholera to combating global warming. Whether you study mechanical engineering or music, bioinformatics or business, Rensselaer is a place for those who yearn to fulfill their dreams, and change the world in the process.

ADMISSIONS REQUIREMENTS

Students may apply to Rensselaer using one of three applications—the Common Application, the Universal College Application, or the Candidate's Choice, Rensselaer's official application. Students using the Common Application or Universal College Application should submit the required supplemental form.

—Patrick Heider '07

For the 2009–2010 academic year, Rensselaer received more than 12,000 applications, which represents a jump of nearly one hundred percent over three years. Most applicants are top students who excel in mathematics and the sciences; many (but not all) apply with Advanced Placement credit or credit from an International baccalaureate program. Rensselaer accepts scores from AP exams and Higher Level IB exams, which can allow students to place out of as many classes as they are eligible for.

The applicants who are best suited for Rensselaer will have completed four years of English, four years of mathematics through pre-calculus, three years of science, and three years of social studies and/or history. Additionally, the admissions committee pays particular attention to candidates who demonstrate qualities and talents that will contribute to the richness of the Rensselaer community.

Standardized Test Requirements

All standardized tests for Rensselaer must be taken by December 31. Students are required to submit official scores from the SAT (critical reading, math, and writing) or ACT (which must include the optional writing component). SAT Subject Tests in a math and a science are required only for applicants to accelerated programs (or ACT, which must include the optional writing component, in lieu of SAT and SAT Subject Tests). The TOEFL is required for international applicants (minimum 230 CBT/88 iBT/570 PBT).

Application Deadlines

Rensselaer offers three application deadlines—Early Decision I, Early Decision II, and Regular Decision. Early Decision I and II offer students the opportunity to apply earlier and hear back from Rensselaer one month later, but are binding decisions (they require the student to attend the university if admitted, barring financial considerations). The Early Decision I deadline is November 1, and decisions are released December 5. The Early Decision II deadline is December 15, with decisions being released on January 16. The Regular Decision deadline is January 15, with admissions decisions becoming available on March 14.

ACADEMIC LIFE

The research leaders who work, study, and innovate at Rensselaer share a common focus: unearthing new opportunities for solving the world's most challenging problems. As our society becomes more interconnected and independent, solving complex problems requires the skills, drive, and imagination needed to approach life's puzzles in more innovative ways. Tackling those problems requires both exceptional resources and curious minds.

Schools

The university offers programs across our five schools; the School of Engineering, the School of Science, the School of Architecture, the School of Humanities, Arts, and Social Sciences, and Rensselaer's business school, the Lally School of Management and Technology. The university was also one of the first in the nation to offer an interdisciplinary degree in Information Technology, offered across all five schools. Rensselaer operates an environment with "low walls," meaning students are free to change majors and participate in classes across the breadth of the university's offerings.

World-Class Facilities

In recent years, Rensselaer has invested hundreds of millions of dollars to build world-class facilities that allow our research leaders to advance the frontiers of human possibility. For example, at our Center for Biotechnology and Interdisciplinary Studies, students and faculty members collaborate to make breakthrough discoveries in the life sciences. One team at the center is conducting pioneering research on peptide imbalances that could help unlock the mystery of Alzheimer's disease.

Rensselaer's extraordinary Experimental Media and Performing Arts Center (EMPAC) incorporates a range of art and performance spaces under one roof, including a concert hall with a "tunable" ceiling and a studio containing one of the world's only 360-degree projection screens for virtual environments. In addition to serving as a world-class performance venue, EMPAC also functions as a platform for simulation and visualization research.

At the Computational Center for Nanotechnology Innovations, researchers perform simulations at speeds approaching two trillion calculations per second using one of the world's most powerful university-based supercomputers. Our Geotechnical Centrifuge Center can produce a force 200 times the force of gravity for earthquake engineering simulation, and our engineering students also study the unique properties of atomic particles at the Gaerttner Linear Accelerator Laboratory on campus.

East Campus Athletic Village

In 2009, the Institute officially unveiled the new East Campus Athletic Village—the most extensive athletic construction project in Rensselaer history, offering athletic and recreation facilities that will change the student experience dramatically. ECAV,

as the new $92 million complex is known, is the latest in a decade-long physical transformation of Rensselaer. The project involves two phases: the grand opening signified the end of Phase 1, which includes a multipurpose lighted stadium with field turf and seating for 5,200 and a 1,200 seat basketball arena. Also, a fully equipped 4,800 square-foot strength and conditioning center connects to a professional-caliber sports medicine suite, and within the arena are offices for athletics administrators and coaches, numerous meeting spaces, a new Athletics Hall of Fame, a pro shop, and a café. Renovations to the Houston Field House were also made.

Multidisciplinary Research Constellations

Rensselaer also structures research activities in ways that help spark new and dazzling insights. As the name implies, our research constellations bring together some of the brightest stars in academia in teams that include undergraduates as well as faculty members and graduate students. The Tetherless World Research Constellation, for example, focuses on radically expanding the capabilities of the World Wide Web. Other constellations, organized around topics such as "future chips" and "biocomputation and bioinformatics," pursue—and realize—equally heady goals in areas that range from unleashing the awesome curative powers of stem cells to transforming organic diodes into light-emitting "wallpaper."

> *I've been involved in research at RPI since my freshman year, working in a lab in the biology department. It's great because I get the opportunity to learn, firsthand, techniques that are only taught in upper-level or graduate courses.*

—Katie Mahoney '07

Projects like these reflect key facets of the Rensselaer philosophy: embracing discovery, creativity, and imagination for its own sake, while always keeping an eye toward how ideas can serve humanity. From creating a synthetic replacement for the blood-thinner Heparin to examining the design of the New Orleans levees, our researchers and students continue to honor the vision of our founders.

> *RPI has the resources available to give you what you want and need from the college experience.*

—Amanda Feather '07

Study Abroad

Maintaining a global perspective is a critical component of the Rensselaer mission. Every undergraduate can participate in an overseas program such as REACH; Rensselaer Engineering Education Across Cultural Horizons. Through this program, students study at locations ranging from Denmark to Singapore. The School of Architecture maintains a robust study abroad requirement that can include trips to Italy, China, and Turkey. Other students choose to participate in their own study abroad programs, that are coordinated with and facilitated by the Rensselaer Office of Undergraduate Education.

SOCIAL LIFE AND ACTIVITIES

The Rensselaer Student Experience

The Rensselaer First-Year Experience program, recognized as one of the best in the nation, is rich in resources and activities that help students make a successful transition to college life. A variety of campus living choices are available, including special-interest theme housing options such as Leadership House and a living and learning community focused on earth, energy, and the environment.

Clustered Learning, Advocacy, and Support for Students (CLASS)

In 2010, the Institute built on the success for the award-winning First-Year Experience program by formally launching the Clustered Learning, Advocacy, and Support for Students (CLASS) initiative. CLASS aims to transform the student experience at Rensselaer by elevating the quality of support for students throughout the undergraduate years. Clusters of residence halls are being developed in order to create smaller, more tightly-knit student communities. These commons will be supported by faculty, student life professionals, and upper-class and graduate student assistants living in or near each of the clusters of residence halls. Additionally, the CLASS initiative will support students who are living off-campus or in Greek life residences.

RPI students put as much passion and drive into extracurricular pursuits as they do into their academics. We encourage students to lead fulfilled and balanced lives by exploring interests ranging from ballroom dancing and improvisational comedy to playing in our pep band or writing for the school newspaper, *The Rensselaer Polytechnic*. There are 164 student-run clubs and organizations—from Habitat for Humanity to the ski club—help fos-

---

ter teamwork and leadership skills. The fraternity and sorority community at Rensselaer, which dates back to 1853, provides opportunities for both leadership development and service programming in more than thirty Greek-letter organizations.

> *" Rensselaer will provide you with the ability to benefit fully from your undergraduate experience in a place where your individual contribution truly matters. The people of Rensselaer are exceptional bridge builders; our graduates masterminded the bridges going in and out of Manhattan and completed the Panama Canal. That tradition is embodied in the Rensselaer undergraduate experience, where students' academic pursuits are fully integrated with residential, athletic, arts, and student activity programs. "*

ATHLETICS AT RENSSELAER

Rensselaer is an NCAA Division III school with two NCAA Division I teams:

Men's Varsity Sports
- Baseball
- Basketball
- Cross Country
- Football
- Golf
- Ice Hockey (Division I)
- Indoor Track and Field
- Lacrosse
- Soccer
- Swimming
- Tennis
- Track and Field

Women's Varsity Sports
- Basketball
- Cross Country
- Field Hockey
- Ice Hockey (Division I)
- Indoor Track and Field
- Lacrosse
- Soccer
- Softball
- Swimming
- Tennis
- Track and Field

Athletics

More than seventy percent of Rensselaer students participate in some form of athletics. In addition to our NCAA Division I women's and men's ice hockey teams, students can choose from among twenty-one other varsity teams and fifty intramural and club sports. The scholar-athletes at Rensselaer are among the best in the nation, with a record number of National Academic All-Americans. Rensselaer continues to elevate our athletic opportunities with the construction of the East Campus Athletic Village, adding a new football stadium, basketball arena, and sports medicine facility to our athletics complex.

FINANCIAL AID

Rensselaer offers a comprehensive and robust financial aid program with more than ninety-five percent of students receiving some form of assistance. More than $135 million in aid is distributed to undergraduates each year. The university has committed $80 million of its resources for need-based and merit scholarships, including the $60,000 Rensselaer Medal Scholarship for superior high school achievements in math and science.

To simplify the financial aid process, Rensselaer also provides each student/family with a financial aid counselor to provide guidance and assistance. All applicants for admission are given full consideration for all of the merit awards available at Rensselaer. Selection of awards is made after a thorough review of the information that has been included as part of the admissions application. No separate application is required for merit scholarship consideration. Entering freshmen must complete the Free Application for Federal Student Aid (FAFSA) and the College Scholarship Service (CSS) Profile to apply for institutional and federal need-based aid. More information on these applications is available on the Rensselaer Financial Aid Web site.

The Rensselaer Medal

For more than ninety years, the university has awarded the Rensselaer Medal in conjunction with high schools around the world. It was first presented in 1916 with two purposes: to recognize the superlative academic achievement of young men and women, and to motivate students toward careers in science, engineering, and technology. The Rensselaer Medal is awarded to promising secondary school juniors who have distinguished themselves in mathematics and science. Responsibility for selecting the Rensselaer Medalist belongs to faculty and staff within the participating secondary school. This $15,000 per year merit scholarship is guaranteed for four years (five years for the School of Architecture program) to be applied to the tuition for each medalist who is accepted and chooses to enroll at Rensselaer.

GRADUATES

Entrepreneurial thinking lies at the heart of Rensselaer's philosophy. As a result, the university has helped our graduates launch many successful businesses including Union Carbide, Texas Instruments, Level 3 Communications, and NVIDIA. The video game giant

Vicarious Visions once operated out of a Rensselaer residence hall. Drawing one-third of its employees from Rensselaer's graduate pool, the company creates such successful video games as *Guitar Hero III, Tony Hawk's Pro Skater 2,* and *Spider-Man 3.*

> 66 *The faculty and course work at Rensselaer have taught me to take on problems from many different angles, and to continually strive for success. I feel confident and ready to join the global workforce after I graduate.* 99

—*Will Manning, '07*

PROMINENT GRADUATES

- Marshall Brian, Class of '83, Creator, "How Stuff Works"
- Dr. Myles Brand, '64, Former President, NCAA
- Gary Burrell, '63, Founder and Chairman Emeritus of Garmin Ltd.
- Bruce A Carbonari, '93, Chairman and Chief Executive Officer Fortune Brands Inc.
- James Crowe, '72, President and CEO of Level 3 Communications
- Wanda Dension-Low, '78, Sr. Vice President, Boeing Company
- George W. G. Ferris, 1881, Inventor, Ferris Wheel
- Claire Fraser, '77, Director of Institute for Genome Science
- J. Erik Jonsson, '22, Co-founder and Former President of Texas Instruments Incorporated, Former Mayor of Dallas
- John E. Kelly III, '78, Sr. Vice President and Director of Research, IBM
- Washington Roebling, 1857, Engineer-Builder, Brooklyn Bridge
- Dennis Tito, '63, Founder, Wilshire Associates

Rensselaer alumni have also launched dozens of businesses in engineering and the sciences. Osborn Engineering, which has designed more than 100 U.S. sports stadiums, including the original Yankee Stadium and Fenway Park, was established by a Rensselaer alumnus. Gary Burrell '63 co-founded Garmin International, a world-class manufacturer of GPS navigation systems.

On average, more than seventy percent of Rensselaer graduates report that they have secured a job by graduation, and another twenty percent go on to attend top graduate schools for advanced degrees. The top employers of Rensselaer graduates annually include General Electric, Lockheed Martin, the Boeing Company, Accenture, Deloitte Consulting, BAE Systems, and IBM.

The Rensselaer alumni network consists of 90,000+ alumni from Switzerland to Venezuela, and from Florida to California. The Rensselaer Alumni Association operates dozens of local groups to assist alumni in connecting and networking, as well as providing special lectures and unique events, such as a "behind the scenes" tour of the North American Aerospace Defense Command (NORAD) in Colorado. Rensselaer alumni are always willing to assist recent graduates with job opportunities and contacts, and understand the tremendous rigor and thoroughness of a Rensselaer education.

SUMMING UP

As a top-tier research university, Rensselaer has produced some of the foremost entre-preneurs, innovators, and visionaries in the world. The undergraduate experience provides our students with the opportunity to walk in the footsteps of our distinguished graduates, and equips them to be driving forces behind the world's next great innovations.

Our campus culture supports an environment that encourages discovery, creativity, innovation, and diversity. Students learn and grow inside and outside the classroom through myriad opportunities to explore new interests and passions while forming lifelong friendships and social connections with their peers. The robust living-learning experience students find at Rensselaer prepares them for academic achievement, entrepreneurship, creative expression, and global leadership. This is where great adventures begin.

❑ *Raymond Lutzky, B.S.*

RHODES COLLEGE

Courtesy of Rhodes College

 Rhodes College
Memphis, TN 38112-1690

 (901) 843-3000
(800) 844-5969

 E-mail: *adminfo@rhodes.edu*
Website: *www.rhodes.edu*

 Enrollment

Full-time ❑ women: 983
       ❑ men: 730

INTRODUCING RHODES COLLEGE

    Located in vibrant Memphis, Tennessee, Rhodes College offers a traditional liberal arts education in a beautiful residential learning environment. Nestled in a quiet historic neighborhood on a 100-acre wooded campus dominated by giant oaks and Collegiate Gothic architecture, Rhodes is home to around 1,700 students from across the country and throughout the world. With its 10:1 student-to-faculty ratio, the college delivers hands-on attention in all aspects of student life. From financial aid to academics, and internships to postgraduate study, Rhodes, if anything, is personal.

If you choose Rhodes, here are just a few of the things you can anticipate.

- As a student, you should expect to work incredibly hard. The academics at Rhodes are challenging to put it mildly, but the supportive environment, extraordinary faculty, and the opportunity to embrace and explore your academic passions make it more than worth it.
- Students, faculty, and staff are all expected to live by the Honor Code. It's not just an idealized value, but a way of life that applies to everything from doing your own academic work to using your own laundry detergent in the community laundry facilities.
- You will likely spend at least one or two days a week volunteering in some capacity— it's the unofficial pastime of choice for most Rhodes students. In fact, in fall 2010 Rhodes was selected *Newsweek's* Most Service-Minded School in America.
- Because Rhodes is located in a major metropolitan area, students have internship opportunities at world-renowned institutions such as St. Jude Children's Research Hospital, and at FedEx and other Fortune 500 companies.
- At Rhodes, you will need to be ready to sing (and shout) "Roll on, Lynx Cats!" for all sorts of situations, including sporting and other events. As a Division III college, athletics are not the primary focus, but Lynx pride is everywhere on campus. Rhodes is perhaps the only college in the country with a Lynx as its mascot.

Rhodes is a remarkable college in many ways, but the thing that most sets it apart from other liberal arts schools is the people it attracts and retains. At Rhodes, you will find the most incredible, dedicated staff members who go out of their way to make you feel at home from the minute you walk on campus. From the grounds crew members to the president, Rhodes is filled with friendly, accessible people who are eager to know you on a personal level. It's not uncommon for a food service employee at the refectory to inquire how your senior thesis is coming, or if you'll be studying abroad next semester. Likewise, the president of the college, the popular Dr. Bill Troutt, is likely to know your Greek affiliation and the campus organizations you belong to, as well as who your RA or roommate is. At Rhodes, college is personal.

Rhodes is also a campus full of friendly students. It's uncommon to walk to class without exchanging greetings with everyone—most are familiar faces, but students are also eager to approach and engage those who are outside their immediate social circle. Professors also help to encourage this behavior. Outside of class, professors can be found at the coffee shop in the library, at the Lynx Lair snack bar, or catching a performance of the current production at McCoy Theatre. Not only are Rhodes professors friendly, they truly go out of their way to immerse themselves in the lives of the students and the overall campus culture.

The Environment

The sheer beauty of the Rhodes campus can be overwhelming. It's a truly inspiring environment in which to study and live. The Collegiate Gothic architecture, including thirteen buildings on the National Register of Historic Places, feature colorful stained glass windows. (The young students at neighboring Snowden Elementary School refer to Rhodes students as those who "live in the castles!") Despite the great beauty of the school, Rhodes is no ivory tower. More than seventy percent of current students are actively involved in some type of volunteer activity, many in leadership roles. In fact, volunteering is part of the cultural makeup of the campus, as well as an integral part of the social scene. Many Rhodes students get together with friends, classmates, and members of their Greek affiliation to participate in volunteer activities. And many new friendships are made as well.

MEMPHIS

The idyllic Rhodes campus is located just four miles from downtown Memphis. The rich history of the city, coupled with the thriving cultural scene, will provide the ultimate collegiate experience. From exploring blues clubs on Beale Street to attending art openings in the Cooper-Young district just minutes away from campus, you will be able to partake in a wide variety of experiences to loosen up after a long day.

And then there's the food. Memphis is home to some of the world's best barbecue, from mild to tangy and hot to spicy. It's a favorite pastime of students to search out "their" barbecue place, although it will take you at least a couple of years to try all of them!

Rhodes has a strong, interconnected relationship with the Memphis community that is unique among "town and gown" relationships. This bond of mutual respect is deeply valued by students, faculty, and staff, and it fosters a rich experience for everyone concerned.

Rhodes students are held in high esteem throughout the community, which can lead to privileges such as in-depth internships that provide real access and relevancy, as well as a plethora of networking opportunities. The bond between Rhodes and the community is strengthened even more by students' commitment to outreach, which has consistently served as an integral element of the college's core values. Students are expected to lead by example, frequently heading up large-scale service efforts to address local needs. It would be easy to peg Rhodes as the ivory tower of Memphis, but it's simply not the case. Because the Rhodes learning experience extends outside the gates, it's hard to find a corner of the city that hasn't been touched by the college.

ADMISSIONS REQUIREMENTS

Admission to Rhodes is highly selective, but some of the criteria may be a little different from what you expect. Rhodes looks at your previous accomplishments as well as the promise you show. While more than half of the entering students in 2010 were in the top ten percent of their class, students are admitted for a variety of reasons. You must show a demonstrated ability to complete the rigorous academic program at Rhodes, yet the college also looks for what you will contribute to the campus. Specifically, Rhodes looks for passionate individuals who truly care about the community and are deeply involved in a few key areas of interest. Serving as a leader of a community or school-based organization, or having a deep commitment to a particular cause or group, are more important to the Rhodes admission process than being a part of every club, team, or community organization. The theory is that students who show a deep commitment to a personal passion will likely continue to pursue that passion while at Rhodes. Whether you serve as a mentor to children in the community or learn everything there is to know about Russian literature, you will know that Rhodes values and honors your passions.

That being said, Rhodes does value applicants with strong academic backgrounds, and the requirements are highly competitive:

- More than half of the entering class typically has a GPA of 3.6 or higher.
- Median SAT score for accepted applicants is 1220–1370.
- Median ACT score for accepted applicants is 26–30.

Don't meet these numbers? Take heart. Each application to Rhodes is individually evaluated to determine a student's preparedness to tackle the coursework, as well as what the student will contribute to the campus as a whole. The essay portion of the Rhodes application is also a great way to distinguish yourself from the rest of the applicant pool. While giving you an opportunity to show off your writing skills, the essay also gives you a chance to show some personality and share some of your life experiences that would enhance the Rhodes community.

Rhodes also emphasizes the value of lifelong learning, so it is essential for potential students to possess a curiosity about the world and a willingness to engage in a wide array of experiences in an increasingly global community.

Applying to Rhodes

When applying to Rhodes, you have the option to apply through either the Early Decision, Early Action, or Regular Decision programs. The Early Decision program is an excellent choice if you know you want to attend Rhodes and are ready to make the commitment if selected. Early Decision applicants turn in applications by November 1, and notifications regarding acceptance are mailed out by December 1. The benefits of applying Early Decision are numerous:

- The application review process is accelerated, minimizing the time you spend waiting for an answer.
- Students who are not accepted under Early Decision will still be considered with regular fall applications. This also gives you a chance to speak more in depth with an admission counselor about ways to improve your chances of acceptance, such as re-taking standardized tests, improving grades, or planning additional visits to Rhodes.
- Applicants who are not accepted under Early Decision have additional time to prepare applications for other schools.
- Accepted applicants have additional time to plan the transition from high school to college.
- Applicants who apply Early Decision have the advantage of a full pool of scholarship money, which may up your chances of receiving a scholarship to Rhodes, although there is no official stance from the college on this matter.
- If accepted, you can celebrate early and enjoy your senior year!

"Applying Early Decision gave me the peace of mind that I had secured a spot at the school of my dreams and allowed me to enjoy the rest of my senior year in high school, while planning out the details of the transition and becoming better acquainted with Memphis."

Early Action is different from Early Decision in several ways. It's the best option if you want to know if you are accepted at Rhodes early in the game, but aren't ready to make a commitment to attend if accepted. With Early Action, you send in your application by November 15 and are notified of acceptance, financial aid, and scholarship offers by January 15. You can then decide to commit to Rhodes at that time, or wait until May 1 to make a commitment. Early Action provides more flexibility than Early Decision and has some of the same benefits. However, Early Decision does show a seriousness of purpose and a strong desire to attend Rhodes, which likely tips the scale in favor of Early Decision students. That said, both groups seem to have an advantage over those who apply via the Regular Decision process. In short, if you feel strongly that Rhodes is the school for you, it's best to apply through Early Decision or Early Action to enhance your chances of acceptance.

You can also increase your chances of being accepted to Rhodes by visiting the campus. Serious consideration is given to students who demonstrate a strong interest and commitment to the college. It's important to schedule an interview with an admission counselor, because it's a good way to determine your strengths and weaknesses in the application process, and it gives you an opportunity to address any areas of concern with your application, transcript, or standardized test scores. The admission counselors want to fully understand your background in order to facilitate the admission process. The counselors can also be excellent resources for students who are still considering Rhodes but are unsure of whether it is the right choice. The counselors excel at pointing students to different on-campus resources and setting up opportunities for potential applicants to chat with current Rhodes students who have mutual interests. While you're on campus visiting, make sure to take some time to talk with students, all of whom tend to be exceedingly friendly and willing to talk about the Rhodes experience. You should definitely sit in on a class as well.

SOCIAL LIFE AND ACTIVITIES

Rhodes is a campus full of leaders, evidenced by the wide variety of clubs, sports, and activities that are available. If anything, Rhodes students are overly involved in their activities and commitments, constantly juggling academics, work, volunteering, and socializing. Such involvement better prepares students for life after college.

Greek Life

There are more than eighty student-led organizations at Rhodes, and more than half of the student body participate in Greek life. Greek life at Rhodes is a little different from other schools in that the organizations are inclusive of the entire campus, frequently hosting open events and parties. The nonresidential Greek system encourages mingling with different groups, making a Greek affiliation only one aspect of social life, not an entire social identity.

Kappa Delta All Sing is a good example of what Greek life is like at Rhodes. It is held annually at the Bryan Campus Life Center (BCLC), and all groups on campus are invited to participate in a dance-off of sorts, the prize being bragging rights for the year and a chance to show off moves in front of an audience packed to the rafters. The event is held during fall Parent/Family Weekend, which only adds to the fun and festivities that come with dancing, singing, and cheering loudly with a group of your best friends, both new and old. All Greek groups participate, as do many other student organizations, from the BSA (Black Student Association) to Rhodes Service Scholars to a diverse group of students known as Crunk. It's definitely an evening to remember and one of the highlights of the fall semester on campus.

Community Service

With more than eighty percent of the student body actively involved in or leading service-oriented activities through the Kinney Program, Rhodes is so well known for volunteering that it was named the Most Service-Minded School in America by *Newsweek*.

THE KINNEY PROGRAM

The Kinney Program is synonymous with community service at Rhodes. Affiliated with more than 100 different service programs and organizations in Memphis, the Kinney Program is a one-stop shop for volunteering. Rhodes students are well known for being dedicated to community service, partly because of personal passion, partly because of campus culture, and partly because Rhodes makes it so easy to find the perfect volunteer opportunities. Students can meet with Kinney service coordinators to learn about a variety of opportunities, ranging from service work focused on health care to homelessness, mentoring youth, to spending time with seniors. There is truly an opportunity to fit every interest and time commitment—and if there's not, the Kinney service coordinators are happy to arrange special projects or extend new affiliations to enhance the service opportunities for every student.

Rhodes students view volunteering as an opportunity to invest in the lives of those around them and expand the classroom experience. You will have the opportunity to choose a volunteer experience based on your major or future career. For example, premed students have the chance to volunteer at St. Jude Children's Research Hospital, while future educators are provided an opportunity to tutor struggling students in the community. It all comes down to the same thing: Rhodes students truly care about the community on both a local and global level.

Rites of Spring

Rites of Spring, an outdoor concert series hosted by the Rhodes Activities Board, is one of the most loved and anticipated events of the year. With winter but a distant memory, students shed overcoats for familiar jeans and Ts, and celebrate the rebirth and beauty of spring by enjoying the sounds of several well-known musicians and bands.

Homecoming

Homecoming is a special time for reconnection and for fostering new friendships. It's also a time to party. The Rhodes Homecoming experience includes a series of parties, mixers, and brunches. Most students kick off the party on game day at the Greek houses (including both Greek and non-Greek students, as well as many young alums!) and move to the bleachers just before the football game begins. After the game, students filter into the Lynx Lair to continue the festivities.

The Rat

The Rat is an affectionate name for the Catherine Burrow Refectory. But rest assured, the name does not reflect the quality of the food that is served there! The Rat offers an all-you-can-eat experience with a wide variety of cuisines, including something for the meat lover and your garden-variety vegan. A cousin to Rhodes's other prime eatery, the Lynx Lair, the Rat is a favorite for early-morning breakfasts and as a place to meet up for an informal study session.

The Rat is also the location for another Rhodes tradition—the late-night pancake study breaks during midterms and finals, when faculty members cook pancakes for the students. Adding to the beauty of this situation is that it is completely free and is late enough in the evening to give even the most exhausted student the much-needed sugar rush to push through.

Athletics

With more than ninety-one percent of students participating in an athletic activity on the varsity, club, or intramural level, there's a lot of Lynx pride at Rhodes. An NCAA Division III member, Rhodes has excellent facilities for student athletes and for those who just want a little activity. The Bryan Campus Life Center (BCLC) is home to a three-court, multi-use gymnasium, which typically is used for intramurals, club sports, and practices, as

---

BIG DIEHL

The Big Diehl is truly a "big deal" at Rhodes. Its unusual spelling is in honor of Charles Diehl, a former president of the college, whose statue presides over the courtyard outside Burrow Hall. The Big Diehl is designed to provide students with engaging, low-cost–or free–weekend programming. Now in its fourth year, the Big Diehl includes weekend ski trips for $20, cheap events at FedEx Forum, free movie tickets, whitewater rafting adventures, affordable excursions to St. Louis and Atlanta, and the ever-popular Redbirds baseball games and Memphis Grizzlies NBA action in downtown Memphis. Big Diehl events are organized by a committee of staff and students, who plan and host around ten events each semester. Big Diehl programs are open only to Rhodes students and allow them to get out and enjoy some of the amazing activities that Memphis has to offer, while also encouraging students to mingle and make new friends. The events and excursions are so popular that long lines form each time event registration opens, and event tickets frequently disappear within twenty minutes.

---

well as a "performance" gym for basketball and volleyball games. The BCLC also includes a 7,000-square-foot training gym and weight room, including cardio equipment. In addition, there's also an indoor track that overlooks the multi-court gymnasium.

Rhodes offers the following varsity sports:

- Baseball (Men only)
- Basketball
- Cross-Country
- Field Hockey (Women only)
- Football (Men only)
- Golf
- Lacrosse (Men only)
- Soccer
- Softball (Women only)
- Swimming
- Tennis
- Track & Field
- Volleyball (Women only)

Club sports at Rhodes offer diverse kinds of recreation, including:

- Badminton
- Cheerleading
- Crew
- Cricket
- Dance Team
- Fencing
- Women's Lacrosse
- Net Footbag
- Quidditch
- Ultimate Frisbee

The Rhodes Outdoors Organization also falls under the heading of a club sport, and includes hiking, rafting, and rock climbing, among other outdoor activities.

Intramural sports are the most relaxed athletic activities at Rhodes, but also some of the most competitive. Student organizations, dorms, and Greek organizations compete to win a variety of tournaments, from Wiffleball to volleyball. The vast majority of students participate in intramural sports at some point. You may not win every time, but you will definitely have fun!

Intramural sports at Rhodes include:

- Basketball
- Flag Football
- Soccer
- Volleyball
- Wiffleball

ACADEMIC LIFE

Academics at Rhodes are second to none, with programs and courses of study that will truly engage and immerse you, while also providing exposure to a wide variety of disciplines true to the liberal arts tradition. While the faculty at Rhodes is very nurturing and supportive, you will ultimately be expected and required to take responsibility for your own learning and development, and to seek out opportunities for academic and personal growth as an extension of classroom experiences. The special thing about Rhodes is that students here actually do just that. With a foundation of mutual respect between professors and students, you'll be equipped with the tools and the confidence needed to pursue academic passions outside of the classroom, whether it's applying for postgraduate fellowship programs, starting a new tutoring program, or publishing research.

Faculty

In truth, the best thing about Rhodes is the faculty. With a 10:1 student-to-faculty ratio, professors can custom tailor curriculum to address the specific interests of the class and to meet the needs of individual students. Professors at Rhodes really exemplify what it means to be a lifelong learner. More than ninety-seven percent of the Rhodes faculty hold the highest academic degree in their field and all are committed to incorporating their own scholarly pursuits and interests into the classroom. A true testament to the value of a Rhodes education is in the college's ability to hire and retain professors who have studied and worked at top universities, but who are committed to their role as educators, not just scholars.

❝Rhodes professors demand a great deal of their students, but offer the support needed for students to grow and meet the high standards set before them. ❞

Learning at Rhodes is not a solitary pursuit. Classes are extremely challenging and rigorous and require long hours of study; yet, the college provides a strong system of support for students, both on an institutional level and at a more casual, social level. The entire campus is equipped to make scholarly activities a cohesive part of student life. Barret Library offers a multitude of quiet study areas, lounges, quiet nooks, and coffee bars, which provide opportunities for group study in special "conference"-style rooms and plush, over-stuffed chairs complete with footrests and sweeping views of the campus. In other locations, there are several computer lounges and separate desks for those who require a bit more structure to churn out their term papers.

The Library

Built in 2005, Barret is a state-of-the-art, world-class college library that truly caters to the needs of students. The library offers incredible volumes of information, as well as a café/study lounge known as the Middle Ground, which features a Starbucks coffee bar, granite counter tops, comfortable chairs and tables for study or conversation, six computers for checking e-mail, and four more for general use. Students can take a break and gaze up at the twenty-four-foot ceiling to view a painting of the constellations as they appeared the year that Rhodes was founded back in 1848. With carpet that features the Rhodes seal, along with the great Gothic chandeliers, Barret is nothing short of inspirational, imbuing students with a sense of purpose and history.

Majors and Courses

There are twenty-four departmental and eight interdisciplinary majors at Rhodes, as well as thirty-five minors. Available degrees include a Bachelor of Arts, Bachelor of Science, and a Master's in Accounting. The most popular majors are Biology, History, English, Business, and Psychology, but students get to try a bit of everything by fulfilling the Foundations Curriculum requirements.

At Rhodes, you will be required to enroll in one of the college's two signature interdisciplinary humanities courses: "Search for Values in the Light of Western History and Religion" or "Life: Then and Now," both of which involve three semesters of study. "Search" is an interdisciplinary study of the ideas, beliefs, and major developments that formed western culture. Established in 1945, "Search" draws faculty from ten departments. The "Life" program is designed for those who want to study the origins and practice of Christianity (a nod to Rhodes's Presbyterian roots).

In addition, you will be required to take at least two years of a foreign language, reflecting Rhodes's emphasis on empowering students to be global citizens and leaders of the next generation.

More than forty percent of students participate in academic and paid internships. Opportunities abound, with more than one hundred local, national, and international businesses looking to bring on Rhodes interns. The academic internship experience is highly encouraged at Rhodes and is seen as an essential tool for building professional skills, learning outside of the classroom in a "real world" setting, and connecting students with professionals in their interest. Internships also provide the chance to gauge different career paths.

> The Fellowship Program at Rhodes will provide an opportunity to gain solid research experience in one's area of interest by working alongside professors, leaders in the field, and other students. Through Rhodes programs such as CODA (the Center for Outreach in the Developments of the Arts), Crossroads to Freedom, Rhodes St. Jude Summer Plus, the Rhodes Institute for Regional Studies, and the Rhodes Summer Service Fellowship Program, students will have the chance to extend the learning experience beyond the classroom.

FINANCIAL AID

College is expensive, but more than seventy-five percent of Rhodes students receive financial aid, and more than eighty-five percent receive some form of financial assistance through fellowships, scholarships, grants, loans, and work-study. The average aid package for students with demonstrated need is more than $32,035. Of the class of 2013, more than fifty-one percent received four-year competitive scholarships, fellowships, and awards.

The total cost of a Rhodes education is $43,060 a year for residential students, which includes tuition, fees, dual-occupancy housing, and twenty-one meals per week at the Rat or Lynx Lair. Rhodes provides a variety of free services, including Internet access, cable TV, computer labs with full software packages, free laundry facilities, and free parking, among other benefits.

Many students participate in the work-study program and use it as a way to help pay for college. The most popular locations for work-study tend to be the campus coffee shop, assisting staff at Barret Library, and working at the BCLC. The various academic departments also have a steady complement of work-study students.

GRADUATES

Rhodes is really a training ground for students who go on to serve in remarkable ways. The majority of graduates pursue postgraduate degrees, with applicants to medical school having twice the national average acceptance rate. Rhodes grads also enjoy a more than ninety-five percent acceptance rate to business, divinity, and law schools.

Many graduates choose to dedicate the first year or two out of school to service work through a variety of programs, the most popular of which is Teach for America, a dual degree/service program with participants earning a master's degree while teaching on-site at at-risk schools.

SUMMING UP

Rhodes is an excellent school that is truly different from other liberal arts colleges because of its metropolitan setting, which provides students with unlimited community service, academic internship, study abroad, and employment opportunities. If you choose to attend Rhodes, you'll graduate with a sense of pride for the college, a deep affinity for Memphis, a longing to return to the beautiful grounds, and a true appreciation for the students, staff, and faculty who relentlessly pushed you to pursue your goals.

❝ I can't recommend any organization in any sector more than I recommend Rhodes. It was a truly life-altering experience for me and for many students. ❞

❑ *Kristine Page, B.A.*

RICE UNIVERSITY

	Rice University **Houston, TX 77005**	**Enrollment**
	(713) 348-RICE; (800) 527-OWLS Fax: (713) 348-5952	**Full-time** ❏ women: 1,567 ❏ men: 1,695 **Part-time** ❏ women: 28 ❏ men: 29

INTRODUCING RICE

Established in 1912, Rice University is one of the youngest and most dynamic of America's highly competitive universities. Although it may not boast the lengthy history of many of its peer institutions, it has taken advantage of the unique opportunity to create an ideal college environment by analyzing and emulating the successful attributes of its predecessors. Well before the first students matriculated, Rice's founders commissioned a study of the premiere educational institutions of the world. After visiting seventy-eight institutions in fifteen countries, the traveling party returned to Texas and combined the best attributes of each into their own vision of a utopian university on the outskirts of the young city of Houston.

The Rice of today has achieved international prominence among educational institutions by adapting itself to the needs of the twenty-first century while remaining loyal to the well-crafted vision of its founders. That vision focuses on three guiding principles:

- A focus on *undergraduate* teaching and research led by world-class faculty.
- A commitment to making the Rice educational experience affordable to all qualified students.
- Development of a vibrant yet close-knit academic and social community based on an inclusive residential college system.

As a result, Rice students benefit from an atmosphere of learning that infuses the campus, both within and outside of the classroom, and that allows them to stimulate their intellectual curiosity while forging lifelong friendships with classmates and faculty alike. Perhaps what makes Rice most revered by its students, however, is its ability to provide a challenging and rewarding academic environment without stifling the fun-loving nature of its 3,319 undergraduates. The administration is known for being particularly tolerant of the mischief that often results from the collaboration of some of the nation's most creative young minds.

The intensity and frivolity of the Rice experience are combined on a 300-acre wooded campus in the heart of Houston, the nation's fourth largest city. The campus itself, which is closed to through-traffic and is bounded by an eight-foot hedge and live oak trees, is surrounded by the world's largest medical center; an impressive museum district (offering student discounts); a city park that is home to a zoo, an outdoor amphitheater, and a public golf course; an upscale residential neighborhood; and a lively pedestrian shopping district that includes both conventional and quirky shops and a diverse array of restaurants and pubs. Though students do not have to set foot outside of the campus or the adjacent neighborhoods for learning opportunities or weekend entertainment, they do not hesitate to venture out to exciting venues throughout the lively and very navigable city of Houston. Whether students are enjoying the city's internationally-recognized performing arts scene, internship opportunities at Fortune 500 companies, research projects in the medical center, or live music at the city's numerous concert venues, they consider the city of Houston to be a very important partner in their Rice educational experience.

ADMISSIONS REQUIREMENTS

Rice prides itself on having a student body that is diverse in every sense—from ethnic, religious, and geographic backgrounds to socioeconomic status and political tendencies to musical and athletic prowess. As a result, admissions at Rice is a very individualized process that endeavors to compile a class of unique individuals who will challenge and learn from each other during their four years at Rice and throughout their lives.

First and foremost, Rice seeks to admit students who are intellectually prepared for and eager to participate in the Rice community. Although grades and test scores can be helpful in determining a student's likelihood of success, other factors that illustrate a student's motivation, such as course selection, teacher recommendations, and extracurricular involvement, are equally important. In fact, in its attempts to compile a diverse but symbiotic class, the Admission Committee may forgo a technically superior candidate in favor of another qualified individual with the capacity to make a unique impact on campus life. Thus, strong academic candidates who use their applications to tell their personal stories and demonstrate commitment and perseverance within and outside of the classroom typically have the best chance for success. Nonetheless, the competition is rigorous: of the 12,393 applicants for a recent freshman class, only 2,639 (twenty-one percent) received an offer of admission.

Rice requires its applicants to submit the customary application components: SAT plus two SAT Subject Test scores, or the Act with writing: an official high school transcript, recommendations from high school teachers and counselors, the Rice application, and a $70 application fee. An interview is also recommended and can add a personal touch to an application while providing the candidate an opportunity to learn more about life as a Rice student. Applicants to the schools of Architecture and Music are also required to submit a portfolio or perform a live audition, respectively.

Rice uses the Common Application, which collects basic information, and, like many selective colleges, also requires a Common Application Supplement. The Common Application Supplement provides students with multiple opportunities to express themselves, including several short-answer questions, a thought-provoking essay, and an empty two-dimensional box that applicants are asked to fill with something that appeals to them (an excellent opportunity to make an impression on a reviewer!).

Note: Each component of the application receives a thorough review, so be sure to answer each question carefully, choose conscientious teachers to write your recommendations, and watch those typos!

Decision Plans

To help alleviate the anxiety surrounding the college admissions process, Rice offers two decision plans for its applicants.

1. Students who are confident that Rice is their first choice school and would like to complete the application process early may apply via the Early Decision Plan by November 1. While awaiting the December 15 notification date, students may continue to prepare and submit applications to other schools as long as no other early decision applications are filed. Students admitted under the Early Decision Plan are required to either commit to Rice or withdraw their applications by January 2. Nonadmitted students may be deferred for later consideration or denied admission.

2. Students using the Regular Decision Plan must postmark their applications by January 2 and will receive notification by April 1. Regular Decision offers of admission must be accepted by May 1. In most years, a small number of talented applicants are also placed on the waiting list, and later, some may receive an offer of admission, filling spaces if they become available in May and June.

Rice/Baylor Medical Scholars Program

Each year, Rice and the Baylor College of Medicine offer a select group of students concurrent admission to an eight-year combined undergraduate and doctoral degree program. Admitted students enjoy access to special programs at Baylor during their four years at Rice and are offered automatic acceptance (i.e., no MCATs!) to Baylor College of Medicine upon their graduation. Interested students must submit the Common Application with the Rice Supplement and the Rice Baylor Medical Scholars Application by December 1.

Getting to Know Rice

One cannot fully appreciate the beauty and intimacy of the Rice campus without paying a visit to the university, so prospective students and their families are encouraged to schedule a trip to Houston if at all possible. The hospitable Admissions Office is open year-round, but visits during the school year can provide the best insight on campus life.

Visitors will quickly learn that one of the biggest indications of Rice students' love for their school is their enthusiastic participation in campus recruiting activities. Each year, hundreds of undergraduates volunteer to host prospective students on overnight visits, lead campus tours, and visit high schools to share information about Rice. In addition, students play a key role in the annual "Owl Days," when all admitted students are invited to spend a day and night on campus to experience life as a Rice student. While you are considering Rice, these student volunteers will be one of your best sources of information, so be sure to ask the Admissions Office about these student-sponsored programs.

> *With less than two weeks remaining to make my college decision, I headed to Houston for Owl Days, utterly confused about my future. I was fortunate enough to have been admitted to several universities, but deciding among them seemed to be an even more monumental task than completing the applications. Once I reached the campus, however, I relaxed and allowed myself to become immersed in the Rice experience. I became fast friends with other prospectives, met enthusiastic students and professors, attended stimulating classes, and learned about the endless opportunities for campus involvement. It didn't take long for me to realize that I felt at home in the Rice community. The next morning, I called my mom and asked her to cancel my reservation at another college recruiting event that weekend—I had decided on Rice! Thanks to Owl Days, I was able to make a truly informed college decision that I have never regretted.*

ACADEMIC LIFE

The aim of the Rice education is not simply to increase students' knowledge but to improve their capacity to learn and ability to think critically through teaching, research, testing, and experience. Whether students are studying in the schools of Engineering, Architecture, Music, Humanities, Social Sciences, or Natural Sciences, they are pushed toward this objective by accomplished faculty members who have come to Rice because they enjoy and are challenged by the exchange of ideas that takes place in its classrooms. A recent quote by Nobel Prize winner Professor Robert Curl typifies the attitude of the Rice faculty: "Teaching strengthens and nourishes research . . . [by] forcing one to think and rethink the very foundation of one's discipline, year after year."

The Rice Curriculum

The focus on producing well-rounded graduates who think independently is enhanced by the flexible Rice curriculum. Although students are asked to indicate a preferred area of concentration upon entrance to the university, Rice recognizes that intellectual development often leads to new ideas and new interests. Thus, the Rice education is designed to provide undergraduates with the maximum amount of flexibility to change their courses of study or pursue multiple and/or novel majors during their undergraduate careers.

> **“**I came to Rice fairly intent on majoring in political science and economics, and I entered my first academic advising session with a schedule full of poli and econ classes ready for the professor's approval. While acknowledging my eagerness, the professor shared with me the Rice philosophy of intellectual exploration and encouraged me to take a more diverse course load. Thanks to his advice, I broadened myself by enrolling in Introduction to Art History, Survey of African American Literature, Contemporary Moral and Legal Issues, and Sexuality and the Social Order, and developed a newfound appreciation for Rice's flexible curriculum. **”**

Students are particularly encouraged to explore the university's diverse course offerings during their first two years on campus. In fact, they are not required to declare a major until the spring semester of their sophomore year, and many change majors well after that time. With the exception of the Architecture and Music schools, there are no special entrance requirements, so changing majors can be as simple as submitting a form to the registrar. Even after students have declared a major, the relatively flexible degree requirements (particularly in the social sciences and humanities) allow them to continue to take classes in a broad array of disciplines or, in many cases, pursue a second or third major in other subjects. Other students find themselves intrigued by a multitude of interrelated fields and choose to pursue (or create!) an interdisciplinary major. As an added incentive to seek out academic challenges, Rice allows undergraduates to take up to four courses under the pass/fail designation.

Regardless of their chosen field of study, all Rice students are required to complete at least twelve hours in each of the general disciplines of science, social science, and the humanities. Most satisfy this requirement effortlessly.

Student-Faculty Relationships

Rice's esteemed faculty members teach ninety percent of undergraduate classes, and students benefit from a student-faculty ratio of five to one and a median class size of fifteen students. However, student-teacher interactions are certainly not limited to the classroom. The majority of professors are also affiliated with one of the residential colleges, thereby fostering more personal relationships between students and faculty. It is common to find faculty members playing on college softball teams, lunching in the college dining halls, inviting students to their homes, and bringing their children to campus on Halloween night to trick-or-treat. In addition, professors' affiliations with the colleges facilitate academic advising for underclassmen. During orientation, freshmen are assigned to faculty members from their colleges who teach in their areas of interest and will counsel them on course selection and other scholastic matters until they declare a major at the end of their sophomore year.

Rice professors also collaborate with their students in the many research laboratories on campus. The university's size, resources, and reputation combine to create ample opportunities for undergrads to complement their classroom experiences with firsthand research opportunities in a variety of disciplines. Professors and students alike frequently work closely with researchers from the Texas Medical Center, NASA, other governmental agencies, and numerous private companies. Because so many research opportunities exist on campus, many students find that all they have to do to get involved is volunteer.

Largely because of the factors cited above—small classes, the residential colleges, and research opportunities—the faculty are integral members of the Rice community and are uncommonly accessible. Few students leave Rice without having connected with one or more professors either through classes, the college system, or research opportunities. Thus, most students have several academic mentors to consult for advice on course selection, recommendations for graduate school, and career guidance.

The Honor Code

The Honor Code is a distinct feature of academic life at Rice. All undergraduates are schooled in the expectations of the Honor Code during orientation, and they are required to sign a pledge to refrain from giving or receiving unauthorized aid on each assignment. The success of the Honor Code provides Rice students with uncommon freedoms, including unproctored tests, take-home examinations, and self-scheduled finals. To most students, the Code is indispensable because of the trusting, accommodating environment it produces.

The success of the Honor Code depends entirely upon student enforcement of its tenets. In the rare instances when students observe others violating the Code, they are required to report the infraction to the student-led Honor Council. The Council considers all alleged violations and imposes appropriate punishments, ranging from loss of credit on an assignment to suspension from the university.

Grades

The grade inflation that has been widely reported at other universities is unknown at Rice. However, while students should enter Rice expecting to work hard, they can also expect to find every possible resource to help them succeed, including a flexible curriculum, accessible professors, and a trusting environment. In addition, students will find a network of support among their peers, for the Rice environment has always favored collaboration over competition. In the end, Rice graduates are rewarded with the admiration of top-notch graduate schools and employers who recognize that a Rice degree is a symbol of aptitude for success.

SOCIAL LIFE AND ACTIVITIES

The Colleges

The Rice community revolves around and is distinguished by its unique residential college system. The colleges serve as Rice's alternative to the Greek organizations and social clubs typically found on other American campuses, which are expressly forbidden by the Rice charter.

The inclusive college system randomly assigns all new students to one of the eleven colleges upon their acceptance to the university. In any given year, seventy to seventy-five percent of Rice students reside in their residential college, and the remaining students enjoy the benefits of membership despite their nonresident status. Since each college reflects the diversity of the entire student body, the system encourages friendships among students of different ages, races, backgrounds, and interests.

Each college is a separate physical structure similar to a dormitory that houses its own dining hall, computer lab, library, recreational lounges, and laundry room. In addition, a college is a self-governing body that provides opportunities for student leadership, innovation, and artistic expression through student government organizations, theatrical productions, athletic teams, social committees, and other activities.

The college system also facilitates student-faculty interaction. In addition to the non-resident faculty affiliates described above, each college has two resident associates and a college master who are members of the faculty or staff of the university. The RAs live in modified dorm rooms within the college itself, and the master, along with his or her family, lives in an adjacent house. All are present on a daily basis to enhance and participate in the college experience, not to patrol the activities of the residents.

> **"** *My parents loved Rice almost as much as I did. They anxiously awaited the annual Families Weekends so they could attend classes, mingle with my professors at social events, and get to know my friends over dinner at Houston's fabulous restaurants. However, they first realized the true importance of the Rice community during the middle of my freshman year when my grandfather passed away unexpectedly. Having met the Resident Associate at my college several times before, they knew they could call on him to be there for me when I heard the news, provide transportation to the airport, and inform my professors of my absence. My Rice 'family' made that difficult time a little easier for all of us.* **"**

From the minute Rice students set foot on campus during orientation week, they feel like part of their residential college family. Upperclassmen eagerly welcome their new "siblings" to Rice and coach them on their respective college traditions. The college bond continues to grow over the course of the Rice experience because members eat, study, compete, and relax together on a daily basis. Not surprisingly, the rivalries among the colleges are deep-rooted and fierce. The antagonism always begins with friendly pranks (called "jacks") that frequently occur between rival colleges during orientation week and continues through the annual spring ritual of Beer Bike, a bike-racing, beer and water (for underage competitors) chugging contest among the colleges.

Campus Clubs and Organizations

Rice is home to over 200 campus clubs and organizations, and because of the school's size, there are endless opportunities for campus involvement. It is not at all unusual to see motivated students assuming important campus roles such as newspaper reporter, radio disc jockey, or student association representative within just weeks of enrollment. Rice students also enjoy the advantage of an administration that expects and encourages student involvement in campus decision-making processes.

Athletics

Athletic events are some of the most popular activities on campus for both participants and spectators. Rice has the distinction of being one of the smallest universities to compete in Division I-A athletics but remains competitive despite its size. In recent years, the baseball team has won fifteen consecutive conference titles, made seven trips to the College World Series, and won the NCAA National Championship in 2003. The women's track team has garnered several individual national titles, and the Owls have generally finished in the top tier in Conference USA, in the sports in which they compete including basketball, cross-country, football, golf (men), track, soccer (women), swimming (women), tennis, and volleyball (women).

Rice also offers varying levels of competitive sports for nonvarsity athletes ranging from the casual competition of intramurals to intra-college contests that aggravate rivalries to the club teams that compete against other universities. Spectating remains a popular sport as well—friendships developed in the residential colleges translate into support on the field, whether for a roommate in a championship game or a neighbor in his or her first intramural match.

Other Student Interest Groups

In addition to athletics, many campus activities revolve around traditional student interest groups such as religious and social groups, political affiliations, service organizations, and academic and artistic pursuits. However, students also busy themselves throughout the year with such off-the-wall traditions as the Marching Owl Band, the school's satirical *non-marching* marching band; Baker 13, a bimonthly campus run led by shaving cream-clad daredevils; the legendary Rally Club, the unofficial, raucous cheering squad for the Owl athletic teams; and elaborate theme parties, including the infamous Night of Decadence ("NOD") at Halloween.

Social Activities

Social life at Rice is as varied as the students themselves. On a typical weekend, a host of activities keep students entertained without ever leaving the campus, such as a theme party thrown by one of the colleges, a theatrical production, live music at the coffeehouse, a pool tournament at the campus pub, or an Owl athletic event. One reason why social life revolves around the campus is that students of legal age are allowed to drink alcohol at Rice. Although unusual, the "wet" alcohol policy is consistent with the school's emphasis on student responsibility and is supported by the Rice community because it discourages drunken driving. In addition, many students believe the open policy results in less peer pressure to drink.

When students do venture off campus, the dance clubs, theaters, sporting and concert venues, restaurants, and art galleries of Houston provide them with limitless choices for quality entertainment. On long weekends or special occasions, students are inclined to take road trips to the beach (less than an hour away), nearby state parks, or a college-student haven such as Austin or New Orleans.

FINANCIAL AID

Rice is committed to attracting and retaining talented students regardless of their financial backgrounds, and it has established a three-pronged strategy to support this aim. Rice uses its large endowment to discount tuition for all students gaining recognition on a national level as being one of the best values in higher education. Rice administers a need-blind admission process so that students' applications for admission and financial aid are considered separately. Rice meets 100 percent of a student's demonstrated financial need through a combination of loans, grants, work-study programs, and scholarships. For families with less than $80,000 in total income, Rice meets all demonstrated need with grants and work-study—no loans.

GRADUATES

After four years of hard work, students graduate from Rice with a sharpened intellect, a true sense of accomplishment, and outstanding prospects for future success. Regardless of whether they elect to pursue graduate studies, international scholarship competitions, or employment opportunities, Rice grads can be sure that their undergraduate records will be held in high regard.

Graduate Studies

Past records show that approximately forty-four percent of graduates continue their studies immediately after Rice in some of the most prestigious graduate schools in the country. Often with the help of the preprofessional advising programs at Rice, these students have compiled impressive applications for graduate admissions and completed an undergraduate course of study that will enhance their graduate experiences. In fact, in a recent study, more than seventy percent of continuing students received an offer of admission to their first-choice graduate program, and ninety-three percent of medical school applicants were accepted to at least one program. In addition, Rice students are becoming increasingly successful at winning prominent national and international scholarships such as the Rhodes, Fulbright, Marshall, and Watson scholarships.

Employment Opportunities

Other students choose to pursue employment opportunities after Rice, and the university helps them to be equally prepared for the demanding interview process. Each year, more than 250 companies and organizations come to the Rice campus to recruit, and hundreds more alumni volunteer to mentor graduates in their disciplines. Within months of graduation, Rice students discover that their classmates have spread across the globe to pursue their varied interests in computational engineering, nonprofit organizations, business, environmental research, and other worthwhile pursuits.

Regardless of where the road to success might take them, however, most graduates remain in contact with their beloved Rice throughout their lives.

SUMMING UP

Rice students enjoy many luxuries during their undergraduate careers, including small classes, personal interactions with professors, first-rate research opportunities, an inclusive social structure, and a collaborative student environment. But what students come to appreciate most during their years at Rice is the culture of personal responsibility and self-determination that pervades the campus. The Rice administration treats its students like adults from the very first minute of orientation week through the end of graduation day. This trusting environment is evidenced throughout all aspects of student life, from the Honor Code and the flexible academic curriculum to the emphasis on student government, and the absence of hall monitors and curfews in the residential colleges. Such freedoms provide students with the ideal environment to mature and develop as intellectuals and as human beings. Although there will certainly be stumbles and challenges along the way, Rice students leave campus as some of the happiest and most self-aware, confident, and capable college graduates in the country.

❏ *Michol McMillian Ecklund, B.A.*

PROMINENT GRADS

○ E. Fay Jones, '51 Architect, American Institute of Architects Gold Medal Winner; Buildings Listed on National Register of Historic Places

○ Ken Kennedy, '67 Served as Cochair of the Federal Advisory Committee on High-Performance Computing and Communications, Information Technology, and the Next Generation Internet, Directs the GRADS Project

○ Larry McMurtry, '60 Author of more than twenty books including Lonesome Dove (1987 Pulitzer Prize), Terms of Endearment, and The Last Picture Show

○ Seth Morris, '35 Architect, numerous public buildings including Astrodome in Houston

○ Jim Newman, '84 NASA Astronaut

○ Hector Ruiz, '73 President and CEO Advanced Micro Devices, Fortune 500 Company in Sunnyvale, California

○ Frank Ryan, '58 NFL Quarterback (1958–1970); Former CEO of Contex Electronics; Former Professor of Computational and Applied Mathematics at Case Western, Yale, and Rice

○ Robert Wilson, '57 Nobel Laureate in Physics

SCRIPPS COLLEGE

Scripps College
Claremont, CA 91711

Main Line: (909) 621-8000
(909) 621-8149 or (800) 770-1333
Fax: (909) 607-7508

E-mail: *admission@scrippscollege.edu*
Website: *www.scrippscollege.edu*

 Enrollment

Full-time ❏ women: 946

INTRODUCING SCRIPPS COLLEGE

The motto of Scripps College is *Incipit Vita Nova*, Here Begins New Life, and nothing could be closer to the truth. From their first academic day (usually spent listening to a required interdisciplinary Core I lecture) to their last (spent finishing the required senior thesis), Scripps students are challenged to grow intellectually and personally by faculty and fellow students alike.

> **❝** *Founded in 1926 by newspaper publisher and philanthropist Ellen Browning Scripps, Scripps College is a top-ranked liberal arts college, and the women's college of The Claremont Colleges.* **❞**

The foundation of Scripps College's liberal arts education rests on the Core Curriculum in Interdisciplinary Humanities, a rigorous three-course exploration of critical thinking and engagement with contemporary issues. The College is distinct for its unique interdisciplinary approach, small size, opportunities for undergraduate research, and its membership in The Claremont Colleges, a consortium of seven undergraduate and graduate institutions located within one square mile.

The mission of Scripps College is to educate women to develop their intellect and talents through active participation in a demanding community of scholars. Students at Scripps College major in humanities, fine arts, social sciences, and science, and many choose majors that explore the interconnectedness of several academic disciplines. All students are required to complete a senior thesis before graduation. After graduation, Scripps alumnae go on to contribute to society through public and private lives of leadership, service, integrity, and creativity.

Claremont Consortium

Scripps is also one of the founding members of the Claremont Colleges Group Plan, the initial vision of creating a group of independent colleges that share key resources. Today, the Claremont Consortium includes five undergraduate colleges and two graduate institutes. Claremont Consortium resources include the Honnold/Mudd library (housing over two million volumes) and the Student Health Services building. Students are welcome to eat at any of the dining halls and are free to enroll in courses in any of the five undergraduate colleges.

The consortium approach gives each college its own unique social and academic flavor, but it also allows for students to meet people with vastly different experiences and views. Weekend socializing frequently crosses campus boundaries with parties and events advertised across the five undergraduate colleges.

ADMISSIONS REQUIREMENTS

Gaining admission to Scripps becomes more and more competitive each year with over 2,097 applications sent in for the 263 spots in the class of 2014. Even before being admitted, however, each student is thought of as an individual who has the potential to enhance the Scripps community. The admission committee looks over each application a minimum of three times before any final decisions are made in hopes that the students admitted will become a truly unique and cohesive class come fall.

Scripps enrolls students from all over the world, including women from Botswana, China, India, Japan, Korea, Singapore, Thailand, Venezuela, and others. This speaks to the commitment the college has made to establish a campus of diverse identities and ideas. The admission committee seeks out women with different cultural, economic, and political backgrounds in hopes that each woman's unique perspective will enhance the community as a whole.

While there are no hard and fast rules when it comes to securing a spot, applicants should show what they have to offer the campus intellectually and personally. Successful applicants usually have taken a rigorous high school course load including four years of English, three or more years of social sciences, at least three years of one or two foreign languages, three years of science, and three years of math. Students with a special talent or skill are encouraged to submit writing samples, art slides, or other additional materials that show off their abilities.

In addition to the standard application materials, Scripps requires two letters of recommendation from teachers and one from a guidance counselor. These should be written by teachers who know the student on a more personal level and can relate what she has to offer the collegiate community. To get a better sense of who an applicant truly is, the admissions committee also asks each student to list all the books she has read over the past year. This gives the committee a chance to see what engages a student and what she enjoys learning about.

Of course, applicants must also submit their SAT or ACT scores and are encouraged to submit any SAT II subject tests they may have taken. Scripps has twenty-five National Merit Scholars in the class of 2014.

Prospective students interested in experiencing life as a Scripps student are welcome to stay overnight in a residence hall and attend classes with a current Scripps student in addition to the standard student-led tour of the campus. Interviews with an admissions counselor are not required but are strongly encouraged and are available for scheduling at both on- and off-campus locations.

Early Decision

Scripps offers two Early Decision deadlines, the first on November 1 and the second on January 1. Those applying under the earliest deadline should be notified as to their acceptance no later than December 15, while students applying under the January 1 deadline should hear from Scripps by February 15. Applicants accepted under the Early Decision program are expected to withdraw their applications for other colleges and enroll at Scripps.

Merit Scholarships

In order to be considered for one of many merit scholarships, including the James E. Scripps Scholarship worth half tuition for four years, applicants must submit their materials by November 1. This deadline is separate from the Early Decision deadline and is completely nonbinding. When choosing recipients of these scholarships, the admissions committee looks for students who will become leaders and contributors to the Scripps community.

ACADEMIC LIFE

Forget what high school teachers say about college courses: Attendance *does* matter at Scripps. When a class has only sixteen students (the average class size at Scripps), the professor knows when someone goes missing. In fact, regular participation usually accounts for at least ten percent of a final grade. This helps facilitate the process of students becoming more than just passive recipients of information and instead helps them become active agents in their own learning.

The small class sizes also ensure that the faculty creates meaningful connections with the students. It's not uncommon to see students and faculty enjoying a cup of coffee together in the Motley. Professors are also known to invite their classes to their houses for an end of the year barbeque or dessert celebration. Nearly sixty percent of Scripps professors are women, and ninety-nine percent of the faculty holds a Ph.D. or equivalent terminal degree.

> **"**I came to Scripps because of the people. The professors genuinely care about the students; they will gladly answer questions or simply offer their support. The students themselves are intelligent, strong, and fun. At Scripps, we are free to studiously discuss our classes and act silly with our friends. The Scripps environment is the best and most supportive I have ever encountered. **"**

—Lauren Becker, '14

While students take many if not all of their classes at Scripps, students also enroll in courses across the other five colleges. If Scripps does not offer a particular major that another college does offer, students are allowed to fulfill the major requirements of the other institution. Students are also allowed to fill their general electives with courses at the other colleges.

Core

The interdisciplinary focus of Scripps starts early with all first-year students required to take Core I "Histories of the Present" in the fall semester. It is a course unlike any other in the country in that it brings together eighteen professors and the entire first-year class to focus on the relationship of critical thinking to contemporary problems and debate.

"Histories of the Present" examines both the values and categories that we often take to be obvious, and the ways in which conventional or accepted understandings of them may prevent us from seeing the world in other ways. Among these values, we include profound and deep contemporary commitments to freedom, autonomy, equality, rights, justice, belief, and toleration.

Core II, the second semester of the program, offers small seminar sessions—usually team-taught by two members of the faculty—that explore a tightly focused interdisciplinary topic or problem. In spring 2011, there are 21 professors teaching Core II courses. Six of these courses are newly developed team-taught courses. Then, in the first semester of the second year, students choose from an even wider array of different Core III seminars. These emphasize independent research and projects, and help prepare students for future work, especially the work students will do in their senior theses.

> ❝ The Core program is an invaluable part of the Scripps College education. The major debates, concepts, and readings of Core not only prepare you for the rigors of college-level work, but also carry over to apply to many different classes and real-life situations. Core essentially provides students with an ever-growing wealth of knowledge from which to draw. ❞

—Susan Bryant, '13

General Electives

Besides the rigorous three-semester Core program, students are also expected to take a wide variety of general elective courses, including at least one course in letters, social sciences, natural sciences with a lab, fine arts, women's studies, and race and ethnic studies. Many students find they can count most courses for up to two requirements (for example, the course "Women and Music" would count for both women's studies and fine arts).

Students must also take at least three semesters of foreign language and pass a precalculus or statistics math course. During first-year orientation, entering students take placement tests and can pass out of one or both of these requirements. While some find the requirements to be daunting at first, some students take a course they wouldn't have otherwise taken and end up minoring or majoring in that very subject.

Joint Science Program

As a women's college, Scripps prides itself on encouraging its students to pursue scientific knowledge, whether that be in a nonmajor course such as "Energy and the Environment" or through a major field of study such as chemistry, biology, physics, or neuroscience. Students may also combine science majors or create one with a specific focus, including bioethics or environmentalism. Courses are offered through the unique Joint Science Program, linking the resources of Scripps, Pitzer, and Claremont McKenna Colleges to offer an outstanding, comprehensive education in the sciences.

The high level of thought that occurs in the science program can be seen through the Scripps students who produce award-winning research projects at conferences across the country. The projects undertaken by science majors ensure that upon graduation, students are more than prepared to pursue higher education in the sciences or continue on to medical school.

Majors

One of the strengths of the Scripps academic program is the ability for students to dual or double major in vastly different fields. Interested in neurobiology and studio art? Not only can a student major in both, but she would be expected to explore relevant connections between the two. Students also take advantage of the ability to create their own majors, with recent conceptions like bioethics and art conservation, which combines science and art.

No matter what their majors, all students must complete a senior thesis. For a chemistry major, this could mean undertaking a major experiment and then writing and presenting the results. English majors usually write at least sixty pages on any topic in literature. Requirements across disciplines vary, but in all cases the thesis must be a substantial undertaking, bringing together the knowledge and know-how of the previous three years of study.

THE SCRIPPS COLLEGE HUMANITIES INSTITUTE

Knowledge knows no bounds when it comes to the Scripps College Humanities Institute. The institute is focused around interdisciplinary studies, focusing specifically on a different theme for each semester. Each theme brings prominent scholars and speakers to campus. The Humanities Institute brings documentary filmmakers, authors, think tank founders, activists, and artists to speak at the College.

While most institutes restrict their fellowships to graduate students, the Scripps Humanities Institute is unique in inviting undergraduate students to become Junior Fellows for a semester. Between ten and fifteen students are selected, meeting every week to discuss aspects of the theme as well as meeting with the speakers personally. While other classes may dally on what exactly an author meant in a sentence, Junior Fellows get the chance to ask the author themselves.

Off-Campus Study

Sixty percent of Scripps students choose to study off-campus sometime during their junior year for one or both semesters. The Office of Off-Campus Study offers approved programs in every continent (with the exception of Antarctica). While some programs require a certain language proficiency, many others teach language skills in the host country. Foreign language majors must study abroad for at least one semester in order to meet their graduation requirements.

The Office of Off-Campus Study guides students throughout the whole process from narrowing down continent and country options to deciding on whether a home-stay or dorm life is the best option for any particular student. Because of the extensive application process that Scripps requires, almost all Scripps students are accepted to their program of choice.

No matter what program a student chooses, she pays Scripps tuition, room, and board and in return the Office of Off-Campus Study covers the host program's tuition, room, and board as well as the cost of airfare to the host city. The Off-Campus Study program is anything but a semester long vacation—not only must students enroll in the equivalent of a full course load at Scripps, but all grades earned at the host institution are transferred as letter grades on the Scripps transcript. All the hard work generally pays off, and students come back more independent, mature, and culturally aware than they were before they left.

SOCIAL LIFE AND ACTIVITIES

Activities

The center of Scripps activities is in SARLO (Student Activities and Residential Life Office). SARLO is the hub of Scripps Associated Students, or student council, as well as many of the other student organizations. It's also the place to go if you want to start your own club and need the paperwork to get it approved in order to receive funds from the College.

SARLO regularly organizes trips to Pasadena, Disneyland, the beach, and musicals in L.A., all usually at reduced prices. Students who file their driver's license on record can also apply to check out one of the two Scripps vans to organize their own excursions around Southern California.

Plenty of outdoor activities like hiking and horseback riding are offered by SOAP (Scripps Outdoors Activities Program) and are open to all Scripps students. Outdoor gear like tents and cooking supplies can be checked out from the SOAP office for a small refundable deposit for students interested in taking weekend camping trips to the local mountains or the beach.

Students are also free to make use of the five-college resources such as the Office of Black Student Affairs, the Chicano Latino Office of Student Affairs, and the Office of the Chaplains, which offers weekly Catholic, Protestant, and Jewish services. Each office plans events throughout the year and offers mentoring and advising to any student who requests it.

RUTH CHANDLER WILLIAMSON GALLERY

The Ruth Chandler Williamson Gallery is appropriately housed in a stucco building near the art department building on the Scripps campus and houses 8,000 art pieces. Selections from the collection, including works by impressionist artist Mary Cassatt and Japanese artist Chikanobu, are put on view throughout the year in conjunction with themed gallery shows.

Every year the gallery hosts the Scripps College Ceramics Annual, the longest running exhibition of contemporary ceramics in the country. Artists' works are selected from across the country, and students are always invited to the opening reception and encouraged to attend the gallery throughout the year.

Scripps art students also make use of the gallery in April during the annual senior art show, showcasing the significant projects that senior art majors have worked on throughout the year.

Residential Life

Housing on campus has been cozy over the past couple of years in part because the Scripps residence halls are consistently named some of the most beautiful in the country and attract most students to live on campus year after year. Of the nine residence halls, four are listed in the National Register of Historic Places. Some students prefer the storage space and bathroom amenities and air conditioning of the newer dorms, but many can't resist the charm and mythology of the older buildings.

THE EUROPEAN UNION CENTER

Dedicated to expanding the knowledge and understanding of the countries of Europe, the European Union Center of California is based at the Scripps campus and brings influential speakers to discuss foreign policy and international affairs involving the European Union. The center hosts an annual state of the EU address and offers internships and research grants to students interested in working in the field of European studies.

Accommodations vary from standard-issue double rooms, to suite-style living, to apartments for students who want to try their hand at cooking. Most first-year students live in double or triple rooms, but juniors and sometimes even sophomores can land a single room. Almost every room has its own sink, and many rooms on campus have an attached bathroom.

Students who are particularly interested in Spanish, French, German, or Italian have the option of living in one of four language corridors. Most of the rooms in the language halls are single rooms, but residents must sign an agreement to speak only the specified language when interacting with anyone else in the corridor.

Sports

The Southern California weather provides the perfect environment for students of all athletic inclinations. NCAA Division III varsity sports are offered in conjunction with Claremont McKenna and Harvey Mudd Colleges, with students from all three schools coming together to form a joint Claremont-Mudd-Scrips team. In total, nineteen teams comprise the CMS program. Female sports teams use the Athenas, while the male teams are known as the Stags. Since the inception of the CMS women's teams into the Southern California Intercollegiate Athletic Conference (SCIAC), the program has won seventy-five SCIAC titles, tied for the most out of all SCIAC schools. The other two Claremont Colleges, Pomona and Pitzer, also share an athletic program, which creates quite the rivalry when CMS plays the Pomona-Pitzer team around homecoming.

Pick-up intramural sports are offered across the five colleges and have proved to be a reliable way of getting to know other students at the Claremont Colleges. Thanks to a revitalized interest in the program, the intramural program has become more than just volleyball and flag football and has started to include Texas Hold 'Em tournaments and bowling championships each semester. The program coordinator is also always open to student suggestions and is constantly adding new activities to interest participants.

Students that like to do their own athletic activities can make use of our new 24,000-square-foot recreational athletic facility. The Sallie Tierman Field House contains cardio machines, weight rooms, an aerobics studio, and a yoga room, as well as a lacrosse field and underground parking.

Many students run in the open space trials just north of the colleges and others enjoy swimming in the 25-meter outdoor pool, regularly staffed with lifeguards.

Dedicated to expanding the knowledge and understanding of the countries of Europe, the European Union Center of California is based at the Scripps campus and brings influential speakers to discuss foreign policy and international affairs involving the European Union. The center hosts an annual state of the EU address, and offers internships and research grants to students interested in working in the field of European studies.

Weekend Social Life

While the small town of Claremont has plenty of boutiques and coffee shops to fill any Saturday or Sunday afternoon, many students find the nightlife of Pasadena and Los Angeles more compelling. But for those without access to a car, the Claremont Colleges provide plenty to do on campus. Every weekend, one of the Claremont Colleges hosts at least one party, often focused around a seasonal theme. Popular at Scripps is the candlelight dinner held in fall for students and alumnae.

Outside of the party scene, each campus regularly has film screenings, performances, concerts, or college-organized weekend excursions to satisfy any taste. One of the five-college favorites is the improv group Without a Box that puts on monthly shows on Friday or Saturday nights at a different campus for each performance.

Even with all the activities available, many students find the weekend a perfect time to catch up on homework or just relax at the Motley or the pool.

Ellen Browning Scripps, the founder of the college, wanted desperately to visit the first entering Scripps class in 1927. But by that time, she was ninety-two years old and in no condition to travel. So instead, the first Scripps class each wrote their names and hometowns in a book and sent it down to La Jolla where Ms. Scripps lived.

That tradition has continued with entering students signing their name and hometown in a hand-bound book in the Denison library. The main steel doors of the library are only opened twice a year, once for new students to enter and sign, and again at graduation when students leave through the doors, glancing at their signed name on their way out. The ceremony represents the four years spent inside an institution of learning, and concludes with students exiting more enriched and enlightened than before they entered.

FINANCIAL AID

Sixty percent of Scripps students receive at least some type of financial aid, usually awarded in a combination of grants, loans, and work-study funds. The average grant or scholarship award for the 2010–2011 year was $28,483, with over $14 million awarded in grants or scholarships. Scripps students shoulder less debt than many other colleges with similar price tags.

Work-study jobs are very common on campus, and students have no trouble finding a job that fits into their course schedule. Many jobs are actually great resume builders, including internships in the Offices of the President and the Dean of Students, as well as the Development offices. The Motley Coffeehouse and Student Store are also both completely student run and primarily work-study, offering managerial and product development positions that can serve as great business experience.

To be considered for financial aid, students need to submit the CSS/Financial Aid PROFILE and the Free Application for Federal Student Aid (FAFSA), as well as signed copies of the most recent federal income tax return and W-2 forms for both the student and the student's parents. The PROFILE only needs to be completed once, but the FAFSA must be completed each year for financial aid consideration.

Scripps offers a monthly payment plan that allows tuition payments to be made over the course of eight months.

GRADUATES

With a useful and resourceful Career Planning Resources (CP&R) office, Scripps gives its students the chance to get a head-start on post-Scripps life. The office offers tips on searching for jobs and applying to graduate schools and even provides the opportunity for a student to participate in a videotaped mock interview so she can get an idea of how she is presenting herself to prospective employers. The conference "Life After Scripps" is presented for all students to get a glimpse of future possibilities. The CP&R Office also offers an alumnae networking service called "Life Connections" that allows any current student to contact alumnae who may be working in her particular field of interest.

A number of Scripps students are awarded the most prestigious national fellowships each year, including the Watson Fellowship, the Barry M. Goldwater Scholarship, the Rotary Ambassadorial Scholarship, and the Fulbright Scholar Program.

Many seniors apply to graduate programs across the country and are accepted into some of the most prestigious Masters and Ph.D. programs in the world. Scripps women are also accepted to law and medical schools in high numbers. Recent grads are currently working on pursuing graduate degrees at Brown University, Caltech, George Washington University, Harvard University, Johns Hopkins University, MIT, Stanford, and UC Berkeley.

Scripps students are successful with full-time employment as well. According to the survey that the CP&R office sends out to recent graduates, approximately sixty percent of alumnae enter the workforce within three months of graduation.

Scripps College also has an energetic and active alumnae association that plans reunions and social events throughout the year. Alumnae are always opening their doors to each other and current Scripps students, providing homes away from home worldwide.

SUMMING UP

Scripps is a college where an independent and open-minded woman can thrive. She is sure to be challenged each and every day, and any obstacles she may encounter make her a stronger person. Students are constantly stretched to the full breadth of their ability and then urged to share their knowledge with others. Learning at Scripps never ends and continues long after a student dons her green graduation gown.

The campus is a community built on sharing ideas and expanding the scope of knowledge in every field. Students are not directed to choose a single interest but are encouraged to explore every area of interest. The staff and faculty encourage students to take these interests beyond Scripps walls by studying off campus or conducting research in the surrounding community. The learning process is only limited by what a student is willing to explore during her four short years at the college.

The residence halls are built to encourage community and the sharing of resources, and it is a daily occurrence to hear students carrying on a conversation about the Core I film, or any other interdisciplinary subject, from lunch until dinner. Of course, Scripps women also know how to relax from time to time and are skilled at finding the perfect spots across Southern California from the local mountains to the Pacific Ocean.

Scripps alumnae enrich the world with their critical thinking skills and ability to communicate clearly and confidently. No matter where they may go in life, Scripps women pursue their dreams with a drive to make a difference.

❏ *Lindsey Galloway, B. A.*

Photo by Jim Gripe

Smith College
Northampton, MA 01063

(413) 585-2500
Fax: (413) 585-2527

Website: *www.smith.edu*

👫 **Enrollment**

Full-time ❏ women: 2,571

Part-time ❏ women: 17

INTRODUCING SMITH COLLEGE

Sophia Smith, namesake and pioneer of Smith College, bequeathed her fortune in 1871. In her will she declared the need for "facilities of education equal to those which are afforded to young men," and insisted that by educating women, "their 'wrongs' will be redressed, their wages adjusted, their weight of influence in reforming the evils of society will be greatly increased...." In short, Ms. Smith thought everything would be better if ladies had the spotlight for a change. She was right.

Smith remains a women's college for a variety of reasons—first and foremost because the culture and traditions are so strong. Smithies recognize the value of a co-educational college but wouldn't give up their unique experience at Smith for anything. It's hard to say precisely what, but without a doubt Smith women share something irreplaceable.

Every year more than 2,500 women choose to study at Smith for a range of reasons as diverse as the college itself. Some women select Smith for the engaging, accessible faculty (which includes men), state-of-the-art engineering facilities, or the innovative, competitive curriculum. Some fall in love with Smith's idyllic Ivy-League feel: the professors in tweed, the long wooden tables piled high with books, the ivy-laced brick buildings, and the traditions—candle-lit Thursday dinners and house tea every Friday are among the most-loved.

> **66** *I chose Smith for the pond, and the boathouse. It's true! When I first saw the campus it was springtime, and flowers were blooming in the greenhouse gardens, and from the top of the hill I saw girls reading on the deck and checking out canoes. The water was beautiful. I couldn't believe it was actually called 'Paradise Pond.' Why not study with an incredible view of paradise?* **99**

—*Andrea Buglione, '09*

ADMISSIONS REQUIREMENTS

Smith accepts the Common Application exclusively, and the application fee ($60) is waived if you apply online. Any applicable supplements (listed on CommonApp.org) are recommended, but not required, except the homeschooler's supplement, which is required. Two teacher evaluation forms are required, all your high school grades (no avoiding it!), and a mid-year academic evaluation are also required. If you are applying Early Decision, include the appropriate Early Decision supplement, and turn in your application by November 15. The deadline for Early Decision II, or Winter Early Decision, is January 1. For both, you agree to attend Smith if accepted. Regular Decision candidates must submit their applications by January 15.

The good news: you have to submit your grades, but SATs, SAT IIs, and ACTs are not required for admission to Smith. This stems from Smith's holistic approach to learning and personal development in general; tests don't necessarily represent the best of each applicant, depending on that student's unique interests and learning styles. Scores will be reviewed if they're submitted, but they can't make or break your application.

International Students

In 2010 Smith accepted over 200 international students from fifty-eight countries. Admissions requirements for international students vary only slightly: the SAT I, ACT, TOEFL, or IELTS are required, as is the international supplement to the Common Application.

Non-Traditional Students: Ada Comstock Scholars

In 1975 Smith began the Ada Comstock Scholars program, yet another way for Smith to impact the women of the world. Applicants who are twenty-four or older, or who will turn twenty-four during their first year at Smith, are invited to apply to the Ada program. Affectionately called "Adas," these women are dedicated, intelligent, and bring a much-needed spectrum of life experience to the classroom. Adas attend classes with traditional students, and in some cases eat and live in the same houses. Varied housing options are available for Adas who bring children, families, or spouses with them to Smith, and over half live off campus and commute to campus. A special application is provided (again, if you apply online, the $60 fee is waived), and additional requirements include two references, a résumé, and an autobiographical essay. Applicants are also expected to include college transcripts with at least thirty-two credits.

WHO ARE ADAS?

Adas, or Ada Comstock Scholars, are women who come to Smith later in life. In Fall 2010, there were 114 Adas attending Smith—some with families, some with partners, and some alone. They range in age from twenty-four to sixtyish, and are an incredibly diverse, intelligent group of women. One common thread among all the women is an interruption in their education and the desire to finish it: some took a break from college to travel, others to begin a career, still others to raise families. Now these women are looking to round out their life experience, and they all feel the need to nurture their intellect. They come from a range of different states and even from countries as far-flung as Burma, Romania, and Japan. Adas enjoy all the resources and take all the same classes as traditional students, but with a more flexible approach designed to accommodate individual needs: reduced course loads, specialized academic advising, and career counseling are all advantages Adas enjoy. Women in the Ada Comstock Program can participate as much as they like in campus activities; some join student government, attend talks and screenings, or play club sports.

Smith is a gathering place for world-renowned academics and bright, competitive young women. In your choice of more than 1,000 courses, you'll learn how to read, write, think, and present yourself to the world. It's a weighty claim, but it's true—that said, the workload at Smith is not for the faint of heart. You will find yourself trucking to the library late into the night, poring over books, digging through research, and conducting experiments until you're forced into bed. But you'll want to continue because you'll be working on things that you care about, for professors who care about you, surrounded by students who are excited to discuss the same readings, share results from shared experiments, or work through problem sets together.

> **❝** *If there was one aspect of Smith I could be confident in during my four-year attendance, it would be that I was experiencing a top-notch education. I was taught to think differently about the world and intellectually challenged in ways that I had never been before.*
>
> *I learned to look at the world in the context of connections. The material I worked with in my Design of Experiment Statistics class somehow managed to correlate to what I was learning in my Political Philosophy class. Smith taught me to understand these connections and articulate my thoughts in a cohesive and intelligible manner. Thanks in part to the professors, of course, but thanks also to my fellow classmates: they were a challenge and a joy in themselves.* **❞**
>
> —*Ellen Daoust, '09*

There is only one required course, a first-year seminar designed to teach everyone Smith's particular style of discussion and writing, and even that course comes in a variety of flavors, from geology-based research to reading poetry. Any curriculum restrictions are designed to keep your studies balanced; extra incentive is given in the form of Latin Honors if you manage to take a course in every discipline, and every major requires taking several classes outside your course of study.

Faculty

Smith professors are downright smart, and tough. There's no getting away with skipping class, or readings, or turning in late work. Every professor keeps track of his or her students and is wholly dedicated to helping each student reach a high level of success. Of course it's your responsibility to get work done, but helpful nudges from your professors can be game-changers.

> 66 *As a first-year, I took a basic English class. We read all sorts of short stories I'd already read in AP English, in high school, and I got frustrated with the discussions and the professor—I thought, I've already learned all this! Eventually I simply quit participating, and soon after I got an e-mail from my professor. She said, 'I've noticed a change in your work. Do you have time to come chat with me?' I went to her office, and she asked me directly why I quit participating. I told her I'd already read everything, and that I was bored. Of course she said: 'It's your own fault you're bored. If you've read it, you have double the perspective and even more to share than everyone else. I suggest you begin participating. It was a tough pill then, but it was a much-needed wake-up call. Good thing someone was paying attention.* 99

Professors are intuitive and demanding, but they're also available for advice and guidance whenever you need them. It's common to meet with professors at any point during the semester: everyone posts their office hours, but if your schedule doesn't mesh, professors are more than willing to set up individual appointments. Collaborations are common, especially on large final projects, and a special event (aptly titled "Collaborations") was devised for the sole purpose of displaying the work professors and students produce together.

The Classroom

Discussions are a vital aspect of learning throughout Smith, both in the sciences and the humanities. The ability to express yourself clearly and persuasively is highly valued, and this talent is cultivated throughout your four years. Classroom discussions at Smith are unusually intimate and foster the kind of thought you could never reach on your own. Part of this is thanks to the all-women environment: you'll certainly find yourself in a classroom full of only women while at Smith, and it's a surprisingly fulfilling, "depthy" experience, as one student put it. At the same time you'll find yourself in mixed classrooms, because many Smithies take classes at Amherst, Hampshire, UMass, and Mount Holyoke, and students

Smith Seniors (and other years, too) are encouraged to pursue a special studies—an independent project guided by a professor that explores a student's carefully focused interest. It tends to represent the pinnacle of their various studies and takes the form of a paper, art piece, story, project, or any appropriate medium. These projects (and other student-professor endeavors) are shared with parents, students, and professors at a presentation and project fair called "Collaborations." Last year, Vanessa Calderon (2010) presented her work with Leslie King, associate professor of sociology, titled "Confronting Consumption." Kaitlyn Krauskopf (2010) titled her project "Sports Nutrition for Strength Training Women," a special studies she developed with Barbara Brehm-Curtis, professor of exercise and sport studies. A few years ago Lila Dodge (2009) performed "The Place It Takes," her site-specific dance deriving from a thesis with Susan Waltner and Rodger Blum, both professors of dance. She and four other girls dressed in red and danced their way through campus, rolling down stairs and climbing walls, wrapping themselves around buildings and out the front gate of campus.

from these colleges come to Smith for classes frequently. Every combination provides a different experience, and you'll value each more for knowing the other.

Studying Abroad

Nearly fifty percent of all students spend time abroad, in places as far-flung as Mongolia and as close to home as Mexico. Four programs founded and run by Smith host students in Geneva, Paris, Hamburg, and Florence. Students in Switzerland focus on European and International Studies, students in Italy on Art and Architecture, and those in Germany and France a variety of language and cultural studies.

In partnership with a consortium of colleges and universities, Smith students can opt to spend a year or a semester in India, Mexico, Spain, or Japan. The options don't end here; if a Smith student admires a certain program or focuses on a particular language, the Office for International Study will consider an application to any other program.

If concern about money is keeping you at home, Smith offers a variety of grants and subsidies for research and study abroad. The International Experience grant is most often used for January term or summer travel, and often extends research begun in the classroom. Blumberg Traveling Fellowships allow students on a Smith program (Florence, Geneva, Hamburg, and Paris) to extend their year abroad and carry out research throughout Europe.

Smith understands the enduring value of an international education, so you'll find considerable support among the faculty and plenty of avenues through which you can navigate your international options.

A Women's College. Really?

Do you ever see boys? Are there parties? Is it weird with only girls? New and prospective students wonder the same things every year, and the best answer is simple: At Smith, the world is… well, still the world. Just across the street Northampton bustles with coffee shops and diners, bars, concert venues, and bookstores. A free fifteen-minute bus ride takes Smithies to Hampshire College, Amherst College, or the University of Massachusetts, all co-ed institutions and members of the Five-College consortium. Smith students can sign up for any class offered at any campus, and vice versa. For even bigger adventures, Boston is two hours away, and New York is only four. You can meet whomever you like and learn whatever you like in a challenging, dynamic environment that doesn't stop at Smith's gates.

> **66** *I loved how my professors encouraged us to reach out and see what was happening in the world beyond campus. My art professor constantly suggested art shows and exhibitions to augment our in-class work—there's tons to see at Smith's own museum, but we were encouraged to visit shows in Boston at the Museum of Fine Arts and at the Clark Museum in Williamstown, just an hour away. Getting off campus is a great way to refresh your brain and (of course) meet fascinating new people. Actually, while at Smith I made a pact with myself and two other friends to take a mini-trip every two weeks. Amherst didn't count; we went there too often anyway. We did things like tour local farms and visit friends at Trinity, Middlebury, Williams, Boston.* **99**

—*Mika Maekawa, '09*

Activities and Organizations

Smith has every activity imaginable: from Ultimate Frisbee to Al-Iman to five *a capella* groups, plus all the standard student government organizations, a radio station (which is anything but standard), a bike club, a Christian fellowship group, and a newspaper—there's nothing Smith doesn't have. But if you don't find what you're looking for, you apply to student government for funding and start your own group.

Northampton is brimming with unforget-table food. Cafe Amanouz offers rich, com-plex Mediterranean (amazing humus), Hungry Ghost Bread has a brick oven and produces thick loaves of tangy, chewy sourdough and long, skinny French "batons." The Green Bean is arguably the busiest and tastiest brunch spot (in close competition with Sylvester's). You can get a killer espresso, hot jazz, and share a big table at Northampton Coffee, but Haymarket is Northampton's staple coffee shop, forever filled with professors and students tip-tapping and sipping away sunny afternoons. A favorite weekend trip is the Montague Bookmill ("books you don't need in a place you can't find") for the long drive and a beautiful, meandering Victorian house chock-full of books. The cupcakes at Café Evolution in Florence should not be missed, and neither should the traditional fall visit to Hadley farms for cider donuts and pumpkins.

Athletics

The Smith Pioneers claim a respectable bevy of victories each year—all manner of serious-minded sports are played, plus a collection of intra-murals, which can be very serious in their own right. Each year Smith hosts a 5k run for Northampton res-idents and Smith students, faculty, and staff. A pro-gram titled Get Fit Smith offers classes on a come-when-you-can basis, and they're all incredibly popular. With classes like yoga and kickboxing, Pilates, and Awesome Abs, there's certainly good rea-son to take a break and work up some endorphins. The facilities are beautiful—wide glass windows and tall, open spaces make going to the gym a real treat. Smith's tree-filled, grassy campus and the trails along the river make for an inviting bike or run, too.

Housing

No one at Smith lives in a dorm. That's incredible, right? Smith is well-known for gorgeous, spa-cious rooms, most of which feature huge bay windows, window seats, and sparkling wood floors. Though first years usually have a roommate, all stu-dents live in single rooms for their last three years (barring any unique living situations you might encounter abroad). House life is a big part of campus, and the women you meet in your dorms will most likely be your friends for the rest of your life. Based on your requests, you are placed in a dorm after you're accepted, but you can apply to switch houses if you like, because there are certainly distinct characters associated with certain parts of campus. Green street is a quiet, studious neighborhood, whereas the Quad can get fairly rowdy.

FINANCIAL AID

Smith pledges to meet the needs of any admitted students, and can be very generous thanks to donations from alumnae and others. There are three types of aid available to

○ Margaret Mitchell '22, Author of *Gone With the Wind*

○ Julia Child '34, Star of TV's *The French Chef*

○ Madeleine L'Engle '41, Award-winning Author of *A Wrinkle in Time*

○ Betty Friedan '42, Author of *The Feminine Mystique*

○ Nancy Reagan '43, Former First Lady of the United States

○ Barbara Bush '47, Former First Lady of the United States

○ Xie Xide '49 Physicist and Former President of Fudan University in China

○ Sylvia Plath '55, Poet; Author of *The Bell Jar* and *Ariel*

○ Gloria Steinem '56, Founder of *Ms.* Magazine and Noted Feminist Writer

○ Jane Yolen '60, Award-winning Children's Book Author

○ Marilyn Carlson Nelson '61, Chairman of the Carlson Companies and Former Chair of the National Women's Business Council

○ Sally Quinn '63, Author and Commentator

○ Victoria Chan Palay '65, Neurobiologist and Former Olympic Athlete

○ Molly Ivins '66, Political Columnist and Commentator

○ Jane Harman '66, U.S. Representative from California

○ Juliet Taylor '67, Casting Director for more than 60 movies, including Woody Allen's films

○ Laura Tyson '69, Professor at the Haas School of Business at the University of California at Berkeley; Former Head of the National Economic Council

○ Shelley Hack '70, Actress (*Annie Hall, Charlie's Angels*)

○ Julie Nixon Eisenhower '70, Author of *Special People and Pat Nixon: The Untold Story*

○ Yolanda King '76, Actress, Producer, Lecturer

○ Pamela Craig '79, Partner in Accenture, the World's Largest Management Information Consulting Firm

○ Lauren Lazin '82, Award-winning Independent Filmmaker (*Tupac: Resurrection*) and Vice President for News and Specials at MTV

○ Tammy Baldwin '84, U.S. Representative from Wisconsin

○ Kathleen Marshall '85, Tony Award-winning Broadway Choreographer and Director

○ Sherry Rehman '85, Member, Pakistan National Assembly

○ Thelm Golden '87, Director and Chief Curator at the Studio Museum in Harlem

○ Farah Pandith '90, Special Representative to Muslim Communities, U.S. Department of State

○ Simran Sethi '92, Environmental Journalist

○ Devin Alexander '93, Chef, Cookbook Author and Host of TV's *Healthy Decadence*

○ Sharmeeen Obaid-Chinoy '02, Investigative Television Reporter and Documentary Filmmaker

prospective Smithies. Need-based, Merit, and Outside Aid. To apply for any kind of aid, you must fill out the financial aid application at the same time you submit your common app—don't forget, or you won't receive aid. Need-based aid is any kind of loan (which you must pay back), grant (which is a gift you don't have to pay back), or campus employment you're awarded. Students who work on campus can do almost anything from library work to washing dishes in dining halls, to working for public relations. Merit aid is awarded based on merit rather than need; all applicants for admission are considered and there are no special applications. Outside aid is any scholarships or awards you receive from sources other than Smith; applicants are highly encouraged to apply for any federal, state, or local scholarships they can.

GRADUATES

Women who graduate from Smith do whatever they please—that's the whole idea. They go on to write epic novels, like Margaret Mitchell's (1922) *Gone With The Wind* or Madeleine L'Engle's (1941) *A Wrinkle in Time*. Win a Pulitzer prize like Margaret Edson (1983) did for her play *Wit*. Or become the CEO of one of the world's largest advertising agencies, like Shelly Lazarus (1968). Or you could change the face of modern cuisine like Julia Child (1934), whip up politics like Molly Ivins (1966), or direct a museum in Harlem like Thelma Golden (1987). These days, lots of Smithies continue their studies at graduate schools around the nation, take time off to travel following their graduation, or jump right into a career. Some Smithies even start families! Whatever you choose, the Smith alumnae network is one of the strongest available, and at the click of a button you can reach women around the globe, all of whom are dedicated to strengthening their relationship with other Smithies, especially young alums. We'll make sure you get where you need to go.

SUMMING UP

Smith is a powerful institution. Living and working among women fosters invaluable relationships impossible to create elsewhere and builds an unparalleled support system both during your four years and forever-after following graduation. College isn't a lifetime, but a four-year experience at Smith will change yours.

❏ *Rachel Miller, B.A.*

Photo by Stanford News Service

Stanford University
Stanford, CA 94305-3020

(650) 723-2091
Fax: (650) 725-2846

E-mail: *admission@stanford.edu*
Website: *http://admission@stanford.edu*

 Enrollment

Full-time ❏ women: 3,405
❏ men: 3,473

INTRODUCING STANFORD

Life at Stanford is about unlimited possibilities. Stanford students roam the art-filled halls in Paris's famed Musée d'Orsay, form part of the White House's work force, and command the attention of sixteen Nobel Laureates on the faculty. As a Stanford undergraduate, you can make the Galapagos Islands your classroom, or stay on campus and enjoy the more than eight million volumes in our libraries, not to mention the technical facilities that advance our nation's scientific knowledge daily. Stanford channels the world's resources into its students, transforming them into tomorrow's innovators. Stanford alumni are responsible for such household names as Yahoo!, Google, the laser, GPS Technology, Kova Netflix (EA) Electronic Arts, and *One Flew over the Cuckoo's Nest*. The boundless resources at Stanford create a vibrancy on campus, infecting students with a sense of purpose and intellectual freedom. Stanford students have wildly differing interests: a single group of friends may include a computer scientist, a budding novelist, and a dedicated public servant, all of whom would be well served by Stanford's curriculum and extracurricular possibilities.

Balancing the unparalleled academic possibilities are Stanford's extracurricular activities. Stanford has received sixteen consecutive Directors' Cups, an award recognizing the top all-around Division I athletic program in the NCAA Division I. Stanford's stellar sports program not only injects its undergraduate body with some of the most dedicated and talented athletes in the country, but it also creates a powerful feeling of Stanford pride and unity among its students. Aside from its sports program, Stanford students have created more than six hundred and fifty student-led organizations, including hip-hop dance groups. Each academic quarter ninety-nine percent of the 6,800 undergraduates either reside on campus or are participating in one of thirteen off-campus studies programs sponsored by the university; residence life is an essential aspect of the Stanford experience. Grouping so many young adults together leads to a rich variety of activities, clubs, and social events, guaranteeing that undergraduate life is anything but dull.

Best of all, Stanford students never have to put their activities (academic or extracurricular) on hold. Thanks to its gloriously mild weather, students literally enjoy Stanford every day of the year. Stanford's perennial sun also serves to highlight its beautiful 8,180 acres located in the foothills of the Santa Cruz Mountains and less than an hour from San Francisco and the Pacific Ocean. Students also relish being near attractions such as Lake Tahoe, Monterey Bay, Big Sur, and Yosemite National Park.

ADMISSIONS REQUIREMENTS

Every year Stanford's Office of Undergraduate Admission assembles a freshman class of roughly 1,600 students out of about 33,000 applicants. Needless to say, getting admitted to Stanford is a complicated and layered process. The selection process weighs everything from extracurricular activities to personal qualities, but academic excellence is far and away the single most important criterion for admission to Stanford.

Each application is reviewed by a committee of admission officers. The goal of the admission staff is to create a freshman class with a myriad of strengths; every student should contribute a valued talent or life experience to Stanford's undergraduate body, as well as proven academic excellence. The Office of Undergraduate Admission seeks to admit those students whose distinctions, whatever they may be, prove they would flourish at a place like Stanford. Stanford values both well-rounded and specialized students; it is important to remember that there is no cookie-cutter recipe for admission to Stanford. Stanford's admission process is truly a personalized one. The application relies heavily on short essays, which allow students to present themselves fully: their motivations, passions, and ideals should resonate throughout the application. Stanford admission officers thus have the privilege of getting to know applicants' personal strengths as well as their academic achievements and intellectual passions.

Examinations

All applicants, including transfer students and international students, must present official scores from either the SAT Reasoning Test or the ACT with the Optional Writing Test. Stanford also strongly recommends that students submit SAT Subject Test scores. Stanford has no minimum thresholds for grade point average (GPA), test scores, or rank in class. Although there will be plenty of students with perfect test scores and GPAs in its applicant pool, Stanford is looking beyond numerical figures: Stanford seeks to admit intriguing and passionate individuals who will contribute to campus life and take full advantage of the opportunities available to them, and who demonstrate an intellectual vitality that clearly states they derive pleasure from learning for learning's sake.

Stanford also values exceptional ability in both the arts and athletics. If you are interested in having these talents evaluated in the admission process, consider submitting samples of artwork or auditioning in music, drama, or dance, or communicating with a coach to see if your abilities are competitive within the Stanford Division I athletic program. For information on pursuing these options, visit *http://admission.stanford.edu*. Please keep in mind that these talents will enhance your application only if you are otherwise well qualified; they will not earn you admission in and of themselves.

High School Rank in Class	Percent of Applicants	Admit Rate	Percent of Admitted Class
Top 10% of Class	81%	7%	92%
Top 11–20% of Class	12%	3%	5%
21% and below of Class	7%	2%	3%

Sat Critical Reading	Percent of Applicants	Admit Rate	Percent of Admitted Class
800	9%	17%	18%
700–799	35%	11%	48%
600–699	38%	6%	29%
Below 600	19%	2%	5%

Sat Math	Percent of Applicants	Admit Rate	Percent of Admitted Class
800	15%	12%	23%
700–799	44%	9%	53%
600–699	29%	6%	22%
Below 600	11%	2%	2%

Sat Writing	Percent of Applicants	Admit Rate	Percent of Admitted Class
800	8%	19%	20%
700–799	38%	10%	51%
600–699	36%	5%	25%
Below 600	17%	2%	4%

While Stanford accepts both the ACT and the SAT, we do not provide data for ACT results here, as the number of applicants submitting ACT scores is not statistically significant.

Restrictive Early Action

Stanford offers a Restrictive Early Action option for those students who know clearly that Stanford is their first-choice school and have completed a thorough and thoughtful college search. This option will best serve students who are ready to be evaluated in terms of their high school career by the beginning of November of the senior year. Early candidates should feel confident in their sophomore and junior year performance, and should complete their standardized testing by October of the senior year. Those offered admission have until May 1 to consider where they will enroll.

Admission Statistics

The previous chart gives some statistics on Stanford's entering freshman class for a recent fall. Keep in mind that these statistics do not quantify many of the criteria Stanford values in the admission process, including personal qualities, intellectual curiosity, and many other areas of excellence as described above.

Stanford admits students of any race, color, religion, sexual orientation, or national and ethnic origin to all the rights, privileges, programs, and activities generally accorded or made available to students at the university. It does not discriminate against students on the basis of race, color, handicap, religion, sexual orientation, or national and ethnic origin in the administration of its educational policies, scholarship and loan programs, and athletic and other university-administered programs.

ACADEMIC LIFE

Stanford prides itself on its quality of education at the undergraduate level. More than seventy-five percent of undergraduate classes have twenty or fewer students, so the undergraduate experience is extremely personalized. Exclusive to freshmen and sophomores are more than 200 small-group seminars where students can enjoy close interactions with professors. With a 6:1 student-to-faculty ratio, it's easy for both students and faculty to get to know each other. There are more than seventy majors from which to choose, including several interdisciplinary majors, and you can create your own major with the help of a faculty member. This freedom to explore beyond undergraduate classes allows students to get a glimpse into what graduate school might be like, thus letting them make informed decisions about their academic futures.

Overseas Programs

Stanford students can choose from among eleven Stanford campuses around the world. Beijing, Berlin, Brisbane, Capetown, Florence, Kyoto, Madrid, Moscow, Oxford, Paris, and Santiago all host a Stanford campus complete with Stanford faculty. Students earn full Stanford credit while studying at these centers. Each center provides unique research and/or internship opportunities: While Florence and Paris are prime centers for art history research, Kyoto and Berlin offer engineering students great hands-on skills.

A Research Institution for Undergraduates

Stanford is a premier research institution, responsible for MRI technology, gene splicing, global positioning systems, DNA micoarray technology, and a host of other inventions contributing significantly to the world. As an undergraduate at Stanford, you will be invited to participate in this innovative research. Student research grants sponsored by the Undergraduate Research Programs provide undergraduates with over $4 million each year to pursue their intellectual passions. As with any researcher, students must submit a research proposal in order to receive these grants. Faculty members assist students in the organization and development of the project, but students have full ownership of their project.

With more than 130 research centers, Stanford provides students with the opportunities and resources to research just about any topic, anywhere. Some of the most renowned centers include:

- Hoover Institution on War, Revolution and Peace. Hoover boasts one of the largest collections of twentieth-century political materials.
- Hopkins Marine Station. Located ninety miles south of the campus, students can supplement their marine biology courses with research in this marine laboratory.
- Jasper Ridge Biological Preserve. Twelve hundred acres within a short walk of campus, where protected flora and fauna can be appreciated or studied.
- Stanford Humanities Laboratory. Interdisciplinary humanities laboratory on campus.
- SLAC National Accelerator Laboratory: Operated for the U.S. Department of Energy, conducting astrophysics, photon science, accelerator and particle physics research.
- Stanford University Medical Center. Includes dozens of specialized clinics. Located on campus, undergraduates are free to attend classes at the medical school, and frequently become research assistants.

- Woods Institute for the Environment. An interdisciplinary center that serves as the hub for all environmental resaerch and education on campus.

SOCIAL LIFE AND ACTIVITIES

Residential Life at Stanford

More than ninety-nine percent of Stanford students live in Stanford housing or at a Stanford-sponsored off-campus study program each quarter. That translates into a community of 6,300 people under the age of twenty-six all living within a relatively small radius. Because of this, Stanford's campus is a vibrant residential campus, full of every imaginable student-led organization, from Greek life to political groups, to recreational clubs, to ethnic-cultural organizations and many more.

Stanford guarantees housing for the four years of a student's undergraduate career. Stanford's small-house system includes seventy-eight residences all located within ten minutes walking distance from the center of campus. The houses vary in size and theme, and include: academic and all freshmen houses, four-class houses, upper-class houses, apartments, cross-cultural theme houses, and a handful of Greek houses. Approximately fifteen percent of students participate in the Greek system, making it a fun option for those who are interested, but not letting it command the undergraduate social scene.

Stanford Athletics—Go Cardinal!

Athletics flourish at Stanford. The glorious California weather, the 8,180 acres of open fields, and the Olympic caliber facilities all contribute to widespread popularity of athletics at Stanford. Not only has Stanford's athletic department captured the Directors' Cup for sixteen years in a row, but also eight out of ten Stanford students participate in the athletic programs, whether it be at the varsity, intramural, or club sport levels. Stanford's expansive campus and idyllic location also provide the perfect setting for hikers, campers, runners, or rock climbers.

CARDINAL CHAMPIONSHIPS

- ○ Total National Championships: 114
- ○ Total Individual NCAA Championships: 409 (most in the nation)
- ○ Total NCAA Championships (NCAA rank): 99 (No. 2)
- ○ Total Men's NCAA Championships (NCAA rank): 60 (No. 3)
- ○ Total Women's NCAA Championships (NCAA rank): 39 (No. 1)
- ○ NCAA Team Championships Since 1980: 82 (most in the nation)
- ○ NCAA Team Championships Since 1990: 59 (most in the nation)

○ **Football Players:** John Elway, former Denver Broncos quarterback; John Lynch, Denver Broncos wide receiver; and Jim Plunkett, Heisman Trophy-winner and former Oakland Raiders quarterback.

○ **Olympic Medalists:** Janet Evans, Eric Heiden, Misty Hyman, Bob Mathias, Pablo Morales, Summer Sanders, Debra Thomas, and Jenny Thompson

○ **Basketball Players:** Jennifer Azzik, Jason and Jarron Collins, Kristen Folkl, Brevin Knight, Mark Madsen, Kate Starbird, Jamila Wideman, and Brook and Robin Lopez

○ **Baseball Players:** Mike Mussina, and Cy Young-winners Jack McDowell and Jim Lonborg

○ **Golfers:** Notah Begay, Casey Martin, Tom Watson, and Tiger Woods

A quick list of Stanford's major athletic facilities includes: Stanford Stadium, Arrillaga Family Sports Center, Avery Aquatic Center, Cobb Track and Angell Field, Maples Pavilion, Stanford Golf Course, Taube Family Tennis Stadium, twenty-six tennis courts, an artificial turf field, a driving range, riding stables, and plenty of outdoor basketball and volleyball courts scattered throughout campus.

Stanford home games also provide a welcome release for students who relish the idea of showing Cardinal pride, often screaming themselves hoarse to the music of the most irreverent and colorful band in college sports, the Leland Stanford Junior University Marching Band.

Traditions

Stanford traditions are priceless in their sheer wackiness. Incoming freshmen are accepted into the Stanford fold in the freshman right of passage, Full Moon on the Quad. During the first full moon of the quarter, departing seniors welcome incoming freshmen to Stanford with a kiss. The sight of more than 3,000 people kissing under a full moon is unforgettable. Serenaded by the crazy Leland Stanford Junior University Marching Band, Full Moon on the Quad is one raucous night.

> **❝** *Stanford traditions are rooted in irreverence.* **❞**

—*Libusha Kelly, '97*

Every Sunday night, Stanford students put down their books to go enjoy a movie at Flicks, a student-run movie house. You can expect a rowdy paper fight during the movie's beginning credits as well as dorm chants and sporadic hissing from the crowd. Every student looks forward to the last flick of their undergraduate career, a free showing of Dustin Hoffman in *The Graduate*.

The Leland Stanford Junior University Marching Band traditionally dons wild, colorful costumes and sports uniquely decorated instruments. Known for their irreverent halftime shows, the Band is one Stanford tradition that keeps Stanford jumping. Backed by the B-d's ever-energetic mascot, the Tree, these students participate in the sound of Stanford's wackiest traditions.

GRADUATES

Stanford students go on to accomplish whatever they set their minds to. Stanford's broad liberal arts education imbues its students with an education applicable to any number of disciplines. Among Stanford's alumni are world leaders, technological innovators, and people of great influence.

Career Development Center

While a tremendous number of Stanford young alumni go on to pursue graduate studies, some set off into the real world with the help of Stanford's Career Development Center (CDC). The CDC provides individual counseling at all stages of a student's career planning and hosts a strong recruiting program, where industries and employers come to campus each quarter to recruit new graduates. Stanford alumni are also a fantastic resource for young alumni and recent graduates.

Stanford Alumni Association

The personal and academic connections students enjoy at Stanford continue to flourish after graduation. For those alumni who wish to continue their academic growth after graduation, the Stanford Alumni Association (SAA) offers an education series entitled "The Stanford Book Salon." Designed to connect Stanford alumni throughout the world, "The Book Salon" includes an online book designed and hosted by a Stanford professor. For those alumni who wish to reconnect with their Stanford peers in recreational ways, there is a yearly Reunion Homecoming weekend full of Cardinal activities, as well as opportunities to vacation with fellow alumni in various locations around the world. These Stanford vacations have included such destinations as the Arenal Volcano of Costa Rica, the Amazonian rain forests, and the mountains of Tibet.

FINANCIAL AID

The total cost of attendance at Stanford costs approximately $55,000 annually. Stanford is need-blind in its admission process, meaning that applying for financial aid does not affect the admission decision. This policy applies to students who are U.S. citizens or permanent residents of the United States. International students should refer to the following section. Stanford is committed to providing a financial aid package that will meet the full demonstrated financial need of every admitted U.S. student or permanent resident of the United States.

In the spring of 2008, Stanford announced significant enhancements to its financial aid policies. Parents whose total annual income is less than $60,000 a year will not be expected to contribute toward educational costs. Parents with income between $60,000 and $100,000 will receive enough scholarship to cover the cost of tuition at a minimum. All families are encouraged to visit financialaid.stanford.edu/calculator to receive an approximation of what a family might be expected to pay.

Beyond traditional work-study opportunities. Stanford also allows students to earn a portion of their financial aid package through community service. This alleviates incoming students' concern that they will be placed in unfulfilling jobs. Instead, Stanford's service organization, the Haas Center for Public Service, helps students find rewarding part-time jobs. The popularity of these community service job accounts for the more than 3,000 students who participate in Haas-sponsored activities. In fact, Stanford has ranked first among top universities in dispensing federal work-study money for community service. The Haas Center also works with faculty to combine community service with classroom teaching. These school-based service programs complementing a student's curriculum include the School of Engineering Precollege Program, the East Palo Alto Community Law Project, the Stanford Medical Youth Science Program, and the School of Education's Stanford/Schools Collaborative.

Financial Aid for International Students

Stanford does not practice need-blind admission for international students, which means the need for financial aid is a consideration in admission. Some international students may be offered admission on the condition that they finance their Stanford education. Financial aid is available to international students on a limited basis.

For more information on Stanford's financial aid program, visit *http://financialaid. stanford.edu*.

SUMMING UP

Stanford is committed to offering its undergraduates an education that is unrivaled among research universities. Recognized as one of the world's leading research and teaching institutions, Stanford has one of the most renowned faculties in the nation. Stanford's extraordinary students—men and women of all races, ethnicities, ages, and experiences—are distinguished by their love of learning and desire to contribute in a significant way to the greater community. From their first day on campus, students explore virtually limitless opportunities that fuel their intellectual passions and help them fulfill their academic and personal promise. They are encouraged to share their interests with members of all campus communities, resulting in a vigorous intellectual life outside the classroom as well as inside.

" Let us not be afraid to outgrow old thoughts and ways and dare to think on new lines as to the future work under our care. "

—*Jane Stanford*

The entrepreneurial spirit that inspired Leland and Jane Stanford to establish the institution and that later helped shape the discoveries and innovations of Silicon Valley, located right at Stanford's doorstep, cultivates an environment of intense creativity. Students at Stanford learn from policy makers, inventors, entrepreneurs, and scholars involved in the most pressing issues facing the world and in turn become involved themselves in discovering new knowledge that will inform the future.

Simply put, the ways you will think and live tomorrow are being shaped at Stanford today.

❏ *Gabriela Gutierrez, B.A.*

STATE UNIVERSITY OF NEW YORK AT GENESEO

Courtesy of SUNY at Geneseo

 State University of New York at Geneseo (SUNY Geneseo)
Geneseo, NY 11040

 (585) 245-5211
Fax: (585) 245-5550

 E-mail: *admission@geneseo.edu*
Website: *www.geneseo.edu*

 Enrollment

Full-time ❏ women: 3,050
     ❏ men: 2,328

Part-time ❏ women: 63
     ❏ men: 44

INTRODUCING GENESEO

Considered by many as "New York's Public Honors College," Geneseo is a premier liberal arts college with a tradition of academic excellence. Founded in 1871, Geneseo combines a close-knit and supportive community with excellent academics and a very high quality of life.

Geneseo offers a true liberal arts education. The school offers majors in the arts, humanities, natural and social sciences, business, and education. The number of different academic areas allows students from all over the college to take classes in their sections. It is common for students to take classes outside of their major, mixing many different disciplines together to form a well-rounded overall education.

From your first moments on campus, you will quickly realize that Geneseo *is* community. With its smaller student body and low student-teacher ratios, Geneseo prides itself on building relationships. Geneseo is big enough that you will meet new people every day, but small enough that you will see the people you know on a regular basis. Students represent different ethnic, religious, racial, and socioeconomic backgrounds. In addition, it is common for professors to extend the learning past the confines of the classroom, often resulting in an invitation for dinner or an extended conversation about a particular academic topic on the quad. Professors are often seen eating lunch with students, and many students report long and lasting relationships with their professors. Everything about the quaint and historic town exudes community. The many cafés, restaurants, and unique stores provide many places for students to relax, mingle, and develop relationships. Many students look back at their time at Geneseo fondly with warm memories of the friendships, partnerships, and connections that they have developed.

> **" ** *At Geneseo you are not a number, you really feel like you are somebody. I remember the personalized attention the admissions officers gave me when I applied to the school. First, there were students waiting to talk with me before my tour in the admissions lobby and before I met with the warm and friendly counselors who followed up with me to make sure that I had all the information I needed. As a student nothing changed; professors were incredibly approachable, college staff went out of their way to engage me in programming and make sure I was not only happy but getting the most out of my experience.* **"**

From Habitat for Humanity builds, to Relay for Life, to concerts and comedians, there is never any shortage of things to do at Geneseo. Besides the wonderful array of student-run extracurricular activities, the school is constantly putting on programing for its students. The Geneseo Late Knight program operates every Friday and Saturday night offering everything from foam parties to midnight movies to game-show competitions. In addition there are over 200 clubs, organizations, and teams that represent the student body's various interests and range from professional societies; to ethnic, religious, and cultural groups; to preprofessional clubs; to sports; and even to special-interest groups, like the humorously entitled juggling group, Geneseo Throws Up, and the student government. Students even gather for semiregular outdoor movie events where students bring their chairs, blankets, and popcorn to enjoy a recently released movie.

○	Applications	9,885
○	Enrolled	1,008
○	H.S. Average	middle 50%, 91/96
○	SAT	middle 50%, 1220/1390
○	ACT	middle 50%, 27/30

ADMISSIONS REQUIREMENTS

Admission to Geneseo is highly selective. Each year the admissions office selects an even more outstanding class than the last. The admissions office knows, however, that each student is hand picked based on his or her talents, experiences, and skills as part of the Geneseo community. Students are specifically selected based on their record of achievement in high school and the unique perspectives they can bring to the campus. The key to admission at Geneseo is to demonstrate that you possess the essential qualities necessary for success at a demanding university, namely, intelligence, motivation, dedication, and talent. While each individual application will be different and may succeed on its own merits, all students must take the SAT or the ACT. In addition, applicants must be graduates of an accredited secondary school or have a GED certificate. The academic program must have included four years each of English, math, science, and social studies, and three years of a foreign language. An essay is required as part of the application. Certain programs, however, require a portfolio or audition and an interview. Geneseo accepts AP and CLEP credits depending on your individual scores. Important factors in admissions decisions are the existence of advanced placement or honors courses in a student's transcript, a proven record of leadership, and an ability to finance a college education.

Generally, freshmen are admitted in the fall and spring. Entrance exams should be taken during the spring of the junior year of high school. There are Early Decision and Deferred Admissions plans. Early Decision applications should be filed by November 15; regular applications, by January 1 for fall entry and October 1 for spring entry. Notification of Early Decision is sent December 15; Regular Decision, March 1. Applications are accepted online.

ACADEMIC LIFE

Geneseo has a wide range of academic departments and course offerings for students to sample. As a liberal arts college, Geneseo promotes students choosing from a variety of majors and allows students to take classes in any of the schools without being a part of that school. Geneseo further promotes well-rounded students with its core curriculum, which ensures that graduating students are prepared for any experiences they may face. The core curriculum consists of taking two courses each in humanities, fine arts, social sciences, and natural sciences. In addition, each student must take one course each in non-Western tradition, critical writing/reading, numeric and symbolic reasoning, U.S. history, and foreign language proficiency.

> **"** *Being undecided, I was worried that I would be unable to choose a major. However, once I had worked my way through the core curriculum, I had a great sense of exactly which courses I liked best.* **"**

ACADEMIC STUDY FACTS

- ○ Geneseo is one of only 280 four-year colleges in the nation to have a chapter of Phi Beta Kappa, the oldest and most prestigious honor society in the nation.
- ○ 820 students presented results of research projects at campus seminars on G.R.E.A.T Day (Geneseo Recognizing Excellence, Achievement and Talent) in April 2010.
- ○ International study programs sponsored by SUNY—600+
- ○ Geneseo students who study abroad annually—300+
- ○ 2010 graduates who studied abroad—30%

Because Geneseo stresses a well-rounded education, students can receive a bachelor's degree in any of seven major areas, which are: Natural Science (biochemistry, biology/biological science, and biophysics, applied physics, chemistry, geochemistry, geology, geophysics, mathematics, and physics), Business (accounting and business administration), the Arts (art history and appreciation, music, musical theater, performing arts, and theater design), Education (early childhood education, elementary education, and special education), Humanities (English), Comparative Literature, French, Philosophy, and Spanish, Social Science (African-American studies, American studies, anthropology, communication, economics, geography, history, international relations, philosophy, political science/government, psychology, and sociology).

Special Programs

Geneseo offers a special 3-2 engineering degree with Alfred, Case Western Reserve, Clarkson, Columbia, Penn State, and Syracuse Universities, SUNY at Binghamton and Buffalo, and the University of Rochester, as well as a 3-3 degree with Rochester Institute of Technology and Upstate Medical University. Cross-registration is available with the Rochester Area Colleges Consortium. Geneseo offers internships, study abroad, a Washington semester, dual majors, and work-study programs. There are fifteen national honor societies, including Phi Beta Kappa, a freshman honors program, and nine departmental honors programs.

The Classroom

Class sizes vary depending on the type and composition of the class. While some of the initial "freshman lecture classes" may be larger (75–100 students), the class sizes drop significantly to a median class size of twenty-four students. The small faculty-to-student ratio (20 to 1) also helps to ensure that students have access to their professors. Particularly interesting is that, unlike many other universities, teaching assistants do not teach classes, only professors do!

FACULTY

- Full-time faculty—244
- Ph.D. or equivalent —89%
- Student/Faculty ratio—20:1
- Classes taught by full-time faculty—83%
- Classes taught by teaching assistants—0
- Median class size—24

> *I'll never forget my tour at Geneseo; I was amazed by the many different types of classrooms. There was everything from classrooms with individualized desks to lecture halls to laboratories to dance halls.*

Faculty

Professors at Geneseo are scholars in their field who have graduated from excellent institutions worldwide and bring their varied experiences into the classroom. The dedicated and learned faculty are the backbone of the excellent education at Geneseo.

Professors are incredibly accessible. They each have their own office hours and they make time for students. It is very common for students to be seen at lunch with a professor or to even be invited to a professor's house for dinner. Because of this Geneseo is a true learning environment where learning extends far beyond the walls of the classroom. Many students develop meaningful relationships with their professors that continue far beyond their time at Geneseo. In fact, I worked so closely with some of my professors that we became friends and still talk on the phone!

> *" Professors at Geneseo are teachers first and professors second. By that I mean that they take their job as educators extremely seriously! Unlike some universities where professors are there merely to do their own research, Geneseo professors love to teach. They do their own research and win all kinds of awards, too, but they are teachers, which makes learning at Geneseo an amazing experience! "*

The Student Body

The real Geneseo experience, however, comes from other students. Students work together to take learning to the next level. Students support each other by helping students in need. One time when I missed class, I had six different classmates offer to photocopy their notes for me. It is very common to see students working together in groups. Students often volunteer their time to tutor other struggling students. In fact, each department operates "learning centers" where fellow students come to tutor their struggling peers in the subjects they have in common. It is this level of interactivity that creates such a wonderful learning environment.

SOCIAL LIFE AND ACTIVITIES

Geneseo offers a highly competitive athletic department with eight intercollegiate sports for men and twelve for women. Geneseo's sports are Division III. Geneseo is best known for its hockey team. In fact, attending sporting events is one of the best and most enjoyable activities at Geneseo. Hockey games fill the void that one might expect from the lack of a football team. Hockey games offer students a chance to interact with other students and show off their school spirit, often with cries of "More Cowbell!" Many organizations make banners and have special cheers for the games.

Athletics

Geneseo's athletic offerings include Division III men's and women's soccer, basketball, lacrosse, cross-country, track, swimming, and diving as well as women's volleyball, equestrian, field hockey, softball, and tennis, and men's ice hockey. In addition to the intercollegiate Division III sports, there are a number of club sports teams that are highly organized and still compete but are not in the NCAA; these include men's and women's rugby, crew, Ultimate Frisbee as well as men's tennis, baseball, and water polo and women's cheerleading. Finally, the school offers intramural sports for those who are not looking for the time-commitment or level of commitment inherent in Division III or club sports. Intramural sports allow students to play a few rounds against other teams of similar athletic level and include most sports, but feature Broomball, a sport played in sneakers on the ice rink, much like hockey but with a ball. Broomball is a must-do activity for all students in their time at Geneseo.

> *I remember my first time playing, I was very unsteady on the ice and I think my team even had bets on how long I could stand between falls on the ice. It was incredibly fun!*

Other Activities

One of Geneseo's strengths is its ability to organize relevant, inspiring, and truly entertaining programming for its students. In addition to the over 200 clubs, organizations, and activities, Geneseo offers a program called Geneseo Late Knight (GLK), which not only offers a pun on Geneseo's mascot, the Knight, but also puts on late-night programming every weekend. Programing ranges from foam parties to Nerf-gun battles to midnight movies to dance-offs in the Knight Spot, an on-campus dance club. The phenomenal late night coordinators plan a range of programming to ensure that all students have something fun to do on the weekends from craft-like programs, game-show type affairs where students can win prizes, comedians, hypnotists, and even the occasional magician.

> **❝** *I still remember my first weekend at Geneseo when GLK brought out inflatable bouncy houses, sumo wrestling, and bungee cord races in a spectacular welcome carnival celebration. GLK helps turn every weekend into a fun, exciting celebration.* **❞**

The clubs, organizations, and activities range from student government organizations like the Student Association, the Activities Commission, and the Student Senate to cultural and similar interest organizations like the Black Student Association, the Jewish Student Association, and the French and Spanish Clubs. There are some common-interest clubs like the Geneseo Gaming Guild and the juggling club (Geneseo Throws Up!) to academic-based clubs like the business and marketing clubs. There are also a bunch of mass media organizations such as the student newspaper (*The Lamron*), the local radio station (WGSU), and the closed circuit television studio (GTV). Of particular interest is the ease with which groups of students can create clubs to address their particular interests. I know my friends and I thought of starting an underwater basket-weaving club.

There are many well-received events that occur annually. Many students look forward to the Latin American Student Association's (LASA) annual dance/fashion show. Each year the residence life department organizes Halloween and holiday gatherings in the Student Union. The school constantly brings guest lecturers, speakers, comedians, debates, and performances. There are two major concerts annually as well as many minor concerts throughout each semester. Geneseo also organizes a number of off-campus trips to many locations throughout Western New York, including Darien Lake Six-Flags, Canada, and other prominent and entertaining locations or events throughout the region. Blake, the arts school, constantly has shows and performances from musicals to small-scale black-box dramatic performances, as well as gallery exhibitions showing off the high-quality work of students.

Greek organizations also provide a social outlet for students despite the fact that only about twelve percent of the campus actually belongs to one. In total, there is one national and seven local fraternities for men and seven local and five national sororities for women. The Greek organizations sponsor activities on campus and throw off-campus parties as well. Greek-sponsored events include various walks for charity as well as Greek Week and GreekFest! The Greek Tree (now called the painted tree) is a tree painted in the colors of one of the campus's Greek organizations and is one of Geneseo's oldest traditions.

The Campus

Geneseo students must live on campus during their first and second years. This helps create the wonderful campus community and provides an opportunity to make some great friends. Most students start out in one of the all-freshman buildings (there are two) and then move into suites with their friends in their sophomore year. There are two main residence clusters: north side and south side. There is a slight rivalry between the two sides as to which is better. Being biased, I will only say that while North Side is closer to the academic section, South Side provides a real community experience where students get a chance to develop really meaningful relationships that they will take with them throughout the rest of their time at Geneseo and into the rest of their lives.

The campus itself is beautiful. While the campus is large, every residence hall is within a fifteen-minute (at the extremes) walk to the academic buildings. All of the academic buildings are grouped by subject area (the science buildings are all together, the arts building houses all the arts programs, etc.) so students do not have to spend valuable time between classes walking a great distance. The MacVittie Student Union has a number of small café areas that are great for getting a snack while studying or relaxing between classes. The Union also has a recreational area with pool tables, air hockey, video games, table tennis, and other forms of entertainment for students to enjoy during the school day and on weekends. All over campus are benches and gazebos for students to enjoy nature.

> **❝** I love how beautiful the campus is! I love just walking around the campus. With the rustic, ivy-clad buildings, I just can't help feeling like I've fallen into the perfect little picture, but it's real! **❞**

Perhaps the most enjoyable part of campus are the two main academic quads. The first has an area called simply "The Green," which is a wide expanse of grass where students go

The 220-acre campus is in a small town 30 miles south of Rochester. Including residence halls, there are 54 buildings.

Special learning facilities include
○ A learning resource center
○ Art gallery
○ Planetarium
○ Radio station
○ TV station
○ Arboretum
○ Greenhouses
○ A particle accelerator
○ Dance studios
○ Sound-proof music practice rooms, and 4 theaters

to study outside and play Frisbee in between classes. The other main academic quad has Geneseo's prominent clock tower, the painted tree, and the "Dr. Seuss Tree."

FINANCIAL AID

Because Geneseo is a public institution, many students receive some form of financial aid. In fact, in 2009–2010, seventy-two percent of all full-time freshmen and seventy-six percent of continuing full-time students received some form of financial aid. Sixty-two percent of all full-time freshmen and sixty-five percent of continuing full-time students received need-based aid. The average freshman award was $10,631, with $3,846 ($9,850 maximum) from need-based scholarships or need-based grants; $4,837 ($7,000 maximum) from need-based self-help aid (loans and jobs); and $2,164 ($6,000 maximum) from other non-need-based awards and non-need-based scholarships, sixteen percent of undergraduate students work part-time. Financial Aid counselors really help to ensure that each student receives aid based on his or her particular financial situation. The average financial indebtedness of the 2009 graduate was about $19,000.

GRADUATES

Geneseo graduates go forth and pursue myriad career paths. However, graduates leave knowing that they are prepared for their lives postgraduation because of the phenomenal education they have received. Geneseo works to maintain positive relationships with each of its alumni through a strong alumni network and a tri-annual magazine as well as its monthly alumni newsletter.

Graduates of Geneseo go on to do a great many things from postgraduate degrees, right into the actual working world. Of the 2008 graduating class, forty-one percent were enrolled in graduate school within six months of graduation, and an additional forty-nine percent were employed.

○ Ysaye Barnwell ('67), Vocalist and Executive Director of the Grammy Award-Winning All-Woman African-American A Cappella Ensemble "Sweet Honey in the Rock"

○ Joseph Bucci ('67), Vice Chair, American Rock Salt Co.

○ Jeffrey Burkard ('89), President and CEO of DesignPac Inc.

○ Christa Carone ('90), Vice President, Marketing and Communications and Chief Marketing Officer, Xerox Corp.

○ Glenn Caron ('75), Executive Producer/Owner, Picture Maker Productions Inc.

○ Jeffrey Clarke ('83), President and CEO of Travelport Inc.

○ Paul Furcinito ('88), Independent Investment Management Professional, Florek Financial

○ Andrew Hamingson ('90), Executive Director/Trustee The Public Theatre

○ Gregg "Opie" Hughes ('86), "Shock-jock" Opie and Anthony Show

○ My Hang Huyng ('91), Synthetic Organic Chemist and Winner of a prestigious MacArthur Fellowship

○ Bruce Jordan ('66), President, Cranberry Productions

○ Peter Kaczorowski ('78), Theatrical Lighting Designer, Winner of Tony Award for Lighting for "The Producers"

○ Raymond Kotcher ('73), CEO and Senior Partner, Ketchum Public Relations

○ Jack Kramer ('76), Senior Vice President, SunGard Higher Education

○ James Leary ('75), Executive Director of Washington, D.C., Law Firm Akin Gump Strauss Hauer & Feld LLP

○ Thomas Moser ('60), Thomas Moser Cabinetmakers

○ Jackie Norris ('92), Senior Policy Adviser to the Corporation for National and Community Service; Former Chief of Staff for First Lady Michelle Obama

○ Gregory O'Connell ('64), Real Estate Developer who has helped revive Brooklyn's Red Hook Area

○ Matthew Rozell ('81), Hudson Falls High School Teacher, Global Studies

○ Brian Saluzzo ('92), Managing Director, Goldman Sachs & Co.

○ Christine Sconzo Munnelly ('86), Vice President, Women's Merchandising, Aeropostale Inc.

○ Curt Smith ('73), Author, Radio/TV host, Former Speech Writer for President George H. W. Bush

○ John Tournour ('87), Sports Talk Radio Host, FOX Sports Radio, "JT The Brick Show"

○ Anthony Wiederkehr ('87), Founding President and CEO of AeroMech Inc.

○ Diane Willkens ('75), President and CEO, Development Finance Intl. Inc.

○ Dr. Pamela York Klainer ('71), Financial Expert, Author, Klainer Consulting

SUMMING UP

Geneseo is a phenomenal place to get an education that will assist you in your life moving forward into the world. From its rustic beauty and small-town feel to its incredible diversity of activities and numerous course offerings, Geneseo offers a community to support and develop your interests. In addition to its reputation as the honors college of the

SUNY system, Geneseo is a truly warm, welcoming, and encouraging community. Geneseo has a small professor-to-student ratio meaning smaller classes and more individualized attention from committed and engaging professors. Geneseo is a college where you will make friendships and partnerships that will last you a lifetime! With its broad range of academic programs and outstanding core-curriculum, students leave Geneseo prepared for whatever life throws their way. Geneseo makes your college years some of the most memorable of your life giving you memories that will last your whole life through.

Leaving Geneseo I was completely prepared for everything I have done since. Not only did I gain a phenomenal network of intelligent and committed friends, alumni, and professors, but I gained the technical and intellectual skills that can only come from a stimulating academic environment.

Be warned, however, that this article is just an introduction to Geneseo and cannot replicate the value of visiting Geneseo. While many visitors indicate that they immediately feel at home and fall in love with Geneseo, not every school is right for every person. I strongly recommend vising Geneseo and deciding for yourself if it is the best choice for you!

❏ *Jared Chester, B.A.*

 Swarthmore College
Swarthmore, PA 19081

 (610) 328-8300

 E-mail: *admissions@swarthmore.edu*
Website: *www.swarthmore.edu*

 Enrollment

Full-time ❏ women: 783
          ❏ men: 727

Part-time ❏ women: 12
           ❏ men: 3

INTRODUCING SWARTHMORE COLLEGE

Founded by Quakers in 1864, Swarthmore's grounds comprise the Scott Arboretum. The campus is located about ten miles southwest of Philadelphia in southeastern Pennsylvania. It is a coeducational liberal arts and engineering college. It offers a robust and diverse academic program across many different disciplines and subject areas with limited distribution requirements across fields. At the core of the school lies its dedication to the value of a liberal arts education, and a belief in the limitless boundaries of its students' intellectual capacity.

&&Upon stepping out of my family's car on my first visit to Swarthmore, I found myself overcome with the urge to wander its verdant grounds. Rather than head immediately to the Admissions Office, I found myself following Swarthmore's various circuitous paths that lead through carefully manicured lawns and gardens. As if transported, I stopped at the Lilac Garden, examined the buds of the famous Dean Bond Rose Garden, and sat in the warm summer air in the cloistered and pungent Fragrance Garden. Upon approaching the grand Scott Amphitheater I became aware of a different part of the campus. Enrobing the Amphitheater's lush grass terraces and stately canopy of branches was the Crum Woods, a rich wilderness through which trickles the Crum Creek. Dotted throughout this idyllic 357-acre campus were dozens, if not hundreds, of spots designed for reading, thinking, and embracing the academic, the personal, and the peaceful. As I trotted back to the Admissions Office with my father in tow, I found myself feeling something I hadn't yet experienced at the other colleges I visited: I yearned to belong to Swarthmore and have Swarthmore belong to me.

It was not until a year later, in my first semester at Swarthmore, that I understood how appropriate its grounds are as a reflection of the broader institution. The juxtaposition of overflowing wilderness with artfully sculpted order is an ideal frame for a school where classes and professors provide intellectual structure, yet also encourage and, indeed, force students into the wilderness of knowledge. For four years, I was constantly pushed into the academic forests with the expectation that I would return and, together with my fellow students, create my own ordered academic garden. Through passionate arguing, furious research, and marathon late-night writing sessions, my peers and I plunged into the tangle of knowledge ostensibly looking for an answer, but learning that the search was equally valuable.99

Swarthmore's student body includes residents of forty-eight states, more than thirty-five countries, and innumerable backgrounds, traditions, ethnicities, identities, and orientations. Despite these impressive statistics, it is still a small school by any standard, having a student body of approximately 1,500. This small size has its downsides. Although it is an easy twenty-minute train ride into the United States' sixth largest city—Philadelphia—for some applicants it may be too secluded and suburban. Additionally, the small student body lends itself to an intimate knowledge of many (if not most) of one's fellow students. The size also has its benefits, however, and most students agree that these outweigh the negatives. The student:faculty ratio, for example, is an almost unheard-of 8:1 supported by 173 faculty members. This lends itself to an average class size of fifteen in regular courses, and an emphasis on small, seminar-style learning built on strong student-faculty relationships. Additionally, Swarthmore has close ties to the nearby colleges of Haverford and Bryn Mawr, creating the Tri-College Consortium. Students are able to co-mingle both inside and outside the classroom with students of these two other colleges, thus expanding the social and academic circles to a much larger population.

Most students choose Swarthmore for its academic reputation: rigorous, high-quality, graduate-level study takes center-stage of life at the college. Yet, unlike large, impersonal research universities, Swarthmore is fiercely noncompetitive. Learning occurs not for ranking or status, but rather for the fun of it; students enthusiastically grapple with their academic work individually and communally, both inside and, importantly, outside the classroom. There is a genuine desire on the part of the student body to help each other learn, the collective exploration and understanding being greater than the sum of its parts.

ADMISSIONS REQUIREMENTS

It has occasionally been remarked that some top-ranked schools don't actually have an admissions department; they have only a PO Box where applications sit, since nobody knows anyone who actually gets accepted, and nobody ever hears back from the admissions departments. Swarthmore, however, is incredible in its highly personable admissions process, priding itself on communication and assistance at every step along the application process. Phone calls from the dean, coaches, professors, and admissions officers are common, as Swarthmore makes every effort to ensure that the applicant is the right fit for Swarthmore and, perhaps more importantly, that the college is the right fit for the applicant.

To dispense with the tedium of scores early on, here are the quick facts on the current first-year class's SAT scores: sixty-five percent scored a 700 or higher on the critical reading sections, fifty-eight percent scored a 700 or higher on the math sections, and fifty-two percent scored a 700 or higher on the writing section. It would be foolish, however, to base one's admissions likelihood or "fit" to the school on these scores alone. The author of this piece, for example, would not have made the cut if the above scores were the sole factor in the application. Swarthmore accepts either the SAT with two subject tests, or the ACT with writing. Interviews are highly recommended.

To some, Swarthmore is well known, but many people will still ask when it went coed (clearly confusing Swarthmore with Skidmore; Swarthmore has been coed since its founding). Given some of its national rankings in the popular press that may seem surprising, it is important to remember that Swarthmore has no football team, is extraordinarily rigorous academically, has limited Greek life, and is small at only 1,500 students. These facts, while appealing to many, also make for a self-selective applicant pool—folks tend not to apply to Swarthmore simply to add another name to their school list.

Most readers of this chapter will probably want to know what Swarthmore wants in an applicant. The answer is short: it depends. Swarthmore admissions staffers read each application as a whole; there is no "magic bullet" to acceptance. That said there are certain attributes that are desirable. The Admissions staff wants to see that the applicant is a hard worker, a dedicated student, a creative and broad thinker, and open to new ideas and challenges. Primarily, however, they want to see if the applicant is the right "fit" for the school. There isn't much sense in trying to strategize through the application; if you are excited by the thought of a small, rigorous, resource-rich four-year-long academic thrill-ride then you belong at Swarthmore. Use the application to highlight those abilities and interests.

Campus Visits

If you're serious about Swarthmore, it is certainly worth visiting the campus for a couple of days first as a "spec" (short for "Prospective Student"). These frequent visitors are warmly included in the social fabric of the school when they visit. They shadow their hosts from class to the dining hall to social events, and are always jovially included in whatever their host may be doing. By staying for a day or two (and particularly a night or two) in a Swarthmore dormitory, an applicant can get a real flavor of the school and its citizens. Swarthmore's dorms are, with one exception, coed and have a mix of all different class years, so getting a sense of life on the halls is very important if you're really interested in the school.

ACADEMIC LIFE

At Swarthmore it can often feel like one's academic life (the title of this section) is just that: life. Indeed, it is that quality that attracts Swatties to the school: they want to be academically challenged, intellectually broadened, and rigorously examined. Fortunately there are plenty of course offerings to choose from, and Swarthmore students typically plunge into their academics with an eye toward achieving academic breadth in the first two years, and academic depth in the last two years.

> **❝** *In this course, we will consider psychoanalytic, phenomenological, and poststructuralist theories of the subject that offer varying ways of understanding who we are, why we do what we do, and the kind of changes in collective practices that might constitute a reworking of what some theorists we consider call the 'cultural imaginary' that informs us.* **❞**

> *—Description of the course INTP 091: Reworking the Cultural Imaginary, the Interpretation Theory capstone seminar*

Study Abroad

As anyone who has gotten this far has figured out, Swarthmore can be an academic pressure-cooker. For this reason (as well as its relatively small size), many students choose to spend a semester or two abroad in their junior or senior years. Swarthmore covers its students' financial aid when they go, and has a terrific foreign study office that assists in choosing the right program and country, and coordinating the study abroad experience. Students return to Swarthmore from abroad rejuvenated, enthusiastic, and energized for their last semesters.

Core Degree Requirements

Swarthmore does have some core degree requirements, but these are typically easily filled out of sheer curiosity about the possible courses. In addition to taking at least twenty courses outside their major, students must also take three classes in each of the three divisions: humanities, social sciences, and the natural sciences. Three of these classes must be writing (W) courses, and those three must include work in at least two divisions. Additionally, students must take a lab course.

Facilities

To support the academic life of its students, Swarthmore has seven libraries/special collections with more than 850,000 volumes, more than 26,000 CDs/DVDs, and it subscribes to more than 10,500 periodicals and databases. Additionally, Swarthmore students have easy and almost immediate access to the libraries of Bryn Mawr College and Haverford College, as well as the global system of interlibrary loan. While there is not an explicit "learning resource center," there are many resources for the curious or the struggling. The Writing Center offers students trained advice and critiques on writing for any class, and many classes organize into study groups and review sessions. In addition, there are Student Academic Mentors (SAMs), and the faculty encourages communication and discussion outside of the classroom.

Degrees

Swarthmore offers B.A. degrees in more than two dozen fields in the arts and sciences and a B.S. degree in engineering, which about five percent of the student body takes. This signifies both the great breadth of course offerings, as well as the diversity of interests within the student body. It also demonstrates one of the greatest strengths of Swarthmore's academic programming: class size, and professor/student engagement. The top three most popular majors among the 2008 graduates were biology, economics, and political science.

Class Size and Professors

Swarthmore's class size is a point of pride for the college. Boasting a remarkable 8:1 student-to-faculty ratio, the core of learning at Swarthmore is direct, personal, and sustained engagement with the professors. This means that Swarthmore students are privileged to work closely with the professors, not with teaching assistants. Students are frequently asked to help professors with their research and lab work, and these relationships often lead to summer internships, postgraduation jobs, and even publishing opportunities. It is not unheard of for students to attend conferences in their own right, and be respected contributors to journals and books.

Typical class size ranges from up to thirty in the first year to anywhere from two to ten as a junior or senior. Classes are discussion- and question-oriented with professors emphasizing debate and conversation as a critical aspect of education. Of course there has to be material to talk *about* and Swarthmore professors never shy away from loading it on. Along with the great freedom of learning-through-conversation comes the great responsibility of knowing the texts and theories before class. A typical syllabus for a seminar may be forty pages single-spaced, and students are frequently asked to read not selected articles but entire books (plural) for class. Students must also prove their competency in writing, and four or five papers a weekend is the norm rather than the exception. Upon leaving Swarthmore, some students compile all their papers and put them in one document to see how many pages they have written in their four years. Needless to say, high three-digit numbers are to be expected.

Honors Program

A distinctive feature of Swarthmore's academic programming is its honors program. Modeled on the Oxford tradition of small discussion-based tutorials, the honors program exemplifies that kind of intense learning process the Swarthmore prides itself on. Students who choose to enter the honors program take four seminars in their last two years of college—one in their minor and three in their major. Sometimes held in intimate seminar rooms and sometimes in professors' living rooms, seminars meet once a week for several hours. Seminar students know not to schedule anything directly after a seminar is supposed to end, as they frequently extend several hours past their assigned stop-time. The format is simple and effective: students typically have one week to read many articles, books, critiques, reviews, and arguments, write a paper (generally five to fifteen pages single-spaced), and then walk the rest of the class through their arguments in seminar, defending their positions the whole time. Although grueling at times, there is also a sense of deep satisfaction when you have successfully defended your paper against critiques from your professor. Discussions are heated, wide-ranging, and academically personal, as the students and professor engage in communal and collaborative learning.

Many students' favorite semester at Swarthmore was the one in which they had only two seminars to make up their four-credit semester workload. With five empty days and only two class meetings per week, students have the time to completely structure their own schedule around personal study habits. Although it may at first appear luxurious, it is important in such a semester not to take on too many extracurricular projects, as the workload of two seminars is like a gas—it expands to fill up the space.

SOCIAL LIFE AND ACTIVITIES

As noted above, Swarthmore is a small school, at roughly 1,500 students. Although this can lead to a lack of privacy, it also lends itself to an incredibly close-knit and supportive community. Social interactions are likely to occur in the lone dining hall and in the library, in the campus newspaper offices, and in the gym; unlike larger schools, if you want to see someone you don't have to make elaborate plans—you'll probably see them in the next couple of hours.

Swarthmore also has a terrific dorm life, presided over by fun, well-meaning, and energetic Residential Advisors (RAs)—seniors and juniors who each have a "hall" that they live on and "lead." While at some schools RAs are merely punitive actors cloaked in the guise of a resource, at Swarthmore they are more typically your friend. At some schools RAs will spend their time patrolling the hallways for signs of drinking and general collegiate foolishness; the Swarthmore RAs take a humane and friendly approach toward their roles: their doors are typically open, they organize hall social events, and they keep an eye out for the student who may be overly stressed or too tired. They also act as an invaluable resource for students to approach and talk to about whatever happens to be on their minds.

Activities and Groups

Swarthmore students are rarely at a loss for what to do with their time. In addition to a full academic load, there are over 138 campus groups, clubs, and organizations ranging from literary arts magazines (a couple) to a hockey club, from the respected War News Radio Station to a fencing team, from dance groups to a debate team, and everything in between. In addition to these clubs, there are a number of cultural support groups and identity clubs that have a robust presence on campus.

In addition to these groups, Swarthmore's student body is very active politically, with groups ranging from organizing international pressure for social justice to advocating for organic food in the salad bar. The political leaning is famously (or infamously) liberal, and some students complain about a lack of a large conservative student base. Occasionally called the Kremlin on the Crum, Swarthmore's student body is politically aware and determined to *do* something about it. Throughout the lifeblood of the college is an insistence that it is not sufficient to simply sit idly by and witness the world's difficulties; Swarthmore students must proactively take charge and get involved in issues. In a recent example, a wide-ranging campus debate centered on whether Swarthmore should end its contract with Coca-Cola due to alleged abuses of employees in their bottling plants in developing countries. For better or for worse, the administration ultimately agreed with the student group and ended its contract. Volunteerism and social activism play important roles in the life of the college and students are frequently and purposefully exposed to new campaigns, new ideas, new debates, and arguments that underscore the classroom learning.

Sports

More than twenty percent of students participate on a sports team. There are twelve outdoor and six indoor tennis courts, six full-length basketball courts, ten outdoor playing fields, a lighted stadium, squash courts, gym, an indoor pool, and a fully staffed sports medicine facility, among other amenities. While Swarthmore's athletics are not the core of the student socialization, and the bleachers are rarely packed, they are also never empty and the school spirit that does exist grows more from supporting one's friends than from following a team. All students who don't participate in interscholastic sports are required to spend several semesters doing phys ed classes that include dance, squash, weight training, or swimming. Additionally, every student must pass a short swimming test in order to graduate.

Social Life

The social life at Swarthmore is a cozy one. In other words, if you are looking for a round-the-clock all-campus party scene complete with Animal House-esque fraternity parties and keggers, Swarthmore is not the place for you.

Students generally enjoy a lower-key level of partying, and during the week, social life is mainly contained in the dorms or, tellingly enough, in the first floor of the main library, McCabe, which acts as a mixing bowl for the student population. During the week most students work on their homework, lab assignments, papers, reading, studying, etc., and are not likely to head out for riotous partying on a Wednesday evening. That said, if you happen to have a schedule without any class on a Thursday or have some free time on Wednesday, there are always places and people to find who are taking a break or cutting loose for a bit. This may involve going to the student-run late-night café, grabbing a movie from the library's DVD stacks, joining one of the ongoing poker groups, or—more often than not—sitting in a dormitory lounge or on the main lawn with some friends, a few beers, and good conversation.

CRUM REGATTA

A popular springtime event at Swarthmore is the Crum Regatta, named after the gentle creek that curls through the campus' backyard. Students spend weeks (and sometimes just minutes) constructing boats and rafts from all sorts of items. On a morning in early April the registrar dresses in a Napoleonic admiral uniform and presides over a race down the Crum in a motley assortment of boats, floats, and rafts. Standing on the shore are the parents (it occurs during parent's weekend) and tables of hot chocolate and coffee. The winning team receives an award and everyone goes home exhilarated from the cold, the caffeine, and the sheer absurdity of the event.

The weekend party scene centers on a few communal party spaces as well as gatherings in students' dorm lounges or rooms. Unlike many other schools, and as mentioned above, the dormitories are monitored by a laid-back social code and a "live and let live" attitude. Of course, sleep and work trump partying in the dorms and the RAs keep the peace by dissolving rambunctious parties when members of the hall are asleep or working, but by and large the gatherings in dorms are mutually acceptable and low-key. They range from watching a football game to playing cards or, again the staple of social interaction at Swarthmore, discussing ideas raised in that day's classes or in the news.

There are two fraternities at Swarthmore that host parties on weekends and throughout the week, and there are a number of parties every weekend hosted by different student groups. As part of the student government, there is a committee that dispenses money for parties and social gatherings. In a relatively easy and painless process, if a student or a student group would like to host a party, they fill out an application and submit it to the committee for review. The committee then assigns a given amount of funding to the group and the party can go forward. The amount of money for any given party ranges from $20 to $500 and goes toward decorations, music, food, and (non-alcoholic) drinks. The only caveat: every student must be admitted to the party.

Drinking

Finally, Swarthmore's administration takes a pragmatic approach to underage drinking on campus. The school realizes that undergraduate students will drink alcohol anyway even if it is prohibited. Thus, the administration has wisely determined that the priority is to prevent students from drinking and driving and from abusing alcohol in unsafe settings. To this end, the school does not drive alcohol out of the dorms or off of the campus, and instead, offers counseling and support services for at-risk students. While it in no way condones, supports, or otherwise encourages drinking by any of its students, and certainly not the underage ones, the school is very open about its pragmatic and health-oriented view of alcohol. As a result, there are comparatively few alcohol-related incidents, and drunk-driving is an almost unheard-of rarity.

FINANCIAL AID

Compared to many other colleges, Swarthmore's financial aid program is generous. Beginning with the 2008-09 academic year, Swarthmore's financial aid awards no longer include a loan component. Instead, additional scholarship is granted in future loan-free awards. With forty-nine percent of the student body receiving some form of financial aid in the 2008–2009 academic year, the loan-free initiative will greatly ease the indebtedness of Swarthmore's upcoming graduates. This helps students choose a major and career path that they want regardless of the salary potential. Thus, Swarthmore deliberately fosters academic and intellectual curiosity by allowing students to pursue degrees in arts and humanities that are incorrectly perceived to be less useful in repaying college loans.

The admissions process is need-blind for U.S. citizens and permanent residents. The Admissions Office is dedicated to recruiting smart students from all ranges of financial backgrounds as a part of its commitment to diversity. The average financial aid award is $33,193 with the vast majority of that ($31,715) being awarded in scholarships or need-based grants. Additionally, there are ample jobs on campus that students can take to make money, with eighty-two percent of the student body working in the libraries, laboratories, academic offices, or other college positions. In a recent year, the tuition, fees, and room and board expenses were $47,804.

Finally, Swarthmore offers two named scholarships: the Evans Scholarships and the McCabe Awards. These are given every year to incoming students with leadership qualities and potential.

GRADUATES

Every June about 350 students join the ranks of the Swarthmore alumni. They go into the world in widely varying fields with vastly different paths and ambitions. Some become dancers while others become neuroscientists, some become community activists, while others become playwrights. There is no one-track path for the Swarthmore graduate and that is exactly what Swarthmore wants: Swarthmore is not a vocational school and does not train its students to perform in a particular field. Instead it provides a much more profound and, ultimately, useful skill: critical thinking and the ability to write complex arguments in a convincing way.

Many alums go immediately or almost immediately into graduate programs at the top universities in the world—within five years more than half of the graduates are back in school—knowing that even if they were pre-med they have the skills to succeed at an art history doctoral program. Although Swarthmore may not be very well known in high-school applicant circles it does command name recognition at graduate schools, and Swarthmore students know that they also have a very active and very committed alumni base upon which to draw advice and support for the next stage of their careers.

Swarthmore's alumni are terrific. They are engaged, involved, and committed to the recent Swarthmore graduates. Active in every imaginable field and at all levels, the alums

○ **Christian B. Anfinsen, Nobel Laureate in Chemistry**

○ **Edward C. Prescott, Nobel Laureate in Economics**

○ **John C. Mather, Nobel Laureate in Physics**

○ **Peter Bart, Vice President and Editor-in-Chief of** *Variety*

○ **David Gelber, Executive Producer, 60 Minutes on CBS**

○ **Kenneth Turan, Movie Reviewer,** *Los Angeles Times*

○ **Neil R. Austrian, Former President of NFL, Interim Chairman and CEO, Office Depot**

○ **Roger Holstein, CEO, WebMD**

○ **Richard Wall Lyman, Former President, Stanford University**

○ **Detlev W. Bronk, Former President, Johns Hopkins University**

○ **Alexander Mitchell Palmer, United States Attorney General (1919–1921)**

○ **Mary M. Schroeder, Chief Judge, United States Court of Appeals for the Ninth Circuit**

○ **Carl Levin, Member, the United States Senate**

○ **Robert Zoellick, President, World Bank**

○ **Antoinette Sayeh, Minister of Finance, Liberia**

○ **Cynthia Leive, Editor in Chief,** *Glamour* **magazine**

○ **Norman Rush, Novelist, winner of the 1991 National Book Award for** *Mating*

recognize that their fellow alumni have been forged in a crucible; painful, joyous, challenging, ecstatic, and ultimately deeply rewarding way. The Swarthmore experience creates bonds and friendships that endure lifetimes. The alumni ranks boast five Nobel laureates, dozens (maybe hundreds) of Fulbright grantees, many Rhodes Scholars, Marshall Scholars, and leaders in business, law, science, and politics. It's an impressive list for a group of just under 19,000.

SUMMING UP

Swarthmore is a unique place in the fullest sense of the word. Certainly there are other small, rigorous, liberal arts colleges with beautiful campuses and high-quality academic programming. But to conclude, I'll end where I began: there is a feeling and a sense about the school that is unlike other colleges in its genre. Quaker meetings meditate on what is known as a "sense of the meeting" in which receptivity to both silence and dialogue leads to communally acceptable consensus. In many ways, although certainly not explicitly, Swarthmore embodies this quiet yet powerful dicta. The sense of Swarthmore is one of purposeful enjoyment of academics and of the pleasures, for four brief years, the thrill and freedom of being young, energetic, and ready to broaden horizons.

Of course, what you get out of the school depends on what you put in. By attending Swarthmore you are not guaranteeing yourself four years of purely positive memories and unhindered intellectual growth. Indeed, you are merely choosing the tool with which to learn; how you use that tool is up to you. There will certainly be times when you are challenged, when you are stretched beyond what you imagine is your breaking point, and when you desire more than anything to leave. Yet almost every student stays because there is something in them that synchs with the sense of Swarthmore. They carry on, knowing that when they graduate they won't have a degree that carries such immediate clout as one from a big Ivy League school. They know that people will often say "where is that again?" or "you'll never find a job if you major in Religion." Swarthmore students know all this yet they carry on because ultimately it is not about how the rest of the world sees us; it is about personal and communal growth, about embarking on a remarkable, if not widely known or recognized, odyssey. And when, in later years, Swarthmore students find each other at reunions or on random street corners, there is an immediate camaraderie and a sense that here stands a kindred spirit.

❏ *Peter Gardner, B.A.*

TUFTS UNIVERSITY

 Tufts University
Medford, MA 02155

 (617) 627-3170
Fax: (617) 627-3860

 E-mail: *admissions.inquiry@ase.tufts.edu*
Website: *http://admissions.tufts.edu/*

 Undergraduate Enrollment

Full-time ❑ women: 2,628
❑ men: 2,483

Part-time ❑ women: 29
❑ men: 24

INTRODUCING TUFTS UNIVERSITY

Founded in 1852, Tufts University has grown from a small, regional college to a world-renowned, major research university whose 5,000 undergraduates come from more than sixty-five countries. Regardless of where they are from, Tufts students, staff, and faculty all share the common goal of using their intellects to better the world, whether it is working in rural Ghana to stop the spread of parasitic diseases found in local water sources or volunteering in Boston as translators for recent Vietnamese immigrants.

> **“** *A Tufts education will inspire [you] to get out into the world and shake things up, tear things down, and make things better.* **”**

—Kyle Halle-Erbe, '10

Referred to by President Larry Bacow as a small university with a sense of intimacy, Tufts nurtures the development of global scholars and leaders by combining the best aspects of small liberal arts colleges—discussion and inquiry-based classes; close relationships with professors—and the best attributes of large research universities—funding and support for undergraduate research; award-winning, internationally recognized faculty. Emphasizing the importance of intellectual exploration and interdisciplinary education, Tufts fosters the growth of poetry-writing engineers, political activist premed students, and environmentally conscious entrepreneurs. Although students are enrolled in either the school of engineering or the school of liberal arts, classes in each school are open to all undergraduates. Undergraduate students also benefit from the resources and research opportunities available at Tufts' eight graduate schools, including the School of Medicine, School of Dental Medicine, School of Veterinary Medicine, Nutrition School, and Fletcher School of Law and Diplomacy, the nation's oldest and arguably most prestigious graduate school in international relations.

A national leader in active citizenship, Tufts is home to the Jonathan M. Tisch College of Citizenship and Public Service. In May 2006, six years after its founding, Tufts alumnus Jonathan M. Tisch's generous $40 million endowment gift ensured the college's future as a university fixture. Integrating active citizenship into the curriculum, Tisch College facilitates collaboration between civic-minded students and faculty who aspire to solve complex real-world problems. Recent student-initiated projects include biomedical engineers utilizing light spectroscopy for breast cancer screening and studio art students examining art and social change as reflected through graffiti.

Located just five miles northwest of Boston, Tufts' beautiful 150-acre New England college campus rests upon Walnut Hill and overlooks the city skyline. The campus is a short walk or shuttle bus ride from Davis Square, a bustling social center that is home to independent coffee shops, live music venues, delicious ethnic food, and one of Boston's best used-bookstores. Davis Square, located on the Red Line of the subway, also provides students with easy access into Boston, where students often grab dinner in the North End (Boston's "Little Italy"), visit the Museum of Fine Arts (where Tufts students receive free admission), or catch a Red Sox or Celtics game.

Although students appreciate Boston's accessibility, the heart of undergraduate life is found on campus, home to 5,000 students and over 200 thriving student-run organizations. Students who live on campus have the option of choosing between single-sex and coed dormitories, on-campus apartments, fraternity and sorority houses, and numerous culture units, including the Africana, Latino, Asian American, International, Jewish, Muslim, Spanish, French, German, Russian, Arts, Crafts, and Substance Free Culture Units. All first- and second-year students are required to live on campus; many third- and fourth-year students choose to live with friends in off-campus apartments immediately surrounding the university.

Construction vehicles and hard hats have been a common site on campus recently. Two major construction projects were recently completed. Sophia Gordon Hall, an environmentally friendly "green" dormitory that houses 125 seniors, opened its doors in the fall of 2006. The university's new music building, home to the music department and a new 300-seat, acoustically engineered, recording-quality auditorium, was completed in January of 2007. Other campus improvements within the past couple of years include the construction of a $2 million boathouse on the Malden River for Tufts' crew teams, the renovation of West Hall, a residence hall since 1872 that is a favorite amongst students and known for its spacious rooms and prime location on the academic quad, and the revamping of Cabot Auditorium and the Fletcher School of Law and Diplomacy.

Tufts is an eclectic and dynamic community of passionate students from a wide variety of geographic, racial, ethnic, socioeconomic, religious, and cultural backgrounds. Students of color and international students make up more than a third of the undergraduate study body. It is not unusual for a first-year student from Chicago to be roommates with a student from Seattle and neighbors with a student from Hong Kong and a student from Texas. The diversity within the undergraduate student body creates a stimulating, intellectual community in which students are constantly learning in the classrooms from their first-rate professors and outside the classroom from their eclectic classmates.

ADMISSIONS REQUIREMENTS

Once a moderately selective regional college, Tufts has transformed itself over the past twenty-five years into a most-selective international university. Students applying to Tufts are required to submit the Common Application and the Tufts Supplement form. Last year twenty-four percent of the 15,433 applicants were offered admission to either the school of liberal arts or the school of engineering. The fact that the admissions process is highly selective should not discourage applicants from applying since the application review process at Tufts is holistic.

As Dean of Admissions Lee Coffin likes to say, a student's application is made up of two parts: the "data" (a student's academic performance) and the "voice" (a student's extracurricular activities, recommendations, and essays). According to the admissions office, the vast majority of Tufts applicants are academically "qualified" to succeed in the classroom. With that in mind, it is important for applicants to realize that although the data certainly does play an important role in the admissions process, the voice is just as, if not more, important.

The data portion of a student's application consists of the high school transcript and standardized test scores. In addition to reviewing students' grades, Tufts evaluates each applicant's curricular rigor and gives preference to students who have challenged themselves by taking AP, IB, and honors classes, or the most demanding classes available to them.

The university also requires students to submit either the SAT exam and two additional SAT Subject Tests or the ACT exam with writing. Students applying to the school of engineering who submit the SAT should submit an SAT Subject Test in math and a Subject Test in either physics or chemistry. For students accepted into the class of 2014, the mid-50 percentile range for the SAT math, critical reading, and writing exams was 690–770, and the mean composite ACT score was 31. Although the admissions committee does take standardized testing into consideration, it is but one of many factors in the admissions process. Students who fall within or exceed the mid-50 percentile are not guaranteed admission and students who score below the mid-50 percentile may not be denied admission. Students who do not speak English as a first language are required to submit the Test of English as a Foreign Language (TOEFL) exam as well.

The voice portion of a student's application is often what distinguishes him or her from the thousands of other Tufts applicants. Admissions officers rely on extracurricular activities, recommendations, essays, and an optional alumni interview to get a better sense of who the applicant is and how he or she would add to the Tufts campus.

Given the importance Tufts places on active citizenship and leadership, admissions officers want to know what students have been up to outside of the classroom. Be it community service, music, athletics, arts, entrepreneurship, or employment, Tufts places an emphasis on the quality of a student's involvement rather than the number of activities in which a student has participated.

Students are required to submit one recommendation from a teacher in a major subject area (math, science, social studies, English, foreign language) that they have had in either their junior or senior year. The best teacher recommendations come from teachers who know students well and are able to share stories, fond memories, and personal anecdotes with the admissions committee. A strong teacher recommendation can carry considerable weight with the admissions committee and almost always strengthens the voice of the application. Additional recommendations are welcomed if the student believes that the extra recommendation will add new information to the application.

Perhaps the most important part of the voice, student essays play a significant role in the application review process. In addition to submitting a 250- to 500-word personal statement, applicants are given the option to write a few short essays in response to creative and innovative questions that change annually. Past prompts include: "A high school curriculum does not always afford much intellectual freedom. Describe one of your unsatisfied intellectual passions. How might you apply this interest to serve the common good and make a difference in society?" and "Create a short story using one of the following topics: The end of MTV; Confessions of a Middle School Bully; The Professor Disappeared; The Mysterious Lab." Students are discouraged from writing essays about banal topics, such as a community service trip, the "big game" or "big shot," or one's love for grandma and grandpa.

All interviews for Tufts are optional and are conducted by local area alumni who are part of the Tufts Alumni Admissions Program (TAAP). After a student submits the Tufts Supplement Form, the admissions office will notify an alumni interviewer in the students' local area who will in turn contact the applicant to schedule an interview. Interviews often take place at coffee shops, bookstores, libraries, and other public locations agreed upon by both the applicant and interviewer. The purpose of the interview is twofold: first, to provide students with another opportunity to add to the voice of their application and, second, to learn more about Tufts through the experiences of the alumni interviewer. In a typical year more than 10,000 interviews are completed by dedicated TAAPers who volunteer hours of their time to remain connected to the university and to advocate for applicants from their local area. Since interviews are optional; students who are not able to complete an alumni interview are not at a disadvantage in the admissions process.

Students have the option of applying to Tufts Early Decision (ED) I, Early Decision (ED) II, or Regular Decision. Both Early Decision rounds are binding, meaning that if admitted the applicant is required to attend Tufts and withdraw any applications to other colleges. The only difference between Early Decision I and Early Decision II is the application deadline (November 1 for ED I and January 1 for ED II). Students who apply Early Decision are notified of their admissions decision approximately one month after the application deadline. The Regular Decision application deadline is January 1, and all applicants are notified of their decision by April 1. The current application fee is $70. Students who are unable to pay the application fee should contact their guidance counselor or the Tufts admissions office to inquire about obtaining a fee waiver.

Whether it is meeting with a student during office hours, grabbing coffee at the library's Tower Café (where beverages are on the house when a student and professor go in together), or inviting students to their houses for dinner or a barbecue, Tufts professors take a genuine interest in the lives of undergraduates, both inside and outside of the classroom. With an average class size of twenty and a student-to-faculty ratio of seven-to-one, classes tend to be discussion- and inquiry-based and require students to come to class prepared and ready to contribute to the learning process.

With an aim of providing students with a broad-based liberal arts and engineering education, Tufts students are encouraged to explore their academic interests by taking classes in any academic department within the university. The most popular majors within the school of liberal arts are international relations, English, political science, and psychology. Tufts is also recognized for its first-rate programs in history, philosophy, child development, biomedical engineering, and community health. Mechanical engineering and electrical engineering are the two most popular majors within the school of engineering, though the biomedical engineering program has experienced tremendous growth and has increased in popularity in recent years. More than forty percent of students—across disciplines—will choose to spend a semester or a year studying abroad on one of the ten Tufts programs or one of the 200 preapproved non-Tufts programs throughout the world. All undergraduates, in both the school of liberal arts and the school of engineering, are encouraged to engage in undergraduate research.

What distinguishes Tufts from many other schools when it comes to research is that rather than doing research *for* a professor, Tufts students play an active role in doing research *with* a professor. Rather than joining an already existing research project, students are strongly encouraged to develop their own projects and to delve deeply into their field. Research takes place across all disciplines, from the sciences to the humanities to the arts. Initiatives such as the Summer Scholars Research Program give undergraduates the opportunity to engage in funded one-on-one research with a faculty member at any of the university's eight undergraduate or graduate schools, including the schools of liberal arts and engineering, the medical school, veterinary school, dental school, nutrition school, and the Fletcher School of Law and Diplomacy. Recent Summer Scholars projects include a drama major that worked with a professor to recreate the costumes and clothing for a PBS documentary on the French and Indian War set in eighteenth-century Pennsylvania, and a community health major who analyzed the problems of asthma and obesity in immigrant populations. Hands-on research is a core element of the undergraduate experience at Tufts and often culminates in a senior honors thesis or further study in graduate school.

> *At Tufts, whether you like it or not, you are going to get to know your professors. For most students, myself included, that is a good thing. My professors, expert scholars and teachers, were all down-to-earth and inspired me to achieve more than I ever thought possible. I formed meaningful professional relationships and friendships with my professors that have lasted well beyond graduation, and I still correspond with many of them on a regular basis, whether it is to ask for advice or just to catch up.*

The Experimental College

Founded in 1964, the Experimental College has been an integral part of the Tufts curriculum for more than forty years. The Experimental College, or ExCollege, is more of an academic department than an actual separate college within the university. Known for offering innovative, imaginative, and interdisciplinary courses that don't necessarily fall into any one academic department, the ExCollege has been a favorite amongst students since its inception.

A unique aspect of the ExCollege is that courses are usually taught by outside professionals rather than university professors. Many of the outside professionals who teach in the ExCollege enrich the learning environment by bringing invaluable real-world experience—and contacts—into the classroom. Recent hits include a course taught by the former general manager of the Celtics on "The Business of Sports: A History of the NBA"; a course on forensic science and crime scene investigation led by a twenty-four-year veteran police inspector of the Connecticut State Attorney's office; and a class on "Producing Films for Social Change" taught by an Academy Award-winning documentary filmmaker. In 2005 Tufts students in the "Producing Films for Social Change" class won a College Emmy Award for *From the Fryer to the Freeway: Alternative Energy Today*. In addition to taking classes in the ExCollege, students also have the ability to teach pass/fail classes in an area of their own personal expertise. All ExCollege courses count for credit toward graduation, and some count as credit toward various majors.

The Dual-Degree Programs

Tufts has two special five-year dual-degree programs with other schools in Boston. The first is a five-year B.A./B.F.A. program with the School of the Museum of Fine Arts, located next to the Museum of Fine Arts in downtown Boston. The second is a five-year

B.A./B.Mus. program in which students earn a Bachelor of Arts degree from Tufts and a Bachelor of Music degree from the New England Conservatory, one of the country's most prestigious conservatory programs. A shuttle bus takes dual-degree students back and forth between campuses, though many opt to ride the easily accessible subway as well.

Both dual-degree options are highly selective and are meant for students who are serious academicians and dedicated and talented artists. To apply for either program, students must submit an application to Tufts and a separate application to the other institution. Students should indicate on each application that they would like to be considered for the dual-degree program.

Early Acceptance to Tufts' Professional Schools

During a student's sophomore year at Tufts, he or she may apply for early acceptance to the Tufts School of Medicine, School of Dental Medicine, or School of Veterinary Medicine. In order to be seriously considered for the program, students must meet two criteria: they must be on track to fulfill the required pre-health science requirements (coursework in biology, chemistry, organic chemistry, physics, etc.) within four years and they must have maintained a high level of academic performance during their first two years.

None of the programs are meant as acceleration programs, though some students may be able to complete the combined dental medicine program in seven years. All students accepted early to the medical or veterinary school, and most of those accepted early to the dental school, will still spend four years completing their undergraduate studies and four years in professional school. The benefit of the early acceptance program is that they will know by the end of their sophomore year whether or not they have been admitted into a top-notch health science graduate program. The early acceptance programs are not binding, and students have until the end of their junior year to decide whether or not they will accept the offer of admission.

Institute for Global Leadership

The Institute for Global Leadership (IGL) provides undergraduates with an opportunity to examine a multitude of complex global issues through course work, on-campus lectures and symposia, and funded in-the-field research. The IGL encourages student-centered learning and pushes students to connect theory to practice by "getting their hands dirty" through funded international research. Recent student trips sponsored by the IGL include a trip to the United Arab Emirates to attend a conference on women's rights and a trip to Zimbabwe to research the problems that country faces as a result of its scarce water resources.

Home to a wide range of initiatives, the IGL's signature program is Education for Public Inquiry and International Citizenship (EPIIC), a year-long colloquium exploring a major global issue. Past EPIIC themes include "Race and Ethnicity," "Sovereignty and Intervention," and "America's Role in the World."

More in depth information about the Institute for Global Leadership can be found at *http://www.tuftsgloballeadership.org/*.

STUDY ABROAD

Did you know that . . .

○ **More than forty percent of students choose to study abroad, placing Tufts among the top ten research universities for percentage of students who study abroad.**

○ **Tufts has a campus at the foot of the French Alps in Talloires, France. During the summer, students have the opportunity to live with a French family while taking six-week-long classes with Tufts professors in an eleventh-century Benedictine priory.**

○ **Tufts' ten study abroad programs are located throughout the world in Chile, China, Germany, Ghana, Hong Kong, Japan, London, Oxford, Paris, and Spain. There are also more than 200 preapproved non-Tufts programs.**

SOCIAL LIFE AND ACTIVITIES

Something that Tufts students understand very well is that a lot of learning in college takes places outside of the classroom. Though students' primary reason for being at Tufts is to excel inside the classroom, a healthy balance exists between coursework, extracurricular activities, and a student's social life.

Even though Boston is just a short T ride away, the heart of the undergraduate social life is found on campus. Students build time into their schedules to participate in some of the more than 200 already existing student organizations, ranging from the Multiracial Organization of Students at Tufts (MOST) to Traveling Treasure Trunk, a children's theater troupe.

Given the university's emphasis on integrating active citizenship into the curriculum, it is no surprise that the most popular student organization is the Leonard Carmichael Society (LCS), an umbrella community service group that is home to nearly forty outreach initiatives. Students interested in media and communications are often active in Tufts University Television (TUTV); Tufts' radio station, 91.5, WMFO; the *Observer*, a biweekly news magazine; and the most widely read publication on campus, *The Tufts Daily*. Tufts is one of the smallest colleges in the country to have a daily newspaper. Performing artists can sing in one of the six a cappella groups, sing in the choir or gospel choir, play in the wind ensemble or the big band, or dance in Spirit of Color, Sarabande, Tufts Dance Collective, TURBO (a breakdance troupe), or one of the university's step teams.

Many students are involved in the cultural organizations that are collectively known as The Group of 6: the Africana Center, Asian/Asian-American Center, International Center, Latino Center, Lesbian Gay Bisexual Transgender Center, and the Women's Center. There are also active religious organizations and groups on campus, including the Protestant Ministry, Catholic Center, Hillel, and the Islamic Center. Students who find that their interests are not met by one of the already existing organizations always have the opportunity to petition to create a new organization.

Athletics

Students interested in participating in athletics at Tufts may do so at the varsity, club, or intramural level. The Tufts Jumbos boast twenty-nine Division III varsity athletic teams that compete in the New England Small College Athletic Conference (NESCAC). Arguably the most competitive Division III conference both athletically and academically, NESCAC foes include Amherst, Williams, Wesleyan, and Middlebury.

Within the NESCAC and also in non-conference play, Tufts varsity teams compete at a very high level. In 2009–2010 Tufts placed sixth out of 311 Division III institutions in the Learfield Sports Directors Cup, an annual ranking of the best over-all intercollegiate athletic programs in the country. Though many teams had great success in 2009–2010, of particular note is the success of the men's lacrosse team and their winning of the NCAA national championship, the women's field hockey team's NESCAC championship and Final Four appearance, and the women's tennis team's Julie Browne and her victory in the 2010 NCAA singles national championship match.

Popular club sports include a nationally ranked Ultimate Frisbee team, rugby, flag football, and table tennis. Those simply looking to stay in shape can take advantage of Tufts' 40,000 pounds of free weights, new nautilus equipment, indoor pool, and the Gantcher Family Sports and Convocation Center's elevated indoor 200-meter track and indoor tennis courts.

Greek Life

Approximately fifteen percent of Tufts students are Greek. With twelve fraternities and five sororities, the Greek system at Tufts is a legitimate social outlet for those interested in taking part in Greek life. At the same time, there is no pressure to join a fraternity or sorority given the numerous opportunities for social stimulation both on campus and in Boston. Even if a student is not directly involved in Greek life it doesn't necessarily exclude him or her from attending parties, dances, fund-raisers, or other events organized by a fraternity or sorority.

Please visit *http://www.tuftslife.com* for more information about student life and a daily listing of campus events.

FINANCIAL AID

One of the first questions on many high school students' and parents' minds is, "How am I going to pay for college?" As the cost of attending college continues to rise, this question gains more and more validity. At Tufts, admissions and financial aid officers work closely with students' families to ensure that finances are not the factor that prevents a student from attending the university. In 2006, President Larry Bacow launched a $1.2 billion capital campaign, with a primary goal of maximizing the university's financial aid resources.

Financial aid at Tufts is need-based and the university is dedicated to meeting 100 percent of a student's financial need, as determined by the Free Application for Federal Student Aid (FAFSA), the College Scholarship Service (CSS) Financial Aid Profile, and the family's tax returns. The only form of merit-based aid are awards from the National Merit Scholarship Corporation. ROTC scholarships are also available to students. Each year students resubmit their financial aid forms so that the university can recalculate and adjust their financial aid package as needed.

Financial aid packages usually include three types of aid: grant, loan, and student contribution. However, the vast majority of aid is in the form of grants, or money that the student does not have to repay. Student contribution, or work-study, provides students with an on-campus job during the academic year. Though a variety of jobs are available, the most highly sought after jobs are those that allow students to study or do work while on the clock. The foreign language lab, gymnasium, and library media center are a few of the most popular places to be employed. In addition to working on campus, some students decide to take advantage of the plentiful job opportunities in Boston to help pay for school.

GRADUATES

Given the geographic diversity of the undergraduate student body and the emphasis on educating tomorrow's global leaders, it is no surprise that Tufts graduates can be found throughout the world. There are more than 80,000 Tufts alumni living in places as close as Boston and New York and as far as Botswana and New Delhi. Current undergraduates and recent graduates greatly benefit from the Tufts Alumni Association, an active network of alumni who are eager to offer advice, resources, and contacts.

Upon graduating from Tufts, around half of all students will go directly to graduate school, though within five years of graduating more than eighty percent of all graduates have already completed a graduate degree or are in graduate school. Approximately a quarter of the graduating class will engage in volunteer opportunities or complete prestigious scholarships and fellowships. Each year Tufts is one of the top schools of its size to send students on to be Fulbright Scholars and Peace Corps Volunteers. Other recent graduates have also been recognized as Marshall Scholars, Truman Scholars, Udall Scholars, and recipients of the Jack Kent Cooke Foundation's Cooke Scholarship. The remaining quarter will enter into the workforce in fields including public service and government, investment banking, consulting, teaching, and journalism among others.

When people ask me what my friends did after we graduated, I usually don't know where to start.

Kate, whom I met during our weeklong freshman orientation community service trip in Boston, won a Fulbright Scholarship to do research on the HIV/AIDS epidemic in sub-Saharan Africa and then went on to work for UNESCO in Paris before doing a master's degree in international public health.

Steve, whom I lived with all four years of college, recently received his master's degree in Islamic and Middle Eastern Studies in Israel and has also been working full-time for a leading conflict resolution nonprofit. Steve's connections at Tufts led to a once-in-a-lifetime opportunity the year after we graduated. That year, he traveled to India as part of a three-person delegation sent to meet with the Dalai Lama and advise the Tibetan government in exile in their dealings with the Chinese.

My other friends are doing equally impressive things across the country and throughout the world, ranging from Ph.D. and professional degree programs to opening up a bookstore on the Greek island of Santorini to working in postconflict areas such as Rwanda and Northern Ireland.

SUMMING UP

Most students are drawn to Tufts because they are looking for a challenge—both inside and outside of the classroom. Tufts provides students with a high-quality education where the learning extends far beyond the walls of the classroom. Tufts students appreciate the diverse student body, beautiful campus, access to a major city, and community in which students take their academics seriously, yet lead healthy and balanced lives.

Originally from the small, rural town of Schulenburg, Texas, Michelle Eilers, '10, chose Tufts because she wanted to attend a school where students learned just as much from their peers during political debates in the dining hall and late-night discussions about global dilemmas in the dorms as they did from their professors. She wrote, "I want to meet people with whom I have nothing in common and argue about values and beliefs. I want to interact with people involved in making real world contributions, because I want to make meaningful contributions of my own." In Tufts, Michelle and many other like-minded students have found a perfect match.

Unlike many other prestigious universities, Tufts is a dynamic and innovative institution of higher learning whose president, professors, and students use academic and social capital to make tangible differences in the world. Under the leadership of President Larry Bacow, the university has heightened an already impressive academic profile by attracting top-notch students and faculty. Robert Sternberg, former president of the American Psychological Association and one of the world's foremost experts on the topics of creativity and intelligence, assumed the position of Dean of Arts and Sciences in 2005. Linda Abriola, a member of the

National Academy of Engineering and a universally recognized specialist in water allocation and water resources, became one of the few female Deans of Engineering in the country when she accepted that position in 2004.

Scholars and students alike recognize that Tufts is a special school—a university on the forefront of both research and teaching, a campus defined by intellectual curiosity and hands-on learning, and a community of scholars and leaders who want to "shake things up, tear things down, and make things better."

❏ *Adam Goodman, B.A.*

TULANE UNIVERSITY

 Tulane University
New Orleans, LA 70118

 (504) 865-5731, (800) 873-9219
Fax: (504) 862-8715

E-mail: *undergrad.admission@tulane.edu*
Website: *www.tulane.edu*

 Enrollment

Full-time	❑ women:	2,936
	❑ men:	2,516
Part-time	❑ women:	1,058
	❑ men:	700

INTRODUCING TULANE UNIVERSITY

You'll know why students love Tulane University the moment you step off of the St. Charles streetcar onto the azalea-filled campus in "uptown" New Orleans. Since its founding in 1834, Tulane, aided by the mystique of the Mississippi River city that surrounds it, has been both educating and entertaining students for generations. Tracing its roots back to the Medical College of Louisiana, Tulane owes its name to a wealthy New Jersey merchant, Paul Tulane, who earned his fortune in the crescent city. After more than a century as one of the most prominent features of the city of New Orleans, Tulane is an even more integral part of the city after surviving the challenge of Hurricane Katrina in 2005. Now, students are flocking to Tulane to experience the rebirth of an amazing cultural center, as well as to be educated in a world-class research environment.

The students at Tulane are diverse, intellectual, and very social. Boasting more than 250 campus groups and situated in the heart of one of the most culturally important cities in the country, Tulane offers students more than just a top-tier liberal arts education, it offers an amazing collegiate experience. "Work hard, play hard" doesn't even begin to describe it. As President Scott Cowen leads the university through the challenges created by Hurricane Katrina, the community of Tulane has come together to embrace what has made the city and school unique and to make sure new students can experience Tulane for years to come. "Only in New Orleans. Only at Tulane" has become the unofficial school motto that is invigorating campus activities, stimulating educational programming, and encouraging the student body to be a part of the rehabilitation of the coastal region.

The culture is just one of the many reasons students love being located in the heart of New Orleans. Public service opportunities, internships with local business and sports teams, full-time employment, and religious communities are all just minutes away. Students can enjoy the history of the French Quarter, the Spanish architecture, the Creole food, and the location of the birth of jazz while surrounded by a university with a renewed focus on educational excellence and a commitment to public service.

At the heart of the campus stands the Lavin-Bernick Center for University Life, the hub of extracurricular activities at Tulane. Under construction until just recently, this brand-new building opened its doors in January of 2007 and puts a fresh face on the forty-year-old University Center. This hub holds dining and meeting facilities, a large bookstore, and the offices of both student programming faculty and student organizations. This building is the heart of the campus and a popular meeting place for groups and individuals alike. Fanning out from the Lavin-Bernick Center is the 110-acre campus, complete with a new business school building—one of the most advanced in the nation—a new $7.5 million baseball stadium, freshly renovated dorm buildings, and lines of historic oak trees that are almost ever-green in the tropical climate of the Deep South. The university has constructed, on average, one new building a year for the past dozen years, with plans in place for further construction among the campus's oaks, magnolias, and occasional banana tree or bamboo grove.

On campus, students study at one of ten schools and colleges, depending on their major and degree. Undergraduates start their Tulane career at the recently reorganized

Newcomb-Tulane College. This undergraduate college was created by joining the H. Sophie Newcomb Memorial College for Women, which was established as part of Tulane in 1886, with the undergraduate men's arm of Tulane College. As the first coordinate college in a university setting to grant degrees to women in the entire nation, Newcomb and Tulane draw students in with their rich history and innovative programming.

Tulane would not be the institution that it is, however, without the philosophies and customs of the city of New Orleans. The charm, hospitality, and pace of the city are undeniably seen in the culture of the university as well. The traditions of both are woven together, and as the leadership and students of Tulane step up and embrace the tasks of rebuilding the city, the futures of the city and the school are inextricably linked. The strength and passion of the city is carried over into the determination and excitement of the students and their educational and personal goals.

ADMISSIONS REQUIREMENTS

Immediately after Hurricane Katrina and the cancellation of the 2005 fall semester, Tulane students were spread to over 600 schools in all fifty states. When the campus reopened in January of 2006, eighty-seven percent of these students chose to return to Tulane to continue their education. This enthusiasm to attend Tulane continues to be very strong in new applicants as well.

Tulane has been growing more and more competitive over the past several years. A trend of increasing applications has continued, despite the interruption of Hurricane Katrina. As a testament to this trend, the 2009 application season presented the largest number of applications in the school's history. Now ranked as one of the nation's most competitive colleges, the last academic year saw 39,887 applications, of which, 7,867 were accepted, leading to a freshman enrollment of just over 1,500. Although the entering class size has become smaller in the past year, the student body has remained a compilation of the nation's top high school graduates. According to university statistics, approximately sixty percent of enrolling freshmen in 2009 were ranked in the top ten percent of their high school classes; nearly eighty-eight percent in 2009 ranked in the top twenty-five percent; and ninety-seven percent in 2009 were in the top half of their class. In addition to being strong academically, Tulane's typical freshman class is both geographically and ethnically diverse. A surprising number of students come to Tulane from great distances—over seventy-five percent of the typical entering freshman class hails from more than 500 miles away from the school. This diversity ensures that students are not only learning from their academic programs, but also from each other.

Application Requirements

Scores from either the SAT or the ACT are required to apply. The average SAT score for a recent freshman class was 1335 (based on 1600) (ACT equivalent of 30), which was more than 300 points above the national average. The ACT Optional Writing test is also required and SAT subject tests, such as math, writing, and science, are recommended for placement purposes. The school recommends taking the SAT, which includes a standard writing section. Equally important for placement and honors program consideration are Advanced Placement (AP) credits, which are enthusiastically accepted. Factors that demonstrate to the admissions team your unique qualities are AP and honors courses, recommendations, and extracurricular activities records, along with a personal essay. For architecture applicants, a portfolio is recommended as well. Students are encouraged to have completed four years each of high school English and math, and three years each of foreign language, social studies, and the sciences.

Campus Visits

Tulane students who visited the campus the spring of their senior year in high school all attest to the power of seeing the campus in bloom and experiencing New Orleans in such beautiful weather. All applicants are encouraged to visit the campus for one of the prospective students activities in the spring, but they will also be accommodated at any point during the year. Daily campus tours are given by passionate Green Wave Ambassadors, often seen on campus walking backwards in flip-flops in front of a crowd of prospective students and parents. Ambassadors also host prospective students on overnight visits where the prospective student can join them in attending classes, meeting friends and professors, and participating in campus activities or sporting events. Efforts are made to make sure that visiting students experience both academic and social life at Tulane before, or after, they make their final decision to attend. To contact an Ambassador, learn more about the visit schedule, or book your tour with the online reservation system, visit *http://admission.tulane.edu.*

Tides

First-year students participate in the Tulane InterDisciplinary Experience Seminars (TIDES) program, which connects them to other students who share similar interests. These seminar courses include speakers, trips, social events, and special programs that link

1. Tulane's Newcomb College, joined to the university in 1886, was the first coordinate college to grant degrees to women.
2. Tulane's study abroad program is one of the oldest in the country.
3. Tulane's School of Social Work has its roots in the very first training program for social workers in the Deep South.
4. The Community Action Council of Tulane University Students (CACTUS) is the oldest and largest student-led community service organization in the country.
5. Tulane's School of Public Health and Tropical Medicine, founded in 1912, is one of the oldest such schools in the country.
6. Founded in 1964, the Tulane National Primate Research Center is one of the oldest and largest of the eight federally funded primate research centers in the United States.
7. The Newcomb College Center for Research on Women is one of the nation's oldest and most prominent research centers of its kind.

to one of fifty chosen topics. Possible choices include: "The Music and Culture of New Orleans"; "Hurricanes, Human Rights, and History"; "Philosophy of Public Service"; "The Cultures of Food"; "Reading and Writing Women"; and many more. These programs were developed to introduce students to the city, the school, and each other by linking them up with faculty, activities, and other new students who share similar personal interests.

ACADEMIC LIFE

Top students come to Tulane to get a world-class education in a unique setting. Academic opportunities, therefore, are embraced by all students. All undergraduates enter through the Newcomb-Tulane Undergraduate College, where a core curriculum ensures academic breadth as they begin their collegiate career, a TIDES course connects them to students with similar passions, and the public service requirement fulfills the mission of Tulane to produce graduates with cultural knowledge who are "good citizens of the world."

Faculty

All courses at Tulane are taught by professors who both teach and conduct research—not teaching assistants. All professors hold open office hours and are more than willing to spend time with students individually. The student-to-faculty ratio of eight-to-one ensures that classes are kept small and students are all given individual attention. The academic environment is influenced by the culture of the surroundings and is more friendly and encouraging than competitive.

Schools, Programs, and Libraries

Outside of the core programs, students will choose majors from the five undergraduate schools: School of Liberal Arts, which awards Bachelor of Arts (B.A.), Bachelor of Science (B.S.), or Bachelor of Fine Arts (B.F.A.) degrees, depending on the choice of major; School of Science and Engineering, which awards a B.S.; A.B. Freeman School of Business, which confers the Bachelor of Science in Management (B.S.M.) degree; School of Architecture, in which students receive the Master of Architecture I degree; and the School of Public Health, where students receive a Bachelor of Science in Public Health. Students may also pursue cross-registration with other universities in the area, and are able to use these additional resources and libraries to their advantage.

Tulane also offers many joint degree programs that combine undergraduate and graduate/professional degrees. Cross-registration in different schools and "4+1" programs are also available. Students can also choose from flexible study options, such as student-designed, dual, and interdisciplinary majors. Because Tulane is nationally recognized in many of its academic programs, a large percentage of students take advantage of more than one academic department for their concentrations.

Academic and research resources available to students are second to none. The main library on campus, Howard-Tilton Memorial, is not only home to five floors of "stacks" and study spaces but also the Latin American Library and the Maxwell Music Library, where students have access to some of the greatest music in the world. Special collections of the university include the Hogan Jazz Archive, Southeastern Architectural Archive, and the Louisiana Collection. Other special libraries on campus span the fields of architecture, botany, business, law, mathematics, natural history, primate research, race relations and ethnic history, and women's studies (home to an impressive collection of historical local cookbooks).

Advisors

Students are assigned to an academic advisor when they arrive at Tulane. These advisors take time to understand a student's goals and passions, and align those with the opportunities and coursework at the different schools. Advisors assist in planning for special programs such as joint degree, personal research, and study abroad. They also suggest courses based on personal interest and coordinate with professors. Once a major is declared, a major advisor is also chosen to assist with field-specific goals, thesis research, and degree planning.

> **❝** *During my junior year at Tulane, I was struggling to find the* perfect *class to fill one of my last elective requirements. My academic advisor suggested that I take a break from my heavy academic workload and sign up for modern dance. At first, I was completely taken aback, but after I attended one class, I was hooked. The opportunity to step outside of my comfort zone and learn something new was amazing. My advisor knew it was exactly what I needed to augment my studies, and I have her to thank for such a* perfect *suggestion.* **❞**

Another advising resource at Tulane is the Career Services Center, which helps students at all levels of their collegiate career. The center advises students on everything from resume writing and interview skills to choosing the right major with resources to help understand not only the curriculum, but also the related career paths. The center offers free workshops, sponsors career fairs, and connects students with internship and job opportunities, as well as offers counselors to critique application essays and cover letters. On-line self-assessments and tools offer advice to students on their schedule.

Tulane's Education Resources and Counseling Center, another facet of the university's advising system, offers both academic and personal counseling services. The center teaches academic skills and tutoring sessions free of charge while also providing personal counseling such as support groups, crisis counseling, and individual therapy.

Beyond the Campus

A significant number of Tulane students participate in the study abroad program. Tulane's Junior Year Abroad (JYA) program is one of the oldest of its kind in the country. Students can choose from full-year or semester programs, Tulane-sponsored programs, or trips coordinated with other schools, or they can develop their own overseas experience with the help of advisors at the Center for International Studies. Tulane has programs in over twenty countries spanning Europe, Latin America, Africa, Asia, and Australia, in addition to a variety of faculty-led summer study-abroad programs for both undergraduates and graduates. Also offered are Washington, DC, semesters for students interested in politics, policy, and public service. All Tulane-sponsored study-abroad programs allow students to keep their specific scholarships and financial aid packages, which removes many barriers often present when studying at another school as a visiting student.

> ❝ Growing up in a small town in the south, I always knew I wanted to travel abroad at some point during my college education. So, it was imperative when I was conducting my college search that I find a school that not only had great academic programs on its campus, but had great programs with other schools around the world. When I learned of Tulane's historic study-abroad programs, the number of students who studied in other countries, and the fact that scholarships and aid would transfer seamlessly, Tulane became one of my top choices. ❞

To complete the public service graduation requirement, students engage with the Center for Public Service to take a service-learning course, coordinate with faculty-sponsored service programs, design a study-abroad experience with a service component, or complete a public service honors thesis. All students at Tulane get outside the classroom to participate in the revitalization of New Orleans and the Gulf Coast. Building houses, painting elementary schools, volunteering for education and health programs, and raising awareness of the region's challenges are examples of ways students get involved.

SOCIAL LIFE AND ACTIVITIES

Tulane University is located in the heart of uptown New Orleans. From listening to world-class musicians at renowned jazz clubs to throwing a Frisbee on the grassy park at the levee, New Orleans offers activities that simply can't be found at other cities. The social life of Tulane, therefore, is inextricably linked with the city that surrounds it. Jazz musicians perform at Tulane events, shuttle bus service takes kids around the city free of charge, students attend professional sporting events, movies shot in the city have their red-carpet premiers on campus, and freshman year officially starts on a paddle boat on the Mississippi River. Throughout a student's years at Tulane, this continues to be the case. Most of the "social life" of the school is rooted in and around the city's activities and big events. Some New Orleans festivals and events most popular with Tulane students include Mardi Gras, the weeks of carnival season associated with large parades throughout the city; New Orleans Jazz & Heritage Festival ("Jazz Fest"), a two-weekend blowout of world famous bands and performing artists, arts and crafts, unique cuisine and late-night concerts; Voodoo Music Experience, a large annual music-festival; and the annual Sugar Bowl college football game.

Student Organizations

On campus, there are over 250 student organizations that create the social scene. Except for a select few, organizations are open to all students and range from activism to sports. The oldest program on campus is the Community Action Council of Tulane University Students (CACTUS), which organizes community service activities of all kinds and involves almost every Tulane student at one point in his or her college experience. In addition to CACTUS, there are honors and professional societies, club and intramural sports, a healthy student government system, and a multitude of multicultural, political, performance, and religious groups. Campus media includes the *Hullabaloo*, the student-run newspaper that is published once a week; a student-managed television channel; and the immensely popular WTUL radio station. Student DJs man the airwaves in two-hour shifts at all hours of the day and night and have shows ranging from rock to folk.

Greek Life

Another dimension to campus life is the Greek system. There are fifteen national fraternities and ten national sororities on campus. Of all students, thirty percent of men and thirty-five percent of women belong to one of these chapters. Greek parties are open to all students, however, and the social scene is not dominated by these events. In fact, fraternities and sororities are some of the most active service organizations on campus and provide a great way to get involved in the community. The Greek recruitment, "Rush," is deferred until a first-year student's second semester on campus, giving the student the chance to make friends, understand the social scene, and join other organizations before committing to a fraternity or sorority. Most students who pledge do not live in organized housing, opting instead to live among friends not involved in the same Greek chapter.

Living on Campus

All freshman and sophomore students at Tulane are required to live on campus and are guaranteed space in one of the university's many dormitories or apartment complexes. Many junior, senior, and graduate students also opt to live on campus, as it provides them with a convenient, safe housing situation. Special living arrangements include female single-sex houses; theme living situations, such as honors, special interest, and international student houses; and the "Leadership Village"—a gathering of the university's top student government and organizational leaders. Campus resources include a plethora of dining alternatives, a barbershop, several bank branches and ATMS, a copy center, post office, bookstore, grocery store, and several laundry facilities.

Campus Programming

Tulane University Campus Programming (TUCP) is a very active group on campus. This student-run club is responsible for bringing chart-topping bands and performers, well-known comedians, and political figures and speakers to Tulane. TUCP also runs a cinema program—which shows new releases on campus for a fraction of the price of movie-theatre admission—and organizes an annual spring carnival.

Mardi Gras

The highlight of every spring semester at Tulane is the arrival of Carnival season. The weeks between Epiphany (January 6) and Ash Wednesday (40 days before Easter) are filled with parades, crawfish boils, parties, and concerts. You will see Tulane students enjoying the parades on St. Charles Avenue, riding on floats with social groups, and marching in parades with the Tulane Marching Band. The university has special programs to maintain the safety of its students during this exciting time of year, including special safety and awareness programs and a registration system to track students visiting campus during Mardi Gras.

Athletics

The Tulane Green Wave is a member of Conference USA in athletics and participates with teams in several NCAA Division 1-A sports, including football, basketball, and track, to name a few. Students receive free admission to all home games of all sports, and transportation is provided. The Louisiana Superdome, home to the Saints Football franchise and the Sugar Bowl, also hosts the Green Wave football team, which has recently produced NFL quarterbacks J. P. Losman and Patrick Ramsey. It is not unusual to be seated at a football game next to President Cowen, who is known to spray paint his hair bright green and paint his face for games!

> ### HULLABALOO CHEER
>
> The Hullabaloo cheer, which is recited, instead of a fight song, every time the Green Wave scores, is one of the strangest of its kind:
> The Hullabaloo
> A One, A Two, A Helluva Hullabaloo
> A Hullabaloo Ray Ray
> A Hullabaloo Ray Ray
> Hooray, Hooray
> Vars Vars Tee Ay
> Tee Ay, Tee Ay
> Vars Vars Tee Ay
> Tulane!

Perhaps Tulane's most successful sports team is men's baseball, which earned its second trip to the College World Series in the 2005 season. The recent renovation of Turchin Stadium, one of the largest and most impressive collegiate baseball fields in the country, was completed in 2007. Tulane's student athletes are also recognized as successful scholars, with one of the largest percentages of graduating student athletes in the country.

FINANCIAL AID

Tulane is committed to offering a great education to all students, regardless of financial situation. In a recent year, eighty-two percent of all full-time freshmen received some form of financial aid. Financial aid packages include grants, government loans, merit-based scholarships and awards, and student employment opportunities both on and off campus. Tulane has a robust work-study program and about forty-five percent of undergraduates work part-time at some point in their college careers. Athletic and ROTC scholarships are also available to students who qualify.

As a member of the College Scholarship Service (CSS), the CSS PROFILE or Free Application for Federal Student Aid (FAFSA) are required to apply for financial aid. The average award for a recent year was $25,224, with an average annual earnings from campus work at $2,500. Upon enrollment, all students are assigned a financial aid counselor, who is committed not only to designing a financial aid award package that is tailored for each student but also to being available on a daily basis for questions about deadlines, forms, procedures, and options.

My freshman year, I was awarded a work-study campus job in my financial aid package. I began doing administrative work for the Levy Rosenblum Institute of Entrepreneurship (LRI) during my free time between classes. After four years at LRI, I had built relationships with local business owners, gotten to know business school faculty personally, and participated in amazing programs. The experience led me into business school at Tulane, where I graduated with an MBA. The experiences I had, consulting for non-profits, improving family-owned regional businesses, and planning events for national figures, could not have been gotten anywhere else.

Merit-Based Aid

The university offers many merit-based scholarships that are awarded based on a student's proven academic record and commitment to community involvement. A special application must be filled out for students applying for the Deans' Honor Scholarship. This merit-based full-tuition scholarship is awarded to a few select students each year. The application includes THE BOX—a blank square on the application that you must fill as creatively as you can. Also requiring a separate application is the Community Service Scholarship, which awards up to full tuition to those students who can illustrate how they have dedicated exceptional time and effort to their communities. All students, regardless of application type or deadline, are automatically considered for other merit-based awards that do not require a separate application, with scholarships that range from $14,000 to $22,000 per year. Financial aid counselors will also work one-on-one with students accepted to Tulane who have received merit-based scholarships from outside organizations or government entities.

GRADUATES

Graduates of Tulane University are equipped not only with a fantastic liberal arts education but also with a great respect for the world's cultures and an understanding of the importance of public service. Tulane produces citizens of the world who are bright and energetic about solving problems, but who are also compassionate and hard-working when it comes to their communities. Tulane grads have pioneered heart transplant and knee reconstruction surgeries; they have changed the world of entertainment; and they have invented software and tools, such as Netscape and Yahoo!, that have transformed our digital world.

In a recent year, 1,405 bachelor's degrees were awarded. Popular majors included business, social sciences, and engineering. In a recent school year, 134 companies actively recruited

PROMINENT GRADUATES

- Lawrence Wright, Staff Writer for *The New Yorker,* Best-Selling Author of *The Looming Tower: A History of al-Qaeda* (2006)
- Patrick Ramsey, NFL Quarterback for the New York Jets
- Michael DeBakey, Heart Surgeon/Transplant Pioneer
- David Filo, Cofounder of Yahoo!
- Neil Bush, Brother of President George Bush
- Amy Carter, Daughter of President Jimmy Carter
- Newt Gingrich, Former Speaker of the United States House (R)
- Francis Cardinal George, Archbishop of Chicago
- Lauren Hutton, Actress
- J. P. Losman, NFL Quarterback for the Buffalo Bills
- Jerry Springer, Talk-Show Host, Former Mayor of Cincinnati (D)
- John Kennedy Toole, Author, Pulitzer Prize Winner
- David C. Treen, Former Governor of Louisiana (R)
- Michael White, Jazz Musician/Jazz Historian
- Bruce Paltrow, Hollywood Director and Father of Gwyneth Paltrow
- Bob Livingston, Former Congressman from Louisiana (R)
- Richie Petitbon, Former Washington Redskins Head Coach

on campus. Since the hurricane, Tulane has revived its commitment to its students to find jobs after graduation. The recent launch of the all-encompassing web site *www.hiretulane.com* helps connect students, employers, counselors, and alumni in a strong network that supports the career paths of Tulane students. Separate career centers for the A. B. Freeman School of Business, the Tulane University School of Law, and the Tulane School of Public Health focus on recruiting, internship, and full-time job opportunities for their students; however, students in these schools are free to use the university career center as well.

SUMMING UP

A Tulane education provides more than just a degree. Academically, Tulane's faculty will prepare you to solve problems, challenge you with new theories, and support your personal research and endeavors. The cultural education you will obtain, however, is like nothing else in the nation. The history of New Orleans, added to the unique cuisine, music, traditions of the city, and the rebuilding process combine to form a truly unmatched collegiate experience. Students who choose to attend Tulane now will not only be studying at a great university, they will be an integral part of rebuilding an American treasure after one of the most devastating natural disasters of our time.

Tulane students all agree that their education is special—architecture students can study Spanish, French, and British influences right in their backyard; English majors can regularly visit places they read about in novels; business students are trusted to invest the school's own money in one-of-a-kind programs; and students studying music have some powerful acts to follow.

The size and location of Tulane make it the perfect combination of opportunity and individuality. Small enough to offer personal support yet large enough to provide research and internship experiences, it offers Southern hospitality coupled with big-city activities to meet the needs of a very diverse student body that hails from all fifty states, and one hundred countries.

❏ *Casey Haugner, B.A.*

UNITED STATES AIR FORCE ACADEMY

Germaine Photography

United States Air Force Academy
Colorado Springs, CO 80840

(770) 757-6784, (800) 443-9266
Fax: (719) 333-3814

E-mail: *Jocelyn.booker@usafa.edu*
Website: *www.academyadmissions.com*
           www.usafa.af.mil

 Enrollment

Full-time ❏ women: 970
            ❏ men: 3,651

INTRODUCING THE UNITED STATES AIR FORCE ACADEMY

The Air Force Academy works to develop officers of character, who bleed excellence, bark the warrior spirit, bellow humility, and above all, personify integrity. Upon graduation, these young men and women have greatly surpassed the mirages they thought were their limitations and overcome challenges that seemed impossible at first glance. More than a student, more than an athlete, each diverse cadet eagerly accepts a distinct four-year experience, yet all of them share the integral core values of integrity, service, and excellence.

> **❝** *I can honestly say that there are very few institutions out there that could have provided me with the skills and experience I earned at the U.S. Air Force Academy. I doubt I will look back and remember it as the most fun I've had over four years, but I will undoubtedly see it as the most I've grown.* **❞**

—2d. Lt. Daniel Walker, '10

As Aristotle once said, "We are what we repeatedly do. Excellence, then, is not an act, but a habit." The prestige of the Air Force Academy stems from a long blue line of extraordinary men and women of valor and a proud heritage of merit. To earn the title of an academy graduate and second lieutenant in the United States Air Force, one must practice and maintain a high level of excellence throughout his or her academy career and beyond graduation. Ready to lead young airmen into battle or major corporations into financial success, academy graduates quickly learn to work efficiently under pressure from the first day of Basic Cadet Training. With a reputation for producing countless pilots, doctors, lawyers, general officers, CEOs, Members of Congress, and astronauts of character, the academy year after year proves why an academy education is world class. Most candidates embrace the opportunity to become an officer of integrity in the world's greatest Air Force; trading in the typical college experience and boldly trekking the road less traveled with nothing more than a flashlight. And so the journey begins as the future leaders of America enter Basic Cadet Training with promising potential, leaving the academy with much more to offer the world.

> **❝** *When so many opportunities present themselves, how can you say no? Ivy league education, world travel, and experiences that I could get nowhere else are what I received at USAFA.* **❞**

—Cadet First Class Carmilya Boykin, '11

ADMISSIONS REQUIREMENTS

The Air Force Academy is one of the most selective schools in the country, not only because of the high number of extraordinary students who apply each year, but also because of an extensive and rigorous application process that challenges the average high school senior. Each year, approximately 13,000 high school students from around the world apply to the Air Force Academy, yet only 1,200 are chosen to accept the challenge of a lifetime, and approximately 1,000 cadets graduate to become officers of character to lead our Air Force and our Nation. To be eligible to attend the academy, you must

- be a citizen of the United States
- be unmarried with no dependents
- be of good moral character
- meet high leadership, academic, physical, and medical standards
- be at least seventeen, but less than twenty-three years of age by July 1 of the year you will enter

Over half of academy cadets graduated in the top ten percent of their graduating classes, with a number of those students graduating as valedictorian/salutatorian. In addition to above-average standardized test scores and grade point averages, USAFA looks at the "whole person" when regarding students' applications. This concept includes students' academic performances, interviews with Admissions Liaison Officers, writing samples, test scores, extracurricular activities, physical performances, and overall physical health.

SCHOLARSHIPS AWARDED TO ACADEMY GRADUATES	
Rhodes	36
Fulbright-Hayes	36
JFK School of Government at Harvard	112
Football Hall of Fame	13
National Science Foundation	75
Hertz Foundation	37
Marshall	9
NCAA	62
Truman	14
Olmsted	76
Albert Bart Holaday	6
Gates Fellowship	1

Grades and Test Scores

The average ACT score for the incoming freshman class, which will graduate in 2014, was 30. The average freshman cadet scored a 660 in the Math section of the SAT and a 640 in Verbal. The average GPA was 3.87. Comparatively, the academy offers an education on par with Ivy League schools, and its students reflect the cream of the crop from America, as well as some international countries. These students took advantage of advanced placement courses, honors, International Baccalaureate programs, and recognized the importance of doing well on their standardized tests. They are accustomed to going above and beyond the average high school student to gain the edge over their peers. Students should contact their high school guidance counselors as soon as possible to begin to prepare for the application process. Interested applicants will also have access to regional Air Force Liaison Officers, or ALOs, who will guide and mentor the applicant at the local level, through the Air Force Academy application process and provide information and insight into ROTC options as well.

Fitness Assessment

Fitness is an essential element in the military and at service academies. The academy requires all of its applicants to pass a fitness assessment, consisting of a basketball throw, pull-ups (flex arm hang for females), a shuttle run, modified sit-ups, push-ups, and a one-mile run. The assessment allows for a two-minute rest in between exercises, and the test, if failed, can render the applicant disqualified. Students are encouraged to practice the assessment as many times as they need.

Congressional Appointment

Each candidate applicant needs to attain a nomination from a United States Senator, Representative, the Vice President, the President, or other military affiliated nomination categories. Nominations are based on merit. Interested high school students should check with their congressperson in their respective districts to verify the correct procedures and deadlines to request nominations. Each congressional office uses different methods to select a nominee, but all use competitive measures to gauge why he/she aspires for admission to the academy.

Personal Essay

This portion of the application process reveals to the academy what standardized test scores and GPAs cannot. Through the personal essay, students have the opportunity to share stories that could make them unique and set them apart from their peers. The student may also embody some of the characteristics of a future leader that can only be expressed in written form. The essay is intended for the selections panel to learn more about the student's personal integrity, leadership, character and overcoming adversity that may not have been illuminated during the rest of the application process.

Extracurricular Activities

The ideal applicant demonstrates his/her ability to manage more than one obligation at a time. Many applicants participate in sports, the arts, scouts, or part-time jobs in addition to their schoolwork. These kinds of activities encourage teamwork, nurture humility, sharpen friendly competition, foster pride, and harness routines that maintain stability. This is not to say that the person with the most after-school programs wins. The Air Force Academy is looking for future leaders with a natural ability to lead their peers. The academy also expects its candidates to practice community service. Such selfless pursuits speak volumes about candidates' character and the willingness to nobly serve their country in the future.

It is important to learn fairly early how to maintain high academic standards and balance studies with family, fitness, and creative interests because an officer sets the standard for excellence in every aspect of his/her life. To practice this competence, the academy will evaluate cadets' abilities to manage multiple activities and expect the completion of all tasks in a timely manner.

ACADEMIC LIFE

The Air Force Academy offers thirty-one majors and two minors. Regardless of the academic major chosen, cadets are required to complete a core curriculum based in mathematical and engineering concepts. Technical and nontechnical majors are both flooded with multiple levels of math, engineering, science, English, history, and foreign language courses, in addition to major's classes. This challenging yet diverse core curriculum exposes cadets to a wide variety of subject matter and adequately prepares them for the opportunity to speak intelligently on a number of different subjects. In turn, graduates earn a Bachelor of Science degree in their chosen field of study and graduate with approximately 140 semester hours.

Faculty Availability

The unprecedented commitment of the Air Force Academy's faculty is invaluable to the 4,400 cadets. The faculty is, hands-down, the most dedicated staff in the country, delivering the most accessible teaching staff available for proactive cadets. Students learn to expect a full-time faculty as the academy's standard and commitment to excellence.

Instructors are devoted to the success of their students by administering their contact information, remaining in their office until the duty day is over to offer extra instruction, and learning the first and last names of every cadet in all their classrooms. The U.S. Air Force Academy's faculty is nationally recognized and officially received its accreditation from the Higher Learning Commission from the North Central Association of Colleges and Schools in October 2009, reaccrediting the school for ten more years. The academy possesses one of the best aeronautical and astronautical engineering programs, as well as the top undergraduate business and management program.

Athletics

General Douglas MacArthur, a World War II hero, asserts that "on the fields of friendly strife are sown the seeds that, on other days and other fields will bear the fruits of victory." In addition to the demanding core curriculum, every cadet is a student-athlete. With twenty-seven NCAA Division I teams, twenty-nine intercollegiate teams, and fifteen intramural sports to choose from, every cadet is engaged in year-round competition. Out of the entire cadet population of about 4,400, twenty-four percent are intercollegiate athletes. The Air Force Academy is number one in the nation for athletic opportunities for women. To further promote teamwork and a commitment to upholding fitness standards, physical education courses evaluate cadets' athleticism, as well as help develop more confidence in their abilities. In addition to regularly engaging in competitive sports, cadets are required to take a physical fitness test and an aerobic fitness test each semester. Cadets' commitment to physical development creates habits that contribute to healthy lifestyles and last a lifetime.

The Honor Code and Oath

The foundation of character and leadership development at the Air Force Academy is the Honor Code and Oath, which every basic cadet trainee takes on the second day of Basic Training. A constant reminder of this oath occupies a wall, just north of the cadet chapel. This oath is arguably the most important fabric of cadet life and sets the academy apart from civilian universities. Every graduate internalizes this oath, not all at once, but gradually and deliberately throughout his/her academy career. To help instill the importance of honorable living, cadets participate in several honor lessons, as well as execute the honor violation review process when a classmate violates the code. Through consistent practice and many tests of their moral fiber, cadets learn to demonstrate integrity and accountability in various interactive scenarios. Leading by example is a dominant theme in cadet life, as is the expectation for every cadet to display a high standard of excellence on and off campus. The Honor Code represents a proud heritage of the Air Force's first core value: Integrity First. The Cadet Honor Oath is as follows:

> **❝** *We will not lie, steal, or cheat, nor tolerate among us anyone who does. Furthermore, I resolve to do my duty and to live honorably, so help me God.* **❞**

Military Development

Each service academy offers a unique undergraduate experience that demands performance from a number of intense, stressful situations in and out of the classroom. Afternoons and weekends are sacrificed for character building and military training. As America's service members and future leaders, the Air Force Academy ensures that cadets take full advantage of every mentoring session. Through purposeful instruction and deliberate practice of the Air Force core values, cadets learn to embody the essential qualities of great leaders.

Basic Training

All cadets begin their excursions the summer after high school graduation, six weeks before their first collegiate academic class. This is Basic Cadet Training, affectionately known as "Beast" for its brutal test of physical and mental limits in several considerably demanding categories. This preparation gradually introduces trainees to the military lifestyle, a memorable transition from high school graduates to military members.

Basic Training is broken up into two periods, each one lasting three weeks long. The first period is spent in the cadet area, or campus dormitories. Here, trainees are introduced to military customs and courtesies, proper table etiquette, marching, wearing the uniform correctly, and military history. The second period is spent in Jack's Valley, an outdoor training facility located on a few of the academy's 18,000 acres. This portion of Basic Training is much more physically demanding with more creative workouts and much more intense field exercises. Throughout Basic Training, cadet cadre strongly emphasize the value of teamwork and effective interpersonal leadership, foreshadowing the fact that it is impossible to graduate from the academy as an individual. The seemingly endless obstacles during Basic Training build character and confidence and are genuinely rewarding.

Upon completion of Basic Cadet Training, trainees are formally welcomed into the cadet wing as fourth-class cadets, or freshmen, during the first parade of the school year. This ceremony marks the beginning of their fourth-class academic year that will prove even more challenging than their brief military introduction to the academy.

Summer Programs

Cadets' summers are full of exciting programs that embolden the warrior spirit. Some will travel across the country to learn about different career opportunities; others will journey to foreign countries and learn about different cultures. Some will fly planes, and others will jump out of them. Summers are divided between three structured, three-week-long periods, not necessarily in any particular order. The Academy uses at least two periods to sharpen cadets' leadership skills, such as serving as cadre members for Basic Training or Instructor Pilots in the Soaring Program. Cadets can choose to go home for a period, or take a summer academic class to alleviate their course load during the school year. Slower-paced summers definitely make up for a rigorous academic year. Still far from lackadaisical, with all the cadets participating in various activities around campus, the Air Force Academy remains busy throughout the summer months.

Combat Survival Training

Combat Survival Training is just one of the many leadership programs the academy offers to train cadets in important wilderness training, survival, evasion, and resistance training. Limited to basic essentials loaded in a heavy backpack in the woods, cadets learn how to forage for food, build fires, and read maps and compasses to navigate through Colorado's intense terrain at an unforgiving altitude. Most cadets fondly remember chasing their dinners (usually rabbits and small rodents) and nursing blisters from long hikes, but all can attest to a challenging, yet rewarding experience.

Flying Programs

As a service academy with the word "air" in its title, the Air Force Academy follows through on its promise of offering the most flying opportunities of any undergraduate institution in the world. Cadets can learn how to fly a fairly large variety of aircraft, including gliders, DA-40s, and a number of remotely piloted aircraft. In as little as ten lessons, some cadets learn to solo in these high-tech vehicles and, in some cases, they are being taught by other cadets. With such a close-knit network of academy alumni, many graduates come back to the academy as instructor pilots and mentors. In addition to flying aircraft, cadets are also awarded the opportunity to jump out of "perfectly good airplanes." As every pilot knows, however, there is no such thing as a perfectly good airplane. Still, cadets who complete the academy's skydiving course and acquire five satisfactory jumps can wear their parachute wings for the rest of their active duty careers.

CLASS OF 2010 ASSIGNMENTS

Combat Rescue	4
Special Tactics	4
Program Analyst	8
Airfield Ops	4
Space/Missile	31
Intelligence	55
Weather	5
Logistics	52
Engineers	17
Security Forces	10
Communications	49
Pilot	516
Navigator	17
Air Battle Manager	9
Public Affairs	5
Services	24
Health Services	4
Aerospace Physiologist	3
Acquisitions	146
Special Investigations	5
Medical School	2
Scientists/Nurses	10

SOCIAL LIFE AND ACTIVITIES

The Air Force Academy is not an institution well known for its college parties or social activities. However, cadets work hard enough during the week to let loose on the weekends. Colorado is full of fantastic outdoor recreation. In fact, the Air Force Academy's recreation center is one of the best in the Air Force. It offers ski/snowboard equipment and passes, car rentals, cycling accessories, and everything to create an entertaining camping trip, from grills and sleeping bags, to tents and fishing poles. The academy's Eisenhower Golf Course offers two 18-hole courses, for players just starting out or looking for a challenge. Down the street, Colorado Springs offers a number of indoor rock-climbing and zip-lining facilities.

1 Congresswoman

3 Chiefs of Staff of the United States Air Force (CSAF)

495 General Officers

Over 700 Chief Executive Officers

500 Doctors

37 Astronauts

○ **Lt Gen Bradley C. Hosmer (1959)**—The Academy's first graduate in the order of merit from its first class, as well as its first Rhodes Scholar. Lt Gen Hosmer later returned to the Academy as Superintendent

○ **Brig Gen Dana H. Born (1983)**—The Academy's first female Dean of Faculty

○ **The Honorable Heather Wilson (1982)**— A Rhodes Scholar and the first graduate elected to the United States Congress

○ **Hila Levy (2008)**—First Puerto Rican Rhodes Scholar

○ **Colonel Gary E. Payton (1971)**—A Spacecraft Test Controller from 1976-1980. Payton traveled over 1.2 million miles in 48 Earth orbits, and logged more than 73 hours in space

Besides all the activities outside of the academy, the institution has seventy-six clubs that cater to each cadet's diverse interests, including Pistol Club, Ski Club, Tae Kwon Do, Tuskegee Airmen, Marathon, Rugby, Wings of Blue, and various language clubs. Each club is headed by an "Officer in Charge," who schedules events and works with other officers in authority to provide budgeted financial assistance. With that being said, upperclassmen still take care of most of the day-to-day coaching, mentoring, leading meetings, and managing club activities.

FINANCIAL AID

The United States Air Force Academy does not offer financial aid, but what it does offer is tuition free, full ride, four-year scholarship. This scholarship includes tuition, room and board, three meals a day, uniforms, and up-to-date laptops for use during class and in dorm rooms to complete homework. The cadets pay this tuition free education back in service to our country following graduation from the academy as a commissioned officer.

SUMMING UP

The Air Force Academy's top-tier tuition free education, hands-on instruction, teacher accessibility, small classes, Division I athletics, networking opportunities, prospective travel, leadership experience, and guaranteed career upon graduation is tempting enough to generate interest among America's best and brightest. The competition is steep, and the most successful start building impressive resumes early. Successful candidates are dynamic in their communities, active in extracurricular activities, and take their standardized tests early and often in their high school careers. Although the academy is among the most challenging institutions in America, it is also among the most unique and rewarding experiences that connects an intimate alumnus of champions in following the traditions of the long blue line.

> 66 *My time at the Air Force Academy stood as one of the most challenging, yet most rewarding experiences of my life. Characterized by hard work, long nights, and the best friendships of my life, I would not trade my time at the academy for anything.* 99

—*2d Lt. Robert Louder, Jr., '10*

❏ *Lieutenant Booker, B.S.*

UNITED STATES MILITARY ACADEMY AT WEST POINT

 United States Military Academy at West Point
West Point, NY 10996

 (845) 938-4041
Fax: (845) 938-8121

 E-mail: *admissions@usma.edu*
Website: *http://admissions.usma.edu*

 **Enrollment**

Full-time ❏ women: 731
❏ men: 3,955

INTRODUCING WEST POINT

If you are ready to change the world through your leadership, vision, and strong sense of duty, honor, and country, then the United States Military Academy at West Point is the place for you. Established by President Thomas Jefferson in 1802, West Point is our nation's first service academy. For more than 200 years it has helped shape men and women of character into leaders who don't wait for others to change the world; they begin to change it from the moment they graduate.

Cadets, as the students at West Point are called, are selected from the most success-ful members of every American community for their outstanding academic, physical, and leadership accomplishments. Valedictorians, team captains, Eagle Scout/Gold Award win-ners, class presidents, and civic leaders from throughout the United States and around the world come together each June to start their forty-seven-month cadet experience. They leave our campus a part of history, members of the "Long Gray Line" of West Point graduates.

> 66 *When I first visited for the Summer Leader's Seminar, I knew immedi-ately that the West Point experience was set a world apart from other universi-ties. Some differences are readily apparent—every student wakes up early, wears a uniform, and stays physically fit—but others are more subtle. Cadets have an incredible sense of duty and commitment to their country and to the profession of arms that motivates them to conquer the forty-seven month experi-ence ahead of them.* 99

Located only fifty miles north of New York City, West Point's 16,000-acre campus is situated in the scenic Hudson Valley. Its proximity to the Hudson River offers breathtaking views and an inspiring setting in which to pursue your higher education. The campus is an historic landmark and a living testament to the military history of the country and the strength of the nation's resolve. Facilities include the Arvin Cadet Physical Development Center, which boasts six floors of high-tech athletic equipment; the Jefferson Hall library and learning center, which provides state-of-the-art research databases; and Eisenhower Hall, the second largest theater on the East Coast and one of the finest performance cen-ters in the country.

One of the world's premier centers for leadership excellence, West Point stresses the academic, military, and physical development of each cadet to best prepare each for the lead-ership challenges and opportunities in the U.S. Army. The academic curriculum has thirty-five Majors and Fields of Study that strengthen cadets' historical perspective, cultivate their cul-tural understanding, structure their military training and leader development, build their critical thinking skills, perfect their social science, and hone their math, science, and engi-neering skills, and address the nature of conflict today from general war to counterinsurgency.

Academics are only the start to a West Point day. After class, cadets focus on physi-cal development by participating in twenty-five NCAA Division I sports, intramural teams and individual sports, and more than 100 club sports such as rugby, triathlon, and crew. The rigorous academic and fitness regimes are designed to test our cadet's mental and physical resilience. Woven throughout is a comprehensive education on officer leadership, discipline, and military drill—a challenging combination that allows cadets to realize their full potential.

> 66 *The officers that will teach you not only come fresh from earning a graduate degree at the nation's top graduate schools, but also full of experience as leaders in the Army. Where else can you learn about differential equations from the same person who can tell you how to lead a company of soldiers?* 99

The final accomplishment is not graduation, but a commission into the United States Army as a 2nd lieutenant, fully ready to serve the nation for five years on active duty followed by three years in the U.S. Army Reserves. West Point graduates have changed the course of history in military campaigns with their tactical, operational, and strategic planning and execution. Those accomplishments in uniform have been mirrored by equally notable achievement in politics, science, education, and business. Are you ready to meet the challenge and become a part of this legendary Corps?

ADMISSIONS REQUIREMENTS

Admission to West Point is about more than your GPA or standardized test scores. The applications of more than 15,000 students are filtered based on academic, physical, and leadership potential to find approximately 1,250 candidates who are ready to be offered the challenge of admission into the Corps of Cadets. With an amazingly high offer-acceptance rate, only the most dedicated, enthusiastic applicants make it to the finish line for the report date each June.

Unlike other top-tier colleges, West Point focuses not only on your academic accomplishments, but also on the whole person. Candidates at the top of their class will also need to qualify medically, excel at the Candidate Fitness Assessment, and earn a nomination from a U.S. Representative, a U.S. Senator, the President, the Vice-President, or the Department of Army (this latter category of nominations is service-related). The four pronged application means that the earlier students start, the more successful they could be since offers are based on rolling admissions.

The Admissions Committee searches for students who stand out from the crowd in their academic merit (sixty percent), physical/athletic success (ten percent), and leadership motivation (thirty percent). The academic strength of a candidate is assessed through high school transcripts, class rankings, letters of endorsement, and standardized test scores. To determine physical fitness aptitude, candidates take the Candidate Fitness Assessment (CFA), which consists of the following six events: a basketball throw, pull-ups (men and women) or flexed-arm hang (women), shuttle run, modified sit-ups, push-ups, and a one-mile run.

Leadership Potential

Because West Point strives to remain the premier leadership institute in the world, the Admission Committee's most salient mission is to determine whether a young man or woman has the leadership potential to take command and be ready to lead the soldiers of our Army. With that in mind, the committee looks for indications of exceptional leadership potential, such as involvement in student government—student body or class president—and participation in Boys/Girls State, scouting, debate clubs, school publications, and varsity athletics. Of particular interest to the committee are applicants who seek out leadership positions in their activities, such as team captains or club presidents. In a typical class of about 1,200 new cadets, more than 1,000 earned varsity letters in high school and about 750 were team captains. Over seventy-five percent of the class graduated in the top fifth of their high school classes. The mean SAT I score for a recent class was 630 Verbal and 647 Math, and 28 on the ACT, and some 237 earned National Merit Scholarship recognition.

> **❝** *Comfort in leadership positions is a quality that will be tried and tested from the first day you show up for Reception Day. I remember being in charge of 20 other plebes and given the task of delivering laundry bundles to upper-classmen's rooms. It seemed an impossible task then, but I could never have imagined that three years later I would be in charge of a whole regiment of cadets doing summer training!* **❞**

Candidates also must be at least seventeen and not older than twenty-three years of age on July 1 of the year they enter the academy. They must also be U.S. citizens, be unmarried, and not be pregnant or have a legal obligation for child support.

Steps in Applying

There are several steps in applying to West Point.

- Make a self-assessment based on the admission criteria detailed on the website and informational brochures. Determine if you qualify for West Point and if this is something you would be interested in doing.
- Start a candidate file online and follow up with the Admissions Office.
- Seek a nomination from the congressional representative from your district and your two U.S. senators.
- You must complete all of your SAT and/or ACT testing, as well as your physical and medical examinations.
- You then have the option of visiting West Point and spending the day with a cadet on a candidate orientation visit. This is optional, but highly recommended; an orientation visit is the best way to get a feel for academy life and a sense of whether it's for you.
- If you complete all these steps and are admitted to West Point, your final step is to enroll in the academy on Reception Day.

For those candidates who consider West Point to be their top college of choice and are interested in applying early, the application is now available as early as the junior year in high school. The Admissions Committee selects students on a rolling admission timeline, so starting and completing all work earlier is paramount to your success. Persistence is key, as about thirty percent of each incoming class is second-time applicants.

ACADEMIC LIFE

West Point's purpose is to produce leaders of character who are equipped to provide selfless service to our Army and the nation. As such, West Point provides a broad-based and balanced curriculum to ensure that graduates acquire knowledge, skills, and attributes necessary for them to effectively address the complex and uncertain challenges they will face in their personal and professional lives. The curriculum draws upon three distinct and yet integrated programs: academic, military, and physical. These programs work in concert to provide challenging experiences that ensure that cadets acquire relevant competencies while, at the same time, contributing to their character development.

A dedicated faculty orchestrates these educational experiences. They serve as inspirational role models and are fully engaged in their students' lives. In addition to this traditional faculty, West Point has a select set of the military faculty who are tactical officers. They have the primary responsibility of integrating the leader development experiences of cadets.

In addition to its formal curriculum, West Point offers its students numerous enrichment opportunities that complement and reinforce the learning and development that cadets undergo in traditional academic, military, and physical settings. These supplemental experiences frequently involve travel to domestic and international locales where, in a real-life setting, cadets apply what they have learned in the classroom, on the playing field, and in training areas.

> 66 *The education you will receive at West Point is second to none. One need only look at the number of Rhodes, Marshall, Truman, and National Science Foundation Scholars that West Point produces year after year to be left with an impression that they are preparing cadets with the right skills and traits to succeed at graduate-level education. My sophomore year, I got involved with the Network Science Center to do extracurricular research on analyzing insurgent networks.* 99

Academic Strengths

The strengths of the Academic Program at West Point are small class sizes, a dedicated and highly engaged faculty, and innovative educational practices. The faculty is made up of a blend of military and civilians who are experts in their fields. They are inspirational role models who are fully devoted to providing their students the most positive and beneficial educational experiences possible. Members of the West Point faculty are readily available to students, providing valuable opportunities for one-on-one interactions.

The West Point academic curriculum incorporates both breadth and depth of study that serves as a foundation for the development of critical thinking and creative problem-solving skills. Breadth is achieved through a substantive set of fully integrated core courses that together provide an appropriate balance between technical topics and the humanities. Cadets choose their area of depth from thirty-five academic majors that span a broad spectrum of academic disciplines.

The academic curriculum culminates with an integrative experience that is often an interdisciplinary and team-based project. Through this senior capstone experience, students draw upon and apply knowledge in their chosen major as well as knowledge gained throughout the course of their studies. Often these projects provide real answers to real-world problems, result in presentations at academic conferences, and bring national recognition to students and the institution.

Physical Program

The physical education curriculum spans the four years, with cadets required to take core courses in military movement techniques, boxing, combatives, survival swimming, and personal/unit physical fitness during a cadet's experience. Additionally, cadets have the option of taking a wide array of physical activity electives. Physical education class grades are incorporated into the cadet grade point average, highlighting the importance of physical fitness in the Army.

West Point cadets also receive graded assessments on two physical fitness tests, both of which also contribute to a cadet's class standing. The Army Physical Fitness Test is designed to measure muscular and cardiovascular endurance, and the West Point Indoor Obstacle Course Test is designed to measure a cadet's functional fitness, to include agility, balance, and coordination.

Finally, every cadet at the academy participates in competitive sports at his/her ability level throughout the academic year. Some compete at the varsity level of intercollegiate athletics, while others are challenged at the intercollegiate club level or in West Point's company athletics program. The physical program challenges cadets every day, but is widely regarded as both rewarding and enjoyable.

Military Program

Military development is a key component of the curriculum. Cadets are graded based on military performance and in military science classes throughout the year. Cadets are immersed from day one in a military environment where they are organized in companies, serve and are evaluated in leadership positions within the Corps of Cadets. The heart of the military training takes place during the summer. During their first summer, new cadets are introduced to the academy through the rigors of Cadet Basic Training, a six-week experience that transforms each new cadet from civilian to cadet, and provides the upper-class cadets opportunities to practice small unit leadership. During Cadet Basic Training—also called "Beast Barracks"—new cadets learn what it means to be a cadet as well as what it means to be a soldier.

The summer after "plebe" or freshman year, cadets participate in Cadet Field Training. At Camp Buckner, sophomores or "yearlings" complete four weeks of advance military training focusing on weapons, urban operations, and combat patrolling. During this training, they apply the skills they've learned in the classroom as they undergo tactical exercises focused on small unit operations. Like Cadet Basic Training, upper-class cadets serve as the cadre for this training. Camp Buckner is also a time for recreation and class bonding.

During the summers of the junior "cow" and senior "firstie" years, opportunities for cadets broaden significantly. During these summers, cadets participate in Cadet Troop Leader Training, which involves being assigned to an active army unit for three weeks and serving as a platoon leader. For most cadets, it is their first experience in the regular army and it is both exciting and rewarding. A cadet also serves as a leader, or cadre member, for either Cadet Basic Training or Cadet Field Training during one of his or her final two summers at West Point.

During the summer of cadets' "firstie" year they also complete Cadet Leader Development Training. Cadet Leader Development Training is a twenty-three-day event that trains and assesses basic leadership skills focusing on the principles of leadership, communication, and tactical decision making under stress. The purpose of this training is to further develop competent, confident small unit leaders that are capable of operating in uncertain, rapidly changing environments.

> 66 *The opportunities for enrichment experiences are simply unparalleled at any other university. I have spent two months at the National Security Agency, been on research to Tanzania, spent a semester abroad in Mexico City, and taken a cultural immersion trip to Puerto Rico. The breadth of exposure that you will get as a cadet to cultural, academic, and professional environments has the potential to prepare you for anything.* 99

Individual Advanced Development

During the summer cadets participate in Individual Advanced Development (IADs). Some military IADs include Airborne School (parachuting), Air Assault School (rappelling out of helicopters), Combat Engineering Sapper School, Mountain Warfare School, and Special Forces Scuba School. There are physical IADs such as training at the U.S. Olympic Center and Outward Bound. Very popular among cadets are academic IADs. These are similar to internships students at civilian colleges might participate in. Some academic IADs include duty with the Supreme Court, Crossroads to Africa, NASA, and the national laboratories.

Perhaps this is a curriculum unlike any you've seen. A cadet's total QPA (quality point average) is based on fifty-five percent academic performance, thirty percent military performance, and fifteen percent physical performance. Cadets must be well rounded to be successful at the United States Military Academy and as future officers in the United States Army. The curriculum is meant to develop "enlightened military leaders of strong moral courage whose minds are creative, critical, and resourceful." It was Thucydides who said "The Nation that makes a great distinction between its scholars and its warriors will have its thinking done by cowards and its fighting done by fools."

SOCIAL LIFE AND ACTIVITIES

One of the toughest aspects of being a cadet is deciding in which activities to participate. From sports to dramatics to religious activities, West Point truly has it all.

Athletics

At the conclusion of World War I, General Douglas MacArthur introduced the phrase "every cadet an athlete, every athlete challenged" and required every cadet to participate in athletic competition because he was "convinced that the men who had taken part in organized sport made the best soldiers. MacArthur's quote, "Upon the fields of strife are sown the seeds that upon other fields, on other days, will bear the fruits of victory" serves as the bedrock philosophy for sports at West Point.

West Point has twenty-five NCAA Division I intercollegiate teams. Eighteen of the teams compete in the Patriot League. Since the inception of the Patriot League in 1990, West Point has either won or finished second for the Patriot League President's Cup a total of thirteen years. The President's Cup recognizes the school with the best overall performance in men's and women's sports. Other West Point teams compete in the Atlantic Hockey Association, Eastern Intercollegiate Wrestling Association, Eastern College Athletic Conference (Gymnastics), Great America Rifle Conference, and the Eastern Sprint Football League. The football team competes as an NCAA Division I Independent. Approximately twenty-five percent of the cadets at West Point participate in NCAA Division I intercollegiate sports.

The competitive club athletics program at West Point is recognized as one of the premier club programs in the nation. Thirty-four West Point club teams have won national championships since 2000. More than 800 cadets compete on twenty-seven competitive club teams.

> *When I first attended club night as a plebe, I was convinced that there were more sports and clubs than there were cadets! If you cannot find a passion or interest, you can find a few friends and start your own club. Participating in clubs and sports is a fantastic way to meet people from different parts of the Corps and build relationships that will last a lifetime.*

The cadet company athletics program has a Fall and a Spring Season with six sports offered each season. Competition in company athletics is based on the military organization of West Point. Each company is represented by one team in each sport. During the regular season, a company competes against other companies in its regiment. At the end of the season, regimental champions participate in a play-off to determine a brigade championship.

Clubs

In addition to sports, there are countless other activities for cadets to enjoy. For instance, there are over 100 recreational clubs available to cadets:

- There are clubs that support the corps such as the cadet spirit band, drill team, glee club, pipes and drums, ski instructors, ski patrol, and WKDT (the cadet radio station).
- Academics clubs include the debate team, the speech team, model UN, amateur radio, astronomy, as well as foreign language clubs, engineering clubs, science clubs, and more.
- There are clubs that are geared toward the arts such as the theater arts guild, staff and ushers, army strings, opera, African-American literature, film forum studio arts, creative writing, and many more.
- Hobby clubs include, bowling, chess, ski, scuba, kendo, fishing, flying, mixed martial arts, snowboard, and kayaking along with a variety of others.
- There are numerous volunteer religious groups and activities. Religion plays a large part in the lives of many cadets and cadets are the backbone of the chapels on post.

There are also many social activities for cadets to attend. There is an on-post movie theater, frequent dances, a golf course, a ski slope, a bowling alley, boat ride, and tailgates. You will never hear a cadet say that he or she is bored.

FINANCIAL AID

The United States Army provides full-tuition scholarship to each and every West Point cadet. Cadets are active-duty members of the United States Army and receive an annual salary of approximately $10,148. Room and board, medical, and dental care is provided by the U.S. Army.

> **"** *Besides, the fact that everyone wears a uniform and has a carbon copy of each others' room, there is no tuition cost and everyone is paid a stipend, so socioeconomic status is never an issue at West Point. Besides, West Point's selection process ensures that there is a representative sample taken from the U.S. population. Where else can you work, live, and play in an environment unencumbered by status and background?* **"**

However, a one-time deposit of $2,000 is required upon admission, in order help pay for the initial issue of uniforms, books, supplies, equipment, and fees. The value of this education and the associated benefits is approximately $200,000 and is on par with the top private school tuitions in the nation.

GRADUATES

Along with developing academically, physically, and militarily, our graduates develop in other ways as part of their preparation to lead this nation's soldiers. Ethical, spiritual, and social development occurs formally and informally throughout your forty-seven months as a cadet. These include formal instruction in the important values of the military profession, voluntary religious programs, interaction with staff and faculty role models, and a vigorous guest speaker program. Cadets also develop ethically by adhering to the Cadet Honor Code, which states "A cadet will not lie, cheat, steal, or tolerate those who do."

Graduates of West Point tend to be very proud of their alma mater; it seems that the older they get, the prouder they become. Alumni weekends are always very inspiring and very crowded. The alumni are known as "old grads" and the funny thing is one becomes an "old grad" the second he or she tosses that hat in the air on graduation day. The common joke is that "old grads" are always complaining that the structure and discipline at West

Point is simply not as rigid as when they were cadets. But most agree, it is the values and traditions that make West Point an enduring national treasure.

West Point has had more than a handful of distinguished graduates. Much of the U.S. Army leadership since the Civil War were members of the Long Gray Line—and the tradition continues. West Point graduates have, and will continue to make wonderful contributions to our nation. West Pointers have served as everything from presidents of corporations to presidents of the United States. Service is what West Point is all about, and our graduates have and will continue to serve our nation well.

SUMMING UP

West Point is indeed a special place. Where else can you eat virtually every meal in less than twenty minutes with the entire student body? Where else can you march into a stadium on national television and be a part of the historic Army-Navy rivalry? Where else can you stop on the way to class and pose for a picture with tourists?

- General Robert E. Lee, 1829
- President Ulysses S. Grant, 1843
- General John J. Pershing, 1886
- General Douglas MacArthur, 1903
- General George Patton, 1909
- President Dwight D. Eisenhower, 1915
- General Creighton Abrams, 1936
- General Alexander Haig, Jr., 1947 (U.S. Secretary of State)
- President Fidel Ramos, 1950 (Philippines)
- Colonel "Buzz" Aldrin, 1951 (Astronaut)
- General H. Norman Schwarzkopf, 1956
- Jim Kimsey, 1962 (Co-founder AOL)
- Secretary Eric Shinseki, 1965 (Secretary of Veterans Affairs)
- Coach Mike Krzyzewski, 1969 (Duke)
- Senator Jack Reed, 1971 (Rhode Island)
- General David Petraeus, 1974
- General Lloyd Austin, 1975
- General Raymond Odierno, 1976
- General Rebecca Halstead, 1981
- Rod Lurie, 1984 (Writer/Director)
- Representative Brett Guthrie, 1987 (Kentucky)
- Amy Efaw, 1989 (Writer/Author)

"I simply could not be more fulfilled that I chose West Point. Like anything that is truly worthwhile, graduating was an arduous and challenging trial that I will never forget. As a graduate employed in the most professional Army in the world, I cannot imagine having gone anywhere else."

❏ *Josh Lospinoso, B.A.*

UNITED STATES NAVAL ACADEMY

 United States Naval Academy
Annapolis, MD 21402-5018

 (410) 293-4361
Fax: (410) 293-4348

 Website: *http://www.usna.edu/admissions*

 Enrollment

Full-time ❏ women: 928
❏ men: 3,675

INTRODUCING THE UNITED STATES NAVAL ACADEMY

The United States Naval Academy was founded in 1845 to provide a place where young men could learn the ways of the sea and the necessary traits of a future combat leader in an environment where a misstep could be tolerated here and there. *Here and there*, mind you. Not often. More than 150 years later, Navy offers both men and women undergraduate degrees in nineteen majors. While math and engineering receive the primary emphasis academically, there are several majors offered in the social sciences and humanities, including history, political science, and English. Everyone who is offered an appointment to Navy is admitted on full scholarship. The Navy pays for your room and board, tuition, medical and dental bills, and even gives you a modest monthly stipend. The academy has baccalaureate accreditation with both ABET and CSAB to go along with its regional accreditation. The Nimitz Library, built in 1973, acts as a second home for many of the academically taxed midshipmen at the Naval Academy. It has 636,500 volumes and subscribes to 2,000 periodicals, as well as possessing such computerized library sources and services as the card catalog, interlibrary loans, and database searching.

> **66** *If life is measured by unique experiences, you just can't pick a better place. In my four years, I went to Navy firefighting school, spent six-weeks of one summer in San Diego training on an amphibious vessel, sang for the president five times as a member of the Men's Glee Club, skippered a forty-four-foot sailboat from Annapolis to Newport, Rhode Island, and back, spent another month one summer with an F/A-18 squadron in Virginia Beach, went to Dublin, Ireland, to watch the Navy football team play Notre Dame, got my scuba qualifications, was in four musical productions, did aerobatics in a T-34 (one of the Navy's training planes) in Pensacola, Florida, and went under the waves in a submarine for a few days. Sound fascinating and eclectic? It was. And I recommend it to any of you.* **99**

Special learning facilities include a learning resource center, planetarium, wind tunnels, radio station, propulsion laboratory, nuclear reactor, oceanographic research vessel, towing tanks, flight simulator, and a naval history museum called Preble Hall.

Mission

The Naval Academy has a unique clarity of purpose, expressed in the school's official mission: "To develop midshipmen morally, mentally, and physically, and imbue them with the highest ideals of duty, honor, and loyalty in order to provide graduates who are dedicated to a career of naval service and have potential for future development in mind and character to assume the highest responsibilities of command, citizenship, and government." That puts everyone—faculty, staff, and midshipmen—on the same wavelength. It also encourages a sense of spirit and pride found at few other schools.

The Campus

The Navy campus, known by the Brigade of Midshipmen as the "Yard" is located in Annapolis, a small Chesapeake Bay sailing mecca and the capital of Maryland. The city is located about thirty miles southeast of Baltimore and thirty-five miles east of Washington, D.C. The Yard covers 338 acres, and is home to twenty-five historic buildings including Bancroft Hall, in which all midshipmen live, which happens to be one of the single largest dormitories in the United States (4.8 square miles of hallway).

Classmates

One thing you can look forward to if you become a midshipman at the Naval Academy is making some of the best friends of your life. Your classmates will hail from all fifty states and more than twenty foreign countries. A recent high school graduate will have classmates here who have spent some time at other colleges or in the operational Navy as enlisted sailors or marines. The diversity is extraordinary, and refreshing. Religiously, many midshipmen practice traditional Judeo-Christian religions. Every major religion in the world is represented within the Brigade. Whatever else may happen, you can be sure that your horizons will expand tremendously.

ADMISSIONS REQUIREMENTS

Requirements for getting into the Naval Academy are much stiffer even than those at many of the nation's other top schools, because, at least in part, Navy looks at other things. While other institutions will examine you closely academically, the academy, because of its affiliation with the federal government and the U.S. Navy, will want to know more about what they are getting. To enter, you have to be between the ages of seventeen and twenty-three, unmarried, with no children, and pass the Department of Defense Medical Review Board physical exam. You must also score high on SAT or ACT. Of the 17,417 applicants for the class of 2014, only 8.4 percent received offers of admission. Of those finally admitted, sixty-eight percent had scored higher than 600 on the Verbal section of their SAT and seventy-eight percent had done at least that well on the Math section (thirty-two percent exceeded 700 on the Math). The combined average of SAT scores for the class of 2014 was 1292.

The Nomination

Once you've met these requirements, the next step is to attain a nomination. This can be done through a couple of different sources, the most common of which is the congressional nomination. This means that you put your name and information in the hands of your congressman and both of your senators, and they decide whether or not to grant you an interview. If you are successful in gaining an interview, you may receive a nomination. If a nomination is offered, it is up to the academy whether or not they will give you an appointment, which is the final acknowledgment of admission. (Note: if you are the child of a career military officer or enlisted person, or if your parent was disabled or killed in the service of our country, there are special categories under which you can be nominated; more information is available on this from the Office of Admissions web site: *www.usna.edu/admissions*). One little hint: you will put yourself in the best position to get a good look from your congressman and senators and the academy if you get your admissions materials in early.

What to Submit

There are a few things that you need to submit. In the spring of your junior year of high school you should go online and fill out a Preliminary Application. If you meet basic qualifications, you will be sent an application letter with information on how to go online and complete the application. Application letters are mailed out weekly, starting in mid-May.

Extracurricular Activities

To make yourself most competitive for a nomination and subsequent appointment to the Naval Academy, there are a few things you can do. First of all—and this is true for all the good schools—get involved in all that you can and do it well. Prove in various activities that you have what it takes to be a leader. Load up your plate with Advanced Placement and Honors courses and perform favorably in them. These courses, along with faculty recommendations from your high school, play a sizable role in the selection process. Also, play varsity sports. The vast majority of each class entering the academy each year lettered in at least one sport in high school. These accomplishments, combined with good grades, show that you are a well-rounded individual, just the kind of person the military is looking for to make up its corps of officers.

Suffice it to say, if you are seeking academic challenge, you won't be at all disappointed by the Naval Academy—it is undoubtedly one of the most stressful and taxing academic programs found in our country. On top of that add the fact that military activities take up much of your free time, and you have a true time-management challenge. Study time simply isn't plentiful, and it takes a great deal of self-discipline to maximize your effectiveness. Over time you learn to cope, however, and are a better person for it.

There is also a great deal of academic opportunity at Navy.

Degrees

The Naval Academy offers the Bachelor of Science degree in three major areas. Engineering, Mathematics and Sciences, and Humanities and Social Sciences. Every midshipman is required to complete 140 semester hours to graduate, and to pass core courses in mathematics, engineering, natural sciences, humanities, and social sciences.

Physical Education

Physical Education is another staple of the curriculum, with everyone taking three semesters of swimming, a semester of boxing and wrestling, a semester of martial arts, and three semesters of free electives. The Physical Readiness Test (PRT) is taken each semester and tests the midshipmen's fitness by measuring their performance in push-ups, sit-ups, and a one-and-a-half-mile run. All midshipmen also take mandatory professional development courses during their four years that include Naval Leadership, Ethics and Law, Seamanship, and Navigation. Class attendance is mandatory for all midshipmen.

Class Size and Faculty

Class size and student-to-faculty ratio are advantages that you will truly appreciate if you attend the Naval Academy. The largest plebe chemistry lecture section may consist of thirty-five people. The average size for an introductory lecture is twenty-three students; for a regular course it's about fifteen, and for a lab, ten. The student-to-faculty ratio is seven to one.

The faculty, you'll find, is impressive in its own right. It is composed of both civilian professors and military officers, with ninety percent of its members holding Ph.D.s.

Educational Options

Last but not least, if you make it through all the rigors of the program and come out with top grades, there are several special options open to you at the academy. First, a group of seniors begin graduate work at educational institutions in the Washington, D.C./Baltimore area like Georgetown and Johns Hopkins each year. This is called the Voluntary Graduate Education Program, and is a great deal for the academically motivated. A small number of midshipmen are also named as Trident Scholars, allowing them to spend their last two semesters doing an independent research project. The Trident program culminates in a presentation given by the Scholars, attended by the faculty of their department, and open to the public. There are ten national honor societies active at the Naval Academy, and five of the departments on the Yard have honors programs in their majors.

SOCIAL LIFE AND ACTIVITIES

Want to be busy? Don't worry about that for a second if you receive an appointment to the Naval Academy. Activities aren't even really an option—they're an imperative. Everyone marches in parades, everyone plays a sport (either intramural or intercollegiate), everyone attends all home football games, everyone attends guest lectures by high-level speakers— everyone takes an active role in the moral, mental, and physical development as a future Navy or Marine Corps Leader of Character.

Sports

On the athletic front, the possibilities are endless. Everyone must participate in a sport, whether at the varsity, club, or intramural level. Navy offers nineteen different intercollegiate sports for men, ten for women, and three coed. Men's and women's basketball, water polo, men's lacrosse, football, and swimming, and crew are some of the sports in which Navy has traditionally been very strong.

In the fall, the football team is the center of all nonacademic activity. Before every home game, midshipmen march to the stadium and conduct a brief parade on the field; after the game they hold tailgaters. But during the game, they sit as a group. There is no sight quite like that of more than 4,000 young men and women in full uniform leaping up and down in celebration of a big play by the team. And keep in mind that the chance to cut loose only comes once in a blue moon at the academy. It gets crazy at Navy-Marine Corps Stadium in the fall, and, in the last couple of years there has been plenty to cheer about. In 2004, the team finished 10–2 and defeated the University of New Mexico in the Emerald Bowl in San Francisco. And since we're on the subject of football, we must mention the annual Army-Navy game. Is it a big event? Read this and you'll see. Both West Point and Navy pack their *entire* student body into buses and cart them to Philadelphia. So you've already got 4,200 plus students from each school there in uniform. Add countless alumni from both schools and national television coverage and you have a truly BIG event. More celebrations of even higher intensity ensue if Navy wins. If it's not a Navy win, the weekend usually takes a major downswing and becomes a time of commiseration with friends. Either way, it's an unforgettable thing to witness. And the game is ALWAYS great. It seems that every year, no matter what the records, rankings, or anything else, the game is a grudge match that comes down to the wire.

Club sports of the more exotic variety like rugby, ice hockey, and karate are also available and are part of some intercollegiate competition as well.

Organizations

Nonathletic activities at the Naval Academy are just as varied as the athletic offerings, if not more so. For the adventurous spirit (as are many that look into attending one of the service academies) there are organizations like the Alpine Racing Club and the Cycling Club, offering basic training sessions as well as more advanced opportunities to their members. Those interested in the fine arts will find the program, especially in the field of vocal music, significantly more rewarding than they might have expected at a service academy. The Men's and Women's Glee Clubs are two of America's best-known and critically acclaimed groups of their type, and Navy's annual winter musical productions are the largest drawing nonprofessional theatrical events in the Baltimore-Washington area. Gospel Choir and Protestant and Catholic Chapel Choirs round out the varied offerings for singers at Navy.

Players of brass instruments and percussion may find a home in the Naval Academy's Drum and Bugle Corps, which generally travels with the football team on road trips and plays every day for a flock of tourists as the Brigade of Midshipmen marches in from noon meal formation.

The Masqueraders are the Naval Academy's thespian troupe; they present a full-length dramatic production in the fall of each year.

If none of this sounds good, maybe mountaineering, cheerleading, competing in triathlons, or one of the host of other options available will. The possibilities are nearly endless.

Social Life

Now to your social life at the Naval Academy. USNA is not a party school. It should be said right off the bat that if your goal at college is to strengthen your liver and go to wild parties five days out of the week, while appearing only to take your exams each semester, Navy is *not* the place for you. Consistently ranked highest in the nation for sobriety and zero tolerance of drugs. Of course, you are reading this book, so this is not presumably the path you have chosen. You won't be highly successful at any of the other schools in this book by modeling your life after John Belushi's character in *Animal House*, but depending on your innate ability and resourcefulness you might be able to graduate. Forget it at Navy. You will be challenged with the restrictions, and the academic demands, accompanied by the fact that you have to stay in pretty darned good physical shape throughout your four years.

With that little disclaimer out of the way, the best way to explain social life at the academy is that you start out with none and it slowly gets better. One of the intentional pillars of the rigid training that one undergoes at the academy is self-sacrifice, and one of the big ways that this is hammered into you is through the withdrawal of many social privileges during your four years. You start out as a plebe (freshman) and go through your summer of basic training (known as Plebe Summer), in which you are not allowed to leave the Yard at all. Then the year starts.

As a plebe during the academic year, you can go out only on Saturday afternoons and evenings. When you do venture away from the Yard, you can't drive, have to wear your uniform, and can only go a certain distance away from the grounds of the academy. Pretty limiting.

66 *An average day as a plebe? How about a morning? Wake up at 5:30, study your rates (required memorization), read the three newspaper articles that you'll be asked to report on at meal, go report your knowledge to your upperclass at 0630, fix your shoes and uniform for formation, do a chow call (stand out in the passageway and scream out the breakfast menu, officers of the watch, and a million other memorized items), and run off to 0700 formation. Morning classes feel more like sanctuary than a grind, since they mark the only time when you can sit quietly. Relax in Bancroft and an upperclassman will gladly remind you of the laundry bags to be delivered, newspapers to be collected for recycling, and various other menial jobs to do. Some plebes escape to the library during their free periods but there aren't any bells there, and fourth class midshipmen are notorious for dozing. Nod off in Nimitz and you might sleep through the rest of your classes for the day…and a plebe on restriction is significantly more unhappy than a plebe delivering laundry. The gist of all this: the kinder and gentler era we live in has had no effect on the level of activity that punctuates an academy plebe's mornings.* 99

During sophomore year, known as youngster year, midshipmen can go out on Saturdays and Sundays. Once or twice a semester, they are allowed to leave on a Friday afternoon and to return that Sunday evening.

Weekday and weekend liberty is granted for first and second class midshipmen, based upon academic, athletic, and military performance.

Social Opportunities

While social life is, to say the least, not traditional, there ARE some social opportunities at the academy that are quite impressive. Every year popular music groups as well as renowned classical musicians come into Alumni Hall, the Naval Academy's arena and theater complex. Popular concerts of the past few years have included shows by Hootie and the Blowfish, Brooks and Dunn, Third Eye Blind, and the Goo-Goo Dolls. The Baltimore symphony, the St. Petersburg State Ballet Theatre, and the Moscow Virtuosi Orchestra, and the traveling company of the New York City Opera have recently appeared as part of the Distinguished Artists Series, a classical program conducted each year in Alumni Hall.

Dances

Some of the traditionally highly anticipated nonperforming arts social events of each year are just as impressive. The Ring Dance, which takes place at the end of the second class year to celebrate the new firsties' right to put on their class rings for the first time, is basically super-prom. It's a formal dance, and the second class midshipmen spend much of the year prior to the event agonizing about who they will bring, often from all the way across the country, to the event. The night includes dancing, a formal dinner, and fireworks to top it all off. Most people arrive in limos and stay at luxurious hotels in Washington, D.C., or Baltimore for the weekend. It's a nice reward for three years of hard work—and good motivation to put up with one more.

Commissioning Week

Then there is Commissioning Week, an indescribably exciting time each year that leads up to the graduation ceremony and the hat toss that mark the end of the road for the departing seniors. It's a week filled with formal parades, concerts, ship tours, a special performance by the Navy's Flight Demonstration Team, the Blue Angels, and many other nice events. Annapolis is so packed with people during Commissioning Week that it is advisable for parents to get hotel reservations at least one year in advance.

FINANCIAL AID

Financial aid at the United States Naval Academy is a given. Everyone at the school has room, board, and tuition paid for all four years by the federal government. Midshipmen even receive a modest (very modest) stipend each month for any extraneous expenses. At the end of the second class year, all members of the Brigade are eligible for the "career starter loan." This loan is currently $35,000 (the ceiling gets a little higher every year) that you pay back at incredibly low (in the neighborhood of one percent) interest rates over the time that you serve in the Navy or Marine Corps after graduation. And that brings up another point: in exchange for these various little perks, all graduates of the Naval Academy owe the Navy or Marine Corps at least five years serving as officers in the operational force.

GRADUATES

The effect that graduating from a place like the academy has on a person is interesting and a bit humorous. You spend four years grousing and complaining at every turn about the limitations that have been put on you and how you wish you could just be "normal" and such. Then you toss your hat up into the azure skies on graduation day and develop an instant and puzzling fondness for almost everything about the place. Navy grads are like a huge extended family. They can be found in all walks of life and are always ready to lend friendship and a helping hand to another alum. And, as it might seem would be the case, they've got more exciting stories to tell than the average grad from a "normal" school. Where the average homecoming gathering at another school will undoubtedly be filled with tales of business deals and house remodelings, a Navy homecoming is filled with

PROMINENT GRADS

- James E. Carter, Thirty-ninth President of the United States
- Admiral William Crowe, Former Chairman of the Joint Chiefs, Ambassador to Britain
- Admiral William "Bull" Halsey, World War II Hero
- Jim Lovell, Former Astronaut, Apollo 13 Commander
- John S. McCain, III, U.S. Senator from Arizona
- Admiral Michael Mullen, Chairman of the Joint Chiefs of Staff
- Admiral Chester Nimitz, World War II Hero
- H. Ross Perot, Entrepreneur
- David Robinson, Member of the Basketball Hall of Fame
- Alan B. Shepard, Jr., Former Astronaut, First American in Space
- Roger Staubach, NFL Quarterback and Heisman Trophy Winner
- Admiral Stansfield Turner, Former Director, CIA
- Vice Admiral James Stockdale, Senior naval service prisoner of war in Hanoi, for eight years
- James Webb, VA Senator, Former Secretary of the Navy, Novelist
- Virtually all of the notable admirals of World War II fame and dozens of Medal of Honor recipients.

anecdotes concerning such topics as night landings on aircraft carriers, being shot at by surface-to-air missiles, or a weekend spent on liberty in Bahrain. It's a whole different world. . . .

SUMMING UP

Attending the United States Naval Academy is a decision that, if you come expecting a challenge, you will never regret. It is a small, insulated, often unforgiving place that pushes you to your limits. For twenty-three hours, fifty-five minutes a day in a regular school week during your four years there you might hate it. But that other five minutes comes about once a day when something happens that reminds you of how much you owe to the place. Maybe it happens walking to class in the morning and looking out at the beautiful campus for a minute, or seeing one of the many close friends you've made there, or going into Memorial Hall and seeing the memorial register of past graduates who sacrificed their lives for our country in all of the major wars that America has been involved in since 1845. Those moments are special. They make it all worthwhile.

> ❝ *What the academy did for my classmates and me was that, through all of its stifling regulations and regimentation, it set us free on the playground of life. It opened up to us a wealth of opportunities that will take some of us to the top of the military profession and to the highest levels of government, and others in altogether different but exciting directions. And we all set out on our journeys armed to the hilt with weapons not often found in our society today: self-awareness, self-reliance, and determination. We were forged in the fire of four years by the waters of the Chesapeake Bay, four years that often hurt, but also purified and strengthened the good in us, and gave us the tools to attack life and its hurdles with gusto and confidence.* ❞

And let's face it...there are more pluses than you could hope for at most other schools: Your education is paid for, you are in a great and historic town, you make lifelong friendships, visit exotic places, try things you've never previously dreamed of, and get a degree out of all of it. You'll have all the tools you need to be a success once you are done here. So how could you really go wrong?

❏ *Ensign Anthony Holds Servidas, B.S.*

UNIVERSITY OF CALIFORNIA, LOS ANGELES (UCLA)

University of California, Los Angeles (UCLA) **Los Angeles, CA 90024**	**Enrollment**
(310) 825-3101 Fax: (310) 206-1206	**Full-time** ❏ women: 14,838 ❏ men: 11,849
E-mail: *ugadm@saonet.ucla.edu* Website: *www.ucla.edu*	

INTRODUCING UCLA

UCLA is like a city within a city, drawing more than 60,000 people daily to its 419-acre campus, nestled in the hills of west Los Angeles five miles from the Pacific Ocean.

The "metropolis" of UCLA includes some ten libraries, two museums and an art gallery, three gardens, an elementary school, day-care facilities, residential complexes and buildings that house nearly 7,000 people, several theaters and performing arts auditoriums, stores, restaurants, gyms, a basketball arena, and a hospital. Additionally, the campus has its own police department, a chiller/cogeneration plant that assures the campus of low-cost power, hot water, and efficient cooling, its own postal system, a fleet of buses, and several newspapers.

> *" I love the view from the top of Janss Steps. Looking west, you can see the residence halls rising above the green athletics field and Drake Stadium. In the distance are the Santa Monica Mountains. Looking east, you face the heart of campus, where Royce Hall and Powell Library, the campus's oldest and most famous buildings, stand majestically. Between them is a beautiful quad area and a brick fountain. Just breathtaking!"*

In fact, UCLA and Los Angeles have nurtured one another through the years, ever since the precursor to UCLA, a two-year teaching college, was established in the little pueblo town of Los Angeles in the 1880s. As Los Angeles grew, so did UCLA. Founded in 1919, the university moved to its current Westwood home in 1929.

From then on, both the school and the city enjoyed phenomenal growth and development. Today, Los Angeles has the second largest population in the United States, and UCLA educated 37,000 students and is the most popular university in the United States among applicants.

In just over eighty years, the university has earned a worldwide reputation for the excellence of its programs and the achievements of its students and faculty. It has distinguished itself as the only campus among the nation's top ten research universities that was established in the twentieth century.

UCLA is a large and complex institution devoted to undergraduate and graduate scholarship, research, and public service. Known for academic excellence, many of its programs are rated among the best in the nation, some among the best in the world.

For more information, please visit *www.ucla.edu*.

ADMISSIONS REQUIREMENTS

There's no one way to gain acceptance into one of the most exclusive colleges in the nation, but UCLA does offer statistics about previous classes. Meeting or exceeding these scores will not necessarily guarantee your admission, but are released to offer you guidance and an idea of who you will be competing with. In 2009, 55,708 students applied to UCLA, and only 12,179 freshman students were admitted. The number of applicants increased to 57,670 students in 2010. This included 18,778 transfer applicants, a thirteen percent increase from the number of transfer applicants in 2009.

Grades and Test Scores

In 2010, the average unweighted GPA of an applicant was 3.55. An unweighted GPA does not include extra points for AP or honors courses. If you take AP and honors courses into account, the average weighted GPA for a UCLA applicant in 2010 was 3.91.

Have you been brushing up on your SAT prep? The average SAT score for the 2010 UCLA application pool was 1,815. And if you are also looking for the average ACT score of UCLA's application pool, take note. In 2010, the average ACT score for UCLA applicants was a 27.

Academic Performance and Achievement

It's also important that you take the minimum required classes that UCLA asks applicants to take. These are all the same across the UC system, and you can visit *http://www.admissions.ucla.edu* or your high school counselor for more information. Make sure you take the "a–g" subject courses, which include everything from history to science to math, and everything in between.

The application also leaves plenty of room for you to fill in all of your accomplishments, awards, and extracurricular activities you took part in during high school. They want to know how you stood out as a leader, how creative you are, or how much you care about your community. This is another element of the application that helps UCLA learn more about you, and what you'll be able to accomplish as a Bruin.

Personal Essay

Aside from your test scores and transcripts, you will also be asked to write a personal statement. Test scores cannot offer a complete picture of what you've achieved, what you've dared to do, or what you aspire to be. Show off what you've accomplished to UCLA Admissions, and give UCLA an idea of who you are.

The application includes two essays that help the individuals reviewing your application paint a picture of who you are. One of the essays is for all applicants, and there is an additional freshman or transfer prompt, depending on what you are applying as.

> **❝***I was so nervous applying to UCLA because I wasn't sure if my grades and test scores would be competitive enough. I really focused on sharing my story in my personal essay, and shared how I impacted my high school as a student leader. And it paid off! Being accepted to UCLA was one of the most exciting days of my life.***❞**

The admissions board encourages you to relax and just be yourself in the essay. This is where you can share more information about a private hardship, offer details about how you are going to make a difference as a Bruin, or pique their interest with a stellar essay. More information is available on the UCLA admissions website.

Application Filing

You'll have from November 1–November 30 to submit your UCLA application. It's a UC-wide application, and you'll specify which schools to send your information to in the process. Make sure you leave yourself plenty of time to get all of the information needed for your application together before November 30!

ACADEMIC LIFE

You've heard the rumors. Attend a large, public university, and you'll be stuck in classes of upward of three hundred students. You'll never interact with professors or world-renowned researchers. You'll be, as some might say, lost in the shuffle. But these rumors? Forget them!

Some of your general education classes or lower division classes will have large lectures, but these are generally accompanied by a smaller discussion section. As you move from lower division requirements to the upper division requirements for your major or minor, you'll notice a significant decrease in class size, including classes with as few as ten students! You'll have plenty of opportunities to meet with your professors in office hours or doing research. Your classes will challenge you, inspire you, and offer you the opportunity to think differently about the world.

Dare yourself to take a class outside your comfort zone, pick a fun class where you can explore a topic like rock and roll or Broadway musicals, and take the time to get to know your teachers. When you get your degree from UCLA, you know that all the hard work you've put into your classes will pay off in graduate school or at your dream job.

The Basics

One of the perks of attending UCLA is its unique quarter system. Students have three quarters to take classes: Fall, Winter, and Spring. Each quarter lasts ten weeks, with an additional week for finals. The structure of the quarter system allows students and teachers to quickly move through materials and cover a broad range of topics.

Classes are structured in a variety of ways, and one of the most exciting things to do before the start of every new quarter is to utilize the class planner to create the perfect schedule. Not a morning person? Try taking classes offered in the afternoon so you can sleep in! Interested in digging your heels into a very specific subject? Try a seminar class that meets once a week, for three hours at a time—and usually has only ten to twenty students in the class.

There are over 100 undergraduate majors offered at UCLA, and thousands of classes offered to fulfill necessary requirements. Most of the majors at UCLA are part of the College of Letters and Sciences, which includes everything from biology to English. There are also eleven other specialized schools for undergraduates for degrees in theater, engineering, nursing, and more. Narrowing down your options might be the hardest thing about choosing a major or deciding which classes to take.

General Education Clusters

Freshman students have the opportunity to take several exclusive courses. The General Education Clusters are a year-long course taught by several accomplished and renowned professors. The overall topic does not change throughout the year, and the third quarter is spent in a special seminar class. GE Clusters include honors credit and are a great way to knock out a couple of general education classes at once, and start your college experience with some of the best professors UCLA offers.

> ❝ The GE cluster I took my freshman year opened my eyes to a topic I had never explored in the slightest, and I loved it. The professors and teaching assistants were so passionate about the class that I couldn't help really enjoying the class just as much, and it was a great introduction to the challenging, and interesting, classes UCLA offers. ❞

Fiat Lux Classes

Fiat Lux classes are also geared specifically toward freshmen, and taught by faculty members considered experts in their field of study. These classes last for one quarter, and are graded on a Pass/No Pass scale. Fiat Lux classes are a great way to round out your schedule as a first-year UCLA student. Recent courses have included classes like "The Economics of Sports" and "Pride and Prejudice: Social World of Jane Austen."

UCLA freshmen get top priority in General Education Clusters and Fiat Lux classes, and you'll quickly notice just how fast they fill up! What's great about these classes, aside from all the reasons listed above, is that you'll be taking them with other freshmen. It's a great opportunity to meet new friends, find a study group, and go through the excitement of your first college classes with other eager, bright students.

Undergraduate Research

A regular in the news thanks to groundbreaking studies and discoveries, UCLA regularly ranks as one of the top universities or colleges in terms of research.

UCLA is known as the birthplace of the Internet, after a computer message was transmitted by a team at UCLA to a computer at Stanford. The fastest barcode reader was developed at UCLA. Cutting-edge research done at UCLA has contributed significantly to studying autism, eye cancer, AIDS, and asthma. Countless lives have been improved and saved thanks to UCLA's Medical Center, considered the "Best in the West" and among the top three ranked hospitals in the nation.

You can jump into the world of research through UCLA's Undergraduate Research Center. It's divided into two areas: Life and Physical Sciences/Care, and Humanities and Social Sciences. The Center makes it easy for students to get started, offering entry-level research courses, seminars, and tutorials. This is the place to go if you want to work toward getting a paper published or want to learn more about research scholarships.

Abroad

Many Bruins choose to spend a quarter studying in an exotic location, and UCLA has an entire office of dedicated staff ready to help you figure out your plans. The Education Abroad Office will help you figure out the cost of your adventure, which is usually comparable to tuition at UCLA since exchange rates are relatively low. They'll also help you figure out which courses you take will transfer back to UCLA and go toward your degree. And there are also financial aid opportunities available!

For students looking to stay a little closer to home, the Center for American Politics and Public Policy is another great option. Students spend a quarter interning and taking classes in Washington, D.C., and opportunities available through the CAPP program are tremendous. Imagine yourself walking through our nation's capital on your way to your internship! Students that have completed the CAPP program rave about the fun they had being a part of United States history serving on Congressional committees or working for a nonprofit organization.

SOCIAL LIFE AND ACTIVITIES

UCLA is a big campus, and thousands of students, staff, and visitors walk around its grounds on a daily basis. Despite its size, however, UCLA feels so much smaller because of its endless opportunities for students to find (or create!) a niche of their own. Whether you plan on taking part on an athletic team, are planning on running for floor president, or looking for a research opportunity, UCLA has something to offer. Getting involved is the best way to make friends, work closely with a world-renowned professor, or make a difference in the UCLA community and beyond.

Dorm and Apartment Life

Have you been dreaming of the day you get to move out of your childhood bedroom and decorate your dorm room? For freshmen or transfer students at UCLA, moving into the dorms is one of the first opportunities for students to bond with their roommates and other students living on their floor. As you put up pictures of your family and friends from home, it's the perfect opportunity to start sharing your history with your roommates, and a starting point for new memories at UCLA.

Ninety percent of new freshmen live in the dorms their first year on campus. And why wouldn't you? You'll meet other freshmen excited to explore the campus and check out all that UCLA has to offer. You'll meet new friends on your floor, in your building, or waiting in line for spaghetti together in the dining halls. UCLA calls the area where all the dormitories are located "The Hill," and it's an appropriate name for residential life as a Bruin. Fine dining just steps away, spacious accommodations, and plenty of quiet areas to study—and that's just the beginning!

UCLA offers a variety of residential options so new students can find the perfect fit for them. As an incoming freshman, you will be guaranteed three consecutive years of on-campus housing, and transfer students are guaranteed at least one year of on-campus accommodations. Many freshmen choose to live in one of the four high-rise residence halls. Residential plazas typically offer two rooms conjoined by a shared bathroom, or one room with a private bathroom. The third option for students is residential suites, where students can live in a two-bedroom facility with its own living room and bathroom.

If you're looking for activities to take part in on The Hill, your RA will be the first person to show you all that dorm life has to offer. From floor dinners to trips to Santa Monica on the Big Blue Bus, your RA will be the go-to person to learn anything and everything about life at UCLA. And if they can't help you, they'll probably direct you to the Office of Residential Life, which offers even more ways to get involved. For parents reading this, RAs and the ORL are also on hand for any emergencies, advice, and making sure you feel safe. Managing a full course-load and extracurricular activities can be a lot for any first-time student, so your dormitory is the place to have fun and kick back.

There's nothing quite like UCLA's dining experience. The menu changes daily at the four cafeteria-style dining options, located only moments from your dorm. You can easily check the menu online to see where you and your friends should head for lunch or dinner. Each dining hall includes a fresh salad bar packed with a variety of toppings, mouth-watering selections from raviolis to sushi, and a tempting dessert selection overseen by an expert pastry chef. If you're in a rush, or looking for something different, there are several cafés, offering a delicious selection of coffee, pastries, and meals to-go. And if you're studying late into the night, late-night options make perfect brain food.

> **"** *I loved living in the dorms, but moved off-campus after my second year. One of the things I miss most about living on The Hill are the dining halls. I'm always calling up my friends that still live in the dorms to swipe me in for Late Night when we're studying, or for dorm brunch on the weekends. My favorite are the omelets, made fresh by a chef while I watch! UCLA made it easy for me to focus on my studies by offering such awesome living accommodations.* **"**

After living in the dorms, many students move into an apartment in Westwood. There are hundreds of options just a short walking distance from UCLA with a variety of pricing options.

Social Life

What's a UCLA student to do to let off some steam after a long week of class and meetings? Enjoy the UCLA and Westwood nightlife of course!

If you're looking for a perfect college town to complement such a vibrant campus, look no further than Westwood. With a variety of dining options from fast food to sit-down options, you can find a restaurant to fit in a quick bite or a date night. Just a quick walk from campus, Westwood also includes a variety of boutiques for a quick shopping trip! There's also a couple of fun, novelty stores, perfect for finding a quick costume for that party you're running to.

Any new UCLA student is quick to learn that Thursday night is favorite night for going out. You'll find plenty of UCLA students enjoying parties at the fraternities on Thursday nights, when Greek life is in full force. Many of the fraternities throw themed parties one or two nights each quarter, and with nearly twenty registered fraternities at UCLA, there's usually something to do every week of the quarter. The parties are generally reserved for members of the fraternity and invited guests, so make sure you get on the guest list!

For the twenty-one and over crowd, there are plenty of options in Westwood. Whether you're in the mood to sing some '90s karaoke with your friends or enjoy a laid-back happy hour, you'll find plenty of places to have a great night with your friends. And stepping just outside of Westwood to Hollywood, Santa Monica, or Malibu, the nightlife seemingly explodes in options. Los Angeles is alive with so many nightlife choices that it's often just a matter of calling a cab or jumping on a bus to get to your destination.

Campus Life

Right after you move into the dorms, and before classes actually start, you'll be given a crash course of life at UCLA during Zero Week. The True Bruin Welcome includes Bruin Bash, an all-school concert and dance that might be one of the first traditions you take part in as a UCLA student. The week also includes the enormous Activities Fair, which offers a slice of some of the roughly 950 student groups that exist on campus.

Passionate about making a difference? UCLA is known throughout the country for its twenty-six-hour Dance Marathon, which benefits the Elizabeth Glaser Pediatric AIDS Foundation. Looking for great networking opportunities? Join one of the dozens of student groups like the Undergraduate Communications Association offering a chance to meet successful individuals in your field of study. There are also plenty of political, cultural, and fitness groups looking for new members and fresh energy.

UCLA is run by a student body government called the Undergraduate Student Association Council, and elections during spring quarter are always exciting. Whether you run for a position on USAC, or serve on a committee for one of the USAC representatives, it's a great way to potentially make a lasting impact at UCLA.

Greek life is another way to get involved on campus, offering a jam-packed calendar of activities every single quarter. Many members of the Greek community cannot imagine their college experience without the friends they made in their fraternity or sorority, and there are also opportunities for serving in a leadership position and networking. Students can "Go Greek" through a national sorority or fraternity, or join a cultural or business sorority or fraternity.

> **❝** *I've experienced more love and laughter than I ever could have imagined by joining a sorority. There are so many great ways to meet people at UCLA, but going Greek was a life-changing experience for me. I know in forty-plus years my sorority sisters and I will still be talking about all the memories we shared at UCLA.* **❞**

Whether you're a freshman or a transfer student, there's plenty of time to get involved and make a difference at UCLA or the greater Los Angeles community. UCLA provides students a solid foundation to be successful in any pathway they choose.

Athletics

There's nothing quite like sitting with all your friends at a UCLA sporting event, wearing your favorite Bruin T-shirt and cheering on your favorite athletes. One of the first things a new Bruin has to learn is the 8-clap, a UCLA cheer that you'll find yourself doing in your sleep, you'll know it so well. There's something about the resounding "fight fight fight" that ends the cheer that gets the fans pumped up and the athletes ready to dominate.

It's no secret that UCLA has the best athletic program in the entire country. The school was the "First to 100," besting every other college program by reaching 100 exciting national championships in 2007. And of course, the athletic program has gone above and beyond, adding on another six national titles in the last three years.

If football is the name of your game, you'd better get your tickets to one of the highlights of fall at UCLA. As summer fades into the crisp fall weather, nothing beats a Saturday game at the historic Rose Bowl stadium, cheering on the boys in Bruin blue and gold. Whether you catch a ride on a UCLA rooter bus or jump in a car with a bunch of your friends, you know you'll spend the short ride to the Pasadena stadium practicing your cheers and deciding which tailgates you're going to stop at first. Your parents will even have a chance do an 8-clap at the Rose Bowl during the annual UCLA Parents' Weekend. When the school year begins with weekend after weekend of football fun, there really is no stopping the tradition of excellence that athletes and fans at UCLA adhere to.

That tradition of excellence was best exemplified by the storied John Wooden, UCLA's legendary basketball coach who passed away on June 4, 2010. He was one of the most revered, and beloved Bruins, who exemplified the finest ideals in coaching and friendship. His record of ten NCAA men's basketball championships, seven of which were consecutive from 1967 to 1973, will likely never be broken (and believe me, there are a million John Wooden fans out there who know these things by heart). Basketball games are played in Pauley Pavilion, but the court is named for John Wooden and his wife, Nell. UCLA basketball makes regular appearances in the Final Four, and has produced basketball legends like Kareem Abdul-Jabbar and Bill Walton, and recent protégés like Kevin Love. Wooden became known as The Wizard of Westwood, and UCLA's student gym is also titled the Wooden Center in honor of the man everyone called Coach.

It doesn't stop with football and basketball, though. Athletes in sports like swimming and soccer don't just excel in the world of college sports. The 2008 Olympics in Beijing featured thirty-three athletes and six coaches from UCLA, and Bruins made up a quarter of the USA Olympic softball team that triumphantly won gold at the games. UCLA has made it really easy for students to support every sports team. The UCLA Den Pass for students guarantees admission to all home football games, and makes it easy for students to get tickets to home basketball games—all for one low price. Included with the pass is admission to all home games for every other sport. All you have to do is flash your Bruin card!

> 66 *When I was a freshman at UCLA, the basketball team made it to the Final Four during NCAA March Madness. There was nothing like cramming into the apartment of one of my friends and cheering the Bruins on as they won game after game after game; it was standing room only, and one of my most cherished memories as a Bruin. Kevin Love and the team that year created such a crazy excitement around campus.* 99

Even if you don't consider yourself the biggest sports fan in the world, you're bound to get swept up in the enthusiasm that sweeps across campus whenever a game is being played at home, or being shown on national TV.

Recreation

What is it about UCLA recreation that stands out? Well, you can start with the John Wooden Center, which includes a mind-boggling number of elliptical machines, a state-of-the-art weight room, squash and racquetball courts—and that's just the beginning! There's a Rock Wall with designated areas for different levels of climbers, volleyball courts that you can reserve for floor-on-floor matchups, and Certified Personal Fitness Trainers on hand. And if you have to run to the gym between classes, spacious men's and women's locker rooms make it easy for you to shower and go.

If you love to work out under the sun, then look no further than the Sunset Canyon Recreation Center, perfectly located near the dormitories on the hill. Take a break between classes to swim laps or challenge your buddies to a game of volleyball on the sand court. During the sunniest months of the school year, you'll find Sunset Recreation packed with students laying out, tanning, or reading for one of their classes under the sun. You're bound to attend a fundraiser or philanthropy here during your time at UCLA. It's the perfect place for a barbecue!

What next? There's also the pool located at the Student Activities Center that's indoors if it gets too cold to swim outside. Drake Stadium (UCLA's track) is also open during selective hours for student use, as well as the IM Field. If you decide to join an IM sport like flag football or outdoor soccer, this is where all your games will be played!

Not enough? Make sure to check out UCLA's Marina Aquatic Center, located in Marina Del Rey for kayaking, windsurfing, and surfing classes. This is also the locale where UCLA's premiere Crew teams practice, but blink and you'll definitely miss them speeding by!

UCLA Recreation is another way to get involved on campus. Take a dance class at the John Wooden Center, join an IM team, or go kayaking with your roommate. There are also plenty of employment opportunities available within UCLA recreation, whether it's working at the gym or running one of the summer camps offered through UCLA rec.

Students at UCLA can use all of these facilities for free! The only thing that will cost you any additional money are classes (like the dance classes), included in a $25 quarterly fitness pass. The pass includes classes from karate to yoga. You will also have to pay additional fees for the outdoor classes, but comparatively, their prices are still pretty inexpensive. Whether you're an intense or casual exerciser, you're bound to find a regimen and location that's right for you.

Greater Los Angeles

There's nothing like going to college in the middle of Los Angeles. Gorgeous beaches for sunning, scenic mountains to hike, Hollywood hot spots to check out, and the potential to spot celebrities anywhere!

Are you a music junkie? There's nothing like seeing a show at the legendary Hollywood Bowl, an outdoor amphitheater framed by the Hollywood hills and the iconic Hollywood sign. From Simon and Garfunkel to Cher to Abbott and Costello, performers know they've "made it" when they can headline a show at the Hollywood Bowl, and recent shows include Phoenix, Earth Wind and Fire, and a spectacular Hollywood Bowl version of the Broadway smash "Rent," directed by Neil Patrick Harris. Other hot music spots you should check out are the Troubadour, the Music Box, Amoeba Music, and the Walt Disney Concert Hall. And that's just the beginning of the Los Angeles music scene.

Beaches are a great place to relax with your friends! Ride the Ferris wheel on the Santa Monica Pier, lie out on one of the sandy beaches in Malibu, or take in the sights on the Venice Beach sidewalks. The Santa Monica Big Blue Bus is easy (and inexpensive) to use, and is a perfect transportation option to get you and your friends to the sand and the surf. A little farther down the coast, Hermosa, Manhattan Beach, and Marina Del Rey are all great day trips for UCLA students looking for a quick getaway.

For anyone interested in shopping in Los Angeles, there are endless options. Start with the Westside Pavilion Mall just down Westwood Boulevard from UCLA, check out Third Street Promenade in Santa Monica, and make a stop at either Westside Pavilion or the Beverly Center, also just a short drive from UCLA. Other great places to check out for shopping and dining include Rodeo Drive in Beverly Hills, The Grove on mid-Wilshire, and the Los Angeles Fashion District located Downtown.

Art aficionados will find plenty of options both on and off the UCLA campus. The Fowler Museum is located centrally on the UCLA campus and The Hammer Museum is located in Westwood. Students in the School of Arts and Architecture or working toward their degree in Design Media Arts often have free art shows throughout the quarter. The Getty Museum is a popular place for UCLA students to picnic and see famous works of art, and is only a short bus ride from UCLA. And the Los Angeles County Museum of Art is known for its must-see Urban Light Exhibit, also a great photo op. There's little chance to get bored attending a school like UCLA!

FINANCIAL AID

There has been plenty of media coverage in recent months about the rising cost of tuition in California, but UCLA wants to make sure students have the opportunity for higher education. When applying to UCLA, don't let the cost factor inhibit you from attending your dream school. There are plenty of options for obtaining financial aid to cover everything from tuition and books to housing costs. A significant number of students that attend UCLA receive some form of financial aid, and many students also find a part-time job. Time management is one of the best things college can teach you, so don't stress about coming up with the dough. UCLA's Financial Aid Office is right on campus to support students, offer advice, and help you figure out exactly what forms you might need to fill out. And here's some of the lingo to help familiarize you with the financial aid available.

- Scholarships: Although competitive, scholarships are generally monetary rewards that you do not have to pay back. How awesome is that? There are many avenues to find scholarships for college, and you can even start looking before you attend UCLA.
- Grants: This is monetary aid rewarded to students based on financial need. You may have heard of Cal Grants, Federal Pell Grants, or the TEACH Grant. These are just a few available to eligible students, and UCLA's Financial Aid Office website offers so many more details to see if you qualify.
- Loans: You've probably heard of these! Parents often take out loans to pay for big-ticket items like cars or houses, and college is no different. UCLA offers several options for students looking to take out loans, and you can pay them off when you land your dream job after graduation.
- Work-study: Many students work part-time jobs as a way to earn extra money during their time at UCLA. This program is specifically designated to ensure that eligible students can find a job at UCLA or in the community to help pay for the cost of their higher education.

Check out *http://www.fao.ucla.edu* for much more information about all kinds of financial aid, scholarship opportunities, and other resources.

GRADUATES

When you are handed your diploma from UCLA, you're definitely joining good company. Some famous UCLA alumni include actor Sean Astin, athlete Kareem Abdul Jabbar, actor and White House employee Kal Pen, and Los Angeles Mayor Antonio Villaraigosa.

Members of Maroon 5 and The Doors attended UCLA. The tradition of excellence at UCLA began when the school first opened its doors in 1919, and has continued ever since.

UCLA's Alumni Association is a great way to network with other alumni, reconnect with old friends, and continue Bruin traditions long after you've graduated from UCLA. UCLA alumni are involved on campus, travel around the world with fellow Bruins, and have made a difference in their chosen careers.

Being a UCLA alumnus is unlike anything else!

SUMMING UP

There's something about being a UCLA student, unlike being a student at any other college. You'll walk to class under the California sunshine on a perfectly temperate day, cheer on the Bruin football team at the historic Rose Bowl Stadium, and be intellectually challenged and inspired with every class you take. The traditions that define the UCLA experience, the strangers on your floor that become your best friends, and the excitement of living in Los Angeles are just a few of the reasons that record numbers of students apply to UCLA every year. UCLA will give you the foundation to begin your academic life and future career, and give you the tools to create something amazing.

❏ *Bethany Powers, B.A.*

 University of Chicago
Chicago, IL 60637

 (773) 702-1234, Admissions: (773) 702-8650
Fax: (773) 702-4199

 Website: *www.uchicago.edu*

Enrollment

Full-time ❏ women: 2,432
❏ men: 2,425

Part-time ❏ women: 27
❏ men: 42

INTRODUCING THE UNIVERSITY OF CHICAGO

As one of the world's leading institutions, the University of Chicago has been shaping higher education and the intellectual lives of undergraduates for more than a century. A private institution chartered in 1890, UChicago and its 211-acre campus on the shores of Lake Michigan has been home to over eighty Nobel Laureates, the largest number affiliated with any American university. UChicago scholars were the first to split the atom, to measure the speed of light, and to develop the field of sociology. The college is the largest academic unit of the university, which encompasses ten graduate divisions and professional schools, including on-campus law, business, and medical schools.

> **❝** *I was going to begin: 'When I look back on my four years at the University of Chicago, they seem to me like a blissful dream.' But that is precisely wrong. I should say: 'When I look back on my four years at the University of Chicago, they seem to me years of waking up and of being intensely awake.' I say 'awake' because the University of Chicago, especially its college, is a community committed to the life of the mind, so that inquiry, whether in laboratories or libraries, tends to be intertwined with life.* **❞**

Carrying on the university's tradition of innovative and provocative thought, the college's 5,000 undergraduates form a community of learners who have discovered the pleasure of exploring, taking risks, immersing themselves intellectually, and determining the direction of their own education. They chose UChicago because they want to live a life with learning at its center, a life of thoughtful action. Such a life attracts the kinds of students who keep discussions going outside of class, who read for fun, whose recreational activities—whether on stage, field, or dance floor—have a certain intensity. They want a liberal education designed by a faculty of renowned scholars and teachers; they seek small classes and spirited engagement (eighty percent of classes have fewer than twenty-five students, and the student-faculty ratio is 6:1); they participate in opportunities on and off campus that nurture and integrate their professional and recreational interests; they want preparation for the most challenging careers and the best graduate schools; and they look to learn outside of the classroom from some of the brightest minds around—other UChicago students.

ADMISSIONS REQUIREMENTS

The Committee on Admissions has no rigid formula for the successful applicant and considers a candidate's entire application—academic and extracurricular records, essays, letters of recommendations, and SAT or ACT scores. A personal interview is encouraged because it provides the candidate with a chance to learn more about the college and lets the college know what may not easily be conveyed in the application.

Though no specific secondary school courses are prescribed, a standard college preparatory program is ideal: four years of English, three to four years of math and laboratory sciences, three or more years of social sciences, and a foreign language. The essays that you are asked to write as part of the application are an opportunity to show your individuality in addition to your ability to write clearly and effectively.

The University of Chicago does not employ numerical cut-offs when evaluating applications for admission. Of the 1,220 students in the Class of 2008, seventy-eight percent graduated in the top ten percent of their high school classes. The middle fifty percent of admitted students had either a combined score between 1360 and 1490 on the SAT or a cumulative score of between 28 and 32 on the ACT. SAT Subject Tests are not required.

Evaluating Applications

The first page of the Chicago application states, "A college application is an imperfect way of communicating your qualifications, talents, and special interests. Still, you should find plenty of room for creativity here as you describe yourself and your accomplishments." The goal in the Admissions Office is to extend its knowledge of a student well beyond a test score or GPA and understand, as much as possible, that student's personal and academic qualities. To that end, each application is read first by a regional counselor, someone who should understand more about the student's high school and its environment. Then, each application is read at least once more (and perhaps three or four times in all), with a final decision rendered by an admissions committee, an associate, or the dean.

> **EXAMPLES OF COMMON CORE COURSES**
>
> ○ Humanities—Human Being and Citizen; Form/Problem/Event; Readings in Literature; Philosophical Perspectives
> ○ Social Science—Classics of Social and Political Thought; Self, Culture, and Society; Wealth, Power, and Virtue
> ○ Civilization Studies—History of Western Civilization; Introduction to East Asian Civilization; Science, Culture, and Society in Western Civilization; Introduction to African Civilization

For first-year applicants, the following information for admission consideration is required:

- Personal information including extracurricular activities
- Essays—two short-answer responses and one extended essay
- High School Report Form including the transcript and the counselor recommendation

- Teacher Recommendations—one from a math or science teacher and one from an English or social studies teacher (substitutions are not allowed, but you may submit additional recommendations)
- SAT or ACT score (test must be taken by the application deadline)
- Midyear Report Form, due by February 15 online, if at all possible
- Students applying for need-based financial aid need to submit the FAFSA, CSS PROFILE and Financial Aid Application Form 4, which is part of the application.

Students are encouraged to interview if possible. Interviews are conducted on campus, but the school is able to accommodate many requests for alumni interviews in the student's home territory. Although it is not required, an interview is an excellent way for students to share information about themselves that is not easily communicated through the application and to gain a greater understanding of the University of Chicago.

ACADEMIC LIFE

An Educational Ideal

The University of Chicago is known for its emphasis on critical and interdisciplinary thinking. Its college classrooms are reputed hotbeds of exhilarating discourse. Students often continue discussions with their housemates in the dorm, over coffee at a neighborhood or campus café, on the playing field, and even while exploring the city of Chicago. As the university's fifth president Robert Maynard Hutchins once wrote, "Education is not to reform students or amuse them or to make them expert technicians. It is to unsettle their minds, widen their horizons, inflame their intellects, teach them to think straight…." Thinking is not confined to the classroom.

> ❝ *The atmosphere of shared intellectual excitement is what I have missed most since I left the University of Chicago.* ❞

A student's UChicago education is comprised of a common core of courses, free electives, in-depth study within a major or concentration, and opportunities for research, internships, and overseas study. This academic program allows for both freedom and flexibility while allowing students to develop shared experiences and languages of discovery.

The Common Core

The Common Core is a UChicago student's introduction to the tools of inquiry used in primary disciplines—science, mathematics, humanities, and social science. Instead of reading "about" Greek philosophers or Western economic theorists, the Core will take you directly to source materials so you can interpret the world for yourself. Designed by faculty and debated over decades, the Core aims to engage all students with the same fundamental questions and help them become familiar with the powerful ideas that shape our world. Not all students read the same texts; they choose among a variety of options in nine areas of study: Civilization Studies, Physical and Biological Sciences, Mathematics, Social Science, Humanities, Arts, Foreign Language, and Athletics. Students continue work in their major having discovered new academic passions and, what's more, having learned how to walk 360 degrees around an idea to understand its nuances and complexities.

Majors

With the help of an academic adviser, students navigate through the Core and begin taking classes in their chosen major. That said, they don't have to declare an official major until the beginning of their third year. UChicago grants the bachelor of science degree in 49 fields in the arts, humanities, natural sciences, social sciences, and in such interdisciplinary areas as biological chemistry, environmental studies, and cinema and media studies. The most popular majors are economics, biology, English, history, and political science. For students wanting even more interdisciplinary scope and flexibility, an interdisciplinary studies in the humanities major is possible. Students also have the opportunity to design personalized courses of study through a major in tutorial studies. Many students write a Bachelor's thesis and graduate with honors.

Electives

Indulge! Rounding out the academic experience are electives that allow students to choose from more than 2,500 classes in any department and, if the spirit moves them, acquire a second (or third!) major, or a minor in one of more than twenty fields. Perhaps you'd like to take an anthropology class about pirates—yes, pirates—and learn all about piracy, from the lore of swashbucklers to today's music industry! Electives are perfect for UChicagoans who crave ideas!

Study Abroad

Through study abroad, The University of Chicago extends its classroom to the ruins of Athens, the temples of Beijing, the mountains of Cape Town, and the museums of Paris. You'll have the opportunity to gain fluency in a local university, or join twenty-four other UChicago students and faculty members as you complete your Civilization Studies requirement. Civilizations programs are in Athens, Barcelona, Beijing, Cape Town, Jerusalem, Oaxaca, Paris, Pune, Cairo, Rome, and Vienna. Together, you and your twenty-five peers will explore the city and region, taste local cuisine, discuss art, hear music, and become lifelong friends in the process. You'll also establish lasting relationships with the faculty, as they share the cities they know and love. Cities with active alumni associations offer further opportunities for engagement.

Study at UChicago's centers in Paris or Beijing. The College and its French counterparts offer a broad range of courses in French and English. A dozen faculty come to the Center in Paris each quarter to teach programs that maintain the high academic standards of the college and integrate students into their learning and city exploration. Yearlong students enroll in French universities, including Sciences Po and University of Paris–Diderot, the largest university campus in the city, conveniently located near the center.

The university's newest center in Beijing promises to link its intellectual community with Asia as the Center in Paris does with Europe. An exciting range of programming is scheduled for 2010–2011, including a Civilization program in partnership with neighboring Renmin University.

If those offerings aren't enough, students can design their own study abroad through a university-funded Summer International Travel Grant. These were born out of the college's commitment to cross-cultural experience, international research, and foreign language acquisitions. In the past, students have conducted research at burial sites from fourth and fifth dynasties in Egypt and learned Chinese to complement their study of biochemistry.

Participants in the study abroad program remain fully registered in the college and retain their financial aid eligibility during the regular autumn, winter, and spring academic quarters. Financial aid packages are extended to take into account the program fee when a UChicago student studies abroad on a college program.

SOCIAL LIFE AND ACTIVITIES

Campus Activities

Even with the delights and demands of academic life, UChicago undergraduates find time to participate in more than 400 Registered Student Organizations (RSOs). *The Chicago Maroon*, one of three student newspapers, got its start in 1892, the year classes began. The Model United Nations Team, Debate Society, and College Bowl Team have all won awards, some at the international level. Model United Nations even hosts an award-winning conference for more than a thousand high school students who descend annually on the Palmer House Hilton for a weekend of intensive meetings simulating the activities of the U.N. Improvisational social satire—the brand of wit made famous on *Saturday Night Live*—got its start here and thrives in the Off-Off Campus improv group. Other clubs range in variety from "anime" to community service, to hot chocolate appreciation. UChicago's extensive intramural and club sports program draws in more than seventy percent of students, and the varsity sports program offers nineteen men's and women's teams at NCAA Division III level.

Another focal point of campus life is the residential house system. Each student is guaranteed housing for four years at Chicago, and students choose from among eleven residence halls.

Fine and Performing Arts

There is no shortage of artistic energy in Hyde Park. Five hundred student actors, playwrights, designers, producers, directors, and technicians stage thirty-five plays annually through University Theater. Any student can audition for any role in any play; a science major can direct a show, and classes on acting and directing are taught by professionals active in the Chicago theater scene. The student-run University Theater has internship programs with two professional theaters: the univesity's professional and critically acclaimed Court Theater and the Steppenwolf Theater. WHPK 88.5 FM, a student-run radio station, offers a dizzyingly eclectic variety of programs, from avant-garde rock to political commentary. The music scene is just as broad; many students join the University Orchestra, the Chamber Orchestra, the University Chorus, jazz and wind ensembles, classical and gospel choirs, and Motet Choir, which makes an annual tour during spring break. There are several student-run *a cappella* singing groups, including Voices in Your Head, Run for Cover, Men in Drag, and Rhythm 'n Jews. The university is home to DOC (Documentary Film Group)—the oldest film society in the country, which shows at least one movie every night and more on the weekends. Fire Escape Productions is the filmmaking arm of DOC. Their productions are mostly shorts, but in 2002, a group of students who were members of Fire Escape Films completed a project they were working on before graduating entitled *A Girl Named Clyde*, which went on to receive critical acclaim at several independent film festivals. Thanks to a generous gift, The Reva and David Logan Center for the Creative and Performing Arts is slated to open in the spring of 2012, ushering in an even more vibrant era for the arts at UChicago.

Festivals and Traditions

Proud UChicago maroons are driven by tradition. There are a number of major festivals during the year, including Blues n' Ribs, The Humanities Open House, Kuviasungnerk, Summer Breeze, and the Folk Festival. Kuviasungnerk, a week during January, is an attempt to beat the cold by getting outdoors at six o'clock in the morning. Hundreds of students attend various activities, including aikido classes led by sociology professor David Levine. On the final day, this class takes place outside on the shores of Lake Michigan. Until 9:00 A.M., one can get free hot cocoa, coffee, and doughnuts from a stand in the center of the quads. Those hardy souls who come every morning earn a T-shirt that proclaims, "I survived Kuviasungnerk!" Summer Breeze, in contrast, is a week of games, dances, and blues and rock performances by acclaimed musicians and bands, and free drinks of all kinds. It is sponsored by the student-run Major Activities Board, which has brought such acts as Kanye West, Nas and Damien Marley, and Cake to campus, as well as comedians such as Demitri Martin, John Oliver, and B. J. Novack. The Folk Festival draws together performers from around the country and students from throughout the university for a weekend of performances, master classes, and jam sessions. The annual Scavenger Hunt, affectionately called Scav, is a huge four-day-long event that has teams, typically whole houses, circling the Henry Crown Field House with paper clips, shaving their heads, and driving to other states to retrieve items ranging from circus elephants to Canadian traffic signs in an attempt to collect over 400 items.

Athletics

From their Big 10 football powerhouse days to their enduring commitment to the scholar-athlete, UChicago boasts a rich history in campus and intercollegiate athletics. Over 400 honors were given to the nearly 600 students who played on their nineteen men's and women's NCAA Division III varsity teams last year. Meanwhile, whether star athletes or novices, all students get in on the action through over 500 intramural teams, sport clubs, and the state-of-the-art Ratner Athletics Center. Rather than distract from the educational experiences, the University of Chicago believes that academic and athletic excellence can complement one another. During the past few years UChicago teams, student-athletes, and coaches have met that challenge. UChicago student-athletes are students first, and maintain grade point averages within a tenth of a point of the average student GPA.

Greek Life

About ten percent of students on campus choose to take part in Greek Life, with fourteen fraternities and six sororities on campus. Students participate in various events on campus, including serving as the judges and coordinators of the Battle of the Bands (the winner opens for the musicians at Summer Breeze), the Inter-Fraternity Cook-off, Mr. University (a male beauty pageant), Anchor Splash (relay races in our Olympic-size swimming pool), and Piano Bar Nights—all to support their philanthropies.

Coffee Shops

Campus coffee shops foster UChicago's distinct conversational social life. The coffee shop in the Divinity School is run by graduate students who use the proceeds to underwrite their expenses and provide scholarships to needy students. Food from many of the ethnic restaurants in Hyde Park, including Thai, Mexican, and Middle Eastern dishes, is served. Being in the basement, the student coffee shop has a close and shadowy feel conducive to heartfelt talk. It also sells mugs and T-shirts that boast: "The Divinity School Coffee Shop—Where God Drinks Coffee." The Classics coffee shop offers its food and drinks in a wood-paneled space that has a very high ceiling and a row of high windows that welcome an abundance of natural light. The Reynolds Club is home to lounges, theaters, a marketplace, offices of numerous student organizations, and pool tables located in the coffee shop, Hallowed Grounds. Hallowed Grounds (formerly Uncle Joes) also functions as a concert venue for local bands, *a cappella* groups, and Open Mic Nights sponsored by the Festival of the Arts student organization. Along with the first floor Einstein's Bagels, which serves milkshakes for one dollar every Wednesday, it is open until 2:00 A.M. for night owls.

Community Partnerships and Service Learning

The university is in the heart of the South Side of Chicago, an economically, ethnically diverse region of the city. The Community Service Center was started by students in the early 1990s. The center links hundreds of students with volunteer opportunities around the city. A tutoring program run by the Blue Gargoyle facilitates weekly one-on-one meetings between university students and children who need help in school. Actors from University Theater perform and lead workshops in local schools. Student-teachers run an after-school program with three local schools, where students teach reading and creative writing in discussion courses that they themselves design.

Habitat for Humanity regularly brings together large groups of students to build or repair homes, and a program called "Turn A Lot Around" puts students to work alongside residents in cleaning up vacant lots and transforming them into gardens. Check the University Community Service Center Website for more details.

Housing

The House System at the University of Chicago is composed of 35 undergraduate Houses spread across ten residence halls. The House is the basic unit of community life; it serves as a "home base" for students, a place where they can relax, study, spend time with friends, and talk big ideas into the early hours of the morning. A House consists of a group of seventy students (on average) sharing a cluster of individual rooms and common areas within the residence hall. Each House has its own designated "House Tables" in one of the campus dining commons, so residents always have a place to sit and dine with friends, if they wish. Weekly House meetings and active House Councils bring students together for cultural activities, fundraising, intramural sports, and activities downtown and in Chicago's myriad neighborhoods.

In addition to House Resident Advisers, each dorm has a Master, usually a senior faculty or staff member, and each House has a Resident Head, usually a senior graduate student. The masters and resident heads host discussions, trips downtown, and study breaks for the dorm. The resident heads, many of whom are married, provide a steadying influence, and if there are children or pets (often house mascots), their goodwill can be great company!

The university guarantees housing for four years. Dorms range from the newest building, South Campus Residence Hall, with its apartment-style living and view of the downtown skyline, to the neo-Gothic Burton-Judson, connected contiguously around grassy courtyards. Max Palevsky, to the North of the Main quadrangle, is one of the largest dorms, with suite-style living, laundry rooms, study rooms, lounges, community kitchens, and a concert venue, although only the latter is atypical for the dorms.

Because students enjoy dining hall menus so much, some students that choose to move off campus will purchase a meal plan. With salad bars, kosher dining, pizza, vegan/vegetarian, and even soft-serve frozen yogurt, campus dining continues to be a viable option for students living both on and off campus.

Chicago—the City

The city of Chicago is yours to explore at all hours, in countless ways. Experience the cultures and cuisines of its seventy-seven distinct neighborhoods. Chicago is one of the original jazz and blues centers of the nation—those with a taste for blues should visit the Checkerboard Lounge. The Chicago Symphony is world class; tickets to concerts at the newly renovated Orchestra Hall are inexpensive and easy to get, whether for full orchestra concerts or intimate chamber music. The major theaters (the Shubert and the grand old Louis Sullivan-designed Auditorium Theater) put on new and classic plays and musicals. The Chicago Shakespeare Theater is widely acclaimed. There is also an array of small inexpensive, experimental theaters, several founded by University of Chicago alumni on the north side, where one can see *Too Much Light Makes Baby Go Blind* or an avant-garde production of Aeschylus' *Agamemnon*. Chicago is also a city that loves to eat: Chinese (try dim sum at Hong Minh in Chinatown) or Japanese, Thai (four restaurants in Hyde Park alone!), Korean, Vietnamese, Polish, Italian, Indian, French, Cajun, or down-home American. Students with a taste for professional sports have options year-round, from the Chicago Bulls to the Bears, the Cubs to the White Sox, and the Fire to the Blackhawks, 2010 Stanley Cup Champions.

> **❝** *It's been years since I left the U of C, but the performances of Shakespeare's* Othello *and Sophocles'* Elektra *that I saw at Court Theater still live in my memory.* **❞**

Hyde Park

Located just seven miles directly south of the loop (downtown Chicago) and along the shores of Lake Michigan, UChicago's neighborhood, Hyde Park, is home to almost all of its students, two-thirds of its faculty, and, unofficially, the President of the United States. Here, you can stumble into independent bookstores, sample a variety of restaurants, catch up with friends over coffee or gelato, and play at parks and beaches. It is the ideal place to branch out on your own while also remaining grounded in UChicago's close knit, diverse, and intellectually vibrant community. Forty percent of students choose to live off-campus during any given year, although they tend to stay within the Hyde Park area, close to campus, as well as to the sixty percent of faculty members who call the neighborhood their home.

Neighborhood cultural attractions, such as the Museum of Science and Industry, the DuSable Museum of African-American History, and the Hyde Park Art Center, complement the rich array of on-campus attractions like the Oriental Institute Museum, the David and Alfred Smart Museum of Art, the Court Theater, and the Renaissance Society. By bus, train, car, or the university's own shuttle service, downtown Chicago is just fifteen minutes away. Whether students are visiting the festivals, shops, and theaters around the city, exploring Hyde Park's tree-lined streets, or absorbing the neo-Gothic architecture of campus, they continue to live the "life of the mind" for which the university is deservedly famous.

FINANCIAL AID

UChicago provides aid according to demonstrated need, the difference between your educational costs and the amount you and your family can afford to pay. Moreover, it guarantees to meet all of your demonstrated need, and it does not consider your financial resources when deciding whether or not you will be admitted to the college. Applicants who are not U.S. citizens, Canadian citizens, or U.S. permanent residents should visit the website to review the university's policies for international students.

Odyssey Scholarships

Odyssey Scholarships replace federal student loans with scholarship funds for eligible students. The program supports all current and incoming students whose families earn less than $75,000 per year. Scholarship awards vary with income. In the class of 2013, nearly half of the students receiving financial aid were awarded Odyssey Scholarships.

GRADUATES

A degree from the University of Chicago can take you anywhere. Graduates work in government, business, law, academia, entertainment, and public service. As students begin to consider their opportunities and ambitions, the Career and Placement Services (CAPS) office helps students make the transition into the wider world. Their career counselors have information about a whole array of opportunities for further study or employment, in the public or private sector, whether for-profit or nonprofit, and they talk with students to help them figure what their ambitions are, what the next step after graduation should be, and how best to present themselves and their credentials. The CAPS website (at *http://caps.uchicago.edu*) provides twenty-four-hour access to a range of information, including an internship database with more than 1,000 listings.

SUMMING UP

Even the very brightest do not run out of challenges at UChicago. Faculty members actually enjoy debating with their students and discovering new knowledge together. The diversity within the university is only complemented by diversity in the city of Chicago: music, theater, shopping, dining, museums, movies, parks, ethnic neighborhoods, night life, and Lake Michigan. These surroundings enliven UChicago's community, where learning, hard work, and thoughtful engagement are celebrated.

❑ *Jonathan Beere, B.A.*

PROMINENT GRADS

- Barack Obama, President of the United States of America
- Ed Asner, Actor
- David Auburn, Tony Award Winner, *Proof*
- Jay Berwanger, First Heisman Trophy Winner
- David S. Broder, *Washington Post* Journalist
- David Brooks, Op-Ed columnist, *The New York Times*
- Henry Steele Commager, Historian, Author
- Katherine Dunham, Dancer, Choreographer
- Milton Friedman, Nobel Laureate in Economics
- Katherine Graham, Former *Washington Post* Chairman and CEO
- Seymour Hersh, Journalist, Author
- Mike Nichols, Director, Actor, Producer
- Carl Sagan, Astronomer, Author
- Susan Sontag, Writer, Critic

UNIVERSITY OF MIAMI

Mike Lovett

University of Miami
Coral Gables, FL 33146

305-284-2211
Fax: 305-284-2507

E-mail: *admission@miami.edu*
Website: *www.miami.edu*

 Enrollment

Full-time ❑ women: 4,877	❑ men: 4,574
Part-time ❑ women: 545	❑ men: 374

INTRODUCING UNIVERSITY OF MIAMI

Palm trees blow gently in the breeze while macaws perch curiously on the branches of giant banyan trees. A manatee, astray from its home, sunbathes in the canal while mischievous ducks chase an ibis looking for food. Inside the buildings nestled in this lush, tropical setting, the serenity disappears into a bustling hotbed of activity. World-renowned geneticists are researching a cure for cancer. Budding journalists are learning to ask the right questions, and musical protégés take advice from Broadway masters including Jerry

Herman and Barry Brown. Located in Coral Gables, Florida, the University of Miami offers the quaint atmosphere of a city rich in history while positioned just ten minutes from a booming metropolis.

Approximately 10,500 undergraduate students call University of Miami (UM) home. Coming from 49 states and over one hundred foreign countries, the university boasts a diverse student population, and a stroll through the Whitten University Center (UC), the hub of student activity, displays this tapestry of cultural pride. On any given day, the UC patio is transformed into a stage for Cuban cuisine, Asian spoken-word poetry, or vibrant hip-hop dancers.

Ethnic heritage isn't the only thing that UM students take pride in. With a tradition rich in athletics, Hurricane sports bond students both on the field and off. "The U," as sports fans fondly call UM, is a powerhouse. Alumni, faculty, staff, and students alike, joined by the whole community, rally for the Hurricanes during baseball and football games, and bleed orange and green when the basketball team takes to the hoops. The university had the unique opportunity to see athletics play out under different stadium lights when UM's on-campus Lowe Art Museum, hosted "Game Face: What a Female Athlete Looks Like." This photographic exhibit was a portrait of women in sports, exemplifying the importance of Title IX and praising the strong, athletic woman.

The university's ability to blend academics with culture provides an environment that breeds higher learning and intellectual growth. With the launch of "UM Presents," an online portal highlighting all the cultural offerings on campus, the university community, as well as UM's neighbors, have a cultural smorgasbord at their fingertips. Promoting events including lectures from UM's renowned faculty to the Frost School of Music's annual extravaganza, Festival Miami, the variety of programs appeals to every taste.

10 Lessons Learned from the Dalai Lama

9 National Football and Baseball Championships—1982, 1983, 1985, 1987, 1989, 1991, 1999, 2001

8 Top States UM Students Hail from: Florida, California, Texas, New York, New Jersey, Massachusetts, Illinois, Pennsylvania

7 Residential Colleges—Mahoney, Pearson, Stanford, Hecht, Eaton, Apartments, University Village

6 Rockin' Concerts—Coldplay, Green Day, All American Rejects, John Mayer, Kanye West, Audioslave and more all have played at the BankUnited Center

5 Presidents in UM History—Ashe, Pearson, King, Foote, Shalala

4 Recent visits from Presidential Candidates—George W. Bush, John Kerry, Howard Dean, Ralph Nader

3 Literary Lectures—Toni Morrison, Maya Angelou, Eli Wiesel

2 Supreme Court Justice Appearances—Chief Justice John Roberts, Justice Edward Breyer

1 Billion Dollars—Raised during UM's Momentum Fundraising Campaign

Giving students the opportunity to learn and grow outside of the classroom is one of UM's best attributes, and it clearly enhances the academic experience. It is not unusual for faculty to offer a Thanksgiving dinner to students not traveling home for the holiday. Creating a home away from home, resident faculty in each of the residential colleges will often provide an oven to bake cookies in or simply help students adjust to life on campus. As seniors, students have created lasting relationships with their professors.

At a school like the University of Miami in a city like Miami, in one day students can learn about DNA or Shakespeare and parasail over Biscayne Bay or snorkel in coral reefs. Learning branches out far beyond the classroom as students explore the city and reach higher.

ADMISSIONS REQUIREMENTS

Applying to the college is an exciting time in any student's life. Perusing college brochures in high school guidance counselor's office and looking at university web sites on the Internet is a good way to research prospective schools. Upon opening an admissions brochure from UM, the bright school colors of green and orange and vibrant photos of college life will immediately spark your attention, as will the text listing all UM has to offer students now and, more importantly, their futures.

Meeting the Faces of UM

The first true step in the admissions process, meeting an admissions counselor, will only make you more eager to apply. UM routinely sends counselors around the country to meet with prospective students, and making an appointment is easy. By joining the mailing list through the admissions web site, high school students can see when the counselors will be in their area.

The Ideal Student

Admissions counselors will talk about UM's ideal student. The profile is someone who demonstrates academic talent and a strong sense of personal integrity and has a well-rounded secondary school experience, inside and outside of the classroom. They will also explain that UM receives approximately 21,845 applications every year but strives to keep the size of each freshman class small, around 2,000. The average weighted GPA of an incoming student is 4.2 and the median SAT scores range from 1220 to 1370 (based on 1600).

Students who took the ACT scored between 27 and 31 and 68 percent of incoming freshmen ranked in the top 10 percent of their high school class.

The numbers may appear a bit intimidating, but the admissions team looks for well-rounded individuals with a strong personal statement and superior recommendations from their guidance counselors.

Down and Dirty with Applications

After the nerves of applying settle; its time to get down to the busy work. By logging on to the admissions web site, students can find a downloadable application. At the university, there are three options to apply. Students can apply for Early Decision if UM is going to be the first choice; Early Action, which allows students to express serious interest in UM but keep their options open; and Regular Decision. The difference between the three is the timeline in which you learn your acceptance status: Early Decision coming in late December and Early Action and Regular Decision coming in mid-April. Here's a hint: Students who choose Early Decision generally get first pick at housing choices because they will have to mail in their enrollment forms and deposits before everyone else. So if you're absolutely sure of the college you want to attend, keep that in mind.

While applying to UM, students can also decide if they would like to enter into the Honors Program which demands a higher level of study and performance. Students who are accepted are required to have an SAT score of over 1300 and must be in the top 5 percent of their class.

The Campus Visit

Even though reading about universities is a good way to get the basics on what the campus has to offer, nothing can compare to the experience of visiting the campus and seeing first-hand the people and places that make up the institution.

After just a fifteen minute taxi ride from Miami International Airport, students arrive at Stanford Drive, the main entrance to UM, and the campus tour begins.

66 Greeted by a row of majestic palm trees, UM's campus looks more like Club Med than the stoic brick and mortar universities I was accustomed to up north. 99

As students explore campus hot spots like the food court, they'll be surprised to see the variety of offerings. Smoothie bars, sushi chefs, salad buffets, Starbucks, and taco stations were bustling with students.

The campus was hopping. Shuttles picked up and dropped off students at several busy locations. The shuttles, aptly named the HurryCanes, not only ran campus routes, but also transported students to and from a neighboring Publix grocery store, Shops at Sunset Place Mall, Crandon Beach, and Coconut Grove, a late night strip popular among college students.

> 66 *After meeting Megan, my admissions counselor, and then seeing the campus myself, I was all Hurricane.* 99

The admissions process at the University of Miami was easy to follow, and admissions counselors create a personal relationship with each prospective student they meet. After the first discussion, it's apparent that their phones, in-boxes, and doors are always open to any questions or comments applicants might have.

ACADEMIC LIFE

At the University of Miami, there are over 10,000 faculty, staff, and administrators whose main goal is to deliver an exceptional higher education experience. The Coral Gables campus, UM's home base, is the location for its two colleges and six schools that house over 120 bachelor's degree programs within eight undergraduate schools. In addition, the Coral Gables campus houses professional degree programs including the School of Law and School of Architecture. The Rosenstiel School for Marine and Atmospheric Sciences and Miller School of Medicine are located on separate campuses. Many schools require students to enroll in a double major. For example, students majoring in motion pictures through the School of Communication may also major in photography through the College of Arts and Sciences. During their time at UM, a 120-credit hour minimum must be fulfilled, which to a student can seem like an eternity, but four years go by fast, and students leave UM prepared to take on the world.

While attending UM, students typically take twelve to eighteen credits a semester, meaning a majority of students are working diligently to graduate in four years. Classes are small, with a fourteen-to-one student-to-professor ratio. Students usually chose credit hours based on the number of activities they might be involved in, hours worked as a student employee on campus, and classes needed to fulfill their requirements. With the help of an academic advisor, picking classes and staying on track became an easy task.

For some students, studying in Miami may seem like traveling to a different part of the world. International food, dance, clothing, and language pop up all over and are celebrated on campus. Researchers at the Miami European Union Center study how Europe's relationships with America, among other counties, shape the world today, politically and economically. Over at the Center for Hemispheric Policy, panels of experts discuss important issues facing Latin America today. Students are given a chance to interact with researchers and attend conferences and lectures that explore the world around them and leave UM prepared to enter the global market.

For students looking for a real international experience, UM's study-abroad program delivers an experience to last a lifetime. Featuring programs in twenty-eight countries, the study-abroad program whisks students away to the Czech Republic, Australia, England, Singapore, Trinidad and Tobago, Iceland, and Monaco to name a few.

The faculty at the University of Miami is among the best in the country. These knowledgeable individuals aren't just people who assign what seems like endless amounts of textbook reading and grade papers with an iron fist; they are movers and shakers in their professions and areas of research. The most interesting aspect of working with professors who are current practitioners is the blending of academics and real-life experience.

In several public relations classes, group projects were assigned where students were paired with a client (usually business members in our local community) and asked to develop a complete media strategy. This meant conducting focus groups and surveys in the community to find out about the public's knowledge of the client, creating promotional material for distribution, and presenting ideas and solutions.

Hands-on curriculum is evident all over campus. Students in the Frost School of Music have recording studios at their fingertips, and several times a year they sit in on master classes where their form is critiqued by leading entertainment professionals. Motion picture majors are required to write scripts, conduct casting calls, and shoot film to produce short movies. At the end of the spring semester, the Cannes Film Festival provides an opportunity for budding directors to showcase their works to the community. Select films are then taken to Los Angeles for a second premiere through a program that matches students to alumni working in the major movie studios in Hollywood.

○ **School of Architecture**
○ **College of Arts and Sciences**
○ **School of Business Administration**
○ **School of Communication**
○ **School of Education**
○ **College of Engineering**
○ **Philip and Patricia Frost School of Music**
○ **School of Nursing and Health Studies**
○ **Graduate School**
○ **School of Law**
○ **Leonard M. Miller School of Medicine**
○ **Rosenstiel School of Marine and Atmospheric Science**
○ **Division of Continuing and International Education**

UM also focuses on giving students a variety of options when choosing classes. This allows individuals to think outside of the box when picking classes. A biomedical engineering major might find him or herself in the actor's studio in Theatre 101. A finance major, opera major, and visual communications major might sit next to each other in an architecture class. Mixing students from all walks of life, with different interests and views, provides students with a melting pot of academic flavors. This classroom recipe increases student productivity as well as the exchange of ideas.

> *" Mixing students from all walks of life, with different interests and views, provides students with a melting pot of academic flavors. "*

SOCIAL LIFE AND ACTIVITIES

Students at the University of Miami will find out fast: New York might be the "city that never sleeps" but Miami is the city that never stops the party. And life at UM keeps that motto alive and well. At UM, students party in a million different ways, continuously redefining the word, and not just in the *Animal House* way. Students involved in Salsa Craze heat things up on the dance floor as they learn how to salsa, meringue, and samba twice a week in the University Center. Members of Delta Gamma, just one of the thirteen sororities on campus, participate in Anchor Splash, their annual fund-raising week by holding contests between different Greek and non-Greek organizations, including a "Mr. Anchor Splash" competition. The Rathskeller, UM's on-campus bar and grill, is the home of Hurricane watch-parties, comedy improv hours, and open mike nights. It's a great place to grab a pitcher and burger and hang with friends.

Campus Activism and Community Service

On the campus activism side of student life, UM offers a number of organizations and activities perfect for the community-service-driven individual. Students can visit the Smith Tucker Involvement Center (also known as The STIC) to look at the list of organizations UM has to offer or pop into the Volunteer Services Center to find out where they can help on campus and in the community.

Over 900 University of Miami students participate each year in the National Gandhi Day of Service. Planned by the Council of International Students and Organizations, this joint effort provides the opportunity to give back to the community. In one of the largest student-led volunteer service events in Miami-Dade County, UM teams up with students from other local colleges to volunteer at a number of locations including Citizens for a Better South Florida, the Community Partnership for Homeless, and Camillus House, a local soup kitchen.

Another initiative at UM is STRIVE (Serving Together Reaching Integrity, Values, & Engagement), a select group of University of Miami students that have formed a living community that focuses on leadership and civic engagement. Originating out of the Butler Volunteer Services Center, thirty-one students live together in on-campus apartments, studying and participating in a number of service- and leadership-driven activities. The program includes an academic component that requires students to take classes with curriculum that focuses on building a strong voice in the greater community and are paired with mentors in the faculty.

Athletics

If anyone has any questions about how much athletics are loved and cherished at the University of Miami, they only need to walk around campus during Homecoming weekend. Almost 3,000 alumni from around the country travel back to South Florida to join current students, faculty, and community members to celebrate the University of Miami's Homecoming festivities. UM's annual homecoming parade kicks off the Friday night pregame parties.

Following the parade is one of UM's most cherished traditions, the boat-burning ceremony on UM's own Lake Osceola, in the heart of campus. The boat-burning ceremony involves setting a wood boat on fire in the middle of the lake. The tradition states that if the mast breaks before the boat sinks, UM will win the Homecoming football game.

Football isn't the only sport Hurricane fans go crazy for. Crowds of students cheer on the basketball team at the state-of-the-art BankUnited Center, and each season the stands are packed as the baseball team takes the recently renovated diamond at Mark Light Field located in the Alex Rodriguez Park. Both venues are located on campus, just a few steps from the residential colleges.

Men's sports have a lot of bragging rights, but the women can definitely do their share of talking. Under the tutelage of Coach Katie Meier, the women's basketball team has made a statement in the Atlantic Coast Conference that they are a force to be reckoned with. Women's track also boasts all-star athletes including Lauren Williams, who was the 2005 World Champion, Olympic medalist, and was also honored as a Visa Humanitarian Athlete of the Year by *USA Track & Field*.

Intramural sports are also of big interest to UM students. Flag football and soccer games are played five days a week on the intramural field. The university's Equestrian Team competes in horse shows, displaying their skills in flatwork and jumping.

Life in the City of Miami

The University of Miami is located in the city of Coral Gables, a suburb of Miami-Dade County. For students, this means easy access to everything Miami has to offer. Downtown Miami, South Beach, Key Biscayne, the Design District, and the upscale shopping center Village of Merrick Park are a twenty-minute drive away. Fortunately for students without cars on campus, Miami and Coral Gables offer a number of safe, easy ways to get around town. With a little planning, students can ride the Metrorail (the university has its own stop), city trolleys, or UM's HurryCane shuttles, or use taxi services to any location in Miami.

> 66 *Students at the University of Miami will find out fast: New York might be the 'city that never sleeps,' but Miami is the city that never stops the party.* 99

Safety On Campus and Off

For parents who may worry about sending their kids away to a big city, they need not be concerned. The University of Miami has a number of programs, policies, and procedures in place to ensure students' safety as they find their way in and around campus.

When walking from residential colleges at night, blue light phones located around campus put students instantly in contact with members of UM's Department of Public Safety. Officers are on call to escort anyone around campus and are a constant and reassuring presence. Students hired through the Department of Residence Halls staff a desk in each residential college at night, checking in visitors, with photo I.D. required. This ensures that only students enter the buildings.

UM also takes a proactive approach toward ensuring students' well-being. Educational programs such as Pier 21, organized by the Center for Alcohol and Other Drug Awareness, teach alcohol awareness and responsibility to students. Through the counseling center, the university has a number of programs for students who might be feeling blue. The Student Health Center is opening for students who are under the weather or may just need a flu shot. The on-campus pharmacy provides quick and easy access to medication for students suffering from a cough or cold.

The Wellness Center provides programs for the mind and body. Students can sign up for yoga, healthy cooking classes, aerobic exercises, and a favorite amongst members, Butts and Guts, designed to tone your abs and behind! The Wellness Center is the best gym in town, and it's all yours if you come to UM. All of the various programs on campus are designed to promote a healthy lifestyle, as well as social and personal responsibility.

Looking tanned and toned in the 80-degree weather that comes during February may be a strong allure to students, especially those coming from the north; however, its important to touch on another weather-related phenomenon unique to Miami: hurricanes.

The University of Miami is well prepared to handle a hurricane of any intensity. Hurricane shutters adorn every residential college. Students are given food and beverage during hurricane warnings as well. Staff and administrators in each of the residential colleges keep students informed and aware of changes in the weather, and updates from the university president are e-mailed as new information arrives. Information is also posted on the school's web site, especially for parents who live outside of Florida. A hotline is in place for students, faculty, staff, and parents to call and find out the latest news.

> **❝** *I have personally been among the trained volunteers who answer the hotline live during and after a storm threatens and can assure prospective students and parents that the university is well equipped and well versed in their hurricane procedures. They go to incredible lengths to ensure that students are well fed and taken care of. Student safety is of the utmost importance.* **❞**

The university administration isn't the only arm of UM involved in hurricane preparation. CERT (Canes Emergency Response Team) is a student-led initiative that serves as a resource for the University and its Coral Gables neighbors during emergency situations such as a hurricane by delivering water and disseminating information to off-campus neighbors. This specially trained group also participates in drills designed to improve basic search and rescue procedures and sharpen the important skills of triaging, treating, and transporting victims. As hurricane season begins, these students are available to even help members of the community put up hurricane shutters.

FINANCIAL AID

It can also be useful to have a finance major sit next to you to tell you how to manage your student loans and financial aid packets each year. That kind of free advice can also be found at UM's Office of Financial Aid or by looking on the department's website.

The university works with students on a number of levels to provide the maximum amount of tuition assistance possible. Academic scholarships are awarded based on merit and are announced in students' acceptance letters. In 2005–2006, 86 percent of all full-time freshmen and 87 percent of full-time upperclassmen received some form of financial aid. The average freshman was given $23,188 to help pay for school. Need-based grants are awarded and need-based self-help aid such as student loans and jobs through college work-study are also available.

GRADUATES

If you think high school went fast, college races by at the speed of light. A blur of late-night cramming sessions at "Club Richter" or the Otto G. Richter Library, spring breaks on

South Beach, and football games at the Orange Bowl come rushing back as you step on stage to receive your diploma on the most important day of a student's life, commencement.

Over 2,400 bachelor's degrees were awarded in 2004 and just over 155,000 people called UM home in the university's eighty-year history. Alumni of the University of Miami are scattered across all 50 states and in 148 countries.

While alumni may have left Miami to make their mark on the world, UM is never far from their hearts. The Alumni Association works as a liaison between UM and alumni, reporting on their successes through the Miami Connection. Alumni groups such as the D.C. Canes, a group of alumni residing in Washington, D.C., hold frequent gatherings to watch athletic events and to network. Alumni weekly news is e-mailed out to subscribers several times a year letting UM grads stay updated on what's happening at their alma mater. Administrators at the university also travel around the country giving lectures and speeches about the vision and future of UM.

It isn't unusual for students to interact with grads who return to campus either. UM alumni often participate in career fairs, recruiting students nearing graduation. For example, when the Public Relations Student Society of America, a student group of public relations majors on campus, holds their biannual mix-ers, a quick glance around the room shows that about half of the attendants are UM grads interested in seeing their fellow Canes succeed in the profession.

If students need assistance jump-starting their career path, the university's Toppel Career Planning and Placement Center is the place to go. Toppel plays host to several major

PROMINENT GRADS

- Rick Barry, '65, Professional Athlete: UM's all-time leading scorer on the court, Barry is the only player in basketball history to win titles in the NCAA, NBA, and ABA. He is also inducted into the Basketball Hall of Fame.
- Gloria Estefan, '78, Entertainer and Producer: An internationally known superstar, Estefan produced No. 1 singles including "Rhythm is Gonna Get You."
- Roy Firestone, '75, Broadcast Journalist: A personality on ESPN's *Up Close*, Firestone hosts a variety of cable network specials as well.
- Jerry Herman, '53, Composer/Lyricist, A revered artist on Broadway, Herman created masterpieces including *Hello Dolly!* and *Mame*. Herman is the recipient of two Tony and Grammy Awards.
- Patricia Ireland, '75, Activist, She is former president of the National Organization for Women.
- David Alan Isaacs, '71, Producer, He created hit sitcoms including *Cheers* and *Frasier*, and also collaborated with writers for *MASH*.
- Duane Johnson, '95, Professional Athlete and Actor, Duane "The Rock" Johnson was a star wrestler in the World Wrestling Federation. He also starred in blockbuster movies that include *The Grindiron Gang* and *The Rundown*.

career fairs throughout the academic year as well as to workshops designed to help students by presenting resume critiques, holding mock interviews, and offering brochures and lectures on job-searching techniques. Toppel also supports CaneZone, an online portal where students can post resumes and search for employment opportunities. If students are exploring graduate school, they can also visit Toppel to research graduate programs, the application process, and admissions exams. These are free services available to students and alumni.

SUMMING UP

At the University of Miami, students will receive an educational experience that lets students dip their feet into political debates, cultural festivals, intellectual lectures, and athletic events, not to mention the Atlantic Ocean. Its dynamic, tropical location, world-renowned faculty, and the exceptional programs designed to enhance student life make UM a place where a high school student grows and matures into an adult ready to enter the professional world with sophistication and creative spark. The unique mix of tradition and innovation instills pride in students and inspires them to leave their own mark the moment they step on campus. When you graduate from UM, you don't become a statistic, you become part of the legacy, part of the UM family that bonds people from every walk of life. Ask any alumni of UM how this university bonds each student who crosses its campus in an indescribable way, and they're sure to say "You wouldn't understand; it's a Canes Thing."

❑ *Melissa Greco, B.S.*

THE UNIVERSITY OF NORTH CAROLINA AT CHAPEL HILL

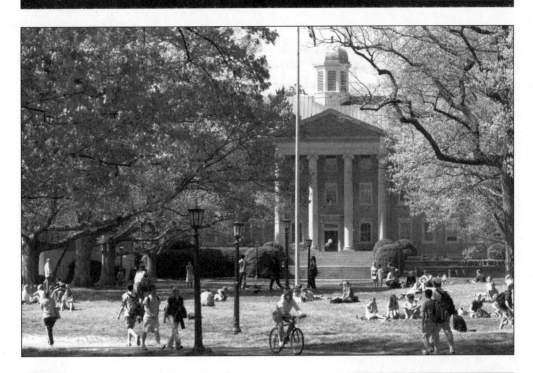

 The University of North Carolina
at Chapel Hill
Chapel Hill, NC 27599-2200

 Fax: (919) 962-3045

E-mail: *uadm@email.unc.edu*
 Website: *http://www.unc.edu*

 Enrollment

Full-time ❏ women: 10,374
❏ men: 7,139

Part-time ❏ women: 565
❏ men: 501

INTRODUCING THE UNIVERSITY OF NORTH CAROLINA AT CHAPEL HILL ▬▬▬

Carolina is a priceless gem, the birthplace of public higher education in America. World-renowned teaching and research, passionate student activism, first-rate athletics, all found at one of America's most beautiful college campuses, has made Carolina a destination for some of the world's best and brightest. In 1789, the same year George Washington became our nation's founding president; the University of North Carolina was chartered. Only four years later, Carolina became the first public university in the United States to open its doors. Now in its third century, Carolina has evolved from the nation's first public university to become a leading global university.

> **❝** *When I was looking at universities to apply to, I was searching for schools whose public service mission was just as strong as its academic mission. My college search came to an end the day I took my first step in the 'Pit,' the unofficial center of campus and heart of student activism, and I witnessed firsthand the student body's enthusiasm and passion for public service, for not only thinking but doing.* **❞**

Carolina recently opened the FedEx Global Education Center, a hub for international studies, and in the fall of 2007 Carolina's own Dr. Oliver Smithies demonstrated Carolina's global reach in winning the Nobel Prize in physiology or medicine. In 2003 UNC became the first university to guarantee that its neediest students would graduate debt-free when it established the Carolina Covenant. More than eighty colleges and universities worldwide have followed suit and adopted similar initiatives.

> **❝** *I love UNC. I love the quad in the spring and the arboretum in the fall. I love the Pit on a sunny day and Graham Memorial Lounge on a rainy one. I love Roy all the time. But what makes UNC truly special is not our beautiful campus, our distinguished reputation, or even our basketball team. It's us—the student body—who make UNC what it is.* **❞**

—*Eve Marie Carson, '08*

While Carolina has earned a reputation as a global leader in higher education, the university is first and foremost an institution of the people. With programs such as the Carolina Covenant, UNC has strived to make a college education affordable and relevant to all worthy students regardless of socioeconomic status. The university's commitment to the people of North Carolina and beyond is evident in not only the diversity of its student body but in Carolina's efforts through ground-breaking research to overcome society's most pressing challenges, from climate change to world hunger.

The Student Body

That commitment to solving the world's most daunting problems originates with the chancellor and the faculty, and permeates throughout the lifeblood of the university, the student body. It is not uncommon at UNC for students to join their professors in patenting an invention or publishing in a peer-reviewed journal. The Carolina environment fosters scholarly breakthroughs that are both bold and entrepreneurial in spirit. UNC consistently ranks among the top universities in the United States and is home to both a world-renowned business school and journalism school. About eighty-five percent of Carolina students graduate within five years after being exposed to a broad-based liberal arts education, completing a rigorous study in their academic major, and often studying abroad for a semester or two.

To say that Carolina students are engaged would be an understatement. Whether sleeping outside in the "Pit" to raise awareness of local homelessness or spending a summer in rural India redeveloping contaminated land, Carolina students serve both locally and globally to improve the lives of those less fortunate. When asked by former student body president Eve Carson to sum up in a phrase what makes Carolina so special, former Chancellor James Moeser replied, "Excellence with a heart." This is the Carolina Way.

The Campus

When not in class, the Pit, or the athletic field, you are likely to find Carolina students enjoying one of the most beautiful college campuses in the nation. While walking the winding brick paths, sitting on the old stone walls, or relaxing in the grassy tree-lined quads it's easy to understand why they call this place the "southern part of heaven." Rested atop North Carolina's rolling Piedmont hills in the college town of Chapel Hill, UNC students enjoy crisp October nights blanketed in the red, orange, and yellow colors of fall. A few light snowfalls are not unheard of during the winter, leaving a dusting of white across campus from the Bell Tower to the historic Old Well. It's not long until the chill of winter gives way to the blossoming of spring and students can be found sunbathing, tossing a Frisbee, or studying in the lush, green quads at the center of campus.

For students at Carolina education has no boundaries and no limits. The college experience is less about prerequisites, blue books, and double-majors, and more about curiosity, engagement, and progress. For those of you looking to spend all of your college years in a dorm room, a lecture hall, or a library, Carolina may not be right for you. Carolina students, faculty, and administrators live life in the fast lane and are engaged around the world. In sum, Carolina is about breaking down old barriers, discovering new truths, and never settling for anything less than "excellence with a heart."

Now that you are convinced you have Tar Heel fever and want to spend the next four years of your life in Chapel Hill, it's time to send in your application. Carolina's admissions process is competitive. Carolina receives freshman applications from roughly 23,000 well-qualified students every year from all parts of North Carolina, the nation, and the world. From this large group of applicants, Carolina chooses a small number of the most competitive students, aiming to enroll a class of roughly 3,900.

For those of you who are not Tar Heel Born or Tar Heel Bred and are instead applying from outside North Carolina, admission to Carolina is even more competitive. Out-of-state enrollment is limited to eighteen percent of the undergraduate class, or about 700 of the freshman spots any given year. Out of the approximately 23,000 students who apply every year for freshman admission at Carolina, more than 13,000 of these students are considered out-of-state for admission purposes. Approximately 2,800 of these students receive admission offers making an out-of-state offer to attend Carolina one of the toughest to come by in the country.

Fortunately, Carolina has a large and experienced staff that pores over applications, reading each application one by one. The admissions staff seeks students who excel not only academically but also in the arts, in athletics, in leadership, service, citizenship, and character. Now that you have a better idea of what you're up against, here's a rough guide on what it takes to get one of those thick envelopes containing your acceptance materials.

Academic Excellence

There is no single profile of an admitted Carolina student. However, if you want to earn an admissions offer from Carolina, a record of high academic achievement is a must. UNC requires that students complete specific high school course units as follows:

- four units of English;
- at least four units of college preparatory mathematics (two algebra, one geometry, and a higher level mathematics course for which algebra II is a prerequisite);*
- at least two units of a single foreign language;
- three units in science, including at least one unit in a life or biological science and at least one unit in a physical science, and including at least one laboratory course;
- two units of social science, including United States history

In order to make yourself a competitive applicant, it is recommended that you enroll in course levels beyond these minimum requirements. To be considered for admission, the university also requires that students have pursued college-preparatory work in high school, and the Admissions Office recommends that students take as many Advanced Placement or International Baccalaureate courses as possible. Carolina requires a high school diploma from an accredited institution and will not accept a GED or high school equivalency degree for freshman admissions.

In evaluating each applicant the Admissions Office also looks at test scores and class rank. Five students with perfect 1600s were among the 3,960 incoming freshmen in 2010. That class, on average, posted an SAT score of 1303, with out-of-state students averaging 1317 and in-state students averaging 1301. The following table provides a more detailed academic profile of Carolina's 2008 freshman class:

Combined SAT Score**	Percent of 2010 Freshmen Class
1500 and higher	5.5 percent
1400 to 1490	19.6 percent
1300 to 1390	30.4 percent
1200 to 1290	25.4 percent
1100 to 1190	13.01 percent
Below 1100	5.9 percent*

*Note: Students with an SAT under 1100 often are admitted because they have demonstrated outstanding ability in an area outside of testing.
**Based on total score of 1600 for SAT.

While the average SAT scores and class rank of the admitted class have been consistently rising, it is important to remember that admissions officers at Carolina don't base their decisions on test scores and grade point average alone. Carolina is unique from any other university in the country due to the energy, activism, and diversity of its student body. Leadership and public service exemplified in extracurricular activities, strong references, and a compelling essay will go a long way in convincing admissions officers you belong in Carolina blue.

ACADEMIC LIFE

Recognized as a "public ivy," Carolina ensures that all of its students receive a well-rounded education exposing students to both the hard sciences and humanities. At Carolina it's not unheard of for Physics majors to discover an appreciation for Bach and Handel while Business majors develop an understanding of evolutionary biology. The new general education curriculum, "Making Connections," was implemented at Carolina in the fall of 2006. The curriculum strives to cultivate the range of skills, knowledge, values, and habits that will enable graduates to excel in the rapidly changing and increasingly interconnected world.

Carolina students do more than sit in lecture theaters and take notes. Undergraduate students are encouraged and even expected to participate in faculty research or projects of their own design. Fortunately, Carolina's fourteen-to-one student-faculty ratio overall means professors are readily available to mentor their students in research. Recently, with the assistance of leaders in student government the Office of Undergraduate Research created the Carolina Research Scholars Program (CRSP). Participants in CRSP who successfully meet the program's requirements will be recognized for their contributions to UNC's intellectual and cultural climate with a designation on their transcript appropriately termed "Carolina Research Scholar."

> *As a sophomore, I took an honors seminar called Morality and Law with Professor Gerald Postema and then became involved in undergraduate research through a Summer Undergraduate Research Fellowship (SURF) from UNC's Office of Undergraduate Research. Since then, I have continued my research via independent study and other research grants and spent this past summer in South Africa conducting interviews with agents involved in the South African Truth and Reconciliation Commission.*

—*Diana Gergel, '09*

First-Year Seminars

If you were expecting to spend your entire first year of college in large 300-person lecture halls you will be surprised to learn that Carolina provides students with the opportunity to connect with faculty by offering dozens of intimate, engaging courses called First-Year Seminars. The classes typically are limited to twenty students or fewer and are available to only first-year students, so you won't have to compete with juniors and seniors for a spot. The seminars are taught by the university's most distinguished researchers and most skillful teachers, and focus on advanced, emergent, and stimulating topics ranging from "Biologists as Entrepreneurs" to "The Economics of Sports." You can check out more online at *http://www.unc.edu/fys*.

General College

Most first-year seminars fulfill course requirements in general education, which is composed of a host of courses students must take in the College of Arts and Sciences. All students spend their first two years in the General College where they must fulfill a number of requirements such as English Composition and Rhetoric, Foreign Language, Quantitative Reasoning, Lifetime Fitness, Physical and Life Sciences, Social and Behavioral Sciences, Humanities and Fine Arts, and a Connections requirement. The courses offered within each requirement are broad and diverse allowing each student the freedom to pursue his or her own unique path of study.

Students also can place out of some courses or use selected Advanced Placement and International Baccalaureate tests to earn credit. General College credits typically are earned during students' first two years, though some upper-level general education requirements are required during junior and senior years. To meet the requirements of the General College and complete their major on time, students typically carry a manageable course load of twelve to fifteen hours. Full-time students must obtain special permission to carry fewer than twelve hours or more than seventeen.

Majors

UNC offers more than seventy undergraduate majors in nine professional schools. Students typically declare a major heading into their junior year, though students who enter Carolina with college credit, place out of courses, or carry especially heavy loads may begin working on a major earlier. When declaring a major, undergraduates either remain in the College of Arts and Sciences or enter one of four professional schools (dentistry or medicine), as well as Kenan-Flagler Business School or the schools of education, information and library science, journalism and mass communication, nursing and public health. Students can double-major at Carolina or can pursue a major and two minors.

TOP TEN MAJORS

Top ten majors (in order of descending enrollment):
- Biology
- Business Administration
- Psychology
- Journalism and Mass Communication
- Political Science
- Exercise and Sports Science
- Economics
- Communication Studies
- History
- International Studies

Going Global

Over the past few years Carolina has made efforts to be recognized around the world as a leading global university. Today, Carolina offers its students the chance to choose from fifty-two different languages and take classes ranging from Mandarin to Swahili. Also, more and more students are taking advantage of the increased opportunities to study abroad or earn joint degrees with highly regarded institutions around the world. The new FedEx Global Education Center has brought international studies, resources for study abroad, and international research centers all under one roof.

For many Carolina students learning about another country or culture in the classroom is not enough. Fortunately, UNC has a strong study abroad program that enables students to tailor foreign experience to their academic pursuits and personal interests. Students can choose from more than 300 credit-bearing programs in seventy countries and can opt for a semester, a year, or a summer session abroad. UNC students have participated in programs all over the world, including China, Jordan, Spain, Cuba, South Africa, and New Zealand. Numerous programs provide internships and service learning opportunities abroad as well as specialized courses taught by UNC faculty or courses taught at a local university.

Carolina has one of the highest percentages among all U.S. public universities of undergraduate students studying abroad before they graduate—thirty five percent. Many students who did not study abroad while at Carolina have pursued international careers and fellowships following graduation from UNC. For instance, a total of 1,092 Carolina alumni have served in the Peace Corps.

Honors

Ranked one of the eight best in the country, the Honors program enables all Carolina students to choose from more than 120 honors courses in 30 disciplines. Accepted applicants are automatically considered for Carolina's Honors Program, which admits around two-hundred incoming freshmen each year. In choosing these students, the Honors Program considers performance on standardized tests (SAT or ACT) as well as high school course selection and grades. If not selected, there are opportunities during the first two years of college to apply to join the Honors Program. Also, students not in the Honors Program may enroll in Honors classes, and although students in the program get first shot at the classes, honors classes rarely fill up before they open to general enrollment. Students not in the program can still graduate with honors by maintaining a high grade point average, usually higher than a 3.2 but determined by individual departments, and by completing an Honors thesis senior year.

Walk around Carolina's campus on a warm April afternoon and you're likely to see dozens of students reading while lounging in the soft grass of Polk Place. Walk a little further to the Pit, the heart of campus, and you will see hundreds of students recruiting members for their student organization, passing out fliers for upcoming events, raising money for world hunger, or just chatting with friends between classes. Located between the student union, the main dining hall, the campus bookstore, and two libraries, the Pit is an ideal place to take a break, chat with friends, publicize a campus event, or just see what's going on at Carolina.

Once class has ended and the sun has set, students can be found walking along the sidewalks of Franklin Street, the main thoroughfare in Chapel Hill, which borders the campus on the north. While the Pit may be considered the center of campus society, Franklin Street is without a doubt the heart of town and campus social life. Whether it's grabbing a bite to eat at one of the dozens of restaurants or taking in the sights while perched on the balcony of Top of the Hill restaurant and brewery, students come to Franklin Street to kick back and have a good time.

Student Organizations

At Carolina students often take their involvement in student organizations as seriously as they do their studies. Carolina has more than 600 officially recognized student organizations, and if you still can't find one that fits your interests, it's easy to start your own. Social and political organizations such as the Young Democrats, College Republicans, and the Black Student Movement are very active on campus and sponsor events and initiatives open to all students throughout the year.

> ❝ It was a big jump to Carolina from my all-girls high school of just 450 students. But I can honestly say that this was never an issue for me. Within weeks of my arrival as a freshman, so many other students, many of them upperclassmen, reached out to me. There is also such a wide variety of incredible groups to join that you often find yourself making lifelong friends even as you are working together for an important cause. ❞

—Monique Newton, '09

The Campus Y, an organization that works to promote social justice, and UNC's independent student government are two of the largest student groups. Student Body President elections, held every February, are often fiercely contested and candidates and their campaign teams have been known to pull out all the stops to earn the student body's support. While Carolina is known for the political activism of its students, groups such as CHiPs, specializing in improv comedy, and the Clef Hangers, an esteemed group of male *a capella* singers, have entertained generations of Tar Heels.

Student Press

Carolina's politically active campus wouldn't be what it is today if it were not for the vigorous student press, namely, *The Daily Tar Heel*, covering every action and reaction on campus. The campus's award-winning, independent student newspaper, commonly referred to as the DTH, circulates 20,000 free copies each publishing day making it one of the largest college dailies in the country. It has produced storied alums such as author Thomas Wolfe and Charles Kuralt of CBS. Carolina also has several publications funded through student fees, including *Blue and White* magazine, *The Carolina Review,* and *BOUNCE,* Carolina's satirical magazine. The journalism school also produces a mostly student-run, award-winning television broadcast program called *Carolina Week.*

Community Service

When students aren't in class, chatting in the Pit, or eating on Franklin Street you may find them hammering nails with UNC's Habitat for Humanity chapter or tutoring local children with one of the Campus Y's many active committees. The APPLES Service-Learning and the Public Service Scholars programs provide students with the opportunity to take courses that require off-campus community service and integrate what they learn in the classroom with the experiences students have while serving the community. Carolina's largest annual student fund-raiser, Dance Marathon, is a twenty-four-hour dance marathon. In 2010, more than 1,000 dancers raised $421,851 for the N.C. Children's Hospital—a record for the event. The marathon involves hundreds of students from across campus, and many fund-raisers are held throughout the year by members of the Greek Community.

Greek Life

The Carolina Greek Community is active both socially and in the local community sponsoring fund-raisers, charity auctions, and other service projects each year. Fraternities and sororities also sponsor various 5Ks and are well known for hosting several large parties thrown on the last day of classes. The Greek system, composed of fifty-four different Greek organizations and approximately 2,900 undergraduate students, draws about fifteen percent of Carolina students. From mixers to semiformals, fraternities and sororities provide students with a great way to socialize and meet new people. However, you don't have to go Greek in order to maintain an active and exciting social life at Carolina.

Athletics

Imagine running with a few thousand other Tar Heels from your Hinton James residence hall past Kenan stadium, through Polk Place, past the Old Well, and finally to Franklin Street. You are quickly joined by tens of thousands of other screaming Carolina fans in the singing of "Hark the Sound," Carolina's Alma Mater. Make it into Carolina and what you have just imagined is likely to become reality following a Carolina victory over Duke in men's basketball. The Tar Heel Nation lives, breathes, and dreams basketball. Led by Hall of Fame Coach Roy Williams, the Tar Heels run an exciting up-tempo offense, which helps create an electric atmosphere while playing at home in the always intimidating Dean E. Smith Center, widely known as the Dean Dome.

With basketball season lasting only a few months out of the year students are fortunate to have a host of other sports to cheer for and play. UNC teams compete in the Atlantic Coast Conference in twenty-eight varsity sports. While the men's soccer team recently competed for a National Championship and the football team has recently secured a top-ten recruiting class, it would be hard for these teams to match the success of the women's soccer and field hockey teams. The women's field hockey team has appeared in the NCAA tournament twenty-six times, while the women's soccer team, led by Hall of Fame Coach Anson Dorrance, has won nineteen national titles and developed athletes such as soccer celebrity Mia Hamm. The program has twenty-one of the most devoted followings of any Tar Heel team, leading the nation in women's soccer attendance five times since 1998.

For those students itching to get out on the soccer field, track, or back into the swimming pool, but are not up to meeting the demands of a varsity team, you are in luck because Carolina has dozens of intramural and club sports teams, including the highly competitive men's and women's club rowing and soccer teams. For those athletes who played competitive sports in high school and enjoy traveling, UNC's club teams offer a wealth of opportunities. Club teams typically have routine practice schedules and are relatively well funded through student fees and fund-raisers. However, for those students who aren't big fans of practice, intramural sports provide additional options. The campus offers numerous well-maintained intramural fields, tennis, volleyball, and basketball courts, ropes courses, a golf course, miles of paths and trails, two pools, and state-of-the-art workout facilities.

Town and Gown

Centuries-old homes, family-run businesses, progressive politics, and a close-knit community of about 50,000 people form what has been deemed a quintessential college town, Chapel Hill. After class many students can be found heading west down Franklin Street to the small neighboring town of Carrboro to retreat to their apartments, lounge on the grass outside Weaver Street Market, or enjoy Carrboro's thriving arts scene.

It's also not uncommon to see students heading east on Franklin Street on their way to Interstate 40. I-40 runs through Chapel Hill and can be used to reach downtown Raleigh, the state capital, in about thirty minutes or in Durham, home of Duke University, in ten minutes. Chapel Hill-Carrboro, Durham, and Raleigh make up what is known as the Triangle region of North Carolina, home to more than one million people. As part of the Triangle, Chapel Hill is located only a short drive from Raleigh-Durham International Airport and the internationally renowned Research Triangle Park.

FINANCIAL AID

Carolina is consistently named a best bargain in national publications, meaning it offers an excellent education for a comparatively low price. While most Carolina students argue they get the best bang for their buck, a Carolina education would still be too costly for some students if financial aid and scholarships were not readily available. Fortunately, UNC is committed to meeting one hundred percent of students' demonstrated financial need in order to ensure that every qualified student has a shot at a Carolina education, regardless of their finances. The university does so with a combination of scholarships, loans, and federal, state, and university grants, and private gifts.

Students who apply for admission are automatically considered for merit-based scholarships. If you wish, you may provide supplemental material for the Robertson Scholarship. UNC also sponsors National Merit Scholars; if you're a National Merit Finalist, you'll need to indicate UNC-Chapel Hill as your first choice in order to qualify. For more information on two of Carolina's most prestigious privately funded merit scholarships, the Morehead-Cain and Robertson Scholarship, please visit *http://www.robertsonscholars.org*

or *http://www.moreheadfoundation.org*. To apply for need-based aid, submit the Free Application for Federal Student Aid (FASFA), and the CSS/PROFILE no later than March 1. Both forms are available online on the FASFA and College Board Web sites.

More information about aid at Carolina can be obtained on the Web site for the Office of Scholarships and Student Aid at *http://studentaid.unc.edu/studentaid*. You can also contact the student aid staff Monday through Friday from 9 A.M. to 4 P.M. at (919) 962-8396. The staff is eager to answer your questions and the office's director, who was a first-generation college student, is a national leader in the effort to increase access for students with financial need.

Carolina Covenant

Carolina set the bar high for universities across the country aiming to provide qualified low-income students with a debt-free education with the establishment in 2003 of the Carolina Covenant. The Carolina Covenant is Carolina's promise that its neediest students graduate without the heavy burden of loans. The Covenant funds the full financial need of each scholar for four years with a combination of scholarships, grants, and work-study jobs. Carolina graduated its first class of Covenant Scholars in May 2008. To be considered for the Covenant, fill out the standard financial aid forms. Students whose parents' adjusted gross income does not exceed two-hundred percent of federal poverty guidelines (based on family size) will automatically qualify for the Covenant. You can find out more and view profiles of Covenant recipients online at *http://www.unc.edu/carolinacovenant*.

GRADUATES

While the more than 250,000 living Carolina alumni are no longer students at UNC, they're Tar Heels for a lifetime. After graduating from Carolina, Tar Heels often look for the next opportunity to learn and grow, whether it's through graduate school at internationally acclaimed universities such as Harvard, Stanford, Yale, or Carolina's own graduate programs. Other students choose to enter the working world and join world-renowned organizations such as SAS, Goldman Sachs, and the National Institute of Health. Forty-five Carolina graduates have gone on to win Rhodes Scholarships, and in 2010, fifty-five graduates joined the ranks of Teach for America, making Carolina the sixth largest source of graduates chosen by the organization.

SUMMING UP

Attending Carolina is not an experience; it's an adventure. Each fall thousands of students from across the country begin their journey from admitted applicant to engaged and impassioned Tar Heel. Carolina students tackle some of the world's most pressing problems through research and debate, service and engagement, leadership and compassion. Always pushing full-throttle, Carolina students are active inside and out, in the classroom and in the lab, on the athletic field, and in the community.

Students at Carolina receive a world-class education, experience collegiate athletics at its finest, and form relationships with classmates who make up one of the most diverse student bodies in the country. As the nation's first public university, Carolina remains committed to being the university "of the people" and therefore educates students from all walks of life at a rate affordable to all those who qualify for admission.

Carolina provides not only an education but rich experiences, unforgettable memories, and life-long friendships. At Carolina expect not only a quintessential college experience but a wild ride full of late night study sessions and even later nights on Franklin Street. Expect to be not only a listener but a debater, not only a thinker but a doer, not only an activist but a leader paving the way for the millions of Tar Heels who have yet to reach the "shining light on the hill" we call Carolina.

❑ *Mike Tarrant, B.A.*

 University of Notre Dame
Notre Dame, IN 46556

 (574) 631-7505

 E-mail: *admissions@ND.edu*
Website: *http://www.nd.edu*

 Enrollment

Full-time ❏ women: 3,865
❏ men: 4,491

INTRODUCING NOTRE DAME

Every year in late August, freshmen converge upon Notre Dame's campus in South Bend, Indiana, rushing from one freshman orientation event to the next. During the many dances, activities, and the Orientation Mass, a certain phrase resonates throughout the campus: "the Notre Dame family." This one phrase, which has a slightly different meaning for each student and alum, is a distinctive element of the University of Notre Dame.

> ❝ *I experienced 'the Notre Dame family' immediately during my initial days at the university. I first sensed the friendliness among the students when my parents and I arrived on campus. As we pulled up to my dorm, a number of my hallmates descended upon our car, fully packed with all the essentials for college, and helped us carry all my stuff to my room. But the Notre Dame family is more than just friendliness; the campus has a sense of togetherness to it. During those first days on campus my parents and I immediately felt at home in my new surroundings and we began to realize that my Notre Dame experience would not only be for me, but would include my parents in many ways as well; they too would become part of the Notre Dame family.* ❞

The phrase "Notre Dame family" embodies three of the main characteristics of Notre Dame: community, tradition, and Catholic heritage.

The campus setting makes it easy to foster a close-knit community. With its tree-lined paths and two lakes, the 1,250-acre campus seems to be isolated from the rest of the world. The university is located ninety miles east of Chicago and has more than 160 buildings on campus. The dorms in particular are an integral part of the campus and enhance the feeling of community. Seventy-six percent of students live on campus, and most remain on campus for three or four years.

Notre Dame's Catholic roots are a vital part of life at the university. Even the buildings on campus, such as Sacred Heart Basilica, the Grotto, and "Touchdown Jesus" on the side of the library, demonstrate the Catholic character and influence at the school. Eighty-four percent of Notre Dame students are Catholic, and the Catholic nature of the school is emphasized in all aspects of life at the university, including classes. In fact, one of the main social activities of the week for dorm residents and off-campus students is Sunday night mass in the dorm chapels.

The Notre Dame family can trace its roots back 165 years to when Fr. Sorin and his fellow Holy Cross religious brothers founded l'Université de Notre Dame du lac (Our Lady of the Lake) in three small log buildings. The campus has grown significantly since that time, but the strong desire to educate students in the classroom and beyond remains. By the time freshmen reach graduation day, they will realize that they are part of a unique group that extends beyond South Bend. And although the students may have different memories of what makes Notre

Dame such a special place, each will have been shaped in some way by the elements of the Notre Dame family.

ADMISSIONS REQUIREMENTS

The University of Notre Dame looks for students who are Renaissance individuals—intellectuals, leaders, athletes, artists, and volunteers. Basically, Notre Dame wants the best all-around students.

In a recent freshman class, 14,356 students applied for entrance, 4,112 were admitted, and 2,064 enrolled. On average, the students who enrolled graduated in the top five percent of their senior class; in fact, thirty-four percent ranked one, two, three, four, or five in their class.

As one recent Notre Dame grad put it:

> **"** *I remember attending a freshman orientation program with my entire freshman class and their families. The Dean of Student Affairs asked those students who had been valedictorians or salutatorians of their high school classes to raise their hands. As I looked around, I was surrounded by a sea of raised arms. That's when I realized my class was packed with students who were all accustomed to being number one.* **"**

So, how does Notre Dame evaluate all of the applications it receives every year? There are five areas on which students are judged: high school record, standardized tests, teachers' evaluations, extracurricular accomplishments, and the essays and personal statement submitted with the application.

From a student's high school record, Notre Dame considers the quality of the school's curriculum. Notre Dame recommends that applying students take four years of English, math, science, foreign language, history, and electives. The admissions counselors especially look at students who have pushed themselves by taking honors and AP-level classes, in addition to courses such as precalculus or calculus, chemistry, and physics.

Notre Dame also considers a student's class rank, grades, and the academic competition at the high school.

Standardized Tests

Notre Dame requires either the SAT or the ACT and candidly admits it places a great deal of emphasis on standardized tests. The mid fifty percent score ranges of entering freshmen are 1320–1500 (SAT, based on 1600) and 31–34 (ACT).

Recommendations

Because Notre Dame does not interview candidates, teacher recommendations are one way for the admissions counselors to learn about the applicants personally. Students should have a variety of teachers, who have worked with them extensively, write their evaluations.

Extracurricular Activities

As mentioned earlier, Notre Dame seeks enthusiastic students who have developed themselves inside and outside of the classroom; therefore, the university weighs extracurricular activities heavily. Students are judged on leadership positions in clubs and student government, school and community involvement, and special talents. Also, because service work is an important aspect of life at Notre Dame, the university looks for students who have volunteered at social service organizations such as nursing homes, soup kitchens, and day care centers.

Personal Statements

Finally, a student's essays and personal statements are thrown into the evaluation mix; these compositions are vital to providing the admissions counselor with an inside look at the student. For instance, one essay asks students to reflect on how a book, poem, play, or piece of music has influenced their lives. Also, Notre Dame requires two long essays and three shorter essays, which is more than many schools' applications.

Application Plans

Notre Dame has two application plans, Early Action and Regular Action. With Early Action, a good option for people who have exceptional grades and standardized test scores, applications are due the beginning of November. If admitted through Early Action, students do not have to withdraw their applications from other schools and they have until May 1 to inform Notre Dame of their decision. Most students still apply Regular Action, however, in which applications are due at the beginning of January.

International and Minority Students

The student body at Notre Dame is geographically diverse, representing all fifty states, more than 100 countries, and five continents. Notre Dame believes international students add a unique perspective to the campus and make the university an international center of teaching and research; however, due to the Catholic heritage of the school, Notre Dame is not as ethnically mixed as it would like to be. Only about twenty-one percent of the student body are minority students.

Similar to many highly competitive colleges, Notre Dame has made a serious commitment to recruiting minority students; for example, Notre Dame hosts two events every year to introduce minority students to life at the school. One is the Fall Open House, which has become a popular event for prospective students. Later in the year, after acceptances are sent out, Notre Dame brings admitted students and their families to Notre Dame for a three-day campus visit to help them with the decision process.

Women

Notre Dame also has increased the number of women in its student body. About five years ago, the ratio of men to women was three to one; now it is almost one to one. To accommodate the increased number of women students, Notre Dame converted some male dorms into female dorms and constructed several new residence halls.

Children of Alums

Part of the reason Notre Dame has maintained its traditions and family feeling is the fact that about twenty-five percent of the students are children of Notre Dame alums. Each year the university aims to admit the appropriate number of daughters and sons of alums to maintain this statistic.

Although it is not unusual to have three generations from one family attend the University of Notre Dame, my grandfather, father, and I share a unique experience in that we all graduated exactly thirty years apart ('34, '64, '94). And while it is true we had individual experiences and memories spanning over half a century, we share a timeless bond with every other member who makes up the much larger 'Notre Dame family': an overwhelming sense of community, tradition, and pride.

Visits

For applying students who wish to visit the campus, Notre Dame will arrange an informational meeting with an admissions counselor and an overnight stay in a residence hall with a student host. To get the feeling of attending Notre Dame, the prospective student sits in on classes and eats at the dining hall. The program is a great way for students to experience the campus and decide if Notre Dame is the right fit for them.

ACADEMIC LIFE

For many students, Notre Dame marks the first time they are required to question and articulate their feelings about their faith, social beliefs, and politics. No longer are students asked to simply regurgitate information as they did in high school; instead, as students learn world history, finance, and calculus, they begin to define themselves and what is important to them. A Notre Dame graduate once stated, "In the Notre Dame classroom, the spirit and the intellect culminate."

As a Catholic school, the university could easily expect that students believe only what the Catholic Church teaches, but often, the required theology and philosophy core classes force students to take a serious look at what they believe and why. The Notre Dame learning environment is a unique combination of faith and questioning.

The Colleges and Majors

Notre Dame is divided into five colleges: Arts and Letters (the largest), Business, Science, Engineering, and Architecture. Overall, the most popular majors are finance, psychology, and political science, with majors such as history and economics growing in popularity. Notre Dame also has a strong preprofessional studies program, which combine medical school prerequisite courses with a liberal arts major or additional science classes. Each college also has its own academic organizations and honor societies, including the Arts and Letters Business Society and the Management Club.

First Year of Studies

Before selecting a college, all students are enrolled into the First Year of Studies (FYS), a program created to help freshmen adjust to college-level academics. The FYS assigns each student an advisor, who guides students with course selection, choosing a college and/or a major, and with concerns about classes. The FYS center also provides students with tutors and study groups if necessary. Students must fulfill the core requirements of the FYS before they can enter sophomore year. Usually, students do not have any difficulty completing the required classes since approximately half of each incoming freshman class receives class credit for AP classes and SAT Subject Test scores.

Although taking calculus for a future political science major might seem like sheer agony, Notre Dame adheres to the philosophy of a well-rounded education, and offers its core classes as a way to achieve this purpose. For example, while in the FYS program, all students must complete one semester of Freshman Seminar and Composition and Literature (Comp and Lit). Freshman Seminar is a literature class that addresses any topic the professor selects, from reading Plato's *Republic* the entire semester to studying the subject of leadership through reading books about Ghandi. Comp and Lit is more of a grammar class that focuses on improving the overall structure of a student's writing through rewriting and peer evaluations.

By the end of their sophomore year, students are required to declare a major, but at this point, most students have created a program of study simply by taking electives that interest them.

College Seminar

If students declare Arts and Letters as their college, they are required to complete a unique course called College Seminar, a semester-long class with approximately thirteen to twenty students, guided by an Arts and Letters professor. Each course is built around the academic specialty of the instructor, but all explore the breadth of the liberal arts.

> 66 *My class was led by Professor T. R. Swartz of the economics department, a man of unmatched energy. The first action he took was to move our class from the uncomfortable, stiff chairs in O'Shaughnessy to the inviting lounge of a residence hall. Next, he limited our writing assignments to one page, exactly, no eight-point fonts and no wide margins. He forced us to write briefly, concisely, and weekly. Our class, a diverse group of students, became fast friends. No one missed class, and it was at 9:00 A.M., which is considered early in college. After an intense year of discussion and thought, T.R. told us, 'Choose a theme for your life. Find a purpose and direct your actions toward it.' Never in my life have such simple words had such a profound effect on me.* 99

Faculty

The majority of classes at Notre Dame have fifteen to twenty-five students. With classes that size and a student-teacher ratio of twelve to one, students and teachers develop close relationships, a crucial element of the educational experience at Notre Dame. Teachers often invite students to their homes for dinner to hold class discussions or simply socialize.

Academics at Notre Dame is a two-part machine, student and teacher, and when they are functioning in sync, they create the spirit of Notre Dame. Professors at the university guide their students, but allow them the necessary freedom to discover their interests and strengths.

Internships

Students have the opportunity to apply for internships that pique their interest, both on and off campus. For example, the local NBC affiliate, WNDU-TV, and the Notre Dame News and Information office offer internships to qualified students. Many students apply to be teachers' assistants their senior year, a rewarding experience that allows upper- and lower-class students to work together closely.

Study Abroad

Many students go abroad their sophomore or junior year. In fact, among research universities, Notre Dame has the sixth highest percentage of students engaged in international study programs. Some of the popular year-long programs are in Angers, France; Innsbruck, Austria; and Toledo, Spain. Students who participate in the year-long programs tend to go during their sophomore year and are required to take intensive language courses before they go. The favorite semester-long programs include London; Santiago, Chile; and Fremantle, Australia. All of the abroad programs are competitive to get into, so often students end up enrolling in other universities' programs, although it does sometimes affect class credit.

Physically Challenged Students

To further diversify Notre Dame academics, the university provides programs to accommodate students with disabilities. For example, students with challenges can get note takers, have extended time on exams, or use textbooks on disk to ensure equal access to all disciplines and facilities.

Libraries

Students also have access to over three million volumes in the ten libraries located on campus. Most of these facilities have late hours and are open twenty-four hours a day during exams. In addition, there are eight computer clusters throughout the campus, many of which are always open.

Because Notre Dame is a highly competitive college that requires students to put in long hours of studying, it is common to see students heading off to the library on Friday and Saturday nights to do class work. Notre Dame students are dedicated to their education and are willing to put in the extra hours on the weekend if necessary, even if they are only going to be studying on the extremely social second floor of the Hesburgh Library.

After four years of intense learning at Notre Dame, students are armed with the tools of the Notre Dame academic environment—independence, questioning, and discipline—and are prepared to commence learning in the real world.

SOCIAL LIFE AND ACTIVITIES

Students at Notre Dame are as busy with club meetings and sports during the week as they are with their normal course load.

Although Notre Dame does not have a Greek system, students reside in the same dorm throughout their stay at Notre Dame and are often identified by the dorm they live in. For example, it is common to hear students refer to each other by saying, "She lives in Walsh" or "He used to live in Carroll Hall." The dorms organize a large number of student activities, including volunteer tutoring at local schools, dinners with Brother/Sister dorms, and residence hall councils.

Athletics

Tradition is an important aspect of life at Notre Dame, and the most famous tradition at the university is football. From the "1812 Overture" played at the beginning of each game's fourth quarter, to the world's oldest marching band, to the legends of Knute Rockne and the Gipper, "Fightin' Irish" football is rich in tradition. Because of the team's national reputation, many believe Notre Dame is much larger than its average enrollment of 8,300 undergraduates. Overall, the Irish athletic programs annually rank among the top twenty in the nation for both men and women.

Intramural sports are very popular. Each dorm usually offers football (men), flag football (women), basketball, and soccer. Since the majority of students played varsity sports in high school, and many were captains of their teams, intramural sports are extremely competitive. In fact, Notre Dame may be the only school where students play intramural football wearing full gear. Women's flag football is equally competitive; injuries such as concussions, broken wrists, and cuts requiring stitches are not uncommon. In line with Notre Dame's love of football, the championship games for both of these football teams are played at Notre Dame Stadium.

After classes, students work out at the athletic facilities available on campus, including the Rockne Memorial (the Rock), the Joyce Center, Rolfs Sports Recreation Center, Rolfs Aquatic Center, and Loftus Center. Students are able to swim, run on tracks and treadmills, ride stationary bikes, lift weights, or participate in aerobics classes at these fitness centers. In addition, Notre Dame has a new Ben Crenshaw-designed golf course for students and alumni to play on from April through October.

The traditions of Notre Dame extend past the football season. Events such as the Keenan Review, a "talent" show performed by the residents of Keenan Hall; An Tostal, the student spring festival; Bookstore Basketball, the world's largest five-on-five outdoor basketball tournament; and the Blue and Gold game, the spring inter-squad football scrimmage, all contribute to traditional life at Notre Dame.

> **❝** *I spent the summer before my senior year living in a Jersey City homeless shelter for women and their children. I was given the opportunity to see the tough realities of the world. One woman I clearly remember was a twenty-year-old mother who was wise beyond her years, struggling to find a job while being supported by the welfare system. Through her I learned what really matters in life: unconditional love, trust, and spirituality. I didn't need to know anything else.* **❞**

Volunteering

On the non-athletic side, the Center for Social Concerns (CSC) runs more than thirty-five community service clubs that offer students the opportunity to participate in volunteer programs in the South Bend area, as well as across the country and around the world. About seventy-five percent of the Notre Dame student body participated in programs coordinated through the CSC, including Big Brothers/Big Sisters, Habitat for Humanity,

Neighborhood Study Help Program, and Recycling Irish. The CSC epitomizes the Notre Dame spirit. The center uses a holistic method by enhancing students' spiritual and intellectual awareness of today's social realities through service opportunities and seminars. The center also identifies volunteer programs to participate in around the country with service trips to areas such as Appalachia and the inner cities. In addition, each summer, more than 125 Notre Dame alumni clubs sponsor 200 Notre Dame students in Summer Service Projects around the United States. Said a recent graduate, who participated in a Summer Service Project while at Notre Dame:

Special Interest Clubs

Notre Dame has more than twenty special interest clubs including College Republicans, College Democrats, and Knights of Columbus. In addition, the university offers twenty-three ethnic organizations such as the African and American Student Alliance, the Hispanic American Organization, and the Korean Club.

Performing Programs

Although Notre Dame historically has not been known as a performing arts school, that is quickly changing, especially with the construction of the new DeBartolo Performing Arts Center, which opened in fall 2004. Students currently have a variety of programs to choose from. There are a range of music groups, from Shenanigans, a song and dance troupe, to the Liturgical Choir, and nine instrumental music groups, including Concert Band. If students are interested in drama, a number of different troupes put on performances throughout the year, including The Freshmen Four, St. Edward's Hall Players, and the Department of Film, Television, and Theatre, which produces four plays. The relocation of Actors From the London Stage to Notre Dame has prompted a surge in Shakespearean productions on campus.

Publications

For future Pulitzer Prize winners, Notre Dame has several student-run publications: *The Observer*, the daily newspaper; *Scholastic*, the weekly news magazine; and *The Dome*, Notre Dame's yearbook. All of these publications have positions for students interested in copywriting, design, and photography. Students with a strong interest in music have the opportunity to be DJs at WVFI-AM, the alternative music station, and WSND-FM, the classical music station.

Additional special annual events on campus include the Notre Dame Literary Festival, the Collegiate Jazz Festival, and the Black Cultural Arts Festival.

Weekend Activities

The weekends offer Notre Dame students plenty of social and recreational activities as well. In the fall, weekends are dominated by Notre Dame football games, both home and away. Students often have family and friends visit on these weekends to tailgate before the game, follow the marching band across campus, and dine by candlelight at the dining halls. Many people say that life at Notre Dame ends after football season, but, since Notre Dame has joined the Big East, other sports, such as men's and women's soccer, volleyball, hockey, lacrosse, and men's and women's basketball games, have become popular events. In fact, women's basketball games average 7,800 fans since winning the 2001 National Championships.

Although traditional dating is not common at Notre Dame, dorms host dances and formals throughout the school year.

Notre Dame does not allow hard alcohol in dorm rooms, and the university has strict penalties if underage students are caught drinking in the halls or carrying alcohol across campus. On-campus parties usually end by 2:00 A.M. when parietals, or visiting hours, end. As a university that is based on Roman Catholic values, Notre Dame has single-sex dorms and enforces visiting hours. If a student is found in a dorm of the opposite sex after parietals, there are serious consequences.

Upper-class students often host parties at off-campus student housing complexes, such as Campus View and Lafayette Square, or hang out at popular bars, such as Corby's and Legends, the restaurant/bar located on campus.

Many students enjoy dining out on the weekends at favorite local restaurants, such as Macri's Deli for sandwiches, Bruno's for pizza, Rocco's for pasta, and CJ's for burgers. Also, the Student Union Board (SUB) and the Snite Museum show recently released films on campus.

FINANCIAL AID

When compared to other Catholic and private universities that are nationally recognized for academic excellence, the overall costs for Notre Dame tend to be lower.

For a recent academic year, Notre Dame expected tuition and academic fees would be around $39,419, and room and board approximately $10,866. For books, students can expect to pay about $950 per year. To cut back on the cost of books, students often purchase course materials from each other or buy used books from Pandora's Books, located on the corner of Howard Street and Notre Dame Avenue, about three blocks south of campus. The university reminds students to expect costs to increase annually in order to maintain Notre Dame's solid academic environment.

As for personal expenses, the overall cost of living in South Bend is less than in other cities, but students typically spent $1,000 to $1,500 per year for incidentals as well as social and weekend activities, such as going out for dinner, movies, and other social activities.

In the last few years, the university has made aggressive efforts to substantially increase its financial aid funding.

According to Joe Russo, Director of Student Financial Strategies:

> **❝** *In 1990, Notre Dame had $5.5 million for financial aid, and in 2007, the amount increased significantly, to more than $78 million. We have now reached the point where every student who gets into Notre Dame can afford to attend Notre Dame and experience the Notre Dame family.* **❞**

This growth in funding stems from generous support from benefactors, programs including post-season football bowl games, the Affinity credit card (each time alums use their Notre Dame credit card, money is donated to Notre Dame's financial aid fund), the NBC contract to televise Notre Dame home football games, and licensing income from Notre Dame paraphernalia sold around the United States.

The Package

When a student receives financial aid from Notre Dame, the university works with the student and his or her family to create a financial aid package, often a combination of low-interest loans (Perkins Student Loans and Stafford Student Loans), scholarship money, and work-study. The university encourages work-study for students on financial aid to help cover their personal expenses. Options for on-campus employment include working in the dining halls, computer clusters, at the athletic department, and in the library.

Also, the Notre Dame alumni clubs across the country provide hundreds of scholarships annually, now totaling more than $2.5 million, to incoming students.

Grants and Other Options

As part of Notre Dame's efforts to increase the ethnic and socioeconomic diversity at the school, the university offers the Holy Cross Grants. These scholarship programs are awarded to students from disadvantaged backgrounds.

Other financial aid options include two-, three-, and four-year ROTC scholarships with the Air Force, Army, or Navy (includes Marines). These scholarships sometimes cover full tuition, and books, and provide a $150 monthly stipend. A little more than five percent of Notre Dame's students are on one of the above ROTC scholarships. In fact, Notre Dame's Navy ROTC unit is the second largest in the country (the Naval Academy is first).

To apply for financial aid, students are required to submit the standard Free Application for Federal Student Aid (FAFSA) and the PROFILE of the College Scholarship Service (CSS) by February 15, but are encouraged to file them as early as possible.

GRADUATES

Every home football game, Notre Dame alumni wander around the campus, remembering the days when the university belonged to them. Wearing their green shamrock-covered pants, they visit the bookstore, stop by concession stands, and stroll past their old dorms. As the current students pass the old alums on their way to tailgate, Notre Dame students promise themselves they will never become sentimental graduates, but when graduation day arrives, they find themselves reminiscing about their time at Notre Dame as well. The recent grads might be wearing jeans instead of plaid pants, but suddenly they also become nostalgic about their alma mater. Notre Dame alums are known for being maudlin when it comes to the university, and are the butt of many jokes as a result, but it is difficult to leave Notre Dame and not realize that it is a special place. Once someone attends Notre Dame, whether it was in the 1940s or in the 21st century, that person is always a member. It isn't a coincidence that Notre Dame boasts one of the largest and most loyal alumni networks of any U.S. college. The university has 218 clubs in the United States and fifty-four alumni clubs worldwide.

After graduating from Notre Dame, alumni locate all over the world and enter a wide array of professions. Every year, Notre Dame sends the largest percentage of its graduates into the career world. The most popular fields graduates enter into include, law, marketing and sales, engineering, medicine, and accounting.

Career Center

To help students secure positions in the business world, Notre Dame's Career Center holds seminars about writing résumés and preparing for interviews, and also counsels students on what professional careers fit their interests. The Career Center invites a range of companies to the campus; however, many of the companies tend to be better matches for business and engineering students than for liberal arts majors.

Advanced Degrees

Many students go on to pursue advanced degrees, in law, medicine, MBA programs, or other graduate programs. Almost half of all Notre Dame grads eventually go on to complete at least one advanced degree.

Service Programs

After graduation, social service continues to be an integral part of many students' lives. In recent years, about ten percent of each graduating class has entered into a one- or two-year service program, domestic and abroad. The Center for Social Concerns, which brings numerous postgraduate service programs to campus, advises students on what programs are available and would be a good match in terms of structure, location, and activity. Some of the more popular programs include Jesuit Volunteer Corps, Alliance for Catholic Education (ACE, a Notre Dame-founded program), Inner City Teaching Corps, and the Peace Corps.

Alumni Support

In terms of alumni annual giving, Notre Dame ranks third in the nation, but alumni are dedicated to Notre Dame more than just financially. Approximately 161,000 alums participate in events organized by the alumni clubs, such as golf outings, happy hours, and vacations. There are also activities meant to enhance the spiritual, educational, and professional aspects of alumni's lives. For example, the Alumni Association has started a program that brings graduates back to South Bend to rehab houses in the area and the Chicago Alumni Club frequently hosts networking meetings for graduates.

When a student graduates from Notre Dame and is unclear what area he or she wants to enter or is looking for a career change later in life, the Notre Dame alumni make up a strong support network. Graduates often look to each other for career guidance, resources, and connections, even if they graduated generations apart.

Alums permeate every field worldwide, from politics and the film industry to medical research and education, yet they all share the moral, ethical, and spiritual framework of the Notre Dame family.

SUMMING UP

The plethora of activities, programs, and facilities at Notre Dame allows students to create their own experience while at the university. As the phrase "Notre Dame family" has a different connotation for each student and graduate, so does the "Notre Dame experience." Although the school encourages students to be involved in all aspects of university life, students can choose if they want to focus more on academics, service, student government, or the arts. It is the same for social activities, where there is something for everyone.

The spirit of Notre Dame students and graduates proves that there is something special about the place. The fact that people affiliated with Notre Dame call it a family shows that students and graduates really care about the school and the people involved with it.

All in all, it is the last lines of the Notre Dame alma mater, "Notre Dame, Our Mother," that truly summarize how its students and graduates feel about the school: "And our hearts forever, Love thee, Notre Dame."

❑ *Meghan Case Kelley, B.A.*

 University of Pennsylvania
Philadelphia, PA 19104

 (215) 898-7507
Fax: (215) 898-9670

 E-mail: *info@admissions.upenn.edu*
Website: *http://www.upenn.edu*

 Enrollment

Full-time ❏ women: 5,100
❏ men: 5,300

Part-time ❏ women: 150
❏ men: 175

INTRODUCING THE UNIVERSITY OF PENNSYLVANIA

Penn was founded in 1749 to provide students with an education based on the ideas of Benjamin Franklin. Franklin's philosophy held that a student's education need not be wholly traditional, but practical as well; he was controversial in his proposal that teaching English was more important than teaching Latin. The resulting curriculum developed during Franklin's forty-year tenure as a trustee included the sciences, mathematics, history, logic, and philosophy. It was later built upon by the creation of the nation's first medical school, business school, and law classes. As America's first university, Penn has remained dedicated to the philosophy under which it was founded, and continues to offer its students and faculty opportunities to achieve in academic, social, and professional worlds.

In 260 years, Penn's student body has grown from a graduating class of seven to a student population of 20,000, half of which are undergraduates. This qualifies Penn as one of the larger schools in the Ivy League; however, the feeling on campus indicates the opposite. The Penn campus is concentrated within a twelve-block area, centered upon Locust Walk, a tree-lined pedestrian walkway that bisects the entire campus in length and connects dormitories, academic facilities, libraries, and recreational spaces. Throughout the campus one can find architectural records of Penn's development in West Philadelphia, tracing from the late 1800s through the present, with buildings by former student Frank Furness, professor Louis Kahn, modernist Eero Saarinen, and Penn graduate Robert Venturi. This mix of old and new gives Penn the easily distinguishable impression that characterizes its campus and sets it off from the city surrounding it.

The campus and its urban setting are major parts of student attraction to Penn. While the campus stands in visual contrast from the rest of the city, Penn is neither detached from Philadelphia nor uninvolved in its community. Penn students regularly explore the city, and many participate in community service and tutoring projects in nearby neighborhoods through the Netter Center for Community Partnerships and the Civic House and Civic Scholars programs. The city provides an excellent complement to Penn, offering more than one hundred museums and galleries, multiple performing arts venues, top-ranked restaurants and bars, historical sites, and a variety of other attractions for students to take advantage of. Students often spend nights and weekends in historic Old City, Center City (Philadelphia's "downtown"), South Street, and other parts of town, but always return to campus to meet up with friends, do schoolwork, or relax at a campus establishment.

Given its setting and the opportunities offered, Penn practically guarantees that a student will find his or her niche. Penn students come from a variety of backgrounds, and are linked by their appreciation for hard work and academics—that is certainly how they earned their place at the university—but are marked by their ability to balance their education with social and extracurricular pursuits. Students come from fifty states and more than one hundred countries (14 percent of students at Penn are international). Registered student groups serving religion, politics, talents, hobbies, geographic origin, ethnicity, culture, sexuality, and other areas number almost 400, and student interests are so broad that this number continues to grow. This exciting mix of personalities fuels the academic and social environment at Penn, where students take a genuine interest in learning on both sides of the classroom walls.

ADMISSIONS REQUIREMENTS

As the college admissions pool becomes increasingly large, acceptance to Penn is becoming more and more competitive. Due to larger Early Decision applicant pools in recent years, Penn has taken up to half of their freshman class from this group. The median SAT falls around 1450, and most freshmen graduated in the top ten percent of their class. In order to remain competitive in this pool, it is necessary to pursue a rigorous high school curriculum.

While the academic program is very important to the application, admissions officers consider more than just letters and numbers. The Penn application gives students a chance to demonstrate personal talents and interests, specific strengths and goals, and any other elements that the applicant feels are important to communicate who they are and what would make them a unique addition to the university. Past essay questions have asked students what fictional character they would most like to meet, what has been one of the greatest challenges they've faced, and of course the one that is most provocative, to include page 217 of one's 300-page autobiography. These questions are deliberately open-ended, allowing students to further demonstrate their personality through their interpretation of the answer.

> **ADMISSIONS PROCESS**
>
> Every year, *The Daily Pennsylvanian* runs an article announcing that Penn's incoming freshmen are the result of its most selective admissions process yet. As a freshman, you read this and gain some confidence for the coming school year—you're more qualified than all of the upperclassmen. Then your sophomore year they have an article about the new freshmen, but the numbers are higher and the accomplishments greater.

Penn looks for a student who has maximized his or her high school experience, meaning that they should be taking the most challenging curriculum offered, and should be doing well. Engineering and Wharton applicants are expected to have taken calculus. Standardized tests are required, and a student must submit either the SAT exam and three SAT Subject Tests *or* the ACT exam. Students are welcome to submit both if they choose. Admissions Officers will consider the highest set of test scores. AP scores may be submitted, and exams may be used for placement or credit.

Note: Though there are no foreign language requirements for application, it is useful to have some background, as there are language proficiency requirements for graduation. This proficiency can be met with one of the more than one hundred languages taught at Penn.

In reviewing all of the required materials, as well as supplementary materials students might have supplied, admissions officers are looking to admit an exceptionally accomplished and diverse student body. This diversity applies to academic and extracurricular interests, life experiences, geographic location, cultural background, and any other number of circumstances that might make for a unique candidate. Admissions officers want students that are right for Penn, but also for whom Penn is a good match, and all applicants are asked to discuss why they feel Penn is best for them.

ACADEMIC LIFE

For many students, the start of freshman year at Penn may be a wake-up call. Most students will come from high schools where they were top students. Take roughly 2,400 of those students and pool them together with 7,500 sophomores, juniors, and seniors, and an incoming freshman can be set for a humbling experience. The upside of this is how much you can learn from your classmates, many of whom may have studied in depth the material you have merely familiarized yourself with. They will have worked in places you'd never thought to work, visited countries you've never thought of visiting, and started clubs and activities unlike any that existed at the school you came from. As a student at Penn, you may learn just as much from your friends as you do in your classes, and they will learn from you.

Penn provides plenty of support for students and makes efforts to acclimate freshmen to their new environment. Students are assigned peer advisors, faculty advisors, and academic advisors from their undergraduate division. These people can help select courses, plan out future semesters, and ultimately guide the student successfully throughout his or her academic career.

Course Selection

Course registration at Penn could not be any easier or more convenient. After out-phasing written and phone-in methods, students can now do their entire course search, request, and registration through PennInTouch, an on-line system that can also be used to manage tuition, transcripts, student voting, and many other student concerns. After establishing a schedule, students are given what is an equivalent to a "shopping period" known as add/drop, during which they may attend various classes to ultimately finalize their course selection by two weeks into the semester.

Faculty

The Penn Faculty includes some of the most knowledgeable, accomplished, and respected teachers in the world. Almost all courses at Penn are taught by full professors, with the exception of some writing and foreign language classes. Though the average class size is small, larger classes break down into recitation sections led either by professors or grad/Ph.D. students. One way or another, professors stay in close contact with their students—they are not at Penn solely to perform private research and teach graduate students—and most professors are extremely accessible and eager to get to know their students. At the first meeting of a class, professors discuss the materials to be covered and dispense syllabi delineating required materials, exams, and assignments, and most important, any contact information, including office location and hours, e-mail, phone number, and additional contacts. All professors are required to keep office hours during which students are invited to stop by with any questions or concerns.

Four Undergraduate Schools

Most students applying to Penn will make their application to one of the four undergraduate schools. These include the College of Arts and Sciences, the Wharton School, the School of Engineering and Applied Science, and the School of Nursing. Dual-degree programs offer students a combination of two of the schools, and students may apply to these highly selective programs as well. As few students are taken into these programs, applicants are given the opportunity to request admission to a single-degree program in one of the affiliated schools should they not be accepted for the joint degree program.

Majors

Undergraduates in the College of Arts and Sciences officially select their majors by the end of their sophomore year. The time before this can be used fulfilling language or general requirements as well as coursework for their intended major. The College has a general requirement, consisting of ten classes taken from seven different academic sectors. In addition, all students must also be proficient in a language and fulfill a writing requirement. Graduates of the College are expected to take full advantage of the liberal arts and sciences.

There are more than fifty majors offered in the College. Special programs such as Biological Basis of Behavior (BBB) and Philosophy, Politics, and Economics (PPE) attract students for their multidisciplinary approach. The Annenberg School sponsors a major in Communications through the College, and the School of Design supports Fine Arts and Architecture majors. Students with specific interests that are not directly addressed by available majors are allowed to find an advisor and create an individualized major. It is not unusual for students in the College to double major or carry multiple minors.

Students in engineering can opt for a Bachelor of Science in Engineering (BSE) or a Bachelor of Applied Science (BAS) degree. Those selecting the BSE are usually on a preprofessional tract, which makes up the majority of students in the undergraduate program. The BAS offers a chance for students with an interest in technology who are less sure about their future career to add a larger liberal arts component to their education. All engineering students take seven courses in the College. The engineering curriculum culminates with a senior design project, which is either an original or continued research project based upon their undergraduate work.

The Wharton School was the first business school in the world, founded with the goal of providing an undergraduate business program that integrated humanities and social sciences. All students in the Wharton School receive a Bachelor of Science in Economics. Students are required to take a set of core requirements including finance, management, accounting, and marketing, and must pursue coursework outside of Wharton as well. Wharton students do not have majors, but concentrations, made up of four course units from one area of study. There are eighteen concentrations offered, and just as in the College, students are permitted to individualize their concentration. Often students will pursue more than one concentration; the most popular is finance.

Nursing students all receive a Bachelor of Science in Nursing, qualifying them to directly enter the professional world or continue in a graduate or professional program. Penn's Nursing program is consistently ranked one of the best in the country. Some nurses use their education as a strong premed preparation. Penn Nursing offers a number of resources not found at most schools, including state-of-the-art simulations labs and clinical experience in the Children's Hospital of Philadelphia and the Hospital of the University of Pennsylvania, two of the nation's best hospitals and both on the Penn campus.

Regardless of which undergraduate school a student chooses to matriculate into, Penn's "One University System" offers the opportunity for students in one school to take classes in any of the other three. In some cases, it is possible to receive a minor or second major in another school. The flexibility of this system allows students to pursue interests outside of their home school, and often eases the concern of students with varied interests. It also enables students, with professor permission, to take graduate-level courses, which can in some cases lead to submatriculation (entry into one of Penn's graduate programs).

Facilities

Students will find that all departments at the university are internationally respected, and that part of the benefit of studying at a large, competitive university is taking advantage of the facilities available. Penn offers sixteen libraries; the two largest and most popular are Van Pelt Library, with its twenty-four-hour study lounge, and the Fisher Fine Arts Library, which is so quiet and beautiful that you'll feel smarter just walking in the doors. In addition to libraries, the university offers a Museum of Archaeology and Anthropology, multiple art galleries, the Institute of Contemporary Art, television and radio stations, performance spaces, an arboretum, and constantly updated computer and science labs. The campus network allows students to have online access from everywhere on campus, including dorm rooms, libraries, classrooms, study lounges, the student union, coffee shops, and wireless access on most of campus.

Study Abroad

Penn offers opportunities for international programs on six continents and nearly fifty countries on a semester-long, full-year, or summer basis. In order to make study abroad a viable option for as many students as possible, Penn's Office of International Programs provides much flexibility in arranging for travel. If you are interested in studying somewhere that Penn does not specifically offer a program, you can find a program through another school, get it approved, and arrange to have your credit from participation in that program transferred back to Penn. If a student is receiving financial aid, that package will be applicable to international programs as well. Most students go abroad at some point, usually in their junior year or at least during the summer. There are programs to suit everyone's schedule and goals, and it is a great way to experience some of the things you have studied in the classroom.

> *❝ I spent the summer between my sophomore and junior years studying in Tokyo. I participated in a language program at a Japanese university, and was able to use those credits toward one of my majors. During that summer, my language skills improved enough that I was able to skip an academic year of language instruction. More importantly, I gained confidence in my language skills and a proper understanding of the practical applications of Japanese. I also had the unique opportunity to travel and explore the culture and sights that I had previously known only in the classroom. ❞*

SOCIAL LIFE AND ACTIVITIES

Everyone says that college is a time to learn about oneself. A large part of this self-discovery is facilitated by the people you meet during these four years. Many of my first friends at Penn were people I met during a preorientation program (PennQuest) or were residents of my dorm floor. With time at Penn, one begins to meet more friends through classes, activities, or at parties and other social events. Freshmen will be happy to know that all first-year students are in the same situation as they are and are eager to make new friends.

Residential Life

Housing is arranged according to a system of eleven individual College Houses each with distinctive characteristics and personalities. They serve as an organizational system as well as a way of breaking students down into smaller groups. Support is found throughout the College House with advising, technical support, and even special residential programs that house people with shared interests. Members of the faculty and staff live within the College Houses as well, operating a host of special events including subsidized trips and activities, study breaks, and educational programs. Within the College Houses, students are divided into groups of about twenty students, each with their own Resident or Graduate Advisor—a current student living in the dorms who provides social support to students and is given a budget to operate small hall functions. The popularity of the College House system and the renovations have made on-campus living more desirable; students frequently retain the room they originally lived in, or stay in their original College House. Many students move off campus as upperclassmen, but can maintain affiliation with the College House they previously lived in.

> **❝** *As a freshman I lived in Penn's oldest dorm, the Quad. I lived in a three-room triple with two other students who were at the time only random names in a packet of housing information. Our freshman hall included students from around the world and of many different backgrounds. It has been interesting to see the different paths that we have explored. There always seems to be some sort of bond between students who have lived together during their first year at Penn.* **❞**

Orientation

Over the past years, Penn's New Student Orientation program has grown into a week-long event, allowing first-year students to get a feel for the campus before classes actually start. Special events planned just for freshmen include tours of campus and the city, introductions to campus facilities, College House meetings, social events, a convocation ceremony, and lots of free food. Many upperclassmen return to campus early to attend a few of the events, such as Freshman Performing Arts Night, which offers a sampling of the many performing arts groups on campus. It is a great way to meet new friends, get your questions about campus answered, and begin the year on a positive note.

> **❝** *Penn offers a few preorientation opportunities, including PENNquest (outdoor experience), PENNacle (leadership), and PENNcorp (community service). I participated in PENNquest, where one hundred students are broken into groups of ten for a four-day hike through the Pocono Mountains. Participation in these programs is limited, and there is an application process that is well worth the effort. The programs offer students a chance to meet other freshmen in a unique environment, and secure friendships that can last through the rest of college.* **❞**

Student Activity Groups

Penn has been dubbed "the social Ivy," a title that it deserves, though not for the fraternity-crazy, non-studying image that it seems to imply. Rather, what distinguishes Penn students is their ability to break from studying to explore personal interests, work on extracurriculars, or just catch up with friends. They approach their out-of-class activities with just as much passion as their academic pursuits.

Students at Penn have their choice of hundreds of student activity groups. Though there is certainly not time to get involved in everything, student groups regularly host events for fund-raising, building student interest or awareness, and showing the talents and culture of the students they represent. There is always something to do on campus, and activities of note are major speakers and performers drawn each year through Social Planning and Events Committee (SPEC)-funded events and many special events organized through the Office of Student Life and the Student Activities Committee. Penn students also get involved in community service, much of which is organized through Civic House, and includes tutoring and mentoring programs for West Philadelphia children as well as other issues ranging from community building to social action.

PENN ATHLETICS FACTS •

○ **The Heisman Trophy is named after Penn Coach John Heisman.**
○ **The Penn Relays held at Penn's Franklin Field every April is the world's largest annual track meet.**
○ **The first black American to win an Olympic gold medal (1908) was a Penn grad, John Baxter "Doc" Taylor.**
○ **Penn's football team was the first in the United States to use numbers on its jerseys.**

Since most groups at Penn are student run, there are opportunities to gain valuable leadership experience as the head of a student group. There are also chances to get involved in all aspects of student life, including student government, and the Student Council on Undergraduate Education. Any students representing a common interest can organize and create their own group, and recruitment by various student groups happens throughout the year at orientation events and along Locust Walk.

Athletics

Penn is Division One and in the Ivy League. Three tiers of athletic involvement offer students the choice of varsity, club, or intramural levels. With these choices, students hoping to continue with sports on a level of high participation and competition can join varsity teams, and those looking for a more relaxed involvement can join club teams (which compete with other colleges) or an intramural team. This allows high school athletes to keep up with their sport, but cut down on time commitment, and also gives novices an opportunity to explore new sports, and take their interests to whatever level they desire.

Penn has three gyms around campus, including the amazing new Pottruck Health and Fitness Center. Other facilities include a tennis pavilion, two pools, squash courts, indoor/outdoor tennis courts, playing fields, an indoor ice rink, rowing tanks, weight rooms, saunas, and a boathouse on Philadelphia's historic Boathouse Row. Athletic facilities are open for use by students with IDs when not reserved by an athletic team. Penn Franklin Field was the nation's first two-tier football stadium, and the basketball teams play in the historic Palestra.

Greek Life

About thirty percent of students at Penn are affiliated with the Greek system. Depending on your interests, Greek life includes members of fraternities, sororities, and coed honors and community service-based fraternities. The official rush for Penn's twenty-nine national fraternities and eight national sororities is in the spring, and pledging begins later in the semester. Because many of the rush activities are fun and a good opportunity to meet people, many freshmen get involved in rush even if they are not interested in pledging, and some realize during the process that they would actually like to pledge. One way or the other, Greek life does not dominate campus, and neither does it determine one's friends. Most fraternity and sorority events are open to all students, non-Greeks included. Given that it is such a relaxed system, membership in a Greek organization comes down solely to a matter of personal preference.

The City and Safety

Students at Penn have the benefit of living in one of the country's largest cities. Situated in the middle of the DC-to-Boston megalopolis, the City of Philadelphia offers a full range of amenities, including wonderful restaurants, rich cultural resources, historic landmarks, and an exciting nightlife. Going to school in the nation's fifth-largest city means that there are always many choices for what to do when you are not in class or doing homework. Attractions such as the Philadelphia Museum of Art, the Franklin Institute, and the Mutter Museum are definitely worth exploring. The city attracts many great performers, and has a lively theater and performing arts scene. Every year the Fringe Festival attracts artists and performers to show off their talents in a week of special events. Also of note is First Friday, during which the art galleries in Old City stay open late. There are many great restaurants and bars in the area as well, and Penn runs shuttles down to the festivities to encourage students to explore.

For students concerned with adjusting to urban life, Penn is very proactive. Students are educated on safety issues when they first come to Penn, and are familiarized with the various levels of security and assistance made available to them. All students are given a photo identification card, which is used to gain access to dormitories, libraries, and other campus buildings.

Free walking and driven escorts are available to take students back to their destination. There are a number of proactive measures taken to make sure students feel safe on campus.

FINANCIAL AID

Like all of the schools in the Ivy League, Penn's admissions process is need-blind (for U.S. citizens, permanent residents, Mexicans, and Canadians), meaning that the admissions decision is made without regard to students' ability to pay for their education. There are no athletic or merit-based awards. The financial aid package is entirely need-based, and the university is committed to fulfilling one hundred percent of "demonstrated need." This figure is calculated using several financial forms, and is unique to each student's situation. Almost sixty percent of undergraduate students receive some form of financial aid. Penn has eliminated loans from their financial aid packages. Students are able to graduate debt-free or use their eligibility for federal loans to help offset their family contribution. Financial assistance packages may include a work-study job and a grant, in addition to funds that might be provided on the federal and state levels. Limited financial aid funds are available to international students from other countries.

PROMINENT GRADS

- ○ Sadie Alexander, First African-American Woman in the United States to earn a Ph.D.
- ○ Harold Prince, Broadway Producer
- ○ Ron Perelman, Financier
- ○ Ed Rendell, Governor of Pennsylvania, Former Mayor of Philadelphia
- ○ Donald Trump, Entrepreneur
- ○ Andrea Mitchell, News Correspondent
- ○ Harold E. Ford, Jr., Chairman of the Democratic Leadership Council
- ○ John Legend, Singer and Song Writer

GRADUATES

On-campus recruiting starts in the fall of senior year, and many students have accepted job offers by the winter holidays. In recent years, as many as fourteen percent of graduates have gone directly to a graduate program, and statistics show that eighty percent of Penn graduates have received a second degree within ten years of graduation.

Graduates of Penn will find that they have received training in more than just their area of study, and many will go on to work in fields very different from their undergraduate studies. If the size of Homecoming and graduation events is any indication of the graduate's appreciation for their alma mater, then applicants should expect great things.

SUMMING UP

The admissions selection process is complex. The best way to know if Penn is right for you is to absorb as much information as possible. Talk to current students, faculty, and alumni, explore the Penn Web site, and if possible, make a campus visit, take a tour, and attend an information session. Go to Penn-hosted events in your hometown.

Penn is always changing, but by adding on and improving, not by replacing and forgetting past success. I invite you to explore what Penn has to offer, partially jealous that I won't be able to experience all of the great new things added every year.

❏ *Erik Frey, B.A.*

UNIVERSITY OF RICHMOND

 University of Richmond
Richmond, VA 23173

 (804) 289-8640 or (800) 700-1662

 E-mail: *admissions@richmond.edu*
Website: *www.richmond.edu*

 Enrollment

Full-time ❑ women: 1,590
❑ men: 1,331

Part-time ❑ women: 4
❑ men: 20

INTRODUCING THE UNIVERSITY OF RICHMOND

Mention to someone that you're a student at the University of Richmond, and most people respond in some variation of "That's the school with the gorgeous campus, right?" or "The Spiders!"—a reference to the school's unconventional and storied mascot.

It's not unexpected: The private liberal arts college sits on 350 acres in Richmond's West End, six miles outside the city on the site of a former amusement park. Its centrally located lake—surrounded by towering Virginia pines, green fields, and flower beds—

makes the campus seem more like an arboretum than the prototypical Academic Gothic college. In other words, it's visually captivating, and especially so when southern springs and summers arrive in full bloom.

The university was founded in 1830 as a Baptist seminary for men and added a program of literary studies in 1840, when it was incorporated as Richmond College. The second-oldest private university in Virginia, it closed in 1861 when most of the student body went off to fight in the Civil War. In 1914, the college moved to its current location and opened Westhampton College, for women.

While the university is integrated, the dual college structure still exists today as the "coordinate college system," which allows separate administrative staffs to attend to men's and women's residential life, student governments, co-curricular programs, and unique traditions.

Richmond is at once small, intimate, and personable—but also rich with opportunities you might expect to find only at large universities: undergraduate research with full-time professors, a large study abroad program, Division I athletics, and award-winning food at the Heilman Dining Center. It also affords the benefits of living a fifteen-minute drive from Virginia's capital city, which provides access to numerous community service opportunities, internships, museums, historic sites, bars, and restaurants.

Academically, Richmond is divided into five schools, offering nearly sixty undergraduate majors in addition to master's and law degrees—the School of Arts and Sciences, Robins School of Business, Jepson School of Leadership Studies, School of Law, and School of Continuing Studies. The school recently finished construction on an international center, showing fresh commitment to international education, and a large addition to the business school.

Required courses are what you might expect from a liberal arts college: Diverse enough to offer student options, but focused enough to give students experience learning deeply about their subjects. Rare is the course at Richmond in which students can coast.

Like any college experience, Richmond's is what students choose to make of it. Few choose to attend classes and study only, and the vast majority of others become active in one (or many) of the dozens of clubs, groups, and organizations.

ADMISSIONS REQUIREMENTS

Richmond admission counselors take a holistic view of student applicants, so asking whether there's a guaranteed formula is impossible to answer. Admission counselors will assess your character, service, creativity, independence, and life experience alongside more conventional measures of academic success.

The admission screening process is highly selective, meaning a solid GPA—between 3.47 and 3.93 unweighted for the middle half of the Class of 2014—strong standardized test scores, and a rigorous course load are extremely important. Admission officers want to see applicants taking the most challenging classes—and doing well in them.

Academics, of course, aren't everything, and the university wants to see you're taking part in activities outside of the classroom. But note that quality counts over quantity, so spreading yourself thin to put a laundry list on your résumé won't win you points.

Doing or accomplishing something that truly sets you apart from others with similar academic ability—a special talent of sorts—will increase your chances of admission. Among the members of the Class of 2014: a peace leader in Cyprus, a dancer who appeared on *America's Got Talent*, nine athletics state champions, and one who performed a solo at Carnegie Hall.

The Class of 2014 submitted 8,661 applications, of which 2,857 were admitted, and 818 enrolled. Thirty-nine percent of those enrolled were admitted during the Early Decision process, fifty-three percent were admitted Regular Decision, and eight percent were admitted from the wait list. Fifteen percent of the class's students are first-generation college students, and 1-in-5 are U.S. students of color. Sixty percent of students come from public schools.

Richmond accepts the SAT and ACT for standardized test scores. For the Class of 2013, the middle fifty percent of admitted students scored between 1270 and 1430 (on a 1600-point scale). Broken down, that's 620–720 for critical reading and 640–720 for math. For the writing portion, the middle half scored between 630 and 720. For the ACT, the middle composite scores were between 29 and 32.

Richmond requires a minimum of 16 units of secondary school coursework, including four units of English, three in college preparatory mathematics (including Algebra I, II, and Geometry), and at least two each in history, laboratory science, and foreign language. Competitive candidates typically go beyond, taking three to four units of science, history, and foreign language at the highest levels available to them.

Early Decision

Two Early Decision options are available for students who know Richmond is their No. 1 choice. Fall Early Decision applicants must postmark their applications by Nov. 15, while winter Early Decision applications must be postmarked by Jan. 15, the same date as Regular Admission. Acceptance rates tend to be higher among the Early Decision pool than the Regular Decision pool.

Students who submit their applications by Dec. 1 are considered for the full-tuition Richmond Scholars program. The school also offers a number of $15,000-per-year merit-based scholarships for the best applicants in the fall Early Decision pool. All Early Decision applicants are considered for the $15,000 Presidential Scholarships, while fall Early Decision candidates are also considered for the $15,000 Trustee Scholarship.

ACADEMIC LIFE

Small classes, high engagement from 309 full-time professors and nearly sixty academic majors among five schools makes Richmond something of an anomaly academically—in a good way. Rare is it that you'll find a liberal arts college with such a well-regarded undergraduate business school—ranked No. 15 nationally by *BusinessWeek*. Plenty of opportunity for academically challenging course study and undergraduate research is available for interested students.

> 66 *A committed student will thrive in Richmond's challenging academic environment, especially if he or she seeks guidance from professors, many of whom will always keep their office doors open. I have had classes as large as 25 and as small as six, and the common thread among all of them is the individual guidance provided by professors. I've gone out to dinner with professors and visited the homes of others. These professors have become mentors, which has become invaluable as I seek out possible careers.* 99

—*Jimmy Young, '11*

School officials also tout the first-in-the-nation Jepson School of Leadership Studies, which in 2010 added former Virginia Governor Timothy M. Kaine to its faculty. Students can also take courses in any of Richmond's schools—regardless of their major.

The academic course load, for the most part, is demanding. As a general guideline, students who put in about 14 hours of work outside of a specific class can expect to get an

"A," depending on the course: Organic Chemistry I will be more rigorous than Introduction to Sociology.

Some first-year courses are larger than advanced courses, but not all the time. The student-to-faculty ratio is 9-to-1 for undergraduates, and classes—none of which are taught by teaching assistants—average about 17 (and rarely exceed 25). The university's president, Edward Ayers, a Southern history scholar, also teaches a course for a handful of freshmen at his house on campus.

Expect professors to know and call you by name, even if you hide in the back of the room. Often they'll schedule meetings outside of designated office hours, and most are always available for extra help. In some cases, professors will provide their cell phone numbers to students.

General Education Program

Richmond, at its core, is a liberal arts institution, and the school works hard to emphasize its integrated academic identity. Accordingly, the general education curriculum comprises four main components: seminars, communication skills, field of study requirements in six areas, and wellness.

Freshmen are generally required to take two first-year seminars on a variety of current topics, team-taught by professors from different disciplines.

Other requirements:

- **Communication skills**, which includes oral communication and proficiency in a foreign language. Advanced high school courses can sometimes help you place out of these requirements.
- **Field of study** requirements in six areas: historical studies, literary studies, social analysis, visual and performing arts, symbolic reasoning, and natural science.
- **Wellness**, which comprises an alcohol awareness program called URAware and two elective mini-workshops on health and wellness topics.

International Education and Study Abroad

Ever since *Newsweek* magazine in 2007 named Richmond the "Hottest School in America" for international studies, Richmond's worn the honor proud—and worked to live up to the acclaim. Most professors, even those outside international education, encourage students to study abroad—sixty percent of the Class of 2009 did. Richmond offers seventy-five study-abroad programs in thirty countries, available for the semester, summer, or full year.

In fall 2010, the Carole Weinstein International Center opened as part of an effort to internationalize their curricula, encourage co-curricular activities, foster collaboration and research between faculty, and prepare students for the increasingly global world and economy.

> **❝** *Spending my junior year studying in France and Cameroon was the best decision I've made as an undergraduate. I've grown as a person, discovered passions, and narrowed my future career path. Richmond highly encourages study abroad, and it provides so many options that anyone can find a program that suits his or her interests* **❞**

—Alex Vlasic, '11

SOCIAL LIFE AND ACTIVITIES

As is the case with many colleges, rare is the Richmond student who has idle time. Students can join some 250 student clubs and organizations, among them: fifteen Greek organizations, various groups for religion, cultures, business, politics, science, music, media, intramural and club sports, student spirit, environment, and diversity. If you don't find one you like, you're encouraged to start your own.

The Campus Activities Board puts on at least one major concert per year and features recently-in-the-theater movies in the Tyler Haynes Student Commons, among other events.

Many other students live off-campus and enjoy downtown Richmond, participate in community service, or hold internships and jobs off-campus during the week.

Athletics and Wellness

Richmond's recent success—particularly in football and men's basketball—has brought athletics back into the national spotlight.

The nineteen Richmond Spider teams compete in NCAA Division I and the Atlantic 10 Conference in most sports, except for football and women's golf, which are with the Colonial Athletic Conference.

- Investiture—First-year men, dressed in suits and ties, are formally accepted into the college and introduced to its history, symbols, and honor system.
- Proclamation Night—Westhampton College Government Association, along with first-year and senior-year women, hold a candlelight ceremony to induct first-year women to the college. First-years write letters to themselves about their thoughts and how they hope to develop over the coming years, then open and read them senior year.
- Ring Dance—Westhampton College women receive their class rings in a ceremony at the historic, five-star Jefferson Hotel in Richmond. Dressed in white, they are presented by their fathers, and then enjoy a formal dance with family and friends.
- First Fridays—Richmond College's dean and associate dean visit students in selected residence halls on the first Friday of each month, part of an effort to build relationships with men on campus (yes, there's free pizza, too).
- Pig Roast—Fraternities open their lodges for partying and roast pig at the end of March, marking the semi-official start of spring: Women wear sun dresses and men wear collared shirts, slacks, and ties.
- Graduation Weekend—Saturday night's candlelight ceremony and resulting fireworks around Westhampton Lake is a sight to behold. The entire graduating class encircles the lake with candles as the president and class representatives speak. On Sunday, graduates gather to walk together—for the last time as students—across campus to the Robins Center for Commencement.

For eighty-one seasons from 1929–2009, football games were played at the run-down City Stadium, about a fifteen-minute drive from campus. But alumni backing and student government leadership combined to bring Spider football back to campus, and the team celebrated its inaugural season at the $25 million, 8,700-seat Robins Stadium in 2010. That same year, the men's cross-country team qualified for its first NCAA National Championship berth and finished the season ranked 24th.

The Spiders established their modern day presence with runs in the NCAA men's basketball tournament in the mid-1980s, becoming known for knocking off top-ranked opponents. In 1991, the No. 15 Spiders upset No. 2 Syracuse in the first round of the NCAA Tournament—at the time the biggest upset in tournament history.

The men's basketball team qualified for the 2010 tournament and finished ranked No. 24 nationally. In 2008, the football program earned the school its first NCAA National Championship, defeating Montana to win the Division I FCS title.

Their success has boosted school spirit on campus to levels not seen for several years. And for its size, the school is remarkable for the competitiveness of its athletics programs and the talent of its athletes. Richmond's student-athlete graduate rate is ninety-three percent.

Other athletics venues include the 9,000-seat Robins Center, where the basketball teams play and commencement and concerts are held; a baseball diamond; lighted intramural fields; the recently renovated and expanded Weinstein Center for Recreation and Wellness; tennis, racquetball, and squash courts; and a natatorium.

School spirit at athletic events seems to hinge greatly on the current success of the teams. If they aren't playing well, expect only the most passionate fans to show for games—the "Richmond Rowdies," the semi-official student athletic spirit group, being the most prominent. Students are known for bailing early from games because of academic and social pressures.

Many other students who played high school sports, but don't want to pursue Division I intensity and time commitments, can join thirty active—and in many cases quite competitive—club sports played by some 600 students. These teams practice regularly, in some cases have their own coaches, and travel to other schools to play other club teams. School officials are moving to increase funding and support for more varsity-level teams—led first in 2010 by men's club lacrosse, which has attracted top talent from high schools across the nation.

For those looking for more casual sports and activities, the recreation center offers soccer, volleyball, football, basketball, and team handball, among others. All students can sign up for free group exercise classes (dance, spinning, yoga, and Pilates courses), fitness and nutritional assessments, and the opportunity to become a certified student personal trainer.

Greek Life

Greek life and its activities are an ever-present part of Richmond's culture and Friday and Saturday night social scene. From recruitment to fraternity lodge parties and the every-Friday-wear-your-Greek-T-shirt ritual, being directly or indirectly involved is a near-given. In spring 2010, thirty-seven percent of undergraduates were Greek-affiliated and involved in one of the seven sororities or eight fraternities. More women join sororities than men join fraternities.

Richmond has no designated housing for Greeks, although students in the same organization will often choose to live in neighboring on-campus rooms and apartments. Fraternities enjoy the benefit of "lodges" along Fraternity Row on the north part of campus, where they host parties on many weekends.

Freshmen aren't permitted to pledge to a sorority or fraternity until the second semester, giving them time to adjust to campus life and form friendships outside of a Greek organization. Relationships between current Greek members and recruits begin to form during the first semester.

Richmond, Virginia

Richmond is a city flush with Civil War history, museums, shopping, parks, and nightlife, including bars and restaurants. Leaving campus is most convenient by car, but in January 2011 the university launched an extensive transportation system that connects the campus with downtown, shopping centers, and the Greater Richmond Transit Company buses. Some key areas of the city:

- **Carytown**—A five-minute drive from campus, Carytown is something of a trendy Main Street USA, and includes a mix of restaurants, boutiques, shops, and the historic Byrd Theatre, which debuted its first film in 1928 and shows movies for $2.

- **The National**—A 1,500-person intimate music venue that draws an eclectic mix of local and national musicians. Every seat in the house is good. Recent acts have included Jimmy Eat World, Lifehouse, Matt Nathanson, Girl Talk, STS-9, and Umphreys McGee.

- **Belle Isle and Pony Pasture**—Belle Isle is a small island in the James River, accessible by a bridge for pedestrians and bicycles. It includes numerous trails, an excellent view of Richmond's skyline, and was once a prison camp for Union soldiers during the Civil War. The island is also a popular spot for seeing wildlife, swimming in the James River, and sunbathing. Pony Pasture, much closer to school, offers a similar experience.

- **Arts and Culture**—The Virginia Museum of Fine Arts, Library of Virginia, American Civil War Center, Landmark Theater, and Science Museum of Virginia are just a few of the city's landmarks. St. John's Church is the site of Patrick Henry's "Give me liberty or give me death!" speech. Hollywood Cemetery is the burial site of two U.S. presidents, John Tyler and James Monroe, as well as Jefferson Davis, the only president of the Confederacy.

- **Sports**—Richmond has no major league professional sports teams, but three minor league teams: the Richmond Flying Squirrels, an AA baseball team; the Richmond Kickers soccer team; and the Richmond Lions rugby team.

GRADUATES

Advisers and professors at Richmond emphasize that your major doesn't determine your job, especially in a liberal arts environment that stresses knowledge on a diversity of subjects. The Career Development Center (CDC) on campus offers daily walk-in hours for help creating a four-year plan for life after graduation, whether that's determining when and where to secure internships or getting help with résumés and cover letters.

The CDC works with alumni and its vast network of employer contacts to place students in internships while in college, and in careers afterward. Each year, it hosts an industry expo for students to meet with potential employers. Its Washington, D.C., Initiative internship connects students with specific internships in the nation's capital.

Despite one of the worst economic climates in decades, ninety-five percent of the Class of 2009 was employed, in graduate school, or involved in scholarly or community work a year after graduation, according to an internal survey with a fifty percent response rate. Average salary a year after graduation was between $40,000 and $44,999. Students find employment everywhere from Goldman Sachs to the American Red Cross to KPMG to Teach for America, a competitive program for students interested in teaching in low-income areas after college.

Here's a breakdown of the Class of 2009's primary fields of employment:

- Business/industry: forty-seven percent
- Government: fourteen percent
- Education: thirteen percent
- Health/medical services: ten percent
- Law occupations: five percent

PROMINENT GRADS

- Melanie Healey—Procter and Gamble's group president for North America. (Currently 13th on Fortune's "most powerful women" list.)
- A.E. Dick Howard—Rhodes Scholar who helped write the constitutions of several former Soviet states in Eastern Europe.
- Mary Sue Terry—First female attorney general of Virginia and first woman to receive the Democratic nomination for governor of Virginia.
- Charles Stanley—Senior pastor of First Baptist Church Atlanta. His sermons and books reach a huge international audience.
- Earl Hamner—Creator of The Waltons TV series, and Author of several *New York Times* Best Sellers
- Leland Melvin—NASA astronaut who played briefly in the NFL
- Robert Dail—Retired three-star general
- Tim Finchem—Current commissioner of the PGA Tour
- Brian Jordan—Two-sport star of MLB and NFL fame
- Sean Casey—Long career in MLB, career .300+ batting average, "Nicest Guy in Baseball"
- Johnny Newman—Long career in the NBA
- Shawn Barber—Long career in the NFL

FINANCIAL AID

Richmond's total cost of education for the 2010–2011 school year—$50,420, which includes tuition, room, and board—is among the higher ones in the country. Including books and supplies, personal expenses, loan fees, and additional costs, the university estimates total yearly costs for an undergraduate to be around $52,520. That, of course, varies by student.

But Richmond's financial assistance programs are also among the most generous. The school doesn't consider a family's finances when making admission decisions—a policy known as "need-blind"—and is among only sixty-six schools nationally that provide one hundred percent of an applicant's demonstrated need, based on the Free Application for Federal Student Aid (FAFSA) and other documents. Through merit-based scholarships, grants, need-based aid, loans, student employment, and a deferred payment plan, numerous ways exist to fund your education.

What's that mean? If Richmond crunches the numbers, and determines your application shows your family can contribute, say, half the total cost of the education, Richmond will—in the form of grants, scholarships, loans, and student employment—make up the difference. Sixty-nine percent of undergraduates at Richmond receive financial aid, with an average award of $33,050.

Scholarships and Jobs

About one-in-thirteen students receive a merit-based scholarship.

Richmond Scholars

Each year, the Richmond Scholars program gives up to 45 full-tuition (some include room and board), merit-based scholarships under four designations: Oldham Scholars, Science Scholars, Artist Scholars, and Boatwright Scholars.

In general, Richmond Scholars demonstrate outstanding and engaged scholarship, leadership, a broad world view, excitement about learning from people different from themselves, a pursuit of self-improvement, and a desire to make the most of the opportunities presented to them, among other qualities.

Oldham Scholars

Up to seven incoming students will be designated as Oldham Scholars, granting them an award equal to the value of full tuition plus room and board. The scholarship is for incoming students who exemplify the highest scholarship, personal integrity, and potential for leadership.

Science Scholars

Up to twelve incoming students who demonstrate passion and excellence in science, mathematics, and computer science can be designated. All Science Scholars must major in the sciences and exhibit a strong potential for the successful pursuit of a career in the above fields.

Artist Scholars

Up to six incoming students who will major or minor in the visual or performing arts and have extraordinary talent are paired with arts faculty mentors as part of this designation. Semifinalists will be asked to submit audition tapes or portfolios for evaluation along with an artist's statement and resume.

Boatwright Scholars

Up to twenty will be designated as Boatwright Scholars and receive full tuition. This award is the broadest, open to students interested in any field of study and is based on academic achievement and personal qualities.

Bonner Scholars

Bonner scholarships aren't awarded based solely on merit or demonstrated need. Applicants who display a strong commitment to community will stand out. That could mean a long-term volunteer position or job experience, but isn't necessarily shown by total hours of service.

Bonner Scholars receive a $2,500-a-year scholarship, renewable for eight semesters of full-time undergraduate study. Scholars are also eligible for summer scholarships, and alumni may be eligible for up to $2,000 in loan reductions.

Virginians

Entering first-year students from Virginia whose total family income is $40,000 or less and who demonstrate eligibility for need-based financial aid receive full tuition, room and board in the form of grants (i.e., no loans). All Virginia residents are also eligible to receive an annual state Tuition Assistance Grant.

Additional scholarship opportunities include the Presidential Scholarship, a merit-based award of $15,000 for students with high grades and standardized test scores. Trustee Scholarships, also for $15,000, are awarded to fall Early Decision applicants exhibiting the same qualities as Presidential Scholarship recipients.

Other awards include the National Merit Scholarships, National Achievement Scholarships, National Hispanic Scholarships, Davis United World College Scholars, Army ROTC, and Music, Dance, and Theatre scholarships—all for varying amounts. A limited number of need-based financial aid grants are offered to international students—non-U.S. citizens—in the incoming class.

Jobs

Students can earn extra money or fulfill work-study requirements working in numerous jobs, including university catering and dining services, Boatwright Memorial Library, the academic departments, and as researchers in the science building, among many options.

SUMMING UP

College advisers, professors, and admissions counselors will tell you that it's not about where you go to college, but what you do with the opportunities presented to you while you're there. At Richmond, it's possible to find your passion at an intimate, beautiful campus with high-achieving students studying under professors who want to see you succeed with the many opportunities afforded—more than you'll ever be able to fully explore in four years.

❏ *Daniel Petty, B.A.*

 University of Rochester
Rochester, NY 14627

 Phone: (585) 275-3221 or (888) 822-2256
Fax: (585) 461-4595

 E-mail: *admit@admissions.rochester.edu*
Website: *www.rochester.edu*

 Enrollment

Full-time ❑ women: 2,625
❑ men: 2,568

Part-time ❑ women: 207
❑ men: 47

INTRODUCING UNIVERSITY OF ROCHESTER

Make no mistake: there are hundreds of outstanding colleges and universities across the country and around the world. However, few schools match the educational opportunities offered at the University of Rochester. Rochester is one of the nation's smallest private research universities. Professors are accessible, classes are small, and one-on-one undergraduate research is the norm.

At Rochester, *there are no required subjects*. There are no general education requirements or core curriculum. You can study what you love, and not spend time fulfilling someone else's concept of education. Rochester has found that students do their best when studying what they love. Rochester students are empowered to make crucial decisions regarding their individual educational experience. From day one students are able to take classes that align with their academic passions. This academic freedom sets Rochester apart from most other colleges and universities. With this freedom, more students are able to double or even triple major if they want to.

The University of Rochester, founded in 1850, is located in Rochester, New York, a city that offers almost everything you would find in a big East Coast city, but without all the traffic. More than a million people call the Rochester area home. The River Campus, the university's main campus, sits on the banks of the Genesee River and covers ninety acres.

AT ROCHESTER...

- ○ you will find students from all 50 states and more than fifty countries.
- ○ there are more than seventy majors in the humanities, social sciences, and natural sciences.
- ○ ninety-six percent of freshmen return for their sophomore year.
- ○ eighty-six percent of all undergraduate students live on campus.
- ○ seventy percent of students are involved in volunteer activities.
- ○ seventy-five percent of students are involved in undergraduate research.
- ○ ninety-six percent of seniors have had at least one career-related experience.

Rochester is a residential campus, and over eighty percent of undergraduate students choose to live in university housing. More importantly, this is not the kind of school where students race home on the weekends. Nearly all students choose to stay on campus and enjoy all that the university has to offer. There are more than 240 student groups, and it seems that every night there is at least one group performance or sponsored event taking place. From *a cappella* shows, to cheap movies, to varsity games, there is always something to do.

The university provides transportation off-campus via free shuttles if you want to experience all that the city has to offer. There are dozens of outstanding restaurants, shops, movie theaters, and so much more just minutes from campus. The world-renowned Eastman School of Music is also just a short ride away. Many concerts at Eastman are free or just a few dollars for all Rochester undergrads. Students can even take free music lessons at Eastman for credit.

Whether it's the open curriculum, outstanding undergraduate research opportunities, a vibrant campus, or a beautiful city, Rochester has a lot to offer. This is a place where you'll define your college experience on your own terms.

Rochester's admissions process is characterized by a comprehensive and holistic evaluation, one that emphasizes academic achievement and sincerely considers the intangible strengths of a prospective student. Applicants are not reduced to a transcript and a test score, but are evaluated as individuals in a highly personalized approach. In this way, it is a process that reveals much about what makes Rochester unique.

Rochester asks that prospective students complete the Common Application along with the Rochester Supplement. Each application includes basic demographic information, a description of achievements and activities, and a college essay. Students should also submit all transcripts, including SAT/ACT scores, and two to four letters of recommendation. For students interested in applying to one of Rochester's combined admission degree programs, an additional supplement is required. Applicants are encouraged to submit writing samples, artwork, musical recordings, and/or any other supplementary materials at their discretion.

All of these documents constitute a completed application and should be submitted to Rochester no later than January 1st (December 15th for international applicants). Students planning to apply to Rochester's binding Early Decision (ED) program should submit their application materials by November 1st. In 2009 Rochester received over 12,000 applications from students competing for approximately 1,000 spots in the freshman class. About 25% of last year's freshman class enrolled through Early Decision.

The Interview

The personal nature of Rochester's evaluative process is evident in the importance that is placed on the admissions interview. While it is not required, prospective applicants are highly encouraged to schedule an interview with an admissions counselor or alumni representative. This provides students with an opportunity to ask important questions and to put a face to what is otherwise a two-dimensional stack of papers in an informal setting. Instead, they are casual conversations; you'll never be asked what kind of tree you would be and why.

Interviews are offered on campus and in more than one hundred cities worldwide each fall. Students may also arrange to have an interview scheduled with an alumni volunteer. Rochester will accommodate any and all students requesting an interview.

Students arriving on the Rochester campus as freshmen can begin studying what they love on day one and do not have to wait until their junior year to have real choices about what classes to take.

Required core classes and general education requirements are seen as a necessary evil by many undergraduate students at other institutions. Often, around the first two years of a student's college career can be spent taking classes necessary to fulfill requirements on a graduation audit, not classes that are chosen because that's what the student wants to study.

The Rochester Curriculum is at the center of the academic experience each undergraduate has. At Rochester, students get to chart their own unique academic path free of limiting, mandatory core classes. If you want to take classes in a foreign language or in the arts, you can, but Rochester will not require you to. If you never want to take a math course again, that's your choice. This freedom of learning and depth of study all take place at one of the nation's leading private research universities.

Majors, Minors, and Certificates

Academic areas at Rochester are divided into three areas of learning: Natural Sciences, Humanities, and Social Sciences. Students must choose a major in one of the three divisions and take at least two different, three-class "clusters" in the academic fields outside their major. Many students take advantage of the cluster system to pick up a minor or a second major more easily, while others just explore an area of study outside their major.

The wide range of seventy-plus majors includes popular programs in Biology, Psychology, and Music, along with unique programs in Brain and Cognitive Sciences, Economics and Business Strategies, and American Sign Language. Programs from the Department of Political Science and the Department of Economics are nationally ranked.

With all the academic freedom afforded Rochester students, minors and certificate programs are a popular choice. Possible minors include areas as varied as Arabic and Medical Anthropology, and you can get a certificate in such topics such as Biotechnology, Medphysics, and Asian Studies.

Faculty

Rochester faculty members are somewhat unusual for faculty at one of America's best research universities: they teach undergraduates and they love doing it. Not only are they an ever-present force in the classroom as early as a student's first introductory class, but ninety-seven percent have the highest degree in their field. Classes are more often small and discussion-based, and faculty members are noted for being available even outside of office hours. With a student to teacher ratio of 9:1 and many faculty winners of the Nobel and Pulitzer Prizes, the Rochester faculty, like the Rochester curriculum, exemplify the reasons Rochester stands out as unique among research universities.

Academic Opportunities

The close relationship with the Eastman School of Music not only offers a great resource for Rochester students, but students can take lessons at the world-renowned music school.

Research as an undergraduate is the norm, not the exception. Seventy-five percent of students participate in undergraduate research, and unlike other research universities, you don't have to wait. You can dive right in during your freshman year, if you choose.

NEW MAJORS
○ Bioethics
○ Health Policy
○ Health, Behavior, and Society
○ Epidemiology
○ Financial Economics
○ Economics and Business Strategies
○ Archeology, Technology, and Historical Stuctures
○ International Relations

Freshman applicants can also apply for one of Rochester's four programs that automatically grant students admission to one of the university's graduate schools. These programs include the Rochester Early Medical Scholars (REMS) program, an eight-year B.A./B.S.-M.D. program, Guaranteed Engineering at Rochester (GEAR), a 3-2 B.S./M.S. program, Guaranteed Rochester Accelerated Degree in Education (GRADE), a five-year B.A./B.S.+M.S., and the Rochester Early Business Scholars Program (REBS), a six-year B.A./B.S.-M.B.A. program. Interested prospective students must fill out an additional supplement to be considered for these programs.

Once at Rochester, many students decide to continue their studies at the graduate level at Rochester by taking part in one of the 3-2 programs in Business Administration, Engineering, Fifth Year in Teaching, Human Development, Optics, Physics, and Astronomy (and Medical Physics), and Public Health.

Take Five Scholars Program and Other Programs

Once you get to Rochester, it's possible you'll find so many areas of study you want to explore that four years simply won't be enough. For these students, Rochester offers the tuition-free Take Five Scholars Program. Through the program, students complete a fifth year of undergraduate study at Rochester in an academic area that is outside of their major concentration.

Another option for students is the Kauffman Entrepreneurial Year, or KEY, Program. Qualified students may propose to devote as much as an entire academic year to internships, special projects, business plan development, research into various facets of entrepreneurship, or analysis of how culture and public policy influence entrepreneurial activity. With the assistance of faculty advisors, KEY students complete their additional study tuition-free.

Study Abroad

If you're looking for a more global adventure, then the study abroad programs at Rochester will satisfy any passion you have. Studying abroad at Rochester is a possibility, no matter what your major is, and Rochester believes that study abroad is an integral part of the undergraduate curriculum. Thirty percent of the students participate in one of seventy-five study abroad programs annually in countries as varied as Australia, Ghana, Italy, Argentina, and China.

SOCIAL LIFE AND ACTIVITIES

Rochester is a place where students can study what they love in a challenging academic environment while still maintaining a life outside of the library. Put simply, Rochester students work hard but still have plenty of time to get involved in the campus community.

If there's one thing you need to know about social life at Rochester, it's that more than eighty percent of undergraduates choose to live on campus. Why do so many students make this decision? Because the dorms are great, the food is good, student activities are numerous, athletics are competitive, and the heart of the city of Rochester is just a quick shuttle ride away. Off-campus housing is inexpensive and accessible, but most students just don't want to give up their on-campus experience.

Campus Housing

Undergraduate housing options are numerous. From corridor-style freshman dorms, to special-interest houses, to suite-style upperclassman buildings, there's a housing option to fit your idea of what college living is supposed to be. The university opened several new upperclassman dorms featuring single bedrooms, a bathroom for every bedroom, and air conditioning. All dorms are just a quick walk from the library, dining facilities, athletic center, and academic buildings; to get from one end of campus to the other takes about ten minutes on foot.

Student Groups

With so many undergrads living on campus, you would expect there to be many active student groups, and there are. In fact, Rochester has more than 240 student groups including varsity, club, and intramural sports teams, *a cappella* groups, religious roundtables, music ensembles, Greek organizations, dance troupes, and so much more.

Athletics

More than 3,400 students participate in varsity, club, and intramural sports at Rochester. In addition to a wide variety of club and intramural sports, Rochester has 23 varsity teams. The university's varsity teams compete in two NCAA Division III conferences, the Liberty League, and the geographically diverse and highly competitive University Athletic Association. Some of Rochester's toughest rivals include Wash U., Chicago, and NYU.

The centerpiece of athletics on campus is the Goergen Athletic Center. This recently renovated facility features an 11,000-square-foot fitness center, four basketball courts, four tennis courts, a twenty-five-meter swimming pool, a two-hundred-meter track, racquetball and squash courts, and several multipurpose rooms used for dance and martial arts classes.

The Arts

Whether you're a classical singer, tuba player, Latin dancer, comedy actor, or mural painter, you'll find your niche at Rochester.

If you play an instrument or sing, you'll find it easy to continue taking lessons or join an ensemble. Whether you audition to take free lessons at Eastman, try out for one of the university's four *a cappella* groups, or take the always popular History of Rock course, you'll always have a musical outlet. If you're not an aspiring musician but still want to listen, the Eastman School offers numerous free concerts for Rochester undergrads throughout the year.

If you dance, you won't have a problem finding a group that suits you. From hip-hop, to tap and jazz, there are several dance groups to choose from.

If you act, direct, or enjoy working behind the scenes, Rochester's International Theatre Program is open to all students regardless of major. Rochester also boasts an outstanding improv comedy troupe.

If you paint, draw, or sculpt, you have an array of Art and Art History courses to choose from. Rochester also has an art center with ample workspace and even a darkroom for student use. In addition, there is a student-run art gallery on campus.

WHERE DO STUDENTS GO IN THE CITY?

- ○ Artisan Works—see local artists at work and enjoy a large collection of eclectic pieces
- ○ Geva Theatre—a professional theater showing everything from musicals to improv
- ○ Memorial Art Gallery—part of the university, free for all undergrads
- ○ Rochester Public Market—offers fresh produce, baked goods, ethnic cuisine, flowers, and much more
- ○ Strong Museum—one of the top children's museums in the country (yes, undergrads go here)
- ○ Susan B. Anthony House—national historic landmark celebrating this women's suffrage movement leader
- ○ Monroe County Parks—more than twenty parks in the metropolitan area
- ○ Eastman School of Music—popular coffee shops and restaurants are nearby
- ○ George Eastman House/Dryden Theater—mansion of the university's leading benefactor; the Dryden has daily showings of classic and contemporary films
- ○ Little Theatre—the city's premier theater for independent films (great student pricing)

The City

As a Rochester student, you'll spend a lot of your time on campus, but when you feel the need to venture into the city for a bite to eat, a game to watch, or a show to catch, the university makes it easy. A university-owned shuttle bus service takes students throughout the city.

More than a million people call the Rochester area home. The city offers the entertainment and culture of a big East Coast city, without the headaches. The city is known for its festivals. From jazz, to local art, to independent film, it seems as if there is at least a festival a week during the warmer months (and no, "warmer months" does not mean July and August only).

Other Options

It is important to note that campus life extends far beyond what has been mentioned above. Rochester students are also politically and religiously active.

College Democrats and College Republicans are popular options for the politically minded. For those wanting to express their faith or learn about the faiths of others, the Interfaith Chapel is a house of prayer for all. Rochester undergrads are also active in the community. More than seventy percent of undergrads volunteer.

There is also an active Greek community on campus; about twenty percent of undergrads join fraternities and sororities. The vast majority of these groups have houses or dorm floors on campus. In addition to providing a vibrant night life for many undergrads, Greek groups organize community service projects and academic programs throughout the year.

FINANCIAL AID

The costs of attending a private research university are high, but the Financial Aid Office works with every admitted student to ensure that the cost of enrollment is not a barrier to attending Rochester. Rochester is committed to meeting the full financial need of every admitted student. Combinations of merit scholarships, grants, low-interest loans, and work study help ninety percent of Rochester students.

For the vast majority of Rochester's merit scholarships, there is no separate application. These scholarships range from $8,000/year to full tuition and are renewable over four years. They are awarded based on the overall strength of a student's application, and are not based solely on standardized test scores or GPA, but if you're serious about competing for merit scholarships, scheduling an admissions interview is strongly recommended.

Both the College Scholarship Service (CSS) PROFILE and the Free Application for Federal Student Aid (FAFSA) are required in order for a student's need-based financial aid to be determined. The deadline for filing these financial aid applications is February 1st, and Early Decision applicants should submit the CSS PROFILE by November 15th.

(Continued)

GRADUATES

Because of their individualized undergraduate experience, Rochester graduates are uniquely qualified and prepared for life after college, whether in the graduate school, an internship, or a career. The Career Center is a valuable resource on campus for students to perfect their résumé, sharpen their interviewing skills, network with employers and alumni throughout the year at on- and off-campus events, and find summer and postgraduate jobs. Ninety-six percent of all Rochester graduates have had at least one career-related experience, and seventy percent of second-semester seniors have found a job, an internship, or have enrolled in a graduate or professional program.

Rochester graduates interested in medical or law school have consistently outperformed national averages. Eighty-two percent of Rochester students with a GPA of 3.6 or higher were accepted to medical school, far exceeding the forty-two percent national acceptance rate. Rochester graduates have an eighty-eight percent law school acceptance rate, well above the national average. With an alumni network nearing 100,000 graduates spanning the globe, Rochester students also have unparalleled opportunities for networking, internships, and career development.

SUMMING UP

As you can see, the University of Rochester has a lot to offer; it's definitely a great place to be an undergrad. Whether it's the unique curriculum, the outstanding research opportunities, or the active on-campus community and engaged student body,

Rochester is a place where you can have an undergraduate experience like no other. Rochester truly stands alone among other research universities and constantly strives to be better, as is evidenced by Rochester's motto, "Meliora," or "Ever Better." This isn't just a saying or catchphrase; it's a philosophy we demonstrate every day. Rochester shows this by adapting to an ever-changing academic landscape in ways that enable students to fully explore their interests and chart their own academic course.

❏ *Ike Howdeshell, B.S.*

UNIVERSITY OF SOUTHERN CALIFORNIA

 University of Southern California
Los Angeles, CA 90089

 (213) 740-1111

 Website: *www.usc.edu*

 Enrollment

Full-time ❑ women: 8,404
      ❑ men: 8,347

Part-time ❑ women: 320
      ❑ men: 408

INTRODUCING USC

Los Angeles is the most vibrant and diverse of cities, and stands as the capital of the Pacific Rim. It is fitting that the University of Southern California is the most global university in the nation, with more international students (7,482 in a recent year) than any other four-year institution. The city is a pulsating nerve of entertainment, commerce, and ideas. USC, located at the southern edge of a re-energized downtown, is, in many ways, a microcosm of the urban giant.

Like Los Angeles, USC offers incredible variation, not only bringing together students of diverse backgrounds, but also nurturing a strong community that encourages innovation and debate. Its current freshman class is among the most ethnically diverse ever enrolled at USC, with twenty-two percent underrepresented minority students. In addition, twelve percent of the entering students are the first in their families to attend college. USC offers more majors and minors than any university in the country. Disciplines intersect across campus, giving birth to many interdisciplinary programs. Each contributes to the culture of the school, making USC a melting pot of theories and principles. Coupled with low student-to-faculty ratios, small class sizes, hundreds of student organizations, and cutting-edge research facilities and an expanding academic medical center, USC boasts an international presence that is expected of a top-tier, private research university.

Los Angeles is the entertainment capital of the world, and USC is firmly connected to that reputation. USC has a long-running commitment to nurturing growth in culture and the arts, and offers five nationally renowned arts schools: cinematic arts, theatre, music, fine arts, and architecture. These schools have trained Emmy and Academy Award-winning directors, writers, producers, and cinematographers; Broadway performers and technical professionals; internationally celebrated artists and architects; and numerous GRAMMY winning musicians.

The various arts programs are simply one of many outstanding offerings of the university. USC has a strong scientific research community, and is one of the top universities in the country in terms of research dollars awarded each year. Moreover, USC has forged innovative programs that encourage undergraduate research. The business programs are equally well known, and USC has developed a national reputation for encouraging entrepreneurship. Likewise, USC has developed programs that combine new technology with new forms of communication, and is a national leader in multimedia and video gaming, thanks to synergies between its strong schools of engineering, cinematic arts, and communication. Its USC Annenberg School for Communication & Journalism is successfully training multimedia practitioners, and has reaffirmed its commitment to journalism, announcing that a $50 million building will be constructed for new media.

The Daily Beast in 2010 named USC "the Hottest College" of the first decade of the 21st century, noting that "USC does a terrific job showcasing its academic assests, particularly the honors science college and the access to its high-tech research facilities. At the same time, its financial aid is among the most generous nationwide." In a recent year, USC increased its undergraduate financial aid budget by eight percent, overall distributing $190 million of university funds.

Despite the great academic opportunities offered by the university, USC is not just about classroom life. One reason that USC was named *Time Magazine's* "College of the Year" in 2000, was because more than half of the student body participates in volunteer programs that help the surrounding Los Angeles community. The city and the school have developed a mutually beneficial give-and-take relationship.

And let's not forget sports. USC has a strong athletic tradition, and has produced more Olympic athletes than any other university in the country, as well as more NCAA championship teams (113) than any other school in America. In a recent year, it had three NCAA champions: women's water polo, men's water polo, and men's tennis. Cardinal-and-gold-colored blood runs thick in the veins of proud alumni who frequent the campus to cheer on their Trojan athletes.

USC is a university that is innovative and forward-looking, bringing its students the best resources to help them become tomorrow's leaders. Yet, as the university has developed and expanded since its founding in 1880, its foundation has remained untouched. At the core of USC stands a united family—the Trojan Family.

The extended family of USC is a global network made up of thousands of alumni, students, faculty, and staff, as well as the parents of students, children, and grandchildren of alumni, the Board of Trustees, the boards of councilors, donors, athletic fans, and neighborhood partners. Indeed, no university is better known for the vastness of support that its alumni and affiliates provide far beyond the campus gates. The uniqueness of the Trojan Family isn't due to its large numbers. Rather, it's the extraordinary closeness and solidarity that is found in this genuinely supportive community. To its members, the term "Trojan Family" is more than a phrase—It represents a promise, a commitment to support that is lifelong and worldwide.

ADMISSIONS REQUIREMENTS

As the Trojan Family has continued to grow and the buzz about USC has spread both nationally and globally, the number of applicants has increased significantly in recent years. In a recent year, the school received 35,753 applications, and was able to admit only 8,724 students, or just about twenty-two percent.

Grades, Test Scores, and Requirements

The median composite SAT score for the 2009 freshman class was 1930–2150. The average GPA was 3.7 (unweighted). Admission to USC is highly competitive. Successful candidates for admission to USC will have completed a rigorous college preparatory curriculum in high school and will have availed themselves of every academic opportunity open to them.

Application Filing

USC does not use any system of Early Decision, Early Action, or Early Notification in its admissions process. There are four deadlines for filing applications:

- October 15: Part 1 application deadline for freshman and transfer students (USC's Part 1 application is optional).
- December 1: Freshman application deadline for scholarship consideration.
- January 10: Deadline for freshman applications.
- February 1: Deadline for transfer student application (scholarship and regular consideration).

Application forms are available from the USC Admission Office, or prospective students may apply on-line at *www.usc.edu*. The application cost is $65. All freshman applicants are notified by April 1.

Transferring

Another way to get into USC is by transferring from a community college. Many partnership programs are in place between USC and community colleges that help facilitate the transfer process.

ACADEMIC LIFE ████████████████████████████

At USC, education can be as unique as you are. "What's your major?" is a question of the past. With more majors and minors offered than at any other American university, many USC students do not settle for just one major. In fact, students are encouraged to pursue double-major and -minor opportunities.

The USC Renaissance Scholars program, launched in 2000, honors students whose broad interests help them excel academically. Like Leonardo da Vinci, who was equally adept in the arts and the sciences, Renaissance Scholars are students whose majors and minors are in widely separated fields of study. Renaissance Scholars are eligible to compete for the $10,000 Renaissance Scholar Prize that has been specially authorized by the Board of Trustees. Up to ten prizes are awarded every year. (I was awarded a Renaissance Scholar Prize for my major in Business Administration with an emphasis in information and operations management and a minor in natural sciences.) Renaissance Scholars have completed hundreds of combinations of majors and minors, ranging from a major in engineering and a minor in cinema to a double major in physics and classics.

Programs of Study

As the Renaissance Scholars program demonstrates, programs of study at USC are both abundant and flexible. With thirty academic departments in the USC Dana and David Dornsife College of Letters, Arts, and Sciences and seventeen professional schools, the university has interdisciplinary programs galore—and if your dream program is not offered, create it yourself.

At the core of any program of study at USC is the general education program. In addition to major requirements, students must take a class from each of six general education categories and take at least two writing classes (one lower-division and one upper-division). The six general education categories cover broad disciplines such as literature, the arts, science, and social issues. Within each category, students may choose from dozens of classes. The program offers students flexibility on two fronts. By having numerous choices to fulfill each requirement, students can tailor their program to their interests and passions. By reducing the total number of courses in the general education program, students have more elective units available to complete a second major or minor, or to take a class for fun.

Elective Classes

When choosing elective classes, Trojan students get to select from some of the best in the country. For example, every semester, Leonard Maltin from "Entertainment Tonight" teaches a weekly cinema class in which he screens a different prerelease motion picture. Following the screening, the class conducts a question-and-answer session with a guest involved in the making of the movie—usually the director, producer, or leading actor.

Every spring, USC President Emeritus Steven B. Sample teams up with University Professor Warren Bennis, leadership guru and author of over thirty books, to teach "The Art and Adventure of Leadership." Forty students, hand-selected by Sample and Bennis, study leadership styles of key figures of the modern era, interact with prominent leaders in the classroom, and are challenged to begin analyzing and developing their own leadership styles.

"The Art and Adventure of Leadership" was the highlight of my classroom experience at USC. Class guests included former Massachusetts governor Michael Dukakis, film director Robert Zemeckis, former Los Angeles mayor Richard Riordan, businessman Eli Broad, and a SWAT team commander. The papers I wrote were read personally by Sample and Bennis and then discussed over small-group luncheons. What other classroom in the country provides students such hands-on access to today's most prominent leaders?

Upper-division Classes

Like general education and elective classes, upper-division classes are also taught by world-renowned faculty. For example, the business school features proven entrepreneurs. And a chief economist for the Securities and Exchange Commission even teaches a class. The USC Viterbi School of Engineering features researchers with many patents on their office walls. The biology department features key contributors to the human genome project. And the music, theatre, cinematic arts, and art schools feature award-winning faculty in their respective fields. Working directly with these distinct leaders provides students access to cutting-edge research in their field of study and connects the classroom community with the outside world.

Collectively, USC's academic programs provide students with the skills, contacts, and knowledge to get their careers off to a running start and help them make significant contributions to their academic, professional, and business communities as they move beyond USC and into the world.

Special Programs

In addition to the broadest selection of academic programs offered by any university, USC also offers several highly selective programs tailored to students with specialized interests. Three of the flagship programs are the Thematic Option program, the Resident Honors Program, and the Baccalaureate/M.D. program.

Thematic Option (TO) has been cited by several college guides as one of the best general education honors programs in the country. Each year, about 200 freshmen participate in the interdisciplinary core curriculum. TO offers small classes with some of the university's best undergraduate teachers and a hand-picked group of writing instructors. The curriculum is organized according to themes rather than by discipline and fulfills all general education requirements.

Resident Honors Program (RHP) allows high-achieving high school seniors to get a head start on their college education. RHP students matriculate into USC a year early and complete their senior year requirements for high school and freshman year simultaneously. Although RHP students attend classes and participate in campus activities like all other students, they are required to stay in the honors dormitory and participate in special group programs to ensure their transition into college is smooth.

The Baccalaureate/M.D. program (BMD) is an eight-year joint undergraduate/medical program designed for students demonstrating a strong interest in pursuing a career as a clinical physician. BMD students are encouraged to pursue "nontraditional premedical" majors and are guaranteed a seat in the Keck School of Medicine of USC upon completion of core classes and passing base GPA and MCAT requirements. While in the program, BMD students participate in medical research projects and attend programs sponsored by the medical school. By reducing the stress attached to applying to medical school and encouraging students to pursue a broad undergraduate education, BMD students have completed many majors in addition to their premed classes.

In addition to these flagship programs, other special programs such as undergraduate research grants and study abroad have a wider reach to students. Undergraduate research is encouraged across campus and is a major requirement in some departments. Most students engaging in research join ongoing projects in large laboratories. However, students may design their own research project and apply for a campus grant. Several dozen grants of $2,500 are dedicated for such projects. For students wishing to leave the beautiful weather of Southern California for a semester or two, USC has partnerships with universities around the world. While most programs satisfy only elective units, some will transfer upper-division credits.

> **❝** *As a member of the Baccalaureate/M.D. program, I majored in Business Administration. My classmates' majors included Theater, Classics, History, and Mechanical Engineering. As part of the program, I participated in plastic surgery and stem cell research projects. The program encouraged me to pursue my passions and build a broad foundation for medical school. The Keck School of Medicine of USC believes such students have the best potential to be great physicians.* **❞**

Faculty and Class Size

USC has the smallest average class size and the low faculty-to-student ratio (ten-to-one) expected of any top-tier private research university. In fact, while the USC faculty have great academic and intellectual horsepower and field recognition, those are not what distinguish it from other universities. What distinguishes USC from other top research universities is the faculty's commitment to undergraduate education and the access granted to students. Most of the faculty who are in the spotlight for their groundbreaking research and best-selling books also teach undergraduate courses. In addition to the normal office hours that professors hold, several programs subsidize lunches with professors to help students build personal relationships. Meeting professors during "nontraditional" hours such as late-night coffee or weekend activities is not uncommon. In short, USC provides its best academic resources directly to its undergraduate students.

SOCIAL LIFE AND ACTIVITIES

USC's rigorous academic programs are accompanied by equally vigorous social activities. On campus, over six hundred organized clubs support interests ranging from archeology to waterskiing. These clubs compete for students' time with conferences, concerts, and special speakers. An extensive Greek system draws participation from approximately seventeen percent of students. Across campus, hundreds of volunteer opportunities await Trojan students in the heart of Los Angeles and across the nation and world in programs such as Alternative Spring Break, where students take part in community service projects. For recreation, students can swim or surf at Southern California's many beaches, snowboard on local slopes, take free Hollywood music clubs, or explore the city's many ethnic neighborhoods and restaurants.

Campus Life

USC has on-campus dormitories and off-campus apartments that house more than 7,000 students. In addition to these, thousands of other students live in apartments and houses in the streets surrounding the campus. USC is becoming much more of a residential campus, with several large on- and off-campus apartment complexes built in recent years.

Several blocks from campus are dozens of large Victorian-style houses that have been converted into student housing. During my sophomore and junior years, nine of my friends and I teamed up to rent a ten-bedroom house.

Campus is always buzzing with activities. One exciting new program is Visions & Voices, a yearlong array of lectures, performances, and screenings—both on- and off-campus—that often include audience talk-backs afterward. This program, begun in 2006, was championed by the then-provost and now newly installed USC President C.L. Max Nikias.

On tap this year are Ira Glass, Michael Pollan, and Eric Schlosser talking about food, trips to the LA Philharmonic and LA Opera, a three-day Chicago literary festival, and dozens of other cutting-edge events on art, politics, and society.

Added to this are student-sponsored Program Board concerts with top national bands. Campus concerts during my campus years included Blink 182, Nelly, Wyclef Jean, and Smash Mouth.

Athletics

Athletic excellence makes the Trojan mascot one of the most recognized in collegiate sports. Trojans have won team national championships, 352 individual NCAA titles, and more Olympic medals than students at any other American university.

Football is perhaps USC's most decorated program: eleven national championships; fifteen unbeaten seasons; six Heisman Trophy winners; and representation in all but two Super Bowls. One football star even won an Oscar for Best Actor! In 1925–26, Marion Morrison played tackle for USC. After graduating, he changed his name and went on to win the award for his performance in *True Grit*. This was none other than screen legend John Wayne.

In baseball, USC has won twelve national championships (no other school has more than five), and produced more than ninety major-leaguers, including home-run specialist Mark McGwire and strikeout ace Randy Johnson.

The women's basketball team has produced many stars including Cheryl Miller, Cynthia Cooper, Tina Thompson, and Lisa Leslie, the first woman to slam-dunk in a professional basketball game.

These championship teams are supported by perhaps the most recognized collegiate band in the country. The Trojan Marching Band has performed nationally and is the only collegiate marching band to have co-recorded a platinum album: Tusk with Fleetwood Mac. The band regularly appears in movies and television shows—most recently in the hit show "Glee."

66 *My dream of playing varsity volleyball faded when I developed a chronic knee injury in high school. Unwilling to completely abandon the idea of playing competitive volleyball at the collegiate level, I teamed up with seven other freshmen to form the USC men's club volleyball team. That year, we scheduled only a few games and had a mediocre record, but we made progress with every season. By my senior year, we had over twenty games scheduled, were sponsored by Nike, traveled Cross-country to nationals, and were ranked in the Top 25 by the governing body of club volleyball.* 99

These achievements help explain why the cardinal-and-gold-colored blood runs thick in the veins of proud students and alumni who fill up stadiums and gymnasiums to cheer their Trojan athletes. On Saturday afternoons in the fall, five generations of Trojans can be found tailgaiting on campus before a football game.

For those wishing to compete on the field, varsity athletics is not always an achievable goal. Two alternatives, intramural and club intercollegiate sports, provide opportunities to play competitive sports. Club sports offer great opportunities to play intercollegiate sports without the demand of varsity schedules. USC has forty-eight official club teams including crew, rugby, softball, soccer, hockey, lacrosse, equestrian, fencing, and polo. But if your favorite sport is not available, form a new team just like we did!

Community Service

More than half of USC students volunteer in community service projects each year. One of the most popular volunteer programs is the Joint Educational Program (JEP). Students participating in JEP teach in local schools once a week, often teaching simplified versions of the material learned in their college classes. Other volunteer opportunities include working in food banks and homeless shelters and the Alternative Spring Break program.

Los Angeles Life

USC's backdrop is Los Angeles, perhaps the world's most diversified and exciting city. The opportunities for fun are endless—the Hollywood nightlife, Santa Monica and Venice beaches, Big Bear and Snow Summit ski slopes, museums, concerts, professional sport teams, and shopping just to name a few. So pick up a map or a travel guide and start exploring!

FINANCIAL AID

With the cost of tuition, room, and board rising, it is not a surprise that more than sixty-two percent of USC students receive some form of financial aid. According to the Office of Admission and Financial Aid, all students applying for aid at USC are required to fill out both the Free Application for Federal Student Aid (FAFSA) and the CSS Profile to establish eligibility for need-based federal, state, and USC grants as well as federal loans and work-study. USC operates one of the largest financial aid programs in the country.

USC has a long tradition of meeting one hundred percent of the USC-determined financial need for those undergraduate students who satisfy all eligibility requirements and deadlines. Entering students are admitted to the university based on academic achievement, test scores, leadership, and community involvement. Financial need is not a factor in the admission decision for freshmen.

> **❝** *I held three part-time jobs during my four years at USC: sports clinician with "Kids In Sports," laboratory instructor for Statistics, and grader for information technology classes. These jobs helped me earn several thousand dollars a year for my school costs, enabled me to apply skills learned in the classroom, and provided a great break from studying. While working these jobs, I averaged eighteen units a semester, played a club sport, and maintained a healthy social life.* **❞**

For those students who apply for financial aid, need is determined by families' income and assets information, collected through the federal FAFSA, the CSS profile, and other required forms. In a recent year, the average freshman need-based financial aid award was $35,653. Such awards are made up of grants, work, and student loans.

Students are encouraged to apply for merit-based awards. The most notable are the Trustee (full-tuition), Presidential (half-tuition), and Dean's (quarter-tuition) scholarships. More than five hundred of these scholarships are awarded annually, providing one of the largest merit-based scholarship programs in the country. In addition to these programs, USC alumni groups and other organizations provide scholarships for our students.

Part-time jobs are also a good way to manage school costs. Working too many hours is discouraged as it distracts from academic focus, but most students can fulfill their work-study requirements with ten to fifteen hours of work per week.

GRADUATES

Many extraordinarily bright people have attended USC. The school has had more than its fair share of successful entrepreneurs, award-winning artists and performers, politicians, and athletes. Simply providing a long list of USC's all-time stars would be interesting, but probably would not tell much about how the average graduate fares.

USC students pursuing postgraduate education have high acceptance rates into medical, law, and other graduate programs. Those entering directly into the business world are highly sought out by both local and global businesses. USC's career advisement centers orchestrate career and job fairs for the more than 600 companies that recruit on campus. In fact, many Trojan students receive job offers before they graduate from USC.

In fact, USC graduates are often better candidates than their counterparts at other top schools because of their internship experience. A benefit of attending school in a large urban setting is that many internship opportunities are available with local companies. These internships are either paid or taken for class credit and often lead to full-time job offers.

Regardless of the paths USC graduates choose to take, the Trojan Family is always there to support them. From mentorship and coaching to interviews and job offers, the Trojan Family is an extraordinarily strong network that is genuinely supportive.

PROMINENT GRADS

- Herb Alpert, Musician, Cofounder of A&M Records
- Neil Armstrong, Astronaut (first man on the moon)
- Art Buchwald, Pulitzer Prize-winning Humorist
- LeVar Burton, Actor
- Frank Gehry, Architect
- Pat Haden, NFL Quarterback, Rhodes Scholar, TV commentator
- Ron Howard, Film Director
- Robinson Jeffers, Poet
- Swoozie Kurtz, Actress
- Marilyn Horne, Opera Singer
- George Lucas, Filmmaker
- Mark McGwire, Baseball Legend
- John Ritter, Actor
- Norman Schwarzkopf, Persian Gulf General
- Michael Tilson Thomas, Conductor, Music director of San Francisco Symphony
- John Wayne, Actor
- Salvatore Ferragamo, Fashion designer
- Will Ferrell, Actor

SUMMING UP

Perhaps it is a cliché, but the four years that constitute an undergraduate education are often the most transformative in a person's life. College is time for learning, growing, changing, and reaching.

When I went to college, I was sure I wanted to be a doctor. Once there, I found USC's premedical training programs to be superb, and my science classes taught me much of what I would need to know in order to pursue my goal. Yet, the classes were just the beginning. Through a hospital and clinical internship program, I got to experience what it would be like to be a doctor, spending time in the hospital, working with patients, and observing surgeries. Then, through another program, I had the opportunity to do original research in a world-class biomedical research lab. While I very much enjoyed the experiences in these programs, ironically it was precisely these programs that helped me to realize that I did not want to be a doctor. Since I was a child, I had imagined myself in medicine, however, when I experienced it up close, I realized it was not for me. Yet, I was only able to learn this about myself, by having such rich and complete experiences in medicine, the kinds of experiences that few places offer undergraduates. Most students have to wait until medical school to find out if they really will enjoy medicine or not.

The change in my perspective largely came from exposure to the abundance of other opportunities available at USC. Things suddenly became interesting to me that I could never have imagined as a high school senior, simply because I did not know that such opportunities were available and viable. Classes in leadership and entrepreneurship opened a whole new perspective of the world to me. Meeting and actually talking to such leaders helped me gain a perspective on how I myself thought about leadership. Working with professors in business classes who were not simply theorists, but practitioners, helped bring the business world alive.

When I think about the transformations I went through at USC, those transformations were not just intellectual, but personal and social as well. When I think of the close friendships I developed at USC, I marvel at their diversity. My close friends included a video-game journalist who was syndicated in many languages, an all-American volleyball player, a keyboard player in a jazz band, a first-generation Indian immigrant, an aspiring orthodox rabbi, a cinema student who had traveled the world, and others who, like me, had grown up in several different countries. Our backgrounds were incredibly diverse, as were our interests. USC fostered an environment where we could learn from each other and enjoy each other, where we came to see our very diversity as a gift in itself.

> 66 *At USC, I learned that I could make a difference. USC's emphasis on community service motivated me to volunteer to organize youth sports leagues in disadvantaged neighborhoods. It was amazing to watch. First, there were a few kids who turned up, then more came. Finally, parents and neighbors came to cheer on the teams. It was wonderful to see people coming together, supporting the kids in their communities, and working to build something special.* 99

Each student's journey through USC is different. Some students come to USC and find that the goals they had in high school are the goals they do pursue, with USC providing a rich and complex background for them to do it. Others, like me, discover that our goals change in response to the abundant intellectual and social opportunities USC affords. USC offers many paths, all of them potentially rewarding.

USC gives its students the world. The university offers a broad selection of highly regarded academic programs taught by world-renowned faculty dedicated to undergraduate education. The student body is one of the most active in the country, with thriving on-campus organizations, a strong involvement in community service, and a broad array of social events. The sports programs are second to none—all in the most vibrant city in the world. Most importantly, once you enter USC you become part of the USC family, a network of friends and support that extend across the world, shaping you and supporting you not only in your college years, but for the rest of your life. The Trojan Family extends its arms to you. Fight On!

❏ *Achi Yaffe, B.S.*

UNIVERSITY OF VIRGINIA

Photo by Dan Grogan

 University of Virginia
Charlottesville, VA 22904

 (434) 982-3200
Fax: (434) 924-3587

 E-mail: *undergradadmission@virginia.edu*
Website: *http://www.virginia.edu*

 Enrollment

Full-time ❑ women: 8,174
❑ men: 6,521

Part-time ❑ women: 436
❑ men: 333

INTRODUCING UVA

In the fall, Thomas Jefferson's village stretches out before you. The tops of the maple and ash trees lining the evergreen lawn burn with the reds, oranges, and yellows of the East Coast fall. The graceful lines of their trunks are echoed in the rows of white colonnades that frame the lawn and announce the historic pavilions and rooms, still living quarters for popular faculty and honored students. Everywhere, the vast expanse of grass is dotted with picnickers, students studying, mini football games, and picture-snapping tourists. Yet your gaze is drawn past all of this to the north end of the lawn, to the building commanding the entire scene, the world-famous Rotunda. Based on the Roman Pantheon, the sparkling marble of its flowing staircase and regal columns and the elegant arc of its majestic dome ensure that the Rotunda is not only a historical landmark, but one of the most beautiful structures ever to grace a college campus.

> **"** *As I walk to my dreaded test, I smile as I remember that by the time I get out of class, the sun will have set and warm yellow light will be glowing within the many windows surrounding the lawn. I know that on my walk home, I'll feel more like a lucky tourist after closing time than an undergraduate headed to the dining hall.* **"**

Amazing aesthetics, however, is not the reason why UVa has long been known as the "Public Ivy," and why it attracts so many exceptional students and professors. Founded by Thomas Jefferson in 1819, UVa remains one of the highest ranked state-funded institutions in the nation. Offering undergraduate programs in architecture, arts and sciences, commerce, education, engineering and applied science, and nursing, the university continues to operate on its founder's belief in the importance of a solid liberal arts education. Of its 20,380 enrolled students, two-thirds are undergraduates, and while offering the opportunities and diversity of a medium-size school, UVa still has a fairly concentrated main campus area, creating a smaller community feel. In other words, it will be virtually impossible to walk to class without recognizing at least a few faces. The central campus area has 1,166 acres and fifteen libraries. (The overall size is 3,392 acres, with 535 buildings.) Many students and professors also take advantage of the extraordinary new Albert and Shirley Small Special Collections Library, which houses numerous rare historical books and items and also boasts one of the most extensive collections of Thomas Jefferson's effects and documents in the world. Although steeped in history and tradition, UVa remains on the cutting edge of technology, offering computerized library services, Internet access, and a variety of resources, including mainframes, minicomputers, PCs, and a network of printers, which are available to students at the many computer labs around grounds. Courses that use a variety of software for collaboration to enhance class communication are quite common. Special learning facilities at UVa include a learning resource center, an art gallery, radio and TV stations, and an art museum.

Attending UVa is more than just going through the motions of four years of tests, papers, and parties. It is an experience that will completely consume you. You will be a first-year instead of a freshman, you will live on-grounds instead of on campus, you will be able to write the honor pledge in your sleep, you will learn "The Good Old Song," and you will come to recognize Thomas Jefferson as some sort of deity. At the end of it all, you will be welcomed into one of the most close-knit, active, and supportive alumni networks in the country. But most important, you will have interacted with top-notch professors and students, will have been a part of Jefferson's still thriving vision of public education, and you will have done it all without you or your parents having to face the increasingly terrifying price tag of a private institution.

ADMISSIONS REQUIREMENTS

You've got the grades and the extracurricular activities. You've taken the toughest courses your high school offers, squared away your recommendations, and conquered the SAT. But in front of you lies one of the most comprehensive college applications in the country. There are several short essays as well as one long, open-ended, and intimidating question. Since you've set your heart on UVa, you've done some research and discovered that sweating over these questions is indeed important. The Admissions Committee will be examining each of your responses in detail, giving your whole application the kind of attention it would typically only receive at a small, private school.

Each year, the qualifications of students applying to UVa are more impressive. SAT I scores for a recent freshman class were Verbal—660, Math—680. The average ACT score was 30.

All applicants must take the SAT or the ACT, as well as two SAT Subject Tests of their choice. Although the GED is accepted, most successful candidates have graduated from accredited high schools and have completed sixteen academic courses including four courses of English, four of mathematics beginning with Algebra I, two of physics, biology, or chemistry (three if they are applying to engineering). AP credits are accepted. Recently about one out of every three applicants was accepted to UVa. You will generally have a slightly better chance if you are from Virginia, or if you fall into the legacy category by being the child of alumni. In any case, if you are seriously considering UVa, then you are probably an excellent student with impressive extracurricular activities, outstanding recommendations, and an eye-catching application essay.

The distinguished majors program is just one example of the outstanding academic opportunities available at UVa. You can take part in internships, study abroad and accelerated degree programs, B.A.-B.S. degrees in biology environmental sciences, dual majors in most arts and sciences programs, student-designed majors and an interdisciplinary major, as well as non-degree study and pass/fail options. A first-year on-grounds honors program and seven national honor societies, including Phi Beta Kappa, are available, as are the departmental honors programs. If you take the time to explore the options and pursue your interests, the university is a once-in-a-lifetime shot at an amazing collection of knowledge, talent, and possibility. Faculty are the recipients of such honors as the MacArthur Award, the Pulitzer Prize, the National Book Award, the Humboldt Award, and Fulbright Fellowships. Graduate students do teach thirty-three percent of the introductory courses. Yet the student–faculty ratio remains fifteen to one, and the College of Arts and Sciences specializes in small, discussion-oriented seminars led by full professors. These courses often involve a significant workload, but they also usually cover the professor's favorite subject, from such topics as Native American poetry to cult studies or Civil War culture, and can be extremely informative, interesting, and entertaining.

> ❝ For more than a year, I have worked one on one with a professor who was an expert in my area of interest. I exhausted every resource in the libraries and university archives. I read, researched, wrote, edited, and rewrote, and though I missed some parties and lost some sleep, I gained something else—the realization that UVa honors thesis is an experience I may never want to relive, but it's also one of which I will always be proud. ❞

Course Requirements

Depending on your major, your flexibility to choose electives and select courses will vary. For example, an English major will always have more decisions to make during registration than a premed biochemistry major. However, because UVa focuses on instilling a broad liberal arts background in all of its students, the distribution requirements insure that everyone gets a chance to sample the wide variety of course material offered. All undergraduates must complete twelve hours of mathematics and science, six hours each of humanities, composition, and social sciences, fourteen credits of foreign languages, three hours of historical studies, and three hours of non-Western perspectives. In total, by graduation, students must complete 120 credit hours, including 18 to 42 hours in their major, with a minimum GPA of 2.0.

Majors

English, history, and biology are the strongest majors academically, while commerce, psychology, and history have the largest enrollments. UVa confers B.A., B.S., B.Ar.H., B.I.S., B.S.C., B.S.Ed., B.S.N., and B.U.E.P. degrees in addition to master's and doctoral degrees.

Echols Scholars Program

An example of academic opportunity at UVa, the Echols program offers talented students the means to make the most of their scholastic experience. Founded in 1960 by university faculty, the program continues to operate under the guidance of tenured or tenure-track professors who act as special advisors and mentors to the scholars. As an Echols scholar, your only requirement at UVa is to graduate with 120 approved credit hours. A scholar is free from the distribution requirements and even from declaring a major at all. Many scholars use this freedom to focus on "concentrations" in several of their areas of interest, to double major, or to truly invest themselves in a distinguished majors program. Echols scholars also enjoy priority in choosing courses from ISIS, UVa's computerized registration process, and a scholar will usually never have trouble adding into a restricted or full class. The Echols program also encourages richness in more than just the educational areas of college life. First-year scholars live together in adjacent dormitories and special group activities, both academic and social, are offered for scholars of all years. Participation in the Echols Scholars Program is usually based on an invitation process. Every UVa applicant is considered, and approximately ten percent of each entering class is chosen.

Honor Code

You will sign and date this statement hundreds of times if you attend UVa, but what exactly does it mean, and why is it so important? Established in 1842 in order to ease tensions between faculty and students, the Honor System was soon adopted and maintained by the students. Although it has changed to reflect the ideals of the ever-shifting student body, the system remains an integral part of the UVa mind-set. The simple principles of honor establish a network of trust rarely found in a college setting, including unproctored tests, take-home exams, and even check-writing privileges throughout the local community. However, violating such significant trust also means significant consequences. If a student commits a willful, serious act of lying, cheating, or stealing, and is found guilty by a jury of peers, the only possible sanction is a permanent dismissal from the university. Since the system is entirely student-run, you may participate in many different facets, perhaps as a randomly selected juror, an honor committee member, or an honor advisor, counsel, or educator. Regardless of whether you seek it out, rest assured that the Honor System, its benefits and responsibilities, will be an important part of your daily student life.

> ❝ *On my honor as a student, I have neither given nor received aid on this exam.* ❞

Pressure and Competition

In general, the students at UVa were serious about academics when they were in high school and by the time they reach Charlottesville, they're even more determined to make the most of their college experience. At the same time though, there is rarely an overwhelming sense of academic pressure and competition. UVa students can usually excel in the classroom without losing their perspective on the larger picture. As one wide-eyed first-year student found out, a sense of humor is often involved in keeping stress under control.

> ❝ *It was 2:00 A.M. in the middle of finals week. I had been buried in my books since early that morning. Despite all my preparation, I was debating not even showing up for my test the next day, I was so sure I was going to fail. Just as I was about to close my book and give up completely, a group of students who had been studying together for hours right next to me suddenly jumped up on top of their table and began an impromptu striptease in the middle of Clemons Library. Pretty soon they had the entire room either participating or cheering them on. When it was over, everyone settled right back down and continued studying. It reminded me that life was not solely about finals. I suddenly realized that I would survive the week. After that, I didn't even mind reopening my books.* ❞

SOCIAL LIFE AND ACTIVITIES

Student Body

With their virtually universal appeal, football games are an example of a UVa social event that draws together all different sections of the student body and the local community, both of which have interesting dynamics. Each year, UVa seems to welcome a more diverse entering class. Of the more than 13,000 present undergraduate students, sixty-nine percent are from Virginia, with the rest coming from all fifty states and Washington D.C. and 120 foreign countries, including Canada. Sixty-two percent of the students are white, nine percent are African American, and eleven percent Asian American. Forty-three percent are Protestant, twenty-two percent are Catholic, and twenty-three percent claim no religious affiliation.

> **"** *At UVa football games, fans of all ages, sporting Cavalier paraphernalia, throng together at the back of the vehicles, imbibing homemade fried chicken, sandwiches, barbecue, beer, and all sorts of other goodies they don't serve at the dining halls. Luckily, my roommate was a legacy student with an entire family of enthusiastic, generous alumni, and I would find myself munching and mingling with the entire clan. A steady stream of students, many showing traditional spirit with their khakis and skirts, others waving banners and various body parts smeared with orange and blue paint, moves through the gates to descend on the bleachers.* **"**

The Town

Charlottesville itself offers a unique mix of long-time residents and ever-present tourists. Although the city and surrounding Albemarle County have a population of almost 200,000, Charlottesville maintains a small, friendly town feeling. At UVa, you are nestled just east of the Blue Ridge Mountains, only minutes from the homes of Thomas Jefferson, James Madison, and James Monroe, as well as the stunning sights of Shenandoah National Park and Skyline Drive. In short, there's never a problem finding activities when the relatives come to visit. As a student, you'll probably spend a significant amount of social time on "the corner," a group of shops, bookstores, restaurants, and bars within walking distance of grounds, or on the historic downtown pedestrian mall, which has movie theaters, local boutiques, plenty of coffee houses, and even an ice skating rink.

University of Virginia

Clubs and Organizations

While major school activities such as football games, the famous annual Virginia Film Festival, and the traditional Foxfield Races bring everyone together, most students find an outlet for their social lives through one or more of the numerous activities offered on grounds. With more than 600 clubs and organizations to choose from, UVa students tend to be as active outside as they are inside the classroom. One of the more popular social opportunities is the Greek system. An example of deeply rooted tradition at the university, there are over sixty social and service fraternities and sororities in which twenty-eight percent of men and thirty percent of women are involved. Many more make treks to Rugby Road (the site of many of the fraternity and sorority houses) on Thursday, Friday, and Saturday nights, where there is never a shortage of parties.

For those who tire of the Greek scene, there is no shortage of alternative extracurricular pursuits. Aside from academic societies and professional clubs (including the oldest debating society for undergraduates in the nation) there are groups related to art, band, cheerleading, chess, choir, chorale, chorus, computers, dance, drama, culture, film, gay interests, honors, international concerns, photography, politics, and sports. There are religious associations and special interest groups, including a UNICEF chapter and ROTC. UVa also has a daily newspaper, a weekly news journal, and plenty of student-run special-interest magazines, as well as two radio stations that broadcast on grounds. Another immensely popular organization is Madison House, through which students participate in a variety of community services.

Sports

Finally, activities that require more coordination, such as intramural sports, are also a favorite way to socialize. More than eighty-five percent of students participate in the thirty different sports available. For the more serious and talented athletes, UVa has eleven intercollegiate sports for men and twelve for women. The university is also a Division I member of the NCAA and competes in the Atlantic Coast Conference. From the recently expanded Scott Stadium and the new John Paul Jones 16,000 seat arena to four recreation centers (including an aquatic and fitness facility), UVa offers students every opportunity to enhance their bodies as well as their minds.

Basically, on those rare occasions when you don't actually have to be studying something (and those more frequent times when you choose not to study something), you'll find plenty of other agendas you want to pursue. The key is to choose which activities are most important to you and to make sure you allot some of your precious nonacademic time to truly enjoying them.

FINANCIAL AID

Approximately forty-six percent of all undergraduates receive some form of financial aid, including Parents PLUS loans. Aside from Athletic Grants-in-Aid, non-need-based loan programs, and special scholarships, all undergraduate financial aid is based on financial need. Five percent of undergraduates are involved in part-time work-study employment and the average earnings from college work for the school year are $2,690. To qualify for financial aid, entering students must complete and submit a Free Application for Federal Student Aid (FAFSA) and a Financial Aid Statement (FAS) by March 1. A new initiative, "Access UVa" offers loan-free packages for low-income students, caps on need-based loans for all other students, and a commitment to meet 100 percent of need for every student.

GRADUATES

In a typical year, UVa awards over 3,000 bachelor's degrees. Among those graduates, the most popular majors are economics, psychology, commerce, history, and English. About 500 public and private organizations recruited on grounds last year.

> *Under a massive oak behind the Rotunda, I, along with the close friends I have made over the last four years, lean together, a blur of caps, gowns, and tassels. The camera snaps one last time before I take my first steps in the procession that marks the end of our undergraduate education. As the May morning stretches lazily towards a steamy afternoon, I descend the steps of the Rotunda and gaze out over the lawn, now overflowing with a colorful mass of proud parents, camera-wielding grandparents, and wide-eyed siblings. Later, at my major ceremony, I hold out my hand and receive the long roll of paper that justifies and attests to all of the cramming, sleepless nights, three-hour finals, and fifteen-page papers of the last few years. Stepping off the stage, no longer a student, I realize that the diploma I clutch is not only a consummation of the past, but what will now also be a powerful key to my future.*

SUMMING UP

So ask yourself, why would you want to attend UVa? Because of its high rankings, its rigorous standards, and its feasible tuition? Obviously. Because you would have the chance to take a poetry seminar with former U.S. poet laureate Rita Dove, or a class on race relations from civil rights activist Julian Bond, or a political science lecture with renowned political analyst Larry Sabato? Of course. Because of the academic opportunities, including honors programs, student-run newspapers, magazines, and radio stations? Absolutely. Or even because of its outstanding Office of Career Planning and Placement, which offers internships, externships, résumé and job search guidance, and even arranges interviews with major companies on grounds? Positively. Maybe because of the richness of UVa's history and tradition, from its creation by one of the most important men in America's past to its unique continuation of distinguished customs such as the student-run honor system or the benevolent and mysterious secret societies? Definitely. Is it because the school is located in the heart of a charming city from which you can drive for ten minutes and be in some of the most beautiful, rural scenery in the country? Certainly. Aside from all of this, you realize that you want to attend UVa because of all the little things, from painting Beta bridge, or attending the Restoration Ball, to working for Madison House, or living in La Maison Française, which make any student who attends this university a member of a community and a part of an experience that stretches far beyond a four-year education.

❏ *Larisa Barry, B.A.*

VANDERBILT UNIVERSITY

 Vanderbilt University
Nashville, TN 37203-1700

 (615) 322-2561; (800) 288-0432
Fax: (615) 343-7765

 E-mail: *admission@vanderbilt.edu*
Website: *www.vanderbilt.edu*

 Enrollment

Full-time ❏ women: 3,513
❏ men: 3,366

Part-time ❏ women: 17
❏ men: 31

INTRODUCING VANDERBILT

Nestled close to downtown Nashville, Tennessee, Vanderbilt University has stood as a stronghold of higher education in the southeastern United States since its founding in 1873 by a gift from railroad and shipping magnate Cornelius Vanderbilt. In recent years Vanderbilt has become one of the nation's most engaging, lively, and balanced undergraduate institutions.

> *Vanderbilt as an institution is very hungry, looking for new ideas, embracing new ideas, new approaches to research, to community engagement, to student education.*

Characterized by a unique balance of academic rigor and social activity, Vanderbilt has always attracted the nation's top students. These students come to learn in an intimate and diverse academic setting; many of them have multiple majors or do research with their professors. Because it is comprised of four undergraduate schools and several renowned graduate programs, Vanderbilt provides unique opportunities for academic exploration.

Students from throughout the States and one hundred countries also bring to campus a buzz of activity. Their wide variety of extracurricular passions range from the more traditional (Division I sports, community service, and student government) to the more obscure (hot air ballooning, bowling, and disc golf). Vanderbilt students traditionally exhibit a thirst for service to the world around them, and nearly three quarters of the student body also participates in volunteer activities while at Vanderbilt. Every year many students travel to destinations ranging from South Dakota to New York City to Toronto, Canada through the Alternative Spring Break program, which was founded at Vanderbilt in 1986.

A walk around Vanderbilt reveals one of the nation's most beautiful campuses. A national arboretum, its 330 acres are densely populated with leafy limbs under which students (and squirrels) habitually nap, snack, or study. The student body lives amidst the various species of trees and classic red brick buildings of Vanderbilt's campus. Students find a fantastic community through residence life, starting with The Commons, a residential living and learning community dedicated to enhancing the first year experience.

Vanderbilt students are only five minutes from flourishing downtown Nashville, and the campus itself rests in the center of the city's trendiest neighborhood. Nashville's population of .6 million people radiates a vibrant mix of cosmopolitan energy and southern hospitality, which students find both welcoming and invigorating. Metropolitan Nashville also offers Vanderbilt students opportunities for community service, employment, internships, and religious life just outside the campus perimeter.

A challenging and energetic university, Vanderbilt continues to seek students who hope to engage in four years of both academic and social learning. These students will play a vital role not only in contributing to Vanderbilt intellectually and socially, but also in shaping the direction of the university.

ADMISSIONS REQUIREMENTS

A highly competitive institution, Vanderbilt has experienced significant increases in the number, diversity, and academic profile of its freshmen applicants for the last few years. In the 2009–2010 application year, 21,811 students applied for 1,600 freshman spots at Vanderbilt. Eighty-five percent of enrolling first-year students were in the top ten percent of their high school class, and these students combined exceptional classroom performance with outstanding leadership accomplishments and community involvement. The mid-fifty percent SAT score for enrolling students was 1360–1530; for ACT scores, the mid-fifty percent range was 30–34.

Application Requirements

An application to Vanderbilt is evaluated on the basis of five components through the common application. The first and most important of these components focuses on a student's academic work in high school. Admissions officers look for a high school curriculum of challenging, academic classes (with an emphasis on rigor of curriculum), rather than simply basing their evaluation on grade point average. Additionally, applicants should submit standardized test scores, academic teacher recommendations, a counselor recommendation, an explanation of extracurricular pursuits, the common application essay, and the Vanderbilt Part 1 Supplement.

Standardized Tests

Vanderbilt accepts both the SAT and the ACT. All ACT students must complete the optional writing tests. SAT subject tests are not required for admission; however, they are evaluated if submitted. These subject tests may also be used for placement into language, math, and writing classes upon entrance to the university (additional placement testing is offered upon enrollment). Vanderbilt additionally requires the TOEFL and/or IELTS for overseas applicants whose first language is not English.

Decision Plans

Vanderbilt offers three decision plans: Early Decision I, Early Decision II, and Regular Decision. Created for students who have decided upon Vanderbilt as their first choice, Early Decision is a binding admission plan. Students who apply Early Decision sign a contract to attend Vanderbilt and agree to withdraw all other applications if admitted. Early Decision I applications are due by November 1 with notification mailed by December 15.

Early Decision II and Regular Decision applications must be postmarked or submitted by January 3. Early Decision II students receive notification by February 15, and Regular Decision students receive notification by April 1.

ACADEMIC LIFE

Under the umbrella of Vanderbilt University lie four undergraduate schools: College of Arts and Science, Peabody College of Education and Human Development, School of Engineering, and Blair School of Music. With its four undergraduate schools and distinguished graduate programs in arts and sciences, law, medicine, business, divinity, nursing, and education, Vanderbilt is uniquely suited to provide its students with lavish opportunity to explore and research many fields of study. Every undergraduate at Vanderbilt has access to the courses and resources of the entire university. At least one-third of Vanderbilt students have multiple majors across schools, and many create their own interdisciplinary programs.

> **❝** *For me, the best part of academics at Vanderbilt was how learning was integrated across the curriculum and even outside it. I had an interdisciplinary major (Public Policy Studies) and minor (European Studies). Having this broad academic background that was an integrated whole rather that a collection of disparate pieces gave me a better leg up in the workplace after graduation, but more than that it prepared me for life in the 'real world.'* **❞**

College of Arts and Science

The oldest and largest undergraduate school at Vanderbilt, the College of Arts and Science offers students a broad, liberal arts education, based on a multidisciplinary curriculum in humanities, natural science, social science, languages, and math. Students begin fulfilling this core curriculum in their first year and are not required to declare a major until the spring of their second year. Thus, broad exploration and multidisciplinary study characterize the Arts and Science student.

Engineering School

The first private school in the South to offer a degree in engineering, the Vanderbilt School of Engineering boasts exceptional facilities to offer every possible learning tool for students in the field of engineering, including wireless connection, interactive computer classrooms, and advanced research and computer labs. Additionally, Engineering students take liberal arts courses and other selected courses from Vanderbilt's three other undergraduate schools. As a result of this breadth of academic experience, Vanderbilt Engineering students are highly sought after by corporations as well as graduate schools for their expertise, intellectual independence, communication skills, and leadership ability. Of those engineering graduates seeking employment in a recent year, approximately ninety percent had jobs within six months of graduation.

Peabody College of Education and Human Development

Ranked the number one graduate school of education for the past three years, Peabody College is home to the education and human development majors at Vanderbilt. With its focus on experiential learning across the lifespan, Peabody requires internship and field placements for most of its majors guaranteeing superb preparation for work upon graduation. The most popular undergraduate major at Vanderbilt—Human and Organizational Development—resides in Peabody College. Peabody has produced several renowned programs, including the progressive Head Start program, and it also boasts the top Special Education program in the nation.

Blair School of Music

The Blair School of Music addresses music through a broad array of academic, pedagogical, and performing activities. Each student auditions as a part of the admissions process and chooses to study performance (including all orchestral instruments), composition/theory, musical arts, or musical arts/teacher education. Both students and faculty enrich the campus with frequent performances at Vanderbilt and in the greater Nashville community. Blair's facility includes a 618-seat performance hall with full staging capabilities, recital hall, and generous rehearsal and studio space, including an impressive 4:1 student-to-practice room ratio.

One of the greatest opportunities I had as a student at Blair was getting to see the Nashville Symphony perform frequently. Seeing my clarinet professor on stage with my music theory professor and the teacher of my ear training class and then being able to dialogue about the performance with them the next day in class was a priceless experience for a music major.

Learning Experience

Vanderbilt boasts an intimate, collaborative liberal arts-based learning experience, including an excellent student-to-faculty ratio (8:1). The learning environment also includes access to over $520 million of funded research each year. With over 97% of classes being taught by faculty who have a terminal degree in their respective field, students get the most of each classroom experience. Professors are known for their accessibility, and goes well beyond just having office hours; they also serve as student academic advisors and mentors. First-year students are also treated to residential heads of houses—professors live with their families in each of the 10 Commons houses. This interaction between professors and students is a hallmark of the Vanderbilt undergraduate experience.

Classes

The learning environment at Vanderbilt feels intimate not only because of the faculty, but also because of the small class sizes. Ninety-one percent of classes have fewer than 50 students, and a majority of them (sixty-four percent) fewer than twenty students. Interdisciplinary and experiential learning are both foundational tenets of the classroom experience at Vanderbilt. Students typically take classes in more than one undergraduate school, and double-majoring across schools is common. In addition, Vanderbilt students often combine classroom learning with internship experience, community service, or study abroad.

Undergraduates at Vanderbilt have regular exposure to teaching and research in cutting-edge fields and have access to some 120 interdisciplinary research centers.

Study Abroad

Approximately one-third of Vanderbilt students study abroad at some point in their Vanderbilt careers. These students take advantage of Vanderbilt's unique partnerships in various countries, usually for one or two semesters of junior year, or for summer study. Vanderbilt offers approximately 100 programs on six continents in over thirty countries. Participants in the Vanderbilt Study Abroad programs are guaranteed that their financial aid packages will translate to the Study Abroad semester or year, and courses in the Vanderbilt programs have been evaluated for transferal of credit. Additionally, Vanderbilt belongs to a consortium of schools through which students can find alternative programs that may be better suited to their interests. Vanderbilt encourages students from all undergraduate schools to pursue studies abroad.

—*Director, VISAGE Melbourne*

Graduate Study

Vanderbilt offers applicants unique academic opportunities for graduate study. Undergraduates have the opportunity to apply early to the Vanderbilt business and medical programs. All four undergraduate schools offer combined B.A./M.A. programs that allow students to earn both an undergraduate degree and a master's degree in five years. The Owen Graduate School of Management admits undergraduates in their junior year at Vanderbilt; these students complete their undergraduate studies in addition to an M.B.A. in five years. Through the School of Nursing Senior Year in Absentia program students can earn a baccalaureate degree from the College of Arts and Science or Peabody College in a non-nursing major and a master of science in nursing in five years. Through the Blair School of Music and Peabody College, students can earn a Bachelor of Music and Master of Education in five years. Also, through the Blair School of Music and the Owen Graduate School of Management, a small cohort of students may earn the B.Mus. and the M.B.A. in five years.

The Honor Code

Today I give you two examinations, one in trigonometry and one in honesty. I hope you pass them both, but if you fail one, let it be trigonometry.

—*M. Madison Garratt*

The Honor Code governs student integrity at Vanderbilt University. A rich tradition at Vanderbilt dating to 1875, the Honor Code allows faculty and students to learn in a flexible and trusting environment.

Commitment to the Honor Code begins with all first-year students participating in a discussion and signing of the Code during fall orientation. The pages of signatures hang in Sarratt Student Center, framed as a reminder to students of their oath and to the Vanderbilt community of its reputation for integrity.

SOCIAL LIFE AND ACTIVITIES

Although Vanderbilt students pursue academic success vigorously, they also pour vast amounts of energy and time into extracurricular pursuits. This balance of academic and social pursuits brings a friendly and energetic feel to campus life.

Student Organizations

Nearly all of Vanderbilt's 350-plus organizations are open to all students, who can join at any point in their Vanderbilt careers. These organizations cater to a variety of interests, and they facilitate speakers, special events, community service projects and various other campus activities.

Sarratt Student Center and The Commons Center are the hubs of campus life. Each houses office space, mailboxes, meeting areas, and even faculty advisors for campus organizations. Additionally, the Sarratt Student Center is a sprawling home to student study spaces, a cinema, several dining options, the bookstore, the post office, and a convenience store called Varsity/Market. Because of the involved nature of campus life at Vanderbilt, the Student Center and The Commons Center daily buzz with activity. On a sunny day, students congregate to advertise events, sell tickets, and socialize. Students can best sum up the undergraduate experience with one word: balance.

" When people ask me to describe my life as an undergraduate at Vanderbilt, I often say 'busy!' From the moment I took my first tour of campus, I loved the fact that Vanderbilt was filled with people who had as much energy as I did. The experience of living, studying, organizing, serving, performing, growing, and relaxing with my fellow students provided me with rich growth and deep friendships, both of which are still part of my life today. "

Athletics

A member of the Southeastern Conference, Vanderbilt offers Division I athletics in addition to club and intramural sports. Vanderbilt University maintains a proud tradition of Black and Gold (the school colors) in intercollegiate sports, including six men's and ten women's varsity teams. Students enjoy attending games to cheer and to socialize, and Vanderbilt Commodore teams often play in front of sold-out home venues. As the smallest and only private member in a conference of giants, Vanderbilt boasts the highest graduation rate among athletes in the SEC and one of the top rates in the country. Vanderbilt teams consistently battle for top honors in the SEC and often advance to NCAA post-season play. Since 2000, Vanderbilt has claimed 16 individual and team SEC championships, and recently posted its first NCAA championship (women's bowling). Also, in recent years, Vanderbilt student-athletes have earned National Player of the Year, SEC Player of the Year, and SEC Freshman of the Year. Complementing the varsity sports, club and intramural sports offer Vanderbilt students many opportunities to continue their high school sport of choice, or to try something new. Whether competing in club soccer or trying out Aiki Ju-jutsu for the first time, students from all backgrounds enjoy the Commodore athletic spirit.

> *Vanderbilt attracted me as an athlete and a student, a combination offering that no other university could match. Challenged daily on the football field, playing against national title contenders, I also relished the chance to compete daily in the classroom against the brightest minds in the country. From a chancellor who strives to 'win' in every aspect of the university, to coaches and players who respect and honor academic commitments and accomplishments, the entire athletic community at Vanderbilt pursues victories on the field without losing sight of other academic and social victories to be won off the field.*

Residence Life

Because all undergraduates are required to live on campus, the students who choose to attend Vanderbilt quickly become integrated into the Vanderbilt community. First-year students live at The Commons, a collection of 10 residence Houses, the Dean of The Commons house, and The Commons Center. This LEED-certified complex facilitates relationships between students and faculty, and among the student body. Students spend just over a week participating in Common VU, an orientation program that begins on move-in day and ends after classes begin. Vanderbilt Visions offers regular small-group interaction throughout the first semester; students are led by a faculty-student VUceptor pair and which helps facilitate the transition into life at Vanderbilt. Vanderbilt Visions allows first year students to discuss issues of transition and the Vanderbilt experience, traditions, and community. Vanderbilt students have a variety of campus living options after freshman year, including traditional dorm living, apartment-style housing, and themed housing, among others. Vanderbilt students take advantage of all parts of campus and enjoy easy access to all academic programs and a myriad of on-campus facilities. In addition, students have walking access to hundreds of shops and restaurants that surround campus. Finally, students take advantage of proximity to downtown and easily venture out for internships, socializing, or dining and entertainment.

Alternative Spring Break

The original program of its kind, Vanderbilt's Alternative Spring Break (ASB) annually sends students into needy communities over spring break. Vanderbilt ASB is also one of the largest programs in the country. Each year, over 400 students travel across the nation and abroad to face issues ranging from Native American poverty to urban violence. The ASB Executive Board states, "Our mission is to promote critical thinking, social action and continued community involvement by combining education and direct service on the local, regional, national and international levels." Vanderbilt now offers Alernative Winter and Alternative Summer Break programs.

Greek Life

While Greek life plays a significant role at Vanderbilt, less than half of the student body participates in fraternities or sororities. Unlike most southern schools, Vanderbilt offers a deferred recruitment process. New member recruitment occurs during the spring semester of freshman year, giving new students a chance to adjust to college life and make friends in the fall semester. Students at Vanderbilt can choose from twenty fraternities and fifteen sororities, including Asian, Hispanic, and historically black Greek organizations. All parties are open to the entire student body, and only officers (usually around six) live in the Greek houses on campus.

Nashville

Students from across the country and around the world fall in love with Nashville soon after arriving. "Music City" has earned its reputation and features musicians from many genres and backgrounds, who can be seen performing all over the city. In addition to its renowned live music scene, Nashville boasts a rich cultural and educational heritage. Sixteen other universities call Nashville home, as do the only exact replica of Greece's Parthenon, the Frist Center for the Visual Arts, the Tennessee government and state capital, the NFL's Tennessee Titans, and the NHL's Nashville Predators. Nashville also features diversity usually reserved for more sizable cities, including the largest Kurdish population in the United States and thriving Asian, Hispanic, and African communities.

Vanderbilt's location near downtown Nashville provides easy access to Nashville's best restaurants and hottest night spots, and students often walk to nearby parks. When Vanderbilt students need to get away for a weekend, Nashville also provides an ideal location from which to travel, as it is served by an international airport featuring service from fourteen airlines, and easy access to three major interstate highways.

FINANCIAL AID

Vanderbilt University's seven-year debt-reduction initiative culminated in the fall of 2009 with the beginning of the Expanded Aid Program. The amount of need-based loans you would have been offered in the past to meet your demonstrated financial need has been replaced with Vanderbilt scholarship and/or grant assistance.

Vanderbilt makes the following commitments to U.S. citizens and eligible non-citizens:

- Since talent and promise recognize no social, cultural, economic, or geographic boundaries, the admissions process is need-blind.
- Vanderbilt will meet one hundred percent of a family's demonstrated financial need.
- Financial aid awards do not include loans. Instead of offering need based loans to undergraduate students, Vanderbilt offers additional grant assistance. Applicants must complete the Free Application for Federal Student Aid (FAFSA) and the CSS PROFILE by February 5.

Over sixty percent of Vanderbilt University students receive some form of financial aid, and the average award in 2010–2011 was $41,835.

GRADUATES

The original gates of Vanderbilt University, still located at the main entrance to campus, have ushered generations of Vanderbilt students into the world with great success. Vanderbilt graduates are equipped with strong analytical, critical thinking and writing skills, and they have many options upon graduation.

The Vanderbilt Career Center assists students in pursuing internships during their Vanderbilt experience and post-graduate employment. The Career Center operates an extensive program connecting students with alumni in particular fields. Additionally, the Center offers career coaching, resume-writing consultation, interview training, and on-campus recruiting opportunities.

On average, about forty-seven percent of Vanderbilt students pursue graduate or professional school immediately after graduation, and approximately fifty-five percent pursue full-time employment at graduation.

SUMMING UP

The perfect blend of social activity and academic rigor, Vanderbilt offers prospective students a chance to explore, engage in, and enjoy the college experience. Its spacious lawns, beckoning benches, and shady branches create a comfortable and lovely home for the university's increasingly diverse and talented student body. In the classroom, students thrive under the expert and personal instruction of Vanderbilt's faculty. Outside the classroom, Vanderbilt students continue to affect the world through involvement and service, both in their years on campus and in their lives beyond the gates of Vanderbilt.

A welcoming community, Vanderbilt University offers all students a chance to experience four years of academic challenge, urban vitality, and community involvement.

❏ *Lauren (Nicole) Shaub, B.A.*

VASSAR COLLEGE

Vassar College **Poughkeepsie, NY 12603**	
(845) 437-7300, (800) 827-7270 Fax: (845) 437-7063	
E-mail: *admissions@vassar.edu* Website: *http://www.vassar.edu*	

 **Enrollment**

Full-time ❏ women: 1,384
 ❏ men: 1,017

Part-time ❏ women: 29
 ❏ men: 16

INTRODUCING VASSAR

When Matthew Vassar decided to open a college for women in 1861, he went big—by erecting the largest building in the entire country.

That's right: when it was first constructed, Vassar's Main Building at the heart of the campus was larger than any other American building. But then, Matthew Vassar was accomplishing something big—the establishment of a college where a woman could obtain an excellent and well-rounded education in a time when few women had access to such opportunities.

Vassar has always been an educational pioneer in its dedication to academic discovery and the spirit of true independence. When it opened, it was the first college in the country to include a museum in its facilities; today, Vassar's Frances Lehman Loeb Art Center has more than 18,000 works in its collection, including pieces by such masters as Picasso, Rembrandt, O'Keeffe, and Pollock. In 1982 Vassar became the first college or university in the world to grant an undergraduate major in cognitive science. Vassar was also the first of the Seven Sisters colleges to become coeducational, when it rejected a merger offer from Yale and instead opened its doors to male students in 1969. Vassar's student body is now forty-two percent male, which is about the national average for a college or university.

But the exceptionality of Vassar does not lie merely in its history, but rather in its ability to balance tradition and cutting-edge modernity. In the new century, its newest additions include a Media Studies major, the Interdisciplinary Robotics Research Laboratory, and the Frances Daly Fergusson Dance Theater. Today Vassar continues to serve as a place where anything is possible.

Here's the rundown on campus residences:

○ **Jewett House:** At nine stories tall, newly renovated Jewett towers over the campus. Legend says that poet Edna St. Vincent Millay threw herself from the top of Jewett once but fell into a nearby oak tree and was saved.

○ **Davison House, Raymond House, Lathrop House, Strong House:** These four quad dorms are the places to be on weekend nights. Strong is also the only all-female dorm on campus.

○ **Cushing House:** Set slightly apart from the other dorms, Cushing provides a tight-knit dorm community behind its ivy-covered walls.

○ **Main House:** Main is at the center of campus, so it's a convenient and happening place to live.

○ **Noyes House:** Its unique curved shape and retro "Jetson" lounge were designed by Eero Saarinen, the architect of the Gateway Arch in St. Louis, Missouri.

○ **Josselyn House:** The first dorm at Vassar that opened with showers (1912), "Joss" has its own green stretch of lawn known fondly as "Joss Beach."

○ **Ferry Cooperative House:** Ferry House provides upperclassmen the opportunity to try out communal living. This cooperative housing environment is completely operated and administered by the students who live there.

○ **Terrace Apartments, Town Houses, and South Commons:** These campus apartments provide Vassar seniors with a chance to move away from dorm living and toward more independent housing arrangements.

A Blend of Old and New

A visit to the famously beautiful campus makes it abundantly clear that the old and the new merge seamlessly at Vassar. Students enjoy some older Vassar traditions (Such as the Daisy Chain, a group of sophomores who carry a chain of daisies and laurel at

Commencement) while creating new traditions of their own, such as Primal Scream, a group howl on the Quad that unofficially kicks off the start of final exams. A recent building such as the Broadway- and Hollywood-grade Vogelstein Center for Drama and Film stands amid genteel nineteenth-century structures without looking a bit out of place. The observatory, opened in 1864 for Maria Mitchell, Vassar's first professor, was succeeded in 1997 by the Class of '51 Observatory, which houses one of the most powerful telescopes in New York State. Students balance traditional subjects such as physics, sociology, and English with courses in Africana studies, German, and environmental studies, and temper study sessions and student group activities with volunteer work and meeting friends at campus hangouts.

Vassar's ability to balance so many different facets of its identity makes it a college of infinite opportunity. The college provides countless paths, all of them exciting and challenging—it's up to a Vassar student to choose!

ADMISSIONS REQUIREMENTS

Don't be scared by the word "requirements" here. In fact, applying to Vassar is a lot like applying to most liberal arts schools—each school has different ways for you to communicate your personality to the folks making the admissions decisions. When reviewing applications, Vassar takes a holistic approach, and considers many aspects: high school program, grades, testing, activities, talents, and drive.

Admittedly, Vassar students are generally a high-achieving bunch: in the class of 2012, the mean SAT average among students was 702 in Critical Reading, 679 in Math, and 691 in writing, with a composite ACT score of 30.4. About ninety-one percent of the class of 2014 had been ranked in the top twenty percent or higher of their high school classes; many of them were National Merit Scholarship finalists or semifinalists. In fact, of the 7,822 applications to the class of 2014 that Vassar received, only twenty-three percent were admitted.

Vassar provides a rigorous academic program, and it expects that its students will have prepared themselves for it to the best of their abilities. Applicants should have taken the most challenging courses available in their high school careers, and typically will have taken English, math, natural science, social science, and foreign language courses during all four years of high school. If applicants have access to Advanced Placement, honors, or International Baccalaureate courses, these should be taken as well.

How to Apply

Early Decision applications (for students who know Vassar is their first-choice school) are due on November 15 with notification in mid-December, or on January 1 with notification in late January; Regular Decision applications are also due on January 1, but don't receive admissions decisions until mid-April. Vassar uses the Common Application, which is accepted at a wide variety of schools across the United States and can be filled out online. Candidates should plan to take the SAT and two SAT subject tests, or the ACT with writing, by no later than January of senior year for Regular Decision applicants; November for ED I or December for Early Decision II applicants.

In addition to the basic application, candidates must include a personal essay and a $65 application fee. Then there's "Your Space," an optional blank space where you can express who you are without SAT scores or biology grades. Some people send poems they've written, some send notes to the admissions office, and some send drawings or sketches. You can do anything for "Your Space"—even leave it blank. Alumni interviews are optional and non-evaluative.

Transfer Students

Vassar accepts a limited number of transfer students each year; most years, only about twenty transfer students enroll. Applicants from other colleges or universities must demonstrate high academic achievement and cannot have taken more than four full semesters of college-level work.

International Students

About 10% of Vassar's student population holds foreign citizenship, and current students represent sixty different nations, with the largest representation coming from Bulgaria, China, India, Korea, Turkey, Japan, Bahamas, Ghana, Singapore, Ecuador, and Romania. International applicants use the same application and must take the same standardized tests as American applicants; however, if English is neither your first language nor the primary language of instruction you have used throughout secondary school, you will need to submit the results of the Test of English as a Foreign Language (TOEFL). Vassar typically expects scores of at least 100 on the Internet-based TOEFL. Vassar also accepts IELTS as an alternative to TOEFL.

For more on applying, check out Vassar's Admissions Web site: *http://admissions. vassar.edu/.*

Vassar's academic curriculum is based upon fierce intellectual curiosity and uninhibited scholastic exploration. Here, course offerings are numerous, professors are often mentors and friends, and classes can be as small as just three or four students. Vassar prides itself on being a place where students can discover new academic pursuits while continuing to study their old favorites. And one of the ways this happens is through Vassar's unrestrictive academic requirements.

> **❝** *In my junior year, Professor Darlington walked into our Romantic Poets class and told me that she thought my paper was 'brilliant.' You don't know what that meant to me—there I was, a small-town girl from Ohio who had worked so hard to get into college, and now my hard work was really paying off. I'd never felt so encouraged before, so completely free to write and think as I chose. To this day, whenever I mess up or feel silly, I think back to what Professor Darlington said to me, and I remember how much I gained from my classes at Vassar.* **❞**

Requirements

One of the most popular aspects of the Vassar curriculum is its flexible graduation requirements. Unlike some other schools where graduation requirements are rigid and intended to force students to follow a one-size-fits-all academic program, Vassar's requirements allow students to choose what they want to study while still exposing them to subjects they might not otherwise have taken.

To graduate from Vassar, students need thirty-four credits (with most regular, semester-long courses worth one credit), including a freshman writing course (a writing-intensive intro course in a particular field), a foreign language credit, and a quantitative course credit. At least 8.5 credits must be taken outside the student's major division. Each student will also have specific requirements for his or her particular major.

Students have until the end of their sophomore year to declare a major. Majors may be declared in either a single department (such as English or biology), an interdepartmental program (such as medieval and Renaissance studies or neuroscience and behavior), a multidisciplinary program that draws from multiple fields and numerous departments (such as cognitive science or media studies), or an independent program, which allows the student to design his or her own major. Students can also choose to declare a correlate sequence (similar to a "minor") in any one of a wide variety of fields. Vassar is known for helping students to customize the curriculum to fit their educational interests and professional goals.

Credit

Vassar credit can also be earned outside the classroom. Last year, more than 500 Vassar students participated in field work internships for credit, in Poughkeepsie and the surrounding Hudson Valley, and many as far as New York City. Vassar's study abroad program is also very popular, with many students studying at other institutions in the United States or abroad during their junior year or over the summer. Vassar has its own programs in Germany, Ireland, France, Italy, Spain, and Russia, but accepts credit from a large number of other study abroad programs.

Studying At Vassar

At Vassar, classes are often intimately small; the average class size is seventeen, but classes can run even smaller. As a result, many students find that they are easily able to get to know their professors and to establish a relationship that goes beyond student-teacher formality. Most Vassar students meet with professors outside the classroom, either for extra help during office hours, to work on a special research project, or just to discuss a particular issue over lunch at the dining hall.

Faculty

Professors at Vassar also serve as academic advisors. Freshman students are assigned temporary "pre-major' advisors in their academic fields or interest; these advisors help underclassmen to decide what courses they should take and what majors might interest them. After declaring a major, a student is given a new advisor from his or her academic department. Students often choose their new advisors based on previous classroom experience or on mutual research interests.

Facilities

Most students spend at least some study time in the fabulous Frederick Ferris Thompson Memorial Library, a cathedral-like building that houses one of the finest undergraduate collections in the country, including a million print volumes, numerous elec-

VASSAR COURSES: A SAMPLER

○ Africana Studies 263: Words of Fire: African American Orators and Their Orations
○ Biology 172: Microbial Wars
○ Computer Science 379: Computer Animation: Art, Science, and Criticism
○ Economics 388: Global Imbalances, Global Consequences
○ English 362: Woven Stories: Medieval and Renaissance Tapestry and Text
○ Film 214: Genre: The War Film
○ German Studies 101: Vampires, Lunatics, and Cyborgs: Exploring the Uncanny Recesses of the Romantic Consciousness
○ History 381: Love and Death in Tokugawa Japan, 1603–1868
○ Music 259: Soundscapes: Anthropology of Music
○ Urban Studies 350: New York City as a Social Laboratory
○ Women's Studies 254: Bio-politics of Breast Cancer

tronic resources, and a computerized learning center known as the Media Cloisters. Also housed there is the Archives and Special Collections Library, a collection of rare and primary sources that can be accessed by appointment. The rare books in the collection date from as early as the fifteenth century, and the manuscript collection includes unique medieval manuscripts, original documents by alumnae writers Mary McCarthy, Elizabeth Bishop, and Edna St. Vincent Millay, and the papers of naturalist John Burrows, astronomer Maria Mitchell, and physicist Albert Einstein.

Of course, if you're looking for a laid-back atmosphere, you could study in the Java City café, where you can grab a snack to keep you focused or a latte to keep you awake during late-night homework sessions.

Because of Vassar's adaptive requirements, engaging faculty, and comfy study spaces, studying at Vassar is often a limitless and adventurous experience. It's a place where you can really explore all your options, discover novel passions, and develop your academic potential in whatever direction you choose.

SOCIAL LIFE AND ACTIVITIES

Let's face it: studying is only a part of college life. And while getting an education is a large part of the equation, your social life and activities are also just as crucial to finding the real you.

So what's life like at Vassar?

For one thing, community spirit runs high. The school is small, with only about 2,450 students, and ninety-eight percent of students live on campus, which makes the college feel homey and intimate. While you won't know everyone on campus by name, you won't be able to walk across the Quad without seeing at least two or three familiar faces. The absence of any fraternities or sororities means that the student body socializes together, rather than in fragmented, isolated groups.

> **❝** *I like the College very much—and think that it is a superior boarding school—nearly everything that could be done is done for the students... I am much better contented than I ever expected to be away from home.* **❞**

—*Letter, dated Nov. 18, 1865, from Mary Coe Tompson, '65–Feb. '66*

Vassar students generally love to have fun, mingle with one another, and get involved with their community. No matter what you love, chances are you'll find someone else who shares that passion at Vassar.

Activities

There are more than 120 student-run organizations at Vassar, and about 1,300 campus-wide events are held each year, including guest lecturers, visiting artists and performers, exhibits, workshops, athletic events, and concerts. Chances are, you won't ever be bored at Vassar.

Theater is definitely big at Vassar. Numerous student performance groups, two intimate black-box theaters, and the 300-seat Martel Theater provide a multitude of opportunities to create and attend shows. There are also improv and comedy troupes, and seven different *a capella* groups, including the Night Owls, the nation's oldest continuing women's collegiate *a capella* group. Students in the Vassar Repertory Dance Theatre (organized by the Dance department) present a fall season and an annual spring weekend of gala performances at the historic Bardavon Theater in downtown Poughkeepsie, and students lead their own dance troupes such as FlyPeople and Vassar Tap. If you play an instrument or enjoy singing, there are plenty of ensembles (both through the music department and independently) that perform throughout the year. And not only are there an abundance of Steinway pianos in the Skinner Hall of Music, there are also a bunch sprinkled throughout the dorms and other social spaces.

Activism

Interested in social activism? Amnesty International, Democracy Matters, Feminist Alliance, Habitat For Humanity, and the Moderate Independent Conservative Alliance are just a few of the groups that are active on Vassar's campus. Vassar also has student political party groups, including the Vassar Democrats, Vassar Republicans, and the Vassar Greens. Cultural groups include the Black Students' Union, the Caribbean Students' Alliance, the Queer Coalition of Vassar College, and Poder Latino, among many others.

Religion

Vassar was founded as a college independent of particular denominational ties, which makes it the perfect space for a variety of religious and spiritual beliefs to coexist. The Office of Religious and Spiritual Life (whose motto actually is "Believe It Or Not") supports and sponsors many student religious groups, including the Vassar Catholic Community, Vassar Christian Fellowship, Buddhist Sangha, the Vassar Jewish Union, and the Pagan Study Group, to name just a few.

Publications

Vassar also has several student-run publications and broadcasts—the *Miscellany News* is one of the oldest student weeklies in the country, and WVKR is one of the most powerful college radio stations in New York State. For creative writers, there is the literary journal *Helicon*; for aspiring Scorseses, there is the Vassar Filmmakers. Every year new student journals, newsletters, and publications spring up, so there's always a fresh new take on current events and artistic goings-on.

And these are all just a slice of the student groups at Vassar. From the Barefoot Monkeys (the student circus troupe that gives fire shows on the Quad) to Hip Hop 101, from PHOCUS (photography and cooperative darkroom) to the Outing Club, there's always something new and challenging to try.

Athletics

Vassar fields twenty-three teams in the NCAA's Division III (no athletic scholarships), and annually boasts athletic and academic All-Americans. In recent years, Vassar's men's volleyball team reached the national championship game; women's rugby competed in the USA Rugby National Championships; and women's tennis played in the NCAA tournament for the seventh time in eight years. As a group, Vassar athletes often maintain an average GPA higher than that of the general student body.

Vassar offers excellent facilities, whether you're a varsity athlete, you play a club sport or in an intramural league, or you just like to work out. The combined Athletics & Fitness Center and Walker Field House include a wood-floor gymnasium, a multipurpose playing surface for everything from tennis to fencing, a six-lane Olympic-size swimming pool and diving well, an elevated running track, several fitness studios, a large exercise room, and a sports medicine facility. The soccer, lacrosse, field hockey, baseball, and track teams are ecstatic over the multimillion dollar renovation and expansion of the Prentiss Field complex. Kenyon Hall features one of the few dedicated volleyball gymnasiums at a U.S. college, and several international standards squash courts. There are varsity and recreational tennis courts behind Josselyn House, the nine-hole Vassar Golf Course welcomes golfers of all levels, and only minutes from campus, Vassar crew teams row across the Hudson River.

Off-Campus Entertainment

Vassar has so much to offer in terms of entertainment that few students feel the need to leave every weekend in order to have fun. There are always plays to attend, films to see, parties to check out at Matthew's Mug (the campus club) or in the College Center, concerts to take in, or friends to see at the Students' Building.

But if cabin fever gets you down, there are plenty of things to do off campus, as well. Student-friendly cafés and restaurants pepper the area around the college, such as Baby Cakes Bakery (a great place to have breakfast on Saturday morning), the tweny-four-hour Acropolis Diner (a Vassar standby), Sushi Village (home of the best spicy tuna roll in the world!) or the Cubbyhole, a great hole-in-the-wall hangout.

Further off is the Galleria Mall and downtown Poughkeepsie, which has the historic Bardavon Theater, the Civic Center, and the Chance Club for touring acts. Poughkeepsie is also surrounded by several nice locations, including artsy Rhinebeck, college-town New Paltz, and Beacon, home to the world-renowned DIA contemporary art museum. And of course, New York City is only an hour-and-a-half train ride away!

FINANCIAL AID

Don't assume that a private, highly selective school such as Vassar is out of your reach. Its financial aid program is strictly need-based, over sixty percent of students receiving some aid and an average Vassar scholarship of $32,861. Vassar is "need blind" for all U.S. citizens and permanent residents. It doesn't take your family's financial situation into consideration when making admissions decisions, and the school meets one hundred percent of the demonstrated need of all admitted students for all four years. Vassar has also recently established a policy that eliminates loans from the financial aid packages of students from low income families, and replaces them with scholarship aid.

If you are awarded financial aid, your aid package will typically include a combination of different sources, including Vassar scholarships, government or private scholarships or loans, and work-study jobs. Work-study allows students to work between eight and ten hours per week at a campus job in a particular administrative or academic department in order to earn money. The Office of Student Employment always gives job priority to financial aid students, which makes it easier to find the right job match for incoming freshmen with financial needs.

In order to receive financial aid, you must apply as early as possible—don't wait to find out if you were accepted! In addition to a Vassar form, applicants must complete the Free Application for Federal Student Aid (FAFSA) and the CSS PROFILE, the College Board's online financial aid application service. For more application information and for specific application deadlines, visit Vassar's Financial Aid website at *http://admissions.vassar.edu/finaid.html.*

GRADUATES

College is an experience in itself, but it also serves to prepare you for a future career. Vassar graduates have gone into so many fields and taken so many different paths that it's easy to imagine that a Vassar education can help you to get virtually anywhere you want to go.

> **❝** *On graduation day, it was amazing to see how far we'd all come. I remember sitting there and thinking about what lay in store for each of my friends as they walked up to receive their diplomas—grad school for some, jobs for others, and for a few, travel or relaxation before starting the next phase of their lives. We were all about to go off on so many different paths, and while it was a scary feeling, it was also incredibly exhilarating.* **❞**

After graduation, you'll have access to a network of more than 3,000 alumnae/i who volunteer as career advisors. You'll have a degree that opens doors to numerous graduate

- Ellen Swallow Richards, 1870, Founder of Ecology
- Crystal Eastman, '03, Coauthor of the Equal Rights Amendment
- Edna St. Vincent Millay, '17, Pulitzer Prize-winning Poet
- Rear Admiral Grace Murray Hopper, '28, Computer Pioneer and Co-inventor of the Computer Language COBOL
- Mary McCarthy, '33, Pulitzer Prize-winning Author
- Elizabeth Bishop, '34, Pulitzer Prize-winning Poet
- Vera Cooper Rubin, '48, Astronomer, proved existence of "Dark Matter"
- Anne Armstrong, '49, Counselor to two U.S. Presidents
- Mary Oliver, '54, Pulitzer Prize-winning Poet
- Elizabeth Titus-Putnam, '55, Founder of the Student Conservation Association
- Sau Lan Wu, '63, High-Energy Particle Physicist, Co-discoverer of Gluon
- Nina Zagat, '63, Co-founder of the Zagat Survey and Guidebooks
- Bernardine Healy, M.D. '65, Director of the National Institutes of Health, Cardiologist
- Ellen Silbergeld, '67, MacArthur Fellow, Public Health Scholar and Advocate
- Lucinda Franks, '68, Pulitzer Prize-winning Journalist
- Meryl Streep, '71, Academy Award-winning Actress
- Jane Smiley, '71, Pulitzer Prize-winning Author
- Vicki Miles-LaGrange, '74, Federal Court Judge, First African-American Woman Named a U.S. Attorney
- Richard W. Roberts, '74, U.S. District Court Judge
- Eben Ostby, '77, Acadamy Award-winning Computer Animator
- Phil Griffin, '79, President of MSNBC
- Rick Lazio, '80, US Congressman
- John Carlstrom, '81, MacArthur Fellow and Astrophysicist
- Matthew Brelis, '80, Pulitzer Prize-winning Journalist
- Lisa Kudrow, '85, Emmy Award-winning Actress and Costar of *Friends*
- Marc Thiessen, '89, Chief Presidential Speechwriter
- Noah Baumbach, '91, Academy Award-winning Writer and Director
- Ethan Zohn, '96, *Survivor: Africa* Winner and Co-founder of Grassroot Soccer
- Sam Endicott, '99, Lead Singer of *The Bravery*

schools, jobs, and career paths. And you'll have four years of amazing memories and friendships that will last for the rest of your life.

Graduate Study

The majority of Vassar students opt for graduate study following the completion of their undergraduate degrees; seventy percent of Vassar grads find themselves in graduate school within five years after graduation. Many alumnae/i opt for professional schools to study law, medicine, or business; in 2009, seventy-five percent of Vassar grads who applied to medical school and eighty-five percent of those who applied to law school were accepted, compared to the national averages of forty-six percent and sixty-six percent, respectively.

And how do they pay for all this? With scholarships and fellowships. Vassar awards $150,000 in graduate fellowships, and every year Vassar students receive Fulbrights, Rhodes, Mellons, Watson, and many more renowned awards. Vassar's Office for Fellowship and Pre-Professional Advising helps students get information on all sorts of grants and awards for graduate school.

Employment

Of course, not everyone chooses to continue with education after completing their undergrad degree. For those with an eye toward immediate employment, Vassar can help you jumpstart your career through the Office of Career Development. It can help you figure out what sorts of jobs interest you, where to find them, and how to get them. The Office can also connect you to alumnae/i in your field or with your interests who can advise and mentor you as you move into post-Vassar life.

Ultimately, though, the best part about graduating from Vassar is knowing that you've got a degree that is applicable in so many different fields and on so many different paths. No matter what you major in, you'll come out of your Vassar experience knowing more about who you are—and where you're going.

SUMMING UP

On the day I graduated from Vassar, I expected to feel miserable. After all, I was moving away from the place that had been, for four whole years, my home, and I was leaving behind the friends I'd grown to love like family. Packing up my stuff the day before had almost reduced me to tears, and so I thought, as I walked across the amphitheater to receive my diploma, that I'd start to feel a terrible sense of loss, a palpable awareness of the end of an era in my life.

But among the sadness at what I was losing, among the fear of the unknown, I actually felt so much excitement, so much anticipation, and so much pride. I knew then that Vassar had really, truly prepared me for my postgraduate life; while I could look back on what I had accomplished at Vassar with a fondness and nostalgia that, even now, never seems to diminish, I could also look forward to putting the experiences I had known, the knowledge I had accrued, and the strength I had gained from Vassar to good use.

> *" Vassar is arguably the most brilliant and beautiful of the Seven Sisters. Clearly, she is the most independent and rebellious, and the only one with enough chutzpah to turn down a marriage proposal from Yale. "*

—*Samuel L. Jackson, Commencement speech to the Class of 2004*

It's an exciting feeling, knowing that you've got a whole big world waiting for you, and an entire life to try and figure it out. And that's what Vassar really gives you: the tools to navigate life, and the courage to go ahead and use them.

❏ *Philosophy Walker, B.A.*

VILLANOVA UNIVERSITY

 Villanova University
Villanova, PA 19085

 Phone: (610) 519-4000
Fax: (610) 519-6450

 E-mail: *gotovu@villanova.edu*
Website: *www.villanova.edu*

 Enrollment

Full-time ❏ women: 3,224
❏ men: 3,192

Part-time ❏ women: 285
❏ men: 277

INTRODUCING VILLANOVA

Villanova's beautiful 254-acre campus is located twelve miles west of Philadelphia, in the famed "Main Line" suburbs. Villanova is the oldest and largest Catholic university in Pennsylvania, and was founded in 1842 by the Order of Saint Augustine. Saint Augustine believed in a commitment to community, and to the connections between the mind and the heart, and between truth and love. The Augustinian values stated on our university seal—*Veritas, Unitas, Caritas*—(translated as truth, unity, and love) still guide " 'Nova Nation" today. Villanova is home to students of all faiths, and tends to attract students who are dedicated to social responsibility, volunteer work, and contributing to the greater good.

> *The most distinctive aspect of Villanova is its sense of community, since this is the aspect of the university that permeates all others and in many ways defines what it means to be a Villanovan. The care that people show for one another, both on our campus and across the world, is tangible and on display constantly. This community focus is central to everything—from coursework to social events to volunteer opportunities. It even flows through our 107,000-strong alumni community. As a recent alumna, I've already gone back to Villanova for several events and I would like to maintain a strong connection to the university for many years to come. During my four years there, I was helped by countless Villanova alumni in all different facets of life and I would like nothing more than to give back as much as I have received.*

Villanova's scenic campus has more than sixty-five buildings—including twenty-six residence halls and a library with more than 1,000,000 volumes. In addition to offering more than forty-five rigorous academic programs, Villanova provides students with a wide range of opportunities to study abroad and to participate in more than 265 campus organizations. Student services are excellent—from the Villanova Laptop program to the Student Health Center, from the award-winning dining services and Holy Grounds coffee shops to the Career Center.

> *Extracurricular opportunities at Villanova definitely appeal to a broad range of student interests. Throughout my four years as an undergraduate, I served as a Villanova School of Business peer advisor, a Villanova Ambassador, a liturgical minister, and president of the National Society of Leadership and Success. I was also involved in intramural sports, including basketball, soccer, and club Frisbee. I led a group of 12 students on a service trip to San Jose, Costa Rica, during my senior year, and spent a summer studying and working abroad in London.*

Villanova is also home to the Davis Center for Athletics, and many intramural and varsity sports teams, including the nationally recognized Wildcat's men's basketball team, which generates a lot of excitement and community spirit on campus. In 2009, Villanova won NCAA national championships in FCS Division I football and Division I women's cross country, and the men's basketball team advanced to the 2009 NCAA Final Four.

ADMISSIONS REQUIREMENTS

Admission to Villanova is competitive. In addition to attracting academically talented, well-rounded students, Villanova seeks applicants who have "compassionate minds" and a desire to transform the world and make it a better place.

VILLANOVA SNAPSHOT: ADMISSIONS STATS

- Number of First-year Undergraduate Applicants: 14,361
- Early Action Application Deadline: November 1
- Regular Application Deadline: January 7
- Number of Applicants Accepting a Place on Waiting List: 2,425
- Wait-listed applicants Admitted: 494
- Transfer Applications Received: 659
- Transfer Students Enrolled: 107
- Tests Required? Yes, SAT I or ACT
- Common Application Accepted? Yes
- Supplemental Forms Required? Yes
- Application Fee: $75
- SAT I Middle 50% Range: 1330–1440/1600
- ACT Composite Middle 50% Range: 30–33
- Freshman Retention Rate: 95%
- Admissions Phone: (610) 519-4000
- Admissions E-mail: gotovu@villanova.edu

Common Application

Villanova is a Common Application member institution. In addition to the Common Application, prospective students are required to complete the Villanova supplement for Undergraduate Admission and submit an official high school transcript and Common Application School Report.

Standardized Tests

Villanova requires applicants to have their standardized test scores (SAT or ACT) reported directly to Villanova by the College Board or ACT.

High School Performance

In the Villanova admissions process, high school performance is an extremely important selectivity factor. Each student's high school record, GPA, and class rank, along with each student's demonstration of character and personal abilities, are carefully considered. Extracurricular and volunteer activities, in addition to outstanding academic work, are helpful to applicants in this regard.

Personal Essay and Recommendations

Another important factor in the Villanova admissions process is the personal essay. Because interviews are not part of the admission process, a well-crafted essay is essential for prospective students to explain who they are and why they should be selected to become Villanovans. (A recommendation from the secondary school counselor is also carefully considered.)

International Applicants

Non-U.S. prospective students are warmly welcomed to apply for admission to Villanova. Applicants who are non-native English speakers countries must take the Test of English as a Foreign Language (TOEFL) or the International English Language Testing Systems (IELTS) test and have scores reported directly to Villanova from the College Board. The Villanova International Student Services Office supports enrolled international students in areas including immigration rights and responsibilities; educational, social, and personal counseling; cultural adjustment issues; and campus and community activities.

Transfer Applicants

Transferring to Villanova is possible, but selective. Students applying to transfer to Villanova must complete a transfer application and submit official transcripts from each postsecondary school attended and a completed Dean of Students Transfer Evaluation form.

ACADEMIC LIFE

Villanova offers degree programs through four colleges: the Villanova School of Business, the College of Liberal Arts and Sciences, the College of Engineering, and the College of Nursing. Graduate degree programs are also offered through the Villanova School of Law. All Villanova colleges are recognized for their academic quality and technological resources, and all are focused on the education and well-being of the *whole* person—intellectually, emotionally, spiritually, culturally, socially, and physically.

Business

The Villanova School of Business, one of the top-ranked business programs in the United States, offers majors in accounting, economics, finance, management, management information systems, and marketing. The school also offers a business honors degree, an

- Accounting
- Arab Islamic Studies
- Art History
- Astronomy and Astrophysics
- Biochemistry
- Biology
- Business Administration: Economics, Finance, Management, MIS, Marketing
- Engineering: Chemical, Civil, Computer, Electrical, Mechanical
- Chemistry
- Classical Studies
- Communication
- Comprehensive Science

- Computer Science
- Criminal Justice
- Cultural Studies
- Economics
- Education (Secondary)
- English
- Environmental Science
- Environmental Studies
- French and Francophone Studies
- Gender and Women's Studies
- Geography
- Global Interdisciplinary Studies
- History
- Honors
- Human Services

- Humanities
- International Business (Co-major)
- Italian
- Latin American Studies
- Liberal Studies
- Mathematical Sciences/Applied Statistics
- Nursing
- Philosophy
- Physics
- Political Science
- Psychology
- Sociology
- Spanish Studies
- Theology and Religious Studies

international business co-major, and minors in entrepreneurship, real estate, and business law and corporate governance. VSB is home to the Applied Finance Lab, which provides students with many of the real-time technological resources available to Wall Street traders. Bartley Hall, with its light-filled, three-story atrium, class- and study rooms, and common areas includes the Bartley Exchange dining hall. The two most popular special programs among VSB students are international experiences and service learning. Nearly half of the student body participates in international academic, internship, and volunteer experiences.

Liberal Arts and Sciences

The College of Liberal Arts and Sciences—one of the few colleges in the country that offers an undergraduate degree in astronomy and astrophysics—provides a wide array of degree programs, concentrations, and majors, along with interdisciplinary majors in the humanities, international studies, comprehensive science, and environmental science. Villanova is one of only eighteen Catholic colleges or universities in the nation to have a chapter of Phi Beta Kappa, the prestigious liberal arts honor society.

Engineering

The College of Engineering, ranked among the best engineering programs in the nation, offers degree programs in the disciplines of chemical engineering, civil and environmental engineering, computer engineering, electrical engineering, and mechanical engineering. The college is home to three research units: The Center for Advanced Communications, The Center for Nonlinear Dynamics and Control, and The Villanova Center for the Advancement of Sustainability in Engineering. The college's home, the Villanova Center for Engineering Education and Research, houses state-of-the-art instructional and research labs. Additional engineering-related facilities can be found on campus in White Hall, John Barry Hall, Tolentine Hall, and the 10,000-square-foot Structural Engineering Teaching and Research Laboratory.

Nursing

A small but very special group on the Villanova campus is the student body of the College of Nursing. A manifestation of the Augustinian spirit of caring in action, Villanova nursing students have opportunities to work closely with community members in need while completing their rigorous coursework.

The College of Nursing is housed in Driscoll Hall, a beautiful 75,500-square-foot building that features:

- a 200-seat auditorium and a 200-seat lecture hall
- future-oriented clinical simulation labs for health assessment, adult health, maternal/child health, anesthesia, and critical care
- simulation labs for standardized patient observation and testing
- a center for nursing research and scholarship
- space for prayer and reflection
- space for global health studies and international student activities
- space for student, faculty, and alumni events and social interaction

VILLANOVA SNAPSHOT: STUDENT BODY

- Minority Students: 20%
- In-State Students: 20.3%
- Students Living on Campus: 70%
- Students Affiliated with the Greek system: 20%
- Students Involved in Varsity or Club Athletics: 21%
- Students who Pursue Graduate/ Professional School after Graduation: 23%
- Number of Official Extracurricular Student Organizations: 265
- Number of States Represented 48
- Number of Countries Represented: 54

Faculty

The student-to-faculty ratio at Villanova is 12:1. The university's 586 full-time faculty members—ninety percent of whom hold the highest degree in their field—teach classes that average twenty-two students. The faculty is accessible and provides the personalized, community-focused educational experience for which Villanova is known.

Technology

The technological resources available to Villanova students are outstanding. Each incoming student receives a new laptop (upgraded at the end of sophomore year), and all residence halls are connected to the campus network. Students can participate in learning experiences across campus; receive curricular advising services; and access tests, webcasts, and library reserves online. Through myNOVA, Villanova's student portal, students keep track of deadlines, class schedules, and financial aid information. Villanova's technology also provides easy access to meal plans, parking registration, laundry reservations, voting processes, ride sharing/carpooling, and basketball ticket lotteries. In addition, students and parents are able to sign up for Nova Alert, the University's emergency notification system.

Career Services

With the help of Villanova's Career Center, students develop their professional skills and gain access to a wide variety of career options. The support resources provided to students include career fairs, career counseling, graduate school counseling, career library, practice interviews, resume critiques, workshops, and seminars.

> 66 *I was challenged by my professors to use my undergraduate accounting degree to pursue an internship with Deloitte & Touche in Manhattan in the spring of 2007.*
>
> *My internship was a phenomenal extension of my classroom learning, and upon concluding my four months in New York, I accepted a job offer from Deloitte & Touche. I am now enjoying my Deloitte & Touche job tremendously, and am grateful to Villanova for providing me with the education that has allowed me to arrive at this point in my life.* 99

More than 4,000 jobs are posted on Villanova's job boards each year and the median starting salary for Villanova graduates is $51,000. More than ninety-seven percent of Villanova graduates become full-time employees or enroll in graduate school within six months of graduation. Internships are also an important source of professional development opportunities for students. Over 400 internships are posted on campus each year, and internships often lead to full-time job offers.

SOCIAL LIFE AND ACTIVITIES

Villanova is a fun, close-knit, caring academic and social community. Filled with endless opportunities to meet new friends, discover new interests, and enjoy campus life, the undergraduate experience at Villanova is most often warmly remembered by alumni as "some of the best years of our lives." In the Augustinian tradition, mutual love, respect, and compassion are paramount values, and Villanova leaders expect these values to guide all interactions among students outside the classroom.

My Villanova experiences provided me with a unique opportunity to learn about myself and others in my community—whether they were my roommates, my professors across campus, the first-graders in West Philadelphia we tutored after school each week, or the host families with whom we stayed in Costa Rica. I accomplished things at Villanova that I'd never imagined I could when I first set foot on campus as a freshman. What I tell incoming students is that you may come to Villanova thinking you know a great deal about yourself and the world, but what you realize by the time you leave Villanova is how much you truly have left to learn! My Villanova experience taught me that it is never enough to settle for what is good right now; our Villanova education instead demands that we constantly strive to be better, in the classroom, at work, in our families, in our communities, and in our world.

To help students transition from high school to college, incoming freshmen have the opportunity to be part of a Villanova Learning Community. Through Learning Communities, students form close friendships as they live together in specially designated residence halls and learn together in courses and cocurricular programs. Learning Communities available to resident freshmen at Villanova include:

- Leadership and Virtue
- Global Community
- Mind, Body, Spirit
- Art and Culture
- Nature and the World
- Pursuit of Excellence

Volunteerism

Service to others through volunteerism and service-learning projects is a fundamental part of the Villanova experience, and seventy-five percent of undergraduates participate. Semi-annual service breaks enable students to choose projects of special personal significance (Habitat for Humanity is especially popular), and Villanova's Special Olympics Fall Festival is the largest annual student-run Special Olympics event in the world. The annual Day of Service matches thousands of Villanova volunteers with service sites across greater Philadelphia. In addition, students have daily opportunities to get involved through student organizations focused on service.

> **"** *One program that sets Villanova apart and truly illustrates the university's sense of community is the Special Olympics, Pennsylvania's Annual Fall Festival, which has been held on campus every November for over two decades. During my freshman year, I was encouraged by my hall-mates to volunteer during the course of the weekend. The experience was so rewarding that I continued to stay involved each year until my graduation. In my senior year, I served as registration chair and recruited my sister, Shannon, a Villanova sophomore at the time, to join the effort.* **"**

FINANCIAL AID

Villanova's Office of Financial Aid breaks the application process down into five straightforward steps for students and parents to follow:

- Step 1: Completion of the FAFSA (Free Application for Federal Student Aid).
- Step 2: Completion of the College Board PROFILE form.
- Step 3: Submit signed copies of the student's and parents' U.S. Federal Tax Returns and all schedules (if files) and all W-2 and/or 1099 or 1099R forms.
- Step 4: A comprehensive review of applications and documents provides results in the student receiving an award letter, detailing all funding offered to the student from Federal, State, and/or Villanova University.
- Step 5: If a student is awarded Federal loans, regulations require that, before any loans are disbursed to a student account, the student must complete an Entrance Interview. This takes about twenty-five minutes to complete at *www.studentloans.gov*. The Entrance Interview is a counseling session that provides information about how to manage student loans, both during and after college.

EXPENSES AND FINANCIAL AID

- ○ Tuition: $39,350
- ○ Room and Board: $10,620
- ○ Books and Supplies: $950
- ○ Financial Aid Forms Deadline: February 7
- ○ Financial Aid Phone: (610) 519-4010
- ○ Financial Aid E-mail: finaid@villanova.edu

Here are some statistics about financial aid at Villanova during the 2006–07 academic year:

- 93 percent of those who applied for need-based aid were eligible to receive some type of assistance.
- 77 percent of those eligible for need-based assistance received Villanova grants for a total of $13 million.
- The average Villanova grant award was $21,322.
- The average assistance package for students with demonstrated financial need (combining grants, scholarships, loans, and student employment) was $29,348.
- 62.9 percent of all matriculating undergraduates received some type of assistance.
- Villanova committed more than $61 million of its resources to grant aid for undergraduate students.

- Madeline McCarthy Bell, 1983, Executive VP and COO, The Children's Hospital of Philadelphia
- Maria Bello, 1989, Golden Globe-nominated Actress
- Stephen J, Furnary, 1972, Chairman and CEO, ING Clarion Partners
- Rear Admiral Christine Bruzek-Kohler, 1974, Executive Director of Healthcare Operations, Joint Task Force-National Capital Region
- Nance K. Dicciani, PhD, 1969, Operating Partner, Advent International
- John G. Drosdick, 1965, Chairman, CEO, and President, Sunoco (ret.)
- Dr. Mary E. Duffy, 1968, Senior Nurse Scientist, Yvonne L. Munn Center for Nursing Research, Massachusetts General Hospital
- William Fallon, 1967, William J. Fallon & Associates, LLC, Retired Four-star Admiral, U.S. Navy, Former Commander of U.S. Central Command
- Dr. Dorrie Fontaine, 1972, Dean, University of Virginia School of Nursing
- Rosa Gatti, 1972, Senior VP of Communication and Outreach, ESPN
- Justin M Gmelich, 1990, Partner-Managing Director, Head of U.S. Credit Trading, The Goldman Sachs Group, Inc.
- John L. Hennessy III, PhD, 1973, President, Stanford University
- Bert Jacobs, 1987, Co-founder and Chief Executive Optimist, Life is Good, Inc.
- Adelene Q. Perkins, 1981, President and CEO, Infinity Pharmaceuticals, Inc.
- Lawrence Waterhouse Jr., 1959, Founder and Chairman Emeritus, TD Waterhouse Investor Services, Inc.
- Robert J. McCarthy, 1975, President, North American Lodging Operations and Global Brand Management, Marriott International
- James V. O'Donnell, 1963, CEO, American Eagle Outfitters, Inc.
- Dr. Rosalie Mirenda, 1959, President, Neumann University
- Thomas Quindlen, 1984, President and CEO, GE Capitol, Corporate Finance
- Sean McDermott, 1988, CEO, Windward IT Solutions

GRADUATES

Villanova is fortunate to have an extremely loyal network of alumni, parents, and friends who are dedicated to the university and return to visit often. There are many "Villanova families," worldwide—those in which several generations or siblings have attended the university, and in which husbands and wives met as Villanova students. There are also many lifelong friendships formed at Villanova.

66 *Villanova University. Whenever the topic of my alma mater is raised, I could speak about the rigorous academic experience, the challenging coursework, and the world-class professors who encourage students to expand their horizons every day. I could speak about the incredible opportunities outside of the classroom, with the hundreds of student organizations that exist on campus. I could talk about the wonderful opportunities afforded to Villanova students through our internship, community service, and international studies programs. But the most distinctive aspect of Villanova is its sense of community, and the genuine care that people show for one another.*

My Villanova experience can be summed up in four words, taken from a speech Villanova University President Father Peter Donohue gave to a group of students during my senior year: 'Take Villanova with you.' Father Donohue was speaking about the challenges facing us as we prepared for the next stage of our lives. He encouraged us to reflect upon our time at Villanova—upon the many experiences that shaped us, helped us mature, and forced us to go beyond our comfort zones. He then challenged us to take Villanova with us. Villanova provided me with the opportunity to do just that, through an education, experience, and community of mentors and friends who will shape the rest of my life. 99

❏ *Maura Topper, B.S.*

Wake Forest University
Winston-Salem, NC 27109

(336) 758-5201

E-mail: *admissions@wfu.edu*
Website: *http://www.wfu.edu*

 Enrollment

Full-time ❏ women: 2,375
       ❏ men: 2,215

Part-time ❏ women: 29
       ❏ men: 38

INTRODUCING WAKE FOREST UNIVERSITY

Wake Forest is a rare find in higher education—a medium-sized university that consistently ranks in the top thirty undergraduate programs nationwide with an active and involved student body and a tight-knit community of professors, students, and administrators. With just 4,657 undergraduates, the university strikes the perfect balance in size. It's impossible to walk across the campus without seeing the faces of your classmates and friends, but there's still the opportunity to meet a new person each day. Only twenty-six percent of students hail from North Carolina, while the rest are transplants from all over the United States and abroad. All these factors combine to create a close, supportive community of students interested in pursuing a liberal arts degree.

Wake Forest students often fondly and with some seriousness refer to their school as "Work Forest." In its defense, they are also prone to say that at Wake, we "work hard and play hard." The academic curriculum is not for the casual student. Core curriculum requirements are extensive, including at least thirty-three credit hours that usually dominate the first two years of the college tenure. Though the classes are hard, the typical Wake Forest student enjoys the challenge and the accompanying celebration that's sure to follow. Students are also able to develop amazing relationships with their professors, all of whom will learn every student's name, meet with students on a regular basis, and probably host a class dinner at their house at least once a semester. The student to professor ratio is small at 11:1. Lecture-style classes tend to top out at thirty students, while more discussion-based seminar classes are limited to between fifteen and twenty students. Larger lectures are virtually nonexistent. The largest classes are perhaps in intro level sciences and they rarely exceed forty-five students. Even with these intimate class sizes, students still experience the perks of a big-time national university in resources, technology, and athletics. The undergraduate school of arts and sciences offers thirty-eight majors, most with corresponding minors, and an additional twenty interdisciplinary minors, which allow students to take a wide variety of courses toward concentrations in journalism, film, Middle Eastern studies, and more. There is also an undergraduate program in the Wake Forest School of Business, which has been consistently ranked in the top twenty-five programs nationwide by *BusinessWeek*.

Wake Forest is situated in the heart of Winston-Salem, the fourth-largest city in North Carolina. Though Winston-Salem is home to four colleges, including the University of North Carolina School of the Arts and Winston-Salem State University, the city does not have the feel of a typical college town. Rather, it is suburban with a bustling art scene downtown and the largest mall in North Carolina, Hanes Mall, just fifteen minutes from campus. Its most impressive attraction is perhaps the plethora of amazing regional restaurants that combine fresh seasonal ingredients with college-friendly budget pricing. There are also a good number of bars for the over-twenty-one crowd, including a nice downtown wine bar, a micro-brewery, and several bustling sports pubs. The city's only social void is perhaps the current lack of dance clubs, which is mostly made up for by frequent on-campus events and open fraternity parties.

It's a common question: What exactly is a Demon Deacon? The original Wake Forest mascot was a tiger, but in the 1920s fans often referred to the team as the "Baptists." After a victory against rival football team Duke University in 1923, the sports editor for the school newspaper, the *Old Gold & Black*, referred to his team as the "Demon Deacons." The athletic directors, coaches, and sports reporters warmed to the moniker and it caught on. Soon, the university adopted the beloved top hat-wearing preacher as their official mascot.

While Winston-Salem is home to the 340-acre campus today, it wasn't the original site of the college. In fact, Wake Forest was established in 1834 by the N.C. Baptist Convention in the town of Wake Forest, N.C. However, the entire campus moved to Winston-Salem in 1956 with the help of a grant from the Z. Smith Reynolds Foundation. In the 1980s the university formally severed governing ties with the Baptist Convention and remains unaffiliated with any religious denomination. Today, the campus is one of the most beautiful in America, bursting with blossoming magnolia trees in the spring and colored with the gorgeous red and gold leaves of maple and ash trees in the fall. The southern Georgian architecture is a repeated motif in each of the buildings, and the campus is compact enough that a brisk fifteen-minute walk will take you from end to end.

ADMISSIONS REQUIREMENTS

In 2008 Wake Forest became the first top thirty university to make standardized testing optional for admission. University officials made the decision based on research that suggested standardized tests are not the best predictors of success in college. There is "a compelling argument that reliance on the SAT and other standardized tests for admission is a major barrier to access for many worthy students," said Jill Tiefenthaler, provost. "By taking this step at Wake Forest, we want to remove that barrier." Students may still choose to submit SAT or ACT scores, but high school curriculum and classroom performance combined with writing abilities, extracurricular activities, and evidence of talent and character have become the most important factors in admission. In conjunction with this change, Martha Allman, director of admissions, now strongly encourages interviews either on campus or with a Wake Forest (alums or graduates) in your hometown. Interviews can be set up through the Office of Undergraduate Admissions. Using a webcam, a microphone, and the Internet, some students applying to Wake Forest can now sit in their living rooms at home and have a "face-to-face" conversation with an admissions counselor. Wake Forest began offering webcam interviews in 2008.

In 2010, about 10,500 students applied to Wake Forest and a little less than forty percent were admitted. Of those admitted, about 1,200 enroll each year. The university has recently explored increasing the size of the undergraduate student body by a few hundred students. However, maintaining the current student-teacher ratio and continuing to provide housing for undergraduates remain high priorities for the administration, so any growth will be slow. Eighty-five percent of entering freshmen rank in the top twenty percent of their high school class. The majority of enrolling freshmen come from southern and mid-Atlantic states, but students enroll from all over the United States and more than twenty foreign countries. A volunteer group of students offers campus tours every day. Prospective freshmen can also sign up to be hosted by a current student for a day. Students take prospectives to their classes and board them in the residence halls for the evening. The university accepts the Common Application, which must be accompanied by a writing supplement. Early Decision applications are due January 1; Wake Forest must be the student's first choice and only Early Decision application. Regular Decision applications are due January 1 and decisions are mailed by April 1.

ACADEMIC LIFE

Curriculum

At its core, Wake Forest is a liberal arts university. This commitment to educating the whole person is reflected in the extensive core curriculum, which is required for all undergraduate students. Most students complete the bulk of the core curriculum, which consists of several basic requirements and additional classes across five divisions, during their first two years. The basic requirements include a first-year seminar, a writing seminar, two courses in health and exercise, and advancing to the 200-level in one foreign language. First-year seminars are often the highlight of the freshman course load. These classes are limited to fifteen freshmen and are offered by faculty in their own area of expertise. In order to meet the foreign language requirement, students may take a placement exam to determine their level of mastery and be placed in a beginning, intermediate, or advanced class. Students with excellent language skills may test directly into the 200-level and take only one class to meet the requirement.

In addition to these basic requirements, students take classes in five divisions: humanities, literature, fine arts, social sciences, and math and natural sciences.

> **❝** *I might have never taken a class in anthropology, sociology, or psychology (all of which I loved) if not for those requirements. You're not only allowed to take classes that aren't part of your major, you're encouraged. That's not a common college experience. A lot of friends who were unsure about what direction to take in college used divisionals to shop around for majors.* **❞**

Majors

Students are not asked to declare a major until the end of sophomore year. Wake Forest offers thirty-eight majors, the most popular being business, political science, psychology, biology, economics, history, communication, English, and health and exercise science. Students are free to declare any major without formal application with only one exception: the Wake Forest School of Business accepts applications for new majors in the spring of the sophomore year. The school offers majors in accounting, business and enterprise management, finance, and mathematical business. Accounting students can earn a bachelor's and master's degree in accounting in five years and the program's graduates have ranked first in the nation for the highest passing rate on the CPA exam for the past four years. The business school has consistently ranked in *US News and World Report*'s top thirty undergraduate business schools and in *BusinessWeek*'s Top 25.

> **❝** *Some of the most meaningful and memorable experiences with my professors were outside of the classroom. My Shakespeare professor invited our whole class to her apartment before the final exam for a study session. We crammed twenty-five students into her tiny apartment, sitting cross-legged on the floor with plates of pizza and salad balanced on couch cushions while we discussed* The Merchant of Venice. *Another of my professors held our final exams in her home. We had pasta salad and homemade iced tea and then presented our projects in her sun room that overlooked a lake. The last such dinner I had at a professor's home was after finishing my senior honors thesis. Our advisor asked us about our postgraduation plans over a whole roasted chicken stuffed with oranges. These are some of my favorite memories of these professors—I was able to see them open up and share a new piece of themselves.* **❞**

Faculty

The undergraduate experience at Wake Forest is characterized by small classes with devoted faculty. Wake Forest maintains a distinguished faculty in which eighty-six percent of the full-time professors hold the terminal degree in his or her field. With a student-teacher ratio of 11:1, students can expect to receive a good deal of individual attention. Classes are anything but impersonal; professors know their students, greet them in the hallways, and often host dinners in their homes for small classes. All professors keep office hours and many make an effort to individually meet with each student during the semester.

Study Abroad

Study abroad is becoming an increasingly common part of the college experience and Wake Forest is no exception. In fact, Wake Forest has one of the highest percentages of students studying abroad. More than sixty percent of Wake Forest students choose to study abroad for at least one semester. Wake Forest has several of its own programs abroad. The university owns houses in London, England; Vienna, Austria; and on the Grand Canal in Venice, Italy. Groups of twelve to fifteen students live in these residences with a Wake Forest professor for a semester. Students take classes for four days a week and often use their long weekends to travel. Wake Forest also has two language emersion programs, one in Dijon, France, and one in Salamanca, Spain. Students in these programs live with native host families and take classes at local universities. In 2011, Wake Forest started a semester-long program in Chile. These programs also organize a good deal of travel around Europe and Asia. Wake Forest also sponsors summer programs in Asia, South America, Africa, and Europe.

Wake Forest students may also choose to study through a program offered by another American university or enroll directly in a foreign university for a semester.

> *My semester abroad in London was spent in a three-bedroom flat with eight roommates. My room, which I shared with one other girl, was literally so small that I could touch both walls with my arms outstretched. I worked for a British guidebook where my coworkers taught me British slang and took me to cheesy dance club nights. I attended a theater class that booked tickets to edgy experimental dramas and sweeping West End musicals. It was the most exciting, unspeakably amazing time of my life.*

Housing

The Wake Forest campus is the heart of the college community, where most of the action takes place. Seventy percent of Wake Forest students live on campus in residence halls. Freshmen mostly live together on South Campus. The majority of these freshman dorms are arranged in hall-style living with fifteen to twenty rooms on a hall. Halls share bathrooms and common rooms. Each room has air conditioning and comes equipped with beds, dressers, desks, and a micro-fridge. All dorms have communal kitchens and free laundry facilities. The residence halls are coed, but separated into male and female halls. Freshmen-year roommates are assigned using a compatibility survey.

With solar panels on the roof to heat water and touch screens in the hallways for monitoring energy usage, Wake Forest's newest residence hall has the latest in green technology. South Residence Hall opened in fall 2010 and reflects the university's commitment to sustainability across campus. The residence hall was designed to meet LEED (Leadership in Energy and Design) certification—silver level standards.

THE PRESIDENT'S BALL

In 2005 Wake Forest welcomed a new university president and in honor of his inauguration, an Inaugural Ball was held for all students, faculty, and staff. The entire Wake Forest community came dressed in cocktail dresses and suits and mingled in the basketball arena that had been transformed into a gorgeous ballroom. President Nathan O. Hatch rode into the arena with the school mascot, seated on the back of a motorcycle as confetti and balloons descended from the ceiling. There were chocolate fountains, ice sculptures, and two excellent local bands. The first event was such a success that a President's Ball is now held every other year.

After freshman year, students move to North Campus into upperclassman dorms. Upperclassmen choose their own roommates and have more diverse housing options. The majority of upperclassman housing is suite-style, meaning that six-to-eight people share a suite with three or four bedrooms and shared bathrooms. Upperclassmen can also move to Polo Residence Hall or student apartments, which offer apartments with private kitchenettes, bathrooms, and living rooms. These usually accommodate two to four people.

Groups of students who share a particular interest may also apply for Theme Housing. These programs are usually located in university-owned houses on the edges of campus or in blocks of rooms in university residence halls. Current theme housing includes the environmental house, foreign language houses, the technology house, and various sports-themed houses such as crew, lacrosse, and soccer. Students must live in university housing for their first three years. Upperclassmen who choose to move off campus often find apartments in one of several nearby complexes that cater to university students or rent homes in the surrounding neighborhood. These rental properties are a short drive from the university and a great option for students looking to save money or get a little more space.

Dining

All students who live on campus are required to have a meal plan. The number of meals required varies based on your type of university housing. Students who have their own kitchens are required to buy fewer meals than students who share communal kitchens. Commuter students are not required to purchase the meal plan. On-campus dining options include two food courts, a buffet-style dining room, a Subway on the Quad, and three coffee shops including a Starbucks in the library. The largest food court is a sunken dining room traditionally referred to as the Pit. The Pit serves three different meals a day, each including a salad bar, pasta station, deli sandwiches, home-cooking station, fresh waffles, world cuisine, and desserts. The dining room itself is spacious, clean, and bright with tons of seating for groups large and small and is fitted with flat screen televisions. There is a carry-out option that allows students to box meals for dining on the go.

A favorite alternative option is the Magnolia Room, a buffet-style dining room that serves southern classics and home-style favorites. Students line up outside the room before its 10:30 A.M. opening and the room stays filled until closing time at 2 P.M. The Benson University Center is favored for quick meals. The recently remodeled dining hall includes a Chick-fil-A, Fresh Market smoothies, and more.

Subway is the number one stop for late night meals. Students can get a sandwich until 2 A.M. Expect long lines when the fresh bread comes out of the oven. Since its opening in 2008, the Starbucks in the library has become a hot spot. The two-level space is comfy and warm; huge study rooms in the back are also a draw. The student-run coffeehouse Campus Grounds also attracts a loyal following for its warm atmosphere and cushy couches.

WINSTON-SALEM'S BEST

- Best Pizza: Burke Street Pizza
- Best 24-Hour Dining: Jimmy the Greek
- Best Burger and Milkshake: Cookout Drive-Thru
- Best Frozen Yogurt: Zack's Famous Frozen Yogurt
- Best for a Date: 6th and Vine Wine Bar and Cafe
- Best Brunch: Breakfast of Course
- Best Sandwich Shop: Simply Yummy
- Best for Parent's Weekend: Village Tavern
- Best Alternative to Village Tavern on Parent's Weekend Because It Will Be Packed: Fourth Street Filling Station

---

Shorty's in the Benson University Center is the only place to pick up beer on campus—try one of the local brews on tap and charge it to your Deacon cash card!

Clubs and Organizations

There are more than 150 student organizations from *a cappella* groups to religious study groups. Two of the largest groups are Student Government, which lobbies for student concerns and allocates funds to clubs, and Student Union, which organizes concerts, performances, movies, and other events. Student Union organizes Wake All Night at the beginning of each semester with free food and poker and other games all night in the Benson University Center. The group is also responsible for Springfest, a weeklong celebration that includes a carnival, the Shag on the Mag spring dance, and a concert. Past performers have included O.A.R, Ben Folds, Guster, and Lewis Black. Student media organizations include a newspaper, television station, radio station, literary journal, and entertainment Web site. The *Old Gold & Black*, the student newspaper, has been publishing weekly since 1916 and has won several national awards. *The Student* Web site is the premiere destination for a calendar of student events and local restaurant recommendations.

Several yearly events drive home the university's commitment to service that is expressed in the school motto, *Pro Humanitate*, which means "for humanity." Every year 1,500 children from community agencies trick-or-treat in the dorms and play games on the Quad during Project Pumpkin. The Brian Piccolo Cancer Fund Drive raises more than $50,000 annually with fun events such as dance-a-thons, silent auctions, and Hit the Bricks. Brian Piccolo's football career with the Demon Deacons and the Chicago Bears and his subsequent battle with cancer are recorded in the film *Brian's Song*. The Volunteer Service Corps and several religious organizations organize a wide variety of service projects both locally, nationally, and around the world. These include yearly service trips to build homes, plant gardens, and teach English in South America, Asia, and Africa.

Greek System

In the tradition of many southern universities, Wake Forest does have a large Greek system. Approximately forty percent of the student body is involved—a little less than fifty percent of females join a sorority and a little over thirty percent of males join a fraternity. However, unlike most universities, Greek housing is not separated from regular university housing. There is no fraternity or sorority row. Rather, students who choose to live in Greek housing do so in residence halls with blocks of rooms dedicated to their respective fraternity or sorority. Members are normally not required to live in Greek housing. Each organization has its own on-campus lounge, in which there are often parties on weekends that are open to the entire student body. In general, the system is very open, partially due to the deferred rush system. Wake Forest's Greek system differs from most others in that students do not rush during their first semester. Formal rush takes place in the spring semester.

Athletics

As the smallest school in the ACC, Wake Forest athletes prove time and time again that big-time athletics can thrive even with a small student body. The proof is in the number of ACC Championships and National Championships the Demon Deacons have won in

the last five years alone. Wake Forest is the third-smallest school in the country to field a Division I football team, but in 2006 the team took the ACC Championship and appeared at the BCS Orange Bowl in Miami, Florida. Since that historic season, the team has won several bowl games and continues to break school and national records. Wake Forest has only recently begun to develop a reputation on the football field, but the school has a long history of dominance on the hardwood. NBA stars Josh Howard, Muggsy Bogues, Tim Duncan, and Chris Paul all got their start at Wake Forest. The women's field hockey team won three consecutive National Championships from 2002 to 2004 and continues to consistently advance to the Final Four. The women's soccer team won the 2010 ACC Championship. The men's soccer team won the 2007 National Championship and was only narrowly edged out of the title again in 2008. The golf program has produced legends such as Arnold Palmer, Curtis Strange, and Jay Haas.

Having great sports teams is only half of the equation; the other half is getting tickets to the games. Unlike large universities that arrange lottery systems for tickets, Wake Forest provides free tickets to all sporting events for all students. The Screamin' Demons fan club arranges student seating and fan gear for football and basketball games. Since the seating is general rather than assigned, students have been known to line up outside the basketball arena days in advance to fight for the courtside seats. The sea of students clad in yellow and black tie dyed shirts, known as the Tie-Dye Nation, is a force to be reckoned with.

Many students participate in club or intramural sports during their time at Wake Forest, whether dodgeball or basketball, tennis or Ultimate Frisbee. With thirty-four club sports teams to choose from and a huge Intramural league, there's something for everyone.

Technology

Each Wake Forest undergraduate receives a laptop computer upon enrollment. Juniors trade in their laptops at the beginning of the fall semester for the latest model. The laptops come fully loaded and include access to some expensive programs such as Photoshop. Resident Technology Advisors (RTAs) live in each residence hall and provide twenty-four-hour computer assistance for the technologically challenged. The entire campus has Wi-Fi accessibility that is so reliable you'll be able to access the Web literally anywhere on campus, even in the middle of the Quad.

GRADUATES

Eighty percent of Wake Forest students graduate in four years. Within six months of graduation, approximately thirty-five percent of graduates enroll in graduate programs and sixty percent are employed. Wake Forest has five professional and graduate schools of its own—the School of Law, the School of Medicine, the Graduate School of Arts and Sciences, the Divinity School, and the School of Business. Students interested in pursuing degrees in medicine and law have historically had great success in enrolling in programs nationwide. Sixty-eight percent of those applying to medical school and about sixty percent of those applying to law school are accepted. With eleven Rhodes Scholars in the past twenty years, the university has a proud history of postgraduate achievement.

The Office of Career Services provides support for students seeking employment. The office hosts career fairs, conducts resume reviews and mock interviews, provides career counseling, and manages a job board and internship posting site. An extensive network of alumni connections is a helpful resource for graduates. The job fairs typically bring more than 170 companies to campus for recruiting. Career Services also offers free seminars and forums hosted by local professionals in which students can explore options in their fields of study.

The Office of Personal and Career Development has been formed to provide valuable opportunities and resources beginning in the freshman year that are essential for career development. Mentoring, professional and career development, entrepreneurship, and academic courses are offered by this innovative office.

FINANCIAL AID

Wake Forest seeks students with high academic standards from a wide range of backgrounds. Students are admitted based on their accomplishments and the unique qualities they bring to the Wake Forest community. Around fifty-two percent of students receive some form of financial aid through scholarships, grants, student loans, or work-study programs. Funds are available through federal and state sources in addition to the university's own financial resources. Students should apply for financial aid even before receiving their decision from the university in order to begin the long process. Applications for need-based financial aid are due March 1.

Merit-based scholarships are available, but the competition for these scholarships is fierce. Several different scholarships, including the Presidential Scholarships, are based on demonstrated aptitudes in certain fields such as theater, dance, music, or community service. Students must apply for these scholarships in January. Recipients of the Reynolds-Cardwell scholarships receive funds to cover tuition costs, allowances for books and living expenses, and summer grants for individual study.

Who should apply to Wake Forest? The right match will be a serious student with the desire and willingness to dedicate himself or herself to academic pursuits. You can't expect things to be easy; students who found high school easy may spend late nights in the library. The right applicant will also follow his or her passions outside of academics. Wake Forest students often dedicate as much time in groups and clubs as they do to school, whether in a fraternity or on the student newspaper. A successful Wake Forest student must also embrace Winston-Salem and the southern culture that's a part of the experience. If you aren't willing to welcome the occasional chicken biscuit or sundress, you may need to rethink your decision. Generally, the student body has a welcoming southern spirit, where everyone can come to appreciate the history and culture. To become a Deac, be prepared to loathe your archrivals at the nearest Carolina schools and come to think of yellow and black tie-dye as an appropriate fashion choice. Expect to sunbathe on the Quad beneath the magnolia trees in the spring and have snowball fights during the two or three snow days each winter.

What defines the Wake Forest experience? The small student body and the dedicated faculty form a tight-knit community and a bond that lasts well after graduation. Alumni feel a special camaraderie, as if Wake Forest is our own personal secret hidden in North Carolina.

❏ *Caitlin Kenney, B.A.*

Washington and Lee University
Lexington, VA 24450

(540) 458-8710
Fax: (540) 458-8062

E-mail: *admissions@wlu.edu*
Website: *http://www.wlu.edu*

 Enrollment

Full-time ❑ women: 876
❑ men: 881

INTRODUCING WASHINGTON AND LEE

On a crisp fall afternoon in Virginia, students walk up the grassy slope to Washington and Lee's colonnade, rows of white columns that define the face of the campus's red brick buildings. The students walk in the shadows of the columns and climb the worn steps of Payne Hall. Just inside their classroom is a bronze plaque commemorating the space where General Robert E. Lee took his oath of office as president of the school in 1865. The open windows frame more students passing along the back campus. Some enter Leyburn Library, a wide complex of concrete and brick. Others open the doors to the Great Hall of the Science Center; vaulted, sky-lit ceilings expose balconies for each of the floors above, where more students move to and from completely modern classrooms and laboratories.

As these students cross Washington and Lee University's picturesque campus, they see its balance of the old and the new—traditions and changes. Founded in 1749, the university boasts a long and rich history. The school won critical support in 1796 when George Washington donated $20,000 to its endowment. (Washington's gift was the largest ever made to a private American school at the time, and the sum continues to pay a portion of every student's tuition.) The school was known as Washington College at the end of the Civil War, when Robert E. Lee assumed its presidency. Lee led the college through far-reaching changes until his death in 1870. Washington and Lee students cherish Lee for his educational reforms: joining the college with a local law school, instituting classes in business and economics, creating the first college-level journalism program, and establishing the seeds of the student-governed Honor System. Those century-old innovations are now traditions that make Washington and Lee the fine liberal arts institution it is today. The university maintains these traditions and follows Lee's example, always initiating change. The last decade has witnessed additions to the curriculum, complete revitalization of the fraternity system, and construction of new facilities for the fine arts, athletics, and the sciences. A new fitness center opened in Fall 2002, along with the newly renovated journalism school, and the new John W. Elrod University Commons opened in Fall 2003. The year 2006 saw the inaugural season of Wilson Hall, the new music and art facility. The renovation of Wilson Field, the stadium for football, lacrosse, and track and field, was completed in 2008, finishing the Richard L. Duchossois Athletic Complex. In the fall of 2010, the Hillel House, a center for Jewish student life, opened its doors, and the first phase of the Colonnade renovation—Newcomb Hall—was completed.

Students at Washington and Lee call their school "W&L," and their love for W&L is extraordinary. One former student admits:

> **“** *I called home crying a few times during my freshman year because I was so grateful to my parents for giving me the opportunity to come to W&L.* **”**

National surveys routinely rank W&L students among the happiest in the country. When naming what makes them happy, every student generation names the same strong traditions:

a small student body of 1,770 that is truly a community, intimate classes averaging around sixteen students, a faculty dedicated to students and to teaching, and an Honor System that creates a society of trust where no student will lie, cheat, or steal.

The small town of Lexington, Virginia forms the backdrop for all of this student bliss. Although only 7,000 residents live in Lexington year-round, students from Washington and Lee and its neighbor, the Virginia Military Institute, add substantially to the town's true population. (The two schools add much to the town through their cultural and athletic programs as well.) One politics major notes:

> **❝** *The scenic, safe surroundings have allowed me to make W&L a home away from home, to enjoy the college experience without the worries and distractions of a big school or a big city.* **❞**

W&L students become active citizens of Lexington as "big brothers" or "big sisters" to local youths, as coaches for Little League teams, as members of church congregations, and as participants in outreach groups such as Campus Kitchen, Habitat for Humanity, and the Nabors Service League.

Although all W&L students call Lexington "home," they journey from all corners of the United States to get there. Only eighteen percent of undergraduates hail from Virginia. Other well-represented states include Florida, Georgia, Maryland, New Jersey, New York, Pennsylvania, and Texas. It surprises many to learn that the student body includes nearly twice as many from California as from Kentucky. W&L truly has a national student body to match its national reputation. An intensified effort to recruit international students has resulted in attracting young men and women of nearly fifty citizenships.

ADMISSIONS REQUIREMENTS

Word is out—magazines rank W&L one of the nation's premiere liberal arts institutions year after year. Its academic reputation, small size, and pure beauty attract an increasing number of applicants with increasingly stronger credentials. Because space in Washington and Lee's student body is limited, gaining admittance to the university has become increasingly difficult.

A glance at Washington and Lee's admissions statistics confirms just how selective the school has become. Of the 6,627 students who applied for admission in 2010, 1,259 were admitted, yielding a first-year class of 472 (238 men, 234 women). These enrolling students achieved remarkable scores on their standardized tests. The middle fifth percent range of their SAT scores spanned 1320–1480; the same range of ACT scores was 28–31. These students earned an average rank in class above ninety-five percent of their high school classmates. Forty-two were valedictorians or salutatorians; twenty-four were National Merit Scholars or Finalists.

These facts certainly portray W&L's selectivity, but they do not illustrate the great care that its Admissions Office takes in reviewing all applications. Washington and Lee believes that the high school record is the surest sign of a student's potential for success in college. Admissions officers read every student's transcript, weighing grades against the difficulty of the curriculum. Successful applicants typically have strong grades in rigorous college-preparatory or Advanced Placement classes. Standardized tests are used as a uniform measurement in comparing students who often come from schools with drastically different curricula and grading scales. W&L also strives to evaluate each student's character and personality through essays and recommendations. In hopes of finding future members of the school's athletic teams, cultural groups, and student committees, W&L's Admissions Office further judges applicants by their extracurricular pursuits.

The Johnson Program

A rare opportunity has been created at Washington and Lee University for a select group of the nation's highest-achieving students. A $100 million gift from an anonymous alumnus, as well as the generosity of numerous individuals and corporations, have allowed W&L to offer scholarships of at least tuition, room and board to approximately ten percent of each incoming class. Students who wish to be considered for a Johnson Scholarship—or any merit-based award—must submit a complete admission application and the separate Johnson Scholarship application no later than December 1. It is not necessary to apply under the W&L binding Early Decision 1 plan in order to be considered for the Johnson Scholarship or other merit-based awards.

After reviewing Johnson Scholarship applications, up to 200 finalists will be invited to campus at the school's expense for the Johnson Scholarship competition. Finalists will be selected on the basis of academic achievement and demonstrated leadership. They will be judged on their potential to contribute to the intellectual and civic life of the W&L campus and of the world at large in years to come. Writing sample, teacher recommendations, and records of leadership, citizenship, and involvement in non-academic activities will be weighed.

Interviews

Proof of Washington and Lee's genuine interest in getting to know applicants lies in the fact that it continues to offer personal interviews. Interviews and student-guided tours may be scheduled by calling the Admissions Office. For students who cannot travel to Lexington for a meeting with an admissions officer, interviews with alumni admissions program representatives are available in most major cities in the United States (*http://admissions.wlu.edu/app*).

Requirements

W&L's admissions requirements are clear and straightforward. Applicants must submit the Common Application (*www.commonapp.org*), or they may use W&L's own paper forms. Those using W&L's paper application should complete Part I of the application for admission, this preliminary application asks for biographical information. After receiving Part I from applicants, W&L then sends Part II of the application. It includes transcript forms, two teacher recommendation forms, and guidelines for the submission of supplemental information (including an essay). Applicants should submit the SAT or the ACT with its writing section, plus two SAT Subject Exams in different subjects. The Regular Decision deadline for submission of applications is January 15. Students can expect replies from Washington and Lee in early April. All application forms are available online at *http://admissions.wlu.edu.*

Early Decision

For students who want to attend Washington and Lee above all other schools, there are two binding Early Decision options. Early Decision applicants must acknowledge that Washington and Lee is their first choice and that they will attend if admitted. Early Decision applications are due by November 15 for Early Decision I or January 2 for Early Decision II. W&L delivers notice by December 22 for E.D. I or February 1 for E.D. II. Admitted students happily claim a coveted place in the freshman class. W&L defers consideration of those who are not admitted until the regular admissions process.

Another admissions deadline remains for applicants who want to vie for the university's many generous Honor Scholarships. These students complete an additional essay and submit their applications by December 15. W&L invites finalists to visit the campus during the late winter; the Admissions Office notifies scholarship recipients in early April.

Nothing shapes life at Washington and Lee more than its Honor System. The Honor System dates back to Lee's simple demand that all of his students act honorably. Today, a committee of elected students (known as the Executive Committee) administers the Honor System, informing freshmen of its guidelines and enforcing its principles. The system is built upon trust; it holds that students who lie, cheat, or steal are not trustworthy and, therefore, not welcome in the Washington and Lee community. For that reason, there is only one sanction for any student found guilty of an honor violation: permanent removal from the student body.

Because the Honor System works so well, Washington and Lee students enjoy freedoms that would be impossible at other universities. All academic buildings on the W&L campus, including the library, remain open twenty-four hours a day. Since professors trust that cheating will not occur, students take unproctored tests and exams. Students even schedule their own exams during week-long exam periods. It is possible that every student in an English class could take the same exam in a different place at a different time; students are trusted not to discuss the content of their exams with their classmates. These freedoms extend beyond the classroom as well.

> **❝** *I constantly leave money in my backpack right in the middle of campus without giving a moment's thought to its security.* **❞**

Classes

If there is one thing that defines all colleges, it must be the classroom. Today, many college classrooms are cavernous, badly lit lecture halls. A professor or, more likely, a teaching assistant speaks through a microphone to hundreds of students seated in row after row of identical chairs. W&L defines the classroom differently. Its students enjoy small, intimate classes that are never taught by a graduate student or a teaching assistant. A large class at W&L might contain thirty-five students. Average classes number fourteen to seventeen. Many upperclassmen take seminar classes with fewer than ten other students. They all might sit around a single table with their professor, creating the kind of personal, in-depth interaction that is a W&L hallmark.

Professors

Small classes allow students to get to know their professors as people, and vice versa.

> **❝** *Teachers here seem to relish the opportunity to get to know the students, even if they realize that that particular student will only be taking that one class from them. Within your major, every professor knows you and begs you to take their classes. It's rather flattering.* **❞**

An alumnus remembers similar experiences:

> **❝** *I never lost my awe of my professors, but I really came to rely on many of them as friends. Of course, that made the stakes higher. I always felt that I had to do my best work because I didn't want to disappoint them.* **❞**

Professors keep long office hours so that they can meet with students outside of class. Most professors do not have strict attendance guidelines, but, because classes are so small, every student learns that an absence gets noticed. Although it may be unheard of at other universities, W&L students enjoy eating dinner occasionally at professors' homes.

Curriculum

Despite Washington and Lee's small size, the university offers a startlingly varied curriculum that a *Washington Post* article described as "the envy of many larger institutions." Committed to the ideal of a liberal arts education, W&L requires all students to meet general education requirements in composition; literature; a foreign language; the fine arts, history, philosophy, and religion; science and mathematics; the social sciences; and physical education. Most students meet these requirements by the end of their sophomore year. They spend their junior and senior years fulfilling a major course of study and exploring elective classes.

Students divide their time between the university's College of Arts and Sciences, which includes the School of Journalism (or "J-School"), and the Ernest Williams II School of Commerce, Economics, and Politics (or "C-School"). W&L's broad curriculum allows it to offer majors in subjects not commonly taught in other top colleges, such as accounting, business, engineering, East Asian languages and literature, geology, and neuroscience. Students may earn Bachelor of Arts or Bachelor of Science degrees, in addition to Bachelor of Science degrees with Special Attainments in Chemistry and Bachelor of Science degrees with Special Attainments in Commerce. The Shepherd Program for the Interdisciplinary Study of Poverty and an interdisciplinary major in environmental studies as well as the Society and the Professions Studies in Applied Ethics are among W&L's distinctive, crosscurricular courses of study, along with formal non-major programs in African American studies, global stewardship, and women's studies. Undergraduates also benefit from the presence of W&L's top-ranked school of law. Some law courses are open to undergrads, and most special events and guest lectures welcome them, as well.

Study Areas

W&L students spread all over the campus to study. Carrels in Leyburn Library may be reserved on the first day of classes. Confident in the Honor System, students leave texts and notebooks in their carrels for the entire school year. Other students study in the libraries located in the Science Center, Journalism School, or Commerce School. Because academic buildings stay open twenty-four hours a day, an occasional student may "pull an all-nighter" while working in a classroom. Every dormitory room is connected to the university computer network, and wireless zones around campus allow students to get online wherever they might be studying.

W&L classes typically demand considerable reading and writing. Students quickly learn that no skill proves more valuable than the ability to write clearly and concisely; professors expect nothing less. Classes and workloads may be tough, but the academic mood at Washington and Lee never becomes cutthroat.

> ❝ W&L may have competitive admissions, but students here enjoy learning more through cooperation and collaboration with peers. ❞

This mood may be due, in part, to the Honor System. Students trust one another. They do not compete against one another; they compete against themselves.

The Academic Year

W&L has an unusual academic year consisting of a twelve-week fall term, a twelve-week winter term, and a four-week spring term. A revitalized spring term was introduced in 2009–10. This new spring term offers innovative, intensive, and challenging student learning experiences in ways that differ markedly from the experience of the two twelve-week terms. Students and faculty benefit from a focused learning environment that allows them to devote undivided attention to the subject matter of one course. Through a range of pedagogies including experimental, interdisciplinary, international, and interactive approaches, the spring term accomplishes the university's stated mission of developing students' critical thinking and promoting their growth in honor, integrity, and civility.

SOCIAL LIFE AND ACTIVITIES

Phil Flickinger, a 1997 graduate of Washington and Lee, has published a collection of his cartoons that appeared in W&L's student newspapers. Entitled *Invasion of the Bug-Eyed Preppies,* the book captures many of the quirks of social life at W&L. Flickinger's most revealing cartoon juxtaposes two groups—"Generation X" and "Generation Lex." "Generation X" is a frowning, shaggy group of tattooed and pierced slackers. "Generation Lex" is a group of Lexington, Virginia's W&L students—straitlaced and smartly dressed. One W&L male in the cartoon asks, "Has anyone seen my Duckheads?"

Like most humor, this cartoon evokes a great deal of truth by use of stereotypes. Of course, every member of Generation X does not have a skateboard and a navel ring. Likewise, every student at W&L does not fit the cartoon's notion of a preppy. For every rule or stereotype, there are exceptions. It may be true that most W&L students are more conservative than their peers at other schools. Nevertheless, W&L's student body contains a strong mix of "ambitious, on-the-ball" individuals who pursue differing interests with differing attitudes. Somehow, they all seem bound by a single thread.

> ❝ *I still maintain that in no other school can one find such a classy group of well brought-up individuals. Everyone respects one another to an amazing degree.* ❞

Residences

All W&L freshmen live in one of four freshman dormitories and take their meals in a contemporary common dining room in the Elrod Commons, the Marketplace. Sophomores live on campus, too, in upperclass dorms and apartments, fraternity houses, and separate residences for groups such as the Outing Club, International Club, and Spanish Club. Juniors and seniors may live on campus, though many choose to live off campus. Apartments above downtown stores provide many options for students, as do legendary student homes with colorful names like Fishbait, Munster, Windfall, the Batcave, Jacob's Ladder, and Amityville. All students enjoy the majestic beauty of the surrounding Shenandoah Valley and Blue Ridge Mountains, which provide every imaginable outdoor activity.

The Greeks

Seventy-five percent of W&L men and women are in one of thirteen fraternities or five sororities. Many fraternities and sororities engage in volunteer efforts, such as tutoring elementary students, cleaning up nature trails, organizing food blood drives, and working for the local emergency services. Their social events aren't exclusive affairs, but welcome all students, Greek and non-Greek alike. Friendships between members of different organizations are common, as are friendships between Greek members and independent students. Fraternity and sorority houses are owned by the university and are clean and well-maintained.

WOMEN'S VARSITY SPORTS

- Cross-Country
- Soccer
- Tennis
- Volleyball
- Basketball
- Swimming
- Indoor Track
- Lacrosse
- Tennis
- Track and Field
- Equestrian
- Field Hockey
- Golf (Varsity in 2012)

Other Organizations

For a small school, Washington and Lee supports an impressive array of civic, cultural, and athletic organizations to meet every student's interests. The Society for the Arts, for example, sponsors dramatic performances and readings of student poetry and fiction. The General Activities Board brings bands and comedians to campus. W&L's many journalism majors contribute to both the independent students' newspaper, the *Ring-tum Phi*, and the department-sponsored online news magazine, Rockbridge Report. The Contact Committee presents debates and lectures by nationally-known visitors. Through club and intramural sports, choral groups, an orchestra, college Democrats, college Republicans, religious organizations, and service groups, any W&L student finds fulfilling diversions and relationships outside of class.

MEN'S VARSITY SPORTS

○ Cross-Country
○ Football
○ Soccer
○ Basketball
○ Swimming
○ Indoor Track
○ Wrestling
○ Baseball
○ Golf
○ Lacrosse
○ Tennis
○ Track and Field

Sports

Many Washington and Lee students also choose to participate in varsity sports. W&L's Generals compete in Division III sports through the Old Dominion Athletic Conference, maintaining sterling academic and athletic records. Recently, 194 of W&L's 400 varsity athletes achieved GPAs of 3.5 or better. In the history of the ODAC, the Generals have won 164 conference championships (83 women, 81 men), the most of any member. For seven consecutive years, W&L teams have won the ODAC Commissioner's Cup for the best all-round athletic program. Football and lacrosse remain the perennial favorites of spectators at W&L, attracting large and vocal crowds.

Popular Events

Among W&L's most popular events are two campus-wide bonanzas: the Fancy Dress Ball and Mock Convention. A black-tie ball attended by students, alumni, and faculty, Fancy Dress (or "FD") is a yearly affair that celebrated its centennial in 2007. A student committee sponsors a concert on a Friday evening, followed by the ball on a Saturday night. Mock Convention (or "Mock Con") occurs with equal flair every four years. Organized to predict the presidential candidate for the political party out of office, Mock Con approximates an actual political convention on a grand scale. Students form state delegations and spend countless hours in research. They succeed in predicting candidates at an uncanny rate. The 1992 Mock Democratic Convention accurately selected Bill Clinton as its nominee. The 1996 Mock Republican Convention garnered live coverage on C-SPAN. House Speaker Newt Gingrich addressed the crowd of Washington and Lee students, and Bob Dole spoke to the assembly via phone when he accepted the convention's nomination. The 2000 mock convention predicted the nomination of George W. Bush, and the 2004 convention correctly chose John Kerry, but the 2008 convention had a rare miss when it incorrectly named Hillary Clinton. The 2012 edition will predict the Republican nominee.

FINANCIAL AID

Income is not a barrier to accessing a quality education at Washington and Lee. Scholarships and need-based awards are offered to applicants at every income level. The university is committed to providing all qualified students an opportunity for an outstanding educational experience. Need-based awards are available to any eligible student who completes the required financial aid documents.

During the current academic year, Washington and Lee will provide more than $29 million in financial aid and scholarships, making it possible for many students to attend who would be unable to do so without the university's help. W&L encourages students to apply for both need-based aid and merit-based aid to ensure that they explore all possible sources of W&L funding. Doing so may increase the total amount of aid a student may be awarded.

In 2008, more than 150 scholarships were awarded through the Johnson Scholarship Program, including the Johnson Scholarship, the Heinz, Lewis, and Weinstein scholarships, and a number of alumni and regional scholarships. Each year 44 enrolling students—nearly ten percent of the incoming class—will receive the prestigious Johnson Scholarship, covering a minimum of tuition, room and board.

To be considered for any form of merit-based aid, students must complete the Johnson Scholarship application and submit it, along with their complete admission application, by December 1. Contact the Office of Admissions with your questions about the Johnson Scholarship Program.

At W&L, all admitted students meeting the need-based financial aid priority deadline will receive an aid package that covers their family's institutionally determined need entirely with grant funds, with no loans. Early Decision applicants should note their preferred financial aid deadlines.

In order to reach its goal of meeting a student's financial needs, W&L's Financial Aid Office requires that a student's family fill out the College Scholarship Service Financial Aid Profile. The CSS Profile may be found online. The Financial Aid Office strongly recommends submission of the profile by mid-January. Doing so will ensure receipt of all student information by mid-February. Additionally, W&L's Financial Aid Office requires a student's family to provide tax returns from the two previous tax years. W&L's priority deadline for submitting all required Financial Aid application materials is March 1st. Applicants and their parents are strongly encouraged to review the detailed instructions about making application for financial aid on W&L's Web site—*http://financialaid.wlu.edu.*

It is Washington and Lee's objective to provide students who are admitted at early decision and who have completed financial aid applications by the priority deadline (Dec. 8 for ED1 and Jan.16 for ED11) a preliminary, estimated financial aid award prior to the submission of the admission deposit fee.

Because any college financial aid process may prove frustrating and confusing, W&L's Admissions office recommends early, careful planning for any student's family. The Financial Aid Office takes great care in addressing each family's personal and individual needs.

GRADUATES

The percentage of freshmen who return to Washington and Lee for their sophomore years stands as a sure, impressive sign of student contentment: typically ninety-five percent of freshmen return to W&L as sophomores. A more impressive sign is the number of W&L students who enter as freshmen and graduate four years later. Typically between eighty-five and ninety percent graduate on schedule. Clearly, Washington and Lee students stay at the university, and they stay happy. In an age when many college students need five years to earn a degree, the vast majority of W&L students find both adequate advising and access to the classes they need in order to graduate in four years.

Traditionally, W&L produces a high percentage of history, biology, and economics majors. That so many students should favor history at W&L, given the university's own long history, should be no surprise. The university's numerous biology majors include many who regularly establish a stellar record in gaining admittance to medical schools. Economics majors typically carry their expert training from W&L's Commerce School into the business world.

All Washington and Lee students receive excellent advice from the Career Services Office. The Career Services Office provides mock interview and résumé-review services. Students use the office's complete resources to research potential employers. The Office welcomes over 100 companies to interview W&L students for jobs and summer internships every year. It further organizes off-campus interviews and enlists students in job fairs through the Selective Liberal Arts Consortium and Big Apple Recruiting Consortium. These job fairs enable W&L students to meet employers in major American cities. The Career Services Office has an internship exchange with twenty-five top liberal arts colleges, which produces over 6,000 internship listings each year.

The Career Services Office also tracks W&L students as they leave W&L for employment and graduate school. Its report for the class of 2009 shows sixty-one percent of graduates in employment, along with twenty-four percent seeking postbaccalaureate degrees. A slim five percent either were seeking employment or were content taking time off after graduation. The report reveals that large numbers of working graduates found positions in business, banking and finance, government, journalism, or education. Of the 2009 graduates who decided to pursue advanced degrees, thirty-three percent entered general graduate schools, thirty-six percent entered law school, and twenty-five percent entered graduate studies in the health professions.

Because students come from all parts of the country to attend Washington and Lee, they also disperse themselves across the map after graduation. Recent trends show increasing numbers of W&L graduates moving to New York City, Washington, Charlotte, and Atlanta for work. In every city, existing alumni association chapters support and welcome new graduates.

Washington and Lee alumni share a unique experience that creates "an immediate bond" between them. They treasure their undergraduate memories and remain fiercely loyal to their alma mater. One graduate describes a revelation about the nature of Washington and Lee alumni this way:

> **"** *I have a W&L trident decal on the back of my car, and I was at the gas station one day when a stranger asked me what it was. I explained that it was the symbol for my school, Washington and Lee University. The stranger said, 'Oh, I thought maybe it was a sign for some kind of cult.' I laughed, and then, the more I thought about it, the more I realized the stranger wasn't necessarily wrong. W&L is a kind of cult—but in a good way. We all believe very strongly in the same ideals and we all have a strong sense of belonging to a very special place.* **"**

Washington and Lee's first-year residence halls are clustered on the edge of campus. With a renovation of the university's historic Colonnade now underway, Baker Hall, a former residence hall for first year students, has been turned into offices and classrooms. So students now live in Davis and Gilliam Halls and in nearby Gaines Hall as well as Graham-Lees, which is across the street. An arched breezeway passes through Graham-Lees; on the left, a marble step between two columns is clearly worn more than the rest. Superstition holds that freshmen must walk up this step, between the columns, or risk failing their first test. Millions of feet have kept that tradition.

Just next door to Graham-Lees dormitory is the Lee House. Robert E. Lee built this home when he was the president of the school, and presidents of Washington and Lee have lived there ever since. Freshman voices can be heard in the Lee House as they echo from the dormitories. A past president joked that, although he preferred classical music, he could not help becoming familiar with the musical tastes of each freshman class.

That the president of the university lives so close to the freshman class demonstrates something wonderful about Washington and Lee: The person who runs the school shares the same block with those who are just learning the school's nuances. There is a continuity from the top of the administration to the bottom of the student body, and this continuity permeates the entire university. There is a sense of familiarity and camaraderie. Washington and Lee students cherish this camaraderie and guard it closely long after they leave the quaint streets of Lexington.

❏ *Cameron Howell, B.A.*

WASHINGTON UNIVERSITY IN ST. LOUIS

 Washington University in St. Louis
St. Louis, MO 63130-4899

 (314) 935-6000, (800) 638-0700
Fax: (314) 935-4290

 E-mail: *admissions@wustl.edu*
Website: *http://admissions.wustl.edu*

Enrollment

Full-time ❏ women: 3,024
❏ men: 3,111

Part-time ❏ women: 581
❏ men: 330

From modest beginnings as a regional university, Washington University in St. Louis has emerged as a national leader in undergraduate and graduate education. The university now draws approximately ninety percent of students from outside of Missouri, with students from all fifty states, three U.S. territories, the District of Columbia, and approximately fifty-five countries. Nearly sixty-five percent of the students come from more than 500 miles away, making this one of the most geographically diverse universities in the world. As a medium-sized university, Wash. U. provides the perfect combination of a friendly smaller campus with the resources of a large university. Visitors will notice a unique spirit of camaraderie. Some might attribute it to midwestern friendliness, but more likely it is the product of the common desire to learn that pervades the campus.

Washington University's Danforth Campus is set on a hill overlooking Forest Park, one of the nation's largest urban parks. The World's Fair brought international ambassadors and exhibits to the park in 1904, and Brookings Hall served as a gathering place much as it does for students today. From this vantage point, seven miles west of downtown St. Louis, the offices, restaurants, theaters, and stadiums nearly blend into the horizon. Known for the majestic Gateway Arch, St. Louis offers a variety of cultural experiences from concerts and theater performances to Cardinals baseball games and the second largest Mardi Gras celebration in the nation.

> **❝***Students here are academic rock stars. They're genuinely passionate about learning.*
>
> *They're also tremendously diverse in their intellectual perspectives, and that diversity has influenced every paper, project, and conversation I've had at Washington U.* **❞**

—*Alex Rosenberg, '10*

Students can choose from four undergraduate colleges: Arts & Sciences, Business, Design & Visual Arts (including Architecture, Art), and Engineering. (There are also graduate programs in these colleges, plus those in Law, Medicine, Occupational Therapy, Physical Therapy, and Social Work.) The choices don't end there. Many students opt to pursue combined studies through double majors, minors, or dual-degree programs. It is easy to pursue multiple interests even if they involve two different undergraduate schools of the university. Flexibility is a key component of an education at Washington University. Faculty advisors guide students on a path that explores a variety of interests.

Wash. U. provides a dynamic, challenging academic environment. Students can choose from unique courses such as "The Cultural History of the Robot" and "Strangers and Savages, Aliens and Outcasts." Opportunities to learn don't end in the classroom either. Research projects are open to undergraduates, and every year many students choose to travel and study abroad through a university-sponsored program.

Technology helps Wash. U. students develop skills for learning that will make them successful later in their careers. In addition to resources located in the libraries, the university offers wireless access to the Internet in most locations as well as computer labs in the residential colleges and other campus locations, and wireless Internet access in each residence hall room. Most courses offer an online element whether it is a home page, tutorials, or one of several interactive online learning tools.

Improvements are also taking place on the campus landscape—new buildings are sprouting up every year. The new South 40 house provides students with state-of-the-art residence space, a wide variety of dining options, a fitness center, a market, and a green "roof top garden." In addition, Stephen F. & Camilla T. Baurer Hall opened in fall 2010. Baurer, which is home to the School of Engineering & Applied Science and Department of Energy, Environmental, and Chemical Engineering, is a Leed Gold Certified Building. Under construction for the School of Engineering is Preston M. Green Hall, which will be home to the International Center for Advanced Renewable Energy and Sustainability.

> *66 My undergraduate research experience has given me great hope. I have watched neurosurgeons implant tiny electrical circuits deep into the brain, observed neurologists program the circuitry, and witnessed the subsequent joy of newfound independence that engineering brought to life. 99*

—*Jennifer Wu, '09*

However, the real value comes from students. At Wash. U., students set high academic standards for themselves, but they also enjoy participating in community service, playing Frisbee in the Swamp, and going to parties at one of twelve fraternities. Social, cultural, political, and religious groups design programs to educate and entertain their fellow students. Ursa's, a corner cafe that accepts university meal cards, offers a patio where students meet on warm afternoons. Issues of *Student Life*, the 130-year-old student newspaper, can be seen on tables and in backpacks all over campus. Whether students choose to live in a Residential College, the Village, a fraternity, or a university-owned apartment, they will enjoy the benefits of a close community.

ADMISSIONS REQUIREMENTS

With nearly 25,000 applications in a recent year, Wash. U. is becoming increasingly competitive. To compete, students must pursue a challenging combination of courses and extracurricular activities. Admissions officers look at course selection and grades, recommendations, essays, extracurricular activities, and standardized tests.

Academic excellence, demonstrated by transcripts and test scores, is only the first step in the admissions process. At Washington U., applicants must also show how they have challenged themselves or pursued a personal talent. Initiative—taking honors, AP and IB courses when available, conducting independent research, or leading a team—separates high achievers. Recommendation letters and essay responses are the best methods for applicants to emphasize their unique qualities.

Admissions Deadlines

Either the SAT or the ACT is required and should be taken in the fall of senior year, if not earlier. Early Decision applications are due by November 15, whereas regular decision applications are due by January 15. Regular admission decisions are mailed by April 1.

Admission Procedures by School

General admission procedures require sending a high school transcript, which should include the following:

- 4 years of English
- 4 years of mathematics (calculus is recommended)
- 3–4 years of history and social sciences
- 3–4 years of laboratory sciences
- at least 2 years of foreign language

High school courses should reflect preparation for the program you are pursuing. For instance, students interested in the sciences, engineering, or the premedicine program should have preparation in chemistry, physics, calculus, and biology. Art and Architecture students have the option of providing a portfolio, which should include drawings from direct observation and a variety of media. A strong academic background is essential for success at Washington University, but it must be combined with a desire to seek out challenges.

> 66 *The diverse student body at Washington U. is a huge plus—for the first time, I know people who are completely different from me. I've learned to think independently and creatively.* 99

—*Samantha Giorgio, '09*

ACADEMIC LIFE

Flexibility is central to academics at Wash. U. Students are encouraged to pursue their interests even when they change; multiple interests are not only tolerated but encouraged. It is common to have a double major, even in different schools of the university. Sixty percent of students earn a major and minor or more than one major. Some students even choose to design their own major. With over ninety programs and 1,500 courses offered, no wonder students get excited about multiple subjects. Wash. U. students experience self-discovery by taking challenging classes in many divisions, working with renowned professors, and using their analytical skills.

Preparation

Many students receive credit for AP, honors, or IB courses taken during high school. In addition, placement exams are offered for areas such as foreign language and mathematics. Even when credit is not awarded, honors courses are beneficial in the admissions process because they represent a student's desire to be challenged.

Unique Opportunities

Many students begin their studies with optional freshman seminars and special programs, such as the Mind, Brain, and Behavior program, which prepares students for research during sophomore year. FOCUS seminars, concentrating on controversial issues in society, are also popular. Wash. U. is a pioneer in combined studies, with majors such as Philosophy,

Neuroscience, and Psychology (PNP) and American Culture Studies. The University Scholars Program in medicine is another unique opportunity, in which students apply for both undergraduate and graduate study at Washington University in its school of medicine. University Scholars work with a faculty mentor who guides them on their path to medical school.

Academic Schedule

The school year is organized into two semesters, with a wide selection of courses also offered during the summer. Students typically take about fifteen credit hours (or five classes) per semester. By junior and senior year, many students are able to schedule classes with Fridays off. One of the only required courses at Wash. U. is Writing 1, a freshman-level writing course. Writing provides the foundation for communication in nearly all disciplines, so its importance is stressed early. Later, course selection is guided by each undergraduate school. In Arts & Sciences, classes are chosen through a cluster system. Core courses cover the following areas:

- Physical and natural sciences and mathematics
- Social and behavioral sciences
- Textual and historical studies
- Languages and the arts

❝I like that you can take classes in any school—art, business, arts and science. I like it open-ended. I came here for a liberal arts education, and that's what I'm doing. ❞

—*Daniel Gealy, '09*

Faculty

Professors at Washington U. are leaders in their fields, engaged in research but also interested in sharing their knowledge with undergraduates. They enjoy teaching. Professors have been honored with awards that include the Nobel Prize and Pulitzer Prize. Yet, professors are approachable and accessible in and out of the classroom. Frequently, students and professors meet to continue a classroom discussion, discuss a paper, or clarify information before an exam. Some undergraduates pursue research, working closely with a faculty mentor. Research is not constrained to laboratory science either. Opportunities exist in a variety of fields, from anthropology to economics.

Classes

As in the selection of a major, class options are numerous and flexible. Students in the undergraduate schools are encouraged to take classes from the other schools. An architecture student may take an engineering class in computer science, while a political science major takes management in the business school.

Classes at Washington challenge students to think analytically, to become problem solvers, and relate ideas to the big picture. More than eighty percent of classes have fewer than twenty-four students, encouraging personal attention from the professor and a prominent role in discussion. Classes can be larger the first year, especially in introductory courses that provide a prerequisite for many majors. By senior year, students find themselves in much smaller classes, among a community of their peers. Classes provide solid preparation for graduate school or a career by emphasizing communication skills and critical thinking.

Advisors

Students are automatically assigned to a four-year academic advisor upon arrival. Advisors are guides and resources for self-discovery. They help students achieve their goals and outline a career path, but they rely on students to challenge themselves. Freshmen also are given a peer advisor, an upper-class student who can provide assistance in making the transition to college. Once a student declares a major, he or she chooses a major advisor. Major advisors have experience and knowledge in their fields and can be especially helpful in discussing career options.

Learning Beyond the Classroom

Outside the classroom walls, experiential learning shapes the Wash. U. experience. Many students participate in internships, whether they are during the summer or the school year. The Career Center maintains relationships with many companies to facilitate internships for students.

Study-abroad programs are available for every discipline, and are typically completed during junior year. Programs include economics at the London School of Economics, business in Hong Kong, and health care in France.

Ultimately, it is the daily experiences of the university—interacting with peers, conducting research, or joining a student group—that complete the learning experience.

Resources

With more than 4.2 million books, periodicals, and government publications, Wash. U. libraries provide excellent resources for research—including wireless Internet access. Electronic resources are also plentiful with subscriptions to many electronic journals and databases available through an Internet connection. In addition, all campus rooms are supplied with wireless Internet access, and each residential college has its own computer lab. Courses in computer science and electronic media are also available for interested students even if they are not students in the School of Engineering.

Campus events such as lectures, readings, and conferences are another asset to an education at Wash. U. The Assembly Series is a regular lecture program during the academic year. In recent years speakers on campus have included NAACP Chairman Julian Bond, former Supreme Court Justice Sandra Day O'Connor, *New York Times* columnist Tom Friedman, the Dalai Lama of Tibet, Hillary Rodham Clinton, Bill Gates, and a number of U.S. Presidents.

Educational services such as the Writing Center, the International House, and the Disability Resource Center offer help to students. Students can discuss an essay with a peer tutor or simply brainstorm ideas at the Writing Center. International students benefit from English Language Programs courses and assistance with the transition to life in the United States. Even a student who breaks a wrist can be assisted with note-takers from the Disability Resource Center ready to fill in while the student heals.

SOCIAL LIFE AND ACTIVITIES

Leadership

Leadership at Washington University is apparent both in and out of the classroom. Students may develop as leaders through group projects in the business school, teamwork in intramural basketball, or as an elected class representative. Avenues for developing leadership skills include meeting with other student leaders in the Student Group Council, attending leadership conferences, or participating in workshops during the Women's Leadership Training Initiative. The most valuable learning experience for many students is simply diving into a leadership position. Advisors in the Office of Student Involvement and Leadership are available for support, but student leaders make the real decisions for their groups.

> **❝** *It's nice because there's always something going on, events to go to with groups and friends and be surrounded by friends. There's variety academically, too. I can do art and East Asian studies at the same time—and whatever else I want.* **❞**

—Jonathan Yukio Clark, '09

Elected positions in the Congress of the South 40 (CS40), the North Side Association, and Student Union (SU) are highly sought after. These governing organizations allow students to influence important issues that shape the Wash. U. community. CS40 and the North Side Association are the government bodies for the residential areas of campus, known as the South 40 and the Village. Student Union, the primary student governmental body, allocates more than $2 million in activities funds to student groups in addition to representing student concerns to the administration. Students here have power to make a difference.

Academic/Preprofessional Organizations

Academic organizations provide an opportunity to meet with students and faculty who share your interests. Groups such as the Biomedical Engineers Society, Pre-Med Society, and American Institute of Graphic Arts allow students to discuss their career interests and learn from a community of their peers. Honorary groups recognize outstanding students and bring them together to help the community. For example, the sophomore honorary, Lock & Chain, hosts the biannual book sale.

Community Service

Surveys indicate fifty-seven percent of students at Wash. U. participate in community service, whether on campus or in the St. Louis community. Volunteer opportunities range from teaching children about environmental issues to serving food to those in need. Community service also means raising money for charities through Greek philanthropies or events such as Dance Marathon, a day of entertainment benefiting the Children's Miracle

Network. The Campus Y offers many programs for students interested in volunteering, including becoming a friend to senior citizens in the community through S.A.G.E. (Serving Across Generations). While some students are enjoying Caribbean beaches, other students choose an alternative spring break, devoting one week to community service projects such as building homes for low-income families.

Greek Life

Fraternities and sororities complement life at Wash. U. by providing social activities, community service, brotherhood, and sisterhood. About twenty-five percent of students belong to one of twelve fraternities or seven sororities. Rush takes place at the beginning of the second semester, so students have a chance to learn about Greek life well before joining. Fraternities have on-campus houses, managed by the university. Sororities have suites to gather for meetings or relaxation, but no traditional living quarters on campus. "Greeks" at Wash. U. are not in an isolated community. Fraternities and sororities provide a supportive social structure for students, but most "Greek" students maintain or develop relationships with "non-Greek" students throughout their time at Wash. U.

> 66 *I have enjoyed my experiences at Washington U. because I have been able to pursue my interests. It's an incredible feeling to win a national volleyball championship and show my designs in Saint Louis Fashion Week—all in the same year.* 99

—Audra Janak, '09

Social Events and Performances

While students at Wash. U. work hard, they also take time to relax. Social events such as concerts, acts by comedians, and a weekly happy hour are popular among students.

Artistic performances are abundant. Wash. U. is known for its excellent *a cappella* groups—male, female, coed, ethnic, cultural, classical, gospel—you name it. The Performing Arts Department puts on up to six productions a year. A battle of the bands called Sounds of the Swamp features student bands in a showcase of Wash. U. talent.

Walk In Lay Down, better known as WILD, is a Wash. U. tradition and the most highly attended event every semester. For one day, the Quad is filled with free food, drinks, games, music, and people. Students, faculty, and staff come together to celebrate both the beginning and end of the academic year. The day culminates with a headlining band, which is kept secret until about a week before the event.

Thurtene

The oldest student-run carnival in the nation, Thurtene, is a Wash. U. community service tradition. A junior honor organization called Thurtene organizes the carnival for one weekend in April each year, complete with a Ferris wheel, cotton candy, and games. Fraternities and sororities team up to build and decorate playhouses, or "facades," to perform plays and musicals written by students. Not only the university's students, faculty, and staff enjoy the carnival, but families from the St. Louis community also join in the fun. All of the proceeds from ticket sales are donated to local charities.

Media

Wash. U. students use media for artistic expression, to convey opinions, or to entertain others, and at the same time they gain valuable real-life experience. The university TV station (WUTV) and radio station (KWUR) are student-run and feature student broadcasters, actors, and DJs. Written publications highlight the talents of student writers. *Student Life*, one of the nation's oldest independent student newspapers, is a forum for dialogue on controversial issues as well as a way to find out what is happening on campus. Literary magazines feature student essays, short stories, poems, photographs, and drawings.

Cultural and Religious Groups

Cultural groups offer a community for people with similar backgrounds while educating others about diverse traditions, values, and lifestyles. Annual performances such as the Indian celebration of Diwali and the Lunar New Year Festival create long lines of students waiting at the box office for tickets.

Religious organizations such as Hillel and the Catholic Student Center create a home away from home for many students. These organizations not only offer religious services, but also fellowship with other students, community service projects, and contact with St. Louis.

Political Activism

Political groups on both sides of the spectrum are active on campus, and they encourage students to discuss issues by sponsoring debates and voting drives. In 2008, the U.S. Vice Presidential Debate, featuring Gov. Sarah Palin and Sen. Joseph Biden, was hosted at the Washington University Athletic Complex. Students participated as volunteers and were admitted into the audience.

> **66** *As a pre-med student, I'm very appreciative of the opportunities to integrate experiences at the medical school. There's even a class that allows you to shadow an ER physician.*
>
> *Pre-medical preparation here is second to none.* **99**

Sports

Wash. U. is an NCAA Division III school and founding member of the University Athletic Association (UAA). No athletic scholarships are offered, which means that athletes are dedicated to both academics and athletics. Student athletes are students first, athletes second. Nineteen varsity sports are offered, and Wash. U. has had championship success in almost every one. In 2007, the women's volleyball team captured a record-setting ninth NCAA Division III national championship. The men's basketball team and the men's golf team also captured NCAA Division III National Championships in 2008.

Club and intramural sports are popular among students because they allow exercise, competition, and camaraderie without the time commitment of varsity sports. More than seventy-five percent of students have participated in at least one intramural sport. Some unusual sports such as Ultimate Frisbee and inner-tube water polo are included in the intramural choices.

Sports and recreation facilities at Washington are comprehensive. The Athletic Complex includes an indoor and outdoor track, a swimming pool, basketball court, tennis courts, racquetball courts, and more. The South 40 Fitness Center provides a place to work out just steps away from most of the residence halls. The tree-lined paths and golf course of Forest Park are just across the street.

St. Louis is known as a great sports city, so even professional sports fanatics can be happy at Wash. U. With teams such as the St. Louis Rams, Cardinals, and Blues, games take place year-round. Busch Stadium is easily accessible from Wash. U. via the MetroLink, and both peer advisors and resident advisors are known to take their groups to sports games on occasion.

On Campus

Freshmen generally live in double or triple rooms on a coed floor of between twenty-five and fifty students. These freshman floors are a learning experience for everyone, and

Washington University in St. Louis   Guide to the Most Competitive Colleges ❑ **1035** become a supportive community. Early in the fall semester, groups of bright-eyed freshmen can be seen walking together on the way to dinner or a party. Sixteen new residence halls have been built since 1998.

Off Campus

Situated near Forest Park, the university provides access to museums, recreational facilities, and the St. Louis Zoo, nearly all of which have free admission. Just on the other side of the park is the Washington University School of Medicine in the Central West End, one of the young, hip areas of St. Louis. Full of vintage clothing stores, every type of ethnic restaurant, and several coffee shops, the Central West End is the perfect place to sit back with friends over a cup of java and discuss the last campus speaker or the results of the chemistry mid-term.

Nearby Clayton, the financial district and county government center, offers opportunities for summer internships or simply a romantic dinner at an Italian restaurant, followed by a stroll through an art gallery. A bit further in the other direction, downtown St. Louis offers history and entertainment. Every student should visit the Gateway Arch sometime during his or her four years, but other attractions such as jazz clubs, Union Station (a historic, restored train station that features a beautiful hotel, shops, and restaurants), and the Anheuser-Busch-inBev brewery (world's largest) deserve some attention.

For students interested in seeing more of St. Louis, the MetroLink light rail system, MetroBus, taxicabs, We Car, and upperclassmen are viable options. Movie theaters, grocery stores, and restaurants are all accessible by train or bus. Areas such as the Loop, a district famous for its shops, restaurants, and bars, is within walking distance of the university. Students can be found at Fitz's—a local root beer brewery—one of the local bookstores, or the famous St. Louis Bread Company (known as Panera everywhere else).

FINANCIAL AID

Most students receive some form of financial assistance through scholarships, student loans, and part-time employment. All scholarships are awarded based on merit, yet some are given on both merit and need. Both the College Scholarship Service (CSS) PROFILE and the Free Application for Federal Student Aid (FAFSA) are acceptable to apply for need-based financial assistance. Army and Air Force ROTC Scholarships are another option. Payment plans with monthly tuition installments and long-term, low-interest loans are available for parents.

Employment

Students have access to numerous campus jobs whether or not they have applied for financial assistance. Approximately half of all students work part-time on campus. These students can be found in laboratories, administrative offices, libraries, theaters, the Athletic Complex, and the bookstore.

Scholarships

The University provides nearly $65 million each year in scholarships to undergraduates, including both merit-based and need-based scholarships. More information is available from the admissions Web site (*admissions.wustl.edu*).

GRADUATES

The most popular majors for a recent year's graduating class included biology, psychology, engineering, and business. Graduates found jobs around the country and around the world. Every year employers seek out the combination of skills developed at Washington University.

Students have access to the Washington University Career Centers, where the staff is ready to critique a résumé, discuss a career search, or provide career resources. Career preparation covers all four years with seminars ranging from "How to Find an Internship" to "Interviewing Skills." Approximately 200 companies recruited on campus in a recent year including Microsoft, Bloomingdales, Teach for America, and Bank of America. Wash. U. also offers an opportunity to build connections with alumni through a database called Career Connections.

An education at Wash. U. fosters a continued desire for learning, and many students choose to continue with graduate study. In fact, thirty-three percent of the Class of 2007 planned to go to graduate school immediately, and eighty-five percent said they planned further graduate or professional education some time in the future. Wash. U. prepares students

FAMOUS GRADS

- Clark Clifford, Former Secretary of Defense
- Ken Cooper, Pulitzer Prize-winning Journalist
- David Garroway, Host of NBC-TV's *Today Show*
- Frank Gladney, Founder of 7-UP
- A.E. Hotchner, Novelist and Playwright
- John F. McDonnell, Former CEO of McDonnell Douglas
- Shepherd Mead, Playwright
- Condé Nast, *Vogue* Publisher
- Mike Peters, Pulitzer Prize-winning Editorial Cartoonist
- Harold Ramis, Screenwriter famous for *Ghostbusters* and *Animal House*
- Earl Sutherland, Nobel Laureate in Medicine
- James Thompson, Former Governor of Illinois
- Tennessee Williams, Playwright
- William H. Webster, Former Director of FBI and CIA

for success in master's degree and Ph.D. programs. Some students even pursue further study in one of the graduate programs offered through the university's seven schools.

> **❝** *I value being able to double major and take other courses I find interesting. I studied Irish literature through a freshman program and attended plays in Ireland. Nothing is watered down. These courses are very substantive and challenging.* **❞**

—*Chase Sackett, '10*

SUMMING UP

From the friendly smiles on the oak-lined paths to the group study sessions in Ursa's Cafe, visitors pick up an atmosphere of community at Wash. U. This atmosphere extends into the classroom, where professors are eager to share their knowledge and students are engaged in active analysis. Flexibility is also prevalent in the selection of classes, majors, and extracurricular activities. Students with initiative can define their own experience, and Wash. U. has the resources to support innovative thinking. Professors who lead in their field, the latest technology, and the surrounding city of St. Louis all create opportunities for learning. Still, much self-discovery takes place outside of the classroom—in residence halls, at student group meetings, and even at social events. The size and location of Washington U. make it a perfect fit for students who don't want to be lost in the crowd but are excited by the opportunities at a medium-sized university.

❏ *Joyce Lawrence, B.S., B.A.*

 Webb Institute
Glen Cove, NY 11542-1398

 (516) 671-2213

 E-mail: *admissions@webb-institute.edu*
Website: *www.webb-institute.edu*

 Enrollment

Full-time ❏ women: 11
❏ men: 68

INTRODUCING WEBB INSTITUTE

The Webb Institute is often described as "a singularity." Ask anybody familiar with the institute to describe the school, and you'll quickly learn that this is no exaggeration: in its rigor, its value, and its culture, Webb stands apart from the status quo of higher education. Let's continue with a few reasons why Webb is one of the best colleges in the world, and without a doubt, one of the most unique learning environments you're ever likely to encounter.

- Webb Institute was founded in 1889 by William H. Webb, one of the preeminent shipbuilders of the mid-nineteenth century, the era of the clipper ships.

- The purpose of the school is to advance the art and science of shipbuilding in the United States by training promising young people for careers in that field.
- Webb confers only one undergraduate degree: a Bachelor of Science in Naval Architecture and Marine Engineering.
- The Webb program is a fully-accredited, four-year, intense engineering education.
- Upon admission, all students receive a four-year, full-tuition scholarship, paid by the school's endowment.
- The school is housed in a mansion on one of Long Island's Gold Coast Estates, with a private beach and twenty-six beautiful, waterfront acres.
- Only about eighty students attend in total, with a maximum of twenty-six in a class.
- Each winter, every Webb student spends eight weeks as an intern in the marine industry or as a shipboard cadet, for a total of at least eight months of practical experience upon graduation.
- Graduates enjoy a one hundred percent placement rate in jobs and graduate schools. Most are recruited for employment as early as freshman year.
- Graduates are regularly accepted into prestigious graduate schools, both domestic (MIT, University of Michigan) and abroad (Delft Technical U, Southampton University), often garnering large scholarships.
- Webb is not a military school; it is a completely private institution, focusing primarily on the needs of the commercial shipbuilding market; therefore, students have no obligations to the school or government upon graduation.
- The Webb degree is readily transferable to a wide range of other engineering disciplines, not only shipbuilding.

If you have never heard of Webb, don't worry—many of the students presently attending didn't know about it either until their junior or senior year in high school, when they received an introductory brochure in the mail! But don't let Webb's small size and apparent obscurity fool you. Webb may be one of the best-kept secrets in academia, but it is certainly no secret in the maritime industry. Read on to learn more about just what makes Webb Institute so singular on the scene of college education.

ADMISSIONS REQUIREMENTS

A school with only eighty students and no tuition invariably prompts the question, "how hard is it to get into Webb?" The answer is, "surprisingly easy," provided you meet the academic criteria and demonstrate a strong desire to become a part of the Webb culture. The application process to Webb is likely to be the easiest of your college applications, weighing in at a scant two pages. The application is used to narrow the applicant pool to about seventy students on the basis of academic performance. Final candidates are selected from this pool and invited to the school for a personal interview with the institute's president, upon which the final admission status is determined. This continues until roughly twenty-five admitted students confirm their enrollment.

Webb does seek a certain type of student; the brightest and hardest-working that America has to offer. Students are held to rigorous academic standards during the preliminary phase of the admissions process. Applicants should have an eighty-five percent or higher average in all core science and mathematics courses, and high school records should reflect a high level of academic achievement. They should be in the top ten percent of their high school class and have a minimum GPA of 3.5. They must also take both the SAT and the SAT Subject Tests in Mathematics Level I or II, and Physics or Chemistry. A minimum score of 600 Verbal and 660 Math on the SAT is required.

Admission considerations extend well beyond scholastic qualification. In such a small school, it is imperative that students be socially compatible with one another. The purpose of the admissions interview is to evaluate this compatibility on an individual basis to ensure that incoming freshmen will perpetuate a historically social, proactive, and familial student body. Furthermore, Webb seeks students with diverse experience; a fact demonstrated by the multitude of well-traveled, musical, mechanical, and/or athletic students on campus.

Applicants with questions or concerns are advised to contact Webb's Office of Admissions for further information.

ACADEMIC LIFE

Webb is a hard school. The 146 credits required to graduate (more than eighteen credits per semester) attest to that. Add multiple field trips, highly respected faculty both in engineering and humanities classes, two months of practical work experience each year, and projects that few other schools dare to attempt—such as the senior thesis and the preliminary design of a large ship—and you begin to get the bigger picture. The incredible amount of learning and work that Webb crams into four years is what makes the school dear to alumni and the alumni dear to employers.

Courses

Webb Institute confers only one undergraduate degree—the Bachelor of Science in Naval Architecture and Marine Engineering. The four-year curriculum is thus mostly fixed, but since Webb is an ABET-accredited school, many of the prerequisites taught in the first two years are common to other engineering colleges. Freshman year focuses on fundamentals such as calculus, physics, chemistry, statistics, and technical communication. Sophomore year builds on this base with dynamics, strength of materials, thermodynamics, fluid dynamics, and humanities. Basic courses in naval architecture and marine engineering are also taught in the first two years. Junior and senior years are filled with upper-level major courses such as hydrodynamics, ship resistance and propulsion, propulsion systems, auxiliary systems, ship structures, and seakeeping. Juniors also study electrical engineering with an emphasis on electronics, motors, and generators. The final two years of Webb are also defined by three major projects: small ship design for juniors, large ship design for seniors, and a yearlong senior thesis. For all its technical focus, Webb makes space in the curriculum for one humanities course each term. These courses not only round out the program, but also they set apart Webb graduates as engineers who can communicate effectively in a variety of different formats—graphically, textually, and orally. You can find the most up-to-date curriculum on Webb Institute's website.

> *" What do you call the guy who graduates last in his Webb Class? A Naval Architect! "*

—*Professor of Marine Engineering*

Disciplines

Naval Architecture and Marine Engineering are examples of *systems* engineering. This means that they are inherently diverse, multidisciplinary areas of study. Consider all aspects of ship design. First, there is the hull moving through the water; the study of this action involves knowledge of hydrodynamics. Next, there is the hull itself; the design of adequate structural integrity requires a good understanding of the principles of civil engineering. Then there are the guts of the ship—all the machinery and electrical equipment. The design of these systems requires, for example, knowledge of combustion and heat transfer (chemical engineering), engines and other auxiliary machinery (mechanical engineering), and ship electrical power distribution and electronic control systems (electrical engineering). Webb is unique in its combinative approach, rolling many engineering disciplines into a comprehensive package. As a result, Webbies find that, during both internships and full-time employment, they are able to engage with engineers of widely ranging backgrounds in intelligent and informed conversations on anything from structures to HVAC systems.

Faculty

The rigor of the Webb education and the respect that Webb graduates earn in the industry are due in no small part to the school's instructors. The Webb faculty is composed of world-class educators, all of whom teach classes themselves (no TAs here!). Most of the professors hold advanced graduate degrees, and because professors do not hold research contracts with the school, they are able to devote themselves to academia, giving the students a more effective learning environment. Students receive an unparalleled level of individual attention, thanks to a student-faculty ratio of about seven to one. Professors are also uncommonly dedicated, frequently staying late to answer student questions, holding evening review sessions, or taking weekend phone calls at home. They are also very personable; many enjoy socializing with pupils at school events or at nearby pubs.

> **"***I enjoy hanging out with the professors. It gives a personality to the red pen!* **"**

Classrooms

Due to Webb's small size, each graduating class has its own classroom. The professors, rather than the students, move from classroom to classroom. The classrooms are partitioned into two sections: the front of the room is the learning space, where students actually sit down and attend lectures given by the faculty, and the back of the room is devoted to personal work space for the students, which becomes a home-away-from-home for most students. Each student has a drafting desk situated in the back of the classroom where each can do homework. Because most students are in the classroom even after classes, the class develops a very close-knit relationship. This is beneficial academically because it allows close access to peers that would not be available at a larger school. If there's dispute or question about an assignment, people who are doing the same exact work are sitting right next to you!

Library, Computers, and Labs

The library at Webb is everything that a naval architecture or marine engineering student could hope for. Books, technical documents, and publications are available in abundance, to suit any research need a student might have. For computerized research, Webb has a lab, equipped with two supercomputers and several up-to-date desktops that are all available for student use. In addition, each student receives his or her own laptop that is loaded with all of the software necessary for work in naval architecture and marine engineering. There are several laboratories, including a chemistry, physics, mechanical engineering, electrical engineering, and fluid dynamics lab, all with up-to-date equipment. There is also a machine shop available for undergraduate thesis work. The most relevant lab, however, is definitely the towing tank, Webb's own facility for model testing. Students can study the hydrodynamic properties of a ship by running a scale model of it down the tank. Towing tanks are often used for professional work, so the fact that students have access to one for their own work is significant. The towing tank is very advanced, with some of the latest tank-testing technology installed for the students' use.

> **"** *The tank is great! Where else will you get to play with model boats in a giant computerized bathtub, all in the name of science?* **"**

Winter Work Program

Possibly the most unique component of Webb's academic requirements is the Winter Work program. To help understand what this program is and how it works, let me first explain the school's somewhat unusual yearly schedule. Webb's fall semester runs the same as most other colleges—beginning in late August and ending with finals just before Christmas—but its spring semester runs significantly later—from early March to late June. This two-month break is not just an extended vacation, however, as students are required to work somewhere in the marine industry during January and February.

The types of places in which students will work during these months vary greatly, depending mostly on what year of school a student is in. For freshmen, the school finds jobs in shipyards around the country, where they will work side-by-side with yard workers physically building the ships they will one day design. The purpose of this work period is to gain hands-on experience in the production of ships, in order to gain a better understanding of the process that goes on after a design leaves an office.

Sophomore year, the school finds students berths on merchant ships around the world. On these ships, students work as cadets, standing watch and performing routine maintenance in the engine room and on deck. This period is intended to give students a better idea of how a ship is operated, so that they can learn to better cater future designs toward efficient and simple operation. This winter work experience also gives students the opportunity to spend time overseas. They will often experience port calls all around the world, including New Zealand, Europe, Singapore, the Philippines, and even Antarctica.

The final two winter work periods—junior and senior year—are a bit more flexible. Students are expected to find their own jobs in the marine industry, working as junior designers in shipyards, consulting offices, and other similar jobs. Webb is fairly flexible toward the internships students can find for themselves, and they are free to find jobs in the field and location of their choice. This also means that if they care to, students have another opportunity to work in foreign countries, something more and more students have been opting for in recent years. Students have worked in a diverse list of countries, including South Africa, Germany, China, Korea, and Dubai.

By the time they graduate from Webb, students have experienced first-hand the design, construction, and operation of a ship. This experience is invaluable to potential employers after graduation and is one of the major reasons for Webb's one hundred percent placement rate, especially when most competing graduates from other naval architecture schools have never even set foot on deck!

SOCIAL LIFE AND ACTIVITIES

Naturally, given its small size, Webb offers an extremely unique social experience. While it is true that the school doesn't exactly offer the immense social diversity that you might find at a big state school, many students will tell you that this is a positive thing. The small, close-knit environment at Webb breeds a distinct "family" atmosphere; and with only three dorm buildings, your closest friends are never more than a stone's throw away. Of course, social life isn't limited to just the Webb community. For just about any social event, most students usually invite friends from local colleges such as Adelphi, NYU, Manhattan College, and a number of others. Line that up with a number of active sports teams, a choral group, a theatrical group, the Long Island Sound, and nearby New York City, and Webb offers tons of attractions and activities for students to enjoy.

The Campus

Webb Institute moved from The Bronx to its current position in 1946. The Webb's twenty-six-acre campus is the former estate of Herbert L. Pratt, overlooking the beautiful Long Island Sound. The campus has been featured in a multitude of movies, most famously, however, as the exterior of Wayne Manor in the movie *Batman Forever*. The main building is Stevenson Taylor Hall, which houses all four classrooms in the wings, the majority of male residences, the dining room, the library, the physics and chemistry laboratories, the lecture hall, laundry room, computer lab, faculty offices, and administrative offices. The second-largest building is the Robinson Model Basin, which holds the model testing tank on the bottom floor and female dormitories on the second floor. Other buildings include Motley Dorm hall, the Luckenbach offices, the student garage, the woodshop, the machine shop, and the marine engineering lab. Although the campus is small, it holds every amenity of being at home and every resource one needs for a good education.

Conveniences

Webb offers its students many services and conveniences. For example, meals are provided three times per day, and the quality of the food is far superior to that of most college food. Students at Webb also enjoy little conveniences including free soap, laundry detergent and bleach, fifty-cent washers and dryers, and ample parking space. Amenities such as a treasury, student kitchen, bookstore, garage, woodshop, and machine shop are particularly helpful. The S.O. treasury allows students to cash checks and make deposits or withdrawals without the hassle of visiting a bank, while the student kitchen provides students with a place to store and prepare their own food. The student kitchen is also stocked with snacks and drinks that are available to students for purchase at any time. Almost anything a student needs to work and live comfortably can be found on the Webb campus.

The S.O.

The Student Organization is another unique part of Webb. The students are given free range to govern themselves with very little oversight from the administration and faculty. By signing a contract at the beginning of their freshman year, every student agrees to abide by the S.O. Handbook and the Honor Code. The S.O. Handbook lays out the chairman-ships and rules, while the Honor Code forbids lying, cheating, and stealing. Most schools have documents similar to these; what makes Webb special is that the students actually enforce and live by the rules set forth by them. As a result of this, the students have adopted habits and ways of living unheard of in any other college situation. Some of these habits include leaving calculators, books, and computers sitting on library tables, having dorm rooms with locks that only lock from the inside, attic-storage of students' belongings, and access to almost every room and building on campus. However, this freedom does not mean that Webb campus is open to the public. A student Officer of the Day is on duty between the hours of 8 A.M. and 10 P.M. to greet guests and to deal with minor problems that may arise during those hours. At night, hired security patrols the campus to ensure the safety of the students. Due to this self-regulation, Webb prevents serious crimes, and all minor offenses are dealt with by the S.O. Honor Council, and the Student Court, allowing students to be able to study without worrying about the safety of themselves or their belongings.

Athletics

Webb offers many sports and activities for students to enjoy during their free time. Webb belongs to the Hudson Valley Men's Athletic Conference, a sports league of small schools in the area. Although it is a men's league, women are welcome to and often do play on the teams. The school has a gymnasium, two tennis courts, and Thorpe Field, where sports including basketball, volleyball, soccer, and tennis are played. Webb also has a successful sailing team that practices on the Long Island Sound. The school owns a fleet of 420s, Lasers, and motor boats that students are welcome to use. Students are also pro-vided with free membership to the Glen Cove YMCA to use its complete weight room, pool, and gym.

" Sporting events are a great chance to get away from the daily grind of homework and projects! "

The general informality of Webb athletics does not mean that the athletes are not dedicated and do not play hard. Students compete fiercely and have fun playing sports at

Webb. The sailing team does particularly well and regularly places highly in regattas, on occasion beating schools such as Cornell and the U.S. Naval Academy. One of the best parts of Webb athletics is how easy it is to get involved. Many students who would not otherwise ever play intercollegiate sports can just show up for practices and then proceed to play in games against teams from schools ten times as large as Webb.

SOCIAL LIFE AND ACTIVITIES

Webb has several major social events throughout the year, both big and formal and small and casual. Small events, which generally occur a few times a month, generally just involve a night of drinking, eating, and hanging out with classmates in the pub. Throughout the year the student-led social committee comes up with ideas and themes for these. Bigger events happen more like once a month, and include the Halloween party, the Christmas party, casino night, and the Gatsby party (people dress like it's the 1920s and the school buys everyone lobster). Last, but certainly not least, is Webbstock. One Saturday every June, Webb will host six or seven bands, free drinks and food, and a number of games, sports, and events (including bouncy castles and dunk tanks) under the warm sun next to the cool green Long Island Sound. Students invite friends from all over the country to this wonderful event, and some will even tell you it's their favorite annual holiday.

Off Campus

When students get a break from work and don't feel like spending their free hours confined to campus, there's plenty to do in the neighboring areas of Long Island. For starters, the town of Glen Cove itself offers a movie theater, a number of restaurants and bars, a bowling alley, a golf course, and a whole lot more—all within five minutes of Webb's front gate. Also less than five minutes from campus is a Long Island Railroad station, giving the students easy access to neighboring New York City. Students head into the city often to see the sights and enjoy everything else the five boroughs have to offer. Just outside of Glen Cove, students often take a ride to Roosevelt Field Mall, one of the biggest shopping malls on Long Island. Just a half-hour south brings you to Long Island's south shore and Jones Beach, which has become a popular surf and swim spot for a number of Webb's water-loving students. Of course, these are only a few of the fun attractions that can be found around Long Island, just a stone's throw from Webb's doorstep.

FINANCIAL AID

Webbies enjoy a unique financial position amongst college students. The cost of attendance is uncommonly low, thanks to the endowment left by Mr. Webb, which covers the entirety of tuition for all students. In fact, student expenditures are limited to room, board, books, and computers. Many students find these costs easy to defray using outside scholarships. If that is not the case, Webb is committed to financial assistance; the school participates in Pell Grants and the Family Federal Education Loan program, which include Plus and Stafford loans. While you cannot call Webb completely free, the school ensures that it remains exceptionally affordable to students from all financial backgrounds. A detailed summary of Webb's expenditures may be found on the school's website.

GRADUATES

So what would you *do* with a Webb degree? It is a reasonable question, and seniors' answers are likely to be as unique and surprising as the school itself is. Usually at least a quarter of Webb's graduating class will enroll directly in another degree program. Harvard Business School and MIT's Transportation Management programs have been popular choices over the years, as have both master's and doctoral degrees in some form of engineering, mechanical, ocean, aeronautical, petroleum, or even advanced studies in naval architecture. Webbies have also gone to law school, medical school, veterinary school, and even divinity school. Webb graduates enjoy high acceptance rates in the programs of their choosing, and they often find their graduate studies to be a breeze after four intense years at Webb.

Seniors who choose to enter the workforce are greeted with a cornucopia of employment opportunities, not just in the United States, but also throughout the world. Some of these opportunities are natural offshoots of junior or senior internships; other opportunities come from exposure to industry figures and alumni. Several prominent engineering firms also visit Webb each term to recruit full-time workers and interns. Enterprising students who pursue their own unique vision of work are often rewarded too. So great is the global demand for defense, infrastructure, transportation, and energy solutions—and so systemic is the shortage of good engineers—that Webb graduates have continued to enjoy one hundred percent job placement even through the depths of the recent Great Recession. Webb's average starting salaries are comparable to those reported by the Ivies.

SUMMING UP

Webb may just be the best school available to the intelligent and motivated student who wants an immersive, rigorous, and value-conscious engineering instruction; a student who prizes a close-knit learning community, where hard work is both expected and rewarded. If that student sounds like you, then do yourself a favor and give Webb a close look. It may not be for everybody, but if Webb turns out to be a match for you, it may be the best four-year favor you'll ever do for your career.

❑ *Casey Harwood, B.S.*

Wellesley College
106 Central Street
Wellesley, MA 02481

(781) 283-1000
Fax: (781) 283-3678

E-mail: *admission@wellesley.edu*
Website: *http://www.wellesley.edu*

 Enrollment

Full-time ❏ women: 2,300

INTRODUCING WELLESLEY

Wellesley's mission statement is to provide "an excellent liberal arts education for women who will make a difference in the world." And if there's one thing a Wellesley education will give you, it's a sense of empowerment that you have the skills, confidence, and know-how to succeed at anything you choose.

Consistently ranked among the top five liberal arts colleges in the nation, Wellesley offers its students a serious intellectual environment combined with a fun, all-women atmosphere. It's not uncommon to find friends gossiping until early morning, baking cookies together while cramming for an exam, or crowded around the dorm television on Thursday nights for a study break.

Wellesley is a college where the emphasis is on you. You'll never be a number at Wellesley; all of your professors will know you by your name and the quality of your work. Student opinions not only count but are actively solicited, from determining which professors receive tenure, to selecting your commencement speaker, to campus and dorm governance issues.

> **66** *My first year at Wellesley, several students were chosen to help select the next president of the college. And our input didn't stop there! The new president asked us to call her by her first name, Diana, and always said hello when we saw her walking across campus or jogging around the lake. She also came to many of the college's activities, from attending school plays, soccer games, and student body meetings, to greeting trick-or-treaters at her home on Halloween. She gave us the feeling she really cared, and she did.* **99**

Part of Wellesley's charm also comes from its surroundings. Nestled in the suburb of Wellesley, Massachusetts, twelve miles outside of Boston, the college is located on a 500-acre campus that boasts one of the most spectacular settings in New England. Students often spend their weekends canoeing on Lake Waban, reading on Green Beach, or "traying" down Severance Green in the snow.

But during the week, students focus almost exclusively on their work. Wellesley is a teaching college rather than a research university, so students receive plenty of individual attention. Professors hold extensive office hours and some will even bake brownies for class or have students over to their homes. Every professor assigns and grades papers and exams; no graduate students compete for your attention or evaluate your work.

English, psychology, and economics are among the most popular majors, although students dabble in everything from economics of Third World countries to sports medicine to Greek art. Many students choose to double-major, while others will select a minor, often a foreign language. Students can take only fourteen of their thirty-two credits in their major, so they are forced to broaden their education beyond a few departments.

Outside of the classroom, students spend much of their time participating in sports, college government, music groups, dee-jaying at the college radio station, and exploring

Boston. While Wellesley is not a party school, social opportunities abound on campus and off. Very few students choose not to participate in an extracurricular activity. And if your favorite activity on campus doesn't exist, simply propose it to college government—chances are, it will be approved.

An open mind is one of the crucial elements of being a Wellesley student, and the colleges stresses racial, ethnic, and religious diversity among its students. While most women call the mid-Atlantic home, students come from all fifty states and hail from more than sixty-five countries. Although everyone is required to take a course from the multicultural curriculum, students often learn best about other cultures and customs from spending time with one another in the dorms.

The dorms each have their own distinct character and it's easy to get to know both older and younger students, since dorms are not separated by class.

All in all, you'll work hard at Wellesley, but you'll never regret it. Wellesley will push you to your intellectual and physical limits, but you'll finish college with excellent preparation for whatever next step you choose to take. Wellesley may drive you crazy as a student, but as an alumna, you'll realize it was the best decision you've ever made.

ADMISSIONS REQUIREMENTS

As Wellesley's profile has risen in recent years, the percentage of students admitted has declined from fifty percent to about thirty-four percent. But if you have a strong academic record, are motivated and enthusiastic, and know you want to attend a top school, Wellesley should be an easy choice.

Since the college believes a diverse student body is important, Wellesley seeks to bring together a group of individuals who enrich the school by their different experiences, races, ethnicities, religions, geographic backgrounds, and interests. Approximately forty-four percent of the student body is white, twenty-five percent is Asian, and thirteen percent is African American, Latino, and Native American, and nine percent are international students. While sixty-three percent have attended public high schools, the other thirty-three percent have gone to private schools, and the rest have been home-schooled or otherwise educated.

Decision Plans

The college offers three decision plans for prospective students, each with different deadlines and each geared toward a different kind of applicant. All, require the standard application fee of $50, although the fee is waived for online applicants and in cases of financial need.

- *Early Decision* is designed for women who are sure they want to attend Wellesley; about one-fifth of incoming students are accepted under this plan. If you think you might fall into this category, it's best to visit the college early, attend a few classes, meet some professors, and arrange an overnight stay with a student in her dorm room. The Early Decision deadline falls on November 1, so you must take the SAT or ACT by October. The advantage of this plan is that you'll know by the winter holidays whether you've been admitted or deferred to the regular application pool. The only disadvantage is that the decision is binding, so if accepted, you must withdraw your applications from all other schools.

- For students who are strongly considering Wellesley but aren't sure they want to commit to the Early Decision program, the *Early Evaluation* plan has a deadline of January 1. You'll receive a letter by the end of February that indicates your chances of acceptance, but the final decision is not sent out until April. Early Evaluation is a smart plan for people who want to know how realistic their chances of admission are without having to pledge to one school.

- Finally, Wellesley offers a *Traditional Regular Decision* plan. Applications are due January 15, so you can take standardized tests through December of your senior year. Again, the Board of Admissions will notify you of its decision in April. Students placed on the wait list will also be notified at this time.

After you've chosen which plan is right for you, it's time to think about assembling your application package.

Application Requirements

Wellesley requires its applicants to take either the ACT (with Writing) or SAT and two SAT Subject Tests (recommended one to be quantitative). In a recent incoming class, first-year students typically scored between 600 and 700 on the Math section and between 600 and 800 on the Verbal section of the SAT I.

Of course, standardized tests are only one part of your Wellesley application. High school grades are equally, if not more, important. Ninety-five percent of incoming students were in the top quarter of their class; all ranked in the top half. You'll also need two academic teacher recommendations. It's best to choose teachers who know you well from the classroom and extracurricular activities, and who can easily talk about your abilities, development as a student, personality, and potential as a Wellesley woman.

Along with the regular admissions paperwork, Wellesley requires a personal essay. The essay is one of the most crucial parts of the application because it tells the admission board who you are, what you think, and why you would make a good candidate for Wellesley. It's also a chance for you to stand out from everybody else and tout your achievements. Remember, students, professors, and admissions officers are reading your essay, so your chances are best if you gear it toward a general audience.

Finally, Wellesley recommends, but does not require, an admissions interview. Try to have the interview on campus, so you can get the flavor of the school. Remember, the interview is not just a chance for the admissions officers to learn more about you, but for you to learn more about Wellesley. If you can't make it up to Boston, you can meet with an alumna in your area.

> **❝** *Applying to college seemed like a daunting process, but the Wellesley students and professors I met were so encouraging I felt as though they really wanted me there. The admissions office also went out of its way. When my parents and I arrived late for the campus tour, a student took us individually to our tour group and showed us sights along the way. The experience was actually symbolic of my years at Wellesley—everyone makes an extra effort to help each other out and is always supportive.* **❞**

A few other points: AP credits (up to a total of four credits) are accepted, provided you score a four or five on most tests. Interviews are required of transfer students, as are high school and college transcripts, and SAT scores. Students applying from abroad must take the college boards and submit scores from their native countries' college entrance exams. Furthermore, a TOEFL exam is strongly recommended for students whose native language is not English.

ACADEMIC LIFE

One of the best things about a Wellesley education is the opportunity to study a broad array of topics. Wellesley's curriculum offers up a plate of anything and everything, but leaves the choice to you. The college provides major and minor programs of study in more than thirty departments and programs.

> *When I was a first-year student at Wellesley, my parents told me they had a few requirements of their own: I should take art history, economics, history, and a course in Shakespeare while in college. I put them off until junior and senior years—what a mistake! I regretted not minoring in history. And now when I go to art museums, I understand so much more—the time period, the artist's purposes, and color schemes.*

Courses

Before students can graduate, they must meet some basic requirements. All students must complete thirty-two units of credits (usually one credit per course), at least eight of which are in your major. You also must maintain a 2.0, or C, average. In addition, all students must elect nine courses drawn from eight substantive and skill-based categories; a multicultural class; an expository writing course; one year of physical education; and demonstrated proficiency in a foreign language. Students must also complete four 300-level, or the most specialized, courses, at least two of which are in your major, to ensure you have in-depth knowledge in several subjects. If this all sounds daunting, it's not. Remember, you have eight semesters to spread these classes out. Most professors would advise, however, that you complete these courses during your first two years at Wellesley, so you can concentrate on completing your major and travel abroad during your junior and senior years.

Beyond the requirements, though, you can break your own academic path at Wellesley, including devising your own major and the courses needed to complete it. It's wise to experiment with a wide variety of offerings; many students find they have strong interests in subjects as different as English and physics, and love spending hours poring over books in the Reserve Room, but also relish nights spent stargazing at the Observatory. The college offers many courses without prerequisites, so you don't have to be a whiz at something before you walk into the classroom.

Faculty

The strongest aspect of Wellesley's academic life is its professors. The 326 faculty members have more women (191) than men (135), a plus for a college focusing on the education of women, all of whom hold degrees in their fields from the top schools. And with a faculty-student ratio of eight to one, you'll not only know but most likely become friends with your professors.

Although research is considered a vital part of any professor's résumé, Wellesley professors are at the college principally because they want to teach, not because they want to do research. This means they'll know you by name and grade your work, and that you'll have valuable personal contacts when it comes time to ask for career advice and graduate school recommendations. They'll also take an interest in your life outside the classroom: how the soccer team did, if your family is visiting for Family Weekend, and when your theater production will be appearing on campus. At Wellesley, the average course size ranges from fifteen to twenty-five students, depending on the type of class.

> **❝** *My parents recently visited Wellesley and had lunch with one of my professors. Even though I graduated several years ago, he jumped at the chance to meet them again and spent an hour and a half reminiscing with them about my years as a student and sharing personal stories. It was a great experience that I doubt would have happened at any other school.* **❞**

Another advantage of such an intimate class setting is that you'll have a unique chance to engage in truly intellectual debates that will often last more than the regular seventy minutes of class time. Professors also go out of their way to bring some of the brightest minds in their field to campus to meet with students in group settings, answer your questions, and spur your curiosity.

Course Load

The course load at Wellesley is not easy, but it is manageable. You can expect to stay up late reading Chaucer, spend your Sunday afternoons in the laboratory running chemistry experiments, and devote your mornings to practicing French in the language lab. But you'll be surprised at how much you come to enjoy each of these experiences, and you'll still have plenty of time left to participate in extracurricular activities and enjoy a healthy social life.

After their first year, Wellesley students are allowed to elect up to five courses a semester; they can also audit classes and take courses pass/fail. The college's Honor Code allows students to schedule their own exams at the end of the semester. While this option allows you to take finals at your own pace, self-discipline in studying is a must.

Honors Program

For those who want to dive deeper into a particular academic area, the college offers an honors program for seniors. Provided students meet a high GPA in their major and choose an appropriate topic for study, they can work with several professors to complete a year-long thesis, thus qualifying for departmental honors. Students can also qualify for Latin Honors, based on their grade point average, which are recognized at graduation.

Exchange Program

Wellesley offers many opportunities for students to study outside the campus borders—ranging from cross-registering for a course at MIT to spending a year or semester at a university in Mexico, Korea, or France. Other programs include exchanges at Spelman College in Georgia, Mills College in California, and the Twelve College Exchange.

A number of intensive courses in other countries are offered during the three-week January winter session.

SOCIAL LIFE AND ACTIVITIES

Clubs

From the rugby team to the Canada Club to the more traditional activities such as the campus newspaper and student government, it's all yours for the taking at Wellesley.

Wellesley prides itself on offering just about any activity its students could want. If you're a dancer or singer, a literary lover, or a philosophy guru, there's a club for you. In all, Wellesley offers about 170 student groups and most have no membership requirements or dues—those are included in your annual student activity fee.

While these clubs will take as much of your time as you let them, they will also comprise some of your fondest college memories. You'll share the experience of running an organization together, from top to bottom, and learn both management and organizational skills far superior to those you'd get out of most internships. Few Wellesley students participate in no clubs at all; on average, students participate in at least one or two groups each year.

Wellesley encourages first-year students to participate in all activities. Most clubs thrive on the energy and enthusiasm new students bring; they're also a great way to meet Wellesley women of all ages. A student activities' night is held at the beginning of each school year, so you can check out clubs that sound interesting. The new Wang Campus Center is the base of extracurricular life, although most activities take students everywhere from campus to the entire northeast corridor.

> 66 *As a resident advisor my sophomore year, I was both the leader on my floor and part of a management team that arranged activities for my fellow dormmates. When the resident advisors met each Wednesday night, we'd talk about our individual problems and successes, and the direction we wanted to help take the dorm in. It was a wonderful chance to be a team player, see the impact our decisions had on our peers, and learn from their feedback.* 99

Sports

Wellesley also offers a variety of sports teams that compete with other Seven Sisters and regional schools, including soccer, basketball, volleyball, swimming, lacrosse, golf, softball, cross-country, and tennis. The college prides itself on graduating well-rounded individuals, so students are encouraged to take part in sports, whether on a varsity or intramural level. And with the Nannerl O. Keohane Sports Center on campus, that's not hard to do. The Keohane Sports Center, named after Wellesley's eleventh president, includes an indoor track, pool, sauna, basketball and tennis courts, and weight room. In the fall and spring, students also canoe on Lake Waban and row on the Charles River in Boston.

Dorms

While clubs and sports are a great way to meet other students, dorms provide the most natural setting for getting to know your Wellesley sisters. Almost all students live in the dorms, and on-campus housing for four years is guaranteed, with most juniors and seniors living in single rooms. Some students live in co-ops, cooking their own food and living in a relaxed residential system. In most dorms, though, resident directors, house presidents, first-year coordinators, and resident advisors plan activities, from showing videos to having leaf-jumping parties, to holding study breaks complete with café lattes and Milano cookies. A favorite activity of the year is Holiday Dinner, where seniors dress in their gowns, students gather to sing songs, and the dining halls prepare a fabulous feast, complete with the college's own peppermint stick pie.

Wellesley does not have a Greek system, but students with interests in art, music, and Shakespeare can join one of the four society houses on campus. The groups arrange campus-wide lectures and events, as well as provide another social outlet for members.

Parties

Keep in mind that Wellesley is not a party school, but that doesn't mean there aren't parties on campus. The opportunities also are there if you want to attend parties on campus or at Boston area colleges and universities each weekend, go clubbing, or be a sister at a fraternity house. While many first-year students do all of the above, older students often spend weekends on campus, listening to comedians and musicians at Punch's Alley, the campus pub; taking advantage of the college theater; seeing classic 1980s movies at the Film Society; and just enjoying each other's company. As with most other things at Wellesley, you create the path you want to take.

FINANCIAL AID

College these days is expensive, but one of Wellesley's most important priorities is maintaining its need-blind admissions policy. More than half of Wellesley students receive some form of financial aid. In 1999 the college boosted its financial aid program by offering more grants instead of loans.

A Wellesley education costs about $49,000 per year, including tuition, room, board, and the student activity and facilities fees. Students in Massachusetts must enroll in a health insurance program. The average yearly financial aid package recently was more than $38,000.

While a financial aid award depends on a student's need, the college provides aid for about sixty percent of first-year students and fifty-four percent of all students.

Payment Plans

Wellesley offers three payment plans to help students pay for their education:

- The semester payment plan allows students and their families to pay tuition and other expenses twice each year; this program is generally recommended for parents who are using savings to pay for college or have loans guaranteed at very favorable rates.
- The ten-month payment plan assists families who are using current earnings to pay for tuition in five installments.

- The prepaid tuition stabilization plan allows families to pay the entire cost of a Wellesley education upon entrance to the school. This program sets the cost of tuition at the first-year rate and will not reflect any subsequent increases during the course of the student's education.

Students who are interested in obtaining financial aid must submit their most recent income tax returns, along with the FAFSA or Wellesley's own financial statement. The deadline for financial aid applications is January 15.

Working on Campus

To raise money for their education, many students work on campus in activities ranging from being a guard in the college's Davis Museum and Cultural Center, to working as an assistant in one of the departments, to working in a dining hall. The average annual intake from these jobs is about $2,000. It's also a great way to meet fellow students, work alongside your professors or administrators, and spend time enjoying the campus.

Loans and Grants

Wellesley also offers four types of loans to incoming students: the federal Stafford Loan, the federal Perkins Loan, the Wellesley College Student's Aid Society Loan, and the Wellesley College Loan program.

The federal Stafford and Perkins loans are repayable starting six months after graduation. While the Stafford Loan has a variable interest rate that is set each summer for the upcoming year, the Perkins Loan has a set interest rate of five percent and is available to students who demonstrate high financial need.

The Wellesley College Student's Aid Society Loan is a low-interest loan that must be repaid within five years and nine months of graduation. The Wellesley College Loan program, which is geared toward international students, requires payments twice a year following graduation.

Wellesley also offers grants from the college's funds and from the federal Supplemental Opportunity Grant Program. In addition, students who think they may be eligible for state grants and the federal Pell Grant should contact the financial aid office, which verifies students' enrollment and eligibility.

Finally, financial awards from outside organizations are calculated into the work-loan-grant program administered by the college. The Students' Aid Society also provides professional and winter clothing, emergency loans, and supplies for students receiving aid.

Chances are you've heard of some of Wellesley's most famous graduates: former First Lady and Secretary of State Hillary Rodham Clinton, former Secretary of State Madeleine Korbel Albright, and screenwriter/director Nora Ephron (of *When Harry Met Sally* and *Sleepless in Seattle* fame), to name just a few. But in truth, whether they're famous or not, most Wellesley alumnae are very successful at (and very happy with) what they do.

Wellesley graduates about 580 to 620 students each year, with about half of them choosing to go on to graduate school or other study, and about half going into the working world. Ninety-three percent of students graduate within six years of enrollment. Many students choose a career in business, often starting out as a management consultant at a high-powered Manhattan or Boston firm. Other popular careers include education, law, journalism, and medicine. Teach for America is the number one employer for recent grads.

More than 150 companies and non-profit organizations, ranging from Microsoft to Smith Barney, recruit on campus each year. Students find that the recruiting process is a great way to learn more about these companies, practice their interviewing skills, and, of course, land that all-important first job. Because Wellesley graduates are so successful, most companies return year after year.

The college also offers a well-staffed Center for Work and Service to assist students about postgraduation plans. From advice on polishing up your résumé to helping you apply for fellowship programs, the center's employees are knowledgeable and accessible. The center also pairs up students and mentors for a day-long "shadow" program in January, and keeps a database with names of alumnae all over the world who have offered to share their professional insights. The Wellesley alumnae network is extensive, powerful, and accessible.

> ❝*I went to the mentoring night my senior year, and sat around an alumna's living room chatting about our common interest in journalism. One alum, Jean Dietz, had been a correspondent for* The Boston Globe. *Another, Callie Crossley, was a producer with the ABC newsmagazine, 20/20. It was great to hear about their experiences as successful women in journalism, and they were genuinely interested in helping me start my career.* ❞

The alumnae association provides several programs for juniors and seniors, too, including a mentoring night, where students share dinner and conversation with alumnae in the Boston area who have similar career interests. In addition, the association sponsors workshops on buying a car, renting an apartment, finding a job, and generally making it on your own.

Many Wellesley alumnae have been pathbreakers in their careers and all of them want to see you succeed; you'll find that this support network of more than 36,000 women worldwide will follow you wherever you go and is always ready to lend a hand.

Once you leave Wellesley, you'll find that all your networks of career support are still available to help you, and that local alumnae clubs throughout the world sponsor events, from happy hours, hayrides, and Sunday afternoon teas to lectures by professors who are visiting the area and pizza nights with prospective students. Graduates also serve on the Board of Trustees, as advisors to various groups, and as admissions representatives. But the best part of being a graduate may be taking part in the reunion parades, where graduates dress in their class colors, take part in Stepsinging—a favorite college tradition—have a chance to revisit the campus in the spring, and catch up with their friends.

SUMMING UP

Although Wellesley women are diverse in their interests, backgrounds, and personalities, all of them share the experience of having attended the top women's college in the country. Wellesley offers its students the opportunity to expand their minds, challenge their limits, and learn to be meaningful leaders in a changing world.

Wellesley women share more than an education, though. From Flower Sunday in September, when sophomores give their "little sisters," or first-year students, a daisy as a sign of welcome and friendship, to commencement, when seniors pop champagne corks together, Wellesley develops in its students a sense of sisterhood, a camaraderie that can only be shared at a women's college. While students may complain about a lack of social life during their four years there, they will also revel in the chance to study without distraction and to be completely in the company of a group of outstanding women. As a favorite campus saying goes, "Not a girls' school without men, but a women's college without boys."

The campus is also a sanctuary, a safe and secure atmosphere, where you will find yourself enveloped by the beautiful Massachusetts environment.

Professors are there to offer a hand as well; many of them have been known to spend an hour or more with each student during office hours. As a student, you'll not only learn facts and figures, but how to analyze and apply that information to other problems. Your professors will challenge you to become active thinkers and participants in and out of the classroom, by sharing your enthusiasm and success, offering advice, and also becoming lifelong friends.

Wellesley is a college where you will be known by your first name, whether you're the college president, a professor, or a student. You can also choose whether to be the student body president or just a member of the student body. You become empowered because you make the decisions and you shape your future.

If you have a preconceived notion of a women's college, chances are it's not true at Wellesley—the college is not a bastion of lesbianism, nor a stronghold of left-wing, radical feminism. It's also not a place for meek-mannered women. What Wellesley is, is a supportive environment that gives its students a sense of self-esteem, accomplishment, and the ability to apply that knowledge and confidence elsewhere. What Wellesley does is to successfully educate women who do, time and time again, make a difference in the world.

❏ *Mary Lynn F. Jones, B.A.*

Photo by Nancy Wolz

 Wesleyan University
Middletown, CT 06459

 (860) 685-3000
Fax: (860) 685-3001

 E-mail: *admissions@wesleyan.edu*
Website: *www.wesleyan.edu/admission*

 Enrollment

Full-time ❏ women: 1,460
❏ men: 1,377

INTRODUCING WESLEYAN

For years, Wesleyan has been one of America's best-kept educational secrets, but it seems that the word is getting out. Increasing numbers of applicants are realizing that Wesleyan's unparalleled academics and unique student body make for a college experience unsurpassed elsewhere. Its top-notch faculty includes some of the best in the country in both research and teaching, and the students are driven by the inner desire to work hard and to have fun. To add to this, Wesleyan is a college on the edge of the future, with an administration and a president, Michael Roth, committed to leading Wesleyan with vision, demonstrating the value of a liberal arts education to the world.

> 66 *Wesleyan students feel a unique bond with one another that goes beyond school spirit. When you meet someone who went to Wes you feel like you know them already, in the sense that you've both shared in the discovery of some wonderful secret.* 99

Three things set Wesleyan apart from the rest: size, academic intensity, and its student body. Wesleyan is a small-to-medium liberal arts college (2,800 undergraduates) set on a beautiful and spacious New England campus, comparable to schools like Amherst and Williams. But as a thriving research university, with a small population of 150 graduate students, the productivity and distinction of Wesleyan faculty in research rival that of faculty at much larger institutions. Because of its unique size, undergraduate students make use of graduate resources and enjoy small seminar-sized classes and opportunities to personally get to know professors.

Many students choose Wesleyan over the Ivy League for its intellectual environment, which differs from other competitive schools in one key quality: While students at other universities are often encouraged to compete against others, Wesleyan students only compete to do better than they did last week. Wes students feel comfortable helping each other with work, and talking about intellectual ideas even (gasp!) outside the classroom.

> 66 *You're in a place where no one tells you how to live, how to dress, or (heaven forbid) what to think—academically or otherwise. I tend to see it as a challenge.* 99

Wesleyan fosters independence—its approach to liberal arts education encourages undergraduates to invest deeply in their courses of study, without mandating a set of core courses that every student must slog through. What students do have in common is *passion*—they are passionate about their studies, passionate about their artistic and athletic endeavors, and passionate about their politics. "The greatest thing that Wesleyan did for me was help me define my own education," said one graduating senior. This might seem daunting to some, but Wesleyan students rise to the occasion.

ADMISSIONS REQUIREMENTS

There is no question that Wesleyan is one of America's "hot" schools. The Office of Admissions has seen a twenty-nine percent increase in applications in the last two years. Under twenty-one percent of those who applied in a recent year were admitted.

What students should apply? Make no mistake: Wesleyan is academically rigorous; in general, applicants have performed extraordinarily well in high school. Of a recent class, sixty-eight percent ranked in the top ten percent of their high school class. Seventy-nine percent took biology, chemistry, and physics in high school. As with many colleges, the high school transcript is considered the most important element of the application, but Wesleyan prides itself on taking the time to get to know each applicant as a person and not as a series of numbers, weighing heavily the personal essay, recommendations, and interview. Median SAT scores are Verbal—700, Math—700, Writing—700, ACT—32. The ACT or SAT with two Subject Tests is required.

Students at Wesleyan are stellar beyond SAT scores, grades, and lists of activities. They are intellectually curious, take initiative, and have proved that they will contribute to the Wesleyan community. A recent freshman class included a student who was the first female member of her high school football team, an award-winning playwright, a nationally ranked chess player, and a student who started a midnight basketball program in his hometown. Every year, there are many students who excel as starting players on varsity sports teams, leaders of high school student bodies, and active volunteers in their communities. Applicants to Wesleyan must prove that they have made use of the resources and options available in high school, and plan to continue to be active and engaged in college.

For the student who is certain about Wesleyan, applying Early Decision provides a slight edge in the application process. It is encouraged only for those who have selected Wesleyan as the top choice. Admittance to Wesleyan ED is binding.

Wesleyan has earned a reputation as one of the finest schools in the country for good reason: its professors are top scholars and teachers, and its students take initiative and have a passion for learning. Wesleyan differs from other top-ranked institutions, however, in the depth of its commitment to fostering the pursuit of individual intellectual interests.

> ❝ It took me a while to get used to the demanding academic schedule at Wesleyan. But when I did, I really came to realize what makes it so special. As well as one-on-one attention from my professors, I really benefited from their scholarship. I began to learn with my professors, rather than from them. ❞

Course Offerings

The breadth of offerings at Wesleyan is outstanding. Typical liberal arts disciplines such as history, English, and physics exist side by side with such departments as molecular biology and biochemistry (MB & B), East Asian studies, and film studies.

> ❝ I was amazed when, in my senior year of high school, I found the Wesleyan course catalog in our guidance center. I thought I might have to go to a huge state university to take the range of courses I was interested in, but Wesleyan had it all—from Oceanography to Linguistics, Archaeology to Film— I felt that I'd finally found a school that would keep pace with my interests. ❞

Wesleyan's unique course offerings include "Commons, Alliances, and Shared Resources," "Politics of Terrorism," "Tropical Ecology and the Environment," and "The Past on Film." Another of Wesleyan's major strengths is its arts curriculum; introductory courses are open to all and most graduating seniors, regardless of their majors, have taken at least one dance, studio art, or music course. Popular choices include Introduction to Drawing, West African Dance, and Worlds of Music.

The free and open aspect of the Wesleyan curriculum goes beyond the arts. Because there are very few classes reserved only for majors, students can follow many interests and not feel blocked out of classes. So how does a student decide which four or five classes a semester to take from more than 900 courses in 40 departments and programs and 47 major fields of study? Upon arrival on the campus, each student is assigned a faculty advisor. The FA works with the student to define an academic mission and choose classes, all via Wesleyan's high-tech and student-friendly on-line course registration system.

FYI Classes

From the very first semester, academic exploration at Wesleyan is encouraged. Freshmen are prioritized for admittance to a host of small, intellectually rigorous seminars known as First-Year Initiatives, or FYI classes. The first two years at Wesleyan are generally reserved for exploration of the wide-ranging curriculum. To fulfill Wesleyan's General Education Expectations (GenEds), students must take at least three courses (from at least two different departments) in each of three categories: humanities and arts, social and behavioral sciences, and natural sciences and mathematics. The vast majority of Wesleyan students fulfill these expectations without ever trying, though it is possible to opt out of the Expectations with a valid academic reason.

Majors

A student's final two years at Wesleyan are when he or she can truly delve into a chosen course of study. Majors are declared at the end of the sophomore year. The most-declared majors at Wesleyan are English, psychology, and government, but double-majoring is common, and more students triple-major than one might imagine. Interdepartmental majors such as neuroscience and behavior, African American studies, medieval studies, and East Asian studies are popular, and the American studies department at Wes is considered to be one of the finest undergraduate programs in the country—housed in the Center for the Americas with Latin American studies. Students may also, with faculty approval, create a university major, joining two or more areas of study not already conjoined under the auspices of an interdepartmental major. Wesleyan also features two special interdisciplinary majors that must be declared during freshman year, the College of Letters (COL), which combines literature, history, philosophy, and foreign languages, and the College of Social Studies (CSS), combining history, government, philosophy, and economics (sometimes called the "College of Suicidal Sophomores," in reference to its demanding sophomore year schedule of a ten-page paper a week). Certificate Programs such as International Relations can be combined with Majors.

Study Abroad

Many students (between forty-five and fifty percent) choose to augment their on-campus experience at Wesleyan by taking one or two semesters abroad or away from campus. With the assistance of the Office of International Affairs, students can study abroad in Wesleyan programs in France, Germany, Italy, and Spain. Wesleyan also has special relationships with programs in Japan and China, and students go to any of the other 145 programs approved by the Office of International Studies. Wesleyan is also part of the Twelve College Exchange Program, a group of prestigious New England colleges that offers exchanges for the semester or year.

The Thesis

The grand finale of a student's academic life at Wesleyan is often the completion of a thesis. Though it is only through the optional thesis process that a student can earn university honors (there is a separate Phi Beta Kappa selection process), many students choose to do a thesis simply to fulfill personal intellectual goals. The most common theses at Wesleyan are year-long research projects, producing papers that range in length from 30 to 45 pages in the sciences to 100 to 160 pages in English or history. Dance, theater, and music majors perform their theses for the Wesleyan community, while studio arts majors participate in a three-week gallery exhibition and the thesis films constitute a special slate of screenings at the end of the semester.

Faculty

The Wesleyan faculty is outstanding and engaging. In recent studies, Wesleyan professors have tipped the scales in scholarship—the science faculty has received more outside funding from prestigious sources such as NSF and NIH than their peers at any comparable institution, and the economics department is renowned as one of the best in the country. Unlike many larger institutions, however, the most productive scholars at Wesleyan are often highly regarded as the best teachers. All of the more than 350 faculty members teach undergraduates. Professors frequently structure classes around their current interests and research, allowing for timely, engaging classroom discussion. Students frequently become involved in helping professors with research and have often co-authored papers with their professors. Professors are generally accessible and meet with their students informally outside of class. The faculty includes jazz musician and MacArthur Fellowship winner, Anthony Braxton; film authority, Jeanine Basinger; 2007 Nobel economist Gary Yohe, who shared the

2007 Nobel Peace Prize as lead author on climate change; experimental music composer, Alvin Lucier; prominent DNA researcher, David Beveridge; leading historian of China, Vera Schwarcz; and noted environmental scientist, Barry Chernoff.

Despite the depth and breadth of the curriculum, students may find they wish to explore a subject not covered by any class offered. In that event, they may, in consultation with a faculty member, design a tutorial to study the subject they are interested in. Recent student-organized tutorials have included topics in Native American studies, literature seminars focusing on American novelists Don DeLillo and Anne Rice, and a survey of "Complexity Theory."

Facilities

It is nearly impossible for any single student to exhaust Wesleyan's academic resources, but it may be even more difficult to exhaust its physical resources. Wesleyan's modern, technologically adaptable classroom space is enhanced by several fine computer labs, e-mail and Internet connections in each dorm room, and more lab space in the Science Center per student than any other science research institution in the country. Olin Library, the university's largest library, has one million volumes including a music library and a rare book collection (including a Shakespeare First Folio). The Smith Room on the first floor is a popular place to meet friends in the evening, and the small, quiet study rooms on the second and third floors are for those who prefer dead silence (many seniors who write honors theses get their own thesis carrels, small private rooms, many with window views). The Information Commons on the first floor is another popular place for students to gather when they work together or individually on various academic projects. Students can use on-site desktop computers and printers or bring their own laptops while having access in a centralized area to library reference resources, information technology, and a network of academic resources on campus. Across the street from Olin, the Science Library houses science-oriented materials along with the Cutter Collection, an eclectic collection of one family's turn-of-the-century books, and a small natural history museum. In 2009, the energy-efficient Allbritton Center opened as the home to two new programs: The Allbritton Center for the Study of Public Life, which links intellectual work on campus to policy issues nationally and internationally, and the Shapiro Creative Writing Center, which brings together students and faculty seriously engaged in writing. Across campus in the Center for the Arts (CFA), the Davison Art Center is a national landmark that houses the art library and 10,000 prints by old masters and modern artists.

SOCIAL LIFE AND ACTIVITIES

The variety of Wesleyan's academic life is equaled, if not exceeded, by the variety of its social life. There is a popular theory at Wesleyan that if you get any students into conversation, you will find that they do something fascinating—from leading the Ultimate Frisbee team to directing a short film. It is a place teeming with students who are interested in living in a charged environment. Each week, the student body hosts a wide variety of activities ranging from dance performances to sports games to live music, and it is not uncommon to attend several of such different events in one day.

Although Middletown is located thirty minutes from New Haven, thirty minutes from Hartford, and two hours from New York City and Boston, Wesleyan students often don't feel the need to venture very far to have fun, and the focus of the social life is located on campus. Middletown has a variety of restaurants popular with students (it can be difficult to get a table at O'Rourke's Diner on a Sunday morning, where students have entertained Clint Eastwood and Allen Ginsberg), but for nightlife Wesleyan sticks close to home. Walk around the campus grounds on a weekend night and you will see bands performing in the West Co Café, plays at the Patricelli '92 Theater, movies at the Goldsmith Family Cinema at the Center for Film Studies, and hip-hop shows at student venues.

Parties

There are as many different kinds of parties as there are kinds of people—gatherings ranging from house parties to all-campus parties to dorm parties to parties sponsored by student groups. Often parties have themes: a costume party in Low Rise, an eighties dance at Psi Upsilon fraternity, or a swing ball to celebrate the Senior Film Festival. Parties range from small and intimate to large and loud, but they are never exclusive, and never focused exclusively around drinking. Often a group such as the Black and Latino Brotherhood or the women's rugby team will sponsor a campus event that attracts a broad cross section of students. Each year, two large musical events—Fall Ball and Spring Fling—attract big-name bands to campus. Recently featured were Andrew WK, Talib Kweli, Saul Williams, Immortal Technique, Cee-Lo, Welfare Poets, and GZA.

The first year at Wesleyan is the only year social activities are arranged; after orientation, students plan their own social calendars. In general, the more adventurous students are, the more events they will attend and the more people they will meet. Friendships grow out of social events, residential life, classes, clubs, and sports teams. While Wesleyan students don't go on traditional "dates," a couple might meet at Klekolo, a local cafe, or drive to the always-open Athenian Diner.

> *I try to go to as many things I can and meet as many people I can, but there's always more—I'm always reluctant to go away for the weekend, because I'm afraid I'll miss something.*

Dining on Campus and in the University Center

Dining on campus underwent a complete renaissance for the fall of 2007. Brand new dining facilities are the anchors of the new 110,000-square-foot Usdan University Center. Two new dining halls that seat more than 300 people each are adjacent to a state-of-the-art dining marketplace with a brick oven pizza oven, a Mongolian grill, a deli, and a salad bar, as well as kosher and vegan serving stations. Students have views of Foss Hill, a popular student hangout, and Andrus Field, where the football and baseball teams play. The University Center also houses a first floor café with soups, sandwiches, salads, and coffee. The third floor features a more upscale dining room for lunches with faculty and staff. Students can still use their meal plan elsewhere on campus at Summerfields and Weswings, or at one of the eating clubs located in the fraternity houses. Always handy is Weshop, the campus grocery store which stocks fresh produce, name-brand foods, and organic and vegan choices; students can make purchases there using their dining points.

Housing

Wesleyan housing is prime real estate compared to some other schools. On-campus housing is guaranteed all four years, and can range from traditional freshman residence halls to small New England houses on tree-lined streets. All undergraduates live on campus. Most first-year students live in residence halls in double or triple rooms. Upperclassmen either elect to stay in the residence halls or live in apartments, townhouses, New England clapboard houses, or two dozen programs, which include everything from The Bayit to Earth House to Well-being House. These houses sponsor educational and social events for the whole campus.

Fraternities and Sororities

Fraternities are an option for housing and also for social life: five percent of students are involved in the six fraternities (some coed) and two sororities on campus. The Skull and Serpent, and secret society located on Wyllys Avenue at the gateway to the Center for the Arts, dates from the early 1900s and is shrouded in mystery, but no one lives here. (We think.)

Organizations

Wesleyan students like to get involved. They serve on every university committee, organize orientation and graduation, and independently allocate funds to more than 200 student organizations, which include groups devoted to politics, athletics, and artistic and cultural interests. Fifteen student publications are sent to press at least once a semester, ranging from the twice-weekly newspaper, the *Argus*, to magazines of fiction, humor, women's issues, activism, and poetry. Students are also responsible for the wide variety of lecturers and artists who visit campus. WESU-FM, the campus radio station, is something to be proud of, not just because it is the oldest continuously operating college radio station in the country, but because it plays cool music and anyone can become a DJ.

Athletics

Although many people do not know it until they visit campus, Wesleyan's Freeman Athletic Center (affectionately nicknamed "The Palace") is one of the finest college athletic centers in New England. Completed in 1990 at the cost of $22 million and recently upgraded with a $13 million addition, the athletic complex has the 7,500-square-foot Andersen Fitness Center, the 1,200-seat Silloway Gymnasium, a fifty-meter pool, a 200-meter indoor track, the Spurrier-Snyder Rink for ice skating activities, the eight-court Rosenbaum Squash Center, and campus also is home to the 5,000-seat Corwin Stadium for football (overlooked by Olin Library), Dresser Diamond for baseball, a new synthetic turf field, sixteen hard-surfaced indoor tennis courts, the 400-meter outdoor Andersen Track, and many fields for practice and play. The Macomber Boathouse on the Connecticut River is home for both men's and women's crew. Athletics at the Wesleyan are first-rate and interest top athletes: fifteen men's varsity and fourteen women's varsity athletic teams compete at the Division III level. About sixty percent of students are involved in some sort of organized athletics with popular club and intramural activities complementing varsity opportunities. In recent years teams in women's basketball, and men's soccer and women's volleyball have all qualified for NCAA tournament play. Numerous other individuals have earned spots at NCAA Championships in swimming, track and field, and wrestling with a handful of All-Americans.

FINANCIAL AID

If you are applying to colleges and are also in need of financial aid, keep this in mind: Wesleyan continues to hold firm to need-blind admissions, meaning that Wesleyan admits students without knowledge of their financial need. Recently, when several schools around the country gave up their need-blind programs, Wesleyan students led the country's college students in protest of this change in policy. Limited aid is available for international and transfer students.

Wesleyan awards aid to all admitted students to the full extent of demonstrated need. Wesleyan is generous with financial aid; most students receiving aid from Wesleyan get a package that includes a grant, student loans, and work-study jobs. However, the university reduced total student-loan debt by thirty-five percent and eliminated loans for most families with a total income of under $40,000 beginning with the class enrolling in 2008. Grants are substituted for the loans.

Tuition at Wesleyan is not cheap. To pay the full amount required—not to mention the other costs in room, board, and personal expenses—about half of the student body receives financial aid, the average grant being $35,300 for 2010–2011.

GRADUATES

Education at Wesleyan is more about learning to live your life than memorizing the vagaries of some obscure academic discipline. Wesleyan is the definitive liberal arts college—here, students learn how to think critically, write clearly, and make informed decisions. Graduates can succeed in any situation; they are flexible, creative, and roll with the punches. It is not uncommon for English majors to become computer programmers, psychology majors to go to law school, economics majors to go to film school, and music majors to become math teachers.

There is no single field of endeavor pursued by the majority of Wesleyan grads. Of a recent class, twenty-one percent of students are in business, seventeen percent are in education, ten percent are in law-related fields, seventeen percent are in grad school, twelve percent are in medicine or health, and eleven percent are in the arts. The top three employers hiring students from the class of 2009 were Teach for America, Deutsche Bank, and Japan Exchange and Teaching Program (JET).

As for continuing education after Wesleyan, about twenty percent of students go to graduate school immediately after graduation. Five years after graduation, about seventy-five percent will have gone to some kind of graduate school, and acceptance rates to professional schools remain close to ninety percent. In addition to formal schooling, Wesleyan graduates have also won more Watson Fellowships for self-designed student projects than any other school in the country. Graduates have recently pursued such topics as "The Practice of Movement: Nomadic Domestic Architecture" and "Understanding Cross-Cultural Health Care for Refugees."

Wesleyan students spend plenty of time visiting the excellent library and friendly staff of the Career Resource Center (CRC), which helps students plan ahead for leaving campus, even in the first year of college. With help from the CRC, many students opt for internships over January break and in the summer, often with Wesleyan alumni or parents in their field of interest. Wesleyan has a tight network of alumni and parents in the field who can also help in the latter years at Wesleyan by providing informational interviews and even offering jobs.

SUMMING UP

So, picture this: It's fall in New England, the air is crisp, your ears are red from the slight bite of the cold, and the leaves of the trees are slowly turning the bright color of fire. You walk from the Campus Center to the steps of Olin Library, one of the oldest buildings on campus, where students have gathered in the afternoon sun to chat and read. You enter the building and follow the hall leading to the front face of the building, the north side of massive arched windows overlooking the football field, and take a seat in the Information Commons.

From here, one has the best view of what Wesleyan has to offer. Across the football field is the old Fayerweather Gymnasium, which has been transformed to house a ballroom and theater and dance rehearsal studios. Beyond that (and beyond the Office of Admission, which has to be seen to be believed), is the Center for the Arts, where generations of students have also learned to play the Javanese Gamelan, an instrument so large it takes twenty people to play. To the west is Foss Hill, a definite social center of campus, and to the east is the scenic and historic college row, where it all began.

Here you can get a vision for Wesleyan's future. The room you are in, the north room of Olin Library, built in 1985, encompasses the original face of the historic building, designed by Henry Bacon in 1831. The addition is more than an architectural element; it is a symbol of the past and future of Wesleyan. Founded as a small Methodist college for men in the early nineteenth century on the principles of community and the value of a liberal arts education, Wesleyan has held fast to these values, at the same time that it has built on, renovated, and transformed the school into a modern small university. It has seen coeducation, racial tension, peace rallies, and firebombings—few American schools have seen as much change. But at the same time, Wesleyan has still remained consistent—just as the old bricks of Olin Library have always faced the football field, the school has always been leading the pack—a place where high-quality students and top-notch faculty gather to learn and explore.

Wesleyan is unique because it attracts vibrant, open-minded, creative students, and because it rewards these students for pursuing intellectual interests and outside pursuits with vigor. At the same time that they engage students in the classroom, Wesleyan's faculty contributes high-level scholarship and is made up of dedicated and caring teachers. Wesleyan has a small-college atmosphere, yet it is a place where students are challenged to make new discoveries about themselves and others. Because of this, it will always be the special place, the undiscovered secret, the definitive liberal arts education of the twenty-first century. Take a moment to discover it for yourself.

❏ *Stacy Theberge, B.A.*

WHITMAN COLLEGE

Photo by Greg Lehman

Whitman College
Walla Walla, WA 99362

(509) 527-5176 or (877) 462-9448
Fax: (509) 527-4967

E-mail: *admission@whitman.edu*
Website: *www.whitman.edu*

 Enrollment

Full-time ❏ women: 886
      ❏ men: 642

Part-time ❏ women: 15
      ❏ men: 12

INTRODUCING WHITMAN

Whitman is a small, private liberal arts college marked by its intimate class sizes, beautiful residential setting, and active student life. It is known for its combination of academic excellence, an unpretentious Northwest culture, and an engaging community. Nestled in Walla Walla, endearingly called "the place so nice they named it twice," Whitman students are able to take advantage of the artsy local wine culture, the farmer's market in hot summer months, and long bike rides through the wheat fields to watch the sunset over scrumptious taco truck dinners. With a student-faculty ratio of 11:1 students get personalized academic attention and ample opportunities to connect one-on-one with their professors. The definition of learning at Whitman also extends beyond the classroom with study abroad programs in over forty different countries, support for internships, fieldwork, research, fellowships, and more.

At Whitman, students are given ample freedom to start their own projects and form groups that speak to their unique interests among the myriad of existing clubs and programming groups that keep the campus calendar packed throughout the year. The 24/7 library is testimony to the fact that many Whitman students tend to balance a busy schedule between rigorous academic standards, cocurricular activities, and an active social life. Having such a small yet dynamic campus fosters a deep sense of community and a network of support systems that make sure every student has the chance to have his or her voice heard and to succeed in whatever the students put their mind to.

A central green space called Ankeny Field is located at the heart of the campus. The windowed facade of Penrose Library—open 24/7 as is the student health center—overlooks the field where there

WESTERN SEMESTER

Semester in the West is one of Whitman's outstanding experiential learning opportunities that extends learning beyond the classroom and into the field through an interdisciplinary curriculum focusing on public land conservation. Twenty-one students are selected to be part of this amazing adventure throughout the American West for an entire fall semester. During this time, they explore the complexities of diverse ecosystems, political-social dynamics, regional public policy, and environmental writing. The environmental issues explored can include water, climate change, restoration, and even elements of social justice. Many students who go through this program claim that it is a life-changing process that gives them a unique lens for the remainder of their experiences at Whitman and beyond.

are intramural sports games and students lounging in the grass. Ankeny is also a central meeting place where friends run into each other and exchange hellos on their way to and from class. Wireless Internet is available virtually everywhere on campus, and dining facilities stocked with healthy eating options are easy to access from the library as well as most academic and residential buildings.

Whitman's reputed college radio station, outstanding student publications, private rehearsal rooms, and the dynamic theater department are just a few of the many creative outlets for students on campus. Further, the strong intramural sport culture, the Outdoor

Program, as well as the newly renovated athletic center and world-class climbing wall are testimony to the physically active culture among students. Altogether, with the myriad of interests and ongoing support of new initiatives and activities, Whitman is a tight-knit community that has plenty to offer undergraduates looking for a well-rounded, personalized learning experience in an atmosphere of collaboration and support.

> 66 *Whitman is often referred to as an "elite" college with an unpretentious, down-to-earth attitude. At a student panel I attended when I was still deciding on colleges, I recall a few people mentioning that at Whitman, nobody wants you to fail and over my four years at the college, I found that to be true. Whitman offers a myriad of opportunities to succeed and, more than likely, it is possible to find like-minded people who want to work together toward similar goals. Within such an intimate campus community, it is possible to initiate and follow through on making visible change through leadership and collaboration.* 99

Whitman is a small school that dedicates a significant amount of individual attention to its students. For this reason, it is hard to feel like just another number or to simply fall through the cracks unnoticed. On an academic and administrative level as well as within the social scene at Whitman, there are a lot of circles of support that allow each student to find a sense of community and craft his or her own unique "Whitman" experience.

ADMISSIONS REQUIREMENTS

Whitman is a highly selective school that seeks students who are actively engaged in extracurricular activities, have a strong sense of intellectual curiosity, and are looking to be part of a rigorous academic environment. Standardized test scores and grades are important factors in the application process but admissions officers are also genuinely interested in learning who the person behind each application is and how that person might be able to contribute to Whitman's vibrant campus community.

The rigor of the classes taken prior to applying, grades, strong writing skills, formal letters of recommendation, and test scores all play a significant role in Whitman's careful selection process. Whitman accepts the Common Application and SAT or ACT test scores are required. Special attention is given to advanced placement or honors courses, a history of involvement in extracurricular activities and the individual merits of each candidate. First-year students are admitted in both fall and spring semesters with options for Early Decision and deferred admission available.

ACADEMIC LIFE

Whitman offers B.A. degrees in the following areas:

- Biological Science
- Communications and the Arts
- Computer and Physical Science
- Engineering and Environmental Design
- Social Science

Biology, psychology, and politics are among the most popular majors at Whitman making them some of the largest departments on campus. Students may also design their own major pending approval from the Board of Review, or choose a combined major study program such as Asian Studies or Biochemistry, Biophysics, and Molecular Biology that involves coursework from two or more departments. Other combined programs in Engineering and Computer Science, Law, Forestry and Environmental Management, Oceanography, and Teacher Education allow students to enter directly into some of the nation's most reputable graduate programs for an accelerated track of study.

Faculty

With an average class size of fourteen, Whitman offers small class sizes and a rigorous academic environment. It is not uncommon to hear about professors inviting a group of students over to their home to have an engaging discussion over dinner or to see an Encounters class being held outside on a sunny day. Professors encourage their students to ask questions, draw parallels between different disciplines, and to take intellectual risks. Faculty members are very accessible and it is generally easy to schedule a time to meet with them individually, even outside of their weekly office hours. Thanks to special research opportunities such as Perry Summer Research Scholarships, students can even have the chance to work in tandem with their professors on specific collaborative research projects. Faculty members also are active contributors in their field and regularly receive highly competitive grants to further their scholarship. The significant breadth and depth of knowledge among Whitman's top-notch faculty is reflected in the college's diverse course offerings and innovative approaches to education that allow students the freedom to really take ownership of their own unique educational experience.

Fellow Students

The fact that Whitman is such a small school fosters a sense of community in which students are able to be supportive of one another. Students exchange notes from class, form study groups, and edit each other's papers, making peer-to-peer support one of the greatest assets of a Whitman education. The Academic Resource Center (ARC) is also an excellent place to go for everything from private tutoring to disability services and individual academic counseling. Each year, first-year students are also assigned to a Student Academic Adviser who lives in their residence hall section and is regularly involved in bonding activities. These Student Advisers help first-years get oriented to their new academic environment, familiarize them with course requirements, and make sure that they are directed to any additional academic support they may need.

WRITING CENTER

Whitman also has an amazing writing center where students across various disciplines can work with expert readers on their papers. Even close to midnight you can find people tying up loose ends on their essays and having serious discussions about how to better structure their paper. A complimentary bowl of candy seems to be perpetually available in the center, keeping spirits high throughout the editing process.

In order to graduate, students must earn a minimum of 124 credits (32 to 36 of which are in their major) and fulfill distribution requirements in the social sciences, humanities, fine arts, science, quantitative analysis, and Alternative Voices.

All first-year and transfer students must take a year-long course titled "Encounters" (previously known as Core) that explores great works such as Homer's *The Odyssey*, Charlie Chaplin's 1931 film *City Lights*, and Galileo's *Letter to Grand Duchess Christina*. This first-year experience becomes a common touchstone that Whitman students across different majors and disciplines can relate back to throughout their college experience.

Senior Project

All majors have to complete an oral exam as well as a thesis or a comprehensive written exam in their final year. Studio Art majors also have the opportunity to present an original body of work at an annual Senior Thesis Exhibition on campus, which includes written artist statements and an oral defense of the work. Senior Research courses and Thesis Classes allow students to bounce ideas off of peers in their major department and develop their final projects over the course of a semester or academic year.

SOCIAL LIFE AND ACTIVITIES

An endless list of activities and a busy social scene on campus make up a significant part of the Whitman experience. Cocurricular activities allow students to make the most of their time at Whitman by striking a balance between the demanding academic curriculum and having fun. Residence life, clubs, the Events Board, and other administrative offices put on countless events throughout the year that keep the campus events calendar packed. The trouble is trying to find downtime with so many interesting things going on!

Housing

Whitman puts a strong emphasis on the holistic experience of living on campus, which is why they replace the term "dorm" with "residence hall" as a way of emphasizing that it's not only a place where students sleep, but where they can work, play, eat, and live. Housing on campus includes single-sex and coed residence halls as well as off-campus apartments. After their first year, students can apply to live in the vibrant Interest House Community close to campus where they stay in beautiful homes related to a specific field of interest. Examples include La Maison Française, the Community Service Co-op, MECCA (Multi-ethnic Center for Cultural Awareness), the Global Awareness House, and La Casa Hispana. By junior year, most students opt for a more independent style of living and move into apartments or share a home in the local area with other Whitties.

Activities

From singing in an *a cappella* group to joining the nationally recognized debate team, or working on the student newspaper, there is something to suit every taste at Whitman. With approximately sixty groups on campus and the possibility of starting a new club, there are countless ways for students to get involved in extracurricular activities. There are also numerous unique opportunities for student leadership and development that span far beyond more traditional positions in Student Government.

Students organize a number of annual events, such as the Renaissance Fair, Choral Contest, and an Interest House Block Party. The Renaissance Fair in particular attracts people and merchants from across the Pacific Northwest to be part of festivities that include live theatrical performances, a life-size maze, medieval costumes, and much more.

Greek life also plays a notable role on campus with almost forty percent of men belonging to one of four national fraternities, and thirty percent of women belonging to one of three national sororities. Whitman has an outstanding reputation in the arts as well, which is reflected in the high-quality theater productions at Harper Joy, the innovative art and literary magazine, *Blue Moon*, and a highly interactive student-run radio station, KWCW. Students' interest in environmental issues and community involvement is illustrated by active groups on campus such as Campus Climate Challenge, the Organic Garden, and the Whitman Mentor Program. Cultural, ethnic, and religious/spiritual clubs such as the Whitman Christian Fellowship, Hillel-Shalom, International Students and Friends, the Black Students Union, and First Generation/Working-Class Students also form additional support systems for students on campus. Within each of these groups, students can find life-long friends, allies, and peer-mentors that will have a lasting impression beyond their years at Whitman.

Athletics

Whitman's varsity teams include basketball, soccer, cross-country, golf, volleyball, baseball, and tennis. Sports facilities at Whitman include a stadium, two high-class gyms, squash and handball courts, saunas, an indoor climbing wall, and aerobic/dance rooms. The

10,000-square-foot athletics center alone houses an eight-lane swimming pool and an array of weightlifting and cardiovascular equipment.

There are fifteen club sports teams at Whitman including teams in cycling, snow sports, rugby, lacrosse, volleyball, tennis, and tae kwon do. There have been national championships in snow sports, cycling, and Ultimate Frisbee, and many outstanding athletes at Whitman have been acknowledged both locally and nationally for their achievements.

While on campus nearly seventy percent of all Whitman students try their hand at Intramural sports, such as flag football, Ultimate Frisbee, and soccer. IMs play a prominent role in campus life, not only for student athletes and coaches but also for spectators who like to cheer them on.

FINANCIAL AID

At Whitman, financial aid comes in the form of scholarships, grants, employment opportunities, and loans. Most awards are based on a combination of demonstrated need and individual merit. Admissions and financial aid staff at Whitman offer outstanding support and even go beyond the call of duty to help students in navigating their financial options. The staff puts forth a serious effort to make Whitman accessible for students from a wide range of socioeconomic backgrounds. Although Whitman cannot fulfill all need, staff members are willing to work closely with students to find the best possible options when it comes to funding their education.

In 2009–2010, eighty percent of all full-time first-year students received some form of financial aid in their first year of college, and of those, nearly half received need-based financial aid. The average award for first-year students in that year was $15,583 and $24,366 for need-based financial aid. Though the combined costs of tuition and room and board total more than $40,000 per year, the average amount of indebtedness for a Class of 2009 graduate was less than $16,000.

PARTNER PROGRAMS

Merit scholarships and need-based financial aid at Whitman can be applied to over forty-two different Partner Programs for off-campus studies in more than twenty countries around the world. Whitman also offers Partner Programs in urban centers across the United States such as Washington, D.C., Chicago, and Philadelphia. Experiential learning is an integral component to a Whitman education, and annually about fifty percent of the junior class study abroad for at least a semester or a full academic year.

GRADUATES

Whitman prepares students to be lifelong learners in whatever field they choose. Whitman's approach to a liberal arts education, supported by a dedicated group of professors and administrators who care deeply about the success of their students, makes a world of difference. Upon graduating from Whitman, students have a solid set of tools that allows them to excel in a myriad of different careers and academic fields, whatever their interest may be. There is also a loyal, strong alumni network that actively seeks Whitman students and alumni for jobs, internships, and other career-related opportunities.

Moreover, Whitman's Student Engagement Center (SEC) is tireless in its work to support students and alumni with professional development. The staff assist with tasks ranging from building a strong résumé to developing useful contacts through the Career Consultant Network. The SEC also offers a series of on-campus workshops addressing important topics such as finding and securing internships, networking, and exploring post-graduation options. One of the most popular events each year is an Etiquette Dinner, which shows students how to make a good impression when networking in a formal dining environment. Students can even apply for career development opportunities outside of the normal academic year such as the Whitman Internship Grant (WIG), which provides funding for unpaid internships at an organization of their choosing during the summer following their sophomore or junior year of college.

Over sixty percent of Whitties decide to continue their education after graduation, and having such a well-rounded liberal arts background, they are able to enter a variety of different disciplines and participate competitively in their area of interest. Whitties move on to forge paths in fields ranging from medicine to law, politics, art, and literature. They find opportunities to earn their master's and doctorate degrees both in the United States and abroad. Others move straight into their career paths after college, bringing a breadth of experience and critical thinking skills to whatever workplace they find themselves in. A number of Whitties also are awarded prestigious grants and fellowships such as the Fulbright, the Marshall, the Rhodes, and the Watson. Whitties travel the world with the Peace Corps and the Foreign Service, serve in Teach for America, and even establish their own nonprofit organizations and businesses. The possibilities are endless, and the ability of students and alumni to excel outside of the college's intimate campus environment is testimony to not only the caliber of a Whitman education, but the amazing support system that propels Whitties forward as they plunge into life after Whitman.

SUMMING UP

Whitman is honored to attract students who represent the Whitman mosaic—down-to-earth high-achievers with diverse interests. The college is a tight-knit community that pushes students to new heights academically and fosters a sense of lifelong learning and camaraderie. Whitman truly invests in each individual student, giving the specialized support and attention he or she needs to thrive and excel. Intellectual curiosity and a sense of social responsibility are promoted both in and outside of the classroom, allowing students to really take the lead in determining how their college experience unfolds. Postgraduation, Whitties can find useful contacts and a sense of community almost anywhere they go as part of an active alumni network that spans a number of different disciplines and career fields. From Walla Walla, Washington to the world, Whitman graduates are prepared to be critical thinkers, leaders, and globally minded citizens who can make a difference through whatever passions they pursue.

❏ *Aisha Fukushima, B.A.*

PROMINENT GRADS

- Dottie Metcalf-Lindenburger '97, NASA Astronaut
- Matthew Ames '70, Director of Research, Mayo Clinic
- Dirk Benedict '67, Actor
- Walter Brattain '24, Nobel Laureate in Physics
- Ralph Cordiner '22, CEO of General Electric
- Ryan Crocker '71, U.S. Former Ambassador to Iraq
- William O. Douglas '20, Supreme Court Justice
- Richard Elmore '66, Harvard University Scholar
- Kathrin Ford '97, Poet
- John Fulton '90, Author
- W. Michael Gillette '63, Oregon Supreme Court Justice
- Shane Johnson '98, Actor
- Craig Lesley '67, Novelist
- Rob Manning '80, Chief Engineer, Jet Propulsion Lab
- John Markoff '71, *The New York Times* Journalist
- Jim Robart '69, U.S. Federal Judge
- John Stanton '77, founder, Western Wireless
- Laura Valaas '06, Member, U.S. Nordic Ski Team
- Adam West '51, Actor (Batman)
- Gordon Winston '50, Williams College Economist
- Gordon Wright '33, Stanford University Historian

WILLIAMS COLLEGE

 Williams College
Williamstown, MA 01267

 (413) 597-2211

 E-mail: *admission@williams.edu*
Website: *http://www.williams.edu*

 Enrollment

Full-time ❑ women: 1,048
❑ men: 985

Part-time ❑ women: 21
❑ men: 13

INTRODUCING WILLIAMS COLLEGE

Nestled in the purple mountains of the Berkshires, Williams College is a small, private, liberal arts institution with an undergraduate population of 2,067 students, brimming with an almost tangible excitement for learning and life. These are students who work hard *and* play hard, devoting serious attention to courses and extracurriculars alike; the result is a campus that hums with activity and academic fervor. After four years, Williams graduates leave the Purple Valley armed with the knowledge and wherewithal to make a difference; their contributions are visible across the spectrum.

Founded in 1793, Williams exemplifies the liberal arts *modus operandi* of experimentation and exploration. Students are encouraged to build strong, broad foundations and then to construct spires soaring into the unknown. In this fashion, students can both pursue familiar interests and discover new ones; it is not uncommon to find a physics major taking music theory, for example, or a political science student spending time in the geology lab. Most students, as well, are vigorously involved in campus life and extracurriculars and don't hesitate to take on several activities in addition to their coursework. With more than 175 student groups on campus, ranging from WUFO, the Williams Ultimate Frisbee Organization, to WCFM, the college radio station, there is always something to pique interest, and students are quick to spearhead new groups as campus interests evolve.

The enthusiasm for learning that pervades the Williams student body is matched by the college's boundless resources, state-of-the-art facilities, and some of the world's premier collections. English majors may fawn over Charles Dickens' original *Pickwick Papers* in the Chapin Rare Books Library, theatre lovers direct plays in the new '62 Center for Theatre and Dance complex, and art history buffs delight over original works at the college art museum and the Sterling and Francine Clark Art Institute just down the road. The college frequently brings in guest lecturers and artists to enrich campus life, and recent years have seen noteworthies like Philip Glass, Werner Herzog, and Salman Rushdie alighting at the lectern.

Williams prides itself on its commitment to excellence and being well rounded, and this promise is most evident in the breadth and depth of the student body itself. Williams students hail from nearly all fifty states and more than forty-five different countries. About a third are American students of color, more than fifty percent receive some type of financial aid, and the division between public and private school students is about 60:40. The spectrum of interests and experiences represented on campus creates a richly diverse environment, where students have great potential to learn from one another and strengthen themselves. Though social groups—as at most colleges—do tend to form based on participation in activities, most Williams students move easily beyond rigid associations, resulting in a friendly, open social atmosphere.

U.S. President James Garfield (class of 1856), speaking of his former professor and early college president Mark Hopkins, once remarked, "The ideal college is Mark Hopkins on one end of a log and a student on the other." To this day, the metaphor lives on; with one of the lowest faculty-student ratios in the country; Williams brings students and professors closer, both in and out of the classroom. Williams professors are not only distinguished scholars but also passionate teachers, and students are top priority. Discussions in class often spill over into debates in the local coffee shop, or a class dinner at a professor's home, and office hours—at all hours—are the norm.

Just as students are central in the college's academic life, so are they in determining the future of the college. When Williams abolished fraternities in the 1960s and then went coed in the 1970s, students participated in the decision-making process. Today, students are a vital part of nearly every administrative committee on campus, helping shape campus social life, enforce the honor code, and even oversee a coffee bar. Students hold real responsibilities at Williams, and it is this trust and partnership, this collaborative climate, that defines the college.

ADMISSIONS REQUIREMENTS

There is no such thing as a "typical" Williams student. As one of the most competitive colleges in the nation, Williams is highly selective, and the Admissions Office prides itself on shaping a class diverse in interests, experience, and ability. The only shared trait—perhaps, even, an archetype—of accepted students is a *joie de vivre*, an enthusiasm for learning and seeking out challenges that electrifies the Williams campus.

Williams requires high school transcripts and standardized test scores from all applicants, including results from either the SAT or the ACT (with writing) and three SAT Subject Tests. If a student submits the SAT, Admissions will consider his or her best score on each section (math, verbal, writing); if he or she takes the ACT, the school will look at the student's best composite score. Although Williams considers grades and test scores to be just two of many admissions criteria, it should be noted that most who are admitted are high achievers, taking the most challenging course load offered at their schools; in a recent class, fifty percent scored 720 or higher on the SAT verbal, and fifty percent scored 710 or higher on the SAT math.

Even so, Williams does not fill its class solely from lists of high school valedictorians and perfect SAT scores. It is rare that a student will get in strictly on academic achievement; the Admissions Committee looks for students who balance academics with a commitment to other pursuits. In the same way that applicants should take the time to get to know the college beyond its statistics, Williams wants a fully realized rendering of its applicants, rather than a schematic of test scores and GPA.

The best way to get to know Williams is to visit and actually spend time on campus meeting students and professors. The Admissions Office offers student-run tours and information sessions every day and will also arrange for prospective students to stay overnight in a dorm to experience residential, social, and academic life at Williams firsthand.

Williams offers both Early and Regular Decision. If Williams is your first-choice school, you may submit your application for early consideration, along with an agreement that, if accepted, you will withdraw all other applications and not apply further. The Early Decision application deadline is November 10, and notification is mailed by December 15.

Applicants not accepted under Early Decision will ordinarily be deferred for reconsideration under the Regular Decision plan. Students with qualifications below Williams's general admission standards, however, will receive final notification in December. Regular Decision applications are due January 1, and decisions are mailed by the first week of April. Accepted candidates must reply by May 1, and acceptances are always contingent upon students finishing the current school year in good standing.

> Williams students use the month of January to take the "work hard, play hard" atmosphere at Williams to a whole new level. During these four weeks, students are required to take a single class, which can range from introductory figure drawing to research projects in molecular biology. Some students plan "99s," or independent studies, and others journey abroad with professors, completing service projects in Guatemala or exploring art and music in Vienna. The possibilities presented by Winter Study are endless, and students enjoy the relief it offers from the normal academic course load.

ACADEMIC LIFE

As a true liberal arts institution, Williams pairs a rich academic tradition with a modern focus on experimental learning. The old disciplines are still evident in the framework, to be sure; one can still read the classics in their original Latin and Greek, play out elaborate rhetorical battles in a philosophy class, and digest the great canonical works of literature and art. Take, for example, the English lecture course "Introduction to the Novel," a survey of some of the classics (Faulkner, Joyce, Nabokov), or the yearlong survey course in Western art and architecture, which, according to rumor, is the most popular selection Williams offers. To supplement this grand academic tradition, however, there are all sorts of new and surprising options: a forensic science class complete with staged crime scenes; an interdisciplinary music/English class explicating the careers of Bob Dylan, Joni Mitchell, and The Beatles; a tutorial on satire.

With a 4-1-4 calendar, Williams divides its year into two twelve-week semesters, with a four-week period in January, Winter Study, sandwiched between. Students must complete four courses per semester and a single class each Winter Study to graduate. There are no specific course requirements (no single class is mandatory); to encourage exploration of different subjects, however, all courses are assigned to one of three academic divisions, and students must pass three courses from each division in order to graduate. Division I includes the arts and humanities; Division II consists of the social sciences, such as economics, history, and psychology; Division III is comprised of the natural sciences, including chemistry, biology, physics, and math. Students must also take one class in a non-Western tradition and complete classes that fulfill specific competencies in writing and quantitative studies.

Students do not declare a major until the end of their sophomore year, affording plenty of time to choose a discipline. The major generally consists of nine to eleven courses, usually culminating in a senior seminar or capstone course. Within the major, students are often given more specific guidelines to diversify their studies; English majors, for example, are required to take courses in three different time periods (pre–1700, 1700–1900, post–1900), to gain a better understanding of literary movements across time.

Williams's lenient course requirements have led to a growing tendency to double major, something now done by about a third of the students. Interestingly enough, most students who double major do so in noncomplementary divisions: history and biology, math and music, English and chemistry. These students believe that double majoring is not only great preparation for the balancing act of the real world but allows for freedom of choice down the road.

There is absolutely nowhere else that can emulate the harmony that comes from this amalgamation of brilliant professors and talented peers. It should be telling that this is a community where it's normal to go to lunch with your professor and debate Kantian ethics with your entry-mates.

—*William Su, '08*

Williams courses are generally small and discussion-oriented, with the exception of a few large, lecture-based introductory courses; even these usually have a separate lab or discussion section that requires student participation. Students are expected to read and learn material outside of class, developing their own take on ideas before coming to lecture. Exams are largely based on problem solving and critical thinking and require students to build upon concepts learned during the course; multiple-choice tests and their ilk are virtually nonexistent.

> **❝** One of the most fascinating things about a Williams workload is the way students respond to it. Certainly, the work is a step up from high school both in terms of the complexity of thought and the sheer number of hours spent working outside class; but the funny thing is there are far fewer complaints about it. Even when a course turns out to more difficult than anticipated, the classes are so interesting and the professors so engaged and willing to help you through that you simply don't mind the extra time you spend. **❞**

—Sean Pegado, '11

Students who wish to pursue honors can complete a senior thesis. Under the supervision of a faculty sponsor, a student works independently for either one or two semesters, completing a substantial written work that must be presented and defended in front of a faculty panel. No senior assignment is required for graduation.

> **❝** This is the best way I can describe the atmosphere at Williams: it's humane. Williams students work hard, but they do so in a genial environment. There's no competition among classmates. Most people are genuine and friendly. The college offers free massages during exam time, places incoming freshmen in surrogate families, and closes the library early on Friday and Saturday nights to encourage students to have fun. And the quaint storefronts and purple mountains mark Williams as something special, like an oasis in the middle of the real world. **❞**

—Alison Hansen-Decelles, '10

Faculty

Williams faculty members are at the college because they primarily want to teach undergraduates, and their motivation invigorates the classroom. Although most of them are brilliant researchers (ninety-five percent have their terminal degree), they put students first and make themselves available both in and out of the classroom. Almost every class is taught by a professor, and teaching assistants are used primarily to help grade routine assignments and help direct review sessions.

The fact that Williams professors are so accessible is sometimes a shock for students who are not used to engaging their teachers. They not only make office hours and appointments available for students with academic questions, but they become advisors on everything from postgraduate plans to personal issues. Professors also keep involved in campus life, some even joining intramural sports.

In addition to teaching, Williams professors produce an impressive amount of scholarship, for which they regularly receive national attention and major grants. Many professors, as well, will take on students to assist them over the summer and during the year, giving students valuable research experience; in recent years, hundreds of students have participated.

Residential Life

The close-knit atmosphere of the college is made even more evident through its housing system. The majority of Williams students live in campus housing—in fact, the option to live off-campus or in a co-operative house is only available to seniors—and the dormitories are kept clean, comfortable, and up-to-date with frequent renovations. Housing is comprised of single and double rooms, arranged in suites, with generous common space.

First-year students live in "entries" of approximately twenty-five students, headed by a pair of Junior Advisors (JAs). Unlike the Residential Advisors of most colleges, JAs are unpaid, are more along the lines of mentors than a police force, and are integral to a first-year student's transition process. Entries often appear cult-like, especially around dinnertime, when large crowds of first-years traipse into the dining halls and commandeer three or four tables at a time, and the connections forged among entrymates are often the strongest of a student's career.

> **"***Rushing to class, submitting a paper, going to practice, printing out homework, grabbing lunch in between, and having a late-night rehearsal; every day at Williams is so dynamic. However, there is always time to grab gelato with your best friend and discuss the latest news on the love front; to tutor a fellow classmate for the bio test tomorrow or just watch a dramatic sitcom in the common room. Williams students are remarkable in multitasking, which makes our life so vibrant and fulfilling.* "**

Williams dormitories and co-ops are further organized into "neighborhoods," a recent housing change aimed to extend the entry experience to upper-class students. Through the neighborhood system, students are assigned to one of four clusters of dorms, geographically located across campus, and live in that cluster over the next three years. Within neighborhoods, students are free to choose where they live and can "pick in" with groups of friends each year in a housing lottery. With diversity across campus as a primary goal, Williams has no fraternities, sororities, or special-interest housing.

SOCIAL LIFE AND ACTIVITIES

With a student body composed of individuals who did *everything* in high school, it is no wonder that the campus is full of an almost frenetic energy. Though the college is small, there is always something going on, and students keep themselves very busy. As Williamstown itself offers few entertainment options (the "town," in students' minds, is often distilled to Spring Street, a one-way thoroughfare located at the heart of campus, crowded with restaurants and shops), social life is student-driven and mostly confined to campus. Few regularly leave town on weekends, so students get to know each other well and support each other in their athletic events, concerts, and performances. The administration contributes to campus life by providing funding for lectures, concerts, parties, and movies to keep the place lively.

Williams students never hesitate to organize new clubs and groups, especially with the help of student activities funding, if they find their interests aren't met. As a result, the number of recognized clubs and student groups on campus grows each year, and now tops one hundred; with so many options to choose from, it's not hard to find something to do in your free time.

Very few teams or clubs restrict membership, and there is no Greek system, so just about everything is open to everyone. Among the largest groups are the swing dancing club and the Williams Outing Club (WOC), which sponsors outdoor activities. The Minority Coalition, comprised of groups supporting students from minority backgrounds, sponsors campus-wide celebrations like Black History Month and Coming Out Days. Students can voice their opinions and spur changes in campus life through College Council and in writing for the weekly campus newspaper, *The Record*, and about forty percent of students regularly do community service. Music is also popular, and students can participate at any level, whether it is through beginners' music lessons or as part of the Berkshire Symphony, a group made up of professional musicians, faculty, and students. Other popular groups include the jazz ensemble, the Kusika African drumming and dance ensemble, and *a cappella* groups.

> **❝** *My biggest fear about leaving for college was being away from my fam-ily. Within a few days, however, I already felt at home at Williams. The unique entry system provided me with the support of 20 brothers and sisters and two caring aunt and uncle-like JAs. Going back to the entry truly gave me a sense of "going home" at the end of the day. After a hard day's work, I enjoyed plopping down on a couch in the common room (essentially a living room) and sharing my day with my entrymates.* **❞**

—*Katie Aldrin, '12*

For those interested in sports (and about forty percent of Williams students are), Williams has over more than thirty-two varsity squads and even more intramural organiza-tions, including an equestrian team, a figure-skating club, and water polo. Moreover, Williams's teams are consistently among the nation's best in NCAA Division III and play a major role in shaping school spirit, drawing huge crowds—especially when Williams is play-ing its nemesis, Amherst.

In terms of a party scene, Williams tends toward smaller parties hosted in dorms, rather than formal all-campus blowouts—except for the big weekends of Homecoming, Winter Carnival, and Spring Fling. Regular weekend parties are hosted in the larger dorms and tend to be standard keg parties with a DJ. A stricter party policy instituted in the past few years has limited the amount of alcohol at these events and has made training with security officers and health counselors mandatory for all party hosts. Still, students who want to drink usually have no trouble finding alcohol, while students who do not drink are not pressured to do so.

FINANCIAL AID

With the annual inflation of tuition prices, college is growing increasingly expensive. Williams, with comprehensive fees totaling $52,340, is one of the nation's priciest, but at the same time Williams goes out of its way to make it financially viable for all accepted students to attend. Williams is one of a handful of schools with a need-blind admissions policy—a student's ability to pay is never factored into an admissions decision—and pledges to meet one hundred percent of the demonstrated need of its students, both American and international.

Williams's financial aid packages are awarded on a need basis; it offers no merit-based scholarships. Instead, the Financial Aid Office evaluates each family individually, considering size, the number of students in college, income, and assets before determining how much the family can pay. The resulting aid package will cover the entire difference between the cost of the student's education and the expected family contribution, in a combination of grants, loans, and campus employment. Students are expected to contribute some of their summer earnings toward their payment.

Being a financial aid student at Williams carries no stigma at all. In a recent year, almost fifty-three percent of the incoming class received some type of financial aid. The average annual award to first-year students in 2009–2010 was $38,524. Many first-year students work in the dining halls, while upper-class students do everything from manning the library reference desks, to working in a professor's lab, to writing news releases for the Office of Public Affairs or the Sports Information Office.

GRADUATES

With today's competitive job market, many might question the value of a broad, liberal arts education. A Williams education, however, in addition to its intellectual perks, carries a lot of weight in the real world, and one's Williams degree becomes a certain kind of pedigree. Williams graduates are seen as movers, shakers, thinkers, communicators, and leaders, and employers recognize that those qualities translate neatly into the ability to learn quickly, meet challenges, and get results—a skill set that is hard to ignore.

A Williams education is good preparation for nearly any career path, and graduates have proven this by making names for themselves in professions as diverse as education, journalism, scientific research, public service, business, and the arts. A Williams degree allows graduates to pursue fields or projects that most interest them, and to switch between fields with relative ease. Many Williams grads go on to more schooling, with many earning professional degrees in law, medicine, and business, and some earning their master's or Ph.D.

On campus, students can research potential career options and build résumés through the Office of Career Counseling (OCC). The OCC hosts a variety of on-campus recruiters, offers mock interview sessions, and assists students with resumes and cover letters. It also puts on alumni panels and career fairs in underrepresented areas, such as nonprofits.

An invaluable asset for graduates is the vast Williams alumni network, often affectionately called the Williams Mafia. Most alumni are incredibly enthusiastic about helping out a fellow Eph, and having contacts in the workforce has proven to be a great help to new graduates.

After leaving Williams, graduates are welcomed into the fold of the Williams Society of Alumni, the first such group in North America. Today, it remains one of the most active alumni associations in the country. Not only do generous graduates donate annually, helping Williams continue expanding and evolving its programs and facilities, but alumni are also active in campus life, often returning to teach Winter Study classes or take on students for summer internships.

SUMMING UP

Williams is built upon and around its students, and they are all the happier for it. The resources available are first-rate, the faculty are among the most distinguished in the nation, and the staff is world-class. But in making lively classroom discussion to organizing nearly all campus events and activities to voicing issues and directing the future of the college, Williams students make the campus the passionate, vibrant place that it is.

Just as there is no "typical" Williams student, the Williams experience is different for everyone who attends; the college is a place where students are expected to create their own paths, both inside the classroom and out. Williams is a place where students seek out and overcome their toughest obstacles, growing and learning with every challenge; they know how to accept help and are generous in offering it to others.

Students work hard and set ambitious goals, but they also know how to put things in perspective, making room for friends and recreation. Even in the face of an all-night study session or hefty research assignment, there is always time for a midnight trip to the snack bar or an hour's respite in the common room. It is these shared moments that are often at the heart of the Williams experience.

In the end, what you get out of Williams is what you put into it: yourself. And even though your time spent in the Purple Valley is, sadly, finite, it is an experience that makes the impression of a lifetime.

❏ *Jennifer Linnan, B.A.*

Photo by Michael Marsland

 Yale University
Office of Undergraduate Admission
P.O. Box 208234
New Haven, CT 06520-8234

 (203) 432-9300
Fax: (203) 432-9392

 E-mail: *undergraduate.admissions@yale.edu*
Website: *http://www.yale.edu*

 Enrollment

Full-time ❑ women: 2,585
❑ men: 2,687

INTRODUCING YALE

If you've decided to attend Yale, "Where are you going to school?" can be a complicated question. If you're like most Yale students, you're so excited about coming to the school that you'll want to jump out and say "Yale!" loud and clear, eyes and cheeks aglow. But answering the question so directly provokes many different reactions, based on Yale's reputation as one of the finest universities in the world. So students and even alumni practice several indirect responses, including "New Haven" (there are a handful of other colleges and universities here;

just read the exit sign for "Yale Univ." and "Albertus Magnus"); "Connecticut" (a state with MANY colleges), and the even more vague "Back East."

Like many of the questions that hold great import before you begin college, this one soon fades into oblivion. A freshman will quickly observe and follow the pattern set by the undergraduate body: Everyone is too busy taking maximum advantage of the university's vast resources to boast or even think about Yale's reputation. The 1998 yearbook is titled *Unlimited Capacity*. Indeed, students are in overdrive most of the time. Yale's unwavering commitment to undergraduate education, the residential college system, and the breadth of academic and extracurricular opportunities are central tenets of the Yale experience. These are the reasons why Yalies have chosen Yale, not for its reputation, and not for its location in the small New England city (though it seems more of a town) of New Haven, Connecticut.

Yalies joke about the question "Where do you go to school?" because Yale is not simply where people go to school. It is a community, and the happiest members of that community are those who actively participate in it. Many students remember being hit with the Yale fever almost immediately upon arriving on campus—that's how tangible the sense of community is.

> 66 *On my first walk around the campus, I just knew that this was where I wanted to go to college. Students were rushing to get to class, while I was struggling to read my campus map that was torn and wrinkled by a strong wind (which I've now come to recognize as a robust sea breeze from the nearby Long Island Sound). Then a student stopped and asked me if I needed directions. I wound up going to his English class, where he introduced me to his professor. Then he took me to Durfee's Sweet Shop, and directed me to other buildings he thought I'd want to see. All his enthusiasm and helpfulness got me hooked. Now I look out for maps blowing in the wind, and am always glad for the chance to talk to prospective students.* 99

ADMISSIONS REQUIREMENTS

Ask students what they know about admissions and you're likely to hear that the hardest thing about Yale is getting in. Look past that casual statement, however, to recognize a deeper truth: There's no set formula for admission to a place that seeks to maintain a diverse student body. As the Admissions Committee says on its Web page (*http://www.yale.edu/admit/*), the two basic questions it brings to the process are "Who is likely to make the most of Yale's resources?" and "Who will contribute significantly to the Yale community?" It's a complex approach, one designed to select a class of motivated, energetic achievers with broad interests and skills, all of whom are enticed by the opportunities Yale offers both in and out of the classroom.

Beyond that stated mission, applicants should be aware of several general facts:

- First, admission is extremely competitive, as the committee aims for a class of approximately 1,250 from over 21,000 applicants.
- Second, while there are no official score cut-offs and applicants' test results vary widely, medians on the Verbal and Mathematics parts of the SAT generally fall in between 700 and 790, and ACT composites in the low 30s.
- Third, the great majority of Yalies (ninety-five percent) placed in the top tenth of their high school class; a distinguished record in a demanding college preparatory program may compensate for modest standardized test scores, but the reverse is usually not true.
- Fourth, the committee is searching for students with some less tangible qualities suggested by the various documents in their applications. Some successful candidates are well rounded, while others have specialized talents, some have displayed leadership capabilities in extracurricular activities while others have shown dedication to an after-school job, but all, hopefully, show a capacity for involvement, commitment, and personal growth.
- Finally, Yale has a need-blind admissions policy for both U.S. and international students, meaning that an applicant's financial circumstances will not be given any weight during the admission process. You won't be rejected because you apply for financial aid, as Yale is strongly committed to the idea of equality of opportunity, seeking to shape a class of students from all parts of the country and all segments of society. In addition, Yale recently announced a $7.5 million increase in undergraduate financial aid, which will reduce the amount that Yale expects a student to contribute to his or her education by $13,780 over four years.

The admissions process produces a class that reflects Yale's interest in diversity, not only in academic and extracurricular interests but also in ethnicity and geographical distribution. Today, minority students comprise nearly twenty-nine percent of the student body, and Yalies hail from all fifty states and over seventy countries. Be prepared to meet people of all cultural, social, and financial backgrounds, and also be prepared to meet people who have worn Yale blue since birth—"legacies" make up around ten percent of each class.

Early Action

Applicants who are certain that Yale is their first choice may want to take advantage of the single choice Early Action program. As with Early Action programs elsewhere, an Early Action application to Yale is not a binding commitment from the student. Interested students should submit a complete application by November 1. In mid-December the committee will respond with an acceptance or denial of admission, or a deferral, which postpones the final decision until April, when all applicants are notified.

Being admitted to Yale signals the Admission Committee's faith in the applicant's ability to be a successful Yale student. Does that mean that admission is, in fact, the hardest part of Yale? Well, all students have to face that question on their own. Yalies tend to make life hard on themselves by pursuing their academics and activities so intensely—clearly they have proven their stamina by the time they graduate.

ACADEMIC LIFE

In 1701 ten Connecticut clergymen met in the town of Branford, each with a gift of books to contribute for the founding of the college in Saybrook on the Connecticut River that would become Yale. From those forty folios, the university's holdings have grown to include over twelve million volumes; the extensive library system is the seventh largest research library in the world. A library is the heart of any learning institution, and the prominence of Yale's collections (not to mention the imposing sight of Sterling Memorial Library's Gothic tower looming over the central campus) reminds students that while they may spend countless hours dashing around to eagerly explore extracurricular interests, their intellectual development is paramount.

To foster that development, Yale has always remained committed to the idea of a liberal arts education. According to one faculty report, "Our object is not to teach that which is peculiar to any one of the professions, but to lay the foundation which is common to them all..." Those words were written in 1828, and they still characterize the Yale philosophy today. Simply put, Yale wants to teach you how to think. The university doesn't have career-oriented fields of study—if you want to major in communications or marketing, for example, look elsewhere—but, instead, aims to provide students with the tools to succeed in any field.

Majors and Workload

What you *can* major in is any of almost seventy disciplines, from astronomy to film studies to Russian. Yale also allows you to double-major and, if you can convince a faculty committee that it's necessary and that you're up to the challenge, to design your own major. In a recent year, there are now over 70 disciplines that students can major in. The most popular majors, in order, are history (358 juniors and seniors), political science (335), economics (320), and biology (185).

Students must take two courses in each of these three academic areas: Humanities and Arts, Social Science, and Science. They must also take at least one foreign language course (or more—depending on the level they start at), and two courses in quantitative reasoning and two that are writing-intensive. To ensure that study is neither too narrowly focused nor too diffuse, the College stands behind the principle of distribution of studies as strongly as it supports the principle of concentration. It requires that study be characterized, particularly in the earlier years, by a reasonable diversity of subject matter and approach, and in the later years by concentration in one of the major programs or departments. A student working toward a bachelor's degree takes four or five courses each term, and normally receives the B.A. or B.S. degree after completing thirty-six term courses or their equivalent in eight terms of enrollment.

It's a lot to grasp at first, and it's no surprise that the structure of a Yale education means things can get pretty hectic and intense at times. However, the system makes perfect sense from a liberal arts perspective, giving students the freedom and responsibility to shape their academic careers, while guaranteeing a certain amount of breadth of study in addition to the depth one experiences in a major. As an added incentive to explore, some courses can be taken Credit/D/Fail, which means that a grade of C or above will show up as a "CR" on one's transcript. Many Yalies grumble about the various distributional requirements, but if you press them, most will admit they're glad they took that English or geology course that initially seemed so unconnected to their interests, because it exposed them to different people and different ways of thinking.

"Shopping" for Classes

These notions of academic exploration, freedom, and responsibility are embodied in Yale's unique shopping period, the first two weeks of each semester, in which students shop for classes. Most colleges require students to preregister for classes, but Yale allows its students to attend any course offered at the start of the semester, filling out their schedules only after hearing the professors and perusing the syllabi. Shopping period is a great opportunity to shape an interesting schedule while trying to balance the various times, demands (tests, papers, problem sets), and sizes (seminars, small and large lectures) of the classes. For some, shopping period can literally be a life-changing experience—one student dropped in on an introductory architecture lecture sophomore year, found himself enthralled by the professor, and spent the next two years immersed in blueprints and models. Many professors dislike shopping period, since they start off the semester with no idea of how many students will eventually take their classes, but students will tell you it's one of the best things about the Yale experience.

Reading Week

The end-of-term equivalent to shopping period is reading week, a week between the end of classes and the start of finals that makes Yale students the envy of their peers at most other institutions. Ideally a time to pause, reflect, and study in preparation for finals, it's more often a time of late-night paper writing and catching up on reading not completed on time. Studying, of course, includes study breaks, and reading week is also a time of catching up with friends before winter break and summer vacation.

Faculty

Yale's graduate schools are well respected, but the college remains the physical, intellectual, and even emotional center of Yale. The student-to-faculty ratio is 7:1 and only nine percent of classes have fifty or more students. As a leading research institution attracting scholars of international renown in every field, Yale expects its faculty to put time and energy into teaching undergraduates. Faculty members welcome the opportunity to share their enthusiasm with students, and many of Yale's most distinguished senior professors teach introductory courses. Some have attained cult status and attract hundreds of students.

Yale is not merely a place for academic excellence. In fact, many students won't even cite the academic environment as the most important aspect of their college years. It is academic excellence, however, that makes the Yale experience and reputation so distinctive and attracts so many applicants each year.

SOCIAL LIFE AND ACTIVITIES

Freshman Orientation

The first few days of freshman year lay the groundwork for a rich and intricate life outside of the classroom. They may begin with a seven-day hiking trip in the Catskills or Berkshires or a two-day retreat at a nearby summer camp. About a third of the class takes part in these programs, known as FOOT (Freshman Outdoor Orientation Trip) and

Freshperson Conference. In addition to FOOT and Freshperson Conference, other pre-freshman programs include Cultural Connections (focus on diversity issues), Harvest (5-day work-stay at organic farms in Connecticut), and Orientation for International Studies. Even though their duration is brief, and students scatter in all directions once classes begin, many alumni of these orientation programs have reunions throughout college. The FOOT program has recently started an electronic listserve for alumni to share their most recent hiking adventures.

The day these programs end, Camp Yale—the official freshman orientation—begins. Wearing navy T-shirts that announce, "Ask me for help," freshman counselors—seniors who have gone through a rigorous training program to serve as peer advisors to the freshman class, and who live with them—stand outside of the entryways on Old Campus to meet their new charges. At convocation, the president addresses the freshman class. This is followed by a reception at his house. Finally, the upperclassmen get their chance to meet and greet, during a bazaar of undergraduate activities. Before classes have even begun, organization leaders line the sidewalks of Old Campus to recruit freshmen. The freshman counselors also hold meetings with their counselees where they go over the course selection process and review many of the resources available to students, from a twenty-four-hour shuttle bus to free condoms to professional counseling.

This flurry of activity during the first few days exemplifies Yale's commitment to its undergraduates. As soon as students arrive, they are part of the community, and are asked to become active in it. There are many different levels of support and orientation; students manage their way through the array of decisions and opportunities differently. Some will visit their freshman counselor every day, while others will turn to upperclassmen or to their faculty advisor. Freedom and choice prevail; Yale expects and relies on students to act responsibly.

Residential Colleges

The primary way to identify new students at Yale is by the residential college. A couple of months before school starts, every incoming student is randomly assigned to one of twelve residential colleges, an affiliation that lasts throughout one's four years at Yale, and beyond. The college system breaks down each class of approximately 1,240 students into much smaller and more intimate units of approximately 100 students who live and eat together. Ideally, during the time students live there, this place feels like home, and has many of the amenities one could wish for: television rooms, libraries, music practice rooms, computer rooms, even performance spaces and printing presses.

Each college has a master, a faculty member who lives with his or her family in the master's house. In addition to their professorial duties of teaching and research, the master oversees the social life of the college—intramural teams, dances, tailgates, and arts festivals, for instance. The master eats regularly in the dining hall and invites students frequently into his or her home, sometimes for the relaxed social interchange of a study break or the chance to meet an author, politician, or other dignitary during a Master's Tea (recent guests have included Denzel Washington, Brian Williams, Hillary Clinton, Tony Blair). The residential college deans also live in the college and oversee the freshman counselors and the academic lives of students. A dean must approve a student's schedule, and is the only person authorized to grant a student a "dean's excuse" for not meeting academic deadlines.

While most freshmen live on Old Campus together, and are encouraged to bond as a class, they also participate fully in residential college life. At the beginning of their sophomore year, students move into their colleges. There they room with classmates, but live in a section or on a hallway with juniors and seniors. In randomly assigning students to residential colleges, Yale's aim is to create twelve microcosms of the larger undergraduate community. Students with different interests and backgrounds—and, outside of the residential college, entirely different lives—live and learn side by side. Students have the option of transferring to another residential college.

About fifteen percent of students decide to live off campus, though Yale recently instituted a new policy that requires undergraduates to live on campus for two years.

The residential college system could be described as part of Yale's infrastructure. During commencement, all students graduate in a ceremony on Old Campus, but return to their residential colleges to receive their diplomas. Most "class notes" in the monthly *Yale Alumni Magazine*, which all graduates of the college automatically receive, identify people by their college. It is an extremely efficient way to give students the best of both worlds at Yale—the resources of a large research university, with the attention, support, and sense of community of a small liberal arts college.

Athletics

The residential colleges also create an infrastructure for students to participate in athletics. Intramurals are recreational and everyone in the college, regardless of previous experience, is encouraged to participate. Competitions between the colleges usually take place in the afternoon or evening, and results are tallied on a weekly basis as residential colleges strive for the Tyng Cup, awarded at the end of the year to the college with the most points. Less publicly fought for but nonetheless a source of college pride is the Gimbel Cup, awarded annually to the residential college with the highest grade point average. Lastly, there's the Tang Cup, awarded to college teams in a one-day competition organized in association with the fraternities. Because of the residential college system, fraternities and sororities are not a major social force at Yale, but they do exist, and provide community service and social outlets for the students who participate.

Clubs and Organizations

Of course, many other communities and affiliations abound at Yale—the ones students create and choose for themselves. There are twelve possible responses to the question, "What college are you in?" There are hundreds of possible responses to the next-important question, "What do you do?" On any given weeknight during dinner, a group of students is planning their next singing jam, magazine deadline, political debate, student rally, chamber orchestra recital, juggling demonstration, Habitat for Humanity project, or play auditions. There's a club for chess players, engineers, anglophiles, and polar bears (those who dare to swim in the Long Island Sound during the winter). There's scripted comedy, improv comedy, and published comedy, not to mention many student-produced comic strips. There's opera, klezmer, and black spiritual music, available live and on CD. It's exhausting to even think of how many options are available—and even more exhausting to recognize that students spend large portions of their time sustaining these organizations. Over 300 groups register with the Yale College Dean's Office, including fifteen *a cappella* groups (from the tuxedoed Whiffenpoofs to the Dylan-inspired Tangled Up In Blue), forty undergraduate publications (including the Yale Daily News, the oldest college daily), and two dozen cultural groups.

You will never lack for something to do on the Yale campus, and if you ever did find yourself in that position, you would do as many have done before you: start your own group for your own hobby. If you're not copyediting final pages into the wee hours of the morning, you're trying to figure out how to see your friends in their three separate productions. Most likely, you'll see the productions back to back and then do your copyediting. One cannot measure a student's devotion, nor can one imagine a limit to a student's energy. The majority of students aren't merely involved in a group, they're leading one. Only during reading period, the week before final exams start, does the campus start to settle down. The kiosks all over campus, usually plastered with posters advertising events, begin to look bare as the libraries swell with students for the first time all semester.

> 66 *Sometimes I wish I could take a semester off from classes, given my other commitments. Blackberries, iPhones, and the like are for professionals, but many people at Yale have them just to keep track of the meetings and dinners they take part in. I try to take my classes on Tuesdays and Thursdays so I have three full free days to work my campus job, do my activities, and study. I feel wired all of the time, but everyone does. There's this frenetic energy or buzz on campus that's very difficult to escape. If I'm not doing something, I feel like a slacker. It's difficult to find time just to hang out, though luckily, I see my friends regularly, since most of them are involved in the same groups. During vacations, I sleep. A lot.* 99

New Haven

New Haven, a moderate-sized port city, is about ninety minutes away from New York. That's far enough away to make New Haven part of New England, and not a New York offshoot. To call it a port city is perhaps misleading, since its days as a prosperous center of shipping and industry are long past. New Haven, designated as an All American City in 2008 and recognized as the cultural capital of Connecticut, would be much worse off without Yale, and while town-gown relations have sometimes been strained in Yale's history, today their interaction is characterized by collaboration and cooperation. Yale is the city's largest contributor of real estate taxes, donates over $2 million a year to the city's fire services, is the city's biggest employer, and the university has joined forces with the city to build a new economic base—the latest goal is to utilize Yale's academic resources to develop a profit-minded Biotechnology center within the city. Completely revitalized Broadway and Chapel Street shopping districts—a component of Yale's community investment program—feature many locally-owned shops and several national anchor stores such as J. Crew, Urban Outfitters, Barnes & Noble, and Au Bon Pain.

The campus is a few miles from Long Island Sound, and refreshing sea breezes can still be felt, even if you have to climb one of the towers on campus to see the water. Beach towns along the Connecticut coast, though difficult to visit if you don't have a car, offer antique shops, fresh seafood, and farms for hayrides and apple picking. East Rock Park is a ten-minute bike ride away. In short, though the campus is adjacent to neighborhoods of different income levels, many of the pastoral diversions completely absent from a big city campus are quite accessible to Yale students. Far from hiding in their dorm rooms in the walled-in courtyards of green lawns and shady trees, students are aware and caring of their surroundings. Over sixty-five percent of the students pursue community service projects in New Haven. The locked gates and visibility of both Yale and New Haven police patrols don't seem to bother students, but do serve to keep students safe.

The Elm City birthplace of President George W. Bush, may not be as nationally recognized as cities that host other Ivy League schools, its charms grow on students, who often decide to stay in New Haven during the summers or attend graduate school at Yale. The small portion of students who do stick to campus life exclusively miss out on a modest but eclectic music and arts scene, and treasures like the first and best hamburger (Louis's Lunch), the best fried donuts and pigs-in-a-blanket (The Yankee Doodle), and, of course, the first pizza in the U.S. (Pepe's, and its rival, Sally's located in Wooster Square—about a twenty-minute walk from campus). The chance to get involved and be useful to the city fosters a civic identity that graduates carry with them. Last year, more than 100 seniors took jobs with Teach for America and the Peace Corps.

FINANCIAL AID

In its admissions process Yale may be need-blind, but no one should be blind to the financial realities connected with attendance. The actual cost of attending college varies from student to student. There are the following usual expenses: tuition and fees, room and board, books, and personal expenses, and a yearly hospitalization coverage fee and other optional and incidental expenses.

The basis of all financial aid awards at Yale is the student's "demonstrated financial need," the difference between the estimated cost of attendance and the expected family contribution. For a recent academic year, more than sixty percent of all undergraduates qualified to receive financial assistance in the form of scholarships, grants, low-interest educational loans, and work-study from all sources. Yale does not offer academic or athletic scholarships or any other type of special scholarship that is not based on demonstrated need. More than $59.9 million in university-controlled need-based aid was offered to forty-five percent of the undergraduate student body.

The expected contribution is determined by the Financial Aid Office, which analyzes the FAFSA, CSS Financial Aid Profile, and other forms submitted by the family, and measures the family's ability to contribute toward Yale's costs.

Packages

After consideration of these factors, the university offers financial aid in the form of a package with two basic components: "self-help" (a combination of term-time employment and educational loans) and "gift aid," which covers any need beyond that covered by self-help. While other types of loans are available, the primary source of long-term, low-interest loans is the federal Stafford Loan Program, for which citizens or permanent residents of the United States are eligible. Students who apply for financial aid will automatically be considered for all types of "gift aid," which consists of scholarships from the university, as well as Yale alumni clubs, and from endowed and federal funds, including federal Supplemental Educational Opportunity Grants, administered by the university. Additionally, Yale participates in a number of financing options that can assist families in paying for college, whether or not the family is determined to have demonstrated financial need.

Jobs

On-campus jobs (available also to students not on financial aid, though aid recipients have priority) offer a wide variety of opportunities. Students fill positions as dining hall workers, library clerks, laboratory assistants, research assistants, and aides to residential college masters. Jobs also abound in various campus offices. Recently, wage rates for university jobs ranged from $10.90 for entry-level positions to over fifteen dollars per hour for dining hall workers. A large number of Yale students balance school and employment.

> **❝** *It helped me pay for college, but my job (in a campus office that doesn't interact much with students) also became something I really enjoyed. The truth is, when you spend your whole day surrounded by eighteen- to twenty-two-year-olds, sometimes it's nice to be around people who aren't students or professors, people who drive into New Haven for the day. It was basic office work, but it was good to have an enforced break from academics and the intensity of the Yale experience.* **❞**

For more in-depth information on financing a Yale education, including an example of a financial aid award, check out *http://www.yale.edu/admit/financing.html*.

GRADUATES

It's difficult enough to describe the intense experience of four years at Yale. Once they enter the world at large, Yalies go off to do a multitude of impressive things. Part of Yale's mission is to train leaders, and Yale's alumni do lead, as U.S. presidents (five attended Yale), company CEOs, academics, journalists, lawyers, and advocates. Living in New Haven, a city where volunteerism can make such a difference, is a life-shaping experience for students, many of whom later gravitate to public service in government or nonprofit organizations. The diversity of Yale's student body, and the breadth of its academic offerings, prepares graduates for diverse careers. A sampling of recent graduates should give you an idea: investment banker, Peace Corps volunteer, reporter in Indonesia, computer programmer, book publicist, teacher. When alumni reach out to one another, they continue to learn from their classmates' endeavors.

The Association of Yale Alumni oversees a network of more than 125 local Yale Clubs and associations that have a mission to connect and reconnect the alumni to the university. These groups also involve alumni volunteers in the admissions process, as they are charged with interviewing students in their area and filling out evaluation forms. Many local groups host receptions for admitted students. Fund-raising is carried out by the Alumni Fund, a separate organization that can boast one of the highest participation rates of the Ivy League. The university recently launched a $3.5 billion capital campaign, largely fueled by the generosity of its alumni. That alumni are devoted and loyal is a good sign of the quality of the experience they had during their time here.

Yalies enjoy coming back to campus. Twice yearly, over 200 alumni, elected as delegates by their local associations, convene in New Haven to address the latest news and developments at Yale and discuss alumni affairs. Some fly in from as far away as Switzerland and Hong Kong.

Reunions bring thousands more back to campus in the spring, for a weekend of dancing, dining, and catching up. Many current students work during reunions, and have the extra treat of meeting alums who lived in their residential college or perhaps took a class with the same instructor. Recently, the university has embarked on "A Day with Yale" program, which puts administrators and faculty members on the road to share their knowledge and talents with the alumni population.

An alumni gathering would not be complete without the spirited singing of the alma mater, "Bright College Years." The lyrics sum up the immense loyalty and nostalgia shared by Yale graduates.

> *Bright College years, with pleasure rife,*
> *The shortest, gladdest years of life;*
> *How swiftly are ye gliding by!*
> *Oh, why doth time so quickly fly?*
>
> *Oh, let us strive that ever we*
> *May let these words our watch-cry be,*
> *Where'er upon life's sea we sail:*
> *"For God, for Country, and for Yale!"*

SUMMING UP

Go to the "front door" of the Yale World Wide Web site (*http://www.yale.edu/*) and you may see a Yale campus scene or famous building. As Yale embarks on its fourth century, the same mingling of past and future is palpable on the campus. For example, students' increasing use of e-mail occurs in the computer center located in the basement of Connecticut Hall, the university's oldest building, and wireless Internet is available in most dining halls and libraries. While the university remains committed to perpetuating its traditional strengths, it also allows its energetic and intellectually enthusiastic student body to lead it toward a new future.

❑ *Amanda Gordon, B.A.*
❑ *Seth Oltman, B.A.*

A MOST COMPETITIVE
COMPARISON

A MOST COMPETITIVE COMPARISON

SCHOOL	NUMBER OF APPLI- CATIONS	ACCEPTED	ENROLLED	M/F RATIO	SAT SCORES CRITICAL READING	MATH	WRITING	COSTS
Amherst College	n/av	n/av	n/av	51/49	n/av	n/av	n/av	$45,000
Bates College	n/av	n/av	n/av	48/52	n/av	n/av	n/av	$51,300 (tuition)
Boston College	30,845	8093	2167	48/52	655	685	665	$52,039
Bowdoin College	5940	1153	494	49/51	710	710	710	$50,900
Brandeis University	n/av	n/av	n/av	44/56	n/av	n/av	n/av	$51,700
Brown University	24,988	2790	1495	48/52	710	720	720	$49,128
Bryn Mawr College	2276	1107	362	All Women	660	630	660	$50,934
Bucknell University	7572	2263	920	49/51	640	670	660	$50,320
California Institute of Technology	n/av	674	252	69/31	n/av	n/av	n/av	$47,739
Carleton College	4784	1459	529	48/52	n/av	n/av	n/av	$50,205
Carnegie Mellon University	14,153	5132	1423	60/40	670	730	680	$51,260
Case Western Reserve University	7998	5599	966	57/43	645	690	640	$47,498
Claremont McKenna College	n/av	n/av	n/av	54/46	n/av	n/av	n/av	$48,000
Colby College	n/av	n/av	n/av	46/54	n/av	n/av	n/av	$51,900
Colgate University	7816	2464	750	48/52	661	680	n/av	$50,930
College of New Jersey	9238	1284	4267	42/58	630	660	630	$22,718 (in-state) $31,404 (out-of-state)

All figures relate to a recent freshman class except the Male/Female Ratio numbers, which reflect the entire undergraduate student body for a recent class. Figures are either as published in *Barron's Profiles of American Colleges, 29th Edition* or in the essay portion of this book.

| SCHOOL | NUMBER OF APPLI-CATIONS | ACCEPTED | ENROLLED | M/F RATIO | SAT SCORES | | | COSTS |
					CRITICAL READING	MATH	WRITING	
College of the Holy Cross	6652	2426	747	44/56	634	647	n/av	$49,342
College of William and Mary	12,110	4058	1391	45/55	n/av	n/av	n/av	$19,182 (in-state) $39,346 (out-of-state)
Columbia University/ Barnard College	n/av	n/av	n/av	All Women	n/av	n/av	n/av	$41,000
Columbia University	n/av	n/av	n/av	53/47	n/av	n/av	n/av	$48,000
Columbia University School of General Studies	n/av	n/av	n/av	51/49	n/av	n/av	n/av	$50,124
Connecticut College	4733	1732	503	40/60	660	650	660	$51,115
Cooper Union for the Advancement of Science and Art	3387	249	193	63/37	660	720	n/av	$15,000
Cornell University	34,371	6565	3181	51/49	n/av	n/av	n/av	$62,274
Dartmouth College	16,538	2228	1095	50/50	n/av	n/av	n/av	$47,469
Davidson College	4495	1185	491	49/51	670	670	680	$45,030
Duke University	n/av	n/av	n/av	50/50	n/av	n/av	n/av	$50,250
Emory University	n/av	n/av	n/av	45/55	n/av	n/av	n/av	$45,000
Franklin and Marshall College	5018	1873	570	51/49	641	654	n/av	$45,654
George Washington University	n/av	n/av	n/av	44/56	n/av	n/av	n/av	$51,000
Georgetown University	18,619	3683	1558	46/54	n/av	n/av	n/av	$47,781
Hamilton College	4661	1376	466	48/52	710	690	n/av	$49,860
Harvard College	n/av	n/av	n/av	50/50	n/av	n/av	n/av	$49,000

| SCHOOL | NUMBER OF APPLI-CATIONS | ACCEPTED | ENROLLED | M/F RATIO | SAT SCORES | | | COSTS |
					CRITICAL READING	MATH	WRITING	
Harvey Mudd College	n/av	n/av	n/av	64/36	n/av	n/av	n/av	$51,037
Haverford College	3403	862	323	46/54	710	690	700	$50,975
Johns Hopkins College	16,123	4318	n/av	52/48	n/av	n/av	n/av	$51,190
Kenyon College	3992	1538	469	47/53	674	645	672	$48,240
Lafayette College	n/av	n/av	n/av	53/47	620	660	630	$50,289
Lehigh University	11,170	3662	1193	39/41	630	670	630	$48,830
Macalester College	4565	2109	565	42/58	720	720	690	$46,942
Massachusetts Institute of Technology	15,663	1676	1072	55/45	715	770	710	$49,142
Middlebury College	6904	1413	603	49/51	n/av	n/av	n/av	$50,780 (tuition)
New York University	37,462	14,159	5000	38/62	658	672	664	$51,993
Northwestern University	n/av	n/av	n/av	48/52	n/av	n/av	n/av	$47,088
Oberlin College	7227	2434	809	45/55	700	670	700	$50,484
Occidental College	6014	2583	576	44/56	650	650	660	$49,702
Pitzer College	4081	828	256	n/av	n/av	n/av	n/av	$50,820
Pomona College	n/av	n/av	n/av	50/50	n/av	n/av	n/av	$48,770
Princeton University	n/av	n/av	n/av	53/47	n/av	n/av	n/av	$47,000
Reed College	3161	1281	368	44/56	710	670	690	$49,950
Rensselaer Polytechnic Institute	12,350	5291	1337	72/28	650	700	630	$50,310
Rhodes College	5039	2113	432	43/57	630	640	620	$42,024
Rice University	11,172	2495	894	52/48	650	670	640	$43,288
Scripps College	2061	678	203	All Women	690	660	690	$50,550

| SCHOOL | NUMBER OF APPLI-CATIONS | ACCEPTED | ENROLLED | M/F RATIO | SAT SCORES | | | COSTS |
					CRITICAL READING	MATH	WRITING	
Smith College	4011	1904	665	All Women	660	640	660	$50,380
Stanford University	30,429	2426	1694	53/47	n/av	n/av	n/av	$49,344
SUNY at Geneseo	10,413	3630	948	43/57	670	630	n/av	$15,876 (in-state) $23,766 (out-of-state)
Swarthmore College	5575	969	394	48/52	720	720	720	$49,600
Tufts University	15,387	4231	1373	49/51	n/av	n/av	n/av	$46,860
Tulane University	39,887	10,563	1502	46/54	665	660	670	$50,190
US Air Force Academy	n/av	n/av	n/av	81/19	n/av	n/av	n/av	n/av
United States Military Academy	n/av	n/av	n/av	85/15	n/av	n/av	n/av	n/av
United States Naval Academy	4644	1464	1251	86/14	n/av	n/av	n/av	n/av
University of California at Los Angeles	n/av	n/av	n/av	45/55	n/av	n/av	n/av	$22,165 (in-state) $44,882 (out-of-state)
University of Chicago	13,564	3708	1335	50/50	723	723	708	$51,078
University of Miami	21,845	9700	2006	47/53	630	650	620	$46,988
University of North Carolina at Chapel Hill	23,224	7345	3958	41/59	640	660	630	$14,296 (in-state) $32,184 (out-of-state)
University of Notre Dame	14,357	4113	2062	53/47	n/av	n/av	n/av	$48,845
University of Pennsylvania	22,645	3628	2397	48/52	n/av	n/av	n/av	$47,638
University of Richmond	n/av	n/av	n/av	49/51	n/av	n/av	n/av	$51,000
University of Rochester	12,111	4686	1087	48/52	650	680	650	$49,890

SCHOOL	NUMBER OF APPLI- CATIONS	ACCEPTED	ENROLLED	M/F RATIO	SAT SCORES			COSTS
					CRITICAL READING	MATH	WRITING	
University of Southern California	35,753	8724	2869	50/50	n/av	n/av	n/av	$50,642
University of Virginia	21,108	6768	3246	44/56	660	680	670	$26,452
Vanderbilt University	19,353	3899	783	48/52	n/av	n/av	n/av	$46,724
Vassar College	n/av	n/av	n/av	42/58	n/av	n/av	n/av	$51,470
Villanova University	n/av	n/av	n/av	50/50	n/av	n/av	n/av	$48,065
Wake Forest University	10,556	3959	1200	49/51	n/av	n/av	n/av	$48,716
Washington and Lee University	6222	1181	472	50/50	690	690	690	$47,287
Washington University in Saint Louis	23,105	5128	1510	49/51	n/av	n/av	n/av	$50,265
Webb Institute	n/av	n/av	n/av	76/24	n/av	n/av	n/av	$8,500 (tuition)
Wellesley College	4156	1463	589	All Women	589	683	693	$49,848
Wesleyan University	10,068	2218	745	50/50	700	700	700	$62,172
Whitman College	3290	1442	396	42/58	680	660	660	$46,200
Williams College	6448	1194	540	50/50	720	710	n/av	$45,140
Yale University	n/av	n/av	n/av	51/49	n/av	n/av	n/av	$45,000

AUTHOR BIOGRAPHIES

❏ AUTHOR BIOGRAPHIES ❏

INDEX

AMHERST COLLEGE ❏ **Katherine Duke,** while a student at Amherst College from 2001 to 2005, Katherine Duke majored in English, earned certification to teach high school, ran the campus vegetarian club, did some acting and dancing, and wrote and edited for several publications. After going to England on an Amherst College Fellowship to get a Master's degree in creative writing, she returned to Amherst, Massachusetts, to work as a writer and editor.

BATES COLLEGE ❏ **Jordan Williams,** African American Studies and Women and Gender Studies Double Major B.A. '08/Phi Beta Kappa, Dana Scholar, Junior Adviser, Residential Coordinator, Student Conduct Committee, Campus Climate Initiative, Admissions Communications Correspondent. In the summer/fall of 2008 he traveled to Germany, Holland, and South Africa, and was preparing to begin a two-year Teach for America commitment teaching high school history in Indianapolis.

BOSTON COLLEGE ❏ **Matthew J. Kita** graduated from Boston College in 1998 with a Bachelor of Arts degree in political science. While at BC, he was a member of several performing ensembles, including the Boston College Marching Band. After graduation, he earned his Master of Arts degree in Higher Education Policy from the University of Maryland, and was working on his Juris Doctorate at the University of Houston Law Center.

BOWDOIN COLLEGE ❏ **Nathaniel Vinton** was an English major at Bowdoin and earned High Honors for his work on Herman Melville. He spoke at his graduation in 2001 and was a candidate for the Rhodes Scholarship. Currently a staff writer at *Ski Racing Magazine* (assigned to the U.S. ski team beat), he is looking for any freelance writing assignments, and can be reached at *nathanielvinton@yahoo.com.*

BRANDEIS UNIVERSITY ❏ **Joshua F. A. Peck**, class of '02, graduated with high honors from Brandeis University. While at Brandeis, he was elected to two consecutive terms as Student Union President. He has worked as a Legislative Correspondent for Congressman Steve Rothman in Washington, D.C.

BROWN UNIVERSITY ❏ **Michelle Walson** graduated from Brown *magna cum laude* in 1999 with an A.B. in English and American literature and honors in creative writing. She served as the arts editor for Brown's weekly newspaper and was a four-year member of the Brown University Chorus. She worked for a PBS documentary series in Boston and is applying to graduate programs in television and film production.

BRYN MAWR COLLEGE ❏ **Sarah E. Caldwell** (Bryn Mawr College, AB 2008) majored in English and Creative Writing, entered the publishing industry as a publicity assistant at Farrar, Straus & Giroux, and recently joined Princeton University Press as a publicist. Sarah has also written op-ed columns for the Philadelphia Inquirer and continues her involvement with Bryn Mawr as an Alumna Admissions Representative.

BUCKNELL UNIVERSITY ❏ **Kristi Johnston**, graduated *magna cum laude* from Bucknell in 2003, with dual majors in English and History. While at Bucknell, she served as Arts & Entertainment Editor of *The Bucknellian* student newspaper. Since graduating, she has been working at Bert Davis Executive Search, an executive recruitment firm in New York City specializing in the publishing industry, where she has served as Marketing & Research Manager.

CALIFORNIA INSTITUTE OF TECHNOLOGY ❏ **Ted Jou**, class of 2003, double majored at Caltech in Applied Mathematics and Business Economics and Management. He contributed to Barron's during his senior year while serving as president of the undergraduate student body. While at Caltech, he served on the student government Board of Directors for two years and was a regular contributor to the student newspaper.

CARLETON COLLEGE ❏ **Erika Lewis** graduated from Carleton in 2006 with a B.A. in English. After graduation, she learned the fine art of making delicious espresso drinks and interned at *MSP Communications*, a magazine firm in Minneapolis, MN. She has been a Teach for America corps member in New Mexico.

CARNEGIE MELLON UNIVERSITY ❏ **Jessica Demers** graduated from Carnegie Mellon in 1999 with a B.A. in professional writing. She is a satellite coordinator at CNN in Atlanta. While at Carnegie Mellon, she worked as a Sleeping Bag Weekend student coordinator through the Office of Admission.

CASE WESTERN RESERVE UNIVERSITY ❏ **Kayla Gatalica** earned a B.A. in English and International Studies from Case Western Reserve University in 2010. She was the editor-in-chief of the *Case Reserve Review*, a SAGES Peer Writing Tutor, and a member of Phi Mu Fraternity and Sigma Tau Delta Fraternity. She currently teaches seventh grade Language Arts in the D.C. region with Teach for America.

CLAREMONT MCKENNA COLLEGE ❏ **Sarah Ciaccia** graduated from Claremont McKenna College in 2003 with a dual degree in Government and Literature. She is the recipient of a Rotary Ambassadorial Scholarship and is currently studying in Bologna, Italy.

COLBY COLLEGE ❏ **Martin Connelly**, Class of 2008 majored in East Asian Studies. He has edited copy for China Central Television, produced content for the Maine Public Broadcasting Network, and written articles for the Chinese design magazine *Urbane*. Connelly is currently based in Maine, ostensibly as a freelance writer and producer.

COLGATE UNIVERSITY ❏ **Jason Kammerdiener** graduated *summa cum laude* from Colgate in 2010 with a history major and an environmental studies minor. He held leadership positions in community service and the club sport groups; was a member of several other campus organizations; volunteered with the Admission Office; pursued studies in Ecuador, Japan, England, and Easter Island; and wrote and edited material for Colgate's communications office. He resides outside Rochester, New York, working as a content editor with Element K.

COLLEGE OF NEW JERSEY, THE ❏ **Nicole Levins** graduated *magna cum laude* from The College of New Jersey in 2007 with a B.A. in Professional Writing/Journalism. She is currently living and working in Arlington, Virginia.

COLLEGE OF THE HOLY CROSS ❏ **Alicia Lincoln**, '09, English major, Creative Writing concentration. Corps member '09, Teach for America, a national program that brings successful college graduates to underserved public school across the country. English teacher, Contemporary Learning Academy High School in Denver, CO.

COLLEGE OF WILLIAM AND MARY ❏ **Matthew Scranton** graduated in 2006 with a B.A. in history with a geology minor. He spent much of his time volunteering in the Office of Admissions as an intern and tour guide. Matt was also the Assistant Director of the Student Mentoring Program, a four-year member of the Rugby team, and the President and Co-Founder of a not-for-profit group and was selected as the student speaker for the 2006 Commencement. He has been a Peace Corps Volunteer serving in Chongqing, China.

COLUMBIA UNIVERSITY ❏ **Adina Brooks** attended Central Magnet High School in Bridgeport, CT and graduated from Columbia College with a B.A. in Urban Studies in 1998. She spent a year teaching English in Osaka, Japan with the JET Program. Career highlights since include working to expand children's health coverage with the Children's Defense Fund and helping to organize a successful campaign to raise the minimum wage with the Working Families Party. She is currently back at her alma mater working as an academic advisor at The Fu Foundation School of Engineering and Applied Science.

COLUMBIA UNIVERSITY/BARNARD COLLEGE ❏ **Catherine Webster** has served as assistant dean at Barnard. She has served Barnard as first-year class dean, associate director of the Pre-College Program, and director of the First-Year Focus Program. She holds M.A. degrees from New York University (in French literature) and Columbia's Teachers College (in College Student Personnel Administration) and a B.A. from Columbia College, where she was a member of the first coeducational class.

COLUMBIA UNIVERSITY, SCHOOL OF GENERAL STUDIES ❏ **Robert Ast** before transferring to GS attended the University of Chicago and worked in the film industry in Los Angeles. At

Columbia he was a columnist and copy editor for the student newspaper, the *Columbia Daily Spectator*, and held a work-study job in the GS Communications Office. In 2008 he graduated *summa cum laude*, with departmental honors in English and comparative literature. He lives in New York and is currently applying to graduate schools.

CONNECTICUT COLLEGE ❏ **Arielle Shipper**, '10, graduated *summa cum laude* and Phi Beta Kappa with a B.A. in sociology-based human relations. While at Conn, she was a staff member of *The College Voice*, an intern for *CC:Magazine*, and a tour guide in the Admissions office. She is currently living and working in Manhattan as an editorial assistant at a national magazine.

COOPER UNION ❏ **Dalia Levine** graduated from Cooper in 2002 with a Bachelor's of Engineering in Chemical Engineering. While serving on the Senior Class Council she helped fund-raise for the Class Gift and helped organize the Senior Bash party. She has also been copresident of Kesher (Hillel) and a vice-president of American Institute of Chemical Engineering. She served on the Resident Hall Association and as a Resident Assistant. Recently, she has worked for Merck & Co., Inc.

CORNELL UNIVERSITY ❏ **Laura Barrantes** graduated from the College of Arts and Sciences in 1997 as a government major. While at Cornell, she was cochair of the Orientation Steering Committee, a member of the Senior Honor Society of the Quill and Dagger, a Cornell Tradition Fellow, a member of Alpha Phi Omega National Service Fraternity, and a Cornell National Scholar. She has served as one of the reunion chairs for the class and has worked in Washington, D.C., with the American Political Science Association.

DARTMOUTH COLLEGE ❏ **Suzanne Leonard** graduated from Dartmouth in 1996 with a double major in English and psychology. While at school, she studied abroad in Madrid and London, had an internship with *Psychology Today*, and was involved with the *Dartmouth Alumni Magazine*. After graduating, she attended the Radcliffe publishing course in Cambridge, Massachusetts. She has worked as an editorial assistant at *Fitness* magazine, lived in Brooklyn, and contemplated a move to graduate school in England.

DAVIDSON COLLEGE ❏ **Page Neubert**, '01, graduated *cum laude* with an A.B. in English and holds an M.A. in creative writing from the Bread Loaf School of English through Middlebury College. She has worked for the Robin Hood Foundation in New York City.

DUKE UNIVERSITY ❏ **Norman Underwood**, '08, graduated *cum laude* with a B.A. in religion with honors. While at Duke, whe as a fraternity member, a first-year advisory counselor, and president of the LGBT student alliance. After having worked in the Duke administration for two years, he is pursuing his Ph.D. in history at the University of California–Berkeley.

EMORY UNIVERSITY ❏ **Brock Cline** received a B.A. in English from Emory University in 2009. While at school, he was active in Greek life, student government, and several philanthropic organizations. Currently, he's an associate at Kilpatrick Advisors, a boutique financial advisory firm in Atlanta. He is planning to pursue an MBA at Georgia State University.

FRANKLIN & MARSHALL COLLEGE ❏ **Nicholas Novack** graduated in 2008 with a B.A. in Philosophy. At F&M he was a leader and contributing chef of the Gourmet Society as well as an avid member of the Kappa Sigma fraternity. He currently operates a small apparel company and edits newsletters for Philadelphia area non-profits.

THE GEORGE WASHINGTON UNIVERSITY ❏ **Brian Hawthorne** earned a B.A. from GW in Geography in 2010, and is currently working on his Masters in Political Management as a Presidential Administrative Fellow. During his time at GW, he served as the co-Founder and President of the GW Veterans Organization, and he earned the 2010 Baer Award for Individual Excellence, the 2010 George Washington Award, and the 2011 Martin Luther King, Jr. Award. He lives in Washington, D.C.

GEORGETOWN UNIVERSITY ❏ **Meaghan M. Keeler** graduated magna cum laude from the Walsh School of Foreign Service with a concentration in International Politics in 2002. She was actively involved in student government, the Senior Class Committee, Leadership Programs, and HoyaSibs Weekend. Meaghan is currently employed as an events coordinator at a non-profit firm, Women in International Security. She plans to return to graduate school for a masters degree in International Affairs.

HAMILTON COLLEGE ❑ **Jennifer Kostka** graduated summa cum laude from Hamilton College in 2004 with a concentration in English and a minor in French. While at Hamilton, she was a member of the Residence Hall Council, secretary of the Emerson Literary Society, copyeditor for *The Spectator,* senior tutor at the Writing Center, and publications intern in the Office of Communications and Development. In addition, she was the winner of the Frederick Reese Wagner prize scholarship in English and was a two-time recipient of the Kellogg Essay prize for excellence in writing. She is currently working at a college textbook publishing company in Boston where she works primarily on English and World Language titles. She has continued to stay connected to the Hamilton community by joining the Boston chapter of Hamilton's GOLD (Graduates of the Last Decade) Alumni Association.

HARVARD UNIVERSITY/HARVARD COLLEGE ❑ **Brooke Earley** received an A.B. in history *magna cum laude* from Harvard and Radcliffe Colleges in 1994 and an M.Ed. from Harvard University in 1998. She has worked as an admissions officer and freshman advisor at Harvard and Radcliffe.

HARVEY MUDD COLLEGE ❑ **Erik Ring** majored in engineering and graduated from Harvey Mudd in 1996. He has lived and worked in Irvine, California, and his work keeps him in front of a computer most of the time. Running, backpacking, tennis, and his pet turtle Curly keep him busy the rest of the time.

HAVERFORD COLLEGE ❑ **Steve Manning** graduated in 1996 from Haverford, where he majored in history and played baseball and basketball. He has worked at the college in the publications office, writing the alumni magazine and maintaining the Haverford home page.

JOHNS HOPKINS UNIVERSITY, THE ❑ **Amy Brokl** graduated from Hopkins in 2003 with a B.A. in English and the History of Art. Over the course of her four years, she served on the

Commission for Undergraduate Education and the Orientation executive staff, alternating with time spent on the lacrosse field and out in Baltimore. She also gave interviews for the Office of Undergraduate Admissions and assisted with its alumni volunteers, a job that proved a natural segue to her current position as an associate director.

KENYON COLLEGE ❏ **Adam Sapp** is a 2002 graduate of Kenyon College. After receiving his B.A. in history at Kenyon, he worked as reporter for a newspaper in northern Ohio for four months before pursuing work at Claremont McKenna College in Claremont, California. He has been the Associate Dean of Admission and Financial Aid at Claremont McKenna College.

LAFAYETTE COLLEGE ❏ **Jodi Morgen**, class of 1997, has worked as an interactive copy-writer and has lived in New York City. After achieving in such challenges as Student Government President and movie critic for *The Lafayette*, Jodi has experienced great success writing advertising on the Internet, most notably banner ads that read "Win! Win! Win!"

LEHIGH UNIVERSITY ❏ **Rebecca Raphael** graduated from Lehigh in 2010 with a Bachelor of Arts in Journalism. She served as a member of the Association of Student Alumni, Panhellenic Council executive board, and hosted the university's Brown & White Minute on WLVR radio reading and announcing Lehigh's top headlines twice a week. In addition, she was a T.A. for Lehigh's only Public Relations course and worked as an intern in the Office of Communications and Public Affairs. Rebecca currently lives and works in New York City.

MACALESTER COLLEGE ❏ **Noah Palm** graduated *summa cum laude* from Macalester College with a Bachelor of Arts in Biology with an emphasis on Immunology and Microbiology. Noah participated heavily in research and teaching while at Mac. He chose to continue his studies in biology by pursuing a Doctorate in Immunobiology at Yale University.

MASSACHUSETTS INSTITUTE OF TECHNOLOGY ❏ **Stacy McGeever**, '93, majored in mathematics and computer science at MIT.

MIDDLEBURY COLLEGE ❏ **Kathryn Flagg** graduated from Middlebury College in 2008 *magna cum laude* with a B.A. in Environmental Studies. She served as the editor in chief of the college's weekly newspaper during her senior year, and was elected to Phi Beta Kappa upon graduation. Flagg has worked as a reporter at the Addison County Independent in Middlebury, VT.

NEW YORK UNIVERSITY ❏ **Eric Muroski** graduated from NYU in 2002 with a double major in playwriting and literature from the Gallatin School of Individualized Study. He is the copresident of a New York City-based theater production company that gives new talent a forum in which to present their art. He also recently held a professional position in the NYU Undergraduate Admissions Office and enrolled in a graduate acting program.

NORTHWESTERN UNIVERSITY ❏ **Kristen Acimovic** graduated *cum laude* and with departmental honors from Northwestern in 2002 with a B.A. in English Literature. While at Northwestern, Kristen was an R.A., an intern, a sorority member, and a volunteer. She has been a freelance writer in New York City.

OBERLIN COLLEGE ❏ **Sue Angell** graduated from Oberlin College with a B.A. in 1999. She majored in English and religion, concentrating on medieval literature and ancient Christianity. Since graduating, she has worked for Oberlin's Office of College Relations as a staff writer and editor.

OCCIDENTAL COLLEGE ❏ **Steven Barrie-Anthony** graduated from Occidental College in 2004 with a B.A. in religious studies and then headed off to work as a staff feature writer with the *Los Angeles Times*. At the *Times* he developed the technology and arts/culture beat, examining the effects of communication technology on person and society, and covered art, architecture, music, the movie business, and literature. In 2006, he returned to Oxy as a research fellow in religious studies, and has served as the journalist-in-residence at NewSchools Venture Fund, a San Francisco philanthropy foundation dedicated to supporting educational entrepreneurship in underserved communities.

PITZER COLLEGE ❑ **Amy Jasper** earned a degree in Political Studies from Pitzer College in 2010. She was honored to speak at the commencement ceremony. During her time at Pitzer, she directed a speaker series that hosted dozens of events and she served as a First-Year Student Mentor for three years, twice as a Lead Mentor. During her senior year, her blog Pitzer Uncovered racked up hundreds of Facebook fans and tens of thousands of page views over her senior year before being hacked by Albanian cyber-terrorists. Before pursuing a Fulbright Scholarship in Cyprus, she completed internships with the Nevada Democratic Caucus in Las Vegas, the Institute of International and European Affairs in Dublin, and the American Civil Liberties Union Jails Project in Los Angeles.

POMONA COLLEGE ❑ **Nick Creech** graduated from Pomona in 2007 with a degree in English and Cognitive Science. At Pomona, Nick was a member of the Glee Club, the men's volleyball team, and Men's Blue and White. He is currently teaching English at Xavier College Preparatory in Palm Desert, California.

PRINCETON UNIVERSITY ❑ **Jessica Arriola Marati** graduated from Princeton in 2008 with a B.A. in History. A member of Mathey College and the Terrance Club, she spent her undergraduate years exploring her Chamorro and Italian backgrounds, writing her senior thesis on the interplay between Chamorro culture and American politics, and studying Italian language and arts while living abroad in Rome. Since graduation, she has filled her time with travel and exploration, and she doesn't plan to stop anytime soon.

REED COLLEGE ❑ **Christopher Moses**, graduated from Reed in 2002, also serving as student body president that year. His senior history thesis investigated Wampanoag Indian and English interactions on colonial Martha's Vineyard. Chris hopes to become a furniture-making, typeface-designing historian, and is currently applying to Ph.D. programs.

RENSSELAER POLYTECHNIC INSTITUTE ❏ **Raymond Lutzky** graduated from Rensselaer Polytechnic Institute in 2002 with a Bachelor of Science degree in electronic media, arts, and communication. After graduation, he earned his Master of Science degree in public relations from Syracuse University. He has served as president of the RPI Young Alumni Council, and is currently vice-president of the Rensselaer Alumni Association. After working in marketing and PR for several years, Ray returned to Rensselaer as Associate Director for Enrollment.

RHODES COLLEGE ❏ **Kristine Page** is an English Literature major, with a minor in Art History. During her time at Rhodes, she was awarded the Buckman Scholarship to study abroad in Italy after studying the Italian language, literature, and Renaissance art. Kristine is an active member of Delta Delta Delta sorority, and she spent time volunteering at St. Jude Children's Research Hospital's Target House and the neighboring Snowden Elementary School. Kristine is married to a fellow Rhodes graduate and works as the Marketing and Communications Manager at the Museum of Photographic Arts in San Diego, California.

RICE UNIVERSITY ❏ **Michol McMillian Ecklund**, a native of Stillwater, Oklahoma, graduated *cum laude* from Rice University in 1997 with a Bachelor of Arts degree and a triple major in Political Science, Economics, and Managerial Studies. While at Rice, she was a varsity cheerleader, Director of the Student Admissions Council, and a statistics tutor. Michol graduated from Harvard Law School in 2000 and has been a senior tax attorney with Marathon Oil Company in Houston.

SCRIPPS COLLEGE ❏ **Lindsey Galloway** recently graduated from Scripps College with a B.A. in English and gender and women's studies, finishing her thesis on historical novels by contemporary women writers. She has interned at *U.S. News and World Report* and Denver's city magazine *5280* and has also written for the Scripps alumnae magazine and college newspaper *Voice*.

SMITH COLLEGE ❑ **Rachel Miller** graduated with a degree in Comparative Literature from Smith College in 2009. After a stint in London and long bike rides through France and Chile, she moved to New York City, where she lives now.

STANFORD UNIVERSITY ❑ **Gabriela Gutierrez** graduated from Stanford in 2002, having majored in Religious Studies, and English and French Literatures. After serving as Assistant Director of Undergraduate Admissions at Stanford, she traveled widely until settling in Mexico.

STATE UNIVERSITY OF NEW YORK AT GENESEO ❑ **Jared Chester** graduated from Geneseo *summa cum laude* in 2008 with dual majors in Philosophy and Communication. He was a tour guide, wrote for the Geneseo weekly newspaper, conducted independent research, and served on the Student Senate. After graduating he joined Teach For America and taught as a fifth grade teacher in Bridgeport, Connecticut for two years before attending law school at Indiana University Maurer School of Law.

SWARTHMORE COLLEGE ❑ **Peter Gardner** '08 was an honors political science major with a minor in history. He was the student body president in his senior year.

TUFTS UNIVERSITY ❑ **Adam Goodman** graduated from Tufts in 2003 with highest honors and a degree in history. While on campus, he participated in the Institute for Global Leadership's EPIIC program, wrote a column for *The Tufts Daily*, and founded the Tufts Table Tennis Club. After spending three years as an Assistant Director of Admissions and Multicultural Recruitment at Tufts, Adam accepted a job in the Rio Grande Valley along the Mexican border, where he has worked as a history teacher at IDEA College Preparatory.

TULANE UNIVERSITY ❑ **Casey Haugner** graduated from Newcomb College of Tulane University in 2005 with a B.A. in English, creative writing. She then went on to graduate from Tulane's A.B. Freeman School of Business with an MBA in finance and management in 2006. She has worked in Washington DC, where she performed marketing and communications duties for Deloitte's global public sector, and misses New Orleans terribly.

UNITED STATES AIR FORCE ACADEMY ❏ **2nd Lieutenant Jocelyn Booker** graduated from the United States Air Force Academy in May 2010, earning a Bachelor of Science degree in Foreign Area Studies, with a focus on Sub-Saharan Africa and a minor in French. She currently serves as an Admissions Advisor in the Diversity Recruiting Office at the United States Air Force Academy.

U.S. MILITARY ACADEMY ❏ **Joshua Lospinoso** was raised in Florham Park, NJ and entered West Point in the summer of 2005. After graduation from West Point in 2009, most of Josh's classmates immediately joined the active Army as 2nd Lieutenants to lead the nation's soldiers. Josh was afforded the opportunity to compete for and win the Rhodes, Marshall, Rotary, and National Science Foundation Graduate Research Scholarships. Josh is currently completing a Doctor of Philosophy degree in Statistics at the University of Oxford, and will serve as a military intelligence officer in the U.S. Army after graduate school.

U.S. NAVAL ACADEMY ❏ **Anthony Holds Servidas**, is a surface warfare officer in the U.S. Navy for 5 years. After his graduation from the U.S. Naval Academy in May of 1997, he worked as the music department coordinator at the academy for seven months. He then completed a stint in Newport, Rhode Island, at the navy's Surface Warfare Officer School. Upon graduation from that training program, he entered the operational fleet as a division officer onboard a navy ship. Servidas appeared on Broadway in the show "Dracula" and was continuing a career as an actor/singer.

UNIVERSITY OF CALIFORNIA, LOS ANGELES (UCLA) ❏ **Bethany Powers** just graduated from UCLA with a degree in American Literature and Culture. An active member of Alpha Delta Pi sorority, Bethany also wrote for *The Daily Bruin* and *UCLA Magazine*. Now jumping into post-grad life, she's looking for a career in social media management or journalism.

UNIVERSITY OF CHICAGO ❑ **Jonathan Beere** graduated from the University of Chicago in 1995 with a concentration in history, philosophy, and social studies of science and medicine. He studied classics at Oxford University as a Rhodes Scholar. He has pursued a Ph.D. in philosophy at Princeton.

UNIVERSITY OF MIAMI ❑ **Melissa Greco** graduated in 2005 with a B.S. in Communication. She currently works for the university's Media Relations Department where she serves as the Media Editorial Coordinator. Like a true Miamian, she enjoys Cuban food and sunny afternoons on the beach. She would like to thank Annette Herrera and Margot Winick for their words and wisdom on all things UM.

UNIVERSITY OF NORTH CAROLINA AT CHAPEL HILL ❑ **Mike Tarrant** graduated from UNC Phi Beta Kappa with a B.A. in Political Science and Communications Studies. While at UNC Mike served as student body vice president and was active in both the Campus Y and the Carolina Athletic Association. In the Spring of 2008 Mike was awarded a Luce Scholarship to live and work in Asia for one year following graduation from UNC. Mike has worked in the Office of University and Global Relations at the National University of Singapore.

UNIVERSITY OF NOTRE DAME ❑ **Meghan Kelley**, '95, was a history and American studies major at the University of Notre Dame and resided in Walsh Hall for three years. While in school, Meghan was active with the Center for Social Concerns, and intramural sports, and studied in London her junior year. After graduation, Meghan volunteered with Boys Hope/Girls Hope and has worked in public relations in Chicago.

UNIVERSITY OF PENNSYLVANIA ❑ **Erik Frey** graduated in 2002 with majors in Architecture and Asian and Middle Eastern Studies and respective concentrations in Design and Japanese. At Penn, he was involved in the Connaissance and Spring Fling committees, the American Institute of Architecture Students, and several other extracurriculars. Since graduation, he has been working, taking post-bac classes, and concentrating on selecting a graduate program.

UNIVERSITY OF RICHMOND ❏ **Dan Petty** graduated from the University of Richmond in 2009 with a Bachelor of Science in biology, a Bachlor of Arts in journalism, and a minor in French. While at UR, he competed on the univesity's Division I cross country and track and field teams, served as news editor and online editor of the student newspaper, *The Collegian*, and interned with The Associated Press, where his stories were published around the world. He now lives and works in Colorado as the social media editor for *The Denver Post* and freelances photography and writing for several publications, including *Running Times* magazine.

UNIVERSITY OF ROCHESTER ❏ **Ike Howdeshell** originally from St. Louis, MO, Ike Howdeshell came to the University of Rochester as a Renaissance Scholar. During his time as an undergrad he served as a campus tour guide, was involved in a fraternity, and was active with both the College Republicans and the College Democrats. He graduated with a major in Political Science and minors in Psychology and Philosophy in 2007. He has lived in the Rochester area where he has enjoyed promoting college access to students from all walks of life.

UNIVERSITY OF SOUTHERN CALIFORNIA ❏ **Achi Yaffe** graduated from USC in 2001 with a B.S. in Business Administration and a minor in Natural Sciences. At USC, he was the cocaptain of the men's club volleyball team, a member of the Baccalaureate/M.D. program, and a Renaissance Scholar. Achi worked as a business analyst with McKinsey & Company, out of their Los Angeles and Tel Aviv offices. He then went on to study for his MBA at Harvard Business School.

UNIVERSITY OF VIRGINIA ❏ **Larisa Barry** graduated with a B.A. from UVa with a distinguished major in English and a minor in French in 1997. She has worked as an assistant editor with an environmental consulting firm in Arlington, Virginia.

VANDERBILT UNIVERSITY ❏ **Lauren (Nicole) Shaub** graduated from Vanderbilt in 2001 with a B.A. in English and Communication Studies. Upon graduation, she worked for two years as an Admissions Counselor at Vanderbilt, and was completing an M.Ed. in Counseling Psychology full-time at Teachers College (Columbia University) in New York.

VASSAR COLLEGE ❏ **Philosophy Walker** graduated from Vassar in 2008 with a degree in English. She is currently a freelance writer and editor and lives in Austintown, Ohio with her husband, Adam, and her two cats, Charlotte Bronte and Lenore.

VILLANOVA UNIVERSITY ❏ **Maura Topper** graduated from Villanova University in 2008 (Summa Cum Laude) with degrees in Accounting and Finance from the Villanova School of Business. She resides in New York City, and is beginning her career as an Audit Assistant for Deloitte & Touche. She is currently working in the Financial Services sector. Maura continues to stay involved with Villanova through her alumni activities and her extended family members, four of whom currently attend the university.

WAKE FOREST UNIVERSITY ❏ **Caitlin Kenney** graduated from Wake Forest in 2008 with a major in English and a minor in journalism. During her time at the university she worked as the editor in chief on the student newspaper, gave weekly tours of the campus, and sang in the choir. She currently works in publishing in New York City.

WASHINGTON AND LEE UNIVERSITY ❏ **Cameron Howell** was born and raised in Columbia, South Carolina. He graduated from Washington and Lee University in 1994 and has resided in Charlottesville, Virginia.

WASHINGTON UNIVERSITY IN ST. LOUIS ❏ **Joyce Lawrence**, B.S., B.A. '04, graduated with majors in marketing and international business and a minor in psychology. She is currently living in San Diego and attending the Masters in Pacific International Affairs Program at University of California San Diego.

WEBB INSTITUTE ❏ **Casey Harwood** is a member of the class of 2011 at the Webb Institute. He is the chairperson of the Webb Institute Public Relations Committee. The student members of the committee who contributed to this work are Brent Morrison ('11), Steven Gugliemoni ('12), Justin Morgan ('12), Colin Spillane ('13), and Amy Zahray ('14).

WELLESLEY COLLEGE ❏ **Mary Lynn Jones** served as editor-in-chief of *The Wellesley News* and graduated from Wellesley College in 1996 with departmental honors in political science. She received her M.S.J. from the Columbia University Graduate School of Journalism in 1997. Mary Lynn has been a staff writer at *The Hill* newspaper in Washington, D.C., covering the Senate and lobbying.

WESLEYAN UNIVERSITY ❏ **Stacy Theberge**, '95, majored in English at Wesleyan, and spent many hours researching an out-of-print novel and rollerblading down Wyllys Avenue. She has lived in Los Angeles, and would like to thank Morgan Fahey, '95, Henry Myers, '95, and Sadia Shepard, '97 for contributing to this article.

WHITMAN COLLEGE ❏ **Aisha Fukushima** graduated from Whitman College in 2009 with honors in Rhetoric and Film Studies and minors in French and Gender Studies. Since then, she has traveled the world as a Thomas J. Watson Fellow exploring "RAPtivism" (rap and hip hop activism) throughout South Asia, Europe, and Africa. Fukushima currently lives in San Francisco, California where she recently completed a human rights fellowship with the mayor's office and enjoys making music on the weekends.

WILLIAMS COLLEGE ❏ **Jennifer Linnan** graduated in 2006 with a double major in chemistry and English. At Williams, she was a copyeditor for *The Williams Record,* wrote news and event releases for the Office of Public Affairs, and performed with the Williams Percussion Ensemble. She has lived in New York City.

BIOGRAPHIES

YALE UNIVERSITY ❏ **Amanda Gordon** has worked as an assistant editor at *Glamour Magazine* and has been active in planning activities and editing a newsletter for New York-area Yale alumni. She graduated in 1994 with a B.A. in English. At Yale she worked in the Admissions Office, the Dean's Office, and the Master's Office of Ezra Stiles College.

❏ **Seth Oltman** graduated from Yale in 1997 with a B.A. in history. At Yale he edited the *Yale Record* (a humor magazine) and *Urim v'Tumim* (a Jewish journal), tutored at a local elementary school, and worked for four years at the Yale University Press. He has been an editorial assistant at *Chief Executive Magazine*.

❑ INDEX BY STATE ❑

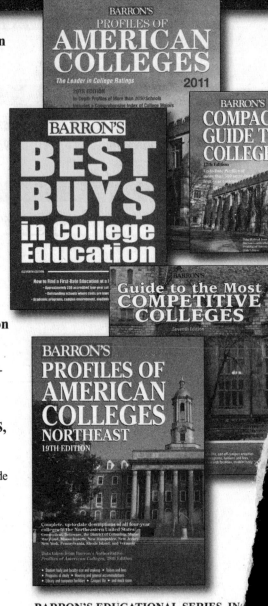